Encyclopedia of

GARDENS

History and Design

Encyclopedia of

GARDENS

History and Design

Volume 3

P–Z

EDITOR

CANDICE A. SHOEMAKER

FITZROY DEARBORN PUBLISHERS

CHICAGO LONDON

Copyright © 2001 by
FITZROY DEARBORN PUBLISHERS

All rights reserved including the right of reproduction in whole or in part in any form.
For information write to:

FITZROY DEARBORN PUBLISHERS
919 N. Michigan Avenue, Suite 760
Chicago, Illinois 60611
USA

or

FITZROY DEARBORN PUBLISHERS
310 Regent Street
London W1B 3AX
UK

Library of Congress and British Library Cataloging in Publication Data are available.

ISBN 1-57958-173-0

First published in the USA and UK 2001

Index prepared by Hughes Analytics, Chicago, Illinois
Typeset by Argosy Publishing, Waltham, Massachusetts
Printed by Edwards Brothers, Ann Arbor, Michigan
Cover design by Chicago Advertising and Design, Chicago, Illinois

Cover illustration: Melissande's Allée, Dumbarton Oaks, Washington D.C., United States. Copyright Eleanor M. McPeck.

CONTENTS

LIST OF ENTRIES

P

Padova, Orto Botanico dell'Università di

Padua, Italy

Location: approximately 20 miles (32 km) west of Venice, in Padua at Via Orto Botanico 15, 1 mile (1.6 km) south of the central train station

Founded in 1545, almost simultaneously with the Pisa and Florence Botanic Gardens, the Orto Botanico dell'Università di Padova (Padua Botanic Garden) is the only early botanic garden that still exists on the spot where it was first created. In structure, function, and layout it has undergone little change since then and is thus a garden monument of outstanding importance for the history of science in general and of botany in particular. It is fitting, therefore, that the Padua Botanic Garden has been included in the World Heritage List of the United Nations Educational, Scientific, and Cultural Organization (UNESCO).

Thanks to numerous studies the history of this institution is well known. Regarded by many as the archetype of a botanic garden, its foundation and early years offer deep insights into university life in the late Renaissance. It is this early period that is here dealt with more fully than the later, less eventful years.

The driving force behind the garden's foundation was Francesco Bonafede, the first *lector simplicium* (reader for simples) of Padua University. He petitioned the senate of the Serenissima Repubblica di San Marco (Venice), to which Padua then belonged, for *una spetiaria* (a pharmacy or spice shop), which would act as a reference collection, making the distinction of genuine from false *cose* (things) possible. This effectively meant plants. Bonafede's proposal must be seen in the context of commerce: Venice was then the most important exchange market for medicinal herbs and spices, notably from the Levant, and an institution was needed for quality control. On 29 June 1545 the senate voted overwhelmingly for the proposal. The founding document speaks of Padua "as an ideal place for planting herbs, putting them into order and conserving them," stresses the universal benefit of such an institution for humankind, and states that the garden should be planted according to the wishes of the university and thus should enjoy some autonomy. Entrance was granted to the learned, and the ultimate goal of this medicinal garden was *per l'utilità pubblica* (for public utility). Simultaneously, rules for the control of pharmacies and their merchandise were set up.

A piece of land with good water supply between Il Santo and Santa Giustina in the center of Padua was leased only eight days after the senate's decision. Daniele Barbaro and Pietro da Noale were responsible for the building works, Luigi Squalerno, called Anguillara, was appointed as the first prefect "to enrich it with plants, supervise, and look after it," and Pier Antonio Michiel, owner of a remarkable private garden in Venice and like Barbaro a wealthy patrician, acted as consultant. Significantly, the function of the prefect was initially independent from that of the *lector* or *ostentor simplicium*. Rules for good behavior were decreed early and became the model for many botanic gardens subsequently founded by other universities. The seven rules of the Padua Botanic Garden decreed are as follows: (1) Do not knock on this gate before the day of Mark the Evangelist [i.e., 25 April], and then not before the XXII hour [i.e., 10:00 A.M.]; (2) Anyone entering through the main gate should not wander from the main avenue; (3) Do not break stems, pick flowers, collect fruit or seeds, or pull up roots in the garden; (4) Do not touch young shoots, and do not stand or leap over flower beds; (5) The gardens are to be respected; (6) Nothing must be done against the will of the prefect; (7) Any contravention of these rules will be punished with fines, imprisonment, or exile. From an early date demonstrations and lectures on *materia medica*, now known as pharmaceutical botany, were given in the Padua Botanic Garden.

A view of the Orto Botanico dell'Università di Padova
Photo by Francesco and Matteo Danesin, courtesy of Università degli studi di Padova, Orto Botanico

The original layout of the garden seems to have consisted of the famous *horto rotondo* (circular garden; also called *hortus cinctus* or *hortus sphaericus*), almost unchanged today, four annexes, a maze, and a largely enigmatic hippodrome. The latter parts may have been only projected; in any case they are not extant and are not well understood. The *horto rotondo* has the form of a circle with an inscribed square, which is in turn divided into four smaller squares by two paths aligned with the points of the compass. The four segments formed by the circle and inscribed square are divided by these paths and thus make up eight triangular beds, so that the circular garden is made up of 12 large beds in all. The four smaller squares included 141, 125, 121, and 117 small beds, respectively, arranged in four different, highly refined geometrical patterns. Parts of the *horto rotondo* were raised, and the large beds had steps leading to them, but they were, many years later, leveled out. Garden archaeology has shown that the original layout of the individual beds is still maintained. All this exemplifies a profound contradiction characteristic of many botanic gardens: although their one and only goal is the transfer of knowledge, their layout—in the case of the Padua Botanic Garden, a sophisticated geometrical arrangement of flower beds—is intended to provoke pleasant sensations in the visitor.

Dated garden plans for this garden drawn in 1571 and 1579 with plant names added have survived (now in Biblioteca Universitaria, Bologna). Because many of these names are found also on the illustrations forming the famous *Codice erbario* of Michiel (now in Biblioteca Nazionale Marciana, Venice), it is possible to determine the contents of the *horto rotondo* in detail. Most of the plants cultivated seem to have originated from the Apennine Peninsula, but some must have been imported from the Balkan Peninsula (e.g., *Syringa vulgaris*), from the Levant (e.g., *Origanum dictamnus*), and of course America (e.g. *Nicotiana rustica*). Some plants clearly had medicinal virtues, but others did not. Nothing is known of how the plants were labeled, but the beds seem to have been numbered with a master list, possibly kept by the prefect. The primary aim of the garden was to provide correctly identified and named medicinal plants to the learned, in particular to students of medicine, but the founding document allowed also for the cultivation of plants without medicinal properties.

A first index to the plants cultivated was printed by Girolamo Porro in 1591, now an extremely rare booklet, which is usually attributed to Giacomo Antonio Cortuso, the third prefect of the garden. It comprises not only precise plans of the garden layout but also a list of plants cultivated. There are also pages with numbered lines referring to the individual flower beds, for the students to fill in the names of the plants cultivated there. The Biblioteca Civica, Padua keeps a partially annotated copy confirming this use. This index was compiled only four years before Lorenz Scholtz's well-known index to the garden in Wrocław. Several later indexes of the

Padua Botanic Garden followed, documenting a gradual increase of species in cultivation and a gradual decrease of medicinal plants. They also testify to the introduction of numerous extra-European species. During this early period at least some visitors were authorized to collect plant samples in the garden. In 1552 it was realized that "the amphitheater of the garden being open, means that anyone can enter and take away plants and simples": the *horto rotondo* was encircled with a wall, but there is no hint of an entrance fee. Little is known about the *speciaria*, but it may have been situated in a small preexisting building on the garden grounds.

From its early days the Padua Botanic Garden was a center for plant introduction, notably from the Levant, then the sphere of interest of the Republic of Venice. Several prefects, among them Anguillara, Melchiore Guilandino (Wieland), and Prospero Alpini, traveled this region and enriched the garden with new living collections: *Rheum rhaponticum* (rhubarb) from contemporary Bulgaria, now widely cultivated, is considered the most famous Paduan introduction; *Cyclamen creticum* and *Campanula saxatilis*, both from the south Aegean area, are other early introductions. Herbarium specimens and plant illustrations also arrived in Padua, then a university enjoying a high prestige among students of medicine, and the knowledge of simples was part of it. The first illustration of a sterile branch of *Coffea arabica* (coffee) was published in 1592 in Alpini's *De plantis Aegypti* in nearby Venice. In 1659 the first conservatory for plants from warmer climates was built; its maintenance became a constant worry just like that of the water supply machinery for the garden.

Following Anguillara a long line of prefects were responsible for this garden, some at the same time being *lector simplicium* or professor of *materia medica* at the faculty of medicine. They all gave their lessons in the Padua Botanic Garden. Although it was several times flooded and hit by storms, the garden was never destroyed by war action and did not suffer from the Napoléonic interlude.

In the early 18th century the garden was ornamented with several pools and fountains, the original wall replaced by a higher one with a balustrade, and the four gateways subsequently embellished with *acroters* (ornamental crowns) in wrought iron representing fruiting *Ananas*, flowering *Fritillaria*, *Lilium*, and *Yucca*. In addition busts of famous botanists were placed on the balustrade. On their grand tour numerous visitors stopped in Padua to see the botanic garden, among them, on 27 September 1786, Johann Wolfgang von Goethe, who many years later wrote in his autobiography, "It is a pleasure and instructive to walk through a vegetation that is strange to us." There is no indication that Goethe met the then prefect Giovanni Marsili, a symbol of stagnation in botany, if not regression, who

is, however, known to have created the small arboretum on the ground near the *horto rotondo*.

Under Habsburg rule since the Congress of Vienna, the Padua Botanic Garden remained a university institution. No less than 5,183 species names are listed in the printed catalog of 1820; a first seed catalog offering living material for partner institutions was printed in 1823. For 43 years Roberto de Visiani was both prefect and professor and enriched the garden with many introductions from his native Dalmatia. By decree of Ferdinand I, emperor of Austria and king of Lombardy and Veneto, a *teatro botanico*—the first lecture hall—was built near the garden and conservatories were added, which were further enlarged by later prefects, among them the famous mycologist Pier Andrea Saccardo. It was only in 1860 that the care for the Padua Botanic Garden passed from the faculty of medicine to the faculty of philosophy. In these years a plant of unknown progeny first cultivated in the Padua Botanic Garden became a considerable horticultural success—*Freesia leichtlinii* from the Cape.

Protected by a conservatory built for this purpose, the oldest living specimen in the garden is now a *Chamaerops humilis* said to have been planted in 1585 and to have inspired Goethe to reflections later summarized in his *Versuch die Metamorphose der Pflanzen zu erklären* (1790; Essay to Explain the Metamorphosis of Plants). A monumental *Platanus orientalis* is only slightly younger.

It could be said that the great days of Padua Botanic Garden have passed with the death of de Visiani. It became one of several similar institutions in what was then the kingdom of Italy and later became the Republic of Italy. Frequented by students today just as 450 years ago, the Padua Botanic Garden is a unique garden monument, a main tourist attraction of the city, and a quiet, shady and well-kept place strongly recommended to visitors.

Synopsis

1545	Garden founded by senate of Republic of Venice, after petition by Francesco Bonafede
1552	Circular wall built to protect plants
1571	First dated manuscript garden plan with plant names
1591	First printed catalog of plants in cultivation, by Giacomo Antonio Cortuso
1659	First conservatory built
1697–ca. 1710	Embellishment with pools, fountains, and *acroters,* and new circular wall built
1786	Johann Wolfgang von Goethe visits
1807–18	Further conservatories added
1823	First *Index Seminum* published

1997   Included in the UNESCO World
                 Heritage List

Further Reading
Azzi Visentini, Margherita, *L'Orto Botanico di Padova
    e il giardino del Rinascimento*, Milan: Polifilo, 1984
Goldblatt, Peter, "Systematics of *Freesia* Klatt (Iridaceae),"
    Journal of South African Botany 48, no. 1 (1982)
Lack, H. Walter, "Die frühe botanische Erforschung der
    Insel Kreta," *Annalen des Naturhistorischen
    Museums in Wien* 98, B Supplement (1997)

Minelli, Alessandro, editor, *The Botanical Garden of
    Padua, 1545–1995*, Venice: Marsilio, 1995
Schiller, Peter, *Der Botanische Garten in Padua:
    Astrologische Geographie und Heilkräuterkunde zu
    Beginn der modernen Botanik; L'Orto botanico di
    Padova: Geografica astrologica e scienza dei semplici
    alle origini della botanica moderna* (bilingual
    German-Italian edition), Venice: Centro Tedesco di
    Studi Veneziani, 1987

H. WALTER LACK

Page, Russell 1906–1985

English Landscape Architect

Russell Page, English by birth and international by choice, was one of the greatest landscape architects of the postwar period and of the 20th century in general. Born in Lincolnshire, Page began his gardening education at 14 with a pot of *Campanula* (Bell flower) bought for one shilling at a country fair. He began to learn its nature and needs, encouraged by his mother, a keen gardener. Books from the public library brought him horticultural knowledge. While a student at Charterhouse, where he took the Leach Prize for Art, Page visited Gertrude Jekyll and her garden. He spent school holidays making rock gardens, finding plants, and learning from whomever he could meet. Mark Fenwick at Abbotswood shared his knowledge and took Page to visit Lawrence Johnston's Hidcote, which Page later acknowledged as having the greatest influence on his work.

Page studied art at the Slade School, University College, London, between 1924 and 1926. He lived in France from 1927 to 1932, supposedly working at the École des Beaux Arts in Paris, but he actively traveled and worked on assorted garden projects while studying European garden architecture. He met and began an important lifelong friendship with Andre de Vilmorin, heir to the great French seed and plant firm.

Page returned to London in 1932 to work in the office of a landscape architect and earn his living. A chance meeting with Henry Bath led to continuing work in the park at Longleat and an association with Geoffrey Jellicoe, with whom Page collaborated on various projects, including Cheddar Gorge and the Royal Lodge, Windsor Great Park. Their partnership ended in 1939 with the start of the war. Page also met during this period the major French decorator Stephan Boudin, of the Paris house of Jansen.

Together they began work at Leeds Castle in Kent and traveled and worked extensively in France and Belgium.

The war years took Page to the United States and to the Near East, where he was stationed in Cairo, which brought him into close contact with the Islamic garden tradition, an early fascination, and to India and Ceylon. From 1945 to 1952 he based himself in Paris at the Vilmorin offices and renewed his work with Boudin. Page continued and increased his work for the French industrialist and racehorse owner-breeder Marcel Boussac at the industrialist's many properties and later revised and replanted the Longchamp racetrack of Paris. Before this, Page's international one-man practice often took him to the south of France and back to England for continual consultation and work at Longleat, Babminton, and Leeds Castle, as well as to landscape the Battersea Festival Gardens of 1951, for which he was given the Order of the British Empire (OBE). Convinced that after the war people in France would want to garden on a popular scale, he encouraged this tendency with his prize-winning Vilmorin garden at the Floralies de Paris in 1957.

Page crisscrossed his years of French residency, as well as the later years after his return to England in 1952 until his death, with working trips to large estates and smaller private country and city gardens in Italy, Spain, Belgium, Switzerland, Egypt, Portugal, Germany, the United States, and the West Indies.

Few landscape architects have had such a vast canvas on which to work and learn. Page's artist's eye and fascination for architecture, whether in stone or with plants, went hand in hand. Every element of the garden, from driveway approaches to paths, retaining walls, swimming pools, and garden houses, took his full attention.

The plantings, within an architectural frame he always favored in order to give strength and unity to a garden, brought grace and harmony. Trees and shrubs, and in many cases sculpture, completed the overall plan. Like André Le Nôtre, Page had the planter's visual feel, the honesty and astringency of the accomplished architect, and a vast horticultural knowledge.

Travels throughout the world brought to Page knowledge of many cultures, their climates, and their corresponding flora. His desire to learn and know was boundless. He traveled with a notebook in which he would sketch an interesting architectural detail and write the name of a plant new to him so as to commit it to memory.

Page calculated that he had designed or worked on over 600 projects from his first in the grand manner at Longleat in England to many smaller private gardens, municipal parks, and city plans for Paris and Iran to a new township in Australia and botanical gardens for Venezuela. These last were never brought to completion. Page made plans for highway landscaping, including the planting around service stations, a private park around a lake in Chile, a Shakespeare theater in the southern United States, a project for the Brooklyn Botanical Park, and the garden of the Frick Museum in New York City. His last great project and masterpiece, accomplished during the last five years of his life, was the design and planting of a sculpture park and series of gardens in upper New York State for the PepsiCo headquarters.

Page's understanding and love of plants began with his youth in England, and his love of trees developed throughout his life. He learned the formality of design in France and Italy and in the gardens of Islam. He designed as an artist with the skill of an architect and the sensitivity of a great plantsman. His only book, the classic *The Education of a Gardener,* was published in 1962. As he stated in a 1984 letter, "Whether I am making a landscape or a garden or arranging a window box I first attack my problem as an artist—my preoccupation is with the relationships between objects, whether it is a wood or a pond, a rock or a plant, or a group of plants."

Biography

Born in Lincolnshire, England, 1906. Started studying gardening at age 14; visited Gertrude Jekyll and her garden, and Lawrence Johnston's Hidcote, while still a teenager; studied art, Slade School, University College, London, 1924–26; worked on garden projects in Paris, France, 1927–32; returned to London and worked in office of a landscape architect, 1932–39; worked in association with Geoffrey Jellicoe, 1935–39; during World War II, traveled to United States and Near East; while stationed in Cairo, was exposed to Islamic garden tradition; established private practice in Paris after the War, 1945–62; returned to England, 1952; traveled extensively, designing private estates and city gardens in Europe, United States, Egypt, and West Indies. Died in London, 1985.

Selected Designs

1932–85	Longleat House and Park, Wiltshire, England
1936	Royal Lodge and Windsor Great Park (with Geoffrey Jellicoe), Windsor, England
1936–85	Leeds Castle, Kent, England
1937–59	Château de Mivoisin, Solonge, France
1949	Creux de Genthod, Vaud, Switzerland
1951	Festival Gardens, Battersea Park, London, England; Frank de Poortere garden, Courtray, Belgium; garden for the Duke of Windsor, Gif-sur-Yvette, France; La Loggia, Piedmont, Italy
1954–	Villar Perosa, Piedmont, Italy; La Mortella, Ischia, Italy
1956	Villa Silvio Pellico, Piedmont, Italy; Kiluna Farm, Long Island, United States
1959	Vilmorin exhibit, Floralies de Paris, France
1964–79	March Sculpture Garden, Majorca, Spain; San Liberato, north of Rome, Italy
1967	Haras de Varaville, Normandy, France; Tor San Lorenzo, south of Rome, Italy
1973	Frick Museum and William S. Paley Gardens, New York City, New York, United States
1975	Reconstruction of gardens, Port Lympne, Kent, England
1976	Project in Santiago de Chile, Chile; Sculpture garden, Columbus Museum of Art, Columbus, Ohio, United States
1980–85	Sculpture park and gardens, PepsiCo headquarters, Purchase, New York, United States
1983	Temple of Flora Rose Garden, U.S. National Arboretum, Washington, District of Columbia, United States

Selected Publications

The Education of a Gardener, 1962

Further Reading

Van Zuylen, Gabrielle, and Marina Schinz, *The Gardens of Russell Page,* New York: Stewart, Tabori and Chang, 1991

GABRIELLE VAN ZUYLEN

Painshill

Cobham, Surrey, England

Location: 1 mile (1.6 km) west of Cobham, off A 245, by River Mole, approximately 15 miles (24 km) southwest of central London

In 1738, at about the same time when estates such as Esher Place, Claremont, Woburn Farm, and Oatlands were transformed, Charles Hamilton, a man who knew those places well, acquired the lease of land for an area of approximately 120 acres (49 ha)—later extended to about 200 acres (80 ha)—next to the River Mole near Cobham in Surrey and started to turn, as Horace Walpole put it, a "most cursed hill" into one of the best-known, most-visited, and influential landscape gardens of the time. Painshill was designed solely by its owner, the youngest son of the sixth earl of Abercorn, a gifted and enthusiastic amateur in garden design who combined antiquarian aesthetics with the qualities of a practical gardener and farmer. Two years after having graduated from Christ Church, Oxford, in 1723, Hamilton traveled the Continent on his grand tour. While in Rome he bought several Roman statues that later reappeared as elements of the scenes created by him at Painshill, among them a statue of Bacchus, more than 2.2 yards (2 m) high, for the Temple of Bacchus.

In contrast to William Kent and Henry Hoare, who designed scenes as a communion of natural setting and architecture, Hamilton began creating scenes by remodeling the landscape and planting trees, shrubs, and evergreens. He experimented extensively with planting, preferring newly introduced species, mainly from North America, to conventional trees. In this he may be considered a pioneer; he not only acquired his seedlings and plants where other garden enthusiasts in Britain did but between 1755 and 1759 he also corresponded and exchanged species with the Abbé Nolin in France, plant collector and advisor to Louis XV and Louis XVI. The trees of North American origin, mainly firs and pines, best suited Hamilton's intention to create a foreign and wild effect in one of his "pictures," in the part of the garden Walpole (*On Modern Gardening,* 1771) later described as the "alpine garden." Visitors to Painshill such as Charles von Linnaeus, son of the famous botanist, commented on the great variety of firs, cedars, and oaks to be found there. Painshill thus differed from other contemporary landscape gardens by its variety of trees, an effect enhanced by another conspicuous element—the use of color or flowering shrubs and plants, some of which adorned a secreted parterre and an orangery during the summer. According to John Claudius Loudon, it was Hamilton who first planted rhododendrons and azaleas in England. By 1750—estate papers and other documents giving accurate dates for the garden's formation are lacking—a lake of 14 acres (6 ha)

with irregular forms and islands had been added, filled with water from the neighboring river by a waterwheel, a horse-operated machine later, and, when the estate had changed its owner, by an iron waterwheel 10.5 yards (9.6 m) in diameter—the first recorded use of cast iron in gardening. Even when integrating elements common to other 18th-century landscape gardens, Hamilton was unique in the way he combined them.

From about 1750 onward, architecture began to assist a nature transformed to provide a series of pictures or scenes with a distinct atmosphere, intended to evoke a specific mood or emotion as, for example, delight or melancholy. It may well be that Hamilton designed some of the buildings himself, which included a Gothic tent or temple, a Roman mausoleum, a Temple of Bacchus—its interior designed by Robert Adam—a cascade, a grotto with artificial stalactites of innumerable pieces of feldspar to catch the sunbeams reflected from the lake's surface, a Turkish tent, and the torso of an abbey next to the lake. There were also several bridges, some in Chinese style, another emulating Palladio's bridge crossing the River Cismone, as well as the waterwheel to fill the lake with water from the River Mole. A watchtower, four stories or 36 yards (33 m), granted a full view of the estate and beyond into neighboring gardens. A hermitage (Hamilton wanted to hire a man to live there for seven years without cutting his hair or fingernails in exchange for food and a considerable sum of money at the end of the term) completed the design of the park as a circuit of three-dimensional pictures reminiscent of Italian *campagna* paintings or paintings by the school of Claude Lorrain, Gaspard Poussin, or Salvator Rosa.

The vineyard at Painshill was a rather uncommon feature for a landscape garden in England. Although a palatable sparkling white wine could be produced after some time of experimenting, the vineyard did not prove the great economic success Hamilton had hoped for to finance his ambitious project. The operation of a tile works on his estate, built for the same reason, failed to produce the necessary results, so that Hamilton had to go on borrowing money, as he had done from his friend Henry Fox and later from the bank of Henry Hoare, who is said to have built a Turkish tent and a hermitage at Stourhead in imitation of the buildings at Painshill. Nevertheless, Hamilton managed to hold out for 17 years after having lost the financial backing of a position at the royal court in 1756. But in 1773 he was finally forced to sell Painshill.

Hamilton retired to Bath but continued to influence the planning of other gardens. For example, he assisted William Petty-Fitzmaurice in designing a cascade for Bowood in 1781 and advised on the planting there—as he had done in laying out the grounds of Holland House in the early 1750s and again in the late 1760s. Fairly often, Painshill changed owners, most of whom did not interfere with the original design of the park. Some, such as Benjamin Bond Hopkins, who added a new house to the property, even continued Hamilton's policy of planting recently available species. However, the heyday of the garden as a magnet for visitors was over. Some of the follies began to deteriorate in the late 19th century, and, when the land was sold off in lots after World War II, the garden suffered further damage from neglect.

It is only since the formation of a group called the Friends of Painshill in the 1970s and the establishment of the Painshill Park Trust in 1981 that 158 acres (63 ha) of the original estate have been bought back in order to restore them as nearly as possible to Hamilton's original design. As only seven of Hamilton's elaborate follies have survived, some of them in poor condition, the trust's aim has turned out an ambitious one. However, much work has already been done to restore the Gothic tent, grotto, Chinese bridge, waterwheel, and even the Turkish tent. In addition, the vineyard has been replanted in order to make Painshill a self-supporting enterprise, the trust's declared intention. Achieving this aim will allow to continue the work that has already been done to restore the grounds to their former state of, in the words of Thomas Whately, writing in 1770, "perfect coalescence of park and garden."

Synopsis

1738	Painshill bought by Charles Hamilton
ca. 1740	Hamilton begins layout of gardens
1748–	Vineyard in cultivation
ca. 1750	Lake laid out
ca. 1764	Grotto by Joseph Lane of Tisbury finished
ca. 1770	Waterwheel replaced by horse-driven machine; Abbey ruin built (facade with tower at each end built of brick and covered in plaster to simulate stone)
1773	Painshill sold to Benjamin Bond Hopkins, who has new house built by Richard Jupp, replacing Hamilton's house
1799	William Moffat, new owner of Painshill, refuses to admit public to grounds
1830s	W.H. Cooper, new owner of Painshill, has large conservatory built at south end of house, which survives until at least 1904
1925	Doric Portico of Temple of Bacchus removed (whole building decays further and is removed about 25 years later)
1939–45	Troops quartered at Painshill; gardens decline, some decorations (e.g., those in grotto) destroyed
1981	Painshill Park Trust begins restoration of park

Further Reading

Hammerschmidt, Valentin, and Joachim Wilke, *Die Entdeckung der Landschaft: Englische Gärten des 18. Jahrhunderts*, Stuttgart, Germany: Deutsche Verlags-Anstalt, 1990

Hodges, Alison, "Painshill Park, Cobham, Surrey (1700–1800): Notes for a History of the Landscape Garden of Charles Hamilton," *Garden History* 2, no. 2 (1973)

Hodges, Alison, "Further Notes on Painshill, Cobham, Surrey: Charles Hamilton's Vineyard," *Garden History* 3, no. 1 (1974)

Jacques, David, *Georgian Gardens: The Reign of Nature*, London: Batsford, and Portland, Oregon: Timber Press, 1983

Sambrook, James, "Painshill Park in the 1760s," *Garden History* 8, no. 1 (1980)

Symes, Michael, "Charles Hamilton's Plantings at Painshill," *Garden History* 9, no. 2 (1983)

Symes, Michael, "Nature as the Bride of Art: The Design and Structure of Painshill," *Eighteenth Century* 8, no. 2 (1983)

ANGELA SCHWARZ

Palermo, Orto Botanico dell'Università de

Palermo, Sicily, Italy

Location: 0.5 mile (0.8 km) east of train station, on Via Lincoln

The principal botanic garden of Sicily, the Orto botanico dell'Università de Palermo (Palermo Botanic Garden) is famous for its fine buildings in a neo-Grecian style. It is the only botanic garden in Europe that grows a large number of subtropical trees in the open, thereby giving an impression of luxuriant, exotic vegetation. It is also important for having introduced several crop plants into the Mediterranean area.

The first public garden in Palermo was the Villa del populo, later called Villa Giulia, situated outside the city walls and very close to the waterfront. Goethe visited this garden in 1786 and praised its beauty. Two years later work started on a rectangular piece of land adjacent to the Villa Giulia, designated to become the Royal Botanic Garden, an institution of the newly founded Regia Accademia degli Studi, soon to become the Royal University of Palermo. Léon Dufourny, a French architect then studying Greek antiquities in Sicily, was chosen to plan the imposing garden buildings—a central *gimnasio* built in neo-Grecian style to house the Schola Regia Botanices (Royal School of Botany), the herbarium, and the professor's residence, flanked by a Caldarium (hothouse) and a Tepidarium (coldhouse). The vault of the *gimnasio*'s cupola shows the goddess Flora in the center and the inscription "miscuit utile dulci" (she mixes the useful with the sweet). Two neo-Egyptian sphinxes at the main entrance to the *gimnasio* were donated by members of the Sicilian aristocracy, and an aquarium at the far end of the garden was financed by Filippo Lopez y Royo, duke of Taurisani, then archbishop of Palermo and Monreale. All this still exists virtually unchanged, with the aquarium, or *ninfeo,* possibly the finest water lily garden in the world. The *gimnasio* is still used to house the historic herbaria and other scientific collections. Garden sculpture has also survived, as did the fine decoration of the *gimnasio,* which has recently been restored.

Ferdinand III, king of Sicily (as Ferdinand IV, king of Naples, later as Ferdinand I, king of both Sicilies) formally opened the Palermo Botanic Garden in 1795 and continued to support the institution.

The layout of the garden followed Linnaean principles, with rectangular flower beds and two main axes crossing at a rectangular angle, now called "the old system." Due to the favorable climate and rich water supply dating back to the city's Arabic period, a luxuriant, subtropical vegetation developed, which makes it an evergreen oasis within an otherwise often hot, dry, and dusty city. Alleys of palms, numerous *Citrus* cultivars, bamboo groves, monumental cycads, a pond full of papyrus, and an extensive collection of aloes and agaves, all grown in the open, make the visitor feel far outside Europe, the wind from the sea adding greatly to this sensation. A huge specimen of *Ficus macrophylla* subsp. *columnaris,* endemic to Lord Howe Island in the Pacific and now spreading over about 1,200 square meters (1,435 sq. yd.) in a banyan habit, gives an idea of evergreen subtropical forests. In addition to being a place of academic teaching, the garden thus became a place of inspiration for many, one of them being the German composer Richard Wagner, who is reported to have frequently visited the Palermo Botanic Garden while finishing his last opera, *Parsifal.*

Originally bought by Maria Carolina, the wife of Ferdinand III, but never erected on the proposed site in Caserta near Naples, a first greenhouse was built in 1823 in the Palermo Botanic Garden. Constructed in England at the end of the 18th century, it survives intact and, due to its old age, is a monument of its own. According to contemporary records, it was only heated on the rare occasions when snow was falling in Palermo. Few greenhouses followed, deemed largely unnecessary due to the site's fine climate. Today they house a large collection of succulents and of miscellaneous plants from the wet tropics.

The September Revolt of 1820 caused considerable damage in the garden, when thousands of pots were used to build barricades or as missiles to launch attacks. A new building to house the botanical institute was built at the beginning of the 20th century. While destruction during World War II was small, the whole institution was under great threat in the 1950s, when plans were discussed to give up the garden and use the land as a construction site and for building a new road.

Substantial enlargements of the garden in both 1820 and 1892 gave additional space for growing more plants, in particular testing crops intended for introduction into the Italian colonies, among them sugar cane, bananas, kapok trees, and notably, cotton. This part of the garden was called the Colonial Garden and fulfilled a role similar to that of the Royal Botanic Garden in Berlin or the Royal Botanic Gardens, Kew. In addition, a systematic section arranged according to Adolf Engler (the "new system") and a plant geography section were planted on the newly acquired space. The fine layout of the original garden was greatly obscured by these changes.

Having acted in the past also as an important gate of introduction for several crops and ornamental plants now widely cultivated in the Mediterranean area, such as mandarins, Japanese medlars, and *Washingtonia filifera* palms, the Palermo Botanic Garden continues to grow a remarkable collection of extra-European plants, often of a size found nowhere else in Europe. The garden offers simultaneously shadow, silence, and peace in an otherwise hectic Mediterranean city.

Synopsis

1789	Work started on piece of land next to Villa del Populo, outside city walls
1795	Inauguration of Royal Botanic Garden, as institution of Regia Accademia degli Studi; construction of Gimnasio, Caldarium, and Tepidarium completed, designed by Léon Dufourny
1797	Addition of aquarium
1820	Heavy damage during September Revolt, and first extension made to garden
1823	Erection of Carolina greenhouse
1892	Second extension of garden

ca. 1920   Garden becomes center for crops
            intended for cultivation in Italian
            colonies
1995   Careful restoration of garden buildings

Further Reading

Fici, Silvio, and Francesco Maria Raimondo, "On the Real Identity of Ficus Magnolioides," *Curtis's Botanical Magazine* 6, no. 13 (1996)

Raimondo, Francesco Maria, and P. Massola, "L'Orto botanico dell'Università de Palermo," in *Orti botanici, giardini alpini, arboreti italiani,* edited by Raimondo, Palermo: Edizioni Grifo, 1992

Raimondo, Francesco Maria, et al., *L'Orto botanico di Palermo; The Palermo Botanical Garden,* Palermo: Editrice Arbor, 1993

H. WALTER LACK

Paradise Garden

The paradise myth or concept of paradise as garden is one of humankind's oldest ideals. Paradise was the secure, ideal, and everlasting garden. The tradition of the Western garden can be traced directly to the continuity of a garden tradition stemming from the ancient empires of the river valleys of the Tigris and Euphrates; the Achaemanians, the greatest gardeners of the ancient world; and Cyrus the Great's garden at his capital at Pasargadae. Later, the Homeric Elysian Fields—a place of perfect bliss and immortality—recalled the Sumerian-Babylonian paradise.

The biblical Eden of the Old Testament was an earthly paradise that rivaled the remote and unattainable celestial abode of God. In the Greek translation of the Old Testament the word *paradeisosi* is used for *garden.* Thus paradise became identified with the Garden of Eden. The Hebrews derived *pardes* (meaning "garden") during their Babylonian captivity. The English word *paradise* is a translation of the Old Persian *pairidaeza* (walled garden), from the Latin *paradisus,* which was derived from the Greek essayist-historian Xenophon in 401 B.C. Xenophon's writings were believed to have inspired Virgil to plant a *paradisus* or enclosed Persian-style garden with groves of trees around a Roman temple.

A mystical feeling for flowers and a love for gardens were considered ancient Persian characteristics. Cyrus the Great built the oldest Persian garden at Pasargadae in about 546 B.C. Only a schematic representation of the original garden is possible; however, it is known that the garden was designed to complement buildings and served to unite the official and residential palaces. Its essential elements included a geometric plan defined by a carved stone watercourse and trees and shrubs planted symmetrically in plots. Within the garden two pavilions stood on raised rectangular platforms of dressed stone. Each building had columned porticoes and consisted of one room with thick walls of mud brick. This design remained the prototype for garden pavilions for centuries.

Greek culture and the concept of the garden as described in Xenophon's writings spread throughout the eastern Mediterranean and far beyond with the conquests of Alexander of Macedonia. Inspiration for Aristotle's Lyceum at Athens, the famous botanical garden, came from the curious plants that Alexander's officers discovered on their Oriental campaigns. The School of Athens, where Plato taught in the tree-planted gymnasium of the Academy, created the association between philosophy and gardens. Later philosophers owned gardens adorned with classical features that included shrines to the muses in the form of a rocky grotto or a *nymphaeum* watered by a fountain or spring, shady porticoes for sculpture display, and tree-lined walks.

Like the royal garden of Cyrus at Pasargadae, the Roman garden was attached to a villa and enclosed with courtyards and colonnades. The garden as a place of inspiration and repose was unknown to the pragmatic Roman world until the second century B.C., when the influence of the Hellenistic world began to penetrate Roman society. Artistic and social associations eventually replaced the early religious ones of the garden as a sacred grove dedicated to a god or goddess or surrounding a tomb. Although the component parts remained the same, the small temples, grottoes, and nymphaeums originally dedicated to the muses and tutelary deities now served as architectural ornaments. An innovative feature common to Roman and Renaissance gardens was the incorporation of *topia,* reliefs, and paintings portraying garden architecture in a picturesque setting of rugged mountains and seaside cliffs or on shores of lakes and rivers, which were used to decorate the walls of porticoes, thereby bringing the gardens themselves right into the buildings.

In *Italian Gardens* Georgina Masson writes that the particular interest of the Pompeian garden of antiquity lies in the fact that despite limited space it contained many of the features of later Roman gardens from which those of the Renaissance drew their inspiration. Two of the most important features in this respect are the relationship of the house and the garden and the use of an axial plan. The main living room usually opened into the courtyard on one side of the axis. The garden was typically accessed from the center of the house. On a wall at one end of this room a painted garden perspective, complete with trees, fountains, and trellises, prolonged this view even farther. This type of trompe l'oeil painting was employed in porticoes and peristyles to give a feeling of greater space and, like the Greek *topia*, seemed to bring the out-of-doors right into the house.

The gardens of the Middle Ages were small cloisters sheltered within the walls of castles and cities. The feudal social system and the constant turmoil and upheavals of the period dictated defensible walled cities of concentrated population densities. Therefore, it was in the monasteries that the tradition of the contemplative garden prevailed. Saint Augustine reinstated the Platonic tradition of teaching in a garden when he first assembled his followers in the African province of Hippo in a garden of a villa given by his friend Valerius. Following Augustine's example, monastic orders established themselves in the ruins of Roman villas in Italy. At the end of the fifth century Saint Benedict established the first monastic order in Western Europe in a grotto of the ruins of Nero's villa at Subiaco. Thus, the monastery cloister evolved from the colonnaded peristyle of the Roman country house. The garden of the Abbey of Casino was described as "a paradise in the roman fashion."

At the early-ninth-century Benedictine monastery of Saint Gall in Switzerland, plants were grown in rectangular beds, each one usually reserved for a separate species. These were further divided into garden simples, which included roses, lilies, gladioli, and scented herbs such as rue, rosemary, and sage; and vegetable gardens, which included leeks, lettuces, garlic, parsley, chervil, and poppies. An orchard, which also served as the cemetery, included pears, plums, mulberries, and fig and nut trees. The secular pleasure gardens of the Saracen emirs and Norman kings first made their appearance in medieval Sicily. Part garden, part hunting enclosure, these "pleasure parks" were modeled on the Oriental paradises. Although their effect on subsequent garden development in Italy was small, they did serve to keep alive the tradition of the pleasure garden.

In the 14th century Petrarch envisaged the garden as a proper setting for the poet and man of learning in the ancient world. By the 15th century Cosimo de' Medici's Platonic Academy was holding gatherings at his villa at Carregi. The study of *humane literae* (classical literature and history) was the precursor of the humanist movement of the 16th century and inevitably ensured Florence's reputation as the cradle of the Renaissance. The humanists' aim was to recapture the spirit of the ancient world by perfecting the ideals of beauty and knowledge in the "complete man" of the Renaissance.

As Stuart Wrede and William Howard Adams point out in their introduction to *Denatured Visions*, technological and economic transformations in the 19th and 20th centuries have had a profound impact on the landscape and attitudes toward nature. The relationship of modern architecture and landscape has been complex and often contradictory. Modern architectural theorists emphasized internal functional requirements and structural logic and seemed to have little to say about building to site (with the notable exception of Frank Lloyd Wright). Yet modern architecture also aspired to a new relationship between buildings, their inhabitants, and nature. This shift was primarily utilitarian, focusing on concern for light, air, exercise, and rest. The implications were most radical in urban design: the traditional city and its cohesive urban fabric were eschewed for freestanding towers in parklike settings intended to achieve an immediate relation between nature and the inhabitants. The dematerialization of the masonry wall into glass also contributed to a radical restructuring of the relations between inside and outside.

The modern park has also increasingly moved away from its landscape roots. With the mass movement to the suburbs and free access to the countryside provided by the automobile, the landscaped urban park seems to have lost its constituency. Recreation and amusement become the defining force, to the point where the city itself has become the park. Parks are now designed as a microcosm of the city.

The private garden, however, became the most problematic landscape type of the 20th century. Associated in earlier eras with aristocracy and wealth, the garden seemed to have no future at a time when the design professions were shifting their emphasis to meeting the requirements of a modern mass society. Yet gardens have mediated the deeper symbolic meanings and myths that nature holds for humankind. The demise in the 20th century of the garden's previous form and the absence to date of any vital new tradition are two of the more troubling aspects of contemporary culture.

Further Reading

Farrar, Linda, *Ancient Roman Gardens*, Stroud, Gloucestershire: Sutton, 1998

Francis, Mark, and Randolf T. Hester, Jr., editors, *The Meaning of Gardens: Idea, Place, and Action*, Cambridge, Massachusetts: MIT Press, 1990

Hartt, Frederick, *History of Italian Renaissance Art: Painting, Sculpture, Architecture*, New York: Abrams, 1969; London: Thames and Hudson, 1970; 4th edition, revised by David Wilkins, New York: Abrams, and London: Thames and Hudson, 1994

Hussey, Chrisopher, *English Gardens and Landscapes, 1700–1750,* London: Country Life, and New York: Funk and Wagnall, 1967

Jackson-Stops, Gervase, compiler, *An English Arcadia: Designs for Gardens and Garden Buildings in the Care of the National Trust, 1600–1990,* London: The National Trust, 1991; as *An English Arcadia, 1600–1900: Designs for Gardens and Garden Buildings in the Care of the National Trust of Great Britain,* Washington, D.C.: American Institute of Architects Press, 1991

Masson, Georgina, *Italian Villas and Palaces,* London: Thames and Hudson, and New York: Abrams, 1959; new edition, London: Thames and Hudson, 1966

Masson, Georgina, *Italian Gardens,* London: Thames and Hudson, and New York: Abrams, 1961; revised edition, Woodbridge, Suffolk: Antique Collector's Club, 1987

Moynihan, Elizabeth B., *Paradise As a Garden: In Persia and Mughal India,* New York: Braziller, 1979

Neckar, Lance M., "The Park: Prospect and Refuge," *Reflections: The Journal of the School of*

Architecture, University of Illinois at Urbana-Champaign 6 (Spring 1989)

Petruccioli, Attilio, editor, *Gardens in the Time of the Great Muslim Empires,* Leyden and New York: Brill, 1997

Price, Uvedale, *An Essay on the Picturesque As Compared with the Sublime and the Beautiful,* London, 1794; new edition, 2 vols., 1796–98

Shepard, John Chiene, and Geoffrey Alan Jellicoe, *Italian Gardens of the Renaissance,* London: Benn, and New York: Scribner, 1925; 5th edition, New York: Princeton Architectural Press, 1993

Woods, May, *Visions of Arcadia: European Gardens from Renaissance to Rococo,* London: Arum, 1996

Wrede, Stuart, and William Howard Adams, editors, *Denatured Visions: Landscape and Culture in the Twentieth Century,* New York: Museum of Modern Art, 1991

PAUL ARMSTRONG

Parc Monceau

Paris, France

Location: 35, Boulevard de Courcelles, Paris, France, 8e arrondissement

The Parc Monceau owns its celebrity to the duc de Chartres and the painter and garden architect Carmontelle (1717–1806), who with this most famous *jardin anglo-chinois* created a typical example of the late 18th-century French variant of the landscape garden. The older, regular structures and the pavilion became part of the irregular landscape garden, which at that time was situated outside of the town on the Monceau plain near the village of Batignolles. Such buildings with gardens (*folies*) could give the illusion of being at the same time in a natural ambience and not too far from urban life, and they were used for social festivities. The character of the so-called Folie de Chartres and its structures are well known from Carmontelle's lavish publication, *Jardin de Monceau* (1779), illustrated with 18 large-size etchings. The author was aware that his creation fit perfectly with the modern French style of his time, and declared it to be a result of French national taste.

The Monceau garden contained many attractions and small buildings (*fabriques*): a famous winter garden and several greenhouses; a mill and a ruined medieval castle; a *ferme ornée;* ruins of an antique Roman temple of Mars; an island with artificial rocks and a Dutch windmill; an Arabian belvedere called Minaret; an Italian vineyard; the famous *Naumachie* or *Cirque,* which imitated the relics of the antique *canopus* in Hadrian's villa (on the border of an oval water basin with an obelisk was set up a row of pseudo-antique Renaissance columns that came from the unfinished funerary chapel for the Valois family, which had been begun in Saint-Denis on command of Catherine de Médicis); a "Wood of Tombs" with a pyramid; Tartarian and Turkish tents; a Chinese *jeu de bague;* a temple; and several statues. Only a few of these *fabriques* have survived.

The idea of combining "tous les temps et tous les lieux" (all times and all places) in one garden, as was realized to a high degree in the Folie de Chartres, is typical of the *jardin anglo-chinois.* It was this feature that was often criticized, both in garden theory and in the special case of the Monceau garden. Already in the

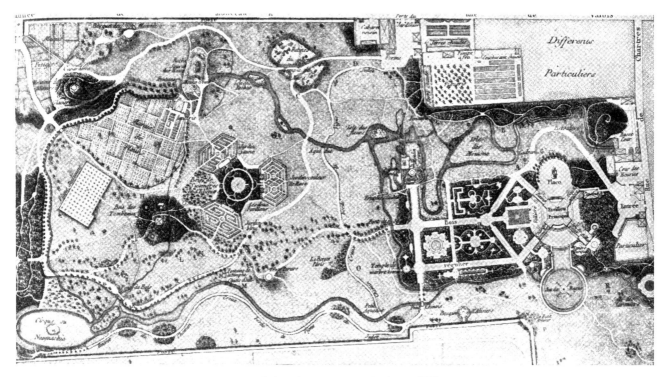

General plan of Parc Monceau, Paris, ca. 1775

1780s the gardener Blaikie changed several parts of the garden and abolished some of Carmontelle's garden structures. Lacking the necessary constant care, others fell into decay. In 1800 propositions for a new use of the park were ruminated—including using it as a cemetery or as exhibition space for Alexandre Lenoir's Musée des Monuments Français—but these were not realized. Festivities and shows took place, such as in 1797 the descent of the first parachutist, André-Jacques Garnerin.

The second important phase of the garden came under Napoléon III during the Second Empire, with Adolphe Alphand (1817–91), who restored the plantations and buildings. The new character of the Parc Monceau, however, was above all due to Georges-Eugène Baron Haussmann (1809–91) and his urban planning. The dimensions of the park were reduced to half of its size, but the new elegant buildings on the east, south, and west border of the park, owned by wealthy citizens, open with small gardens to the public space. The effect is mutual. On one hand the Parc Monceau seems a huge private garden surrounded by private buildings. These, on the other hand, brought a new, urban quality to this park, which Haussmann in his memoirs defined as the "most luxurious and most elegant promenade of Paris."

Synopsis

1769–73	Philippe d'Orléans, duc de Chartres (later Philippe Egalité), commands architect Louis-Marie Colignon to build pavilion in formal garden
1773	Duc de Chartres decides to build much larger landscape garden and buys neighboring plots
1773–79	Garden architect Louis Carrogis (called Carmontelle) designs new landscape garden
1779	Publication of Carmontelle's *Jardin de Monceau*
1783	Scottish gardener Thomas Blaikie takes over direction of garden and changes several features of Carmontelle's garden
1787–88	Construction of Claude-Nicolas Ledoux's *bureau d'observation,* a customs house (called the Rotonde) on garden border; new customs frontier of Paris, established by Fermiers Généraux, includes Monceau garden
1793	Philippe Egalité executed
1794–	Garden opened to public
1802–6	Pavilion replaced by another building

1805	Napoléon I offers garden to his chancellor, Cambacérès (who gives it back in 1808)
1814	Garden restored to d'Orléans family
1848	During 1848 Revolution, garden used for newly established national workshops
1852–60	Controversy concerning property between d'Orléans family and State
1860	Expropriation of garden for Haussmann's urban planning; bought by City of Paris; Haussmann sells more than half of garden plot to banker Emile Péreire, who builds *hôtels* on it; garden thus reduced to about 21 acres (8.5 ha); earned sum used by Haussmann for reconstruction of remaining garden
1861	Adolphe Alphand renovates garden (with help of architect Davioud); opening ceremony of new Parc Monceau and of adjoining Boulevard Malesherbes
late 19th C.	Several monuments and statues set up, including arcade of Renaissance Hôtel de Ville (destroyed by fire during Paris Commune in 1871)

Further Readings

Adams, William Howard, *The French Garden, 1500–1800*, New York: Braziller, and London: Scolar Press, 1979

Lévêque, Jean Jacques, *Jardins de Paris*, Paris: Hachette, 1982

Mosser, Monique, and Georges Teyssot, editors, *The History of Garden Design*, London: Thames and Hudson, 1991

Peterson, Corinne, Françoise Pochon, and Nicolas Le Barazer, *Guide des parcs et jardins de France*, Paris: Éditions Princesse, 1979

Robinson, William, *The Parks, Promenades, and Gardens of Paris*, London, 1869; 3rd edition, as *The Parks and Gardens of Paris*, 1883

Soprani, Anne, *Paris jardins*, Paris: Paris-Méditerranée, 1998

Wiebenson, Dora, *The Picturesque Garden in France*, Princeton, New Jersey: Princeton University Press, 1978

IRIS LAUTERBACH

Park

Rulers of ancient urban societies created parks in their cities or enclosed natural areas for use as parks. However, when discussing these ancient endeavors, it is difficult to categorize them and discuss them in terms of what we now know as parks, gardens, garden orchards, and hunting reserves.

When urban civilizations began in Mesopotamia, Egypt, and China about 3000–1500 B.C., there began a dichotomy between the city and country. The response was to develop natural settings within the urban environment. Large enclosed parks, the privilege of royalty and wealthy individuals, served multiple purposes including providing food for the table, hunting for sport, entertaining guests, and relaxing. Although most parks were private, there are indications that some parks were open to the citizens living in the urban area. Later urban societies also had parks, such as the Greco-Roman societies, Persian and Arabic societies, Aztec and Inca societies, and medieval European societies. Again, these are difficult to distinguish from gardens or from large-scale urban landscaping.

During his travels Gilgamesh (a Sumerian king, Mesopotamia, ca. 2750 B.C.) encountered a city that had one-third of its territory planted as a garden orchard. And while other Mesopotamian kings created parks and gardens, Sennacherib (an Assyrian king, Mesopotamia, ca. 704–681 B.C.) re-created entire ecosystems, including a southern Babylonian marsh and Amanus mountain habitats. One of these was the now famous hanging garden thought to have been in Babylon, but which now appears to have been one of Sennacherib's gardens in Nineveh.

Chinese emperors also had large parks. The *yuan* was an open royal park or hunting reserve, while a *yu* was an enclosed park. Some emperors also had more private parks or gardens to which they gave individual names. One of the best known was the Ling yu (or Lingyou), the "Garden of Intelligence" or, more accurately, the "Garden for the Promotion/Encouragement of Knowledge," which Wen Wang established about 1030 B.C.

Persian *pairidaeza* (*paradeisos* in Greek), or paradise garden parks, greatly influenced Greek, Roman, and

Arabic gardens and parks. Roman parks also included the *therotrophium,* a large wooded area surrounded by a park wall, and the *vivarium,* an enclosed private park. The former became what was known as a chase (which was not enclosed) in Europe about 1460, and the latter became a vivarium or menagerie in Europe in about 1600 and 1712, respectively. The word *park* (or *parke*) appeared in writings during the 13th century. According to the *Oxford English Dictionary,* a park was originally an enclosed tract of land held by royal grant for keeping animals for the hunt (as was the case with the ancient parks). These parks were distinguished from both the chase and forest by being enclosed and by not having any special regulations. Modern European parks for public use were derived from these large royal tracts. However, there has not been a well-defined consensus on what a park is, or what a park is to be used for. Even in recent times the diversity of parks and their use is an indication that the concept has many definitions.

Cortés, in the early 1500s, described large areas surrounding the Aztec capital that were park orchards. They were well planted with trees of many different kinds. These forest gardens were continued through the use of flower gardens in the cities and within private homes. Colonial explorers of the 16th and 17th centuries also found garden parks in India, Southeast Asia, and Indonesia.

Wilderness areas, particularly forests and mountains, were still frightening places to the Europeans during this period. These areas were also considered barren unless cultivated or otherwise used. However, during the 18th century, Europeans began to overcome their fears as they developed these natural areas into rural and urban environments. Wild nature became a place to cherish rather than destroy, and nature was recognized as a healthy environment for recreation and relaxation.

As urban areas became larger and more dense, the need for natural environments within these cityscapes increased. Between the 16th and 19th centuries, European and American cities developed commons, greens, public squares, parade grounds, promenades, and public gardens to alleviate the urban environment. By the 19th century, many European cities were large and industrialized; much of the population lived in these cities, most of the nonurban land was rural, and wild nature was scarce. Natural areas within the cities (what were to become parks) were a civilized re-creation of wild nature and were considered beneficial. While the once scarce and orderly patterns of agriculture and agroforestry had been considered an improvement over the abundant and irregular disarray of nature, now the opposite was true.

Many European countries favored the formal garden, but the British preferred the informal landscape garden with its large fields, rolling hills, winding streams, clus-

tered vegetation, and scattered trees. European public parks began in Paris, Berlin, and Magdeburg during the early 19th century. Existing royal parks and estate properties within the London region were also transformed into public parks. London's St. James, Hyde, Green, and Regent's Parks were open to the public early in the 19th century. Work began on Birkenhead Park near Liverpool in 1844 using public funds to landscape a barren piece of property specifically as a public park. This park had meadows for sports (such as cricket and archery), winding drives for carriages, pathways for pedestrians, lakes, and gentle hills (made from the excavations that created the lakes). Surrounding lands, enhanced in value due to the park, were sold as residences with the money from these sales going to pay for the park. This park, its design, and the methods used to establish it inspired the creation of parks throughout England and the United States.

James Rosier, one of the early New England explorers, remarked on a 1605 visit to the Maine countryside (with its open, hilly, sparsely treed ecology), "It did all resemble a stately Parke." (quoted in Cronon's *Changes in the Card*). This parklike environment was the result of fires set by the region's Native Americans. However, like Europe in earlier years, the United States had extensive wilderness to "conquer" and did not feel the need for large parks. But this was to change, as it had in Europe. Several early American municipal plans incorporated commons, public squares, and public gardens into their urban landscapes. Boston Common was created in 1634; the original 1682 plans for Philadelphia included public squares; and Savannah, Georgia, had public gardens in 1733.

These public areas, however, had relatively little influence on the development of public parks. A more influential precursor to the public park in the United States was the landscaped cemetery. These landscaped rural cemeteries near large cities provided relaxing walks and picnicking; some even produced guidebooks. Examples include Mount Auburn in Boston (1831), Laurel Hill in Philadelphia (1836), and Greenwood in New York (1838). Proponents of public parks, such as Andrew Jackson Downing, used the popularity of these places to convince civic leaders and municipal authorities to develop parks. These individuals felt that parks, like other 19th-century civic improvements (such as better housing, improved sanitation, and "proper" or "moral" recreation), were important to the civil development of urban citizens. Parks were considered to be healthy environments, to produce moral inspiration, to be aesthetically pleasing, and to provide wholesome recreation opportunities. It was also the Romantic period, when managed, picturesque nature brought relief from harsh urban conditions.

In addition, British parks influenced the development of parks in the United States. For example, Frederick Law

Olmsted visited Birkenhead in 1851 while on a trip to England. Olmsted was still a "scientific farmer" and not yet landscaping parks, but the methods used to create this park out of a barren clay farm and its Romantic pastoral scenery greatly impressed him. It was a "people's park," where all classes were admitted: a significant change from the past when only the upper classes enjoyed such amenities. Along with the concept of a park for all citizens came the notion that public parks should be a municipal responsibility and should be supported by taxes.

Several individuals are well known for their landscape gardening during this period, but few were working on the new park concept. Jean Charles Alphand was doing so in Paris, John Nash planned Regent's Park in London, and Joseph Paxton planned Birkenhead Park in Liverpool. An initial effort at creating a similar public, landscaped urban park in the United States was made in Washington, D.C. Andrew Jackson Downing designed a park for the Washington Mall in 1851, but it was left unfinished when he died in 1852. This design for the mall was a continuation of the proposal Pierre-Charles L'Enfant (who laid out the plan for the capital) had made for this area, which he called the grand avenue.

Downing designed the Washington Mall as a "national park," with landscaped gardens and a public museum of living trees and shrubs. By "national park," he meant a park that could serve the national capital's needs and set an example to other cities that might be encouraged to develop their own urban parks. Downing felt that the mall park would inspire other urban parks, just as Mount Auburn Cemetery had inspired other landscaped cemeteries. After work stopped in 1852, the mall's development occurred piecemeal over an extended period. While Downing's efforts at the mall did not inspire other urban parks, his writings on the subject did.

It was New York City that succeeded in developing the first landscaped urban park intended for use by all classes of the population. Proponents for a public park in New York included Downing, William Cullen Bryant, and Horace Greeley. Downing, in addition to being a landscape gardener, was author of *A Treatise on the Theory and Practice of Landscape Gardening, Adapted to North America* (1841) and publisher of *The Horticulturist*. Bryant was the editor of the *New York Evening Post*, and Greeley was the editor of the *New York Daily Tribune*. Other large cities had their own proponents as well; however, a public park in the style of the new British parks was still a novelty.

New York's Central Park was the first of its kind in the United States. An act authorizing the acquisition of land for the park was passed in 1853, and the process of land acquisition continued until 1856. At that time a Board of Commissioners for Central Park was established, which hired a chief engineer, Egbert L. Viele. By 1857 the board was looking for a superintendent and

revising its plans for the park, having disapproved of Viele's preliminary plans. Olmsted became the superintendent and worked with Viele until a new plan for the park could be solicited. A competition was held, and in 1858 the winner was a plan, known as "Greensward," submitted by Olmsted and Calvert Vaux.

Although there was much talk at the time about parks alleviating the harsh urban environments, there were few large cities prior to the mid-19th century. Manhattan, where Central Park is located, was one of the larger cities, but at the time it was still located at the southern tip of the island and had not yet reached the area where Central Park would be located. Nevertheless, Olmsted was a futurist and justified the location, stating:

> The time will come when New York will be built up, when all the grading and filling will be done, and when the picturesquely-varied, rocky formations of the Island will have been converted into foundations for rows of monotonous straight streets, and piles of erect, angular buildings. There will be no suggestion left of its present varied surface, with the single exception of the Park. (quoted in Rybczynski)

Central Park took about 20 years to complete, had as many as 3,600 workers at a time, and cost about $13 million in mid-19th century dollars. It opened to the public gradually as various sections of the park were completed, and each section proved to be immensely popular. Central Park's popularity sparked what Downing had earlier called "parkomania" throughout the United States. During the 1860s parks were being developed in Baltimore, Boston, Brooklyn, Chicago, Detroit, Hartford (Connecticut), and Philadelphia. While other cities followed New York City's example of creating individual parks, Buffalo (New York) began to plan a coordinated park effort. Buffalo was considering three sites for a park in 1868 when Olmsted suggested using all three with connecting "parkways," and Buffalo's park committee agreed. However, it was Boston that established the first American metropolitan park commission and park system in 1892. A few years later, in 1895, Essex County, New Jersey, established the United States' first county park system.

Regional park systems increased in number gradually until they became widely popular around the second decade of the 20th century. The early 20th century was a time of urban decentralization and suburbanization. Many cities were too congested to build anything other than small parks in their downtown areas, but larger parks could often be created in the less-populated suburbs. Many suburban developments were simply extensions of the congested urban areas. A handful, however, were better planned and included large residential lots, tree-lined roads, and parks. Some of these landscaped suburban developments included Evergreen Hamlet near Pittsburgh (early 1850s), Llewellyn Park in New Jersey (about 12 miles (19.3 km) west of New York City, late 1850s), Irving Park at Tarrytown, New York (late 1850s), and Riverside near Chicago (late 1860s). These developments were interrupted during the Civil War and the later economic depression of 1873 but became widespread in the early 1900s and then again after World War II.

At the time Central Park was developed, landscape gardening was popular in Europe and elsewhere; however, it did not apply to what Olmsted was doing at Central Park. Olmsted coined the term *landscape architecture* for the kind of work he was doing. This was not the first time this term was used, which was probably in 1840, with the publication of John Claudius Loudon's *The Landscape Gardening and Landscape Architecture of the Late Humphry Repton, Esq., Being His Entire Works on These Subjects*. Park landscaping in Olmstead's sense was to design a pleasing and relaxing artistic creation using natural materials on existing landforms. Some considered Olmstead a dreamer, and municipalities, developers, and estate owners often rejected his plans as expensive, impractical, or too unusual.

Other landscape architects in the 19th century included Horace W.S. Cleveland (who designed parks in Boston, Chicago, and Minneapolis as well as writing *Landscape Architecture as Applied to the Wants of the West* [1873]), Robert M. Copeland (who designed parks in Boston, New England, New York, and Pennsylvania), Henry A.S. Dearborn (who designed Mount Auburn Cemetery), David B. Douglas (who designed Greenwood Cemetery), Charles Eliot (who designed parks in New England), John Notman (who designed Laurel Hill Cemetery), and James C. Sidney (who, with Andrew Adams, designed Fairmount Park). In 1899 a small number of practitioners, including F.L. Olmsted, Jr., founded the American Society of Landscape Architects. Harvard University established the first academic program in landscape architecture in 1900 with F.L. Olmsted, Jr., the first professor. Thus, the vocation of the 19th century became a profession in the 20th century.

Twentieth-century urban landscaped parks throughout the world have developed out of a combination of historical precedents, modern needs, and cultural influences. The Jardins de Turia (Valencia, Spain) was established in the Turia riverbed that curved through the city after the river had been diverted for flood control purposes. Parque Tezozomoc (Azcapotzalco, Mexico City) was established in a densely populated and polluted section of town in order to relieve both of these conditions. Sutton Place (Surrey, United Kingdom) was designed to revitalize an estate park originally begun in 1525. Le Parc de la Corderie Royale (Rochefort-sur-Mer, France) landscapes a long, narrow rope factory originally used by Louis XIV's navy that also parallels the Charente River. Grand Mall Park (Yokohama City, Japan) creates an urban landscape adjacent to the city's art museum. NMB Bank (Amsterdam, Netherlands) provides a park setting in a heavily urbanized area alongside the country's third largest bank. Brion Family Cemetery (San Vito, Italy) enhances an existing urban cemetery with a park. Joondalup Central Park (Perth, Australia) connects the city with its natural environment and provides a refreshing change from the area's dry savannah.

The 20th century was also a time during which state parks developed, as did national parks, wilderness parks, marine parks, and game parks. Active recreation and conservation became important objectives in park design and use. Yellowstone National Park, established in 1872 as the first national park, was soon followed by other national parks in the United States and throughout the world. These parks were followed by wilderness parks with restricted access and activities. These newer kinds of parks, however, are natural areas that are maintained but not planned or landscaped in any significant way, and therefore are different from the parks considered here, even though some are in urban areas.

Parks have many purposes and serve an increasing number of people. With wilderness and other natural areas decreasing, it is inevitable that urban and suburban parks will assume an increasingly important role in the leisure-time pursuits of future generations.

Further Reading

Birnbaum, Charles A., and Lisa E. Crowder, editors, *Pioneers of American Landscape Design*, Washington, D.C.: U.S. Department of the Interior, National Park Service, Cultural Resources, Preservation Assistance Division, Historical Landscape Initiative, 1993

Birnbaum, Charles A., and Julie K. Fix, *Pioneers of American Landscape Design II*, Washington, D.C.: U.S. Department of the Interior, National Park Service, Cultural Resources, Heritage Preservation Services, Historical Landscape Initiative, 1995

Chadwick, George F., *The Park and the Town: Public Landscape in the 19th and 20th Centuries*, New York: Praeger, and London: Architectural Press, 1966

Cox, Thomas R., "From Hot Springs to Gateway: The Evolving Concept of Public Parks, 1832–1976," *Environmental Review* 5, no. 1 (1980)

Doell, Charles E., and Gerald B. Fitzgerald, *A Brief History of Parks and Recreation in the United States*, Chicago: Athletic Institute, 1954

Forman, L. Ronald, et al., *Audubon Park: An Urban Eden*, Baton Rouge, Louisiana: Friends of the Zoo, 1985

Lancaster, Clay, *Prospect Park Handbook*, New York: Rawls, 1967

Laurie, Michael, *An Introduction to Landscape Architecture,* New York: American Elsevier, 1975; 2nd edition, New York: Elsevier, 1986

Loughlin, Caroline, and Catherine Anderson, *Forest Park,* Columbia: University of Missouri Press, 1986

Olmsted, Frederick Law, *The Papers of Frederick Law Olmsted,* 6 vols., Baltimore: Johns Hopkins University Press, 1977–92

Olmsted, Frederick Law, *The Papers of Frederick Law Olmsted, Supplementary Series,* vol. 1, edited by Charles E. Beveridge and Carolyn F. Hoffman, Baltimore, Maryland: Johns Hopkins University Press, 1997

Pregill, Philip, and Nancy Volkman, *Landscapes in History: Design and Planning in the Western Tradition,* New York: Van Nostrand Reinhold, 1993

Rosenzweig, Roy, and Elizabeth Blackmar, *The Park and the People: A History of Central Park,* Ithaca, New York: Cornell University Press, 1992

Rybczynski, Witold, *A Clearing in the Distance: Frederick Law Olmsted and America in the Nineteenth Century,* New York: Scribner, 1999

Schuyler, David, *The New Urban Landscape: The Redefinition of City Form in Nineteenth-Century America,* Baltimore, Maryland: Johns Hopkins University Press, 1986

Simo, Melanie, *100 Years of Landscape Architecture: Some Patterns of a Century,* Washington, D.C.: ASLA Press, 1999

Thomas, Keith, *Man and the Natural World: Changing Attitudes in England, 1500–1800,* London: Lane, 1983; as *Man and the Natural World: A History of the Modern Sensibility,* New York: Pantheon Books, 1983

Van Erp-Houtepen, Anne, "The Etymological Origin of the Garden," *Journal of Garden History* 6, no. 3 (1986)

White, Theophilus Ballou, *Fairmount, Philadelphia's Park: A History,* Philadelphia: Art Alliance Press, 1975

Zaitzevsky, Cynthia, *Frederick Law Olmsted and the Boston Park System,* Cambridge, Massachusetts: Harvard University Press, 1982

VERNON N. KISLING, JR.

Parkway

A parkway is a linear park containing a road designed for scenic and recreational enjoyment. A variety of recreational opportunities, such as hiking, camping, picnicking, swimming, fishing, museums, history exhibits, lodging, and refreshment, may also be provided in the park. The emphasis of the park, however, is the parkway road and its associated landscape.

Parkways originated in the United States. The era of the American Parkway lasted from roughly 1920 until World War II. Parkways evolved from carriage roads, such as the Approach Road at Biltmore Estate in Asheville, North Carolina, developed in the 1890s. The final work of Frederick Law Olmsted, the road is a carefully orchestrated series of connected landscape experiences. Parkways are comparable to the Biltmore Approach Road in the shared intention of releasing travelers from psychological strain through immersion in landscape scenery. This objective is achieved through careful location of the route, sensitive attention to topography, and manipulation of views. The result is a fluid driving experience that allows concentration to shift from the road to the road's landscape.

In the early 1900s the profession of landscape architecture grappled with issues related to automobile roads. John Charles Olmsted (1915) advocated the adoption of parkways for rural and suburban areas, as "curvilinear pleasure traffic routes, especially such as include or adjoin pleasing natural landscape features, . . . [parkways] frequently serve more or less completely as local parks."

The first parkway, modeled on J.C. Olmsted's "informal, curvilinear pleasure route" was the Bronx River Parkway. The project was initiated in 1906 as a cleanup of land adjacent to the Bronx River. At first the land was to be simply a green buffer/park for the river. In the early 1920s, however, an automobile road was added as a pleasure drive. It was instantly popular. Westchester County, New York, just north of the Bronx, developed a series of interconnected parks and parkways in the mid 1920s and 1930s to lure urbanites to the suburbs. The Westchester County Park Commission established a collaborative approach to solving parkway design problems by employing landscape architects, such as Gilmore Clarke and Stanley Abbott, and civil engineers such as Jay Downer. The results were positive as observable in the Saw Mill River Parkway and others. The federal government adopted the interdisciplinary approach on an even more complex level.

The Great Depression stimulated parkway projects such as the Blue Ridge Parkway (467 miles [752 km]

Curve alignment between road and landscape, Blue Ridge Parkway, United States
Copyright Mary E. Myers

long) and required federal agencies to work together as design and construction partners. This was the peak period for parkway construction. The Taconic Parkway (New York), Colonial Parkway (Virginia), Merritt Parkway (Connecticut), George Washington Parkway (Virginia), Skyline Drive (Virginia), and Blue Ridge Parkway (North Carolina and Virginia) were either designed or built during the 1930s. Although parkways continued to be built after the depression, and some are being built today, government financial support ebbed. Transportation resources since World War II have been directed to the development of state highways and the Federal Interstate System.

Parkways have many design attributes, including characteristics that enhance safety, control speed, strengthen scenic and recreational qualities and provide connections with the regional landscape. Parkways pioneered standards of road safety that came to be the norm for highway design around the world. They were the first roads to be automobile only. Commercial trucks and buses are not permitted on parkways, nor are parkway alignments, tunnels, and bridges designed for these vehicles. The elimination of larger vehicles

makes for a safer driving environment. Parkways were also the first roads to separate directional traffic, thereby reducing the chances of head-on collisions and allowing concentration to shift from the traffic to the landscape. By limiting access to the road, parkways also eliminate the frequent access points that interrupt driving tempo and create safety hazards. Parkways accommodate cross traffic safely with bridges. Their curvilinear layout and changing views of near and distant landscape give an interesting rhythm to the road, a changing tempo that relieves the monotony of driving and keeps drivers alert.

In addition, parkway speed is slower than standard highway speed. High speeds require greater attention to the road, blur foreground detail, and reduce peripheral vision. Scenic parkways such as the Blue Ridge Parkway have speed limits of 45 miles (72 km) per hour, with views adjusted to speed.

Parkways encourage relaxation with scenic overlooks and rest and recreation stops. Overlooks may include short trails for stretching travel-weary legs. National parkways, including the Blue Ridge Parkway and Skyline Drive, offer overnight facilities, food service, cultural and natural history exhibits, camping and picnicking areas, and a variety of trails. Facilities occur at intervals of 25 to 80 miles (40 to 130 km).

Parkway design characteristics include location of the road, vertical and horizontal alignment, medians of varying size, overlook turnouts, rustic bridges and tunnels, signage, and native plants. The work of landscape architect Wilbur Simonson, chief designer of the Mt. Vernon Memorial Parkway, established high design standards for alignment.

Parkway medians vary in size and elevation, thereby reducing disturbance of the surrounding terrain. Bridges and tunnels are considered part of the overall scene and are designed of natural materials to blend with the landscape. The size and graphics of parkway signage are designed to complement the scenery.

Finally, parkways employ native plants to merge roads with their settings. Vistas of distant features, such as mountains, may be framed with trees or seen below tree canopy. Trees may be thinned for views into the woods or of adjoining pastures. Shrub and grass bays are employed to direct attention toward selected views or are sited as parkway highlights. The botany-rich Blue Ridge Parkway emphasizes seasonal change with masses of native dogwood, rhododendron, and mountain laurel. Parkways were among the first national planning efforts to consider ecological ramifications and to stress the use of indigenous plants. In the 1930s designers of the Blue Ridge Parkway adjusted landscape expectations to enhance wildlife habitat.

Parkways, like parks, are works of art and deserve recognition and protection. As the population grows, suburban sprawl, rural vacation homes, and other uses compromise parkway views. Governmental commitment to protection of view sheds is necessary if future generations are to experience roads that convey and work with the beauty of the regional landscape.

The earth expanding right hand and left hand,
The picture alive, every part in its best light,

The music falling where it is wanted and stopping where it is not wanted,
The cheerful voice of the public road, the gay fresh sentiment of the road . . . (Walt Whitman)

Further Reading

Abbuehl, Edward, "A Road Built for Pleasure," *Landscape Architecture* 52 (1961)

Cron, Frederick, et al., *Practical Highway Esthetics,* New York: American Society of Civil Engineers, 1977

Dill, Malcolm H., "Planting in Streets, Parkways, Highways and Byways," *Landscape Architecture* 23 (1932)

Elliot, Charles W., II, "The Influence of the Automobile on the Design of Park Roads," *Landscape Architecture* 13 (1922)

Newton, Norman T., *Design on the Land: The Development of Landscape Architecture,* Cambridge, Massachusetts: Harvard University Press, 1971

Olmsted, Frederick Law, "Street Traffic Studies," *Landscape Architecture* 1 (1910)

Olmsted, John Charles, "Classes of Parkways," *Landscape Architecture* 6 (1915)

Simonson, Wilbur H., "Some Desirable Policies in a Program of Roadside Development," *Landscape Architecture* 25 (1934)

Simonson, Wilbur, "Roadside Planting," *Landscape Architecture* 27 (1936)

Simonson, Wilbur H., and R.E. Rowall, "Roadside Improvement," *Landscape Architecture* 25 (1934)

Visual Character of the Blue Ridge Parkway, Washington, D.C.: United States Department of the Interior, National Park Service, 1997

Zapatka, Christian, *L'architettura del paesaggio Americana,* edited by Mirko Zardini, Milan: Electa, 1995; as *The American Landscape,* New York: Princeton Architectural Press, 1995

MARY E. MYERS

Parmentier, André Joseph Ghislain 1780–1830

Belgian Nurseryman and Garden Designer

The early history of landscape architecture in North America is a story of the marriage of horticulture and design as complementary ingredients that generated the planned landscape. André Joseph Ghislain Parmentier was a key performer, and one of the earliest, in this story. Born in Belgium in 1780, he emigrated to the United States in 1824 where he settled near Brooklyn, New York. There he acquired a roughly 25-acre (10 ha) tract and built one of the earliest nurseries in New York. This nursery became noted throughout the eastern United States and Canada for both its extensive collection of plants and innovative display gardens. The nursery's gardens included features novel in the United States, including a rustic arbor and a pavilion referred to as a French Saloon. The origin of Parmentier's specific interest in plants and design is unclear. He may have attended horticulture and botany lectures at the University of Louvain in Belgium. In addition, he may have had his interests aroused through the professional work of his brother Joseph-Julien, a noted horticulturist in Belgium.

Parmentier's 1824 arrival in New York came at a fortunate time for both himself and landscape architecture. In the post–Revolutionary War period, plant exploration and horticulture experienced rapid expansion in the number of horticulturally related businesses and in their offerings. Most of these concerns focused on plant cultivation and development of new varieties, but Parmentier captured a different segment of the market by offering design services along with plants. His business may have been the first high-style design-build practice in the Americas. Since others offered similar plant material, his real contribution to landscape architecture was as a designer rather than plantsman. The then fashionable English style of naturalistic design, sometimes called the landscape gardening school in England and later the romantic style in the United States and Canada, influenced Parmentier. This approach, which emphasized the use of curvilinear forms adapted to natural landform, the use of plants in irregular masses, and rounded rolling topography, had been popularized in England in the 18th century by William Kent and Lancelot "Capability" Brown, among others. In the early 19th century their design successors, such as Humphry Repton and John C. Loudon, introduced variations to this naturalism that reintroduced geometric garden spaces to certain areas of the landscape. It is this later approach to landscape design that Parmentier's known works appear to follow, thus making him a very stylish designer for his day.

Few existing works by Parmentier are known from archival plans or documents, and none survive in their original form. The best-documented project is Parmentier's own nursery near Brooklyn, a project for which both a description and plan were published in *New England Farmer* during his lifetime. In plan the layout had two major sections separated by a tree-lined avenue: the south section of planting beds, laid out in rectilinear form; and the north section, a smaller naturalistic area that included curvilinear paths between planting beds, plant displays, and ornamental structures. Most of his other works were large residential grounds. These included the Hyde Park Estate on the Hudson River (home of Dr. David Hosack, himself a noted horticultur-

ist and founder of the Elgin Botanical Garden), Elisha King's estate at Pelham Manor, New York, and Moss Park, the Toronto, Ontario, home of William Allen.

Parmentier's design work was not limited to residential grounds. In the late 1820s he developed a plan for the grounds of the University of King's College in Toronto (now the University of Toronto). To what extent this was a true master plan for a campus rather than merely a planting and site design is unclear. If it were a site plan, then Parmentier's effort ranks as one of the earliest planned campus designs on the continent, equal in significance to Thomas Jefferson's plan for the University of Virginia or John Jacques Ramee's plan for Union College in Schenectady, New York.

Whether for an estate, nursery, or campus, Parmentier's schemes followed certain design characteristics that demonstrate his design skill and the evolution of his ideas from what was an unsophisticated romantic-style design at his nursery to the sophisticated incorporation of natural topography, with naturalistic and geometric plan patterns at Moss Park. In particular Parmentier's work merged curvilinear naturalism with more structured formal garden spaces in ways that made each seem particularly appropriate for their specific place in the overall plan of the site. This characteristic was especially evident in his plan for Moss Park. There a curving plant mass edge and pathway mirrored the natural topography that they overlooked, while the ornamental and utilitarian gardens to one side of the residence repeated the rectilinear geometry of the house itself.

Parmentier's lasting contributions to the development of landscape architecture in North America are difficult to assess because of his early death in 1830 at age 50. Certainly his nursery was well known both from the publication of its plan and from visits by perspective customers. His other projects, particularly the extensive residential work, were likely seen by only a few. Yet his influence was significant in the formative years of the mid-19th century. Andrew Jackson Downing, himself the most influential design authority after Parmentier, wrote that Parmentier was the "only practitioner of the art [of landscape gardening] of any note. . . . [W]e consider M. Parmentier's labours and example as having effected, directly, far more for Landscape Gardening in America, than those of any other individual whatever" (*Treatise on the Theory and Practice of Landscape Gardening Adapted to North America* [1841]).

Biography

Born in Belgium, 1780. May have studied horticulture and botany at the University of Louvain; emigrated to United States, 1824; set up nursery and display garden near Brooklyn, New York; offered design services in United States and Canada; designed estates, parks, and at least one college campus; his designs were influenced by contemporaneous theory and practice in England; his work was highly regarded by Andrew Jackson Downing. Died in New York, 1830.

Selected Designs
1824 Parmentier's Horticultural Garden, Brooklyn, New York, United States
1827 Elisha King estate, Pelham Manor, New York, United States
1829 Moss Park, Toronto, Ontario, Canada
1830 University of King's College, Toronto, Ontario, Canada

Publications
"Landscapes and Picturesque Gardens," in *New American Gardener*, edited by T.G. Fessenden, 1828

Further Reading
Crawford, Pleasance, and Stephen A. Otto, "André Parmentier's 'Two or Three Places in Upper Canada,'" *Journal of the New England Garden History Society* 5 (1997)

Downing, Andrew Jackson, *A Treatise on the Theory and Practice of Landscape Gardening, Adapted to North America,* New York and London, 1841; reprint, Washington, D.C.: Dumbarton Oaks Research Library and Collection, 1991

Gager, C. Stuart, "The Four Botanic Gardens of Brooklyn," *The Long Island Historical Society Quarterly* 2, no. 1 (1940)

Hedrick, Ulysses Prentiss, *A History of Horticulture in America to 1860,* New York: Oxford University Press, 1950

Stetson, Sarah P., "André Parmentier: Little-Known Pioneer in American Landscape Architecture," *Landscape Architecture* 39, no. 4 (1949)

Zaitzevsky, Cynthia, "André Parmentier," in *Pioneers of American Landscape Design: An Annotated Bibliography,* edited by Charles A. Birnbaum and Lisa E. Crowder, Washington, D.C.: National Park Service, 1993

Zaitzevsky, Cynthia, "André Parmentier: A Bridge between Europe and America," in *The Landscape Universe: Historic Designed Landscapes in Context,* edited by Charles A. Birnbaum, Bronx, New York: Wave Hill, 1993

NANCY J. VOLKMAN

Parque Güell

Barcelona, Spain

Location: off Calle de Olot, approximately 1 mile (1.6 km) northwest of Barcelona city center, between Gràcia and Horta quarters

Parque Güell is considered by many to be a mature expression of the provocative ideas of the well-known Catalan architect Antonio Gaudi (1852–1926). Throughout his life, Gaudi experimented in his designs. As his work yielded positive results, he would incrementally incorporate them into his new designs. During the course of its 14 years of construction and development, Parque Güell allowed Gaudi to synthesize and execute many of his ideas about nature, landscape, architecture, planning, and Spanish tradition. In this park one finds the application of Gaudi's lifetime of exploration into design and construction.

Between 1882 and 1889 Gaudi completed several successful architectural commissions for Don Eusebi Güell, a wealthy Spanish businessman. Güell, a well-traveled and well-read gentleman, was aware of 19th-century planning projects, especially the British garden cities that were just coming into vogue. The fact that many of these projects were largely left unbuilt motivated Güell to purchase 37 acres (14.5 ha) of property high on the hillside of Montanya Pelada and ask Gaudi to design a suburban development in line with the prevalent garden-city ideas. In 1900 the Parque Güell was outside urbanized Barcelona in what was considered to be suburban land. The site rose to between 450 feet (137 m) and 630 feet (192 m) above sea level, offering a spectacular view of Barcelona below and of the harbor beyond. Today, the property offers a view of Gaudi's ongoing project—the Sagrada Familia—and other important Barcelona landmarks. Parque Güell was intended to be a housing development offering communal services that the future residents would share. An esplanade, market, school, chapel, security system, and a common infrastructure of roads, water, and electricity were integrated into the design. The project's aim was to foster a communal spirit. It would follow a set of strict codes to

Palm columns at Parque Güell
Copyright Stephany N. Coakley

enhance the communal aspect as well as ensure that house heights would not hinder the view or the access to sunlight. Only two houses were ever built.

The mountainous topography was the initial concern for Gaudi. He had a deep respect for nature and particularly admired Montserrat, a mountain monastery near Barcelona. His experience designing the Stations of the Cross for the monastery together with frequent visits to Montserrat offered inspiration. Gaudi sought to maintain the integrity of Montanya Pelada by fitting all architectonic elements into the site. Free-flowing patterns of roads and pedestrian ways were carefully switchbacked and snaked throughout the site. In order to maintain these patterns, the roads were placed on viaducts supported on a system of angled columns that resembled tree trunks. The quarried material gathered from the construction was used to build the column supports and retaining walls as needed to protect the mountain. Planters of this same stone are repeated along the edge of the roads. Gaudi provided stone

benches between these planters so that strolling residents could sit and take advantage of the magnificent view down to Barcelona.

At the lowest elevation of the park, off Calle de Olot, Gaudi provided a clustered grouping of communal facilities: a wall enclosing the site, an entry, two service pavilions, a dragon fountain, a market, and a large terraced open space. This cluster is the heart of Parque Güell. Gaudi's incredible genius for integrating function with aesthetic expression is easily seen in many of the design's elements. The entry wall keeps vagrants out with its height and a rounded decorative ceramic cap that is difficult to grip. An entry gate made of iron for security is enriched with its bars that are carefully sculpted into palm branches. The retaining walls holding back the soil for a curving stairway also provide a decorative alternating pattern of colorful and textural convex and concave squares.

The terraced open space at the upper level is where children play, parents watch, and people jog, play chess, or read. It is lined with a colorful serpentine bench. The undulating S shape of the long bench reflects Gaudi's fascination with nature and ideas derived from British painters, writers, and architects who also shared a similar fascination with nature. The S curve has a naturally derived aesthetic providing a serpentine curve that is also highly stable as an engineered wall. The design of the large open space provides a spectacular view down to Barcelona and its harbor and of the colorful tile patterns that decorate its curves. The colorful patterns defining the wall's textures were made by adhering broken tiles or glass to the bench in a traditional Catalan art known as *trencadis*. The bench was a collaborative effort with Josep M. Jujol, another Catalan architect.

Gaudi's work was, in general, greeted with negative reviews. It was considered repulsive and inappropriate for the period in which it was built. In its day it was openly criticized and the subject of many newspaper editorial cartoons. Today, his ideas and work are considered visionary for the unique character of architec-ture, landscape, and furniture design produced. Parque Güell exemplifies Gaudi's emphasis on adapting structure to function, experimenting with aesthetics through technical innovations, and nurturing nature in the public landscape. Barcelona is enriched with Parque Güell's valuable contribution as a public park.

Synopsis

ca. 1900	Don Eusebi Güell purchases land for garden city project
1900–1903	Main buildings, staircases, pavilions, walls, roads, and porticos constructed, designed by Antonio Gaudi
1903	Barcelona Association of Architects visits to examine project
1906–6	Gaudi builds house in Parque Güell
1910–12	Jujol collaborates on long bench
1914	Work suspended on Parque Güell with only two of projected 60 houses completed

Curling Wave pathway at Parque Güell
Copyright Stephany N. Coakley

1923   Parque Güell purchased by City of
        Barcelona and dedicated as municipal
        park
1926   Gaudi dies 10 June; Parque Güell
        acquired by city of Barcelona
1969   Spain declares Parque Güell national
        monument
1984   UNESCO declares Parque Güell a World
        Heritage site

Further Reading

"Antonio Gaudi, 1852–1926," *Architecture and Urbanism* no. 86 (extra issue) (1977)

Casanelles, Eusebi, *Nueva visión de Gaudí*, Barcelona: Ediciones La Polígrafa, 1965; as *Antonio Gaudi: A Reappraisal*, Greenwich, Connecticut: New York Graphic Society, 1965; London: Studio Vista, 1967

Cirlot, Juan Eduardo, *Introduccion a la arquitectura de Gaudi*, edited by Luis Marsans and the Marquis de Aguilar de Vilahur, Barcelona: Editorial RM, 1966; as *The Genesis of Gaudian Architecture*, translated by Joyce Wittenborn, New York: Wittenborn, 1967

Descharnes, Robert, and Clovis Prévost, *La vision artistique et religieuse de Gaudí*, Lausanne, Switzerland: Edita, 1969; as *Gaudí: The Visionary*, translated by Frederick Hill, New York: Viking Press, and London: Stephens, 1971

Güell, Xavier, *Guide Gaudí: L'exaltation de Barcelone*, Paris: Hazan, 1991; as *Gaudi Guide*, Barcelona: Gili, 1991

Martinell, César, *Gaudí: Su vida, su teoría, su obra*, Barcelona: Colegio de Arquitectos de Cataluña y Baleares, Comisíon de Cultura, 1967; as *Gaudí: His Life, His Theories, His Work*, translated by Judith Rohrer, edited by George R. Collins, Cambridge, Massachusetts: MIT Press, 1975

Permanyer, Lluís, and Melba Levick, *El Gaudí de Barcelona*, Barcelona: Ediciones Polígrafa, 1996; as *Gaudi of Barcelona*, adapted and edited by Sarah Underhill, New York: Rizzoli International, 1997

Perucho, Juan, and Leopoldo Pomes, *Gaudi: Una arquitectura de anticipacion*, Barcelona: Ediciones Polígrafa, 1967; as *Gaudi: An Architecture of Anticipation*, New York: Tudor, 1967

Sweeney, James Johnson, and Josep Lluis Sert, *Antoni Gaudi*, New York: Praeger, and London: Architectural Press, 1960

FERNANDO MAGALLANES

Parterre and Plate-Bande

The word *parterre*, which is derived from the French *par terre* (on or along the ground), encompasses all types of geometric pattern making in box, grass, flowers, or water. It connotes the sense of a feature best enjoyed from the upper windows of a palace or house. The origins of the parterre are thought to date back to Claude Mollet's work at Anet in the 1580s, when Etienne du Pérac returned from Italy and showed him a method of laying out a decorative design as a unified figure. The parterre as an ornamental entity in box thus replaced disparate compartments of herbs interwoven as knots. These patterns in box soon acquired the name *parterre en broderie* because of their likeness to embroidery. However, not until the publications of Jacques Boyceau (1638) and André Mollet (1651) was the finest interlacing of organic forms manifest as *parterre de broderie*. By then, the *compartiment de gazon*—winding strips of turf and flowers—emerged as a second type of parterre. Other forms that developed in the 17th century range from water parterres to *boulingrin*—a sunken grass parterre derived from the English "bowling green."

The parterre was codified in A.-J. Dézallier d'Argenville's seminal work *La Théorie et la pratique du jardinage* (1709; *The Theory and Practice of Gardening*). He ranked the *parterre de broderie* as the "finest" type. It differed from the *parterre de compartiment* in its one-sided symmetry along the central axis (as opposed to bilateral symmetry). Colored inorganic materials were used in the spaces between the box arabesques. The "plainest" *parterre à l'anglais* was distinguished by the dominant use of English lawn, while the *parterre d'Orangerie* employed grass and water as a background for displaying orange trees in tubs. The *parterre de pièces coupées pour des fleurs* (cutwork parterre) or *parterre fleuriste* was devoted to flowers in geometric beds that recall the Renaissance flower garden. Its cutwork forms correspond to *gazon coupé*—lawn cut into geometric figures against a sand base as a variation on simple English grass plats. Both are inspired by decorative strap work, while *broderie* (as an elaboration of the earlier knot) correlates to contemporary embroidery on waistcoats and dresses.

Using these prototypes, designers could create complex hybrids, for example J.-F. Blondel's 1738 design for

Parterres at Moseley Old Hall
Copyright Paul Miles Picture Collection

a *parterre de broderie melé de gazon entouré de plate-bandes de fleurs*. By this date *broderie* was beginning to lose its preeminent status in the parterre adjacent to palace or mansion; it was challenged by both grass and flowers in the shift to "naturalness" in the Régence and rococo periods. In time the box parterre died out entirely (although the term *parterre* survived into the Picturesque period) only to be revived in transfigured form in 19th-century formal gardens. In that revival A.-J. Dézallier d'Argenville's plates offered the most frequently copied motifs.

Dézallier d'Argenville's retrospective codification of 17th-century forms has obscured a degree of complexity in evolving parterre types. Thus, for example, the radiating mélange of *broderie*, grass, and flower beds that occurred in designs in Boyceau's *Traité du jardinage* of 1638 (and in designs by Jacques Mollet or John Evelyn) seems to bring the radial symmetry of the florists' flower garden (e.g., Pierre Morin's Paris garden designed like a daisy's petals) into the realm of the decorative parterre.

This mixed form also finds echo a hundred years later in Blondel's use of *broderie melé de gazon,* even though his asymmetrical rococo style is entirely removed from those radial forerunners.

The term *plate-band*, which Blondel employed in his description, was usually applied to the flower border that surrounded and framed the parterre. Typically from three- to six-feet (0.9 to 1.8 m) wide and edged by low box, a *plate-band* was planted in a checkerboard pattern that, when viewed from above, resembled "a Cloth of Tissue of divers Colours" (*The Retir'd Gard'ner* [1706], the George London and Henry Wise translation of Louis Liger's *Le Jardinier fleuriste et historiographe* [1704]). Dézallier d'Argenville likened the effect to an "enamelled mixture of all the colours."

There were different ways of organizing plants within this grid pattern. A common arrangement was to place the medium or taller flowers along the center between clipped evergreens and flowering shrubs, the margins on either side being reserved for small bulbs or low flowers.

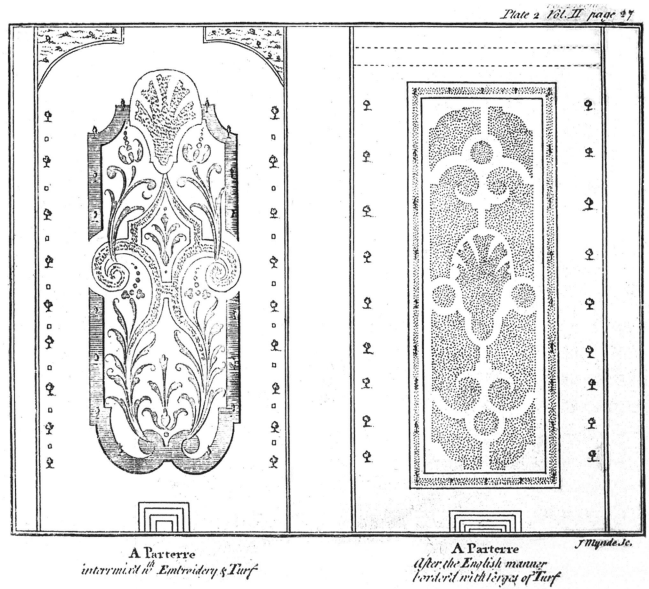

Plate 2 *Vol. II page 27*

J Mynde Sc.

A Parterre
intermixed with Embroidery & Turf

A Parterre
After the English manner bordered with Verges of Turf

Plan of an 18th-century garden depicting parterres
Courtesy of Mary Evans Picture Library

This created a degree of graduation toward the middle that was accentuated by a mounding of earth. Such earth "risings" were likened to an ass's back or carp's back and were meant to show off the flowers to better advantage than a flat border. André Le Nôtre sometimes even used giant hollyhocks and sunflowers to elevate the centers of his *plate-bandes*. An alternative arrangement involved distributing flowers in a grid across the entire border, often without shaped evergreens or flowering shrubs along the spine. A tendency to eliminate both topiary and taller flowers is apparent after Le Nôtre's death in 1700. Notable examples of this flatter profile are Dominique Girard's design for Nymphenburg and

Johann Conrad Schlaun's layout at Nordkirchen (both ca. 1720).

It has been generally accepted that the Dutch *plate-band* differed from the French in its sparse display of rare flowers. The pictorial evidence of Het Loo, Clingendael, and Zeist certainly indicates a single row of specimen flowers at the center of the border, sometimes disposed between shaped evergreens and climbers on stakes. Yet paintings of Versailles and Chantilly from the period of Le Nôtre support the argument that a single line of flowers (or flowers with topiary) was sometimes favored in France, even if there was more massing than in the sparse style of the Low Countries. On the other hand, the French invention of a lattice for setting out plants suggests a prevailing checkerboard manner.

An English variant on these continental models has been postulated for the Privy Garden at Hampton Court. In the replanted *plate-bandes* of 1995, bulbs and flowers were confined to a single dense row along the margins, with a tall row of shaped evergreens and free-growing shrubs as a dominant central motif. Further archival research may clarify whether this was the common practice followed by George London and Henry Wise.

Typically, a spring, summer, and autumn planting palette orchestrated seasonal display. But in very rare cases (notably at the Trianon), the flowers might be changed more frequently by a method of "plunging" pots directly into the *plate-band*. The attempt to reduce such costs and artifice are apparent as the English flower border began to develop as a feature independent from the parterre. The specification for planting borders at Goodwood in 1735, attributed to Philip Miller, suggests an integrated planting scheme for spring to late summer. If it was still indebted to the *plate-band* in its graduated rhythmic structure, its successional blooming and horticultural complexity anticipate the herbaceous border of the 19th century.

Further Reading

Boyceau, Jacques, *Traité du jardinage selon les raisons de la nature et de l'art,* Paris, 1638; reprint, Nördlingen, Germany: Verlag Dr. Alfons UHL, 1997

Dézallier d'Argenville, Antoine-Joseph, *La théorie et pratique du jardinage,* Paris, 1709; as *The Theory and Practice of Gardening,* translated by John James, London, 1712; reprint, Farnborough, Hampshire: Gregg, 1969

Gentil, François, *Le jardinier solitaire,* Paris, 1704; as *The Retir'd Gardener,* translated by George London and Henry Wise, London, 1706; reprint, New York: Garland, 1982

Hansmann, Wilfried, "Parterres: Entwicklung, Typen, Elemente," in *Gartendenkmalpflege: Grundlagen der Erhaltung historischer Gärten und Grünanlagen,* edited by Dieter Hennebo, Stuttgart, Germany: Ulmer, 1985

Karling, Sten, "The Importance of André Mollet and His Family in the Development of the French Formal Garden," in *The French Formal Garden,* edited by Elizabeth B. MacDougall and F. Hamilton Hazelhurst, Washington, D.C.: Dumbarton Oaks Trustees, 1974

Laird, Mark, "Parterre, Grove, and Flower Garden: European Horticulture and Planting Design in John Evelyn's Time," in *John Evelyn's "Elysium Britannicum" and European Gardening,* edited by Therese O'Malley and Joachim Wolschke-Bulmann, Washington, D.C.: Dumbarton Oaks Research Library and Collection, 1998

Laird, Mark, and Hugh Palmer, *The Formal Garden,* New York: Thames and Hudson, 1992

Laird, Mark, and John H. Harvey, "'A Cloth of Tissue of Divers Colours': The English Flower Border, 1660–1735," *Garden History* 21, no. 2 (1993)

Mollet, André, *Le jardin de plaisir,* Stockholm, 1651; reprint, Paris: Éditions du Moniteur, 1982; as *The Garden of Pleasure,* London, 1670

Whalley, Robin, and Anne Jennings, *Knot Gardens and Parterres: A History of the Knot Garden and How to Make One Today,* London: Barn Elms, 1998

Woudstra, Jan, "The Planting of the Privy Garden," in *The King's Privy Garden at Hampton Court Palace, 1689–1995,* edited by Simon Thurley, London: Apollo Magazine, 1995

MARK LAIRD

Pathways and Paving

In 1712 John James in *The Theory and Practice of Gardening* claimed that

> Walks in Gardens, like Streets in a Town serve to communicate between Place and Place, and are as so many Guidances and Means to conduct us throughout the Garden: Besides the Agreeableness and Convenience they constantly afford in Walking, they make one of the principal Beauties of Gardens, when they are well executed and well kept.

James thus highlighted both the practical and aesthetic aspects of pathways.

Pathways provide a sense of direction and structure to designed landscapes. A more practical consideration is the provision of a dry surface to walk on, free from dirt and dust. Besides these main functional considerations, some sort of hierarchy is achieved by design or materials. For example, main walks may be emphasized by greater widths, associated planting, or particular paving materials, whereas other types are used in subservient

Paths at Hestercombe
Copyright Clay Perry/The Garden Picture Library

walks. Alternatively it may be possible to unite a disparate design by means of materials. Materials generally provide scale and texture, and they may also create a pattern.

The traditional procedure of creating walks was by removal of the topsoil, after which time drainage was frequently incorporated, either in a drain or gully underneath or in channels along the sides. Sometimes drainage was achieved by means of a cambered base. The top surface of the subsoil or subgrade after completion of the excavation became known during the 20th century as the formation level. The foundation or sub-base was invariably formed with some coarse material and served to spread the load. On top of this a surface layer was applied, with a camber—rounded in the center—or a

crossfall, drained to specific gullies. The edges might be contained by edging boards or stones or by a curbstone associated with open channels and gullies. The majority of garden walks were laid with a simple camber and drained into grass edging or planting. Great attention was paid to providing the correct profile for a specified purpose, best represented in models provided by Edward Kemp in *How to Lay Out a Garden* (1864).

The surface layer depended on what was available in the region and was generally provided by a local material. Transport of materials has always been the most expensive element in making paths; architects generally refer to the 400-yard (366-m) rule as a limit for the range of transporting local materials, which also applies to materials used in creating paths. In areas with cheap transport—boats or later, trains—materials might come from further afield. Besides locality, construction of and materials for pathways depend on tradition and fashion; for example, in English parks and gardens, gravel walks were prevalent until the 20th century (they were also commonly found in public parks in the United States). Since the end of the 19th century, stone paving in gardens was associated with the Arts and Crafts movement. In France consolidated sand was normally used, while in the Netherlands earth walks were common inland and shell paths in coastal areas. During the 19th and 20th centuries, options for path surfaces proliferated with a great variety of possibilities, and now there is a wide range of different manufactured alternatives.

Historic path materials include organic materials such as cockle shells or tanners bark. Historic mineral materials include stone, cobbles, ragstone, sets, pebbles laid in mosaics, gravel, compacted sand, earth or garden soil, and brick. The most common material in England was gravel, which would be excavated as a mixture with clay, which acted as a binder. This was compacted by rolling and provided a solid surface. It was one of the aspects for which English gardeners were renowned from the 17th to the 19th centuries, when an owner's status was often measured by the condition of the walks, which was frequently commented on by visitors. The compacted gravel walk became so famous and identified with the contemporary landscape style that there were even some instances where gravel was exported to complete an English garden abroad, such as at Casserta in Italy. During the 19th century alternatives to gravel were explored, ranging from wood blocks and coal ashes to asphalt from the Seyssel deposits in France (from 1827 onward), and gas tar, the forerunner of tarmacadam of the 1880s, of which one form was trademarked in 1903 as tarmac. Other materials included pitch and bitumen as bonding agents for path surfaces since the 1830s.

During the 20th century even more materials were being explored, including concrete, both in situ and as blocks or tiles. At the same time brick and York stone went through a phase of popularity in the wake of the Arts and Crafts movement. Traditional gravel (nowadays referred to as *hoggin*) was gradually phased out due to new production methods, whereby gravel was dredged rather than dug in dry pits. The dredged material was graded and in the process lost the fines, which provided the binding qualities; the resulting material was loose and uncomfortable to walk on but was nevertheless frequently used in gardens. Processed gravels, such as Breedon gravel, produced from crushed limestone, have been produced since the 1970s to provide solid path surfaces, but these lack the texture of the historic materials. Inventiveness has seen fashions with walks created from cut logs, railway sleepers, and board

walks, which had the disadvantage in wet climates of being slippery and having a relatively short life span. Lately there have been experiments with plastic surfaces and even olive stone walks.

The latest trends in public parks and gardens have been in favor of more durable hard-wearing surfaces, which are easy to maintain, are nonslip, and are easily accessible for wheelchairs. At the same time, there has been a move toward a more solid base, which has become less impervious. In the Anglo-Saxon world, paving has long been laid on a lean concrete mix, and recent practice even includes a layer of tarmac underneath granite. This encourages water runoff to end up in drains instead of percolating through a permeable surface, which totally contravenes the issue of sustainability. The practice on the European continent continues to be paving on sand, which enables a good degree of permeability.

There have been significant developments in the diversity and implementation of paved surfaces, which saw a proliferation of manufactured products, including concrete pavers, from the 1950s and resin-bound surfaces in the 1980s and 1990s. It is encouraging to note that, due to greater concerns about our environment, there is a return to more traditional materials and methods of construction that are potentially more sustainable while also responding to and supporting regional character and diversity.

Further Reading

Beazley, Elisabeth, *Design and Detail of Space between Buildings,* London: Architectural Press, 1960; revised edition, as *Beazley's Design and Space between the Buildings,* edited by Angi and Alan Pinder, London: Spon, and New York: Van Nostrand Reinhold, 1990

Blanc, Alan, *Landscape Construction and Detailing,* London: Batsford, and New York: McGraw Hill, 1996

Cochrane, Timothy, "Hard Surfaces," in *Techniques of Landscape Architecture,* edited for the Institute of Landscape Architecture by A.E. Weddle, New York: American Elsevier, and London: Heinemann, 1967

Elliott, Brent, "Paths," in *The Regeneration of Public Parks,* edited by Jan Woudstra and Ken Fieldhouse, London and New York: Spon, 2000

Hennebo, Dieter, et al., *Gartendenkmalpflege: Grundlagen der Erhaltung historischer Gärten und Grünanlagen,* Stuttgart, Germany: Ulmer, 1985

Dézallier d'Argenville, Antoine-Joseph, *La théorie et la pratique du jardinage,* Paris, 1709; as *The Theory and Practice of Gardening,* translated by John James, London, 1712; reprint, Farnborough, Hampshire: Gregg, 1969

Kemp, Edward, *How to Lay Out a Small Garden,* London, 1850; 4th edition, as *Landscape Gardening:*

How to Lay Out a Garden, edited and adapted by Frank A. Waugh, New York: Wiley, 1912

Lyle, William Thomas, *Parks and Park Engineering,* New York: Wiley, 1916

Miller, Philip, "Walks and Gravel," in *The Gardener's Dictionary,* by Miller, London, 1731

Woudstra, Jan, "The Planting of the Privy Garden," in *The King's Privy Garden at Hampton Court Palace, 1689–1995,* edited by Simon Thurley, London: Apollo, 1995

JAN WOUDSTRA

Pavlovsk

Pavlovsk, St. Petersburg Oblast, Russia

Location: approximately 17 miles (27 km) south of St. Petersburg

Pavlovsk takes its name from Pavel, the son of Catherine the Great. As a young man Pavel enjoyed hunting in this area, situated a few miles from the empress's summer residence of Tsarskoye Selo. On the occasion of the birth of her first grandson in 1777, Catherine offered this area to Pavel and his wife, Grand Duchess Maria Feodorovna. Various projects concerning the grounds were initiated the following year, and works continued up till Maria Feodorovna's death in 1828. As early as the 1780s, Pavlovsk gained an international reputation as a distinguished and poetical landscape garden. Today, it ranks as the finest work in this genre in Russia.

The Pavlovsk ensemble clearly bears the marks of Maria Feodorovna, allowing both her taste for antiquity and her horticultural interests to come to the fore. A series of architectural and botanical motifs in the garden testifies to her strong family involvement, and during the first quarter of the 19th century, she was the driving force behind Pavlovsk's status as a highly esteemed meeting place for poets, artists, and musicians. Over the years a personal and sentimental iconography came into being in the Pavlovsk garden. One mid–19th century source relates that every corner of the garden bears witness to Maria Feodorovna's "taste, her preferences, and her memories from travels abroad."

As was traditional at the imperial Russian Court and among the Russian nobility since the days of Peter I, foreign architects, artists, and gardeners were engaged to create the new and fashionable summer residence at Pavlovsk. Catherine the Great took the initiative to let the Scottish architect Charles Cameron work not only at Tsarskoe Selo but also at Pavlovsk. He worked at Pavlosk in two periods, 1779–96 and 1800–1803. Prior to his work on the classically inspired architecture, part of the forest had been cleared and two wooden houses, Paullust and Marienthal, had been constructed. A small Dutch-inspired flower garden was also laid out, and some artificial ruins were erected next to the Slavyanka River, along with a Chinese kiosk and some Chinese bridges.

Cameron began his work on the terrain. He was involved with the landscaping of the grounds and over the years designed a dozen large-scale structures for the Pavlovsk garden, including the so-called Temple of Friendship (1779–83), which Maria Feodorovna dedicated to Catherine, and the Apollo Colonnade (1780). Just as happy events were commemorated (e.g., the Family Grove), so too was death, by the urns, tombs, sepulchral monuments, and ruins in the landscape garden. Several motifs alluded to Maria Feodorovna's memories from her childhood and youth in the duchy of Württemberg. The Dairy (1782) was in fact copied after the one in the family's pleasure garden at Étupes, near Basel. Impressions gained during a journey to France in 1781–82 furthered her taste for such vernacular garden motifs. All elements were carefully integrated with the natural slopes, the waters, and the plantation, such as the obelisk commemorating the foundation of Pavlovsk (1782) and the column erected on the garden periphery and named the End of the World (1783).

Paullust and Marienthal were not replaced until several of the new appointments of the landscape garden had been finished. The Pavlovsk Palace (1781–86) remained Cameron's largest commission. The building was in the Palladian manner, cherished since the mid-1720s by English country-house owners; Pavlovsk's interiors were also furnished according to the prevailing neoclassical paradigms of the time. Following Catherine's death in 1796, Pavel I appointed Vincenzo Brenna, an Italian-born architect, to head the enlargement of the palace (1796–99). The original proportions suffered severely from this remodeling, yet Cameron's virtuosity

Pavlovsk, St. Petersburg Oblast, Russia
Copyright Paul Miles Picture Collection

in the handling of the palace corpus and in the interiors is still recognizable. Brenna also left his mark on the garden design, adding alleys, parterres, terraces, and formal bosquets near the palace area and installing a large number of bronze and marble sculptures in the areas called the Old (1793) and the New Sylvia (1800). A preference for Dutch- and then Italian-inspired garden patterns thus marked the projects dating to the 1790s.

After Pavel's death in 1801, Maria Feodorovna directed a unique suite of landscapes to be created on the extensive grounds surrounding a core consisting of the Great Star, the White Birches, and the Parade Ground. Here, the Italian-born theatrical painter and designer Pietro Gonzago transferred his painterly aesthetics to nature. His orchestration of the vast area called the White Birches (1803–25), consisting of a radial pattern formed by eight roads that lead up to a big circle of birch trees, stands out as a true, yet still poorly known, masterpiece in landscape art. A mausoleum devoted to Pavel (by Thomas de Thomon, 1803–10) was placed in a som-

ber part of the garden, and firs were planted to emphasize the melancholic atmosphere, as recommended in the garden literature of the time.

Along with her comprehensive knowledge of art and architecture, Maria Feodorovna was also a horticulturist, her father having been her first mentor in this field. She supervised all the plantings at Pavlovsk and took an active part in the care and protection of the flowers and trees. She not only had the ambition to duplicate scenes from some of Europe's landscape gardens but was also determined to overcome the restraints the northern climate put on planting. She ordered seeds and cuttings, bulbs, and trees from many countries, including Germany and Holland; in 1795 a special delivery, including new plant discoveries from the South Seas, arrived from the Royal Botanic Gardens, Kew. The wealth of pots in the palace interiors and in the luxuriant parterres of the so-called Privy Garden reflected Maria Feodorovna's passion for flowers. Her vast botanical knowledge often permitted her to specify the varieties she wanted, and she was also familiar with many of the new theoretical works of the period.

The Russian Revolution put an end to Pavlovsk's role as an imperial summer residence. The palace was turned into a museum and opened to the public in 1918. Pavlovsk suffered severely during World War II. The larger part of the structures was ruined, and the grounds and the plantations were also devastated. Large-scale restoration has been performed on a continuous basis, and Pavlovsk now appears as one of a series of grandiose historic palace and garden ensembles surrounding St. Petersburg.

Synopsis

1777	Work begun on summer residence for Grand Duke Paul, son of Catherine the Great, and his wife, Grand Duchess Maria Fyodorovna
1778	Construction of formal gardens
1779–83	Temple of Friendship constructed, designed by Cameron
1779–96	Scottish architect Charles Cameron lays out garden, including design and integration of garden pavilions, bridges, and walks, with landscape scenery
1780	Apollo Colonnade built, designed by Cameron
1781–86	Construction of Pavlovsk Palace, designed in Palladian style by Cameron
1790s	Construction of terraces, parterres, and formal bosquets, designed by architects Brenna, Rossi, Voronikhin, and others
1795	Special delivery of newly discovered South Seas plants received from Royal Botanical Gardens, Kew, ordered by Maria Fyodorovna
1796	Pavlovsk became imperial summer residence of Paul I
1796–99	Redesign of palace by Italian-born architect Vincenzo Brenna
1801	Paul I dies and Maria Fyodorovna hires Italian theatrical designer Pietro Gonzago
1803–25	Layout of White Birches by Gonzago
1828	Death of Maria Fyodorovna
1918	Following Revolution, Pavlovsk opened to public as museum
1941–44	Severe damage during World War II
after 1944	Continuous restoration of palace and garden

Further Reading

Belanina, V.A., *Pavlovsk: Dvortsovo-parkovyi ansambl'* (Pavlovsk: The Palace and Park Ensemble), Leningrad: Lenizdat, 1989

Floryan, Margrethe, *Gardens of the Tsars: A Study of the Aesthetics, Semantics, and Uses of Late 18th Century Russian Gardens*, Aarhus, Denmark: Aarhus University Press, and Sagaponack, New York: Sagapress, 1996

Likhachov, Dmitrii Sergeevich, *Poeziia sadov: K semantike sadovo-parkovykh stilei* (The Poetry of Gardens: On the Semantics of Garden and Park Styles), Leningrad: "Nauka," 1982

Massie, Suzanne, *Pavlovsk: The Life of a Russian Palace*, London: Hodder and Stoughton, 1990

Shtorkh, Platon, and V.A. Zhukovskii, *Putevoditel' po sadu i gorodu Pavlovsku* (Guide to the Garden and Town of Pavlovsk), St. Petersburg, 1843

Vergunov, A.P., and V.A. Gorokhov, *Vertograd: Sadovo-parkovoe iskusstvo Rossii: Ot istokov do nachala XX veka* (Vertograd: Garden and Landscape Art in Russia: From the Beginning to the Early 20th Century), Moscow: Kultura, 1996

MARGRETHE FLORYAN

Paxton, Joseph 1803–1865

English Architect, Gardener, and Writer

Joseph Paxton—a landscape designer, architect, writer, and entrepreneur—has had great influence in the areas of landscape design, garden structures, and their unique construction. Despite humble beginnings as a gardener, Paxton was recognized as an intelligent and knowledgeable young man by William Spenser Cavendish, the sixth duke of Devonshire. At age 23 Paxton became the superintendent of the gardens at Chatsworth, the duke's Derbyshire estate. Here he created a pinetum, an arboretum, and a rockworks with naturalistic waterfalls. He displayed his entrepreneurial spirit in the efficiency of his position and his creative solutions. Paxton's work reached beyond Chatsworth's grounds with his enlargement of the great house. This alteration necessitated moving part of the village of Edensor in order to provide the house with an unobstructed view. Paxton was key in the redesign of the village as well as many of the homes.

At Chatsworth, Paxton designed and built a conservatory of glass and iron in 1840 and a lily house for the duke's Victoria Regia (*Victoria amazonica*) in 1850. This rare Amazon River water plant was brought back and failed to bloom until Paxton obtained it and recreated its native conditions. To solve this problem, the lily house included a tank (11 yards [10 m] in diameter), heating, lighting, a slotted floor to allow ventilation, and a waterwheel to keep the water agitated. His design details included roof supports of iron columns that were used as drainpipes and a wooden glazing bar that channeled exterior rainwater. Similarly an interior glazing bar collected and channeled interior condensation into troughs, nicknamed the "Paxton gutter." These buildings are a summary of his work, composed of standardized units—light, economical, and simple.

The exhibition building for the Great Exhibition, more commonly known as the Crystal Palace, is considered by most to be Paxton's crowning achievement, if not his most well known. With over 245 designs submitted to the design competition (originally international in scope) by April 1850, all of the schemes were seen as expensive and impractical to build in the time allotted since opening day was to be 1 May 1851. Paxton feared that a mistake would be made and was encouraged to submit his own design. His Crystal Palace, a building 1,848 feet (565 m) long and 408 feet (124 m) wide with a transept 72 feet (22 m) wide and 108 feet (33 m) high, was completed in a little over six months and made with prefabricated materials. Assembled in Hyde Park in London, the Crystal Palace was four times the size of St. Peter's Basilica in Rome. From a design standpoint, it is a direct descendent of the conservatory and lily house but on a grander scale. The use of steel and glass is reminiscent of the conservatory at Chatsworth. He also borrowed from his railroad experience; examples of these modes of construction allowed for three columns and two girders to be erected every 16 minutes and 76 trolleys running on gutters with two glaziers to fix the glass in place.

Many believe that from the beginning Paxton envisioned this structure to remain permanently, despite the intention for the Great Exhibition to be only temporary. His pamphlet titled "What Is to Become of the Crystal Palace" received great praise and additional support from *The Times* and *Punch*; however, Prince Albert and the House of Commons voted for removal. Paxton prepared for this decision by creating a public company to buy the building and eventually to move it to Sydenham, southeast of London. He hoped that with the addition of a rail line, this would become a place of leisure and entertainment for years to come.

In 1831 Paxton started a monthly magazine called the *Horticultural Register* and three years later another periodical entitled *Paxton's Magazine of Botany and Register of Flowering Plants*. In 1835 he gave up the editorship of the *Horticultural Register* but continued to write into the middle point of his life. In 1838 *Practical Treatise on the Cultivation of the Dahlia* was successful and was translated into several European languages. He later collaborated with John Lindley on two projects: in 1840 on the *Pocket Botanical Dictionary* and again in 1850 for *Paxton's Flower Garden*. Also in the early 1850s, he penned the *Calendar of Garden Operations*.

Paxton was also responsible for several newspapers. The *Gardeners Chronicle* was a weekly that still is in existence. With three other gentlemen, he founded the *Daily News*. They had hired Charles Dickens as editor, but this arrangement lasted for only three weeks. After a short time Paxton seemed to withdraw as well.

While under the duke's employ, Paxton was able to open his own private practice; the details and arrangements of much of his work during this time may never be known. However, he was commissioned to work on several urban public parks, such as Birkenhead Park. Several of the design criteria have great importance and influence. The plantings and design of the lakes are informal with interior spaces left largely open for formalized games and to create a variety of contrasting views. Circulation within the park consists of a footpath system that surrounds the lakes and links them to the various entrances, directing them to important views within the park. The circulation system is further designed so that the pedestrian and vehicular experiences do not conflict. The vehicular system allows for a circuit of the park giving one experience, while the pedestrian allows for a more intimate experience, allowing the visitor to reach more of and farther into the park. This articulation of circulation systems had an influence on Fredrick Law Olmstead, the "father" of landscape architecture. One can see in the design of Central Park in New York City the separation of vehicular and pedestrian systems with vehicular underpasses for the conveniences of the park user. This was a direct result of early visits to Birkenhead and discussions with Paxton.

See also Birkenhead Park; Chatsworth Gardens; London Parks

Biography

Born in Milton Bryant, Bedfordshire, England, 3 August 1803. Gardener for sixth Duke of Devonshire; held position of head gardener for Duke at Chatsworth, Derbyshire, England, 1826–58; built Great Stove (iron and glass conservatory), 1840; built lily house for the Duke's Victoria Regia *(Victoria amazonica)*, 1850; designed what was widely known as Crystal Palace, for Great Exhibition, 1851, from prefabricated components in only six months; influential in moving of Crystal Palace to Sydenham, London, where it remained until destroyed by fire, 1936; wrote landscape and botanical books and periodicals; designed several public parks; served as member of parliament. Knighted, 1851. Died in Sydenham, London, 8 June 1865.

Selected Designs

1836–40	Great Stove (conservatory), Chatsworth, Bakewell, Derbyshire, England
1842	Prince's Park, Liverpool, Merseyside, England
1843–47	Birkenhead Park, Birkenhead, Merseyside, England
1850	Crystal Palace, Great Exhibition of 1851, Hyde Park, London, England
1852–54	Crystal Palace re-erected, Sydenham, London, England

Selected Publications

editor, *Horticultural Register,* 5 vols., 1831–35

editor, *Paxton's Magazine of Botany, and Register of Flowering Plants,* 16 vols., 1834–49
Practical Treatise on the Cultivation of the Dahlia, 1838
Pocket Botanical Dictionary (with John Lindley), 1840
Gardeners Chronicle (with John Lindley), 1841
Calendar of Garden Operations, 1850
Paxton's Flower Garden (with John Lindley), 3 vols., 1850–53

Further Reading

Anthony, John, *Joseph Paxton: An Illustrated Life of Sir Joseph Paxton, 1803–1865,* Aylesbury, Buckinghamshire: Shire, 1973
Chadwick, George F., *The Works of Sir Joseph Paxton, 1803–1865,* London: Architectural Press, 1961
Chadwick, George F., "Paxton's Design Principles for Birkenhead Park," *Landscape Design* (March 1990)
McKean, John, *Crystal Palace: Joseph Paxton and Charles Fox,* London: Phaidon, 1994
Thorne, Robert, "Paxton and Prefabrication," *Architectural Design* 57, nos. 11–12 (1987)

JOSEPH C. BLALOCK, JR.

Peets, Elbert 1886–1968

United States Landscape Architect

Born in Ohio, Elbert Peets received his basic education in the Cleveland public school system and as a teenager worked for H.U. Horvath, a local landscape architect and nurseryman. Peets graduated with high honors from Cleveland's Western Reserve University in 1912 and received a Master's of Landscape Architecture (MLA) degree from Harvard University three years later.

While attending Harvard Peets taught horticulture and completed the manuscript for a book, *Practical Tree Repair: The Physical Repair of Trees—Bracing and the Treating of Wounds and Cavities* (1913), based on his MLA thesis. He also prepared subdivision plans for landscape architects Pray, Hubbard, and White, whose firm was headquartered in Cambridge, Massachusetts. In 1916 Peets began a collaboration with the German expatriate and internationally known city-planning consultant Werner Hegemann, who was residing in Milwaukee, Wisconsin, during World War I. Between 1916 and 1923 Hegemann and Peets prepared plans for numerous communities in Wisconsin, including the model industrial village of Kohler (1916) and the large, but only partially completed, subdivision of Lake Forest (1916–20), located in Madison. Their most notable Wisconsin project was a subdivision plan for Washington Highlands (1916–20), situated just outside Milwaukee in Wauwatosa. The Highlands' plan reveals the consultants' efforts to avoid excessive land cuts and fills, to develop easy street grades around steep hills, to reserve primary vantage points as the most desirable building sites, to preserve large trees, and to design the entire community as a secluded residential park.

After U.S. entry into World War I, Peets served two years as a civilian planning engineer in the U.S. Army (1917–18) and later collaborated with Hegemann and Henry Hubbard on a plan for the new community of Wyomissing Park (1922–23), near Reading, Pennsylvania. Peets also spent much of 1920 in Europe, when he was finally able to use the Charles Eliot Travelling

Fellowship awarded to him by Harvard in 1917. Another collaboration between Hegemann and Peets resulted in their monumental volume *The American Vitruvius: An Architects' Handbook of Civic Art,* which originally appeared in 1922. Hegemann and Peets described The American Vitruvius, one of the classic design manuals of the 20th century, as "a thesaurus, a representative collection of creations in civic art . . . [that would] bring out the special significance of each design."

After returning to Cleveland in 1923, Peets developed a private practice, specializing in the design of gardens, parks, and subdivisions. During the 1920s he also established a reputation as a leading design critic. Several of his articles concerned Washington, D.C., a city he loved, but two submissions, both published in the *American Mercury* (then edited by H.L. Mencken), are well known because they present his iconoclastic views about the deficiencies of New York's Central Park ("Central Park," March 1925) and the shortcomings of the United States's "landscape priesthood" ("Landscape Priesthood," January 1927).

When the number of private commissions available to landscape architects declined during the Great Depression, Peets found employment with the Cleveland City Planning Commission in 1933. Two years later he moved to Washington, D.C., where he served as the principal planner for the U.S. Resettlement Administration community of Greendale, Wisconsin, one of three suburban greenbelt towns sponsored by the federal government during the Great Depression. The plan he prepared for Greendale displayed his awareness of European Renaissance towns and squares, midwestern villages and small cities, and the reconstruction of Williamsburg, Virginia. Designing a community that was built around a line instead of a point, Peets developed a grid plan with a central boulevard that terminated at Greendale's Village Hall—a building modeled on Williamsburg's government buildings. He also employed English Garden City principles in the form of parks and pathways, residential streets that ended in dead-end courts or culs-de-sac, and accessibility to a 2,000-acre (809-ha) greenbelt that was later reduced to a river parkway because of residential expansion. During the early planning of Greendale, Jens Jensen, a midwestern landscape architect noted for his use of native plants in landscape design, derided Peets's recommendations calling for the use of some nonindigenous flora throughout the community. Despite Jensen's complaints, Peets's planting list prevailed after he argued that residents wanted to "see the trees and shrubs that have been made dear to them by familiarity." According to Peets, the people who moved to Greendale regarded golden-twig willows, apple and cherry trees, lilacs, and hollyhocks as their "old friends."

Peets prepared a plan for California's Santa Catalina Island in 1938; one year later, after becoming chief of the Site Planning Section of the Federal Public Housing Agency, he wrote a report on city planning and housing for San Juan, Puerto Rico. Following World War II he continued to serve as a consultant to the federal government. His major postwar project, undertaken as a private commission, was a design for the planned community of Park Forest, Illinois (1946–50), situated just south of Chicago. Peets adapted the layout to the rolling terrain of the site and used design principles derived from the English Garden City, Radburn, New Jersey, and the U.S. Greenbelt towns. At Park Forest these concepts were manifested in the form of a large park located at the center of the community, as well as neighborhoods that featured schools with adjacent open space areas and recreational facilities. Compared with other early post-World War II planned communities, the most unusual aspect of Park Forest was its centrally located shopping plaza. Park Forest received further notoriety when William Whyte used the community as the locus for his book *The Organization Man* (1956), a classic study of postwar Americans adjusting to suburban life.

Peets continued to provide planning recommendations for Greendale until 1957, was a member of the Fine Arts Commission in Washington, D.C., from 1950 to 1954, and lectured at Yale and Harvard Universities between 1950 and 1960. A gifted designer and illustrator, he had a rare ability to understand relevant historical principles of civic design and apply them to the communities of his time. With increasing emphasis being given to "new urbanism" and "neotraditional" community planning, Peets's early contributions as a civic designer and author are today assuming even greater importance.

Biography

Born in Hudson, Ohio, 1886. Apprenticed to landscape architect and nurseryman, H.U. Horvath, in Cleveland, Ohio; graduated with high honors from Case Western University, Cleveland, Ohio, 1912, and Harvard University, with Master's of Landscape Architecture, 1915; collaborated with German expatriate planner Werner Hegemann in preparation of plans for model industrial village of Kohler, Wisconsin, and suburban subdivisions, 1916–23; coauthor with Hegemann of *American Vitruvius,* 1922; served as civilian planning engineer for U.S. Army, 1917–18; studied in Europe, 1920, after receiving Charles Eliot Traveling Fellowship from Harvard, 1917; maintained private office in Cleveland, Ohio, 1923–33; wrote many seminal articles on civic design and landscape architecture; worked for Cleveland City Planning Commission, 1933–35; employed by U.S. Resettlement Administration, 1935–38; served as primary designer of Greendale, Wisconsin; prepared planning reports for Santa Catalina Island, California, 1938, and San Juan, Puerto Rico, 1939; chief of Site Planning Section in Federal Public Housing Authority, 1939–45; after World War II, continued as consultant to federal government; principal designer of Park Forest, Illinois, 1946–50. Died in Ohio, 1968.

Selected Designs

1916	Model village of Kohler (with Werner Hegemann), Wisconsin, United States
1916–19	Washington Highlands subdivision (with Werner Hegemann), Wauwatosa, Wisconsin, United States
1916–20	Lake Forest subdivision (with Werner Hegemann), Madison, Wisconsin, United States
1922–23	Community plan for Wyomissing Park (with Werner Hegemann and Henry Hubbard), Reading, Pennsylvania, United States
1935–57	Federally sponsored greenbelt town of Greendale, Wisconsin, United States
1938	Development plan for Santa Catalina Island, Los Angeles county, California, United States
1939	Housing and city plan for San Juan, Puerto Rico
1946–50	Plan for new community of Park Forest, Illinois, United States

Selected Publications

Practical Tree Repair: The Physical Repair of Trees— Bracing and the Treating of Wounds and Cavities, 1913

"Some Trees in the Built-up Districts of Large Cities," *Landscape Architecture* (October 1915)

American Vitruvius: An Architects' Handbook of Civic Art (with Werner Hegemann), 1922

"Central Park," *American Mercury* (March 1925)

"Landscape Priesthood," *American Mercury* (January 1927)

"New Washington," *American Mercury* (August 1926)

"Famous Town Planners I—Haussmann," *Town Planning Review* (June 1927)

"Famous Town Planners II—Camillo Sitte," *Town Planning Review* (December 1927)

"Famous Town Planners III—L'Enfant," *Town Planning Review* (July 1928)

On the Art of Designing Cities: Selected Essays of Elbert Peets, edited by Paul Spreiregen, 1968

Further Reading

Alanen, Arnold R., "Elbert Peets: History As Precedent in Midwestern Landscape Design," in *Midwestern Landscape Architecture,* edited by W.H. Tishler, Champaign: University of Illinois Press, 2000

Alanen, Arnold R., "Peets, Elbert," in *Pioneers of American Landscape Design,* edited by Charles A. Birnbaum and Robin S. Karson, New York: McGraw Hill, 2000

Alanen, Arnold R., and Joseph A. Eden, *Main Street Ready Made: The New Deal Community of Greendale,* Wisconsin, Madison: State Historical Society of Wisconsin, 1987

Alanen, Arnold R., and Thomas Peltin, "Kohler, Wisconsin: Planning and Paternalism in a Model Industrial Village," *Journal of the American Institute of Planners* 44 (April 1978)

Collins, Christiane Crasemann, "Hegemann and Peets: Cartographers of an Imaginary Atlas," in *The American Vitruvius: An Architects' Handbook of Civic Art* (1922), by Werner Hegemann and Elbert Peets, edited by Alan J. Plattus, New York: Princeton Architectural Press, 1988

Randall, Gregory C., *America's Original GI Town: Park Forest,* Illinois, Baltimore, Maryland: Johns Hopkins University Press, 2000

Shillaber, Caroline, "Elbert Peets, Champion of the Civic Form," *Landscape Architecture* 72 (1982)

Spreiregen, Paul D., "Elbert Peets," in *American Landscape Architecture: Designers and Places,* edited by W.H. Tishler, Washington, D.C.: Preservation Press, 1989

ARNOLD R. ALANEN

Père Lachaise Garden Cemetery

Paris, France

Location: approximately 2 miles (3.3 km) east of the Louvre museum, in the 20th arrondissement, on the Boulevard de Ménilmontant

Père Lachaise cemetery established both the concept and practice of such places as "a burial place in a garden." Today 46 hectares (115 acres) large, the original site was a rural retreat of 17 hectares (42.5 acres), purchased by Parisian Jesuits at the beginning of the 17th century. Among their members was Father François Aix de la Chaize, a man of exceptional learning who in the latter part of the century became the confessor of King Louis XIV.

As royal confessor, La Chaize's contacts and resources allowed him to embellish considerably the Jesuit retreat. With subdued splendor, he replicated the residence of his royal penitent at Versailles, laying out extensive gardens, enhancing bucolic vistas, decorating the retreat house, and encouraging an avian paradise. Visited by many socialites, including the cleric's mistresses, the locale was a noted pleasure grounds.

After La Chaize's death the site declined, and with the suppression of the Jesuits, it passed into various hands. At the same time the emerging Enlightenment, with its emphasis on the orderly and rational organization of society, held among its followers many who were concerned about public health and sanitation in Paris. Uppermost in their minds was the foul-smelling and grotesque overcrowding of the city's medieval cemeteries. Putrefying corpses surfaced out of the ground, and the areas were used as convenient refuse dumps and latrines.

With the rise of Napoléon and his concern for orderly government, large cemeteries outside the city were planned. Only one, to the east, came to be established. This was on the site of Father La Chaize's pleasure garden, his name still associated with the locale.

The architect Alexandre Brongniart was instructed to design the cemetery respecting its original bucolic character, the low rolling hills planted with thousands of trees frequented by numerous songbirds. Both Enlightenment and Romantic ideas regarding the centrality of nature to man combined to create this type of cemetery. It comprised a new way of entering into one's final rest, settling into the serenity of a rustic garden.

The secularization of French society produced a further singular characteristic for the cemetery. A pantheon for the heroes of the Revolution and modern French history had been designed in Paris, to be filled with heroic statuary and paintings. The cemetery too came to be considered an appropriate place to memorably commemorate one's entry into immortality. Furthermore, since the cemetery was also a real estate venture, the bodies of famous Parisians—Abelard and Héloïse, Moliére, and La Fontaine—were reburied in the locale under appropriate monuments. Thereby others were attracted to buy plots, acquiring grandeur by association. Buying a plot in a cemetery as a piece of property was itself a further innovation, an indication of the emerging dominance of bourgeois resources and values. Burial in this pastoral locale dotted with classical sculpture associated one with heroic antiquity.

By the middle of the 19th century, the cemetery expanded, acquiring adjacent areas. It lowered neighboring property values and thereby facilitated its own enlargement, an ironic self-perpetuation. Rather than rolling hills, however, the new areas were flat. Curving lanes and stairway paths gave way to a grid pattern of byways.

The area continued, however, to be dense with trees: ash, beech, black walnut, cedar, cherry, cypress, linden, plane, and sycamore. Some of these were planted in rows along the sides of lanes. The branches bent over the road, forming a solemn arch shading passing processions of mourners. A few species of trees did not survive, their roots not enduring the clay soil of the area. The trees attracted numerous types of birds, including blackbirds, jays, magpies, nightingales, and woodpeckers. These birds, along with small rodents, accounted for the hundreds of cats who progressively occupied the cemetery.

By the end of the 19th century and throughout the 20th, the cemetery increasingly changed from an area of trees and grassy hills to a dense sculpture garden. Over the past hundred years, statuary surrounded by small garden plots have come to dominate the character of the grounds. These tiny gardens are planted with every variety of flower, from the ubiquitous rose to the symbolic forget-me-not and the evocatively fragrant lilac. Planted over the generations, flowers have blossomed and withered as a floral resonance to the mortality of the area they grace. The passing sweetness of their fragrance has also heightened the strong air of melancholy and reverie so striking about Père-Lachaise. Some have, perhaps startlingly, even observed an erotic character to the locale. This may be due to the floral perfume wafting around the writhing forms of statues heightening the senses of a viewer.

By the end of the 20th century, over a million people had been buried in Père-Lachaise. Such a number indicates the high density of this sculpture garden, although monumental sculpture has not been allowed for some time. Noted sculpture includes the reclining figures of Abelard and Héloïse, characters from the tales of La Fontaine etched on the bronze sides of his tomb, a mourning female figure over the tomb of Chopin, a bust of Balzac on a pillar, and the magnetic stare of a blackstone bust of the spiritist leader, Alan Kardac. One of the most emotional funerals in recent times was that of the popular singer Edith Piaf, the "little sparrow."

Synopsis

early 1600s	Jesuits establish rural retreat
1600s	Father Françoise Aix de la Chaize, confessor of Louis XIV, lays out extensive gardens
late 1700s	Cemetery designed by Alexandre Brongniart

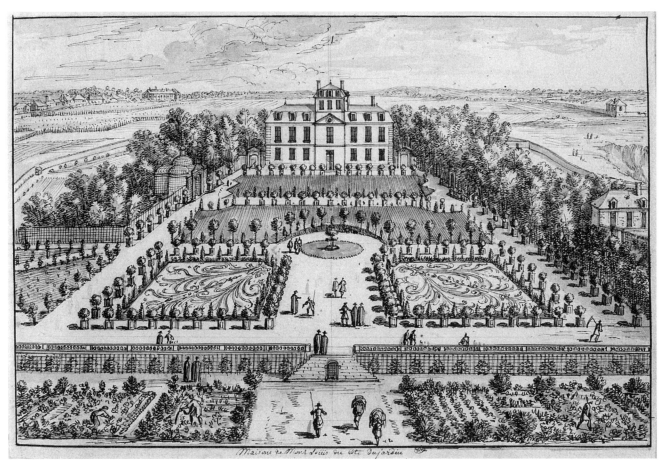

Maison de Mont-Louis of Père Lachaise, as seen from the garden, pen and ink drawing by Israel Silvestre the Younger
Copyright Rèunion des Musèes Nationaux/Art Resource, New York

1804	Père Lachaise cemetery inaugurated, situated in low hill country just east of Paris
1850	Acquisition of adjacent areas to cemetery more than doubled its size
1860	Annexation of suburbs brought Père Lachaise into Paris
1871	Against southeast wall of cemetery, Republican forces defeat last remnants of partisans of Paris Commune, burying 700 victims here, an event commemorated in monument Mur de Fédérés, with adjacent area becoming popular place for interment of laborers
1881–85	Jews and Moslems allowed burial in cemetery
1934–68	Political debates between Right and Left over who can be buried in Père-Lachaise

Further Reading

Brown, Frederick, *Père Lachaise: Elysium as Real Estate*, New York: Viking Press, 1973

Culbertson, Judi and Tom Randall, *Permanent Parisians: An Illustrated Guide to the Cemeteries of Paris*, Chelsea, Vermont: Chelsea Green Publishing Co., 1986

Dansel, Michel, *Au Père Lachaise: Son histoire, ses secrets, ses promenades*, Paris: Fayard, 1973

Dansel, Michel, *Les lieux de culte au cimetière du Père - Lachaise*, Paris: Guy Trédaniel Éditeur, 1999

Etlin, Richard, *The Architecture of Death: The Transformation of the Cemetery in Eighteenth-Century Paris*, Cambridge, Massachusetts: MIT Press, 1984

Tartakowsky, Daniel, *Nous irons chanter sur vos tombes: Le Père-Lachaise, XIXe–XXe siècle*, Paris: Aubier, 1999

EDWARD A. RIEDINGER

Perennials

Perennials are plants that live longer than two growing seasons, as opposed to annuals, which complete their life cycle within one growing season, or biennials, which have a life span of two years. Perennials can be classified into two categories: those with a permanent woody structure, which are defined as trees and shrubs, and those that have an underground storage or perennating organ, in the form of stem and root tubers, bulbs, corms, and rhizomes, from which each year the plant produces new stems, leaves, and flowers, which are usually followed by seeds. These are known as herbaceous perennials. According to this definition all plants that live longer than one year can be classified as perennial, but in horticultural terms it is usually applied to herbaceous plants. Herbaceous perennials normally undergo a dormant season each year, usually the season with the harshest climate. Although for most plants this is winter, some have had to adapt themselves to their environment by going dormant during summer. Examples of this summer dormancy can be found in *Papaver orientalis* (oriental poppy), which is inactive during the hot, dry period when little water is accessible, and *Doronicum orientale* (leopard's bane), which has too little water and sunlight available under the dense tree canopy of its native woodland environment. Certain perennials overwinter showing small basal leaves or dormant buds, some retain a woody base, and others completely die down to ground level. With their ability to adapt themselves, many herbaceous perennials are quite tolerant of a wide variety of growing environments, although different climatic conditions can equally affect the plants' performance.

Perennials play a vital role in gardens as well as in native landscapes. The woody structures of trees and shrubs provide the permanent backdrop, like a stage setting, in front of which the herbaceous perennials will emerge, flower, set seed, and disappear again like actors in a performance. They provide seasonal variety and character, each season having dominant plant types and colors. Spring is the time for the bulbous plants, available in a wide range of riotous colors, welcome after the long, gray winter months. Early summer is the time when the tender greens are accompanied by clean and fresh-looking whites, pinks, blues, and purples of delphiniums, peonies, and geraniums. As summer progresses and the days get hotter, the colors reflect the heat: August is the month of the *Compositae*, with rich yellows, velvety reds, and rusty oranges, as the heat shimmers on the horizon. When fall arrives, with its first autumnal colors, the asters and chrysanthemums display their dusty pinks, faded blues, and mauves, as well as the coppery tones that reflect the fall colors of the trees, all of which blend into the melancholy of the season.

Not until the latter part of the 19th century did herbaceous perennials become an important group of garden plants in their own right. Medieval illustrations show peonies, hollyhocks, columbines, irises, carnations, lilies of the valley, and primroses. Most plants grown in the Middle Ages would have been either symbolic or functional plants, grown for medicinal, culinary, or domestic purposes. Monastic establishments played an important role in the cultivation, development, and spread of these plants. The second half of the 16th century saw the introduction of many new plants into northern Europe, mainly from the Middle East. Dedicated botanists such as Carolus Clusius, founder of the Leiden Botanic Garden in the Netherlands in 1590, distributed these different plant varieties to Europe's flourishing botanic gardens. John Parkinson's *Paradisi in Sole, Paradisus Terrestris* (1629; The Terrestrial Paradise of the Park in the Sun) shows that the proportion of exotic bulbous plants available at that time was still much higher than any other plant type. This was largely because dormant bulbs and tubers could be carried over great distances by land or sea, whereas plants such as perennials, trees, and shrubs were less likely to survive these long journeys unless they were transported in the form of seed. As a result plants were rare and valuable and would be planted in small numbers, widely spaced. The tulip became particularly sought after, especially the virus-infected bulbs, which produced the most unusual color patterns on the petals. The collecting craze known as tulipomania reached its height in the 1630s, when Dutch speculators would bankrupt themselves by speculating on exorbitantly expensive bulbs. While the affluent could afford to grow plants for their ornament, plants for the herb garden continued to be the dominant plant group found in gardens; almost half the plants listed in Johann Sigismund Elssholtz's 1684 account in *Vom Gartenbau* (From Horticulture) were intended for the herb garden, many being herbaceous perennials.

During the 18th century there was a gradual increase in new plants reaching European gardens, but it did not come to a climax until the 19th century. This was a century of horticultural excellence, during which technology flourished, an unprecedented range of plants was introduced, and the nursery trade boomed. All continents became accessible, including Asia, and with the help of the newly invented Wardian case, a small, enclosed portable greenhouse, the survival rate of nontuberous plants during the long, treacherous sea journeys increased dramatically. The abolishment of the window tax meant that English gardens could suddenly afford greenhouses, and with labor being cheap and plentiful, the greenhouses could be used to grow the latest craze: the tender perennials that had come from more exotic climates. Begonias, calceolarias, salvias, and pelargoniums were some of the many brightly colored flowers that invaded most gardens. Herbaceous perennials were still present, but only in the background. They could be found in pleasure grounds, planted along shrubbery edges, or in walled gardens, where they were often found in long borders, flanking the paths, bringing a decorative touch, while being useful as a source of cut flowers for the house.

From the mid-19th century onward the range of perennials available to gardeners increased rapidly as nurseries began taking an interest. Commercial growers printed in their nursery catalogs sample planting plans for herbaceous borders, encouraging people to buy their special selections. New cultivars were rapidly introduced into the booming market, often to be withdrawn from catalogs within a few years as newer and better forms became available. Because the selection process was not very rigorous, popular species such as peonies and delphiniums could have a dozen or more new cultivars on the market each year. This work continues today, but at a more restrained pace. The selection process has become much more rigorous, and restricted budgets mean that not every nursery can afford to dedicate large areas of land to the lengthy process of elimination to obtain a good new cultivar. Although many of the early introductions have vanished, we still benefit from the early selection work as the reliable cultivars have survived. Most species are now available in a large range of carefully selected cultivars of strong, healthy plants, varying in height, color, and flowering period. The huge color range available to modern-day gardeners makes it possible to arrange plants in very sophisticated and distinctive color schemes.

Boosted by the increasing range of herbaceous perennials available, the first half of the 20th century could be considered as the highlight period for perennials. It was the time when some of the greatest designers and plantsmen were at their most creative and when a great exchange of ideas was taking place. It was also the period during which some of the most successful planting styles were developed. In Britain the gardens created by Gertrude Jekyll and Sir Edwin Lutyens were at their height and had, thanks to Jekyll's publications, a great following. In addition there were passionate amateur gardeners, such as Lawrence Johnston and Vita Sackville-West, who planted their gardens at Hidcote and Sissinghurst, respectively. These gardens were formally designed, divided into geometric rooms, but planted with a billowing abundance of flowers according to distinctive color schemes, creating spaces with unique character and mood. Plants chosen for color, shape, and texture were used in groups, positioned so as to show them off to their best effect. Beds or borders thus planted were quite labor intensive, as the plant groups had to be kept as upright entities, carefully staked and regularly deadheaded. These passionate gardeners planted mainly for optical effect.

The end of World War II brought an end to many herbaceous borders. Labor was scarce and expensive, and most gardens could not afford to reinstate these elaborate schemes. It was not until the 1980s that many amateur gardeners tired of the ground-covering shrubs, conifers, and heathers, as well as the rose beds that had replaced many herbaceous beds and borders.

The last decades of the 20th century saw a distinct revival of herbaceous perennials, with many gardeners exploring new ways of using them. Especially influential were the more naturalistic planting styles practiced by the Germans, Dutch, and Americans. While Britain was under the artistic influence of the Jekyllian school of thought, Germany developed a much different approach to planting, which has left an equally important international legacy. German gardeners were treated to a vast array of excellent, sturdy, healthy new garden plants put on the market by their famous plantsmen Georg Arends and Karl Foerster, who was also responsible for bringing the value of ornamental grasses to the attention of gardeners worldwide. Foerster was a plantsman rather than a designer and was concerned with planting the right plant in the right place. He was one of several gardeners who since the middle of the 19th century used nature as inspiration for planting schemes. Richard Hansen, one of his close followers, classified plants according to their habitat, enabling designers to plant according to the specific environments. A distinctive naturalistic planting style has evolved from this way of using herbaceous perennials, including grasses, that grow in the same habitat but originated from different parts of the world, planting them in similar communities as they would naturally grow. The style consists of a matrix of ground-covering vegetation out of which arise seasonal highlights. The vegetation is managed so that plant communities can evolve. Whereas the British were gardening for optical effect, the Germans were letting logic dictate their planting. Both styles have had many followers, but it is clear that the labor demands of the proper English herbaceous border has turned it into a luxury that few can still afford. The less-demanding, more environmentally sensitive approach developed by the Germans has gained in popularity, as it fits in more with modern-day gardening expectations, partly because of its ecological implications and partly because it of its lower labor implications.

Similar movements have developed in other countries. In the Netherlands the work of Mien Ruys, influenced by Foerster's philosophy as well as the aesthetic approach she encountered while working in Britain, produced her own distinctive planting styles but has now been overtaken by a new generation of designers. The

Heemparks, where only native plants are used, present one extreme, but the distinctive work of Piet Oudolf, with bold naturalistic drifts of herbaceous perennials and grasses, still reflects on his predecessor's artistic approach to gardening. Likewise in the United States, where at the start of the 20th century Beatrice Farrand was creating her own highly structured masterpieces, inspired by the ideas of her English counterparts, there is now a much stronger movement toward naturalistic planting schemes, allowing perennials to be the main features in major planting areas. James van Sweden and Wolfgang Oehme were instrumental in breaking with old traditions, introducing large numbers of perennials in their schemes. The work of others such as Neil Dibbol is even closer to nature, creating prairie meadows with native flowers selected according to habitat, which provide great wildlife havens and form an important feature of the traditional American landscape. Although each country has created distinctive planting styles to suit various trends and moods, they also tend to suit the country's climatic conditions. Prairie planting, for example, works well in the hot, dry summers created by a continental climate but would fail in milder, more temperate maritime environments where there is too much competition from lush grass growth throughout the season. On the other hand, this mild climate is ideal for the English herbaceous border, where a wide range of plants tolerate the mild, wet winters and the mild moist summers.

Further Reading

DiSabato-Aust, Tracy, *The Well-Tended Perennial Garden: Planting and Pruning Techniques*, Portland, Oregon: Timber Press, 1998

Hansen, Richard, and Friedrich Stahl, *Stauden und ihre Lebensbereiche in Gärten und Grünanlagen*, Stuttgart, Germany: Ulmer, 1981; as *Perennials and Their Garden Habitats*, translated by Richard Ware, Portland, Oregon: Timber Press, 1993

Jellito, Leo, and Wilhelm Schacht, *Die Freiland-Schmuckstauden*, 3 vols., Stuttgart, Germany: Ulmer, 1985; as *Hardy Herbaceous Perennials*, 2 vols., translated by Michael E. Epp, Portland, Oregon: Timber Press, 1990

Phillips, Roger, and Martyn Rix, *Perennials*, 2 vols., London: Pan, 1991

Pope, Nori, and Sandra Pope, *Colour by Design: Planting the Contemporary Garden*, London: Conran Octopus, 1998

Thomas, Graham Stuart, *Perennial Garden Plants*, London: Dent, 1976; 3rd edition, London: Dent, and Portland, Oregon: Timber Press, 1990

Trehane, Piers, *Index Hortensis: A Modern Nomenclator for Botanists, Horticulturists, Plantsmen, and the Serious Gardener*, Wimborne, Dorset: Quarterjack, 1989

ISABELLE VAN GROENINGEN

Pests and Diseases, Combating of

The battle against pests and diseases in the garden is age old, but gardeners have always had a wide choice of weapons at hand, in categories as diverse as their own hands, practical devices, poisons, and biological controls.

A large majority of plant diseases and disorders are caused by parasitic fungi, but this was only recognized in the mid-19th century, thanks to research on potato blight. The cure—a combination of lime and copper sulfate known as Bordeaux mixture—was the first universal fungicide. Until then, it was supposed that rot, rust, canker, and mildew, as well as complaints known as "freezing and scorching," were due (if not to the wrath of God or the stages of the moon) to insects, bad weather, or a combination of the two. Without a full understanding of plant pathology, successful treatment was chancy; it was also sometimes extremely toxic.

Most of the pesticides recommended in the Roman husbandries are nonresidual and comparatively harmless to warm-blooded creatures. Sticky, bitter, or smothering substances such as tar and bitumen, soap and soap ashes, dung, soot, ammonia (made from sal ammoniac, urine, or spirits of hartshorn), lime, and salt disposed of small pests. Steam, fumes, and smoke from a sulfurous pesticide brewed in the open in copper pots appeared to benefit Roman gardens, orchards, and vineyards, but with no understanding of what was, in effect, a forerunner of Bordeaux mixture.

Classical gardeners also had more lethal pesticides, such as amurca, a dangerous by-product of olive oil production. Early gardeners also used arsenic, mercury, and strychnine, mainly to kill ants, wasps, rats, mice, moles, and rabbits. By 1886 gardeners were using cyanide, hellebore, and pure nicotine as insecticides, often as fumigants and at considerable risk to themselves. All these substances are as deadly to humans, fish, birds, and animals as they are to insects, fungi, and viruses, and some remain toxic for weeks or months.

Spraying pests, ca. 1891
Courtesy of Mary Evans Picture Library

Later, less harmful pesticides included the relatively innocuous tobacco refuse (stalks and the parts too tough to smoke in pipes, a 17th-century introduction) and paraffin oil (introduced in the mid-19th century); West Indian quassia chips and Dalmatian pyrethrum powder (both used for centuries in their countries of origin but not imported to England for use as insecticides until the late 19th century); and tar oil and derris dust, two 20th-century pesticides.

Combined with one another or used singly, the pesticides were applied as drenches, washes, pastes, and powders with syringes, watering cans, sponges, brushes, or bellows. Drenches of brine, lime, and copper were sprayed on seed corn and potatoes. Washes made from infusions of bitter leaves, urine, alumroot, and vinegar with the addition of soft soap smothered aphids, mealy bugs, and unspecified "blights." Irritant powders of lime, soot, ash, sulfur, or tobacco dust deterred slugs and caterpillars; disinfectants based on cow dung or mud, ashes, and lime were plastered over tree wounds

and grafts. Fumigants of bonfire smoke, sulfur, and tobacco were used in orchards and greenhouses.

Many of the most lethal pesticides date only from the end of the 19th century. They are made from synthetic poisons—chlorinated hydrocarbons—which are based on organochemical compounds. Some have since proved so dangerous that they are now banned. The first such compound—formaldehyde, sold as Formalin—was produced in 1885. An organomercurial compound (chlorphenol-mercury) followed in 1913 and was sold under various trade names. Later discoveries—all used in gardens in the 1950s and 1960s—include the now notorious insecticides aldrin and dieldrin (first used 1948); calomel (another mercurial compound); two powerful organophosphorous insecticides—parathion benzene hexachloride (also known as BHC or lindane) and dichloro-diphenyl-trichloro-ethane (DDT); two selective, long-term, synthetic organic weed killers, smazine and monuron (discovered in 1942); and the fungicides thiram and captan (invented 1937 and 1951, respectively).

Toward the mid-19th century, commercial pesticides became available; before then gardeners made their own. The ingredients were cheap and easy to obtain. Soot, elder leaves, dung, urine, and ashes cost nothing; soft soap, lime, sulfur, tobacco, and so on were bought from itinerant tradesmen. Today, treatment relies increasingly on palliatives invented in laboratories. Virtually all pesticides, herbicides, insecticides, and fungicides are now bought ready-made.

Manual and mechanical pest controls are usually harmless to creatures other than the intended victims. They deal with sizable insects, caterpillars, snails, and slugs or small creatures such as mice and birds. They include powerful hoses for syringing infested leaves with water; agitating and removing affected branches; moth and butterfly nets; protective fencing, hairlines, netting, and tar bands; and lures and traps, scaring devices, and so on.

For many centuries, children, weeding women, and garden boys were employed in the destruction, by hand, of the eggs, caterpillars, and larvae of cabbage butterflies, and gooseberry, currant, and codling moths. Wasps nests were destroyed with squibs of gunpowder; snails were lured overnight with baits of bran and swept up by the hundreds in the morning.

The earliest forms of biological control were simple: a garden cat caught mice and scared birds; captive tomtits, toads, hedgehogs, and guinea pigs ate the slugs and wood lice in greenhouses and mushroom sheds; tame seagulls and ducks were allowed in kitchen gardens to eat slugs and snails. Today, benign insects are introduced into closed environments such as frames and hothouses in order to eliminate less desirable insects. Another ancient pest deterrent, known to the Greeks, is companion planting, whereby certain plants appear to release toxins that control pests on neighboring plants or in the soil. The old remedies were not totally ineffective, but gardeners who were ignorant of the true causes of blight, disease, and infestation—and helpless in the face of tempests, droughts, frosts, and floods—also put their faith in a wealth of superstitions.

Some of these superstitions are remembered even now, for not all the old beliefs are as daft as they seem. People without calendars or clocks planted and reaped by phases of the moon, or on certain saints' days, and measured short time spans with repetitive incantations. Classical kitchen gardeners placed effigies of the gods and goddesses of fertility in their gardens, primarily to make sure of bounteous crops, although statues of Priapus, with his rampant private parts, were intended to scare intruders as well.

Further Reading

Bush, Raymond, *A Fruit-Grower's Diary*, London: Faber and Faber, 1950

Cato, Marcus Porcius, *On Agriculture*, translated by William Davis Hooper, revised by Harrison Boyd Ash, Cambridge, Massachusetts: Harvard University Press, and London: Heinemann, 1934

Columella, Lucius Junius Moderatus, *On Agriculture and Trees*, 3 vols., translated by E. S. Forster and Edward H. Heffner, Cambridge, Massachusetts: Harvard University Press, and London: Heinemann, 1955

Evelyn, John, *Kalendarum Hortense: The Gard'ners Almanac*, London, 1691; edited by Rosemary Verey, London: Stourton, 1983

Forsyth, William, *Treatise on the Culture and Management of Fruit-trees*, New York and London, 1802; 7th edition, London, 1824

Gardeners Companion, 7th edition, London, 1795

Hill, Thomas, *The Gardeners Labyrinth*, London, 1577; edited Richard Mabey, Oxford and New York: Oxford University Press, 1987

Jones, William, *The Gardener's Receipt Book*, London, 1845; 5th edition, 1861

Lawson, William, *A New Orchard and Garden*, London, 1618; reprint, New York: Garland, 1982

Loudon, John Claudius, *An Encyclopaedia of Gardening*, 2 vols., London, 1822; new edition, 1835; reprint, New York: Garland, 1982

McIntosh, Charles, *The Practical Gardener, and Modern Horticulturist*, 2 vols., London, 1828; 6th edition, 1851; as *The New and Improved Practical Gardener, and Modern Horticulturist*, London, 1865; see especially vol. 1

Mellanby, Kenneth, *Pesticides and Pollution*, London: Collin, 1967; 2nd revised edition, 1970

Morton, Alan G., *History of Botanical Science*, London and New York: Academic Press, 1981

Palmer, Ray, and W. Percival Westell, *Pests of the Garden and Orchard, Farm and Forest*, London: Drane, 1922

Pliny, the Elder, *Natural History*, 10 vols., translated by H. Rackham, W.H.S. Jones, and D.E. Eichholz, 1938–63

Theophrastus, *Enquiry into Plants and Minor Works on Odours and Weather Signs*, 2 vols., translated by Arthur Hort, Cambridge, Massachusetts: Harvard University Press, and London: Heinemann, 1916; reprint, 1980

Theophrastus, *De Causis Plantarum*, translated by Benedict Einarson and George K.K. Link, 3 vols., Cambridge, Massachusetts: Harvard University Press, and London: Heinemann, 1976–90

SUSAN CAMPBELL

Peterhof. *See* Petrodvorets

Peto, Harold Ainsworth 1854–1933

English Architect

Harold Peto was born into a large family, the fifth son of Sir Samuel Morton Peto, a successful Victorian entrepreneur in railways and the construction industry. At the age of 17, Harold Peto began his architectural training with J. Clements of Lowestoft before going to work in London, where in 1876 Peto went into partnership with Ernest George. Together they developed a successful practice responsible for a number of important mansions in London and a considerable number of country houses throughout England. During this time Peto traveled regularly to Europe and developed a keen interest in gardens; diaries of his visit to Spain in 1888 give a vivid impression of his delight in the Alhambra and Generalife in Grenada and the Alcázar gardens in Seville, all of which served as inspiration for much of his later work as a garden designer. His diaries reveal not only his pleasure in plants and gardens but also his increasing frustration at living in London and his desire to move to the country. As a result, in 1892 he gave up his partnership with George and moved to a house in Kent. For the next seven years, while he searched for a permanent dwelling in the country, he continued to travel, his most ambitious journey being to sail around the world in 1898. During this trip he was in Japan for several months, where he spent much time exploring their gardens. His diary is full of enthusiasm and delight in the landscape and the plants of Japan, many of which he had sent back to England.

In 1899 Peto's search for a country house ended when he bought Iford Manor near Bath, where he settled for the remainder of his life. From 1900 to 1914, he undertook his major landscape commissions. One of the earliest, starting in 1902, was an ambitious scheme for the countess of Warwick at Easton Lodge in Essex, which included a magnificent pergola, a balustraded lily pond, a Japanese teahouse by the lake, and even a tree house. The water garden for Lord Faringdon at Buscot Park, Berkshire, was another early commission, for which Peto designed a series of linked pools descending from the house to the lake with canals, fountains, and bridges. Crichel House, Dorset; Bridge House, Surrey; Wayford Manor, Somerset; and Hartham Park and Heale House, both in Wiltshire, were all commissioned before 1910 and are evidence of his distinctive style, which includes the use of Italianate pavilions, terraces, balustrades, and ornamental bridges. He has been primarily associated with an English interpretation of Italian gardens, and although undoubtedly they were a strong influence on his work, Moorish and Japanese gardens were equally an inspiration. Combined with his skillful use of plants, his manipulation of these influences contributed to the success and praise that he enjoyed during his lifetime from such important garden makers as Gertrude Jekyll.

In 1910 Peto began one of his most extensive schemes at Ilnacullin (Garinish Island) (see Plate 28), in southwest Ireland, where he was commissioned to design a house and garden on a barren rocky island in Bantry Bay. All the soil had to be imported before planting could begin, but by the 1920s Peto's pavilions were set among a renowned plant collection. Other major gardens abroad include those on the Riviera near Menton: the Villa Sylvia for his American friend Ralph Curtis and a palatial house and garden, Villa Maryland, for the Englishman Arthur Wilson.

Peto's own garden at Iford Manor remains today one of his major achievements. The garden, laid out on a steep hillside, is given its distinctive form with long flights of steps leading up to the great terrace, which runs across the hillside from a curved stone seat at one end to a garden house at the other. The terrace is lined with antique sculpture, and the view over the valley is framed by openings in a long colonnade that Peto built alongside the terrace. He built a stylish summerhouse, the casita, at the foot of the hanging wood. At the far end of the garden is the Cloisters, a building that shows the influence of his early visit to Spain and that he built in part to house his numerous sculptures. As well as being a pre-eminent garden designer of the Edwardian period in England, Peto was a great collector of early sculpture. The Byzantine scholar Thomas Whittemore praised Peto's collection of Byzantine reliefs as one of the largest west of the Veneto. Peto was also a friend of the Boston collector Isabella Gardner, and his contacts in Italy helped in the purchase of sculpture for her collection at the Gardner Museum.

Regrettably, Peto left few records of the most active part of his landscape career, and apart from the *Boke of Iford* (1993), which gives a personal history of the making of the garden at Iford, the most useful sources for visual material on his commissions are to be found in the pages of *Country Life*.

Biography

Born at Somerleyton Hall, Suffolk, England, 1854. Began architectural training with J. Clements of Lowestoft, Suffolk, England, 1871; went into partnership with Ernest George, London, 1876–92; during period with George, worked on large number of architectural commissions in London and elsewhere in England; traveled widely in Europe, 1876–92, and visited America, 1887; traveled to Spain, 1888; left partnership in 1892 and moved out of London, living first in Kent, then Hampshire, finally settled at Iford Manor near Bath, 1899; further travels in Europe and around the world, 1898; carried out most important landscape work, 1899–1914, mostly in England, major commission in Ireland at Ilnacullin and several important works on Riviera around Menton, France; major work was own garden at Iford Manor; after World War I, appears to have carried out few new commissions. Died at Iford Manor, 1933.

Selected Designs

1899–1933	Iford Manor, Wiltshire, England
1902	Easton Lodge, Essex, England; Wayford Manor, Somerset, England
ca. 1903	Bridge House, Weybridge, Surrey, England; Hartham Park, Wiltshire, England
1904	Water garden, Buscot Park, Oxfordshire, England

ca. 1904   Villa Maryland, Alpes-Maritimes, France
1906–11   Heale House, Wiltshire, England
ca. 1907   Crichel, Dorset, England
1910–20s   Ilnacullin, Garinish Island, Glengariff,
    County Cork, Ireland

Selected Publications
Boke of Iford, 1993

Further Reading
Moore, Graeme, "Renaissance d'Azur," *Country Life* (7
    July 1988)

Ottewill, David, *The Edwardian Garden,* New Haven,
    Connecticut: Yale University Press, 1989
Quest-Ritson, Charles, *The English Garden Abroad,*
    London: Viking, 1992
Whalley, Robin, "The 'Plantsman' of Iford Manor?"
    Wiltshire Gardens Trust Journal 31 (Spring
    1995)
Whalley, Robin, "Harold Peto's Japanese Diary,"
    Hortus 36 and 37 (Winter 1995 and Spring
    1996)

ROBIN WHALLEY

Petri, Bernhard 1767–1853

German Landscape Designer

A man of many interests, Bernhard Petri was one of the most important designers of the classic English landscape style in central Europe. He studied science and economy, and the elector of the Palatinate sent him abroad, first to England, for a study trip. He spent his years of study with Ludwig von Sckell, who drew up his journeyman's certificate in 1785 after three years of practice. Petri traveled throughout England, France, Belgium, the Netherlands, and Germany, returning home to become the chief director of buildings and gardens in Zweibrücken.

After the French Revolution the Palatinate was occupied by France, and Petri had to flee his homeland. Afterward he worked as an independent landscape architect, first in Vienna beginning in 1791, where he designed several gardens for the nobility. In 1794 he designed for the sovereign, Emperor Leopold II, a project for a national garden. The proposed garden, meant for Brigittenau in Vienna, aimed to foster patriotic feelings and love and fidelity toward the monarch and the homeland, but the plans were never executed. The Temples of Peace, Victory, and Homeland were to house historic paintings, while the proposed temple on the Island of Elysium would have contained statues of noteworthy Austrians, an idea likely inspired by the Temple of British Worthies at Stowe in England. Petri's plan called for leaving large open grass-covered areas around the buildings. He intended to incorporate the sight of the surrounding landscape, the Danube, and the city into the garden.

Petri accepted the invitation of the Hungarian Palatine, Archduke Alexander Leopold of Habsburg,

and about 1793 went to Hungary. His invitation was probably in connection with the reshaping of the gardens of the royal palace at Buda Castle. Although he spent less than ten years in Hungary, he was highly influential as the first designer of the classic English landscape style there. He also recorded his principles of landscape design in his descriptions of his Hungarian creations.

Petri worked concurrently on the different gardens executed in Hungary. His first design was probably made for Hédervár, where he transformed a formal garden into the landscape style with the help of massive earthworks and heavy plantations. He planted *Robinias,* poplars, and fruit trees in large areas. His garden at Vedrőd was also a transformation into an informal garden. He led a nearby creek to the garden in a curving line and formed a lake from it. He built an obelisk, a hermitage, and artificial ruins in the garden as well. A quotation from Carl Hirschfeld referring to the work of the garden's designer was engraved into the obelisk. The Orczy Garden in Pest was Petri's best-known creation. Being in the capital and open to the public, the garden was also famous for the circumstances of its creation. It was established on a sandy desert, where successful plantation provided a particular challenge for the landscape designer. Petri created his fourth garden in Hungary at Ásványráró on a charming rural landscape.

Petri always kept in mind the situation of the place and its connection to the neighboring landscape. He attached the sight of the characteristic and worthy elements of the surroundings into the garden. He placed special emphasis on the selection of plant ensembles, particularly on the harmony of colors and sizes. To create contrast between the large open grassland and the surrounding woods, he used certain dark-leafed trees such as *Aesculus hippocastanum, Fraxinus americana, Rhus typhina,* and eight other carefully chosen species. He created picturesque arrangements, treating the garden as an ensemble of different images, and incorporated the sight of farm buildings, animals, and utilitarian plantations into his garden designs. He was a follower of two principal figures of the English landscape style, the designer Lancelot "Capability" Brown and the theoretician Carl Hirschfeld. Brown's style inspired the generous space arrangement, the use of belts and clumps, and the creation of lakes. Petri was equally influenced by Hirschfeld's theories, aspiring to create various atmospheres with the different garden scenes and to make strong contrast between them.

Petri arrived at the Lichtenstein estate of Loosdorf (Lower Austria) in the service of Prince Johann by 1796, where he later also designed the transformation of the garden. In the course of this process he created a lake, built temples and a hermitage, and planted a great quantity of trees. The trees were expected to bring profit as well, and 1 million *Robinias* were planted to be exploited in due time. After 1803, when Prince Johann became the head of the family, Petri designed several other gardens at Lichtenstein estates. The most significant among these is Lednice-Valtice in Moravia; others include Adamov, Nove Zamky, and Rossau near Vienna.

In the park of Lednice Petri had to deal with the regular floods over the site. He solved the problem by digging lakes and using the extracted earth to create islands and to heighten the surface of the rest of the territory. Development of the massive earthworks continued based on his designs even after he left in 1808, until the park's completion in 1811. In the last phase of the site's transformation, a new bed was created for the river Dyje outside the park to avoid further damage in the gardens.

Petri's discovery and description of a fungus that grows in water pipes, as well as a register on the native ligneous plants of Hungary, exemplify his botanical interest, and his article on the acclimatization of southern plants to colder climates proves his horticultural skills. He performed many scientific experiments and observations to determine the cold tolerance of various plants. After his retirement in 1808 he turned to the breeding of merino sheep and published several articles on various economic and agricultural matters.

Biography

Born in Zweibrücken, Palatinate, Germany, 1767. Father was Johann Ludwig Petri, head gardener of Schwetzingen. Traveled to England, France, Belgium, Netherlands, and Germany, as part of studies; returned to Palatinate, 1785; received journeyman's certificate, 1785; worked in botanical garden of Elector and became chief director of buildings and gardens in Zweibrücken; due to French occupation, had to leave country; worked as independent landscape architect, Vienna, from 1791; went to Hungary to serve as landscape architect under Archduke Alexander Leopold of Habsburg, ca. 1793; designed gardens in Lichtenstein for Prince Johann, ca. 1796–1808; became financial director of Lichtenstein's estate of Loosdorf, 1803; retired, 1808. Died in Theresienfeld bei Wien, Austria, 1853.

Selected Designs

1791	Gardens for the nobility, Vienna, Austria
ca. 1793–96	Garden, Hédervár, Hungary; garden, Vedrőd, Hungary; Orczy Garden, Budapest, Hungary; garden, Ásványráró, Hungary
1794	National Garden project, Vienna, Austria
1803	Garden, Loosdorf, Austria
1805–8	Lednice-Valtice, Moravia, Czech Republic; garden, Nove Zamky, Moravia, Czech Republic; garden, Rossau, Austria

Selected Publications

"Beschreibung des Naturgartens zu Vedröd in Ungarn," in *Taschenbuch für Garten Freunde,* edited by W.G. Becker, 1797

"Entwurf zu einem Nationalgarten," in *Almanach und Taschenbuch für Garten-Freunde,* edited by W.G. Becker, 1798

Further Reading

Galavics, Géza, *Magyarországi angolkertek* (English Gardens in Hungary), Budapest: Balassi, 1999

Novák, Zdenek, "Eisgrub-Feldsberg in Mähren: Ein bedeutendes Dokument der Landschaftsgestaltung in Mitteleuropa," *Die Gartenkunst* 6 (1994)

KRISTÓF FATSAR

Petrodvorets

Peterhof, St. Petersburg Oblast, Russia

Location: approximately 14 miles (22.5 km)
southwest of St. Petersburg, on southern
coast of Neva Bay, Gulf of Finland

With its dramatic view of the Gulf of Finland, Petrodvorets, the summer palace of Peter the Great, truly personifies Russia's "window into Europe," celebrating a victory that launched Russia's status as an imperial power and assured its control of the Baltic Sea. Known as Peterhof until 1944, Petrodvorets (the "fountain capital") was formally unveiled in 1723 to celebrate the defeat of the Swedes in the Great Northern War and the consequent acquisition of strategic Finnish borderlands. Although the construction of the estate spanned two centuries, the foundations were laid in 1704 when Peter the Great built a wooden house on the Gulf of Finland while supervising construction of the nearby Kronstadt naval fortress. By 1709 he had focused his energies on an official summer residence, and his visit to the French court later that year motivated him to transform his new palace and grounds into an eastern version of Versailles, thus reinvigorating plans for the architectural nexus of the estate, the Grand Palace (Bolshoi Dvorets).

The architect Domenico Trezzini received the commission to draft designs for the grounds and structures. He took advantage of the dramatic views and terraced topography by constructing the palace on a plateau approximately 12 meters (13 yd.) above the Baltic Sea, thereby separating the two gardens that were planned about the same time. The czar summoned other international artisans and engineers as well, among them the Dutchman G.W. Henin, who was enlisted to construct a system of dams for the estate, and several renowned French landscape designers, including Alexandre-Jean-Baptiste Le Blond, a student of André Le Nôtre. Le Blond faithfully replicated the French grand style that Peter had so admired at Versailles, using radiating avenues, geometric patterns, and a complicated waterworks system that for the most part overshadowed the natural landscape and any emphasis on plant collections. After Le Blond's death in 1719 Niccolo Michetti pursued Le Blond's designs for the baroque pavilions and collaborated with the talented hydraulic engineer V. Tuvolkov on the fountain designs.

The recherché fountains of Petrodvorets, as its Russian name suggests, are its most identifiable characteristic. Incredibly, the 144 fountains on the estate all operate without the use of pumps and instead rely on gravity and the differing levels of the ponds and fountains. The Grand Cascade, the focal point of the fountain system, flows downhill from the palace through two staircases to a large basin holding a statue of the biblical Samson wrestling with the lion. The statue is a clear allegorical reference to Russia's military might; the Nazis looted the original—crafted by Mikhail I Kozlovsky in 1802—during World War II, and a replica now stands in its place. The Grand Cascade, which also contains a grotto and 64 fountains, ultimately forms a large, decorative channel descending to the sea, where tourists arrive from neighboring St. Petersburg in hydrofoils and boats.

The Upper and Lower Parks neatly divide the estate, providing ten museums and three smaller parks within their scope. Originally designed by Johann-Fredrich Braunstein (who was quickly replaced by the more famous Le Blond), the Upper Park lies on the south side of the Grand Palace and is centered by a fountain of Neptune purchased in later years by Czar Paul (1796–1801). Erected in 1798, the Neptune fountain was constructed in Nürnberg more than a century before and like the two other main fountains, resides in a central stall while the auxiliary fountains lie within square ponds on opposing sides of the Grand Palace's side wings. Nearby, manicured lime trees, statuary, allées, and a large parterre complete the baroque formal garden, an arrangement somewhat overshadowed by the estate's elaborate waterworks system.

Three smaller palaces separated by bosquets and fountains form the chief attractions of the Lower Park. Of the three, Peter's preferred residence was the Monplaisir residence, a conservative, Dutch-styled country house and a point of contrast to the more extravagant quarters of the Hermitage Pavilion and the Chateau de Marly, both specifically designed to accommodate royal family and visiting dignitaries. In later years additional guest quarters and elegant garden pavilions were built throughout the remainder of the Lower Park, including the Znamenka estate, the personal dacha, and the stately Alexandria Park. Constructed for Nicholas I in 1831, the Alexandria Park holds a farm house, the much-visited Cottage House, and a neo-Gothic chapel—a later stylistic counterpoint to the baroque design of the bulk of the estate.

Remodeling plans were initiated in 1745 under the guidance of Bartolomeo Rastrelli, the architect behind St. Petersburg's winter palace. Rastrelli completed much of the cornice work, in the process enlarging the Grand Palace over a ten-year period and enhancing the rudiments of Trezzini's original design. The park benefited from smaller additions throughout the years, and by the

Grand cascade, Petrodvorets (Peterhof), St. Petersburg Oblast, Russia
Copyright Ellen Rooney/Garden Picture Library

early 20th century Peterhof had emerged as one of the most popular summer residences for the imperial Romanov family. With the advent of the Bolshevik Revolution, the palace and grounds were commuted to public property, falling under the jurisdiction of the socialist state. The doors were soon opened to the first Soviet workers' group on 18 May 1918, and for the next few decades Peterhof was celebrated as a cultural symbol of the new Communist regime.

A new era began when the Germans invaded Russia in 1941 and quickly penetrated St. Petersburg and its environs, entering Peterhof on 23 September. The gardens suffered much abuse: trees were razed, the fountain complex torn up, and many bronze monuments plundered. For nearly two-and-a-half years Nazi troops desecrated the area despite the efforts of caretakers who had hurriedly transferred some museum valuables and sculptures underground prior to the invasion.

With liberation in 1944, Peterhof (German for "Peter's house") was subsequently renamed Petrodvorets. Yet the fountains celebrated in its new Russian name had been largely destroyed and the palace itself devastated. Restoration began in earnest soon thereafter with the reconstruction of 172 fountains, three cascades, and 15 monuments. Russian architects V. Savkov and Y. Kazanskaya assisted in overhauling the damage and organized efforts to fortify the vandalized structure of the Grand Palace. In 1947 a duplicate statue of Samson was transplanted in the Grand Cascade, and within the next 11 years the palace had been gracefully restored. Periodic improvements continued throughout the years, and in 2000 a refurbished Grand Cascade and Chinese Garden were unveiled to the public.

Synopsis

1704	Czar Peter the Great builds wooden house on Peterhof site
1709	Peterhof founded after Peter the Great visits Versailles
1714	Construction of official summer residence started, designed by J.F. Braunstein
1716	Peter the Great summons French landscape designer Alexandre-Jean-Baptiste Le Blond to Russia to replicate French grand style
1719	Le Blond dies and Niccolo Michetti continues work
1720–21	Waterworks built by engineer Vasily Tuvolkov
1721	Treaty of Nystadt signed between Russia and Sweden
1723	Opening festivities for Peterhof
1728	Peter the Great dies
1745	Remodeling plans begun under Bartolomeo Rastrelli
1750	Several royal residences constructed for dignitaries
1798	Neptune Fountain erected
1802	Mikhail Kozlovsky sculpts Samson Rending the Lion's Jaws, for basin of Grand Cascade
1831–33	Alexandria park designed by A.A. Menelas for Czar Nicholas I
1918	Grand Palace visited by first Socialist workers' group
1941	German troops enter Peterhof and cause extensive damage
1944	Peterhof liberated from Nazis and renamed Petrodvorets
1946–55	Grand Cascade and water avenue restored
1947	Samson sculpture reconstructed in Grand Cascade
2000	Chinese Garden, Upper Garden House, and Grand Cascade renovated

Further Reading

Adams, William Howard, *Nature Perfected: Gardens through History*, New York: Abbeville Press, 1991

Egorova, Kira Mikhailovna, *Leningrad: House of Peter I, Summer Gardens, and Palace of Peter I*, Leningrad: Aurora Art Publishers, 1975

Floryan, Margrethe, *Gardens of the Tsars: A Study of the Aesthetics, Semantics, and Uses of Late 18th-Century Russian Gardens*, Aarhus, Denmark: Aarhus University, and Sagaponack, New York: Sagapress, 1996

Gaynor, Elizabeth, and Kari Haavisto, *Russian Houses*, New York: Stewart Tabori and Chang, 1991

Hobhouse, Penelope, and Elvin McDonald, editors, *Gardens of the World: The Art and Practice of Gardening*, New York: MacMillan, 1991

Shvidkovsky, Dmitri, and Alexei Reteyum, "Botany in a Cold Climate: Moscow's Botanical Garden Is Restored and Discovers a New Role," *Historic Gardens Review* (Winter 2000)

KRISTIN WYE-RODNEY

Petzold, Eduard 1815–1891

German Landscape Gardener

Eduard Petzold is one of the most important landscape gardeners of the late 19th century, whose fame and work went well beyond the boundaries of Germany. His positions as court gardener of the grand duke in Weimar, as well as that of princely garden inspector and, later, garden director of the Netherlands, supplied Petzold with important contacts to the ruling representatives of the aristocracy as well as to the bourgeoisie. In addition to his official obligations in Weimar, in Muskau from 1852, in Silesia (Heinrichau), and periodically also in the Netherlands, he designed, redesigned, restored and supervised approximately 170 public and private gardens and parks in several European countries.

Petzold strove for spaciousness, used nature as his guiding principle and model, and was committed to the "landscape style" without exception. He was always concerned with a balanced concept of space, which, however, also permitted differentiation in both design and function. On the basis of his extensive botanical knowledge, he used a much richer range of plants, with a greater subtlety of nuance, than, for instance, Prince Hermann Pückler-Muskau. Petzold, unlike Gustav Meyer, another leading German landscape designer of the day, placed the pleasure ground around the house generously. Vistas, visible not only from the buildings but especially from the circular paths and in combination with the landscape, were meant to create virtual "picture galleries." Ponds and lakes, as well as artificial rivers, were considered by Petzold to be important elements of a park. He designed lakes, for example, with deep inlets and protruding banks, as well as integrating islands, all of which made the water's surface appear more extensive than it actually was. The system of development typical of Petzold is extensive, and, unlike that of his contemporaries Peter Joseph Lenné or Meyer, characterized by a conspicuous restraint regarding the number of paths. Like Pückler, Petzold strove for systems in the sense of a *ferme ornée* (ornamental farm) whenever possible and concerned himself very much with measures that beautified the landscape.

Petzold's creations, such as Sondershausen, Zwickau, De Paauw, Heinrichau, Zypendaal, Salaberg, Finckenstein, Rhederoord, Greiz, Altdöbern, Josephstal, Sandrowo, and Twickel received international attention, as did the 55-hectare (136 acres) complex of the Arboretum Muscaviense (designed in collaboration with Georg Kirchner). Some of the sites, such as the Weimar Ilmpark, the parks of Tiefurt and Muskau, the Brühlpark in Quedlinburg, or the Volkspark Bosch in The Hague, Petzold was required to treat "in the spirit of the park"—that is, according to the rules of preservation.

Some of Petzold's apprentices and assistants, such as Max Bertram in Saxony, achieved considerable success in their careers and thus promoted Petzold's knowledge and principles. His reputation, enhanced by his work as a co-editor of the journal *Gartenflora*, became so firmly established that he was appointed to preside as chairman and serve as a jury member of many international exhibitions, including those in Vienna (1873), Amsterdam (1877), and Berlin (1885). In park planning he occasionally competed with colleagues such as Lenné, Heinrich Siesmayer, Eduard André, and Leonard Springer.

Petzold published approximately 30 writings, which covered virtually all current topics in the field of garden architecture, including its foundations, principles of design, and elements. He passed down some expert opinions, for example, passages on cemeteries and public gardens from Friedrich Ludwig von Sckell's *Beiträge* and some works by Pückler. One of Petzold's major achievements was his translation into German (working initially with Friedrich Wilhelm Döll, the princely court gardener of Eisenberg) of the writings of the English landscape designer Humphry Repton, whose basic principles Petzold largely adopted but implemented in a highly independent way. In comparison to Meyer's *Lehrbuch der schönen Gartenkunst* (Textbook on the Architecture of Beautiful Gardens), Petzold's *Landschaftsgärtnerei* (Landscape Gardening) provides something new, namely, pronouncements on matters of perspective and ideas about the design of cemeteries and avenues. As early as the 1860s, Petzold had acquired some experience in the designing of cemeteries (Zwickau). In 1888 he presented and discussed exemplary cemetery complexes in London, Paris, and Berlin, as well as those in the Orient, which he had studied on a trip to Constantinople. The activities of his son Max under Adolph Strauch at the Spring Grove Cemetery in Cincinnati, Ohio, may have finally motivated him to support to a greater extent the establishment in Germany of landscape cemeteries like those in Boston, New York, and Philadelphia.

Natural observation informed his written works. His explanations on planting consider location, plant properties, and their possibilities for use in parks. Tree-lined avenues are another topic Petzold took up in a number of books, in which he suggested possibilities for combining different species of trees when laying out new avenues. He preserved old avenues in landscape parks as much as possible but frequently disguised them with new plantings or partly broke them up in order to achieve groupings of trees.

View from the terraces with water pool and flower bed to the group of trees, which were planted by Petzold in Rhederoord, Netherlands, ca. 1900
Courtesy of Kasteel Rhederoord

Petzold developed the basic principles of the theory of color and perspective for landscape gardening and was the first German garden architect to formulate the principles of park preservation—in other words, the beginnings of the movement to conserve the old avenues and gardens laid out in the symmetrical style. His specialist books, particularly the two editions of his *Landschafts-gärtnerei* and the *Arboretum Muscaviense,* a reference book on woody plants (written with Kirchner), were internationally known. His influence exerted itself on park owners, assistants, and professional colleagues, such as Hermann Jäger, Wilhelm Hentze, and Springer; he also influenced those in related fields—for example, the philosopher and botanist Ernst von Hallier and his studies on the aesthetics of nature; the architect Hermann Wentzel; and the forest aesthetic of the forestry

engineer Heinrich von Salisch. Occasionally a close bond developed between Petzold and his clients and employers, as evidenced in the dedications of his publications. His biographical works are proof of his personal relationships with others in the field; they include a translation of J.C. Loudon's book on Repton; a biography of Döll; and volumes on the garden inspector and head of the botanical garden of Jena, Franz Sebastian Baumann, the garden director of the electorate of Hesse, Wilhelm Hentze, and, last but not least, Pückler. His books on Pückler also contain detailed descriptions of the prince's garden style.

Biography
Born in Königswalde, east of Frankfurt, Germany, 1815. Completed thorough apprenticeship under Jacob H.

Rehder in garden nursery and park of Prince Pückler-Muskau, 1831–34; after assistantship, employed by Georg Riedesel Freiherr zu Eisenbach at Park Neuenhof, Thuringia, 1838; leave for six months annually in order to take educational trips throughout Europe, where he studied park systems and nurseries and came into contact with experts such as Peter J. Lenné, Hermann Sello, Sebastian Rinz, Philipp F. von Siebold, and Eduard A. von Regel; active as court gardener in Ettersburg and Weimar, Germany, for eight years, from 1844; under Prince Friedrich of the Netherlands, garden inspector of park systems of Muskau, Germany, which he completed and extended to 600 ha, 1852; regeneration and planning for Prince's properties in the Netherlands; simultaneously ran own tree nursery in Silesia and designed for over 130 parks throughout Europe; supervised parks in Heinrichau (Silesia) for Grand Duchess Sophie Wilhelmine von Sachsen-Weimar-Eisenach, until 1890; park and garden director of the Netherlands in 1872; resigned Netherlands position in 1878, but continued as chief director in charge of Muskau Park, Germany, until 1881; moved to Dresden, Germany, 1882; continued to work freelance and write; received commission in Bulgaria and Constantinople, Turkey, in 1884. Died in Dresden-Blasewitz, 1891.

Selected Designs

1844–48	Complex of Ettersburg, near Weimar, Thuringia, Germany
1844–50	Park Tiefurt, Weimar, Thuringia, Germany
1847–59	Park Eisenbach, Lauterbach, Hesse, Germany
1848–52	Goethe's Ilmpark (with Julius Hartwig), Weimar, Thuringia, Germany
1850–51	Park Sondershausen (executed through Karl Arlt), near Gotha, Thuringia, Germany
1850–66	Schwanenteichpark (Swan Pond Park) and Stadtpromenade (Town Promenade) Zwickau (executed through Julius Hartwig), Zwickau, Saxony, Germany
1852–81	Park Muskau, including Arboretum Muscaviense, Bad Muskau, Saxony, Germany
1854–81	De Paauw and park systems in Wassenaar (partly together with architect Hermann Wentzel and Japan expert Philipp Franz von Siebold), Wassenaar near The Hague, Netherlands
1855–79	Feudal estate Boersdorf, near Jauer, Silesia; today, Targoszyn near Jawor, Msciwojów, Legnica, Poland
1856	Park Buchwald, near Schmiedeberg, Silesia; today Bukowiec near Ksostrzyca, Myslakowice, Jelenia Góra, Poland
1856–60	Park Dobrau, near Kappritz, Silesia; today Dobra, near Krapkowice, Strzeleczki, Opole, Poland
1858–66	Park Langenstein near Halberstadt, Sachsen-Anhalt, Germany
1863	Stadtpark Liegnitz, Silesia; today Park Miejski in Legnica, Legnica, Poland
1863–90	Park Heinrichau, Heinrichau near Münsterberg, Silesia; today Henryków near Ziebice, Ziebice, Walbrzych, Poland
1864	Park Salaberg, Haag near Linz, Austria
1866–68	Park Finckenstein, near Rosenberg, East Prussia; today Kamieniec, Susz, Elblag, Poland
1867	Stadtpark Brühl, Quedlinburg, Sachsen-Anhalt, Germany
1868	Park Rhederoord near Arnheim, Netherlands
1869	Park Bodelschwingh, Dortmund, Nordrhein-Westfalen, Germany
1870	Park Weinrich in Dobrenitz near Chlumetz, Bohemia; today Dobrenice near Chlumec, Czech Republic; Park Planitz near Zwickau, Saxony, Germany
1871	Volkspark Bosch, The Hague, Netherlands
1872	Park Karnitten near Osterode, East Prussia; today Karnity, Zalewo, Olsztyn, Poland
1873–76	Park Amtitz near Starzeddel, Niederlausitz; today Gebice near Gubin, Gubin, Zielona Góra, Poland
1874	Summer Residence Hummelshain as landscape beautification, near Kahla, Thuringia, Germany
1877–80	Park Oud-Wassenaar, Wassenaar, Netherlands
1879–81	Park Ruurlo near Zytphen, Netherlands
1880–82	Park Altdöbern near Cottbus, Brandenburg, Germany
1880–83	Park Klitschdorf near Bunzlau, Silesia; today Kliczków near Boleslawiec, Osiecznica, Jelenia Góra, Poland
1883	Park Josephstal near Jungbunzlau, Bohemia; today Josefuv Dul near Mladá Boleslav, Czech Republic
1883–84	Park Elswout and Duinlust, Haarlem, Netherlands
1884–86	Princely Park Sandrowo near Varna, Bulgaria
1884–91	Park Twickel, Delden, Netherlands
1888	Park Clingendaal (executed through Leonard Springer), Den Haag, Netherlands

Selected Publications
Beiträge zur Landschafts-Gärtnerei, 1849
Zur Farbenlehre der Landschaft. Beiträge zur Landschaftsgärtnerei, 1853
Die Landschaftsgärtnerei; Ein Handbuch für Gärtner, Architekten, Gutsbesitzer, und Freunde der Gartenkunst, 1862; enlarged 2nd edition, 1888
Arboretum Muscaviense, with Georg Kirchner, 1864
Fürst Hermann v. Pückler-Muskau in seinem Wirken in Muskau und Branitz, 1874
Die Anpflanzung und Behandlung von Alleebäumen, 1878
Erinnerungen aus meinem Leben: Für die Familie als Handschrift gedruckt, 1890

Further Reading
Gresky, Walter, *Eduard Petzold, der Geisteserbe des Fürsten Pückler, als Hofgärtner in Ettersburg und Weimar,* Erfurt, Germany: Stenger, 1940
Irrgang, Walter, *Bemerkenswerte Parkanlagen in Schlesien,* Dortmund, Germany: Auslieferung Forschungsstelle Ostmitteleuropa, 1978
Oldenburger-Ebbers, Carla S., *De tuinengids van Nederland,* Rotterdam: De Hef, 1989
Rohde, Michael, "Eduard Petzold: Weg und Werk eines deutschen Gartenkünstlers im 19. Jahrhundert," Ph.D. diss., University of Hannover, 1998
Rohde, Michael, *Von Muskau bis Konstantinopel: Eduard Petzold, ein europäischer Gartenkünstler, 1815–1891,* Dresden: Verlag der Kunst, 1998
Stappenbeck, Ilse, *Der Park zu Greiz: Seine Geschichte, seine künstlerische Entwicklung und ihre Vollendung durch Eduard Petzold,* Zeulenroda, Germany: Sporn, 1939
Wijck, Henri W. van der, *De Nederlandse buitenplaats: Aspecten van ontwikkeling, bescherming en herstel,* Alphen aan den Rijn, The Netherlands: Canaletto, 1982

MICHAEL ROHDE

Philosopher's Garden

The term *philosopher's garden* designates a villa garden in the Italian Renaissance that was used for the enjoyment of the garden and for philosophical conversation. The humanists associated gardens with Socratic dialogues, and this was in turn taken up by the Renaissance patrons who sought to re-create the ambiance of a Greco-Roman academy or a Roman villa. In the early 15th century, as urban life flourished, the villa became the site of *villeggiatura,* a seasonal retreat to a country residence for leisure and cultural pursuits. In Tuscany numerous villas were built on the hills surrounding Florence, overlooking mountains, valleys, vineyards, and plains. The villa garden was inspired by Leon Battista Alberti's *De re aedificatoria libri X* (Ten Books of Architecture), which was completed in 1452 and printed in 1485. Alberti drew upon designs from Persia, Arabia, Greece, and Rome, notably the Roman gardens of Pliny the Younger. Pliny's gardens were open to the varied landscape yet had some enclosed elements for entertainment, pleasant walks, and solitude. The gardens were intimately linked to the villas and held numerous fountains and waterworks, terraces, cypress, topiary formed of box and scented evergreens, obelisks of box, and fruit trees. Such elements would recur in the Renaissance. The Villa Medici at Careggi, converted by Michelozzo Michelozzi from a fortresslike manor into a villa, had a garden that was an imitation of a Roman garden, with cypress, bay, box, myrtle, and flower beds. This was the meeting place of the Florentine Academy led by Marsilio Ficino. The academy then moved to the Villa Medici at Fiesole, located on a hillside chosen for visual, social, and climatic considerations. There were two terraces and a secret garden, with panoramic views of the Arno valley. This was the first true Renaissance villa that employed the new concepts of nature, geometry, and space. The great innovation of Alberti was in the development of ideas on geometry and proportion based on the analysis of the classical concept that beauty comes from a harmony of all the parts.

Whereas the enclosed medieval garden denied the physical space and directed thoughts to God, the Renaissance garden was open, projected out onto the landscape, and sought to celebrate and control nature. The garden, interrelated to the landscape and villa, was where the imitation of nature and its regulation took place. Geometric topiary gardens were designed to reveal the hidden patterns of nature, to create meaning and beauty out of chaos through human skill. Topiary was emblematic of a confidence in the human ability to discover and experience nature. At the same time the Renaissance pleasure garden shared some of its symbolism with monastic gardens; both the soul and the fields were to be cultivated. The garden was an outstanding place for contemplation because the geometry of the garden reflected the cosmic, divine order.

Gardens for philosophical discussion tended to be small and intimate so that they would foster conversation, contemplation, and amusement rather than surprise and delight. This is different from the secret garden, which was reserved for privacy, family activities, and love, and as such was hidden. In a garden of philosophy, nature was contained in an Arcadian world that Virgil had invoked, yet its boundaries blended into the larger landscape. The harkening back to the mythical golden age, associated with the Christian concept of paradise and humanistic theories of the pastoral life, was fundamental to the ideology of the Medici family and other patrons whose gardens would increasingly represent their greatness.

In 1499 a book appeared that was to singularly influence the 16th-century Renaissance garden in architecture, symbolism, and iconography. *Hypnerotomachia Poliphili* (The Dream of Polyphilo), attributed to Francesco Colonna, portrays a fantastic landscape strewn with extraordinary architectural hybrids with a strong classical component. Here the hero, Polyphilo, searches for his love, Polia. Polyphilo's unquenchable desire for Polia is intertwined with the desire to enjoy the landscape that was simultaneously sensuous, in its splendor and variety, and mysterious with its geometric shapes. Colonna's ideas are resonant in the garden of the Villa Brenzone, a typical 16th-century humanistic villa. The humanist philosopher Agostino Brenzone was a leading member of the cultural life in the Veneto. Whereas most of the villas of the Veneto were agrarian villas located on flat, fertile land, the Villa Brenzone was on a foothill overlooking a lake. There were three gardens of intimate scale that combined elements of botany, classical mythology, astrology, and Christianity. The first was the Garden of Love, with a statue of Venus that was full of myrtles and lemon trees. In the Garden of Apollo, or Parnassus, were orange and cedar trees, a laurel, and a fountain that emanated from a stone statue of Petrarch. The third garden was the Garden of Eden, with trees mentionedin the bible. A double colonnade and a rotunda of the ancients surrounded by cypresses enhanced the classical ambiance of this land of seclusion and dream akin to Colonna's gardens.

In the 16th century learned conversation continued to be a favorite pastime at villa gardens. Gardens also became highly complex and lavish. The 16th-century gardens, such as the magnificent Belvedere Court of the Vatican, often associated images of antiquity with spectacular arrangements of manipulated nature on vast scales. They displayed botanical and material collections and ingenuous inventions including waterworks. Relatively uncultivated *boschi*, or groves, were employed to provide a transition from the formal beds to the outer landscape or elements of surprise in the wilder areas. Ovid's *Metamorphoses* provided important sources for such transitions between nature and artifice. At the mannerist garden of the Villa Lante, Ovidian transformation is embodied in the mutation of water, from stream to canals to fountains. As gardens became more public, different levels of iconography were employed so that the initiated and the occasional visitor would enjoy and understand different aspects. Increasingly the *bosco* was used as a symbol of free nature that undermined the rational hierarchy of the Renaissance garden and the idea that the hidden order of nature was knowable. At the Villa Lante, labyrinthine elements, randomly intersecting paths, and manipulated perspectives provided an escape from order into the realm of ambiguity.

Further Reading

Castell, Robert, *The Villas of the Ancients Illustrated*, London, 1728; reprint, New York: Garland, 1982

Coffin, David R., *The Villa in the Life of Renaissance Rome*, Princeton, New Jersey: Princeton University Press, 1979

Coffin, David R., "'The Lex Hortorum' and Access to Gardens of Latium during the Renaissance," *Journal of Garden History* 2, no. 3 (1982)

Coffin, David R., editor, *The Italian Garden*, Washington, D.C.: Dumbarton Oaks, 1972

Colonna, Francesco, *Hypnerotomachia Poliphili*, Venice, 1499; as *Hypnerotomachia Poliphili: The Strife of Love in a Dream*, translated by Joscelyn Godwin, London: Thames and Hudson, 1999

Comito, Terry, *The Idea of the Garden in the Renaissance*, New Brunswick, New Jersey: Rutgers University Press, 1978

Hunt, John Dixon, *Garden and Grove: The Italian Renaissance Garden in the English Imagination, 1600–1750*, London: Dent, and Princeton, New Jersey: Princeton University Press, 1986

Hunt, John Dixon, editor, *The Italian Garden: Art, Design, and Culture*, New York: Cambridge University Press, 1996

Lefaivre, Liane, *Leon Battista Alberti's "Hypnerotomachia Poliphili": Recognizing the Architecturial Body in the Early Italian Renaissance*, Cambridge, Massachusetts: MIT Press, 1997

Masson, Georgina, "The Gardener's Art in Early Florence," *Apollo* 81 (1965)

Masson, Georgina, *Italian Gardens*, New York: Abrams, and London: Thames and Hudson, 1961; revised edition, Woodbridge, Suffolk: Antique Collectors' Club, 1987

Mosser, Monique, and Georges Teyssot, editors, *L'architettura dei giardini d'Occidente*, Milan: Electa, 1990; as *The Architecture of Western Gardens*, Cambridge, Massachusetts: MIT Press, 1991; as *The*

History of Garden Design, London: Thames and Hudson, 1991

Van der Ree, Paul, Gerrit Smienk, and Clemens Steenbergen, *Italian Villas and Gardens: A coso di disegno,* Munich: Prestel, 1992

Woods, May, *Visions of Arcadia: European Gardens from Renaissance to Rococo,* London: Aurum Press, 1996

HAZEL HAHN

Picturesque Style

Picturesque has, since the early 18th century, been a recurrent term in English gardening, especially landscape gardening. In a short but historically momentous period from around 1790 to 1815, its scope and significance increased to denote a powerful and controversial cultural movement, the Picturesque. The Picturesque extended beyond landscape gardening to the realms of literature, fine art, fashion, aesthetics, architecture, agriculture, town planning, and travel literature and so made landscape gardening central to the social concerns of polite society.

As adjective or abstract noun in 18th-century gardening, *picturesque* denoted the making of views in the manner of paintings. The paintings in question ranged from the idyllic Italianate landscapes of Claude Lorrain and Gaspard Dughet, with their framing plantations, planar vistas, and classical temples, to the more vernacular, foreground-focused scenes of Jacob van Ruisdael and Meindert Hobbema, with cottages, old trees, wildflowers, and streams. It also included the works of 18th-century painters such as Thomas Gainsborough and Antoine Watteau. The very word *picturesque* was first deployed in English as a translation from the French *pittoresque* or the Italian *pittoresco* and, perhaps for this reason, quickly achieved a cultural currency in English that it originally lacked in those languages but attained when it was reintroduced along with the fashion for English gardening.

Picturesque gardening was never purely painterly. Some variants incorporated a scenic vividness, an intricacy, and a train of associations derived from a range of sources from theater design to rustic poetry and topographical prints of exotic or antiquarian curiosities such as Chinese gardens or medieval ruins. Picturesque gardening could be strictly academic and highly planned or ad hoc and eclectic and could combine highly cultivated, even formal, areas with more naturalistic-looking scenes. The relationship between gardening and painting was close, complex, and controversial. Picturesque gardens were not just modeled on painting but, as prime sites for landscape appreciation, provided arenas for the development of new forms of drawing and description.

Not all landscape gardens were Picturesque, and there was as strong a movement to maintain a distance between painting and gardening as there was to entwine them.

William Gilpin popularized Picturesque tastes in his tourist books on parts of Britain. Some aristocratic parks and gardens feature in his tours, and he likened the power of tourists or painters to compose the scene they observed to that of a landowner improving his property. He found many such parks un-Picturesque, however, and extended the scope of the category to less polished landscapes and its cultural associations to more popular forms of visual culture. Gilpin made Picturesque sensibilities a fashionable accomplishment for anyone in polite society, not least those from the professions and commerce. Gilpin influenced the English landscape designer Humphry Repton's theory and practice of landscape gardening. Repton's style was more pictorial than that of the English designer Lancelot "Capability" Brown and his followers, and Repton's "Red Books" of designs were illustrated by charming watercolors. With the aid of a hinged overlay page, Repton contrasted the dull scene in the existing garden with the delightful one he envisaged, a smart sales device for those trained to look at scenery Picturesquely, as Gilpin had prescribed. While angling for aristocratic patronage, Repton also successfully marketed his work to a range of clients, commerical and professional.

Picturesque landscape gardening became a highly contentious issue with the publication in 1794 of two manifestos, *Essay on the Picturesque* by Uvedale Price and *The Landscape: A Didactic Poem* by Richard Payne Knight. Price and Knight reformulated the Picturesque in terms of two horizons of knowledge: day-to-day estate management by resident landowners and connoisseurship of Old Master paintings. They made the Picturesque the preserve of the gentleman-amateur and deployed it as a weapon to oppose professional landscaping in general and Repton's practice in particular. They also activated the agrarian reputation of their home county of Hertfordshire to make the Picturesque a more productive aesthetic than it had been in Gilpin's writings, but this aspect was rarely recognized by their critics, who saw their version of the Picturesque as a recipe for neglect and disorder and, as such, politically suspect at the outset of the war with France and the threat of sedition at home. In response Repton drew a strict division between painting and gardening, although his own work continued to be highly pictorial. The "Picturesque controversy" drew in many other writers and extended to many other spheres of polite culture.

The controversy cooled in the 19th century. The Picturesque aesthetic informed town planning schemes, which incorporated gardens such as those of John Nash and Decimus Burton for the West End of London. In the 1820s and 1830s, William Sawrey Gilpin, nephew of the travel writer and a disciple of Price, developed a professional practice of what he called "picturesque gardening." This was characterized by tree planting and terrace walks, but like many Picturesque designers, he had little knowledge of smaller plants and flowers. Indeed the popularity of botanically informed gardens, with their emphasis on specimens and habitats, helped displace the Picturesque as a commanding aesthetic. By the mid-19th century the term had lost much of its scope and power in British gardening, being confined to places such as rockeries and meaning little more than pretty or quaint. Along with the fashion for English landscape gardens, the Picturesque style was, however, exported overseas, to continental Europe, the United States, and the British empire, where it gained in power as it was deployed in new settings.

Picturesque gardening saw a revival in the 20th century. Christopher Hussey's book *The Picturesque: Studies in a Point of View* (1927) was inspired by the realization that the landscape of his family estate, Scotney Castle, was not natural but had been carefully planned by William Sawrey Gilpin a century before. Through his editorship of *Country Life*, Hussey exerted a powerful influence on preservationist tastes. The Picturesque was also revived in Britain through the writings of Nikolaus Pevsner in the modernist *Architectural Review* to influence post–World War II town planning and the role of gardens within it.

Further Reading

Arnold, Dana, editor, *The Picturesque in Late Georgian England,* London: Georgian Group, 1994

Copley, Stephen, and Peter Garside, editors, *The Politics of the Picturesque,* Cambridge: Cambridge University Press, 1994

Daniels, Stephen, *Humphry Repton: Landscape Gardening and the Geography of Georgian England,* New Haven, Connecticut: Yale University Press, 1999

Daniels, Stephen, and Charles Watkins, editors, *The Picturesque Landscape: Visions of Georgian Herefordshire,* Nottingham: University of Nottingham, 1994

Garden History 22, no. 2 (1994) (special issue on the Picturesque)

Hussey, Christopher, *The Picturesque: Studies in a Point of View,* London and New York: Putnam, 1927; reprint, Hamden, Connecticut: Archon Books, and London: Cass, 1967

Pevsner, Nikolaus, editor, *The Picturesque Garden and its Influence outside the British Isles,* Washington, D.C.: Dumbarton Oaks Trustees, 1974

Wiebenson, Dora, *The Picturesque Garden in France,* Princeton, New Jersey: Princeton University Press, 1978

STEPHEN DANIELS

Pisa, Orto Botanico dell'Università di

Pisa, Tuscany, Italy

Location: two blocks south of the Leaning Tower, between Via Santa Maria and Via Roma

The Pisa Botanic Garden is the oldest university botanic garden in Europe. It was founded in 1543 by Luca Ghini after he was appointed to the Chair of Botany (professor) at Pisa University. A physician and botanist from Croara, Ghini had been professor of medicine at Bologna, but the grand duke of Tuscany (Cosimo I de' Medici) persuaded him to come and teach botany at Pisa. Ghini realized the necessity of having a garden to show his students live plants as well as a herbarium of dried plants. There has always been some dispute as to whether the garden at Pisa came before the garden at Padua or vice versa. However, a letter written by Luca Ghini dated 4 July 1545 implies that the garden at Pisa was well established by this time and ready to receive plants that had been collected by Ghini and others on the Apennines. This date was only five days after the decrees of the Venetian state that founded the garden at Padua. The original garden was situated on the right bank of the river Arno near the shipyard and was known as the Arsenal Gardens.

In 1563 the botanic gardens had to move when Cosimo I needed to enlarge the shipyard to boost Pisa's defense system. Andrea Cesalpina, Ghini's successor and one of the first botanists who attempted to order or classify plants based on similarities and differences of morphological, physiological, and phenological characteristics, supervised the move to a site northeast of the city. Unfortunately, no traces remain of the garden's time at either of these sites.

The garden was on the move again in 1591, when it relocated to its present site between Via Santa Maria and Via Roma near the cathedral square and the Leaning Tower. Joseph Goedenhuitze (or as he is better known in Italy, Giuseppe Casabona) oversaw the move, which took until 1595 to complete. Lorenze Mazzanga and Casabona laid out the new garden in the Renaissance fashion of the day, and soon it became the center of scientific interest and culture. Even at this time exchanges of views and information between the Pisa Botanic Garden and other universities took place, confirming Pisa's importance in the world of botanical research. There was even a well-stocked library.

The original Botanic Institute building commissioned by the grand duke of Tuscany is still standing, and its interesting facade decorated with shells and mother-of-pearl has been preserved. The old main gateway is still visible, but out of eight original ornamental fountains only six are still in existence.

Many changes have taken place since the original design, and the garden is now laid out in various sections. The oldest part of the garden is the "Botany School," which was planned during the second half of the 19th century. It was laid out in plant systematic order for the university botany students and contains examples of historic and scientific interest (e.g., a *Gingko biloba* planted in 1811 and a *Platanus occidentalis* planted in 1808).

The Cedar Garden was named so because until 1935 there was a massive cedar of Lebanon (*Cedrus libani*) growing there, which had been planted in 1787. This part of the garden was acquired just over 200 years ago, a donation from the Grand Duke Leopold to the garden.

A walled garden called the "Myrtle Garden" is named after an old and very large *Myrtus communis*, which was planted in 1815. It is in this part of the garden that the medicinal plants or "simples" are grown. These are plants, some of which are poisonous, that are grown for pharmaceutical purposes.

The glasshouses, one of which is among the earliest examples of iron-framed hothouses built in Italy, house exotics from hot climates. Another glasshouse has many varieties of succulents from deserts all over the world and a section housing Tuscan wetland plants. Some of these plants are no longer growing in the wild; others are under threat from water pollution and land reclamation. One example of these is the marsh hibiscus (*Hibiscus palustris*).

On the north side of the garden is the arboretum. Among the trees of note here are two cedars (*Cedrus deodara* and *Cedrus atlantica*) and an ash (*Fraxinus excelsior*). A copse of mainly evergreens including a yew (*Taxus baccata*) is sited near a clump of papyrus (*Fatsia papyrifera*), the plant used in the East to produce high-quality writing paper.

Further north of the arboretum is the most recently acquired part of the garden. It contains a winter garden, a rockery, and a pond that is covered in lotus plants (*Nelumbo nucifera*).

Probably one of the most interesting plants in the garden is the bald cypress (*Taxodium distichum*), which has pneumotophores arising from the root system. Another tree that merits attention is a camphor tree (*Cinnamomum camphora*), introduced along with several Australian araucarias (*Araucaria bidwilli*), which grow extremely well in the climatic conditions at Pisa. These are probably the oldest living examples of this plant in Europe.

The botanic garden's herbarium is among the most important in Italy. The earliest herbarium collections, *hortus sicci*, were in Pisa and Padua in the 16th century. Pisa's original herbarium has been dispersed, and it is no longer known where Ghini's herbarium is, if it still exists as a complete collection. The current herbarium collection was begun toward the end of the 18th century and now comprises some 300,000 dried plant specimens, with approximately 300 new specimens being added each year.

Besides having an interest in the plant families *Liliaceae* and *Amaryllidaceae* (mainly Italian species), the garden also carries out research into the ecological problems in the nearby areas of the Apuane Alps, the Tuscan-Emilian Apennines, the Pisan Hills, and the Tuscan Archipelago.

Synopsis

1543	Pisa Botanic Garden founded by Luca Ghini, near River Arno
1563	Garden moved to north of city
1591–95	Garden moved again, to current site near Cathedral Square, and laid out by Lorenze Mazzanga and Giuseppe Casabona
1723	Tilli, director from 1695 until 1740, cataloged all 5,000 plants in garden

1787   Oldest trees still living in the garden
            planted (a *Magnolia grandiflora* and a
            Gingko biloba)

Further Reading

Chiovenda, Emilio, *Note sulla Fondazione degli orti Medici di Padova e di Pisa,* as *On the Foundation of the Botanical Gardens at Padua and Pisa,* Pisa: Lischi, 1931

Ferri, Sara, and Francesca Vannozzi, *I giardini dei semplici e gli orti botanici della Toscana,* Perugia, Italy: Giunta Regionale Toscana, 1993

Garbari, Fabio, "The History and Present Role of Pisa Botanical Gardens," in *Network of Botanic Gardens,* edited by Madhavan P. Nayar, Calcutta: Botanical Survey of India, 1987

Garbari, Fabio, Lucia Tongiorgi Tomasi, and Alessandro Tosi, *Giardino dei semplici: L'orto botanico di Pisa dal XVI al XX secolo,* Ospedaletto, Italy: Pacini, 1991

Hyams, Edward, *Great Botanical Gardens of the World,* London: Nelson, and New York: Macmillan, 1969

L'orto Botanica di Pisa, Pisa: Azienda di Promozione Turistica, 1991

Meda, Pia, *Guida agli orti e giardini botanici,* Milan: Mondadori, 1996

JANE HUTCHEON

Pits. *See* Frames and Pits

Plants in Garden Design and Gardens

Throughout history plants have been cultivated because they provide shade or shelter, can yield a useful product such as food or medicine, or have aesthetic value. The emphasis on these aspects varies from culture to culture and at different points in history. Planting designs differ, as does the variety of plants grown.

The development of a garden as a decorative or ornamental place dates back to the ancient gardens of Babylon, Mesopotamia, and Egypt, where plants were grown for their cultural or religious significance and for their usefulness as well as their beauty. The Romans continued Western garden development. Inspired by earlier and contemporary cultures, they developed gardens with a strong sense of design. Plants had mainly a functional role, used as a material within the formal garden. As the Roman Empire expanded in the first century A.D., their influence on garden layout spread throughout Europe. The next development was in the Islamic gardens that emerged in the eighth century. Again formal in design, the gardens were meant to represent paradise on Earth. Plants were used to create a sense of coolness and serenity heightening the spiritual aspect of the garden. Flowers were grown in sunken beds adjacent to raised pathways, creating the impression of walking on a Persian carpet.

During the period known as the Dark Ages in Europe, horticultural skills and plant usage did not develop further. The medieval garden that then emerged developed from a functional plot in the early gardens to a much more sophisticated design. Descriptions and illustrations of both monastic and secular gardens provide indications of planting design. Gardeners had only a limited range of plants from which to choose and often used selected forms of indigenous plants. Plants that were cultivated had several uses, such as their culinary, medicinal, or symbolic value. They were rarely used simply for their aesthetic value within the garden setting. However, the design of gardens developed, and while plants continued to be useful, they were set out in a more definite design. Planting in patterns became evident, for example, in the knot garden, which also yielded clippings to be strewn on house floors.

The ideas of the Renaissance culture slowly spread throughout Europe in the 16th and 17th centuries. Humankind imposed itself upon nature both in design and plant use. Formal gardens incorporated features such as the parterre, hedge maze, and avenues of clipped trees. Plants were treated as a material to be clipped into a designated space, and flower color was limited. Fruits and vegetables were now segregated from the main ornamental composition. There was great interest in botanical study, leading to the creation of separate botanical gardens.

The 18th century witnessed a revolution in garden design, with a shift from the rigid formal garden style to an informal parkland landscape. Fruits and vegetables were still grown in separate kitchen gardens, and indigenous trees were largely favored over exotic introductions. In England designers such as Lancelot "Capability" Brown used clumps and belts of trees such as oak (*Quercus robur*) and beech (*Fagus sylvatica*), with the occasional exotic specimen tree such as the Lebanon cedar (*Cedrus libani*). Many large country estates took to the new style, sweeping away the previous formal landscapes. However, small domestic gardens continued with the style of cottage-garden plantings associated with earlier medieval gardens.

Toward the end of the 18th century, the taste for the landscape movement began to wane. Garden features and flowers reappeared around the house, pushing the parkland back. The rise of suburban gardens during the 19th century further enhanced the divide between park and garden. In England Humphry Repton and later John Claudius Loudon were leaders in the new style. During the 19th century the range of plants for garden use rapidly expanded. Plant hunters, such as Ernest Henry Wilson and Robert Fortune, working in China, Japan, and the Americas, introduced many new plants into cultivation. Plants became a status symbol, and the role of the head gardener was crucial at this time. Skills and facilities were needed to produce cut flowers, fruits, and vegetables in and out of season. Opulent plant displays were created both in the garden and in the conservatory. Carpet bedding, mosaiculture, and seasonal flower beds were used on a large scale in both private gardens and the newly created public parks. Topiary was popular, as was the lawn, a feature aided by the invention of the lawn mower, which was patented in 1830. The density of planting was much greater than in previous centuries, a trend that continued into the 20th century.

The overexuberance of the High Victorian gardens of the 19th century provoked sharp criticism and a call for a more restrained and tasteful style. William Robinson advocated a naturalistic planting style, such as the planting of bulbs in grass. Claude Monet's garden at Giverny in France is a good example of this informal style, although it was created as a dynamic palette to support the artist's work.

Plants and garden design style from China came to Europe from the mid-18th century and a hundred years later from Japan, although in both cases designs were interpreted very much in the Western tradition. The Oriental planting style is in sharp contrast from those seen in Western gardens, with much more controlled use and positioning of plants. Plant growth may be manipulated to achieve a deliberate plant form, and in both China and Japan the age and maturity of plants is highly regarded. Despite there being a wealth of Chinese and Japanese native plants that are extensively used in Western gardens, the range of plants used in Oriental gardens is limited since their selection is influenced by the symbolism attached to individual plants. In China, for example, the peony is associated with happiness and the bamboo with a person's moral character (tall and bending, yet not breaking). In Chinese gardens plants are often inextricably linked with the hard landscape. In Japan the greenness of foliage is regarded as just as important as the color of flowers. Also, curiosities such as plants with variegated leaves are highly valued and are grown in individual containers on display benches.

The end of the 19th century saw the emergence of a design style that has remained popular to the present time. The Arts and Crafts style united strong structural design with informal planting and is exemplified in the work of the architect Sir Edwin Lutyens and garden designer Gertrude Jekyll. The garden was divided into a series of "outdoor rooms," each with themed plantings, many of which were based on plant color. Herbaceous perennials were widely used. The White Garden at Sissinghurst, created by Vita Sackville-West, is one such example. Others include Hidcote in England and Dumbarton Oaks in the United States.

As the 20th century progressed, gardens became smaller, and many more people took an interest in growing fruits, vegetables, and flowers in their own gardens. The 1960s and 1970s saw an emphasis on labor-saving designs and low-maintenance plants; ground-cover planting became popular. High-maintenance planting such as herbaceous borders and rose gardens became unfashionable. However, herbaceous perennials regained popularity in the 1990s, but have been used in a more creative style, for example in the work of designers Wolfgang Oehme and James van Sweden in the United States. Beginning in the 1990s, with environmental issues underpinning many areas of activity worldwide, there has been a trend toward ecological and naturalistic plantings, with an emphasis on grouping plants together based on natural habitats. The wildlife value of plants is also considered in plant selection. Plant breeding has provided designers with a wealth of new plants to use, but the issue of genetically modified plant material is set to cause many debates in the early part of the 21st century.

Further Reading

Billington, Jill, *Planting Companions,* London: Ryland Peters and Small, and New York: Stewart Tabori and Chang, 1997

Brickell, Christopher, editor, *The Royal Horticultural Society Gardeners' Encyclopedia of Plants and Flowers,* London: Dorling Kindersley, 1989; revised edition, London and New York: Dorling Kindersley, 1994

Brookes, John, *The Country Garden,* London: Dorling Kindersley, and New York: Crown, 1987

Carpenter, Philip L., Theodore D. Walker, and Frederick O. Lanphear, *Plants in the Landscape,* San Francisco: Freeman, 1975; 2nd edition, 1990

Clouston, Brian, editor, *Landscape Design with Plants,* London: Heinemann, and New York: Van Nostrand Reinhold, 1977; 2nd edition, Oxford: Heinemann, and Boca Raton, Florida: CRC Press, 1990

Cox, Jeff, *Landscaping with Nature: Using Nature's Design to Plan Your Yard,* Emmaus, Pennsylvania: Rodale Press, 1991

Dirr, Michael A., *Manual of Woody Landscape Plants,* Champaign, Illinois: Stipes, 1975; 5th edition, 1998

Druse, Kenneth, and Margaret Roach, *The Natural Habitat Garden,* New York: Clarkson Potter, 1994

Fisher, John, *The Origins of Garden Plants,* London: Constable, 1982; revised edition, 1989

Gent, Lucy, *Great Planting,* London: Ward Lock, 1995

Gorer, Richard, *The Development of Garden Flowers,* London: Eyre and Spottiswoode, 1970

Hansen, Richard, and Friedrich Stahl, *Die Stauden und ihre Lebensbereiche in Gärten und Grünanlagen,* Stuttgart, Germany: Ulmer, 1981; as *Perennials and Their Garden Habitats,* translated by Richard Ward, Cambridge: Cambridge University Press, and Portland, Oregon: Timber Press, 1993

Hobhouse, Penelope, *Plants in Garden History,* London: Pavilion Books, 1992; as *Penelope Hobhouse's Gardening through the Ages,* New York: Simon and Schuster, 1992

Hobhouse, Penelope, and Jerry Harpur, *Penelope Hobhouse's Natural Planting,* London: Pavilion, and New York: Holt, 1997

Jekyll, Gertrude, *Colour Schemes for the Flower Garden,* London: Country Life, 1908; reprint, Woodbridge: Antique Collectors' Club, 1994

Lloyd, Christopher, *The Well-Tempered Garden,* London: Collins, 1970; New York: Dutton, 1971; new and revised edition, London: Viking, and New York: Random House, 1985

Lloyd, Christopher, *Christopher Lloyd's Flower Garden,* London and New York: Dorling Kindersley, 1993

Oehme, Wolfgang, James Van Sweden, and Susan Rademacher Frey, *Bold Romantic Gardens: The New World Landscapes of Oehme and Van Sweden,* Reston, Virginia: Acropolis, 1990; revised edition, Washington, D.C.: Spacemaker Press, 1998

Robinson, Nick, *The Planting Design Handbook,* Aldershot, Hampshire, and Brookfield, Vermont: Gower, 1992

Robinson, William, *The English Flower Garden,* London, 1883; 15th edition, London: Murray, 1933; reprint, Sagaponack, New York: Sagapress, 1995

Thomas, Graham Stuart, *The Art of Planting; or, The Planter's Handbook,* London and Melbourne: Dent, in association with The National Trust, and Boston, Massachusetts: Godine, 1984

Verey, Rosemary, *Good Planting,* London: Lincoln, 1990

SANDRA NICHOLSON

Plant Training

Throughout history, human beings have attempted to dominate nature, attempting to "civilize" it. Hedges, parterres, topiary, and espalier are plant training techniques that provide good examples of this attempt. Training is used to alter a plant's shape in order to make it more decorative, to emphasize a special feature of the plant, to obtain more fruit or leaves, or to improve the quality of the fruit.

When the Greeks marched into the heart of the Persian Empire under Alexander the Great, they found mature and splendid gardens that included hedges of clipped myrtle and screens of plane, cypress, and pines. By Roman times such hedges and screens were ornamental features of the garden, used to emphasize the outline of the design. The use of hedges continued throughout the Dark Ages primarily in monasteries, especially those of enclosed orders. Private cells for solitary prayer and contemplation were arranged around a cloistered courtyard of small individual gardens, such as at Va di Ema, Florence, or Certosa di Pavia, where low clipped hedges divide the cloister garden into small units. In the 15th and 16th centuries in Italy and France, more elaborate hedges, used to surround beds and to create patterns or knots within them, were developed. In England hedges were familiar in Anglo-Saxon times and increased through the Middle Ages. In Germany hedge theaters were formed, as at Herrenhausen and Veitshöchheim. Excavations at Williamsburg, Virginia, in the United States have shown that gardens during colonial times included hedges as well as parterres and other forms of plant training.

Hedges at Chatsworth, Derbyshire, England
Copyright Clay Perry/Garden Picture Library

Hedges were originally used in place of a wall or fence to keep out human intruders and animal pests. Planting a hedge as a boundary around a garden satisfies the natural instinct to enclose one's property, but it also outlines the garden's edges, turning it into a kind of outdoor room with defined structure and character. Hedges can also provide shelter from wind or strong sun, screen unsightly views, and filter out noise and dust.

A parterre (from the French for flowerbed) was historically a separate formal section of the garden, divided into a balanced pattern of beds in geometrical shapes surrounded by a wall or dwarf clipped hedge. The parterre garden was a popular form of garden from the

Middle Ages to the early 19th century. Despite its French name, the parterre is not exclusively part of the gardening tradition of France. Already by the middle of the 14th century gardens of Florentine houses included areas of ornamental beds arranged in patterns, an idea that might be traced back to the Roman custom of edging beds with low box hedges. These early Italian parterres do not seem to have yet developed the balanced patterns typical of the formal gardens of 17th-century France.

The knot garden is an older and specifically English concept using a single bed or pattern of beds, each laid out to contain an intricate design of dwarf hedges. Sometimes the hedging was made from a single species

Espalier
Copyright Chicago Botanic Garden

as a framework for colored gravel, herbs, or flowering plants grown in the enclosed spaces, but often the various strands of the design were themselves contrasted by using hedging plants with different colored or textured foliage.

Another use of hedges closely related to parterre gardens are mazes or labyrinths. Their origins are lost in prehistory, as early pictorial maze art and ancient earthworks attest. The hedge maze, however, is a relatively recent development, probably of the 17th century. The best known example is that at Hampton Court, dating from about 1690.

Many shrubs and some trees, both evergreen and deciduous, can be used for hedging. The plant used depends on the style of the garden and the size, position, and purpose of the hedge. Box (*Buxus sempervirens*) and yew (*Taxus baccata*) have been and continue to be widely used. Yew is typically used in hedges that include elaborate shapes such as cones, balls, or figures of animals and birds because it is more dense and firm. Hawthorn (*Crataegus*

monogyna) was for centuries a favorite for outer hedges because of its hardiness, strength, and impenetrable spiny growth. Lawson cypress (*Chamaecyparis lawsoniana*) and Leyland cypress (x *Cupressocyparis leylandii*) are vigorous growers that behave well as formal hedges and both have green- and yellow-leaved varieties. Beech (*Fagus sylvatica*) is an excellent tree for a deciduous formal hedge as well as hornbeam (*Carpinus betulus*). Herbaceous plants often trained into a hedge are rosemary (*Rosemarinus officinalis*) and lavender (*Lavandula angustifolia*).

The art of topiary—shaping trees and shrubs by clipping, pruning, and training—dates from at least the days of Pliny the Elder, who lived in the first century A.D. In his *Historia naturalis* he describes a hunt scene, fleets of ships, and other images all shaped out of cypress (*Cupressus sempervirens*). Box, shaped into various forms, was also used during Roman times. Sometime about 100 A.D., Pliny the Younger makes references in his letters to the topiary at his two country

Fruit trees displaying plant training
Copyright Linda Oyama Bryan, courtesy of Chicago Botanic Garden

villas. By the Middle Ages plants were trained and clipped into simple nonrepresentational shapes, often on wire frames. During the Italian Renaissance a major topiary revival took place. *Hypnerotomachia*, a book dating from 1499 by a monk called Francesco Colonna under the pseudonym of Polyphilius, contains illustrations for various basic topiary forms including spherical, mushroom, and ring forms as well as more sophisticated renderings of human figures, urns, and other architectural motifs.

Despite the widespread occurrence of topiary in all its forms in Renaissance Italian gardens, usually it seems to have existed only as a structural element or decorative accent within a geometrical overall plan. Very rarely was a garden devoted entirely to a collection of topiary. At Castello Balduino, however, a medieval castle at Montalto di Pavia on the high slopes of the Appenines, a beautiful topiary garden of remarkable symmetry has survived the centuries. The bulky evergreens that fill the garden are clipped into simple abstract shapes and arranged in a simple yet bold pattern. Another surviving

Italian topiary garden is at the Villa Garzoni near Collodi in Tuscany. This garden was constructed in the middle of the 17th century and seems to show the liberating influence of baroque ideas.

With the 17th century French-inspired garden of parterres, topiary became the primary component of garden design. Rather than the figurative topiary found in the Italian gardens, French designers used clipped trees as elements in the intricate parterres. In the Netherlands, where gardens were likely to be small, the individual qualities of specimen topiary were appreciated. In Germany and other parts of Europe, the French manner was also evident with elaborate patterned parterres supplemented with shrubs trimmed into abstract shapes and potted topiaries.

England also felt the influence of France but in quite an un-French manner, English topiaries were in more eccentric forms. The English topiary skill was most admirably exercised in the gardens at Hampton Court Palace. According to the writings of a German traveler, the topiary at Hampton Court in 1599 contained

Side view of trees displaying plant training
Copyright Linda Oyama Bryan, courtesy of Chicago Botanic Garden

centaurs, servants with baskets, and figures of men and women. George London and his partner Henry Wise, the most famous nurserymen of the period, were notorious for their devotion to topiary. They deemed bay (*Laurus nobilis*), pyrancantha, *Arbutus unedo,* laurel (*Prunus laurocerasus*) and species of *Phillyrea* all worthy of topiary treatment. The publication in 1662 of John Evelyn's *Sylva* did much to promote the use of yew for topiary; previously box had predominated.

By the 18th century the craze for topiary had run its course, and it became associated with all that was old-fashioned and in bad taste. Joseph Addison expressed his opinion about topiary in *The Spectator* (1711 and 1712) saying that the "marks of the scissors" are "upon every bush" and works of nature were "more delightful than artificial shows." Alexander Pope supported the offensive urging in an essay on gardening in the *Guardian* (1713) a return to the "amiable simplicity of unadorned nature," rejecting the balance, regularity, and artificiality of formal gardens and elaborate topiary work. The extensive execution of the new landscape style of William Kent, Lancelot "Capability" Brown,

and their many disciples destroyed countless examples of topiary.

In 1803 Humphry Repton challenged the whole philosophy of this movement and revived the use of topiary in the antiquarian garden he designed for the duke of Bedford at Aspley Wood Lodge, Woburn Abbey. But it was the Arts and Crafts movement that was topiary's savior. Its followers idealized the rural skills of "olde" England, which included the art of garden making. Its use was recommended in works by J.D. Sedding (*Garden Craft Old and New,* 1891) and Reginald Blomfield (*The Formal Garden in England,* 1892).

Many plants are suitable for use in topiary, including traditional, long-lived evergreens such as yew, bay, and box, and less common ones such as *Osmanthus, Berberis,* and *Phillyrea.* Simple, short-lived shapes can be created using *Artemisia abrotanum* or *Santolina chamaecyparissus.* The impatient gardener can achieve almost instant topiary effects by training climbers, such as ivy, on wire forms.

Espalier, a method of training trees or other plants to grow on one plane, has been used since Roman times, primarily in the cultivation of fruit trees. It has also been used decoratively, however, to soften large blank spaces on walls or fences or as a focal point in a garden. There are many forms of espalier—fan, candelabrum, single cordon, double cordon, palmette. Many climbing plants and a great number of shrubs can be trained to grow successfully against walls and fences. For many of the same reasons fruit trees were grown as espalier, and ornamental vines and shrubs that are not hardy enough to thrive in the open garden may be grown successfully close to a sunny, sheltered wall. Also, in a small garden, training or tying in against a wall allows shrubs to be accommodated that might be too large grown as freestanding specimens.

Coppicing is the regular, sometimes annual, cutting back of a tree to ground level to obtain vigorous, new young stems. Traditionally the cuttings were made in winter to be used for firewood, basketwork, barriers, and as poles. There is evidence of coppicing dating back to Neolithic times; in England and northern France, where this type of woodland management was popular, coppice survives that is at least 600 years old. Pollarding is another method of having only annual growth on a tree, but here the shoots arise from the head of a clear tree trunk from which all branches have been cut away. These methods of plant training were initially used in woodland management but were quickly adapted to use in the garden as the resulting vigorous plant growth was often of considerable ornamental value.

Pleaching is the weaving together of the branches of a row of trees. Combined with formal trimming, it creates a hedge with an intricate branch structure on a freestanding row of clear trunks. In Tudor England, pleached avenues were status symbols, showing off the number of gardeners the landowner was able to employ. Trees commonly used for this most labor-intensive form of tree training are lindens, hornbeams, beeches, and hollies (*Ilex* spp.), although most trees that tolerate clipping are suitable.

Although developing and maintaining these various forms of plant training is very labor-intensive, all are still used in gardens. The baroque parterre gardens at Het Loo in Appledorn, the Netherlands, has been accurately restored to its 17th century conception. Near Lisbon, Portugal, at the Palace of the Marquez de Fronteira, an Italian parterre garden has a splendid planting of precisely trimmed box that is accented with yew topiary and transverse gravel paths. At Beloiel, Belgium, towering columns topped with urns, all sheared from hornbeam and beech, form an impressive arcade. Longwood Gardens, in Kennett Square, Pennsylvania, United States, also has a fine collection of architectural topiary.

Further Reading

Brickell, Christopher, editor, *American Horticultural Society Pruning and Training*, London and New York: DK Publishing, 1996

Clarke, Ethne, *English Topiary Gardens*, New York: C.N. Potter, 1988

Clevely, A.M., *Topiary, Its History and Planning*, Topsfield, Massachusetts: Salem House, 1988

James, Theodore, *Specialty Gardens*, New York: Stewart, Tabori and Chang, 1992

CANDICE A. SHOEMAKER

Plate-Bande. *See* Parterre and Plate-Bande

Platt, Charles A. 1861–1933

United States Landscape Architect

Charles Adams Platt exerted a major influence on the development of historically based design styles during the American Country House era of the first quarter of the 20th century. He was born to an affluent and cultured family in New York City. Studying chiefly at home, he discovered talents as a painter and etcher that he perfected during a five-year residence in France in the early 1880s. Later in the decade, he returned to the United Stat1001es and innocently began his career as an architect by designing summer homes for himself and

Maxwell Court in Rockville, Connecticut, created by Charles A. Platt, ca. 1901, from Charles A. Platt, *The Architecture of Charles A. Platt*, 1913

several friends at the artists' colony in Cornish, New Hampshire. His skill at treating masses, his ability with symmetrical organization, and especially his sensitivity to site are evident even in these initial designs.

In 1892, Platt had the opportunity to study first hand the gardens of Italy with his brother, William, who was preparing to join the office of Frederick Law Olmsted. Although William died before the year was out, Charles Platt remained profoundly affected by his visit to Italy and assembled his photographs, watercolors, and sketches into a series of articles for *Harper's Magazine,* which later received wide circulation in book form as *Italian Gardens.* Published in 1894, *Italian Gardens* treated 19 major villas dating from the 15th to the 18th centuries. Platt produced neither an anecdotal guidebook nor a collection of art historical details. What gave the work its freshness was his analysis of the design elements of the sites with the intent that the methods of the Italians in the treatment of their gardens might be adopted in the United States. The rightness of Italian villas as precedents for U.S. residential architecture and landscapes became a central theme in his limited writings on design theory. Assuming that the United States lacked its own architectural tradition, New World architects were obliged to model their work on

an Old World inheritance, where the "eternal verities" of design had long ago been discovered.

Italy, and to some extent England, offered the preferred examples. The Renaissance villa tradition suited the outdoor lifestyle of the U.S. family in the country, where daily activities occurred in the gardens as much as in the house, and residence and landscape needed to function as a whole. Italians had discovered the best principles of siting a house in its landscape, which frequently established a clear relationship to a distant view. The gardens, of course, were an encyclopedia of specific design ideas for benches, balustrades, pergolas, and pavilions that might find a proper place in a U.S. context. Neither in matters great nor small, however, did imitation take the place of inspiration, for Platt assumed that adapting these "best models" to conditions unique to the United States would result in a distinctly U.S. style.

Although some associated with the traditions of Frederick Law Olmsted, such as Charles Eliot, were not impressed by this call for formal designs, Platt seems to have had the right message at the right time. Within a few years others, including the novelist Edith Wharton, were writing in praise of Italian gardens. The resulting books and articles did much to promote Italianate design as certified good taste. Logically, Platt's first commissions came for landscapes in the Italian style. Both "Faulkner Farm" for Charles F. Sprague in Brookline, Massachusetts (1897–98) and the Italian Garden on the neighboring estate, "Weld," for Larz and Isabel Anderson (1901) were enthusiastically received by the press and given extensive coverage in both professional journals and shelter magazines. Composing with simple curves and rectangles organized along clear axes and set within walled spaces, Platt developed original designs that suited both the needs of his clients and the demands of the sites. He also filled the gardens with colorful plants, since, unlike most of his contemporaries, Platt believed that early Italian gardens had been filled with flowers. Even given his original turn of mind, he directly quoted details found in the Italian gardens featured in his book: a casino from the Villa Lante at Bagnaia for the Spragues, stone benches and balustrade from the Villa Borghese for the Andersons. While these gardens launched Platt's career, neither allowed him to explore fully the crucial relationships between residence and landscape. At both sites he dealt with existing houses. Soon, however, the ideal commission was secured.

"Maxwell Court" (1901–3) for Francis T. Maxwell in the mill town of Rockville, Connecticut, was entirely Platt's creation: interior decoration, architecture, and landscape. Its basic disposition of residence, outbuildings, and gardens recalled the Villa Gamberaia near Florence. From the wrought iron gates at the road, the drive ran straight past the service area and into a walled arrival court by the front door. An axis from this shaded court at the north door ran through the width of the house to the south facade's expansive, sunny terrace, which afforded views across lawns to the valley below. This offered, in a short distance, dramatic changes in experiences: exterior, interior, and exterior. Placed on a longer cross axis, the principle living rooms were alined with a major garden walk, thus again integrating interior and exterior spaces. With only minor changes in details, an unidentified plan of "Maxwell Court" became the archetypal formal house and garden for the thousands of students who saw it in the principal 20th-century textbook for landscape architecture courses in the United States, Henry Vincent Hubbard and Theodora Kimball's *An Introduction of the Study of Landscape Design* (1917).

Platt created numerous other grand country houses and landscapes that refined and adapted the basic concepts originated in his early work. As his practice grew, he collaborated increasingly with other landscape designers, such as Warren H. Manning and Ellen Shipman, apparently leaving many decisions about the gardens in their hands. In the 1920s and 1930s, Platt's activities as a landscape architect were restricted largely to the planning of educational institutions. He held posts as consulting architect at Johns Hopkins University in Baltimore, Maryland; Dartmouth College in Hanover, New Hampshire; and the University of Rochester in Rochester, New York. At none of these campuses did he design any of the buildings, and, given the collaborative nature of the work, his specific contributions are difficult to assess. However, his role at the University of Illinois, Urbana-Champaign, was significant. Platt confronted the problems of a campus rapidly but chaotically expanding. In addressing these problems, he was inspired by the City Beautiful movement and the Daniel Burnham plan for the development of Chicago. Visual harmony was encouraged by adopting a uniform Georgian architectural style with long coordinated facades, which emphasized the horizontal. All were executed in red brick with limestone trim and slate roofs. The structures played against allées of trees. New buildings were arranged on three sides of a long mall running north and south. He designed the library for the south end of the mall, but rather than using it to terminate the north-south axis, he placed it with the other buildings on the west side of the mall. Mirroring the library to the east was the Morrow Rotation, the oldest agricultural experimental fields in continuous use in the United States. Thus he symbolized the process of learning both from books and from practice. This thoughtful siting and the willingness to do the unexpected marks most of Platt's design work.

Biography

Born in New York City, New York, 1861. Perfected talent for painting and etching while resident in France, early 1880s; returned to United States; began career in architecture by designing summer homes for friends and himself, 1889–90; toured gardens of Italy, 1892, and recorded impressions in *Italian Gardens,* 1894, widely circulated book that introduced him to wealthy clients planning country houses back in United States; designed series of grand houses and gardens and occasional commercial or public buildings (Hanna Building, Cleveland, Ohio; Freer Gallery of Art, Washington, D.C.), 1900–1920; design practice turned more to master planning, especially for universities (University of Illinois, Johns Hopkins University) and independent secondary schools (Phillips Academy, Andover, Massachusetts). Died in New York City, New York, 1933.

Selected Designs

1890–1912	Charles A. Platt residence and gardens, Cornish, New Hampshire, United States
1897–98	Charles F. Sprague garden, Faulkner Farm, Brookline, Massachusetts, United States
1901	Larz and Isabel Anderson Italian garden, Weld, Brookline, Massachusetts, United States
1901–3	Francis T. Maxwell residence and gardens, Rockville, Connecticut, United States

1902–3	George Maxwell Memorial Library, Rockville, Connecticut, United States
1907–20	William G. Mather residence and gardens (with Warren H. Manning and Ellen Shipman), Cleveland, Ohio, United States
1908–10	Russell A. Alger residence and gardens (with Ellen Shipman), Grosse Pointe Farms, Michigan, United States
1908–18	Harold F. McCormick residence and gardens, Lake Forest, Illinois, United States
1909–24	William Fahnestock residence and gardens, Katonah, New York, United States
1913–23	Freer Gallery of Art, Washington, District of Columbia, United States
1919	Hanna Building, annex and theater, Cleveland, Ohio, United States
1919–33	Johns Hopkins University, consultant for Homewood campus plan, Baltimore, Maryland, United States
1921–33	University of Illinois, campus master plan, design or consultation on 12 major buildings, Urbana-Champaign, Illinois, United States
1922–33	Phillips Academy, campus master plan and landscape (with Olmsted Associates), design for six buildings, Andover, Massachusetts, United States
1929–33	Deerfield Academy, consulted on campus master plan, design for three buildings, Deerfield, Massachusetts, United States

Selected Publications
Italian Gardens, 1894
"Villa," in *Dictionary of Architecture and Building*, edited by Russell Sturgis, vol. 3, 1901
"Where We Get Our Ideas of Country Places in America," *Outing* 44 (1904)
Monograph of the Work of Charles A. Platt, 1913

"A Renaissance Villa near Rome with Photographs and Sketch Plan by Charles A. Platt," *Architectural Review* 3, old series no. 20 (1915)

Further Reading
Cortissoz, Royal, "Charles A. Platt, F.A.I.A.: Etcher, Landscape Painter, Landscape Architect, Mural Painter, and Architect," *Pencil Points* 14, no. 11 (1933)
Cortissoz, Royal, "Charles A. Platt," *American Magazine of Art* 27, no. 7 (1934)
Croly, Herbert, "The Architectural Work of Charles A. Platt," *Architectural Record* 15, no. 3 (1904)
Croly, Herbert, "An American Landscape Architect: An Explanation of the Work of Mr. Charles A. Platt," *House Beautiful* 20, no. 5 (1906)
Embury, Aymar, II, "Charles A. Platt: His Work," *Architecture* 26, no. 2 (1912)
Kenworthy, Richard G., "Published Records of Italianate Gardens in America," *Journal of Garden History* 10, no. 1 (1990) (with bibliographic references to many individual landscape architecture projects)
Morgan, Keith N., "The Patronage Matrix: Charles A. Platt, Architect, Charles L. Freer, Client," *Winterthur Portfolio* 17, nos. 2–3 (1982)
Morgan, Keith N., *Charles A. Platt: The Artist as Architect*, New York: Architectural History Foundation, and Cambridge, Massachusetts: MIT Press, 1985 (a complete catalog of Platt's architectural and landscape commissions)
Morgan, Keith N., *Shaping an American Landscape: The Art and Architecture of Charles A. Platt*, Hanover, New Hampshire: Hood Museum of Art, Dartmouth College, and University Press of New England, 1995
Price, Charles Matlack, "The Art of Architecture: Notes on Some Phases of the Work of Charles A. Platt," *Arts and Decoration* 4, no. 3 (1914)

RICHARD KENWORTHY

Pleasance

A pleasance is, in simplest terms, a place of pleasure; the term is derived from old French and medieval words for pleasure or delight. Pleasure gardens may be created close to a dwelling or sometimes in a secluded part of the larger landscape around it. The pleasance was distinguished from functional gardens, such as orchards and kitchen, herb, and physic gardens that provided food for the table or plants for medicinal and other purposes. The idea that these special gardens were created for pleasure is clear in the descriptions that emphasize the impact on and the reaction of the senses: the sight of beautiful flowers; the sound of birds, bees, and splashing fountains; the smell of fragrant herbs and flowers; the taste of fruit plucked from vines; and the coolness or warmth associated with touch. The first pleasure gardens are recorded at monastic complexes, and later at royal palaces and aristocratic private dwellings. By the end of the Middle Ages, pleasure gardens were associated with even fairly modest dwellings.

The word *pleasance* itself does not occur frequently in early documents. It was used in the late 19th and early 20th centuries as an evocative term for medieval and Tudor gardens, at a time when there was a revival of these early garden styles. Typical is Eleanour Sinclair Rohde's *The Old-World Pleasaunce: An Anthology* (1925), which includes poetic and horticultural references to the pleasures of, especially, Tudor gardens. A more recent interpretation of the word includes the idea that pleasances were a sort of prototypical landscape garden.

The idea that a garden could be purely for pleasure is implicit in the early description of a garden in the monastery of St. Swithun's, Winchester, as "Le Joye." Increasingly, abbots or priors created private pleasure gardens, mentioned in accounts, as well as poetic descriptions. Almost always enclosed—either by walls, wooden palings, or hedges—the gardens were planted with grass, sometimes interspersed with wildflowers (the "flowery meads" depicted in medieval manuscripts and tapestries). Long tunnel arbors and rounded bowers provided protection from sun or rain. Seats—often planted with turf or sweet-smelling herbs—provided resting places. Delicate and exotic floral specimens were planted in ornamental pots. The finest gardens had wells or fountains to provide water, as well as for ornamental purposes.

Medieval palaces and mansions also had pleasure gardens, usually situated within the palace grounds, near the private lodgings of the family. One of the rare documented uses of the word *pleasance* appears in connection with the medieval palace at Greenwich, enlarged in Tudor time. It was such a favorite of Henry VIII and his daughter Elizabeth I that it became known as "Placentia" or "pleasance."

Pleasances could also be set away from the dwelling, sometimes surrounded by a moat or series of moats. Although possibly originally a defensive concept, it soon evolved into one of pleasurable escape. The most famous was at Kenilworth Castle in Warwickshire, where Henry V had a "pleasance" laid out from 1414 to 1417 (another example of a documented use of the word) about a half mile (approximately 0.8 kilometers) from the castle itself. The pleasance at Kenilworth was a square, double-moated enclosure of about ten acres (4 ha). Within the

enclosure was "a praty banketynge house of tymbre" that was later dismantled by Henry VIII and reerected in the castle grounds. The site of the pleasance is still evident in the landscape near the castle today.

Another early water garden, known as Rosamund's Bower because it was said to have been created for clandestine meetings between Henry II and his mistress Rosamund Clifford in the 12th century, was created at Woodstock Palace in Oxfordshire (today on the site of Blenheim Palace). Within a walled enclosure (entered through a gatehouse) were a small pleasure palace with chambers overlooking "three Baths in trayne," as John Aubrey described them in the mid-17th century. Possibly an early form of cascade, this water garden and retreat were among the most famous in the medieval period. The well that supplied it with water is still visible. Richard II built a retreat on an island in the Thames with special barges to transport his guests from the palace at Sheen (later called Richmond) to the island garden. Thus, the idea of a pleasance seems also to have been associated with more complex water gardens as well as the private pleasure gardens near the dwelling.

That enclosed pleasances were created in the open landscape has led some scholars (notably John Harvey) to conclude that they were associated with an early appreciation of natural landscape, a sort of prototype of the 18th-century English landscape garden. Parks, of course, were primarily used for hunting, but they were also carefully planted, and their aesthetic qualities were valued from the beginning. Perhaps the most famous was Hesdin (in modern France), created by Robert of Artois in the late 13th century. So large that it included villages as well as hunting grounds, the park was filled with wild and tame birds and animals, ponds, and smaller, enclosed pleasure gardens with highly sophisticated automata and pavilions.

Further Reading

Harvey, John Hooper, *Mediaeval Gardens,* Beaverton, Oregon: Timber Press, and London: Batsford, 1981

Landsberg, Sylvia, *The Medieval Garden,* New York: Thames and Hudson, 1996

McLean, Teresa, *Medieval English Gardens,* New York: Viking Press, 1980; London: Collins, 1981

Rohde, Eleanour Sinclair, *The Old-World Pleasaunce: An Anthology,* New York: Dial Press, and London: Jenkins, 1925

Thacker, Christopher, *The Genius of Gardening: The History of Gardens in Britain and Ireland,* London: Weidenfeld and Nicolson, 1994

PAULA HENDERSON

Pleasure Garden

According to Gertrude Jekyll, "a garden is for its owner's pleasure and whatever the degree or form of that pleasure, if only it be sincere, it is right and reasonable, and adds to human happiness in one of the purest and best of ways."

The fragmentary documentation that exists indicates that during the medieval and Renaissance periods, along with gardens for medicinal herbs, kitchen produce, fruit, and altar flowers, pleasure gardens existed on the estates of nobles and church officials. Except in parks designed for hunting or for spectators, the typical pleasure garden of the period, which was most often designed for the monarch, courtier, or churchman, was of modest size and usually consisted of a level lawn surrounded by flowering trees, such as pear, cherry, or medlar. Under the Tudors, the pleasure garden in England became an essential part of palace planning. A good example of this is the French-influenced Richmond Palace, whose gardens were laid out as a series of enclosures linked by covered walks and galleries. During the reign of Henry VIII, the king's rivalry with Francis I of France resulted in the creation of royal gardens at Hampton Court Palace, Whitehall, and Nonsuch Palace.

During the Elizabethan period the pleasure garden became an important feature of the country house, and by the 18th century the definition of the term *pleasure garden* was more specific: a simple grid pattern of sand or gravel walks with grassed or wooded areas between them. Such private pleasure gardens were evident at Buckingham House (later Buckingham Palace), Burlington House, Marlborough House, and the New Spring Gardens at Vauxhall, which intersected its allées at right angles through a grove of cultivated elm and sycamore trees.

Garden at Moor Park, ca. 1908
Courtesy of Mary Evans Picture Library

Although many public pleasure gardens in England were not originally designed as such, an exception is Ranelaugh, where in 1741 the owners commissioned architect William Jones to redesign the entire garden after the original layout by George London and Henry Wise had fallen into decay after years of neglect. Although the garden at Ranelaugh was designed to focus attention on Jones's rotunda, it became, along with the New Spring Gardens at Vauxhall, a model for 18th-century pleasure gardens. During this period landscapers introduced various design features into pleasure gardens, including curved walks, pebble mosaic paths, and various architectural structures such as pavilions, temples, grottoes, and obelisks. Toward the end of the 18th century, public pleasure gardens featured structures as varied as Chinese pagodas, Moorish temples, Venetian gondolas, and hermitages, the most outstanding features of which were that they did not depend on any unifying theme or relation to the garden but instead reflected the fashionable influences of the time.

Public pleasure gardens continued to be established and maintained in England throughout the 19th century. Often places of public entertainment, they frequently served as the settings for concerts, banquets, fireworks displays, and special attractions of public interest.

Further Reading

Adams, William Howard, *Nature Perfected: Gardens Through History*, New York: Abbeville Press, 1991

Gibbs, Nancy R., "Paradise Found," *Time* (20 June 1988)

Myers-Cooke, Brodee, *Gardens for Pleasure*, Sydney: Angus and Robertson, and London: HarperCollins, 1996

Scott-James, Anne, and Osbert Lancaster, *The Pleasure Garden: An Illustrated History of British Gardening*, Ipswich, Suffolk: Gambit, 1977

MARTIN J. MANNING

Pliny Family

Roman Scholars and Writers

The surviving works of the Pliny family provide a great wealth of information on Roman life and society. Although writing on different themes, both Pliny the Elder and Pliny the Younger influenced later generations: the elder through his scientific study and the younger for his collection of letters covering a variety of topics.

Pliny the Elder was considered the most learned man of his age. He was incredibly industrious: every spare moment would be spent in study; books were read to him and copious notes taken. His masterpiece, *Naturalis historia* (A.D. 77; *Natural History*), is the first encyclopedia, a vast compilation of "20,000 noteworthy facts" in 37 books, dealing with information on all subjects relating to ancient science and "knowledge of the world." The work contains his own observations and those from numerous sources, which are cited (including Theophrastus and Varro), thus providing information on many lost works; there are many interesting digressions, but no critical analysis is given. Books 1–11 of Pliny's *Natural History* are concerned with astronomy, geography, ethnography, anthropology, and zoology; books 12–19 are devoted to botany; books 20–32 to pharmacology; and books 33–37 to mineralogy, art and architecture, and art history. In book 36 he includes celebrated statues displayed in the gardens of Servilius at Rome.

The botanical sections of *Natural History* are particularly useful, for Pliny the Elder differentiates between wild and cultivated plant species. Although many were grown in a *potager*, or rustic kitchen garden, he does include species with decorative qualities, which could be found in ornamental gardens. An index of plants mentioned has been added to the Loeb edition of *Natural History* (volume 7; 1951–56). In book 12 Pliny informs about different trees, their use in gardens, and some exceptional specimens. Book 13 lists plants used in the production of perfumes. In book 14 he names those plants used in the production of cordials and wines. Book 15 deals with fruit trees, grafting, the introduction and improvement of forms, and the extensive use of myrtle and laurel; book 16 looks at ornamental trees and noteworthy specimens; books 17–18 include ways to improve the soil, horticultural and agricultural techniques, and climatic observations; books 19–20 contain information on kitchen garden plants—vegetables, herbs, and spices—plus some remedies against garden pests; book 21 enumerates the flowers and shrubs used in the making of chaplets and garlands, followed by those planted near beehives; book 22 covers wild and cultivated medicinal plants; and book 23 gives information on medicines obtained from cultivated trees.

The letters of Pliny the Younger reveal a man of refined tastes, who corresponded with a wide circle of friends of literary note, such as Tacitus, to whom he dedicated his *Epistles* (ca. 98–113; *Letters*). Pliny the Younger was a generous benefactor and highly respected. He wrote lively and vivid descriptions of two of his villas, one on the seashore at Laurentum, the other in the Tuscan hills. Other Roman writers, such as Cicero, Varro, and Seneca, make brief references to their villas and gardens, but the lengthy details in the letters of Pliny the Younger provide a valuable insight into landscaped gardens during the Roman Empire. His villas were surrounded by extensive gardens and terraces, some of an open nature and others enclosed. Pliny the Younger also shows that, although these were luxurious dwellings, space was still reserved for a rustic kitchen garden. Views were important, and the surrounding farmlands, woods, and vineyards were not hidden from view but incorporated into the overall design. At Laurentum two prospect towers provided a view of the sea, his gardens, the woods, and mountains. One passage in his letters mentions a colonnade opening onto a *xystus*, or terrace, "scented with violets." Another part of the villa looked onto a circular drive lined with hedges of box and rosemary, the inner part containing a shady vine-covered pergola, while the garden beyond was planted with mulberry and fig trees. The buildings themselves incorporated colonnaded garden courts. One at his Tuscan villa was shaded by four large plane trees with a fountain in the center; a room leading off this open area was painted with a verdant fresco with bubbling fountain, which by its light and cool refreshing colors brought the garden into the house.

Pliny the Younger's Tuscan villa was situated on a sloping hillside, and gardens were designed on a series of terraces. A portico on the uppermost level opened onto a terrace decorated with topiary figures of box, some being animals facing each other. There was a bed of acanthus on a lower level, and paths lined with trained bushes. An island bed contained more box figures and clipped trees. Tiers of box disguised the enclosing stone garden wall so the eye could encompass the view of a continuing landscape of meadows beyond. In addition Pliny the Younger describes the beauty of his hippodrome garden, which, according to him, surpassed that of the buildings. This garden form is also found at Tivoli and on the Palatine, but Pliny in his letters provides information on how they would be planted and indicates some of the garden furnishings they might contain. The design mimicked a race track with tree-lined walks around the perimeter, in this case, of box, laurel, and plane festooned with ivy, with cypress on the curve. The inner part contained paths lined with box hedges, topiary, fruit trees, beds of roses,

and acanthus. Benches and fountains were placed at intervals, and a small stream gently flowed throughout the glade. An al fresco dining area was created in the midst of the garden, under a vine-covered pergola. Diners reclining on a curved couch were served food from dishes placed on the edge of a decorative pool, or from vessels floating on the water near flowing fountains; after the feast guests could rest in the little pavilion opposite.

Over the centuries Pliny the Younger's descriptions have given rise to numerous interpretations by architects seeking to design a classical-style villa. Their plans and elevations, sometimes including areas of landscaped garden, vary greatly and to a certain extent reflect fashions during the various architects' careers. We therefore can witness the changes made through the decades and centuries, from Félibien (1699) and Castell (1728) to Schinkel (1841) and Huet (1989).

Pliny the Elder (Gaius Plinius Secundus) A.D. 23 or 24–79

Biography
Born at Novum Comum, Como, Italy, A.D. 23 or 24. Studied in Rome; career as advocate, saw military service on Rhine frontier, and rose to rank of cavalry commander; believed to have been procurator in Gallia Narbonensis (southern France), A.D. 70; held similar posts in Africa, Gallia Belgica, and Hispania Citerior (southern Spain); final post as commander of fleet stationed at Misenum, Italy, across the bay from Pompeii; wrote many works (on use of javelins by cavalry, life of Pomponius Secundus, wars in Germany, study of oratory, reflections on literature) but only encyclopedic books on natural history *(Naturalis historia)* survive; interest in science led to investigation of eruption of Mt. Vesuvius, A.D. 79. Died in Stabiae, Italy, A.D. 79.

Selected Publications
Naturalis historia, A.D. 77; as *The Historie of the World,* translated by Philemon Holland, 1601; as *Natural History,* 10 vols., translated by H. Rackham and W.H.S. Jones, 1938–63

Pliny the Younger (Gaius Plinius Caecilius Secundus) A.D. 61 or 62–113

Biography
Born at Comum, Como, Italy, A.D. 61 or 62. His father, L. Caecilius, died early, and young Pliny was adopted by his maternal uncle, Pliny the Elder, who made him heir to his estate; continued education in Rome, studying rhetoric under Nicetes Sacerdos and Quintilian; aged 18, was at Misenum when eruption of Mt. Vesuvius claimed life of his uncle, and later in life wrote an

eye-witness account of the catastrophe (*Epistles*, 6.16 and 20); became advocate at 18 years old, specializing in cases of inheritance and property and acting in several high profile cases of corruption, and became known as great orator; passed through *Cursus Honorum*, the Roman career structure, consisting of regular series of official administration and military posts; wrote history of his own times, a book of poetry, and published his speeches and orations, a panegyric on the emperor Trajan, and a collection of letters *(Epistles)*, of which only the latter two have survived. Died in office while governor of Bithynia, Asia Minor, A.D. 113.

Selected Designs

ca. A.D. 90–109   Landscaped villa gardens, Laurentum, near Ostia, Italy; Hippodrome garden and landscaped villa gardens, near Tifernum Tiberinum (modern Città di Castello), in the Tuscan Hills, Italy

Selected Publications

Epistles, ca. A.D. 98–113; as *The Letters of the Younger Pliny*, translated by Betty Radice, 1963

Further Reading

Daubeny, Charles, *Essay on the Trees and Shrubs of the Ancients*, Oxford, 1865

Duff, John Wight, *A Literary History of Rome in the Silver Age*, New York: Scribner, and London: Unwin, 1927; 3rd edition, edited by Arnold Mackey Duff, London: Benn, and New York: Barnes and Noble, 1964

Du Prey de la Ruffinière, Pierre, *The Villas of Pliny from Antiquity to Posterity*, Chicago: University of Chicago Press, 1994

Farrar, Linda, *Ancient Roman Gardens*, Stroud, Gloucestershire: Sutton, 1998

Tanzer, Helen H., *The Villas of Pliny the Younger*, New York: Columbia University Press, 1924

Von Albrecht, Michael, *Geschichte der römischen Literatur*, 2 vols., Bern, Switzerland: Francke, 1992; as *A History of Roman Literature*, Leiden and New York: Brill, 1997

Whalley, Joyce Irene, *Pliny the Elder: Historia Naturalis*, London: Victoria and Albert Museum, and Sidgwick and Jackson, 1982

LINDA FARRAR

Pniower, Georg Béla 1896–1960

German Garden Architect

Georg Béla Pniower was an outstanding garden architect in Germany from 1925 until his death in 1960. He learned gardening in Silesia and then worked as a journeyman in nurseries and held positions in municipal parks departments elsewhere in Germany. He graduated from the state school for fruit growing and horticulture at Proskau, Silesia, in 1920 and took another exam in horticulture in Berlin in 1923. Since there were still no university courses for garden and landscape architecture, Pniower was anxious to improve his skills elsewhere. He attended lessons at the school for decorative arts in Hanover and the Technical University of Hanover in architecture and city planning while he served as garden technician and personal assistant to parks director Hermann Kube in the city of Hanover, Lower Saxony. He also took courses at the state academy of art in Düsseldorf, while working in that city for the well-known landscape architect Josef Buerbaum. Pniower himself also taught courses in science and garden design at the Israelitic school for horticulture at Ahlem near Hanover. Pniower's outstanding design qualification in garden architecture is reflected in two positions he held before he became a freelance landscape architect in 1925. In 1922 he received one of the few top jobs in landscape architecture in Germany in those days, becoming head of the design department of the firm of Ludwig Späth in Berlin, the largest tree nursery on the European continent in those days (some 900 acres [364 ha]). In 1924 he switched to Hermann Rothe, who operated the largest horticultural firm in Berlin. Pniower, a member of the Association of German Garden Architects (Bund Deutscher Gartenarchitekten) and Reichs Association of Forming Artists (Reichsverband bildender Künstler), was about to start an international career. His winter-garden design for the famous Gourmenia restaurant in Berlin was published in the Italian journal *La Casa Bella* in 1930. The Italian government invited him as the only German landscape architect to contribute to the Triennale in Milan, in February 1933. Early on, in the last years of the democratic government before the National Socialist takeover in 1933, Pniower served as representative of the Association of German Garden Architects in the Committee for Reichs Motorways (Ausschuß für die Reichsautostraßen, later, Reichsautobahnen) and realized the job opportunity for landscape architects that the construction of the new motorways (Autobahnen) offered.

Pniower's kleine Landschaft (little landscape) design for the 1935 Berlin fair and exhibition was a striking success. Shortly after the opening of the exhibition, the National Socialist press celebrated it as an example for German volkish design. When it became known only a few days later that Pniower was not a German volkish designer and did not want to be regarded as a blood and soil artist, he was forbidden to continue to work as a garden architect by the National Socialist Reichs Chamber of Forming Arts (Reichskammer der bildenden Künste), where every professional artist had to be accredited during National Socialism. Furthermore, the kleine Landschaft on the exhibition site was leveled. According to the Nuremberg racial laws, Pniower was considered half-Jewish. Pniower consequently transferred his business to his wife and tried to continue to work, but he ran into increasing difficulties with Nazi authorities, who ultimately forced him to work illegally. In the spring of 1938 he accepted an invitation to work in England, mostly in Surrey and in London, and was received as guest of the Royal Society of British Architects. Due to pressure on his family, however, he was forced to return to Germany for compulsory military service on 1 September 1939 and was drafted in the summer of 1940. Late in 1940 the Reichs Chamber for Forming Arts decreed that his "Aryan" wife could not join this chamber as a member. The reason given was that her application was an attempt to circumvent the Nuremberg racial laws. Pniower then established a horticultural business and tried to continue to work as landscape architect secretly. He was caught by the secret state police and had to work in a factory for textile fabrics as a compulsory worker from September 1944 until the end of World War II. Together with his brother he rebuilt his business in 1945 and by the end of July received the commission for the design of the Kleist Park, where the building of the Allied Council in Berlin was located. Shortly afterward he was commissioned for the design of the U.S. headquarters in Berlin.

On 1 July 1946 Pniower received the chair and became director of the Institute for Landscape and Garden Design at the Faculty of Agriculture at the University of Berlin. He succeeded Heinrich Friedrich Wiepking-Jürgensmann, who had been an adamant follower of National Socialism and had left his position in Berlin when the Russians came to town. In 1947 Pniower delivered a pathbreaking modern design for the completely destroyed Tiergarten park in Berlin west of the Brandenburg Gate. It showed his excellency as a designer and caused considerable public debate. It was not implemented, not the least because the Tiergarten park was located in West Berlin and Pniower decided to stay with Humboldt University, which was based in East Berlin. Aware of the urgent need for housing, Pniower took a position as president of the Selbsthilfe-Verband zur Bekämpfung der Wohnungsnot in Groß-Berlin (self-help association to fight the need for housing in greater Berlin) in 1948 and thus cooperated with the president of the Berlin allotment holders association, Wilhelm Naulin, who had been deprived of his position during National Socialism. This association dissolved itself in 1949.

In order to signal the new professional emphasis, Pniower changed the name of the institute at the University of Berlin from Institut für Landschafts- und Gartengestaltung (Institute for Landscape and Garden Design) to Institut für Gartenkunst und Landschaftgestaltung (Institute for Garden Art and Landscape Design). He felt that the earlier name, used by Wiepking-Jürgensmann during the era of National Socialism, reflected a politically tendentious program for the restructuring of Europe according to the views of National Socialism. The institute's buildings were located in the borough of Berlin-Dahlem, which now belonged to West Berlin, whereas Humboldt University and its administration were located in the borough of Berlin-Mitte, which now belonged to East Berlin. Although Pniower seems to have worked hard to re-create "his" institute, he had to face political distrust, as he had had to do during National Socialism. The state authorities in the German Democratic Republic knew that he did not approve of the political system and that he privately criticized it. They also knew that he occasionally visited the America House, which was located not far from where he lived in the borough of Berlin-Zehlendorf, which was part of West Berlin.

On 30 September 1950 Pniower was dismissed from his post by the Berlin Magistrate Department of People's Education, which was located in West Berlin but served all of Berlin. Pniower decided to stay with Humboldt University and created a new institute in Berlin-Mitte beginning in 1951. As of May 1952 he named it the Institut für Garten- und Landeskultur (Institute for Garden and Land Culture). He also moved from Berlin-Zehlendorf in West Berlin to Berlin-Grünau in East Berlin.

Pniower initiated a number of research projects at this institute. Most remarkable was the research on Beispiellandschaften (exemplary landscapes), which are meant to follow a design that fights soil erosion and at the same time increases agricultural productivity by biological means. This research was carried out in the Huy-Hakel area east of the Harz mountains. Other research related to the need for green spaces of various kinds as part of socialist city planning. Another project looked at the flora in big cities, while others tried to research the impact of plants on climatic conditions in cities and study the greening of rubble and debris areas in cities, a pressing problem in many cities in Germany after World War II. The institute directed specific research toward the dust-filtering capacity of plants, to economic aspects of green space maintenance, and to the improvement of recultivation measures for waste dumps from brown coal mining. Pniower also tried to improve the conditions for willow growth. Pniower himself took his doctoral exam shortly before his death in 1960.

Biography

Born in Breslau, Germany, 1896. After apprenticeship in gardening enterprise of Ernst in Glatz, Silesia, Germany, 1911–1913, worked for tree nursery Guder in Breslau, tree nursery Wagner in Echternach, Luxemburg, rose nursery Lambert in Trier, Germany, municipal parks department in Trier, and municipal parks department, Beuthen, Silesia, 1913–16; attended state school for fruit growing and horticulture, Proskau, Silesia, 1916–17 and 1919–20, and during this time practiced as student in garden and landscape contractor's firm of Jacob Ochs, Hamburg, Germany; worked as garden technician and personal assistant to parks director Hermann Kube in city of Hannover, Lower Saxony, Germany, 1920–21; attended school for decorative arts in Hannover and Technical University of Hannover in architecture and city planning; worked with landscape architect Josef Buerbaum in Düsseldorf and at same time attended classes at state academy of art in Düsseldorf, Germany, in 1921 and 1922; became head of design department of firm of Ludwig Späth, Berlin, Germany, 1922–24; took exam as diploma-horticulturist, 1923, at Prussian school for fruit growing and horticulture at Berlin-Dahlem; head of department for garden design in firm of Hermann Rothe, Berlin, 1924–25; freelance landscape architect and landscape contractor, 1925; invited by Italian government as only German landscape architect to contribute to Triennale in Milan, Italy, February 1933; forbidden to work as landscape architect, 1935, because considered "half-Jewish" by National Socialist Reichs Chamber of Forming Arts; worked in England, spring 1938; forced to return to Germany for compulsory military service on 1 September 1939; worked in factory for textile fabrics as compulsory worker from September 1944 until end of World War II; rebuilt landscape contracting business with help of brother, 1945; received chair and became director of institute for garden art and landscape design on faculty of agriculture at University of Berlin, July 1946 (successor to Heinrich Friedrich Wiepking-Jürgensmann); dismissed from post by Berlin magistrate department of peoples education, located in West Berlin, 30 September 1950; built up new institute for garden and land culture located in East Berlin, 1951 on, at Humboldt University, Berlin; initiated several research projects, such as research on "exemplary landscapes" (*Beispiellandschaften*); took doctoral exam shortly before his death. Died in Berlin, 1960.

Selected Designs

1926	Garden of Georg Pniower's house, Berlin, Germany
1928	Tropical "winter garden" for Gourmenia restaurant, Berlin, Germany
1932	Kleiner Garten für hohe Ansprüche (small garden for high claims), Berlin fair exhibition, Berlin, Germany
1935	Kleine Landschaft (little landscape), Berlin fair exhibition, Berlin, Germany
1945	Kleist park, in front of building for Allied Council, Berlin, Germany; former Telefunken area, then U.S. headquarters in Berlin, Germany; Soviet memorial, Berlin, Germany; French Quartier Napoleon, Berlin, Germany
1947	Tiergarten park, Berlin, Germany
1949	"Exemplary landscapes," Huy-Hakel area, east of Harz mountain, Germany
1950	Concept for recultivation of extensive brown coal-mining areas, Niederlausitz area, Germany
1959	Landscape design along railroad line, Potsdam and Saarmund, Germany
1959–60	Inner courtyard, Humboldt University, Berlin, Germany

Selected Publications

"Schafft Automobilstraßen!" *Deutsche Gartenarchitekt* 8 (1931)

"Übergang vom Haus zum Garten," *Gartenschönheit* 16 (1935)

"Von den Aufgaben des Institutes für Gartenkunst und Landschaftsgestaltung an der Landwirtschaftlich-Gärtnerischen Fakultät der Universität Berlin," *Neue Berliner Gärtner-Börse* 1 (1947)

"Ein Vorschlag zum Berliner Tiergarten," *Die neue Stadt* 2 (1948)

"Rund um den Kleistpark," *Garten + Landschaft* 60 (1950)

"Über die Entwicklungsgeschichte und landeskulturelle Bedeutung der Dendrologie," *Referate der Ersten Zentralen Tagung für Dendrologie in Dresden-Pillnitz vom 29. bis 31. August 1953* (1954)

"Wirtschaft und Naturschutz," *Märkische Heimat* (1956)

"Grundgedanken zur Gestaltung von Kinderspielplätzen," *Deutsche Gartenarchitektur* 1 (1960)

Further Reading

Gandert, Klaus-Dietrich, "Professor Dr. Georg B. Pniower zum Andenken," *Beiträge zur Gehölzkunde* (1985)

Giese, Helmut, "Zur Erinnerung an Georg Pniower," *Garten und Landschaft* 100, no. 12 (1990)

Gröning, Gert, and Joachim Wolschke-Bulmahn, "Zum 90. Geburtstag des Gartenarchitekten Georg Bela Pniower," *Das Gartenamt* 35, no. 12 (1986)

Gröning, Gert, and Joachim Wolschke-Bulmahn, *Grüne Biographien: Biographisches Handbuch zur Landschaftsarchitektur des 20. Jahrhunderts in Deutschland*, Berlin: Patzer, 1997

GERT GRÖNING

Poetry, Garden in

The garden has been represented in poetry in many cultures throughout the ages. Although it is often seen as a symbol of beauty and repose, it can take on a whole variety of meanings, including work and pleasure, life and death, hope and sadness, and love and deprivation. The garden can evoke memories; it can be viewed as a haven for wildlife and beautiful plants; and it can stimulate humor and wise sayings.

Some religions portray the beginning and end of life in a garden—Eden and Paradise. The Aztec heaven, for example, was envisaged as a place to revel among the rich blossoms and odors of the gardens of paradise. In *Paradise Lost* John Milton (1608–74) depicts Eve in the Garden of Eden discussing with Adam the fact that a gardener's work is never done:

> Adam, well may we labour still to dress
> This garden, still to tend plant, herb, and flower,
> Our pleasant task enjoin'd: but till more hands
> Aid us, the work under our labour grows,
> Luxurious by restraint; what we by day
> Lop overgrown, or prune, or prop, or bind,
> One night or two with wanton growth derides,
> Teeming to wild.

Likewise, in "Digging" the Irish poet Seamus Heaney (1939–), who won the Nobel Prize in literature in 1995, writes of his father working in the garden:

> Under my window, a clean rasping sound
> When the spade sinks into the gravelly ground:
> My father, digging. I look down
>
> Till his straining rump among the flowerbeds
> Bends low, comes up twenty years away
> Stooping in rhythm through potato drills
> Where he was digging.

Rudyard Kipling (1865–1936), in "The Glory of the Garden," contrasts the beauty of the garden with the hard work of weeding that needs to be done in order to maintain it:

> Our England is a garden, and such gardens are not made
> By singing: 'Oh, how beautiful!' and sitting in the shade,
> While better men than we go out and start their working lives
> At grubbing weeds from gravel-paths with broken dinner-knives.

Other poets concentrate on the pleasure and productivity of the garden, as in Alexander Pope's (1688–1744) translation of Homer's *Odyssey* when he describes the garden of Alcinous:

> Close to the gates a spacious garden lies,
> From storms defended, and inclement skies:
> Four acres was th'allotted space of ground,
> Fenced with a green enclosure all around.
> Tall thriving trees confessed the fruitful mold;
> The red'ning apple ripens here to gold,
> Here the blue fig with luscious juice o'erflows,
> With deeper red the full pomegranate glows,
> The branch here bends beneath the weighty pear,
> And verdant olives flourish round the year.

Similarly, Andrew Marvell (1621–78), in "The Garden," luxuriates in the fruitful produce of the garden:

> What wond'rous life is this I lead!
> Ripe apples drop about my head;
> The luscious clusters of the vine
> Upon my mouth do crush their wine;

The nectarine, and curious peach,
Into my hands themselves do reach;
Stumbling on melons, as I pass,
Insnared with flowers, I fall on grass.

Samuel Taylor Coleridge (1772–1834), in *Kubla Khan*, describes the magnificence of Chinese royal gardens:

So twice five miles of fertile ground
With walls and towers were girdled round:
And there were gardens bright with sinuous rills,
Where blossomed many an incense-bearing tree;
And here were forests ancient as the hills
Enfolding sunny spots of greenery.

The natural seasons in the garden give rise to poetic images of life and death, and to feelings of hope and sadness. In "To Blossoms," for example, Robert Herrick (1591–1674) expresses the fragility of the blossoming tree:

Fair pledges of a fruitful tree,
Why do ye fall so fast?
Your date is not so past
But you may stay awhile
To blush and gently smile
And go at last.

John Donne (1573–1631), in "The Blossom," warns of the danger of a late frost:

Little think'st thou, poore flower,
Whom I have watchd six or seven dayes,
And seene thy birth, and seene what every houre
Gave to thy growth, thee to this height to raise,
And now dost laugh and triumph on this bough,
Little think'st thou
That it will freeze anon, and that I shall
To morrow finde thee falne, or not at all.

Autumn brings the process of decay, as the American poet Alice Cary (1820–71) conveys in "Autumn":

The Rose has taken off her tire of red—
The mullein-stalk its yellow stars have lost,
And the proud meadow-pink hangs down her head
Against earth's chilly bosom, witched with frost.

The popular Chinese poet Po Chu-i (772–846), in *The Chrysanthemums in the Eastern Garden*, likens this seasonal change to growing old:

The days of my youth left me long ago
And now in their turn dwindle my years of prime.
With what thoughts of sadness and loneliness
I walk in this cold, deserted place!

In the midst of the garden long I stand alone;
The sunshine, faint; the wind and dew chill.
The autumn lettuce is tangled and turned to seed;
The fair trees are blighted and withered away.
All that is left are a few chrysanthemum-flowers
That have newly opened beneath the wattled fence.

For the American poet Ester Popel (1896–1958) in "October Prayer," however, this autumnal laying bare is seen as glorious:

Change me, oh God,
Into a tree in autumn
And let my dying
Be a blaze of glory!

Drape me in a
Crimson, leafy gown,
And deck my soul
In dancing flakes of gold!

And then when Death
Comes by, and with his hands
Strips off his rustling garment
Let me stand

Before him, proud and naked,
Unashamed, uncaring,
All the strength in me revealed
Against the sky!

Oh, God
Make me an autumn tree
If I must die!

Similarly, Emily Brontë (1818–48) smiles through the dreary autumn:

Fall, leaves, fall; die, flower, away;
Lengthen night and shorten day;
Every leaf speaks bliss to me
Fluttering from the autumn tree.
I shall smile when wreaths of snow
Blossom where the rose should grow;
I shall sing when night's decay
Ushers in a drearier day.

When spring comes again, the reclothing of the trees is celebrated, as in the poem "A Date with Spring" by the Guyanese poet John Agard (1949–):

What's the good of being a tree
if you can't flaunt your beauty?

Winter, I was naked.
Exposed as can be.
Me wardrobe took off

with the wind.
Life was a frosty slumber.
Now, Spring, here I come.
Can't wait to slip in
to me little green number.

Flowers from the garden are often used in poetry to represent love, as in this sonnet (XLIV) by Elizabeth Barrett Browning (1806–61):

Beloved, thou hast brought me many flowers
Plucked in the garden all the summer through
And winter; and it seemed as if they grew
In this close room, nor missed the sun and showers.

The red rose in particular has long been a symbol of love, as when the Scottish poet Robert Burns (1759–96) writes "O my luve's like a red, red rose,/That's newly sprung in June." William Morris (1834–96), in "The Life and Death of Jason," uses the flower in the same way:

I know a little garden-close,
Set thick with lily and red rose,
Where I would wander if I might
From dewy morn to dewy night,
And have one with me wandering.

But in *Othello*, William Shakespeare (1564–1616) reminds us of the rose's mortality:

When I have pluck'd the rose,
I cannot give it vital growth again,
It needs must wither: I'll smell it on the tree.

The fruitfulness and joy associated with the garden can be spoilt and stunted. For William Blake (1757–1827), in "The Garden of Love," it was the oppression of organized religion that could destroy the garden:

I went to the Garden of Love.
And saw what I never had seen:
A Chapel was built in the midst,
Where I used to play on the green.

And the gates of this Chapel were shut,
And Thou shalt not, writ over the door;
So I turned to the Garden of Love,
That so many sweet flowers bore,

And I saw it was filled with graves,
And tomb-stones where flowers should be:
And Priests in black gowns, were walking their
    rounds,
And binding with briars, my joys & desires.

The German poet and playwright Bertolt Brecht (1898–1956), in "The Plum Tree," uses the barren tree

to symbolize social deprivation, which prevents human beings from achieving their full potential:

In the yard stands a small plum tree
Though you'd hardly believe it was one.
It has a railing round it
So no one can knock it over.

It can't grow any bigger
Though that's what it wants to do.
That's out of the question—
It gets too little sun.

You'd hardly believe it was a plum tree
For it never bears a plum.
But it is a plum tree
You can tell by the leaves.

The Irish poet Oliver Goldsmith (1728–74) also draws attention to social factors in gardening. "The Deserted Village" examines how 18th-century enclosures of land by the wealthy led to a "garden" for the rich and a "grave" for the poor:

the man of wealth and pride
Takes up a space that many poor supplied;
Space for his lake, his park's extended bounds,
Space for his horses, equipage and hounds.

Gardens outlive human beings. In "Tamarind Flower" the Indian poet Rabindranath Tagore (1861–1941), who won the Nobel Prize in literature in 1913, reminds us how much a tree may have seen:

In our town house there is
an aged tamarind tree I've know since childhood,
standing in the north-west corner
like a guardian-god
or an old family servant
as ancient as Great-grandfather.
Through the many chapters of our family's births
    and deaths
quietly it has stood
like a courtier of dumb history.

The names of so many of those
whose rights to that tree through the ages were
    undisputed
are today even more fallen than its fallen leaves.
The memories of so many of them
are more shadowy than that tree's shadow.

Memory is a theme of much garden poetry, as the Japanese poet Matsuo Basho (1644–94) illustrates:

Many things of the past
Are brought to my mind,

As I stand in the garden
Staring at a cherry tree.

In "Childhood" the Northamptonshire "peasant poet" John Clare (1793–1864) recalls making a garden:

Our little gardens there we made
Of blossoms all arow
And though they had no roots at all
We hoped to see them grow.

In a similar vein Thomas Hood (1799–1845) remembers his childhood garden:

I remember, I remember
The roses, red and white,
The violets, and the lily-cups—
Those flowers made of light!
The lilacs where the robin built,
And where my brother set
The laburnum on his birthday,—
The tree is living yet!

In "An Old-Fashioned Garden" the American lyricist Cole Porter (1891–1964) also reminisces:

One summer day,
I chanced to stray
To a garden of flowers blooming wild.
It took me once more
To the dear days of yore
And a spot that I loved as a child.

There were the phlox,
Tall hollyhocks,
Violets perfuming the air,
Frail eglantines,
Shy columbines,
And marigolds everywhere . . .

For William Wordsworth (1770–1850), in "Intimations of Immortality," the associations of flowers are almost beyond expression: "To me the meanest flower that blows can give/Thoughts that do often lie too deep for tears."

Poets have added to our appreciation of plants in the garden by their use of metaphor. The American poet Emily Dickinson (1830–86), for example, writes of the "dandelion's pallid tube," and Matthew Arnold (1822–88) looks forward to seeing the "gold-dusted snapdragons." John Keats (1795–1821), in "I Stood Tip-Toe upon a Little Hill," imagines sweet peas ready to take off:

Here are sweet peas, on tip-toe for a flight:
With wings of gentle flush o'er delicate white,

And taper fingers catching at all things,
To bind them all about with tiny rings.

In "The Lodging-House Fuchsias" Thomas Hardy (1840–1928) describes the garden fuchsias giving a shower to passersby:

Mrs Master's fuchsias hung
Higher and broader, and brightly swung,
Bell-like, more and more
Over the narrow garden-path,
Giving the passer a sprinkle-bath
In the morning.

She put up with their pushful ways,
And made us tenderly lift their sprays,
Going to her door:
But when her funeral had to pass
They cut back all the flowery mass
In the morning.

Olive Senior (1943–), a Jamaican poet who lives in Canada, describes the generosity of the guava:

Than guava fruit
nothing sweeter
so free in its wild simplicity
so generous
it makes itself available to all comers
—even the worms.

Some poets have been intrigued by wildlife in the garden. D.H. Lawrence (1885–1930), for instance, describes the mosquito as a "pointed fiend" with its "hateful bugle in my ear." In "Don't Cry Caterpillar" the Guyanese poet Grace Nichols (1950–) muses:

Don't cry, Caterpillar
Caterpillar, don't cry
You'll be a butterfly—by and by.

Caterpillar, please
Don't worry 'bout a thing.

"But," said Caterpillar,
"Will I still know myself—in wings?"

The comic poet Edward Lear (1812–1888), in "Nonsense Alphabet," rails humorously against the rabbit:

R was a rabbit
Who had a bad habit
Of eating the flowers
In gardens and bowers.
r!
Naughty fat Rabbit!

Many common sayings referring to the garden have a poetic ring, such as the Chinese saying, "Too many flowers dazzle the eye," meaning spoiled for choice, or "Different flowers strike different eyes," meaning beauty is in the eye of the beholder. There is a Japanese saying, "Happiness is to hold a flower in both hands," and in Jamaica is the expression, "Little bush sometime grow betta dan big tree."

Many popular garden rhymes are about predicting the future, such as the medieval English proverb, "He that would live for aye/Must eat Sage in May." A saying from Northamptonshire predicts, "A bloom upon the Apple-tree when the Apples are ripe/Is a sure termination to somebody's life." On a lighter note is this Scottish rhyme: "Snailie, snailie, shoot out your horn,/And tell us if it will be a bonny day the morn."

Further Reading

Adams, Estelle Davenport, *Flower and Leaf: Their Teachings from the Poets*, London, 1884

Beretta, Ilva, *The World's a Garden: Garden Poetry of the English Renaissance*, Uppsala, Sweden: Uppsala University, 1993

Clare, John, *The Poems of John Clare*, 2 vols., edited by John William Tibble, London: Dent, and New York: Dutton, 1935

Folkard, Richard, Jr., *Plant Lore, Legends, and Lyrics*, London, 1884; 2nd edition, London, 1892

Gardner, Rose, editor, *The Garden Anthology*, London: Routledge, and New York: Dutton, 1906

Grindon, Leopold Hartley, *The Shakspere Flora*, Manchester, 1883

Hollis, Jill, compiler, *Come into the Garden: A Treasury of Garden Verse*, London: Ebury, 1992

Hoyles, Martin, *The Gardener's Perpetual Almanack*, London: Thames and Hudson, 1997

Hunt, John Dixon, editor, *The Oxford Book of Garden Verse*, Oxford and New York: Oxford University Press, 1993

Osgood, Irene, and Horace Wyndham, *The Garden Anthology*, London: Richmond, 1914

Richardson, John, *In the Garden of Delight*, London: Harrap, 1912

Rohde, Eleanour Sinclair, *Shakespeare's Wild Flowers: Fairy Lore, Gardens, Herbs, Gatherers of Simples and Bee Lore*, London: Medici Society, 1935

Senior, Olive, *Gardening in the Tropics: Poems*, Toronto, Ontario: McClelland and Stewart, 1994; Newcastle upon Tyne, Northumberland: Bloodaxe, 1995

A Treasury of Garden Verse, Edinburgh: Canongate, 1990

Waters, Michael, *The Garden in Victorian Literature*, Aldershot, Hampshire: Scolar Press, 1988

Wood, Arthur Denis Blachford, compiler, *Poets in the Garden: An Anthology of Garden Verse*, London: Murray, 1978

MARTIN HOYLES

Poland

The cultivation of gardens has a long-standing tradition in Poland. Initially gardens of the elite dominated, then they gradually extended to the peasants. The style of gardens followed European trends in garden art, especially Italy, France, Holland, England, and Germany. The peculiarity of Polish culture, climate, and orography has expressed itself in the variety of Polish garden styles. Foreign styles were usually adapted to suit the local conditions, contributing to the richness of European garden art.

Since the Middle Ages garden art in Poland developed from local cultivation traditions. Decorative trees, shrubs, and flowers were gradually introduced to orchards, vegetable gardens, and greeneries. Development of monasteries began in the second half of the 11th century. Gardens of the cenobite order differ from the eremitic. Cenobite gardens included areas surrounded by a wall fence encompassing orchards, vegetable gardens, vineyards, fishponds, and mills. The contemplation garden, called *viridarium*, was arranged in the form of a cross. Only a few of these remain (Wąchock, Kamień Pomorski, Mogiła, Oliwa, Pelpin, Sulejów, Koprzywnica, Henryków, Jędrzejów, Bielany near Cracow, Bielany near Warsaw, and Kartuzy).

Small greeneries or decorative gardens called *hortus conclusus* were usually set around castles within the fortification. No examples of such gardens have remained, but they existed in Chojnik in the 14th century, at the Wawel in Cracow, and Melsztyn. Animal parks and flower meadows were set outside the fort and used as playgrounds (Bolkow, 13th century).

In the 16th century (during the reign of Queen Bona [r. 1518–56]) Renaissance gardens, called Italian gardens, were introduced with the participation of Italian architects and gardeners. These were elite gardens around palaces, villas, castles, and the homes of rich patricians. The nearest examples of such are in the southern regions around hilly areas with panoramic views; for example, single terraces such as Mogilany, Zator Balice, Prądnik Biały, Niepołomnice, and Łobzów (on a plain near Cracow, it had to remain as a view hillock) or multiterraces such as Pieskowa Skala, and Wola Justowska. The Renaissance gardens near Warsaw are situated on a hillside with a panoramic view of the postglacial valley of the Vistula (e.g., Ujazdów). The possibilities of constructing fountains, cascades, and other hydraulics were limited; only pools were built. The gardens in Baranów and Brzeg are situated in a valley plain. Beech (*Fagus*), linden (*Tilia*), ash (*Fraxinus*), and other native trees dominated. Gradually Mediterranean plants were introduced, such as box (*Buxus*), myrtle (*Myrtus*), oleander (*Nerium*), lombardy poplar (*Populus nigra* 'italica'), walnut (*Juglans*), horse-chestnut (*Aesculus*), and lavender (*Lavendula*). Concurrently various Italian vegetables and herbs were introduced. Polish Renaissance gardens were both decorative and practical, encompassing animal parks.

The baroque palace-garden ensembles seen in the 17th and 18th centuries and protective forts of barons were most characteristic of the first half of the 17th century. Small gardens were functionally connected to fortification (e.g., Krzyżtopór [currently a ruin], Przecław, and Podhorce [Ukraine]). In the second half of the 17th century, ensembles of the *entre cour et jardin* type became widely disseminated. Examples of these include Nieborów, Wysock, Sieniawa, Mała Wieś, Wilanów, and Rogalin, which are still extant.

The French influence became marked in the 18th century. Garden-town ensembles were built, for instance, in Warsaw, the Saska and Stanisławowska axes made up of richly decorated gardens and an urbanized system of avenues and squares. Numerous residences of the rich followed the same garden style, coupled with fields, housing estates, animal parks, and gardens trailed by avenues. Examples are Rydzyna, Białystok, Otwock, and Łańcut. Earlier baroque gardens such as Wilanów and Nieborów were enlarged according to this system. Small baroque gardens appeared at town palaces in the form of garden salons with little bosquets.

The so-called Italian gardens were built at modest palaces in the countryside, especially around the classical residences of gentries. In these gardens the Renaissance tradition kept changing, connecting the medieval tradition and *all 'italiana* style with its compositional solutions. Such a garden usually had a garden salon with a manor house on the northern side and hedges forming the western and eastern walls. The southern side was left open. They were often called Sarmatian gardens, using the *all 'italiana* and *pallazo in fortezza* tradition. This type of garden survived in typical forms as Polish "Italian garden" until the 19th century.

In the 18th century baroque gardens gradually became open to the public, such as the Saski garden in 1727. The first urban green areas were introduced, for example, the Great Avenue in Gdańsk and generally accessible calvary landscape parks dating as far back as the beginning of the 17th century (e.g., Zebrzydowska Calvary in 1601).

In the second half of the 18th century, sentimental, classical, and romantic landscape parks were introduced. Sentimental conceptions with extended literary programs conformed to English-Chinese solutions, for example, the Arcadia, near Nieborów. Outstanding and existing classical conceptions include the Łazienki Park and Królikarnia in Warsaw, Dęblin, Jabłonna, and Lewków. The first romantic park was Zofiówka (1795–1800, presently Ukraine), which had an Arcadian program.

Romantic parks in the first half of the 19th century had a profound emphasis of patriotism. Among the best parks from this period are Puławy, Skierniewice, Dowspuda, Opinogóra, the Belvedere garden in Warsaw, and Natolin. Such parks sprung up next to, or around, baroque gardens, for example, Wilanów, Rogalin, and Mała Wieś. Changing fashion and "modernization" meant destruction of regular gardens, which, however, was criticized as anglomania. Besides European trends, such as historical picturesque and beautiful styles, the traditional Polish Italian garden was still popular. In the second half of the 19th century, new compositions were introduced and old ones were enlarged using earlier styles, which led to numerous eclectic solutions: for example, the baroque Wilanów with a neo-Renaissance Italian garden, the neo-Renaissance Posadowo, the great neo-Renaissance terraces leading into a landscape park in Samsotrzel, in Łańcut the neobaroque garden as formal garden joining the romantic park with a naturalistic dendrological descent, and the neobaroque garden in Koztówka. Gothic Revival solutions could also be found, for example, Sobota and Bedlewo. Dendrological parks also appeared, including Medyka, Gołuchów, Pszczyna, Racot, Romanów, and especially Kórnik. Polish gardening has benefited from the dendrological wealth of North America and Asia.

In the late 19th century, compositions such as ornamental farms were created with filial attachments, animal parks, and protective green belts; for example, Wilanów, Łańcut, and Złoty Potok, or modest ones such as Zarzecze and Turew. Concurrently naturalistic trends became popular. These tendencies were associated with nature conservancy movements that were springing up at that time. Toward the end of the 19th century, outer-drive landscape parks became widely known. Different forms of urban green areas were introduced, such as city parks, town squares, boulevards, cemeteries, tree-lined roads, health resorts, and children's gardens, according to the ideas of Dr. H. Jordan, a physician from Cracow.

In the 20th century more types of town parks (stylistically informal), garden cities, and national parks emerged. People's parks and parks for culture and recreation in the mixed style (the so-called William and Mary garden style) were established in towns. Generally the increased need for town greens led to the development of protected green areas, employment allotments, garden cities, settlement greens, adventure playgrounds, botanical gardens, protection zones, and finally urban ecological systems. Rehabilitation of devastated areas inclined toward formation of recreation parks instead. Environmental protection and the formation of protected cultural landscapes has led to the establishment of forest parks, forest-protection green belts, extensive landscape parks, and areas of protected landscape that account for about 30 percent of the Polish territory.

The number of gardens in the late 1990s reached about 11,000, among which about 10,000 have been classified as historical; more than 5,700 have been added to the register of monuments. The state of historical parks and gardens is rather discouraging, however. The degradation of palaces and gardens begun during World War II was continued during the communist rule when after nationalization they became ideologically obsolete. Most became premises of various institutions, for example, headquarters of state farms, village schools, homes for aged people, or healthcare centers. Others that could not be used were left unattended. Only seven palace-garden ensembles were taken over by the government as national museums (Łańcut, Kozłówka, Łazienki, Wilanów, Nieborów, Oliwa, and Rogalin). Currently there are trials to find solutions for the restoration and protection of historical gardens. Some of the ensembles are being sold or returned to their previous owners. Specialists in garden restorations are being trained at all levels. People are gradually becoming aware of the cultural value of historical gardens. New parks, some private, and villa gardens are being built, presenting a new form of cultural landscape protection.

See also Arkadia; Łazienki Park; Nieborów; Puławy; Wilanów

Further Reading

Ciołek, Gerard, *Ogrody polskie,* Warsaw: Arkady, 1954; 2nd edition, 1978 (summary in English)

Jankowski, E., *Dzieje ogrodonictwa w Polsce,* Warsaw, 1923

Majdecki Longin, *Historia ogrodów,* Warsaw: Panstwowe Wydawnictwo Naukowe, 1978

Siewniak M., and Mitkowska A., *Tezaurus sztuki ogrodowej,* Warsaw, 1999

MAREK SIEWNIAK

Politics of Gardening

In China there is a tradition of seeing gardening as an alternative to politics, as in the Soochow garden called the Garden of the Unsuccessful Politician. In Europe Voltaire's reference to cultivating one's garden means to escape from politics and worldly affairs. Yet there are many ways in which gardening and politics are connected, the word *politics* here referring to the relationships of power in society and how they are played out.

The Shorter Oxford English Dictionary (1973) defines a garden as "an enclosed piece of ground devoted to the cultivation of flowers, fruit, or vegetables." Enclosure is essential to gardening, and this raises the important questions of who is doing the enclosing, who owns the land, and who is being kept out. Between 1760 and 1867 in England, a small group of wealthy landowners enclosed 7 million acres of common land that had been the property and livelihood of the common people of the country. People were often evicted from their houses, and whole villages were destroyed or moved in order to create the famous landscape gardens of the 18th century. The work at Milton Abbas in Dorset, for example, which was carried out between 1773 and 1786, led to the destruction of a small town with its own market, grammar school, almshouses, shops, four inns, and a brewery. The owner, Joseph Damer, later earl of Dorchester, employed Lancelot "Capability" Brown to landscape the new park and also to try to stop the pillaging carried out by local children.

Centuries earlier in Rome hundreds of people were ousted from their homes to create the Emperor Nero's gardens, which contained vineyards, woodlands stocked with game, a large lake, and waterfalls. Similarly in 17th-century France, André Le Nôtre's design for Nicolas Fouquet's gardens at Vaux-le-Vicomte included destroying three hamlets, diverting rivulets, and transplanting whole woods. Some 18,000 men were employed in the construction work. At Versailles over 22,000 men and 6,000 horses were used.

The owners sometimes spent vast sums of money on their parks and gardens, which were often resented. The

Women gardeners at the Royal Botanic Gardens, Kew
Copyright Royal Botanic Gardens, Kew

royal park of the Han emperor Wu Ti (140–87 B.C.) at his capitol Chang-an, in the west of China, extended for 50 square miles. It aroused so much indignation that he was forced to release the land back for cultivation.

The example of Wu Ti indicates that the power of land ownership can be resisted. From medieval England came the legend of Robin Hood and his outlaws opposing the privatization of the forests. In the 16th century the Norfolk rising against the whole system of enclosures took place. It was led by Robert Kett who in 1549, with an army of 20,000, captured Norwich, the second most important city of England. In the uprising the Earl of Surrey's newly enclosed gardens at St. Leonard's Priory near Norwich were destroyed.

Attempts by King James I in the 17th century to enclose Northwood Common in south London were met with prolonged and successful resistance. It was led by the Lewisham parish priest, Abraham Colfe, and involved tearing down the illegal fences and sending a deputation to the king. In 17th-century England the Diggers argued that the land belonged to the whole people. In the 19th century public campaigns in England were necessary to stop Hampstead Heath and Wimbledon Common from being enclosed for development.

Another key political issue in gardening is the division of labor—the distinction between those who own the garden and those who work in them, as well as between those who design them and those who do the manual labor. According to garden-history books the famous English landscape gardens were made by William Kent, Capability Brown, and Humphry Repton, but little mention is made of those who undertook the actual physical work. There is a marked division between those who did the mental work and those who carried out the manual work of construction. A similar division exists between those who produced the gardens and those who enjoyed them.

Upkeep of the gardens was labor intensive. In 1831 at Chatsworth, Derbyshire, 22 men were employed in the kitchen garden. During the same period the earl of Harrington employed 90 gardeners at Elvaston Castle, near Derby. Great care had to be taken to keep everything looking perfect. It would take three men with scythes a whole day to cut an acre of grass. They would be followed by lawn women who gathered up the grass cuttings. In 1721 at Canons Park in Middlesex, home of the duke of Chandos, the grass was scythed two or three times a week and weeded daily.

The gardener's work has always been hard and badly paid. In the winter, during periods of frost and snow, many gardeners would be laid off. In the 19th century groups of gardeners could be found begging in the streets, holding aloft the tools of their trade. They were often fired, the reasons given being lack of intelligence, pilfering, fighting, or getting drunk.

The job of gardening was so poorly paid and precarious at the beginning of the 19th century that gardeners often had to beg for charity in the gardening press. Living conditions were often atrocious; in some parts of the country the bothy system operated, in which families were split up and consigned to separate bothies. The bothy was a shed usually built on the north wall of the kitchen garden, a dark and damp place to live.

At the end of the 19th century a ten-hour day was normal. A 60-hour week was common, with unpaid Sunday duty, and holidays consisting of three feast days a year. Sometimes a half-day was granted to visit a flower show, but the time usually had to be made up.

Every famous garden has been dug, planted, weeded, and pruned by workers such as these, usually without any protection from a trade union. Theophrastus had slaves to dig his garden in Athens, the Aztec king Nezahualcoyotl (1403–74) had men from the provinces tending his Texcotzingo gardens as a tribute, and medieval monks employed casual laborers to cultivate their monastery gardens. The botanic garden in Rio de Janeiro was worked by slave labor up until 1860, and the Calcutta Botanic Garden used to be cultivated by convicts in chains.

Plants themselves also reflect the political nature of gardening. For centuries they have been part of the economy of societies, used in trade and subject to conquest. Queen Hatshepsut of Egypt, for example, had incense trees brought from Somalia, and Tiglath-Pileser, king of the Assyrians around 1100 B.C., records that he carried off trees such as cedar and box from the countries he conquered and planted them in the parks of Assyria.

The famous British plant hunters of the 18th and 19th centuries were part of an imperial enterprise. In 1768 Joseph Banks, later to become the president of the Royal Society, set sail with Captain Cook and brought back from Australia 30,000 specimens of plants, which could be divided into 3,500 different species, more than half of them unknown in Europe. One of the key aims was that of economic botany: to find plants that would be profitable. Banks saw the commercial value, for instance, of cultivating New Zealand flax, which could be made into stronger canvas for the British navy to maintain its power in the world.

In 1772 the king placed Banks in charge of Kew Gardens. He soon turned it into a botanic garden that became the center of world plant exchange for the benefit of the British Empire. In the 19th century plants were brought to Kew from all around the world and then sent out to British colonies for cultivation, where the trade could be controlled: Robert Fortune took tea plants from China to start the Indian tea industry, William Hooker arranged the illegal transfer of cinchona (used to make quinine for treating malaria) from South America to India, and rubber seeds were smuggled out of Brazil for his son Joseph Hooker to initiate the rubber plantations of Malaysia.

These celebrated plant hunters carried their racist ideology with them on their botanical expeditions. Banks portrays the Australian aborigines as savages and uncivilized; Fortune calls the Chinese deceitful, lazy, and stupid; and Joseph Hooker describes the Nepalese as savage and the Tibetans as lazy and filthy.

Another consequence of European expansion and colonialism has been the naming of plants after European men. Usually these were scientists or men of the Church. Sometimes they were both, such as Rev. Adam Buddle (1660–1715), the English botanist after whom *Buddleia* is named, Georg Joseph Kamel (1661–1706), a pharmacist and Jesuit priest from Moravia who spent his life as a missionary in the Philippines and gave his name to *Camellia,* and Father Armand David (1826–1900), a French zoologist who went to China as a missionary in 1862 and from whom *Clematis armandii* got its name. There is clearly great value in an international language for plant classification, but botanical Latin is also an example of the impact of politics on gardening, and it is clearly more difficult for Chinese or Japanese people to learn than it is for Europeans.

The history of gardening also reveals another important political issue—that of gender. It has generally been a story about men, written by men. Women are usually either completely absent, in a supporting role to men, or relegated to weeding.

The earliest English records of women working as paid laborers in a garden are the entries in the 14th-century rolls of Ely Cathedral, wherein women appear in the wages list for digging the vines and weeding. The number of historical references to weeding women is remarkable, and in the 14th century they were paid twopence half-penny a day, half the male gardener's wage. Later, in the 19th century, while a jobbing gardener would earn about five or six shillings a day, his weeding-women helpers would only get paid between eight and ten pence a day, about a seventh of the male wage.

There are hardly any gardening books written by women until the 19th century. In England women were not trained at horticultural college until 1891. They were not allowed to become gardeners at Kew until 1895, and then they were ridiculed for the bloomers they were forced to wear. Yet women have always gardened. In ancient Greece and Rome women took care of gardens. The same was true of England in the Middle Ages. Today women produce at least half the world's output of food. In Africa they perform 60 to 80 percent of agricultural work. Despite this, it has often been maintained that gardening is too hard for women.

One of the most absurd myths that has been perpetuated about women is that their very presence can injure plants. In his 16th-century *Herbal* William Turner quotes Pliny as saying that if women touch young gourds, or even just look at them, it will kill them. Similarly Thomas Hyll in *The Gardener's Labyrinth* (1577) quotes from Columella, who himself was citing the Greek Florentinus, that the same thing can happen to cucumbers if the woman is menstruating. In the fifth century B.C. Democritus extended to all plants the withering effect caused by women.

More scientifically proven is the damage done to women by gardening. Some 40,000 women working in the Colombian flower industry suffer from rheumatism, eczema, damaged embryos, miscarriages, leukemia, bronchitis, asthma, epilepsy, and cancer because of the pesticides that are used. Carnations, roses, and chrysanthemums are exported from Colombia to Europe, particularly Aalsmeer, just south of Amsterdam, which is the site of the most important flower market in the world. Millions of flowers are sold there each day, but as one Colombian woman put it, "We die because of the flowers."

Gardens have often been considered an essential ingredient of political utopias. In these imagined societies many of the forms of oppression and inequality historically associated with gardens disappear. In his *Utopia* of

1516 Thomas More envisages a city in which property is banished and all things are held in common. The utopians value their gardens highly, combining pleasure and use, cooperation and friendly rivalry. Likewise in *Pilgrim's Progress* (1678) John Bunyan describes the Celestial City, in which each house has access to orchards and vineyards. Lands and their produce are rent free.

Bunyan's contemporary, the English revolutionary Gerrard Winstanley, wanted to produce this type of heaven on earth. He attacked enclosures, arguing instead for common ownership of the land and cooperation in its cultivation. In that way everyone could enjoy the produce of the earth and there would be no need for wars, prisons, or gallows. In the 19th century William Morris also claimed that the ideal was not impossible to achieve. He argued the case for skilled cooperative gardening for beauty and for use. Even factories would be set in beautiful grounds, tended voluntarily as a form of open-air relaxation. As William Wordsworth writes in *The Recluse* (1806):

Paradise, and groves
Elysian, Fortunate Fields—like those of old
Sought in the Atlantic Main—why should they be
A history only of departed things,
Or a mere fiction of what never was?

In the middle of the 19th century, England became the first country in history to have a larger population of its people living in towns rather than in the countryside. The loss of easy access to the country was keenly felt, especially by factory workers, and the 1840s movement to establish public parks was one response to this deprivation. At the end of the 19th century, the garden city movement, initiated by Ebenezer Howard, was another attempt to marry town and country and build a pleasant living environment. Today access to parks and gardens is still a political issue, as is their maintenance and the degree of safety people feel when using them.

In her utopian novel *Woman on the Edge of Time* (1976), the American Marge Piercy symbolizes the combination of use and beauty in the mixing of vegetables and flowers and the integration of the gardens with the buildings. Young and old work together in the gardens, combining intellectual and manual work. Education takes place in the garden, where theory and practice are combined.

Another crucial political issue related to gardens is pollution. In the middle of the 19th century London was so polluted with smoke that many garden plants simply would not grow. This was one cause of the fundamental change in garden style to bedding schemes during this period. Bedding plants could be safely grown under glass until they were planted out for the few months that they needed to survive. The reason that there are so many plane trees in London is because of their ability to shed their bark and so survive the polluted atmosphere. *Rhododendron ponticum* and privet are also resistant to the smoke. In the second half of the 20th century, after the clean air acts, pollution came more from lead than smoke. All land in inner London was found to be contaminated by lead, coming mainly from vehicle exhaust pipes.

Much more catastrophic pollution is caused by the political act of war. In Vietnam the soil was so contaminated by the U.S. use of the defoliant Agent Orange that eating the fruit and vegetables now grown in Vietnamese gardens and fields is leading to children being born with mental and physical deformities.

One of the strangest places to find people gardening is in prison, yet there have been many examples of political prisoners gardening. William Cobbett, the famous English radical who also wrote books on gardening, was sentenced to two years in Newgate Gaol, ostensibly for criminal libel, but really for opposing the government. From his prison cell he carried on running his farm and garden with the help of his eldest son and daughter, who brought him a hamper of produce every week, including flowers that were in season such as violets, primroses, cowslips, and bluebells.

Another famous political prisoner was Leigh Hunt, poet and journalist, who made a garden when he was imprisoned for seditious libel in 1813. He fenced off part of the prison yard and filled it with flowers and young trees. He grew scarlet runner beans up a trellis and planted an apple tree from which, in its second year, he had enough apples to make a pudding.

The most famous political prisoner of all, Nelson Mandela, made a garden in a dry and rocky courtyard in his prison on Robben Island. He sowed tomatoes, chilies, and onions and gave some of his best produce to the warders. He ordered books on gardening and horticulture and saw his garden as one of the few things he could control in prison. The small patch of earth offered him a small taste of freedom during his 27 years in captivity.

In the last few decades of the 20th century, there has been a political movement to make gardens and gardening more accessible to disabled people. This involves, among other things, making safer paths, with tapping rails, handrails, and tactile junction indicators; constructing raised beds; providing braille labels, audio cassettes, and embossed maps; and producing long-handled, lightweight tools. There are two demonstration gardens in London for disabled people run by the Disabled Living Foundation, one at Battersea Park and the other at Syon Park. Another in Dulwich Park was begun in 1986, planned and in part built by disabled people. There is also one at the Royal Horticultural Society's gardens at Wisley, near Woking in Surrey.

The Advisory Committee for Blind Gardeners, working with the support of the English South Regional

Association for the Blind, has produced guidelines to keep in mind when designing gardens. They make it clear that they do not support the idea of gardens exclusively for people with visual impairment but explain that all gardens should be designed with the enjoyment of everyone alike in mind. Attached to the guidelines is a list of fragrant plants recommended by the Royal Horticultural Society.

Despite the widespread belief that gardening has nothing to do with politics, these examples demonstrate that in fact gardening is in various ways inextricably linked to politics.

Further Reading

Balmori, Diana, and Margaret Morton, *Transitory Gardens, Uprooted Lives*, New Haven, Connecticut: Yale University Press, 1993

Brockway, Lucile H., *Science and Colonial Expansion: The Role of the British Royal Botanic Gardens*, New York and London: Academic Press, 1979

Carter, Thomas M., *The Victorian Garden*, London: Bell and Hyman, 1984

Crouch, David, and Colin Ward, *The Allotment: Its Landscape and Culture*, London: Faber, 1988

Howard, Ebenezer, *Tomorrow: A Peaceful Path to Real Reform*, London, 1898; new revised edition, as *Garden Cities of Tomorrow*, Eastbourne, East Sussex: Attic Books, 1985

Hoyles, Martin, *The Story of Gardening*, London and Concord, Massachusetts: Journeyman Press, 1991

Kellaway, Deborah, editor, *The Virago Book of Women Gardeners*, London: Virago, 1995; revised edition, as *The Illustrated Book of Women Gardeners*, London: Virago, and Boston: Little Brown, 1997

Mack, Maynard, *The Garden and the City: Retirement and Politics in the Later Poetry of Pope, 1731–1743*, Toronto, Ontario: University of Toronto Press, and London: Oxford University Press, 1969

McLean, Teresa, *Medieval English Gardens*, New York: Viking Press, 1980; London: Collins, 1981

Prest, John, *The Garden of Eden: The Botanic Garden and the Re-Creation of Paradise*, New Haven, Connecticut: Yale University Press, 1981

Rowson, N.J., and P.R. Thoday, *Landscape Design for Disabled People in Public Open Space*, edited by P.M. Croft, Bath, Avon: University of Bath, 1985

Shoard, Marion, *This Land Is Our Land*, London: Paladin Grafton Books, 1987

Turner, James, *The Politics of Landscape: Rural Scenery and Society in English Poetry, 1630–1660*, Oxford: Blackwell, and Cambridge, Massachusetts: Harvard University Press, 1979

Warner, Sam Bass, Jr., and Hansi Durlach, *To Dwell Is to Garden: A History of Boston's Community Gardens*, Boston: Northeastern University Press, 1987

Williams, Raymond, *The Country and the City*, London: Chatto and Windus, and New York: Oxford University Press, 1973

Williamson, Tom, *Polite Landscapes: Gardens and Society in Eighteenth-Century England*, Baltimore, Maryland: John Hopkins University Press, 1995

MARTIN HOYLES

Polonnaruwa Gardens

Polonnaruwa, North Central Province, Sri Lanka

Location: approximately 100 miles (161 km) northeast of Colombo

The strategic advantages of the site of Polonnaruwa, a United Nations Educational, Scientific, and Cultural Organization World Heritage Site near the Mahaweli River in central Sri Lanka, determined its selection as a capital by the South Indian Chola dynasty in the 11th century. It is approximately 134 miles (216 km) northeast of Colombo and 46 miles (75 km) southeast of Anuradhapura.

The city, with its palace enclave once walled with an approximately four-mile (six km) perimeter rampart, reached its peak under Parakramabahu I (r. 1153–86), who created huge buildings and magnificent parks. Parakramabahu's successor, Nissanka Malla (r. 1187–96), tried to outdo him in the creation of a magnificent agglomeration of monumental structures and gardens, but the complex eventually proved vulnerable to Indian invasion, and by the early 14th century it was abandoned, and the capital moved to the west. A huge 2,400-hectare (5,931-ha) water-storage and irrigation lake known as the Parakrama Samudra (Parakrama Sea) had been built at Polonnaruwa, although it probably is not coterminous with the lake that exists today and whose reestablishment together with its 11 channels directing water into the irrigation canals for the purposes of local agriculture led to the discovery of the ruins of ancient Polonnaruwa and their partial restoration. The ruins are scattered along approximately four miles (6 km) of the main north-south road of the old town, north of the modern new town, although a concentration of important constructions covers an area not much more than 1.4 square miles (3.6 sq km).

The main interest of the restored Polonnaruwa focuses on the buildings and carvings, which are of immense archaeological and historical significance. Such gardens as have been laid out beneath the giant trees served primarily to set off the buildings and have had to be re-created from the scrub and jungle. Many of the ruined buildings served religious purposes, while others were given over to the administrative, leisure, and religious needs of the monarch and his court. Among the more memorable monuments is the Gal Vihara, about 1.6 miles (2.5 km) north of the central quadrangle and part of the northern monastery. Carved from a single enormous granite boulder or cliff are four images of Buddha, of which three represent the high point of Sinhalese rock carving. The best of the imposing series is a seven-meter (7.7-yd.) tall standing Buddha. One of the sitting Buddha statues is in an artificial cavern carved from the rock, and the reclining Buddha entering Nirvana is 14 meters (15.3 yd.) long.

At the south end of the central compound is an enclosed complex of buildings, including the royal palace of Kramaharabahu, where the 11th-century walls of the main hall stand among the ruins of about 40 interconnecting rooms. The palace, measuring 31 by 13 meters (33.9 by 14.2 yd.), has three-meter thick walls and once probably had seven stories, of which the top four would have been wooden. The audience chamber contains exquisite carvings and a frieze of elephants, with each animal in a different position. Its royal entrance is approached by two flights of steps with moonstones and lion portals. Beyond is the Kumara Pokuna, or bathing pool, which still has one of its crocodile-mouth water spouts.

Halfway up the western wall of the central compound is the raised and walled "quadrangle" completed by Nissanka Malla and which contains the seventh-century Vatadage, a roofed circular stupa house whose outermost terrace is 5.5 meters (6 yd.) in diameter and whose second terrace has four entrances with particularly fine guard stones (sculpted king cobras). The entrances lead to the four seated Buddha figures guarding the sacred relics in the dagoba (vertical set of solid hemispheres rising to a spire containing relics of the Buddha). In the

quadrangle is also the Thuparamaya, an image house sometimes said to date from the third century B.C. but built in the style characteristic of Polonnaruwa and more likely dating from the 12th century A.D. It is barrel-vaulted and domed, with thick brick walls covered with painted stucco.

The Gal Pota (stone book) within the quadrangle is an enormous stone representation of a palm-leaf book, 9 meters long, 1.5 meters wide, and between 40 to 66 centimeters (15.75 to 26 in.) thick. The text extols Nissanka Malla, and an inscription relates that the 25-ton stone was dragged from nearly 62 miles (100 km) away. Three tooth relic chambers of different sizes, shapes, and degrees of elaboration are found in the quadrangle: the Atadage, Hatadage, and Vatadage. The Atadage, similar to the Hatadage in purpose and construction, was the first tooth temple built by Vijayabahu. Rectilinear in its inner and outer lines, the Hatadage and the circular Vatadage are the largest buildings within the quadrangle, which also accommodates a strange construction, the Satmahal Prasada, of Cambodian design, originally made of seven diminishing stories in the form of a stepped pyramid. Also within the quadrangle is Nissanka Malla's Latha-Mandapaya, with a latticed stone face imitating a wooden fence and surrounding columns in the form of lotus stalks with unopened buds, which themselves surround a small *dagoba*.

North of the large walled compound are the various, more scattered ruins of the monastic complex. Within the old Jetavanarama monastery is the lotus pond in the shape of an open lotus nearly eight meters (8.75 yd.) in diameter. Descent into the empty bath involves stepping down five concentric rings of eight petals each. The most important of the monastic ruins is the Tivanka image house, the Pilima Geya, named for the image of Buddha in the antechamber in the *tivanka*, or thrice-bent position, normally seen only in female statues.

Polonnaruwa is an extended site of vast historical importance and considerable antiquity within which much meticulous archaeological restoration has already taken place. The gardens, mostly rectilinear forms within low-clipped topiary borders, serve as ornamental paths between the widely separated monuments to which they are ancillary and are not themselves reconstituted from the antique. The entire site is in the middle of a wilderness made fertile again by the restored irrigation system.

Synopsis

368	Residence of Ceylon kings
1070	Sinhalese king Vijayabahu I drives Indian Cholas out of Sri Lanka and makes Polonnaruwa his capital
1153–86	King Parakramabahu I creates parks for palace enclave

early 14th C. Pressure from Indian incursions forced capital to be moved west and palace abandoned

Further Reading

De Silva, K.M., *A History of Sri Lanka,* Delhi: Oxford University Press, and Berkeley: University of California Press, and London: Hurst, 1981

Ludowyk, Evelyn Frederick Charles, *The Story of Ceylon,* London: Faber and Faber, 1962; New York: Roy, 1963; revised edition, New Delhi: Navrang, 1985

Samarasinghe, S.W.R de A, and Vidyamali Samarsinghe, *Historical Dictionary of Sri Lanka,* Lanham, Maryland: Scarecrow Press, 1998

Sri Lanka Ministry of Cultural Affairs, *A Guide to Polonnaruwa,* Colombo: Sri Lanka Ministry of Cultural Affairs, 1982

ANTHONY H.T. LEVI

Pope, Alexander 1688–1744

English Poet, Garden Designer, and Garden Theorist

The poet Alexander Pope is notable in 18th-century garden history for a variety of reasons. He is the author of some of the most influential garden poetry of the early 18th century; his own small garden at Twickenham was a significant early example of the new, less formal garden style; he was friend and adviser to a number of the owners of great gardens, such as the earl of Burlington at Chiswick and Lord Bathurst at Cirencester; and he was well acquainted with many of the best-known garden designers of his day, including William Kent and Charles Bridgeman. The classical foundation of Pope's own ideas about nature and gardens is clear in his 1713 essay on gardens in the *Guardian,* which includes a translation of a passage from Homer's *Odyssey* describing the garden of Alcinous. His many comments on gardens were often repeated, and his friend the Rev. Joseph Spence published many of them.

Pope was born in London in 1688. As a Roman Catholic, he was barred from attending university in England and was therefore largely self-taught, with a keen knowledge of modern and classical language and letters. A childhood illness, probably tuberculosis of the spine, left him with curvature of the spine and an adult stature of only four feet six inches. Entering the London literary scene in 1704, Pope became known primarily as a poet and satirist. His general interest in landscape is apparent in the *Pastorals* of 1709 and *Windsor Forest* of 1713.

In 1719 Pope settled into a villa with five acres (2 ha) by the river Thames at Twickenham, not far from London. Here he began his career as amateur gardener and garden adviser to the owners of many large estates. Although his garden was considerably smaller than other famous gardens of the same time period, it exhibited most of the features associated with their design. It was carefully planted to hide the boundaries, it had a serpentine path, it incorporated into its overall design views out of the garden, and it included classical references as well as statues and temples intended to encourage moral contemplation. And with its inclusion of a monument to Pope's mother, his garden also shared the funerary references that could be found in many of the great gardens of the time.

During his lifetime, the garden was chiefly known for the grotto that cleverly transformed a passage under a road between house and garden into a key garden feature. Encrusted with geological specimens brought to Pope from many parts of the globe, the grotto recalled both Italian garden grottoes and cabinets of curiosities, which were often found in aristocratic homes and housed collections of small and precious objects and works of art. Denuded of its rock ornamentation, the grotto is the only element of Pope's garden still in existence.

Pope's most famous poetical contribution to garden theory was the 1731 "Epistle to Burlington." The poem praises the architectural and garden building programs of Richard Boyle, third earl of Burlington, contrasting them with the tasteless designs of the fictional Timon, an ostentatious aristocrat. Pope's contemporaries associated Timon with various wealthy garden builders of the day and lambasted Pope for such ungenerous attacks on his friends and patrons, although Pope continued to deny that Timon was modeled on any particular person. The public uproar may have diverted attention from the basic messages of the poem, which celebrates Burlington and encourages garden designers to follow his example, consult the "Genius of the Place," and follow "Sense" as a guide to beautiful garden design. Pope also makes it clear that gardens laid out on these principles would display the characteristics of variety and naturalistic disposition of parts that were becoming important in English garden design:

> He gains all points, who pleasingly confounds,
> Surprises, varies, and conceals the Bounds.

More than once, he also notes that garden building and maintenance contribute to the economy by providing gainful employment to laborers.

Among the great gardens of his day on which Pope seems to have had considerable influence are, in addition to Chiswick and Cirencester, Henrietta Howard's (Countess of Suffolk) at Marble Hill, Ralph Allen's at Prior Park, Lord Bolingbroke's at Dawley Farm, and Robert Digby's at Sherborne Castle. Pope's fame put him in a position to offer ideas and develop sensibilities through conversations, letters, and the repetition of his views by others, and he probably had an indirect influence on many gardens and designers even where he did not formally participate in the garden design.

In all of his garden pursuits, both actual and poetical, Pope was concerned with pictorial effects in garden layouts, as well as with their poetical or allusive character. Spence quotes him as maintaining that "All gardening is landscape-painting, just like a landscape hung up." In the "Epistle to Burlington," Pope writes that the genius of the place "*Paints* as you plant, and as you work, *Designs.*" While often advocating plantings, statues, temples, and other features, he was always sensitive to both specific landscape features and the historical associations of particular landscapes.

As writer and garden owner, adviser, and visitor, Pope was one of the most prominent thinkers determining the direction of garden design in early 18th-century England. His contribution was frequently downplayed by historians following the lead of Horace Walpole, who chose rather to see a clear lineage from William Kent to Lancelot "Capability" Brown, bypassing the intellectual content that was so important to Pope and many of his friends. Scholarship of the late 20th century, however, has returned him to a well-deserved place of prominence as one of the foremost garden designers and theorists of his age.

See also London Parks

Biography

Born in London, England, 1688. As a Roman Catholic, Pope barred from attending university in England, and was therefore largely self-taught, with keen knowledge of modern and classical languages and letters; childhood illness, probably tuberculosis of spine, left him with curvature of spine and adult stature of only four feet six inches; entering London literary scene in 1704, known primarily as poet and satirist; general interest in landscape apparent in *Pastorals* of 1709 and *Windsor Forest* of 1713; in 1719, Pope settled into villa with 5 acres (2 ha) by Thames at Twickenham, not far from London; began career as amateur gardener and garden advisor. Died in Twickenham, London, 1744.

Selected Designs

1719–44   Alexander Pope's Villa, Twickenham, London, England

Selected Publications

Correspondence, 1704–44; edited by George Sherborne, 5 vols., 1956
Pastorals, 1709
Windsor Forest, 1713
"Essay" [On Gardens], *Guardian* 173 (29 September 1713)
An Epistle to the Right Honourable Richard Earl of Burlington, 1731
A Master Key to Popery; or, A True and Perfect Key to Pope's Epistle to the Earl of Burlington, unpublished manuscript, 1732; in *The Prose Works of Alexander Pope*, edited by Rosemary Cowler, 1986

Further Reading

Allen, Beverly Sprague, *Tides in English Taste (1619–1800): A Background for the Study of Literature*, 2 vols., Cambridge, Massachusetts: Harvard University Press, 1937
Andrews, Malcolm, "A New Description of Pope's Garden," *Journal of Garden History* 1, no. 1 (1981)
Brownell, Morris R., *Alexander Pope and the Arts of Georgian England*, Oxford: Clarendon Press, 1978
Brownell, Morris R., *Alexander Pope's Villa: Views of Pope's Villa, Grotto and Garden: A Microcosm of English Landscape*, London: Greater London Council, 1980
Charlesworth, Michael, "Alexander Pope's Garden at Twickenham: An Architectural Design Proposed," *Journal of Garden History* 7, no. 1 (1987)
Fabricant, Carole, "Binding and Dressing Nature's Loose Tresses: The Ideology of Augustan Landscape Design," *Studies in Eighteenth-Century Culture* 8 (1979)
Hunt, John Dixon, "Pope's Twickenham Revisited," in *British and American Gardens in the Eighteenth Century*, edited by Robert P. Maccubbin and Peter Martin, Williamsburg, Virginia: Colonial Williamsburg Foundation, 1984
Mack, Maynard, *The Garden and the City: Retirement and Politics in the Later Poetry of Pope, 1731–43*, London: Oxford, and Toronto, Ontario: University of Toronto Press, 1969

Malins, Edward Greenway, *English Landscaping and Literature, 1660–1840,* London and New York: Oxford University Press, 1966

Martin, Peter, "Intimations of the New Gardening: Alexander Pope's Reaction to the 'Uncommon' Landscape at Sherborne," *Garden History* 4, no. 1 (1976)

Martin, Peter, *Pursuing Innocent Pleasures: The Gardening World of Alexander Pope,* Hamden, Connecticut: Archon Books, 1984

Sambrook, James, "The Shape and Size of Pope's Garden," *Eighteenth-Century Studies* 5 (1972)

Serle, John, *A Plan of Mr. Pope's Garden,* London, 1745; reprint, New York: Garland: 1982

Spence, Joseph, and Edmund Malone, *Observations, Anecdotes, and Characters of Books and Men,* London, 1820; new edition, 2 vols., edited by James M. Osborne, Oxford: Clarendon Press, 1966

LINDA CABE HALPERN

Portugal

The Portuguese have had some ambivalence in adopting anything high style, especially if it is foreign. Portuguese individualism may give their gardens less classic purity than those of, for example, France, but on the other hand they can be readily enjoyed, and as Rose Standish Nicols notes, the pleasure of viewing their country's gardens is not dependant upon the weight of one's intellectual baggage. This view echoes Sir George Sitwell's belief that the real beauty of any garden lies in its relation to the individual, that it should be a background for life, not a glittering museum piece.

Portuguese garden making was easy because plants—especially the exotics imported from its colonies—grew readily in its frost-free Mediterranean climate. The dry, sometimes arid summers, however, demanded irrigation, and the wide variety of soils encountered called for above-average horticultural skills.

Roman, Moorish, and medieval gardens are all part of Portugal's garden heritage. The partially restored Roman peristyle houses at Conimbriga give a sense of their glory. Here and there in modern gardens can be found echoes of the tile and water gardens of the Moors (e.g., St. George's Park, Lisbon). The form of the medieval *hortus conclusus* survives in the architectural spaces of cloisters (e.g., Alcobaça, Bathalia, Tibäes, Tomar) but usually lacking their original furnishings of fruit trees, useful herbs, and graves. Medieval traditions were tenacious and only reluctantly were Renaissance ideas accepted. Thus the spatial revolutions of Renaissance garden art born in 15th-century Italy did not appear in Portugal until the middle of the 16th century, and these were passed casually by word of mouth or through translations of Renaissance books.

An exception was the garden at the Quinta de Bacalhôa (1528), where the diplomat Braz de Albuquerque introduced a highly individualistic vision of the Florentine Renaissance to his country manor. The happy mingling of top fruits and flowers recalls the Italians' easy integration of agriculture with country pleasures (such as the Villa Medici, Fiesole). Delicately turned arcaded loggias on the first floor afford multiple views. Internally, they provide an overview of the geometry of the topiary garden and beyond to glimpses of family and guests strolling the flower- and tile-bordered promenades. More distant prospects are of orchards and vineyards, giving way to fields and distant Lisbon, all recalling the Tuscans' emphasis on view sheds. A large rectangular pool provides irrigation water, resembling the Medici *vasca* or water tanks (for example, at Villa Petraia). Mirrored in the water is an arcaded pavilion topped with steep pyramidal roofs. Internal facings are of 15th-century polychrome tiles or *azulejos*.

The Palácio Fronteira, Benfica (1679), possesses the finest of 17th-century gardens exhibiting high Renaissance and mannerist features found in Italy a century earlier (as in the Villa Medici, Rome). The form of the palace follows Italian stronghold designs (such as at St. George's Castle, Mantua) with architectural embellishments culled from published designs by Sebastiano Serlio (ca. 1540) and G.B. Ferrari (1638). It was built by the first Marquess of Fronteira, João Mascarenhas, a hero, who was instrumental in freeing Portugal from Spanish rule. Not surprisingly, the obligatory classical mythology is here interwoven with aspects of Portuguese history and romance.

A variety of spatial experiences provide interest and delight, bringing permutations on spaces that are open and closed, bathed in sun or proffering shady refuges. The open lower garden is expansive, sunny, and of extreme formality, with complex topiary inspired by Muslim geometric patterns, accented vertically with stone sculpture and fountains. To one side rises the unique Galeria dos Reis (Gallery of the Kings), its rich decoration reflected in a large rectangular pool. Blind arcades are faced with blue-on-white *azulejos* with representations of mounted knights from the *Lucidas;* three openings reveal grottoes, the center dedicated to Apollo who with his diminutive Muses and Pegasus sits atop Parnassus. To either side rise broad flights of stairs to the actual Gallery of the Kings, where niches contain busts of Portuguese kings, including the bust of João IV (r. 1640–56), king of the Restoration and a confidant of Mascarenhas. The whole is faced with brilliant blue and molded *azulejos.* From the gallery, kings and visitors gaze down on the sunny geometry below.

A retaining wall, an extension of the palace garden facade, defines an upper garden, the shady Garden of Venus, its focal point a central star-shaped fountain accented with a representation of the goddess. The nearby Chapel Promenade is backed by a curious composition of blind arcades and niches housing statues of gods, topped by roundels filled with busts. *Azulejos* are much in evidence with blue-and-white representations of the Muses. Beyond is a water garden with elaborate baroque arabesques and Masonic symbols, terminated with a grotto faced with shells and fragments of rare Chinese export porcelain that was smashed, according to local legend, after a banquet for João IV. Above, on rising topography, is an extensive garden in the English landscape style, shaded by specimen trees.

Baroque extravaganzas deriving from France, Hungary, and, naturally, Italy are anticipated in the Palácio Fronteira's arabesques and in the Jardim do Paço Episcopal, Castelo Branco. Around Oporto one finds the complex architectural silhouettes introduced by the Tuscan architect Nicolau Nasoni accompanied by new and exotic foliage plants from the colonies. Nasoni's Solar de Mateus (1743, 1750) exhibits many aspects of the mature Portuguese baroque style, with stucco walls framed in gray stone, capped with an exuberance of scrolls, pinnacles, and statuary: a fantastic vision mirrored in a (modern) pool. Four levels of parterres with boxwood curlicues descend the hillside; interest is added by a tunnel of cypress trees, a rare survivor of a once popular garden feature.

Water stairways, a feature of Italian baroque gardens (e.g., Villas Lante, Aldobrandini, Torlonia, and Cicogna), are represented by monumental ones at Buçaco and Tibães. The pilgrim staircase is another application of the dramatic sequential possibilities of baroque landscape space found at Buçaco, the Via Saacra, at Nossa Senhora dos Remédios, Lamego (1750–60), and at Bom Jesus do Monte, Braga (1723), the latter having a remarkable sculpture-enriched scissor stair.

The 18th century was a period of great prosperity due to Portugal's profitable colonial possessions. Many country manors or *quintas* attest to this affluence. They follow an amiable vernacular style—small, with comfortably long and low proportions, whose random addi-

tions add a pleasing asymmetry. Gardens likewise follow the vernacular, planted with useful trees and plants and framed by walls capped with balustrades that on occasion can be found accented by a chubby Neptune or comically proportioned mythical or historical figures (e.g., Paço Episcopal, Castelo Branco). Paths and water features casually integrated with the geometry of architecture (Quinta dos Conegos, Barreiros, and Casa de Recareio, Oporto), disregarding the classical rule that building and garden geometry should be as one.

In the Portuguese there is an inherent love of plants engendered as much from the mild climate and the broad range of rich and indifferent soils as from the abundant exotic plants brought home by returning mariners and colonials. The island of Maderia was a revictualing stop for vessels on the route to and from the Far East, and cuttings and seeds found their way into the rich native flora. The volcanic soils of the Jardim Botânico da Maderia (formerly the Quinta do Bom Sucesso) contain a rich collection of natives as well as the ancestors of the exotics discovered in Portugal's East and West African colonies.

Plant love inevitably led to plant collection. By the mid-18th century, random collections gave way to botanical gardens organized precisely according to the Linnaean system of scientific botany. An early collection is that at Buçaco. From the sixteenth century this forest on the western slopes of the Buçaco mountains was sought out for its peace and seclusion. In the 17th century it attracted papal attention and protection. In 1622 its precincts were defined by Gregory XV, and a Bull forbade women entry to them. In 1626 Carmelites built a monastery and enclosed 260 acres (105 ha) with a high wall. A Bull of Urban VIII added conservation restrictions, forbidding the cutting of trees under pain of excommunication. To the native mountainous forest flora of oak, pine, and evergreens such as laurustinus (*Viburnum tinus* sp.) and phillyrea, the friars introduced exotic trees from the colonies, notably the tender *Cupressus lusitancia* or cedar of Goa, actually a native of Mexico and Guatemala. João de Melo, count-bishop of Coimbra, added the Via Sacra and its baroque chapels to the Cruz Alta.

The plant collections at Buçaco were vastly extended when the land became state property in 1859. Dom Rodrigo de Morais Soares planted the still comparatively bare lands around the former monastery with an outstanding collection of plant material from the Americas, the Orient, and Africa. From Australasia came the outstanding Valley of the Ferns, which included tree ferns such as the *Dicksonias* and *Cyatheas.*

The earliest of the scientific collections are at Lisbon and the University of Coimbra. Coimbra's Jardim Botânico was founded by the Marquês de Pombal, part of his policy to eject the religious orders from Portugal and from their stranglehold on higher scientific education. In common with the university gardens at Padua, Leiden, and Oxford, Coimbra's botanical garden is planted within an overall architectural plan. This is amiably enriched by statuary and fountains, by retaining walls holding back the terraced slopes, by wrought iron balustrading, and by several splendidly ornate entrance gates set into the high walls guarding the precincts. By 1791–1811 the garden contained more than 4,000 types of plant. About 1870 a friendship between director Júlio Henriques and Baron von Mueller, director of the Melbourne Botanical Garden, led to the acquisition of a huge collection of Australasian flora.

Dr. Félix de Avelar Brotero, director at Coimbra during its prime in the early 19th century, was concurrently director of another garden, the Real Jardim Botânico da Ajuda at Belém, founded in 1768 by Dom José I. Belém was the first port of entry to Lisbon and a natural collecting place for those vessels carrying plant materials. This was a new type of garden, whose goal was the study of the empire's plants for their commercial potential. It had a checkered life lasting until 1874, when it rapidly declined in competition with two new gardens, the Jardin Botânico at the University of Lisbon and the Jardim Tropical in Belém, which like the Royal Garden was founded to study the economic aspects of colonial trees.

The 19th century was one of social and economic disasters. First was Napoléon's invasion of 1807–10. Then came the economic crisis of 1822 that followed Brazil's declaration of independence, which lost Portugal its trading monopolies. Civil war and years of unrest were abated somewhat with the accession of the constitutional monarch Luís of Savoy (r. 1861–89).

For centuries Sintra's cool humid summers had attracted the rich, who built summer places there. The end of the 18th century saw the arrival of wealthy Englishmen, encouraged by the amiable relations between Britain and Portugal, who built summer retreats with gardens that followed the richer garden styles being popularized in England by Humphry Repton and John Claudius Loudon. Of these Monserrate is typical, rebuilt in 1856 with an exotic garden designed by William Stockdale, assisted by the botanist William Nevill of the Royal Botanic Garden, Kew.

In the 20th century revivals of traditional styles continued to be built, and the fascination for tropical plants continued unabated. These are displayed in the wild jungle of the Estufa Fria (Cool Greenhouse) collection, established in Lisbon (1910).

In the public garden at the Casa de Serralves, Oporto is a rare example of an Art Deco mansion and garden. The house was designed by Marques da Silva, the gar-

dens by the French landscape architect Jacques Greber (1937). The style is chiefly apparent in the detailing, whereas the form pays homage to Portugal's lost Moorish heritage, evident in the long canal of azure blue tiles that bisects the garden and symbolically irrigates it via a number of lateral channels, each marking a step down of the slope. Built as a residence for the mistress of the second count of Vizela, it now houses the national collection of contemporary art.

In like manner Calouste Gulbenkian built his Center (completed in 1984) for the city of Lisbon. The Center's gardens occupy the old Parque de Santa Gertrudes in one of the city's poorer districts. Like the London parks it is a social place, providing a green refuge from the hectic city life. Snug niches accommodate the old and very young; open spaces accented by water are a delight for all ages.

High above Lisbon's Alfama district is the old Moorish fortress St. George's Castle, which houses a brilliantly designed social park formed within the walls of the vacated military base. The needs of both the elderly and the young are happily catered to as are those of teenagers. An underlying philosophical theme echoes the Moorish preoccupation with water as the essence of life.

These latest public parks integrate new social and spatial ideas but never lose sight of Portugal's rich garden heritage. Roman sensitivity to urban needs is joined with a Moorish love of water (Caldas da Rainha, Quinta das Torres, Setubal); there is also the Renaissance delight in prospects (St. George's Castle, Lisbon, Quinta da Bacalhoa). The rich palette of plant materials provides canopies and defines spaces to enrich the public experience, while color and textural accents stimulate or soothe the eye (Guimares, Braga's Sta. Barbara Garden, Bom Jesus, Buçaco).

See also Frontiera, Palácio

Further Reading

Azevedo, Carlos de, *Solares portugueses*, Lisbon: Livros Horizonte, 1969; 2nd edition, 1988

Berendsen, Anne Albertina Johanna, et al., *Fliesen*, Munich: Keyser, 1964; as *Tiles, a General History*, translated by Janet Seligman, New York: Viking Press, and London: Faber, 1967

Binney, Marcus, et al., *Houses and Gardens of Portugal*, New York: Rizzoli, and London: Cartago, 1998

Nichols, Rose Standish, *Spanish and Portuguese Gardens*, Boston: Houghton Mifflin, and London: Constable, 1924

JOHN MARTIN

Potager (Kitchen Garden)

Kitchen gardening is as old as civilization itself, and, as its prime purpose is to provide culinary plants for the household, it has been practiced continuously (until the recent past) throughout the history of gardening.

The ideal kitchen garden is a warm, sheltered enclosure sited close to a source of water, in a fertile spot. Its traditional division into four quarters, often with a central pool, well, or fountain, was dictated by an ancient system of irrigation that relied on a gridlike arrangement of beds and channels; the channels also acted as paths between the beds.

Most culinary plants have wild ancestors, which tended to be small, tough, and either bitter or insipid. The earliest gardeners "improved" these plants by watering them, feeding them, and taking advantage of accidental mutation and hybridization; by classical times the skills of seed selection, propagation with vegetative slips, layering, and grafting were well established. The Romans practiced regular crop rotation, trenching, marling, and manuring, as well as pest control by various means. Tender exotic plants or plants grown outside their natural season were protected from bad weather with shelters of reed or mica. The garden was secured against thieves, animals, and the worst of weather by walls, palings, or thick thorn hedges.

Classical and medieval kitchen gardens provided culinary herbs, fruits, and vegetables as well as plants and flowers for medicinal, veterinary, domestic, and recreational or decorative use. One garden served both for beauty and utility; this type of garden still survives as our modern *potager*. The variety of produce depended on the wealth of the owner; onion, brassica, and pulse tribes predominated, with orchards devoted to apples, pears, quinces, cherries, and mulberries. Herbs, nuts, and soft fruits such as gooseberries, raspberries, and strawberries were gathered from the wild. Melons, gourds, lettuces, cucumbers, figs, vines, and peaches were grown in Mediterranean gardens. A surplus of summer and autumn produce provided food for the winter months. Some of this produce was preserved by the housewife, but the kitchen gardener has always had charge of all the outdoor storage places, ranging from root cellars to fruit rooms and lofts.

The discovery of the Americas widened the choice of edibles; potatoes, tomatoes, maize, Jerusalem artichokes, capsicums and peppers, and new varieties of squash and bean were introduced, cautiously and as botanical curiosities at first, to European gardens. At the same time advances in fruit-tree growing and training in France and the Netherlands popularized dwarf trees grown in formation and espaliers trained on walls. Stone, brick, or cob walls became a necessity, with the longest sides of what was now advisedly a rectangular garden, facing south.

Heat was supplied by hotbeds of fermenting manure, innovations that, combined with an antipathy toward the sight of vegetable beds disrupted by cropping, resulted, in the early 17th century, in the separation of the kitchen garden from the flower garden and the pleasure grounds.

The best kitchen gardens of the late 17th century were equipped with new, glass-fronted stove houses heated by subterranean flues. They were built as lean-tos against ever taller, south-facing walls, upon which grew peaches, nectarines, apricots, dessert grapes, figs, and cherries. Extra, freestanding fruit walls were often built within the existing walls. The layout was still four-square, but the bed-and-channel system was discontinued in favor of flat, open beds. Hotbeds, which were largely used to raise melons, were placed within a separate, hedged, fenced, or walled compartment. To make the best of a kitchen garden wall, both sides were clad with fruit. The area outside was also cultivated and was known as the slip garden.

A passion for pineapples—a fruit introduced from the tropics of South America—gave 18th-century hothouse development its impetus. By the mid-18th century top-class kitchen gardens had at least one fully glazed, lean-to pinery on the sunniest walls, heat being provided by hot-air flues in the back wall. Similar flues were built inside south-facing "hot walls" for the best outdoor fruits. With the open quarters for hardy, outdoor plants, glasshouses for more tender productions, a row of sheds behind them for furnaces, storerooms, and workrooms, slip gardens for soft fruit, nursery beds, and the coarser sorts of produce, and frameyards for early forcing, the modern layout of the kitchen garden was now established.

By the end of the 18th century the walled kitchen garden of a grand house could cover several acres. Hothouses supplied hundreds of pineapples a year, thanks to a series of succession houses, which also provided melons and muscat grapes, salads, out-of-season beans and roots, exotic herbs and aromatics, and even bananas, loquats, or mangoes. In England the landscaping of parks meant that kitchen gardens were frequently resited even further from the house, to a place where their high walls could not obstruct the view and where traffic between kitchen and garden would not disturb the peace. Smoke from hothouse or hot-wall chimneys, combined with the odors of manure and rotting vegetation, encouraged their removal, sometimes to over a mile (1.6 km) away.

The kitchen gardens of the 19th and early 20th centuries reached the peak of horticultural perfection. As in Tudor times, they were still walked in and visited, and they were still laid out four-square, with ornamental, standard, or cordoned fruit trees and herbaceous beds lining the main walks. But now up to a third of their

Villandry recreated potager garden
Copyright Garden Matters

area might be taken up with glass. With the invention of steam boilers, cast iron, and sheet glass, hothouse management became more efficient, and a year-round supply of fruit, vegetables, salads and culinary herbs, ornamental potted plants, cut flowers, epergnes, posies, and buttonholes was taken for granted. Even when the family was away, produce was packed by the gardeners and sent on, a tradition going back several centuries.

Plant breeders, seedsmen, and nurserymen supplied an ever-improving variety of fruits and vegetables to suit every situation. Fertilizers, pesticides, and mechanized garden tools were readily available from gardeners' sundriesmen. By the Edwardian era the kitchen gardens of England were arguably the best in the world.

After World War II, however, both fuel and labor became expenses few could afford; moreover, fruit and vegetables were to be had more cheaply in the stores. The use of glass was inevitably the first component to be stopped. The open quarters usually followed. Swimming pools, tennis courts, and bungalows were built within the great walled enclosures, or the space was used for market gardening, garden centers, and tree nurseries.

Nevertheless, here and there walled kitchen gardens are being restored. Lost horticultural skills are being rediscovered; labor is augmented by volunteers; watering, feeding, shading, and ventilating is computerized; and visitors pay to see these relics of the past and buy old varieties of produce that, when guaranteed fresh and organic, are sold at a premium. The kitchen garden lives on. Its role as a museum is helping it to survive.

Further Reading
Bradley, Richard, *A General Treatise of Husbandry and Gardening,* London, 1721–23
Campbell, Susan, *Cottesbrooke: An English Kitchen Garden,* London: Century, 1987
Campbell, Susan, *Charleston Kedding, a History of Kitchen Gardening,* London: Ebury Press, 1996
Campbell, Susan, *Walled Kitchen Gardens,* Princes Risborough, Buckinghamshire: Shire, 1998
Cobbett, William, *The English Gardener,* London, 1829; new edition, edited by Peter King, London: Bloomsbury, 1998
Davies, Jennifer, *The Victorian Kitchen Garden,* London: BBC Books, 1987
Langley, Batty, *New Principles of Gardening,* London, 1728; reprint, New York: Garland, 1982
La Quintinie, Jean de, *Instruction pour les jardins fruitiers et potagers,* 2 vols., Paris, 1690; as *The Compleat Gard'ner,* translated by John Evelyn, London, 1693; reprint, New York: Garland, 1982
Laurence, John, *The Clergy-Man's Recreation,* London, 1714; 5th edition, 1717
Laurence, John, *The Gentleman's Recreation,* London, 1716; 3rd edition, 1723
Loudon, John Claudius, *An Encyclopaedia of Gardening,* 2 vols., London, 1822; new edition, 1835; reprint, New York: Garland, 1982
McIntosh, Charles, *The Book of the Garden,* 2 vols., London, 1853–55
Meager, Leonard, *The English Gard'ner,* London, 1670; 9th edition, 1699
Miller, Philip, *The Gardeners and Florists Dictionary,* 2 vols., London, 1724; 8th edition, as *The Gardener's Dictionary,* London, 1768
Morgan, Joan, and Alison Richards, *A Paradise out of a Common Field,* London: Century, and New York: Harper and Rowe, 1990
Reid, John, *The Scots Gard'ner: In Two Parts,* Edinburgh, 1683; reprint, as *The Scots Gard'ner: Published for the Climate of Scotland,* Edinburgh: Mainstream, 1988
Stuart, David C., *The Kitchen Garden: A Historical Guide to Traditional Crops,* London: Hale, 1984
Switzer, Stephen, *The Practical Kitchen Gardiner,* London, 1727
Wilson, C. Anne, editor, *The Country House Kitchen Garden, 1600–1950,* London: Sutton, 1998

SUSAN CAMPBELL

Prague Castle Gardens

Prague, Czech Republic

Location: central Prague between Malá Strana and Hradcany

The gardens of Prague Castle form part of the green belt that surrounds Prague Castle—which since the ninth century has been the seat of the Czech rulers and, later, presidents. In view of their position in the middle of historic Prague, these gardens and parks are extremely important for the environment of this city of about 1.5 million people. At the present time there are altogether 13 gardens and other green areas belonging to Prague

Castle, covering an area of some 30 hectares (74 acres). The oldest is the Royal Garden, founded in the 16th century beyond the northern fortifications of the castle after members of the House of Habsburg ascended the Czech throne. In the 1920s and 1930s traditional garden layouts were built in front of the castle's southern facade (the Garden on the Ramparts and Paradise Garden) as well as inside the castle grounds (Garden on the Bastion), designed by the castle architect Josip Plečnik.

The Royal Garden (3.6 ha [8.9 acres]) has undergone several transformations since the 16th century, and its

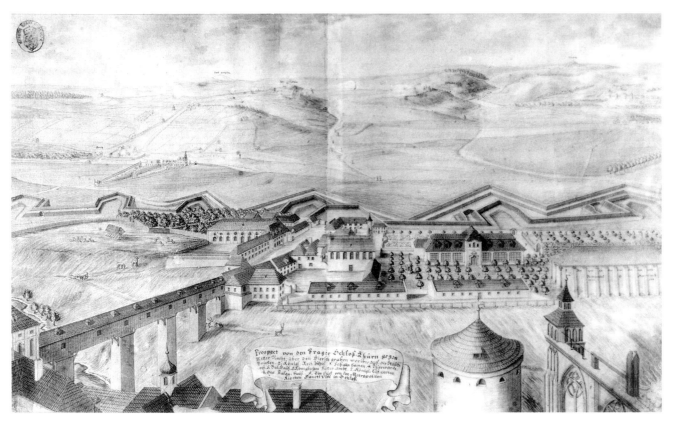

Rendering of the Prague Castle viewed from the south with the Paradise Garden and the ramparts, late 16th century
Courtesy of Věra Vávrová

development has, from the very beginning, been recorded in written documents and from the end of the 17th century, also in consecutive iconography (plans, drawings) that have been preserved in the archives. The founder of the Royal Garden, the Czech king and Roman emperor Ferdinand I of the Habsburgs, and later his son the Archduke Ferdinand took a personal share in creating the garden, influenced by gardens in southern Europe. The garden was laid out on the site of vineyards beyond the castle's northern fortifications and a natural ravine (the Stag Moat), across which a bridge was built (the Powder Bridge). After initial failures in finding a suitable place for cultivating plants and a fire that engulfed the royal seat, a remarkable Renaissance garden emerged. Rudolph II, who, like Ferdinand I, lived in Prague, extended the garden and bought neighboring plots of land. The Royal Garden became a subject of admiration among people of the day. The western part of the garden was divided into two terraces. On the upper terrace was a parterre consisting of ten fenced-in fields, with a place by the northern wall for cultivation of rare plants, especially bulbs, herbs, and aromatic plants. On the lower terrace there was a pitch for ninepins, a shooting range, and summer playground. In the eastern part was an orchard, and the *gia-rdinetto* in front of the Royal Summer Palace was composed of four flower beds around a fountain by Francesco Terzio. Besides the floral plants, rare bushes, and trees, the garden was decorated with statues. There were also several buildings: the Royal Summer Palace, the Ball-Game Hall, and the Fig House can still be admired today.

From its beginnings the garden was created not only by builders and architects but especially by gardeners and botanists. Among the important builders were Giovanni Spatio, Paolo della Stella, Bonifac Wolmut, Ulric Aostallis, Giovanni Gargiolli, and Hans Vredeman de Vries. Such natural scientists as Hugo Vennius, Pietro Andrea Mattioli of Siena in Italy (the author of a well-known herbarium), and perhaps even Rembert Dodoens gave advice. The gardeners brought practical experience from countries in southern and western Europe, including Italy, Germany, and the Netherlands. Besides trees, flowers, and other plants common in these latitudes, the garden was gradually enriched with heat-loving plants from the south of Europe, such as fig trees, orange and lemon trees, and pomegranates. Valuable rarities also came to the imperial court through the ambassador A.G. Busbecque from the steppes of Turkey and from Syria. There were narcissi growing in the garden at that time,

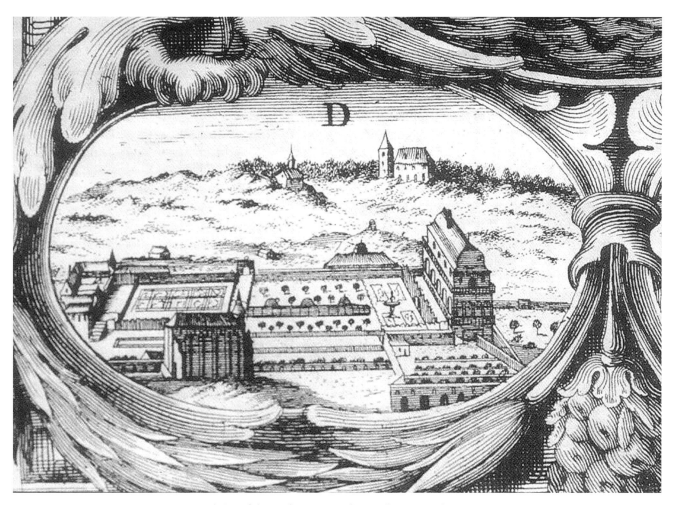

Rendering of the northern surrounding garden area, 18th century
Courtesy of Věra Vávrová

as well as hyacinths, fritillaries, and lilacs. It is thought that it was here that tulips were first grown in Europe that later became famous in the Netherlands.

The garden was turned from a Renaissance to a baroque one in the 1720s and 1730s. At that time Prague had not been the seat of the Habsburgs for a hundred years, which had an unfavorable impact on the level of work put into Prague Castle. The gardening family of the Zinners were the ones mainly responsible for creating the garden's new look. Three generations of the Zinner family worked for Prague Castle, followed by the important court architect K.I. Dientzenhofer and the builder's scribe, J.H. Dienebier. Plans and drawings that have been preserved document the appearance of the Royal Garden at the time. A parterre with cut box hedges was made on the upper terrace, while on the lower terrace there was a central pool surrounded by shaped lime trees. A growing archway of twigs ran along the central axis from the Hercules fountain east-

ward to the Royal Summer Palace, in front of which was a baroque-style *giardinetto*. The garden also included an extensive orchard, an herb plot, and kitchen garden. It was decorated with a number of baroque statues. Useful buildings, such as greenhouses, were built beside the Renaissance buildings. The varieties of plants are recorded in descriptive inventories beginning in the 18th century.

The new style that came to garden architecture from England at the end of the 18th century and spread to other countries began to appear in Prague Castle only in the first half of the 19th century. Both the Royal Garden (transformed by the Weppl gardening family) and other green areas to the south and east of the royal seat were laid out in the new landscape style. Some of the trees that were newly planted then are still growing as precious examples in the Royal Southern Gardens today. The absence of the ruler in Prague—he had his seat in Vienna—influenced the varieties of plants cultivated.

The orchard was abolished in the Royal Garden, as well as the herb plot and kitchen garden. The greenhouses continued to be used for the cultivation of heat-loving plants, and the growing of fig trees, with its tradition of almost 350 years, continued through the beginning of the 20th century.

The present appearance of the Royal Garden is the result of arrangements made in the 19th century. After the founding of the Czechoslovak Republic in 1918, historical building research was carried out in the rather neglected Prague Castle, followed by the reconstruction of its individual parts. In the Royal Garden the trees were revitalized, as were the lawns and flower beds, and work was started on repairing the buildings. The *giardinetto* in front of the Royal Summer Palace, with the Singing Fountain in the middle of it, was renewed in 1937–39. In the 1920s and 1930s attention was devoted mainly to the gardens below the southern facade of the Prague Castle grounds. Owing to various circumstances the proposal put forward by the experienced gardener F. Thomayer was never realized, nor were any of the plans that had been entered for a competition on the best garden layouts. Later the Slovene architect Josip Plečnik was invited to find a solution. His design resulted in a completely new conception of the southern gardens—the Garden on the Ramparts and Paradise Garden. The vast garden area respects the historic building elements and the full-grown trees and emphasizes the panoramic views of the city. The oldest plant is a European yew (*Taxus baccata*) in the Paradise Garden that is about 400 years old. Owing to their protected position, unusual trees do well here, such as the paulownia (*Paulownia tomentosa*), catalpa (*Catalpa bignonioides*), Japanese pagoda tree (*Sophora japonica*), and even the elm (*Ulmus*), which has become rare. The flowers grown in the southern gardens are restricted mainly to pot plants in the summer season. In the 1960s the garden of the baroque Hartig Palace was joined to these gardens.

The Garden on the Bastion, designed by Plečnik, is on two levels. The upper terrace by the entrance to the impressive Spanish Hall is conceived as a modern garden inspired by the traditional *giardinetto* of Italian gardens and Japanese gardens. The white gravel creates a good contrast with several rows of thujas. Stepping stones on the lawn lead to a pergola over the medieval bastion. The lower terrace is paved with small round stones. From this garden one can go down into the Upper Stag Moat. Plečnik planned a symbolic vineyard on its southern slopes and what is called Masaryk's Prospect, in the middle of which is a beautiful lime tree (*Tilia cordata*), the Czech national symbol.

Most of the gardens and parks in Prague Castle were closed to the public before 1989, and the Royal Garden was considered to be part of the residence of the president of the Republic. After the Velvet Revolution, President Václav Havel decided to open the Royal Garden. In 1993 the southern gardens were opened to the public, and since 1999 people may walk through the whole Stag Moat.

It is only in the past few years that the work of Josip Plečnik at Prague Castle has been appreciated. This rehabilitation was helped along by the reconstruction of the gardens, carried out from the end of the 1980s. The positive evaluation of his work was demonstrated by the exhibition of his works at the castle in 1996, for which the gardens were themselves part of the exhibition.

On the basis of new projects other parts of the northern surrounding garden area of Prague Castle have gradually opened to the public, such as the Pheasantry and Lumbe's Garden. A project is also in preparation to reconstruct the St. Wenceslas's vineyard in Opyš, on the hillside in front of Prague Castle as approached from the east. There is a remarkable scheme under way at present to revitalize the old water system in the castle— the main pipes date from the 16th century—that will improve the method of watering the castle gardens and other green areas and will increase the flow of water in the Brusnice stream, which runs through the Stag Moat.

Synopsis

1534	King Ferdinand I, Holy Roman Emperor, founds Royal Garden
1535	First consignment of seeds from Vienna, and arrival of first gardener, Francesco (Francisco)
1538	Further consignment of seeds from Genoa, grafts from Trieste
1539	Arrival of new court gardener from Flanders, Dr. Hugo Vennius (Velius)
1540–62	Two new experienced gardeners, Reinhardt brothers, work in Royal Garden
1541	Fire in Prague Castle burned wooden bridge joining garden to royal palace; first ornamental parterre laid out
1554	Tulips said to have flowered for first time in Europe, in Royal Garden
1559	Archduke Ferdinand of Tyrol establishes private garden under his palace windows (later called the Paradise Garden)
1563	Consignment of bulbs of tulips, hyacinths, and fritillaries, and tubers of irises arrived from Asia Minor
1564	Royal Summer Palace completed, under supervision of Bonifac Wolmut
1564–75	Reign of Maxmilian II, big and small Ball Game Halls built, as were Singing Fountain and Fig Tree House with roof that could be dismantled

1576–1611	Reign of Rudolph II, Royal Garden enlarged, the *giardinetto* in front of Royal Summer Palace founded, and walled-in menagerie built (Lion's Court)
1648–49	Royal Garden damaged during invasion by Swedish soldiers
1657–1705	Reign of Leopold I, arbor path laid out, J.J. Bendl makes Hercules fountain, and theater built in garden
1701	Oldest inventory of plants in Royal Garden
1725–40	Royal and Paradise Gardens renovated in baroque style
1742	Northern surrounding garden area of the castle occupied by the French army
1757	Bombardment of Prague Castle by Prussian army caused great damage in newly renovated Royal Garden in baroque style
1755–75	Prague Castle altered by Empress Maria Theresa, wooden bridge to north replaced by embankment, alley On the Ramparts (later Garden on the Ramparts) laid out on adapted terrain beneath new southern castle facade
1820	*Giardinetto* in front of Royal Summer Palace abolished due to landscaping of Royal Garden
1833	Public park founded to east of Royal Garden, known as Chotek's Orchard
1861–63	Royal Garden redeveloped as landscape park, abolishing orchard in eastern part
1918	Czechoslovak Republic came into being
1920–35	Foundation of southern gardens (Garden on the Ramparts and Paradise Garden), and Garden on Bastion and vineyards with view over Upper Deer Moat (Masaryk's Prospect), designed by architect Josip Pleènik
1937–39	Renovation of Renaissance *giardinetto* in front of Royal Summer Palace, which was again reconstructed in 1955
1945–55	Reconstruction of big Ball Game Hall after fire in 1945, baroque summerhouse (originally greenhouse) rebuilt as house for president, new garden founded on terrace of Riding School, all designed by castle architect Pavel Janák
1960s	Hartig Palace Garden joined to southern gardens
1989	17th November beginning of Velvet Revolution
1990	President Václav Havel decides to open Royal Garden to public
1993	Completion of reconstruction of southern gardens; opened to the public
1996	Exhibition on architect Josip Pleènik, in Prague Castle
1997–99	Upper and Lower Stag Moat opened to public and New Orangery built from plans by architect Eva Jiøièná

Further Reading

Bašeová, Olga, *Pražské zahrady* (Prague Gardens), Prague: Panorama, 1991

Birnbaumová, Alžběta, "Naše zahrady v minulosti (Our Gardens in the Past)," *Salon* 18, no. 8 (1938)

Horáková, Ljuba, editor, *Zahrady Pražského hradu* (Prague Castle Gardens), Prague: Poláček, 1993

Krčálová, Jarmila, "Die Gärten Rudolfs II," *Leids Kunsthistorisch Jaarboek* 1 (1982)

Lukeš, Zdenek, Damjan Prelovšek, and Tomáš Valena, *Josip Plečnik—Architekt Prazského hradu,* Prague: Správa Pražského hradu, 1996; as *Josip Plečnik: An Architect of Prague Castle*, Prague: Prague Castle Administration, 1997

Morávek, Jan, "Z počátků královské zahrady (From the Beginnings of the Royal Garden)," *Umění* 11 (1938)

Morávek, Jan, and Zdeněk Wirth, *Pražský hrad v renesanci a baroku, 1490–1790* (Prague Castle in Renaisssance and Baroque Times), Prague: Praze, 1947

Pacáková-Hoštálková, Božena, et al., *Zahrady a parky v Čechách, na Moravě a ve Slezsku* (Gardens and Parks in Bohemia, Moravia, and Silesia), Prague: Libri, 1999

Valena, Tomáš, "Plečnik's Gardens at Hradèany: In Search of the Modern Architectonic Gardens of the 20th Century," *Architektov bilten* 20, nos. 107–8 (1991)

Vávrová, Věra, "Zahrady Pražského hradu (Prague Castle Gardens)," *Prague Castle: Programme Quarterly* (1998–99)

Vávrová, Věra, and Martina Drbalová, et al., *Zahrady Pražského hradu a zámecké zahrady v Čechách a na Moravě* (The Gardens of Prague Castle and Castle Gardens in Bohemia and Moravia), Prague: Správa Pražského Hradu a Národní Galerie v Praze, 1996

Wirth, Zdeněk, *Pražské zahrady* (Prague Gardens), Prague: Poláček, 1943

VĚRA VÁVROVÁ

Prairie Style

In architecture the Prairie style was defined by the Prairie School, which encompasses the period from 1900 to 1915. The highpoint came in 1914 and was based in the American Midwest. During its formative years the Prairie School architects focused on suburban Chicago, but the style would also reach into rural Illinois, Minnesota, Iowa, and Wisconsin. Emphasizing horizontality of design, the Prairie School was a regional manifestation of a more general, international revolt and reform occurring in the visual arts.

Critics linked the emphasis on horizontal lines in this style to the prairie that defined the American Midwest. Symbolically, the architects found the prairie to represent democracy and basic American liberty. In terms of its composition, however, the stability derived from a firmness of "line." Architectural historian Irving Pond defines this emphasis on line as "the disposition of the single mass or composite massing." This can be seen in the shape of the low, long hipped or gable roof, the horizontal banding of windows, the emphatic belt course or shelf roof between the stories—which often continued on one side as a lateral porch—and the broad, forward-set foundation. The continuity of line, edge, and surface lent horizontal unity to the design; against these horizontals a spirited interplay was established with short vertical accents, such as piers, mullions, and subsidiary masses.

Beyond the aesthetics of appearance, the Prairie buildings often worked extremely well. Functionality grew from sophisticated spatial arrangements. Designers generally not only sought to enhance the human experience but also to devise the maximum sense of space in a restricted area. The spiritual leader of the school was Louis H. Sullivan, who designed the Wainwright Building in St. Louis as well as banks and other buildings throughout the Midwest. Younger architects turned to him for inspiration and instruction. The ideas that he disseminated grew out of what was commonly called the Chicago School. This work sought a more complex vocabulary than the simplification and elimination that characterized Chicago's tall commercial structures. Sullivan, who began designing after 1889, is credited as the inventor of the first modern architectural style in the United States and as a leader of a younger group of radical architects that assured him of an esteemed position in American cultural history. The Prairie School followed Sullivan's desire and succeeded in devising a mode universally applicable to residential, ecclesiastical, and civic design.

The Prairie style followed two different tacks of development. One portion sought to house the masses, while another remained committed to artistic purposes that required wealthy patrons. The seeds of the style were rooted in an appreciation of nature and a dedication to the freedom and individuality inherent in democracy. Frank Lloyd Wright, Sullivan's most gifted pupil, added connections to artistic creation and literature of the day that informed him about the Aesthetic and Arts and Crafts movements as well as transcendentalism. From these influences arose a common theme of unity, harmony, simplicity, and respect for the nature of materials and the uniqueness of individuals. Wright's proven ability, unquestioned genius, and aristocratic presence soon brought matters into focus and caused a reorientation and consolidation within the group. Uniformity of expression temporarily superseded experimentation, as many sought guidance and training from Wright. While only a few Prairie-style designs were built in the 1920s and 1930s, some of Wright's work as late as 1950 reflect his Prairie School heritage. Wright's influential Prairie work includes the Bradley House, Willits House, Fricke House, Dana-Thomas House, and the Robie House, among others.

For Wright the horizontal mimicking of the landscape allowed the form to become organic, concealed in the landscape, and satisfied his modernist desire for simplification. He and Sullivan had wished to develop an American architecture especially suited to the Midwest. Wright felt that the "whole exterior was bedeviled, that is to say, mixed to puzzle-pieces with corner-boards, panel-boards, window-frames, corner-blocks, plinth-blocks, rosettes, fantails, and jiggerwork in general." He yearned for a simplicity in architecture that he saw in the prairie: "I had an idea that the horizontal planes in buildings, those planes parallel to earth, identify themselves with the ground—make the building belong to the ground."

The link between structure and landscape was further stimulated by the management of inner and exterior space. The Prairie homes were designed to bring the inside of the home out and the surroundings inside. Patios, gardens, and windows were designed to facilitate this connectedness, and building materials were selected in order to include natural elements of the surroundings, such as wood, stone, stucco, brick, or the elemental sand, gravel, cement, and water that make up concrete. This was also true of the plants and landscape design of the elongated gardens and courtyards. The linking device between such spaces was often the stone fences that extended wall lines outward, but most often the most responsible element was the elongated roof lines. These over-hanging roofs acted as a protecting shelter that allowed the house "to associate with the ground and become natural to its prairie site," according to Wright.

As modern architecture veered in other directions, some scholars referred to the Prairie style as conservative or reserved. In many ways the style upheld the values of their time and place while interpreting them into something contemporary in spirit and uniquely American. Among the other architects of the Prairie School were Walter Burley Griffin, George Grant Elslie, William Gray Purcel, Barry Byrne, Hugh M.G. Garden, Richard E. Schmidt, Robert C. Spenser, Jr., William E. Drumond, and Marion Mahoney.

A product of cultural taste, the Prairie style's popularity waned as preferences changed. *House Beautiful* illustrated its last Prairie house in 1914. Stickley's journal ceased publication in 1916 as the Arts and Crafts movement also lost popularity. Each year prior to 1914 the Prairie School had gained strength; thereafter, the commissions fell off sharply. The Prairie style's great achievement is a mode of design universally applicable to every building type. Its influence can be seen in many other types of architecture of the 20th century, particu-

larly in gardens and courtyard designs. Many suburban homes, including the ubiquitous ranch house, strive for a similar link between the horizontal exterior space and the domestic living environment.

Further Reading

Brooks, H. Allen, *The Prairie School,* New York: Norton, and Toronto, Ontario: University of Toronto Press, 1972
Garner, John S., editor, *The Midwest in American Architecture,* Urbana: University of Illinois Press, 1991
Legler, Dixie, and Christian Korab, *Prairie Style: Houses and Gardens by Frank Lloyd Wright and the Prairie School,* New York: Stewart, Tabori and Chang, 1999

BRIAN BLACK

Pre-Columbian Gardens

Pre-Columbian is a term that pertains to the Americas before Christopher Columbus came into contact with the Caribbean region. In its broadest sense, however, the term *pre-Columbian* is affiliated with the time period related to a multitude of nations across the Americas predominately before extensive contact with the many immigrants and explorers from other areas of the globe. The term can also be used to describe European nations before they were vastly influenced by Native American nations, or First Nation people—for example, before the significant introduction of the tomato to Italy. During this pre-Columbian period the many nations of the Americas developed a vast array of fascinating gardens, planned open spaces, civic monuments, earthworks, cities, and preserved sacred spaces that in many ways are only just beginning to be recognized for their important contributions to the human experience in landscape architectural planning and design. Throughout the Americas one can find a rich tradition in site planning, site development, and natural resource management by the pre-Columbian nations that includes some Euro-Asian-like garden design and certainly gardenlike features. The volumes of research, description, and knowledge are extensive and rapidly expanding, deserving numerous texts to describe the range of efforts. This discussion highlights only a few of the well-documented plans and designs associated with pre-Columbian landscape design in the Americas.

Before describing some noteworthy sites, it is worth mentioning a few ideas expressed by Lewis Binford, a noted ethnographer who studies First Nation people. Binford stresses that the descriptions and notions presented by an authority concerning the interpretations of another culture and its people may reveal more about the culture and beliefs affiliated with the person conducting the study than about the culture being studied. Such a statement has certainly held true about the many interpretations of the people and cultures of the pre-Columbian Americas. For example, Europeans and Euro-Americans often focus their attention to geomantic concepts, architecture, and spiritual concepts, while ignoring opportunities to describe gardens, site organization, and oral traditions. In the literature there can be wild speculations, misinformation, and misguided characterizations addressing pre-Columbian people and their culture. As another example, the names commonly employed to describe a particular nation often are not the names that a particular group of people have used to identify themselves (for example, the Chippewa or Ojibway are actually the Anishinaabeg). There is much to relearn about the First Nation people of the Americas. In addition, it is important to remember that the descendants of these pre-Columbian people retain vibrant and intact functioning cultures. The artifacts, sites, and bones of ancient cultures are not the property of scientists or others not affiliated with these ancestors. Contemporary First Nation people have a right to keep their culture and activities private and for others to respects their wishes; learning about pre-Columbian cultures and present-day traditions is a privilege to be respected.

Native American three-sisters method of growing corn, beans, and squash
Copyright N.Carter/North Wind Picture Archives

Central America is an appropriate place to discuss some of the designed spaces of First Nation people. Incipient agriculture, writing, and state architecture for much of the Americas originated in this region. Also, the oldest known designed space, Gheo-Shih, dating from 5000 to 4000 B.C., is found in the Oaxaca valley of Mexico. At this site several bands of hunters and gathers (a macroband) seasonally arrived from June to August to harvest an abundance of mesquite pods along the Rio Mitla. Adjacent to the mesquite trees two parallel lines of flat-topped boulders are aligned in what is believed to have been a ceremonial and social space. The interior of this space is relatively free of archaeological artifacts, while the immediate surroundings are littered with flint tools, firecracked rocks, and beads. Is Gheo-Shih a garden? In the strictest European and East Asian sense, probably not, but in the broader definition whereby designed spaces are created or made possible in association with vegetation, probably yes.

Central America was the site of many ancient civilizations and cultures, some of which scholars have not yet studied in great detail. However, we know much more about the Olmec, Zapotec, Mixtec, Mayan, Teotihuacano, Toltec, and Aztec cultures. The Olmec civilization is credited with having the first city-states in the Americas. The culture is known for its large monumental stone heads in the near plaza-like village spaces placed upon small mounds or raised areas. These plaza spaces (the valleys) and associated platforms and eventually pyramids (the mountains) would become a standard organizational structure within much of Mesoamerica. While these spaces generated interesting and functional urban design, architecture, and hardscape exterior landscapes, there is little evidence that plants played an important design role in the city center. Nevertheless, in residential palaces there were significant gardens. For example, in the early 16th century the leaders of Iztapaplan had a residential garden organized in a rectangular pattern, with small canals and aqueducts for irrigation. The plants were arranged via a scientifically based classification system. Like a modern arboretum collection, the plants found in the garden were from various regions in Mesoamerica and included fruit trees, shrubs, vines, and herbaceous ornamentals. In addition, there were zoological and botanical gardens such as the more elaborate terraced garden that existed further inland at Tezcoinco, near Tezcuo. Water was diverted in substantial aqueducts and canals to support ornamental waterfalls and pools as well as to irrigate the plants. Besides the botanical character of the site, this garden was also zoological in nature, containing fish and aviaries. Unfortunately, the garden was destroyed during the Spanish conquest.

In contrast, the rural landscape contained some important functional and aesthetically interesting garden landscapes. Archaeologists have discovered a wide variety of Mayan garden types spreading across Honduras, Guatemala, Belize, and southern Mexico including the Yucatan Peninsula. Much of the landscape may have been more intensively farmed than the modern Red River Valley of the north (Minnesota, North Dakota, Manitoba) or the Sacramento Valley in California. The Maya developed a variety of terraced and raised fields to support agronomic production. The raised or ditched fields in lowland areas may have supported fish, root crops, fruit and nut crops, fiber crops, and medicines. These raised fields are similar in concept to the ancient raised fields of New Guinea. These islandlike gardens surrounded by water may have supported somewhat high rural and urban population densities. It is believed that multiple crops were often harvested from the raised fields of Belize. The remnants of a similar system can be visited today in the southern portion of greater Mexico City, at Xochimilco, a Toltec refuge, eventually conquered by the Aztecs. The raised gardens of Xochimilco are called *chinampas* (Chinampanecs is the name of Toltec refugees), supporting a vast diversity of vegetation and at one time numerous fish in the canals. *Chinampas* are known for their functionality as well as for their beauty. At one time pre-Columbian people within the region grew ornamental herbaceous plants in terraced gardens and transplanted fruiting plants found across the region. Horticulture, ecological applications, and intentionally created landscapes were directed activities in Mesoamerica.

To the north of the Mesoamerican cultures reside the Puebloan cultures of the American southwest. Today the ancestors to the contemporary Puebloan people are called the Anasazi. However, as in Mesoamerica, there was a broad array of people spread across the landscape, forming a dynamic complex of people and artifacts. Some of these people and cultures are just beginning to be studied. Currently, the Puebloan cultures are the most well known and studied; yet every year, new sites, structures, ancient roads, and artifacts of the Anasazi are being discovered. As in Mesoamerican cultures, the use of plants by the Puebloans may

have been confined primarily to agricultural and other functional uses. Nevertheless, many Puebloan people evolved and adopted a recognizable spatial organization to their residential setting, in which a central plaza contained kivas, to the north of the plaza were the pueblos, and to the south were the middens (trash piles). This spatial arrangement can be observed in numerous landscape settings such as the Yellow Jacket site (on a plateau), the cliff-dwelling Mesa Verde sites, and the Chaco Canyon sites. These plazas can be considered large patios or piazzas located in a beautiful landscape setting, thus enabling an appreciation of the gardenlike nature of these elegant pre-Columbian hardscapes.

Even farther north, in the northern Great Plains, reside the Numangaki (Mandan), a culture living in the Missouri River Valley. They built small fortified villages that were carefully sited adjacent to timber lands, agricultural lands, landscape settings useful for recreational games, and appropriate places for cemeteries. Whenever a village moved, the elders would conduct site investigation reconnaissance and carefully select a new site, using certain landscape-planning and site-design principles. Numangaki women designed their food production gardens around some general principles. The size of the garden was from one to three acres (0.4 to 1.2 ha), depending on the number of women tending each garden. The edges of the garden were ringed with sunflowers. One portion of the garden was designated for a patch of squash, and the second portion was composed of hills of corn and beans. When horses became prevalent on the Great Plains, an outside row of wattled willows and red-twig dogwood was employed as a barrier. Manure was not used as a fertilizer because it contained numerous weed seeds. During the work day Numangaki women sang in their gardens. Among the gardens several small trees were kept, containing platforms for teenage boys to stand watch and signal a warning if they observed raiding warriors (Dakota, Cheyenne, and others), who might kill a Numangaki woman maintaining her garden. This spatial arrangement of scattered trees with somewhat circular vegetable gardens and women singing their traditional songs could be considered a functional as well as an aesthetic experience and is worthy of merit. The Potowatomi of Michigan, the Wyandot and Neutral First Nation people of southern Ontario, the Iroquois of New York, and numerous East Coast cultures are examples of people with traditions somewhat similar to the Numangaki, who often had distinct village configurations and utilitarian garden designs.

In the design of spaces, the use of earth forms and earthworks is a common feature from Minnesota, Wisconsin, Iowa, and Illinois southward and eastward to Florida. When these mounds and berms were first encountered by Euro-Americans, a great controversy arose concerning the builders of the mounds. Since that time it has been widely recognized that a variety of First Nation cultures built different types of mounds. Berms were used to surround ceremonial spaces. Some mounds were burial mounds (conical and elongated cones), while other mounds were ceremonial platforms (flat-top mounds). Although the Adena and Hopewell mounds in the Ohio River watershed, such as Serpent Mound, are widely known, there are many more mounds in the surrounding region. A major Mississippian mound site called Cahokia, near Collinsville, Illinois, is spectacular in size and diversity of mounds but is not well known. This mound site dating from about A.D. 900 to 1250 was part of the largest pre-Columbian city north of the Aztec capital Tenochtitlan. Cahokia had an estimated population ranging from 8,000 to 42,000 people, at the time comparable to the city of London. A wooden palisade circled approximately 205 acres of a 1,600-acre (647.5-ha) site. Cahokia included a wooden henge aligned to use the largest mound as a calendar. Many more of these village and city mound clusters can be found from Wisconsin to Florida. In contrast to platform mounds, effigy mounds were often burial mounds affiliated with the shapes of animals associated with a specific family. The best-preserved examples can be found in Iowa, along the Mississippi River. Many mounds across the eastern United States have been destroyed by agriculture and urban development.

In South America the Inca civilization is probably the most well known pre-Columbian people. In many respects this civilization operated like the Roman Empire, conquering neighboring people and adopting the best of what each conquered people had to offer. A network of roads, administrative centers, and conscripted mercenaries helped to keep the empire together. The potato was a staple of this area. Machu Picchu is a famous site within the Incan Empire, containing terraced and integrated agricultural gardens incorporated into a citadel design. In many respects their principles predate the similarly organic nature of the Prairie School designers in the American Midwest, who carefully integrated structures and landscape. There is little documentation concerning the development of gardens in South America during pre-Columbian times. This does not, of course, mean that South America lacked a contribution; instead it probably means that either no one has yet looked at (a very common problem in the Americas and Africa) or documented South American contributions. With further interest, research, and scholarship, the pre-Columbian contribution to garden design and landscape architecture may be expanded and embellished.

Further Reading

Binford, Lewis Roberts, *Debating Archaeology,* San Diego, California: Academic Press, 1989

Burley, Jon, "Gheo-Shih: An Ancient Pre-Columbian Plaza," *Landscape Research* 17, no. 2 (1992)

Coe, Michael D., *Mexico,* London: Thames and Hudson, 1957; New York: Praeger, 1962; 4th edition, as *Mexico: From the Olmecs to the Aztecs,* New York: Thames and Hudson, 1994

Coe, Michael D., "The Chinampas of Mexico," *Scientific American* 211 (1964)

Coe, Michael D., *The Maya,* London: Thames and Hudson, and New York: Praeger, 1966; 6th edition, New York: Thames and Hudson, 1999

Ferguson, William M., and Arthur H. Rohn, *Anasazi Ruins of the Southwest in Color,* Albuquerque: University of New Mexico Press, 1987

Flannery, Kent V., editor, *Maya Subsistence: Studies in Memory of Dennis E. Puleston,* New York: Academic Press, 1982

Fowler, Melvin L., *The Cahokia Atlas: A Historical Atlas of Cahokia Archaeology,* Springfield: Illinois Historic Preservation Agency, 1989; revised edition, Urbana: Illinois Transportation Archeological Research Program, University of Illinois, 1997

Mallam, R. Clark, *The Iowa Effigy Mound Manifestation: An Interpretive Model,* Iowa City: Office of the State Archaeologist, University of Iowa, 1976

Pohl, Mary DeLand, editor, *Ancient Maya Wetland Agriculture: Excavations on Albion Island, Northern Belize,* Boulder, Colorado: Westview Press, 1990

Silverberg, Robert, *Mound Builders of Ancient America,* Greenwich, Connecticut: New York Graphic Society, 1968; abridged edition, as *The Mound Builders,* 1970

Vizenor, Gerald Robert, *The People Named the Chippewa: Narrative Histories,* Minneapolis: University of Minnesota Press, 1984

Weatherford, Jack McIver, *Indian Givers: How the Indians of the Americas Transformed the World,* New York: Crown, 1988

Weatherford, Jack McIver, *Native Roots: How the Indians Enriched America,* New York: Crown, 1991

Will, George F., and George Hyde E., *Corn among the Indians of the Upper Missouri,* St. Louis, Missouri: Miner, 1917; reprint, Lincoln: University of Nebraska Press, 1964

Woodward, Susan L., and Jerry N. McDonald, *Indian Mounds of the Middle Ohio Valley: A Guide to Adena and Ohio Hopewell Sites,* Newark, Ohio: McDonald and Woodward, 1986

JON BRYAN BURLEY

Prior Park

Bath, Avon, England

Location: approximately 2 miles (3.2 km) southeast of Bath city center, and 100 miles (161.3 km) west of London

Prior Park is a villa within the boundary of the city of Bath. It was designed for Ralph Allen between 1735 and 1750 by John Wood, the Elder, but completed, after a dispute in 1748 between the two, by the clerk of the works, Richard Jones. The house, which in 1830 became a Catholic boarding school, has a complicated history, twice being badly damaged by fire, first in 1836 and then again in 1991. Much of what is there, therefore, especially the interiors, has been either restored or altered. The estate itself is at once like that of the traditional Palladian villa, a house standing isolated within a park, and a landscape that asks to be seen as a part of the city, above it but looking out over it, or as a visitor in 1788 put it, "which sees all Bath and which was built for all Bath to see."

The house is large, 15 bays wide, finished with the usual hexastyle, Corinthian portico, two columns deep. The ground-floor windows have alternating pediments above a rusticated floor that serves as the basement. Connected to the house by a range of one-storied arcades are pavilions. A grand staircase was added to the portico in 1834, at which time the east wing was also enlarged. At the west end the large and majestic church of St. Paul (1844–63) was added, designed by Joseph Scoles. Allen's original chapel in the house is preserved, but much else is changed, most obviously the entrance hall and the drawing room, both restored after the fire of 1836.

Beyond and around is the garden. The sight to the north faces Bath, the view so admired by Allen's many visitors. Indeed, Allen and Prior Park were the models for Squire Allworthy and his home in Henry Fielding's *Tom Jones* (1749). The house and its grounds are still perhaps the most pleasing surviving Palladian landscape in Britain, in style standing somewhere between the classicism of Stowe and the later, more romantic vistas of Stourhead. Although Wood was quickly dismissed from this project, in the scheme finally carried out there may be traces taken from his notion of Palladio's account of the Roman theater plan—filled out with his own extensive antiquarian and historical researches—to establish a relationship between the house at one end and the ever-opening vista to Bath beyond. Indeed, Daniel Defoe, writing in 1726, spoke of plays being put on in the afternoons, the city being used, he suggested, as the backdrop for the stage.

The area of the park itself is small, some 28 acres (11.3 ha) in all. Behind the house are formal lawns, but on the side toward Bath there is a path, now restored and cleared, leading down past a cultivated wilderness to the Palladian bridge and the ornamental fishponds around it. The bridge, possibly designed by the amateur Thomas Pitt, first Baron Camelford (1737–93), on the pattern of that at Wilton, was constructed by Jones in 1755–56. The narrow path continues beyond, cut into the hillside and built up at times with walls of stone. Each part of the path was meant to give the traveler a particular view back—to the chapel, to the house reflected in the lake, up to the house itself, and then to the bridge. All this was designed by Allen around the pattern of the landscape already there. He was helped in his ideas and organization by his friend Alexander Pope. Indeed, it has been suggested that it was Pope who suggested the wilderness area to Allen, so clearly a contrast to the formal area on the other side of the house. In the wilderness area were set a number of fancies, a sham bridge, a grotto, a lake, and a statue of Moses standing over a cascade.

The vogue for Gothic later led to Richard Jones setting a Gothic lodge here. A generation later a rock garden in the Chinese style was added, as was a thatched house, now almost completely gone. The garden itself was also extended, finished down the valley to the lakes below, which were also made larger. There was a third stage of development in the 1760s, perhaps from the now growing influence of Lancelot "Capability" Brown: a number of the outbuildings were removed and the lawns and plantings at each side were made to seem more natural. After Allen died in 1764 nothing further was done and the garden was neglected. At some point an obelisk in honor of General George Wade was removed, and in 1921 the Gothic house was transferred to the nearby Ranch Wood House. In 1836, at the time of the other additions, a driveway had also been laid, leading up to the front of the house, in effect dividing the grotto from all else there in the wilderness area.

The fire of 1991 lead to an extraordinary and costly renovation of the interior, financed by English Heritage and the Bath Preservation Trust. In 1993 the National Trust took over Prior Park from the Order of Christian Brothers. Much has been done to bring the garden back to its original forms, with clearing and replantings of yew, ash, and lime trees to fill the gaps. There is more to be done, especially around the wilderness, but the grandeur of Prior Park and its garden is once again discernable. The grotto is in restoration, and there are also plans to excavate and restore the cascade that flowed from the lake and perhaps even bring back the lake itself to its original serpentine shape.

Synopsis

1735–50	Villa and Palladian landscape garden built, designed by John Wood the Elder
1748	Wood the Elder dismissed after dispute with owner, Ralph Allen
1748–64	Allen designs wilderness and ornamental fishponds
1755–56	Palladin bridge constructed, designed perhaps by Thomas Pitt
1760s	Gardens redesigned under influence of Lancelot "Capability" Brown
1830	House taken over as Catholic boarding school
1836	House badly damaged by fire
1991	House again badly damaged by fire
1993	Prior Park taken over by National Trust

Further Reading

Haddon, John, *Portrait of Bath,* London: Hale, 1982
Hart, Vaughan "One View of a Town: Prior Park and the City of Bath," *Res* 17–18 (1989)
Wood, Anthony, "Prior Park, Bath," *Country Life* (18 May 1995 and 19 September 1996)

DAVID CAST

Průhonický Park

Průhonice, Bohemia, Czech Republic

Location: approximately 8 miles (13 km) southeast of Prague city center

The foundation of a natural and landscape park next to the capital of Prague dates back to the turn of the 20th century. A key person in the history of the park was the owner of the estates and the founder of the park, the count Arnost Emanuel Silva Tarouca, who purposefully reshaped the original forest growths (the area of which was 250 hectares [618 acres]) along a creek and reworked them into a work of art. The key point is the building of a Renaissance château erected on the foundations of a Middle Age stronghold, with a chapel of the Birth of the Virgin consecrated as early as in 1187. Three ponds were designed gradually on the creek: Podzámecký in the first section, Labeška in the other section called Preserve, and the Bořín, the youngest among the waterworks whose surroundings were newly reshaped and replanted.

Silva Tarouca descended from ancient noble families of Portugal (Silva) and Spain (Tarouca). The first ancestor was a court councillor at Vienna and an adviser to the empress Maria Theresia. Later, in 1768, he purchased estates at Čechy pod Kosířem in Moravia, where a château was also situated in the middle of a natural park.

The elder brother of Silva Tarouca, František, as the firstborn son, kept the native château, around which he developed a natural park. He published his findings on the development of parks (1894) and wrote a paper on the importance of horticulture.

Through a marriage with Maria Antonia Nostiz Rhineck, Arnošt Emanuel Silva Tarouca acquired several estates and a generous basis for the development of the park at Průhonice. At his time, the use of parks and gardens was combined with the fondness for nature, landscaping, and gamekeeping, which may be documented by the affinity to the family of the successor to the Austrian throne, Ferdinand d'Este, who, in the same era, supported the landscape and garden development at his château Konopiště.

Průhonický Park preserves significant features that were described by its founder in detail in the framework of an edition on parks and gardens (*Die Gartenanlagen Österreich-Ungarns in Wort und Bild,* 1909–14), comprising six books and describing significant parks across the empire. In Vienna, the Dendrological Society was founded, and Silva Tarouca provided support and land at Průhonice for its Club and Introduction Garden.

The general secretary of the society was Camillo Schneider, who was sent on an exploration expedition to Caucasus in 1908 and China 1914 (however, the latter expedition was suspended because of World War I, and therefore Schneider was invited by Alfred Rehder to work at the Arnold Arboretum in the United States).

Many newly discovered plants were grown in Průhonický Park, in particular in its alpine section, which was developed on a large natural rock (seeds

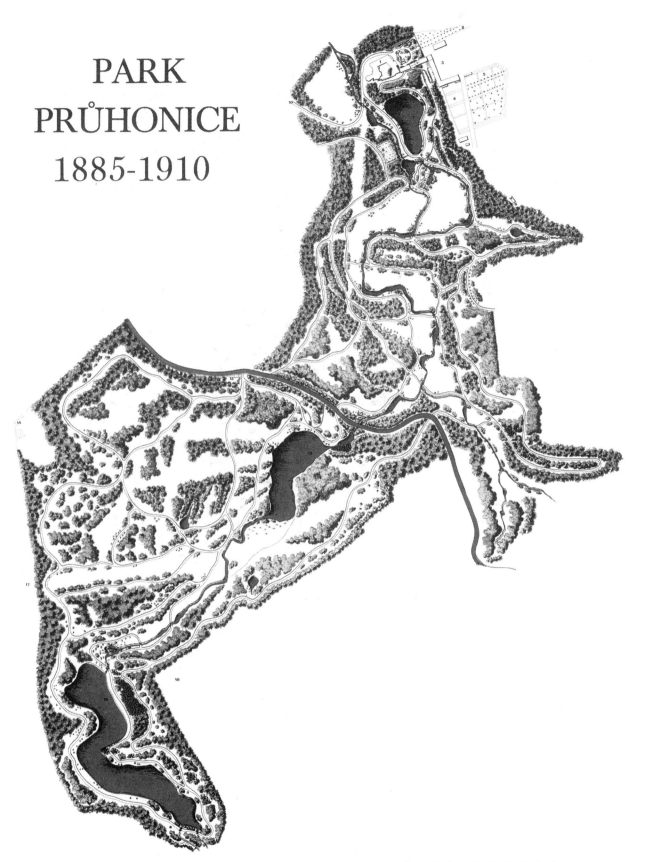

PARK
PRŮHONICE
1885-1910

Plan of Průhonicý Park, originally drawn by Silva Tarouca, ca. 1908, redrawn by Antonín Marián Svoboda
Courtesy of A.M. Svoboda

were brought back from expeditions, e.g., those led by Wilson and Rock, and also in cooperation with Wilhelm Kriechbaum of Gratz).

Details about the park are described in the publication issued by the founder, as in the manuals (*Handbücher*) prepared with Camillo Schneider, and are still a popular reference literature, dealing with coniferous, broad-leaved, perennial, and mountain species (alpine plants). The whole park was thoroughly described several times. Of extraordinary importance is the original plan (1908), which shows all significant details and the layout of paths, ponds, and weirs on the creek and which distinguishes broad-leaved growths and all newly planted coniferous growths along the border of the park. Silva Tarouca was familiar with the work of the park's developer, Hermann Pückler of Muskau (Lusatia), as well as with the publication on parks called *Andeutungen über Landschaftsgärtnerei* (1834, reprinted 1986). The founder studied his concepts and considerations and accepted his views concerning the development of a natural and landscape English park in Europe. The manuscripts of both brothers on the park and garden development remained unfinished. The owner of Průhonice and Čechy pod Kosířem died in the same year in their family's château in Moravia (1936).

All of Průhonický Park lies in an extensive deep valley along a watercourse, wide valley meadows, and adjacent steep slopes with natural rocks. In the wood growth are a number of original time-honored oaks and a number of other original tree species, such as linden, ash, maple, elm, buckthorn, and alder buckthorn among shrubs. Tree species significant in terms of forest husbandry were gradually added, such as pine, spruce, and European larch. Distant vistas of the château, meadows, and ponds were developed at elevated viewing points. Several of these are fan shaped and located next to Labeška pond.

Exotic species, both trees and shrubs, are dominant in specific sections of the park. The total numbers of taxa and individual units are in the thousands. Among the coniferous trees the following species are represented: Douglas fir; hemlock; various species of pines, firs, junipers, and cedar; and European larch. Among the broad-leaved trees of special interest are magnolia, tulip tree, beech, and oak. Shrubs are numerous, the most important being azalea and rhododendron, including many species from around the world as well as by many cultivars. Of extraordinary importance is a group of Czech decorative varieties grown at Průhonický Park, most often by the crossbreeding of the cultivar Cunningham's White or *Rhododendron smirnowii*.

The general layout of such a large park allows visitors to enjoy the heterogeneity of viewing points and the enormous range of trees species from various continents.

Historical Development

Over the centuries, widely conceived botanical and gardening research has been developed at Průhonice. Průhonický Park has become a basis for the Decorative Gardening and Landscaping Research Institute, which conducts research on greenhouse and bulbaceous plants, among others. The château contains a valuable herbarium owned by the Botanical Department of the National Museum in Prague. Another department located at the site is the Botanical Garden (1962–69), founded by the Czechoslovak Academy of Science, which continues to study domestic and introduced tree species. Currently, it forms a department of the Botanical Institute of the Academy of Science of the Czech Republic (since 1969).

In the vicinity of the park, within the limits of Průhonice, experimental gardens were founded such as the Dendrological Garden, which is open to the public. This garden was developed on the foundations of the original Club Experimental and Introduction Garden of the Dendrological Society (founded in 1908) and originally was situated within the park but has now been extended beyond the Prague-Brno motorway.

The modern design of the garden makes it possible to present groups of species in individually designed sections (e.g., coniferous and broad-leaved trees and climbing and alpine plants). There are rich collections of decorative cultivars (e.g., *Pinus, Abies, Picea,* and *Juniperus*) and broad-leaved trees (e.g., *Acer, Fagus,* and *Magnolia*). The total number of plants installed since 1980 (on an area of 80 hectares [197 acres]) amounts to thousands of taxa, species, and cultivars.

In the framework of the increasing popularity of gardening design and landscaping, a documentation center was founded in compliance with the United Nations Educational, Scientific, and Cultural Organization (UNESCO) concept of world cultural and natural heritage preservation and based on the 1972 Paris UNESCO Charter in order to collect documents on domestic sites. These include parks already registered, such as the Lednice-Valtice park area, Podzámecká and Květná gardens at Kroměříž, Prague castle and palaces gardens, Telč Château park, and baroque gardens in Český Krumlov. This contribution to international cooperation includes similar research centers across Europe and worldwide.

Synopsis

1885	Count Arnošt Emanuel Silva-Tarouca acquires Průhonice estates through marriage to Maria Antonia Nostitz Rhineck
1885–92	Development of park and reconstruction of Renaissance château
1908	First layout of Průhonický Park, designed by Silva Tarouca

1928 Sale of estates to Czechoslovak Republic, with administration entrusted to Ministry of Agriculture and newly founded Gardening Research Institute

1936 Decorative Gardening and Landscaping Research Institute established here for research into greenhouse plants

1949 Prague National Museum herbaria relocated to château

1962–69 Foundation of Botanical Garden of Czechoslovak Academy of Science

1978 Development of Dendrological Garden of Decorative Gardening and Landscaping Research Institute

1985 Conference devoted to centenary of Průhonický Park

1989 Conference on occasion of 80th anniversary of foundation of Dendrological Garden

2000 Development of Průhonický Park by Botanical Institute of Academy of Science of Czech Republic

Further Reading

Ludvík, Helebrant, *100 let Pruhonickeho parku a zahradnickych tradic v Pruhonicích* (100 Years of Průhonice Park and the Tradition of Horticulture in Průhonice), Prague: Výzkumný a Spechtitelský Ústav Okrasneho Zahradnictví Pruhonicích v Nakladatelstvi Novinár, 1985

Ludvík, Helebrant, *Význam zahradnických tradic v Pruhonicích: Dendrologická Spolecnost a její introdukcní spolková zahrada 1909 (k 80 výroci zalozeni)* (Tradition of Horticulture in Průhonice: The Dendrological Society and Its Club Introduction Garden, 1909: The 80th Anniversary of Its Foundation), Prague: Sluzba Výzkumu, 1989

Silva Tarouca, E.E., "Der Průhonicer Park (Boehmen)," in *Die Gartenanlagen Österreich-Ungarns in Wort und Bild*, edited by Camillo Karl Schneider, 6 vols., Vienna: Tempsky, 1909–14

Svoboda, Antonín Marián, *Der Park Průhonice: Ein Naturwissenschaftlicher und instruktiver Führer durch seine Geschichte, Architekturdenkmäler und botanische Forschungen*, Průhonice: Botanisches Institut der Tschechoslowakischen Akademie der Wissenschaften, 1969

Svoboda, Antonín Marián, *Introdukce okrasných listnatých drevin: Mapové prílohy*, Prague: Academia, 1981

Tábor, Ivo, and Marie Soucková, *Dendrologická zahrada výzkumného ústavu okrasného zahradnictví Průhonice*, Průhonice: Naše Vojsko, 1995

ANTONÍN MARIÁN SVOBODA

Puławy

Lublin, Poland

Location: approximately 30 miles (50 km) west-northwest of Lublin and 70 miles (116.6 km) southeast of Warsaw

Puławy is one of the most famous Polish landscape gardens, and it significantly influenced Polish country mansions. It is also known as the birthplace of Polish museums. Puławy was given a vast scale by Princess Izabela Czartoryska at the turn of the 17th century. The princess was a great lover and creator of gardens; she also produced a very popular and pioneering manual on laying out parks, *Myśli rózne o sposobie zakładania ogrodów* (1805; *Thoughts on the Manner of Planting Gardens*), in which the theory and practice of English landscape gardening are adapted to Polish habits and customs. The result of her experience and observations while building a park in Powązki near Warsaw and that in Puławy, and reprinted a number of times until the mid-19th century, the book was a model and source of inspiration for many owners and creators of gardens in Poland.

By the end of the 1780s the baroque residence in Puławy, with its geometrical garden with poplar alleys and bosquets, as well as decorative flower beds, was transformed according to the English style. The basic principles of landscape gardening were demonstrated here. Princess Izabela Czartoryska popularized the English term *clump* (Polish, *klomb*). The gardener James Savage, brought from England, was the main creator of the park. Set in a widely varied landscape, with a high escarpment above the old riverbed of the Vistula, with ravines and an isle, the garden was soon to become

Illustration of the Gothic House at the gardens of Puławy
Photo by Marek Studnicki, courtesy of Czartoryski Foundation, Crakow

the place where the most fashionable park elements adapted to the Polish climate and biological conditions were displayed. Grottoes (one transformed into a chapel) were located in the escarpment in front of which a sculpture of a reclining sleeping puma was placed. Further elements were added later, including bridges, fountains, a sarcophagus commemorating the late parents of the prince, a little altar, and the English Staircase, as well as a number of pavilions such as the Fisherman's House (unpreserved), Chinese Arbor, Greek House near a decorative farm called Żulinki, and the Yellow House; moreover, boulders with inscriptions (e.g., a stone dedicated to Jacques Delille) were spread around.

Among the garden pavilions the Temple of the Sibyl and the Gothic House surpassed the limits of garden art. They are considered now to have given a start to the history of museums in Poland. The Temple of the Sibyl was designed by Chrystian Piotr Aigner (1801), following

the Temple of the Vesta in Tivoli. Dedicated to Polish tradition and history, the pavilion displayed historical mementos of some famous Poles, including kings and military commanders, as well as Nicolaus Copernicus and the Renaissance poet Jan Kochanowski; the inscription "The Past for the Future" was placed above the entrance to the room that was to commemorate Prince Józef Poniatowski, who had suffered a heroic death while struggling for the liberty of his home country. The temple was opened with a special key (kept today in the Czartoryskis's Museum in Cracow) in the shape of the staff of Hermes, himself the guide of souls, with the Greek words "I open the Temple of Memory." Throughout the century after the Temple of the Sibyl's construction, thousands of Polish pilgrims converged on the pavilion, seeking there a sense of national renewal after the collapse of the Polish-Lithuanian Commonwealth.

The Gothic House guarded a collection of European art and historical mementos connected with European

Illustration of the Temple of Sybilla in Puławy by Johann Schumann after an engraving by Ema Potocka, 1807
Copyright Muzeum Narodowe w Warszawie

history. It was rebuilt to acquire a picturesque pseudo-medieval appearance after Chrystian Piotr Aigner's design (1809). Princess Izabela Czartoryska, who personally wrote the list of pieces of art and objects collected there (published as *Poczet pamiątek zachowanych w Domu Gotyckim* [1828; *The List of Mementoes Preserved in the Gothic House*]), called the pavilion a place of "memory of the World," a place for reflection over the passing of time and memory that can overcome death and the collapse of ideas. Contrary to the Temple of the Sibyl, the Gothic House was a place that cherished European culture, particularly the elements of medieval knightly tradition. Many sculptural and architectural details of ancient, medieval, and Renaissance origin (as well as "twenty bricks from the Bastille" and a "part of the frieze of a Druid temple in Scotland") were inserted in the outside elevation of the Gothic House. This building, too, could be opened with a special key only (preserved in the Czartoryskis's Museum). Princess Izabela Czartoryska and her son Adam Jerzy, a great lover of the Middle Ages, devoted much effort to arranging an appropriate "medieval" outside setting for the pavilion. "Grim" spruces were planted to harmonize with the ogival arches of the colonnade of the building, and a "Gothic alley" of a double line of lindens with branches forming sharp arches was created. The opening of the Gothic House in 1811 was highly ceremonious and included the so-called *visions gothiques*, in which the public participated together with the actors in the illusionary medieval world. The construction of the pavilion brought into the natural setting of the park a number of games resembling medieval tournaments, as well as *tableaux vivants* referring to definitive events in Polish history.

Czartoryska was in favor of composing the plants of the park from the local species. A forested part of the old zoological garden, consisting of oaks, elms, poplars, and alders, was connected with the park. However, she also introduced exotic plants among the Polish trees. Still growing in Puławy is a special Weymouth pine (*Pinus strobus*) that she brought from North America. Puławy became the center of conscious propagation of horticulture, the knowledge of plants, and the promulgation of varieties of good fruit trees.

The palace park, according to the English theory the princess had acquainted herself with so well during her extensive tour of all the major parks in England and Scotland, was united with a vast purposefully shaped landscape. The park was adjacent to a little palace, called Marynki, belonging to the daughter of the princess, Maria Wirtemberska, who was a writer. The island opposite Marynki was a place of outdoor entertainment stylized to resemble country work. Farther afield, Czartoryska established an ideal village for her subjects, Włostowice. Farther still, among scenic ravines, the so-called Parchatka was arranged; it was to serve as a place

of rest during the excursions in the neighborhood, with a house, a chapel, and sculptures, from where a magnificent view could be admired. In Góra, on the opposite bank of the river, groups of trees were planted around a small palace and a church in such a way as to offer a magnificent view from the palace windows. At the same time, the view of the palace from Góra itself was impressive, since it was set on the edge of a high escarpment overlooking a spacious park.

The form and symbolism of the park were permeated with the influence of artists and poets associated with the court of the Czartoryskis, mainly the painter Jan Piotr Norblin de la Gourdaine, who also executed many drawings of the park. A number of poets praised the beauty and patriotic significance of Puławy (e.g., F.D. Kniaznin, J.U. Niemcewicz, J.P. Woronin, and M. Sokolnicki). Together with the princess they developed pre-Romantic motifs of the symbolism of trees and praised the new landscape character of gardens as an equivalent of the freedom of humankind. The Puławy garden quickly achieved fame. Jacques Delille included a description of Puławy in the second edition of his poem *Jardins* (1801). Many visitors to Puławy in the 19th century wrote descriptions of the park in their travel diaries and articles published in magazines.

After the failure of the November Uprising, in which Prince Adam Jerzy Czartoryski, the elder son of Princess Izabela Czartoryska, played a major role, the Puławy residence was confiscated by the Russians to be transformed into the Alexandrian Institute of the Education of Maidens in 1840. Out of this came a valuable album of lithographs showing the park and executed by a drawing teacher at the institute. Later, an agriculture institute, famous for the great patriotism of its students, had its seat in the palace. At the same time both the buildings and the stand of trees began to deteriorate. After World War II some garden sculptures saved during the czarist times were returned to Puławy; the stand of park trees began to be reconstructed under the supervision of Gerard Ciołek, the most illustrious expert on garden history in Poland. Currently, the palace is the home of the Institute of Agriculture, Fertilizing, and Pedology. At the bottom of the escarpment is the experimental field of the institute, together with a precious botanical collection.

Synopsis

1671–78	Building of palace, designed by Tylman van Gameren
ca. 1785	Puławy became principal abode of Prince Adam Kazimierz and Princess Izabela Czartoryska
1788	Beginning of construction work on orangery (Greek House); layout of private garden for Princess Izabela

Czartoryska by the side wing of palace, with little altar bearing inscription "To God for My Children"

1788–89   Grottoes in escarpment built

1790   Beginning of construction work on Marynki palace (palace of Princess Maria Wirtemberska), designed by Chrystian Piotr Aigner

1791   Arrival in Puławy of gardener James Savage from England

1796–1809   Major work on planting park

1798–99   Construction of second orangery, adjacent to palace, designed by Aigner

1798–1800   Construction of Temple of Sibyl, designed by Aigner

ca. 1800   Sculpture of Puma, by Italian master, placed at entrance to grottoes

1811   Opening of Gothic House, rebuilt by Aigner

1831   Confiscation of Puławy complex by Czarist authorities, after fall of November Uprising

1840   Palace became seat of Alexandrian Institute of Education of Maidens

1862   Palace became seat of Polytechnical, Agricultural, and Forestry Institute

1917   Palace became seat of State Institute of Farming (since 1950, Institute of Agriculture, Fertilizing, and Pedology)

1948   Regional Museum of PTTK (Polish Tourist Country-Lovers' Association) arranges expositions in Temple of Sibyl and in Gothic House

1998   Foundation established to reconstruct park

Further Reading

Aleksandrowicz, Alina, *Izabela Czartorzska: Polskosc i europejskosc,* Lublin: Wydawnictwo Uniwersytetu Marii Curie-Sklodowskiej, 1998

Jaroszewski, Tadeusz S., *Chrystian Piotr Aigner: Architekt warszawskiego klasycyzmu,* Warsaw: Panstowowe Wydawnictwo Naukowe, 1970

Kseniak, Mieczyslaw, *Rezydencja Czartoryskich w Pulawach,* Lublin: Krajowa Agencja Wydawnicza, 1986; as *The Czartoryski Family Residence in Puławy,* Lublin: Idea Media, 1998

Lorentz, Stanislaw, editor, *Puławy,* Warsaw: Arkady, 1962

Szafrańska, Malgorzata, editor, *Ogród: Forma-Symbol-Marzenie* (exhib. cat.), Warsaw: Zamek Królewski w Warszawie, 1998

MALGORZATA SZAFRAŃSKA

R

Rambouillet

Yvelines, France

Location: approximately 30 miles (48 km) southwest of Paris

The château and grounds of Rambouillet reflect the tastes of its numerous owners and designers through the centuries. A monastic property from the 8th to the 14th centuries, the name evolved from the hamlet of "Rumbelitum" located in the forest of Yvelines. Portions of the building date to the 14th century when Jean Bernier purchased it and began to construct a château in the style of the day. These medieval beginnings give the present structure a confusing plan. After Bernier's death Regnault d'Angennes purchased Rambouillet in 1384, and the property stayed in his family until 1699.

Rambouillet is located in a vast hunting park, rich in vegetation and game, and is on the route from Paris to Chartres. Consequently, aristocratic and royal visitors were numerous. In 1547 François I was traveling in the vicinity and, having fallen ill, stopped at Rambouillet. He died in the tower there that still bears his name. In the 17th century the Angennes expanded the palace, creating a three-sided court at the entrance; the courtyard was flanked on one side by the François I tower.

In 1700 Jean-Baptiste Fleurian d'Armenonville began to improve the grounds; he wanted to create a little Versailles. There were formal gardens on each side of the château containing two water basins: the Rondeau on the left and the Miroir on the right. At the edge of the formal gardens a terrace was constructed along a canal running parallel to the building and perpendicular to the main axis. Fleurian extended the canal on axis with the château. This grand canal was flanked by two islands and two more canals at angles so that the canal system formed a *patte d'oie,* or goose-foot shape. Two circular islands, Île des Roches and Île des Festins, were located at the ends of the canals set at angles. The central axis was further expanded beyond the grand canal

with the addition of a *tapis vert,* a swath of lawn, extending the vista to the horizon.

In 1706 Louis XIV purchased the property for the comte de Toulouse, one of Madame de Montespan's children. The count continued to embellish the landscape, planting a quincunx, creating more canals and islands, and cutting avenues through the forests for hunting. He enclosed more than 12,000 hectares (29,640 acres) of the park. After the count's death his widow and her son, the duc de Penthièvre, continued to improve the park in the picturesque manner. Inspired by Rousseauist attitudes toward the landscape, the duke added an English garden to the right of the *tapis vert.* The park featured a rockery, a thatched cottage, and farm animals. The English garden at Rambouillet is an example of the preoccupation of the French in the 18th century with designing sites that imitated nature. Usually located in remote areas away from the formal gardens, these idyllic settings provided contrasting experiences in the landscape. Some of the best known, besides Rambouillet, were the Petit Trianon at Versailles and Chantilly.

Louis XVI enjoyed hunting at Rambouillet and bought it in 1783. He hired Hubert Robert to bring the standard of the château and gardens up to royal status. Marie-Antoinette did not like Rambouillet, so Louis added some amenities to please her, including an experimental farm, with merino sheep from Spain, and a dairy that provided fresh milk and cheese.

During the Revolution Rambouillet became property of the state and fell into ruin. Napoléon I acquired it in 1800 and used it until his abdication. He was fond of Rambouillet, and although he only spent one month and 14 days there, both the château and the gardens underwent extensive restorations while he was in power. Trepsat served as the official architect of Rambouillet and was later replaced by Flamin.

Rambouillet, central axis
Copyright John F. Webster

When restorations began, Trepsat wanted to demolish the entire château and succeeded in removing one wing before Napoléon stopped him from any further destruction of the palace. The loss of that wing created an entrance courtyard enclosed on only two sides. The Miroir was filled with rubble from the demolished wing and planted with a bosque of trees; basins and canals were cleaned. The English gardens were restored and enlarged. Seeds of Louisiana cypress trees in the Rambouillet nurseries that had been forgotten during the Revolution were found, and a magnificent allée was planted.

After his marriage to Marie-Louise in 1810, Napoléon had an iron balcony constructed to join their apartments. The promenade, designed by Fauconnier, was 90 meters (98.5 yd.) in length, running along the south facade of the château. Flamin, Trepsat's replacement, added statuary to the gardens and restored the pavilion on the Île des Roches. Two avenues were cut through the parterre and planted with rows of lindens, tulip trees, and poplars. Some of the canals were filled,

and the islands forested. During this time over 10,000 trees were planted. When Napoléon first began restorations at Rambouillet, he removed the furnishings from the dairy and had them installed at Malmaison for Josephine. Later, after his marriage to Marie-Louise, he brought them back to Rambouillet for her enjoyment.

Although he initiated extensive restorations at Rambouillet, Napoléon considered it to be a hunting lodge rather than a residence and preferred spending more time at his other country places. Toward the end of his reign Marie-Louise and their son, the king of Rome, sought refuge at Rambouillet and received there the news of Napoléon's abdication and exile to Elba. No longer safe in France, the empress and her son were escorted to Austria by her father. A year later Napoléon spent his last night in France at Rambouillet before being escorted to his second and last exile on the Island of St. Helena.

The property went through a series of owners, both royal and aristocratic, during the 19th century. It remained a setting for historical events; in 1830 Charles

Rambouillet, garden side
Copyright John F. Webster

X abdicated there. In 1850 it was used as a restaurant and two years later, a military orphanage. The building and landscape slowly declined. During the Second Empire Napoléon III rescued the château and restored its dignity. It became the summer residence of the presidents of France in 1870.

Synopsis

768	Rumbelitum given to the Monastery of St. Denis
1368	Jean Bernier acquires the estate of Rambouillet
1384–1699	Property held in the d'Angennes family
1700–1705	Owned by Jean-Baptiste Fleurian d'Armenonville
1700	D'Armenonville lays out formal gardens imitating Versailles
1706–38	Louis XIV purchases the property for the Comte de Toulouse
1737–83	Duc de Penthièvre inherits Rambouillet and begins the English Park
1783–90	Louis XVI owns the property
1800–1815	Napoléon I owns the estate
1815–30	Louis XVIII and Charles X own the estate
1830–70	Various owners and uses, including an orphanage and a restaurant
1870	Becomes domain of the State and the president's summer residence

Further Reading

Adams, William Howard, *The French Garden: 1500–1800*, London: Scolar Press, and New York: Braziller, 1979

Arneville, Marie Blanche d', *Parcs et jardins sous le premier émpire: Reflets d'une société*, Paris: Tallandier, 1981

Biver, Marie-Louise, *Pierre Fontaine: Premier architecte de l'émpéreur*, Paris: Éditions d'Histoire et d'Art, 1964

Bottineau, Yves, *Le château de Rambouillet*, Paris: Caisse Nationale des Monuments Historiques, 1980

Guerrini, Maurice, *Napoléon et Paris: Trente ans d'histoire*, Paris: Téqui, 1967; as *Napoleon and Paris: Thirty Years of History*, translated by Margery Weiner, London: Cassell, and New York: Walker, 1970

Hautecoeur, Louis, *Histoire de l'architecture classique en France*, 7 vols., Paris: Picard, 1948–57; see especially vol. 5, *Revolution et empire*, 1953

Miltoun, Francis, *Royal Palaces and Parks of France*, Boston: Page, 1910

Nicot, Guy, *Le château de Rambouillet*, Paris: Nouvelles Éditions Latines, 1974

Péan, Prosper, *Jardins de France*, 2 vols., Paris: Vincent, 1925; see especially vol. 2

CONSTANCE A. WEBSTER

Rastrelli, Bartolomeo Francesco 1700–1771

Italian Architect

Bartolomeo (elsewhere Bartolommeo) Francesco (Varfolomei Varfolomeevich) Rastrelli was the main exponent of the so-called Petersburg baroque, also known as Rastrellian baroque, one of the most evident elements of the Romanov dynasty's vision of St. Petersburg as an imperial capital. From the time of its foundation, brought about by Peter the Great in 1703, St. Petersburg experienced moments of magnificence alternating with periods of decline and neglect, days of grandeur and times of poverty, to be followed again by resurrection. Rastrelli was a leading light in one of the most important periods of this Russian city located on the Neva River delta. After the death of Peter the Great in 1725, and of his widow, Catherine I (r. 1725–27), St. Petersburg faced a turbulent half-century that witnessed the capital's return to Moscow under Peter the Great's grandson Peter II (r. 1727–30). St. Petersburg was restored as the capital by Anna (Peter the Great's niece, who reigned for ten years), but it was during the reign of Peter the Great's daughter Elisabeth (r. 1741–62) that St. Petersburg was embellished with its famous baroque masterpieces, of which Rastrelli was one of the prominent creators.

Rastrelli arrived in Russia from France in 1716 with his father Bartolomeo Carlo, a sculptor and occasional architect. His father's family was Italian, probably from Veneto (other sources say Tuscany). He studied in Paris, but this circumstance, as with other facts of his life before the St. Petersburg period, is extremely uncertain. His first renowned architectural works date to the 1730s. During this period he designed buildings in Latvia (the most significant are the Biron Palaces at Rundale and at Jelgava). In the next two decades, when Rastrelli became a chief architect and supervisor of civil and religious buildings for St. Petersburg, commissioned primarily by Elisabeth, he achieved fame by defining the characters of his personal baroque view, which permeated St. Petersburg and reached other parts of the Russian Empire.

The sources of Rastrelli's style are as uncertain as his education. His father, a sculptor who made a statue of *Peter the Great* in St. Petersburg among other sculptures, probably sent him to Europe at the age of 25 to make a sort of grand tour. He visited Italy for the first time only in 1762, at the end of his career, with a pension from Catherine II (r. 1762–96), and again in 1768. Evidently, his knowledge of Italian and European architecture, widely visible in his works, could not have derived totally from personal contacts with historical and contemporary buildings. More probably, he was directly or indirectly inspired and educated from a scrupulous and talented observation of prints, engravings, illustrated books, and drawings. Other sources included meetings with the many Russian- and European-trained architects who collaborated with the Romanov court in St. Petersburg at that time.

Rastrelli's limited knowledge of historical architecture, particularly that of the Italian baroque and French rococo, stupefies some critics of his works. Cesare Brandi describes him as more embedded in the Italian tradition than in the middle European one. Rastrelli seemed more influenced by what was built in Italy than in France, Saxony, Bavaria, or Vienna. Rastrelli had a remarkable ability to learn lessons from the Roman baroque architecture of Francesco Borromini, Carlo Rainaldi, and other baroque architects of the 17th century. Another influence was Filippo Juvarra, creator of the Stupinigi Palace in Turin and the Real Palace in Madrid. French rococo is another visible component of Rastrelli's language. He selectively applied its formal dictionary, adapting it to his personal and independent view. Other influences derived from the mannerism of

Giovanni Antonio Viscardi, the Swiss architect who mostly worked in Bavaria where his famous Mariahilfkirche in Freystadt, reproduced in a well-known engraving in 1708, surely inspired Rastrelli for the Smol'nyi monastery (1748–64). Viscardi's attitude toward scenography, which was typical of other European court architects of that time and of the previous century, emerges in a composed and controlled way in Rastrelli. It is evident in many of Rastrelli's works that he managed the exterior with great ability, enlivening the presentation of the facades, rather than the interiors, which are often disappointingly flat compared to the external space.

Petrodvorets (Peter's Palace), formerly known as Peterhof, is a huge palace-and-park complex situated 18 miles (29 km) outside St. Petersburg. Peter the Great personally chose the site when he saw it for the first time in 1705. His idea was to use the natural features of the terrain for the garden layout (the Lower and the Upper Gardens) and buildings; he wanted to link into a unique landscape different built elements with the sea and the parks. In 1710 a small wooden palace was erected. The construction of the ensemble started four years later, when the building of the Palace of Monplasir began simultaneously with that of the Upper Mansion. This great effort was due initially to the participation of several architects from Germany (Johann-Friedrich Braunstein), France (Jean-Baptiste Alexandre Le Blond), and Italy (Niccolò Michetti). To follow the Romanov grandeur there were also engaged a hydraulic engineer from Russia (Vasily Tuvolkov), a garden designer from Holland (Leonard van Harnigfelt, who played a major role in the landscaping), sculptors (including Rastrelli's father), painters, wood-carvers, and fountain builders. Rastrelli worked at Peterhof beginning in the 1740s. His most significant work was the extension of Peter's Upper Mansion and the conversion of the Great Palace. Between 1745 and the mid-1760s he constructed two trellis summerhouses, a brick building close to Monplasir for the Empress Elisabeth (now known as Catherine House), and the new Roman Fountains. He contributed to the enhancement of the Upper Gardens, widening them to match the altered facade of the Great Palace and building a monumental railing broken by the main gate.

Tsarskoye Selo (Tsar's village), now named Puskin after the Russian poet, is another palace and park complex; its construction began in the 1720s and continued uninterrupted for more than 150 years. Located 15 miles (24 km) south of St. Petersburg, the palace hosted the court during the summer. During Elisabeth's reign many of the existing palaces were substantially reconstructed, first under the direction of Mikhail Zemtsov and other Russian architects and then under the supervision of Rastrelli. In 1751 Rastrelli integrated the separate architectures into a solid block. The decorative scheme gave an astonishing appearance to the Catherine Palace, with white columns set off by the sky blue of the walls and gilded stucco decors.

The Winter Palace (1754–62), now known as the Hermitage, represents both the apotheosis and the end of Rastrelli's predominance on Russian architecture. In 1761 a project of Rastrelli for the St. Petersburg market was rejected. The influence of the new Academy of Fine Arts, founded in 1759 and oriented to neoclassical architecture, definitively ousted Rastrelli and the baroque during the reign of Catherine II.

See also Petrodvorets; Summer Garden

Biography
Born in Paris, 1700. Received first education in France; moved to Russia in 1716 with father, sculptor Carlo Bartolomeo Rastrelli, who worked at French court; sent on grand tour to Europe (but not Italy) by father, ca. 1725; designed buildings in Latvia, 1730s; became court architect at Romanov court, Russia, 1736; under Empress Elizabeth of Russia became one of chief architects for all imperial projects, 1741–62; also designed many private palaces and mansions in St. Petersburg; sent by Catherine II to Italy for medical treatment, 1762; left royal service and was given pension, ca. 1763; traveled to Latvia, Italy, and Germany, 1764–70; elected honorary member of Academy of Fine Arts, St. Petersburg, 1771. Died in St. Petersburg, Russia, 1771.

Selected Designs

1721–27	Cantemir Palace, on Neva river, Russia
1736–40	Biron Palace, Rundale, Latvia
1738–40	Biron Palace, Mitau (now Jelgava), Latvia
1744–46; 1749–56	Hermitage Pavilion, Catherine's Park, Tsarskoye Selo (now Pushkin), St. Petersburg Oblast, Russia (with Mikhail Zemstov)
1745–mid 1760s	Peterhof, St. Petersburg Oblast, Russia
1748–57	St. Andrew church, Kiev, Russia
1748–64	Smol'nyi monastery (or Voskresenkij Novodevicij), St. Petersburg, Russia
1749–58	Voroncov Palace, St. Petersburg, Russia
1749–61	Grotto Pavilion (Morning Hall), Catherine's Park, Tsarskoye Selo (now Puskin), St. Petersburg Oblast, Russia

1750s	Interiors, Catherine Palace, Tsarskoye Selo (now Puskin), St. Petersburg Oblast, Russia
1752–54	Stroganov Palace, St. Petersburg, Russia
1752–56	Catherine Palace, Tsarskoye Selo (now Puskin), St. Petersburg Oblast, Russia
1754–62	Winter Palace (now the Hermitage), St. Petersburg, Russia
1755–60	Parterres (with Bernhard Fock), Lower Park, Peterhof, St. Petersburg Oblast, Russia

Further Reading

Belyakova, Zoia, *The Romanov Legacy: The Palaces of St. Petersburg*, New York: Viking Studio Books, 1994

Brandi, Cesare, "Rastrelli, Quarenghi e Rossi a Leningrado," in *Struttura e architettura*, edited by Cesare Brandi, Turin, Italy: Einaudi, 1967

Cuppini, Giampiero, editor, *Gli architetti italiani a San Pietroburgo*, Bologna, Italy: Grafis, 1996

Gubanov, Gennady, and Leonid Zykov, *Leningrad: Iskusstvo i arkhitektura*, Leningrad: Izd-vo "Avrora," 1985; as *Leningrad: Art and Architecture*, translated by William Freeman, Yury Nemetsky, and Bella Vlader, Leningrad: Aurora Art, 1990

Kennett, Audrey, *The Palaces of Leningrad*, London: Thames and Hudson, 1973

Lemus, V.V., *Pushkin: Palaces and Parks*, Leningrad: Aurora Art, 1984

Malinovskii, Konstantin, *Architetti italiani a San Pietroburgo, e l'edificazione della città nel Settecento*, Milan: Edizioni il Polifilo, 1996

Raskin, Abram, *Petrodvorets (Peterhof): Palaces and Pavillions, Gardens and Parks, Fountains and Cascades, Sculptures*, Leningrad: Aurora Art, 1978

Shvidkovskii, D.O., *St. Petersburg: Architecture of the Tsars*, New York: Abbeville Press, 1996

DANILO PALAZZO

Real Alcázar, Seville. *See* Seville, Real Alcázar

Red Fort

Delhi, India

Location: in Old Delhi, approximately 4 miles (6.5 km) northeast of the Presidential Residence in New Delhi

Delhi, with its historical and geographical eminence spanning 3,000 years, has been home to seven major cities. Situated between the Aravalli Hills and the Jumna River, it falls along specific strategic routes. Of all these cities, the most prominent was Shahjahanabad, designed and constructed by Emperor Shah Jahan, after he decided to shift the capital from Akbar's Fatehpur Sikri. At the east end of the principal axis and an important commercial thoroughfare called Chandni Chowk lies the Red Fort, or Lal Quila, as it is locally called. This prominent massive red sandstone structure remains the primary landmark of the capital city of India.

Delhi, with its turbulent history, has not spared the Red Fort. Situated in less picturesque settings than its Agra counterpart, its palaces and gardens have suffered extensive damage. Ample areas have been carefully restored, with portions of the fort housing army garrisons.

An irregular octagon in plan, the Red Fort was designed on the concept of a great water palace. At the northeast corner a marble chute drew water from the river into a scalloped basin. It contained several gardens, interlacing palaces, and public courts with a network of water channels. The water drawn into the Shah Bagh, the pavilion housing the water chute, then flowed into the palace buildings along the river edge of the fort and other chambers, courtyards, and gardens in the form of cascades, fountains, pools, and waterfalls. Thus water formed an important component of the gardens here.

Red Fort, Old Delhi
Copyright Johann Scheibner/Das Fotoarchiv

The largest of the gardens are to the north of the fort campus. They are the Hayat Bakhsh Bagh (Life-Giving Garden) and the Mahtab Bagh (Moonlight Garden). Although *bagh* essentially means garden, the paramountcy of water as a landscape element is evident through the naming of the pavilion commanding the river bank housing the water chute as Shah Bagh. The pavilion was meant to protect the fort's only source of this life sustaining element.

The Red Fort is accessible through two imperialistic gateways—the Lahore Gate on the west face and the Delhi Gate at the southeast corner. The Lahore Gate leads to the Chatta Chowk, a vaulted arcade flanked by 32 enclosures serving as the noble bazaar. This leads to a square proceeding to the Nakkar, or Naubhat Khana, a musical hall measuring 30 by 24 meters (33 by 26.4 yd.) and approached through a finely carved sandstone dado gateway. Music was played here five times a day during

Namaaz (daily ritual prayer). Farther beyond lies the Diwan-i-Am, or Hall of Public Audience. It stands on an elevated plinth, its interiors originally covered with ivory polished limestone. The Diwan-i-Am led to the Imtiaz Mahal, one of the private palace quarters, enclosing a garden court for the women. A gate on its northern side led to the Diwan-i-Khas, or Hall of Private Audience, which seated the emperor on the famed and precious Peacock Throne. The interiors are similar to the Diwan-i-Am, divided into square or oblong spaces by intersecting arcades of arches, except that massive piers replace smaller ones to support the arches, thus reflecting its hierarchy. North of the Diwan-i-Khas lie the royal baths, or *hammams*, with three principal chambers. Floors and dado throughout the bath area were of marble inlaid with floral patterns of multicolored stones. A hot vapor bath was provided in the bath while the dressing room to the east contained a fountain that sprayed rose-scented water.

To the west of the baths lies the Moti Masjid, or Pearl Mosque, constructed by Emperor Aurangzeb, Shah Jahan's successor in 1662, for his personal use and for the ladies of the zenana. To the south of the Diwan-i-Khas lies the Khass Mahal (1639–48), housing the royal residential quarters. It consists of three chambers—the Khwabgah, or Sleeping Room, the Tasbih Khanah, or Private Chapel, and the Baithak, or Sitting Room. Farther south is the Rang Mahal, the main building of the royal zenana, which is now used as the mess gall of the army officers stationed at the fort.

This conglomeration of arcades and palace quarters culminates in the royal palace gardens to the north of the Diwan-i-Khas. The imperial gardens and pavilions offered the royal family total seclusion from the public world. Only the most privileged ambassadors, foreign princes, and favorite guests were allowed entry. These gardens formed two separate enclosures treated as one design format.

The larger garden, the Hayat Bakhsh Bagh, is situated at a level 1.5 meters (1.6 yd.) below the private apartments from where the water flows down to serve the garden. It is a courtyard approximately 18 meters square (21.5 sq. yd.)(originally 46 meters square [55 sq. yd.]), with the Shah Burj bastion at the northeast corner. This garden was laid on the square chahar-bagh principle and consisted of a broad central platform with fountains and cross bridges, flower beds, and walkways. Only the central pavilion and basin remain of the garden. The center was occupied by a large bathing tank with a baradari (fountain pavilion) surrounded by fountains in its midst. Four canals radiated from this reservoir, two of them being filled at their far ends by streams running in through two charming little marble pavilions. These pavilions, the Bhadon and Sawan, are so called because the sheets of water flowing over lighted recesses suggested showers and lightning of the monsoon. Water cascaded over chini-khanas (niches) that were decorated with flower-filled gold and silver vases during the daytime, replaced with wax candles and scented flowers at night. Along the terrace walk on the ramparts ran a water parterre, with a fountain in each of its little beds.

The Mahtab Bagh, originally the same length as the Hayat Bakhsh and approximately 91 meters (100 yd.) wide, no longer exists. It was originally planted with pale flowers such as lilies, narcissus, and jasmine.

The trees found in the garden were cypress, sycamore, mulberry, and almond. Fruit trees included peach, plum, mango, and cherry.

The Red Fort was witness to the decline of the Mogul Empire; it was the final large-scale project commissioned. No contemporary Mogul garden manual has been found, resulting in a lack of knowledge concerning their nomenclature, dimensions, and proportions. Even the Bayaz-i-Khwushbu (The Sweet-Smelling Notebook), an unpublished early household manual from the Shah Jahan period, concerns itself entirely with architecture, dimensions, and ratios and does not mention a single flower or tree.

Synopsis

1638	Mogul Emperor Shah Jahan decides to shift empire's capital back to Delhi from Fatehpur Sikri and creates designs for city of Shahjahanabad (now Old Delhi)
1639–48	Shah Jahan constructs Red Fort
1659–62	Moti Masjid (Pearl Mosque) built by Mogul Emperor Aurangzeb
1739	Peacock Throne seized by Persian invader, Nadir Shah
1857	Rang Mahal defaced
1909	Diwan-i-Am restored by British viceroy Lord Curzon
2000	Red Fort restored and became in part housing for contingents of Indian Army

Further Reading

Brown, Percy, Indian Architecture, vol. 1, The Islamic Period, Bombay: Taraporevala, 1942

Edwardes, Michael, Indian Temples and Palaces, London: Hamlyn, 1969

Fanshawe, Herbert Charles, Delhi Past and Present, London: Murray, 1902; reprint, as Shah Jahans' Delhi: Past and Present, Delhi: Sumit, 1979

Gascoigne, Bamber, The Great Moghuls, London: Cape, and New York: Harper and Row, 1971

Hambly, Gavin, Cities of Mughal India: Delhi Agra and Fatehpur Sikri, London: Elek, and New York: Putnam, 1968

Lehrman, Jonas Benzion, Earthly Paradise: Garden and Courtyard in Islam, London: Thames and Hudson, and Berkeley: University of California Press, 1980

Mehta, Rustam Jehangir, Masterpieces of Indo-Islamic Architecture, Bombay: Taraporevala, 1976

Mitchell, George, and Philip Davies, The Penguin Guide to the Monuments of India, 2 vols., London: Penguin, and New York: Viking Press, 1989; see especially vol. 2, Islamic, Rajput, and European, by Davies

Moore, Charles Willard, The Poetics of Gardens, Cambridge, Massachusetts: MIT Press, 1988

Nath, R., Shah Jahan, New Dehli: Abhinav, 1985

Peterson, Andrews, Dictionary of Islamic Architecture, London and New York: Routledge, 1996

Petruccioli, Attilio, editor, Gardens in the Time of the Great Muslim Empires: Theory and Design, Leiden, The Netherlands, and New York: Brill, 1997

Smith, Edmund, W., *Moghul Architecture of Fathpur-Sikri*, 4 vols., Allahabad, India, 1894; reprint, Dehli: Caxton, 1985

Toy, Sidney, *The Fortified Cities of India*, London: Heinemann, 1965

Villiers-Stuart, Constance Mary, *Gardens of the Great Mughals*, London: Black, 1913; reprint, New Delhi: Cosmo, 1983

KARTIK RAM GANAPATHY

Regency Gardening

Regency gardening brought about a revived interest in horticulture in England. It took its name from the Regency period in British history, usually calculated as roughly 1810–20, when George, prince of Wales, oldest son of George III, was designated prince regent of England due to his father's increasing bouts of insanity and poryphria. As regent and then as George IV (r. 1820–30), the prince was a compulsive builder, altering and remodeling a series of palaces, houses, and gardens, including parts of Carlton House, Brighton Pavilion, Windsor's Royal Lodge (in the first phase), and Buckingham Palace. Not since Charles I had there been a king in whom exquisite taste and refined connoisseurship combined so potently. His passions, in order of importance, were building, interior decoration, and gardens, which although rarely innovative were highly fashionable.

George's garden making was dominated by two people, the architect John Nash, the person most closely associated with the style of Regency England, and William Townsend Aiton, the royal gardener. Nash was a partner of Humphry Repton, the exponent of garden design during the late 18th century who transformed the estates of the landed gentry into a series of Romantic pictures. Nash ended his partnership with Repton in 1802, but the latter continued to do projects for the prince regent. With Nash, Aiton carried out what became one of the prince's most lasting memorials, Regent's Park, London, once part of the Royal Chase but mostly fields and pastures prior to 1811. Nash redesigned it as an elaborate architectural complex embracing a park with buildings in the form of villas and surrounding terraces. He also laid out parts of Carlton House, Brighton Pavilion, Windsor's Royal Lodge (the first phase), Kensington Palace, and Buckingham Palace. Nash was director of the Royal Botanic Gardens, Kew, in Surrey, and was one of the founders of the Royal Horticultural Society.

The first meeting of the Royal Horticultural Society was held at Hatchard's bookshop in Piccadilly in 1804 for "the improvement of horticulture." The seven founders consisted of four amateur and three professional gardeners, a combination still reflected in its membership, which is currently about 92,000. The main activities of the society, which became "Royal" in 1861, were in the pursuit of better horticulture and included shows, demonstrations, education, and publications. At the first modest meetings of members, papers were read and plants exhibited. The society's first garden was obtained in 1818, expressly to grow and propagate new fruits and vegetables and to grow a collection of garden plants from China. A second, much larger garden was purchased in 1821 in Chiswick, where there was more room for the trials and collections of exotic plants. Between 1820 and 1825 six young men were sent to the Far East, North and South America, and Africa to collect new plants for the society. Its first publication was an irregular periodical that started soon after the society was established.

During the Regency period cottages ornes became quite fashionable. These small, usually asymmetrically designed buildings contained elaborate rustic elements, such as decorated weatherboarding. They were used as a feature in a park, as a lodge, or for housing, an architectural expression of the upper classes for the "simple life." The accent was on the interaction of house and garden with flower-filled conservatories and creeper-covered veranda columns in the manner of Endsleigh, Devon, England, which was designed by Repton. The precedent for the Regency picturesque shrub plantations and island beds had been set by William Mason, English poet and landscape gardener, at Nuneham Park, Oxfordshire, England, to which Mason claimed he brought both "Poet's Feeling and Painter's Eye." Nuneham's enclosed garden, a rare feature in the 18th century, was based on Julie's garden in Rousseau's novel *Julie; ou, La nouvelle Héloïse* (1761; *Julie; or, The New Heloise*). Mount Edgcumbe, Cornwall, England, with one of the most beautiful sites in Great Britain (with Dartmoor in one direction, Plymouth in another, and the sea visible in a third), displayed an interesting juxtaposition of a French parterre garden, an Italian garden with fountain and stairway, and an informal English flower garden along with landscaped gardens enclosed not by walls but by natural flowing shrubberies.

Henry Phillips used the term *Sylva Florifera* in his book of the same name (1823) to describe the type of planting seen at Mount Edgcumbe, which was viewed as a natural development from Picturesque landscape gardening, an 18th-century trend strongly influenced by the idea of making landscapes in the manner of pictures, in particular the drawings of Claude Lorrain and Gaspar Poussin, with flowers being "amenable to the rules of composition," according to William S. Gilpin. Picturesque shrub plantations drew inspiration from scenery observed in the New Forest by Gilpin, who found "frequent tufts of sweetbriar, box or thorn steal on the greensward" of the forest lawns breaking the spaces into a "mossy maze," according to Mason. Shrubberies with serpentine paths and mixed flower and shrub plantations were particularly suitable for perambulations in public parks and were extensively used by Nash in his metropolitan schemes and in his designs for the Royal Pavilion. Scotney Castle, Kent, England, is an outstanding example of the late Regency Picturesque; the new house and the design of its grounds were created at the same time with a site that created eastward views over a wide pastoral valley.

Perhaps the most enduring monument to Regency gardening is the exotic Royal Pavilion, Brighton, East Sussex, England, which was built for the prince regent beginning in 1787 and based on Nash's ideas on landscape gardening. Nash was influenced by his former partner Repton, whose proposals were rejected but published in 1808. The limited size of the pavilion grounds allowed the landscape style to be adopted to the growing taste for floriculture. Nash's overall plan allowed for paths and shaped shrubberies and beds while Aiton, superintendent of the Royal Botanic Gardens, Kew, which received plants from China, the Cape, and Australia, provided the planting lists. The gardens were arranged in the Picturesque style, with irregular beds, thick set with evergreens, flowering shrubs, climbers, roses, and herbaceous plants such as foxgloves and delphiniums, and they are lasting testament to the Regency passion for a profusion of flowers.

Further Reading

Hyams, Edward, *Capability Brown and Humphry Repton,* London: Dent, and New York: Scribner, 1971
Strong, Roy C., *Royal Gardens,* New York: Pocket Books, 1992

MARTIN J. MANNING

Reggia di Caserta, La. *See* Caserta, La Reggia di

Reistad, Karen 1900–1994

Norwegian Landscape Architect

Karen Reistad was one of the most influential landscape architects in Norway. She designed numerous private gardens, cemeteries, hospital areas, residential areas, and playgrounds in the pioneering age of the profession. She was also a writer and critic, a founder and leader of landscape architecture organizations of great importance, and a teacher at the department of landscape architecture at the Agricultural University of Norway. Her most important contribution is in the field of cemetery design. She was the first National Cemetery Consultant (from 1945 to 1970). Her style has been named "poetic functionalism"; it is characterized by a careful use of earth form, vegetation, and sometimes water, and an almost seamless transition from the designed to the natural.

Reistad was born and raised on a small farmstead near Hamar, Norway. Her main interest was drawing and painting, and she decided to become a garden architect at a very early age. She studied at the Oslo School of Fine Arts (1917–21) and in 1923 graduated from the State Gardening College in Oslo. She studied at the Hoheren Lehranstalt für Gartenkunst in Dahlem, Berlin, from 1923 to 1925. She claimed that her choice not to study at the then newly established Department of

Soviet War Cemetery, Tjøtta, Norway, designed by Karen Reistad
Copyright Karsten Jørgensen

Garden Art at the Agricultural University of Norway was a deliberate one: she disliked agriculture and felt secure that the profession she was about to enter belonged to the fine arts. She kept up her painting all her life and held several exhibitions.

Reistad worked for the parks department of Aker municipality from 1925 to 1942 (in 1948 Aker became a part of Oslo). She designed several cemeteries and cemetery extensions during this period: Høybråten, Nordstrand, Bekkelaget, Grorud, and Ullern. At the same time she worked as a private consultant designing gardens for the rapidly growing number of one-family houses in the Oslo area. She established her own studio in 1942, and after that many private gardens, cemeteries, hospital areas, residential areas, sports fields, urban parks, and squares in virtually all parts of Norway came from her hand.

A columnist for the magazine *Vi selv og våre hjem* in the 1930s and editor of the journal *Form og Flora* in 1937–38, Reistad also published articles in *Byggekunst, The Norwegian Review of Architecture, Hagetidend, Havekunst,* and *Kirkegårdskultur* throughout her career. She was an active member of the Norwegian Association of Landscape Architects from its establishment in 1929, both as director, secretary general, and professional editor. In 1945 she was appointed as the first National Cemetery Consultant, a position she held until her retirement in 1970. From 1953 to 1970 she was responsible for the teaching of cemetery design at the department of landscape architecture at the Agricultural University of Norway. In 1966 she initiated the establishment of the National Association of Cemetery Culture and became the first director of this organization. In 1971 she received the golden royal honorary medal for her contribution to Norwegian landscape and cemetery culture.

Both in her projects and her published lectures and articles, Reistad presents a subtle kind of functionalism in landscape architecture. The gardens, parks, and cemeteries foremost invite the people to use them, and they are able to endure a proper use. But in all her designs there is also an underlying poetic tension that gives each project a special value. At, for example, the central hospital in Akershus County at Lørenskog (1962–64), there is an apparently seamless connection between the strictly designed areas close to the house and the natural surroundings. In addition, many of her private gardens have this kind of silent obviousness and simplicity. In Askim Folkepark (1954; People's Park in Askim) she integrated meadows, sports fields, a sculpture garden, a central area with a pond, and two amphitheaters in a natural-looking forest with meandering footpaths.

Reistad's most important works are in the field of cemeteries, especially the many war cemeteries for which she was responsible in the late 1940s and early 1950s. She designed many Russian war cemeteries; the largest one, from 1953, is situated in Tjøtta, Nordland, where many of the more than 8,000 Russian soldiers killed in Norway during World War II are buried. The plan is extremely simple—two divisions symmetrically on each side of the main axis, one with small plates in the grass with the names and dates, the other with anonymous graves. The axis rises from the main entrance toward a tall monument at the highest point. Outside the stone walls the axis continues as a treeless area all the way down to the coast, as a vista from the shipping lane to the monument. Inside the cemetery there is a fringe of a few small native birch trees scattered around. In this way she relates her design to the impressiveness of nature with its shifting seasons.

In 1970 another war cemetery was consecrated at Tjøtta, just next to the Russian one. Reistad was asked to design a new international war cemetery, for the 2,500 who drowned in one of the largest ship disasters in the world, which happened in 1944. A German prisoner-of-war ship, Riegel, was bombed by the British Air Force in the narrow inlet between Tjøtta and the nearest island. The bodies were not rescued until the late 1960s. Here Reistad used some of the same elements, but this cemetery is in a sense more isolated. There are more trees, and the graves are placed in a sunken rotunda, like an old ship's grave. From the outside, the walls are identical with those surrounding the Russian cemetery. Seen from the inside they are formed as grass-covered slopes, planted with the same kind of trees, almost like a modern version of the ha-ha from the English landscape garden. The result is peaceful isolation, and at the same time there is contact with the sky and far mountains through a transparent curtain of low birch trees.

The two cemeteries today form a harmonious whole and together show the strength of Reistad's design: the interplay between clear and functional simplicity and the nature of the Norwegian landscape—in effect the Norwegian version of Mies van der Rohe's "less is more."

Biography

Born 1900. Raised on small farmstead near Hamar, Norway; studied at Oslo School of Fine Arts, Oslo, Norway, 1917–21; graduated from State Gardeners College, Oslo, 1923; studied at Hoheren Lehranstalt für Gartenkunst, Dahlem, Berlin, Germany, 1923–25; worked for parks department of Aker municipality, Norway, 1925–42; established own studio, 1942; appointed first National Cemetery Consultant, 1945, a position she held until retirement in 1970; responsible for teaching cemetery design in department of landscape architecture, Agricultural University of Norway, Ås, 1953–70; initiated establishment of National Association of Cemetery Culture, in 1966, and became first director. Died 1994.

Selected Designs

1952	Soviet War Cemetery, Vestre Gravlund, Oslo, Norway
1953	Soviet War Cemetery, Tjøtta, Nordland, Norway
1954	Lovisenberg Hospital, Oslo, Norway
1954	Peoples Park, Askim, Østfold, Norway
1954	Lillestrom Torg (central plaza), Lillestrom, Akershus, Norway
1958	Egenes Cemetery, Stavanger, Rogaland, Norway
1959	Eidsvoldsbygningen, Eidsvoll, Norway
1962–64	Central hospital, Lorenskog, Akershus, Norway
1965	Kråkerøy Cemetery, Fredrikstad, Norway
1965	Student residential areas, Kringsjå and Sogn, Oslo, Norway
1969	International War Cemetery Tjøtta, Nordland, Norway
1958–72	Modum Bad Nerve Sanatorium, Vikersund, Norway

Selected Publications

"Almindelige regler ved anlegg av hage," *Form og Flora* (1937)

"Privathage i Nordbergveien," *Form og Flora* (1937)

"Frokost på solterrassen," *Hus og hage* 1 (1950)

"Bedriftshage i Oslo," *Havekunst* 32 (1951)

"Kirkegården," *Havekunst* 45 (1964)

Om gravplasser og kirkegårder, 1970

"Kirkegårdskultur - kirkegårdskonsulent i Norge," *Landskap* 52 (1971)

"Krigsgravplasser på Tjøtta i Nordland," *Kirkegårdskultur* 1 (1973)

Planlegging av gravplasser - historisk oversikt, 1977

Further Reading
Jørgensen, Karsten, "Karen Reistad: Grand Old Lady i norsk landskapsarkitektur," *Byggekunst* 2 (1986)

Jørgensen, Karsten, "Equality and the Modern Way of Death," *Topos: European Landscape Magazine* 2 (1993)

KARSTEN JØRGENSEN

Religion, Garden in

At a fundamental level the "garden in religion" must have religious content or meaning. Such gardens may exist autonomously. More often, they are found as part of many types of religious architecture, including temples and shrines, halls of congregational worship, monasteries, tombs, and cemeteries. Traditionally, even so-called secular architecture such as palaces and houses may contain gardens with ritual or sacred aspects. With or without accompanying religious buildings, a garden, or natural elements such as rocks, mountains, springs, or groves, may be associated with a theophany or the proximity of spirits. Yet in a broader sense such auspicious places are evidence not simply of numinous presence but of a world of divine invention and sustenance.

The prevalence of a garden in the foundation accounts of diverse cultures attests to it as a manifestation of the primary ground of the divine, and whether regarded as eternal or created, it is archetypal. Human beings can be regarded as fully integrated with, and part of, nature; yet the natural world is also the vessel for all human endeavor. In the Greek coupling of *physis* (nature) and *nomos* (law or convention, i.e., culture), there is a reciprocity that expresses a basic continuity between humans and the natural world that varies according to specific cultural and religious interpretations. Only in modern secular thinking is there the attempt to polarize and oppose nature and artifice.

The garden as a temporal creation represents humanity's encounter with nature, always incorporating some level of human fabrication, as in the paradigmatic Genesis account where expulsion from Eden requires that Adam begin to cultivate the land. Thus, although many creation myths focus on a natural event or element, such as the monolith Uluru (Ayer's Rock in Australia), believed by the Aborigines to be a trace left by mythic ancestors, we may in a more specific sense understand the garden in religion not as an aspect of sacred nature found but as that which is in some way designed and made by human hand to mimetically represent the transcendent.

Gardens may act as settings for rituals and carry meanings particular to each faith. These vary tremendously: for example, the tea ceremony in the Zen Buddhist gardens of Japan, pilgrimage to Christian gardens that mark scriptural events, the naming of Confucian scholars' gardens, and funerary practices at Islamic garden tombs. Generally speaking, Western gardens that stem from Arcadian and Edenic utopian traditions may be contrasted to the gardens of China and Japan that are devoted to the ongoing reconciliation of the individual within the cosmos. Despite major differences, however, certain key areas overlap and common themes occur; these include the cosmological, paradisiacal, temporal/regenerative, and dialectical.

Traditionally, the garden was understood to embody order within wider chaos. This normally entails some sort of domain or demarcation, and in many religions the garden is regarded both as retreat and as world. As a living cosmos it is represented in remarkably different ways. Symbolism of the cosmos in a fourfold division of the land is found in the premonotheistic gardens of the Near East and Persia; it is an image well known from the narrative of the four rivers of Eden in the Hebrew Bible. The fourfold is commonly manifested in both Christian and Islamic gardens: monastic cloisters represent, in a nature/culture reformulation, the city and garden of the book of Revelation's Heavenly Jerusalem; in Islam the quadripartite garden, known as a *chaharbagh*, is associated with Paradise and Judgment. Life-giving, purifying water normally marks the center point and source of a cross-shaped plan; in practice a fountain or pool at the intersection of two channels structures the garden symmetrically into four planted beds. In many religions reciprocity between the source or center and its dispersion or periphery is a widespread and enduring cosmic theme; elements such as a single tree—symbol of celestial phenomena, life, and knowledge—may function as an *axis mundi* (world axis), or in Vedic and Puranic creation accounts, a lotus flower floating on water represents the center of the divine cosmos.

Chinese and Japanese gardens are organized with certain places or points of focus, representing a scaled-down cosmos by the incorporation of distant landscape into the garden in the notion of "borrowed scenery" (in Japanese, *shakkei*, literally "captured alive"). In these gardens remote topographies are represented in miniature: a rock may symbolize a Chinese mountain pilgrimage destination, or a small mound in the middle of a pond may reflect the island aspect of Japan; the principle is summarized in a 16th-century book on gardens called *Ka Senzui No Fu* by Tessen Soki, a Zen priest, who describes the garden of Ryoan-ji in Kyoto as "the art of reducing 30,000 miles to the distance of a single foot." Within the microcosmos of Eastern gardens human beings are present, but their situation varies. The elements of a Daoist garden may be described as existing in mutual deference to each other; through such relationships—dynamic and meandering paths punctuated by gates, pavilions, and views (in the notion of *de* as "focus")—the individual is thrust into creation to live in unity with cosmic laws. On the other hand, the abstracted dry gardens of Zen are viewed with more distance, fostering contemplation in order to escape the world of illusion to find truth.

In such cosmic visions of nature eternity is understood implicitly. But more specifically the notion of paradise as a perpetual and atemporal garden may be found in many religions. Both Virgil's Arcadia and Ovid's Golden Age were lands of everlasting spring; the Hebrew *pardes* (literally, "walled grove," and etymologically related to the Persian *pairidaeza,* from which comes the English word *paradise*) is seen symbolically as a reference to the constancy of divine wisdom; and the Daoist Isles of the Blessed were inhabited by immortals. In designed landscapes there have been attempts to fabricate different kinds of paradise on earth: the medieval Hangchow gardens symbolized the promise of paradise to the virtuous; the early Western botanical gardens were considered Edenic in their attempt to contain every known species of plant. In monotheism paradise takes on eschatological significance. Islam most explicitly promises a garden, the Koranic *djanna,* to the righteous at the end of days. In tomb gardens, such as the Taj Mahal, the dead lie waiting for judgment, with the implication that this paradise on earth is a prefiguration of what is to come.

In reciprocity with their paradisiacal and eternal character, gardens also exhibit constant change. Buddhist and Hindu concerns for the passing of time are reflected in nature, where metamorphosis is constant: quickly in the blossoming and death of flowers, slowly in the gradual erosion of rocks. Decay is ultimately regenerative, leading to a new and fecund season. In ancient Greco-Roman religion gardens were often developed around dark and wet caves or grottoes that were deemed sacred, dedicated to divinities of fertility and water sources or adopted as places of initiation and healing. The primary paradigm of rebirth in Christianity involves the resurrection of the crucified Christ from a cave in a garden at Jerusalem. Christ is known as the "true vine," a regenerative theme reinterpreted from the earlier pagan cult of Dionysius that finds itself repeated throughout Christian theology, art, and thought.

Regenerative decay is a cyclical process incorporating the dialectic of life and death that is found in various ways in many religions. In its life-affirming aspects the garden is often regarded as a place of virtue, yet darker powers are always at hand: Eden is God's creation but also the scene of the fall of humankind. Symbolic meanings attached to plants reflect this double edge: for example, Christianity knows the color and perfume of the rose as a symbol of divine love along with its thorn, which mortifies the flesh. The proximity of evil in the sacred world is explicitly brought into play in the 16th-century Sacra Bosco at Bomarzo in Italy, where the Gates of Hell are depicted as a howling stone jaw in the earth. And perhaps most pervasive in the monotheistic religions, the desert endures as a barren place of temptation, loss of faith, and death—seemingly the opposite of a garden—and yet it functions in many ways as the birthplace of these religions. Rather than the possibility of true nothingness that afflicts modern secular thought, the void is regarded as having inherent potential for creation and life. Such a notion appears in certain minimal gardens from various religions: spare and arid mosque courtyards common throughout much of the Islamic world may recall the latent fertility of the desert and foreshadow a lush paradise; the gravel yard in front of the main hall of Shinto shrines is a purified ground, empty except for a pair of trees.

Dialectic is clear in the Chinese word for "landscape," *shan shui,* two signs meaning "mountain" and "water." The garden was seen to balance the two complementary essences of the world, *yin* (female, passive, dark, water) and *yang* (male, active, sun, mountain); in Japan *in* and *yo* are similar ideas. In the gardens of China and Japan, unseen forces—friendly and unfriendly genies—traditionally reside together in the garden and are incorporated into all aspects, inorganic as well as organic. In the Chinese practice of *feng shui,* or geomancy, the design of gardens focuses on the propitiation of the genies through their proper spiritual embodiment in the water, earth, rocks, and mountains. Unlike in the West, the aim is for coexistence rather than reconciliation.

Further Reading

Comito, Terry, *The Idea of the Garden in the Renaissance,* New Brunswick, New Jersey: Rutgers University Press, 1978

Cooper, J.C., "The Symbolism of the Taoist Garden," *Studies in Comparative Religion* 11, no. 4 (Autumn 1977)

Delumeau, Jean, *Une histoire de paradis,* 3 vols., Paris: Fayard, 1992; as *History of Paradise: The Garden of Eden in Myth and Tradition,* translated by Matthew O'Connell, New York: Continuum, 1995

Eliade, Mircea, *Traité d'histoire des religions*, Paris: Payot, 1949; as *Patterns in Comparative Religion,* translated by Rosemary Sheed, New York: Sheed and Ward, 1958; reprint, Lincoln: University of Nebraska Press, 1996

Gibb, L., "Djanna," in *The Encyclopedia of Islam*, new edition, vol. 2, Leiden: E.J. Brill, 1958

Glacken, Clarence J., *Traces on the Rhodian Shore: Nature and Culture in Western Thought from Ancient Times to the End of the Eighteenth Century*, Berkeley: University of California Press, 1967

Gothein, Marie Luise Schroeter, *Geschichte der Gartenkunst*, Jena, Germany: Diederichs, 1914; 2nd edition, 1926; as *A History of Garden Art*, 2 vols., edited by Walter P. Wright, translated by Mrs. Archer-Hind, London: Dent, and New York: Dutton, 1928; reprint, New York: Hacker Art Books, 1979

Graham, Dorothy, *Chinese Gardens: Gardens of the Contemporary Scene: An Account of Their Design and Symbolism,* New York: Dodd Mead, 1938

Hall, David L., and Roger T. Ames, "The Cosmological Setting of Chinese Gardens," *Studies in the History of Gardens and Designed Landscapes* 18, no. 3 (1998)

Hayakawa, Masao, *Niwa*, Tokyo: Heibonsha, 1967; 2nd edition, 1979; as *The Garden Art of Japan*, translated by Richard L. Gage, New York: Weatherhall, 1973

Isaac, Erich, "The Act and the Covenant: The Impact of Religion on the Landscape," *Landscape* 11 (1961–62)

Isaac, Erich, "God's Acre," *Landscape* 14 (1964–65)

Ito, Teiji, *Koto no dezain shakkei to tsuboniwa*, Tokyo: Tankosha, 1965; as *Space and Illusion in the Japanese Garden,* translated and adapted by Ralph Friedrich and Masajiro Shimamura, New York: Weatherhill, 1973; 2nd edition, 1980

Ito, Teiji, *Nihon no niwa*, Tokyo: Chuo Koronsha, 1971; as *The Japanese Garden: An Approach to Nature*, Tokyo: Zokeisha, and New Haven, Connecticut: Yale University Press, 1972

Keswick, Maggie, *The Chinese Garden: History, Art, and Architecture*, London: Academy Editions, and New York: Rizzoli, 1978

Ledderose, L. "The Earthly Paradise: Religious Elements in Chinese Landscape Art," in *Theories of the Arts in China,* Susan Bush and Christian Murck, editors, Princeton, New Jersey: Princeton University Press, 1983

MacDougall, Elisabeth B., and Richard Ettinghausen, editors, *The Islamic Garden,* Washington, D.C.: Dumbarton Oaks Trustees, 1976

Makeham, John, "The Confucian Role of Names in Traditional Chinese Gardens," *Studies in the History of Gardens and Designed Landscapes* 18, no. 3 (1998)

McLean, Teresa, *Medieval English Gardens,* London: Collins, and New York: Viking Press, 1981

Miller, Naomi, *Heavenly Caves: Reflections on the Garden Grotto*, New York: Braziller, 1982

Moore, Charles Willard, William J. Mitchell, and William Turnbull, Jr., *The Poetics of Gardens,* Cambridge, Massachusetts: MIT Press, 1988

Moynihan, Elizabeth B., *Paradise as a Garden: In Persia and Mughal India,* New York: Braziller, 1979

Pearsall, Derek Albert, and Elizabeth Salter, *Landscapes and Seasons of the Medieval World,* London: Elek, 1973

Prest, John M., *The Garden of Eden: The Botanic Garden and the Re-creation of Paradise,* New Haven, Connecticut: Yale University Press, 1981

Sirén, Osvald, *Gardens of China,* New York: Ronald Press, 1949

Thacker, Christopher, *The History of Gardens,* London: Croom Helm, and Berkeley: University of California Press, 1979

Van der Heide, A., "Pardes: Methodological Reflections on the Theory of the Four Senses," *Journal of Jewish Studies* 34 (1983)

Williams, George Huntston, *Wilderness and Paradise in Christian Thought: The Biblical Experience of the Desert in the History of Christianity and the Paradise Theme in the Theological Idea of the University,* New York: Harper, 1962

WENDY PULLAN

Renaissance Garden Style

The Renaissance garden embodied, among many things, the medieval view of the garden as sacred space. Enclosing the monastic garden on all four sides by walls served to define it as a sacred space, bounding it in such a way that it was a guarantee of integrity, as "virtue's barrier against the wild boar of the world" (Comito). Both the ancient Roman city and the medieval city were also ritually bounded as sacred space in defense of the surrounding wilderness. This is exemplified in the well-known story of Romulus, who murdered his own brother for not honoring the sacred wall of the Roman city. In the description of the nature of the monastic life as virtue's barrier can be heard resonances of the monastic garden itself: the solitude of the cloister life is sacred and distinct from the profanity of life outside. This distinction between potent and powerless space is both literally and symbolically represented in the walls of the garden and monastery, which itself is a self-sufficient community with aspirations toward being a heavenly city on earth.

The medieval monastery garden was best if it was square. Divided into four quadrants, the garden made visible the symbolic structure of the cosmos, representing the four rivers, the four seasons, the four elements, the four humors, the four cardinal virtues, and the four gospels—in other words, "all the co-ordinates of man's physical and spiritual cosmos . . . the inner reality of the world" (Comito). The crossing at the center of the four quadrants marked a sacred space, wherein a fountain or a tree of knowledge was placed. The Renaissance garden incorporated this quartering of space and also recalled the classical precedents of the Roman town planning structure of the primary and secondary cross-axiroads called *Roma Quadrata* and the *Cardo Decumanus*. These roads divided the city into four quarters for both practical (military) purposes and cosmological reasons in line with the north-south and east-west axes, ensuring that the city was in harmony with the gods through the seasons and the four directions, and so on. In this way not only was the garden a microcosm of the city but both the garden and the city were microcosms of the cosmological order of the world.

Many aspects of the medieval garden are embodied implicitly in the Renaissance gardens. At the same time there is a radical departure. The 15th-century architectural theorist Leon Battista Alberti discussed the Italian villa garden as integral to the house in that the spaces of the garden extend from those of the house. Alberti may have been influenced by Plato's analogy of the city as a house: "If men are to have a city wall at all, the private houses should be constructed right from the foundations so that the whole city forms in effect a single wall: . . . A whole city looking like a single house will be quite a pretty sight" (*The Laws*). Following on from this, the citizens would be considered as members of one big family of the city. Alberti not only makes the analogy between the city and the house but broadens it to include outside spaces:

For if a city according to the opinion of philosophers, be no more than a great house, and, on the other hand, a house be a little city; why may it not be said, that the members of that House are so many little houses; such as the court-yard, the hall, the parlour, the portico, and the like?

Given that the Renaissance garden was an extension of the villa (and indeed often upstaged the villa itself), Alberti extended the analogy to include the outside spaces such that the villa and garden were as one. It follows that the rooms of the garden would be equally contributing members as the rooms of the house, which he perceived as the many buildings that make up the fabric of the city. Like Plato's analogy of the city as a single house, here the villa is a little city. Alberti's ideal Renaissance city sounds as much like a garden as it does a city:

A harmonious enclosure separated from the ordered terrestrial world outside, which within it has the principles of nature, philosophy, and intellect, and of God's harmony, order, and wonder clearly revealed to the sight in its design and ornament. . . . [One] is surrounded by the evidence of the harmony of the cosmos provided by the art of the architect. (Westfall)

Influenced by the Roman statesman Pliny the Younger in his condemnation of the trivial business of the city and love for serene repose of the garden as intellectual and physical respite, Alberti associated the real city with vice and the garden with virtue.

Two specific gardens demonstrate these aspects of Renaissance design principles.

Villa Lante

Cardinal Giovan Francesco Gambara's Villa Lante in Bagnaia, designed by Giacomo Barozzi da Vignola and completed in 1578, was influenced by Albertian principles. It is located approximately 50 miles (80.4 km) from Rome and just 3 miles (4.8 km) from Viterbo. Cardinal Gambara exhibited the virtuous qualities of Alberti's ideal citizen, owing to his intellect and his noble, powerful, and famous family from Brescia, which dated back to the tenth century. This 16th-century garden addition to the town of Bagnaia was designed for summer visits by the bishops of Viterbo.

The walls surrounding the grounds of the Villa Lante enclose two distinctly different landscapes: the formal garden and the adjacent hunting park called the *bosco*. The iconographic theme of the garden expresses the relationship between nature and culture as depicted in the allegorical and juxtaposed themes of the Golden Age of Saturn (the *bosco*) and the Age of Jupiter (the formal garden). The natural state of the Golden Age is brought out in the *bosco*, representing a virtuous existence of people who lived in freedom and peace with no laws. The state of nature was not altered by plowing the land, cutting the trees, mining the earth, or slaughtering the animals. They ate what was produced by nature, shared the land, and lived without wars, cities, and other such institutions of civilization. The Age of Jupiter is the age of discovery of the arts, the invention of tools with which to implement the ideas, and the gaining of knowledge that accompanies civilization. Consequently, the "art" of civilization is embodied in the formal garden. The two contrasting landscapes represent the natural state of ideal existence and civilized society, freedom from limitations versus restraints, and instinct and nature versus reason and art (Lazzaro).

The formal garden is composed of a series of five terraces arranged in a linear progression ascending the slope of a hill. The terraces are connected by stairs and ramps bridging the "garden rooms." The water is turgid at the top of the garden, and the vegetation at its most lush. The water and plantings become increasingly calm and formal toward the lower terraces. The grotto, at the top of the formal garden, bridges the two distinct gardens and is a symbol of the transition from chaos to form, an idea that the Renaissance associated with the story of the deluge and its aftermath. Water is a dominant theme and the life source of the garden. It connects each terrace and fountain in a variety of ways, flowing along the central perspectival axis that serves to invite and persuade people into the garden. Alberti speaks of perspective as a persuasive device that can lead people toward a virtuous life. This fits well into the symbolism of the Renaissance garden as ideal city that encourages its inhabitants toward an ideal existence.

From the grotto begins the process of civilization. This is depicted through the gradual introduction of the arts—the decrease of the natural vegetation on the successive terraces—until in the final terrace geometry and symmetry prevail. The water in the grotto bursts forth from the seemingly natural springs of the earth, gradually decreasing in pressure until it culminates in the placid pools of water in the fish ponds of the lowest terrace, where nature is ultimately subdued by art.

The division of the square of this highly formal and geometrically organized space of the final terrace recalls both the monastic garden's cosmological quartering of space and the quartering of the ancient Roman city. Here, the sacred crossing at the center of the quadrants is marked by Gambara's family device (a crayfish), reflecting Renaissance transitions from a God-centered to a human-focused world.

The grotto, the mythological themes, the dramatic representation of the cosmological order embodied in the quartering of space, the perspectival axis, and the transformations of the water and plantings from natural to ordered all express the ideas of nature and culture. What emerges is a theme common to the Renaissance garden and the ideal city: the creation of settings that inspire a virtuous existence. The garden as an ideal city was a stage for the expression of virtue.

The spatial structure of Villa Lante finds its precedent in the Cortile del Belvedere in Rome. In both gardens there is a highly significant plateau at the lowest level with adjacent twin buildings that act as a proscenium backdrop to this primary space and also give definition to the perspectival axis of the garden. The ascending plateaus are common to both gardens, as is the U-shaped architectural configuration at the top, a form marking the ultimate place of arrival.

It is interesting to note, too, that there is a significant urban space in Rome that comprises a similar spatial structure—the principal processional route involving the Piazza del Popolo, the Corso, and the Campidoglio. Entering first through the triumphal arch gate in the ancient city walls, one then moves into the grand entry space of Piazza del Popolo. Initially established in the third century A.D. as the northern entry gate to Rome from the rest of Europe, Piazza del Popolo has a long tradition of ceremonial arrivals deriving from the triumphal entry ceremonies of ancient Rome. This was revived during the Renaissance and baroque periods and was accorded to royal, papal, and political visitations. The entry procession to the Piazza del Popolo contained a clear sense of sequentially ordered ceremony, comprising a procession through layers of gates into the inner sanctum of the heavenly city.

Making one's way across the piazza, the eye is drawn to the perspectival view of the Corso, which persuasively draws the participant into the city. Passing between the twin churches S. Maria di Montesanto and S. Maria dei Miracoli (completed by Bernini in 1679 and designed to reinforce the Renaissance trident), one travels along the ancient processional route into the heart of the city (near the Roman Forum) and ascends up the steps to the Campidoglio. The entrance to the Campidoglio piazza is framed by two literal twins, Castor and Pollux. The Campidoglio piazza is defined by the U-shaped configuration of the senate house and palace. This existing urban topography is less malleable and therefore less ideal than that of the garden, However, it does comprise the spatial structure shared by both the Belvedere and Villa Lante: significant stage at lowest level, perspectival axis, ascension, and U-shaped space at top. In his writings, Alberti allows for less than ideal translations to be made into existing urban conditions. In comparing ideal and actual space, it was much easier to construct the ideas of an ideal city into a garden than into an existing city, as we see at Villa Montalto.

Villa Montalto

The trident extending away from the Piazza del Popolo is a Renaissance invention that was first established there on a grand scale. The three perspectival axes radiating from the Piazza del Popolo persuasively invite people to venture forth along the routes into the depths of the city. The Villa Montalto in Rome incorporated this newly invented Popolo trident into its structure of paths in the garden.

Villa Montalto was designed and built between 1580 and 1590 by Pope Sixtus V and his architect Domenico Fontana. Destroyed in 1888, it was located where the Rome train station, the Termini, now stands. While creating this paradise out on the Esquiline Hill, Sixtus V and Fontana were also carrying out an overly ambitious papal project on the eastern arm of the Popolo trident in the city, which had intriguing structural parallels in the Montalto garden.

Sixtus V became pope following a succession of popes who had been revitalizing the city with design projects of their own. They had all inadvertently set the stage for Sixtus V's subsequent vision of linking all the pilgrimage churches, palaces, monuments, and significant piazzas of the city by the placement of Egyptian obelisks at terminus points of significant axial routes. The location of obelisks created a large-scale urban structure that not only expressed the power of the papacy but also marked the perspectively persuasive invitation through the city toward the principal churches of Christian worship along the pilgrimage procession, including Sixtus V's favorite church, Santa Maria Maggiore. The pilgrimage route represented a dramatic reenactment of the sacred journey of Christian devotion, in this most "heavenly paradise" of Rome (Westfall).

Sixtus V's particular urban enthusiasm was that of connecting the Piazza del Popolo to Santa Maria Maggiore and developing this eastern area of the city, which was near his villa. The pope provided this part of the city with roads and water, thus developing it through large-scale urban design and the revitalization of the ancient aqueduct, the Aqua Felice. Like gardens, fountains were replenishing theatrical celebrations of water as a life-giving substance.

The Montalto garden, located just east of Santa Maria Maggiore, was enclosed in 1587 by walls and six prominent portals. The plan of the Monalto garden included certain elements common to the urban axis upon which the Pope was focusing. This was the Via del Babuino axis of the Piazza del Popolo trident, which extended to the Piazza di Spagna, the Trinita dei Monti, the Quattro Fontane, and Santa Maria Maggiore. Such an immense project could be realized more immediately and ideally in the smaller-scale version of a garden.

The elements from this urban axis that are recalled within the Montalto garden include the Piazza del Popolo, the trident, Santa Maria Maggiore, and the Quattro Fontane, although in a different order. This can be seen in a significant entry piazza and trident that radiates into the garden. The pope's own villa stands on the principal axial route of the trident. Just behind the villa was the circular fountain that was placed at the intersection of the garden's primary and secondary axes, similar to Quattro Fontane's strategic position within the city. The organization of the Montalto garden parallels aspects of the structure and elements of the pope's vision for the city, which proved impossible to make actual in its ideal form.

The primary influences embodied in Roman Renaissance gardens have origins in the philosophy and architecture of the ancients, the symbolic conception of space of the Middle Ages, the early Renaissance treatises for ideal cities, and the use of perspective and theater as political and religious tools of persuasion. The planning of gardens and of cities involved similar underlying principles and structural orders that reinforced the metaphorical relationships between them.

Further Reading

Alberti, Leon Battista, *De re aedificatoria*, Florence, 1485; as *The Architecture of Leon Battista Alberti in Ten Books*, translated by James Leoni, London: 1755; reprint, as *The Ten Books of Architecture: The 1755 Leoni Edition*, New York: Dover, 1986; also translated as *On the Art of Building in Ten Books*, translated by Joseph Rykwert, Neil Leach, and Robert Tavernor, Cambridge, Massachusetts: MIT Press, 1988

Coffin, David R., "Some Aspects of the Villa Lante in Bagnaia," in *Arte in Europa: Scritti di Storia dell'Arte in Onore di Edoardo Arslan*, 2 vols., by Edoardo Arslan, Milan: Artipo, 1966

Comito, Terry, *The Idea of the Garden in the Renaissance*, New Brunswick, New Jersey: Rutgers University Press, 1978; Hassocks, Sussex: The Harvester Press, 1979

Eliade, Mircea, *Das Heilige und das Profane: Vom Wesen des Religiösen*, Hamburg: Rowohlt, 1957; as *The Sacred and the Profane: The Nature of Religion*, translated by Willard R. Trask, New York: Harcourt Brace, 1959

Krautheimer, Richard, "The Tragic and Comic Scene of the Renaissance: The Baltimore and Urbino Panels," *Gazette des Beaux-Arts* (1948)

Krautheimer, Richard, *The Rome of Alexander VII, 1655–1667*, Princeton, New Jersey: Princeton University Press, 1985

Lazzaro, Claudia, *The Villa Lante at Bagnaia*, Ph.D. diss., Princeton University, 1974

Lazzaro, Claudia, *The Italian Renaissance Garden: From the Conventions of Planting, Design, and Ornament to the Grand Gardens of Sixteenth-Century Central Italy*, New Haven: Yale University Press, 1990

Plato, *The Laws*, translated from the Greek by Trevor J. Saunders, Harmondsworth, Middlesex: Penguin, 1970

Pliny the Younger, *The Letters of the Younger Pliny*, translated by John Delaware Lewis, London: Trübner,

1879; translated by Betty Radice, Harmondsworth, Middlesex: Penguin, 1963

Westfall, Carroll William, "The Two Ideal Cities of the Early Renaissance: Republican and Ducal Thought in

Quattrocento Architectural Treatises," Ph.D. diss., Columbia University, 1967

LORNA ANNE MCNEUR

Repton, Humphry 1752–1818

English Landscape Gardener

Humphry Repton was the leading landscape gardener in later Georgian England. In a career spanning 30 years he prepared more than 400 reports for commissions and published four books on the theory and practice of landscape gardening. He worked for a variety of clients, from dukes to lawyers, and saw his profession as helping to fashion the cultural consensus of polite society. Repton worked at a number of sites the length and breadth of England and at a few in Wales, although there is a high concentration of commissions in the eastern counties and around London, close to his home at Hare Street in Essex.

Repton took up landscape gardening as a career in 1788, aged 36, after a series of unsuccessful ventures as a textile merchant, a country squire, a private secretary, an art critic, an essayist, and a transport entrepreneur. Repton claimed to have coined the term *landscape gardening*, although the term had a currency earlier in the century that it may have lost. What Repton did was to refashion landscape gardening from a range of paid skills and amateur accomplishments, some of which he had practiced in his former occupations—watercolor drawing, essay writing, poetry, estate management, planting, and farming—and to transform it into what he called a "polite art." The basis of Repton's art was the so-called Red Book, a report bound in red morocco. This document described the projected improvements in sometimes meticulous detail and in a fine copperplate script, which broke into verse, literary quotation, and passages of theory. The improvements were illustrated by a unique device, a hinged overlay that, when covering a page, would show the present scene and when taken up would reveal the proposed one. The illusionism of Repton's style owed much to the theater and was distrusted as such by some of his rivals. It turned "rural improvement" into "rural pantomime," complained William Marshall, a rival landscape gardener.

On properties of all sizes, from great country estates to suburban villas, Repton tended to work on a modest area, focusing on the pleasure grounds around the house and in the vicinity of lodges, approaches, walks, and drives, although the scenic transformations entailed might be grand, in views and vistas within and beyond the property and in its impression from the public highway. Repton's designs were finely detailed, horticulturally and architecturally, making use of such features as balustrades, trelliswork, and baskets for flowers; in his later years such detail became more intricate and brilliant, the focus of the design rather than a frame for the landscape at large.

In the first few years of his career Repton enjoyed dramatic success through valuable clients of all kinds. He secured aristocratic patrons such as the duke of Portland, who offered him influential company as well as a good deal of direction on commissions, and lesser figures who gave him the money and independence to establish his practice. Repton was keen to gain the support of women and flatter their tastes, for the arena and style of his art were considered feminine. Repton sought both to professionalize this arena and extend its social range. Aesthetically and morally, he offered a vision in which the entire family of a client could participate. He designed an arena for the cultivation of domestic virtues, which were promoted throughout polite society.

Repton prepared two Red Books for the duke of Portland's estate at Welbeck, Nottinghamshire, in 1790 and 1793. These formed the "groundwork," as he called it, for his first published treatise, *Sketches and Hints on Landscape Gardening* (1794). The culmination of a first, highly successful phase of his career, this book also marked the beginning of controversy and disappointment that dogged Repton thereafter. He was forced to delay issuing the book until 1795, to add an appendix to reply to a pre-emptive, coordinated attack on his work in two manifestos, *Essay on the Picturesque* by Uvedale Price and *The Landscape: A Didactic Poem* by Richard Payne Knight. Price and Knight were connoisseurs and Hertfordshire squires; they objected to professional landscape gardening on the grounds that it commercialized an endeavor they believed landowners themselves should practice with the knowledge of their property and of Old Master paintings and the help of their estate staff. Repton represented a metropolitan movement that threatened virile ideals of rural virtue. Repton replied vigorously and established his practice in his antagonists' home county, but for the next few years he was embroiled in what became known as the "Picturesque controversy."

From the outset of his career, Repton collaborated on some commissions in association with architects, notably William Wilkins and James Wyatt. Wilkins was little known outside Norfolk and became increasingly gout ridden; Wyatt was nationally renowned but unreliable. From around 1796 Repton formed a partnership with the architect John Nash, which he thought would transform his practice and bring him enduring fame and fortune. Nash took Repton's sons John Adey and George Stanley into his office as assistants and agreed to pay Repton part of the percentage on work he secured. In design terms the partnership worked most successfully at Luscombe in Dorset, for the banker Charles Hoare, where Nash's architecture and Repton's landscaping were pleasingly integrated and well executed. Professionally and personally, the partnership proved to be a failure. Nash terminated the partnership in 1800, refusing to pay Repton anything, claiming the money had been absorbed by the cost of accommodating his sons. An embittered Repton took John Adey out of Nash's office and into partnership with himself, whereupon his son's architecture decisively shaped particular designs and his theory of landscape gardening. They developed a domestic style called "Queen Elizabeth's Gothic," loosely based on manor houses in Norfolk, which combined an antique-looking exterior with a characteristic internal arrangement, including view-framing windows and accommodating the "Comforts of Modern Life." (George Stanley Repton stayed with Nash and developed a talent for the design of cottages and minor estate buildings, notably Blaise Hamlet.)

Repton's second treatise, *Observations on the Theory and Practice of Landscape Gardening* (1803), reflected the increasing alignment of landscape and architecture in his work. By this time he was also aware of how his designs had been ignored or abandoned by clients or spoiled by estate stewards and workmen, and he wanted to make his books—rather than the places where his designs were implemented—the main showpiece of his work. *Observations* was reprinted in 1805. The publisher also requested a new edition of *Sketches and Hints*, which had become so scarce it was fetching four times its original price. Repton decided not to reissue this expensive book but to extract some passages for a new and much cheaper one, *An Enquiry into the Changes of Taste in Landscape Gardening* (1806). Intended to reach a less affluent audience (perhaps in response to the sales suc-

cess of his rivals in the Picturesque controversy), this small, unillustrated octavo included extracts from recent Red Books, a "History of Landscape Gardening," and a response to a recent book by Knight, *An Analytical Inquiry into the Principles of Taste.*

The year 1805, wrote Repton, was the "pinnacle of my ambition." He had begun a prestigious and lucrative long-term commission for the sixth duke of Bedford at Woburn Abbey and secured his most promising commission of all, the refashioning of the Royal Pavilion, Brighton, for the Prince of Wales. From the outset of his career, Repton had sought royal patronage. When Thomas Sandby died in 1798, he tried unsuccessfully to secure, through his aristocratic contacts, the position of deputy ranger of Windsor Great Park, which Sandby had used to pursue landscaping and architecture. Repton worked on the commission for Brighton Pavilion with his three sons, John Adey, George Stanley, and Humphry the younger. They chose an Indian style, explicitly modeled on the illustrations in volume one of William Daniell's *Oriental Scenery* (1805), and prepared a sumptuous Red Book. Repton was again disappointed. His design was not implemented, nor was he paid for his work; moreover Nash prepared another design loosely based on Repton's, which was eventually built. Repton tried to salvage something from the commission by publishing *Designs for the Pavilion at Brighton* (1808).

Repton blamed the decline of his fortunes on developments during the Napoleonic Wars, especially the imposition of taxes (both on himself and potential clients) and the dramatic inflation and unregulated increase in paper money, which he thought encouraged a spirit of speculation unsympathetic to his art of landscape gardening. By 1808 he was finding commissions difficult to secure, and those that he did obtain tended to be brief consultations for the nouveaux riche he despised, men of modest beginnings who had made fortunes during the wars and possessed none of the cultural accomplishments he valued in more established clients. In January 1811 his career was further blighted by a road accident, when his carriage overturned one icy night returning home from a ball. He suffered a spinal injury from which he never fully recovered. His heart was affected, and he endured frequent and painful attacks of angina pectoris.

From 1811 Repton found work scarce, and his fears of personal bankruptcy made him morbid about his own condition and that of the country. When he did secure prestigious commissions he lavished enormous attention on them. That for Sheringham (from 1812) he considered his favorite work because it was in his home county of Norfolk and because his young client, Abbot Upcher, shared his social and scenic views. Upcher's death in 1817 left it unfinished, however. Repton prepared Red

Books to landscape the work of architect Jeffry Wyatt-tville at Ashridge, Hertfordshire, for the duke of Bridge-water, in 1813 and Endsleigh, Devon, for the duke of Bedford, the following year. By this time Repton was in a wheel chair and finding movement of any kind, from travel to a site to getting around the grounds, a very painful experience.

From 1814 Repton spent most of his time at home at Hare Street reading, corresponding with friends and family, and writing his memoirs and his last treatise *Fragments on the Theory and Practice of Landscape Gardening* (1816). *Fragments* is a valedictory work, charting the break-up of landscape gardening and the society that sustained it. It focuses on small flower gardens and ornate Gothic buildings. He wondered whether landscape gardening would revive in peacetime or whether it would be seen as a lost art. The postwar economic depression and Repton's worsening health brought his practice to an end. He died suddenly, probably of a heart attack, on 24 March 1818.

From the Picturesque controversy of 1794, Repton had suffered a good deal of ridicule, much of it provoked by his early success. He was dubbed a "coxcomb" by aristocratic men for his vanity and conceit and for his reputation for flattering feminine tastes. Professional rivals such as William Marshall and John Claudius Loudon did not hesitate to launch public criticism while adopting Repton's ideas. In public Repton parried criticism, but he was bitter in private. Toward the end of his life, as he retreated from public view, he was caricatured in Jane Austen's *Mansfield Park* (1814) as a generic name—"Repton, or any body of that sort"—for the fashion-conscious to commission and in Thomas Peacock's *Headlong Hall* (1816) as the obsequious advocate of "picturesque gardening." In 1840, over 20 years after his death, Loudon edited all of Repton's published works on landscape gardening in a cheap edition with crude line engravings of the original aquatints; in the preface he claimed his former adversary as a precursor of his own patented style, the "gardenesque."

Repton's reputation spread beyond Britain, through influential travelers such as the German prince Hermann Pückler-Muskau, who observed his works on the ground, and his son John Adey, who was commissioned by Pückler-Muskau during a working trip to Germany and Holland in 1821–22. Repton's principles were given an exposition in the German landscape gardener Eduard Petzold's *Landscschaftsgartenerei* issued in Leipzig in 1862. Repton's writings were a strong influence on the work of the U.S. landscape architect Andrew Jackson Downing, notably his *Treatise on the Theory and Practice of Landscape Gardening* (1841). The first two of Repton's treatises were edited and published in the United States as *The Art of Landscape Gar-*

dening (1907) without many of the original illustrations and supplemented by modern photographs of English landscape parks, not all Repton sites. In Britain Repton was rediscovered as a theorist in Christopher Hussey's *The Picturesque* (1927) and as a commissioned designer in accounts of country houses in issues of *Country Life*. The first modern biography, *Humphry Repton* by Dorothy Stroud, was published by *Country Life* in 1962.

Biography

Born in Bury St. Edmunds, Suffolk, England, 1752. Apprenticed as textile merchant, Norwich, Norfolk, England, 1768–73; in business, 1773–76; retired to Sustead, Norfolk, to be a country squire and gentleman amateur, 1776–83; private secretary to William Windham at Dublin Castle, Dublin, Ireland, 1783; professional watercolorist, art critic, and essayist, living in Bath, Avon, and on Hare Street, Romford, Essex, 1783–88; landscape gardener, 1788–1818; prepared over 400 reports for commissions, known as his Red Books, including those for Welbeck (1790, 1793, 1803), Kenwood (1793), Longleat (1804), Woburn (1805), the Royal Pavilion, Brighton (1806), and Sheringham (1812); published three major treatises on the theory and practice of landscape gardening in 1794, 1803, and 1816; collaborated on occasional basis with architects William Wilkins and James Wyatt, 1790–94; formed partnership with John Nash, 1796–1800, then one with his son John Adey Repton, which lasted until his death. Died in Essex, England, 1818.

Selected Designs

1789   Brandesbury, Middlesex, England, for Hon. Lady Salusbury

1790   Welbeck, Nottinghamshire, England, for Duke of Portland

1793   Port Eliot, Cornwall, for Reginald Pole Carew

1801   Magdalen College, Oxford, England (never executed)

1805   Woburn Abbey, Bedfordshire, England, for Duke of Bedford

1806   Royal Pavilion, Brighton, East Sussex, England, for Prince of Wales

1810   Armley, Yorkshire, England, for Benjamin Gott

1812   Sheringham, Norfolk, England, for Mr. Abbot Upcher

1814   Ashridge, Hertfordshire, England, for the Duke of Bridewater

Selected Publications

Sketches and Hints on Landscape Gardening, 1794

Observations on the Theory and Practice of Landscape Gardening, 1803

An Enquiry into the Changes of Taste in Landscape Gardening, 1806

Designs for the Pavilion at Brighton, 1808

Fragments on the Theory and Practice of Landscape Gardening, 1816

Red Books of Humphry Repton, 4 vols., edited by Edward Malins, 1976

Further Reading

Carter, George, Patrick Goode, and Kedrun Laurie, *Humphry Repton, Landscape Gardener, 1752–1818,* Norwich, East Anglia: Sainsbury Centre for Visual Arts, 1982

Daniels, Stephen, *Humphry Repton: Landscape Gardening and the Geography of Georgian England,* New Haven, Connecticut: Yale University Press, 1999

Repton, Humphry, *The Landscape Gardening and Landscape Architecture of the Late Humphry Repton, Esq.,* edited by John Claudius Loudon, London: Longman, 1840; reprint, Farnborough, Hampshire: Gregg International, 1969

Repton, Humphry, *Humphry Repton: The Red Books for Brandsbury and Glemham Hall,* with an introduction by Stephen Daniels, Washington, D.C.: Dumbarton Oaks Research Library and Collection, 1994

Stroud, Dorothy, *Humphry Repton,* London: Country Life, 1962

STEPHEN DANIELS

Restoration, Landscape

Since the Middle Ages or earlier, it has been possible to create landscapes by clearing forest land for cultivation or by reclaiming land from the sea, as in the low countries. Certainly since the 18th century, landscapes have possessed an aesthetic value, a value that needed to be actively preserved. It also became reasonable to seek to restore the landscape wherever neglect had allowed it to deteriorate or its aesthetic qualities had been destroyed by human agency. Landscape restoration has therefore come to cover a vast range of activities, from the re-creation of lost gardens known only from descriptions or paintings, as at Painswick in the English Cotswolds, to projects for the reclamation of fenland in Schleswig-Holstein. It is concerned chiefly with the return of landscape to some former desirable state for any of a whole variety of reasons, including the provision of a habitat for endangered species of fauna, the different sorts of aesthetic qualities that attract tourists, the educational value of making visually apparent historical interest, and different kinds of scientific study.

The Standards for Historic Preservation of the U.S. secretary of the interior, as promulgated in 1976 and revised in 1992, distinguishes restoration from preservation, rehabilitation, and reconstruction. Its defining feature is that it allows "cultural landscape," here understood as any landscape of historical interest, to be reinstated as it was at any given historically important moment by the retention of whatever materials connect it to that moment and the removal of everything else. Such a definition is plainly of practical use primarily where battle sites or particularly important periods of industrial or urban history are concerned. Some historic cities, such as York in England, have reconstituted period shopping precincts that fall within the scope of the restoration of cultural landscape. The best-known example of this type of urban landscape restoration is Williamsburg, Virginia, where in 1926 John D. Rockefeller, Jr., afforded financial assistance to allow 700 buildings to be removed, 83 to be renovated, and 413 to be rebuilt on their original sites.

On a much smaller scale, the Painswick garden restoration represents an activity of the same type. Here in the 1740s Benjamin Hyett transformed a small valley behind his country mansion into a spectacular pleasure garden, painted in 1748 by a local artist, Thomas Robins. The garden was first reduced in size and transformed to grow fruit and vegetables and then abandoned and planted with trees. It became a wood. Only after an exhibition of Thomas Robins's paintings in 1976 was it realized that the painter, in an ostentatiously rococo painting, had left the only complete record in existence of an English garden from the rococo period, and in 1984 restoration of the garden from scratch was begun. Now virtually complete, the six-acre (2.4-ha) reconstitution, with its vistas, geometric patterns, off-centered design, and garden buildings restored according to original 18th-century designs, has been transferred to a charitable trust and opened to the public. A maze was opened in 1999 to celebrate the painting's two and a half centuries, and a children's nature trail has been added with a café, a gift shop, and a nursery offering an unusual range of plants. Like York, but unlike Williamsburg, the Painswick restoration is in fact a "reconstitution," justified by aesthetic considerations, rather than a restoration. Only the shape of the terrain is authentic.

Authenticity is the sensitive point in landscape restorations. Debate centers on what started as the concept and has now become the discipline of ecological restoration, which seeks to restore the original plant and animal community in its historical complexity. The task has not proved easy. In his 1995 paper "Is Landscape Preservation an Oxymoron?," Robert Cook of the Arnold Arboretum of Harvard University points out that even the often-cited Henry Green Prairie at the University of Wisconsin, Madison, has not in 50 years been totally successful in restoring the 50-acre (20.2-ha) cornfield to its precultivation state.

While it supports over 200 native plant species, the absence of green snakes, upland sandpipers, Franklin's ground squirrels, elk, and bison in the Henry Green Prairie makes it necessary to undertake frequent intense burns, cutting, and the application of herbicides to keep out weeds and woody species, sweet clover, and wild parsnip. The meadow requires quite intense gardening to maintain even the appearance of authenticity, and its form of restoration has even been referred to as forgery and worse. Cook advocates an approach governed by the principles put forward by S.T.A. Pickett and V.T. Parker in 1994 that there is no single reference state on which an ecological restoration can be based and that ecological restoration can never be regarded as a single event but must continue into an ongoing intervention. The reference point has moved from "the balance of nature" to "the flux of nature," and ecological restoration is now seen increasingly as an interpretative cultural activity, governed by changing cultural aims.

Where the aim of landscape restoration is primarily the provision of habitat for birds and other wild species and the preservation of plant species, as in Schleswig-Holstein, it may still be hoped that science can achieve a better control of the dynamics of soil change and eventually promote the provision of adequate nutrients and nesting conditions for present populations on smaller surface areas. It is clear from work being undertaken at the Kiel Ecology Center (Ökologie Zentrum) that fen vegetation can be controlled by adjusting the water table. Raising it reduces peat mineralization and consequently augments the nutrient content of the ground. Wet meadow plants have been successfully reintroduced by extensive land use without fertilization and by a single annual mowing with lightweight machinery when the water table is at its lowest.

It has been possible in Western cultures to alter landscapes for many centuries, notably by draining, flooding, controlled irrigation, and changing the course of rivers. Recently it has become economically beneficial to alter landscapes by the creation of dams to generate electricity. By the 17th century it had become routine for grand landscape projects in France, such as that envisaged by Armand-Jean du Plessis, Cardinal de Richelieu, for the family château in the hamlet of Richelieu, to move earth in sufficient quantities to reverse the slope of a large landscape garden. The technology for changing or preserving domestic landscape, unless against such uncontrollable forces of nature as tornado, earthquake, or rising sea level, is available. Even the provision of funding in economically advanced societies normally depends only on the existence of political will.

Achieving a balance between the reinstatement of landscapes, whether or not motivated primarily by aesthetic concerns, and addressing the considerations of the local economy can be problematic. A healthy local agricultural economy or other industry may suffer if desirable recreational or aesthetic features of landscape are to be restored or even if a given species of bird or plant is to be preserved from extinction. In the end these are political decisions, dictated by the cultural values of a society. Debate stimulates awareness of the issues, both promoting informed techniques in the management of landscape restoration and showing what the society as a whole regards as the ideological excesses that may creep into restoration movements as into all conscious efforts to advance cultural change.

Further Reading

Baldwin, A. Dwight, Jr., Judith DeLuce, and Carl Pletach, editors, *Beyond Preservation: Restoring and Inventing Landscapes*, Minneapolis: University of Minnesota Press, 1994

Birnbaum, Charles A., *Protecting Cultural Landscapes: Planning, Treatment, and Management of Historic Landscapes*, Washington, D.C.: U.S. Department of the Interior, National Park Service, 1994

Cook, Robert E., "Is Landscape Preservation an Oxymoron?" in *Balancing Natural and Cultural Issues in the Preservation of Historic Landscapes: Selected Papers from the National Association for Olmsted Parks Conference*, edited by Charles Birnbaum and Sandra L. Tallant, Hancock, Michigan: George Wright Society, 1996

Pickett, S.T.A. and Parker, V.T, "Avoiding the Old Pitfalls: Opportunities in a New Discipline," *Restoration Ecology* 2, nos. 75–79 (1994)

Trepel, Michael, *Aims and Problems of Fen Restoration in a Cultural Landscape: Planning, Treatment, and Management of Historic Landscapes*, Washington D.C.: 1994

ANTHONY H.T. LEVI

Rievaulx Terrace

Helmsley, North Yorkshire, England

Location: approximately 2 miles (3.2 km) northwest of Helmsley, and 20 miles (32 km) north of York

The turf terrace at Rievaulx is an elaborate example of the mid-Georgian taste for broad terrace walks in gardens with commanding views over natural scenery. It was constructed for Thomas Duncombe III about 1758 as an extension to the pleasure grounds of Duncombe Park, Helmsley, Yorkshire. The designer of the terrace, an impressive piece of landform engineering, is not known. Remarkably, Duncombe Park already had a great turf terrace walk, laid out ca. 1715, immediately east of the house. Rievaulx Terrace appears to have been laid out as a similar, but contrasting, feature on another part of the estate, taking advantage of dramatic topography, as well as a rich variety of scenery, and bringing some fashionable ideas into the new design. It can thus be seen as a revised, refined, and updated successor to the Duncombe Terrace.

Remote from the house and now in separate ownership, the Rievaulx Terrace consists of a broad turf walk, half a mile (0.8 km) in length, carefully leveled and modeled but essentially following the contour of the valley edge of the River Rye. At either end of the terrace are classical temples, and a backdrop of wood lines the inner edge of the terrace. The terrace permits extensive views into the rural scenery of Ryedale, and sight lines are cut through the dense wood on the slope below the terrace to provide changing views of the ruins of the Cistercian abbey of Rievaulx in the valley below.

The Rievaulx Terrace represents a further development of a design feature characteristic of mid-18th-century English gardens evolving from formal, inward-looking layouts to a less geometric approach guided by natural contours and looking out to carefully selected rural views. Such views might include evocative features such as medieval ruins (Duncombe Terrace looks out over Helmsley Castle) or battlefields (as at Farnborough, Warwickshire). Early terraces such as those at Bramham Park, Yorkshire, tended to be straight, with bastions projecting into the surrounding fields. These bastions were sometimes decorated with statues, as at Castle Howard, Yorkshire. Opportunities for vista closers were soon exploited. These features were sometimes very grand, such as the column and chapel at either end of the Grand Walk at Gibside, Tyne, and Wear.

The terrace at Rievaulx adapted an established formula to new tastes, presenting varied scenery as picturesque incidents evoking a range of sentiments: viewing "sub-

lime" nature from the safety of a "beautiful" setting; the contrast between the ordered regularity of classical architecture and the rambling, romantic qualities of the Gothic; the mixed emotions provoked by ruins, especially when shown as tantalizing framed views, as here and at Studley Royal, Yorkshire, where a garden seat views the ruins of Fountains, another Cistercian abbey ruin.

The visitor arrives, guided by an enclosed woodland walk, at a pair of gate piers halfway along the terrace. The luxurious turf walk is revealed for the first time at this point. Turning to the left, the terrace curves gradually toward the Tuscan Temple, a circular *tempietto* attributed to Sir Thomas Robinson. The interior features reused medieval floor tiles, as well as stucco work attributed to Giuseppe Cortese.

Returning along the front of the terrace, the ingenuity of the design begins to reveal itself. As the visitor advances along the walk, the sight lines cut through the wood begin to display a succession of framed views of the abbey ruins far below. As the terrace curves round, so each view presents the ruins from a different aspect and focuses on a separate part of the buildings. The wider view above the treetops also reveals changing views of the valley and the uplands beyond: hanging woods above the river, agricultural fields, scattered cottages, little changed since the terrace was laid out.

At the far end of the terrace is the Ionic Temple. Similarly attributed to Sir Thomas Robinson, this rectangular temple, perhaps intended to remind the visitor of the Maison Carrée at Nîmes, is the culmination of the terrace. The visitor arrives here having seen the full sequence of 13 views to the abbey and valley and enters the temple to discover the interior presented as a banqueting house, for use as an exquisite place of refreshment and summer entertainment. The ceilings and cove are decorated with frescoes by Giuseppe Mattia Borgnis, copying mythical scenes by Caracci and Guido Reni in Rome. The temple includes a basement for servants to prepare the refreshments.

Returning to the columned portico, the visitor looks back along the terrace. The woodland backdrop, unlike the Duncombe Terrace, advances and recedes in a serpentine line, reflecting the taste for this rococo "line of beauty" to which William Hogarth devoted his *Analysis of Beauty* in 1753. The sheltered bays created by the waving line of trees provide additional resting places along the walk, and ornamental shrubs line the woodland edge, where an earlier generation would have maintained a defining hedge. The edge of the slope is covered in wild flowers, merging into the woodland below.

The "learned and ingenious" agriculturist and observant tourist Arthur Young described the pleasure of the scene unfolding before him in 1771 in picturesque terms, referring to "the enjoyment . . . which results from contrast and unexpected pleasure." Catching sight of the abbey ruins through the wood, he writes, provides "a casual glance at a little paradise, which seems as it were in another region." Young describes the countryside itself as a painterly composition: "The scattered trees, hay stacks, houses and hedges, all together form a pleasing landscape. Two distant hills give a proper termination to the view." Trees grow among the abbey ruins "in a stile too elegantly picturesque to admit description." Young's experience is still to be had today.

Rievaulx Terrace is in excellent condition and is regularly open to the public.

Synopsis

1131	Rievaulx Abbey founded by Walter l'Espec, lord of Helmsley
1538	Dissolution of monasteries
1689	Sir Charles Duncombe purchases Helmsley estate
1713	Building of Duncombe Park
ca. 1715	Duncombe Terrace laid out
1758	Completion of Rievaulx Terrace for Thomas Duncombe III
1771	Arthur Young's description
1963	Rievaulx Terrace acquired by National Trust

Further Reading

Burke, Edmund, *A Philosophical Enquiry into the Origin of Our Ideas of the Sublime and Beautiful,* London, 1757; edited by Adam Phillips, Oxford and New York: Oxford University Press, 1990

Hogarth, William, *The Analysis of Beauty,* London, 1753; new edition with corrections, edited by Ronald Paulson, New Haven, Connecticut: Yale University Press, 1997

Lemmon, Kenneth, *Yorkshire and Humberside,* London: Batsford, 1978

Young, Arthur, *A Six Months Tour through the North of England,* 4 vols., London, 1770; 2nd edition, 1771; reprint, New York: Kelley, 1967

STEVEN DESMOND

Rio de Janeiro, Jardim Botânico do

Rio de Janeiro, Brazil

Location: Rio de Janeiro city center; southeast corner of Parque Nacional Tijuca

One of the oldest botanical gardens in the New World, the Jardim Botânico do Rio de Janeiro is an exotic combination of Amazonian jungle and landscaped gardens, containing not only specialized greenhouses, statuary, and majestic avenues of palms but also an abundance of history. The garden was founded in 1808 as the Portuguese royal family, fleeing persecution from Napoléon Bonaparte, shifted headquarters from Lisbon to Rio de Janeiro. Once relocated, they soon established several industries under the aegis of the imperial crown, including manufacturing and agricultural enterprises. One of these early factories was located on the estate of Rodriguo de Freitas, who had focused his energies on sugarcane production, and it was not long before his sugar mill and the surrounding grounds were sold to the crown's administrative arm, the *Junta de Fazenda e Arsenais,* and earmarked for garden preparation and planning by Prince Regent Don Joaõ VI. First called the *Real Horto* (real garden), the land was initially designated for the cultivation of both medicinal and commercially viable plants, mostly those of East Asian origin. It was Don Joaõ's intent to create a "garden of acclimatization" that would serve as a repository for spices from the Orient—a profit-minded design at the time. Tea crops were quickly introduced as well as superior strains of sugarcane, clove, cinnamon, and pineapple, all popular nonindigenous plants.

The garden's first donation of seeds arrived from an unlikely source: a Portuguese naval officer, Luiz de Abreu Viera y Silva, who had been captured by the French following a shipwreck off Goa, India. De Abreu was held as a prisoner of war on Île de France, where the successful and famous *Jardin Gabrielle* was housed. It was from this garden that he purloined samples of seeds and roots (including the now-famous royal palm as well as breadfruit and avocado seeds) that he later delivered as a gift to Don Joaõ after devising his escape. With these and other developments, the *Real Horto* slowly began to flourish, and 11 years after its dedication it was renamed the Royal Botanic Garden, with funds mandated for similar gardens in Bahia, Minas, Pernambuco, and São Paulo.

Sadly, during the years of Brazil's struggle for independence, the gardens were neglected and almost abandoned until a later caretaker, the Carmelite botanist Frei Leandro do Sacramento, began planting what would eventually be the famous avenues of trees and expanding the cultivated garden areas. Indeed do Sacramento was the first of several visionary and progressive directors who guided the park through its development. During his term as director he also began construction of an artificial lake—today called the Lago Frei Leandro—that was to become a centerpiece of the garden complex, marking the beginning of plans for other lakes and ponds to support aquatic flora, such as lotus, papyrus, water hyacinth (*Eichornia crassipes*), and water lettuce (*Pistia stratiotes*). In later years the Macaco River was canalized to flood a large portion of the garden, and the wetland topography subsequently drained into a series of ditches feeding into ornamental canals and an aqueduct—all linked by a serpentine system of paths within the garden complex. Perhaps one of do Sacramento's most valuable contributions was to implement a policy of seed exchanges with other international gardens (including the botanical garden in Cambridge, England), enriching not only the collection of the Jardim Botânico but other satellite gardens in Brazil as well. Systematic classification began in earnest some years later through the stewardship of another friar, Alves Serraõ, in 1859. These efforts were continued during the tenure of one of the garden's most famous directors, João Barbosa Rodrigues, who not only compiled a full catalog of the garden's plants but also established a botanical library that is today considered a singular research institution with more than 66,000 volumes and 3,000 rare works. As the Jardim Botânico evolved in later decades, it developed importance as a research facility, with several laboratories and a staff of researchers and technicians.

Before his death in 1909, Rodrigues introduced a herbarium and an arboretum as well as the first greenhouse. Today the garden complex occupies roughly 339 acres (137 ha) with the gardens extending about five miles (eight km) from the center. One hundred thirty-three acres (54 ha) of this area is cultivated, with the remainder native jungle. The cultivated area suggests a strong French influence with its carefully plotted, transverse avenues of palms reaching close to 33 yards (30 m). Certainly, Royal Palm Avenue is one of the garden's most recognized features, and all 12 genera of *Palmae* are represented in the garden. The figs, also large and compelling, include several species (*Ficus elastica* and *F. clusiaefolia*), and bamboo, particularly the mammoth *Dendrocalamus giganteus*, exerts a strong presence as

well. Other arboreal genera are *Artocarpus* (comprising jackfruit and breadfruit trees) and *Couroupita* (cannonball tree), both of which flower and bear their heavy fruit on the trunk and main branches. Groups of the boldly colored *Couroupita guinanensis* form another allée through the park, and the wood-mulatto and brazilwood (*Caesalpinia echinata*) trees act as special points of interest because of their endangered status. Other indigenous trees include the *Aroids*, whose beauty served as inspiration for legendary landscape architect Roberto Burle Marx.

The enormity of the collections is staggering. The garden holds impressive groupings of bromeliads, orchids, cacti, insects, medicinal plants; 5,500 trees and shrubs (including philodendron, hibiscus, mimosa, and euphorbia); six lakes; 11,000 global specimens; 8,000 classified vegetable species with a herbarium holding 330,000 samples of dehydrated plants; a xiloteca with 8,000 wood samples; and a carpoteca with a large dry fruit collection. Moreover, 138 species of birds from 34 families reside within the park's parameters, making it a popular and worthwhile destination for birdwatchers. Other greenhouses include a *cactario* (cactus hothouse), created during the administration of Paulo de Campos Porto (1951–61). The first cacti collection was assembled in 1910 in combination with an exchange program among other institutions for seeds and seedlings. These acquisitions were augmented in later years through the addition of Mexican and other North American flora. Nearby a greenhouse for African violets (formerly the Maranthas greenhouse) was begun in 1942 and renovated in 1991.

Fountains, statues, and architecture are representative of two centuries of the garden's history but stylistically recall French neoclassic influences. An ornate melted-iron fountain dominates the center of the garden; purchased in 1895 by then-director João Barbosa Rodrigues, it was imported from England and bears four allegorical images: music, poetry, science, and art. Scattered throughout the garden's cultivated areas lie other striking sculptures, including works by Master Valentim, perhaps the most important Brazilian sculptor and architect of the second half of the 19th century, whose statues of Ecco and Narcissus were the first large pieces to be cast in the country. Others include a ceramic rendering of Ceres (1887) and a sculpture of Thetis rising out of the Lake of Frei Leandro. French influence is particularly obvious in the Fine Arts Academy Portal created by Auguste Henri Victor Granjean de Montijn; razed in 1938, it was reconstructed nine years later.

A Japanese garden and an unusual sensory garden are several of the thematic gardens within the Jardim Botânico. The Japanese garden—a staple of many botanical collections—was constructed in 1935 for a visit by the Japanese Ministry of the Economy and reinaugurated 60 years later for the arrival of Princess Sayako. Filled with beautiful bonsai and cherry trees, the garden also holds groves of bamboo and lakes stocked with carp. In March 1995 the nearby sensory garden was dedicated to visitors with disabilities; its plants were selected to both provoke and soothe the senses with both scents (honeysuckle and gardenia) and exotic textures (*Kalanchae laxiflora* and *Gasteria verrucosa*).

Modest improvements and modernization efforts were initiated before the 1992 Earth Summit, including the construction of a new *orquidário* (orchid greenhouse). Within the *orquidário* there are about 2,500 specimens from 708 different species of orchids, including *Oncidium flexuosum* and *Scuticaria adwenii*. An orchid program was developed in 1996 to promote studies in reproduction, biology, and diversity for these epiphytic plants, which have been a perpetual source of interest for visitors and collectors worldwide.

Synopsis

1808	Real Horto founded by Don Joaõ VI
1809	Luiz de Abreu Viera y Silva provides first donation of seeds
1812	Shipment of Asiatic plants arrives from Portuguese India
1819	Renamed Royal Botanic Garden
1824–29	Frei Leandro do Sacromento reorganizes garden and establishes seed exchange programs
1859–61	Alves Serraõ serves as director; begins classification system for plants
1890–91	João Barbosa Rodrigues serves as director; library, central fountain, and herbarium introduced
1895	Main fountain purchased from England
1910	Cacti collection begun
1915–31	Director Antônio Leão enlarges collection with samples from Amazon basin
1935	Japanese garden dedicated
1942	Maranthas greenhouse for African violets begun
	Garden made part of Ministry of Environment; improvements initiated in preparation for Earth Summit
1995	Sensory garden dedicated
1996	Orchid program developed

Further Reading

Adams, William Howard, *Nature Perfected: Gardens through History*, New York: Abbeville Press, 1991

Adams, William Howard, *Roberto Burle Marx: The Unnatural Art of the Garden* (exhib. cat.), New York: Museum of Modern Art, 1991

Cavaliero, Roderick, *The Independence of Brazil*, New York: St. Martin's Press, and London: Tauris, 1993

Eliovson, Sima, *The Gardens of Roberto Burle Marx*, Portland, Oregon: Sagapress/Timber Press, New York: Abrams/Sagapress, and London: Thames and Hudson, 1991

Hyams, Edward, *Great Botanical Gardens of the World*, New York: Macmillan, and London: Nelson, 1969

McQueen, Jim, and Barbara McQueen, *Orchids of Brazil*, Portland, Oregon: Timber Press, and Melbourne: Text, 1993

Pio Vorreia, Manuel, *Dicionário das plantas úteis do Brasil e das exóticas cultivados*, 3 vols., Rio de Janeiro: Imprensa Nacional, 1926–52; as *Brazilian Palms: Notes on Their Uses and Vernacular with Updated Nomenclature and Added Illustrations*, translated and edited by Claudio Urbano Pinheiro and Michael J. Balick, New York: New York Botanical Garden, 1987

KRISTIN WYE-RODNEY

Robinson, William 1838–1935

Irish Writer and Gardener

William Robinson was a champion of the naturalistic garden and an unswerving advocate for hardy perennials at a time when bedding-out with annuals was the accepted practice in British gardens. The author of more than a dozen books and the founder of eight gardening periodicals, Robinson was a major figure in the garden world from the 1870s through the early 20th century. In comparison with his idolized contemporary, Gertrude Jekyll, Robinson's reputation has suffered somewhat due to a number of factors. Even though his publications were revolutionary in their day, they lack the elegant writing style that characterizes Jekyll's books. Consequently, Robinson's books are largely unfamiliar today. Unlike Jekyll and other figures associated with

Arts and Crafts gardens, Robinson designed scarcely a handful of gardens. In addition, he continues to be bedeviled by an undeserved reputation as an irksome, opinioned personality, based in part on a biographer who perpetuated myths.

Robinson's main contribution to the history of gardens is the incomparable array of publications he either wrote or edited, in particular *The Wild Garden* (1870) and *The English Flower Garden* (1883). *The Wild Garden*, the first book to promote the use of native plants in naturalistic settings, was a reaction against what Robinson regarded as wasteful bedding-out. Driven by improvements in greenhouse technology during the Victorian era, bedding-out was a response to the wide variety of brightly colored tender plants that could be grown. Robinson's book, with its sensible plea for using hardy perennials, made a profound impact on garden designers such as Jekyll, whose woodland garden at Munstead Wood was laid out on principles put forth in Robinson's book. Henry Francis du Pont's garden at Winterthur, Delaware, also owes much to the study of *The Wild Garden*.

Robinson's most popular book, *The English Flower Garden,* which was in print for 50 years during the author's lifetime, appealed equally to small cottage gardeners and landed gentry who managed large estates. The core of the book is an alphabetical encyclopedia of hardy plants, with cultural information and recommendations for their use in gardens. Robinson compiled here information drawn from the many horticulturists who contributed to his periodical *The Garden,* founded in 1871. For illustrations he secured leading artists and photographers of the day, such as Henry Moon (renowned for his watercolors of orchids), Alfred Parsons (who illustrated *The Wild Garden*), and Jekyll (who supplied many of the photographs). Each of the 15 editions of *The English Flower Garden* included an ever-changing selection of essays on garden design.

Robinson maintained a wide-ranging circle of professional friends around the world, whose expertise he drew upon in his various publications. In 1870, when he was 31 and already a highly regarded horticultural authority, he visited the United States. During this visit he called upon the important figures of the day, such as Frederick Law Olmsted and Asa Gray of Harvard, and visited notable American gardens, such as the H.H. Hunnewell estate in Wellesley, Massachusetts, which was renowned for its pinetum and outstanding collection of rhododendrons and azaleas.

In the 1890s Robinson was embroiled in a controversy known as the Battle of the Styles, which pitted formalist architect-garden designers against the horticulturally inclined naturalists, such as Robinson. The controversy was sparked by the publication of two books—John Sedding's *Garden Craft Old and New*

(1891) and Reginald Blomfield's *The Formal Garden in England* (1892)—that provoked Robinson's ire. He felt that they undermined his accomplishments and promoted all that he had fought against for years: topiary, pleaching, figurative statuary, unnatural terracing, and all manner of "foreign" ideas from Italy and France. From his standpoint there was nothing English about any of his adversaries' ideas. In his rebuttal, published in *Garden Design and Architects' Gardens* (1892), Robinson complained:

> Everywhere . . . the too frequent presence of stupid work in landscape gardening offers some excuse for the two reactionary books which have lately appeared—books not worth notice for their own sake, as they contribute nothing to our knowledge of the beautiful art of gardening or garden design.

He unkindly referred to Sedding's book as "Vegetable Sculpture" because it promoted unnatural clipping of trees, a practice Robinson referred to as "barbarous, needless, and inartistic."

Robinson's work as a garden designer, a subject that has not been fully investigated, played only a small role in his career. His commissions include North Mymms Park, Hertfordshire; Shrubland Park, Suffolk; and Killerton, Devon; as well as Jekyll's first garden at Munstead House, Surrey. Robinson's greatest garden, in some ways comparable to Jekyll's at Munstead Wood, is his own at Gravetye Manor, in Sussex. He acquired hundreds of acres of the farmland surrounding Gravetye, eventually raising cattle and managing the woodlands as a country squire. He wrote about these activities in later publications such as *Home Landscapes* (1914) and *Gravetye Manor* (1911).

Over the years Robinson's ideas about garden design mellowed to the extent that Gravetye had spectacular "formal" gardens in the stone terraces surrounding the house. Dozens of beds filled with roses and perennials, enclosed on several sides by pergolas festooned with dozens of varieties of clematis, for which Gravetye was renowned, made Gravetye the subject of many artists' paintings. Gravetye Manor is presently a hotel. Once again the terraces are ablaze with Robinson's favorite perennials, and the surrounding meadows are filled with sweeps of daffodils in the spring.

Biography

Born in County Down, Northern Ireland, 15 July 1838. After working as gardener on several large Irish estates, moved to England, 1861, where he took up work at Royal Botanic Society, Regent's Park, London, 1861–67; traveled extensively in England, France, and Switzerland; published *Gleanings from French*

Gardens, 1868; founded weekly publication, *The Garden,* 1871; edited seven publications, including *Gardening Illustrated* (1879) and *Flora and Sylva* (1903–5); purchased Gravetye Manor, an Elizabethan manor house in Sussex, 1884, and established extensive gardens. Awarded the George Robert White Medal by Massachusetts Horticultural Society, 1916. Died at Gravetye Manor, East Grinstead, Sussex, 12 May 1935.

Selected Designs
1884–1935   William Robinson's gardens, Gravetye Manor, East Grinstead, Sussex, England

Selected Publications
Gleanings from French Gardens, 1868
The Parks, Promenades, and Gardens of Paris, 1869; 2nd edition, as *The Parks and Gardens of Paris,* 1878
Alpine Flowers for English Gardens, 1870
The Wild Garden, 1870
The Garden (1871–99) (periodical for which Robinson was founder and initial editor)
Gardening Illustrated (1879) (periodical for which Robinson was editor)
The English Flower Garden, 1883
Garden Design and Architects' Gardens, 1892
Flora and Sylva (1903–5) (editor)
Gravetye Manor; or, Twenty Years' Work Round an Old Manor House, 1911
Home Landscapes, 1914

Further Reading
Allan, Mea, *William Robinson, 1838–1935: Father of the English Flower Garden,* London: Faber and Faber, 1982
Duthie, Ruth E., "Some Notes on William Robinson," *Garden History* 2 (1974)
Helmreich, Anne L., "Re-presenting Nature: Ideology, Art, and Science in William Robinson's 'Wild Garden,'" in *Nature and Ideology: Natural Garden Design in the Twentieth Century,* edited by Joachim Wolschke-Bulmahn, Washington, D.C.: Dumbarton Oaks, 1997
Massingham, Betty, "William Robinson: A Portrait," *Garden History* 6 (1978)
Ottewill, David, *The Edwardian Garden,* New Haven, Connecticut: Yale University Press, 1989
Tankard, Judith B., "A Perennial Favourite: William Robinson's 'The English Flower Garden,'" *Hortus* 17 (Spring 1991)
Tankard, Judith B., "William Robinson and the Art of the Book," *Hortus* 27 (Autumn 1993)

JUDITH B. TANKARD

Rococo Style

The French term *rococo* is derived from *rocaille* (shellwork) and originally described the ornamental style of the mid-18th century, based on shellwork as one of its characteristic elements. The shellwork was linked to scroll-like forms and shapes (C and S), asymmetry, and generally a sense of lightness and playfulness. It was regarded as a "feminine" style. The term can also be applied to the other arts of this time, including poetry, sculpture, music, painting, architecture, and garden design. In architecture it is characterized by a lightening of solidity and heaviness, a replacing of grandeur with elegance. The rococo can be regarded as a transitional style between the baroque style, which preceded it, and the neoclassicism that followed. There was a field for experiment and new, free forms after the long-prevailing fixed rules of the Renaissance and baroque periods. Now amateur gardeners could be their own garden designers. Like the term *baroque,* the term *rococo* was first used in a pejorative sense in the 1840s, referring to its playful, nonclassical, overdone attitude.

Applied to garden matters, the term was still being used as late as the second half of the 20th century. The German garden historians Alfred Hoffmann and Ingrid Dennerlein have contributed the best discussions of this period. English garden historians have also applied the term *English rococo garden* since the 1970s.

The style originated in France in the period after the coronation of Louis XV in 1719. In France, therefore, the style is also referred to as Louis XV. The foregoing period from the death of Louis XIV in 1715 is called Régence after the regency of Duke Philippe of Orleans. The Régence garden style, however, had already been introduced in the last years of Louis XIV after the death of his master gardener André Le Nôtre in 1700. A celebrated forerunner was Antoine Watteau, who painted dreamlike Arcadian scenes that served as a model for translation into garden design. The surreal neglected gardens of Watteau's paintings were decorated with sculptures and pavilions surmounted by greenery. The rococo painters François Boucher, Honoré Fragonard,

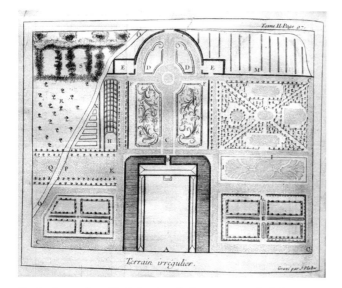

Garden layout from Noel-Antoine Pluche, *Les spectacle de la nature*, 1735
Copyright C.A. Wimmer

and Hubert Robert borrowed ideas from Watteau later in the century. The 18th century books on garden design by Louis Liger and Antoine-Joseph Dézallier d'Argenville in his early editions are the best sources of this type of design. Stonework and sculptures were mostly avoided and replaced by natural features such as grassy slopes and clipped trees or hedges. The *parterre de gazon* or *à langlais* was invented at this time and gradually replaced the baroque *parterres de broderie*.

Most European nations copied the French rococo style. In Britain, however, this movement did not make much headway. The most famous British rococo craftsman was the cabinetmaker Thomas Chippendale. The use of the word *rococo* in this period presents some problems. Some art historians have also applied the term to the curves and serpentine lines of paths and lakes in the landscape gardens, but the rather great scale of such gardens may be contradictory in spirit to the rococo love for smallness. Many features of the rococo garden were borrowed from earlier times—for example, grottoes, trelliswork, rockwork, and labyrinthine paths. On the other hand, features of the rococo garden, such as Chinese and Gothic buildings, appear in later gardens. Michael Symes has distinguished between rococo gardens, which are small in scale and very scarce today, and rococo elements within larger gardens or parks, which have been well documented and preserved.

Rococo gardens are largely regular in design, although irregular details may be included in the smaller parts of the geometric layout. In poetry and painting, however, irregularly designed gardens had already been depicted. The garden at Clarens described by Jean-Jacques Rousseau in his *Nouvelle Heloise* (1762) may be cited as a famous example of a literary rococo garden quite unexecutable at the time.

Rococo gardeners used more plant species than their predecessors. Flowers and flowering trees and shrubs were highly esteemed. The assortment, enriched by new introductions from North America, was grouped into a regular grid. Philip Miller published such a planting scheme in the article "Wilderness" in his *Gardener's Dictionary* (1731). The earliest flowerbeds, clumps, and shrubberies date from this period. The clipping of trees was more and more avoided, and useful plants were not restricted to the hidden kitchen garden. Some gardeners looked at the several tints of greenery using them in a picturesque manner. Also the variegated-leaved cultivars were much esteemed in these times. Among those who included new, exotic plants in their planting schemes were Archibald, duke of Argyll at Whitton, Scotland; the Duchess Beaufort at Badminton; Lord Petre at Thorndon Hall; the earl of Essex at Cassiobury; Charles Hamilton at Painshill; Philipp Southcote at Woburn Farm; and Horace Walpole at Strawberry Hill.

Few gardens from this period have been preserved. Famous rococo gardens existing today are Veitshöchheim, Eremitage, and Sanspareil in Bavaria, Sanssouci at Potsdam, Painshill in Surrey, Painswick in Gloucestershire, Nuneham in Oxfordshire, and Petit Trianon at Versailles.

A neorococo movement occurred from the 1820s to 1850s. The figures of Dézallier d'Argenville's treatise were reprinted in John Claudius Loudon's *Encylopaedia of Gardening* (1822). In 1853 the Scottish gardener Charles M'Intosh adopted designs by Dézallier for flower gardens proposed in his *Practical Gardener*.

Further Reading

Blondel, Jacques-François, *De la distribution des maisons de plaisance*, 2 vols., Paris: Jombert, 1737–38; reprint, Farnborough, Hampshire: Gregg Press, 1967

Chambers, Douglas, *The Planters of the English Landscape Garden: Botany, Trees, and the Georgics*, New Haven, Connecticut: Yale University Press, 1993

Dennerlein, Ingrid, *Die Gartenkunst der Régence und des Rokoko in Frankreich*, Worms, Germany: Werner, 1981

Dézallier d'Argenville, Antoine-Joseph, *La théorie et pratique du jardinage*, Paris, 1709; as *The Theory and Practice of Gardening*, translated by John James, London, 1712; reprint, Farnborough, Hampshire: Gregg, 1969

Harris, John, *Gardens of Delight: The Rococo English Landscape of Thomas Robins the Elder*, 2 vols., London: Basilisk Press, 1978

Harris, John, "The Flower Garden 1730–1830," in *The Garden: A Celebration of One Thousand Years of British Gardening*, edited by John Harris, London: Beazley, 1979

Hoffmann, Alfred, "Rokoko," in *Geschichte der deutschen Gartenkunst,* by Dieter Hennebo and Alfred Hoffmann, vol. 2, Hamburg: Broschek, 1965

Langley, Batty, *New Principles of Gardening,* London, 1728; reprint, New York: Garland, 1982

Pluche, Noël Antoine, *Le spectacle de la nature,* vol. 2, Paris: 1732; as *Spectacle de la nature; or, Nature Display'd,* London, 1735

Symes, Michael, *The English Rococo Garden,* Princes Risborough, Buckinghamshire: Shire, 1991

CLEMENS ALEXANDER WIMMER

Roman Gardens

The Roman Republic and Empire flourished for many centuries, from the days when Rome emerged as a power in central Italy to its domination of most of Europe and all the lands around the Mediterranean Sea, extending from Britain to Morocco, Portugal to Syria. Rome was initially influenced by its neighbors the Etruscans and Samnites; after expansion it came into contact with the settled communities of Greeks in southern Italy and Sicily. Following the wars with Carthage, new lands to the south, west, and east were conquered and absorbed. Rome was the capital of the empire, the heart and center of government, administration, and society. Colonies and municipal settlements in the provinces were modeled in its likeness, and many of the fashions set in Rome permeated outlying regions. In the third century A.D. the power and wealth of the empire started to decline; it was beset by economic difficulties, and constant battles on its borders took its toll on the standard of life within the empire.

Information on Roman gardens can be found in ancient literature, inscriptions, contemporary art such as sculpture mosaics and frescoes, and by archaeological discoveries made throughout the Roman Empire. Of the literary sources many briefly mention aspects of gardens relating to wealthy properties, but only Pliny the Younger describes his gardens in detail. Pliny the Elder and Dioscorides provide details of plants grown, and methods of agriculture and horticulture survive in manuals written by Cato (second century B.C.), Varro (ca. 36 B.C.), Columella (ca. A.D. 60), and Palladius (fourth century A.D.).

Early Roman gardens were rustic in nature and were essential in an economy largely devoted to subsistence farming. The *hortus,* the Latin word for garden, was then an enclosed area in which kitchen garden plants and fruit trees were grown and was primarily designed to meet the needs of the family. It was situated close to the home so that valuable produce and beehives could be protected. Virgil, in *Georgics,* relates the joys of a simple country garden that also contains herbs and some flowers for bees to make honey.

Villas in the country would originally have contained a *hortus rusticus;* decorative elements were added later, commencing late second to first century B.C. Larger villas then comprised three distinct groups of buildings: the rustic portion—which would still contain a *hortus rusticus*—a storehouse, and the *villa urbana,* or the owner's house, which was finished to a higher standard. The change was influenced by an increase in wealth stemming from conquests in Sicily and the east. Booty including sculpture was sent to beautify public buildings in Rome, indirectly triggering a desire to beautify home and garden as well. The opulence of eastern rulers influenced many; and the subsequent hedonistic lifestyle of one of the returning generals, Lucullus, became proverbial. On his return he built a grand villa with landscaped gardens on the Pincio hill overlooking Rome (ca. 60 B.C.). This was the first project on such a scale, and its beauty was admired by all. The new garden form contained elements derived from Persian *paradeisoi,* the pleasure gardens and game preserves of eastern rulers, and the sacred groves of Hellenistic Greece. Gardens varied greatly in size, then as now, but there are two distinct forms; one of an open nature, the other enclosed. Both are found in domestic and public contexts, in urban or rural areas. Large villas would contain enclosed garden courts and light wells, whereas some had semi-enclosed areas between residential wings, as well as extensive landscaped grounds.

In towns and cities, gardens were more limited in size, but many owners included aspects of a luxurious country villa, to provide a little *rus in urbe.* Houses and gardens were designed to fit into an *insula,* or block of housing. Each house was built adjacent to its neighbor's boundary so that the dwelling was inward facing around a light well; the sloping roofs also enabled rainwater to be collected from roofs into a cistern. In Italy the houses were generally on an axial plan with the street entrance passage leading into an atrium, a partly roofed hall surrounded by rooms. The garden was usually sited to the rear of the house and in the early days was probably more rustic than decorative. At Cosa and Pompeii archaeological excavations have detected this phase of housing from an early date, the late fourth or early third century B.C. At some time during the second century B.C., a new fashion emerged, which involved inserting a peristyle, or series of porticoes, around the old *hortus*. This development is believed to have come from the east, but unlike the paved courts of Greek cities, the open area inside the Roman peristyle was planted. If the garden was small and there was insufficient room for a full peristyle encircling the rectangular garden, only one, two, or three porticoes were built. An illusion of a complete peristyle was sometimes attempted with painted or applied stucco columns and frescoes of a garden or landscape painted in the intervening spaces. These trompe l'oeil works of art effectively created a much larger garden.

There was often a deliberate line of sight through the dwelling to the garden beyond. The Romans were proud of their gardens and appear to have liked to demonstrate the fact that they possessed fine garden furnishings or garden frescoes, for it was part of life to show one's status and prosperity. These displays were often deliberately placed so that they could be seen from the entrance door of the house, as well as from important reception or dining rooms.

Houses were sometimes enlarged, often by absorbing part of an adjacent property; this allowed a second garden to be installed or a larger one created. A few houses grew so large that there were only one or two properties in an entire block of housing. This rise in prosperity can be seen at Pompeii and elsewhere, such as Italica in Spain. The Italic atrium house is found in other provinces, but a further development, more often seen outside Italy, was the introduction of a central peristyle in which a vestibule or passage led straight to the internal peristyle garden. This served as a light well for surrounding rooms.

Gardens relying solely on water drawn from a cistern were mostly planted with only a small range of trees and shrubs that would not need frequent watering. However, the building of aqueducts indirectly brought about a revolution in garden design: water primarily piped to bath complexes was frequently extended to houses and villas, and this constant supply suddenly gave more freedom of choice in planting. More delicate species could be added, and formally planted bedding schemes became possible. Water features were introduced, and at times there was a lavish display of water consumption.

Fountain houses or *nymphaea* (a shrine of a nymph) were built in gardens. Some were fitted into an *aedicula*, a recess with a pediment roof, the more decorative versions being covered in shells and brightly colored mosaic. Another form comprised multiple fountains in a series of niches that mimicked a Roman theater facade. Fountain figures were added and in some cases the water was made to tumble down a short flight of stairs into an ornamental pool. Some pools were evidently stocked with fish and had fish refuges inserted into side walls. The rectangular pool was most common, but many decorative forms exist, all formal in character and geometrically inspired, containing a combination of either internal or external recesses based on the rectangle or semicircle. There was never a desire to have irregular natural-shaped fishponds. The most elaborate pool types contained watertight caissons that could be planted; these islands of greenery were also decoratively shaped. Several houses at Conimbriga, Portugal (second to third century A.D.) had water gardens of this type: in the House of the Water Jets, 400 arcs of water played around its perimeter and between each of the six island beds.

Altars and shrines were often sited in gardens for religious purposes and played an important role in the everyday life of the Romans. Divinities associated with nature were invoked or propitiated to ensure the successful cultivation of plants. For instance, Flora was sought to ensure that flowers bloomed in their proper season, and crops would need protection from Robigus, the god of rust. The most powerful garden deities were Priapus, whose rustic ithyphallic image was used to protect produce from thieves, and Venus, who was responsible for the garden's fertility. Cupid and statuettes of playful *erotes* or *amorini* are also found in garden contexts. Vines were grown in many gardens, and sacrifices to Bacchus, the god of wine, were made before al fresco meals. All the retinue of Bacchus can be found in garden statuary: satyrs, maenads, fauns, centaurs, and Pan. As creatures strongly associated with nature, they would be at home in the greenery of the garden. Other figures found in gardens were connected to their environment by myth. For example, a scene from one of Hercules' exploits—the Garden of Hesperides—could be re-created in a garden. The Muses and Apollo could also foster contemplation and inspiration, gained from a walk through the garden or after repose on a well-chosen bench seat under a shady tree.

Sundials were sited in gardens that did not have too much shade. Some had a flat dial, but the majority were engraved into a concave surface. The sundials functioned in a different way from ones in the present day, however, for the hours of the day were not of equal lengths throughout the year; those of summer were longer than in winter. Other sculptural items could include Herms, a bust on a short shaft. These were popular garden ornaments throughout the Roman period, whereas *pinakes* and *oscilla* appear up to the third century A.D. *Pinakes* were rectangular relief panels mounted onto a post; *oscilla* were smaller relief panels suspended from a tree or colonnade. There was a vogue for rustic genre figures such as an emaciated fisherman holding his catch; the related theme of a shepherd continued into later Christian iconography. Most statuary could be thought of as both decorative and sacred, and although some pieces were of outstanding quality, many were mass produced expressly for gardens. Statues, however, were status objects kept by families over many years. Some were made out of bronze, but as these were expensive to make and because the material could be melted down, few survive. At Pompeii, in the House of the Vettii, a pair of bronze *amorini* holding ducks once poured water into a tablelike fountain basin. Because these garden furnishings are still in situ, this house is the best example of a decorative Roman peristyle garden; most sculpture surviving from this period is now in museums.

Statuary was also displayed in public parks and in the large public portico gardens seen in cities. Many of these were donated by wealthy individuals and were of a more monumental size to suit their public nature. These areas of greenery were an act of benevolence and a welcome refuge in overcrowded urban areas. The first portico garden was constructed in Rome by Pompey the Great in 55 B.C. This was placed next to his theater to provide a pleasant walk between plays. Details of this garden and four others survive on fragments of a marble map of Rome made under the emperor Septimius Severus. The gardens were usually square or rectangular in shape with a portico on three or four sides. Many contained *exedrae,* recesses for bench seating. Writings of poets from this time reveal that there was a double grove of plane trees in Pompey's portico, box trees in the portico of Europa, and laurels in the garden of Agrippa. Portico gardens graced many public buildings such as libraries where scrolls could be read in good light; planted areas could be found in the exercise yards of bath complexes; and sacred groves were planted in temple precincts. At Mérida (Spain) the large theater portico garden has been replanted.

Gardens were occasionally constructed on a lower level and would have provided cool areas in hot weather. These gardens were usually designed to be seen from above. At the Casa di Ancora Nera, Pompeii, a narrow staircase of nine steep steps led down to the sunken garden. Statues were placed in arched niches on either side of the garden, and the focal point at the end comprised two ornamented recesses flanking an elegant shrine. A palatial example exists on the Palatine, Rome, in the so-called stadium garden. This conceit is more frequently called a hippodrome garden, recalling a race track; in this example two semicircular pools marked the turning points of the "racecourse." Hippodrome gardens are also found on level terrain.

Romans preferred to build and create gardens on flat ground and would therefore terrace land and insert stairways between different levels. Remains of terracing can be seen on the hills around Tivoli, which was a pop-

ular area for building large luxurious villas. At least one of the many garden areas in the grounds of the emperor Hadrian's villa (A.D. 118) at Tivoli was constructed on a terrace (the large Poikile garden); and the *cryptoporticus* below is still preserved at one end of the garden where the land drops sharply. Everything in this villa is suitably imperial in size, but scaled-down versions would also have existed.

Hadrian's villa provides many examples of landscape garden features, including a beautiful Doric temple and two belvederes, or prospect towers. There is still a wonderful panorama of surrounding countryside. Hadrian named several areas after particular places of note, a practice that was not too unusual. These locations had made such an impression on his travels throughout the Roman Empire that he sought to re-create their atmosphere. There was the Poikile, a painted colonnade in Athens, which he recalled in a long garden ambulatory opening onto a large terraced garden, and an Athenian-style academy or lyceum, the haunt of philosophers (also re-created at an earlier date by Cicero, mid-first- century B.C.), which was translated as a promenade through a grove of plane trees. A nearby valley was altered to appear like the beautiful Vale of Tempe in Thessaly; a grotto representing Hades was built into a hillside; and a fabulous open-fronted dining hall was made to overlook a likeness of the Canopus Canal of Egypt.

Large sheets of water, usually in an elongated rectangular shape, were not only named after the Canopus Canal but were also called a Nile or Euripus (a narrow tidal race off the Greek coast). A famous *euripus* built in Rome ca. 19 B.C. had little bridges crossing its course; those water features added to the houses of Julia Felix and Loreius Tiburtinus at Pompeii may have sought to re-create the example seen in the capital. The philhellenism of high society led to two other named Roman garden concepts: the *xystus,* which was approached through a colonnade and was effectively a garden terrace with promenades, and the *gestatio,* a drive sometimes of a circular form.

Gardens enhanced the beauty of many buildings and were a means to link different sections. Surviving frescoes depict another aspect of gardens not often found by archaeology because of their ephemeral nature: the use of trelliswork and low ornamental walls to partition areas or make garden rooms. Decorative panels often contained open sections to relieve their linear form, and recesses were formed to highlight statuary or a specimen tree. Most of the fencing comprised low panels, but there are also examples of tall latticework. Wooden pergolas and arches were added to provide height, and life was brought to the scene with several marble urn fountains, which often appear to entice wild birds. Birds were actively encouraged into gardens, and many Romans also possessed an aviary somewhere on their estate. Varro, for example, describes a highly ornamental yet functional example.

Large complex villas also existed in the provinces. Some of the major sites are Piazza Armerina (Sicily), Montmaurin (France), and Fishbourne (Britain). Only a few have been excavated using modern techniques of garden archaeology to ascertain details of their surrounding landscape gardens. At the palace at Fishbourne (A.D. 75), however, three garden forms have been detected: a landscaped southern garden with a pond and views out to sea, a large formally planted courtyard, and small light-well courts. In the large formal garden, a good loamy soil in bedding trenches was preserved in the poor subsoil, revealing the outline of a topiary box hedge with a complicated, architecturally inspired design of alternating rectangular and semicircular recesses. The most elaborate sections bordered a wide central path, and to one side near the colonnade a line of post pits indicates an alignment of espalier trees. Plant beds have also been identified at modest-sized winged villas such as at Bancroft and Frocester Court (Britain), and box clippings have been found on site. Details of the actual planting schemes, however, are not known; in general the survival rate of pollens is rare unless found in anaerobic conditions, such as in a sealed clay or waterlogged deposit. In towns and cities in the provinces, the items more often encountered are the foundations of architectural garden furnishings and fishponds, paths, post or plant holes, and areas of friable soil that show garden cultivation over many years.

In Pompeii, however, the eruption of the volcano Vesuvius in A.D. 79 covered the area with a thick layer of volcanic fallout that immediately preserved details of the way of life in a Roman town. When archaeologists removed the ash and lapilli, they uncovered numerous houses. A survey of these houses' gardens (totaling 450) undertaken by Wilhelmina Jashemski has revealed much more information. When the original ground surface of A.D. 79 had been reached, the raised edges of plant beds were detected and root cavities were explored. Root casts were made and compared with modern varieties to identify any diagnostic characteristics. A detailed scientific analysis of the soil could then be made and surviving pollen grains and macrofossils studied to indicate which plant species are represented. One of the latest gardens explored, by Ciarallo at the House of the Chaste Lovers, reveals a pathway delineated by a simply erected reed fence; at either side juniper alternated with rose bushes. This garden also contained plants with contrasting foliage, but as in many cases, the genus rather than the variety is known. These include *Artemisia, Myrtus, Malva, Campanula, Lychnis,* and *Cerastium.*

Just as today no two gardens are exactly alike, the gardens of Pompeii have their own individual characteristics.

Formal garden designs are suspected at a number of houses, where rows of former plant roots are set in a symmetrical pattern indicative of topiary hedges. Some of the small gardens, however, were more informal; many were almost completely shaded by large fruit- or nut-bearing trees, with some trained against a wall. Also in one part of the town there appears to have been several small market gardens sited behind the living quarters of a shop; these *horti* are rustic in style with clearly defined rows of bedding trenches. One had broken amphorae along the top of the garden wall to repel thieves. Some had been kept as a vineyard, where salad or vegetable crops would have grown between rows. These rustic *horti* often included an outdoor dining area, or summer triclinium, most of which were permanent fixtures made of brick covered with stucco. The sight of the ripening fruit was clearly thought very satisfying; the fact that these were productive gardens and not ornamental did not matter. Within the town there were also gardens attached to some taverns and eating establishments where diners could have al fresco meals under the shade of a vine-covered pergola.

Summer triclinia are found in domestic town gardens at Pompeii and elsewhere in the provinces, including Vienne (France), Ostia (near Rome), and Italica (Spain). The dining couches were usually grouped into three (a *triclinium*), two (a *biclinium*), or a single large curved couch to accommodate several people (a *stibadium*). In all three of these provincial locations, the al fresco dining area had been sited beside an ornamental pool, and it is possible that the pool acted as a water *mensa*, or table, on which light dishes could be floated on the water surface, a scenario described by Pliny the Younger in his Tuscan garden. Clearly, the garden was for enjoyment and was designed to delight the senses.

Gardening in the provinces was in many ways similar to that practiced at Rome. In very hot regions there was a divergence that stemmed from a lack of sufficient water for plants, and in dry areas large cisterns were built beneath the dwelling. Plants were ringed by mounded earth so that when watered all the liquid would be contained for the plant's roots; no water was wasted. Another method, seen in dry rocky terrain, was to excavate and fill a plant pit with fine soil; this would also restrict water loss and provide sufficient room for root growth. Any ornamental pools that were constructed tended to be small in size and designed so that their outflow would irrigate the garden, again conserving water. In northern regions, in contrast, protection from winter frosts was needed, and some of the tender southern plant species could not survive.

The plants of this period are basically those originating from provinces bordering the Mediterranean Sea. Over the centuries numerous plants were acclimatized and introduced to gardens in different provinces, and the dissemination of plant species is one of the enduring legacies of the Roman Empire. Pliny the Elder, in his *Naturalis Historia* (A.D. 77; *Natural History*), gives a great deal of information on garden species (he mentions 139). Pliny discusses each plant's usefulness to humankind and the way in which each was grown. He also recounts which plants had a medicinal use and which were grown for the table; some were used to make wines and cordials, others to make honey (in the absence of sugar, this was their natural sweetener). Aromatic plants were also grown to make perfumes, and many flowers were picked for making garlands.

The Romans were practical by nature, which is demonstrated by the fact that so many of the plants had a particular use. After time, however, some ornamental species were added to gardens; of these the otherwise poisonous oleander is perhaps the most spectacular, with its abundance of bright pink flowers. This colorful addition is illustrated in several of the verdant frescoes from Pompeii. Another ornamental example is the plane; literary sources suggest that this was the most widely planted large tree. With its large leaves and broad canopy, it provided ample shade under which one could sit. Some censured its use, because it was a sterile tree, compared to the fruitfulness of walnut or chestnut.

The nettle tree (*Celtis australis*) was admired for its graceful habit, and some trees and bushes, such as the jujube (*Zizyphus jujuba*), were included in gardens for their novelty value. Roman horticulturists regularly pruned, layered, or grafted trees, experimented, and produced new cultivars; in some cases even several branches of different fruits were grafted onto one tree. A variety of fruit trees was grown, including some not of commercial value today, such as quince, mulberry, medlar, and service trees. Exotic fruits were prized; the peach and apricot were introduced to Rome, but the citron/lemon (the orange was not yet known), which originated from Asia Minor, took considerable efforts to establish in the warmer areas of Italy. Even here the plants needed attention to help them survive winter frosts, but the effort was considered worthwhile, for this attractive yellow aromatic fruit had medicinal properties. These fruits are occasionally seen in frescoes and mosaics.

Frescoes are an important source of information because, where descriptions are brief and not sufficiently clear as to which variety of plant is discussed, an actual illustration can confirm a plant's existence at a particular date. Some of the frescoes are simplistic in style, hampering classification, but many are so well drawn that a more positive identification is possible. The decorative Roman garden was planted with a variety of evergreen shrubs and trees. The most common appear to be myrtle, bay, laurustinus, oleander, strawberry tree (*Arbutus*), pine, cypress, box, and fruit trees.

The laurel, or bay, was sacred to Apollo, just as the myrtle was to Venus, and both were popular garden shrubs due to their scented foliage. They are the most frequently painted shrubs, filling either the midground or background of garden scenes; their distinctive leaf pattern is discernible in even the most rudimentary compositions. Pliny mentions that the *tinus,* with its blue berries, was considered another form of laurel, and their tightly grouped white flowers identify these bushes as the laurustinus. The strawberry tree was also a decorative addition, and its small fruit, inedible to humans, was relished by thrushes.

Ivy was one of the main plants used for making swags of garlands that decorated the home and shrine. It was allowed to grow up trees and would link tree to tree, as it did the columns of a peristyle. It was also draped over statues to make them more alluring. Frescoes show that ivy was also grown and trained into the shape of a mound, so that it would resemble a compact evergreen bush. There were several forms of ivy, with dark, pale, or variegated leaves.

Scented flowers were highly regarded; the most popular were the rose, violet, lily, narcissus, and sweet marjoram. There were single and double roses, but only white, pink, and red forms were known. The late-flowering Praeneste rose was the most favored, closely followed by the twice-flowering rose of Paestum. A species with "a hundred petals" was also planted. The rose species represented were *Rosa gallica, R. phoenicea, R. damascena, R. moschata,* and *R. centifolia.* Of the lilies the white flowers of *Lilium candidum* are well recorded, and those with red flowers are thought to be of *L. martagon.* The violet was described as having three different colors, and this represents an instance when a particular term for scented flowers in general, such as *gilliflower,* was used for more than one plant species. Today it is believed that the small blue violet was *Viola odorata,* the yellow form possibly a wallflower, *Cheiranthus cheiri,* and those with scented white flowers, stocks, *Matthiola incana.* Pliny informs us that the sweet scent of *Hesperis matronalis,* the dame's violet, was also appreciated in gardens at night or dusk.

Many of the culinary herbs known today were grown in Roman gardens, and the majority were also considered decorative. The florets of parsley, for example, have a delicate scent, and it produces numerous pliant stems for weaving or plaiting into a floral crown. It is mentioned in a dance called "The Flowers," during which revelers sang to the chorus of "Where are my roses, where are my violets, where my beautiful parsley?" The glossy-leafed acanthus, *Acanthus mollis,* lent a statuesque touch to a garden and like the periwinkle was often used as ground cover in large beds; the latter was "at times filling the gap when other flowers fail" (Pliny the Elder).

A pleasing leaf shape certainly had an appeal; in this class were the hart's tongue fern, maidenhair fern, cynoglossum, iris, and plantains. The hart's tongue fern and plantains are often depicted in frescoes on low garden walls or in the dado zones of larger Roman frescoes. A number of frescoes depict a cluster of orange or white daisylike flowers, which are thought to be marigolds, wild chrysanthemum, or chamomile; these freely seeding plants would have given added color to bedding areas.

A pine tree is central to the composition of several frescoes; of these trees the stone pine was the most favored, chiefly because the nuts were added to many food dishes. Slender juniper and cypress were also grown; the latter is mentioned for use in topiary work. In dry areas rosemary was an alternative to cypress or box.

The word *topiary* derives from *topiarius*, a person specifically employed as a gardener of ornamental gardens. He clipped the hedges and created *topia*, or landscapes. His work, *opus topiarium*, was in effect that of a landscape gardener. There was no all-embracing term for a gardener; instead, individuals would have been known by their specific duty. Therefore, a *hortulanus* was someone who worked in a market garden; an *olitor* was employed to cultivate vegetables; an *arborator* tended trees in and out of the orchard; a *vinitor* was a vine dresser; and an *aquarius* was one who watered the plants.

With the decline and fall of Rome, garden art in the West suffered greatly and may have survived in a greatly reduced form in palatial residences. In the East the empire continued for a time under the Byzantine emperors. Ornamental gardens were largely confined to the residences of wealthy governors, bishops, and courtiers based in Constantinople and other large eastern cities. A form of garden could be found in the forecourt of some of the early Christian churches; interestingly, these green areas were often referred to as a Garden of Eden or Paradise. The peristyle was preserved in monastic cloister gardens, but these increasingly were used as herbaria rather than as ornamental gardens. Byzantine gardens were to some extent an influence on later Islamic garden design, as seen in their use of pools and fountains.

Further Reading

Andreae, Bernard, *Am Birnbaum: Gärten und Parks im antiken Rom, in den Vesuvstädten und in Ostia*, Mainz, Germany: Von Zabern, 1996

Barton, Ian M., editor, *Roman Domestic Buildings*, Exeter, Devon: University of Exeter Press, 1996

Ciarallo, A.M., "The Garden of 'Casa Dei Casti Amanti' (Pompeii, Italy)," *Garden History* 21 (1993)

Cunliffe, Barry W., *Fishbourne: A Roman Palace and Its Garden*, London: Thames and Hudson, and Baltimore, Maryland: Johns Hopkins Press, 1971; revised and updated edition, as *Fishbourne Roman Palace*, Stroud, Gloucestershire: Tempus, 1998

Farrar, Linda, *Ancient Roman Gardens*, Stroud, Gloucestershire: Sutton, 1998

Gleason, K.L., "Porticus Pompeiana: A New Perspective on the First Public Park of Ancient Rome," *Journal of Garden History* 14 (1994)

Grimal, Pierre, *Les jardins romains à la fin de la république et aux deux premiers siècles de l'empire*, Paris: Boccard, 1943; 2nd edition, Paris: Presses Universitaires de France, 1969

Jashemski, Wilhelmina F., *The Gardens of Pompeii: Herculaneum and the Villas Destroyed by Vesuvius*, 2 vols., New Rochelle, New York: Caratzas, 1979–93

Lawson, James, "The Roman Garden," *Greece and Rome* 19 (1950)

Lloyd, R.B., "Three Monumental Gardens on the Marble Plan," *American Journal of Archaeology* 86 (1982)

MacDonald, William Lloyd, and John A. Pinto, *Hadrian's Villa and Its Legacy*, New Haven, Connecticut: Yale University Press, 1995

MacDougall, Elisabeth B., and Wilhelmina F. Jashemski, editors, *Ancient Roman Gardens*, Washington, D.C.: Dumbarton Oaks Trustees for Harvard University, 1981

MacDougall, Elisabeth B., editor, *Ancient Roman Villa Gardens*, Washington, D.C.: Dumbarton Oaks · Research Library and Collection, 1987

Tomei, M.A., "Nota sui giardini antichi del Palatino," *Mélanges de l'École française de Rome: Antiquité* 104 (1992)

LINDA FARRAR

Romania

Bordered by the Black Sea and several newly independent republics, Romania is a modest-sized country, whose location on the turbulent Balkan peninsula has left it disadvantaged, politically and economically, for much of its history. Both the Ottoman and Austro-Hungarian empires alternately marauded and occupied the area, and the former Soviet Union retained a firm grip until 1989 through a system of shadow dictators. Because of these conditions Romania's abundance of natural resources has proven of little use, and horticultural development was as a result stunted by autocratic regimes. Nevertheless, the topography is dramatic. The Carpathian Mountains arch along the central and eastern part of Romania and enclose the large plateau region of Transylvania. Stretching outward from the mountains lie fertile tablelands and arable slopes that eventually merge into lowlands occupying most of Romania, including the Tisza Plain—also known as the Banat—and the plains of Walachia, cradled between Bulgaria and the Transylvanian Alps. Wooded steppe dominates most of the topography through a composite of beech and mixed forest, juniper tree bushes (*Juniperus tiberica*), and bilberry (*Vaccinium myrtillus*). While endowed with these hardy woodlands, Romania also possesses a sufficient system of waterways. The Danube and its tributaries constitute the most important river network, with much of the rich Dobruja corridor near the Black Sea consumed by the Danube delta—a 5,000-year-old region of serpentine channels within 25 distinct ecosystems. Freshwater lakes are common in the mountainous areas, but the saline shallows along the littoral are usually considered the nation's largest bodies of water. The country's temperate climate, moderate rainfall, and four-season cycle have traditionally been conducive to grain and vegetable farming, as well as grape cultivation, and vineyards and orchards are plentiful in the higher regions. While natural circumstances have proven beneficial to attempts at gardening in Romania, political situations have frequently discouraged such expressions. Private gardens were modest, and only in the 19th century did organized state-sponsored gardens begin to make an appearance.

The capital of Bucharest lies to the south on a level plain. Divided by the Dîmboviţa and Colentina Rivers, the city drew from French tradition in its early 20th-century urban planning and landscape development, eventually earning reference as the "Paris of the Balkans." The last Soviet-era dictator, Nicolae Ceauşescu, leveled a sizable portion of the city to build a civic center in the 1980s. Despite this methodical destruction Bucharest is still known as a "green city," filled with lime and horse chestnut trees, renowned for its decorative and historical parks, and buffeted by a lush system of suburban woodlands. Near the center of the city is Cismigiu Garden, a well-attended public retreat wherein gardens are partitioned into regional collections, each exhibiting the flora of a particular country district, and host to noteworthy groupings of trees (magnolias, planes, and oaks) and striking ornamental flowers. Developed on a former swampland by a German developer, Cismigiu traces its history to 1845, when the owner, a Turkish water inspector, bequeathed the private lands and lake to the town. By 1850 landscaping had begun, and the main path and peripheral routeways plotted and dug within what would be the central garden. Later an artesian well was built in the center of the lake, which today holds rowboats that provide a popular warm-weather pastime. The park's statues, scattered throughout the grounds, celebrate the nation's culture and include busts of historic Romanian writers and other luminaries.

Nearby Herestrau Park is the largest garden in the city at 461 acres (187 ha). Situated along the Colentina River, the park was founded as a seasonal pleasure resort, and by 1936 a 25-acre (10-ha) open-air museum showcasing traditional Romanian buildings had been added. Also within city limits, the botanical garden (*gradina botanica*) of Bucharest formed in 1884; by 1891 landscapers had plotted the principal garden design, and the first greenhouses opened. Although some of the original greenhouses and structural elements were destroyed in both World War I and II, they were eventually reconstructed as repositories for exotic, southern plants, while indigenous and Mediterranean plantings were arranged on the outside grounds. A spacious botanical museum adjoins the gardens with rooms dedicated to regional flora (including a large exhibit on Danube delta vegetation) augmented with exhibits of painted botanical illustrations, manuscripts, and specimen collections.

Other organized botanical collections exist in Iasi, close to the border with Moldova. These include a municipal botanical garden and the Copou Garden, which contains the oldest public forum in Romania. Timişoara, a city to the east near Serbia and Romania's third-largest city, is also celebrated for its parks and gardens. Cluj-Napoca, capital of the Cluj district in central Romania, houses a garden that enjoys large attendance as both a well-respected research institution and beautiful landscape park. Although at 35 acres (14 ha) smaller than the municipal gardens in Bucharest, the Cluj-Napoca garden is considered the most comprehensive in Romania with more than 12,000 species of plants, including an impressive cactus collection. It is a more scientific garden than many, with a large team of researchers who maintain the sophisticated hothouse system of six greenhouses in which Amazonian and Mediterranean plants, orchids, and tropical ferns are carefully cultivated. Founded in 1872 by two professors, the garden established its collection on European flora, and in 1920 Professor Alexandru Borza purchased more land to create a larger facility that stressed scientific classification. Appropriately, the city's botanical institute shares space with the garden, whose features include a richly landscaped Japanese Garden and a Roman Garden (subdivided into vegetable and flower gardens and a museum for archaeological artifacts from the Roman occupation of the Napoca municipium). The ornamental section of the garden holds hundreds of varieties of ligneous and herbaceous plants, but the most scientifically valued and educational section is certainly the assemblage of phylogenetically arranged plant species.

Like its counterparts in Bucharest, the Cluj garden contains abundant samples of Romanian flora characteristic of the mountain regions (including a replicated microclimate), Transylvanian plain, and Danube delta.

General attempts at private gardens within Romania have been crippled over the centuries by the uncertain geopolitics of eastern Europe. References to fledgling royal gardens may be traced to the Walachian prince Constantin Brancoveanu (r. 1688–1714), who was a tremendous promoter of art and culture. Enthused by Byzantine, Renaissance, and baroque decorative motifs, the prince created a large Italian garden with an arbor in the Old Princely Court of Bucharest. This garden, improved by successive generations, is perhaps one of the first documented forms of garden expression within the capital. Other private garden endeavors have been negligible and strictly the provenance of the wealthier class. One Romanian traveler in 1824 lamented the lack of developed Romanian gardens and, following a tour of other European estates, set about creating his own garden retreat outside Bucharest in hopes of replicating the styles he had admired elsewhere.

As Romania emerges from its troubled past it is hoped that the nation can begin to look inward to more home-wrought inspiration as it develops a sustainable garden tradition of its own.

Further Reading

Barbu, Gheorghe, *Arta vindecarii în Bucurestii de odinioara*, Bucharest, Romania: Editura Stiintifica, 1967

Beattie, William, *Danube: Its History, Scenery, and Topography*, London: Virtue, 1844

Grigorescu, Dan, *In the Danube Delta*, Bucharest, Romania: Meridiane, 1967

King, Charles, *The Moldovans: Romania, Russia, and the Politics of Culture*, Stanford, California: Hoover Institution Press, 1999

Lupan, Petre, editor, *Bucharest: Museums of Art*, Bucharest: Meridiane, 1977

Petranu, Adriana, compiler, *Black Sea Biological Diversity: Romania*, New York: United Nations Publications, 1997

Polunin, Oleg, *Flowers of Greece and the Balkans: A Field Guide*, New York and Oxford: Oxford University Press, 1980

KRISTIN WYE-RODNEY

Roof Garden

Today's roof gardens have antecedents in the ziggurats of ancient Mesopotamia, the Hanging Gardens of Babylon, and the roof gardens of Tenochtitlan in Mexico. The Kremlin in Moscow and the Hermitage in Saint Petersburg also had extensive roof gardens. In modern times the roof garden built by Karl Rabbitz in Berlin, exhibited in scale model at the Paris World Exposition of 1867, and the Munich roof gardens constructed by King Ludwig II of Bavaria, were forerunners of the theater roof gardens of the 1890s, including the Winter Garden and Madison Square Garden in New York City. Oscar Hammerstein's Olympia Music Hall garden in New York (1895) included mountain crags and a lake. Interest continued in the 20th century: Charles-Edouard Jeanneret, better known as Le Corbusier, considered roof gardens one of the five tenets of modern architecture, and Frank Lloyd Wright made roof areas important parts of his work. The Derry and Toms Department Store garden in London (1938) was immensely influential.

During the post–World War II era, roof areas whose principal use had been as smoking sections for servants were eagerly appropriated by new generations of city dwellers. Urban dwellers in recent years have discovered that roof areas have their own microclimate, ideal for growing tomatoes, for example. The potential was obvious: in New York City there are an estimated 20,000 usable roof acres (8,094 ha), or 23 times the size of Central Park. This can be conspicuous gardening; the roof gardens of Rockefeller Center, for example, are overlooked by an estimated 100,000 windows.

While Le Corbusier will be remembered as one of the architects of the 20th century intrigued with roof gardens—and he designed several, which he compared with the hanging gardens of Semiramus—his designs offer little room for plants: for example, his design for Cote Charles de Beistegu's Paris penthouse, an experiment in what has been called "denatured nature." Indeed, in a 1929 *House Beautiful* article, Fletcher Steele castigated Le Corbusier, Robert Mallet-Stevens, and other modern architects for their inability to handle the gardens of their buildings, which "might have been carried out by the most commonplace and conventional of garden makers."

Union Square in San Francisco in the early 1940s was one of the first combination roof gardens and garages in a major city and inspired Yerba Buena Gardens, Crocker Terrace, and Ghirardelli Square in the same

Roof garden for Safra Bank by Roberto Burle Marx, São Paulo, Brazil
Copyright Michel Viard/Garden Picture Library

city, Mellon Square in Pittsburgh, and many other similar projects. The roof garden (1959) of the Kaiser Center in Oakland, California, made pioneering use of lightweight soil mix as well as lightweight pumice stone, which, along with ingenious planting of large trees directly over supporting columns, has resulted in an amazingly mature landscape: horizontal mugho pines and gnarled cork oaks are a testimony to the thoughtfulness of the original design. The wise choice of specimens with fibrous root systems rather than those with tap roots has avoided drain trouble. The successful plantings include olive, Japanese maple, magnolia, and arbutus trees. Part of Kaiser's success is the ingenious use of a four-inch (10 cm) layer of expanded shale over the entire roof. When shale is baked at a temperatures over 2,000 degrees Farenheit (1,093 C), it turns into hard balls full of air pockets that are excellent for retaining water.

The architect of Kaiser, Theodore Osmundson, came to be regarded as the doyen of modern roof-garden designers, and his courses on the roof garden at the Harvard School of Design were a major factor in increasing the popularity of such gardens after World War II. The soundness of his approach contrasts with that at nearby Oakland Museum roof gardens, built later. They have been a disaster, with many leaks and much of the soil being washed away.

The Pusey Library at Harvard, in Cambridge, Massachusetts (1976), set the pace for a large number of university buildings with roof gardens in order to save open space. Also notable are the Haupt Gardens of the Smithsonian Institution in Washington, D.C., which enhance the surrounding Victorian architecture and sit comfortably on top of the Asian and African galleries. Haupt is extraordinary for its deep soil beds of up to eight feet (2.4 m).

Almost any roof area can be turned into a garden; great results (with proper plant selection) have been had with even six inches (15 cm) of soil. The major problems with roof gardens are largely weight and water, along with unimaginative and repetitive screening material, too many pots, ubiquitous brass telescopes, and a chronic overuse of birch and maple trees. For plantings there are many possibilities to be considered, such as sweet gum, honey locust, little-leaf linden, ginkgo, and weeping purple beech. Surprisingly often overlooked in planning is the need for a maintenance center for fertilizers, tools, and trash.

A number of tragedies have led to some cities passing ordinances that parapet walls should be a minimum of 1.2 meters (1.3 yd.) tall; regardless of legal requirements, this is simply common sense, as is getting professional advice about the amount of load the roof will bear. Parapets are not only safety devices but also give welcome protection against wind. Care about root penetration of membranes and drains is essential since it can present a major problem years after construction. For example, experiments with sprayed-on asphalt waterproofing instead of more expensive rubber membranes have proved disastrous. At least two complete systems for roof gardens have been developed in Europe, the Bauder and the Sopranture. These involve various layers of material that prevent condensation in the building below, prevent roof penetration, and handle exceptional rainfall. Complete cooperation between the general architect and the landscape architect is a must.

One of the most ambitious new roof gardens at the beginning of the 21st century is the project of Chicago's mayor Richard Daley for its City Hall. The intention is to inspire the creation of gardens on top of other Chicago buildings, helping to clean the air and cut energy bills. More than 20,000 plants of 150 different species were used. Weight and water retention were priority problems, solved by a special light soil mixture. The temperature of the new garden is to be monitored and compared with buildings without roof gardens, with the hope of demonstrating savings in energy bills. The designer, William McDonough, also created roof gardens for the Gap's corporate headquarters in San Bruno, California, and at Oberlin College in Ohio. Chicago

officials pointed out that in a number of German cities roof gardens are required for new buildings.

Although many roof gardens become asphalt beaches or outdoor storage closets, they seem to be flourishing as never before, with trompe l'oeil, an enthusiasm for exotic fragrance, and ingenious lighting extending their vistas. Among the more recent urban retreats the gardens on the top of Trump Tower in New York City stand out, designed by architect Thomas Balsley with an extraordinarily lavish use of teak, copper, and plantings. Connecting roofs with bridges to provide a park in the skies, proposed but never implemented for Rockefeller Center, is an idea whose time may have come, exemplified by the Bunker Hill Gardens in Los Angeles and the Chicago City Hall project.

Further Reading

Busch, Akiko, *Rooftop Architecture: The Art of Going through the Roof,* New York: Holt, 1991

Colby, Deidre, *City Gardening: Planting, Maintaining, and Designing the Urban Garden,* New York: Simon and Schuster, 1987

Hendy, Jenny, *Balcony and Roof Gardens: Creative Ideas for Small-Scale Gardening,* Alexandria, Virginia: Time-Life Books, 1997

Imbert, Dorothée, *The Modernist Garden in France,* New Haven, Connecticut: Yale University Press, 1993

Osmundson, Theodore, *Roof Gardens: History, Design, and Construction,* New York: Norton, 1999

Pierce, Nona P., *Garden Getaways: Northern California: Public Gardens and Special Nurseries,* Palo Alto, California: Tioga, 1989

Pool, Mary Jane, *Gardens in the City: New York in Bloom,* New York: Abrams, 1999

Zevon, Susan, *Outside Architecture: Outdoor Rooms Designed by Architects,* Gloucester, Massachusetts: Rockport, 1999

PAUL RICH

Rose, James 1910–1991

United States Landscape Architect

James C. Rose was a key innovator in the development of the modern movement in landscape architecture. He began his formal training at Cornell University and in the 1930s studied at Harvard University, with fellow classmates and modernist advocates Garrett Eckbo and Dan Kiley. The three were educated according to the

Beaux-Arts classical landscape tradition, which employed axial layouts and symmetrical balance through Italian and French Renaissance-style garden prototypes. According to some contemporary academic thinking, landscape design could not be part of the avant-garde modern movement in art and architecture since its materials (plants, earth, water) were timeless and not conducive to the new tear-drop forms of industrial design or the experimental materials and methods of construction characterized by modern "machine-age" architecture. Rose argued against this view and presented his modernist perspective through a progression of articles published in 1938 and 1939 for *Pencil Points* magazine (now *Progressive Architecture*).

Rose's early exploration in modern landscape architectural forms cost him a Harvard degree; he was expelled in 1937 for his passionate pursuit of modernism and blatant discard of neoclassicism. He especially resented the modern architect's notion that landscape was a mere foil for architecture. His many provocative articles, including not only the *Pencil Points* essays but also four books, as well as a series for *Architectural Record* coauthored with Eckbo and Kiley, present an evolving thesis for the development of modern gardens that helped to advance the theory and practice of landscape architecture as an art form. Modern art, particularly the Cubist paintings of Pablo Picasso and Georges Braque, as well as the constructivist sculpture of László Moholy-Nagy, inspired his thinking and work. He was also influenced in this regard by Ludwig Mies van der Rohe, Le Corbusier, Christopher Tunnard, Lewis Mumford, and other modernists.

Rose expertly carried the abstracted forms of his gardens into three-dimensional complex spatial structures. The paintings and sculpture of Moholy-Nagy show a striking similarity to his gardens. Rose wrote in "Freedom in the Garden" (1938) that "Landscape design falls somewhere between architecture and sculpture." He presented in the same essay the idea that landscape is not an object but "outdoor sculpture . . . to surround us in a pleasant sense of space relations." In time he expanded on this idea and wrote of the need to create gardens for experience and to promote self-discovery by client-users.

Rose explored the notion of interlocking forms and three-dimensional spatial volumes in order to create a "oneness" of landscape volumes as sculptural form. He wrote in *Creative Gardens,* "This oneness evolving from the fusion and interplay of materials is characteristic of good form anywhere." A stream became his theoretical metaphor and visual model for the idea of oneness. Imagery of the widening and narrowing of a meandering stream through a flat field transformed (through Rose's description) into an interconnected pattern of water and land blended into one object. Concepts of positive and negative spatial fusion were a major focus of his modern style, characterized by organic abstracted patterns composed of triangular forms that appear to have been derived from an abstraction of natural forms such as topography or rock outcropping made into a series of occult geometric volumes. These patterns, or modern "free form" concepts as he called them, are often described as irregular forms, which perhaps unfairly implies randomness. His gardens were not arbitrary or random but highly controlled deliberate, yet flexible, outdoor rooms, in which he responded strongly to the distinctive qualities of the site.

Rose was employed with the New York design firm Tuttle, Seelye, Place, and Raymond in 1941. During this employment he designed a staging area to house 30,000 men at Camp Kilmer, New Jersey. He continued briefly in New York, establishing his own firm, engaged in the design of large-scale public and corporate projects. Quick to follow his true creative spirit, he moved to New Jersey to focus his efforts on private gardens primarily located in northern New Jersey and New York.

During World War II Rose was stationed in Okinawa; while there he developed the design for his home in Ridgewood, New Jersey, which was built in 1953. *Progressive Architecture* published the design in December 1954, highlighting Eastern inspiration and Rose's ability to integrate interior and exterior spaces. The design concept included provision for ongoing change and design evolution. Rose used a study model to represent his concept; he later criticized the extensive use of plan drawings to create gardens, pointing to the false sense of security that can be built up concerning the value of such drawings, which require skillful interpretation in moving from the two-dimensional drawing to the three-dimensional garden. He argued that such drawings have the same limitation for the garden as they would for sculpture. This conviction led him to practice in a "design-build" capacity where he could manipulate the raw materials on site through "spontaneous improvisation," therefore controlling the artistic vision and intricacies of the garden.

Rose traveled to Japan in 1970 as an invited participant in the World Design Conference. As a result of this trip and many others to follow, he became interested in Japanese garden design and Zen Buddhism. Eastern influence on his work can be seen most strikingly through his integration of interior and exterior spaces both visually and physically. Moveable screens, garden walls, regionally handcrafted materials, use of transparent and overlapping techniques, hanging vines, and delicate plant textures such as the mountain ash became features he used to create his gardens. Exploring garden design as an art form, Rose was interested in developing flexible gardens that could change over time. He created modular systems through movable paving and translucent shojis (paper screens) and often used recycled materials rich in texture and light. Usually walled for privacy, his gardens were sculptures of continuous spatial volumes, not unlike the experimental movement and spatial patterns of modern dance; indeed, Rose made comparisons between modern dance and his experiments.

Rose has been referred to as a miser, a recluse, a maverick, and an angry poet possessing a prickly persona. But any contradictions between his personality and the beautiful gardens he created should be set aside. Rose said it best himself in his own handwritten acknowledgments for *Creative Gardens* (1958): "For all my faults, of any kind whatever, I beg full credit for myself; after living with these so long, I have come to value imperfections."

Biography

Born in 1910. Completed early training at Cornell University, Ithaca, New York, and Harvard University, Cambridge, Massachusetts, 1930s; expelled from Harvard for failing to cease his pursuit of modern landscape forms, 1937; wrote series of critical articles for *Pencil Points* magazine promoting modern gardens and landscape architecture, 1938, 1939; employed by New York design firm Tuttle, Seelye, Place, and Raymond, 1941; established own firm in New York and then New Jersey with a focus of private modern gardens. Died in 1991.

Selected Designs

1953   James Rose's residence, Ridgewood, New Jersey, United States, now the James Rose Center for Landscape Architectural Research and Design, under the direction of Dean Cardasis

Selected Publications

"Freedom in the Garden," *Pencil Points* (1938)
"Integration," *Pencil Points* (1938)
"Modular Gardens," *Progressive Architecture* (1947)
Creative Gardens, 1958
Gardens Make Me Laugh, 1965
Heavenly Environment, 1965
Modern American Gardens Designed by James Rose (writing as Marc Snow), 1967

Further Reading

Birnbaum, Charles A., and Robin Karson, editors, *Pioneers of American Landscape Design*, New York: McGraw Hill, 2000

Eckbo, Garrett, *Landscape for Living*, New York: Architectural Record, 1950

Treib, Marc, editor, *Modern Landscape Architecture: A Critical Review*, Cambridge, Massachusetts: MIT Press, 1993

Treib, Marc, and Dorothée Imbert, *Garrett Eckbo: Modern Landscapes for Living*, Berkeley: University of California Press, 1997

Tunnard, Christopher, *Gardens in the Modern Landscape*, London: Architectural Press, 1938; 2nd edition, New York: Scribner, and London: Architectural Press, 1948

Tunnard, Christopher, *The City of Man*, New York: Scribner, 1953; 2nd edition, 1970

Walker, Peter, and Melanie Simo, *Invisible Gardens: The Search for Modernism in the American Landscape*, Cambridge, Massachusetts: MIT Press, 1994

LAURI MACMILLAN JOHNSON

Rose Garden

Since ancient times, roses (such as *Rosa gallica, Rosa damascena,* and *Rosa alba*) have been cultivated in European gardens, but their isolation into a rose garden, called a *rosarium* or *rosery,* is a 19th-century practice. This is partly due to the popularity of the gardenesque style, which displayed plants individually according to their kind, and to the introduction of the repeat-blooming China rose (*Rosa chinensis*) in the 1780s. Hybridization of the China rose to produce Bourbon, Noisette, Boursault, and Hybrid Perpetual roses capable of flowering from June to October enabled roses to become plants for "modern" flower gardens.

Rose garden design through most of the 19th century was done in the massed or "modern" style. In his prolific *Encyclopaedia of Gardening* (1834), John Claudius Loudon contrasted the mingled flower garden with the massed style. A mixture of flowering plants was displayed according to each plant's individual size in the mingled flower garden. "The object is to mix the plants, so that every part of the garden may present a gay assemblage of flowers of different colors during the whole season." In the more common massed flower garden, flowers were planted in masses of one kind, either in separate beds or in separate divisions of the same bed. "It must be confessed that, whether the principle of arranging flowers in masses of one colour be applied to borders along walks, or in beds on lawn or gravel, the effect is striking and brilliant beyond that of any other manner of planting." Sweet scented and crimson China roses, such as Slater's Crimson China, and varieties of standard noisette roses were frequently massed together.

Loudon's circular flower garden (design 864 in *Encyclopaedia of Gardening*) was planted on the lawn. The central circle, 10 feet (3 m) in diameter, contained a collection of China roses, including purple noisette standards in the center, interspersed with bulbs and margined with a line of mixed hyacinths. The other beds were planted with herbaceous and showy greenhouse plants.

According to Loudon, when roses are grouped by themselves in beds surrounded by lawn or gravel and edged with common boxwood or wire, they constitute a rose garden or rosery. Generally, roseries were part of a comprehensive ornamental garden complex that could have included a flower garden, arboretum, American garden, and occasionally a grotto or rockwork. In Loudon's rosery, one kind of rose was introduced and planted with varieties that closely resembled it so that their distinctions could be easily seen. Particular compartments of the rosery were devoted to one species, such as the Scotch or Burnet-leaved Rose (*Rosa pimpinellifolia*), the China Rose (*Rosa chinensis*), or the Yellow Rose (*Rosa foetida*). Sometimes a piece of rockwork covered with creeping roses was placed in the center compartment. On other occasions the creeping roses were trained into trellis work to form a fence or hedge of roses. Standard roses may have been introduced into this hedge at regular distances. A grove of standards was also frequently found in the center of the rosery or here and there throughout the beds.

It was popular for a rosery to contain "baskets of roses"; that is, circular rose beds edged in wire to imitate basket work. The soil within the wire margin was prepared and graded into a convex mound, which increased the surface area to be planted. Strong rose shoots were pegged down into the soil until they rooted. This reduced plant height and increased the density of roses on the surface of the basket.

Loudon's gardenesque sentiments immigrated to America through the books and periodicals of Andrew Jackson Downing. Downing's modern flower garden echoed Loudon's: it was planted on turf and massed with low growing flowers that filled the whole bed or part of the bed. He also concurred with Loudon that "This produced a brilliancy of effect quite impossible in any other way." Plants such as petunias, portulacas, and pelargoniums that bloom for most of the summer were specifically chosen. "Next to these, the greatest ornaments to the flower garden are the everblooming roses, those China roses known under the name Bourbon, Bengal, and Noisette."

The finest effect from everblooming roses, Downing proposed, would occur when they were planted in small round beds, three to four feet in diameter and surrounded by turf. Each bed should be planted with roses

Plan of a rose garden, from *Journal of Horticulture and Cottage Gardener* 1 (1881)
Courtesy of Richard Iversen

of a single color; for example, one bed of white, another of red, a third of rose-color. Branches should be pruned and pegged down along the surface of the soil, so that the entire bed is covered with foliage and bloom.

In *The Horticulturist* of May 1848, Downing adopted Loudon's design for a small arabesque flower garden. It was to be created on a plot of smooth, level lawn that was surrounded by a boundary walk, making it a complete scene by itself. The four larger beds were to be filled with everblooming roses, "the gems of all flower gardens, unsurpassed in beauty of form, colour, and fragrance." To enable the eye to see the whole group of beds all at once, Downing instructed readers to peg rose stems down to the soil surface so that no soil would be visible.

Everblooming roses became indispensable to American flower gardens by 1848; over 70 varieties were listed in *Cottage Residences*. Downing praised the Bourbon roses, a variety first hybridized in 1817 on the Isle de Bourbon from *Rosa chinensis* and *Rosa damascena bifera*. 'Souvenir de la Malmaison'—with its constant blooming habit, large size, exquisite flesh color, and charming fragrance—was his favorite.

Despite worthy new rose varieties, there was still an absence of distinguished rose gardens in England at mid-19th century. The September 1861 *Journal of Horticulture* included the accompanying plan for a rosery in hopes of raising "the queen of flowers . . . to her regal rank." "There exists scarcely a garden of any pretensions where the introduction of roses *en masse* might not advantageously be effected." This rosery design was secluded within a shrubbery of American plants and enclosed by a colonnade of climbing roses. In its center, a pool was surrounded by a parterre of China roses on gravel walks. Throughout the garden, vases were planted with miniature, Provence, pompon, and dwarf Chinese or 'Fairy' roses.

By 1902, Gertrude Jekyll had grown impatient with the usual rose garden, "generally a target of concentric rings of beds placed upon turf, often with no special aim at connected design with the portions of the garden immediately about it, and filled with plants without a thought of their colour effect or any other worthy intention." Jeykll advocated a background of dark shrubs and trees to enclose a rose garden, which often combined both formal and free elements. It was a secluded, gated garden, a sanctuary where the queen of flowers reigned supreme.

Further Reading

Beales, Peter, *Classic Roses: An Illustrated Encyclopaedia and Grower's Manual of Old Roses, Shrub Roses, and Climbers,* London: Collins, and New York: Holt, 1985; revised and enlarged edition, New York: Holt, 1997

Downing, Andrew Jackson, *Cottage Residences,* London and New York, 1842; new edition, New York: Wiley, 1873; reprint, as *Victorian Cottage Residences,* London: Constable, and New York: Dover, 1981

Downing, Andrew Jackson, "A Chapter on Roses," *The Horticulturist* 3, no. 2 (August 1848)

Hibberd, Shirley, *The Amateur's Rose Book,* new edition, London: Groombridge, 1874; new edition, London: Collingridge, 1894

Jekyll, Gertrude, and Edward Mawley, *Roses for English Gardens,* London: Country Life, and New York: Scribner, 1902; reprint, Woodbridge, Suffolk: Antique Collectors' Club, 1990

Loudon, John C., *An Encyclopedia of Gardening,* 2 vols., London, 1822; new edition, 1835; reprint, New York: Garland, 1982

Thomas, Graham Stuart, *The Old Shrub Roses,* London: Phoenix House, 1955; Boston: Branford, 1956; 5th edition, London: Dent, 1980

Wright, Walter Page, *Roses and Rose Gardens,* London: Headley, and New York: Stokes, 1911; 3rd edition, London: Allen, 1940

RICHARD R. IVERSEN

Rousham House

Rousham, Oxfordshire, England

Location: approximately 11 miles (17.8 km) north of Oxford, and 60 miles (96.8 km) northwest of London

Rousham House, near Oxford, England, is one of the few country estates that has kept its final layout, as designed by William Kent, largely unchanged. In 1738 General James Dormer commissioned the artist to enlarge the Jacobean house, to decorate the newly built rooms, and to transform the garden, which had been laid out by Charles Bridgeman in the middle of the 1720s, into a continuum of scenic natural vistas. The first stage of work removed all the structures and walls that had lent an architectural character to the site. Following his own basic principle that nature has no straight lines, Kent allowed the Cherwell River at the foot of the garden to flow freely, did away with the geometrical division of the garden into quarters, and transformed the terraces into fluid formations. He had devised a plan to blend together the garden and the landscape into one artistic whole. The Cherwell Valley fulfilled the aesthetic conditions of embracing the countryside promoted by the poet Alexander Pope only a few years earlier.

Kent's landscape designs went far beyond the narrow confines of the garden. He extended the area in several directions. Toward the north, for example, he expanded the design in order to include in the garden the medieval bridge over the river. He transformed an old water mill standing outside the garden farther toward the north

William Kent's drawing for the Cascades at Rousham House, from Osvald Sirén, *China and Gardens of Europe of the Eighteenth Century,* [1950], 1900
Copyright Dumbarton Oaks

into a Gothic structure. The existing architectural elements expanded into a triple-axis wall that Kent erected artificially on a distant hilltop. All these structures blended in the landscape into one vista that Kent skillfully arranged on the garden side of the house and framed with side plantings. A visitor stepping outside the house, which Kent also decorated with Gothic elements, would get the impression that the garden reached far beyond the meadow landscape by the river out to the farthest horizon. Linked to such a reversion to medieval forms, initiated by the 18th-century Gothic Revival, was the notion of an architectural style rooted in England's own history, representing a patriotic picture of the Middle Ages.

In the innermost part of the garden, however, Kent designed structures in a purely classical style. In the eastern portion he erected a pyramid, which he answered in the western part with a small temple of Tuscan origin. Between them arose a sevenfold arcade reminiscent of the famous temple terraces of Praeneste.

The numerous statues that Kent arranged on grassy knolls and in several hollows evoke the image of a sacred shrine from ancient days. Horace Walpole, while visiting the garden, fancied himself transported to Daphne, the legendary sacred grove of Apollo outside the gate of Antioch. One 18th-century scholar compared the garden with Tempe and hailed it as "locus amoenus" (Cicero: "a most pleasant place"). The many pools of water and the lush green vegetation contributed substantially to this image, especially in the largest enclosed space of the garden, the Venus Vale. Kent modeled the clearing in flowing waves, using the existing pools as a reservoir to flood the masonry cascades his plan called for. Jets of water rose from the ponds. In the greenery along the sides, dividing the valley from the neighboring fields, he placed statues of nature gods, which seem to be moving toward the Venus statue, here depicted as a nymph, in the center of the enclosure, as if to carry the visitor off to Arcadian rest. Turning a landscape into such a literary stage production points to the guiding influence of Pope, who counted both the owner and the artist among his friends.

In order to unite the various scenes of nature in the garden with the landscape, Kent laid an enclosed walkway around the periphery. The visitor following this silent guide found the views and scenes unfold in a continuity of space and time. Of course, this presupposed a spatial pattern such that the succession of vistas reveal an orderly whole. In addition to the topography of the site, the vegetation in the garden played a decisive role in shaping this structure. The legend on a plan sketched in 1739, probably prompted by Pope's visit, includes three notes for various types of vegetation. There are symbols for deciduous trees and conifers, as well as a type of shading indicating thick shrubs, which cover most of the garden. The tree symbols illustrate the spatial framework supplied by the vegetation. Scattered areas indicate grove-like plantings, with darker areas showing clumps or perhaps frame plantings. The Venus Vale, for instance, is encircled with a continuous row of conifers, which the landscape gardeners hid behind an inner circle of rows and small groups of deciduous trees. This ensured on the one hand that even during winter the basic spatial structure would be maintained and on the other hand that the garden visitor would not be able to see into the valley from the surrounding paths. The same procedure was useful for focusing the visitor's views onto the wider landscape and not into neighboring parts of the garden.

Around the pyramid and the garden temple Kent placed bell-shaped beds to correspond with the angle of sight from the buildings. When visitors made their way around the pathways and caught sight of them, the beds acted like a parabolic reflector to gather the beams of light and direct the eye to the structures.

A description of the garden from 1750 confirms that the primary consideration in planting was variety. In addition to groves of "Oak, Ash, Alder, Beach, and Horsechestnuts" and side plantings of "Scotch and Spruce firs," there were "deferant sorts of flowers, peeping through the deferant sorts of Evergreens, here you think the Laurel produces a Rose, the Holly a Syringa, the Yew a Lilac, and the sweet Honeysuckle is peeking out from under every Leafe, in short they are so mixt together, that youd think every Leafe of the Evergreens produced one flower or a nother." This description contradicts the opinion that the early landscape gardens of the 18th century had no flowering plants at all.

Synopsis

after 1635	Erection of manor house on site of previous building, constructed by local architect commissioned by Sir Robert Dormer
1677	Published description of hanging terraces below house by Robert Plot
1721	Edward Grantham's survey of Rousham mentions New Garden
ca. 1725	Garden designed and laid out by Charles Bridgeman
1738–42	Entire estate altered according to design by William Kent
1860	House enlarged by James Piers St. Aubyn

Further Reading

Müller, Ulrich, *Klassischer Geschmack und gotische Tugend: Der englische Landsitz Rousham*, Worms, Germany: Wernersche Verlagsgesellschaft, 1998

ULRICH MÜLLER

Royal Botanical Gardens, Ontario.
See Ontario, Royal Botanical Gardens

Royal Botanic Garden Edinburgh.
See Edinburgh, Royal Botanic Garden

Royal Botanic Gardens, Kew. *See* Kew, Royal Botanic Gardens

Royal Botanic Gardens Sydney. *See* Sydney, Royal Botanic Gardens

---

Ruins

One of the earliest descriptions we have of ruins in the landscape dates from 1359, in which Petrarch reflects on the ruinous architectural residues of splendor in Rome and finds in them romantic inspiration. Another early description of ruins in the landscape dates to 1499 with the publication of Francesco Colonna's "Aesthetics of Ruins" in his book *Hypnerotomachia Poliphili*. Colonna lists plant materials to be associated with ruins—herbs, weeds, and exotic species.

The first designed and constructed ruin was commissioned in 1510 by the duke of Urbino at Pesaro, Italy. Girolamo Genga, an architect, archeologist, stage designer, painter, and sculptor, designed the ruin. It was built in a residential study that on first glance seemed chaotic and abandoned, but with further examination proved to be a pragmatic, carefully planned working environment.

In the 17th century a more ideologically developed, romantic perception of ruin arose. Ruins were a topic for writers, critics, designers, and landscape painters. The baroque landscapes of Claude Lorraine, Nicolas Poussin, Jacob van Ruisdael, and especially Salvator Rosa centered on an erosion of nature and the impermanence of human constructions and flesh. John Donne wrote of the crumbling mountains of the English and Scottish countryside and allied this emotive landscape with mortality. Anthony Wood, an antiquarian of the 17th century, described the medieval abbey at Eynsham as venerated and stately, though much lamented. This early response to ruins, and the arising individualistic and humanistic perception of the world in the late 17th century, led to a more enlightened view of ruins in the 18th century.

In 18th-century England and continental Europe, existing monastic and dynastic ruins or constructed, artificial ruins were used as architectural follies or eye-catchers in the Picturesque landscape. The formality of André Le Nôtre's Versailles and Vaux le Vicomte reflected the self-aggrandizing ideals of the aristocracy, which was beginning to lose control of a repressed and increasingly educated proletariat. The socio-industrial conditions at the time gave rise to this newly wealthy middle class who, while rejecting the totalitarianism of Louis XIV, sought to establish a sense of history within their own estates. These ruins styled as medieval or gothicized structures came to represent a mythicized past for the new rich. Also, the bourgeoisie built ruins to simulate a relationship with the natural world, which was idealized later in the philosophical musings of Goethe and Rousseau, stressing interaction with nature in order to transcend material culture and gain a verdant education through romantic contemplation.

The grand tour exposed the youth of English gentry to the dramatic landscapes of the Italian Alps. Among these tourists were Thomas Gray, an English poet, and Horace Walpole, the son of the first prime minister of England. Walpole and Gray helped to define the new picturesque aesthetic in landscape design by promoting the sublime landscapes of Salvator Rosa. Ruin was, for the picturesque, an exemplar of the newly celebrated "irregular," the "accidental," and the "natural." The new aesthetic of the ruin as folly or eye-catcher allowed the viewer a transcendent experience and a voyage through history without having to leave one's estate.

These images of decay and worldly experience were in high demand and stimulated the construction of many false ruins, artificial grottoes, Chinese pagodas, bark huts, and other structures that harkened back to a more primitive, idealized condition of humanity. These follies popped up throughout the English countryside, propelled by the publication of Batty Langley's *New Principles of Gardening* in 1728. Langley, a garden designer and critic, included designs for ruins that, he wrote, could either be painted on canvas or built with brick and covered with plaster in imitation of stone. Examples of artificial ruins from this time include a neoclassical

Artificially ruined Roman arch in the Royal Botanic Gardens, Kew, designed by William Chambers

arch erected in 1732 at Alfred's Hall; Cardinal von Schonborn's hermit's huts built on the foundations of actual Roman ruins; and a Gothic hermitage built at Richmond in 1733, consisting of a heap of disordered stones and planted with mosses and shrubs to create the effect of a wild, disordered raw nature.

Langley again published Gothic designs in 1742, and a wave of ruinous construction followed in England with Sanderson-Miller's Folly of Edgehill (1743) and Hagley Park Castle (1745), William Kent's satirical Temple of Ancient Virtue, Walpole's Gothic Strawberry Hill, and the Duke of Cumberland's Virginia Water (1746), which used ancient columns augmented with artificial parts. The building of ruins in England climaxed with William Chambers's artificial Roman "ruined" arch in 1759 at Kew Gardens.

The constructed ruins were commonly accompanied by plantings of exotic species such as Italian cypress (*Cupressus sempervirens*), Lebanon cedar (*Cedrus libani*), and Windmill palm (*Trachycarpus fortunei*). Along with these newly imported exotic species were planted herbs and weeds.

Ruins in the 18th-century English landscape fulfilled a need to present the past free of a dogmatic, scientific perspective. Individuals lost faith in the objective, analytic viewpoint of the clergy and aristocracy and sought an emotive release from autocratic power. The common view of history among the 18th-century English gentry was that the classical age was the pinnacle of human achievement, and the works of classical writers such as Homer and Virgil were familiar to all educated gentry. The construction of classical ruins alluded to this common thread in elite society and created strong associations to a celebrated past. An example of the neoclassical ruin is Chambers's ruined arch at Kew Gardens. These designed ruins complemented well the austere forms of Palladian architecture.

The crumbling abbey or decaying castle stood for freedom from oppression at the hands of the clergy and land barons. At the end of the 18th century, ruins were no longer charming indulgences but became a source of intellectual stimulation and caused reflection on the passage of time, the meaning of history, and the destiny of humankind. With the image of the ruin, the revolutionary had tangible proof that all things come to an end and that Eliade's cycle of destruction and regeneration may be applied to a social apparatus. In 1795 John Carter, an English antiquarian, protested the fabrication of ruins as shallow dissimulation. Constantin-François Volney elevated the ruin to a universal symbol with his text *Ruins* (1791) and saw them as a tangible warning of the impermanence of stone and flesh.

The artificial ruin meshed well with the naturalistic landscape gardening style of Kent and Lancelot "Capability" Brown in England. These same images, when applied to the formal French landscape, served as rococo ornamentation. Continental Europe used ruins in the landscape and garden on a more detached philosophical plane. At Ermenonville (1776) the Temple of Philosophy represented the modern human condition of existential angst and disconnection. At the Desert de Retz the massive neoclassical ruined column was a commentary on the vastness of ancient architectural achievement as compared with modern practice. These varied commentaries differed with the mostly emotional, dynastic, or clerical associations of ruins in England.

In Germany during the late 18th century, Christian Cay Lorenz Hirschfield's theories concerning garden art, along with the *Naturphilosophie* of Goethe gave rise to constructed ruins at Worlitz, Weimar, Potsdam, Nymphenburg, and Schonbrunn. These royal gardens provided a withdrawal from worldly pleasures and cares. The ruins constructed in Germany referenced ancient castles on the Rhine or Danube. Rather than abstracting a classical past, however, the Germans found romantic impetus in their own history, stimulating sentimentalism and reflecting a strong sense of nationalism.

In the 19th century ruins in the landscape continued to provide emotional stimulation. At Woodbridge Lodge in England, the landscape was dotted with Gothic relics and ruins. The lodge was an amusing, somewhat trivial museum that stimulated the viewer with shocks of discovery but lacked the ideological depth of previous ruinous construction.

The revolutionary spirit of the 19th century was reflected in the mannerist use of fragmented sculpture in the garden, which represented the physical state of the aristocrats and celebrated the victory of the proletariat in France and the United States. The fact that mutilated torsos and heads were the preferred garden ornaments may reference directly the guillotine and the practice of quartering aristocrats in France. The ruin of a social structure was thus represented materially.

Modern thoughts on ruins are broad and not easily defined. Ruins may be seen as a process of erosion and an awareness of organic change. They may be viewed as a stimulation for restoration and as a place of pride in a regional or vernacular landscape. Ruins may also represent a ghostly reminder of the postreligious individual's loss of faith. The wide-ranging perceptions of a ruin in modern culture signify a need for places of meaning that parallels the philosophical needs of the past.

Further Reading

Hadfield, Miles, *Pioneers in Gardening,* London: Routledge and Kegan Paul, 1955

Harbison, Robert, *The Built, the Unbuilt, and the Unbuildable: In Pursuit of Architectural Meaning,* Cambridge, Massachusetts: MIT Press, and London: Thames and Hudson, 1991

Lowenthal, David, *The Past Is a Foreign Country,* Cambridge and New York: Cambridge University Press, 1985

Piggott, Stuart, *Ruins in a Landscape: Essays in Antiquarianism,* Edinburgh: Edinburgh University Press, 1976

Saudan, Michel, *De folie en folies: La découverte du monde des jardins,* Geneva: Bibliothèque des Arts, 1987; as *From Folly to Follies: Discovering the World of Gardens,* New York: Abbeville Press, 1988

Zucker, Paul, *Fascination of Decay,* Ridgewood, New Jersey: Gregg Press, 1968

PETER BUTLER

Russia

The earliest evidence of Russian gardens dates to the mid-12th century. It is known that Saint Antony Pechersky established a garden at the Pechersky Monastery in Kiev. He probably was inspired by the monastic gardens he saw in Byzantium during his pilgrimage to the Christian East. Between the 11th and the 17th century the typical Russian medieval garden took shape. In addition

to the monastic gardens five different types of princes' gardens are known: large regular gardens of fruit trees and vegetables; water gardens located at the country residences of the aristocracy; hunting parks; small, enclosed gardens for women (a type probably of oriental origin); and the gardens of the city estates, which were common in Moscow by the end of the Middle

Ages. The plants used during this period were predominantly local varieties of trees and shrubs. Oak trees were very popular as the compositional center of the landscape; groves of birch and willow trees were also popular, usually planted along the shores of artificial lakes. Among the fruit and berry types the red currant and black currant, gooseberry, raspberry, cherry, and pear were grown. In the 17th century apple trees were brought from Ukraine and cedar and larch trees from Siberia. The rose, hawthorn, elder, and lilac were used as ornamental shrubs. Among the medicinal herbs sage, chicory, mint, poppy, fennel, and parsley were known. Melons, watermelons, and pumpkins were grown in greenhouses and moved to the garden in the summer months to serve as decorations.

As a rule the monastic complex, such as the Troitse-Sergievskaya Lavra, Savvino-Storozhievsky, and Novo-Jerusalimsky monasteries near Moscow, consisted of a main group of buildings surrounded by a wall and often situated on a hill. Small gardens of flowers and fruit trees were situated inside the walls, sometimes with a pond where fish caught in nearby lakes and rivers could be kept. Larger fruit gardens and orchards were situated outside the walls. Very often artificial lakes with running water were created near the monastery.

In many cases the landscapes created by the monks covered vast areas, especially in northern Russia. Solovetsky Monastery changed the landscape of a whole archipelago of islands in the White Sea, while Valaamsky Monastery transformed the islands in Lake Ladoga. A similar process of transformation of enormous areas of land occurred on the continent, Kirillovo-Belozersky Monastery being the most evident example. In the 17th century these artificial landscapes began to be given allegorical meanings. The complex of Gefsimania—inspired by the New Testament sites of Golgotha, the garden of Gethsemane, and the Cedron River—was created near the Novo-Jerusalimsky Monastery.

From the 14th to the 17th century the gardens at the residences of the great princes and tsars constantly grew in size. They were similar in layout to the monastic lands, including small flower gardens near the palace and larger formal fruit gardens, with groves of trees and systems of lakes around the core of the estate. Vast hunting parks dominated in the tsar's estates near Moscow, in Kolomenskoye, Sokolniky, and Izmaylovo.

Foreign travelers were constantly surprised by the number and size of gardens in Moscow in the 15th century through the 17th century. Within Russian cities, gardens and pastures covered a much greater proportion of the land than elsewhere in Western Europe. The reason was the traditional practice in Russia of city-dwellers' growing a majority of their own vegetables and keeping their own cows. Even in the heart of Moscow, on the right bank of the Moscow River opposite the Kremlin, the tsar maintained a large fruit garden and orchard; to this day that part of the city is called Sadovniki—"the Gardens."

By the end of the Middle Ages in Russia, garden designs were becoming more and more elaborate as a result of Polish and Dutch influences. The decorative character of gardens was strengthened, and complex layouts appeared featuring concentric circles, labyrinths, and the first complicated parterres. At the same time the diversity of plants, especially medicinal herbs, grew, and physic gardens became more important.

The hanging gardens constructed on the roofs of the tsars' palaces were the most unusual Russian gardens of the late Middle Ages. The roof vaults, sheathed with thick layers of lead, were covered over with soil. Apple and pear trees and berry bushes were grown in these gardens; flowerbeds planted in large wooden boxes included such exotic "foreign" plants as peonies, tulips, lilies, and gillyflowers. These hanging gardens had allegorical meanings connected with the legendary gardens of Babylon and the garden of Eden.

Gardens of the Russian Baroque

With the reign of the first Russian emperor, Peter the Great (1682–1725), the European way of life was installed in Russia. The transformation of Russian culture extended to the art of gardening. The emperor had spent his childhood in the royal residences situated around Moscow, which included in addition to their regular gardens a special "playing garden" created for his education. Thereafter educational gardens became very common in Russian estates of the 18th century. During his first trip abroad in 1697–98 Peter the Great studied the German, Dutch, and English gardens. After the establishment of St. Petersburg in 1703, he ordered the creation of large gardens in the Dutch style in the new capital and at his seaside residences Peterhof (Petrodvorets) and Oranienbaum (Lomonosov). His taste in gardens changed after his journey to France in 1714, where he visited Versailles, Saint-Cloud, and Marly. The emperor wrote that he wanted to organize the gardens to rival those of Versailles. To carry out this project the French architect Alexander Le Blond was invited to St. Petersburg; he designed the plan of the city as well as the most important gardens at the imperial residences in the suburbs.

By the 1720s Peter the Great had conceived of a garden that embodied the ideology of the new Russian Empire. As a result of the activities of Le Blond, the Dutch gardener Jan Roosen, and the Italian architect Niccolo Miketti, Dutch, French, and Italian features were included in this model. According to a treatise from Peter the Great's time, preserved in manuscript form, the emperor's garden should incorporate the landscape styles of many different countries, creating the

View of the lake in the garden at Pavlovsk, from a late 18th-century engraving
Courtesy of Moscow Institute of Architecture

impression of the whole world contained in a single garden. This internationalism is the most typical feature of the early gardens of the Russian Empire. The principle was also applied to the choice of plants, which came from different parts of Russia and other countries around the world.

In the first quarter of the 18th century, many plants were imported for use in the emperor's gardens. First, from Holland, came the Dutch lime, box, and yew. Flowers included the narcissus, tulip, lily, gillyflower, and peony. Aromatic herbs such as sage, majoram, basil, and mint remained very popular.

With time it became clear that many of the imported plants would not grow well in the severe northern climate of Russia, and local trees—fir, birch, mountain ash, and bird cherry—were used instead. The fashion for planting low parterres of red bilberry (*Vaccinium myrtillus*) came from Sweden. The first Russian botanical gardens were founded during the reign of Peter the Great in Moscow (1709) and St. Petersburg (1712).

From the 1730s to the 1760s, during the reign of the empresses Ann I and Elisabeth I, the gardens of Russia flourished. Enormous baroque compositions were created at the imperial residences near St. Petersburg. At Peterhof the garden included a system of water channels, fountains, and cascades; the garden at Tsarskoye Selo had a vast menagerie, while that at Ropsha featured an outstanding system of cascades. Annenhof, in Moscow, was the largest regular park of the period. All of these were designed by Bartolomeo Rastrelli.

At the same time other, smaller types of gardens appeared. The first was the private gardens of the city estates with their decorative parterres. These were located mainly along the embankments of the Moika and Fontanka Rivers in St. Petersburg. Another type of garden was that of the private country residence of the wealthy aristocratic families. Usually these gardens included a large lake and a cut lawn behind the palace (Kuskovo, Arkhangelskoye, Studinets near Moscow). Both imperial and private gardens shared certain elements: axial designs based on strict mathematical principles and a penchant for allegory. Elements of the rococo—labyrinths, hills, and follies—began to appear in the gardens of the mid-18th century.

Landscape Park

The Enlightenment came to Russia in 1762 with the beginning of the reign of Empress Catherine the Great. During the early years of this period the rococo style dominated the imperial gardens, which abounded with complicated, ornamental parterres punctuated with numerous pavilions and galleries. The architecture of these buildings reflected the growth of interest in chinoiserie. The park of the Chinese palace in Oranienbaum and the new parts of the park in Tsarskoye Selo

were designed in this manner in the first half of the 1760s.

By the end of that decade Catherine the Great had developed an enthusiasm for English gardens. She sent to Britain for garden books and commissioned from Wedgwood the famous "Green Frog" china service, which featured 1,244 views of English landscapes, estates, and garden pavilions. In the 1770s many British gardeners and architects were invited to St. Petersburg: John Busch and later Charles Cameron to work in Tsarskoye Selo; James Meaders to design the English park in Peterhof; William Gould—a pupil of the great Engish garden designer Lancelot "Capability" Brown—to the estates of Prince Potyomkin; and others. The empress wrote to Voltaire in 1772 that "anglomania rules my plantomania." In the gardens of the Russian Enlightenment the English influence was connected with other features typical of Russian culture, but there is no doubt that British gardeners brought to Russia the fashion for creating natural landscapes. One of the most outstanding landscape parks of 18th century Russia is Pavlovsk, created by Charles Cameron for Prince Paul, the son of Catherine the Great. In his *Encyclopaedia of Gardens* (1822), J.C. Loudon remarks that, upon seeing Pavlovsk in 1813, he felt certain the park could have been created only by Brown. Catherine the Great was interested not only in copying nature, in seeking "the genius of the place," but also in creating architectural structures like those that appeared in the English garden. She was impressed by the possibility of using the artistic "language" of garden pavilions in different tastes, including the antique manner, Eastern exotic style, and romantic Gothic. The creation of complicated ideological systems became typical of Russian imperial gardens of the second half of the 18th century: the glorification of victories, plans for future political successes, sentimental memories, extravagant caprices, historical and geographical associations. The most interesting example of the combination of all these themes—Tsarskoye Selo of 1770 to the 1790s—still survives to a considerable extent.

The second half of the 18th and early 19th century was a period during which garden culture flourished in the country estates of the Russian gentry. In 1762 the gentry were freed from obligatory governmental service. With this event many thousands of gentlemen left the army and became full-time residents of their country estates, preoccupied with looking after the prosperity, comfort, and beauty of their ancestral homes. Provincial estate gardens of the day were described by Andrei Bolotov, the creator of the famous garden in Bogoroditsk near Tula and publisher of two magazines devoted to country life, "Economical Magazine" and "Country Gentlemen." In his magazines Bolotov published hundreds of recommendations for the making of

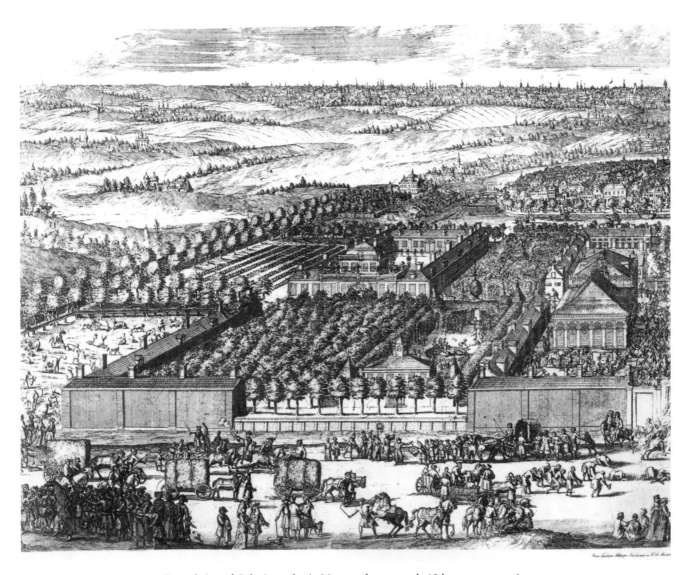

General view of Golovin garden in Moscow, from an early 18th-century engraving
Courtesy of Moscow Institute of Architecture

gardens, based first of all on the works of Christian Hirschfeld and also on his own experience adapting European ideas to the Russian climate and flora.

The typical Russian estate garden of the second half of the 18th and early 19th century was based on the example of the English garden but included some features of early 18th century French and Italian gardens, as well as features from the previous medieval period. Usually the country garden had a system of geometrically precise axes, surrounded by other more picturesque elements. It always had certain formal elements, for example the straight main alleé leading to the palace and small parterres near the main house. Very often the house was situated on a hill or high bank of a river, and the garden had terraces going down the slope. As in the Russian

medieval gardens, water played an important role in garden compositions: usually a large lake was situated in the center of the estate, while the cascades of the fishponds with running water were near the agricultural lands. The landscape garden allowed the use of a variety of local trees. Compositions of birch, maple, and fir were the most popular because of their autumn colors.

At the same time a growing interest in botanical and agricultural science was apparent in both imperial and private gardens of the Russian Enlightenment. Some country estates, for instance, Gorenki and Neskuchnoye near Moscow and Trostjanets in Ukraine, were transformed into vast private botanic gardens with as many as 7,000–9,000 types of plants. Also at this time nearly all of the exotic plants brought to Europe from America and India began to appear in Russia. To Pavlovsk alone in the period from 1730 to the 1750s, about 20,000 plants were brought from abroad. In addition, these rich botanic collections received many new examples of Siberian flora.

Gardens of the 19th Century

The 19th century was the heyday of public gardens in the cities and towns of Russia. In Moscow systems of boulevards were created in place of medieval walls—the Boulvarnoye and Sadovoye circles made up a chain of green parks. The Scottish architects William Heisty and Adam Menelaws introduced the small public garden into town planning, a practice that became widespread nearly everywhere, not only in St. Petersburg (e.g., the garden near the Admiralty, Mikhailovsky garden) and Moscow (Petrovsky Park) but in the cities of Ukraine, Siberia, and elsewhere. A system of botanical gardens was developing as well. The apothecary gardens in Moscow, St. Petersburg, and Kiev were given to the universities. New botanical gardens were founded in Tomsk in Siberia, in the Crimea near Yalta (Nikitsky Botanichesky Sad), and in Tiflis and Batumi in Georgia.

During the first half of the 19th century country estate gardens continued to develop according to the same principles as in the epoch of Catherine the Great, including both landscape and formal elements. By the end of the century picturesque features were being combined with the ideas of the Arts and Crafts movement on the estates of the richest Russian industrialists and entrepreneurs (e.g., Abramtsevo near Moscow, Talashkino near Smolensk, Kutchuk-Koi in the Crimea).

An important new type—the garden of the dacha, or small summerhouse of the middle classes—appeared around the turn of the century. In composition they reflected the estate garden on a smaller scale, having short, straight alleés, small lawns surrounded by shrubs, flowerbeds with a broad variety of annuals, and the obligatory vegetable garden and orchard. The dacha garden became widespread after the socialist revolution in 1917, when large private gardens were confiscated.

Gardens of the Soviet Period

After 1917 all the former imperial gardens were transformed into public gardens. The majority—about 80 percent—of the country estates were destroyed; those that survived became sanatoriums and rest houses. The network of scientific botanical gardens became well developed.

In Soviet garden art the creation of large public parks, usually called "the parks of culture and rest," is perhaps the most interesting development. In general they had formal plans with both their overall composition and

pavilions in the neoclassical style; among the best-known examples of the "Park Kulturi" is Gorki Park in Moscow.

From 1960 to the 1980s many memorial parks were created to commemorate events of World War II. Symbolic sculptural and architectural groups play a key role in these parks—for example, "Mamayev Kurgan" in Volgograd (Stalingrad), the "Circle of Glory" in Leningrad, and the "Park of Victory" in Moscow, the latter finished after the dissolution of the Soviet Union.

See also Archangelskoye; Gatchina; Komarov Botanical Institute Botanic Garden; Kuskovo; Moscow University Botanic Garden; Oranienbaum (Lomonosov); Pavlovsk; Petrodvorets; Russian Academy of Sciences, Main Botanic Garden; Summer Garden; Tsarkoye Selo; Victory Gardens: Russia

Further Reading

Carter, Harold Burnell, *Sir Joseph Banks and the Plant Collection from Kew Sent to the Empress Catherine II of Russia, 1795,* London: British Museum (Natural History), 1974

Cross, Anthony, "Russian Gardens, British Gardeners," *Garden History* 19, no. 1 (1991)

Dubiago, T.B., *Russkie reguliarnye sady i parki,* Leningrad: Gos. Izd-vo Lit-ry po Stroitel'stvu, Arkhitekture i Stroit. Materialam, 1963

Floryan, Margrethe, *Gardens of the Tsars,* Aarhus, Denmark: Aarhus University Press, and Sagaponack, New York: Sagapress, 1996

Hamilton, George Heard, *The Art and Architecture of Russia,* London and Baltimore, Maryland: Penguin Books, 1954; 3rd edition, New Haven, Connecticut: Yale University Press, 1983

Hayden, Peter, "British Seats on Imperial Russian Tables," *Garden History* 13, no. 1 (1985)

Hayden, Peter, "Russian Stowe," *Garden History* 19, no. 1 (1991)

Kennett, Audrey, *The Palaces of Leningrad,* London: Thames and Hudson, and New York: Putnam, 1973

Loudon, John Claudius, *An Encyclopaedia of Gardening,* 2 vols., London, 1822; new edition, 1835; reprint, New York: Garland, 1982

Massie, Suzanne, *Pavlovsk: The Life of a Russian Palace,* Boston: Little Brown, and London: Hodder and Stoughton, 1990

Orloff, Alexander, and Dmitrii Olegovich Shvidkovskii, *Saint Pétersbourg: L'architecture des tsars,* Paris: Menges, 1995; as *St. Petersburg: Architecture of the Tsars,* translated by John Goodman, New York: Abbeville Press, 1996

Roosevelt, Priscilla R., *Life on the Russian Country Estate,* New Haven, Connecticut: Yale University Press, 1995

Shvidkovskii, Dmitrii Olegovich, *The Empress and the Architect: British Architecture and Gardens at the Court of Catherine the Great*, New Haven, Connecticut: Yale University Press, 1996

Shvidkovskii, Dmitrii Olegovich, and Jean-Marie Pérouse de Montclos, editors, *Moscou: Patrimoine architectural*, Paris: Flammarion, 1997

DMITRY SHVIDKOVSKY

Russian Academy of Sciences, Main Botanic Garden

Moscow, Russia

Location: between Botanicheskaya Street, Kamenka River channel, and All-Russia Exhibition Center, approximately 7 miles (11.2 km) north of Kremlin

As the outcome of World War II became evident and was nearing an end, the Soviet Union gradually began redirecting its economy to more peaceful goals. The government, the Soviet of the People's Commissars, made immense postwar plans, and one of its first resolutions (21 January 1945) concerned the development of the most peaceful science—botany. The new large-scale botanic garden of the USSR Academy of Sciences was to appear in Moscow soon, to serve as headquarters for the work of all botanic institutions in the country. After the breakup of the Soviet Union, the Russian Academy of Sciences inherited the garden. It remains the leading and largest botanic garden in the country. By area it is the largest in Europe and one of the largest in the world.

On 14 April 1945 the presidium of the USSR Academy of Sciences received a comprehensive program for the construction of the garden, and the name "Main Botanic Garden of the USSR Academy of Sciences" was heard for the first time. This is considered the date of the garden's foundation. On the same day the small Moscow botanic garden of the Academy of Sciences on Sparrow Hills, founded in 1936, was officially replaced.

The goals of the new institution were announced: (1) to develop the theoretical foundations and methods of maximal use of plant resources in the Soviet Union and other countries for the needs of the national economy and culture; (2) to develop the scientific basis and practical methods of planting trees and shrubs in cities, construction projects, communications, and buildings and housing, as well as advance decorative horticulture and floriculture; and (3) to organize educational methods and disseminate botanic knowledge and methods for the practical use of plants in the economy and culture. In May 1945 the territory of the Ostankino oak forest

(361.35 hectares [892 acres]) in northern Moscow was designated for the construction of the garden.

The main territory of the garden forms a figure approximating a triangle, confined on two of its three sides by man-made topographical elements older than the garden itself. These are Vladykino Road (now Botanicheskaya Street, traversing the two parts of the garden), the cascade of ponds along the Kamenka River channel, which separates the garden from the forest preserve belonging to the Ostankino museum country estate, and the territories of the All-Russia Exhibition Center, founded in the 1830s on parts of the Sheremetevs' land. The road went from Moscow to the north through oak forests. Our earliest knowledge about the part of these indigenous forests nearest to Moscow—the Ostankino oak forest—dates from the 16th century, when the territory belonged to the czar's valet, I.M. Veshniakov. In the 18th century the forests west of the road were granted to the Vladyka (the patriarch of the Russian Orthodox Church), who razed them and leased the land to peasants. Today, the part of the garden territory situated on the patriarch's former holdings is completely treeless.

The vast forests to the east of the road were awarded to Count Boris Sheremetev in 1743. On the southern half of his land—that is, on the right bank of the Kamenka River, in the Ostankino Grove—the count, one of the most enlightened Russians of his time, built a country estate park in the English landscape style, named after the village of Ostankino. The count set aside a forest range to the north of the Kamenka River (Erdenevo Grove, now part of the botanic garden territory) as a preserve, with a number of regulations that were unique, if not revolutionary, for the 18th century: (1) do not chop down trees for wood, (2) do not mow hay or herd cattle, (3) do not remove anything from the forest (including mushrooms and berries) or clear out fallen tree trunks, (4) do not sow exotic species of plants, and (5) do not allow in "strollers" and hunters. Under this regimen of protection and care, the country estate park and the adjoining groves were preserved in wonderful condition through the beginning of the 19th century. Later selective chopping was carried out only on the outskirts of the estate. By the end of the 19th century, the environs had become a dacha region. In the middle of the forest range, however, an ancient virgin oak forest was still preserved.

The landscape composition of the new botanic garden developed around this forest. Here and there on the garden territory one can see the remains of a ditch surrounding the count's property, within which his enforced safety regime took place. In essence, it was the first preserve in Russia. Under Soviet rule one of the first decrees to appear after the transfer of the government from St. Petersburg to Moscow in 1918 concerned the establishment around Moscow of a wooded park zone. The decree, which prohibited indigenous breeds within this zone from being felled, protected these areas from decimation in the early part of the 20th century.

The choice of this place for the botanic garden essentially saved the historical indigenous oak forest ecosystems in its territory up to this day. The forest was provided with reliable surroundings and scientifically planned care at the same time that Moscow, having experienced an unprecedented population growth in the second half of the 20th century, urbanized and incorporated all surrounding territories (the garden, originally established on the outskirts of Moscow, is now located closer to the center than to the edge of the city). The excellent soil under the broad-leaved tree forests represented a further advantage for the establishment of a botanic collection. In addition, the garden became one of the most important parkland ranges in the north of the city, and its recreational value only grows from year to year.

Owing to the efforts of the country's best botanical scientists and landscape architects, several layout schemes and project sketches for the garden were developed in the summer of 1945. The landscape architect I.M. Petrov, the academician N.V. Tsitsin (the inspiration behind the project and the first director of the garden, a position he held until 1980), and his deputy P.I. Lapin, who directed the work, developed the final layout. The well-known architect A.V. Shchusev also participated in the project's early stages.

The presidium of the USSR Academy of Sciences examined and approved the technical project (General Plan of Construction) in May 1952. The methodological significance of this multivolume work, with its botanic sections and layout worked out in detail, turned out to be so great that its basic propositions were applied in the designing of many other Soviet and foreign (in Poland, Czechoslovakia, and China) botanic gardens.

The creation of the first permanent displays began in 1953. Many of them were quite complicated in terms of

landscaping. By 1954 the present layout of the territory had for the most part taken shape. In 1958 the construction of the laboratory building (begun in 1954) was finished. Upon the completion of the basic structure, the garden opened to the public in July 1959. At present the living collections of the garden consist of more than 21,000 taxa of plants, which are continually expanded.

The core of the garden is the indigenous oak forest, with an area of about 56 hectares (138 acres). It has been surrounded by a grating since 1965 and remains closed for any human use or trespassing. Along with oak (*Quercus robur*), the most plentiful large trees here are birch (*Betula verrucosa*), pine (*Pinus sylvestris*), linden (*Tilia cordata*), and maple (*Acer platanoides*). In the underbrush are mainly hazel (*Corylus avellana*), honeysuckle (*Lonicera xylosteum*), viburnum (*Viburnum opulus*), warty-barked spindle tree (*Euonymus verrucosus*), rowan (*Sorbus aucuparia*), and buckthorn (*Rhamnus frangula*). In the herbaceous covering lungwort (*Pulmonaria obscura*), weaselsnout (*Galeobdolon luteum*), ferns, goutweed (*Aegopogium podagraria*), sedge (*Carex pilosa*), and water avens (*Geum rivale*) predominate. The remaining territory of the garden serves as a buffer zone for this preserve. All the displays and collections are arranged in a ring around the central nucleus, in the less pristine sections of the forest and in the open areas.

The garden territory is a distinct closed landscape ensemble. The layout employs the traditions of Russian park architecture as well as some of the better models of world park design. The garden is constructed according to the principle of a circular chain of gardens in one large natural garden. The links of this chain constitute separate thematic layouts. Five entrances to the garden are arranged around the perimeter of the entire territory at a sufficient distance from one another to allow the viewing to begin and end at any of the linked expositions on the circular path.

The arboretum (75 hectares [185 acres]), designed in a landscape style, fits well into the natural scenery of the old forest range. Its open spaces alternate with groves and spurs of the main body of the oak forest (L.E. Rozenberg suggested the landscape-architectural solution). The collected shrubbery plantings (approximately 2,000 taxa) are distributed according to the demands of the given indigenous plants, in open spaces, along the edges of the forest, or under the canopy of thinned-out forest sections.

The banks of the cascade of ponds along the plot of the southern border of the garden are designed as exhibitions of coastal and water plants. The rose garden (the part that is open for visitors) is set up on a gentle slope of the southern exposition. The forest protects it from northern winds, creating an appropriate microclimate. In the best years of the garden, up to 2,500 kinds of roses were found here, including many old varieties from the 18th and 19th centuries, the material of which was received between 1946 and 1950 from Germany. The perennial garden is designed as an enormous open garden (7.5 hectares [18.5 acres]). Within its free landscape composition all of the best types of decorative herbaceous perennials and beautifully flowering shrubs from the garden's special collection are represented.

The collection of useful plants (about 3,000 species) is organized in such a way as to demonstrate the evolution of domestically useful plants from their wild ancestors to the newest kinds, as well as the methods of their cultivation. The exposition of natural flora of Russia and neighboring countries (in all, approximately 30 hectares [74 acres]) was basically completed in 1953 and is set up according to the botanic-geographical principle. Here, the idea of arranging representatives of every floral complex of one region or another in one plot with the goal of external imitation of typical plant communities was carried out with varying degrees of success. Flora of the European part of Russia, the Caucasus, central Asia, Siberia, and the Far East are set up in this manner.

The garden's greenhouse collections are concentrated chiefly under the roof of the main greenhouse, with an area of 0.5 hectares (1.2 acres) and a maximum height of 14.5 meters (15.8 yd.), where the plants are arranged by the ecological-geographical principle. The first exhibits were brought in together with the greenhouse building itself, transported piecemeal from Sanssouci in Potsdam (Germany) in the capacity of postwar reparations from 1948 to 1950. The plants brought over at that time included veritable rarities, such as specimens of *Encephalartos altensteinii* more than two hundred years old and still living today. The 19 climatic greenhouse sections contain a total of about 5,700 taxa. The greenhouses are distinguished particularly by the fullness of their collections of orchids (more than 1,000 taxa), Proteaceae (more than 100 types), Ericaceae, and tropical herbaceous plants, among which are collected several full generic complexes, a large collection of succulent plants, and inhabitants of tropical coasts and bodies of water. In 1989 the construction of a new greenhouse with an area of more than 6,000 square meters (7,176 sq. yd.) was begun. At the present time construction has been halted temporarily due to financial difficulties.

In 1987 the only Japanese garden in the country, and probably one of the northernmost in the world, was completed (2.7 hectares [6.6 acres]) with the participation of Japanese landscape architects (K. Nakajima, T. Adachi). Local and other non-Japanese species were used in this landscape-botanic composition along with imported plants for the creation of the typical effects of a Japanese garden (in all, about 130 taxa). To form the picturesque rocky relief, 250 tons of huge boulders were brought in from the Transcarpathians. Traditional small architectural forms, among them a 150-year-old 13-meter-long (14.2 yd.) stone pagoda brought from Japan and numerous other elements were used. Exhibits of bonsai from the garden collection (whose foundation consists of bonsai donated in 1976 by the Japanese embassy) and elsewhere are presented here in the stylized pavilions, along with exhibits of other traditional Japanese art and theatrical tea ceremonies.

The garden paths are extremely long. The main roads are asphalt; a chain of small paths (including all those in the oak forest) was constructed with a graveled surface system. The Main Botanic Garden of the Russian Academy of Sciences, undoubtedly the most outstanding work of landscape architecture of the first half of the 20th century, has become over the years of its comparatively short existence an object of study and imitation as a brilliant and unified landscape composition.

Synopsis

1743	Count Boris Sheremetev acquires land, builds English landscape park, and sets aside portion for forest preserve
1945	Soviet of People's Commissars of USSR establish Botanic Garden of USSR Academy of Sciences in Moscow; Ostankino oak forest in northern Moscow designated as site for garden; plan for garden completed by I.M. Petrov and N.V. Tsitsin; approval of structure of garden
1948	Botanic layouts begin
1948–50	Greenhouse and part of its collection moved from Sanssouci, Potsdam, Germany
1949	Arboretum construction begins
1952	General Plan of Construction examined and approved by Presidium of USSR Academy of Sciences
1953–54	Layout of garden completed
1954–58	Laboratory building constructed
1959	Basic garden construction completed and garden opened to public
1965	Enclosure of oak forest preserve
1987	Opening of Japanese garden
1989	Construction of new greenhouse begins

Further Reading

Andreev, L.N., *Introduktsiia rastenii v Glavnom botanicheskom sadu im. N.V. Tsitsina: K 50-letiiu osnovaniia* (Plant Introduction at the Main Botanic Garden: On the Fiftieth Anniversary of Foundation), Moscow: Nauka, 1995

Lapin, P.I., "Glavnyi botanicheskii sad (The Main Botanic Garden)," *Vestnik sel'skokhozyaistvennoi nauki* (Bulletin of Agricultural Science) 2 (1960)

Lapin, P.I., "Glavnomu botanicheskomu sadu A.N. SSSR 30 let (The Main Botanic Garden of the USSR Academy of Sciences on the 30-Year Anniversary)," *Vestnik Akademii nauk* (Bulletin of the Academy of Sciences) 10 (1975)

Lapin, P.I., "Otkrytie Glavnogo botanicheskogo sada (The Opening of the Main Botanic Garden)," *Vestnik Akademii nauk SSSR* (Bulletin of the USSR Academy of Sciences), 8 (1959)

ARTYOM PARSHIN

Ruys, Mien 1904–1999

Dutch Landscape Architect

Mien Ruys was born into a family of horticulturists, and like most of her siblings she made this her professional interest. Her father, Bonne Ruys, had founded the Moerheim Nursery in 1888, which specialized in perennials. The nursery became an international center of excellence, visited by many of the renowned horticulturists of the day, including Karl Foerster and Camillo Karl Schneider, with whom the Ruys family became good friends. This stimulating environment influenced Mien's choice of career, and at an early age she decided that she would become a garden architect. Working at the nursery she gained practical experience and profound plant knowledge and started her own experimental gardens at a corner of the orchard of her parents' garden in 1924. Through her access to international contacts Ruys was able to gain an unconventional informal training. She spent some time with the nursery and garden design firm Wallace and Son in England and took the opportunity to meet the best-known gardeners, including Gertrude Jekyll, whose ideas made a lasting impression on Ruys. She then undertook some training at a newly founded garden architecture course in Berlin. On her return she headed the garden design department of her father's nursery, but in the recession there was little work and she found time to take a course on architecture at the Technical University in Delft.

Ruys's informal education encouraged her critical capacities, and she distanced herself from her orthodox Christian family background and actively expressed communist and socialist tendencies. The type of work she became involved with reflected these interests, including communal gardens for social housing schemes, in which she cooperated with architects she had met in Delft. Most of her work, however, consisted of the design and layout of private gardens, designed by her and carried out by the contract department of the nursery. Her prewar work clearly shows English Arts and Crafts influences. She was influenced by the architectural style in Germany as expressed in the work of Erwin Barth and Hermann Muthesius. Particularly after her connection with the International Congress of Modern Architecture (CIAM), she developed her ideas on landscape and garden design, providing modernist design solutions that were asymmetric and functional. This was reminiscent of the work of the artists of the De Stijl movement with whom she had become involved.

Following World War II her designs responded to the Danish influence, with its emphasis on diagonal lines. Later she would return to a more rectangular and playful approach, for which she became so well known. Many of her best-known commissions in the postwar era were in association with modernist architects. While she always stressed form foremost she paid much attention to the use of materials and the planting with perennials, creating accomplished schemes with perennials in borders or naturalizing them in woodland gardens, signifying the influence of Jekyll and William Robinson. Ruys's postwar work shows the proliferation of naturalistic treatment in planting, promoted by the ideas of Jac. P. Thijsse and by the Germanic way of planting perennials in large swathes throughout the design, rather than in borders.

Ruys's postwar career was greatly assisted by her husband, Theo Moussault, a press photographer and publisher, who published much of her written work. Most of her books were directed to the amateur, and dealt with technical subjects: for example, ponds, rock gardens, and roses. The use and care of perennials was a recurring subject; one of her books, entitled *Spelen met planten* (1977; Playing with Perennials), clearly demonstrates her philosophy of experimentation and belief that gardens should be allowed to develop. In 1955 her husband commenced a quarterly gardening magazine *Onze Eigen Tuin* (Our Own Garden), which she edited and in which she wrote about her schemes. Within a three-year period this magazine had achieved a circulation of 100,000, evidence of the degree of Ruys's success. Of her many publications her best-known work is *Het nieuwe vaste planten boek* (1973; *The New Perennial Book*), an updated version of *Het vaste planten boek* (*The Perennial Book*), which had first appeared in 1950. This book, which sums up a lifetime of experience with plants, is engaging and authoritative. Her popular books were reprinted several times, and her more professional texts, coauthored with others, received no less attention. Her essay "De keuze van het terrein" ("The Choice of the Plot") in J.J. Vriend's *Bouwen en wonen* (1953; *Building and Living*) still makes worthwhile reading, and her section in *Leven met groen* (1960; *Living with Greenery*), written with J.T.P. Bijhouwer, in which she addresses the idea of and practicalities of the garden and criticizes the environmental impact of planning policies, was well in advance of her time. *Van vensterbank tot landschap* (1981; *From Windowsill to Landscape*), written with Rosette Zandvoort, provides a beautiful summing up of the range of work of the landscape architect and environmental challenges facing the population.

Ruys was also concerned about good-quality materials and always tried to find different solutions. In order to reduce individual orders to the nursery, she developed the idea of standard borders. These were promoted by a descriptive catalog published by Moerheim in 1953. Plants were arranged according to soil type and exposure, with borders drawn to scale, which might be ordered as a group. These were also shown as standard borders at her experimental gardens. Together with a manufacturer she developed a concrete and gravel slab based on an old one in her father's nursery, which was larger than the usual Dutch concrete tiles. They became a commercial success after they had been renamed as Grion tiles. She later abhorred the way in which manufacturers tidied up and regularized the Grion tiles, as well as their widespread popularity. While working on a garden in 1960, she used railway sleepers in order to bridge differences of level within a garden and later on used them as edging or paving. Published in her garden magazine, this soon became a very popular trend and earned her the nickname "Bielzen Mien" (Railway Sleeper Mien). She was always looking for new applications of materials. During the 1980s she and her colleagues became interested in alternative uses for recycled plastic materials instead of wood in the experimental gardens in Dedemsvaart.

Mien Ruys was the best-known Dutch landscape architect of the 20th century. She was responsible for a tremendous output, and her inventions reached popular acclaim. Moreover, she showed how garden making and planting could be fun. Her experimental gardens now survive in trust.

See also Pathways and Paving

Biography

Born in Dedemsvaart, Overijssel, Netherlands, 1904. Daughter of renowned nurseryman Bonne Ruys, of Moerheim Nursery; worked at garden-design department of father's nursery; began experimental gardens, Dedemsvaart, 1924; practical experience at garden-design department of Wallace and Son, Tunbridge Wells, Kent, England, 1928, and met Gertrude Jekyll; at advice of Camillo Karl Schneider, studied garden architecture at Berlin-Dahlem, Germany, under Erwin Barth, and enjoyed cultural life in Berlin, 1929–30; became head of garden-design department at Moerheim; followed lectures on architecture at Technical University, Delft, Netherlands, 1931–32; moved garden-design department of Moerheim Nursery to Amsterdam, 1937, and spent summers in Dedemsvaart and winters in Amsterdam; joined De 8, the Amsterdam branch of the International Congress of Modern Architecture, 1943; worked mainly on designs for private homes and also social housing schemes; met press photographer and publisher Theo Moussault, 1947; married Moussault, 1950; taught at Wageningen Agricultural University and Delft Technical University, 1951–52; continued course on urban greenspace in Delft, 1953–55; published gardening magazine *Onze Eigen Tuin*, 1955 (circulation by 1958: 100,000); made regular study visits abroad, from 1960; extended office with partners Hans Veldhoen (1968), Arend Jan van der Horst (1969–81), and Anet Scholma (from 1985); total number of commissions well over 3,000. Died in Dedemsvaart, 1999.

Selected Designs

1925–99 Experimental gardens, Moerheim Nursery, Dedemsvaart, Overijssel, Netherlands
1949–51 Communal gardens for new housing scheme, Frankendael, Amsterdam, Netherlands
1952 Public garden, De Eenhoorn, Oostburg, Netherlands
1955 Grounds of the Tomado Factory, Etten-Leur, Netherlands
1956 Cemetery (with architect H. Hartsuyker), Nagele, Noordoostpolder, Netherlands
1960 Hospital grounds (with architect J.P. Kloos), Almelo, Netherlands
1962–63 Private garden for architect Abe Bonnema, Pollesingel 2, Hardegarijp, Netherlands
1967 Private garden for architect O. Greiner, Amstelveen, Netherlands
1967 School grounds (with architect professor P.H. Tauber), Higher Technical College, Alkmaar, North Holland, Netherlands
1970 Grounds of retirement home (with architect A. Bonnema), Emmeloord, Netherlands
1976 Public garden Festhalle (with architect O. Greiner), Biberach, Germany

Selected Publications

Borders: Hoe men ze maakt en onderhoudt, 1939

Rotsplanten in de tuin, 1940

Vijvers in de tuin, 1941

Het vaste planten boek, with J.D. Ruys and T. Ruys, 1950; 2nd edition, as *Het nieuwe vaste planten boek*, 1973

"De keuze van het terrein," in *Bouwen en wonen*, edited by J.J. Vriend, 1953

Onze Eigen Tuin, 1955–99 (editor)

Rozen voor iedereen, 1956

Het gebruik en verzorging van vaste planten in onze tuin, 1959

Leven met groen: In landschap, stad en tuin, with Jan Thijs Pieter Bijhouwer, 1960

Zo beplanten wij onze tuin, 1965

Spelen met planten; De 18 voorbeeldtuinen van Mien Ruys, 1977

Playing with Perennials, 1977

Van vensterbank tot landschap, with Rosette Zandvoort, 1981

Mijn tuinen, 1987

Zo verzorgen wij onze tuin, n.d.

Further Reading

Geertsema, Reinko, *Mein Ruys: Beschrijving van haar beroepspraktijk*, Wageningen, Netherlands: Department of Landscape Architecture, Agricultural University, 1982

Jellicoe, Susan, and Geoffrey Alan Jellicoe, *Modern Private Gardens*, London and New York: Abelard-Schuman, 1968

Mercer, Frank Alfred, editor, *Gardens and Gardening: The Studio Gardening Annual*, New York: Rudge, and London: The Studio, 1932

Pearson, Dan, "Dutch Treat," *Sunday Times* (5 March 1995)

Salomonsen, Hein, "House near Apeldoorn," *The Architectural Review* 112 (1952)

Shepheard, Peter, *Modern Gardens*, London: Architectural Press, 1953

Vroom, Meto J., *Buitenruimten: Ontwerpen van Nederlandse tuin- en landschaps-architecten in de periode na 1945; Outdoor Space: Environments Designed by Dutch Landscape Architects in the Period since 1945* (bilingual Dutch-English edition), Amsterdam: Thoth, 1992

Zijlstra, Bonica, *Mien Ruys: Aspecten van leven en werk van een Nederlandse tuin- en landschapsarchitecte*, Amsterdam: Nederlandse Tuinenstichting, 1990

JAN WOUDSTRA

Ryōan-ji

Kyoto, Japan

Location: approximately 5 miles (8 km) northwest of Kyoto Station

The word *Ryōan-ji* has come to mean one particular example, some would say the supreme example, of the Japanese dry landscaping style called *kare-sansui*. More accurately, Ryōan-ji is a temple of the Rinzai sect of Zen Buddhism. Its extensive grounds still include a pond from the Heian period (794–1185), when the site was a summer palace for a branch of the Fujiwara clan. The famous rock garden occupies one small strip, approximately 9 by 24 meters (10 by 26 yd.), along the south side of the abbot's quarters.

Across this space 15 rocks are arranged into five groups in a ground of white gravel, itself raked into clean lines. A skirt of moss surrounding each rock group is the only plant matter in the whole ensemble, although old records indicate a cherry tree once grew near the right-hand corner of the building. Today, the presence of trees is only felt from those beyond the mottled patina of the enclosing wall. The temple veranda provides the viewing area. Beyond this inventory of the garden's elements, everything else about Ryōan-ji is contentious, including its date, its designer, and its meaning.

There are two possible dates for the placing of the Ryōan-ji rocks, either the late Muromachi period (ca. 1499) or the late Edo period (late 1790s). After its early history as a Fujiwara estate, the site passed into the hands of Hosokawa Katsumoto in 1450. He was responsible for the founding of Ryōan-ji as a subtemple of Myōshin-ji, one of Kyoto's five main Zen temples. After being razed by fire, the temple was rebuilt in the late 1490s by his son, Matsumoto. This event offers a possible date for the creation of the garden. Whether it was precisely the garden as it stands today cannot be

Ryoan-ji, Kyoto, Japan
Copyright Marc Treib

determined; early descriptions from the 1680s mention a garden with nine stones, not 15.

Fire again destroyed the temple in the late 1790s, providing the second moment of focus in the garden's obscured history. Some argue that the rock placing as we see it today could have occurred at this time, as part of yet another rebuilding.

Of course, speculation concerning who designed Ryōan-ji is implicated by the choice of date. If the earlier date is accepted, Soami, the renowned painter and garden designer, can be advocated. Although not supported by firm documentation, this is the traditional attribution. Katsumoto himself was also credited with the design in old manuscripts. This earlier date also permits the theory that two *kawaramono* (people who lived along the riverbank), whose names are carved into one of the rocks, were responsible for the rock placing. Given that this lower class of laborer was engaged in such manual tasks, this seems plausible. One Japanese

scholar (Teiji Ito), however, has difficulty with this solution, for such signing of their work would have been highly unusual.

Kuitert argues a strong case for the later date, believing the late 18th-century garden designer and author Akisato had a hand in the final positioning of the 15 rocks as part of the temple's second major reconstruction. The implications of this attribution are significant, for it runs counter to the popular view that Ryōan-ji is a product of the Muromachi period, the high point in Japanese Zen culture.

Even more speculation has ensued over the significance and meaning of Ryōan-ji. Some praise the garden for its formal qualities alone. Early modernists embraced Ryōan-ji's economy of design as an affirmation of what they themselves were seeking. Some went so far as to claim that the garden manifested a nascent modernism, despite the inherent anachronism in this argument. More recent attempts to fathom Ryōan-ji's aesthetic secrets similarly give priority to formal analysis and make note of the direction of movement suggested by the rock groups. This is usually read as flowing from left to right, although Slawson discerns a critical countermovement from the three groups on the right back into the defined rectangle.

Others seek more historical sources to explain Ryōan-ji's seemingly groundbreaking play of solids and voids. The Chinese art of *bonseki*, the arrangement of small stones across a sand-filled tray into a miniscule landscape, is proffered by some as a likely model. The "beauty of emptiness" (*yohaku-no-bi*)—the aesthetic decision in some Chinese landscape painting to leave large areas of silk free of ink—suggests another source for Ryōan-ji's composition.

Others see in Ryōan-ji more than its formal attributes, believing the garden to be of the highest spiritual order, to transcend its own materiality. Old Japanese texts spoke of the arrangement of the rocks in figurative terms—tiger cubs crossing a stream, mountains above mist or islands in the sea. Since the 1930s, however, Western chroniclers have eschewed these representational readings as inadequate. By 1940 the harmony in the Ryōan-ji landscape, between the rock groups and their setting and within themselves, was seen to be a statement of "that Harmony which underlies the universe" (Kuck, 1940). Ryōan-ji had become a site for cross-cultural spiritual expression.

With the increasing popularity of Zen in the West since the 1950s, Ryōan-ji's status has grown to that of a quintessential expression of Zen. According to this position, only the practitioner of *zazen* (the discipline of sitting in meditation) is privy to the garden's metaphysical dimension, a dimension that one writer describes as "the 'experience' of nothingness, of the void, emptiness" (Nitschke). Some commentators, however, take issue with the underlying premise of this reading—that Ryōan-ji was designed to be a site for meditation (see, for instance, Keane).

There is a popular middle ground that acknowledges Ryōan-ji's design and senses its profundity beyond the merely physical yet is reticent to presume complete grasp of why or how this is achieved. Moore and his fellow scholars concluded "the fifteen stones . . . induce in the rapt observer a concentrated calm. Precisely why, we don't pretend to know" (Moore et al.).

These readings are but a sampling of the efforts to do justice to the experience of Ryōan-ji's rock garden. It is important that their variety and quantity does not drown out the silent stillness that is Ryōan-ji.

Synopsis

12th century	Pond garden, for summer palace belonging to Fujiwara clan
1450	Site taken over by Hosokawa Katsumoto, who later founded Ryōan-ji temple
1488	Temple destroyed by fire
1490s	Temple rebuilt, and rock garden laid out (perhaps by the renowned garden designer Soami)
late 1500s	Hideyoshi visits to view cherry blossoms
1680–82	Written descriptions of rock garden with nine rocks in front of main hall
1797	Garden may have been altered to present form in temple reconstruction after another fire, and rock garden may have been laid out by Akisato
1799	Publication of Akisato Rito's *Celebrated Gardens and Sights of Kyoto*, with print showing 15 rocks arranged as they are today
1930s	First Western accolades published
1961	Construction of temporary replica begun at Brooklyn Botanical Gardens, New York, United States, with Takuma Tono as consultant

Further Reading

Bring, Mitchell, and Josse Wayembergh, *Japanese Gardens: Design and Meaning*, New York: McGraw Hill, 1981

Hayakawa, Masao, *Niwa*, Tokyo: Heibonsha, 1967; 2nd edition, 1979; as *The Garden Art of Japan*, translated by Richard L. Gage, New York: Weatherhill, 1973

Ito, Teiji, *The Gardens of Japan*, Tokyo and New York: Kodansha International, 1984

Keane, Marc Peter, *Japanese Garden Design*, Rutland, Vermont: C.E. Tuttle, 1996

Kuck, Loraine E., *One Hundred Kyoto Gardens*, London: Kegan Paul, Trench, Trubner, and Kobe, Japan: Thompson, 1935

Kuck, Loraine E., *The Art of Japanese Gardens*, New York: Day, 1940

Kuitert, Wybe, *Themes, Scenes, and Taste in the History of Japanese Garden Art*, Amsterdam: Gieben, 1988

Moore, Charles W., William J. Mitchell, and William Turnbull, Jr., *The Poetics of Gardens*, Cambridge, Massachusetts: MIT Press, 1988

Nitschke, Günter, *Gartenarchitektur in Japan: Rechter Winkel und natürliche Form*, Cologne, Germany: Taschen, 1991; as *Japanese Gardens: Right Angle and Natural Form*, translated by Karen Williams, Cologne, Germany: Taschen, 1993

Shigemori, Kanto, *Japanese Gardens: Islands of Serenity,* Tokyo and San Francisco: Japan Publications, 1971
Slawson, David A., *Secret Teachings in the Art of Japanese Gardens,* Tokyo and New York: Kodansha International, 1987
Treib, Marc, and Ron Herman, *A Guide to the Gardens of Kyoto,* Tokyo: Shufunotomo, 1980

FRAN NOLAN

S

Sackville-West, Victoria (Vita) Mary 1892–1962

English Poet, Garden Writer, and Garden Designer

Victoria Mary Sackville-West was a deeply passionate and unconventional woman whose twin loves were poetry and gardening: "My garden all is overblown with roses,/My spirit all is overblown with rhyme . . . / And, undetermined which delight to favour,/On verse and rose alternately carouse." Vita, as she was known, would like to have been remembered as an important poet but instead is probably better known as the creator of one of the most celebrated and best-loved gardens of the 20th century—Sissinghurst Castle, Kent, now in the care of the National Trust.

Sackville-West was born at Knole, Sevenoaks, the 16th-century stately home of one of England's great families. She had a privileged childhood and developed a strong sense of heritage and belonging both to the family home and the Kent countryside. When her grandfather died in 1908, the property became entailed to her uncle and cousin, and she realized that she would never inherit the home she passionately loved. This had a profound influence on her life and was perhaps the spur for her striving for recognition as a poet and novelist and the need to create her own miniature country estate at Sissinghurst Castle.

Sackville-West traveled extensively during her early life, absorbing the beauty of the landscape and gardens of Italy, France, Spain, and Russia. On her return from Russia in 1910, she met the diplomat and writer Harold Nicholson, whom she married in 1913. After a year in Constantinople, where Nicholson was posted, she returned to England, pregnant with her first child. In 1915 the couple acquired the Long Barn, Sevenoaks Weald, their first home in Kent, within walking distance of Knole. It was at the Long Barn that Sackville-West began to garden seriously, with Nicholson as the designer and Sackville-West planning the planting. Influences included William Robinson, Gertrude Jekyll,

and the architect Sir Edwin Lutyens, who later designed a Dutch garden for the Long Barn.

Sackville-West fell in love with the landscape of Persia on her visits there during Nicholson's posting, her journeys being recorded in her traveler's diary *Passenger to Tehran* (1926). At this time she also completed her epic poem *The Land* (1926), a tribute to the Kent countryside, for which she won the Hawthornden Prize in 1927. The most evocative lines from this 2,500-line epic are those describing one of her close friends, Dorothy Wellesley, to whom the poem is dedicated: "She walks among the loveliness she made,/Between the apple-blossom and the water–/She walks among the patterned pied brocade,/Each flower her son, and every tree her daughter."

In 1930 Sackville-West and Nicholson bought Sissinghurst Castle, a dilapidated property with a 16th-century tower and 10 acres of walled and moated ground surrounded by agricultural land. It was here that they created their "garden of rooms," each enclosure marked by the classical architecture of Nicholson's design and the romantic profusion of Sackville-West's planting. Sackville-West adopted the life of a country lady, rather eccentrically dressed in corduroy breeches and boots topped by a silk blouse and pearls. She eventually spent all her time at Sissinghurst, gardening and writing, returning to London only occasionally, her deliberate seclusion being described in one of her many poems, *Sissinghurst* (1931).

Sackville-West was a prolific writer, completing a number of biographies, essays, short stories, and poems as well as 11 full-length books, two epic poems, and several travel books. She wrote regularly for the *New Statesman,* continuing her "Country Notes" feature during World War II. During this period she also continued work on *The Garden* (1946), her second epic poem, a brilliant dialogue between reality and dreams,

Rose garden at Sissinghurst
Photo by Dave Parker

chronicling the garden through the seasons. Although *The Garden* won the Heinemann Prize, it did not receive critical acclaim from Sackville-West's literary contemporaries, and it was the last poem she published. She is remembered by many, however, for her regular gardening columns in the *Observer*, to which she contributed for 14 years, beginning in 1946, and which were published initially as four individual volumes and then as a compendium.

After the war, the gardens at Sissinghurst were restored and re-opened to the public. Sackville-West continued to garden, write, and lecture and to support the activities of the Royal Horticultural Society and the National Trust, being a founder member of the Gardens Committee from 1946. She became ill in the summer of 1959 and was later diagnosed as suffering from cancer. She died at Sissinghurst on 2 June 1962; her ashes were placed in the Sackville crypt at the church of St. Michael and All Angels, Withyham, Sussex.

See also Sissinghurst Castle Garden

Biography

Born at Knole Castle, Sevenoaks, Kent, 9 March 1892. The only child of Lionel and Victoria Sackville-West; traveled extensively to Italy, France, Spain, and Russia; returned from Russia, 1910, and met Harold Nicholson, whom she married, 1913; in Constantinople, Turkey, 1914; acquired the Long Barn, Sevenoaks Weald, Kent, England, 1915, where she began to garden seriously; traveled to Persia and was deeply influenced by its landscapes, before 1926; bought Sissinghurst Castle, Kent, 1930, and with her husband began to create their "garden of rooms"; contributed regular gardening columns to the *Observer*, 1946–60; won the Hawthornden Prize for *The Land*, 1927, and the Heinemann Prize for *The Garden*, 1946; awarded RHS Veitch Memorial Medal, 1954. Died at Sissinghurst Castle, Kent, 2 June 1962.

Selected Designs

1915–30   Gardens, Long Barn, Sevenoaks Weald, Kent, England

White garden at Sissinghurst
Photo by Dave Parker

1930–   Gardens, Sissinghurst Castle, Cranbrook,
         Kent, England

Selected Publications

Passenger to Tehran, 1926
The Land, 1926
Sissinghurst, 1931
"Country Notes," *New Statesman* (1938–41)
English Country Houses, 1941
The Garden, 1946
"In Your Garden," *Observer* (1946–60); as *In Your
   Garden,* 1951, *In Your Garden Again,* 1953, *More
   for Your Garden,* 1955, and *Even More for Your
   Garden,* 1958; collected edition, as *V. Sackville-
   West's Garden Book,* edited by Philippa Nicolson,
   1968

Further Reading

Brown, Jane, *Vita's Other World: A Gardening
   Biography of V. Sackville-West,* London and New
   York: Viking Press, 1985
Brown, Jane, *Sissinghurst: Portrait of a Garden,* New
   York: Abrams, and London: Weidenfeld and
   Nicolson, 1990
Glendinning, Victoria, *Vita: The Life of Vita Sackville-
   West,* New York: Knopf, and London: Weidenfeld
   and Nicolson, 1983
Nicolson, Nigel, *Portrait of a Marriage,* New York:
   Atheneum, and London: Weidenfeld and Nicolson,
   1973
Scott-James, Anne, *Sissinghurst: The Making of a
   Garden,* London: Joseph, 1974

BARBARA SIMMS

Saiho-ji

Kyoto, Japan

Location: 2.5 miles (4 km) west of Arashiyama, northwest of Kyoto

The garden of the Saiho-ji Temple in Kyoto is one of the oldest surviving gardens in Japan. It was built in 1339 during the transition from the Kamakura and Muromachi periods, and as a modified paradise garden it represents an important transition in Japanese garden design. The Saiho-ji garden is credited to the famous Zen priest and garden designer Muso Soseki (1275–1351), also known as Muso Kokushi (the priestly title granted to him by the emperor). Although many believe that the original garden of Saiho-ji was created in 1190, Muso was responsible for creating the details and character for which it is famous.

The Saiho-ji garden is also referred to as the Kokedera, or Moss Garden, because of the many varieties of moss that carpet the ground of the lower garden. The moss was not necessarily part of Muso's design; during the Meiji period (1868–1911) in Japan the temple could not afford to keep up with the maintenance of the garden. This neglect, combined with the garden's rich, clay soils and shaded location, resulted in the luxurious and profuse growth of as many as 100 varieties of moss.

The Saiho-ji Temple was a seminary for the Zen Buddhist priesthood. Japanese Zen temples were originally created as places to study religion and were built and offered to Buddha by high-ranking officials and nobles. The gardens connected to these temples were created as an extension of the deep religious atmosphere of the temple and used as an aid in meditation and prayer.

The garden is divided into the upper and lower gardens, which are viewed by a winding path and rocky steps. These two distinct areas reveal the dual nature of this garden by displaying a shift from the otherworldly concept of a paradise garden to one that focuses on the more earthly beauty of nature, resulting in a modified paradise style. The lower garden of Saiho-ji centers around the *ogonchi,* or golden pond, which is roughly in the shape of the Chinese character *shin.* This was a favorite character of the Zen Buddhists and means "heart, soul, spirit." The pond was inspired by the Pure Land of Amida concept of paradise. Amida was a Buddhist deity whose paradise was a place of purity and goodness, often represented by a lake garden. Amida's garden lay to the west and was often referred to as the Western Paradise. Saiho-ji's name originally translated to "Temple of the Western Direction," which refers to this Pure Land. Later in the 14th century Zen monks changed the Chinese characters to mean "Temple of the

Western Fragrance," a Zen allusion. Although the pronunciation remained the same, this change is further evidence of Saiho-ji's place as a transitional garden.

When entering the lower garden, one is surrounded by what seems to be an undulating sea of green moss that flows uninterrupted from the hillside to the banks of the lake, over ground, rocks, and tree trunks. The garden seems vast, covering approximately 4.5 acres (1.8 ha), and is deeply shaded by broadleaf evergreen trees overhead, with occasional spots of light penetrating the canopy to the floor of moss. The garden is relatively open at eye level, increasing the sense of depth created by the rhythm of tree trunks drawing one's eye into the distance. Most of the trees in the garden grow naturally instead of being trained into specific shapes, as is often associated with Japanese gardens. The trees consist mainly of pines, maples, evergreen oaks, cypress, firs, podocarpus, osmanthus, and cryptomeria. Bamboo, Japanese winterberry, azalea, camellia, and holly are among the other plant species that contribute to the character of the garden. Early on, the garden was famous for its showing of cherry blossoms, but in keeping more with the Zen Buddhist spirit, these flowering trees were not replaced when they died. The only color that contrasts the sea of green in the lower garden today are the few Japanese maples that flash leaves of orange and crimson in the autumn. The pathway in the garden provides guests with an opportunity to stroll in the garden instead of being confined to boats and viewing the garden only from the lake, as was typical of gardens up to this point. This concept of the pathway of movement became a central component in later Japanese gardens, including the Zen Buddhist tea garden and the stroll gardens of the Edo period.

The upper garden of Saiho-ji is separated from the lower garden by a ceremonial gateway, the *kokojan,* which marks the separation between the older paradise concept of the lower garden and the later Zen practices and style of the upper garden. A further distinction of the upper garden is the lack of maples; it was thought that their bright fall color was contrary to the Zen tenet of restraint. The upper garden contains Japan's oldest existing *kazan* rock work. Translated as "miniature mountains," *kazan* is a dry landscape gardening style, in which mountain scenery is depicted by the arrangement of rocks, often in a small space.

One of the rock compositions at Saiho-ji is designed as a large, cascading waterfall that suggests the rushing and tumbling of water, despite the fact that water has never been a part of the scene. Over time the moss has

Saiho-ji
Photo by Elizabeth R. Messer Diehl

assumed the role of water, spilling over the rocks' flat edges and flowing downhill. Rock work suggesting calmer pools of water is found below the waterfall composition, along with a large, flat stone said to be used for meditation. Farther on is another rock composition that represents an island in the shape of a tortoise. This arrangement refers to the Chinese myth that speaks of an island paradise of immortality that rests on the backs of gigantic tortoises. The rock work has been interpreted in different ways, however, any of which are valid when one understands that the Zen garden emphasizes the individual's contemplative experience, rather than the understanding of any particular representation.

The beauty and serenity of Saiho-ji have inspired garden makers for centuries, as have specific elements within the garden. Features such as streams, springs, and even buildings were copied and used in other gardens, and it is said that adoration of the garden had taken somewhat the form of a cult. The main hall at Saiho-ji, the *shariden*, was duplicated at two later temples, Kinkakuji, or the Golden Pavilion, and Ginkakuji, or the Silver Pavilion. The garden of Ginkakuji was based on that of the Saiho-ji Temple. Ashikaga Yoshimasa, a shogun in the Muromachi period and the grandson of the designer of Kinkakuji, built the garden at Ginkakuji and visited Saiho-ji many times before starting it in 1482. It is similar in its design, also being divided into two parts with a pond, maple trees, and buildings in the lower garden and a spring and stone arrangement in an upper garden.

Muso designed many other gardens, including Nanzenji and Tenryuji in Kyoto, Gyukoji in Tosa, and Yorinji in the province of Kai. It is said that Muso built the Saiho-ji garden for Fugiwara no Chikahide, a powerful member of the Japanese government in the middle of the 14th century. Muso himself served as a government advisor and was deeply respected. This was a time of civil unrest in Japan, and the Saiho-ji garden represents the increasing popularity of the paradise garden as an escape from this civil strife. Muso occupied a transitional position as a garden designer, and despite enjoying extremely high rank as a spiritual figure, he was strongly criticized for his increasing secularism, a shift that can be seen in the design of Saiho-ji.

Synopsis

1190	Original Saiho-ji Temple and garden created
ca. 1300	Saiho-ji becomes Zen Buddhist Temple
1339	Saiho-ji garden reconstructed by Muso Soseki (Kokushi)
ca. 1395	Kinkakuji (Gold Pavilion) built
1469	Saiho-ji's original buildings destroyed during Onin Civil Wars
1482	Ginkakuji (Silver Pavilion) built
1868	Saiho-ji garden neglected, and mosses, which later became well-known feature of garden, established themselves
ca. 1868	Founders' Hall built (the current main building)

Further Reading

Bring, Mitchell, and Josse Wayembergh, *Japanese Gardens: Design and Meaning*, New York: McGraw Hill, 1981

Charlé, Suzanne, "Temple of Moss," *Connoisseur* 212, no. 849 (1982)

Engel, David Harris, *Japanese Gardens for Today*, Tokyo and Rutland, Vermont: C.E. Tuttle, 1959

Fukuda, Kazuhiko, *Japanese Stone Gardens: How to Make and Enjoy Them*, Tokyo and Rutland, Vermont: C.E. Tuttle, 1970

Holborn, Mark, *The Ocean in the Sand: Japan from Landscape to Garden*, London: Gorden Fraser, and Boulder, Colorado: Shambhala, 1978

Ishimoto, Tatsuo, *The Art of the Japanese Garden*, New York: Crown, 1958

Ito, Teiji, *Nihon no niwa*, Tokyo: Chuo Koronsha, 1971; as *The Japanese Garden: An Approach to Nature*, translated by Donald Richie, New Haven, Connecticut: Yale University Press, 1972

Jellicoe, Geoffrey Alan, and Susan Jellicoe, *The Landscape of Man: Shaping the Environment from Prehistory to the Present Day*, New York: Viking Press, and London: Thames and Hudson, 1975; 3rd edition, expanded and updated, New York: Thames and Hudson, 1995

Kuck, Loraine E., *The World of the Japanese Garden: From Chinese Origins to Modern Landscape Art*, New York: Walker/Weatherhill, 1968

Schaarschmidt-Richter, Irmtraud, *Japanische Garten*, Baden-Baden, Germany: Holle, 1977; as *Japanese Gardens*, translated by Janet Seligman, New York: Morrow, 1979

Takakuwa, Gisei, *Meien hyakushu*, Kyoto: Mitsumura Suiko Shoin, 1959; as *Gardens of Japan*, translated by Saijiro Akita, Kyoto: Mitsumura Suiko Shoin, 1959

Thacker, Christopher, *The History of Gardens*, Berkeley: University of California Press, and London: Croom Helm, 1979

ELIZABETH R. MESSER DIEHL

Sakuteiki

Sakuteiki (Records of Garden Making) was written in the mid-11th century in Heian (present-day Kyoto), Japan, making it the earliest extant treatise on aesthetic garden making. The purported author of the *Sakuteiki* was Tachibana no Toshitsuna (1028–94), son of the imperial regent Fujiwara no Yorimichi (992–1074). Both Toshitsuna and his father are recorded as well-known garden makers, Yorimichi being the owner of Kayanoin, a particularly splendid and well-documented palace within the Heian capital, as well as Byōdō-in, a temple south of Kyoto in Uji, the main hall of which still exists after nearly 1,000 years.

The *Sakuteiki* undertakes to explain the gardens of aristocratic *shinden* residences, specifically the *nantei,* or Southern Court. The Southern Court included a sand-covered courtyard, *tei* (Chinese, *ting*), to the south of the main hall that served as an entry court to the main hall and a stage for accommodating various ceremonies, as well as a pond garden that was constructed just south of the *tei*. The *Sakuteiki* was not written as an encyclopedic record but reads rather like a series of notes on sundry garden-design related topics that the author had come to experience in the course of his life; it is written in the tone of a cultured aristocrat discoursing on gardens for the benefit of others of his ilk. There are many aspects of Heian-period gardens that can be surmised from other literary references, contemporary paintings, and archeological digs that are not mentioned in the *Sakuteiki* at all, for instance, the tiny enclosed courtyard gardens, *tsubo,* of *shinden* residences and the concept of building a garden to symbolize the Western Paradise of Amida Buddha (Sanskrit, Amitābha). The treatise was not meant for widespread distribution but rather was intended as a supplement to secret oral teachings, *kuden*. While the treatise is not rigidly divided into chapters, there is a basic grouping of material: fundamental concepts, southern courts, ponds and islands, stones, gardening styles, islands, waterfalls, garden streams, taboos, trees, wellsprings, and miscellany.

The explanations of these various aspects reveal certain attitudes toward garden design that were prevalent in the Heian period (and reflective of aristocratic life at the time) and can be grouped into five categories: technical advice, nature imagery, geomancy, Buddhism, and taboos. Primarily the treatise is a technical manual that overtly tries to explain various details of garden layout and construction. Examples of specific technical advice include how deep, from north to south, to make the *tei,* how far below the veranda of the garden arbors to set the water level of the pond, how to use a piece of bamboo split lengthwise and filled with water to create a level with which to properly adjust the heights of stones being set in an as-yet-unfinished pond area, and how to seal an underground pipe or wellspring with clay to prevent leaks.

Nature imagery was an important motif in aristocratic life in general. In particular it was central to writing poetry, the premier art form of the time. The imagery of nature that was woven into the gardens was undoubtedly derived to some extent from the large body of poetry that existed, and connoisseurship of gardens was certainly informed by knowledge of poetry. It is also known that aristocrats (depending on their rank and thus freedom of movement) made excursions to the countryside surrounding the Heian capital and even went on plant-collecting trips. Perhaps the favorite nature image mentioned in the *Sakuteiki* that could easily have been drawn directly from the environment of Heian was the meadow, *nosuji*. Others, such as the rocky-shore style, *araiso,* which evoked the image of an ocean beach, were drawn from farther afield. The design of waterfalls, streams, mountains, wetlands, and islands—all images drawn from nature—is also mentioned in the text.

Geomancy is a catchall term used to describe several theories developed in ancient China to explain the order of the physical world, as well as that of human society. The primary geomantic components revealed in the *Sakuteiki* are yin and yang (Japanese, *in* and *yō*), opposing yet integrated negative and positive forces; Five Phases (Japanese, *gogyō*), namely, wood, fire, earth, metal, and water; Four Guardian Gods (Japanese, *shijin*); and Twelve Directional Animals (Japanese, *jūnishi*). The author of the *Sakuteiki* applies these systems to explain various aspects of garden design, including the flow of river water into, through, and out of the garden; the placement of stones within the garden, especially those of large size or particular colors; and the placement of certain species of trees in specific cardinal directions.

Four aspects of Buddhism are mentioned in the *Sakuteiki* in connection to garden design, some of which relate to the esoteric Buddhist sects, such as Shingon and Tendai, which were widely supported by the aristocratic class, and others simply indicative of Buddhism in general. The four are Gion shōja (Sanskrit, Jetavana), a monastery built for Shakamuni (Sanskrit, Śākyamuni), the Living Buddha, the tale of which was used as a model for the solemnity desired in aristocratic gardens; Fudō myōō (Sanskrit, Acalanātha), a deity dedicated to purging evil from the mortal world whose form was correlated with waterfalls; Buddhist Trinities, *sanzon-butsu,* which were expressed by setting three stones in a triangular form; and the Eastern Flow of Buddhism, *buppō tōzen,* which was related to the eastern flow of water in sacred spaces.

Taboos governed a great deal of aristocratic life in the Heian period, from the directions allowed for travel to the dates for washing one's hair. In the *Sakuteiki* many expressions are couched in the language of taboo, threatening the onslaught of sickness, poverty, or death to those who violate the warning. Taboos included using a stone in a position other than as it was found in nature, setting large stones near a residence in line with its columns or in the northeast quadrant, building a mountain form in the southwest quadrant, and setting a Buddhist Trinity arrangement so that it faced directly on a residence.

Further Reading

Keane, Marc Peter, *Japanese Garden Design,* Rutland, Vermont: C.E. Tuttle, 1996

Kuck, Lorraine, *The World of the Japanese Garden: From Chinese Origins to Modern Landscape Art,* New York: Walker/Weatherhill, 1968

Kuitert, Wybe, *Themes, Scenes, and Taste in the History of Japanese Garden Art,* Amsterdam: Gieben, 1988

Nitschke, Günter, *Gartenarchitektur in Japan: Rechter Winkel und natürliche Form,* Cologne, Germany: Taschen, 1991; as *Japanese Gardens: Right Angle and Natural Form,* translated by Karen Williams, Cologne, Germany: Taschen, 1993

Takei, Jiro, and Marc P. Keane, *The Sakuteiki, Vision of the Japanese Garden: A Modern Translation of Japan's Gardening Classic,* Boston: C.E. Tuttle, 2001

MARC PETER KEANE

Sanctuary Garden

It is said that the Latin word for sanctuary (*sanctuarium*) is closely connected to the idea of holiness; thus sanctuary is the "holy place," the place to restore our emotional and spiritual balance. Following this thread, the sanctuary garden is that holy place on this earth where we retreat to restore harmony in our lives, and thus gardening, whether creating or enjoying, becomes an instrument of grace, a sacrament, if you will. Thomas Moore, in *The Re-Enchantment of Everyday Life* claims that the garden is the external model of our hearts and that the soul within is a garden enclosed. The garden is both our desire for and our opportunity to re-create a bit of the original Garden of Eden. It is precisely this desire that gave rise to the gardens of the ancient East and the *paradeisos,* or paradise gardens, of Dar-al-Islam and medieval Europe and that also finds expression in the modern "sanctuary garden." It would not be wrong to say that all gardens are "sanctuary gardens"; however, not all gardens are designed specifically to be a bit of paradise on earth. Sanctuary-garden design, as a specific type of garden design, flows from a purposeful desire to reclaim a sense of harmony with both the Creator and creation, a desire that requires a devotion to peace, place, and most of all stewardship: the idea that one must give nurture in order to be nurtured.

Although seemingly a modern phenomena, the sanctuary garden is deeply rooted in the ancient histories as well as in the myths of both the East and West. The word *paradise* comes from the ancient Persian *pairidaeza* and literally means "fenced-in garden." Fence implies boundary; a fence cuts us off from the outside world, yet the gate still allows us access to it. In a spiritual sense the sanctuary garden becomes both the end and beginning of pilgrimage—the place of restoration as well as the place from which we begin our pilgrimage back into the world to share the blessing of our spiritual restoration. As a place of spiritual restoration the sanctuary garden is akin to the Greek *temeno,* from which we get the word *temple,* a sacred enclosure suspended in time. Of significance, too, is the use of the primitive root *daez* in *pairi-daeza. Daez* refers to primordial Creator God, *dis* in European myth.

Medieval garden writers, while touching on the spiritual aspects of garden design, were more content to dwell on sociological needs and how they influenced garden design, thus giving plenty of practical advice and little spiritual direction. This was not true, however, in the East. These same ideas were developed in the Oriental garden. In fact, the gardens of the East flow from an ancient oriental mystical theology of harmony. Who is not familiar with the Zen garden?

In the context of Buddhism, "obtaining Paradise," or *Gokurakujō,* did not mean getting back to the primordial spirit of nature but rather to a nature created by man, a garden. In Shinto the unusual in nature is venerated as *go-shintai,* the abode of the deity, and in time these unusual features came to be re-created in Japanese gardens as a focal point, recognizing that the life spirit resides in nature, and hence the garden is above all else a holy place, a sanctuary. It is taught in Buddhism that the Buddha lives in a garden, the holy *Gokurakujō,* just as it is the intent of the Islamic *pairi-daeza* to create a place for Allah to dwell among his creatures.

In Taoist myth, far to the East lay five garden islands—sanctuaries—populated by humans who have reached immortality and reside in harmony amid unspeakable beauty. These islands are known as "The Isles of the Blest." From each isle rises the mystical Mount Horai-zan (Chinese, *Pieng-lai*). The Oriental garden is seen as a re-creation of these mystical islands. The central focus of the Tao garden is what the Japanese call *Horai,* either a miniature mountain or an island in a "sea" that symbolizes these holy isles. In Hindu cosmology the holy mountain is the *axis mundi,* the center of the universe, from which all life flows. This is the Japanese *Horai;* more than a garden appointment, it is the very center where harmony is to be found. The oldest of the Japanese chronicles, *Kojiki* (A.D. 712; Record of Ancient Matters) and *Nihon shoki* (A.D. 720; Chronicle of Japan) cover the history of Japan from prehistorical times to A.D. 697, and in the chronicles there are several references to the *Horai,* or sanctuary garden, both mythical and to their influence on Japanese history.

All of this suggests that the sanctuary garden, at least in original concept, is sacramental, a place that nurtures and heals our very being. In its Buddistic context paradise is nevertheless a place that humans create. As a human creation certain characteristics are essential to the design of the sanctuary garden: (1) the garden must provide for solitude and reflection, (2) the garden must provide for celebratory communion, and (3) the garden must provide for cocreative stewardship.

For the fundamentals we can draw parallels from the Shinto concept of garden design, a design that is finding revival in the renewed interest in using the ancient principals of *feng shui* in sanctuary garden design. *Feng shui* literally means "wind and water" and is about connecting us with the spirit, or harmony, of a particular place. In gardening it is about the gardener and garden being in partnership not only with each other but also with the earth. *Feng shui* teaches us that gardening, or specifically the design of the sanctuary garden, is more about emotional and spiritual attitude than actual design.

Feng shui, along with other Eastern sanctuary garden design, draws on three ancient Shinto archetypes, each of which enter equally into the design. In other words, there is an inherent balance intentionally built into the design. The first of these archetypes is *shime,* the "territorial archetype." *Shime* is about the garden plot itself. The word literally means "a bound artifact." Thus the garden plot is that land that is "taken possession of," much in the same concept of the *pairi-daeza.* In the *pairi-daeza* and the *horai* garden, "possession" is not about owning but about setting apart, literally "sanctifying," or making it holy by becoming one with it— being "bound" to it. Such thinking gives rise to a whole

"theology of gardening," which should be considered in planning a sanctuary garden. The second and third archetypes are also about binding. *Iwakora* and *iwaraka* refer to mystically binding rock, and speak to the significance of garden appointments, both in their selection and placement. Appointments should not be selected and placed for eye appeal alone but primarily for their "heart appeal," their resonance within us. As in the *Paradiso,* a significantly placed bench, a small pond of water with an island, or a large rock as its *horai* all contribute to a sense of sanctity. The third archetype, *shinzen,* is about the "binding of agriculture," such as in the binding of sheaths of grain. In the design of sanctuary gardens, it is important that the plants and the gardener each nurture the other. The particular choice of plants is relatively insignificant as long as the choices have spiritual value, in that they offer something to the heart. An unusually shaped or exceedingly beautiful or fragrant tree or bush can become the garden's *go-shin-tai,* the symbol of both holiness and the One from which holiness flows. In Western garden design, a plaque of the face of the Celtic Green Man (Cernunnos, the Lord of the Forest) or a statue of St. Francis serve the same purpose. Thus, plot, appointment, and plants must all be in balanced relationship to each other and the gardener, which can be considered the fourth archetype as the "one who binds."

From an Oriental perspective sanctuary gardens are said to be endowed with what Zen Buddhists call *yugen,* which can roughly be translated as signifying a "tranquility with mysterious depth," or a "lingering resonance." The Zen monk Shōtetsu described *yugen* in 1430 as that which is "suggested by the sight of a thin cloud veiling the moon or by an autumn mist swathing the scarlet leaves on a mountainside." It is this sense that sanctuary gardens seek to convey.

A classic example of *yugen* is to be found in the *karesansui* garden found in Saihō-ji. *Karesansui* comes from *kare,* meaning "dry," *san,* meaning "mountain," and *sui,* meaning "water"; thus a *karesansui* is a "dry mountain water garden," what we know as the Zen garden. The garden, stones raked into ripples around the *shinzen* and *iwaraka,* was designed by Musō Kokushi, the "father of Japanese contemplative garden design," in the early 1500s and predates the rest of Saihō-ji by 400 years; it is said to be the first *karesansui* garden built.

The early Celtic church performed a ritual, borrowed from the druids, in Gaelic called *do-foirdea,* literally the making of boundaries with song. The monks would circle in clockwise fashion the monastic territory, marking off its mystical boundaries through singing as they walked. The same ritual was also applied to marking off the boundaries of agricultural fields and kitchen gardens alike, in effect making them a sanctuary of holiness. Such is the idea of creating a sanctuary garden, and the practice of *do-foirdea* is a fitting element in "binding," or sanctifying, the sanctuary garden to its holy purpose.

In a practical sense the sanctuary garden must be designed so as to touch upon all of the senses: smell, taste, sight, hearing, touch, and a sense of balance. The organization of the garden, whether natural or architectural, must convey harmony, not fragmentation. A stroll through the garden needs to be a pilgrimage, centering upon the garden's *axis mundi*. It is not insignificant that many of the larger medieval and Victorian gardens contained a labyrinth with a place to sit in solitude in its midst. Even many herb gardens contained miniature knot-work labyrinths with a significant appointment at the center.

As the pilgrimage unfolds the incidents and discoveries along the way need to be savored. A strategically placed plant here, a bit of water there, or perhaps an appointment hid among the plants all contribute to the journey. Scale also is important. As the Japanese *horai* was Mount Horai-zan on a smaller scale, the features of the sanctuary garden need to be scaled to give us a new perspective of the larger picture. Never, however, should the scale be overwhelming. There is something to be said about motion that engages the viewer, and the sanctuary garden's design should incorporate motion, perhaps in a small waterfall or bubbling fountain, or the gentle swaying of a weeping willow, or even a glimpse of the moving clouds through the branches of a tree. Reminiscent of Eastern *karesansui* garden design, contemplative garden designer Julie Moir Messervy suggests that there are seven landscape archetypes that appeal to the mind, and that at least a few should be worked into the sanctuary

garden in a scale that is balanced to the garden. They are the sea, the cave, the harbor, the promontory, the island, the mountain, and the sky.

Whatever the style of sanctuary garden, whatever the features, a garden only ultimately becomes a sanctuary garden when it enables the gardener to enter the harmony of transcendence as a creative participant.

Further Reading

McDowell, Christopher Forrest, and Tricia Clark-McDowell, *The Sanctuary Garden: Creating a Place of Refuge in Your Yard or Garden*, New York: Simon and Schuster, 1998

Messervy, Julie Moir, *Contemplative Gardens*, Charlottesville, Virginia: Howell Press, 1990

Moore, Thomas, *The Education of the Heart: Readings and Sources for Care of the Soul, Soul Mates, and the Re-enchantment of Everyday Life*, New York: HarperCollins, 1996

Nitschke, Günter, *Gartenarchitektur in Japan: Rechter Winkel und natürliche Form*, Cologne, Germany: Taschen, 1991; as *Japanese Gardens: Right Angle and Natural Form*, Cologne, Germany: Taschen, 1993

Streep, Peg, *Spiritual Gardening: Creating Sacred Spaces Outdoors*, Alexandria, Virginia: Time-Life Books, 1999

Wydra, Nancilee, *Feng Shui in the Garden: Simple Solutions for Creating Comforting, Life-Affirming Gardens of the Soul*, Chicago: Contemporary Books, 1997

FRANK MILLS

Sanspareil

Bavaria, Germany

Location: approximately 15 miles (24.2 km) west of Bayreuth, 5 miles (8 km) north of Hollfeld, and approximately 40 miles (64.5 km) north of Nuremberg

*S*anspareil is the French word for "unparalleled," and there could hardly be a more appropriate name for this idiosyncratic garden. It is situated on the crest of a hill near the medieval castle of Zwernitz. The remodeling of the former hunting grounds began in 1744 under the Margrave Frederick and Margravine Wilhelmine of Bayreuth. Quite contrary to contemporary German

taste for formal garden design, they adopted wholesale, with only minor alterations, the bizarre limestone rock scenery in a beech grove. Art historian Erich Bachmann has characterized the garden as a rare example of the genre of rock garden.

In 1745 four buildings were erected around a sunken *parterre de broderie* to the west of the grove. One of them, the Morgenländische Bau (oriental building), was one of the first Moorish follies in Germany, at a time when chinoiserie was predominantly fashionable. To the rear, the rock grove extends over an area of approximately 160 by 650 meters (175 by 711 yd.). At no point could the garden be viewed in its entirety; the scattered buildings and rock formations were only revealed in succession. The serpentine paths followed the natural topography without any formal relationship to the residence, and some walks led into the adjacent fields. Wooden follies crowned several crags from where one could view the surrounding landscape. Some of the buildings were faced with bark and quarry stone; others were decorated in the interior with scenic mosaics of moss and stone.

Joseph Saint-Pierre designed the buildings and supervised the work in Sanspareil. Having worked as a set decorator and architect in Germany and France, he took over the post as the court architect of Bayreuth in 1743. The works in Sanspareil were probably initiated by Margrave Frederick (r. 1735–63). After educational years in Geneva, France, and Holland, he returned to Bayreuth in 1731. That year he married Wilhelmine of Prussia. Wilhelmine, sister of Frederick the Great, must have been one of the most accomplished and cultured women of her time. Having at one time been promised to the Prince of Wales, she was well versed in English culture. After her marriage to Frederick, the country house of Monplaisir, situated in the grounds of the Eremitage of Bayreuth, was given to her as a place of retreat. The respective contribution of Frederick and Wilhelmine to the design of Sanspareil cannot be clearly defined. It is probable that Frederick influenced the early stages of the works and that Wilhelmine was the driving force especially behind the creation of the rock garden.

Wilhelmine connected the different garden parts by literary allusions. The didactic moral messages could perhaps have been evoked by her marital problems at that time. She may have also been inspired by the educational novel *Les Aventures de Télémaque* (1699) by Archbishop François de Salignac de la Mothe-Fénelon, the tutor to the French dauphin. Fénelon narrates the adventures of Telemach in his search for his father, Odysseus. Resisting all temptation of sensual pleasure and flattery, Telemach finally returns home to Ithaka, where he is reunited with his father. In the last stages of the garden construction, some rocks and follies were metaphorically assigned to the island of Ogygia, one of the stations of Telemach's journey. However, some scenes found in Sanspareil but not in Fénelon's novel give reason to believe that the garden iconology was based on Pierre de Marivaux's satirical novel *Télémaque travesti* (1736).

Neither Fénelon nor Marivaux could have inspired the famous ruined or grotto theater in Sanspareil, which was begun in 1746 at the eastern corner of the grove (see Plate 29). A natural grotto shelters the entrance and auditorium. Four stone arches vault the stage, and a window in the walled backdrop allows views into the sur-

rounding beech wood. The theater is built in a rustic style, using undressed stone and tuff and decorated with pebble work and classical sculptures. Temporary theaters were common in European baroque gardens, whereas stone theaters remained a rarity. An early example is the natural stage set in a rock face at Hellbrunn in Salzburg built in 1612. A ruined garden theater in classical style was begun in 1743 under the direction of Saint Pierre in the grounds of the Eremitage in Bayreuth. The theater at Sanspareil is remarkable for it is a unique synthesis of both types: the ruined theater and the natural stage.

After Sanspareil was completed, Wilhelmine wrote that "Nature herself was the master builder." Indeed, the creation of a garden with only minor alteration to the existing rock scenery was a notable exception in contemporary German garden design. It thus differs from Betlehem at Kukus (now Czech Republic), which was laid out from 1726 to 1733 by Franz Anton Earl of Sporck, or Bomarzo in Italy (ca. 1580) by Duke Vicino Orsini. There, as in Sanspareil, serpentine paths followed the natural terrain through a wooded and rocky landscape. But at Kukus and Bomarzo the rocks were transformed by sculptors. One cannot categorically define how much Sanspareil's design was influenced by English examples or whether in fact it was still the lingering baroque ethos of the juxtaposition of nature and architecture that was the predominating theme instead of elevating nature herself as the decisive element. Typical components of the landscape garden such as corresponding lines of sight or vistas are lacking, and the scattered courtly amusements seem more rococo in spirit. According to Hennebo and Hoffmann the development of the landscape garden on the Continent did not receive much of an impulse from the creation of Sanspareil. It was, however, still a topic for illustrations and travel descriptions into the 19th century.

In 1769 Margrave Alexander (r. 1756–91) inherited the territory of Bayreuth. Apart from adding a few more follies, he maintained Sanspareil as it was. Bayreuth became part of the Bavarian kingdom in 1810, and after years of neglect several buildings were demolished in the 1830s. By the time the Bavarian Administration of Public Castles, Gardens, and Seas took over Sanspareil in 1942, only the ruined theater, the Morgenländische Bau, and the kitchen building had survived. After a comprehensive restoration program the garden, theater, and the Morgenländische Bau are once again open to the public.

Synopsis

1290	Purchase of castle of Zwernitz by Hohenzollern dynasty (who owned it until 1810)
1744	Erection of first follies and remodeling of hunting grounds as rock garden, under

	Margrave Friedrich and Margravine Wilhelmine of Bayreuth
1745	Work starts on residential buildings, designed by Joseph Saint-Pierre, including Morgenländische Bau (Oriental Building)
1746	Work started on ruined theater; renaming of Zwernitz to Sanspareil
1748	Sanspareil near completion; different parts of garden connected by means of literary allusions
1769	Margrave Alexander of Ansbach inherits Sanspareil; addition of more follies
1810	Sanspareil comes under jurisdiction of Bavarian kings
1835–39	Several follies and two residential buildings demolished
1942	Sanspareil comes under jurisdiction of Bavarian Administration of Public Castles, Gardens, and Seas
1951	Start of restoration program
1984–87	Reconstruction of parterre in front of Morgenländische Bau (Oriental Building)

Further Reading

Bachmann, Erich, "Anfänge des Landschaftsgärtens in Deutschland," *Zeitschrift für Kunstwissenschaft* 5 (1951)

Bachmann, Erich, *Felsengarten Sanspareil,* 2nd edition, Munich: Bayerische Verwaltung der staatlichen Schlösser, Garten und Seen, 1962; 3rd edition, 1970

Buttlar, Adrian von, *Der Landschaftsgarten,* Cologne, Germany: DuMont, 1989

Habermann, Sylvia, *Bayreuther Gartenkunst: Die Garten der Markgrafen von Brandenburg-Culmbach im 17. und 18. Jahrhundert,* Worms, Germany: Werner, 1982

Hansmann, Wilfried, *Barocke Gartenparadiese,* Cologne, Germany: DuMont, 1996

Hennebo, Dieter, and Alfred Hoffmann, *Geschichte der deutschen Gartenkunst,* Hamburg, Germany: Broschek, 1962– ; see especially vols. 2 and 3

Kammerer-Grothaus, Helke, "Les Aventures de Télémaque: Ein literarisches Programm für den markgräflichen Felsengarten in Sanspareil und die klassizistische Bildtapete von Dufour, Paris, 1823," *Zeitschrift des deutschen Vereins für Kunstwissenschaft* 51 (1997)

Kluxen, Andrea M., "Die Ruinentheater der Wilhelmine von Bayreuth," *Archiv für Geschichte von Oberfranken* 67 (1987)

Köppel, Johann Gottfried, *Die Eremitage zu Sanspareil*: *Nach der Natur gezeichnet und beschrieben,* Erlangen, Germany, 1793; reprint, Erlangen, Germany: Palm and Enke, 1997

Krückmann, Peter Oluf, *Das Bayreuth der Markgräfin Wilhelmine,* Munich and New York: Prestel, 1998

Pfeiffer, Gerhard, "Markgräfin Wilhelmine und die Eremitagen bei Bayreuth und Sanspareil," in *Archive und Geschichtsforschung: Studien zur fränkischen und bayerischen Geschichte, Fridolin Solleder zum 80. Geburtstag dargebracht,* Neustadt, West Germany: Schmidt, 1966

Toussaint, Ingo, editor, *Lustgarten um Bayreuth: Eremitage, Sanspareil und Fantaisie in Beschreibungen aus dem 18. und 19. Jahrhundert,* Hildesheim, Germany: Olms, 1998

Volland, Gerlinde, "Wilhelmine von Bayreuth als Gartenarchitektin," *Stadt und Grün* 46, no. 11 (1997)

TILMAN GOTTESLEBEN

Sanssouci

Potsdam, Brandenburg, Germany

Location: immediately adjoining northwest Potscam City, 12 miles (19.3 km) southwest of Berlin

In 1715 King Friedrich Wilhelm I laid out a kitchen garden at the western end of the town of Potsdam, called Marly-Garten, signifying that his "Marly" was to be more modest than the one owned by Louis XIV. Until 1843 this garden was used as a royal kitchen gar-den. Following the death of the last kitchen gardener, who happened to be garden designer Peter Joseph Lenné's father-in-law, it was redesigned into a small and precious landscape garden by Lenné's master student, Gustav Meyer. Its original walls still exist. The royal architect August Stüler built the Romantic Peace Church (Friedenskirche) on the bank of an adjoining artificial lake, its courtyard reminiscent of an Italian

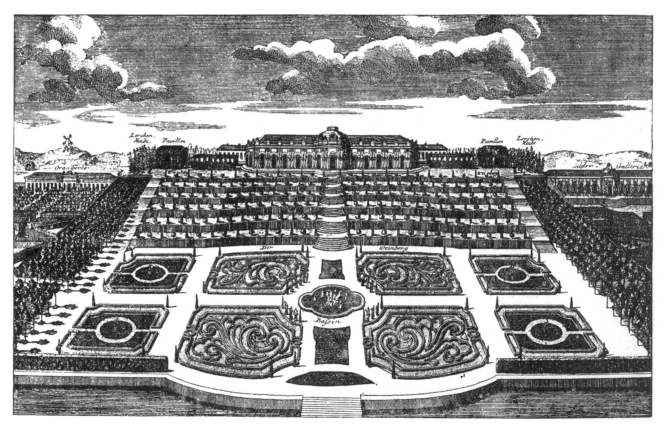

The terrace garden of Sanssouci, from Robert Dohme, *Barock-und Rokoko-Architektur*, 1887

monastery. This was the private church of Friedrich Wilhelm IV and his domestic staff.

Not far from this garden Friedrich Wilhelm I's son Friedrich II (Frederick the Great) created a vineyard in 1744, consisting of six parabolic curved terraces. There are many different opinions concerning the true originator of the principal layout and the original model it followed. It is known, however, that the king strongly exerted his influence on his architects and occasionally even drew up simple sketches himself. Such a royal sketch for Sanssouci exists, but it only shows five terraces instead of six, and it is not known whether this is just a draft or an incorrect situation plan.

The small castle crowning the uppermost terrace was conceived somewhat later, when the construction of the terraces was well advanced. It was built in 1745–47 by Gerg Wenzeslaus von Knobelsdorff. The castle, situated on top of a terminal moraine from glacial times, would have offered a splendid view over the Havel valley at the time it was built. Because of the mature size of the trees of the park and the addition of several high buildings, the river can no longer be seen.

To the south of the terraces Frederick the Great had a parterre constructed, comprising eight compartments surrounding a water basin with a gilded *Thetis* group in the middle. Little is known about the inner structure of the main compartments. The plans dating from the king's time show different *broderie* ornaments, but they are not very precise. The four outside compartments were simple lawn parterres, so popular with rococo gardeners. The basin is surrounded by French marble statues. The short lime tree alley running southward is guarded by two marble sphinxes, inspired by those on the Parterre du Sud at Versailles.

The top terrace, originally only covered with gravel, was redone by Lenné with lawn, flower beds, and marble fountains (after 1840). At the same time the former eight compartments of the parterre, then united to only two, were decorated with hedges, marble benches, and precious sculptures. The basin was widened and the main axis cut off behind the basin. The glazed windows in the terrace walls were replaced by large panes that hid the wall completely. These operations were directed by Ludwig Persius, Friedrich Wilhelm IV's architect. Beginning in 1922 the Prussian Administration of Castles and Gardens swept away many of the alterations dating from the 19th century. Today the terraces look about the same as they did during Frederick the Great's days. While the eight compartments have been reconstructed, the basin and the marble benches are still the ones Persius created.

This central garden was originally bordered by five rows of chestnut and walnut trees, which never blossomed (they have now been replaced by lime trees). Behind these trees two hornbeam-lined bosquets are to be found, richly decorated with marble sculptures and basins. Special attractions in these areas are the charming Neptune grotto (1751–57; by Knobelsdorff) and the former Dutch *parterre de broderie* in front of the Picture Gallery (1764–66). Today this is a lawn parterre only, but reconstruction of the original is expected.

The cross axis starts on the eastern side with the Obelisk Gate by Knobelsdorff (1747) and stretches westward to the New Palace, approximately 1.2 miles (2 km) away. It is quite narrow in relation to its length. Originally it divided a *Rehgarten* (game preserve). The head gardener, Friedrich Zacharias Saltzmann, redesigned this area into a rococo park in the 1760s with hedged serpentine walks. The Chinese Tea Pavilion (1754–57; after a model in Lunéville) originally stood in a bosquet *salle*. In front of the New Palace, built in 1763–69 as a symbol of victory after the Seven Years' War, a semicircular lawn parterre of classical style is laid out. Nearby are two neoclassical temples, hidden behind groups of trees (1768). The older part of the park in the east was laid out in the rococo style. The present appearance of the *Rehgarten* dates back mainly to Lenné, who modernized it in the landscape style. Emperor Wilhelm II had a number of rhododendrons planted, but only some of their formerly grafted stocks survived.

The manor of Charlottenhof, adjoining the Rehgarten in the south, was given to the future Friedrich Wilhelm IV by his father in 1825. Lenné and Hermann Sello designed a charming landscape park, while Karl Friedrich Schinkel transformed the old manor house into an Italian villa. On the eastern side of this building, an elevated terrace offers a view over the wide park to the cupola of the New Palace. It is enclosed by an exedra bench, originally covered by a tent. In the middle of the terrace gentle water splashes from a marble fountain. To the east is the recently restored rosarium and a nearby lake that Sello, the first head gardener at this place, created by damming a small river. The rose garden contains only ancient roses that were bred before 1860.

At the northern end of the lake is an assembly of Italianate buildings, consisting of Sello's home, a tea pavilion, the Roman Baths, and a boarding house for Sello's journeymen (1829–36). Small but lavish flower gardens are hidden in the courtyard, while the western front is accentuated by a large Italian bedding of subtropical plants.

To the west of the main villa is the Poets' Grove, based on ancient models and furnished with herms of European poets and a cast-iron fountain. An *Ildefonso* group leads westward to the next area, a vast open space called a hippodrome. The distance between the rosarium in the east and the hippodrome in the west was meant to symbolize the way of human life from birth to death.

The nearby New Palace contains several enclosed gardens, designed from 1863 onward by Crown Princess Victoria, a daughter of Queen Victoria. This princess, later an empress for a mere 99 days, was an ambitious gardener and garden designer. Today, only a few fragments of her gardens are preserved, but restoration work has begun.

On the northern boundary of the Sanssouci park is a sequence of remarkable gardens. First, the grand orangery, 1,300 meters (1,430 yd.) long and built in 1851–60 by Friedrich Wilhelm IV, has two Italianate towers inspired by the Villa Medici, Rome. In addition to two large rooms to store plants, the orangery comprises several other splendid rooms, including the Salle Raphael with paintings by this master, which originally opened to a shady sunken parterre on the north side and allowed for vistas into the scenic country outside Sanssouci.

Ample stairways lead down the southern facade into the park. The oblong lawn parterre on the lower level, called Jubilee Terrace, was created as late as 1913 by Emperor Wilhelm II. This late origin also applies to the little park and bridge in the northwest of the orangery, as well as the cropped lime tree alley (1906) leading westward from the orangery to the newly restored Belvedere dating from 1770–72. On the terraces across the slope below the Belvedere were magnificent glasshouses and glass-plated walls to force exotic fruit for the royal table (until 1918). Not far from the Belvedere is a Chinese Pagoda (1770), originally built as the vine gardener's home.

Two smaller but equally attractive gardens, created by Lenné and Meyer (1857), are on the slope. The Sicilian Garden includes hornbeam tunnels, a vine arbor, marble vases and basins, ancient bronze statues, formal flower beds, and palm tubs. Opposite to the north is the so-called Nordic Garden, with strong yellow brick walls and pergolas. This garden is dominated by evergreens and conifers, as well as some notable ginkgo trees.

The entire park is interwoven with rare and precious dendrological specimens, collected by several generations, mostly in the 19th and 20th centuries.

Located behind the orangery is the little village of Bornstedt. The poor inhabitants used to serve as workmen in the royal gardens since Frederick the Great's time. In 1841 Friedrich Wilhelm IV decided to renew most of the village in his beloved Italianate style. He purchased the manor house and rebuilt it, while Lenné designed a garden between the house and the Bornstedt Lake. Later, the church and school were rebuilt with

Italian campaniles. The churchyard became the preferred burial ground for the higher servants and head gardeners of the court. Sello established a private cemetery to be used by his own family, which produced quite a number of gardeners, and by the royal architect Ludwig Persius. In addition, Lenné was buried here in 1866. This cemetery has been preserved and well maintained. Sello's intimate "place of refuge" is surrounded by a public cemetery. The manor garden is being redone in the form originally given by Crown Princess Victoria (1873).

Beyond Bornstedt an area of agrarian landscape stretches out as far as the former royal estate of Bornim and the Havel River. Although agrarian land, it was nevertheless styled and adorned by Lenné and Sello. The curved lime alley between Bornstedt and Bornim laid out by Sello (1844) and a crossing mulberry alley just recently restored are most impressive. The Bornim manor house at the end of the alley was completely destroyed after World War II.

East of Bornstedt is a hill crowned with artificial ruins (Ruinenberg) built up by Frederick the Great and nearly in line with the main axis of Sanssouci. A Norman Tower was added by Persius in 1845. To the north a large modern park was laid out for the Federal Garden Exposition (Bundesgartenschau), which opened in 2001.

Synopsis

1715	Marly Garden laid out by King Friedrich Wilhelm I of Prussia, as royal kitchen garden
1744–47	Sanssouci garden built and terraces laid out by Friedrich II
1747	Obelisk Gate built by Georg Wenzeslaus von Knobelsdorff
1751–57	Neptune Grotto completed by Knobelsdorff
1754–57	Chinese Tea Pavilion built
1763–69	Rehgarten Park and gardens around New Palace
1826–36	Charlottenhof Park and gardens by Peter Joseph Lenné
after 1840	Top terrace redone by Lenné
1845–60	Marly Garden redesigned
1851–60	New Orangery built
1857	Sicilian and Nordic Gardens created by Lenné and Meyer
1906–8	Bridge, alley, and park to west of Orangery constructed
1913	Jubilee Terrace created by Wilhelm II
1922–	Restoration work

Further Reading

Ostergard, Derek E., and Ilse Baer, editors, *Along the Royal Road: Berlin and Potsdam in KPM Porcelain and Painting, 1815–1848*, New York: Bard Graduate Center for Studies in the Decorative Arts, 1993

Potsdamer Schlösser und Gärten: Bau- und Gartenkunst vom 17. bis 20. Jahrhundert, Potsdam, Germany: Stiftung Schlösser and Garten Potsdam-Sanssouci, 1993

Wimmer, Clemens Alexander, *Parks und Gärten in Berlin und Potsdam*, Berlin: Nicolaische Verlagsbuchhandlung, 1985; 5th edition, 1992

CLEMENS ALEXANDER WIMMER

Sargent, Charles Sprague 1841–1927

United States Botanist

Charles Sprague Sargent established and guided the Arnold Arboretum of Harvard University, located in the Jamaica Plain section of Boston, Massachusetts, for almost 55 years. As arboretum director, Sargent was responsible for some of the best plant offerings to American horticulture during the second half of the 19th century and the beginning of the 20th. Introducing plants; writing and editing numerous plant-related articles, books, and periodicals; and mentoring young botanists and plant hunters established him as one of the most influential individuals in the plant world at that time, along with his former teacher Asa Gray (1810–88)—author, creator of the botany department at Harvard University, and director of its botanic gardens—and his friend, colleague, and collaborator Frederick Law Olmsted (1822–1903)—the father of American landscape architecture.

Sargent was born in 1841 to Boston banker Ignatius Sargent and Henrietta Gray Sargent and grew up in the wealthy suburb of Brookline. Sargent initially showed little interest in plants, botany, or horticulture and did not study with Professor Gray during his student days at

Harvard College. Several months after graduating in 1862—graduating 88th in a class of 90—he enlisted in the Union Army during the Civil War and was discharged with rank of brevet major in 1865. Consistent with his contemporary lifestyle, Sargent commenced a three-year grand tour of Europe and Britain. There is little evidence to show whether this was a gentleman's pleasure trip or whether Sargent set about to learn about European banking. Some archivists surmise that he visited gardens and country estates suggested by his horticulturally motivated cousins H.W. Sargent and H.H. Hunnewell. Sargent himself dated his beginning study of trees after his return to the Boston area in 1868 at age 27.

After almost three decades of seeming horticultural disinterest, Sargent took over management of the family estate Holm Lea, and his latent talents emerged. Almost certainly influenced by his cousins, Sargent finished in the early 20th century what his father had begun at Holm Lea in the late 19th, making it a horticultural showplace.

Despite a lack of academic qualifications and a solid plant or gardening background, Sargent was appointed a Harvard professor of horticulture in May 1872 and in June was appointed curator of the yet-to-be-built Arnold Arboretum. Subsequently, in November 1873, he became its director and simultaneously succeeded Asa Gray as director of the Harvard Botanic Garden in Cambridge. Sargent's appointments by the Harvard Corporation may have been due to powerful and wealthy sponsors coupled with his own wealth and position in society. Nevertheless, he brought the same characteristics of hard work and purposefulness to these appointments that his father had dedicated to his business pursuits.

When Sargent took over the Harvard Botanic Garden, it was partnered with a herbarium, library, and laboratories, comprising the best-known botanic complex in the United States. Unfortunately, the living collections in the garden were disorganized and congested, while the physical plant needed attention. Sargent, while studying the plant material under Gray, resourcefully and quickly turned the situation around, making the botanic garden an attraction to both students and casual visitors. His duties at Harvard Botanic Garden ended in 1879, allowing him to devote his full time to designing, developing, and operating Arnold Arboretum.

In the late 19th century, naturalistic public pleasure grounds were designed and implemented, and one of Sargent's overriding concerns in designing the arboretum in a scientific format was to ensure that it would also be easily accessible to the public, both physically and aesthetically. Consequently, he sought a collaboration with Frederick Law Olmsted, the United States's leading landscape architect, on the overall design and master plan of the arboretum. Foreseeing the continuing need for money to build and maintain this design, Sargent set out to persuade the City of Boston and Harvard College to

forge a joint financial venture in which the arboretum would become part of the City of Boston park system. The unique thousand-year agreement—which calls for the city to construct and maintain driveways and boundary fences and for the university to organize the arboretum, expand programs, and enhance and maintain the plant collections—was signed on 20 December 1883. Interestingly, there was never an opening-day or ribbon-cutting ceremony for the arboretum. Its development was, like Sargent himself, orderly and systematic.

Sargent proceeded to execute his mandate to plant and cultivate on the Jamaica Plain site every tree capable of withstanding the New England climate. Gray's observations about similarities between plant species and climate in eastern Asia and eastern North America helped form Sargent's earliest acquisition plans. Cuttings from existing eastern Asian introductions were acquired from the Hunnewell Estate in Wellesley, and plantings were obtained by W.S. Clark in Amherst from the Boston City Park System and from European gardens, including Kew in London.

To facilitate plant identification, verification, and documentation, Sargent began an herbarium to complement the living collections. He also initiated a broad-based reference collection in his own home with books often purchased with his own funds. To bring contemporary horticultural thought together, Sargent established, guided, and edited the weekly periodical *Garden and Forest: A Journal of Horticulture, Landscape Art, and Forestry* from 1888 to 1897. After the demise of *Garden and Forest,* Sargent initiated the *Bulletin of Popular Information* in 1911, superceded by *Arnoldia.*

With work well under way at the arboretum, in August 1892 Sargent embarked on his first Asian exploration to Japan's two principal islands, Honshu and Hokkaido (which most closely approximates New England's climate). He returned with 1,225 sets of herbarium specimens and seeds of about 200 species and varieties of plants. Included among these were the Nikko maple (*Acer nikoense/A. maximowiczianum*), known in Europe but new to North America, and several that were new to cultivation on both continents: the anise-leaved or willow-leaved magnolia (*Magnolia salicifolia*), the flame or torch azalea (*Rhododendron obtusa* var. *Kaempferi*), and the long-stalk holly (*Ilex pedunculosa*). A flowering cherry (*Prunus sargentii*), one of the earliest to flower with fiery red autumn leaves, and a crabapple (*Malus sargentii*) were new to both botanical and horticultural science. His interpretation of Japanese woody plants is emphasized in *Forest Flora of Japan.*

Sargent's horticultural insight led to his persistence in recruiting well-known plant hunter Ernest Henry Wilson to carry out the arboretum's first plant exploration into China. Wilson's discoveries, coupled with Sargent's commitment to developing the arboretum's living collections, enhanced its reputation as a center of plant introduction and distribution. Wilson's discoveries in western China in 1907, 1908, and 1910 are detailed in three volumes edited by Sargent. His 50-year report on activities at the arboretum reports between 5,000 and 6,000 species and varieties of trees and shrubs belonging to 87 families and 325 genera growing on the property in 1922. Also listed are 1,932 taxa that Sargent believed the arboretum first introduced into cultivation in North America, 778 of which were original horticultural introductions. The scholarly publication *Journal of the Arnold Arboretum* was begun in 1919 and continued until 1990; it was absorbed into the *Harvard Papers in Botany* in 1996.

Apart from his arboretum responsibilities, Sargent advised and encouraged many working in American horticulture. Gifford Pinchot and Sargent advised Frederick Law Olmsted on forestry practices and growing of both native and imported trees at the Biltmore Estate in North Carolina, where Olmstead envisioned an arboretum that would be the largest in the world. Beatrix Farrand, in an unusual practice for garden designers of that time, used native deciduous trees over exotics in some of her schemes and demonstrated Sargent's influence by her interest in the positioning and maintenance of woody plants. During the garden restoration of George Washington's Mount Vernon in 1914, Sargent was responsible for replanting of native trees along the symmetrical yet natural looking west front.

Sargent also accepted significant commission and committee work dealing with trees and forestry. He finished the government census report on American forests in 1884 and then completed his 14-volume work on trees of North America in 1905. An offshoot of these volumes was an illustrated two-volume tree manual in 1905 that was revised and enlarged in 1922. Sargent was appointed to the committee that would bear his name as the Sargent Commission and recommend establishment of the Adirondack Forest Preserve in New York.

See also Arnold Arboretum

Biography

Born in Boston, Massachusetts, April 1841, into prominent New England family. Early years spent in Brookline, Massachusetts; began traditional education, 1858, at Harvard College; sandwiched tour of duty with Union Army between Harvard graduation, 1862, and three-year grand tour of Britain and Europe; upon returning took over management of Holm Lea; dated study of trees; appointed professor of horticulture, Harvard University, curator of Arnold Arboretum, 1872; named director of Harvard Botanic Garden,

succeeding Asa Gray, and of Arnold Arboretum, 1873; accepted commission and completed census report on American forests, 1884; appointed Sargent Commission, and recommended establishment of New York Adirondacks Forest Preserve; plant hunted in Japan, 1892. Selected for Horticulture Hall of Fame of American Society for Horticultural Science, 2000. Died in Boston, Massachusetts, 22 March 1927.

Selected Publications

The major repository for Sargent's papers is the Archives of the Arnold Arboretum Library, Jamaica Plain, Massachusetts.

Report on the Forests of North America (Exclusive of Mexico), 1884
The Silva of North America, 14 vols., 1891–1902
Forest Flora of Japan, 1894
Manual of the Trees of North America (Exclusive of Mexico), 2 vols., 1905; 2nd edition, with additions and revisions, 1922

Further Reading

Alexander, Edward Porter, *The Museum in America: Innovators and Pioneers,* Walnut Creek, California: AltaMira Press, 1997
Connor, Sheila, "The Arnold Arboretum: An Historic Park Partnership," *Arnoldia* 48, no. 4 (Fall 1988)
Connor, Sheila, *New England Natives,* Cambridge, Massachusetts: Harvard University Press, 1993
Hay, Ida, *Science in the Pleasure Ground: A History of the Arnold Arboretum,* Boston: Northeastern University Press, 1995
Spongberg, Stephen A., *A Reunion of Trees: The Discovery of Exotic Plants and Their Introduction into North America and European Landscapes,* Cambridge, Massachusetts: Harvard University Press, 1990
Sponberg, Stephen, A., et al. "Gardens and Forest: A Journal of Horticulture, Landscape Art, and Forestry, 1888–1897: Excerpts and Editorial Interpolations" *Arnoldia* 60, no. 2 (2000) and no. 3 (2001)
Sutton, Sylvia Barry, *Charles Sprague Sargent and the Arnold Arboretum,* Cambridge, Massachusetts: Harvard University Press, 1970
Wilson, Ernest Henry, *Plantae Wilsonianae: An Enumeration of the Woody Plants Collected in Western China for the Arnold Arboretum of Harvard University during the Years 1907, 1908, and 1910,* 3 vols., edited by Charles Sprague Sargent, Cambridge, Massachusetts: Harvard University Press, 1913–17; reprint, Portland, Oregon: Dioscordies Press, 1988

GEORGENE A. BRAMLAGE

Sceaux

Hauts-de-Seine, France

Location: south of Paris, about 6 miles (9.7 km) south of the Porte d'Orléans

Sceaux is one of the finest historic parks on the fringes of Paris. It has undergone several major phases of change, but the gardens still retain much of their 17th-century layout, designed by André Le Nôtre. They also contains some fine garden buildings.

In 1670 Jean-Baptiste Colbert, Louis XIV's Surintendant des Batiments, acquired the barony of Sceaux from the duc de Gesvres and employed the architect Claude Perrault to enlarge the existing modest château. The result was a straightforward classical building around three sides of a court, approached from the east by a double avenue and outer court. The court artists, Charles Le Brun, François Girardon, and Antoine Coysevox, decorated the château. Colbert's new château and gardens were a proud demonstration of his great status and wealth. However, mindful of the jealous eye of the king and of his own role in the downfall of Nicolas Fouquet's Vaux-le-Vicomte, Colbert made sure that Sceaux was more restrained. This did not prevent him from plundering the gardens of Vaux-le-Vicomte for plants and statuary for Sceaux, however.

The gardens were laid out for Colbert by Le Nôtre, who cleverly exploited the site's sharp differences of level. A great deal of leveling was needed to achieve his design; 10,000 cubic meters (13,080 cu. yd.) of earth had to be moved. To the west of the château, where one might have expected to find the majority and main axis of the gardens, the area then available was restricted: it only reached as far as the present terrace with two circular fountains. The steeply sloping ground below was not then part of the property. Le Nôtre made three shallow terraces, dropping from east to west, laid out in *parterres de broderie,* and a rectangular basin.

The chief axis of Le Nôtre's garden layout runs southward, at right angles to the château, where the ground drops steeply and then rises again. A contemporary illustration shows that the axis, flanked by woodland, began with a great allée, flanked by tall, clipped hornbeam hedges (*charmilles*), at the end of which was a fountain. On the steep slope to the south were wide steps, below which were a pool and fountains flanked by more steps. Below this was the great cascade, in three sections, flanked by beds, plants in tubs, strips of grass, and wide sloping paths. The cascade was designed by Le Brun and was originally ornamented with statues by Girardon and Coysevox, but these are now gone, replaced by *mascarons* (grotesque sculptural masks) by Auguste Rodin, dating to 1900. The cascade itself survives, in altered and restored form. At its foot was, and is, a large octagonal basin, the Bassin de l'Octogone, ornamented with a single, high central jet. This is as far as Colbert's grounds reached south of the château. Around the basin are four copies of classical statues and two large, bronze stag groups by G. Gardet flanking the main axis. Beyond, this axis continues up the hillside opposite the cascade as a grass slope.

One of the outstanding features of Colbert's layout to survive is the Pavillon de l'Aurore, designed by Charles Perrault. It is situated to the northeast of the château, originally in the center of the *potager,* or kitchen garden, which, together with the orchard, was designed by the royal gardener, La Quintinie. The area was later converted to a formal flower garden. The design of the pavilion is considered by some to be a perfect example of academic classicism; built on a terrace, with steps on either side and a marble fountain in front, it has a central circular salon flanked by two *cabinets* (small rooms). Inside the salon are paintings of seasonal gardening tasks after Le Brun designs; the cupola is decorated with a fresco of *Aurora Leaving Cephalus to Bring Light to the World,* also by Le Brun. This small building both symbolized Colbert (the decoration includes his emblem, a grass snake) and was his favorite retreat. Here, he received the king in July 1677 and the Academie Française in October 1678.

The grounds were further embellished and extended after 1683 by Colbert's son, the marquis de Seignelay. He added a sumptuous orangery on the south side of the entrance court in 1685, designed by Jules Hardouin-Mansart, inaugurated by Louis XIV, and now used for exhibitions and events. In 1695–1700 land acquisition to the west and southwest of the château enabled the gardens to be extended. To the west were laid out a further terrace and a long sloping lawn, the Plaine des Quatre Statues. A huge canal, the Grand Canal, designed by François Leclerc, was built parallel to and to the west of the cascade and Bassin de l'Octogone, to which it was linked by a lesser canal. The stately poplar trees lining the Grand Canal were all blown down, as were many other trees in the park, in the great gale of 26 December 1999. To the west of the canal a large area was laid out. Later altered, it now has axial rides, a lawn on the east-west axis of the Bassin de l'Octogone and minor canal, and two flanking bosquets. An unusual feature is the north-south avenue of huge cedars of Lebanon.

The marquis lived and entertained lavishly at Sceaux from the moment he inherited it. Extravagant fetes were held on the premises, including the famous *Idylle de Sceaux*, in the summer of 1685, at which Louis XIV and the dauphin were entertained. The fete was designed by the brilliant and versatile artist Jean Berain, whose "set" for the entertainments broke new ground for its ingenuity. The entertainment was thought "la plus belle jamais donnée au Roi" (the most beautiful ever given to the king).

In 1699 Sceaux passed to the duc du Maine, son of Louis XIV and Madame de Montespan. During this time few significant changes were made to the gardens; the old *potager* was converted to a garden of flowering *plate-bandes*. The duchesse was much given to theatricals and treated Sceaux as her private playground, with performances in the Pavillon de l'Aurore, the orangery, and on makeshift stages, always with herself in the leading role. Among the entertainments, which included works by the playwrights Molière and Racine and the composer Lully, were the infamous *Nuits Blanches de Sceaux*. By 1785 the domaine had reached its present extent of 152 hectares (375.6 acres).

Sceaux then passed to the duc de Maine's nephew, the duc de Penthièvre, upon whose death in 1793 it was confiscated and deserted. The château was demolished during the Revolution. Revival came in the 1850s, when the new owner, the duc de Trévise, who acquired Sceaux through marriage, built an undistinguished château, smaller than Colbert's and designed by the architects Quantinet and Le Soufaché, on the same site in 1856–62. The gardens were restored at the same time. For the most part Le Nôtre's structure was followed; only the area west of the canal now differs significantly from the original layout. It centers on the Pavillon d'Hanovre. In 1932 this small, elegant garden pavilion, originally a wing of the Duc de Richelieu's Hôtel d'Autin, was moved from Paris and re-erected at the west end of the axis of the minor canal and the Bassin de l'Octogone. It was designed by Jean-Michel Chevotet for the duc de Richelieu in 1760 but had been moved to make way for the Berlitz building on the Boulevard des Italiens.

In 1923 Sceaux was sold to the Département de la Seine. The château now houses the Musée de l'Île-de-France, and the park, particularly popular with runners, is open to the public.

Synopsis

1597	Potier de Gesvres family builds first château
1670	Jean-Baptiste Colbert acquires Sceaux; château enlarged and transformed by Charles Perrault, and grounds laid out by André Le Nôtre; cascade designed by Charles Le Brun
1685	Orangery designed by Jules Hardouin-Mansart
1695–1700	Gardens enlarged, and Grand Canal built by François Leclerc
1699	Sceaux passed to duc du Maine, son of Louis XIV
1793	Sceaux confiscated, château demolished during Revolution
1798	Bought by Jean-François Hippolyte Lecomte
1856–62	Duc de Trévise builds present château on site of demolished earlier one and restores gardens
1870	Occupied by Prussians; east end of orangery destroyed
1923	Sold by Princesse de Faucigny-Cystra, daughter-in-law of second duc de Trévise, to Département de la Seine, and opened to public
1932	Pavillon d'Hanovre moved to park from Paris
1992–94	Château and cascade restored
1999	Poplars lining Grand Canal and many other trees blown down in gale

Further Reading

Adams, William Howard, *The French Garden, 1500–1800*, New York: Braziller, and London: Scolar Press, 1979

DeLorme, Eleanor P., *Garden Pavilions and the 18th Century French Court*, Woodbridge, Suffolk: Antique Collectors' Club, 1996

Hazlehurst, F. Hamilton, *Gardens of Illusion: The Genius of Andre Le Nostre*, Nashville, Tennessee: Vanderbilt University Press, 1980

Woodbridge, Kenneth, *Princely Gardens: The Origins and Development of the French Formal Style*, New York: Rizzoli, and London: Thames and Hudson, 1986

ELISABETH WHITTLE

Schinkel, Karl Friedrich 1781–1841

German Architect

Karl Friedrich Schinkel was the most important architect of 19th-century Prussia and one of the most important in German history. His work reveals his particular interests in the neoclassical (Greco-Roman) style as well as the Gothic revival. His buildings served a wide range of functions, including country houses, garden buildings, public and institutional buildings, and churches; he also designed a wide range of furnishings and monuments. In addition to his architectural achievements, Schinkel was a painter and theater set designer of the first rank.

Schinkel's architectural thinking was influenced at an early stage by the neoclassical designs of his mentor David Gilly, and his fascination with the world of antiquity was the impetus for his tours of Italy in 1803–5 and 1824. The Napoleonic occupation brought an end to country-house commissions, and Schinkel turned instead to painting. His paintings, emotional in character, often feature scenes from German legends, with Gothic buildings (the "German" style) in idealized countrysides, and reflect a growing interest in native sources of inspiration, as well as the influence of his contemporary Caspar David Friedrich. During this period Schinkel became closely associated with the romantic poets of the day.

Schinkel's equal facility in Gothic and Greek modes is indicated in his proposals for a mausoleum for the young Prussian queen Luise, whose death in 1810 had caused a wave of national grief and patriotic feeling. The completed building is a Greek temple, but Schinkel also presented alternative Gothic proposals. The mausoleum is carefully sited in the grounds of Charlottenburg Palace, Berlin, and the associated atmospheric planting scheme emphasizes the architect's sensitivity to the setting of his work.

The conclusion of the wars of liberation led to Schinkel's appointment to senior public office in Berlin in 1815. His versatile and experimental approach led to a series of buildings and monuments in neoclassical and Gothic styles, often promoting new technologies such as the decorative use of cast iron or the large-scale use of brick in high-quality buildings, as he established himself as the architect of the new Berlin.

In his later career Schinkel resumed his early interest in the design of country houses in ornamental settings. One early such project was Schloss Neu-Hardenberg, designed for the Prussian chancellor Prince Hardenberg, east of Berlin. Schinkel recast the existing house in neoclassical style and for the first time collaborated with the landscape gardener Peter Joseph Lenné. Lenné's style, based on English precepts of grass, wood, and water, controlled views, and an air of studied informality, drew on the work of F.L von Sckell, a pioneer of the English style in Germany. Neu-Hardenberg was also the venue for Schinkel's first encounter with Prince Pückler-Muskau, Hardenberg's son-in-law, who advocated a more vigorous and detailed approach to estate design, favoring the ideas of Humphry Repton in particular.

Concurrent with his work at Neu-Hardenberg, Schinkel secured another important country-house commission, the reconstruction of Schloss Tegel for Wilhelm von Humboldt. Lenné again provided an ornamental park as the setting, into which Schinkel introduced a family burial ground, including a semicircular seat characteristic of much of his work in the country-house context.

Schinkel's villa format now found royal favor. His New Pavilion was constructed in the grounds of Charlottenburg Palace for King Friedrich Wilhelm III of Prussia, a "Neapolitan" villa where the king could retire to cultivated surroundings free from the grandeur of state apartments. Schinkel's close relationship with the Prussian royal family led to a series of country-house projects, which remain his most important contribution to landscape design. In these he worked closely with his pupil Ludwig Persius, as well as Lenné. Together these three developed ornamental estates for three sons of Friedrich Wilhelm III in the countryside around the royal residence town of Potsdam, forming a designed landscape on a huge scale, rich in variety and of exceptional quality.

The first of these projects was at Schloss Glienicke, acquired by Prince Carl from the Hardenberg family in 1824. The park was extended, refined, and replanted by Lenné, and Schinkel introduced the house and ornamental buildings in a manner that enhanced the existing relationships with the rural landscape on the banks of the Havel looking across to Potsdam. The house and garden are carefully integrated, and Schinkel catered to the prince's antiquarian and Mediterranean tastes by providing a series of garden features including the Grosse Neugierde (Great Curiosity), a circular pavilion based on the Choragic Monument of Lysicrates in Athens, and a "Casino" consisting of a pavilion with flanking pergolas overlooking the Havel and the Glienicke Bridge. Characteristic seats by Schinkel adorn the garden, which also features work by Persius, all seamlessly integrated into Lenné's garden and the wider landscape setting.

Schloss Babelsberg, for Prince Wilhelm, was built immediately to the south of Schloss Glienicke, but here Schinkel responded to his client's wish for a house in the Gothic manner, with a varied, picturesque roofline. The house was later extended by Schinkel's pupils. Lenné provided an informal parkland backdrop for the undulating terrain, but found himself ousted in the garden by Pückler-Muskau. The estates of Babelsberg and Kleinglienicke reflect each other across their riverside parks in contrasting styles.

For the crown prince, later Friedrich Wilhelm IV, the new composition of Charlottenhof was laid out to the south of the royal park of Sanssouci from 1826 onward, and it represents the culmination of Schinkel's country house work. At Charlottenhof Schinkel, Persius and Lenné worked together to produce an ornamental park of superb quality: villa, gardens, subsidiary buildings, and parkland are immaculately blended. Everywhere individual features are skillfully integrated, so that from different viewpoints the neoclassical villa looks out onto a poets' grove of trees, a "prehistoric" burial site, a geometric flower garden, and the court gardener's house with its secondary complex of "Roman" baths and courtyard garden evoking the warm south.

Schinkel's versatility in designing buildings and ornaments of uniformly high quality in a wide range of distinctive media and styles, decorated and furnished with his own objects and schemes, would in itself make him the subject of general admiration. His concern to integrate his creations into a network of visual relationships with their designed and natural surroundings entitles him to a special place in the history of the country-house garden, park, and estate.

Biography

Born in Neuruppin, Prussia, Germany, 13 March 1781. Studied with David Gilly in Berlin, 1798; completed early designs for country houses, 1800–1803; toured Italy, 1803–5 and 1824; traveled to Britain, 1826; worked as painter, set-designer, and interior designer, 1806–13; employed by state of Prussia, from 1815; responsible for public buildings in Berlin, Potsdam, and elsewhere; designed series of country-house estates for private and royal clients, from 1820 onward, often collaborating with Ludwig Persius, Peter Joseph Lenné, and others. Died in Berlin, 1841.

Selected Designs

1810–12	Mausoleum for Queen Luise, Charlottenburg Palace, Berlin, Germany
1818–21	Cast-iron gothic war memorial, on Kreuzberg (now Viktoriapark), Berlin, Germany
1820–22	Schloss Neu-hardenberg, Brandenburg, Germany
1820–24	Schloss Tegel, Berlin, Germany
1824–25	New Pavilion, Charlottenburg Palace, Berlin, Germany
1824–37	Schloss Glienicke, Berlin, Germany
1826–33	Schloss Charlottenhof, Potsdam, Brandenburg, Germany
1832–	Schloss Babelsberg, Berlin, Germany

Selected Publications

Sammlung Architektonischer Entwürfe, 1820–40; as *Collection of Architectural Designs*, 1981
Vorbilder für Fabrikanten und Handwerker (with Peter C.W. Beuth), 1821–30

Further Reading

Bergdoll, Barry, *Karl Friedrich Schinkel: An Architecture for Prussia*, New York: Rizzoli, 1994
Krieger, Peter, "Schinkels Gemälde," in *Galerie der Romantik* (exhib. cat.), Berlin: Nationalgalerie, 1986
Potsdamer Schlösser und Garten (exhib. cat.), Potsdam, Germany: Potsdamer Verlagsbuchhandlung, 1993
Schinkel, Karl Friedrich, *The English Journey: Journal of a Visit to France and Britain in 1826,* edited by David Bindman and Gottfried Riemann, translated by F. Gayna Walls, New Haven, Connecticut: Yale University Press, 1993
Snodin, Michael, editor, *Karl Friedrich Schinkel: A Universal Man,* New Haven, Connecticut: Yale University Press, 1991
Trost, Heinrich, editor, *Die Bau- und Kunstdenkmale in der DDR: Bezirk Potsdam,* Berlin: Henschel, 1978

STEVEN DESMOND

Schleissheim

Bavaria, Germany

Location: 8.6 miles (14 km) north of Munich

Built in stages over the course of two centuries, the extraordinary palace complex at Schleissheim bears both the imprint of three generations of Bavarian monarchs and the legacy of French Versailles. Wilhelm V, duke of Bavaria, ruled his duchy in a turbulent post-Reformation Germany until the year 1597, when he

Parterre and park from the castle terrace at Schleissheim, from Giovanni Francesco Guernieri, *Delineatio Montis*, 1706

then resigned his kingdom to his eldest son, Maximilian I of Wittelsbach. Construction slowly began on the site of Wilhelm's old hermitage a year later, and between 1616 and 1623 Maximilian initiated an energetic series of plans for the Old Palace (Altes Schloss), originally intended as a retreat for his father, who died shortly after its completion. The Thirty Years' War, which broke out in 1618, interrupted further work for several decades, but at the war's end Maximilian was honored for his military victories on behalf of the Catholic cause and appointed as the first elector of Bavaria.

Maximilian's grandson Max Emanuel inherited his title and was a celebrated military general in his own right. He commissioned the Lustheim Palace (1684–88) at Schleissheim for the occasion of his marriage to Maria Antonia, the daughter of Emperor Leopold I, and later a stately summer palace (Neues Schloss), designed in 1701 and completed 20 years later. One of the largest baroque palaces in Germany, the Neues Schloss was erected to celebrate Max Emanuel's victory over the Turks in 1688, with a style that drew heavily on Versailles, in both the palace's architectural plans and the

baroque gardens. The Versailles model was a touchstone for not only Schleissheim but also Sanssouci in Postdam, Petrodvorets outside St. Petersburg, and the nearby Nymphenburg (Max Emanuel's more famous summer home). Yet it was not the German intent to replicate the gardens completely but rather to import a general design modified by a distinct regional cachet. Max Emanuel continued his grandfather's construction efforts at Schleissheim on a lavish scale, in part hedged on hopes of securing a strategic political marriage for his son, but he was constrained by a shortage of finances. Although the elaborate blueprints for the Neues Schloss included a four-wing building, modest revisions downsized the scope of the structure. Even so, at its completion the facade of the palace was more than 335 meters (366 yd.) long, embracing the gardens along their entire span.

Fiscal concerns fortunately did not preclude Max Emanuel from recruiting Enrico Zuccalli, a highly regarded Swiss architect who had a large work portfolio including other residences and parks in Europe, among them Slavkov Castle in Moravia and Nymphenburg.

His plans for the Lustheim Palace positioned both this structure and the Neues Schloss to form an axial relationship with the Altes Schloss. Working with colleague Joseph Effner, Zuccalli created a large, geometric baroque garden, with the Lustheim in turn enclosed by a Dutch-style ring canal segregating both palace and its gardens onto themselves.

Although Zuccalli was commissioned as the original landscape planner, Dominque Girard (who also planned the gardens at Nymphenburg and Schloss Augustusburg) and his colleague Carbonet executed most of the early garden designs, plotting the lively arrangement of flower beds, canals, and waterfall that surround the three palace structures. Both were French designers who had trained at Versailles under the tutelage of André Le Nôtre, and this influence demonstrates itself in many places throughout Schleissheim. The gardens were laid out in a circular pattern, and the main parterre cushioned in a sunken area of the land between the rear of the Neues Schloss and the cascade. Small woods, hedges, river basins, glades, and flower borders punctuate the park grounds merging into woodland on the periphery. An eight-pointed double ring serves as the centerpiece of the ornamental shrubbery between the Lustheim and the Neues Schloss with the center canal forming the vertical diameter.

Additional clusters of shrubbery along the main mall were planted in the late 18th and 19th centuries. A nursery garden and orchards stand on one side of the central mall bracketed by a large nature area that was only completed in 1965. While some original features disappeared, others were added later: a parterre between the Altes Schloss and the Neues Schloss was finished in 1881 during the reign of King Ludwig, and a hedge border has since replaced the orangery along the circumference of the Lustheim Palace. It is worth noting that the orangery had a special place in many German gardens, providing both a venue for entertainment and protection for some of the more delicate garden plants.

Work for both the gardens and the extensive canal system commenced in 1689. Feeder canals were also dug with the additional purpose of transporting building materials. Some historians suggest that Max Emanuel intended to import a Dutch character to the flat topography of the Bavarian countryside with a canal network engineered to tap the Wurm and Isar Rivers, probably a carryover from his tenure as governor of the Spanish Netherlands. Nevertheless, the central canal is perhaps the focal point of the park, forming the axis of the Neues Schloss with bosquets on each end and the cascade at its terminus. Although the dramatic cascade, finished in 1733, originally featured statuary, little remains at present. Two lateral canals neatly surround the central waterway, and elegant linden avenues planted by Zuccalli parallel these twin canals throughout the course of the entire garden.

World War II levied considerable destruction on all three palaces and the gardens; the Altes Schloss, in particular, was badly damaged and only fully reconstructed in 1971. Restoration efforts are still incomplete, and although the estates and gardens have been capably preserved, it is unfortunate that Schleissheim has lost some of the 18th-century splendor that once earned its nickname as the "Bavarian Versailles."

Synopsis

1597	Wilhelm V, duke of Bavaria, succeeded by son, Maximilian I
1598	Construction begun on Altes Schloss under Maximilian I, duke of Bavaria
1618–48	Thirty Years' War interrupts work on gardens
1623	Altes Schloss completed
1684–88	Lustheim Palace built under Maximilian II Emanuel, elector of Bavaria, with palace and gardens designed by Enrico Zuccalli, and further garden design by French designers Dominique Girard and Carbonet
1689	Work begun on canal system and gardens
1690	Lateral canals completed
1700	Ornamental shrubbery planted
1701	Construction of summer palace Neues Schloss begun
1704	Neues Schloss work halted because of financial constraints
1717	Main parterre completed
1718–27	Construction of Neues Schloss resumed and completed
1733	Cascade completed
1781	Central canal completed
1881	Parterre between Neues Schloss and Altes Schloss completed
1940s	Severe damage to all three palaces and gardens
1965	Nature area completed
1971	Restoration efforts finished for Altes Schloss

Further Reading

Hager, Luisa, *Schleissheim: Neues Schloss und Garten, amtlicher Führer*, Munich: Bayerische Verwaltung der Staatlichen Schlösser, Gärten und Seen, 1965

Hansmann, Wilfried, *Gartenkunst der Renaissance und des Barock*, Cologne, Germany: DuMont, 1983

Richthofen, Christa von, *Germany: Architecture, Interiors, Landscape, Gardens*, New York: Abrams, and London: Weidenfeld and Nicolson, 1992

Schopf, Regine von, *Barockgärten in Westfalen*, Worms, Germany: Wernersche Verlagsgesellschaft, 1988

Ursula, Gräfin zu Dohna, Philipp, Graf Schönborn, and
Marianne, Fürstin zu Sayn-Wittgenstein-Sayn, *Private
Gartenkunst in Deutschland,* Herford, Germany:
Bosse-Seewald, 1986; as *Private Gardens of Germany,*

translated by Ted Gang, New York: Harmony Books,
London: Weidenfeld and Nicolson, 1986

KRISTIN WYE-RODNEY

Schönbrunn

Vienna, Austria

Location: approximately 3 miles (4.8 km) southwest
of Vienna city center

Embodying the greatness and the fate of the Habsburg
dynasty, Schönbrunn constitutes the Austrian counterpart to Versailles. The palace is Austria's most visited
tourist site, and the gardens are a popular recreation
area for the people of Vienna.

The gardens of Schönbrunn are an important creation
of landscape architecture. Their present-day appearance
was mainly formed in the period of the imperial couple
Maria Theresa (r. 1740–80) and Franz Stephan, when a
rococo garden was laid out (1750–60) in the style of J.-
F. Blondel, which was furnished with sculptures and follies (1772–80). The pleasure garden, orangery, botanical
garden, and menagerie are parts of a baroque *Gesamt-
kunstwerk.* The special quality of the park derives from
the allées and bosquets, which have been continuously
maintained since the mid-18th century, as well as from
the almost completely preserved furnishing, including
sculptures, fountains, and garden buildings.

In 1569 the Emperor Maximilian II acquired the
estate and manor house of Katterburg and installed a
hunting preserve. The grounds already comprised the
major area of today's gardens. In 1642–43 the manor
house was extended into a small *château de plaisance*
with a modest pleasure garden. In 1642 the name
Schönbrunn was first mentioned, deriving from a spring
with excellent water, which had been discovered about
1600 on the Katterburg grounds. In 1683 Turkish
troops devastated the estate.

In 1686 the emperor Leopold I became the owner of
the estate. About 1688–90 Johann Bernhard Fischer von
Erlach presented "Schönbrunn I," a plan for a monumental palace—larger than Versailles—on the top of Schönbrunn Hill, with terraced gardens on the slope. Probably
this utopian project was never intended to be realized but
was designed as an ideal representation of imperial power.

About 1693–96 Fischer von Erlach designed a second
palace, "Schönbrunn II," on the northern end of the

grounds for the crown prince Joseph (emperor
1705–11). On the southern hill Fischer planned to build
a belvedere. The gardens between the palace and the
belvedere were only sketched in rough outlines, but the
conception of the central axis, especially, extending
from the palace to a large fountain at the foot of the hill
and further up to the belvedere, remained important for
later development.

The construction of the palace started in 1696, but in
the previous year the French garden designer Jean Trehet had already begun to lay out the gardens. Trehet
established the actual width of the Great Parterre by
planting wooded sections on both sides, which were
crossed by octagonal allées. The Great Parterre
extended roughly half of its eventual length. In 1700 the
exterior of the palace was more or less completed. Subsequently, the works were reduced and finally came to a
halt due to war and the early death of Emperor Joseph I
in 1711. In the following years the gardens were
attended to, but no major alterations were carried out.

In 1743 Maria Theresa decided to transform the
unfinished palace into her summer residence. Franz
Stephan's interest focused on the gardens. He commissioned a team of artists from his native Lorraine, among
them the architect Jean Nicolas Jadot, the garden architect Louis Gervais, and the engineer and geodetic surveyor Jean Brequin de Demenge. In addition Franz
Stephan employed the Dutch gardener Adrian von
Stekhoven. Before 1750 the *Kammergärten* (Giardini
Segreti, or Secret Garden) on the east and west flanks of
the palace were readapted and furnished with corridors
and pavilions of trelliswork. Between 1750 and 1760
the gardens underwent a profound transformation. A
new radial system of avenues was created, incorporating
most of the existing older allées. The two major diagonal axes of the new network converge in the center of
the palace as the focus of the ensemble. The Great Parterre was expanded to the foot of the Schönbrunn Hill.
It was divided into six elaborate *parterres á l'angloise*
with *gazon coupé* (cut turf), palmette ornaments in box,

and small bowling greens, as can be seen on Bellotto's view of the gardens about 1760 in Vienna's Kunsthistorisches Museum. In the subsequent years the bosquet areas created by the new network of allées were planted with walks, cabinets, and *salles de verdure* (green rooms) in rococo style as well.

The circular menagerie was constructed in 1751–52 following a design by Jadot. Only the central pavilion was completed in 1759. In 1753 Franz Stephan acquired a piece of land on the western border of Schönbrunn. A geometrically structured botanical garden was laid out there; it was called the "Dutch Garden" because of the nationality of its designer Adrian van Stekhoven and his assistant Richard van der Schot. In order to extend the botanical collection and also the animal stock of the menagerie, an expedition was sent to the Caribbean from 1755–59 under the command of the eminent botanist Nicolas Jacquin. In 1755 the orangery (186 meters [203 yd.] long) and the adjoining rotunda were completed.

The plain areas of the gardens had been completed before Franz Stephan died in 1765. In 1772 Maria Theresa decided to proceed with the embellishment of the slope. The architect Johann Ferdinand Hetzendorf von Hohenberg designed a generous project for the Schönbrunn Hill and the Great Parterre, with a belvedere on top and numerous terraces, fountains, and sculptures on the slope and the plain. The scope of this project had to be reduced in 1776–77 because there was not a sufficient water supply. The elements of the plan that were realized included the reservoir on the hilltop (1773), the Gloriette as the crowning belvedere (1775), the terraces and the zigzag paths on the slope, the Neptune Fountain (1780) (see Plate 30), and the remodeling of the Great Parterre into eight beds, with 32 statues aligned on the flanking bosquet walls. In the eastern bosquet area Hohenberg erected the Obelisk Fountain (1777) and the artificial ruin (1778); the circular aviary was also probably constructed in these years.

In 1773 the sculptor Wilhelm Beyer was commissioned to create the 32 statues for the Great Parterre. More statues were added later. Beyer was assisted by several collaborators, among them Johann Baptist Hagenauer and Benedict Henrici. Beyer also created the sculptures for the central Neptune Fountain, the two naiads for the basins of the eastern and western allée crossings, and the particularly fine statue of the nymph Egeria for the *Schöne Brunnen*.

In 1779 the emperor Joseph II (son of Maria Theresa) opened the major part of the gardens to the general public. When Maria Theresa died in 1780 the main features that characterize the park today had been laid down.

After Maria Theresa's death her successor's interests focused on the scientific gardens on the western side of the grounds. The emperors Joseph II and Franz II (Franz I of Austria) both acquired additional land for the enlargement of the botanical garden in 1788, 1802, and 1817, and they sent out expeditions to the Caribbean and to South Africa in 1783–88 and to Brazil in 1817–21 to collect exotic plants and animals. In 1814 Sir Joseph Banks described Schönbrunn as "the only rival of Kew I am acquainted with."

From 1828 to 1850 first the geometric Dutch Garden and then the other sections of the botanical garden were transformed into a natural *jardin anglais*. The southwestern part of the botanical garden has retained this form up to the present.

In 1880–82 the Great Palm House designed by Franz Xaver Segenschmid was erected on the site of the former Dutch Garden and a historic ornamental garden was laid out around it, replacing the landscape garden from 1828. In 1904 the Sundial House, a glass house in the manner of the Jugendstil designed by Alfons Custodis, was constructed west of the Great Palm House.

From 1869 to 1886 the garden director Adolf Vetter carried out a substantial regeneration of the baroque gardens, replanting and trimming trees and hedges. About 1896 the garden director Anton Umlauft redecorated the eight beds of the Great Parterre with neobaroque ornaments, which still exist in slightly modified forms.

In 1918, with the end of the Habsburg monarchy, Schönbrunn became the property of the Republic of Austria. Several new buildings were constructed and new functions designated for older garden structures and areas, especially in the part south of the Gloriette (barracks 1938–39, Gardening Academy 1949–51, Research Institute for Forestry 1952, etc.).

In 1945 the palace, the Gloriette, the Great Palm House, the Sundial House, and the menagerie were hit by bombs. From 1986 to 1990 an overall renovation of the Great Palm House was carried out, and in the 1990s several restorations and renovations of garden structures were begun. Much of this work is still in progress.

Synopsis

1569	Emperor Maximilian II acquires estate and establishes hunting preserve
1642–43	*Château de plaisance* built from manor house and pleasure gardens created
1683	Siege of Vienna, Turkish troops devastate estate
1686	Emperor Leopold I inherits estate
1688–90	Schönbrunn I, Fischer von Erlach's first design completed
1693–96	Schönbrunn II, Fischer von Erlach's second design
1695	Jean Trehet begins to lay out gardens
1696–1700	Construction of palace according to Fischer's second design

1743	Empress Maria Theresa decides to develop Schönbrunn as summer residence
1750–60	Rococo garden laid out, with extensive redesign of gardens by Emperor Franz Stephan and artists from Lorraine
1751–52	Menagerie created, from design by Jadot
1753	Botanical garden (the Dutch Garden) laid out on newly acquired extension of gardens
1755	Orangery completed; botanist Nicolas Jacquin sent to Caribbean to gather plants for garden's collection
1772–80	Terracing of Schönbrunn Hill completed, fountains and follies by Hetzendorf von Hohenberg, statuary by Wilhelm Beyer and his team
1779	Gardens opened to public
1788–1817	Enlargements of Botanical Garden in three phases (1788, 1802, 1817)
1828–50	Transformation of Botanical Garden from geometric to landscape garden
1880–82	Construction of Great Palm House
1896	Neo-baroque flower ornaments in beds of Great Parterre
1904	Construction of Sun Dial House
1918	End of Habsburg monarchy, Schönbrunn becomes property of Republic of Austria
1945	Damage by bombs
1985	Start of several restorations in gardens and renovations of zoo, still in progress

Further Reading

Glaser, Josef, *Schönbrunner Chronik*, Vienna: Schloßhauptmannschaft Schönbrunn, 1969; 4th edition, 1987

Hajós, Beatrix, *Die Schönbrunner Schloßgarten*, Vienna: Böhlau, 1995

Hajós, Beatrix, and Brigitte Mang, "Schönbrunn," in *Historische Garten in Österreich*, edited by Géza Hajós, Vienna: Böhlau, 1993

Hajós, Géza, *Schönbrunn*, Vienna: Zsolnay, 1976

Hajós, Géza, "Schönbrunner Gartenkonzepte zur Zeit von Kaiser Franz Stephan I.," *Kunsthistorisches Jahrbuch Graz* 25 (1993)

Kronfeld, Ernst Moriz, *Park und Garten von Schönbrunn*, Vienna: Amalthea, 1923

Morachiello, Paolo, "Schönbrunn: A Theatre of Fragments," in *The Architecture of Western Gardens: A Design History from the Renaissance to the Present Day*, edited by Monique Mosser and Georges Teyssot, Cambridge, Massachusetts: MIT Press, 1991

Raschauer, Oskar, *Schönbrunn, eine denkmalkundliche Darstellung seiner Baugeschichte: Der Schloßbau Kaiser Joseph I.*, Vienna: Schroll, 1960

BEATRIX HAJÓS

Schwetzingen

Schwetzingen, Baden-Württemberg, Germany

Location: approximately 12 miles (19 km) south of Mannheim and 50 miles (80.5 km) south of Frankfurt

The gardens at Schwetzingen were laid out during the second half of the 18th century at a time when court life in the Palatinate was briefly a center of artistic excellence. The completed layout comprises a baroque centerpiece with a unique circular parterre, a suite of rococo compartments of considerable richness and refinement, and an early Continental example of a landscape garden. The designers of the layout and features were of the front rank, and the garden is in excellent condition following extensive restoration work in the years after 1970.

The Elector Palatine Carl Theodor, ruler and patron during this golden age, took office in 1743. His court was based at the great palace in Mannheim, but Schwetzingen was his principal summer residence and thus the scene of a great deal of creative activity and achievement.

The castle is a tall, plain structure rebuilt in the early years of the 18th century following the destruction of its medieval predecessor during the Thirty Years' War. The approach from the town square, through a *cour d'honneur* flanked by lodge pavilions, gives little hint of the

Park of Schwetzingen Palace, built by Carl Theodor, with statues of river gods Rhine (left) and Danube (right)
Copyright Erich Lessing/Art Resource, New York

splendor to come on the other side of the castle, where the great garden was laid out from about 1750.

The centerpiece of the garden is the great circular parterre, laid out according to a plan by Johann Ludwig Petri in 1753, with later modifications by the court architect Nicolas de Pigage. The principal axis is a continuation of the line from the village street through the castle arch; this line continues the length of the garden toward the Rhine. Looking back toward the east, the hills beyond Heidelberg form the horizon. A cross-axis runs north and was formerly terminated by a view of the palace at Mannheim. The circle is framed on the east by the curving pavilions built in 1748 to house the orangery and festive suite and on the west by answering tunnels of clipped lime. Barthélemy Guibal's Arion Fountain occupies the center of the circle, which is completed by a parterre pattern of box arabesques against a ground of colored gravel.

The eye is then drawn westward along the broad axial walk. Emblematic statuary, focused on Peter Anton Verschaffelt's Stag group, is set out at the head of the walk, which proceeds to a lake. In the original design this was a rectangular pond, but it was gradually given a more "natural" appearance, the present outline reflecting the work of Johann Michael Zeyher in the early 19th century. Beyond the lake the baroque arrangement, for state and parade, falls away entirely to be replaced by a remarkable design in the English landscape style by the court gardener Friedrich Ludwig von Sckell from 1776; it is one of the earliest layouts in this style in Germany. Sckell was a significant innovator in the landscape style in Germany and was later responsible for the English Garden in Munich.

Sckell's design, cleverly added to the baroque layout without appearing to contradict it, curls around the lake along sinuous paths. The visitor is drawn along the route by unfolding views of decorative features in a swelling and swooping landscape of turf, trees, and water. The ornamental buildings, largely designed by the adaptable Nicolas de Pigage, include some of exceptional quality, including a dramatic mosque complete with prayer corridors, and the convincingly "ruined" Temple of Mercury. These two buildings admire one another across a pond with studiously serpentine margins. Statues and bridges lead through this ideal landscape to the extraordinary "Roman" fort with adjoining aqueduct and obelisk, another conceit by de Pigage and Sckell, completed in 1779. The structure, one of the most elaborate follies in Europe, stands in a grove called the Arboricum Theodoricum after its patron. The informal layout was complete by 1795, but its intimacy and presentation as a series of theatrical episodes recalls the work of William Kent and his contemporaries in England in the mid-18th century. Further ornamental buildings, also by de Pigage, include the Temple of Botany, with its "organic" exterior, and the Temple of Minerva, isolated in a grove near the central parterre.

The rococo garden is a complete contrast to the expansive atmosphere of Sckell's landscape garden. It consists of a series of randomly connected small, immaculate spaces, each with a separate theme and each precisely and ingeniously formed. The Grove of Apollo features the temple of that god, silhouetted above a cascade flowing from a grotto (representing Parnassus) into an elliptical green space. The Bath House, by de Pigage, is a riot of decoration with rails in the form of serpents, and it leads the visitor to the pool beyond with its water-spouting sculpture birds in a space surrounded by decorative aviaries. Beyond this is the optical illusion of the "End of the World," achieved by viewing a painted curving wall bearing a glimpse of Paradise along a trelliswork tunnel. In a shady walkway is a dramatic statue of Pan overlooking a pond of a writhing outline, one of the most delicate achievements of rococo garden design. The whole layout of this section, hidden from immediate view in a maze of green bosquets and salons, evokes the rococo in a brilliant and refreshing fashion.

The garden at Schwetzingen remains among the best sites in Europe for understanding and comparing the baroque, rococo, and landscape styles alongside one another, each vigorously expressed and well presented.

Synopsis

1715	Reconstruction of *Schloss* completed
1743	Carl Theodor takes office as Elector Palatine
1748	Building started of curving pavilions to house the orangery and festive suite
1749	Orangery wing completed
1750	Garden lay out begun
1753	Corresponding festive wing completed; Johann Ludwig Petri's plan for the baroque garden
1764	Grove of Apollo in rococo garden constructed
1766–72	Bath House
1766–73	Temple Grove of Minerva
1776	English landscape design by Friedrich Ludwig von Sckell
1776–79	Temple of Botany and "Roman" fort and aqueduct completed
1780–95	Mosque completed
1784–87	Ruined Temple of Mercury constructed
1799	Death of Carl Theodor
1823	Remodeling of lake by Johann Michael Zeyher from rectangular pond to a more natural shape
1970s	Extensive restorations return gardens to excellent condition

Further Reading

Cowin, Andrew, "Schwetzingen Castle Garden: The Long Road from Pleasure to Enlightenment," *Hortus* 24 (Winter 1992)

Goulty, Sheena Mackellar, *Heritage Gardens: Care, Conservation, and Management*, London: Routledge, 1993

Reinhardt, Helmut, "German Gardens in the Eighteenth Century: Classicism, Rococo, and Neo-Classicism," in *The History of Garden Design: The Western Tradition from the Renaissance to the Present Day*, edited by Monique Mosser and Georges Teyssot, London: Thames and Hudson, 1991

Reisinger, Claus, et al., *Der Schloßgarten zu Schwetzingen*, Worms, Germany: Werner, 1987

STEVEN DESMOND

Sckell, Friedrich Ludwig von 1750–1823

German Landscape Designer

Friedrich Ludwig von Sckell was one of the first great German landscape designers to incorporate elements of the English landscape in his designs for both royal and public gardens. He was the eldest son of a court pleasure gardener, Johann Wilhelm von Sckell. As a young man Friedrich Ludwig studied primarily in England, where he was influenced by the work of Lancelot "Capability" Brown and Sir William Chambers. Sckell's first commission was the redesign of the baroque gardens at Schwetzingen for Palatine Elector Karl Theodor. At Schwetzingen, Sckell designed the outer landscape of the residence in the English landscape style. In the spirit of Capability Brown, he transformed an existing rectangular pond into a larger, "naturelike" lake. With director of gardening Nicholas Di Pigage, Sckell also developed a series of thematic gardens and structures. These thematic elements included a Chinese bridge, Turkish mosque, Roman water tower, trompe l'oeil *Ende der Welt*, and an Egyptian quarter with a copy of the obelisk of the pharaoh Sesostris.

In 1784, upon the advice of Schwetzingen visitor Christian Hirschfeld, Sckell made modifications to these thematic designs and omitted the Egyptian quarter. Hirschfeld criticized the use of exotic structures and plants in landscape gardens and proposed that landscape designs should accentuate characteristics of the existing countryside. Sckell's interaction with Hirschfeld marked a turning point in his work toward a more restrained English landscape style. As the court and pleasure gardener for almost 30 years, Sckell continued to refine his German adaptation of the English landscape style at Schwetzingen and other princely estates. Sckell was also influential at estates such as Herrsheim at Worms and later with the design of the Seegartens at Amorbach. Sckell embarked on his first public work when he was asked by Karl Theodor to redesign the town fortification at Mannheim into a public promenade.

When Karl Theodor became ruler of Bavaria, he moved his residence from Mannheim to Munich, where he opened to the public the *Hofgartens* adjacent to the royal palace. Influenced by the French Revolution and social reformer Benjamin Thompson, a refugee from the American Revolution, Theodor ordered that the grounds be designed as a public park. This park, the Englischer Garten, would contain commercial, recreational, and cultural programs in an English landscape setting. In 1789 Sckell began work on the Englischer Garten with Thompson. The Englischer Garten was formally opened as a public park in 1792, and it is still used by residents of Munich today.

In 1803, after much hesitation, Sckell left Schwetzingen and moved to Munich, where he took full responsibility of the garden. Using indigenous plant material and existing water courses, Sckell created a park of pathways, streams, expansive meadows, and tree groupings in the English landscape style. The landscape imagery for the Englischer Garten was based on the aesthetic criteria established by the poet Shenstone for his farm at Leasowes, England. Garden structures were similar to those found in well-known English gardens, such as the pagoda based on Sir William Chamber's pagoda at the Royal Botanic Gardens, Kew.

Sckell also redesigned the baroque gardens at Nymphenburg, the summer residence of the Bavarian electors and the largest palace in Germany. Leaving the baroque parterre, central canal, and side canals in front of the palace untouched, Sckell sought to open up views to the surrounding countryside with the implementation of lakes in front of the Badenberg and at the Pagodenburg. The landscape gardens at Nymphenburg represent one of Sckell's most mature works. Synthesizing a restrained palette of expansive lawns, meadows, lakes, and indigenous plant grouping as trajectories from the earlier baroque garden spaces, Sckell was able to harmonize the baroque and English landscape styles on an uncompromising and grand scale.

After Karl Theodor's death, Elector Maximilian IV Joseph appointed Sckell director of gardening in Rhineland-Palatine and Bavaria. During this time Sckell began to articulate his thoughts concerning the design of landscape parks. In a memorandum of 1807 Sckell expressed how the *Volksgarten* (people's garden) must not only be a grand landscape but also be instructive for both the body and spirit. In 1818 he published *Beitrage zur bildenden Gartenkunst, für angehende Gartenkunstler und Gartenliebhaber* (Contributions to Forming Garden Art, for Beginning Garden Artists and Garden Lovers). Reprinted many times after his death, this garden primer helped introduce German landscape designers to the English landscape style. Sckell also revealed many of his techniques, such as his use of optical illusions to create the appearance of topographical change in the garden. Sckell continued to consult on Nymphenburg and other gardens in Bavaria until his death in 1823.

See also Nymphenburg, Palace of; Schwetzingen

Biography
Born in Weilburg, Hessen, Germany, 1750. Worked as garden apprentice and journeyman in England and France; from 1776 to 1804, commissioned as Court and Pleasure Gardener at Schwetzingen, summer residence of Palatine court in Baden-Württemberg, Germany; worked with Benjamin Thompson on Englischer Garten in Munich, Germany, 1789, one of first public parks in Germany; became fully responsible for design of Englischer Garten, 1803; redesigned baroque gardens at Nymphenburg, Munich, 1804; director of gardening in Rhineland-Palatinate and Bavaria. Died in Bavaria, 1823.

Selected Designs
1776–1804	Schwetzingen, Baden-Württemberg, Germany
1788–92	Herrsheim, Worms, Rhineland-Palatinate, Germany
1789–1804	Englischer Garten (with Benjamin Thompson), Munich, Bavaria, Germany
1804–23	Nymphenburg, Munich, Bavaria, Germany

Selected Publications
Beitrage zur bildenden Gartenkunst, für angehende Gartenkunstler und Gartenliebhaber, 1818

Further Reading
Goecke, Michael, "Der englische Garten in Munchen—Aspekte seiner Entstehung," *Garten und Landschaft* 99, no. 11 (1989)

Hanwacker, Volker, *Friedrich Ludwig von Sckell: Der Begründer des Landschaftsgarten in Deutschland,* Stuttgart, Germany: Deutsche Verlags-Anstalt, 1992

Neubert, Sigrid, *Der Park: Die Gartenanlagen zu Nymphenburg,* Hamburg, Germany: Knaus, 1980

Siemon, Gerhard, "Friedrich Ludwig Sckells Entwurf für den Seegarten in Amorbach," *Die Gartenkunst* 9, no. 2 (1997)

SUSAN HERRINGTON

Scotland

Scotland occupies Europe's northwestern extremity; its latitude is moderated by maritime influences, particularly that of the North Atlantic Drift on the west coast and Hebridean islands. Thus, in winter, parts of Scotland may be as warm as the Mediterranean, but in summer it is one of the coolest places in Europe. A remarkably wide range of plants, therefore, can survive in Scotland, although their growth rate may be much slower than elsewhere. Apart from local variations in climate, the major challenge for plant cultivation is exposure to winds, which are frequently salt laden. The response throughout history has been to make sheltered gardens and utilize southern aspects where possible. This approach reached its most sophisticated expression in the walled gardens developed from the 17th century to the early 20th century, a principal feature of Scottish garden design.

From prehistoric times the landscape of Scotland has been marked out with special places, the evidence for which remains as standing stones and megalithic monuments whose full purpose remains obscure. These include the henge at Cairnpapple Hill (ca. 3000 B.C.) and the stone circle at Callanish on Lewis (ca. 2000–1500 B.C.). The earliest known evidence of an enclosed gardenlike space is probably a tiny courtyard between houses at

Walled garden at Edzell Castle, Howe of the Mearns, Scotland
Copyright Catharine Ward Thompson

Skara Brae, Orkney, dated as early as 3100 B.C. Thousands of years later, Iron Age brochs, unique to northwest Scotland, show evidence of small, walled houses and enclosures developed around the central, circular tower, for example, at Gurness, in Orkney (ca. A.D. 100–400). Similar enclosed spaces, making use of any readily available stone or timber to respond to the need for shelter, were probably used as gardens throughout Scotland across many centuries. The *planticrues* (tiny vegetable plots surrounded by low walls) of Shetland, still in use in the 20th century for cultivating *Brassica* seedlings, show a refinement of this tradition, using *drystane dikes* (dry stone walls) with gaps in the upper courses, permeable to the wind, to create shelter without turbulence.

Records of the first centuries of the Christian era are scant, although gardens were evidently part of Celtic religious establishments in the Western Isles, for example, from as early as the sixth century. In the later Anglo-Norman period, elaborate herb gardens and orchards, as well as more extensive agricultural enterprises, were associated with the great medieval monasteries. Large forest clearances in the 12th century marked the creation of new farm settlements, particularly in the Lowlands, and by the 15th century timber was being imported from Scandinavia. Royal deer parks at this time were mainly heathland and scrub woodland rather than fully afforested. Designed gardens probably continued to be walled enclosures or "yards," adjacent to or within monasteries or the protective walls of castles and fortified houses and following patterns similar to the *hortus conclusus* of the rest of medieval Europe. Gardens continued to combine utility with ornament well into the 17th century, often containing *doo'cots* (dovecotes), orchards with an impressive variety of fruits including peaches, apricots, and figs, and *stanks* (fishponds). Extant remnants of early secular gardens include the King's Knot at Stirling, laid out for James VI, apparently (and unusually) on a open site to the west of the castle, and Edzell Castle, in the Mearns, whose sophisticated 1604 walled pleasure garden (the planting is modern) indicates French, Dutch, and German design influences.

John Reid's pioneering book *The Scot's Gard'ner* (1683) demonstrates a continued advocation of walled gardens and the need for shelter: "There is no way under the sun so probable for improving our land as inclosing and planting the same." By the end of the 17th century, concern over the almost complete clearance of trees from the Scottish landscape for commercial purposes led to an enthusiasm for new planting promoted by both government and landowners. The landscape began to be marked with square fields surrounded by shelterbelts, and by the early 18th century wealthy landowners had established extensive baroque parklands around their houses, with vistas focused on distant mountains or monuments. Sir William Bruce's designs for Kinross (ca. 1685–92) used the ruin of a castle on the island in Loch Leven as the terminus for the main vista, for example, and a 1730s panorama of Taymouth Castle shows a layout of extraordinary power and wealth extending far into the landscape.

The economic and political revival in the Lowlands after the early 18th century Acts of Union between Scotland and England saw the emergence of a lively interest in agricultural improvements. For the politically astute following the defeat of the 1745 Jacobite rebellion, estate improvements in the Highlands also became possible, and land enclosure was accompanied by (sometimes ruthless) clearances for sheep, and later deer, grazing on the hills. An educated and increasingly wealthy group of "Improvers" developed design principles, based on the philosophies of the Scottish Enlightenment, for the policies (parklands) around their houses in parallel with enclosure and development of their agricultural estates. Sir John Clerk of Penicuik laid out a number of landscapes, most famously at Mavisbank with the help of William Adam (architect/landscape designer) and William Boutcher (nurseryman). Clerk described his design ideas in a didactic poem *The Country Seat,* published in 1727, reflecting a growing interest in the wilder features of the natural landscape and Alexander Pope's "genius of the place." Other landowners of the time trying new methods and layouts included the duke of Atholl, who had established the Society of Scotch Improvers in 1723 and the Haddingtons at Tyninghame, East Lothian.

By the mid-18th century, the writings of Sir John Dalrymple and Lord Kames had established the connection between garden design, the senses, and the emotions, Kames promoting a poetic approach to the beautiful and the sublime particularly suited to Scottish topography. This was in contrast to designs for lowland and borders estates such as Duddingston by pupils and followers of Lancelot "Capability" Brown, which reflected a smoother, English pastoral aesthetic. The woodlands of the Blair Adam Estate, for example, were developed between 1748 and 1792 to take advantage of rocky crags, picturesque walks, and panoramic views, very

much in the spirit of Kames's suggestions. The Picturesque movement that developed toward the end of the 18th century was particularly appropriate to Scotland, whose naturally rugged terrain matched Picturesque ideals and was promoted by writers such as Sir Walter Scott and the Rev. William Gilpin. John Claudius Loudon, the great Scots writer, noted in 1822 that the gardens of Scotland "excel those of England in the prominence of their natural features; being generally backed by hills or mountains; encompassed by a river or stream; or situated on a lake or on the sea shore."

At the same time that romantic ideas were developing about the layout of the pleasure ground, the challenges of creating productive gardens in such latitudes led to a tradition of skilled Scots gardeners who became renowned well beyond their homeland; if they could produce ripe peaches for the table in Aberdeenshire, they could surely produce wonders in Kent. The superior Scots' education and skill was commented on by Switzer in 1718: "A Scot could learn more in 12 months than a south countryman in seven years." Beginning in the 18th century Scottish head gardeners were appointed to many of the great houses in England and abroad, for example, Thomas Blaikie was appointed to Bagatelle, France, in 1776 and nurserymen such as Veitch established international reputations. Scotland also provided a succession of famous plant collectors, including Archibald Menzies in the late 18th century, David Douglas in the 19th century, and George Forrest in the early 20th century, who traveled to all parts of the world and supplied seed and specimens for cultivation in botanical gardens and private estates throughout Britain, Europe, and North America.

Loudon was a prolific writer on matters from farming to horticulture, providing detailed technical advice as well as aesthetic guidance, and, with his wife Jane, he established the first gardening and architecture magazines in the 1820s and 1830s. He recorded the work of otherwise forgotten designers such as James Ramsay and promoted an extreme form of the Picturesque—the "gardenesque"—in his own designs. Other writers followed suit, such as Sir Henry Steuart, whose *Planter's Guide* (1828) championed root pruning and transplanting of large trees for instant effect. In the 19th century arboreta and pineta became increasingly popular, benefiting from the enthusiasm of plant collectors and the skill of nurserymen. Many gardens contained extensive informal pleasure grounds to display collections of exotic plants. Inverewe, initiated by Osgood Mackenzie in the 1860s with an essential shelterbelt plantation as a first step, is one of many famous gardens established to take advantage of the acid soils and moist, warm climate of the west coast especially suited to conifers and Asiatic rhododendrons.

A parallel Victorian enthusiasm was a return to the formal terraces and parterres of the 17th century (of varying historical accuracy), together with elaborate greenhouses for tender plants and forced production of herbaceous plants for carpet bedding. By the end of the 19th century, a revivalist interest in baronial architecture led to re-creations of the walled pleasure garden, such as at Earlshall, Fife, by Sir Robert Lorimer.

A number of public parks were established in towns and cities during the 19th century and proved enormously popular; they were known for their elaborate bedding displays and curious tree specimens, such as the Camperdown elm, as well as for their neat orderliness. Winter gardens such as the People's Palace in Glasgow Green added to the attraction, and by the 1880s such parks could be visited by tens of thousands of people on a single day.

Many of Scotland's larger estates and gardens became impossible to maintain after World War I and have fallen into disrepair or suffer from lack of maintenance, although there have been some recent attempts at renewal or reconstruction. Recent gardens of fame are few, and the broader landscape reflects contemporary concerns with productive forestry plantation, after the establishment of the Forestry Commission in 1919, and reclamation of industrial spoil in the wake of extensive oil shale and coal extraction in the Central Lowlands; both have involved the professional skills of landscape architects. Two private gardens of note are Little Sparta, created in Lanarkshire in 1967 by the poet Ian Hamilton Finlay, and a later garden in Dumfries based on themes of ancient oriental tradition and modern chaos theory, created by the architectural critic Charles Jencks and his late wife, Maggie Keswick.

See also Edinburgh, Royal Botanic Garden; Little Sparta, Stonypath

Further Reading

Anderson, Mark Louden, *A History of Scottish Forestry,* 2 vols., London: Nelson, 1967

Bown, Deni, Alan P. Bennell, and Norma M. Gregory, editors, *4 Gardens in One: The Royal Botanic Garden, Edinburgh,* Edinburgh: HMSO, 1992

Cox, Euan Hillhouse Methven, *A History of Gardening in Scotland,* London: Chatto and Windus, 1935

Debois Landscape Survey Group, *Designed Landscapes in Scotland: Notes on Their Planting and Management,* Edinburgh: Scottish Natural Heritage, 1997

Desmond, Ray, *Dictionary of British and Irish Botanists and Horticulturists, Including Plant Collectors and Botanical Artists,* London: Taylor and Francis, 1977; revised edition, by Desmond and Christine Ellwood, London and Bristol, Pennsylvania: Taylor and Francis, and London: Natural History Museum, 1994

Dingwall, Christopher, *Researching Historic Gardens in Scotland: A Guide to Information Sources,* Edinburgh: Scottish Natural Heritage, 1995

Goulty, Sheena Mackellar, *Heritage Gardens: Care, Conservation, and Management,* London: Routledge, 1993

An Inventory of Gardens and Designed Landscapes in Scotland, 5 vols., Perth: Countryside Commission for Scotland, 1987

Little, G. Allan, editor, *Scotland's Gardens,* Edinburgh: Spurbooks, 1981

Loudon, John Claudius, *An Encyclopaedia of Gardening,* 2 vols., London, 1822; new edition, 1835; reprint, New York: Garland, 1982

MacLeod, Dawn, *The Gardener's Scotland,* Edinburgh: Blackwood, 1977

Millman, R.N., *The Making of the Scottish Landscape,* London: Batsford, 1975

Reid, John, *The Scots Gard'ner,* Edinburgh, 1683; reprint, Edinburgh: Mainstream, 1988

Skinner, David Neave, *A Woody Plant Selection Guide for First and Second Year Students,* Edinburgh: Edinburgh College of Art, and Heriot-Watt University, Department of Landscape Architecture, 1987

Tait, Alan Andrew, *The Landscape Garden in Scotland: 1735–1835,* Edinburgh: Edinburgh University Press, 1980

Verney, Peter, *The Gardens of Scotland,* London: Batsford, 1976

Whyte, Ian D., and Kathleen Whyte, *The Changing Scottish Landscape, 1500–1800,* London: Routledge, 1991

CATHARINE WARD THOMPSON

Sculpture Garden

Sculpture has been an important element in gardens throughout history. During the last part of the 20th century, however, the concept of a "sculpture garden" emerged as distinctly different from a garden with sculpture. In the sculpture garden sculpture is seen not merely as ornament but as taking a primary role in the garden.

For nearly 3,000 years sculpture has been incorporated into the design of buildings, gardens, tombs, and public spaces as expressions of a particular society's religious, political, and artistic ideals. Many of these ancient sites have been pillaged or destroyed, but archaeologists have been able to determine much of the extent and location of the use of sculpture. Among the oldest of these sites is Queen Hatshepsut's funerary temple in Egypt near Thebes. Built about 1480 B.C., the design incorporated numerous figures (most of which represented the queen) carved from stone and arranged in rows approaching the temple. Other Egyptian temples were approached by way of long avenues of carved sphinxes protecting the temple precinct.

Between 650 and 80 B.C., ancient Greeks incorporated impressive statues into their temple complexes that commemorated the gods. The Acropolis in Athens, for example, housed an approximately nine-meter-high (9.8 yd.) statue of *Athena* that would be carried from its location in the Parthenon out into the open area of the Acropolis on special occasions. The *Athena* would have been an impressive and startling sight for visitors and enemies approaching Athens from the sea. Greek marketplaces contained sculptures honoring political and military heroes.

The Roman Empire included many uses of sculpture during its reign from the third century B.C. to the fifth century A.D. Many statues were found in the Roman Forum, the central district of Rome, as well as in courtyards of private residences. From palace courtyards to those of the middle class, statuary was an essential component of homes in Pompeii. A peristyle walkway surrounded the enclosed courtyards, which often included plantings, a water feature, paintings of imaginary landscapes, and statuary. Statues usually defined the edges of pools and terraces and paid homage to patrons, ancestors, or household gods. Hadrian's Villa in Tivoli was filled with statues illustrating Hadrian's extensive travels; the emperor often re-created buildings and gardens at his vast estate as a sort of souvenir of his favorite places. Sculpture was an essential component of these tributes.

In other parts of the world sculpture was being created in different forms and for different reasons. In pre-Columbian America narrative and symbolic carvings and reliefs were composed for temples and gods. The Mayans are known for their ceremonial complex at Teotihuacan (A.D. 100–750), which contained pyramids covered with relief carvings and sculptural elements. The Mayans believed that these carvings expressed and helped to maintain their partnership with the gods, on which they depended for survival. Many of these sculptural elements were of feathered serpents and frightening faces representing the rain god. Chichen Itza was another Mayan complex, taken over by the Toltecs in the ninth century; it too displays abundant sculpture. The Toltecs were a more militaristic people, a characteristic illustrated in their sculpture. Images depicting lines of marching warriors and row after row of human skulls can be found at Chichen Itza. Carved figures on their backs called *chacmools* served as altars to hold human hearts during sacrificial rites.

Hindu and Buddhist cultures created statuary and reliefs that narrated the journey to enlightenment. The Stupa of Barabudur in Java, which dates from about A.D. 750, was such a place. People from far away would make a pilgrimage to physically enact this experience of ascension. The Stupa, a rock temple mountain, served as a symbolic pillar between heaven and earth. The monument was covered with sculpture that narrated the pilgrims' journey as they moved through the monument. The upper levels were terraces filled with 72 stone Buddhas representing the cosmos and the way to enlightenment.

Sculptural stones of diverse sizes and character held prominent positions in Chinese and Japanese temples and gardens and were seen as sculptures of nature. Trees and shrubs were trained to specific shapes, and as with stones, they were strongly sculptural and symbolic, creating sanctity, mood, and balance in the garden.

The use of stone sculpture during the Middle Ages was not common, but toward the end of the period the use of topiary, the decorative shaping of shrubs, hedges, and borders, became quite popular. As gardeners became more adept at creating these sculptural and often architectural forms from plants, designs became increasingly complex.

The birth of the Italian Renaissance in the 15th century marks the beginning of a dramatic increase of the use of sculpture in the garden. Looking back at the Roman models of antiquity, designers of the Renaissance period created prominent positions for statues and sculpture in both public plazas and private gardens. The great plazas in Rome, Florence, and many other Italian cities are centered on monumental statuary. The Villa d'Este in Tivoli was a marvel of fanciful sculpture and waterworks interwoven with the gardens. Some statuary represented mythological figures, while other sculpture told of the history of Rome. It is said that the Villa d'Este was heavily influenced by nearby Hadrian's Villa and that some of the sculpture was actually taken from the ancient Roman estate. The Villa Orsini in Bomarzo is an excellent example of the mannerist response to the Renaissance garden; the garden is inhabited by numerous bizarre and primitive stone creatures. Among them are giants, two-headed dogs, and monsters whose open mouths serve as passageways; all of them play with notions of reality, scale, and fantasy. The element of mystery and surprise is strong in this garden, and the sculpture seems to take on a life of its own.

The use of sculpture in the French baroque garden can be seen most clearly in the gardens of Versailles (ca. 1668) and Vaux-le-Vicomte (1661), both of which were designed by André Le Nôtre. Gardens and their details were designed on a heroic scale, and the domination of nature was evident throughout. Statuary was used in the garden to create focal points, terminate axes, punctuate space, and create rhythm in the garden along the wide, long walkways. These sculptures depicted allegorical and mythological figures meant to create dignity in the garden, thereby elevating the status of the patron.

The English landscape style that emerged at the beginning of the 18th century turned its back on the Italian and French Renaissance styles and created wholly different landscapes. The use of sculptural elements in the garden was also quite different and took the form of "follies" or "incidents" that were set out in the landscape for guests to discover. These follies were often created to appear as ancient ruins and temples, to provide focal points, and to modulate movement in the various parts of the pastoral landscape. The gardens of Stourhead, created in the middle of the 18th century, are an excellent example of this style. Structures with allegorical references offered political commentary and delighted distinguished guests, who were encouraged to move through the garden and discover each folly.

The use of sculpture in outdoor spaces in the United States can first be recognized in conjunction with the development of the city plaza and public park. Starting in the mid-19th century, monuments of stone and bronze were commissioned to decorate these types of spaces. Most were dedicated to classical figures that represented ideals such as courage and freedom, but later, more realistic portraits of political and cultural heroes emerged. Evidence of this trend can be found in the numerous statues of victorious generals astride their horses in cities and towns throughout the United States.

Two influences that developed in the 1960s clearly affected the creation of sculpture gardens as they are understood today. One was the requirement imposed by many local and federal governments on developers to dedicate a percentage of their project budget to public art. As a result, numerous sculptures have been designed for public outdoor spaces, most of which are more abstract in form than the previous figure compositions. Using modern materials and often bright colors, sculptors have moved away from the typical commemorative piece and toward creating pieces that express an idea, convey a message, or explore the relationship between the artwork and its surroundings.

The other significant influence that developed during the 1960s was the emergence of environmental art, following the minimalist movement. During this time artists began to question the concept of the art "object." The interior spaces of museums and galleries were viewed as limiting and homogenizing because they usually assumed a frontal engagement with the art piece.

Artists who wanted to explore the spatial and behavioral aspects of their work found the conventions of interior space restrictive. In attempting to avoid this confining environment, many artists looked to the outdoors as a new setting for their work. The living landscape was a growing, changing entity that offered an entirely different experience than that of the gallery, for both artist and viewer. The environmental artist Robert Morris compared the spatial qualities of traditional gallery art and environmental art as noun- and verb-type spaces. The gallery, or noun-type space, treats art as an object that is almost always disconnected from its surroundings. The open field, or verb-type space, treats the art as a changing, living form that confronts and integrates itself with its specific site.

In the contemporary sculpture garden the placement of artwork takes into consideration its natural surroundings as background as well as the relationships between pieces. The more successful sculpture gardens influence viewers' perceptions of the artwork by defining the space and creating views and approaches. These controlled perspectives heighten curiosity and suggest potential discovery, extending the experiential aspects of the garden. The mystery of the three-dimensional object and its relationship to the landscape increases the viewer's desire for understanding of the artist's intention. The sculpture may also suggest a literary, mythological, or historical narrative that increases the viewer's interest and appreciation and enhances the sense of place in the garden. The outdoor conditions of weather, light, season, and time also extend the experience of the garden by offering different experiences with each visit.

Brookgreen Gardens in South Carolina, founded in 1931, is said to be the oldest sculpture garden in the United States. Among the most successful sculpture gardens around the world is the Millesgården in Stockholm, which contains the work of artist Carl Milles. The Kröller-Müller Museum in Otterlo, Netherlands, presents a number of experiences through the creation of a variety of enclosures and views related to various pieces. The Storm King Art Center in suburban New York is perhaps the largest sculpture garden, covering a 500-acre (202-ha) site. The art pieces in the Henry Moore Sculpture Garden in Kansas City, Missouri, seem to inhabit the landscape and respond to Moore's belief that sculpture should be viewed with nature. Ian Hamilton Finlay's garden Stonypath in Scotland combines sculpture with poetry and guides the viewer through the garden by way of a series of spaces and narratives. At Grizedale Forest in Cumbria, England, artists are invited to create artworks, many of which have a fleeting existence, within the forest using materials found on site.

The number of sculpture gardens is continually rising, with new ones being developed regularly in both public and private realms. More and more museums consider the sculpture garden to be a major and indispensable exhibit area, hoping to attract new and varied audiences. The relaxing and natural setting combined with the creative and skilled display of artwork helps to achieve this objective by facilitating the introduction of large numbers of visitors to the imaginative forms and ideas of contemporary sculpture.

Further Reading

Crosby, Theo, "Bomarzo," *Architectural Design* 50, nos. 1–2 (1980)

Fletcher, Valerie J., *A Garden for Art: Outdoor Sculpture at the Hirshhorn Museum,* edited by Jane MacAllister, Washington D.C.: Hirshhorn Museum and Sculpture Garden, 1998

Gartner, P., "Murphy's Secret Garden," *Artnews* 84, no. 1 (1985)

Gillette, J.B., "Pure Design, Pure Image," *Landscape Architecture* 88, no. 10 (1998)

Lewis, Roger, "In This Sculpture Garden, Construction Melds with Nature," *Museum News* 68, no. 5 (1989)

Messer, Elizabeth, "Art and The Landscape: Designing for Natural Interactions," in *International Federation of Landscape Architects Symposium Proceedings,* Athens: IFLA, 2000

Osmundson, Theodore, "Sculpture Garden Garden Sculpture: Designing the Difference," *Landscape Architecture* 73, no. 1 (1983)

Sonfist, Alan, editor, *Art in the Land: A Critical Anthology of Environmental Art,* New York: Dutton, 1983

Thacker, Christopher, *The History of Gardens,* Berkeley: University of California Press, and London: Croom Helm, and Sydney: Reed, 1979

Treib, Marc, "Sculpture and Garden: A Historical Overview," *Design Quarterly* no. 141 (1988)

ELIZABETH R. MESSER DIEHL

Sculpture in the Garden

Sculpture has long been the seasoning of the garden. Its use to focus, enlarge, or even shrink space was well known in ancient Greece and Rome. "Of the many ways of directing or compelling attention in a garden," notes Hugh Johnson, "the most peremptory is the statue." There was limited garden making in the Middle Ages, but Renaissance and baroque gardens revived the ancient principles, and the writings of Ovid, Virgil, and Lucretius helped provide inspiration for the re-creation of Olympus. Statues of Venus, Pan, and Bacchus were ubiquitous in gardens.

Holland in the early 17th century embraced sculpture to the exclusion of flowers until bulbs came in vogue. Isola Bella in Italy became a floating garden of sculpture, ornamenting Lake Maggiore. The Bomarzo sculpture garden at the Villa Orsini in Lazio, Italy, was regarded with wonder. The Herrenhausen Royal Gardens at Hanover remain an extraordinary example of a sculpture-dominated garden. In the use of sculpture in gardens perhaps nothing can surpass France, with its great trinity of the Tuileries, Fontainebleau, and Versailles. Nonetheless, the 18th-century projects in Spain at La Granja of Philip V and the parks designed at the Palace of Caserta by Luigi Vanvitelli for the king of Naples remain extraordinary examples of the integration of sculpture with landscape.

Although the gardens of the Westover Plantation in Virginia incorporated sculptures as early as 1726, the expense of lead and stone limited the amount of garden sculpture in the United States. With the invention of Coade stone in 1769, there was a marked increase in the use of sculpture in gardens. A notable forerunner was the garden created by Governor John Eager Howard at Belvedere in Baltimore in 1783, which was inspired by the Vatican Belvedere (1504) of Julius II. The Italian Renaissance had been marked by extensive garden construction, which Americans were copying by the end of the 18th century. Representations of the continents, four seasons, and five senses competed for pedestals with grazing animals, satyrs, unicorns, and other heraldic beasts.

Brookgreen Gardens in South Carolina claims to be the first public sculpture garden in the United States. It was founded by sculptor Anna Hyatt Huntington and her husband Archer in 1931 on over 9,000 acres (3,642 ha) of unspoiled land. The property is situated on the coast of South Carolina near Myrtle Beach and has more than 500 sculptures on display.

The trend toward temporary exhibits, despite the obvious physical difficulties in moving large sculptures, is seen at Cedarhust Sculpture Park near St. Louis, Missouri, where many of the pieces are on display for just two years. A highlight of its permanent exhibits is Martha Enzmann's *Dancers,* floating sculptures of a man and woman dancing that are manipulated by underwater cables to change the pace and directions of the figures as the wind velocity and direction changes.

Today, sculptures in gardens are no longer an affair of smoothly finished and instantly recognizable lions, centaurs, pineapples, nymphs, and dryads; they are just as likely to be scarred, pitted, and enigmatic. Auguste Rodin's Impressionism marked a watershed, although it was admittedly followed by a reaction epitomized in the sculptures of Carl Milles. The previous standard gardening advice to bring sculpture "down to earth" by plantings of bleeding heart or Virginia creeper around the base seems old-fashioned; the scope of garden sculpture has been extended to include almost any scheme involving three-dimensional space and to move away from permanent exhibits. Some collections, such as Hat Hill Copse in England, try to make changes every year. The David Smith collection at the Storm King Art Center in Mountainville, New York, has experimented with a three-year cycle drawn from its permanent collection and from other collections.

The Vigeland display in Frogner Park near Oslo deserves special mention. Gustav Vigeland, Norway's greatest sculptor, created this 75-acre (30 ha) park over a period of many years (1924–42) to feature more than 200 granite and bronze statues. A 1.9-mile (3 km) walk is intended to parallel life's journey, with sculptures to match, highlighted by an approximately 16-meter-high (17.5 yd.) monolith carved with more than 125 figures.

There are many other noteworthy sites. Cranbrook Academy in Bloomfield Hills, Michigan, demonstrates how sculpture and gardens can be integrated successfully. Rodin's *The Walking Man* and David Smith's *Two Circle Sentinel* are among the sculptures displayed there. The Museum of Fine Arts in Houston, Texas, has a small but choice garden. Ellsworth Kelly was commissioned to create *Houston Triptych* in 1986. A triangular granite freestanding wall there is by Isamu Noguchi. The Houston garden is liberally endowed with seats, which is something often forgotten in such installations. The Kykuit Gardens surrounding the former home of Nelson A. Rockefeller in North Tarrytown, New York, include more than 70 sculptures by Jean Arp, Alexander Calder, Jacques Lipchitz, Henry Moore, and Pablo Picasso.

Artists such as Stephen De Staebler, J.B. Blunk, and Roger Bolomey, who appear to be placing natural rocks in patterns, also create sculpture for gardens, as do Lloyd Hamro, Jerome Johnson, and Kenneth Capps, whose work in another era might have been considered as follies. Andy Goldsworthy's projects have included a traveling arch that has appeared in dialogue with city centers and sheepfolds. All of Heather Donaldson's sculptures incorporate a water feature, such as *Water Dance* for the garden plaza of the Saratoga (California) City Hall.

Much of modern garden sculpture has the advantage of not having been endlessly copied and thus stale.

Unlike past work, in which conventional figures often dominated, modern garden sculpture often works well in small spaces. At its best, new garden sculpture suggests that plants be looked at as sculpture as well.

Nonetheless, the green of lawns can still be relegated to acting as the carpet of a gallery garden, or the equivalent of the white of museum walls, with plants excluded; the growth of minimalism in architecture often has seen plants relegated to a secondary role at best. This is not a new phenomenon; the 1925 decorative arts exposition in Paris included the celebrated garden created by Robert Mallet-Stevens and Jan and Joel Martel on the eastern section of the Esplanade des Invalides. Four concrete trees dominated, with slabs of concrete at 45-degree angles suggesting leaves. Some called this the triumph of Cubist sculpture in the garden, while others suggested the trees were substitutes for real ones that had died. This was an ultimate statement for the constructed/sculpted or "rationalized" architectural garden. Another significant example of this viewpoint is the garden Mallet-Stevens created at the Villa Noailles in southern France, dominated by the sculpture of Jacques Lipchitz known as *Joy of Life*. The sculpture rotated every four minutes, and critics felt it was out of place as a focal point, especially since the garden ignored the magnificent views of the Mediterranean. In defense, Charles de Noailles described "statues [as] an excellent thing in the garden, they are halfway between man and matter, a perfect intermediary between nature and humanity" (quoted in Imbert).

More recently, sculptures such as Herbet Bayer's *Mill Creek Canyon Earthworks* in Kent, Washington, and Isamu Noguchi's *Water Source, California Scenario* in Costa Mesa, California, provide excellent examples of the continuing tension between landscapes dominated by sculpture and landscapes where nature rules. The sculptor Henri Olivier is a particularly forceful exponent of the dominance of sculpture, as Allen Weiss explains:

A certain minimalism gives rise to thought, but abhors allegory, as in the case of Olivier's site-specific garden sculptures, which often constitute microcosmic elements of landscape architecture: canals devolved into mirror slits, pools condense into puddles of rainwater filling out hollowed sculptural spaces, orchards nominally reduced to a word or a name.

While much outdoor sculpture seems indifferent to its surroundings, Henry Moore was aware of the effect of trees as frames for his pieces and considered the sky to be an essential background for his work. His piece *Large Totem Head*, commanding a pool and ribbon of water in the courtyard of the Salk Institute in La Jolla,

California, is an example of how extremely stark landscaping can be emotionally moving.

Minimalism and gardens are not as easily paired as minimalism and sculpture, as H.B. Dunington-Brubb makes clear:

> We need only once glance at the modernist's pitiful efforts out of doors to know that he is stuck. In most cases he has thrown up his hands and done nothing. The few examples where any serious effort has been made are of such severity, or of such grotesqueness, as to have little resemblance to anything we should recognize as a garden. (quoted in Imbert)

Just as minimalism was a reaction to the excesses of the *jardin horticole*, there has been a reaction to minimalism and sometimes the happy combination of sculpture and flowers.

The best way to form opinions about these controversies is by viewing, and many opportunities exist for visiting sculpture gardens that will give ideas to even those gardeners with small yards. The impeccably curated Frank D. Murphy Sculpture Garden at the University of California at Los Angeles, designed by Ralph Cornell, demonstrates how a university campus can be enhanced by the use of "man-made works set into the sculpture of nature." The National Sculpture Garden on the Mall in Washington, D.C., is one of the newest. A further sampling includes the now restored Vizcaya Museum and Gardens at Miami, the sculpture gardens created by Peggy Guggenheim at the Palazzo Venier di Leoni in Venice with the help of the architect Giorgio Bellavitis, the Heriberto Juarez courtyard at the University of the Americas in Cholula, Mexico, the Edward James Wilderness Sculpture Garden in Xilitla, Mexico, and the Auguste Rodin Garden at Stanford University in California.

Further Reading

Bowe, Patrick, *Gardens in Central Europe*, edited by Ptolemy Tompkins, New York: M.T. Train/Scala Books, 1991

Bradley-Hole, Christopher, *The Minimalist Garden*, New York: Monacelli Press, and London: Mitchell Beazley, 1999

Ceysson, Bernard, and Antoinette Le Normand-Romain, *Sculpture: From the Renaissance to the Present Day: From the Fifteenth to the Twentieth Century*, Cologne, Germany, and New York: Taschen, 1999

Damaz, Paul F., *Art in Latin American Architecture*, New York: Reinhold, 1963

Enge, Torsten Olaf, and Carl Friedrich Schröer, *Gartenkunst in Europa, 1450–1800*, Cologne, Germany: Taschen, 1990; as *Garden Architecture in Europe, 1450–1800*, translated by Aisa Mattaj, Cologne, Germany: Taschen, 1990

Goldsworthy, Andy, and David Craig, *Arch*, New York: Abrams, and London: Thames and Hudson, 1999

Goldwater, Robert John, *What Is Modern Sculpture?* New York: The Museum of Modern Art, 1969

Henry Moore in La Jolla: Tasende Gallery and Select Locations, the Salk Institute, Ellen Browning Scripps Park (exhib. cat.), La Jolla, California: Tasende Gallery, 1982

Imbert, Dorothée, *The Modernist Garden in France*, New Haven, Connecticut: Yale University Press, 1993

Israel, Barbara, *Antique Garden Ornament: Two Centuries of American Taste*, New York: Abrams, 1999

Johnson, Hugh, *The Principles of Gardening: A Guide to the Art, History, Science, and Practice of Gardening*, New York: Simon and Schuster, 1979; as *The Principles of Gardening: The Science, Practice, and History of the Gardener's Art*, London: Beazley, 1979

Meyers, Marilyn, editor, *Sandsong: Ephemeral Sculptures*, New York: St. Martin's Press, 1983

Neubert, George W., *Public Sculpture/Urban Environment* (exhib. cat.), Oakland, California: The Oakland Museum, 1974

Pereire, Anita, *Gardens for the 21st Century*, London: Aurum Press, 1999

Phillips, Emily, *Decorative Accents for the Garden*, New York: Sterling, 1996

Plumptre, George, *Garden Ornament: Five Hundred Years of History and Practice*, London: Thames and Hudson, 1989; New York: Doubleday, 1990

Smith, Candida N., and Irving Sandler, *The Fields of David Smith*, New York and London: Thames and Hudson, 1999

Smith, Linda Joan, *Smith and Hawken Garden Ornament*, New York: Workman, 1998

UCLA Art Council, *Franklin D. Murphy Sculpture Garden: An Annotated Catalog of the Collection, 1976*, Los Angeles: UCLA Press, 1976; revised edition, as *Franklin D. Murphy Sculpture Garden, University of California, Los Angeles: An Annotated Catalogue of the Collection, 1984*, Los Angeles: Fredrick S. Wright Art Gallery, 1984

Valentiner, Wilhelm Reinhold, *Origins of Modern Sculpture*, New York: Wittenborn, 1946

Weiss, Allen S., *Unnatural Horizons: Paradox and Contradiction in Landscape Architecture*, New York: Princeton Architectural Press, 1998

PAUL RICH

Seifert, Alwin 1890–1972

German Landscape Architect

Alwin Seifert was one of the two most influential 20th-century German landscape architects. The other was his colleague and rival Heinrich Friedrich Wiepking-Jürgensmann. Seifert had a significant impact on garden design in Germany between the 1930s and 1960s. He was particularly influential in extending the scope of professional tasks from the garden to the landscape—that is, from garden design to landscape architecture and landscape planning. Such interests had already begun to shape professional activities during the Weimar Republic, when garden architects such as Leberecht Migge and Georg Bela Pniower attempted to similarly broaden the scope of professional interest. Wiepking and Seifert rode on the surging wave of National Socialism and introduced Nazi ideas such as "blood and soil" to landscape architecture. Seifert was a fanatic anti-Semite and strongly promoted the National Socialist blood-and-soil ideology. Numerous documents and his own publications give evidence of this.

Seifert started his professional career as a mason's apprentice. As a student of architecture (1909–13) he was pupil of Theodor Fischer and German Bestelmeyer. In his youth he had joined a nationalistic group of the Wandervogel, an important section of the bourgeois youth movement. From 1915 to 1918 he served as a soldier in World War I. From 1918 to 1921 he was head of his father's building firm. From 1920 to 1923 he was an assistant at the architecture department of the Technical University, Munich. In 1923 he began working as a freelance architect and landscape architect in Munich. He held a teaching assignment in garden and landscape design as well as in rural architecture at the Technical University of Munich from 1932 to 1944; in 1938 he was appointed an honorary professor.

In addition to his career as a garden designer, Seifert was especially influential as a garden writer. From 1929 on he published numerous articles about natural, or as he called it, "rooted-in-the-soil" (*bodenständige*), garden and landscape design. Very likely earlier writings of the garden writer Willy Lange had inspired Seifert. His concept of rooted-in-the-soil garden design had a strong ideological and political background and was oriented toward a strengthening of nationalistic ideas. In 1930 he stated his intentions: "I wanted to bring garden art into the struggle in all living spaces which has broken out in our present days between 'rootedness in the soil' and 'supra-nationality.'" According to Seifert, this struggle was "a fight between two opposing world views: on one side the striving for supra-nationality, for equalization of huge areas, and on the other the elabo-ration of peculiarities of small living spaces, the emphasis which is rooted in the soil." In 1933, immediately after the takeover of the Nazi regime, Seifert urged gardeners to "ban all that until now has pleased the heart of the gardener: everything high-bred, overfed, conspicuous, foreign, everything that just is unable to establish intimate bounds with the flora of our garden, which has been apportioned by nature."

Seifert still tolerated the use of some so-called foreign plants in the garden, but where the larger landscape was concerned, he became more and more radical. In 1937 he called for a "destiny determined" poverty of species in plant use. In the landscape "nothing foreign" should be added, "but nothing native must be left out." According to Seifert, the determining factor for the landscape architect had to be the "harsh country" that one "was born into." Seifert was a follower of biodynamic husbandry and gardening, which had been promoted by Rudolf Steiner, the leader of the Anthroposophical movement in Germany.

Seifert was able to implement his ideas about landscape design under National Socialism. He had connections to Rudolf Hess, the deputy of Adolf Hitler, and other leading Nazis. In 1934 Seifert became the decisive adviser to Fritz Todt, the inspector general of German roads, in charge of the landscape design of the state's motor highways (*Reichsautobahnen*). He established a group of landscape architects, the so-called landscape attorneys (*Landschaftsanwälte*), who were involved in landscape planning for the highways. Each of them was responsible for a specific section of the highways. On the occasion of Seifert's 50th birthday in 1940 Hitler appointed him state landscape attorney (*Reichslandschaftsanwalt*). Scientific evidence for the exclusive use of so-called native plants was sought by Seifert and his colleagues in the emerging discipline of "plant sociology."

In 1934 Seifert published his ideas about landscape design for the German highways in the newly established magazine *Die Strasse* (The Road):

> We are not allowed to let our new roads be separated from the living organism of landscape, we have to integrate them harmoniously. Therefore they have to participate in the laws that have formed our country over millenia; therefore they should not be more appropriate for a Sarmatian steppe than for the landscape of German peasants.

Seifert promoted the concept of the *Heckenlandschaft* (landscape of hedges) as the ideal landscape for the

Comparative examples of highway construction from Alwin Seifert, *Ein Leben für die Landschaft*, 1962
Courtesy of Heinrich Hugendubel Verlag

various regions in Germany. He also developed ideas for the design of the landscape in the areas of Poland taken by the Nazi army at the beginning of World War II. He published them in 1941 under the title *The Future of the East German Landscape*.

Seifert had some knowledge of the Nazi concentration camps. Together with landscape attorney Max Müller he visited the Dachau concentration camp, where Heinrich Himmler's SS forced prisoners to cultivate medicinal herbs. According to Seifert's correspondence, another landscape attorney, Werner Bauch, worked for Himmler at Auschwitz. It seems characteristic of landscape architecture in Germany in the second half of the 20th century that many landscape architects and garden historians have prefered to ignore Seifert's anti-Semitism and his strong sympathy for the Nazi blood-and-soil-ideology and its impact on his ideas about landscape design.

Despite his involvement in Nazi landscape planning activities, Seifert successfully continued his career after World War II. The help of landscape architects such as Herta Hammerbacher, who wrote a letter of reference for Seifert to the denazification agency, was decisive. After 1945 Seifert worked as a freelance landscape architect for various power stations in Bavaria and for the state of Bavaria and as an adviser for the expansion of the river Mosel. As senior lecturer he taught garden and landscape design at the Technical University, Munich and retired in 1955. In 1960 Seifert was awarded the Fritz-Schumacher prize of the Technical University of Hannover, and in 1969 he received the Friedrich-Ludwig-von-Sckell ring of the Bavarian Academy of Fine Arts. He died in 1972 in Dießen, Bavaria.

Biography

Born in Munich, Germany, 1890. Apprenticed as mason and studied architecture at Technical University, Munich, 1909–13; after World War I, directed his father's building firm, 1918–21; established practice as freelance landscape architect and architect in Munich, 1923; taught garden and landscape design at Technical University, Munich, 1932–44; appointed professor, 1938; strong promoter of Nazi blood-and-soil ideology and he became landscape adviser to Fritz Todt, Inspector General for German Road Affairs, 1934; established group of landscape architects (the so-called landscape attorneys), who were responsible for landscape planning of specific section of German highways; on occasion of 50th birthday, Seifert appointed by Adolf Hitler as Reich landscape attorney (Reichslandschaftsanwalt); after World War II, continued career as freelance landscape architect and as teacher of garden and landscape design; taught as associate professor at the Technical University, Munich, and retired as teacher, 1955. Died in Dießen, Bavaria, 1972.

Selected Designs

1920s	Open spaces for Borstei, Munich, Germany
1925	Garden Hentig, Munich, Germany
1931	Garden Karlin, Meersburg, Germany
ca. 1934	Garden Rudolf Hess, deputy to Adolf Hitler
1936	Garden Dr. Beck, Munich, Germany
1937	Gardens for exposition Schaffendes Volk (Creating People), Düsseldorf, Germany
1934–43	Landscape planning for Reich motor highways, Germany
1947	Garden Kraemer, Munich, Germany
1948	Garden Niedermayr, Rosenheim, Germany
1951	Garden Ludowigs, Wülfrath, Germany; garden Flachsenberg, Wülfrath, Germany
1952	Garden Färber, Munich, Germany
1954	Garden Rupf, Heidenheim, Germany
1958	Garden Seifert, Dießen, Germany
1960	Garden Winkler, Munich, Germany

Selected Publications

"Die Stuttgarter Weißenhof-Siedlung in gartenkritischer Betrachtung," *Die Gartenkunst* 41 (1928)

"Gedanken über bodenständige Gartenkunst," *Die Gartenkunst* 42 (1929)

"Bodenständige Gartenkunst," *Die Gartenkunst* 43 (1930)

"Der kommende Garten," *Deutsche Bauzeitung* (1933)

"Natur und Technik im deutschen Straßenbau," *Naturschutz* 18 (1937)

Im Zeitalter des Lebendigen: Natur, Heimat, Technik, 1941

"Die Zukunft der ostdeutschen Landschaft," *Leib und Leben* 8, no. 11 (1941)

Die Heckenlandschaft, 1944

Der Kompost in der bäuerlichen Wirtschaft, 1950; as *Compost*, translated by E.M. Hatt, 1962

Further Reading

Gröning, Gert, and Joachim Wolschke-Bulmahn, *Die Liebe zur Landschaft*, Münster, Germany: Minerva, 1986; see especially vol. 1, *Natur in Bewegung*

Gröning, Gert, and Joachim Wolschke-Bulmahn, *Grüne Biographien: Biographisches Handbuch zur Landschaftsarchitektur des 20. Jahrhunderts in Deutschland*, Berlin: Patzer, 1997

Gröning, Gert, and Uwe Schneider, "Nachlässe von Gartenarchitekten des 19. und 20. Jahrhunderts als Grundlage freiraumplanerischer Forschung," *Die Gartenkunst* 8, no. 1 (1996)

Nietfeld, Annette, *Reichsautobahn und Landschaftspflege: Landschaftspflege im Nationalsozialismus am Beispiel der*

Reichsautobahnen: Diplomarbeit, Berlin: Institut für Landschaftsökonomie der TU Berlin, 1985

Wolschke-Bulmahn, Joachim, "The Fear of the New Landscape: Aspects of the Perception of Landscape in the German Youth Movement between 1900 and 1933 and Its Influence on Landscape Planning," *The Journal of Architectural and Planning Research* 9, no. 1 (1992)

Wolschke-Bulmahn, Joachim, "Political Landscapes and Technology: Nazi Germany and the Landscape Design of the Reichsautobahnen (Reich Motor Highways)," in *Selected CELA Annual Conference Papers, volume 7, Nature and Technology,* Washington, D.C.: Council of Educators in Landscape Architecture, 1996

Wolschke-Bulmahn, Joachim, and Gert Gröning, "The Ideology of the Nature Garden: Nationalistic Trends in Garden Design in Germany during the Early Twentieth Century," *Journal of Garden History* 12, no. 1 (1992)

JOACHIM WOLSCHKE-BULMAHN

Semenov, Vladimir Nikilayevitch 1874–1960

Russian-Soviet Landscape Architect and Urban Planner

Vladimir Nikilayevitch Semenov was born in 1874 in the town of Kislovodsk, in the northern Caucasus. In 1898 he graduated from the High School of Civil Engineers in St. Petersburg and started to work as assistant to the chief architect at Gatchina, the imperial residence near St. Petersburg, with its palace and large gardens from the 18th and 19th century. A year later he joined a troop of volunteers and left for Transvaal, southern Africa, where he took part in the Boer War fighting on the Boer side. He then returned to Russia and worked until 1908 in his native spa-resort district of Mineral Waters in the Caucasus, where he designed the hotel Bristol in Piatigorsk, the country estate of Emir Bukcharski in Zheleznovodsk, and other buildings. In 1904 he won the first prize in the design competition for a new opera and ballet theater in Ekaterinburg.

From 1908 to 1912 Semenov lived in London. In Britain he studied the problems of modern city planning and became interested in the garden-cities movement. During this period he worked in the British Library, visited garden cities and suburbs in England, and traveled to Paris, Vienna, Brussels, and many German cities. This "English period" greatly influenced the rest of his career. In 1912 Semenov returned to Russia and published his book *The Good Accommodation of the Cities,* which aroused considerable interest in Russian intellectual and architectural circles. In this monumental work Semenov reviewed the general history of city planning, discussed its current state, and introduced a number of fundamental ideas connected with the theories of the English city planner Ebenezer Howard, the founder of the garden-cities movement, and other city planners of the time. Semenov's own theoretical system was fully adapted to the Russian situation. He emphasized the importance to urban planning of accurate population projections. His own estimates of the future population growth of the world's capitals, although received skeptically at the time, appeared by the middle of the 20th century to have been quite accurate. Raising the problem of optimal type and size of a settlement within the garden cities paradigm, Semenov further developed Howard's idea of the establishment of interrelated groups of garden cities. An important feature of Semenov's work was his emphasis on the need to achieve a balance between social needs and aesthetics. He felt strongly that town planning should take into account the physical landscape of every site, and he formulated the idea of "an elastic plan—i.e., the plan for [a] gradually developing city." Semenov's book, full of specific information and calculations on cities' economies, infrastructures, parks and gardens, and sociology and composition, became the primary source of ideas and guidelines for Russian town planning in the 20th century.

In 1913 Semenov designed one of the first garden cities in Russia, the town of Prozorovka, near Moscow, for the workers of the Moscow-Kazan railway. This project provided him with a rare opportunity to put his ideas into practice, and he showed himself to be a talented, professional planner. The development of Prozorovka was unique in Russian town planning of the early 20th century. Up to this time the majority of new suburbs or towns had been planned not by architects but by surveyors. Semenov chose a regular composition of three radial axis-avenues arising from the railway station. The middle axis-boulevard led to the town's main square, which accommodated a variety of administrative and public buildings. The network of smaller curving streets was more irregular in layout. Special attention was paid to public transportation, parks, and public buildings for specific uses, including a library, theater, indoor swimming pool, and others. Of the total 680 hectares (1,680 acres), 170 (420 acres) were reserved for "outer parks" around the town and 53 (131 acres) for "inner parks." Well-known Russian architects, including A.I. Tamanyan, A.V. Shusev, and others, designed the public buildings and one- and two-story brick-and-wood houses. Residential buildings had between one and eight flats and included gardens ranging in size from 1,400 square meters (1,674 sq. yd.) to 2,300 square meters (2,751 sq. yd.). The development of Prozorovka began in 1914; work was stopped with the outbreak of World War I but was partly resumed in the 1920s. Although Semenov's plan was never fully realized, it became the model for architects of the period. By the early 1920s Semenov was widely known as a landscape architect and city planner.

Between 1920 and the 1950s Semenov helped to formulate the basic principles of city planning in the Soviet Union and carried out many commissions, usually as head of the design group. In 1922 he started to teach, first at the Moscow technical high school, later at the Moscow Architectural Institute, and from 1926 in Giprogor, designing the city planning institute. From the mid-1920s on, he worked in most of the important cities of the Soviet Union. For Stalingrad (1929–31) Semenov created the underlying plan of four separate industrial towns, standing along the Volga River, divided by parks. Among his most interesting works closely connected with landscape and garden art was the design for the famous spa-resort district of Mineral Waters in the northern Caucasus (1935–37). A detailed plan was created for the district as a whole, along with individual designs for the resorts of Kislovodsk, Zheleznovodsk, and others. The resorts were connected by a single transportation and services infrastructure. In town plans for each resort, informal picturesque elements, inspired by the mountain landscape, was combined with more formal elements, including neoclassical-style sanitoriums.

From 1934 Semenov headed the department of city planning and landscape architecture at the Academy of Architecture. In 1944 he prepared *Rules on Architecture and City-Planning for Designs of Urban Settlements,* the document that guided the state program of reconstruction of cities destroyed during World War II. In the 1940s and 1950s he made the design for the reconstruction of Rostov-on-Don and consulted on the designs for Minsk, Stalingrad, and Leningrad. In designs for Moscow in the early 1930s and the 1940s Semenov formulated the main principles of reconstruction and development of the capital, paying special attention to the organization of a system of public parks

and "green zones" on the city's outskirts. In the 1940s and 1950s he designed a number of small rural settlements and groups of villages, so-called agro-cities. He also edited *The Organisation of Green Spaces in Soviet Cities* (1954), a textbook for designers.

Biography

Born in Kislovodsk, Northern Caucasus, Russia, 1874. Graduated from High School of Civil Engineers, St. Petersburg, Russia, 1898; took part in Anglo-Boer War, South Africa, 1899–1900; designed numerous buildings in spa resorts of Northern Caucasus, Russia, including hotel Bristol, Piatigorsk, and country estate of Emir Bukcharski, Zheleznovodsk; studied modern city planning, London, England, 1908–12, and became interested in the garden-cities movement; traveled to Paris, Vienna, Brussels, and Germany; returned to Russia and published *The Good Accommodation of the Cities,* 1912, which became an important source of ideas and guidelines for Russian town planning in the 20th century; designed one of first garden cities in Russia, the town of Prozorovka (near Moscow), for workers of Moscow-Kazan railway, 1913; took part in working out basic principles of city planning in Soviet Union, 1920–50s, and headed special institute Giprogor for city planning; worked on city plans for Stalingrad, 1929–31, and Baku, 1932–34; design for famous spa resort district of Mineral Waters in Northern Caucasus, 1935–37; prepared official *Architectural and Planning Rules for City Designs,* 1944, the basic document in the State program of reconstruction of Soviet cities destroyed by fascists during World War II; made numerous pattern designs for small rural settlements, collected into groups of villages (so-called agro-cities), 1940–50s; wrote textbook for designers, *Organisation of Green Spaces in Soviet Cities.* Died 1960.

Selected Designs

1904	Estate of Emir of Bukchara, Piatigorsk, Northern Caucasus, Russia
1913	Prozorovka garden town, near Moscow, Russia
1926	Design of red-lines in city plan for Minsk, Belorussia
1926–27	City plan for Vladimir, Russia
1926–28	City plan for Bezhitsa, industrial suburb of Briansk, Russia
1929–30	City plan for Stalingrad, Russia
1930	City plan in competition for Magnitogorsk, Russia; sketch design of reconstruction of Moscow, Russia
1930–31	Living quarters, Stalingrad, Russia
1931	Detailed plan of Tractor factory district, Stalingrad, Russia
1932	Sketch design of city plan, Moscow, Russia

1932–34	District plan of Apsheron peninsula (with V.N. Obraztsov), Azerbaijan
1935–37	District plan, Mineral Waters spa resort district, Northern Caucasus, Russia; city plans for Piatigorsk, Yessentuki, Kislovodsk, and Zheleznovodsk, Mineral Waters district, Russia
1944–45	Plans for rural villages, Russia
1944–46	City plan, detailed plans of city center, main squares, and embankments for post-World War II reconstruction of Rostov-on-Don, Russia
1949	Plans for reconstruction of center, Moscow, Russia

Selected Publications

The Good Accommodation of the Cities, 1912
"The Greenery in the City," *Krasnaya niva* 19 (1924)
"About the Construction of Socialist Stalingrad," *Kommunalnoye delo* 2 (1930)
"Architectural Reconstruction of Moscow," in *Voprosi architekturi*, 1935

"The Planning of District and Resorts of Mineral Waters" (with D.I. Shejnis), *Socialist City* 6 (1937)
The Rules on Architecture and City-Planning for Designs of Urban Settlements, 1944
"The Basic Principles of Planning for Reconstructed Cities," *The Problems of Modern City-Planning* 1 (1947)
The Organisation of Green Spaces in Soviet Cities, 1954

Further Reading

Belousov, Vladimir Nikolaevich, and O.V. Smirnova, *V.N. Semenov*, Moscow: Stroiizdat, 1980
"The First Garden-City in Russia," *Gorodskoye delo* 22 (1912)
"The Russian: Russian Responses to the Garden City Idea," *Architectural Review* 168, no. 96 (1978)
"Urbanism et planification regional dans l'URSS des années trente," *Metropolis* 3, nos. 31–32 (1978)

EKATERINA SHORBAN

Seville, Real Alcázar

Seville, Andalusia, Spain

Location: southeast of the Cathedral of Santa María, in the Santa Cruz quarter of Seville, southeast of the city center

The Real Alcázar of Seville reveals the history of Spain in an eclectic layering of Islamic, Gothic, mudejar, Renaissance, and baroque works. Originally, it was the location of the Roman port and market forum. An early Christian basilica was erected at the site in 426.

In Islamic times there were gardens, orchards, and military grounds in the Mary al-Fidda (Silver Meadow), an esplanade that spread during the 10th and 11th centuries beyond the Umayyad Dar al-Imara (House of the Prince) and the 'Abbāsid Qaṣr al-Muārak (Palace of the Blessed) to the Tagarete, an affluent of the Guadalquivir.

The Almohad walls erected in the 12th century divided the esplanade into the outer Huerta del Parque and inner Huerta de la Alcoba, so called in reference to its oratory or garden pavilion with *al-qubba*, or dome.

Orange (*Citrus sinensis*), lemon (*C. limon*), lime (*C. aurantiifolia*), and citron (*C. medica*) trees were cultivated in the orchards, irrigated from a basin fed by an aqueduct developed on the Roman waterworks called Cañas de Carmona. Sugarcane (*Saccharum officinarum*) was also grown, probably by the Tagarete.

The royal house of the 'Abbāsid Qaṣr al-Muārak, built in the 11th century, looked upon a garden that was later transformed into the Patio del Crucero by the Almohads in the 12th century. This Islamic paradise court is sectioned into four sunken parterres by two pools that cross under a circular path at a central jet fountain. Orange trees were probably planted, as they are now, on the lower ground, with the fruit within easy reach along the paths.

The Patio del Yeso (Court of the Plaster) is a remnant of an Almohad palace built in the 12th century. It consists of a courtyard with a central rectangular basin, hedged by myrtle (*Myrtus communis*) and flanked originally by two, presently one, arcades. The fine plaster tracery supported by the columns reflects on the water, which flows in a runnel from a circular jet fountain inside the Sala de la Justicia (Hall of Justice), built by Alfonso XI over the Islamic palace in 1340. The patio typologically reflects the traditions of Córdoba and ornamentally anticipates the plaster works of Granada.

In the 12th century the Almohads constructed their main palace within the Dar al-Imara. It had a two-level *crucero* (cruciform) patio with crossing and bordering paths above and a central basin, quadrant orange trees, and perimetrical galleries below. The *crucero* patio was likely influenced by the Roman *cryptoporticus,* an enclosed gallery with windows for air and light that was often built partially underground for the moderation of temperature, such as the one at the House of the Exedra in Itálica near Seville.

After 1252, when Alfonso X el Sabio built his palace, which later became known as the Gothic Palace or Halls of Charles V, the courtyard underwent alterations. The covered lower level of the courtyard became the Baths, and the exposed upper level became the Patio de María de Padilla (lover of Peter the Cruel), which consists of four parterres edged by myrtle hedges.

From 1364 to 1366 Peter the Cruel built his Mudejar palace, enlisting artists, masons, and artisans from Toledo, Córdoba, and Granada to reflect the architecture of al-Andalus. Its layout revolves around two patios: one courtly, the Patio de las Doncellas (Court of the Maidens); the other private and intimate, the Patio de las Muñecas (Court of the Dolls).

The *jardines antiguos* or old gardens were developed within the Huerta de la Alcoba in the Renaissance and baroque periods, spatially into compartments of Islamic origin and aesthetically in the style of the Italian mannerism. The vitality and fantasy of mannerism encountered fertile ground for eclectic expression in the sensuality and refinement of the Islamic heritage.

This amalgamation sustained the refreshing ambience of the Islamic tradition in the development of the orchards and *corrales* (pens and yards) as gardens. The gardens are individually sheltered by walls and efficiently irrigated with water that runs from reservoirs along runnels into deep planters. Benches and fountains are clad with *azulejos* (colored and patterned glazed ceramic tiles) in the typically Sevillian manner.

The first old garden to be developed was the Jardín del Príncipe on the west between the Corral de los Puercos and Corral de las Piedras. On the east inside the wall, Charles V began the Jardín del Conde, Jardín de la Alcobilla, and Jardín Antiguo del Cidral, which were later enhanced by Philip II. These three eastern gardens, which had simple layouts with fountains, myrtle, and fruit trees, eventually became two.

Juan Fernández constructed the Cenador de la Alcoba (Pavilion of Charles V) between 1543 and 1546 at the site of the ancient *al-qubba* among the citrus trees. This garden pavilion, a mixture of Mudejar and Italian Renaissance sensibilities, is considered a masterpiece of 16th-century Spanish architecture.

When Philip II renovated the Jardín del Príncipe, Roman topiary was reintroduced to Seville in the form

Patio de las Doncellas at Real Alcázar, Seville, Spain
Copyright J.A. Bueno

of a myrtle *galera* or ship. Mannerist grottoes were also built in the lower level of the Almohad Patio del Crucero, Jardín de las Flores (formerly the Corral de los Puercos), and Jardín de las Damas. At the site of the Corral del Estanque on the east, the Jardín del Chorrón and the Jardín del Estanque were constructed. At the latter, the basin was developed as a pool garden that was later overlooked by the Mirador and Galería del Grutesco designed by Vermondo Resta.

Topical gardens were developed, but later altered, along the *corrales* from the Jardín del Estanque down to the Jardín de las Flores. In the Jardín de la Danza a topiary circle of myrtle nymphs and satyrs appeared to dance. The Jardín del Laberinto probably included a representation of the labyrinth of Crete and the myth of the Minotaur. In the Jardín de la Galera topiary galleys decked with water cannons simulated a naval battle.

Patio del Crucero at Real Alcázar, Seville, Spain
Copyright J.A. Bueno

Philip II developed the Jardín de las Damas (later enlarged) and Jardín de la Santa Cruz (later destroyed) in the Huerta de la Alcoba. In the 17th century, during the reigns of Philip III and Philip IV, the Jardín de las Damas became the paradigm of mannerist gardens in Spain, when it was enhanced with grottoes, fountains, and a water organ, as well as frescoes, sculptures, and grotesque galleries.

The *jardines nuevos* or new gardens were developed beyond the Galería del Grutesco in the Huerta del Parque (later, Huerta del Retiro) at the beginning of the 20th century. These gardens, which were begun by the Marqués de la Vega Inclán and finished by Gómez Millán, include the Jardín Inglés, Jardín del Marqués, and Jardín de los Poetas.

The Jardín del Marqués is a Sevillian garden with Renaissance elements and Granadine waterworks. The Jardín de los Poetas is a Romantic garden aligned on two long rectangular basins that are edged by boxwood (*Buxus sempervirens*)—centered on a circular fountain and anchored by a column at each terminus. The rest of the Huerta del Parque was ceded to the city and enhanced as the Jardines de Catalina de Rivera, popularly known as the Jardines de Murillo.

Synopsis

913–14	'Abd Allāh ibn Sinān builds Dar al-Imara for Umayyad 'Abd ar-Raḥmān III
929–1031	Mary al-Fidda made site of Umayyad gardens, orchards, and military grounds
1023–90	'Abbāsid al-Mu'taḍid and his son al-Mu'tamid build Qaṣr al-Muārak; royal house is developed with patio or garden
1147–1232	Mary al-Fidda divided into Huerta del Parque and Huerta de la Alcoba; Almohad Patio del Crucero developed on Qaṣr al-Muārak patio or garden; Patio del Yeso developed, and Patio del Crucero developed on Dar al-Imara site
12th century	Almohads construct main palace within the Dar al-Imara
1248	Ferdinand III captures Seville, and Alcázar becomes royal Spanish residence

Patio de las Muñecas at Real Alcázar, Seville, Spain
Copyright J.A. Bueno

Patio del Yeso at Real Alcázar, Seville, Spain
Copyright J.A. Bueno

1526	Charles V, Holy Roman Emperor, marries the infanta Isabella of Portugal at the Alcázar
1539	Start of mannerist *jardines antiguos* (old gardens) in Huerta de la Alcoba
1543–46	Juan Fernández builds Cenador de la Alcoba (Pavilion of Charles V) at site of *al-qubba*
1610	Vermondo Resta builds *mirador* overlooking Jardín del Estanque
1612–21	Vermondo Resta builds Galería del Grutesco
1700	Alcázar essentially reaches present layout
1987	UNESCO designates the Alcázar of Seville a World Heritage Site
1993	Patronato del Real Alcázar established

Further Reading

Bonet Correa, A., "El Renacimiento y el Barroco en los jardines musulmanes españoles," *Cuadernos de la Alhambra* 4 (1968)

Bueno, Juan Antonio, "The Patio: Origin, Development, and Transformation of the Hispanic Courtyard," in *Annual Meeting Proceedings*, Washington, D.C.: American Society of Landscape Architects, 1997

Caro, Rodrigo, *Antigüedades, y principado de la ilustrísima ciudad de Sevilla*, Seville: Grande, 1634; reprint, Seville: Alfar, 1982

Chueca Goitia, Fernando, *Historia de la arquitectura española: Edad Antigua y Edad Media*, Madrid: Dossat, 1965

Dickie, James, "The Islamic Garden in Spain," in *The Islamic Garden*, edited by Elisabeth B. MacDougall and Richard Ettinghausen, Washington, D.C.: Dumbarton Oaks, 1976

Marín Fidalgo, Ana, *El Real Alcázar de Sevilla*, Madrid: Aldeasa, 1995; as *Guide to the Real Alcázar of Seville*, translated by Nigel Williams, Madrid: Aldeasa, 1998

Marín Fidalgo, Ana, "Sevilla: los Reales Alcázares," in *Jardín y naturaleza en el reinado de Felipe II*, edited by Carmen Añón and José Luis Sancho, Madrid: Sociedad Estatal para la Conmemoración de los Centenarios de Felipe II y Carlos V, 1998

Newton, Norman T., "The World of Islam: Córdoba, Seville," in *Design on the Land: The Development of Landscape Architecture*, by Newton, Cambridge, Massachusetts: Harvard University Press, 1971

JUAN ANTONIO BUENO

Shalamar Bagh, Lahore. *See* Lahore, Shalamar Bagh

Shalamar Bagh, Srinagar. *See* Srinagar, Shalamar Bagh

Shepherd, Thomas 1779–1835

Scottish Landscape Gardener and Commercial Nursery Owner

Thomas Shepherd was trained as a landscape gardener in Scotland and England. He operated as a nurseryman and landscape gardener in England first under Thomas White, a popular landscape gardener at the end of the 18th century. Shepherd worked as a landscape gardener in his own right according to his own writings between 1800 and 1825, but no gardens designed by him have been identified. His plant nursery at Hackney and later in Sussex supplemented his income and served as a source of plant material for his landscape work.

Shepherd sailed with his family for New Zealand in March 1826 and surveyed a site for a new colony on Stewart Island. This place was unsatisfactory and the settlers sailed for Sydney, where they arrived late in 1826. Shepherd was persuaded by the governor of the colony of New South Wales to settle in Sydney and set up a plant nursery, which was badly needed by the young colony. Given a grant of land, Shepherd spent money and labor to clear the land and prepare the nursery. He received assistance of plant cuttings, roots, and seeds from Alexander McLeay's Elizabeth Bay Garden, which Thomas may have assisted in designing, and from William Macarthur at Camden Park. Both of these gardeners, important and wealthy men of the colony, imported new plants from all parts of the world. Mr. Frazer, the superintendent of the Sydney Botanic Gardens, was another colleague who assisted Shepherd.

The greatest influence exerted by Thomas Shepherd came from his two books. Each comprised a series of lectures prepared to be delivered at the Mechanics School of Arts in Sydney. The first was *Lectures on the Horticulture of New South Wales* given in 1835 and published that same year by the local bookseller William McGarvie. There was a great need for a gardening book specifically related to the conditions and climate of the colony, not to mention the simple complication of the reversal of seasons for the Southern Hemisphere. There had been some gardening guides published in the *New South Wales Almanack* since 1806, but something more substantial was needed. Shepherd's book was just what was required to instruct local gardeners in the growing of vegetables. Shepherd included, for example, the method of growing plants from seeds in a country of uncertain rainfall and discussed the need to keep soil sufficiently damp for the seeds to germinate, describing his own method.

Having succeeded with his first book, Shepherd set out to write another. This was *Lectures on Landscape Gardening in Australia* (1836), which was the first book on the subject to appear outside Britain and five years before the first such book was published in the United States. His ideas for landscape were for the laying of large estates, which was not possible or likely in the young small colony at that time. Shepherd discussed the importance of siting the house and including the surrounding countryside in his landscape concept. His only design in the colony was a plan for Hyde Park in Sydney, which was not carried out. Shepherd was more sensitive to the beauty of the countryside than were many later gardeners and especially recommended the preservation of the eucalyptus or gum trees. He argued against completely clearing land.

Shepherd was very involved in the growing of grapevines for a proposed wine industry. He wrote articles in the newspapers on the subject and was the leader of a committee of investigation reporting on the large collection of grape cuttings growing in the Sydney Botanic Gardens brought from France and Spain by James Busby.

Biography

Born in Kemback, Scotland, 1779. Father was head gardener on estate of Lord Crawford and Lindesay; educated in local school and early in life had ambition to become landscape gardener; learned landscape painting together with David Wilkie; apprenticed to well-known landscape gardener Thomas White; moved to England and designed gardens (but no garden designed by him known), 1800–1825; established nursery at Hackney near London; later moved to south of England, but his wife died leaving him with a young family; landscape business difficult after Napoleonic Wars, and in 1826 accepted offer to take group of settlers to establish settlement in New Zealand; arrived at Stewart Island, New Zealand, but it was found unsuitable, and they sailed on to Sydney, Australia, 1826; established first commercial nursery in colony, in New South Wales, Australia, called Darling Nursery, on government grant of land; wrote and published book *Lectures on the Horticulture of New*

South Wales; became involved in controversy about blight in grape vines (grape-growing for wine production was a matter of importance in the colony at that time); prepared series of lectures entitled *Lectures on Landscape Gardening in Australia*, but died before they could be delivered (published after his death); son-in-law and young sons carried on nursery and also became important figures in horticultural community of New South Wales. Died in Sydney, New South Wales, Australia, 1835.

Selected Publications

Journal of the Brig Rosanna on the Coast of New Zealand 5 March to 12 November 1826, MSS, Sydney, Mitchell Library, 1826

Lectures on the Horticulture of New South Wales, 1835
Lectures on Landscape Gardening in Australia, 1836

Further Reading

Crittenden, Victor, *A Shrub in the Landscape of Fame: Thomas Shepherd, Australian Landscape Gardener and Nurseryman*, Canberra: Mulini Press, 1992
Price, Una Shepherd, *My Family of Shepherds*, Scone, New South Wales: s.n., 1989

VICTOR CRITTENDEN

Shipman, Ellen Biddle 1869–1950

United States Landscape Architect

Ellen Biddle Shipman, one of the leading landscape architects of the early 20th century, specialized in the design and planting of flower gardens. Throughout her long and productive career in the United States (1912–47), Shipman designed hundreds of small residential gardens on Long Island and in suburban New York, northern Ohio, Michigan, Texas, and the South. Today Shipman is recognized as an important pioneer designer; her name is often linked with Marian Cruger Coffin, Beatrix Jones Farrand, and Martha Brookes Hutcheson. With few exceptions, however, Shipman's commissions were limited to the residential arena, while the work of her colleagues encompassed campus or community planning. This can be explained in part by Shipman's insularity at the time of her training. Unlike other women designers of the period, Shipman did not become a professional until midlife when, as a single parent with sole responsibility for three children, she embraced garden design for financial reasons.

Thoroughly versed in gardening and horticultural skills acquired while working in her own garden, Shipman was informally tutored in design and construction by the architect Charles A. Platt about 1910. Both Shipman and Platt lived (and gardened) in the artists' colony in Cornish, New Hampshire, nationally renowned for its vernacular or old-fashioned gardens. Sculptor Augustus Saint-Gaudens, etcher Stephen Parrish, illustrator Maxfield Parrish, and artist Thomas Wilmer Dewing were among the many resident artists whose gardens served as inspiration for Shipman.

Platt, first as a landscape architect and later architect, had executed several pivotal commissions in the Cornish colony that elucidated his ideals of integrated house and garden based on the Italian Renaissance villa. His ideology served as a springboard for Shipman, who used copious quantities of layered plantings and simple ornamental features in place of rigid architectural layouts to achieve privacy, enclosure, and the harmonious relationship of house and garden.

Shipman began collaborating with Platt in 1912, but her responsibilities were often limited to replanting gardens designed by him years earlier. Laverock Hill, the Isaac T. Starr estate in Chestnut Hill, Pennsylvania, dating from 1915, represents a highly successful early Platt and Shipman collaboration, done in the spirit of the partnership gardens designed by Edwin Lutyens and Gertrude Jekyll in England at the turn of the century. Platt's symmetrical design for the walled garden at Laverock Hill was perfectly balanced by Shipman's robust planting of ornamental trees, shrubs, and perennials that created a sense of enclosure. Her scheme for four densely planted flower beds, edged in boxwood and linked with one another across intersecting paths with rose arches, was suggestive of Cornish gardens. Masses of lilacs, flowering cherries, magnolias, and weigelia planted on the exterior walls provided a fragrant and lush background.

Shipman's early independent commissions were inspired by the traditional New England colonial revival garden, a rectangular layout with an informal mix of

Rynwood, estate of Samuel A. Salvage, Glen Head, Long Island, New York
Courtesy of Division of Rare and Manuscript Collections, Cornell University Library

hardy perennials and traditional annuals accented with sundials, fountains, and other simple features. By the early 1920s, after having worked with Platt on a dozen projects, as well as numerous ones on her own, Shipman had developed an identifiable personal style that she rarely deviated from throughout her career. Mattie Edwards Hewitt's evocative photographs of Shipman's gardens from this era, which appeared in *House and Garden, House Beautiful,* and *Garden Magazine,* captured the imagination of countless new clients. Shipman's planting prowess reached its apogee in the long-vanished garden on Long Island designed for the Pruyn sisters, which Fletcher Steele praised for its delicate balance of formality and informality. Eight rectangular beds, divided by axial brick or dirt paths, brimmed with sophisticated plant combinations, in which abstract drifts were planted in response to each plant's character and habit. Shipman's ability to create perpetual bloom (a rigorous replacement of plants requiring teams of trained gardeners) was based on her deep knowledge of horticulture.

Even though most of Shipman's early gardens have disappeared due to lack of maintenance or destruction, the recently restored walled garden at Stan Hywet Hall in Akron, Ohio, is an excellent example of her planting artistry. Shipman's replanting scheme of 1928 (the garden was originally laid out by Warren Manning) called for abundant perennials and annuals densely planted in fan-shaped drifts. She arranged them in sparkling color contrasts rather than in English-style drifts of muted color; white lilies sparkled against masses of dark yew, and ornamental trees created a flowering overhead canopy.

Shipman used this same planting style in the Sarah P. Duke Memorial Gardens at Duke University in North Carolina, one of the largest commissions that the landscape architect undertook in her career. Designed in 1937, it has been continuously open to the public since then. Shipman's design was based on a large bowl-shaped amphitheater, with thousands of plants arranged in seven descending curvilinear terraces, but even in its day it was challenging to maintain such dense residential-style plantings. Also, Shipman was not as conversant with southern plants and growing conditions as she was with a New England plant palette.

Shipman's laurels rest on a commission that she undertook in the 1930s, Longue Vue Gardens in New Orleans, for Edith and Edgar Stern. This imaginative project is perhaps the best surviving example of Shipman's skills as a designer, planting artist, and interior designer. Her large, complex scheme entailed a series of linking garden compartments, including a majestic camellia allée. Soon after installation it became apparent that the garden far outshone the house. Shipman's role in conceiving the replacement house (designed by William and Geoffrey Platt, Charles Platt's sons) was

critical and extended to overseeing the interior furnishings, making Longue Vue the only known example of Shipman's work as an interior designer.

Shipman is also hailed as an advocate for women in the field of landscape architecture. During the 1920s and 1930s she trained dozens of women in her New York City office, many of whom established firms across the country. In the latter part of her career, Shipman was a highly sought after lecturer for garden clubs (most of her clients were garden-club women) and an ardent proponent of victory gardens during the war. The fragile nature of Shipman's delicate and sensual gardens, however, accounts for the near eclipse of her career after her death, but the recent restoration of several of her gardens has brought her name to the forefront again. Shipman's archives can be studied at Cornell University.

Biography

Born in Philadelphia, Pennsylvania, 5 November 1869. Attended Miss Sarah Randolph's School, Baltimore, Maryland, then Harvard Annex, Cambridge, Massachusetts, 1892–93; married playwright Louis Evan Shipman, 1893; trained informally with Charles A. Platt, 1910; established own office in Cornish, New Hampshire, 1912, and began collaboration with Platt; opened office in New York City, early 1920s; between 1912 and retirement in 1947, carried out nearly 600 residential commissions, ranging geographically from New York and New England to South and Midwest. Died in Bermuda, 27 March 1950.

Selected Designs

1912 Fynmere, estate of J.F. Cooper, Cooperstown, New York, United States
1915 Laverock Hill (with Charles Platt), estate of Isaac T. Starr, Chestnut Hill, Pennsylvania, United States
1917 Grahampton (with James L. Greenleaf), estate of Henry W. Croft, Greenwich, Connecticut, United States; The Moorings (with Charles Platt), estate of Russell A. Alger, Jr., Grosse Pointe, Michigan, United States (now Grosse Pointe War Memorial)
1919 Estate of Mary and Neltje Pruyn, East Hampton, New York, United States; Halfred Farms (with Warren Manning), estate of Windsor T. White, Chagrin Falls, Ohio, United States
1924 Chatham Manor, estate of Daniel B. Devore, Fredericksburg, Virginia, United States (now part of the Spotsylvania and Fredericksburg National Military Park)
1925 Estate of Mrs. Holden McGinley, Milton, Massachusetts, United States

1926 Rynwood, estate of Samuel A. Salvage, Glen
      Head, New York, United States; Penwood,
      estate of Carl Tucker, Mount Kisco, New
      York, United States
1928 English Garden (with Warren Manning), Stan
      Hywet Hall, estate of Frank A. Seiberling,
      Akron, Ohio, United States
1929 Cottsleigh, estate of Franklin B. Lord, Syosset,
      New York, United States; Estate of Ralph
      and Dewitt Hanes, Winston-Salem, North
      Carolina, United States
1930 Aetna Life, Hartford, Connecticut, United
      States
1931 Rose Terrace, estate of Anna Dodge, Grosse
      Pointe, Michigan, United States
1935 Longue Vue, estate of Edgar and Edith Stern,
      New Orleans, Louisiana, United States
1937 Sarah P. Duke Memorial Gardens, Duke
      University, Durham, North Carolina, United
      States

Selected Publications

"How I Teach My Own Children," *Ladies Home
  Journal* (September 1911)
"Window Gardens for Little Money," *Ladies Home
  Journal* (September 1911)
"The Saint-Gaudens Memorial," *Garden Club of
  America Bulletin* (May 1948)

Further Reading

Close, Leslie Rose, "Ellen Biddle Shipman," in
  *American Landscape Architecture: Designers and
  Places,* edited by William H. Tishler, Washington,
  D.C.: Preservation Press, 1989
Karson, Robin S., *The Muses of Gwinn: Art and Nature
  in a Garden Designed by Warren H. Manning,
  Charles A. Platt, and Ellen Biddle Shipman,*
  Sagaponack, New York: Sagapress, 1995
Meador, Deborah Kay, "The Making of a Landscape
  Architect: Ellen Biddle Shipman and Her Years at the
  Cornish Art Colony," M.L.A. thesis, Cornell
  University, 1989
Nevins, Deborah, "The Triumph of Flora: Women and
  the American Landscape, 1890–1935," *The
  Magazine Antiques* 127, no. 4 (April 1985)
Tankard, Judith B., *The Gardens of Ellen Biddle
  Shipman,* Sagaponack, New York: Sagapress, 1996
Tankard, Judith B., "The Artistry of Ellen Shipman
  (Ohio's Stan Hywet Hall)," *Horticulture* 94, no. 1
  (1997)
Tankard, Judith B., "Ellen Biddle Shipman's New
  England Gardens," *Arnoldia* 57, no. 1 (1997)
Tankard, Judith B., "Shipman in Seattle," *Pacific
  Horticulture* 58, no. 2 (1997)
Tankard, Judith B., "Ellen Biddle Shipman," in *Pioneers
  of American Landscape Design,* edited by Charles
  Birnbaum and Robin S. Karson, New York: McGraw
  Hill, 2000
Van Buren, Deborah E., "Landscape Architecture and
  Gardens in the Cornish Colony: The Careers of Rose
  Nichols, Ellen Shipman, and Frances Duncan,"
  Women's Studies 14 (1988)

JUDITH B. TANKARD

Shisen-dō

Kyoto, Japan

Location: approximately 6 miles (9.5 km) northeast of
  Kyoto station

Early in Japan's Edo period (1603–1867) the samurai
Ishikawa Jōzan, who had once served the great
Tokugawa Ieyasu, deliberately turned his energies to the
quite different realm of the arts. Shisen-dō, or the Hall
of the Poetry Immortals, was his creative refuge from
the constraints and conformity of urban life. Together
with its small upper garden, it represents a now rare
expression of a mid-17th century Japanese intellectual's
taste.

In 1600 Ieyasu, with Jōzan in his retinue, quelled the
last of his opponents at the battle of Sekigahara. With
this decisive victory the Tokugawa clan came into
power. After decades of civil war, stability was now
attained through the imposition of Chinese neo-Confu-
cian principles of social and political order. As the century progressed, however, a certain class of scholars
were influenced in other ways by the continent. This literati, known as the *bunjin,* avidly absorbed and emulated
Chinese classical poets and artists. Jōzan (1583–1672)
was among their number. For these cultivated gentlemen, the arts offered avenues of self-expression and

Shisen-dō, Kyoto, Japan
Copyright Marc Treib

informality that were not found in the highly conventional society of their day.

Released from his obligations as a samurai in 1635, Jōzan was free to nurture his artistic persona. In 1641 he began to create Shisen-dō, taking as his model the secluded retreats of Chinese poets such as T'ao Ch'ien and Lin Pu. Jōzan lived out the remaining years of his life at Shisen-dō, writing verse in the Chinese style and perfecting his Chinese calligraphy. The building and garden have been altered since his time, yet what remains is sufficient to evoke Jōzan's retreat, the world of the *bunjin*. This was a place where the arts enriched each other—a painted scroll with calligraphy, a garden with a poem. Accordingly, Shisen-dō's garden was one facet of the aesthetic milieu Jōzan created around himself for the very purpose of evoking his own aesthetic expression.

Jōzan's own name for his retreat was *Ōtotsusō*, the Trompe l'oeil Nest. He composed it around a number of

features and gave each a poetic name. From the Lesser Paradise Cave, the humble entrance gate at the street level, a narrow shaded pathway takes the guest toward Jōzan's secluded enclave. Another threshold, the Old Plum Gate, gives access to the rear court behind the simple, unostentatious dwellings. The first room entered is the Hall of the Poetry Immortals (the *Shisen-dō*), the source of the site's modern-day name. This was Jōzan's study, the most important room in the residences of the *bunjin*. Here Jōzan surrounded himself with imaginative portraits of the Chinese poets he revered most, 36 in all. The originals by Kanō Tan'yū have since been replaced with fresh images by the 20th-century artist Shūsei. From this room Jōzan and his privileged guests could ascend the stairs of the Tower for Whistling at the Moon to enjoy views of the garden and beyond.

To the left of Jōzan's study, looking towards the garden, he had another room for reading called the Nest for Hunting among the Rue. Today in front of these two rooms closely planted azaleas, carefully trimmed into perfect rounds, all but hide the Shallow of Floating Leaves, the small stream that flows through them. A pagoda, barely taller than the shrubs, catches the eye. In contrast to this area's close planting, the space to the right is mostly comprised of an empty expanse of brushed sand; rounded azaleas at its far edge serve to accentuate its two-dimensionality. The branches of a beautiful old white camellia reach out over the space.

The sound of the garden's Waterfall for Washing away Ignorance is intermittently punctuated by the clacking of bamboo on rock. This is made by the water mortar (*sōzu* or *shishi-odoshi*) just beside the path leading to the lower garden. This simple device was originally used in rural areas to scare away any creatures that might otherwise linger to eat the crops. Water is made to flow into a length of bamboo sealed at one end and attached to a crossbar. When it is filled, the bamboo tips over and spills its contents. Once empty, it swings back up, bouncing on a strategically placed rock as it does so. Its auditory contribution to the garden was not lost on the poetic ear of Jōzan.

While the upper garden adjacent to the building is thought to still reflect Jōzan's intentions, the lower garden is more recent and quite different in mood. Here a pond surrounded by irises and an arbor of wisteria provide color that Jōzan would have likely enjoyed, for in his time there was an Embankment of a Hundred Flowers that is no longer evident today. The Chinese poets whom he admired used to enjoy long debates over the relative merits of different flowers.

Jōzan imagined his retreat in relation to the landscape beyond his own domain. He commissioned the painting of a scroll, *A Pictorial Record of Twelve Scenes at the Ōtotsusō*, to give form to his abstract conception. Some of the scenes in the scroll could indeed be seen in or from the garden, such as "Cherry Blossoms Filling the Path" and "Plowing in the Rain at the Village Out Front." Others, however, could only be imagined: Shisen-dō's location made a view of "Leisurely Clouds Above the Peak of Mount T'ai" (i.e., Mount Hiei, north of Kyoto) or "The City Walls of Osaka" physically impossible. Sites such as these, however, held much cultural and historical significance. Perhaps with this schema the reclusive Jōzan was tacitly acknowledging his wider cultural context and locating his aesthetic stance within it.

Shisen-dō is a place where many arts lived in creative rapport. This is perhaps best felt in one of its fruits, the poem by Jōzan titled *An Autumn Night: Depicting Activity Within Quiescence:*

White hairs in autumn—I am moved by the scene.
In the mountains I live, companion to the moon,
  passing what's left of my life.
Late at night, the ten thousand sounds of nature
  have all given way to silence—
I can only hear the sound of the water mortar
  knocking against the rock.
(translation by Chaves, 1991)

Synopsis

1583	Ishikawa Jōzan born
1600	Tokugawa Ieyasu victorious at the Battle of Sekigahara, with Jōzan in his service
1635	Jōzan leaves his posting with the Asano clan and resides at the temple of Shōkoku-ji, Kyoto
1641	Jōzan begins to create Shisen-dō (Hall of the Poetry Immortals)
1672	Death of Ishikawa Jōzan
1716	Shisen-dō placed in the care of the Shingon Buddhist sect
1743	In the care of the Sōtō Zen Buddhist sect to the present day
1825	After a period of neglect, some rebuilding of the garden carried out
1945–	Lower garden levels added

Further Reading

Bring, Mitchell, and Josse Wayembergh, *Japanese Gardens: Design and Meaning*, New York: McGraw Hill, 1981

Chaves, Jonathan, "Jōzan and Poetry," in *Shisendō, Hall of the Poetry Immortals*, by J. Thomas Rimer et al., New York: Weatherhill, 1991

Hayakawa, Masao, *Niwa*, Tokyo: Heibonsha, 1967; 2nd edition, 1979; as *The Garden Art of Japan*, translated by Richard L. Gage, New York: Weatherhill, 1973

Kuck, Loraine E., *The World of the Japanese Garden: From Chinese Origins to Modern Landscape Art*, New York: Walker/Weatherhill, 1968

Rimer, J. Thomas, "Ishikawa Jōzan," in *Shisendō, Hall of the Poetry Immortals*, by J. Thomas Rimer et al., New York: Weatherhill, 1991

Suzuki, Hiroyuki, "The Garden of the Shisendō: Its *Genius Loci*," in *Shisendō, Hall of the Poetry Immortals*, by J. Thomas Rimer et al., New York: Weatherhill, 1991

Treib, Marc, and Ron Herman, *A Guide to the Gardens of Kyoto*, Tokyo: Shufunotomo, 1980

FRAN NOLAN

Shi Tao (1642?–1707?)

Chinese Artist

Shi Tao was not only a great painter and calligrapher but also an excellent art theorist. Scholars are still confused about Shi Tao's dates; different sources give his date of birth as 1630, 1636, 1640, 1641, and 1642. Similarly, his death is given as 1707, 1713, 1718, and 1720. Shi Tao also has innumerable assumed names, both artistic and Buddhist. Even though he is well respected and his works are highly appreciated, much about his life is uncertain.

Shi Tao was born in Quanzhou City, Guangxi Province, and was a descendant of a prince's family. After his father's death, a palace coup forced Shi Tao, then four years old, into exile with his servant, and he became a Buddhist monk. Then a lifetime of wandering, homelessness, and misery began. He was active in Anhui Province, Nanjing, and Yangzhou, and in his later years he settled in Yangzhou.

Shi Tao's life can be divided into five periods. The Wuchang period (1642–62), during which Shi Tao was protected and sponsored by an anonymous guardian, involved studies of the Buddhist scripture, literature, painting, and calligraphy. Few works of this period have survived. During the Xuancheng period (1666–79), Shi Tao traveled through South China to visit the famous Buddhist masters and persons of virtue. He visited Yellow Mountain several times, which gave him inspiration for his career as an artist. From 1667 he lived in the Guangjiao Temple of Jingting Mountain and called himself Xiaoshengke (Guest of Hinayana). His works of this period were deeply influenced by the master of the Yellow Mountain school, Mei Quing (Yuangong, 1623–97), and his personal style of painting was formed.

During the Nanjing period (1680–89), Shi Tao was famous, and he spent four years in solitude. He then rejoined society and became acquainted with many scholars, artists, and members of the upper class. In 1684 and 1687, he was received by Emperor Kangxi. At that time, his landscape painting was in its mature period, and he also started to create his flower-and-bird paintings. Shi Tao was leading a new school of painting, and nearly half of his surviving paintings are the works of this period.

During his Beijing period (1689–92), at the invitation of a prince, Shi Tao went to Beijing, the capital, and painted for the nobility. Finally, during the Yangzhou period (1692–1707), Shi Tao resumed secular life and became a professional painter. He named himself Dadizi (A Great Cleaner).

The works of Shi Tao represent and express fundamental social change. His main works are landscape paintings, but he also excelled at paintings of flowers and plants, especially of orchids and bamboo. He has not left as many figure paintings as landscape paintings. Shi Tao's painting overcomes the limitations of orderly traditional painting methods, and he created his own style. In general, Shi Tao's painting was not constrained by any conventional pattern, and he modeled his works on nature. His landscape paintings have a number of distinguishing characteristics. First, he used his pen freely, and his paintings demonstrate a skillful combination of power, simplicity, and vigor. Second, his works show a rich and varied use of ink. Third, his composition of picturesque scenes in his paintings is always innovative. He paid more attention to imaginative creativity and originality. Fourth, his landscapes are always evocative of an imposing spirit and power. Shi Tao demonstrates his gifted artistry in many ways, and he created his own technique for landscape painting.

Shi Tao left a great deal of literature on the theory of painting, including poems and annotations on the scroll paintings. It reflects his thinking of painting as a discipline. His most famous written works are *Hua Yu Lu* (The Quotation on Paintings) and *Hua Pu* (The Book on Paintings). The manuscript of the former was published in 1728, and it represents some of the most important artistic thinking in the history of Chinese fine art and aesthetics.

See also Ge Yuan

Biography
Born Zhu Ruoji in Quanzhou City, Guangxi Province, China, 1642. Exiled to Wuchang, where he became a Buddhist monk and took styled name of Shi Tao, 1645; painted orchids, 1654; visited Yellow Mountain, 1655; painted first landscape in Wuchang, 1657; settled in Xuancheng City and lived in Guangjiao Temple of Jingting Mountain, where he was given name Xiaoshengke ("Guest of Hinayana"); visited Yangzhou, 1678; moved to Nanjing, 1680; stayed in Yangzhou from 1681–82; from 1683–87, lived in Nanjing; interviewed by Emperor Kangzi in Nanjing, 1684; lived in Yangzhou, 1687–89; interviewed second time by Emperor Kangxi in Yangzhou, 1687; lived in Peking from 1689–92; settled again in Yangzhou, 1692. Died in Yangzhou, 1707.

Further Reading
Li, Wancai, *Shi Tao: A Library of the Chinese Painting Masters of Ming and Qing Dynasty,* Jilin Fine Arts Press, 1996

Xu, Jianrong and Xingyi Cai *Shi Tao: The Encyclopedia of Chinese Masters of Painting, Qing Dynasty,* Shanghai: Shanghai People's Fine Arts Press, 1998

Yang, Chengyin, *The Essence of the Painting Discipline of Shi Tao,* Shanghai: Shanghai People's Fine Arts Press, 1996

ZHENG SHILING

Shi Zi Lin

Jiangsu Province, China

Location: Suzhou, Yuanlin lu No. 23

Shi Zi Lin is a small but exquisite garden in the northwest of Suzhou. It is famous for its design and for the rockeries, built of Tai Hu (Big Lake) rocks. It represents the garden style of the Yuan dynasty (1260–1360) and has a unique position in the history of Chinese gardens.

During the more than 600 years of its existence, the garden has undergone many changes. It belonged to the monastery of the Buddhist Chan sect (Japanese Zen), and it was established in the year 1342 by the monk Tianru in the memory of his teacher Zhongfeng on a Song dynasty (960–1279) garden site. The whole was called the Monastery of the Lion Grove (Shi Zi Lin Si), purportedly because several lion-shaped rocks were found on the site. Another explanation is that the name reminded the founder of his former home, the Lion Cliff in the Xitianmu Mountains in Zhejiang Province. The name had symbolic connotations, as Buddha's seat is called the Lion Seat. The garden, which provided space for quiet life and meditation in the middle of a city, had features in common with the private retreats of the intellectuals and retired officials in Suzhou. In the year 1352 the name of the monastery was changed to Puti Zheng Zong Si (Bodhi Orthodox Monastery).

At the end of the Yuan and at the beginning of the Ming dynasty (1368–1644) the garden was the meeting place of local painters and poets who had close connections with the Chan monks. The monk Weize described the garden and its life in 14 poems. In the year 1373 the painter Ni Zan (1301–74), one of the Four Masters of the Yuan dynasty, who is said to have arranged the rockeries in the garden, was asked by the monk Ruhai to paint Shi Zi Lin. His painting in the form of a horizontal scroll reflects the subdued atmosphere of the garden. Shi Zi Lin was also the main theme of a picture album attributed to Xu Ben (ca. 1399) and other works.

From surviving documents it is evident that the original garden located behind the monastery was quite simple. Its main features were bamboo groves and Tai Hu rocks of fantastic shapes representing mountains. Tall trees provided shade so that summer there was as cool as autumn. There was a Lion Peak (Shi Zi), a lake with a bridge, and several rustic garden structures—a hut for meditation, a place to study, and a hall to receive visitors. Tianru noted in a poem that there he felt as though he were surrounded by thousands of mountains, although he lived in a city. After Ruhai's death the monks scattered in all directions, and the monastery was left to its fate.

Eventually the place was taken over by an influential local family called Shi. There followed a period of decline. In the year 1648 the monastery was restored to its original function. In 1703 the Qing emperor Kang Xi visited the garden on one of his southern tours. At the beginning of the Qian Long era (1736–95) the garden was separated from the monastery by a wall. It was purchased by the Huang family and its name changed to She Yuan. It was rebuilt and when Emperor Qian Long visited the garden in 1762, he was impressed by it. After returning to the capital, he decided to use it as a model for a garden in the imperial park Yuan Ming Yuan (the Garden of Perfect Brightness) and also in the Bi Shu Shan Zhuang (Imperial Mountain Resort) in Chengde. With the decline of the Huang family the garden was neglected, trees and stones were sold, and pavilions and other structures collapsed. In 1917 the garden was bought by a Mr. Runsheng Pei and completely reconstructed. Most of the extant pavilions and halls were built during the next ten years. In 1937 when the Japanese occupied Suzhou, the garden buildings became living quarters for the army. In 1949 Pei donated the garden to the government of the Chinese People's Republic, and after renovation it was opened to the public.

The grounds of the garden are almost square. On a limited space of approximately two acres (0.8 ha) of originally flat ground, the sophisticated methods of Chinese garden art created the illusion of a mountain retreat. The most important feature of the garden is the

A rockery constructed of Tai Hu rocks in the courtyard of Shi Zi Lin garden
Copyright Robert M. Craig

Tai Hu rocks, natural sculptures formed by the waters of nearby lake Tai, where they were submerged for decades. There is rhythm in their lines, softness or roughness on their surface. In this garden they are used in many ingenious ways. Isolated magnificent rocks resembling lions in different postures enhance the contemplative atmosphere of the garden. Grouped together they resemble mountain ranges. Trees grow out of their crevices, and underneath there are caves and tunnels. Carefully selected rocks line the banks of the pond and were also used to make a waterfall. The winding path and covered walkways climbing up and down the artificial hills from the shade of the caves to the full light of a bright day lead the visitor from one scene to another.

While the composition of the rockery, largest in Suzhou gardens, divides the central space, different architectural structures, pavilions, towers, halls, and so on are mostly located closer to the boundaries.

Entering Shi Zi Lin, the first building to be seen is the Banquet Hall for the Honored (Yanyu Tang) and the Small Square Hall (Xiao Fang Ting) behind it. From there, nine Tai Hu rocks shaped like lions can be seen. The nearby veranda Pointing to the Cypress (Zhi Bo Xuan) was used to entertain guests. The bamboo grove to the west and the Five Pine Court Yard (Wu Song Yuan) are part of the original Shi Zi Lin. On the bank of the pond shaded by the drooping willows is the Lotus Hall (He Hua Ting) and the famous Real Interest Pavilion (Zhen Qu Ting) with a horizontal board inscribed by the Emperor Qiang Long. The pond is crossed by a zig-zag bridge leading to the Middle Lake Pavilion (Hu Xin Ting). The Stone Boat (Shi Fang) further to the north has the function of a tea pavilion. A covered walkway leads up the hill to the Flying Water Pavilion (Fei Pu Ting) with an artificial waterfall. The Plum Tower (Wen Mei Ge) surrounded by plum trees was where the Suzhou literati met. The Fan pavilion (Shan Ting) offers a view of all the buildings in the garden. In front of the Standing in the Snow Pavilion (Li Xue Tang) are Tai Hu rocks of different shapes suggesting lions, frogs, and other animals, and there is also the famous group called the Ox Eats Crab While the Lion Watches (Shi Zi Jing Guan Niu Chi Xia). The Sleeping Clouds Chamber (Wo Yu Yun Shi) surrounded by rocks suggests an atmosphere of solitude. Thus the material objects in this garden express abstract ideas that reveal the essence of nature.

Synopsis

1342	Construction of garden and Monastery of the Lion Grove (Shi Zi Lin Si)
1352	Name of monastery changed to Bodhi Orthodox Monastery (Puti Zheng Zong Si)
1373	Ni Zan paints picture of garden
early 15th C.	Site enters period of decline after being taken over by Shi family
1648	Monastery begins functioning again
1703	Qing emperor Kang Xi visits garden
ca. 1740	Garden separated from monastery by wall and purchased by Huang family; garden's name changed to She Yuan
1762	Qing emperor Qian Long visits garden
19th century	Garden again enters period of decline
1917	Architect Runsheng Pei purchases the garden
1926	Reconstruction of garden is completed
1937	Occupying Japanese army uses garden's buildings as living quarters
1949	Pei donates garden to government of People's Republic of China; after renovation, garden opened to public

Further Reading

Hrdlička, Věnceslava, and Zdeněk Hrdlička, *Chinesische Gartenkunst,* Prague: Aventinum, and Hanau, Germany: Dausien, 1998

Hu, Dongchu, *The Way of the Virtuous: The Influence of Art and Philosophy on Chinese Garden Design,* Beijing: New World Press, 1991

Johnston, R. Stewart, *Scholar Gardens in China: A Study and Analysis of the Spatial Design of the Chinese Private Garden,* Cambridge and New York: Cambridge University Press, 1991

Keswick, Maggie, and Charles Jencks, *The Chinese Garden: History, Art, and Architecture,* London: Academy Editions, and New York: Rizzoli, 1978

Ren, Changqiu, and Yanan Meng, *Zhong guo yuan lin shi,* Beijing: Yanshan chuban she, 1993

Zhong, Junhua, *Sights and Scenes of Suzhou,* Beijing: Zhaohua, 1983

Suzhou: A Garden City, Beijing: Foreign Languages Press, 1984

Tong, Bao, *Suzhou Yuanlin,* Shanghai: Tongji daxue chuban she, 1987

Věna Hrdličková

Shoden-ji

Kyoto, Japan

Location: northwestern Kyoto, approximately 5 miles (8 km) north-northwest of Kyoto train station

The Shoden-ji Temple, situated in the hills in the northwestern part of Kyoto, is famous for its elegant and lyrical *kare-sansui* garden (dry landscape garden) laid out in 1653, called Shishi-no-ko Watashi (Lion Cub Bridge). The temple belongs to the Rinzai sect of Zen Buddhism. The garden follows the tradition of monastic Zen gardens of the early Edo period (1600–1868), which were to be viewed from the inside of the temple from a settled point, the composition keenly reflecting the qualities of a painting. As a rule they were positioned on the flat area in front of the abbot's quarters and backed onto a low wall.

The stylistic lineage of the Shoden-ji garden can be traced directly to the garden of the Ryoan-ji Temple; however, it is worked not in rocks but entirely in living clumps of pruned azaleas. On a small stretch of white sand (365 sq. m [400 sq. yd.]) are three groupings of shrubs, the distinct, immaculately rounded shapes

A garden at Shoden-ji
Photo by Agnieskza Whelan

arranged into a configuration of three, five, and seven. They are gently floating over the sand, close to a whitewashed and tiled wall. Beyond the wall a rich background of cedars, bamboo, maples, and pines creates a contrast of colors and dimensions before receding down along the steep slope of the hill, on which the temple is built. A vast expanse of the sky opens up above, adorned with a distant view of Mount Hiei. The view beyond is part of the garden's design as *shakkei*, the borrowed landscape. The garden faces east; a wide vista of the Kyoto plain opens to the front while from behind it enjoys the security of the sheltering hill. A path to the right side of the garden leads over the sand to the ornate gate and out toward utility gardens and a cemetery, both used as part of the religious practices. One more gate, a modest one in the north wall of the garden, exists, although no path leads to it.

With a minimum of means the garden touches on the Buddhist themes of immortality and harmony in the universe. The sand is often interpreted as an ocean bearing the Islands of the Blessed, on which Mount Horai is a prominent feature, while the clusters of shapes refer to the symbolic invocations of Buddha triads or other religious ideas. The meanings of the garden recede in importance before its use as part of the monastic routine, which is dedicated to the search for the true Buddha nature of every individual. In the Rinzai Zen that search involves concentrating on all aspects of human activities in an effort to practice both meditation in action and still meditation. In the context of the garden this would mean practical maintenance and contemplative appreciation.

The Zen rock and plant gardens of the type similar to Shoden-ji were known for a century and a half before this one was built. But what the gardens of the earlier Muromachi period (1333–1568) achieved with an uncompromising austerity of form and spirit, here was realized with soft simplicity, accentuated by rounded outlines of plants and by their seasonal blossom. The sophisticated ease of the garden was further heightened by the noble shapes of surrounding trees, living their separate, untamed lives outside the ordered enclosure, and by the spectacle of the changing sky and the fleeting beauty of Mount Hiei appearing from behind the clouds. These characteristics point to the inspiration of Enshu Kobori (1579–1647), although there seems to be no possibility that he actually designed it.

Kobori was the greatest master of *o-karikomi*, working with topiary, and his were the most celebrated gardens of this technique—Raikyu-ji in Okayama Prefecture and Daichi-ji in Minakuchi, Shiga Prefecture. He was skilled in incorporating aesthetically and symbolically a distant view into the gardens. His designs were characterized by richness of form and color checked by the discipline of Zen thought, an elegant ease, and a gentle spirit. The Kobori connection at Shoden-ji is also reinforced by the presence in the temple's history of Ishin Suden (1569–1633), abbot of Nanzen-ji and a superior of Shoden-ji. Suden furnished Shoden-ji with a new *hojo* (abbot's quarters), a building that he transported from the Fushimi castle, once Hideyoshi Toyotomi's stronghold, destroyed by Tokugawa. A highly influential political figure of the early decades of the Tokugawa shogunate, Suden promoted values of sophisticated, artful, and informed beauty. Enshu Kobori answered these values directly, having served the first three Tokugawa shoguns himself as a consummate mediator of Zen Buddhism to courtiers and lords. Suden commissioned Kobori to design gardens of Nanzen-ji and its subtemple, Konchi-in, Kyoto.

The beautiful forest surroundings had always made Shoden-ji a favorite meditative retreat with the highest elite—the emperors Kameyama and Godai-go were very fond of it, as were the shoguns Ashikaga, Hideyoshi Toyotomi, and Iyeiasu Tokugawa.

Maintaining the shapes of plants was extremely difficult, and few gardens of this type exist. In the late 17th century the temple experienced heavy monastic taxation from which it never recovered. The Kyoto Forest Society restored the neglected garden in 1935. Some rocks added to the garden during the Meiji period (1868–1912) have been removed, and the topiary clumps have been planted with mixtures of *Rhododendron cv.*, *Gardenia jasminoides*, *Aucuba japonica*, *Eurya japonica*, *Nandina domestica*, *Camelia sasanqua*, and *Ardisia japonica*.

Synopsis

1261–64	Foundation and establishment of Shoden-ji in Ichijyo-Idegawa by Chinese priest Funei
1282	Temple moved to present location
1653	Creation of garden
1935	Restoration of garden by Kyoto Forest Society and removal of rocks introduced in Meiji period

Further Reading

Ito, Teiji, *The Gardens of Japan*, Tokyo and New York: Kodansha, 1984

Shigemori, Mirei, et al., *Nihon teienshi taikei* (The Great Compendium of Japanese Garden History), vol. 15, Tokyo: Shakai Shisosha, 1971–76

Nitschke, Günter, *Gartenarchitektur in Japan: Rechter Winkel und natürliche Form*, Cologne, Germany: Taschen, 1991; as *Japanese Gardens: Right Angle and Natural Form*, translated by Karen Williams, Cologne, Germany: Taschen, 1993

AGNIESZKA WHELAN

Shrubbery

The term *shrubbery* seems to have been first used in England in the late 1740s by William Shenstone and Lady Luxborough. Perhaps derived from earlier usages (*shrubbery* might mean "land covered in scrub"), this term developed new meaning in the 1750s. It came to signify a graduated display of trees and shrubs, sometimes with flowers. In large part the feature was generated in the mid-18th-century landscape garden by the influx of new woody species, notably from colonial North America. Importation accelerated after 1735, when Peter Collinson made an agreement with his collector in Philadelphia, John Bartram, to supply seeds and living plants to subscribers in England. In this sense the shrubbery was like other collections of exotica—a reassembling of the botanical riches of the Garden of Eden. Yet the attempt to regiment the shrubbery within the English landscape garden may have gained its potency in counterpoint to the chaos and anarchy that collectors such as Mark Catesby experienced and depicted in the wilderness of the New World.

It was in the English "wilderness" (a hedged plantation laid out in geometric configurations like the French bosquet) that the characteristics of the shrubbery first evolved in the 1720s. Around wilderness quarters gardeners gradually reduced the height of hedges below eye level as they realized that a slope of flowering shrubs could be introduced as a decorative border. This corresponded to William Kent's moves to "informalize"

English gardens in the 1730s. The model of three ranks of shrubs and trees behind a three-foot-high hedge slowly gave way to the shrubbery proper: an irregular plantation of six or seven ranks, in which tall trees formed the apex and a band of low shrubs or a border of flowers decorated the outer margin "encompassing" the clump or belt. Horticultural writers used the analogy of seats in a theater to describe the tiered arrangement. Thus this new fashion of "theatrical" planting became linked to the mania for American shrubs and exotic shrubberies in the consumer-driven world of Georgian England.

While the wilderness was generally a woodland garden pierced by shady walks (both straight and serpentine), the shrubbery varied from a sunny and floriferous feature to a largely shaded one. The American garden with its enclosed labyrinthine paths, for example, sustained the traditions of woodland gardening, while the shrubbery of the *ferme ornée* represented a new type—one-directional, airy, and expansive. Joseph Spence's plan entitled "Order of Planting after Mr. Southcote's manner" (ca. 1749) records a graduated plantation of trees, shrubs, and flowers that was edged by pinks along a sand walk around a field. This sun-filled circuit shrubbery evolved into extensive linear shrubberies—a dominant prototype for pleasure grounds in the second half of the 18th century. Unlike the enclosed wilderness, such one-sided shrubberies afforded views out over the park.

Shrubbery clumps on lawn formed the second important prototype. The clump was first evident in Robert Greening's plans for the pleasure ground at Wimpole (ca. 1752) and in sketches by Thomas Wright. These clumps were the counterpart to larger clumps of trees in the landscape park as well as to smaller clumps of flowers in the Picturesque flower garden first developed by Richard ("Dickie") Bateman in the 1730s. Richard Woods's proposal for the Elysium Garden at Audley End, 1780, represents a unified model: a self-contained world of flowers and shrubs within the wider landscape garden. It was enclosed by linear shrubberies and ornamented by floral and woody clumps. Here the three features often considered distinct within the Picturesque style—the pleasure ground, the shrubbery, and the flower garden—were melded into one.

The shrubbery also served purposes other than display: it could be a utilitarian screen to farm buildings or kitchen gardens, a frame for temples and eye-catchers, or a backdrop to statuary; it could act as a means of enclosure, both pictorial and functional (sometimes, for example, substituting for a hedge around a rare collection of plants, or concealing a path used by gardeners or servants); and it could direct the visitor circuits around the landscape garden, providing shelter from wind and sun. At Painshill Charles Hamilton used shrubbery not merely to display exotics and control the illusions of space but also to reinforce mood—gloomy near the Mausoleum and joyful by the Temple of Bacchus.

Several themes besides theatrical graduation dominated discussion of shrubbery in the 18th century. One was the segregation of evergreen and deciduous species. Inherited from the 17th-century tradition of evergreen groves that John Evelyn called "Perennial-greenes, and perpetuall Springs," the evergreen shrubbery was sometimes regarded as a "Winter Garden." In practice, designers seem to have intermixed the two types of plants as early as the 1740s, but even as late as the 1770s, distinct deciduous and evergreen plantations were favored by James Meader in *The Planter's Guide* (1779). The advocates of separation pointed to the cultural and aesthetic benefits. This was especially true in winter when bare stems could appear a "deformation" amid "perennial verdures."

Another theme was a debate over the merits of composition versus collection. As the number of exotics increased through importation, the realization arose that picturesque compositional balance was being upset by the "excessive variety" of horticultural collections. By the late 18th century, Richard Payne Knight could ridicule the shrubbery in his poem *The Landscape* (1794):

So the capricious planter often tries
By quaint variety to cause surprise;
Collects of various trees a motley host,
Natives of every clime and every coast;
Which, placed in chequer'd squares, alternate grow,
And forms and colours unconnected show.

The alternation of individual plants along rows—the so-called mixed or mingled style of planting, which the 18th-century Picturesque had adopted from the baroque—accentuated the muddle resulting from this overabundance of species. As a response, and in line with changing aesthetics, designers shifted to the massing of the "select or grouped" style of planting. John Nash's shrubberies at the Brighton Pavilion and St. James's Park, London, presented "drifts" of shrubs within an irregular planform. By 1823 Henry Phillips in *Sylva Florifera*, the first work exclusively devoted to the shrubbery, could sum up the shift from mixing to massing in a few words: "A shrubbery should be planted, as a court or stage dress is ornamented, for general effect, and not for particular and partial inspection."

John Claudius Loudon's departure from Picturesque aesthetics, the Gardenesque of the 1830s, reintroduced the idea of specimen planting with a new emphasis on spatial autonomy. In 1852 Joshua Major advocated specimens in an "ornamental fringe" around the shrubbery, while in 1850 Edward Kemp promoted Nash's idea of individual trees as "outliers" on lawns. However, such botanical emphasis did not affect the general movement to drifts and massing within the deep recesses and promontories of Regency and Victorian shrubberies.

The lists of plants ordered at Brighton between 1816 and 1830 also point to the upsurge in new species from the Orient, such as *Aucuba japonica* (Japanese laurel), *Magnolia liliiflora* (Lily-flowered magnolia), and *Ligustrum lucidum* (Chinese privet). These plants would eventually supersede the North American exotics, some of which had proved only partially viable in English conditions. A new wave of importation of early- or late-flowering evergreens from western North America and China—including *Mahonia aquifolium* (Oregon grape holly), *Garrya elliptica* (Silk-tassel bush), and *Osmanthus × fortunei*—also helped foster the return of the Winter Garden. Evergreens had already made a comeback in the Regency period, notably in Mrs. Siddon's residence on the Harrow Road, but by the Victorian period the shrubbery could boast of being not merely perennially green but also almost perpetually flowering.

Further Reading

Kemp, Edward, *How to Lay Out a Small Garden,* London, 1850

Laird, Mark, *The Flowering of the Landscape Garden: English Pleasure Grounds, 1720–1800,* Philadelphia: University of Pennsylvania Press, 1999

Loudon, John Claudius, *An Encyclopaedia of Gardening,* 2 vols., London, 1822; new edition, 1835; reprint, New York: Garland, 1982

Major, Joshua, *The Theory and Practice of Landscape Gardening,* London, 1852

Meader, James, *The Planter's Guide; or, Pleasure Gardener's Companion,* London, 1779

Myers, Amy R.W., and Margaret Beck Pritchard, editors, *Empire's Nature: Mark Catesby's New World Vision,* Chapel Hill: University of North Carolina Press, 1998

Phillips, Henry, *Sylva Florifera: The Shrubbery Historically and Botanically Treated,* 2 vols., London, 1823

MARK LAIRD

Shugaku-in

Kyoto, Japan

Location: at the base of Mt. Hiei, approximately 5 miles (8 km) north-northeast of Kyoto station

Shugaku-in was built and considered to have been designed by Japanese emperor Gomizuno (r. 1612–29). Gomizuno's reign was short, when he abdicated in favor of his eight-year-old daughter. Freed from the demands and tensions of politics, the ex-emperor cultivated the artistic pursuits valued by the imperial class: calligraphy, flower arrangement, poetry (authoring the book *Ososhu*), and garden making. His knowledge of formal garden design probably derived from working with Koburi Enshu, designer of the Sento Gosho Imperial Garden in Kyoto. When Gomizuno was in his forties, he was given permission and provision by the ruling Tokugawa clan (his in-laws), to build a beautiful villa. For 14 years he searched for the appropriate site by traveling the countryside around Kyoto and setting up temporary camps. In 1655 he visited his older daughter Umenomiya at a Buddhist convent situated at the base of Kyoto's sacred Mount Hiei. Delighted with the site, he appropriated it for his villa.

Gomizuno is considered to have been Shugaku-in's primary designer, but he collaborated closely with Ogawa Bojo Shunsho and Horin Shosho and with other craftsmen. It is also likely that he consulted with his wife, Empress Tokufumen, noted for her refined taste and style.

Shugaku-in's landscape maximizes the spectacular natural qualities of its site. It is considered a premier example of *shakeii*, or borrowed landscape. The borrowed landscape incorporates a partial view of the city of Kyoto and at least three mountain ranges to the west. Manicured trees and shrubs comprise the foreground, and a large pond and rice fields the middle ground of the *shakeii*. The designed landscape enhances the distant landscape. The whole gives a sense of expansiveness unusual in Japanese gardens. Although the size of the villa is only 73 acres (30 ha), its view encompasses a river valley (Kyoto's Kamo and Katsura Rivers) and distant mountain ranges.

The design is in three parts: lower, middle, and upper villas linked by a path through rice fields. The lower and middle villa gardens emphasize human scale, with attention to plant form and texture, fish ponds, water falls,

The garden and pond of the Shugaku-in Imperial Villa
Courtesy of Werner Forman Archive with permission of Imperial Household Agency

stones, and paths. There is a sense of intimacy and comfort in these gardens. But they are not very different from other Japanese gardens of this and earlier periods. It is the working, agricultural landscape and the upper villa garden that are exceptional.

Rice fields are ubiquitous in Japan. The dedication of garden space to a common, agricultural landscape, a scene observable nearly anywhere in Japan, seems a curious feature in imperial landscape. It speaks of a love for the everyday, utilitarian and enduring aspects of Japanese culture. Today, as in former centuries, Shugaku-in's fields are worked by hand. This connotes a sense of continuity with the past. The rice fields are experienced as one walks the gravel path and also from the pond path above.

The sequenced progression through the lower villas and fields culminates with an ascent up the steep hillside of Mount Hiei. A steep and lushly planted path leads to a pavilion called Cloud Touching Arbor or Rinun-tei. The pavilion is sited above a large, asymmetrically shaped pond, created by a huge, earthen dam that is concealed by plantings from below, where it appears as part of the mountain. The pond is revealed from the pavilion, and as one pauses in contemplation, the *shakeii* view beyond is revealed. There is a blending of landscape forms. The curves of the large pond (designed in clay model by Gomizuno) harmonize with the arching forms of the distant mountains. Trees are layered and pruned for a windswept effect. The idealization of their natural forms contributes to the *wa*, or harmony, of the overall view.

Shugaku-in is small relative to Western imperial landscapes. It has been compared with Versailles, built about the same time. Owner personalities and cultural sensibilities produced extremely different landscapes, however. Versailles reflects the authority of Louis XIV and a sense of dominion over nature. The ego of Gomizuno is only subtly expressed in Shugaku-in. The garden instead is about eliciting the intrinsic character of the site. The upper villa speaks of a spiritual connection with the larger context. It is comparable in feeling to sacred places throughout the world, such as Monte Alban, Mexico, that have been developed to offer contact with the sky, wind, and mountains.

Synopsis

1618–22 Kobori Enshu, noted landscape designer, works with Emperor Gomizuno on design for garden for Imperial Palace in Kyoto
1629 Gomizuno abdicates throne of Japan at age 34
1641–55 Ex-emperor Gomizuno searches for scenic site on which to build vacation villa
1655 Gomizuno visits Enshogi Nunnery on sacred Mount Hiei and determines to build villa there
1655–58 Design and construction of buildings, ponds, and gardens, by Gomizuno
1818–29 Renovation of Shugaku-in by Tokugawa Iyenari
1883 Shugaku-in comes under supervision of Imperial Household Agency where it remains today

Further Reading

Bring, Mitchell, and Josse Wayembergh, *Japanese Gardens: Design and Meaning,* New York: McGraw Hill, 1981
Mori, Osamu, *Shugakuin Imperial Villa,* Tokyo: Mainichi Newspapers, 1970
Taniguchi, Yoshiro, *The Shugakuin Imperial Villa,* Tokyo: Mainichi Newspapers, 1956
Treib, Marc, and Ron Herman, *A Guide to the Gardens of Kyoto,* Tokyo: Shufunotomo, 1980

MARY E. MYERS

Simonds, Ossian Cole 1857–1931

United States Engineer and Landscape Designer

When the Prairie style of landscape design flourished in the midwestern United States, Ossian Cole Simonds was regarded as one of its leading practitioners. Simonds was born near Grand Rapids, Michigan, to a family with early ties to New England. Growing up amid the woods and fields of his family farm, he developed an early love for the land. He enrolled at the University of Michigan to study civil engineering and worked during the summers along the Lake Michigan shore for the United States Lakes Survey. He also took courses from William Le Baron Jenney, who had begun the university's new program in architecture. Upon graduating in 1878, Simonds moved to Chicago to work as Jenney's assistant.

At the time, Jenney, who had prepared plans for Chicago's West Parks, was working on an expansion of the city's Graceland Cemetery. The new area had extensive drainage problems, and Simonds, with his background in engineering, was assigned to supervise this project. Through this association, Simonds met Byron Lathrop, a prominent and civic-minded landscape-design enthusiast who worked for the Graceland Cemetery Company and whose passion was to bring Chicago's aesthetic standards up to those he had found during his studies and travels in Europe.

Lathrop had a major influence on Simonds, introducing him to the fine art aspects of landscape gardening. Under Lathrop's tutelage, Simonds read extensively about landscape painting and studied major books on landscape architecture to learn new skills, which he combined with his engineering training. The two men traveled to important early cemeteries in the eastern United States, including Mount Auburn, near Boston, and Spring Grove, in Cincinnati, Ohio, where they met Adolph Strauch, Spring Grove's renowned superintendent. While at Graceland, Simonds began to apply his new design expertise.

In 1880 Simonds formed a partnership with William Holabird, who had been a fellow employee at Jenney's office. Two years later Martin Roche joined the firm, which became Holabird, Simonds, and Roche. Their architectural commissions increased, while Simonds continued his work with Graceland. Then he accepted a full-time position as Graceland's superintendent—a title that grew to include landscape gardener, engineer, and surveyor. His work focused on Willowmere, the lake he helped design, plus planting and grading activities at the cemetery. Eventually, to focus more time on his private practice, Simonds resigned as Graceland's superintendent

View in the Edgewood Section of Graceland Cemetery, Chicago, Illinois
Photo by O.C. Simonds, courtesy of Morton Arboretum, Suzette Morton Davidson Special Collections

and became its consulting landscape gardener and a member of its board of managers. In 1903 he renamed his business O.C. Simonds and Company.

By 1887 Simonds was working on Fort Sheridan, situated on a wooded bluff north of Chicago. He also began publishing his first articles on landscape design in the *Michigan Horticulturist,* a journal edited by his cousin. The essays focused on cemeteries, home-grounds design, school plantings, and the use of native plants, based on his keen observations of nature. Eventually his writings were published in widely read magazines and respected professional journals. His book *Landscape Gardening* (1920), which was dedicated to his friend and mentor Byron Lathrop, remains the best expression of Simonds's design philosophy and his belief that landscape design could teach people to see the beauty of nature as "the great teacher."

Simonds's reputation as an authority on landscape gardening grew. Active in numerous professional organizations, he was elected to membership in the Western Society of Engineers in 1886. The following year, fostered by growing interest in "rural" cemetery design, Simonds and a group of cemetery supervisors organized the American Association of Cemetery Superintendents. A familiar figure at their annual meetings, he served as their president from 1895 to 1896 and occasionally delivered papers based on his extensive cemetery planning experience. He was also a member of the American Civic Association, the Park and Outdoor Art Association, the American Forestry Association, the Ethical Culture Society, and the Cliff Dwellers and other clubs in Chicago. In 1899 Simonds became one of the 11 founding members of the American Society of Landscape Architects—its only Midwesterner. Later he served as president of the organization (1913–14) and organized the group's first meeting in Chicago.

In 1908 Simonds began teaching landscape design courses at the University of Michigan, where he was instrumental in initiating its landscape architecture program. At this time his practice began to flourish, and Simonds often referred to himself as a "landscape gardener." Commissions included a wide range of projects, including arboretums, cemeteries, residential grounds, schools, subdivisions, parks, and golf courses. Some of his most important work can be found in his residential projects (many for influential clients) and his many public parks. These include the extension of Lincoln Park in Chicago, Riverview Park at Hannibal, Missouri, and parks in Dixon, Springfield, and Quincy, Illinois, where his efforts succeeded those of H.W.S. Cleveland. In Madison, Wisconsin, he planned several attractive subdivisions and prepared initial designs for three of the "Four Lakes" city's parks. Late in his career, one of his most significant projects was designing the Morton Arboretum near Chicago.

Shortly before World War I Wilhelm Miller, who had worked with Liberty Hyde Bailey at Cornell University, joined the University of Illinois faculty as head of their division of landscape extension. In this capacity Miller began publishing a series of informative circulars espousing rural beautification and the Prairie School philosophy of landscape design. His thesis was based on the heartland's special sense of place qualities, especially its flat prairie landscape, and on principles of landscape painting similar to those used by Simonds. Using photographs in his experiment station circular, the *Prairie Spirit in Landscape Gardening* (1915), he cited the work of Jensen, Simonds, and Walter Burley Griffin as leading figures in this movement. Simonds, however, had reservations about Miller's thesis, noting in a letter to him that Miller was trying to "make facts fit a theory rather than theory fit the facts."

During his 53-year career, Simonds emerged as a leading figure in U.S. landscape architecture. While most of his work occurred in the Midwest, he was involved with projects throughout the United States. Three of his six children carried on his land ethic: Gertrude, an early activist and tour leader with the Prairie Club in Chicago; Robert, who holds a degree in landscape architecture; and Marshall, who continued his father's practice with J. Roy West and then joined the Green Bay, Wisconsin, parks department.

Biography

Born in Grand Rapids, Michigan, 1857. Studied civil engineering at University of Michigan, graduating 1878; began working at Graceland Cemetery, Chicago, 1878, an affiliation he continued throughout his career; partnership with architect William Holabird, 1880, and then with Martin Roche, 1882–83; founding member of the American Society of Landscape Architects, 1899, and first non-East-Coast member to become president, 1913; established firm of O.C. Simonds and Company, 1903, which became Simonds and West, 1925; began teaching at University of Michigan, 1908, and helped establish their landscape architecture program; considered major practitioner of the Prairie School of landscape architecture; worked throughout the United States designing parks, estates, campus plans, subdivisions, and civic and institutional projects. Died in Chicago, Illinois, 1931.

Selected Designs

1878–1931	Graceland Cemetery, Chicago, Illinois, United States
1892–93	Lake Forest College, Lake Forest, Illinois, United States
1895–1913	Quincy Parks, Quincy, Illinois, United States
1897	Glen View Golf Club, Glen View, Illinois, United States
1907	Washington Park, Springfield, Illinois, United States
1908–31	Riverview and Nipper Parks, Hannibal, Missouri, United States
1911	The Highlands subdivision, Madison, Wisconsin, United States
1915	Nakoma subdivision, Madison, Wisconsin, United States; Iowa State University, Ames, Iowa, United States
1921–25	Morton Arboretum, Lisle, Illinois, United States

Selected Publications

The Lakefront Park: A Few Suggestions from the Landscape Gardening Point of View, 1898

"Trees for the Home Grounds," in *How to Make a Flower Garden: A Manual of Practical Information and Suggestions,* edited by Wilhelm Miller, 1903

"The Aesthetic Value of Wooded Areas in Michigan," *Report of the Michigan Forestry Commission for the Years 1903–4* (1905)

Landscape Gardening, 1920

"Nature as the Great Teacher in Landscape Gardening," *Landscape Architecture* 22, no. 2 (1932)

Further Reading

Gelbloom, Mara, "Ossian Simonds: Prairie Spirit in Landscape Gardening," *Prairie School Review* 12, no. 1 (1975)

Grese, Robert E., "Ossian Cole Simonds," in *American Landscape Architecture: Designers and Places,* edited by William H. Tishler, Washington, D.C.: Preservation Press, 1989

Grese, Robert, "The Prairie Gardens of O.C. Simonds and Jens Jensen," in *Regional*

Garden Design in the United States, edited by Marc Treib and Therese O'Malley, Washington, D.C.: Dumbarton Oaks Research Library, 1995

Miller, Wilhelm, "A Series of Outdoor Salons," *Country Life in America* (April 1914)

Miller, Wilhelm, *The Prairie Spirit in Landscape Gardening,* Urbana: University of Illinois Agricultural Experiment Station, 1915

"O.C. Simonds Passes On," *Park and Cemetery* (December 1931)

WILLIAM H. TISHLER

Singapore Botanic Gardens

Singapore

Location: approximately 3 miles (4.8 km) north of the city center of Singapore

The Singapore Botanic Gardens remain today the cornerstone of botanical inquiry in Southeast Asia. Their contribution and role as a conduit for botanical dispersal has had a profound effect on the world. Directors of the Singapore Botanic Gardens throughout the years have included Henry James Murton, Nathaniel Cantley, Henry Nicholas Ridley, Isaac Henry Burkill, Richard Eric Holttum, and Humphrey Morrison Burkill. England's Kew Gardens played a strong role in the life of these individuals, was influential in their appointments, and was the principal repository of their species collections and research outcomes.

Sir Stamford Raffles, the founder of Singapore and a keen naturalist, established the first botanic garden, or "government garden," in Singapore at Fort Canning in 1822, adjacent to his bungalow. The garden was established, with Dr. Nathaniel Wallich's advice and support, mainly to introduce into cultivation economic crops such as nutmeg (*Myristica fragrans*), clove (*Caryophyllus aromaticus*), and cocoa. Raffles's role in establishing Singapore is well recognized, but he also maintained constant communication with numerous botanists, wildlife experts, and scientists of the day. He earned a knighthood for his *History of Java* (1817), which includes an extensive scientific review of the natural environment of Java, and was a founder of the Zoological Society of London serving as its president in 1826. *Rafflesia arnoldi,* the world's largest flower, honors his assiduous collecting and scientific contribution. The garden was closed in 1829, and land parceled out, following Raffles's departure from Singapore in 1823.

In 1859 a new Agri-Horticultural Society agreed for the exchange of the Fort Canning land in return for 23 hectares (57 acres) at Tanglin, which forms the original portion of the present gardens. Supported by "Whampoa," Hoo Ah Kay, the society was chaired by the governor of Singapore and sought to develop a pleasure park with botanic gardens, enlisting the services of former nutmeg plantation manager Lawrence Niven. One of the first actions by the society was the construction of a bandstand-promenade on a high point in the garden, which opened in 1860. Niven laid out much of the circulation structure of this garden, and it progressively became a popular display and acclimatization venue for plants and animals.

By 1875 the Agri-Horticultural Society had overextended itself financially on the gardens, and it was handed over to the government. A new committee sought the advice of the Kew Gardens, and Murton was recommended as the first director. Murton changed the garden from a recreational park to a venue for serious scientific experimentation and display of plants. He established a herbarium, commenced research into economic crops including coffee, and established its Economic Garden. This garden became the experimental station for a wide range of economic species including the Para rubber (*Hevea brasiliensis*) that first arrived in Wardian cases in 1877.

Arriving from the Mauritius Pamplemousses Gardens, the Kew-trained Cantley continued the research begun by Murton and also assumed management of the Forest Department. Within the latter he established the foundation of the forestry reserves in Malaysia, placed the botanic gardens on a firm systematic footing, engaged suitable staff to achieve this objective, reestablished the Penang and Malacca gardens, and introduced Malayan trees into the Economic Garden. He also, although skeptical, continued the *Hevea brasiliensis* cultivation experiments. In addition, Cantley introduced an arboretum to the Economic Garden, built nurseries for ornamental plants, commenced a tree-planting program in Singapore, designed and laid out the "Peoples Park" in Singapore, and started a commercial sales outlet.

Upon Cantley's death in 1888, Ridley, "the father of Malaya's rubber industry," became director. For the next 25 years he worked tirelessly, resulting in the most productive phase in the gardens' history. In the face of ridicule he continued the *Hevea brasiliensis* cultivation trials, gaining the involvement of Malaccan tapioca planter Tan Chay Yan in his vision. By 1920 Malaya was producing over half of the world's rubber. He established the Agricultural Department and developed the Economic Garden into a center for experimental work in tropical agriculture while championing forest conservation in his role as director of forests. Many of the forest reserves extant today in Singapore and Malaysia are a consequence of his conservationist activities. He established the periodical *Agricultural Bulletin*, expanded the herbarium and its library, aided orchid research including the hybridization of *Vanda* 'Miss Joaquim', and completed the authoritative *Spices* (1912), the *Flora of the Malay Peninsula* (1922–25), and *The Dispersal of Plants throughout the World* (1930).

Isaac Henry Burkill, the former economic botany adviser to the Bengal government, succeeded Ridley in 1912. He maintained many of Ridley's initiatives and research programs, notwithstanding the war, and accumulated a formidable amount of data that resulted in his *Dictionary of the Economic Products of the Malay Peninsula* (1935). In 1924 the Economic Garden was excised for the construction of the Raffles College, and Burkill shifted the gardens' direction toward native plant ecology research, taxonomic botany, and horticulture.

When Holttum assumed the directorship in 1925, he set about seeking to improve the appearance of the gardens, promoting horticultural and ornamental plant activities. During this time he commenced much of the orchid hybridization program, resulting in the present free-flowering orchid nursery industry in the region and his credit as "father of the orchid industry." During this time he wrote *Gardening in the Lowlands of Malaya* (1953), the *Malayan Plant Life* (1954), and the *Revised Flora of Malaya* (1953–). During the war occupation Holttum worked closely with the Japanese-appointed director, Kwan Koriba, between 1942 and 1945, to maintain much of the integrity and activities of the gardens. In later years Holttum served as the first professor of botany at the University of Malaya (1949–53) and returned to the University of Cambridge (1949–73), retiring as emeritus professor of tropical botany. Many important publications by E.J.H. Corner, a staff researcher, appeared during this period, including the *Wayside Trees of Malaya* (1940).

Following several short directorships, H.M. Burkill was appointed director in 1957. He led the gardens through the "Malayanization" phase, the split of Malaya and Singapore and President Lee Kuan Yew's "Garden City" agenda. Successive director appointments continue to assert the preeminent role the gardens have established in research, information dissemination, and management of Singapore's national parks.

The herbarium, established in 1880, now accommodates some 600,000 dried and preserved plant specimens collected mainly from the Malay Archipelago. The Plant House, one of the oldest structures in the gardens, was erected in 1882 with an annex added in 1889. These structures shelter aroids, ferns, and other shade plants within their wooden lathes, including the New Guinea creeper (*Mucuna bennettii*), introduced in 1939. In 1969 an elegant Victorian gazebo from the Old Admiralty House gardens was relocated to the gardens. The School of Horticulture was established in 1972 in the former residence of H.N. Ridley. In the late 1970s to early 1990s the gardens went through a redevelopment phase that introduced the Second and Third Lakes and the Orchid Enclosure. It also extended the gardens' grounds northward into the Bukit Timah zone to create an extensive arboretum, increasing the gardens to their present size of 52 hectares (128.5 acres). In 1990 the gardens came under the jurisdiction of the National Parks Board.

The design of the present gardens is segmented into three zones: Central, Tanglin, and Bukit Timah. The original gardens, the Tanglin zone, remain relatively unchanged from Niven's design for the Agri-Horticultural Society. The Central zone includes the main entrance the EJH Corner House, the National Orchid Garden, Ginger Garden, Palm Valley, Symphony Lake, and Heliconia Walk. Orchids have been a significant feature of the gardens since their establishment, and the new Orchid Garden seeks to draw out the various dimensions of the orchid flower—variety, colors, rare and indigenous species—with a gently sloping pathway system to display some 2,000 specimens (see Plate 31). The Bukit Timah zone retains a remnant of the Singapore's original evergreen forest together with a newly designed lake to display the economic values of plants such as timber trees, fruit and beverage crops, spices, herbs, and medicinal plants. Other features include the English Garden, recently designed to display gardens-bred orchids named after luminaries, the Tan Hoon Siang Mist House that hosts rare orchid cultivars, and the Yuen-Peng McNeice Bromeliad Collection, which displays some 20,000 bromeliads donated by Lady Yuen-Peng McNeice that originally formed the collection at Shelldance Nursery in California.

Synopsis

1794   First botanic garden established in Penang by
            Christopher Smith
1822   Singapore Botanic Garden established by
            Stamford Raffles; second botanic garden in

Penang established by George Porter with Raffles's encouragement

1829	Singapore Botanic Garden closed
1859	Singapore Botanic Garden reestablished by Agri-Horticultural Society with land acquired at Tanglin (part of present site)
1860	Bandstand opened in garden
1875	Gardens given to government
1877	First rubber seedlings arrive in Singapore, in Wardian cases from Royal Botanic Gardens, Kew
1879	Land for Economic Garden obtained
1882	Plant House erected
1884	Waterfall Botanic Garden in Penang established by Charles Curtis
1886	Malacca Gardens at Bukit Sabukor established
1893	Vanda 'Miss Joaquim' first reported in Gardener's Chronicle
1896	Malacca Gardens closed
1924	Economic Garden excised from gardens; gardens redirected toward native-plant ecology
1969	Gazebo from Old Admiralty Gardens transferred to gardens
1972	School of Horticulture established
1976	Second Lake completed
1981	Vanda 'Miss Joaquim' selected as national flower of Singapore
1985	Rose garden constructed
1990	Gardens placed under National Parks Board

Further Reading

Banfield, F.S., *Guide to the Botanic (Waterfall) Gardens, Penang,* Penang, Malaya: Sinaran Sdn. Bhd., 1949

Bastin, John, "The Letters of Sir Stanford Raffles to Nathaniel Wallich, 1819–1824," *Journal of the Malaysian Branch of the Royal Asiatic Society* 54 (1981)

Bastin, John, "Sir Stanford Raffles and the Study of Natural History in Penang, Singapore, and Indonesia," *Journal of the Malaysian Branch of the Royal Asiatic Society* 63 (1990)

Burkill, Isaac Henry, *The Botanic Gardens, Singapore: Illustrated Guide,* Singapore: Government Printing Office, 1926

Burkill, Isaac Henry, *A Dictionary of the Economic Products of the Malay Peninsula,* 2 vols., London: Crown Agents, 1935; 2nd edition, Kuala Lumpur: Ministry of Agriculture and Cooperatives, 1966

Corner, Eldred John Henry, *Wayside Trees of Malaya,* 2 vols., Singapore: Government Printing Office, 1940; 3rd edition, Kuala Lumpur: Malayan Nature Society, 1988

The Gardens' Bulletin 9 (1935)(special issue on Henry Ridley)

"Historical Notes on the Rubber Industry," *Agricultural Bulletin of the Straits and Federated Malay States* 9, no. 6 (1910)

Holttum, Richard Eric, *Plant Life in Malaya,* London and New York: Longmans Green, 1954

Jones, David, "The 'Waterfall' Botanic Garden on Pulau Pinang: The Foundations of the Penang Botanic Gardens, 1884–1910," *Journal of the Malaysian Branch of the Royal Asiatic Society* 70, no. 273 (1997)

Jones, David, "The Penang Botanic Gardens, 1794–1905: The Design and Development of a Tropical Botanic Garden," *Studies in the History of Gardens and Designed Landscapes* 18, no. 2 (1998)

McCracken, Donal P., *Gardens of Empire: Botanical Institutions of the Victorian British Empire,* London and Washington: Leicester University Press, 1997

A Pictorial Guide to the Singapore Botanic Gardens, Singapore: Singapore Botanic Gardens, 1989

Purseglove, John William, *The Ridley Centenary,* Singapore: Botanic Gardens, 1955

Raffles, Thomas Stamford, *The History of Java,* 2 vols., London, 1817; 2nd edition, London, 1830; reprint, 2 vols., Kuala Lumpur and Oxford: Oxford University Press, 1994

Ridley, Henry Nicholas, "The Flora of Singapore," *Journal of the Straits Branch of the Royal Asiatic Society* 33 (1900)

Tinsley, Bonnie, *Singapore Green: A History and Guide to the Botanic Gardens,* Singapore: Times Books, 1983

Tinsley, Bonnie, *Visions of Delight: The Singapore Botanic Gardens through the Ages,* Singapore: Botanic Gardens, 1989

Tofield, Anne, editor, *Golden Gardening: Fifty Years of the Singapore Gardening Society, 1936–1986,* Singapore: Singapore Gardening Society, 1985

DAVID JONES

Sissinghurst Castle Garden

Kent, England

Location: 2.5 miles (4 km) northeast of Cranbrook, and approximately 35 miles (56 km) southeast of London

The garden of Sissinghurst, now in the possession of the National Trust through the gift of its owner Nigel Nicholson, is one of the trust's most visited properties. Created effectively as a family garden, it receives many thousands of visitors in the six-and-a-half months of the year when it is open. In 1999, the last year for which full numbers are available, these were 171, 885. Because of the garden's domestic scale, extending over only ten acres (4 ha), numbers are controlled by a timed admission system, which protects the garden and ensures that visitors can see it in reasonable conditions. As it is, the number passing through call for the highest standards of management and maintenance.

The castle itself has a long and checkered history. Settled in the late 12th century by a Norman family, it was for nearly 300 years a medieval moated manor house. At the end of the 15th century a family called Baker acquired it. Sir John Baker rose to eminence in the court of Henry VIII, holding a number of positions, including chancellor of the exchequer, and gaining great wealth. He continued serving the monarchy, fulfilling the same role for Queen Mary. In 1557 the queen was received at Sissinghurst in the course of a royal progress. Sir John's son Sir Richard continued serving the crown and welcomed Queen Elizabeth I and her entourage on a three-day visit in 1573 at what must have been a grand and extensive range of buildings forming the manor. For another hundred years it remained a quiet country property, but in the late 17th century the family, having supported the royalist cause in the Civil War, became impoverished, and it fell into a decline. Writing in the mid-18th century, Horace Walpole described it as "a park in ruins and a house in ten times greater ruin." Later in the 18th century it acquired the title of castle, not as one that provides defense from an outside enemy but in which prisoners of war could be held. It was successively neglected and plundered for a further 150 years until the Nicholsons bought it in 1930. They devoted as much time as they could over the next 30 years to creating the garden; their living accommodation seems to have been spread about in the habitable parts of the ruins. It was only in the 1960s, after the death of his mother, that Nigel Nicholson had the Fore-Building modernized to create a unified "house."

Sir Harold Nicholson was a career diplomat and his wife Victoria a novelist and poet, known by her nickname and maiden name, Vita Sackville-West. A direct descendant of the Bakers, Sackville-West was the principal architect of the garden restoration. She created a series of garden spaces, making use of the walls of the building and the ruins to create the divisions. Sissinghurst's central feature is the Tower, built in brick like the Fore-Building, and which affords views over the whole garden and the surrounding landscape.

Entrance to the garden is from the west through a central arch in the long low Fore-Building. Through this archway is the grass courtyard across which a central path leads to the Tower. Beyond is the Tower Lawn separated from the largest element of the garden, the orchard, by the long Yew Walk running north-south. The orchard is bounded to the north and east by the old moat and to the south by the Moat Walk, next to which, further south, is the nuttery.

The real glory of the garden rests in two areas, the White Garden immediately north of the Tower Lawn, and the Rose Garden to its south. The whole garden complex depends for its form on the strong framework created by the remaining old walls of the original great manor house of the 16th century, with some 20th-century additions and further augmentation by the planting of hedges. The sense of order, enclosure, and intimacy that is created within these walls called for a similar treatment in the outlines of the internal spaces, and all the garden, with the exception of the orchard, conforms to axial rules in its outline. Nonetheless, some interesting accidentals of alignment resulted from site design problems. The design's genius resides in the way this generally uncompromising formality of line is softened by the use of plants. For example, the courtyard's outline is a trapezium and not a rectangle, with the central path at right angles to the Tower and not the Fore-Building. This is not so much a visual problem on entry; on return it is softened by the use of accent planting along the walls and in the corners.

Sissinghurst is often compared to Hidcote, and its style to the work of the owner of the latter property Laurence Johnson, who likewise composed a garden of small scale, enclosed elements with a formal framework, and used soft, flowing plant material. Johnson was almost exactly contemporary with Sackville-West and her husband. It can be argued, however, that both owe much to the earlier work of the partnership of Gertrude Jekyll and Sir Edwin Lutyens.

The Rose Garden is centered on the great Rondel, a circle of grass with a high thick yew hedge that extends beyond the circle along the paths. Although roses were placed throughout the garden, here musk and other old-fashioned roses were massed. At the southern end of

The cottage at Sissinghurst Castle, Kent, England
Copyright John Feltwell/Garden Matters

this is the South Cottage, whose small garden, an extension of the Rose Garden, forms a pivot, which helps to resolve the different alignments of that garden, and the nuttery and lime walk.

The White Garden is two gardens in one, its southern half set out in four simple quarters, and its northern half divided into 16 compartments bordered by box hedging. At least the eastern half of this garden was once the garden of the Priest's House, which stands on its north side. The idea of gardens planted with a single color originated with Gertrude Jekyll, but Sackville-West's ideas, worked out before World War II but not completed until after the war, exceeded everything that had gone before. The White Garden has long been considered one of the most lovely single-color gardens. Greatly admired worldwide, it has been copied many times and has been the inspiration for many gardeners.

Synopsis

late 15th C.	Manor house acquired by Baker family
1535	Gatehouse and arch built by Sir John Baker
1557	Queen Mary visits as guest of Sir John
1573	Queen Elizabeth I visits as guest of Sir Richard Baker
late 17th C.	Bakers support Royalist cause in Civil War and are impoverished; estate declines
1930	Estate purchased by Sir Harold Nicolson and wife, Vita Sackville-West (a direct descendant of the Bakers)
1930s–60s	Vita Sackville-West designs and plants gardens, including Rose Garden and White Garden
1962	Vita Sackville-West dies and bequeaths estate to younger son, Nigel Nicolson
1967	Nigel Nicolson donates garden to National Trust
1968	Harold Nicolson dies

Further Reading

Brown, Jane, *Vita's Other World: A Gardening Biography of V. Sackville-West*, London and New York: Viking, 1985

Brown, Jane, *Sissinghurst: Portrait of a Garden*, London: Weidenfeld and Nicolson, and New York: Abrams, 1990

Hussey, Christopher, "Sissinghurst Castle, Kent: Conversion of the Fore-Building for Mr. and Mrs. Nigel Nicholson," *Country Life* (8 August 1968)

Scott-James, Anne, *Sissinghurst: The Making of a Garden*, London: Joseph, 1974

M.F. DOWNING

Sørensen, Carl Theodor 1893–1979

Danish Landscape Architect

Carl Theodor Sørensen was among the most influential landscape architects in Denmark in the 20th century. He was first of all a designer but also a teacher and writer during the modernist period, 1920–75. Sørensen worked with all the leading architects of Danish functionalism and was a leading figure in the establishment of the close cooperation between the Nordic associations of landscape architects. He was a lecturer from 1940, and from 1954 to 1963 he was a professor at the Royal Academy of Fine Arts in Copenhagen. He is regarded as the father of Danish landscape architecture and also among the greatest of his time in the world.

Sørensen was born in Altona in northern Germany of Danish parents. He was raised in northern Jutland and educated as a gardener. In 1916, after his apprenticeship period at a manor house in Jutland, he worked as drawing assistant in the office of Erik Erstad-Jørgensen, one of the leading landscape architects of the time in Copenhagen. Beginning in 1920 Sørensen started publishing articles in magazines such as *Gartnertidende* and *Havekunst* (Gardener's News and Garden Art). He traveled to Germany and England in 1921 and 1922 on study tours, and in 1922 he established his own practice. Between 1925 and 1929 he worked with G.N. Brandt, the leading theoretician among landscape architects of the time, and through him was introduced to leading architects such as Povl Baumann, Steen Eiler Rasmussen, Kay Fisker, and C.F. Møller, with whom he later worked on many projects.

Sørensen published numerous articles throughout his life, and in 1927 he published his first book (on technical drawing for gardeners). In 1930 he published another book on garden design together with landscape architect Peter Wad, and in 1931 *Parkpolitik* (Park Policy) was published, one of Sørensen's most important books, in which he expressed his ideas on the development of residential areas, especially areas for children. As a result of his work on this topic, he designed the first adventure playground in Emdrup in 1940. Later he published several other books, among them *Europas Havekunst* (1959; History of Garden Art in Europe). In 1940 he was appointed lecturer at the Royal Academy of Fine Arts, following G.N. Brandt's retirement from this position. In 1954 he became professor, a position he held until his retirement in 1963. He continued his practice and designed some significant projects also during the late 1960s and 1970s, among them the Angli Art Center in Herning (1963–68) and the Swedish National Bank in Stockholm (1972–76), one of his very few projects outside of Denmark.

Sørensen's work encompasses a wide range, from private gardens to city parks, large institutions, and residential areas. Many of his more than 2,000 projects seem astonishingly fresh and challenging even today and are indeed among the most loved landscapes in Denmark. His style can be characterized as a playful yet serious transformation of elements from the history of garden art. His style is generally geometrical but most often in combination with organic and asymmetrical shapes. His earlier work shows the influence of Edwin Lutyens and Gertrude Jekyll. Some of Sørensen's later works indicate the influence of his contemporary Thomas Church.

In Aarhus University Park (1931) Sørensen created a kind of landscape style that is an artistic variation of the Danish cultural landscape with oak groves, now fully grown, and an impression of constancy and dignity. The way the university buildings are placed on the fringe of the park, in relation to openings and paths, with no obvious main building, gives an impression of an egalitarian or democratic society quite unlike the traditional university campus concept of the time. The amphitheater and the terrace by the library nevertheless make this a center of gravity in the park.

Sørensen also designed many residential areas. In Klokkergaarden (1937–39) in Copenhagen is an ellipse, with a small sand playground, a small group of trees, and a lawn—symbols of what he called the three ideal environments for children: the beach, the grove, and the meadow. In Høystrup (1948–52) in Odense, the grove theme is developed. The area between the houses consists of a grove of oak trees with a few informal paths. On the street side is a pergola that creates a play of sun and shade on the pavement—simple but elegant.

More sophisticated is the project for the Vitus Berings Park in Horsens (1945). This was supposed to be a "green monument," free from practical purposes, in honor of the great explorer Vitus Bering, who was born in Horsens in 1681. The resulting design was a series of geometrical figures, triangle, quadrate, pentagon, hexagon, heptagon, octagon, circle, and ellipse, called the Geometrical Garden. This is the most striking example of Sørensen's geometrical style, the formal space composition. Sørensen himself called it "the Musical Garden," perhaps referring to the elements of rhythm and composition or to the element of purposelessness. He was very pleased with this project, but the city of Horsens got cold feet and dared not build a park like this. Instead, the landscape architect—on pressing request—designed a new project, built 1954–56. Today the Vitus Berings Park is a beautiful but more traditional rhododendron park.

A scaled-down version of the Musical Garden was later built in the city of Herning—this was eradicated by the end of the 1970s. But after Sørensen's death in 1979, the Danish association of landscape architects, in collaboration with the city of Herning, began to create a full-size Musical Garden—this time as a monument to the landscape architect himself. The site for this garden is the Angli Art Center near Herning.

The communal garden plots in Naerum near Copenhagen from 1948–52 are perhaps the most famous of Sørensen's gardens. The plots are walled by ellipse-formed hedges spread on a meadow, like a stylized part of the Danish cultural landscape, in which the focus is on places more than properties, where the inside is private and the outside a common area. This bold solution creates outside spaces that are wonderful play areas, such as a miniature town with narrow and wide streets and squares. At the same time they create intimate private garden plots for growing vegetables and flowers or for relaxing and enjoying the view of the flowering fruit trees of the neighbors.

Biography

Born in Altona, Germany, 1893. Parents Danish; raised in North Jutland, Denmark; worked as gardener 1908–16, then in drawing office of landscape architect Erik Erstad-Jørgensen, 1916–22; traveled to Germany and England, 1921–22; established his own practice, 1922; became partner in office of landscape architect Gudmund Nyeland Brandt, 1925–29; between 1922 and his withdrawal from practice in 1960s, carried out more than 2,000 commissions, including urban parks (Aarhus University Campus, Aarhus, Denmark, 1931–47) and residential areas (Klokkergaarden in Copenhagen, 1938–39); lecturer in garden art at Royal Academy of Fine Arts, Copenhagen, from 1940; appointed professor at Royal Academy of Fine Arts, Copenhagen, 1954; retired from professorship, 1963. Awarded many prizes and honorary medals, including Peter Joseph Lenné Prize, 1979. Died in Copenhagen, 12 September 1979.

Selected Designs

1931–47 Aarhus University (with architects Kay Fisker, C.F. Møller, and Povl Stegmann), Aarhus, Jutland, Denmark

1937–39 Klokkergaarden, residential area (with architects Povl Stegmann and Knud Hansen), Copenhagen, Denmark

1940–41 Skrammellegepladsen, adventure playground, Copenhagen, Denmark

1942–52 H.C. Andersen-haven, public gardens, Odense, Denmark

1948–52 Naerumvaenge kolonihaver, colony garden plots, Naerum, Denmar; Højstrup, residential area, Odense, Denmark

1950–51 Bellahøj Friluftsteater, open air theater, Copenhagen, Denmark

1954–56 Vitus Berings Park, public garden, Horsens, Denmark

1963–68 Angli Art Center and sculpture garden, Herning, Denmark

Selected Publications

Parkpolitik i Sogn og Købstad, 1931; new edition, 1979
Om Haver, 1939

Europas Havekunst, fra Alhambra til Liselund, 1959
The Origin of Garden Art; Havekunstens oprindelse (bilingual English-Danish edition), 1963
39 Haveplaner: Typiske haver til et typehus, 1966; new edition, 1984
Haver: Tanker og Arbeider, 1975

Further Reading

Andersson, Sven-Ingvar and Steen Høyer, *C.Th. Sørensen: En havekunstner,* Copenhagen: Arkitektens Forlag, 1993

Borgen, Lars, "C.Th. Sørensens skulpturpark," *Landskab* 62, no. 3 (1981)

Borup, Helle, *C.Th. Sørensen: Curriculum vitae,* Copenhagen: Landscape Department, Royal Academy of Fine Art, 1991

Eijofor, Annemarie, and Dennis Lund, "C.Th.-kavalkade," *Landskab* 54, no. 7 (1973)

Jørgensen, Karsten, "Giardini del danese Carl Theodor Sørensen, architetto del paesaggio," in *Il giardino Europeo del Novecento, 1900–1940,* edited by Allessandro Tagliolini, Florence: Edifir, 1993

KARSTEN JØRGENSEN

Sorensen, Paul 1890–1983

Danish Nursery Owner and Garden Designer

Recognized as Australia's "master gardener," Paul Sorensen offered his clients (whom he preferred to call "patrons") a total package that was in his opinion essential for a great garden: superb design, quality construction, and continuing maintenance, and these are features of his surviving gardens.

Danish by birth, Sorensen had a traditional Scandinavian training, being apprenticed to a nurseryman and formally educated at the Horsholm Technical School of Horticulture in Copenhagen. He then worked for many years for some of the best landscape design contractors in Germany, France, and Switzerland until the outbreak of World War I. Initially he contemplated emigrating to South America, but the offer of an assisted passage to Australia was more tempting. The first years in his adopted country were discouraging, however; a major drought and a nation at war meant there was little hope of establishing an ornamental horticulture or landscape design business. He was contemplating moving to New Zealand when the opportunity to redesign the garden at the Carrington, a fashionable tourist hotel in the Blue Mountains west of Sydney, persuaded him to stay. He remained in this locality for the rest of his life.

By 1920 Sorensen, having established his own nursery at the small village of Leura, was beginning to gain a reputation as a garden designer. The timing was perfect—wealthy Sydney businessmen were building weekend retreats in the cool climate of the mountains, and they wanted exotic gardens to complement their new houses. A slightly eccentric Scandinavian, who not only brought the latest design ideas from Europe but who could also construct and plant such gardens, was just what these people were looking for, and Sorensen soon became a household name. Satisfied clients recommended him to others, and requests to design and construct new gardens came pouring in. At no stage did he have to solicit work, and it was rare for him to lose a client. Most remained friends and regularly sought his professional advice, and many engaged him to design second gardens.

The scale of Sorensen's work during the 1920s was relatively modest, and he quickly acquired a reputation as a creator of finely detailed small gardens. Then in 1932 he accepted commissions to work on two much larger gardens: one a rural property at Mudgee, New South Wales, and the second at his hometown, Leura. Over the next two decades he worked sporadically on the latter, and Everglades, as it is called, is considered his finest achievement, now listed as a heritage garden. At Everglades Sorensen perfected the details that became hallmarks of many of his later gardens: splendidly crafted dry stone walls that terminate in massive drumlike "newels" and enclosed beautifully recessed steps, meticulously laid paving, carefully set up axes and perfectly aligned terraces, and tree species selected for both aesthetic effect and longevity—Sorensen became famous for his ability to design with trees. Everglades was a turning point in his career. From then on he had more opportunities to create large gardens not only in the Blue Mountains but also in many other parts of the state.

Sorensen was indeed a master gardener, thoroughly trained in all aspects of his profession. He knew and loved his materials, with which he worked skillfully, and he had the ability to fashion them into works of art. In essence his gardens had all the qualities of the 19th-century Arts and Crafts movement, he himself being both artist and craftsman. He approached his work as a painter or sculptor would, first thoroughly investigating the site with his client and assessing its innate qualities, then pointing out its potential for development and suggesting how existing features could be incorporated into the design. He did not harbor preconceived notions and always respected and responded to existing site qualities, which made each of his gardens unique.

A true craftsman, Sorensen understood the scope and limitations of his materials, always selecting these himself and rejecting anything he considered inferior, including plant material: most of the species used in his designs came from his own nursery, where he even mixed his own potting composts. Like most landscape designers of his day, Sorensen preferred exotic to indigenous species, although he often retained existing native trees, incorporating them into his design. He maintained that, to ensure unity in the design, trees should always form the structural elements throughout a garden, so they needed to be long-lived species. Broad-leaved deciduous species, such as oak (*Quercus*), elm (*Ulmus*), tulip tree (*Liriodendron tulipifera*), London plane (*Platanus* × *hybrida*), and conifers such as fir (*Abies*), cedar (*Cedrus*), spruce (*Picea*), and California redwood (*Sequoia sempervirens*) became some of his signature trees. He used trees and large shrubs not only to provide visual enclosure and shelter from wind but also to create a feeling of mystery, tempting the visitor to explore further. He exploited this technique to make small gardens

appear larger and on large properties to create interlocking and overlapping spaces that eventually led the eye into the surrounding landscape, often by dramatically framing a distant view. When he did use bulbs and herbaceous perennials, these were planted on a grand scale to create broad sweeps of color. He was expert at exploiting existing changes in level by skillful use of retaining walls. He favored stone, which he liked to see exposed, but would sometimes use brick in less important parts of a garden, usually covering it with creepers. Concrete he disliked as a finish but acknowledged its value as a cheap structural material when not exposed.

Although he had no formal qualification, Sorensen styled himself a landscape architect and was one of the first to use this title in Australia. As a professional, however, his methods were somewhat unorthodox. A dislike of drafting and a mistrust of measured drawings meant that he rarely presented plans to clients, preferring instead to discuss every detail with them on site. When drawings were requested, he refused to refer to them, so the finished garden bore little resemblance to the original plan. He worked on every job himself and was highly respected by his workmen. In later years, his youngest son, Ib, began to take over much of the construction work, which disappointed some clients, even though Paul still supervised the job.

Throughout his career Sorensen believed the nursery to be an essential part of his design business. He had built both house—which included his office—and nursery, and one section was used to display examples of walls, steps, paving, pools, and specimen plants for visitors and clients to examine and discuss with him. While Ib Sorensen has continued the design and construction side of the company, he never had any interest in maintaining the nursery, and, sadly, this has been sold.

Unlike his contemporaries Jocelyn Brown in Sydney and Edna Walling in Melbourne, who wrote a great deal about their design work, Paul Sorensen wrote nothing. When asked about this, he replied that he had been too busy learning his craft to write about it, adding, "Edna Walling has left behind many words; I have left behind many gardens!"

Biography

Born in Copenhagen, Denmark, 1890. Trained in horticulture and landscape design, construction, and maintenance, in Denmark, Germany, France, and Switzerland, 1902–14; emigrated to Australia, 1915; worked in Victoria before moving to New South Wales, Australia; by 1920, had established his own nursery and landscape design business at Leura, in the Blue Mountains, west of Sydney, Australia, where he remained for the rest of his life; designed and constructed more than 70 major gardens, chiefly in the Blue Mountains region, but also in the Southern

Highlands, Hunter Valley, Sydney's North Shore, and other parts of New South Wales. His youngest son, Ib, has carried on the landscape business. Died in Leura, New South Wales, Australia, 1983.

Selected Designs

1929	Cheppen, Leura, New South Wales, Australia
1932	Heaton Lodge, Mudgee, New South Wales, Australia
1932–47	Everglades, Leura, New South Wales, Australia
1936, 1968	Invergowrie, Exeter, New South Wales, Australia
1946	Saskatoon, Leura, New South Wales, Australia
1950	Bethune, Orange, New South Wales, Australia; Pine Hills, Bathurst, New South Wales, Australia; Ballantyre, Cassillis, New South Wales, Australia
1951, 1960	Blue Mist, Leura, New South Wales, Australia
1970	Ulinda, Binnaway, New South Wales, Australia

Further Reading

Baskin, Judith, and Trisha Dixon, *Australia's Timeless Gardens,* Canberra: National Library of Australia, 1996

Bligh, Beatrice, *Cherish the Earth: The Story of Gardening in Australia,* Sydney, 1973

National Trust of Australia (N.S.W.), *Everglades, Denison Street, Leura,* Sydney: National Trust, 1962; revised edition, 1968

Ratcliffe, Richard, *Australia's Master Gardener: Paul Sorensen and His Gardens,* Kenthurst, New South Wales: Kangaroo Press, 1990

Tanner, Howard, and Jane Begg, *The Great Gardens of Australia,* Sydney and Melbourne: Macmillan, 1976; new edition, 1983

ALLAN CORREY

Soseki, Muso. *See* Kokushi (Muso Soseki)

South Africa

Two factors have influenced the development of gardens in South Africa. First, in modern times until 1910, the region was dominated by European colonial powers: the Dutch, then the British. The descendants of these European settlers controlled political power until the 1990s. Second, South Africa's climate, with the exceptions of the very southwestern Cape and Kwazulu-Natal, is predominantly hot and dry. Thus, on the high veld of the interior, raked soil rather than grass lawns was often the norm, at least in the dry season. As for the subjugated indigenous population, who had a keen sense of the various properties of local plants, their concern was mostly with subsistence. Travelers' comments about "gardens" at African homesteads or kraals are misleading, for these refer to areas of arable cultivation.

Much of South Africa in modern times was a frontier society, and as such, despite the superb variety of indigenous plants, gardens in the European sense were not plentiful. Though the Dutch enthusiasm for gardening was well established before they landed in South Africa in 1652, this excitement was not transported to the Cape of Good Hope. Settlers' gardens were minimalist and functional, with a kitchen garden and often an extensive herb garden, but the glory of the old Cape Dutch farmsteads was a combination of architecture, rows of vines, frequently a spectacular mountain backdrop, and avenues of trees, usually European oaks. Occasional flowerbeds might be dotted here and there, but they did not contribute much to the colonial Dutch ambiance. In the towns and villages the houses frequently fronted directly onto the street or had only a small grassy patch between the house and the water sluice at the side of the road. To the rear were fruit trees and, perhaps, a vegetable patch.

Only in the Victorian era, when more towns grew up and communities became more settled, did the "pretty

The Victoria Jubilee Conservatory, erected in Durban Botanic Gardens, 1898
Courtesy of Durban Botanic Gardens

flower garden" appear, especially in the western Cape, where older gardens such as Newlands and Bishopscourt came to maturity, and new gardens such as The Hill and Groote Schuur were developed. Nearby, Wynberg and Stellenbosch could boast some lovely small and showy gardens.

In Natal Pietermaritzburg became synonymous with azaleas, and, as in Pretoria, its streets were lined with jacaranda trees. Of Durban one writer in the 1850s commented, "The erven [plots] were crowded with houses [and] no room for gardens." But 30 years later Marianne North enthused about the gardens on Durban's Berea ridge, filled with blue *Ipomoea, Bignonias, Tecomas, Thunbergias,* hibiscus, cycads, and *Stangerias.*

By the early 20th century many of the great homes of the gold-mine owners (the "randlords") in Johannesburg had spectacular gardens complete with pergolas, covered walks, and water features. Sadly, most of the plants grown were exotics, though at the Union Buildings in Pretoria, thanks to the efforts of the botanist I.B. Pole-Evans, indigenous plants were prominent.

For nearly 200 years the words *the garden* meant only one thing at the Cape: the old Dutch East India Company Garden in the center of Cape Town. This had been the raison d'être for Dutch settlement: a garden in which to grow fruit and vegetables to supply Dutch ships plying to and from the East Indies. Another less famous company garden was at Newlands.

Governor Simon Van der Stel (1679–99) transformed the Cape Town garden into a park, and for the next century it was served by botanists and not master gardeners as formerly. It also soon acquired a menagerie. Ironically, at the time of the "Cape heath craze" in Europe at the close of the 18th century, when the European botanical magazines were dominated by newly discovered species from South Africa, the old company garden went into decline.

Only in the late 1840s did botany revive in South Africa, and for the next generation a number of botanic gardens struggled for survival against penury, regular drought, rivalry, hostility from nurseymen, and the ministrations of untrained and often convict labor. These included the gardens at Cape Town (established 1848), Durban (1849), Grahamstown (1850), King William's Town (1865), Graaff-Reinet (1872), Pretoria (1874), Pietermaritzburg (1874), and Queenstown (1877). In addition there were a great number of public parks, which also received government grants and which sometimes termed themselves "botanic gardens."

By the turn of the century interest in botany was again in decline in South Africa, and all the botanic gardens became municipal parks. Only in 1913 when the National Botanic Garden at Kirstenbosch was established along with a Botanical Society of South Africa. Kirstenbosch specialized in growing the indigenous flora of South Africa. Rivalry came from the Transvaal, where a Division of Botany and Plant Pathology (later called the Botanical Research Institute) established a national herbarium in 1923 and the Pretoria National Botanic Garden in 1958. It was not until the 1980s that the two wings of South African botany merged to form the National Botanical Institute, with an extensive network of satellite botanic gardens. By then various municipal botanic gardens were flourishing in Durban and Johannesburg, which grew exotics and indigenous flora. But the exemplar of Kirstenbosch's advocacy of botanical nationalism has since the 1980s made the growing of South African plants a sine qua non for all right-thinking South Africans.

See also Kirstenbosch National Botanical Garden

Further Reading

Cran, Marion, *The Gardens of Good Hope,* London: Jenkins, 1926; reprint, 1933

Fairbridge, Dorothea, *Gardens of South Africa,* Cape Town: Miller, and London: Black, 1924; reprint, Cape Town: Miller, 1934

Gunn, Mary, and Codd, L.E.W., *Botanical Exploration of Southern Africa,* Cape Town: Balkema, 1981

Karsten, Mia C., *The Old Company's Garden at the Cape and Its Superintendents,* Cape Town: Miller, 1951

Lighton, Conrad, *Cape Floral Kingdom: The Story of South Africa's Wild Flowers, and the People Who Found, Named, and Made Them Famous the World Over,* Cape Town: Juta, 1960; 2nd edition, 1973

McCracken, Donal P., "Parks and Gardens," in *Pietermaritzburg, 1838–1988,* edited by John Laband and Robert Haswell, Pietermaritzburg, South Africa: University of Natal Press, 1988

McCracken, Donal P., *A New History of the Durban Botanic Gardens,* Durban, South Africa: Durban Parks Department, 1996

McCracken, Donal P., and Eileen M. McCracken, *The Way to Kirstenbosch,* Cape Town: National Botanic Gardens, 1988

Smith, Alan Huw, *The Brenthurst Gardens,* Houghton, South Africa: Brenthurst Press, 1988

DONAL P. MCCRACKEN

South America

South America comprises a land area of tremendous climatic, geologic, and topographic diversity. The best-known feature is doubtless the Amazonian rain forest, occupying a diminishing 2.3 million square miles (6 million sq. km) of watershed territory, but the region as a whole is much more complex and varied, encompassing both the icy fjords and tectonic glaciers of the Tierra del Fuego and the formidable Andes mountain range that extends down the western flank of the continent. Indeed, South America is a continent of extremes, partitioned into four highland provinces originating from the Atlantic and Pacific coasts with three intervening lowland provinces or basins drained by the continent's principal rivers, the Amazon and the Orinoco. The most northern of the lowland areas, the Orinoco Basin, contains a region of alluvial plains called the llanos. Farther south the Paraguay and Paraná Rivers create another basin that eventually merges with the flat grasslands of the Argentine Pampas. To the west large plateaus—the altiplanos—separate the cordilleras of the Andean range in both Bolivia and southern Peru.

Climatic ranges can be dramatic, although the continent as a whole is generally characterized by a warm belt of equatorial weather. While humidity is typical for most of Argentina and Brazil, east of the Andes is more arid; the best example perhaps is the Atacama desert of Chile, where exceptionally arid temperatures and saline flats classify it as one of the most desiccated areas on the planet. In contrast, heavy rainfall, common in the southern part of the country, originates from fierce storms in the turbulent southern ocean, regularly saturating the southern cone region of Patagonia. Vegetation zones mimic the layout of the climatic zones; correspondingly, rain forest, or *selva*, is dependant on the wet, humid habitat of the equatorial region.

Because of the continent's vast diversity, the botanical collections of South America are singular resources of indigenous flora, including wholly unique varieties of climbers, creepers, lichens, mosses, bromeliads, trees, and flowers. While commercially driven deforestation continues to ravage most of the interior, conservation efforts have reached unprecedented levels through an increasing awareness of the continent's rich and valuable biomass.

Argentina

Second only to Brazil in size, Argentina has a vast territory (1.07 million sq. mi. [2.8 million sq. km]) of multiform climate and topography. Elevation ranges are most dramatic: the warm northeastern area is conducive to tropical plants such as jacaranda, red quebacho, *Enteroblums,* and *Arucaria imbricata,* while the mountainous areas of the Andes to the east and the treeless steppes of the Pampas—less hospitable to garden preparation and planning—host only drought-resistant species of hardy plants.

With the country's independence in 1810, civic pride found its expression in the construction of elegant parks, gardens, and city structures throughout the burgeoning capital of Buenos Aires. In an attempt to create the "Paris of the Americas," formal garden planning became more energized by landscape planner Carlos Thays, who was appointed by the municipality in 1892 to design the entire park system of Buenos Aires and superintend the planting of open areas throughout the city limits.

The most conspicuous of Thays's efforts lie within the aptly named Jardín Botánico Carlos Thays on Avenida Santa Fe, occupying 20 acres (8.1 ha). It was laid out as both an ornamental and a scientific garden to showcase specimens and promote the botanical sciences. An additional mission aimed toward the inclusion of plants representative of all Argentine regions, but initial attempts failed because these imports were poorly adapted to the very different climate of the seasonal capital city. In all, Thays and his colleagues collected more than 700 samples from throughout the country, but few survived the transition. The Thays garden includes small Italian (*jardín Romano*) and French subgardens, but the design was collectively inspired by the English examples of the late 19th century with their admixture of plants, trees, and shrubs, including *Ficus elastica,* and herbaceous plant borders.

Throughout the country's nine provinces are 16 botanical gardens, with a third located within or near the capital of Buenos Aires. Some of the gardens depend on national universities or scientific research organizations, while the remainder are municipal and private gardens. The main botanical garden in the Palermo district of the capital is famous for its beautiful sculptures and ironworks, but it also holds more than 5,000 species of plants, a rose garden, and an Andalusian patio with evocative lagoons. Also within the garden limits is the Jardín Japones, donated by the Japanese community in 1979. Distinguished by its rock gardens (over 1,700 tons of rocks were imported from the rivers of the Cordoba province), the garden is replete with bridges and lagoons stocked with koi.

Brazil

Brazil, the largest country on the continent with a surface area of more than 3 million square miles (7.8 million sq. km), contains almost 15 percent of the world's diversity within its biomass. The nation also shelters the largest portion of the Amazonian rain forest and a profusion of other distinct ecosystems. With its enormous biodiversity, the Amazon region is not homogenous but rather is a grouping of different subzones that host plants and animals specific to only that particular zone, making the wholesale deforestation of this resource even more troubling. But it is not the only region in the country to suffer from exploitation. To the northeast the arid Caatinga region has been mostly destroyed, along with the Araucaria Forest (home to a rare Brazilian pine species) farther south. The swampy Pantanal, near the border of Bolivia and Uruguay, is a much-touted ecosystem the size of Utah with lush grasslands and a distinct vegetation grouping that has adapted to the seasonal, lowland flooding. Farther inland, the central plateau of the country shelters the incredible biodiversity of the Cerrado, where flowers prosper year-round in this six-season habitat.

Coffee production dominated the Brazilian economy from the mid-1880s to the 1930s, and rubber, palm oil, and brazil nuts quickly emerged as important commodities. Yet the feverish exploitation of timber and an aggressive system of slash-and-burn agriculture contributed to a much-documented environmental crisis. In recent years conservation efforts have expanded preservation areas and accelerated the development of botanic research institutions. At present Brazil has 15 established botanic gardens that cover a total area of 2,100 acres (850 ha). Two of the largest gardens in Rio de Janeiro (established in 1808 by the Portuguese monarch Don João VI) and Brasilia account for half of this area, and the remainder may be considered "specialized" gardens. Even so, the current garden collections fall short of representing the exotic range of Brazil's landscape and biota. Most of the institutional gardens are located in the southeast and Atlantic forest areas, but unfortunately the Pantanal has no botanic garden, and only the botanical garden in Belem focuses on Amazonian species and their conservation.

Brazil enjoys a strong history of garden design, which—similar to other Latin American nations—gained full momentum following the nation's independence from Portugal. The first designs commingled natural landscape with an English Picturesque style, using long avenues of royal palm trees, sculptures, and fountains. These early examples were mostly in Rio de Janeiro, but later efforts began to appear in São Paolo, Porto Alegre, and the highlands of Curitiba. Predictably, the early garden designers were Europeans, usually Frenchmen (including François-Marie Galziov, who created the garden of the Quinta da Bóa Vista in 1858), yet native Brazilians began to make serious inroads by the 1940s. Roberto Burle Marx, one of Latin America's most esteemed modernist landscape architects or *paisajistas,* made an enormous imprint on the emerging new capital of Brasilia with a team of other botanists and gardeners including Oscar Niemeyer and Lucia Costa. One of the most exciting aspects of Burle Marx's work was his use of rare and often preternatural-looking plants from his own collections, including the ten species of the *Helicoma* and his eponymous *Philodendron burle-marxii.* His efforts extended to roof gardens and private estates as well, including the Monteiro residence in Correias, Brazil, with its heavy use of flowers and tropical materials, and a number of coastal retreats in Venezuela and abroad. These compelling organic compositions can be traced to Burle Marx's first project in 1932, a private garden for a house designed by Costa and George Warchauchik. Shortly thereafter he began planning the gardens for the Praça da Republica and the water garden of the Casa Forte square in Recife; as with his later work on the waterfront garden in Rio de Janeiro, the designer's use of stone in water settings, although romantically inspired by European examples such as the Royal Botanic Gardens, Kew, was innovative and later copied elsewhere across the continent.

Chile

The slender littoral that is Chile qualifies the nation as one of the most unusually shaped countries in the world, stretching over 2,600 miles (4,184 km) vertically and only 110 miles (177 km) across at its widest point. With such a tremendous latitudinal reach of territory, Chile contains areas as dissimilar as the nitrate-rich desert to the north and the submerged coastal mountains that create the southern archipelagos. The climate as a whole is similar to the Mediterranean, but a hyper-arid belt extending south from Peru creates an unusual condition wherein pockets of vegetation, so-called *lomas* formations, are created by maritime fogs. Yet, like Brazil, Chile struggles with an overharvesting of timber that has endangered its rare cathedral forest—one of the last two extensive temperate rain forests in the world with an assemblage of laurel, magnolia, false beech, and alerce trees (*Fitzroya cupressoides*), the second-oldest living tree species on Earth.

The municipal planning within the capital of Santiago centers on carefully planted city squares of mostly imported species. European influence was pronounced in many aspects of early Chilean garden design, but curiously, Chile achieved a style of its own between the early 1930s and the 1950s through the works of Oscar Prager, a native Austrian considered one of the most important *paisajistas* of his time. Prior to Prager, French and English formal models were the predominant influence in Chilean gardens with an emphasis on Europeanized knolls and lagoons and, for the more privileged and wealthy citizens, the use of exotic plants, which communicated status. Prager, however, prioritized the use of indigenous vegetation. Some art critics later attributed this preference to his alleged past as a spy for the Germans and implied that the Nazi philosophy of racial purification extended to the plant selections in his gardens. Regardless, Prager, like his Brazilian counterpart Burle Marx, placed emphasis on the volume of vegetation and the importance of natural landscape and dramatic vistas. Soon after he settled in Santiago, he developed Providencia Park (1933), followed by plans for parks in San Miguel (1936) and the south slope of the Santa Lucia Hill in 1938. Unfortunately, for the most part these gardens have been left to decline in the wake of encroaching urban development.

State-sponsored botanical collections exist in both the capital and outlying regions. In Valdivia, south of Santiago near Chile's lake district, the Jardín Botánico, created in 1957, contributes to the conservation and study of native Chilean plants. Its collections are housed in a 25-acre (10.1-ha) complex, containing more than 1,000 native species with approximately 800 vascular plants. The Parque Quinta Normal in downtown Santiago was founded in 1830 for the purpose of acclimatizing foreign plants, trees, and shrubs while also exhibiting indigenous specimens; examples of both include the Monterey pine, Babylonian willow, cypresses, poplars, *Peumus boldus, Quillaja saponaria,* and the popular Chile pine (*Aruacaria imbricata*), a member of the family of valuable timber trees that grow as high as 50 yards (46 m).

Colombia

The three cordilleras of the Andes form the dominant topographical feature of Colombia, reaching across the backbone of the nation and dividing the highlands into valleys and basins wherein most of the population resides. The llanos lie to the east with the rain forest. Although the country is situated completely within the torrid zone, temperatures naturally vary with elevation.

The country has several remarkable botanical garden collections, some representative of different altitudes. In the capital, Bogotá, the Jardín Botánico Jose Celestino Mutis in Santa Fe de Bogotá began in 1955 with well-stocked collections of medicinal plants, as well as specimens of Colombian and Andean flora, including those specifically formed within the ruptures of mountain ranges. Nearby in the city, Simon Bolivar's farmhouse, la Quinta de Bolivar, has beautifully kept gardens surrounded by ancient trees.

Other collections in outlying areas include the Jardín Botánico del Quindio in Armenia, located in the town of Filandia at 6,398 feet (1,950 m). It includes 50 acres (20 ha) of well-preserved natural forest, and the garden has also acquired 86 more acres (35 ha) of forest near the city of Calarca. In a unique fashion the garden incorporates collections of several altitudes to display representative areas of the Colombian Andean range, including climbers, creepers, lichens, bromeliads, mosses, and ferns. Coffee plantations have encroached on much of this area, but the sciophilous forest has proven to have excellent regenerative capacity. Farther south toward the border with Ecuador, the Jardín Botánico de Popayan occupies 20 acres (8 ha) adjacent to the colonial city of Popayan and is dedicated to conservation of and research on orchids. In addition, the Jardín Botánico Joaquin Antonio Uribe in Medellin holds not only several acres of landscaped gardens and hothouses but also a noteworthy orchid collection.

Ecuador

Ecuador, a country approximately the size of Colorado, contains one of the most diverse collections of flora and fauna in the continent, with more than 25,000 species of vascular plants (in comparison, North America has approximately 17,000) and a collection of orchids representative of more than 10 percent of the cataloged world varieties. The country is usually cordoned into four distinct geographical areas. The northern part of the Pacific coastline is mostly jungle, and areas girding the Andean slopes are characterized by moist forests. Notably, Ecuador is also the custodian of the mostly arid Galapagos Islands, which contain not only mangrove forests but also a high index of endemic species that reflect unique and well-documented adaptations to the unusual topography.

Southeast of the capital of Quito lies the Pedagogical Ethnobotanical Omaere Park, with its impressive groupings of indigenous plants and vegetation. Located in the Amazon basin province of Pastaza near the city of El Puyo, two-thirds of the 39-acre (16-ha) reserve is secondary forest, and one-third is primary woods. Along three central pathways visitors find collections of not only Amazonian plants but ornamental plants and an orchidarium. On the Pacific coast two cities hold significant botanical collections: Esmeraldas to the north, and the botanical garden at Guayaquil, which houses 3,000 species of plants, including 150 types of indigenous and foreign orchids. Other botanical institutions include the Jardín Botánico Reinaldo Espinsosa at Loja—in the heart of the Andes—an institution with a large collection of regional plants.

One garden model that has proven popular in highland regions not only for aesthetic reasons but for sustainable yields is the forest garden. This garden type typically includes a stacked polyculture of different plant species with layers of canopy, midstory, shrub, herb, ground cover, root, and vining verticals, all composed of edible or otherwise useful plants. These terraces may include fruit trees or other companion plants.

Venezuela

Like Colombia, Venezuela abuts the Caribbean Sea and shares a climate that can be both moist and semiarid, a combination supportive of the forests of palms, mangoes, and brazil wood covering almost half of the country's territory. After the defeat of the Spanish in 1821, Venezuela declared its independence, and Caracas soon became the epicenter of early gardening efforts in the country. Like many other South American capitals, Caracas is perched high (2,999 ft. [914 m]) above sea level in a valley surrounded by coastal highlands and is home to several large gardens, including the Parque del Este, the Los Caobos gardens, and the Jardín Botánico de Caracas. The city's municipal squares were originally designed with an unwavering formal style at odds with the outlying private gardens and their emphasis on natural vegetation. The centerpiece market-square plaza with its rigid avenues parcels the area into eight landscaped rectangles that in turn enclose the sitting areas and fountains of an earlier design. This plaza and others throughout Venezuela honor Simon Bolivar, a lieutenant in the revolutionary forces who has been immortalized as "the liberator," guiding the path toward independence for the Spanish-dominated nations. He is celebrated in other areas of Caracas through vestiges of French classical design within the Carabobo park and El Calvario park, both of which make use of water in the forms of lagoons or fountains.

The conservative symmetry and formal style of the capital is quite different than the private gardens of the periphery, including the paradisiacal retreat of the outlying Hacienda La Vega, begun in 1590. This garden has a distinctive Moorish influence with tiled patios and corridors that allow a continuum between the interior and outside. The main garden includes flowering trees such as jacarandas, acacias, mangos (*Mangifera indica*), cypresses, and royal palms (*Roystonea*), as well as a rich collection of ferns and orchids.

Venezuelan landscape design took a different turn in the middle of the 20th century under the guidance of Brazilian landscape designer Roberto Burle Marx, one of the early proponents of environmental conservation. The trademarks of his designs are often easily identified: a heavy use of outdoor murals, tiles, natural plant groupings, and an obvious appreciation of the drama and vista of the surrounding landscape. Collaborating with two other architects, Burle Marx created some of the most fantastical gardens along the Caribbean coastal region, including the partially completed Parque Nacional del Este, the Palacio residence, and the Delfino Garden.

See also Rio de Janeiro, Jardim Botanico do

Further Reading

Adams, William Howard, *Roberto Burle Marx: The Unnatural Art of the Garden* (exhib. cat.), New York: Museum of Modern Art, 1991

Balslev, Henrik, and James L. Luteyn, editors, *Páramo: An Andean Ecosystem under Human Influence,* London and San Diego, California: Academic Press, 1992

Berry, Paul E., Bruce K. Holst, and Kay Yatskievych, editors, *Flora of the Venezuelan Guayana,* Saint Louis: Missouri Botanical Garden, and Portland, Oregon: Timber Press, 1995

Cobo Borda, J.G., Claudia Uribe Touri, and Cecilia Mejía Hernández, *Gardens of Colombia,* Bogotá, Colombia: Villegas Editores, 1996

Dallman, Peter R., *Plant Life in the World's Mediterranean Climates: California, Chile, South Africa, Australia, and the Mediterranean Basin,* Berkeley: University of California Press, and Oxford: Oxford University Press, 1998

Eliovson, Sima, *The Gardens of Roberto Burle Marx,* New York: Abrams/Sagapress, and London: Thames and Hudson, 1991

Heywood, V.H., and Peter S. Wyse Jackson, editors, *Tropical Botanic Gardens: Their Role in Conservation and Development,* London and New York: Academic Press, 1991

McQueen, James, and Barbara McQueen, *Orchids of Brazil,* Portland, Oregon: Timber Press, 1993

Moore, David M., *Flora of Tierra del Fuego,* Saint Louis: Missouri Botanical Garden, and Oswestry, Shropshire: Nelson, 1983

Pio Correia, Manuel, *Brazilian Palms: Notes on Their Uses and Vernacular Names Compiled and Translated from Pio Corrêa's "Dicionário das plantas úteis do Brazil e das exóticas cultivadas" with Updated Nomenclature and Added Illustrations,* translated and edited by Claudio Urbano B. Pinheiro and Michael J. Balick, Bronx: New York Botanical Garden, 1987

Roth, Ingrid, *Leaf Structure: Coastal Vegetation and Mangroves of Venezuela,* Berlin: Borntraeger, 1992

Ruiz, Hipólito, *Relación del viaje hecho a los reynos del Perú y Chile: Por los botánicos, y dibuxantes enviados para aquella expedición,* Madrid: Tipográfico Huelves y Compañíaas, 1931; as *The Journals of Hipólito Ruiz, Spanish Botanist in Peru and Chile, 1777–1788,* translated by Richard Evans Schultes and María José Nemry von Thenen de Jaramillo-Arango, Portland, Oregon: Timber Press, 1998

Stannard, B.L., and Y.B. Harvey, editors, *Flora of the Pico das Almas: Chapada Diamantina-Bahia, Brazil,* Kew, Surrey: Royal Botanic Gardens, 1995

Tulloss, Rodham E., Clark L. Ovrebo, and Roy E. Halling, *Studies on Amanita (Amanitaceae) from Andean Colombia,* Bronx: New York Botanical Garden, 1992

Vaccarino, Rossana, editor, *Roberto Burle Marx: Landscapes Reflected,* New York: Princeton Architectural Press, 2000

Viveros, Marta, et al., *Oscar Prager: El arte del paisaje,* Santiago, Chile: Ediciones ARQ, Escuela de Arquitectura, Pontificia Universidad Católica de Chile, 1997

Zuloaga, Fernado O., and Osvaldo Morrone, editors, *Catalogo de las plantas vasculares de la república argentina II,* 2 vols., St. Louis: Missouri Botanical Garden, 1999 (introduction in English)

KRISTIN WYE-RODNEY

Spain

Spanish Landscapes

Located in the middle latitudes between the Atlantic Ocean and the Mediterranean Sea, Spain is characterized by its climatic diversity, evidenced by the differences between coastal areas and the interior of the country, the well-defined seasonal changes, and the temperature fluctuations ranging from weak to strong. The humid north, whose weather patterns are governed by the Atlantic, is rich in plant life and differs from the regions influenced by the Mediterranean. The latter regions include the interior, which is predominantly dry and cold; further south the climate is arid, particularly in summer, although moderately less so in the area of the Levant. Spain's location in the extreme southwest of the Eurasian continent, its climate, and its proximity to Africa are reflected in the country's flora. Not including the Canary Islands, there are over 6,000 species of plants and flowers.

The complexity of the Spanish relief and climate gives rise to a variety of landscapes, from the mountains to the low-lying fertile areas near rivers and from the extensive plains of the large inland plateau—the Meseta Central—to the peculiarities of the coast.

The Atlantic region of Spain is covered by deciduous forest and ground vegetation made up of heath and broom. The species here belong to the Euro-Siberian floristic region and include, among others, beech and oak. The rest of the peninsula is characterized by Mediterranean scleryphyllous forest—predominantly consisting of oak—and maquis of rockrose and thyme. Among these, two other formations are characteristic: the marascent forest, predominantly of gall oak, and the conifer (pine and fir) and needle (savin and juniper) forests of the peninsular interior. The holly oak (*Quercus ilex*)—and its cork oak variant (*Quercus suber*)—is able to adapt to a variety of climates and soils, making it the quintessential Mediterranean species. It is found throughout the peninsula in a multitude of landscapes, particularly in the *dehesas,* wide spaces of cleared forest, in the western and southwestern parts of Iberia.

However, it is the conifer forests that are in greatest abundance, encompassing some 54,300 square kilometers (20,970 sq. mi). Reforestation efforts resulting from an interest in woodlands and in the natural environment have produced notable results, such as the recovery of leaf forests. Riverbeds are characterized by bands of deciduous formations of varying size and makeup. The dry riverbeds in the Mediterranean region abound with groves of tamarisk. The ecological importance of the vegetation in the coastal marshlands—La Albufera in Valencia or El Coto de Doñana—has played a vital role in creating a tradition of environmental protection in Spain.

The Canary Islands offer protection to some extraordinary species of plants. The special nature of this vegetation is aided by the pronounced relief of the islands, which is structured in levels. The outstanding forest of laurisilva, with more than 20 species, receives the moisture it needs by its own thickness.

Although the forest is a constant throughout Spain, the predominant feature is shrub land, which exceeds even cultivated land in area. Wide expanses of low population density and the transformation of rural zones make the natural potential of large areas of land more and more evident. A future in which the diversity and wealth of Spanish landscapes provide an alternative to barren lands and the devastating effects of the arid climate may therefore be imagined. This diversity is also cultural. Xavier de Winthuysen, a pioneer in the study of Spanish gardens, declared that despite many years of neglect it was possible to uncover there "the entire history of the art of the garden from the Middle Ages to the present."

Gardens in Muslim Spain

The Mediterranean tradition of the house courtyard was introduced permanently into Spain by Greeks and Romans. This type of courtyard, which joins house and garden, had a traditional and unchanging form and was

View of the Casa de Campo, 17th-century
Courtesy of Museo de Burgos, Burgos, Spain

carried to the Americas over the course of the 16th century. But it was with the arrival of Arab civilizations in the eighth century that the Spanish garden tradition began. Because humans simultaneously adapt to and create their surroundings, this process of development was sensitive to the existing natural conditions. Adept in agricultural techniques, the inhabitants of this civilization introduced species such as rice, the orange tree, the lemon tree, and the date palm. The cultivation of fruits and vegetables also spread. In the vicinity of certain cities, such as Toledo, Córdoba, and Granada, orchards were supplied with water from rivers and canals. The Arab peoples developed a special terminology for gardens: *Burj* (tower) in Almería, *Munya* (object of desire) in Córdoba, or *Manjara* (orchard) in Granada. The names of places mark the Arab culture on the Spanish landscape.

The Patio de los Naranjos at the Mezquita de Córdoba, which was begun in the eighth century and successively expanded, is the oldest enclosed garden still in existence in Spain. The origin of the planting is debatable since it was unusual in the Omayyad tradition. Olive, palm, and laurel trees may have been planted first, while the orange tree was introduced in the tenth century. Today the perfectly aligned rows of orange trees resemble the columns system of the mosque. Other courtyards of orange trees, such as those at the cathedral in Seville and El Palacio de la Generalitat in Barcelona, suggest particularly Spanish features in that they reflect the effects of the exchange between East and West, the creation of a hybrid culture, and the level of diversity that can be reached through simple forms.

James Dickie (1992) describes "the basic components of the Hispano-Islamic garden [as] a raised grid, irrigation under gravitational pressure, central collecting pool or distribution point, and formal walkways incorporating channels by which the irrigation is accomplished." Excavations have proven this, just as they have verified the existence of the eastern influence. The palace of the caliphate at Medina Azahara (the flowering city) demonstrates the quality of the garden tradition in the eighth century, supported by a mastery of hydraulics. Opposite the palace facade was a broad pool; on the other side was a small pavilion encircled by four symmetrical reservoirs edged by stone walkways and small channels. At the Alcázares of Seville and at the Generalife, ancient Almohade gardens based on the quadripartite model have been excavated.

The gardens of the Alhambra and the Generalife are surprising at first for the site chosen and for their relationship to the urban setting, the rugged relief, and the valley below. But they are particularly surprising for the material quality of spaces realized at the late stages of a complex evolutionary process. The Alhambra is the pinnacle of the Mediterranean concept of the villa courtyard, with the power to create its own atmosphere. The garden courtyard is inscribed within the palace itself and acts simultaneously as a room and a distributor of space; this is true both of the Patio de los Arrayanes (Myrtles), which forms an axis with the Torre de Comares, and of the Patio de los Leones (Lions), where the play of shadow and the patterns of water work in service of the newer rooms. The Patio de Riad at the Generalife is the best example of a garden pertaining to a recreational villa.

All the Hispano-Arab gardens have been completely transformed over time. The gardens at the Alcazar palace in Seville are a mix of Arabian and Castillian influences—the Mudéjar style. Moorish craftsmen working for Christian monarchs laid out the gardens over spaces formerly of Almohade rulers; later additions are of Renaissance and baroque styles. Enclosed within a wall, the gardens are a curious blend of styles and periods; beside the fountains, jasmine and orange blossoms give the gardens an almost tropical feel. Without responding to a single guiding idea, the gardens have an identity all their own. But it is the small, simply organized gardens at the Alhambra—such as the Jardín de la Reja and the Jardín de la Daraxa—that resolve spaces in the outskirts of the palace and give an indication of the elements that have been applied systematically in Spanish homes and cities.

From the *Hortus conclusus* to the King's Garden
Medieval Christian Spain was characterized by the enclosed garden—the *hortus conclusus*. As in other European countries, secluded gardens were constructed between the walls of castles, such as the Castle of Olite or the Vergel (Orchard) in Tordesillas. But the gardens at the cloisters of monasteries and convents were most representative of this period. These included the sober Benedictine cloisters such as that at Silos, the gardens of Cistercian

monasteries such as those at Poblet and Santa Creus, and the cloisters of cathedrals such as the one at Tarragona.

The transition to the Renaissance style is evident in some gardens: for example, the small palace and gardens for the retirement of Charles V in Yuste or the courtyard of the Colegio de Fonseca in Santiago. But in Spain there was no great tradition of gardens among the noble society; it was the monarchy that displayed an interest in gardens at royal sites. The monarchs selected their enclaves—whether for pleasure or retirement—carefully choosing the sites. Usually in climax areas, the royal gardens are more-or-less homogeneous ensembles, with a history of magnificence and decay in a complex sequence of events.

Philip II had a great interest in nature, and the gardens created under his reign have their origin in his travels throughout Europe when he was a prince. Unfortunately, they have all disappeared: the small Jardín del Rey at the Alcazar in Madrid; the Casa de Campo, palace and belvedere with beautiful gardens; El Pardo gardens; and the lovely interior garden at Valsaín, in the Segovian forest. They were the places of the royal court's birth and development in Madrid. The gardens at Aranjuez on the banks of the river Tajo still maintain the general form given them by Juan Bautista de Toledo and Juan de Herrera. Under the meticulous supervision of Philip II, Dutch and Flemish artists planted flowers in abundance, trees of all kinds, and meadows of clover, all of which were irrigated by the singular reservoir of Ontígola.

At the Escorial, in the Guadarrama mountain range, the relationship is one of unforced dominance. The gardens, originally laid out with 68 different types of flowers, surround the building in the service of architectural unity. The Cloister of the Evangelists may be the most important garden of the Spanish Renaissance. Its precedent could be the cloister of the Jerónimos in Guadalupe with a central shrine for the lavabo and the quadripartite garden in the Almohade tradition. The central shrine at the cloisters at the Escorial contain four reservoirs—the biblical *fons vitae* (source of life)—which have been surrounded since the 18th century by 12 box hedges. The garden was initially more disordered and populated with flowers and herbs. Father Sigüenza, a royal chronicler, wrote in the 16th century that the gardens recalled the fine carpets brought to Spain from Cairo and Damascus, once again reflecting the hybrid nature of the Spanish garden.

Other important Spanish Renaissance gardens are the Fresneda, near the Escorial and still recognized, the Abadía, designed by Flemish gardeners and promptly abandoned, the Bosque de Béjar, where a reservoir and arbor are preserved, and the garden at the palace of the Marqués de Villena in Cadalso de los Vidrios, a square garden enclosed within walls. The palace of the dukes of Medinaceli in Seville, known as the Casa de Pilatos, retains two gardens on either side of a large central courtyard where a fountain, sculpted by Aprile de Carona,

dominates the scene. The main garden is rectangular, with *cortiles* (lateral arcades) and classical statuary brought from Rome, Capua, and Naples aligned in a row against a backdrop of bougainvillea. Other Andalusian palaces, such as the Palacio de las Dueñas in Seville and the Palacio de las Rejas in Córdoba, also contain attractive gardens.

In 1636 Philip IV had constructed the Palacio de la Zarzuela, which preserved the Italian-style garden over terraces. A fire devastated this palace, as in other unfortunate cases, causing a series of renovations in several royal sites.

The year 1700 tends to be considered the line of demarcation between the Habsburg and Bourbon dynasties and therefore between the Renaissance and the baroque in Spain. This division is represented by the gardens at La Granja, where the French taste was introduced. Philip V and his wife, Isabella Farnese, promoted new and old gardens. Artists such as Boutelou, Marchand, Bachelieu, and Bonavía remodeled the gardens at Aranjuez. Here, in the middle of dry Castille, trees that are hundreds of years old provide leafy vegetation to the area. At La Granja, a blending of the French and Italian tastes of the monarchs, the gardens, laid out by R. Carlier and E. Boutelou, extend from the palace facade to a natural cirque at the foot of the sierra. Today La Granja is essentially a wooded park in which the fountains, the sculptural elements, and the water effects combine to form an impressive spectacle.

The gardens at the Buen Retiro in Madrid were the last ones to be created by the Spanish Habsburgs, although there were later additions by the Bourbons. In 1628 Philip IV summoned Cosmo Lotti, who had collaborated on the Boboli Gardens. The estate, which was used as a retreat by the royal family in times of mourning, was transformed into a vast park dotted with hermitages and gradually took on a variety of forms. Reenactments of naval battles, called *naumaquias*, were carried out in the park's large reservoir; in the gardens great spectacles and feasts of the court were celebrated. At the beginning of the 18th century, French artists such as Robert de Cotte tried in vain to renovate the dilapidated gardens. A certain amount of their former splendor was recovered under Ferdinand VI and Charles III. Deeply bound to the history of Madrid, the park was turned over to the Spanish people after the revolution of 1868, thus becoming the first great urban park.

Toward the end of the 18th century, the sons of E. Boutelou and Juan de Villanueva created at Aranjuez the Jardín del Príncipe, thus completing the gardens. El Laberinto de Horta in Barcelona, begun in 1794 by Doménico Bagutti, and the Alameda de Osuna in Madrid are other notable examples of neoclassical gardens. The latter, referred to as "my whim" by the duchess, was changed to a Romantic garden by M. López Aguado in 1834. Abandoned for many years, it is today undergoing a process of restoration.

The reservoirs, small temples, grottoes, and diversity of vegetation at these gardens are reminders of a lost time in Spain, when, as a result of the difficult times during the 19th century, neither the State nor the owners of gardens were able to care for them to any great extent.

Garden and Science in the Spanish Enlightenment

Philip II was in possession of a copy of Dioscorides's *De materia medica* (ca. A.D. 50–80; *The Greek Herbal of Dioscorides*), which had been translated into Spanish and illustrated by Dr. Laguna (1555), the former private physician of Pope Julius III. Laguna would later organize for the king the first modern botanic garden at Aranjuez.

The discovery of the Americas led to Spain's greatest contribution to the field of botany. Christopher Columbus and Hernán Cortés had begun to realize the importance of this new knowledge, as evidenced by their references to the cacao and the tomato plant, in addition to other plants. Philip II later sent his personal doctor, Francisco Hernández, to Mexico to study the plant life of these new lands. The result, the monumental *Rerum Medicarum Novae Hiapaniae Thesaurus,* is a pioneering scientific work.

The introduction of the botanic garden into Spain was due to Ferdinand VI, who invited Carl Linnaeus to the country. Linnaeus's disciple Peter Loeffling arrived in Spain in 1751 and went to America. In 1755 José Quer and Juan Minuart began the facilities for the first botanic garden to be established in Madrid. Charles III initiated the activity at the new site in 1781, which was located next to the present-day Prado Museum, formerly the Museum of Natural Science. Its first director, Casimiro Gómez Ortega, ably organized the scientific structure of the site and its relationship with the Americas. A number of expeditions were undertaken, particularly in the 18th century. Between 1779 and 1788 Hipólito Ruiz and José A. Pavón journeyed through Chile and Peru and investigated an enormous number of plants, including the cinchona—which Linnaeus named *Chinchona officinalis* after the countess of Chinchón—the coca, and the araucaria, among many others. Sent to America, Martín Sessé between 1795 and 1804 organized a great journey of discovery in New Spain, and the Malaspina expedition to South and Central America and the Philippines resulted in a herbarium with 10,000 plants.

Among the botanists of this time, the work of José Celestino Mutis stands out. Linnaeus recognized Mutis's greatness, classifying the *Mutusia* in his honor, and Alexander von Humboldt dedicated two books in recognition of his studies on the vegetation of Colombia and Ecuador, collected in the monumental *Flora de la Real Expedición Botánica del Nuevo Reino de Granada.* Mutis's scientific training aided Linnaeus in the investigation of the medicinal properties of cinchona and in the discovery of tea, cinnamon, and a great number of plants.

Gardens were also established to acclimate the plants brought from the Americas. Valencia, where a botanic garden had existed since 1632 thanks to Dr. Villena, and La Orotava in Tenerife stand out in this regard. In the Canary Islands the climate has aided in the survival of many tropical plants and is today an area of great interest.

Houses and Gardens

The adaptation of residential structures to the landscape by including garden spaces is characteristic of Spain. The complex mix of influences blends with the harmonic reality of a landscape that can only be identified as itself. Rising up from the hillsides of the valley of the Darro opposite the Alhambra emerges an extraordinary garden city, the Albaicín, which has a unique form of villa garden called the *carmen*. In the vegetable and fruit gardens here, rosemary and lavender blend with flowers, fruits, and vegetables. The Andalusian *cortijos* (isolated single farms) include garden courtyards surrounded by fields.

The *pazos*—"palace" in the language of Galicia—are characterized by a baroque style of architecture that typically includes granite and by shady and lush gardens that in these humid lands give them a romantic air. Valuable gardens have been preserved here, as at the Pazo de Castrelos, which has been transferred to the city of Vigo. The best known is the Pazo de Oca, whose garden was created in the 18th century by the Marqués de Camarasa. Magnificent stonework is found there, and the age of some of the vegetation reaches a hundred years. There is a stone ship with figures of fishermen at the extremes. Located in the middle of a large reservoir that is crossed by a lovely bridge, the ship provides a touch of melancholy to the scene.

Proceeding from the Arabian tradition, the *cigarrales* that rise up from the land in the area around Toledo can be seen from the bank of the river Tajo opposite the city. The *cigarrales* are estates that contain gardens designed for recreation and rest around small houses. The gardens are located on hillsides and surrounded by aromatic plants, as well as olive, almond, and fruit trees. Many *cigarrales,* such as the Cigarral de La Cadena, belonged to religious orders; others are notable for the people who have owned them.

The Majorcan *sones* (rural houses with gardens and orchards) also show an Arabian influence, inasmuch as the knights who reconquered the island in 1229 installed themselves in former Moorish houses. The *sones* are nearly always located in areas of rugged terrain. Through the irrigated gardens, they maintain a relationship with the water; attractive vistas provide a connection to the horizon. With its walkway covered by vines and wisterias, its courtyards and its fountains, the Alfabia in Majorca, today a public park, gives an inkling of what the *sones* were like. At Son Fortuny, formerly a Cistercian convent, the water effects stand out, as does the architecture, which opens out onto the garden through a loggia. The same is true at Son Raxa, which was altered in the 18th century by its owner, Cardinal Despuig, to conform to the Italian taste. At the Son Berga, the Mediterranean form of the *sones* becomes clear, as does its essential role of a family home adapted to the hillside. The small palace occupies a central position above the pine forest and pastures on the estate. The hillside itself has been transformed into terraces and parterre gardens; rows of orange trees form a cross, and there is an orchard of olive trees. On the highest part of the slope, the ensemble terminates in a vineyard.

Parks, Cities, and Contemporary Spanish Landscapes

Since the middle of the 16th century, tree-lined walkways and avenues have been a feature on the outskirts of Spanish cities. These were conceived of as open-air urban salons and were deeply rooted in the social life of the city. Examples include the Paseo del Prado and the Paseo de Recoletos in Madrid, the Paseo de Gracia in Barcelona, La Alameda in Valencia, and La Florida in Vitoria. According to Pascual Madoz, in 1835 there were 487 localities in Spain that had such walkways and avenues. Elm, poplar, and black poplar trees were predominant, although cypress, willow, orange, chestnut, and cedar, among others, were also common. Benches generally lined the walkways as well as, on occasion, aviaries, arbors, reservoirs, and fountains.

The transformation of formerly open spaces on the outskirts of cities, the transference of aristocratic gardens, the confiscation of convents, and the tearing down of city walls gave rise to new public open spaces. The origin of these spaces is evident in the toponyms applied: *prados* (meadows), *campos* (fields), *eras* and *ejidos* (commons), *dehesas* (pastures), *arenales* (sandy areas), *espolones* (retaining walls often used as walkways), *bulevares* (boulevards), etc. Parks of high quality began to appear; these were replanted with vegetation and structured as romantic or neoclassical parks. Some had the features of a botanic garden. Examples are the Campo Grande in Valladolid, with a nursery of over 30,000 plants, the Huerta del Cura in Elche, with a palm grove (*phoenix datilifera*) that is unique in Europe, the Taconera in Pamplona, and the Jardín de San Carlos in La Coruña. In Catalonia and the Levant, walkways—called *Ramblas*—were built over streams in the city and on the outskirts.

In the 19th century Narciso Pascual y Colomer, in an attempt to recover a tradition that had nearly been lost, designed several parks in Madrid and executed two palaces with gardens—one in the city and one in the outskirts—for the influential Marqués de Salamanca. Vista Alegre outside the city has a picturesque garden that recalls the gardens both the Marqués and his architect had seen in Rome. In Barcelona Josep Fonserè designed in 1872 the Parque de la Ciudadela to celebrate the occasion of the world fair.

The history of Spanish parks is also marked by the presence of the French landscape architect J.C.N. Forestier. In 1929 Forestier designed parks to celebrate the occasion of the International Exposition in Seville and in Barcelona. He was adept at incorporating local cultures into the landscape design, and in 1911 Seville entrusted him with the Parque de Maria Luisa. Forestier designed the park respecting the preexisting spaces around the duck pond and the small temple. At the park attractive, peaceful areas have been laid out on an orthogonal design, some of which were inspired by Arabian influences. In 1915 Barcelona charged Forestier with the job of landscaping various areas of the hillside in Montjuich. Forestier designed a lovely rose garden edged by orange trees and hedges of pittosporum and containing a rectangular pond replete with water lilies. The area is enchantingly Mediterranean, with a style resembling the Catalonian *noucentisme* (a Catalonian artistic movement in reaction against the Art Nouveau at the beginning of the 20th century). Forestier's activity was intense. Assisted by his friend and disciple Nicolás Rubió i Tuduri, who would later continue the work of his teacher, Forestier designed Parque Guinardó and the garden at the Palacio de Pedralbes. He also executed gardens in a number of other areas of Spain, but it was in Seville and Barcelona where a singular rebirth of the garden took place, with an intense activity in private gardens that would continue up until the Civil War in 1936.

One singular example of a garden, the Parque Güell, was designed by Antonio Gaudi and constructed in Barcelona between 1900 and 1914. Despite the fact that the garden was left unfinished—or perhaps for that very reason—the architecture at the park stands out for its use of raised platforms, columns, and galleries over the city. A romantic association exists in Spanish gardens that cannot be precisely classified. Forestier captured this in private gardens such as the one at Moratalla in Córdoba. This is also evident in other contemporary gardens such as Santa Clotilde in Lloret de Mar, designed by Rubió, as well as the garden of the Fundación Rodríguez Acosta in Granada, an atypical *carmen* designed by Teodoro de Anasagasti in 1920, with sculptural elements inspired by those of ancient Rome.

The city of Barcelona stands out for its program of gardens and parks, which have been incorporated into urban renovation and development plans on a citywide scale. Three new gardens were designed in 1970 for the area of Montjuich, dedicated to three important Catalonian poets: Mossèn Jacint Verdaguer, Joan Maragall, and Miquel Costa i Llobera. Designed by architects, the Parque del Clot, the Parque de Besós, and the Parque de Crueta de Coll are verification of the evolution from the geometrically modeled park-plaza to a rediscovery of nature and a use of types of vegetation that are capable of providing a sense of place. This may be seen in the rediscovering of the sea front and in parks such as the Park of Dunes de Poblenou and the new Botanic Garden of Catalonia.

Other gardens, such as the Jardín del Turia in Valencia and the Jardín de Juan Carlos I in Madrid, are contradictory manifestations of the model of the urban park as a more natural space. In rare cases, such as the Marimurtra Botanical Garden in Gerona or in the work of César Manrique, whose gardens have been adapted to the landscape of the Canary Islands, a deeper idea of nature is recognizable.

See also Alhambra; Aranjuez; Córdoba, Great Mosque of; El Escorial; Generalife; Islamic Gardens; La Granja; Madinat al-Zahra'; Parque Güell; Seville, Real Alcázar

Further Reading

Añón Feliú, Carmen, and José Luis Sancho, editors, *Jardín y naturaleza en el reinado de Felipe II,* Madrid: Sociedad Estatal para la Conmemoración de los Centenarios de Felipe II y Carlos V, Unión Fenosa, 1998

Brown, Jonathan, and John H. Elliott, *A Palace for a King: The Buen Retiro and the Court of Philip IV,* New Haven, Connecticut: Yale University Press, 1980

Casa Valdés, Teresa Ozores y Saavedra, *Jardines de España,* Madrid: Aguilar, 1970; as *Spanish Gardens,* translated by Edward Tanner, Woodbridge, Suffolk: Antique Collectors' Club, 1987

Dickie, James, "The Islamic Garden in Spain," in *The Islamic Garden,* edited by Richard Ettinghausen and Elisabeth B. MacDougall, Washington, D.C.: Dumbarton Oaks, 1976

Dickie, James, "The Hispano-Arab Garden: Notes towards a Typology," in *The Legacy of Muslim Spain,* edited by Salma Khadra Jayyusi, Leiden, Netherlands, and New York: Brill, 1992

Dominguez Pelaez, Cristina, "Los jardines en España," in *Jean Claude Nicolas Forestier, 1861–1930: Du jardin au paysage urbain,* edited by Bénédicte Leclerc, Paris: Picard, 1994

George, Michael, and Consuelo M. Correcher, *The Gardens of Spain,* New York: Abrams, 1993

Harvey, John H., "Spanish Gardens in Their Historical Background," *Garden History* 3, no. 2 (1975)

Iñiguez Almech, Francisco, *Casas reales y jardines de Felipe II,* Madrid: Consejo Superior de Investigaciones Científicas, 1952

Kubler, George, and Martin Soria, editors, *Art and Architecture in Spain and Portugal and Their American Dominions, 1500 to 1800,* London and Baltimore, Maryland: Penguin, 1959

Navascués Palacio, Pedro, *Arquitectura española, 1808–1914,* Madrid: Espasa Calpe, 1993

Remón Menéndez, Juan F., "The Alameda of the Duchess of Osuna: A Garden of Ideas," *Garden History* 13, no. 4 (1993)

Sancho, José Luis, *La arquitectura de los sitios seales: Catálogo sistórico de los palacios, jardines, y patronatos reales del patrimonio nacional,* Madrid: Patrimonio Nacional, 1995

Soto Caba, Victoria, "Jardines de la ilustración y el romanticismo en España," in *Der Landschaftsgarten: Gartenkunst des Klassizismus und der Romantik,* by Adrian Von Buttlar, Cologne: DuMont, 1989

Torres Balbás, Leopoldo, *La Alhambra y el Generalife,* Madrid: Editorial Plus-Ultra, 1953

Villiers-Stuart, C.M., *Spanish Gardens: Their History, Types, and Features,* London: Batsford, 1929

Wilkinson-Zerner, Catherine, *Juan de Herrera: Architect to Philip II of Spain,* New Haven, Connecticut: Yale University Press, 1993

Winthuysen, Xavier de, *Jardines clásicos de España,* 2 vols., Madrid: Real Jardín Botánico, CSIC, and Aranjuez, Spain: Doce Calles, 1990

JUAN LUIS DE LAS RIVAS SANZ

Srinagar, Shalamar Bagh

Srinagar, Jammu and Kashmir, India

Location: on the lake road at northeast end of Dal Lake, approximately 400 miles (644 km) north-northwest of Delhi

Located at the foot of the Pir Panjal Mountains along a lagoon that connected to Lake Dal, the Shalamar Bagh was the most renowned and praised of the 777 (by Mogul estimates) summer estates built and seasonally inhabited by successive generations of Mogul rulers and members of their family. At 4,921 feet (1,500 m) above sea level, these imperial and nonimperial Kashmiri garden estates were a refreshing retreat from the intense heat

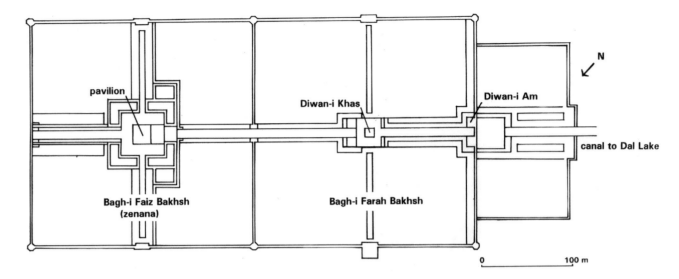

Plan of Shalamar Bagh, Srinagar, Kashmir
Courtesy of D.F. Ruggles

of Delhi, Agra, and the cities of the plains. The Shalamar Bagh was converted from an older garden of the same name to its present form in 1620 when Prince Khurram (the future Shah Jahan; r. 1628–57) dammed a stream near the site at the behest of his father, Emperor Jahangir. Typically one reads that the young patron was coached by his father, but Jahangir's abilities were impaired by his addictions, and it is more likely that Jahangir's wealthy and educated wife, Nur Jahan, was the principal advisor.

The complex was laid out in three stepped terraces and built in two stages, encompassing 40 acres (16 ha) at its completion. The first terrace was reached by boat through a canal flanked by poplars and extending north from the lagoon. This small rectangular garden was a semipublic space where the emperor gave audiences seated on the black marble throne of the Diwan-i Am (public audience hall), which straddled a water channel. The two terraces above and north of this were laid out in classic *chahar bagh* (quadripartite garden) style. The lower one was called the Bagh-i Farah Bakhsh (Garden of the Bestower of Pleasure), and in the contemporary texts the entire Shalamar Bagh was often referred to by this name. This terrace was centered around the Diwan-i Khas, an audience hall where a more privileged class of nobles and court officials was entertained. All that remains of this building, which also bridged the water channel, is the platform, which seems to float in a large water tank. At the west end of the east-west axis of this terrace, a bath hall still stands.

The uppermost level, called the Bagh-i Faiz Bakhsh (Garden of the Bestower of Plenty), was built in 1634 when Shah Jahan ordered that the garden be extended toward the mountain's base and more pavilions added. This garden was the harem quarters (*zenana*) reserved for the private use of the female members of the emperor's family. Commanding a central position, a

large black marble pavilion (*baradari*) still stands amid a large (now empty) tank of water linked to the surrounding walkways by arcuated causeways. Originally domed with black marble, its wooden roof is an unfortunate replacement. Within the tank a multitude of gravity-driven jets that one visitor described as a "forest of silver lances" shot water skyward while on three of its sides water flowed over a bank of recessed niches (*chini-khanas*), which at night could be illuminated with flickering oil lamps for a dazzling effect.

A stream coursed down the center of all three terraces, and as it fell from each level to the one below, it cascaded over chutes (*chadars*) whose rippled textures sent the water into a dynamic dance. The fine mist that rose from the cascades refreshed the viewer, and the sound of its descent joined the trilling of birds to add music to the garden. This central waterway was flanked by water jets that spouted water back into the stream and likewise produced a cooling spray and pleasant sound.

The historians of the period paid more attention to the architecture of these estates than the plantings, which is regrettable since, although many of the pavilions still stand, water is now scarce and the original plantings have long since been replaced by turf and modern-style beds. Contemporary historians described abundant orchards and especially cherry trees, once rare in Kashmir but planted in abundance around Lake Dal by Shah Jahan's day. We know specifically that cypress (admired for its sandalwood-like scent), willow, poplar, quince, almond, apple, date, peach, and jujube trees, as well as grapes, tulips, and clover, were also planted there. References to Kashmiri gardens in general also mention roses, lilies, hyacinths, violets, narcissus, blue and white jasmines, lotus, and anemone. In the Shalamar Bagh the Mogul love of ordered nature—the garden with its waterway imitating a natural stream—was contrasted against a dramatic setting of high mountains. Indeed, the garden was the means by which the calm lake and vertiginous snow-capped mountains were united.

Initially the Shalamar Bagh was the emperor's private property and limited to those members of the court who had business with the emperor. (The Mogul rulers actually resided in Akbar's Hari Parbat fort, across the lake.) But gardens such as these were ephemeral creations and too soon were replaced by new garden estates along the lake. As a garden passed hands from owner to owner, it often declined in value and eventually became a semi-public garden.

Synopsis

pre-1620	Garden laid out during the Mogul period
1620	Stream dammed and garden rebuilt by Shah Jahan
1634	Garden extended toward the mountain by Shah Jahan and additional pavilions built in area called the Bagh-i Faiz Bakhsh (Garden of the Bestower of Plenty)

Further Reading

Asher, Catherine, *Architecture of Mughal India,* Cambridge and New York: Cambridge University Press, 1992

Brookes, John, *Gardens of Paradise: The History and Design of the Great Islamic Gardens,* New York: New Amsterdam, and London: Weidenfeld and Nicolson, 1987

Crowe, Sylvia, et al., *The Gardens of Mughul India,* London: Thames and Hudson, 1972

Habib, Irfan, "Notes on the Economic and Social Aspects of Mughal Gardens," in *Mughal Gardens: Sources, Places, Representations, and Prospects,* edited by James L. Wescoat, Jr., and Joachim Wolschke-Bulmahn, Washington, D.C.: Dumbarton Oaks Research Library and Collection, 1996

Jellicoe, Susan, "The Development of the Mughal Garden," in *The Islamic Garden,* edited by Elisabeth B. MacDougall and Richard Ettinghausen, Washington, D.C.: Dumbarton Oaks Trustees, 1976

MARG Pathway 26 (1972) (special issue on Mughal gardens)

Moynihan, Elizabeth B., *Paradise As a Garden in Persia and Mughal India,* New York: Braziller, 1979

Petruccioli, Attilio, "Gardens and Religious Topography in Kashmir," *Environmental Design* 11, no. 1–2 (1991)

Thackston, W.M., "Mughal Gardens in Persian Poetry," in *Mughal Gardens: Sources, Places, Representations, and Prospects,* edited by James L. Wescoat, Jr., and Joachim Wolschke-Bulmahn, Washington, D.C.: Dumbarton Oaks Research Library and Collection, 1996

Villiers-Stuart, Constance Mary, *Gardens of the Great Mughals,* London: Black, 1913

D. FAIRCHILD RUGGLES

Stadtpark

Vienna, Austria

Location: just outside the Ringstrasse, approximately 0.3 mile (0.5 km) southeast of Vienna city center

No doubt less famous in Anglophone regions than Vienna's older Prater amusement park with its enormous Ferris wheel, the Stadtpark (or town park) is historically the most interesting of all the 800 parks in Vienna. Officially measured at 11.4 hectares (28.17 acres), it was the city council's first public park and remains the largest of the parks bordering the Ringstrasse (one of Europe's most well known boulevards), which, with the Danube canal to the northeast, forms a circular enclosure containing the inner city. The Stadtpark, longer than it is broad, runs along an axis from southwest to northeast on the outside of the southeast portion of the Ringstrasse. The Stadtpark is both less formal than the other principal Viennese gardens and more heavily used because there is excellent public transportation to the park and because of the way in which it links the inner city to the desirable residential area southeast of the street bordering its far side, known as Am Heumarkt.

In 1862–1863, the Stadtpark was laid out on the site of what used to be a moat protecting the Karolinentor, one of the town's gates, in the English landscape style to create "an artificial landscape in the city," according to a modified version of draft plans by the landscape painter Josef Selleny under the direction of Vienna's first garden director, Rudolf Siebeck. The park, at first restricted to the left bank of the Vienna River, was to be given "the friendly character of a pleasure garden, with clumps of bushes, open vistas, sunken paths and flower beds," and was opened on 21 August 1862. The following year a children's park with more shade was opened on the right bank of the stream and joined to the main park by the iron Karolinen bridge, named after the original town gate at the site.

In 1862 the city council bought the famous cast-iron pavilion, which had been exhibited at London's Great Exhibition of 1851, and in 1867 Johann Garben erected the Kursalon at the west end of the park, originally a venue for *thé dansant,* in the heavy neo-Renaissance style of the rest of the Ringstrasse building exteriors. It is still used for summer concerts of light Viennese music, but it is scheduled to become a restaurant in 2005. The original layout of the park, with shrubberies, lawns, and flower beds, was completed in 1872, and the park was arranged to optimize the display with blooms lasting as far as possible throughout the year while toward the Ringstrasse rows of trees form imposing avenues at the edge of the park. In 1906 a plan by architects Friedrich Ohmann and Josef Hackhofer for bridging and covering part of the Vienna River was partially adopted.

The landscape concept has been respected with winding paths and a serpentine artificial lake. Some of the trees and bushes were made subject to preservation orders on account of their rarity in 1941 and 1973. Today the park is most noted for its concentration of Art Nouveau constructions, such as the café Hubner, the municipal garden directorate, and the garden's monuments to half a dozen of Vienna's artists and to some of its most renowned musicians, including Franz Schubert and Franz Lehar. There is a bronze of Anton Bruckner and a marble bust of the Viennese mayor responsible for the park, Andreas Zelinka, as well as a modern steel sculpture by Donald Judd.

Most famous of all are the monuments to "the kings of waltz," Johann Strauss the elder and his one-time rival, Joseph Lanner, and the 1925 monument to Johann Strauss the younger by Edmund Hellmer. The Hellmer statue of the younger Strauss, standing with violin to chin, is framed by a stone arch of naked naiads. Gilded all over, it is illuminated at night and is an important tourist attraction, being on the route of many guided tours. The park is popular and is still used by Viennese painters to exhibit their work. On the right bank of the river are playgrounds for children, and in the interests of the disabled and mothers with baby strollers, access to the park by lift directly from the underground system was arranged in 2000. Except along the path beside the river, dogs are forbidden.

Synopsis

1858–60	Demolition of Vienna's town wall and creation of Ringstrasse
1861	Josef Selleny's draft plan accepted, Rudolf Siebeck employed as municipal gardener
1862	Cast-iron pavilion purchased from Hermann Bergmann and installed; park opened to public
1862–63	Stadtpark laid out as English landscape style garden
1863	Children's park completed
1865	Opening of Ringstrasse
1867	Kursalon concert hall installed by Johann Garben
1872	Park layout completed
1906	Covering over of Wien river completed, designed by Friedrich Ohmann and Josef Hackhofer
1907	Installation of Vienna's garden directorate in Art Nouveau building in park
1941	First tree preservation order, to protect rare species
1973	Second tree preservation order

Further Reading

Berger, Eva, and Ralph Gläzer, *Parkpflegekonzept: Stadtpark Wien,* Vienna: Institut für Landschaftsplanung und Gartenkunst der TU Wien, 1989

ANTHONY H.T. EVI

Stanford University

Palo Alto, California, United States

Location: approximately 20 miles (32 km) southeast of San Francisco

Frederick Law Olmsted's design for the campus of Leland Stanford Junior University was a critical element in his attempt to address the problems of the semi-arid western United States. It was intended as a powerful regionalist statement that would correct the prevailing and, in Olmsted's view, inappropriate stylistic eclecticism. The latter took the form of a broad array of popular architectural styles and the use of turf and non-native plants that could survive in the semi-arid climate only with the liberal use of nonseasonal water. The executed design was a compromise considerably affected by the opinionated Leland Stanford, former chairman of the Central Pacific Railroad Company, governor of California, and U. S. senator from California.

The partial realization of Olmsted's proposals reflects the power of culturally determined architectural and landscape preferences. However, the collaboration between client, landscape architect, and architect was of great significance in the subsequent development of American campus design, a burgeoning interest in California missions as a source for a new architectural style, and an adoption of formalism in architectural design.

Stanford, one of the richest and most powerful Californians in the second half of the 19th century, purchased 650 acres (263 hectares) of the Spanish-Mexican Rancho San Francisquito Palo Alto as a country home in 1860. The ranch was on the San Francisco Peninsula and included softly rounded foothills, gently sloping meadows, and extensive groves of California live oak trees. The impetus was to provide a suitable country home for his only child, Leland Stanford, Junior. The property was named the Palo Alto Farm; it also contained the Palo Alto Stock Farm, an elaborate livestock-breeding farm. By the early 1880s Stanford had increased its size to more than 8,000 acres (3,237 ha).

Stanford enlarged the existing house and surrounded it with a naturalistic garden planted with a large collection of exotic non-native plants. In 1880 an elaborate radial plan was prepared centered on a new house, where the mausoleum was subsequently built. This unfashionably formal plan has been attributed to Stanford's fascination with monumental effects. The only element executed was an oval "Arizona Garden" designed by Rudolph Ulrich, a German gardener who had worked on several estates in the area. Ulrich collected plants for this garden from deserts in Arizona and New Mexico.

The plan's implementation was prevented by the early and unexpected death of the younger Stanford from typhoid fever in 1884, which prompted his grieving parents to found a university in his memory in 1885. The Stanfords visited several eastern universities and hired General Francis A. Walker, the president of the Massachusetts Institute of Technology, as an adviser. He in turn urged Stanford to employ Olmsted.

Olmsted's advocacy of an irregular Picturesque scheme on a site in the rolling foothills commanding picturesque eastward views was rejected because Stanford apparently insisted on a symmetrically monumental layout and landscape treatment. This disturbed Olmsted, who wrote, "I find Governor Stanford bent on giving his University New England scenery, New England trees and turf, to be obtained only by a lavish use of water." Stanford insisted on selecting a level area that had been his son's favorite riding place.

Both Walker and Olmsted agreed that the buildings should be consolidated into a courtyard scheme with the structures linked by arcades. Contemporary popular literature associated this type of design with the Spanish missions of California, a concept that can be directly attributed to Stanford. The Boston, Massachusetts, architectural firm of Shepley Rutan and Coolidge employed the Richardsonian Romanesque style in a honey colored stone that matched the color of the grassland in the long dry summers.

The first proposal for a long east-west oriented quadrangle facing the mountains, with a large memorial church on one side, was rejected by Stanford. The quadrangle was rotated on a north-south axis with provision for expansion with further flanking quadrangles at the sides on the cross axis. The long axial drive from Palo Alto railway station provided a monumental approach focused on a memorial church beyond the massive entrance archway. The main quadrangle was to be paved and contain eight circular beds filled with low-growing plants rising from shrubs to low trees, above which palm trees would provide an effect of "gloria in excelsis."

The monumental axiality of this scheme contradicted Olmsted's Picturesque inclinations, but his proposals for an arboretum exemplified his beliefs in the uplifting power of science and design to change inappropriate practices. Above the quadrangle he proposed the development of a large arboretum of native and non-native trees that would flourish in the semi-arid climate. His superintendent Thomas Douglas was instructed to plant 400–500 acres (162–202.5 ha) with drought-tolerant trees and record how they grew. The initial planting included sugar pine (*Pinus lambertiana*), western yellow pine (*P. ponderosa*), Monterey pine (*P. radiata*), redwood (*Sequoia sempervirens*), giant fir (*Abies grandis*), Monterey cypress (*Cupressus macrocarpa*), Douglas fir (*Pseudotsuga menziesii*), and white cedar (*Chamaecyparis thyoides*). But by 1889 Stanford had completely lost interest in the arboretum, possibly because he did not want the hills covered with extensive plantings of trees.

Olmsted was kept in continual suspense over the campus work. Stanford changed his mind over the paving in the central courtyard, and the planting of the circles was halted, and turf installed in the sunken panels in front of the quadrangle. By 1892 the Olmsted firm was no longer employed at Stanford. After Stanford's death his wife initiated a change in architectural style with the design of the art museum. Yet up to 1919 the Olmstedian concept of arcaded quadrangles was accepted as the basic unit of expansion. After World War II, however, Stanford completely abandoned the courtyard concept and celebrated the free-standing structure.

Olmsted's plan for Stanford University never transformed landscape design in California, as he had hoped, but it succeeded in initiating a new formalism nationally in campus design that lasted for decades and played a critical role in promoting the mission revival style in architecture. By contrast Californian garden design continued to exploit the use of plants from a wide range of temperate and semitropical zones in loosely naturalistic settings. By the 1910s stylistic eclecticism prevailed and formal garden design was common.

Synopsis

1860	Leland Stanford purchases Palo Alto Farm
1880	Garden design completed
1884	Leland Stanford, Jr., dies at age 15
1885	Leland Stanford, Sr., founds Stanford University and hires General Francis Walker, president of MIT, as advisor, and Frederick Law Olmsted, Sr., to design campus landscape; later, Shepley, Rutan, and Coolidge, architects of Boston, were hired
1886–91	Construction of quadrangle completed
1889	Construction of Mausoleum completed
1892	Art Gallery completed
1906	Earthquake severely damages structures on the quadrangle
1919	Main library completed
1921	Stadium completed
1930	Golf course laid out
1937	Frost Amphitheater completed, designed by E. Leslie Kiler
1959	Stanford University Hospital Garden, designed by Thomas D. Church
1986	Inner quadrangle refurbished
1999	Iris and B. Gerald Cantor Center for Visual Arts and Rodin Sculpture Garden, designed by SWA, landscape architects

Further Reading

Beveridge, Charles E., "Introduction to the Landscape Design Reports: The California Origins of Olmsted's Landscape Design Principles for the Semiarid American West," in *The Papers of Frederick Law Olmsted,* vol. 5, *The California Frontier, 1863–1865,* edited by Victoria Post Ranney, Baltimore: Johns Hopkins University Press, 1990

Elliott, Orrin Leslie, *Stanford University, the First Twenty-Five Years,* London: Stanford University Press, 1937

Joncas, Richard, *Building in The Past: The Making of the Iris and B. Gerald Cantor Center for Visual Arts at Stanford University,* Stanford, California: Stanford University Press, 1999

Lettieri, Linda Hittle, "Updating Stanford's Inner Quad," *Landscape Architecture* 76, no. 6 (1986)

McGuire, Diane Kostial, "Early Site Planning on the West Coast: Frederick Law Olmsted's Plan for Stanford University," *Landscape Architecture* 47, no. 2 (1957)

Turner, Paul V., Marcia E. Vetrocq, and Karen Weitze, *The Founders and the Architects: The Design of Stanford University,* Stanford, California: Department of Art, Stanford University, 1976

DAVID C. STREATFIELD

Steele, Fletcher 1885–1971

United States Landscape Architect

Fletcher Steele, landscape architect and author, was a transitional figure between traditional and modern landscape design in the 1920s and 1930s. Well versed in plantsmanship and traditional site design, he advocated a modern landscape architecture that reinterpreted Beaux-Arts design principles in response to modern garden functions, an expanded palate of materials, and new construction techniques. His built designs experimented with new forms, and his writings opened new possibilities of form and materials to the next generation of landscape architects.

Steele began training in landscape architecture at Harvard's new masters program in 1907. He left a year later to intern with Warren H. Manning, where he quickly developed as a plantsman, designer, and planner. Steele took his first grand tour of Europe in 1913, with partial financial support from Manning. In return Steele compiled his extensive collection of notes, sketches, and photographs in a detailed report of landscape design. This collection and additions from later excursions to Europe, Russia, and China became important resources for his design work and writings. The modern French garden experiments of the 1920s and 1930s proved the most influential.

In 1914 Steele established an office in Boston just as thousands of newly wealthy industrialists were entering the country-home market. The country-place era (1890–1925) was part of an unparalleled period of economic growth and unrestrained displays of wealth. Steele and his contemporaries reveled in developing an American landscape style, borrowing a mix of European and Asian design elements in an exuberant celebration of place. Initially influenced by the École des Beaux-Arts, they transferred balance, symmetry, and spatial hierarchies in architecture directly into the landscape and related them back to the house. Steele was unique among his peers, striving to incorporate modern function, whether use or beauty, into the framework and detailing of his gardens. He was soon recognized for reinventing tradition in landscape design. An eclectic designer, he tested innovative forms, materials, and construction techniques.

The gardens Steele first saw at the 1925 Exposition des Arts Decoratifs and Industriels Modernes in Paris heavily influenced his writings and how he regarded his design work. Gabriel Guévrékian, Pierre LeGrain, Albert LaPrade, and André and Paul Vera emphasized the composition of spatial volumes using fractured axes, as well as geometrical three-dimensional elements and patterns in asymmetrical combinations. The work was spatially balanced and composed. Unlike many of his peers, Steele did not regard the use of traditional or nontraditional materials as a central issue; rather, he admired the functional qualities incorporated into the spatial composition of the gardens. The gardens and their implications for U.S. landscape architecture were the center of discussion in articles he wrote for *Landscape Architecture, House Beautiful,* and *Country Life.* A 1930 article entitled "New Pioneering in Garden Design," helped establish a national discussion on the future of landscape architecture and modernism in the United States. Daniel Kiley and Garrett Eckbo cite Steele's importance in developing their ideas about landscape architecture.

The 1920s was also a period of change in the profession of landscape architecture. Among others, John Nolen and Warren Manning were developing metropolitan park systems, community plans, and residential neighborhoods for private and public clients. A division developed between those seeking a larger market for landscape architectural services and those focused on garden design. Steele was an ardent proponent of landscape architecture as a fine art and publicly lamented the profession's move toward "landscape engineers and conservers." He denounced public employment as a corruption of the profession's artistic base and refused to consider any public work.

Steele's garden-design work evolved as he experimented on the large estates and suburban gardens of some of the country's wealthiest clients. Naumkeag (1926–55), Mabel Choate's Stockbridge, Massachusetts, estate, ties together a series of playful and expressive gardens. The Afternoon Garden (1926) borrows floor patterns from Persian carpets; the Chinese Temple Garden (1937) features a sparseness typical of Chinese courtyards; and the Blue Steps (1938) uses cinder block, metal piping, paper birches, and bold color to create spatial volume within the hillside planting. In Charlotte Whitney Allen's Rochester, New York, garden (1915–67), Steele fully succeeded in tying multiple garden rooms into a unified three-dimensional composition. He transformed the flat, quarter-acre (0.1 ha) suburban lot into a highly tailored, richly textured green backyard garden. The garden's structural framework started with a series of space-shaping devices. Walls and grade changes define three separate but related outdoor garden rooms. The fractured axes and architectonic plantings reflect French garden influences. A restrained palette of plantings, carefully selected and placed, establishes strong regular rhythms unifying each room. Design elements such as the pool, arch, and sculptures provide a sense of order, permanence, and clarity. Steele continued experimenting with materials. Because Allen regarded flowers as disorderly, Steele used polychrome, cast-bronze flowers to fill the poolside flowerpots permanently. A Gaston Lachaise nude and Alexander Calder's first outdoor mobile were also commissioned as axial features of the garden. The pool house is the most striking feature. Resembling a Moor campaign tent, it is enclosed with bronze chain mail.

Steele was a prolific writer and through the height of his career contributed to many popular publications as well as professional magazines. A popular lecturer, he spoke regularly at meetings of the influential Garden Club of America and the American Society of Landscape Architects. Although his client list primarily consisted of large-scale estates, he was aware of the growing small-house movement. Many of his articles and talks, as well as his books *Design in the Little Garden* (1924) and *Gardens and People* (1964), addressed middle-income home owners seeking to develop a beautiful and functional garden to fit their needs and income. He provided detailed advice on planning, plant selection, and constructing suitable suburban landscapes for the growing middle class.

During the later half of Steele's long professional career, landscape architects saw him as out of touch with their professional directions. Only during the 1990s, when historians began to review modern landscape architecture's history, was Steele recognized for the significant contributions he provided through his writings toward giving new meaning to landscape architecture as a design art.

Biography

Born in Pittsford, New York, 1885. Attended Harvard University, Cambridge, Massachusetts, for graduate studies in landscape architecture, 1907–9; apprenticed with Warren H. Manning, 1908–14; toured Europe, 1913; opened consulting firm in Boston, 1914; completed more than 500 commissions for such private gardens as Naumkeag in Stockbridge, Massachusetts, 1926–55 and Charlotte Whitney Allen garden in Rochester, New York, 1915–67; traveled extensively to Europe and Asia, which heavily influenced his built work; wrote over 100 articles and two books on garden design and landscape architecture. Died in Pittsford, New York, 1971.

Selected Designs

1915–67	Atkinson and Charlotte Whitney Allen garden, Rochester, New York, United States
1925–48	Angelica Gerry garden, Ankrum House, Lake Delaware, Delhi, New York, United States
1926–55	Mabel Choate garden, Naumkeag, Stockbridge, Massachusetts, United States
1928–32	George and Mary Doubleday garden, Westmoreland, Ridgefield, Connecticut, United States
1928–41	Bok Amphitheater, Camden Public Library, Camden, Maine, United States
1928–42	Standish Bachus garden, Grosse Pointe Shores, Michigan, United States
1929–40	Standish Bachus garden, High Cliffe, Manchester, Massachusetts, United States
1936–53	Harry Stoddard garden, Bass Rocks, Gloucester, Massachusetts, United States
1946–49	Robert and Helen Stoddard garden, Worcester, Massachusetts, United States
1948–54	Catherine and John Bullard garden at Seminole, Nonquitt, Dartmouth, Massachusetts
1963–68	Richard and Nancy Turner garden, Pittsford, New York, United States

Selected Publications

Design in the Little Garden, 1924
"Design of the Small Place," in *House Beautiful Gardening Manual,* 1926
"New Styles in Gardening: Will Landscape Architecture Reflect the Modernistic Tendencies Seen in the Other Arts?" *House Beautiful* (March 1929)
"New Pioneering in Garden Design," *Landscape Architecture* (April 1930); and in *Modern Landscape Architecture: A Critical Review,* edited by Marc Treib, 1993
"Modern Gardens: Europe Blazes a New and Spectacular Trail in Horticulture," *Country Life* (November 1930)
"Landscape Design of the Future," *Landscape Architecture* (July 1932)
"Modern Landscape Architecture," in *Contemporary Landscape Architecture and Its Sources,* 1936
"China Teaches: Ideas and Moods from Landscape of the Celestial Empire," *Landscape Architecture* (April 1947)
Gardens and People, 1964

Further Reading

Birnbaum, Charles A., and Robin S. Karson, editors, *Pioneers of American Landscape Design,* New York: McGraw Hill, 2000

Calkins, Carroll C., *Great Gardens of America,* New York: Coward McCann, 1969

Fitch, James Marston, and Frederick Frye Rockwell, *Treasury of American Gardens,* New York: Harper, 1956

Karson, Robin S., "Fletcher Steele's Last Vista," *Garden Design* 3 (Spring 1984)

Karson, Robin, "Fletcher Steele's Places to Dream," *Landscape Architecture* 78 (December 1988)

Karson, Robin, "Clarity and Elegance: Fletcher Steele's Masterpiece of Design, a Garden Room in Rochester, New York," *Garden Design* 8 (Spring 1989)

Karson, Robin S., *Fletcher Steele, Landscape Architect: An Account of the Gardenmaker's Life, 1885–1971,* New York: Abrams, 1989

Mann, William A., *Landscape Architecture: An Illustrated History in Timelines, Site Plans, and Biography,* New York: Wiley, 1993

Pregill, Philip, and Nancy Volkman, *Landscapes in History: Design and Planning in the Eastern and Western Traditions,* New York: Van Nostrand Reinhold, 1993; 2nd edition, New York: Wiley, 1999

Tobey, George B., *A History of Landscape Architecture: The Relationship of People to Environment,* New York: American Elsevier, 1973

Van Valkenburgh, Michael, "Fletcher Steele," in *Built Landscapes: Gardens in the Northeast: Gardens by Beatrix Farrand, Fletcher Steele, James Rose, A.E. Bye, Dan Kiley,* edited by Valkenburgh, Brattleboro, Vermont: Brattleboro Museum and Art Center, 1984

TERRY L. CLEMENTS

Stourhead

Stourton, Wiltshire, England

Location: in the village of Stourton, 3 miles (4.8 km) northwest of Mere, 10 miles (16 km) south of Frome, and approximately 30 miles (48.2 km) southeast of Bristol

Although he succeeded his father in 1724 at age 19, Henry Hoare II, "The Magnificent," did not take up residence in the house designed by Colen Campbell for Henry Hoare I until his mother died in 1741, after he had spent three years in Italy. A year after this his first wife died in childbirth, and it was after the tragic death of his second wife in 1743, leaving him with a son and two daughters, that Hoare began seriously to make the garden and landscape at Stourhead in the emerging English landscape style.

The garden evolved progressively over about 30 years, beginning with the Temple of Flora (1745), which overlooked a rectangular basin until the great dam was com-

Stourhead, Wiltshire, England
Copyright Ken Gibson/Garden Matters

pleted, along with the zigzag walk through the shades to the Wooden Bridge, and then the Grotto (1748) and the Pantheon; all was completed by 1754. This first phase also included the formal Fir Walk terminated by an obelisk that overlooked the lake and pleasure ground from the east, until it was obscured by the trees.

The return route via the dam overlooking Turner's Paddock Lake, the Rock Arch (1765) to the Temple of Apollo (1765) and the grotto underpass, seems to have been a distinct second phase from 1760, indicating that the landscape evolved piecemeal in the way of the 18th-century dilettante, rather than arising from any preconceived master plan. It seems that creating a view from the far side of the lake to the Stone Bridge (1762), Bristol Cross (1765), and the village and church did not occur to Henry Hoare until he could stand in front of his Pantheon to compose "a charm[in]g Gasp[ar]d picture at the end of the water."

Apart from the Bristol Cross, which was salvaged from a road junction in that city, Henry Hoare employed Henry Flitcroft, a protégé of Lord Burlington and associate of William Kent, architect for all his buildings. But in the development of Hoare's ideas for the landscape as a whole, his friend Coplestone Warre Bampfylde of Hestercombe had an important influence. Bampfylde's panoramas of the garden ca. 1770 (Victoria and Albert Museum) are valuable records, and he is known to have collaborated with making the Cascade, presumably based on the one at Hestercombe. Hoare also extended the Fir Walk to create a terrace ride to Alfred's Tower (1771) and back via the Convent (1760–70).

Although highly significant in the development of the English landscape style, especially for pleasure grounds, Stourhead represents changing attitudes, both in the 18th century and after. Its importance is greatly enhanced by the contributions of successive generations of the family and the strong thread of continuity over more than 200 years. Now it is the responsibility of the National Trust.

Within Henry Hoare II's concept the garden has absorbed progressive adaptations and enrichment to give it an ever-broader significance and appeal. It remains a great work of art, accessible on a variety of levels, which annually raises the spirits of many thousands of visitors.

Synopsis

1722–41	Stourhead house designed by Colen Campbell, for Henry Hoare I with formal garden and Fir Walk
1741–54	Henry Hoare II creates lake, circuit walk, Temple of Flora, Obelisk, wooden bridge, Grotto, rock-work bridge
1760–71	Henry Hoare II creates the Temple of Apollo, grotto underpass, Stone Bridge, Bristol Cross, and Alfred's Tower
ca. 1770	Coplestone Warre Bampfylde creates his panoramas of the garden
1791–1838	Sir Richard Colt Hoare adds wings to house, remodels the drive and the park near the house, builds Terrace Lodge, removes several buildings, lays gravel paths, and introduces many exotic trees and the first rhododendrons
1838–94	Henry Hugh Hoare and Hugh Richard Hoare (third and fourth baronets) add the portico to the house, build the Iron Bridge, and continue planting exotic trees and shrubs, especially conifers
1857	Sir Henry Ainslie Hoare succeeds
1894–1946	Sir Henry Hoare restores the house after a fire in 1902, renovates the garden and many garden buildings, increases the range and variety of trees, shrubs, and conifers, and plants rhododendrons extensively after 1927; gives property to the National Trust
1946–97	Woodlands replanted, buildings repaired, garden renovated, historic vistas reopened, many rhododendrons resited and regrouped
1997	Conservation plan under review; bridge built over road to give access to restored walled garden

Further Reading

Gilpin, William, *Observations on the Western Parts of England*, London, 1798; reprint, Richmond, Virginia: Richmond, 1973

Hoare, Richard Colt, *A Description of the House and Gardens at Stourhead*, Bath, 1818

Hussey, Christopher, "The Gardens of Stourhead," *Country Life* 133 (1938)

Hussey, Christopher, *English Gardens and Landscapes: 1700–1750*, London: Country Life, and New York: Funk and Wagnalls, 1967

Lees-Milne, James, *Stourhead, Wiltshire: A Property of the National Trust*, 5th edition, London: Country Life, for The National Trust, 1958

National Trust, *The Conservation of the Garden at Stourhead and Parts of the Park Relating to It*, Bath, Avon: Bath University Press, 1978

Parnell, John, "Stourhead in 1768," *Journal of Garden History* 2, no. 1 (1982)

Pevsner, Nikolaus, *Wiltshire: With Notes on the Prehistoric and Roman Antiquities*, London: Penguin, 1963; 2nd edition, 1975

Plate 28. Garden at Ilnacullin, Garinish Island, Southwest Ireland
Copyright Robin Whalley

Plate 29. The theater at Sanspareil, Erlangen, Gemany

Courtesy of Staatsbibliothek Bamberg

Plate 30. Neptune fountain at Schönbrunn Palace, Vienna, Austria

Plate 31. Orchids and palm trees at Singapore Botanic Gardens
Copyright Rex Butcher/Garden Picture Library

Plate 32. Contemporary view of the tomb garden (*chahar bagh*) and the mausoleum and flanking buildings as seen from the gateway of the Taj Mahal, Agra, India
Courtesy Ebba Koch

Plate 33. View of the orangery, Versailles, France

Plate 34. Garden painting from the House of Venus Marina, Pompeii
Copyright Stanley A. Jashemski

Plate 35. Garden at Wisley, Surrey, England
Copyright Paul Miles Picture Collection

Plate 36. Himeji Japanese garden of raked gravel, moss, and stone
Copyright Steven Wooster/Garden Picture Library

Turner, James, "The Structure of Henry Hoare's Stourhead," *Art Bulletin* (March 1979)

Walpole, Horace, *Journals of Visits to Country Seats,* Oxford: University Press, 1928; reprint, New York: Garland, 1982

Woodbridge, Kenneth, "Henry Hoare's Paradise," *Art Bulletin* (March 1965)

Woodbridge, Kenneth, "The Sacred Landscape: Painters and the Lake Garden of Stourhead," *Apollo* (September 1968)

Woodbridge, Kenneth, *The Stourhead Landscape,* London: National Trust, 1971; new edition, 1982

Woodbridge, Kenneth, "The Dream of Aeneas: A Rosa Source for Cheere's River God at Stourhead," *Burlington Magazine* (December 1974)

Woodbridge, Kenneth, "The Planting of Ornamental Shrubs at Stourhead: A History, 1746 to 1946," *Garden History* 4, no. 1 (1976)

JOHN SALES

Stowe

Stowe, Buckinghamshire, England

Location: 3 miles (4.8 km) northwest of Buckingham, approximately 50 miles (80.5 km) northwest of London

Stowe has one of the most famous 18th-century landscape gardens in England. In particular it helped to develop the naturalized classical landscape garden, later idealized as *le jardin anglais*. Stowe is significant for many other reasons, too, but especially for the combination and scale of factors involved: the garden alone covers 250 acres (101.2 ha); it was at the forefront of development for over 70 years, involving many leading architects and artists of the time; and it still has the largest collection of 18th-century garden buildings in England.

At Stowe, beginning in 1719, Charles Bridgeman developed one of his first uses of the ha-ha to join the garden to its surroundings in a continuous vista. Thus, the fortified ditch around Home Park allowed garden visitors to overlook cattle grazing in the enclosed park with little visual barrier. Lord Perceval remarked in 1724 that the replacement of walls by the ha-ha "leaves you the sight of a bewtifull woody Country, and makes you ignorant how far the high planted walks extend." In this way the new landscape garden formed a "landskip" around the house, stretching from the garden itself out into the neighboring countryside, just as the villas and temples of Rome and Greece seemed to nestle within their own pastoral settings. The natural successor of Stowe's Home Park, almost enclosed with a ha-ha and garden walks by 1727, was the *ferme ornée*, such as Philip Southcote later developed at Wooburn (Surrey, England) from 1734.

If Stowe is famous for its early use of the ha-ha, so important for the setting of landscape gardens, it is also important for an even more significant change within the garden. Once the countryside could easily be seen from within a garden, it was soon realized that the old formal layouts did not suit the wild nature outside its boundary. Thus, in Horace Walpole's memorable phrase, William Kent led the second revolution in landscape design: "He leaped the fence and saw all nature was a garden." "Nature," it was now assumed, "abhors a straight line." By 1734 Sir Thomas Robinson described Kent's new notion as laying out a garden "without either level or line." He added that Stowe, like a few other gardens, was now full of laborers modernizing the expensive works only just finished. At this time the valley below the parish church was being turned into the exquisite Elysian Fields. The scale there is much smaller than Home Park to the west or Hawkwell Field to the east, both enclosed by an inward-facing ha-ha. During the 1740s Lord Cobham and Lancelot "Capability" Brown, for ten years his head gardener at Stowe, went on to develop this principle on a far larger scale in the Grecian Valley to the north. In turn, from 1751 after leaving Stowe, Capability Brown went on to export elsewhere this ideal of the English landscape garden, with its sweeping lawns of grass and carefully positioned clumps and belts of trees and shrubs, punctuated by sinuous lakes and eye-catching buildings.

As a landscape garden Stowe has always been noted more for its trees and shrubs than for smaller flowers. Many of the garden trees were new introductions to England, such as the large maidenhair tree (*Ginkgo biloba*) beside the Grecian Valley. Some of Brown's fine old cypresses, cedars, and acacias survived into the 1830s, although by this time the garden was not keeping pace with the nurseries in new and rare plants. The cedar of Lebanon (*Cedrus libani*), surviving close to the Temple of Ancient Virtue, must also date from Lord

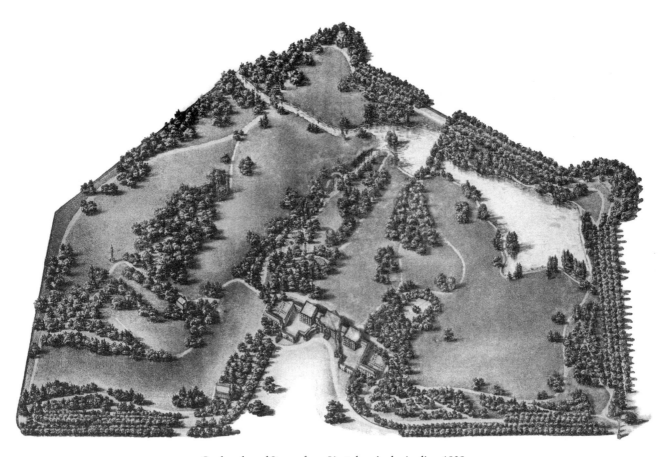

Garden plan of Stowe, from *L'art de créer les jardins*, 1839

Cobham's time. He was the major plantsman at Stowe, although in the 19th century the first duke of Buckingham and Chandos brought in James Brown as gardener, and the third duke replaced many trees lost in his father's sales. By 1989, however, only 5 percent of the garden's trees were more than 70 years old. The original trees were carefully sited—Brown was famous for his machine, probably first used at Stowe, to move semimature trees; in 1770 plantations of deciduous trees were set behind borders of predominantly evergreen trees and shrubs such as laurels, hollies, and magnolias. Not all tree types have continued to be planted at Stowe: the original elms, for instance, which formed the avenues on the Straight Course and Stowe Avenue, have had to be replaced with other species.

Beyond the garden lay the Northern Park, including part of Stowe Woods, a much earlier layout of rides unconnected with the garden. They were important for the income generated by the timber and for the vistas from the garden. During the 19th century the Northern Park became home to the Bucks Yeomanry when the first duke created a new park to the south of the garden. He built a gentle carriage drive through part of the Southern Park as a short cut to Earl Temple's spectacu-lar approach from his Corinthian Arch to his Oxford Bridge. The marquess added a large walled kitchen garden at Dadford; it was later updated extravagantly, but only for a few years, by the second duke.

The 70 years that it took Lord Cobham and Earl Temple to create most of the garden and park, together with their great wealth and personal interest, meant that they were able to call on many of the leading architects of landscape and buildings of that time. Thus, Bridgeman, Vanbrugh, Gibbs, Kent, Leoni, Brown, Miller, Borra, William Pitt, Blondel, Thomas Pitt, Robert and James Adam, and Valdre all supplied advice or plans. Subsequently, other well-known names have been drawn to Stowe, such as Soane, Blore, Williams-Ellis, Blomfield, Lorimer, and Fielding Dodd, making its many layers an informative cross section of landscape history and ideas on restoration.

Stowe's unique collection of over 30 neoclassical buildings or temples adorning its landscape can be matched by few other gardens. Under Lord Cobham and, to a slightly lesser extent, Earl Temple, it led the way in several early flowerings of the neoclassical movement. Thus, it could claim two early classical *rotondos*, a rare rostral column and a trend-setting Grecian temple (now the

Temple of Concord and Victory), however inaccurate in detail at first. This use of innovative buildings has always been one of the most memorable features of Stowe and the one most frequently copied elsewhere. Other original but nonclassical features, such as the Egyptian Pyramid, Witch House, and Chinese House, were removed by Earl Temple as he carefully purified the classical nature of the landscape.

The series of temples began, of course, as a play on the Temple family name and motto (*templa quam dilecta*—how delightful are thy temples) and developed into a complex iconographical program with clear political messages, especially following Cobham's break with Walpole's Whigs over the Excise Bill in 1733. This feature soon lost significance, but it was replaced by Earl Temple's more widespread iconography of liberty and Bacchus. It was aided in part by the significance of over a dozen paintings decorating the garden buildings, along with their magnificent groups of associated sculpture and dozens of inscriptions, mostly in Latin. The result was a complex set of intellectual and aesthetic experiences rarely matched in other gardens.

Stowe's significance was deliberately enhanced by a series of publications designed to promote the fame of the garden. Publicity was intended from the start, since in 1717 Lord Cobham had the New Inn built on the main route from Buckingham and close to the visitor entrance at Bell Gate. From here was sold the unique series of some 35 editions of the *Descriptions* started by Benton Seeley in 1744. Even before this, in 1731, Alexander Pope, a friend of Cobham and a frequent visitor to Stowe, had singled out Stowe for praise in his *Fourth Epistle, to the Earl of Burlington;* the following year Gilbert West had published a whole poem in Stowe's honor. Defoe and Boyse followed with more detailed accounts, and soon Bickham and Wasey competed with Seeley. Meanwhile, in 1733 Rigaud drew and engraved a magnificent series of views of the garden. By 1753 a further three sets of engravings of the grounds and buildings were published, spreading Stowe's influence far abroad. As a result many of Stowe's buildings were soon imitated, with copies from Hagley Park to St. Petersburg.

In the early and middle years of the 18th century, Stowe was renowned as a meeting place for many of the leading literati of the time, including Lord Cobham's Kit-Cat friends such as Vanbrugh and Congreve, Pope, Gay, Swift, West, Lyttelton, Pitt, Hammond, and Thomson. Many of them shared his passion for gardening. The position of Stowe, close to Blenheim and some other north Oxfordshire seats such as Ditchley and Rousham, helped it become part of a regular tour, aided by its proximity to London and to main stagecoach routes.

Stowe's fame as a garden, however, cannot be disassociated from the significance of the family that made Stowe one of the powerhouses at the center of 18th-century British politics. There were four prime ministers connected with the family within the last 50 years or so of the century, and it has been argued that family rifts were partly responsible for the loss to Britain of its American colonies. The sinecures that formed the spoils of high office at the time helped finance the vast expenditure necessary to keep furnishing and rebuilding the house and physically moving over a dozen of the garden buildings.

The family not only sought fame through its house and garden but deliberately aimed at acquiring a dukedom, which they finally did in 1822, just before they lost much of their political influence in the Reform Act. They also achieved the longest surname in the country, quintuple-barreled. The second duke of Buckingham and Chandos could even claim, through his Plantagenet inheritance, a descent from King Henry VII similar in some respects to that of Queen Victoria. At one stage Stowe claimed more visits by royalty than any other private house.

Another factor in Stowe's fame was the family's notorious financial crash just two years after Queen Victoria's visit of 1845. The contents of the house were sold and many trees in the grounds were felled. The money had began to run out in 1805, however, which meant that much of the important 18th-century garden escaped major change after Earl Temple's death in 1779. The direct male line of the family died out in 1889 and ever greater costs led to the estate's sale in 1921.

The year 1923 saw the foundation of Stowe School, a British public school founded with a distinctive philosophy under J.F. Roxburgh, a major figure of 20th-century education in the United Kingdom. The school's first architect, Clough Williams-Ellis, ensured the careful conversion of the building and sympathetic treatment of the grounds. He was personally responsible for helping to save Stowe Avenue. Had the house and grounds not been purchased for the new school, it is probable that the buildings and garden would have been lost. The work of Williams-Ellis at Stowe is particularly interesting, revealing elements of his growing concern for conservation mixed with a delight in siting new buildings in sympathy with the existing landscape, a trait later developed at Portmeirion.

In the fields of restoration and conservation Stowe has often been at the forefront. In 1933 the Stowe School began the first of many campaigns to restore the garden buildings, house, and landscape. In 1954 the school was one of the first two private estates to receive government money for the restoration of garden buildings, and in 1985 the National Trust purchased the Oxford Avenue, the first time it acquired property to enhance an estate that it did not own, although the school had given covenants to the National Trust for over 221 acres (90 ha) of the garden in 1967.

The surveys undertaken by the National Trust, following the Stowe School's gift of most of the garden and park in 1989, have set new standards for detail and thoroughness. They included surveys of the garden buildings, archaeology, and biology, as well as a garden survey by land use consultants, leading to a draft management plan in 1993. In parallel scholars of Stowe's history, led by George Clarke, have begun to research the thousands of documents in the Huntington Library in San Marino. These are being entered into a computerized database to facilitate historically accurate restoration of both landscape and buildings. Especially impressive have been the restoration of the Temple of Concord and Victory under the architect Peter Inskip and the transformation of its surrounding landscape of the Grecian Valley. Silt has been removed from eight of the lakes, and many thousands of shrubs and trees have been planted. Even the Chinese House has been returned to Stowe after an absence of over 240 years.

The house, the key garden temple, was transferred to the Stowe House Preservation Trust in 2000 and is planned to be restored in six phases. With generous financial help the result should be that, by the second decade of the 21st century, the garden and house will be in as good a state as at any time since Earl Temple's death in 1779.

Synopsis

1676–83	New Stowe House built, from design by Cleare, and new Parlour Garden and Abele Walk to south of new house laid out for Sir Richard Temple, third baronet
1711–17	Grand Parterre, replacing Parlour Garden, and area west of house laid out for Lord Cobham
1714–26	Charles Bridgeman involved in laying out garden
1717–24	Lord Cobham develops area north of house and south of Grand Parterre down to Octagon Lake; near main entrance he builds New Inn; Vanbrugh adorns landscape with garden temples, including Nelson's Seat, Temple of Bacchus, Rotondo, and Lake Pavilions
1719	Bridgeman develops one of his first ha-has to join garden to surrounding countryside in continuous vista
1724–32	Garden extended southwest into and around Home Park; Vanbrugh's Pyramid, built in 1724, was turned into his memorial at his death in 1726; James Gibbs adds first Temple of British Worthies and Boycott Pavilion; William Kent adds Hermitage and Temple of Venus
1733–45	East of house, valley near church developed: southern part as Elysian Fields, with buildings by William Kent (Temple of Ancient Virtue, second Temple of British Worthies, and Congreve Monument), and northern part as secluded Alder River flowing from grotto; further east, Hawkwell Field enclosed as rough pasture with buildings by Gibbs (Temple of Friendship and Gothic Temple), linked by Palladian Bridge
1746–49	Lord Cobham, with head gardener, Lancelot "Capability" Brown (employed at Stowe 1741–51), lays out Grecian Valley, with Grecian Temple, Captain Grenville's Column, and Lord Cobham's Pillar
1749	Death of Lord Cobham
1749–62	Earl Temple continues to naturalize landscape, flattening most inward-facing ha-has around Home Park and Hawkwell Field and moving and altering many buildings with help of Borra; on approach from Oxford, builds Oxford Bridge and adds pair of lodges
1762–79	Felling of Abele Walk led to development of grand approach from Buckingham, with Pitt's Corinthian Arch on southern horizon, and rebuilding of South Front of house to Adam's design, as amended by Pitt and possibly Valdre; North Front also rebuilt
1779	Death of Earl Temple
1779–1813	Marquess of Buckingham adds to approaches, while wife has Menagerie built
1813–39	First duke of Buckingham and Chandos completes physical extent of garden by purchase of Lamport Manor, which he replaces with picturesque rock and water garden; adds Queen's Drive and Silverstone Lodges
1839–44	Blore adds several lodges for second duke and moves many statues
1862–1922	Third Duke and his descendants replant some avenues
1921	Harry Shaw purchases most of Stowe estate
1922–49	Harry Shaw sells most of Stowe estate to Governors of Stowe School; some Old Etonians save Stowe Avenue; under J.F. Roxburgh, first headmaster, and Williams-Ellis, school's first architect, new buildings sited west of house
1923	Stowe becomes a school
1933	Stowe School starts program of restoration of historic buildings and landscape

1949–67	New campaign of repairs to historic buildings and landscape started by Stowe School with help of Historic Buildings Council and others
1967	Stowe School covenants 221 acres (90 ha) of garden to National Trust
1967–86	Replanting program drawn up, and over half of garden buildings repaired
1986	Stowe Garden Buildings Trust established, starting work on Temple of Ancient Virtue
1989	Stowe School gives most of garden and park to National Trust, which undertakes detailed surveys and begins ten-year campaign of restoration of buildings and landscape
1995	National Trust buys Home Farm with help from National Heritage Lottery Fund
2000	Stowe School transfers Stowe House to Stowe House Preservation Trust (established 1997)

Further Reading

Beckett, John V., *The Rise and Fall of the Grenvilles: Dukes of Buckingham and Chandos, 1710 to 1921*, Manchester and New York: Manchester University Press, 1994

Bevington, Michael, *Templa Quam Dilecta*, 11 vols., Stowe, Buckinghamshire: Capability Books, 1989–93

Bevington, Michael, *Stowe: The Garden and the Park*, Stowe, Buckinghamshire: Capability Books, 1994; 3rd edition, 1996

Bridgeman, Charles, Jacques Rigaud, and Bernard Baron, *Stowe Gardens in Buckinghamshire; Les jardins de Stowe dans le comte de Bucks* (bilingual English-French edition), London, 1746; reprint, as *Stowe Gardens in Buckinghamshire*, edited by George Clarke, London: BW, 1987

Clarke, George, editor, *Descriptions of Lord Cobham's Gardens at Stowe (1700–1750)*, Aylesbury, Buckinghamshire: Buckinghamshire Record Society, 1990

Clarke, George, and Michael Gibbon, "A History of Stowe: I–XXVI," *The Stoic* 22–27 (1966–77)

Cornforth, John, "Achievement and Challenge: The Preservation of the Stowe Landscape," *Country Life* 189 (April 1986)

Eyres, Patrick, editor, "The Political Temples of Stowe," *New Arcadian Journal* 43/44 (1997)

Gowing, C.N., and George Clarke, editors, *Drawings of Stowe by John Claude Nattes in the Buckinghamshire County Museum*, Aylesbury, Buckinghamshire: Buckinghamshire County Museum and Stowe School, 1983

Hall, Michael, "Stowe Landscape Gardens I–II," *Country Life* 190 (February 1996)

Haslam, Richard, "Concord Restored and Victory Assured," *Country Life* 191 (August 1997)

Knight, George Wilson, *The Dynasty of Stowe*, London: Fortune Press, 1945; 2nd edition, 1946

Macdonald, Alasdair, *Stowe School: An Illustrated History*, London: Dalton Watson, 1977

Pevsner, Nikolaus, and Elizabeth Williamson, *Buckinghamshire*, London and Baltimore, Maryland: Penguin, 1960; 2nd edition, London and New York: Penguin, 1994

Robinson, John Martin, *Temples of Delight: Stowe Landscape Gardens*, London: National Trust, 1990

Stowe Landscape Gardens, London: National Trust, 1997

Sutton, Denys, editor, "The Splendours of Stowe," *Apollo* 97 (June 1973)

Whistler, Laurence, Michael Gibbon, and George Clarke, *Stowe: A Guide to the Gardens*, London: Country Life, 1956; 3rd edition, Milton Keynes, Buckinghamshire: Hillier Designs, 1974

MICHAEL J. BEVINGTON

Studley Royal and Fountains Abbey

Studley Royal, North Yorkshire, England

Location: 2.5 miles (4 km) west of Ripon, 25 miles (40 km) north of Leeds, and approximately 190 miles (306 km) north-northwest of London

Studley Royal, Yorkshire, near Ripon, is one of the most perfectly preserved early 18th-century semiformal or natural gardens in England, together with Hackfall and Kirkby Fleetham, one of three laid out by John Aislabie.

In 1983 it was acquired by the National Trust from the West Riding County Council, to whom ownership had passed from family descent in 1966. Recently discovered account books have allowed a new history to be written of its design and of its once notorious owner who, as chancellor of the exchequer, was disgraced when in 1720 he was involved with the South Sea Bubble. Aislabie came from a prosperous landowning family, and he inherited the estate, about 700 acres (283.3 ha), through his mother's side. In 1651 his uncle, the poet Edmund Waller, began the Hall Barn garden. Work had also been done on the river Skell, which flows down through the landscape from the foothills of the Pennines. It was only after 1693, when Aislabie became full owner, however, that anything on the scale of what is there now was begun.

In some ways the plan of the garden, which was laid out by the gardener William Fisher, is difficult to describe, tracing as it does the irregular line of the river Skell, running essentially south-north from the area around Fountains Abbey through the long canal to a lake at the end. The first reference to the canal comes from 1718; it was a remarkable piece of hydraulic engineering, based perhaps on the manual by A.C. Dézailleurs d'Argentville or that of John James to which Aislabie was a subscriber. The canal follows the natural fall of the ground to cascade past two fishing tabernacles, small classical pavilions, and into the lake at the northern end. The vista along it, now obscured by trees, ended in the sight of a gaming tower on How Hill, the first of the several buildings placed in the garden. To one side of the long straight line of the canal is a small semicircular-shaped pond; to the other is the water garden with its so-called moon ponds, across which, on the center axis, is a small hexastyle Doric temple dedicated to Piety. Below, on the level of the water gardens, is a group of lead sculptures of various classical figures by the French sculptor Andries Carpentière, who was first employed in England by the duke of Chandos at Canons and then at Ditchley and Castle Howard. On one side, on the hill above, is the Octagon Tower, reached by a path that goes through a long grottolike tunnel, a building in the Gothic style with pointed arches, pointed quatrefoil decoration, and pinnacles; to the south is the Temple of Fame, an open rotunda, made of wood.

Across the canal on the other side, and across the Coffin Lawn, is the Banqueting House, completed in 1731 perhaps on design by Colen Campbell, who had done other work for Aislabie at Waverley Abbey. The Banqueting House was the original center of social activity in the garden, and it had some of the most dramatic views, especially toward the Octagon Tower and then to a site behind the Temple of Piety, where there was perhaps another sculpture, set on a platform of which traces remain. Beyond this, to climb southward, the route leads to what is called High Walk and Tent Hill, which opens up a view on one side back to the water beds and to the

fishing tabernacles and the large lake. On the other side it opens to the ruins of Fountains Abbey, a Cistercian monastery, which was at the time of its dissolution in 1538 one of the richest foundations in England.

Aislabie had long wanted to take possession of the abbey site and its ruins, but it was not till 1768 that his son William was able to persuade John Michael Messenger, the owner, to sell him the estate, together with the adjoining Fountains Hall, which had been built about 1611 by Sir Stephen Proctor from the stones of the abbey. By the middle of the 18th century, ruins of this kind were considered the most perfect culmination for the vista of such landscapes, seen perhaps best at a distance and approached, as here, on a long axis, framed by a line of trees. William was careful to preserve what was left, tidying up the ruins, and turning the garden into a Gothic garden, laying out a parterre in the cloister and joining together fragments of tracery rescued from the site. Yet this regularization of the Gothic was criticized by some, for by then taste was turning away from the essentially semiformal design of such a garden as this, with its classical figures and temples, to something more sublime and mysterious; the ruins at Fountains being thought best seen by moonlight, so that, as Arthur Young said in 1770, they might impart "a kind of religious melancholy."

A medieval house on the site, rebuilt in 1748 after a fire and in 1762 given a Gothic portico, was destroyed by fire in 1948. The stables remain, completed about 1731, again with the possible help of Campbell, in a neo-Palladian style, with square turrets at the corners. Scattered also on the estate are gates, an obelisk erected in 1815, and some lodges, built about 1840. Nearby is St. Mary's, built by William Burgess (1871–78). For all these changes, the plantings at Studley Royal were not altered in the 19th century. Although Kirkby Fleetham and, most recently, Hackfall, have disappeared or fallen into ruin, Studley Royal is preserved still; and the forestry program now being carried out will clarify the original plantings of Aislabie using evergreens as framing devices for the vistas, deciduous trees higher up the slopes, keeping the garden its original green. Yew hedges give a program of episodes, or tunnels, connecting the various areas and either muffling or opening up the sounds of the cascading waters.

Synopsis

1651	Poet Edmund Waller begins Hall Barn garden
1693	John Aislabie inherits estate
1693–	Garden laid out by William Fisher
1720	Aislabie, chancellor of the exchequer, disgraced by collapse of South Sea Bubble
1722	Aislabie retires to Studley Royal to devote himself to building garden

1725	Aislabie completes Moon Ponds
ca. 1729	Banqueting House completed, perhaps designed by Colen Campbell
1768	John Aislabie's son William purchases adjacent ruins of Fountains Abbey
1966	Studley Royal acquired by West Riding Council
1983	Studley Royal taken over by National Trust

Further Reading

Bradford Art Galleries and Museums, *Mr. Aislabie's Gardens*, Bradford, West Yorkshire: New Arcadians, 1981

Fleming, Laurence, and Alan Gore, *The English Garden,* London: Joseph, 1979

Haslam, R., "Studley Royal, North Yorkshire," *Country Life* 179 (March 1986)

Hussey, Christopher, *English Gardens and Landscapes, 1700–1750,* London: Country Life, and New York: Funk and Wagnalls, 1967

Richardson, T., "Studley Royal, Yorkshire," *Country Life* 191 (May 1997)

Somerset Fry, Plantagenet, *Fountains Abbey: North Yorkshire,* London: HMSO, 1981

DAVID CAST

Summer Garden

St. Petersburg, Russia

Location: center of the city of St. Petersburg on left bank of Neva River on Kutuzov Embankment near Troitsky Bridge

The Summer Garden, the first garden of St. Petersburg, was founded in 1704, almost simultaneous with the start of the development of the new capital of the Russian Empire. In 1710 the two-storyed Summer Palace was built by Domenico Trezzini. Here a new style of garden art was developed as a part of the program to re-create Russian culture according to the European taste.

During the first years (1704–16) the Summer Garden was designed in the manner of the Dutch gardens Peter the Great had visited during his first travels. The emperor inspected the works himself until his death in 1725. During this period a number of different gardeners were employed, including Ivan Matveev, a Russian, Jan Roosen, a Dutchman, the French architect Alexander Le Blond, and the Russian architect Michael Zemtsov. In the very beginning Matveev made the square plan, divided into bosquets by a rectangular grid of allées. Roosen twice enlarged the garden's territory, adding two additional parts with diagonal roads. At this time too the flower parterres and fountains made of slate were added. The trees were large specimens taken from the nearby forests.

In 1717 Le Blond created the grandiose design for the Summer Garden, combining two existing areas and adding new ones. He laid out the enormous field with the star-shaped system of allées (now the Mars Field, or Marsovo pole) and two large parterres, one in a very complex design, the other more simple. The design by Le Blond was not fulfilled, however, with the exception of the new bosquets near the Summer Palace.

In the 1720s Zemtsov built the second palace in the garden, "the Glorious Banquetting Hall," the grotto with numerous gilded sculptures, and the big labyrinth decorated with the figures of characters from the tales of Aesop. The complicated system of architectural and sculptural decoration expressed the new ideology of the Russian Empire by means of mythological language— the themes of Victory, Peace, Justice, and Enlightenment. Today, 89 allegorical sculptures survive of the original 250, made mainly in the beginning of the 18th century. In the Summer Garden an outstanding system of fountains was created, which worked with the help of a steam-powered engine (1717), the first in Russia.

After the death of Peter the Great the Summer Garden began to deteriorate. In the 1730s it was reconstructed by the Italian architect Bartolomeo Rastrelli with the use of an old design. In the first half of the 18th century it played the role of the court's pleasure garden. By the end of the century it became a public garden. In 1777 a flood destroyed the fountains, which were never restored. In 1773–86 the famous metal fence was constructed along the bank of the Neva by George Felten. In the 19th century the old pavilions of the Summer Garden were rebuilt in a neoclassical style: the coffee house, the teahouse (both in 1837), and others.

Today the Summer Garden preserves the features of Peter the Great's epoch: the main plan and the sculpture. Its greenery is not of special interest and represents

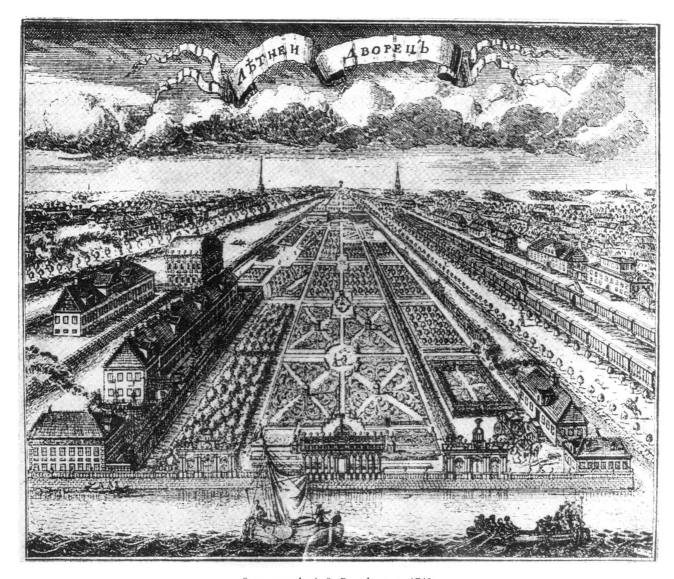

Summer garden in St. Petersburg, ca. 1740s
Courtesy of Moscow Institute of Architecture

the Summer Garden as it was in the late 19th century, but with diminished flower beds. Restoration was begun after World War II.

Synopsis

1703–4	Foundation of Summer Garden by Peter the Great
1704–11	Layout of gardens by Russian gardener Ivan Matveev
1710	Construction of Summer Palace by Domenico Trezzini
1711–25	Gardens developed by Dutch gardener Jan Roosen
1717	Steam-powered machine installed to work fountains; design of garden by French architect Alexandre-Jean-Baptiste Le Blond (never built)
1720s	Second palace (Glorious Banquetting Hall) built by Michael Zemtsov
1723–25	New design of garden by Michael Zemtsov
1732–38	Reconstruction of garden according to design by Bartolomeo Rastrelli
1773–83	Construction of metal fence in neoclassical style, according to design by George Felten
1777	Destruction of fountains by flood
late 18th c.	Garden becomes public
1825–26	Rebuilding of pavilions in neoclassical style

1945–46	Restoration of Summer Garden after World War II

Further Reading

Dubiago, Tatiana, *Russkie reguliarnye sady i parki* (The Russian Regular Gardens and Parks), Leningrad: Gos.

Izd-vo Lit-ry po Stroitel'stvu, Arkhitekture i Stroit. Materialam, 1963

Matsulevich, Zhannetta, *Letnii sad i ego skul'ptura* (The Summer Garden and Its Sculpture), Leningrad: Leningradskoe Otd-nie, 1936

DMITRY SHVIDKOVSKY

Sutherland, John 1745?–1826

Irish Architect and Landscape Designer

John Sutherland's early life is still obscure, the earliest known reference to him being to his design of the landscape park and lodge (1776) at Derrymore, County Armagh, for the lord chancellor of Ireland, Isaac Corry. Sutherland later designed major landscape settings for five Irish country houses that were designed by the important English architect John Nash: Caledon, County Tyrone; Rockingham, County Roscommon; Shane's Castle, County Antrim; Lough Cutra Castle, County Galway; and Gracefield, County Laois. Other important works include the extensive landscape parks at Slane Castle, County Meath; Ely Lodge, County Fermanagh; Ballyfin, County Laois; and Mount Shannon, County Limerick (the last for another lord chancellor, the earl of Clare). Sutherland also designed smaller parks around lesser country houses such as Mountainstown, County Meath, and at Killester, Peafield, and Annesley Lodge, all in north County Dublin. The one urban park that can be assigned to him is that of Mountjoy Square in Dublin.

Sutherland also worked as an architect, in which profession he is listed in the Dublin directories between 1819 and 1826. He designed greenhouses for Charleville Castle, County Offaly, and for Caledon, County Tyrone, a bridge at New Park, County Roscommon, a stable block at Donard, County Wicklow, and a complete range of buildings, including the house as well as the garden, at Oakpark, County Roscommon.

Considerable documentation survives about Sutherland's involvement in two of the best-known personal controversies of the Ireland of his day. He arbitrated when Lord Kingston accused his mother of wasting his inheritance on elaborate landscaping projects at Mitchelstown Castle, County Cork. Sutherland also helped resolve the problem of the bigamy of his client Lord Annesley, to which he had unwittingly contributed by recommending the gardener whose wife eloped later with Lord Annesley and married him bigamously.

Sutherland landscaped in the style of Lancelot "Capability" Brown, and contemporary literature abounds with references to his celebrated taste and skill. One reference attests to the fact that "some of the most splendid places in the kingdom acknowledge him for their founder and reformer." He was criticized by a younger generation of landscape gardeners, including James Fraser and Edmund Murphy. Designers in the later picturesque, or more natural, style of gardening, they felt that Sutherland did not harmonize his designs sufficiently with the surrounding natural landscape. Sutherland retired in 1826, handing over his practice to Arthur Snow, his assistant for nearly 30 years, and died later that year.

A full-length portrait by Martin Cregan, the prolific Irish portrait painter, shows Sutherland at work in the park at Shane's Castle, County Antrim. It survives in the collection of the present Lord O'Neill.

See also Edinburgh, Royal Botanic Garden

Biography

Born ca. 1745. Professional landscape gardener, first known commission was for Derrymore, Armagh, Ireland, ca. 1776; practice consisted mainly of designing landscape parks in "Capability" Brown style around aristocratic country mansions, including five houses designed by famous English architect John Nash; known to have designed one urban park (Mountjoy Square, Dublin, Ireland) and to have practiced also as architect; portrait painted by Martin Cregan, ca. 1820; practice continued by his assistant, Arthur Snow. Died in Dublin, Ireland, 1826.

Selected Designs

1776	Estate of Isaac Corry, Derrymore, Armagh, Ireland
1787	Slane Castle, Meath, Ireland

1803   Garden, Mountjoy Square, Dublin, Ireland
1807   Caledon, Tyrone, Ireland
ca. 1810 Rockingham, Roscommon, Ireland
ca. 1813 Shane's Castle, Antrim, Ireland
ca. 1818 Lough Cutra Castle, Galway, Ireland

Further Reading

Bowe, Patrick, "Mr. Sutherland's Elegant Taste," *Country Life* (14 July 1977)

Bowe, Patrick, "Some Irish Landscape Gardeners," in *National Trust Studies: 1981*, edited by Gervase Jackson-Stops, London: Wilson, and Totowa, New Jersey: Sotheby Parke Bernet, 1981

Lamb, Keith, and Patrick Bowe, *A History of Gardening in Ireland,* Dublin: National Botanic Gardens, 1995

Malins, Edward Greenway, and the Knight of Glin, *Lost Demesnes: Irish Landscape Gardening, 1660–1845,* London: Barrie and Jenkins, 1976

PATRICK BOWE

Sweden

Sweden, one of the four Scandinavian countries, is not clearly defined either in terms of the history of gardening or its geography, climate, botany, or culture.

The topography of Sweden has characteristics that broadly resemble those of Norway and Finland. Danish topographical characteristics can only be found in the southwestern part of the province of Skåne. The boundary between northern and Central Europe passes through Skåne in the south, while the Arctic Circle cuts through the country in the north. However, all of Sweden is characterized by its proximity to the sea. There are relatively small differences between temperatures in the summer and those in the winter. Westerly winds are predominant, bringing areas of low pressure along the North Atlantic polar front that in turn result in very unstable weather conditions. The Swedish climate can be described as humid-temperate. An arctic climate can be found in the mountains, and there are semiarid conditions on the large islands of Öland and Gotland in the Baltic.

The Swedish garden has been developed with these physical features as a distinct background: large distances, vast forests, ample waterways, and few people. It is from the combination of nature (mountains, forests, lakes) and cultivated land (forest meadow, pastureland) on the one hand and imported gardeners, architects, and expressions of form and plants on the other hand, that Swedish landscape gardening and landscape architecture has obtained its distinctive character.

Since the Middle Ages, Sweden has been divided into three areas. Götaland (in the south), Svealand (on a level with Stockholm), and Norrland (in the north), areas that are the results of physical geographical conditions as well as culture-historical circumstances. The Scandinavian mountain chain (the Caledonian mountains) stretches out in the far north and west. The divide, with summits above 2,000 m (2,187 yd.), forms a boundary with Norway. Large continuous forests with spruce and pine (*Picea abies, Pinus sylvestris*) that make up part of the boreal pine-forest region, the taiga, cover most of Norrland. Most of the settlement in this area is along the coast and the major rivers. Svealand and Götaland are primarily part of the boreal-nemoral zone. Pine forests also predominate in this area, but there are features of valuable deciduous forest in the central Swedish plains. The forest oak (*Quercus robur*) also grows abundantly here in forests and enclosed pastures. The area around Lake Mälaren, with waterways in Lake Mälaren and Lake Hjälmaren west of Stockholm, and the plains that are part of it, makes up one of the oldest Swedish districts with cultural traditions and is at present one of the most populated areas in the country. The southern end of Sweden and its coasts is a part of the boreal deciduous forest area (*Tilia cordata, Acer platanoides, Fraxinus excelsior, Ulmus glabra*) with a major streak of beech (*Fagus sylvatica*). In addition to the Stockholm area, the Öresund area (including surrounding areas of Denmark and Skåne, Sweden) today makes up the most expansive region in the country.

Sweden was completely covered by the inland ice during the last ice age. The ice started melting in the south some 13,000–14,000 years ago, and by approximately 7,000–6,000 B.C. the whole country was ice-free. However, there are still glaciers remaining in the Scandinavian mountain chain. The oldest known traces of people (remains of settlements) in today's Sweden (Skåne) can be dated back to around 11,000 B.C. These people were reindeer hunters, fishermen, and gatherers, and arrived in Skåne via the causeway from Själland (Zealand) during the summers, approximately at the same time as the birch tree (*Betula pubescens*) and the pine tree (*Pinus sylvestris*) found their way into Sweden. There are coastal settlements, as well as graves and grave-fields dating back to Mesolithic time (8,200–4,000 B.C.). The yew tree (*Taxus baccata*) also found its way into Sweden during this time (around 7,000 B.C.).

The first large monuments in the Swedish landscape, such as dolmens and passage graves, were erected during early Neolithic time (4,000–3,300 B.C.). The beech (*Fagus sylvatica*) colonized the country from the south during middle Neolithic time (ca. 3,000 B.C.), as did the hornbeam (*Carpinus betulus*) half a millennium later.

The conspicuous rock carvings (agricultural carvings) on flat rocks and boulders, for example in Tanum in the province of Bohuslän, were most likely part of a fertility cult and date from the earlier Bronze Age (1,800–1,100 B.C.). Spruce (*Picea abies*) also starts its colonization through the country at this time, spreading from the north and from Finland toward the south. The grave in Kivik in Skåne (ca. 1,000 B.C.), a grave with ten stone slabs under a mound of stones several meters high and 75 meters (82 yd.) in diameter, forms a mighty landmark by the coast. We know of major settlements with houses built with three large naves from the later Bronze Age (1,100–500 B.C.).

The later Iron Age (400–550 A.D.) brought fortifications, so called ancient castles, that were partly natural and situated at high points in the landscape. The custom to erect memorial stones with runic inscriptions began ca. 300 A.D. and culminated during the period 950–1,100 A.D. More than 3,000 runic inscriptions have been discovered and are now protected in Sweden. Birka in Lake Mälaren was from the 8th century to the beginning of the Middle Ages an ancient Swedish "city" or trading center. The largest tumulus in Sweden, Ales stenar (Boulders of Ale, 67 m [73 yd.] long, 59 boulders) at Kåseberga on the south coast, has been dated back to the Viking Age.

The question concerning the oldest garden in Sweden, where it was situated or what it looked like, cannot be given a definitive answer. The problem is partly an etymological one. The Old Swedish concept *trægarper*, which now is *trädgård* in modern Swedish, is more than 1,000 years old. It is a compound based on the two nouns *träd* (tree) and *gård* (yard). In its original meaning the word *trädgård* only referred to an enclosed area surrounded by trees, in most cases fruit trees, but also valuable lopped deciduous tree. Today the word *trädgård* is a Swedish comprehensive term for any yard with garden contents.

The greater problem, however, is how to define the phenomenon of the garden in the context of Swedish history and landscaping, and where to draw boundaries for the definition of the garden. Through spatial reconstructions of the landscapes from as early as during the Stone and Bronze Ages, as seen from ever more numerous and sophisticated archaeological research findings, what we see is a constantly and dynamically changing mosaic landscape. For example, there are cultivated manmade forest landscapes with arable strips of land, no larger than gardens, that appear in a manner we today might call a park, where there was grassland; thinned out, burnt down, and grazed forests; lopped and ringbarked trees; stumps with rootsuckers; and deliberately spared useful trees and bushes, such as linden, crab-apple, hawthorn, sloe, dog rose, and hazel. Archeologists in Sweden today very carefully use the concept of garden during this period. We can no longer ignore the possibility that from early on many plants could have been found in something resembling vegetable gardens or herb plots.

"The Primeval Garden," in a traditional sense, is best described as a small utility plantation, a fruit or kitchen garden in a small square or rectangular enclosure or bed. We know of such cabbage, onion, and angelica gardens from the Viking Age (800–1050 A.D.), for example in Birka, through archaeological findings and from medieval law texts. The oldest garden phenomenon mentioned in Scandinavian literature is the herb garden in which the Norwegian queen Ragnhild had a dream ca. 850 A.D.

Another expression of the northern European garden is older, however. It is the forest meadow (*lövängen*), and it reflects the whole Scandinavian culture of infields with broad-leaf gathering, hay-making, and a very deliberate utilization of useful and bearing trees in meadows as well as in pasture lands. It originated chiefly as a consequence of the dramatic deterioration in the climate in the 6th century B.C. Both because of the cold weather and the snow-covered ground, it was no longer possible for the animals to graze all year round. Instead they had to be put into stables, and consequently there was a need to harvest their feed (hay and leaves) the year before. The meadows, shaped by farmers to get just enough light to the ground for an optimal grass harvest but to still have enough trees to lop and as many bearing trees and bushes as possible, became comprehensive landscaping expressions. A profusion of flowers was obtained into the bargain. For that reason it can be said that the forest meadow is the Swedish farmer's most original garden. In some areas of Sweden it took until the late 19th century and the early 20th century before "the common garden" gained ground. Today most of the remaining forest meadows can be found along the east coast of Sweden and on the islands of Öland and Gotland, for the most part as nature reserves. Nordic folk songs have their origin in the forest meadow landscape.

The history of Swedish gardens during the Middle Ages (1050–1550 A.D.) is traditionally described as closely linked to the establishment of the monastic system in the country from the beginning of the first half of the 12th century, with its new cloisters and herb gardens. The introduction of new horticultural plants as well as new methods of cultivation and growing is often credited to the Order of St. Benedict and the Cistercian Order. Some 20 of the Cistercian monasteries were built in the country during the second half of the 12th century. Some of the important monasteries were Herrevadskloster (1140s) in the province of Skåne, Nydala (1143) in the province of Småland, Varnhem (1150) in the province of Västergötland, Alvastra (1143) in the province of Östergötland, Vårfruberga (1160s) in the province of Sörmland, Roma (1164) on the island of Gotland, and Riseberga (1195–1200) in the province of Närke. A visit to the partly reconstructed monastery in Alvastra still recalls a full medieval monastic environment to the attentive observer. Sister Botilda of Vårfruberga, who worked during the 12th century, is Sweden's first female gardener known by name.

Sweden's first deer park may have been Dalby Hage in the province of Skåne. It is connected to the Dalby church, the oldest stone church still standing on the Scandinavian peninsula from ca. 1060 and an early episcopal see. Important documentary evidence of the introduction of plants during the Middle Ages can be found in the works from ca. 1300–1450 of the Danish physician and canon Henrik Harpestreng from Roskilde. Some 120 different horticultural plants were introduced in southern Scandinavia from ca. 1050 until the end of the 15th century. The oldest and possibly the largest tree in Sweden (trunk circumference is greater than 13.50 m [15 yd.]), also dating back to the early Middle Ages, is the Rumskullaeken (*Quercus robur*) in Norra Kvill in the province of Småland, growing in an old pasture landscape.

St. Bridget's Abbey and its extensive gardens in Vadstena originated in the mid-14th century. They were designed in part by one of Sweden's first gardeners known by name, Johan Päterson, at the request of St. Bridget herself. The garden lives on in an unbroken tradition of space and atmosphere, with possibly partly authentic middle age plants, mostly the carpets of spring snowflakes (*Leucojum vernum*) under the fruit trees. No abbey grounds have yet, however, been excavated by archeologists with respect to the design and contents of Swedish gardens. We still know very little about the gardens of the secular medieval manor houses and princely manors. There are, however, some traces of gardens on the island of Gotland and at Alsnöhus (the 13th century) on the island of Adelsön in Lake Mälaren.

From the beginning of the 16th century the Vasa kings, like Nordic Renaissance princes, took over the role of the monasteries in the design and administration of horticulture. The Reformation was a lengthy process in Sweden and continued during most of the 16th century. The general cultural influences at this time mostly originated from Holland and Germany. The new gardens were laid out around the castles of Uppsala, Svartsjö, Gripsholm, Stockholm, Linköping, Strängnäs and Kalmar, built by King Gustaf I (Gustavus Vasa) and his sons, and were designed by imported architects, gardeners, and artists.

It is possible that the gardener Hans Friese, sent for in 1545 from Friesland (Holland), was the first to introduced box (*Buxus sempervirens*) in Sweden, a plant that became standard for all new border hedges, embroidery parterres, and topiaries of the new North European Renaissance style. Apart from working at the castles, Friese was also active in the Kungsträdgården, the court cabbage garden, as early as the 1430s; today it is the oldest preserved park in Stockholm, together with Humlegården. Jean Allard, a French gardener hired by King Erik XIV in 1563, gave Kungsträdgården a rectangular shape and an overall architectural design and transformed it into a pleasure garden. According to some information the first wintering house for frost sensitive plants (orangery) was built here in 1565.

The oldest preserved Swedish garden design is an herb garden on a grassy bastion at the castle of Uppsala. It was designed by the architect of King Johan III, an Italian by the name of Fransiscus Pahr, around 1572. The large gardens of Nyköpingshus in the province of Sörmland, shaped as squares, crosses, and diagonals and constructed during the 1580s and 1590s, were the chief contribution of King Karl IX to Swedish landscape gardening during the turn of that century, with the assistance of the gardener Hans Gardinär. The free-standing gardens were arranged into regular designs during this time and included bird houses and game courts. The utility cultivations of King Karl IX were also considerable.

The finest Renaissance garden in Scandinavia from the 16th century can be found at the castle of Uraniborg on the island of Ven, in Öresund, at that time part of Denmark and owned by the world famous astronomer Tycho Brahe (1546–1601). The garden, like the whole construction, blossomed during the 1580s and 1590s in a strict geometric composition of circles, crosses and squares; a cosmic projection on earth of heavenly conformities to law. The construction presents great similarities with the botanical garden of Padua (1545), and the main building itself has been modeled after Andrea Palladios' Villa Rotunda outside Vicenza. Even from a European perspective, Uraniborg constitutes a unique and harmoniously composed construction of different buildings, outer gardens, and inner herb gardens together with ramparts. It was re-inaugurated in 1992 after a reconstruction of one fourth of the garden. An ongoing project of tracing, supporting, propagating, and reintroducing a historically authentic plant life is associated with the establishment.

In the 17th century, Sweden became a great power. One of the results of this change can be seen in the dramatic advances in garden culture. Between the middle and end of the 17th century, the country advanced from the position of a European bystander to that of a leader. Many new manors and estates were built and established during this time. Between 1630 and 1650 many Renaissance manors and castles were built in Scania, which at that time was part of Denmark.

In the middle of the 17th century, the Germanic style of Renaissance building lost its importance and was no longer a source of inspiration in Sweden; this was the era of French design art. In 1648 Queen Christina of Sweden requested that the French gardener André Mollet (ca. 1600–1665) attend the Swedish court. At about this time two of Sweden's foremost architects returned from their travels through France and Italy, Jean de la Vallée (1623–96) and Nicodemus Tessin the Elder (1615–81). Both architects had been inspired by André Le Nôtre and his creations at Vaux-le-Vicomte on the outskirts of Paris.

In 1681 Nicodemus Tessin the Younger (1654–1728) was charged with managing Drottningholm's palace and gardens as well as other royal residences such as Strömsholm and Ekolsund. The axial style with main axis and adjacent groups of gardens reached its perfection in Sweden through the work of Tessin the Younger. Drottningholm is one of Sweden's most important landmarks in garden art and is named on the United Nations Educational, Scientific, and Cultural Organization (UNESCO) World Heritage List.

Johan Hårleman (1662–1707), one of the most able baroque gardeners in Sweden, worked with Tessin the Younger on Drottningholm and many other sites. A few decades into the 18th century, his son Carl (1700–1753) became a prominent garden architect as well. Although Carl Hårleman remained faithful to the French style, he replaced the graceful boxwood ornamentation with elegantly contoured grass and lawns. He was also responsible for giving the kitchen garden more prominence, for "enlightenment and housekeeping." The kitchen garden was given more space and featured more clearly in the general plan of a garden by being regular and distinct. Carl Hårleman was also active in Svartsjö, Ulriksdal, Övedskloster in Scania, and the botanical gardens of Uppsala and Lund in the 1740s.

It was generally the lords of the manors and the owners of large estates, the so-called gardening lords, who introduced the English park to Sweden. These parks were to take over from the more formal gardens around many manor houses and castles during the late 17th and early 18th centuries. The most important Swedish landscape gardener of the new style was Fredrik Magnus Piper (1746–1824). He was greatly influenced by the parks he had visited in England, Stourhead and Painshill in particular. When he returned to Sweden in 1780, he was commanded by King Gustav III to transform the gardens surrounding the palace of Drottningholm and Haga. The king took an active interest in this work and had very clear wishes and diagrams for what he wanted done.

In the middle of the 18th century, Carl von Linné and his followers burst onto the scene in Sweden and throughout Europe at about the same time that the science of botany came of age. A stream of previously unknown plants now came into the country. Sweden's first agricultural society was formed in the 1790s followed by the Royal Swedish Academy of Agriculture and Forestry in 1811 and the Swedish Garden Association in 1832. The elementary schools' charter of 1842 declared in their vision of the future that all teachers should teach garden management, and gardens were successfully established in schoolyards throughout the country.

The theory of gardening was taught by the Royal Swedish Academy of Sciences from 1791 at the Bergianska Trädgården. In 1832 the Royal Swedish Academy of Agriculture and Forestry's School of Gardening was founded on the Proving Ground, and in 1876 Alnarps Horticultural College was established. Following the first major expansion of the Swedish railway network, the Department of Gardens of the Swedish State Railways was established and Olof Eneroth was appointed director. The Swedish State Railways was a pioneer in the promotion of Swedish garden heritage; they had their own planting organization complete with gardeners and nursery.

It can be said that Knut Forsberg (1827–95) was the heir to Piper's ideas. In 1851 he was awarded a prize for his suggestion for the grounds at Bois de Bologne in Paris, France. Gardens drawn by him in the "German style" frequently reflect the central axis with perspective and a degree of symmetry close to the main buildings but with less strict dimensions further away. Berzelii Park in Stockholm, Nääs Slott in the province of Bohuslän, and Gerstorp in the province of Östergötland are typical examples.

Sweden's first city park was laid out in the 1860s and was inspired by both German and English gardens. A period of intensive building and planning followed until the end of the century, with a peak in the 1880s. Kingspark and Slottspark in Malmö are well-known examples. In 1893 the first people's park was laid out in Malmö at the initiative of the labor movement. An earlier people's park, Krokbornspark, had been laid out in 1796 by mining advisor Detlof Heijkensköld in Hällefors. In 1895 the first allotment was laid out in Malmö, adjacent to Pildamm Lake.

In 1921 the Swedish Association of Gardeners was founded, and in 1971 the National Swedish Federation of Landscape Gardeners was established. Many of Sweden's most eminent garden enthusiasts and characters have been members of these organizations. They include Rudolf Abelin (1864–1961), who promoted Norrvikens

Trädgårdar, the women pioneers Ruth Brandberg (1875–1944) and Ester Claesson (1884–1931), Sven A. Hermelin (1900–1984), Walter Bauer (1912–94), the manor house and estate restoration pioneer Ulla Molin (1909–97), the private house garden architect and professor Per Friberg, Gunnar Martinsson, and Sven-Ingvar Andersson, all of whom are currently working on local and international projects.

Further Reading

Broberg, Gunnar, Allan Ellenius, and Bengt Jonsell, *Linnaeus and His Garden,* Uppsala, Sweden: Swedish Linnaeus Society, 1983
Margareta, Crown Princess of Sweden, *The Garden That We Made,* New York: Stokes, 1920
Parker och trädgårdar i Sverige; Parks and Gardens in Sweden (bilingual Swedish-English edition), Lund, Sweden: Tralala Reklambyrå, 1997
Phibbs, John, "Pleasure Grounds in Sweden and Their English Models," *Garden History* 21 (Summer 1993)

KJELL LUNDQUIST
Original part of this essay translated by Gunnar Thander; part of this essay first appeared in "Den Svenska Trädgården: En Kulturhistorisk Skiss" by Kjell Lundquist in Parker & Trädgårdar i Sverige, 1997, *copyright P.A. Norstedts & Söner AB; reprinted by permission of the publisher*

Switzer, Stephen 1682–1745

English Garden Designer and Writer

Stephen Switzer was a gardener, designer, seedsman, and writer. His greatest contribution to garden history and design was his documentation of and advocacy for the shift to a more natural style that was eventually known as "landscape gardening." He and Charles Bridgeman were the first professional gardeners to support and practice this revolutionary new style of design based on irregular shapes and winding paths as opposed to the symmetrical, regular shapes still popular in English gardens at the time. He was opposed to the stiffness in garden design usually associated with the Dutch style—clipped hedges, topiary, formal arrangements of plants, and parterres.

In his first book, *The Nobleman's, Gentleman's and Gardener's Recreation,* published in 1715, Switzer describes his views of forest or rural gardening, calling for the management of large properties as gardens, using no walls and instead planting trees and placing walkways to provide views of long vistas from the house. He said that flowers and decorative elements were suited to town gardens or to the property closest to the house but that the remainder should rely on woods, groves, and agricultural integration. His idea was that actively managing an estate was the key to enjoying and making a profit from the countryside.

In 1718 Switzer published an expanded edition (three volumes) of his first book entitled *Ichnographia Rustica.* This work is his major contribution to the history of garden design. The first volume is mainly a history of garden-ing with additional essays on soil, weather, and raising forest trees. The second is about surveying and features illustrations of garden designs, and the third focuses on agricultural matters and includes more designs.

Switzer's theory of design was based on three main principles, which he described in the preface to *Ichnographia* (taken from a passage in Horace's *Ars Poetica*): *utile dulchi* (careful mixture of pleasure and practical use), *ingentia rura* (genius of the place), and *simplex munditiis* (simple means, combination of symmetry and variety as observed in nature). "The purport, that the whole art of gardening lies in combining use and beauty, extensive countrysides and simple means of ornament, departed radically, by stressing *ingentia rura* and *simplex munditiis,* from the medieval and renaissance tradition of a garden's essentially enclosed and ornate character" (Hussey, 1967).

Switzer praises Wray Wood at Castle Howard in his book for its imitation of nature, "from which the Ingenious may draw the best of their Schemes in Natural and Rural Gardening." His insistence on the interrelationship between gardening and agriculture is rooted in Virgil's *Georgics,* made popular at the time by Dryden's 1697 translation. Switzer also expressed the belief that following nature meant following the ancients. He admired and quoted ideas from his contemporaries—such as Alexander Pope and Joseph Addison—as well.

Other circumstances in the culture at the time contributed to the developing acceptance of the landscape movement. Many of the woodlands in England had been depleted and were in desperate need of being replanted, and the use of enclosure in agriculture was transforming the appearance of the countryside. In addition, the climate of opinion was related to the Whig settlements of 1688 and 1715, which vindicated the principles of democracy, toleration, and freedom as sensible means of reconciling antagonisms. A theme in Switzer's writing is the combining of opposites—pleasure and business, use and beauty, uniformity and variety—which was characteristic of Whig idealism and fundamental to the principles of what was to become the "landscape garden." Switzer did not use that term; instead he described this new approach as "extended or rural and forest gardening."

As an apprentice to George London and Henry Wise, Switzer worked at Castle Howard and Blenheim. London and Wise were among the most noted gardeners of their time and founded the renowned Brompton Nursery of London (1681), which first made the supplying of plants for gardens into a big business, maintaining large reserves of box, yew, hornbeam, and lime. Their designs followed the French style, referred to as *"la grand manier,"* with managed grounds extending far beyond the house and featuring woods and groves with wide pathways intersecting all. Though Switzer embraced the expansiveness of the style, he rejected the straight roads and regular geometric shapes created by equal lengths radiating out from a central axis. He moved away from Wise and London and toward John Vanbrugh, whose ideas about grand simplicity he admired. By 1710 Switzer was no longer associated with London and Wise.

The only full design that is known to be by Switzer is Grimsthorpe. The design included economically viable fields and woods as well as mock fortifications and bastions. An arm of the garden was taken along the ridge of the hill so that fields remote from the house could be viewed. It featured serpentine paths and extensive tree plantations. Switzer published an idealized version of this design in the 1718 edition of *Ichnographia* (volume 2) with the name Manor of Paston. By the 1730s his recommendations for Grimsthorpe had largely been put into practice.

Around the same time, Lord Bathurst created an extensive garden at Riskins in Buckinghamshire. Switzer praised the garden in *Ichnographia* as a grand example of a *ferme ornée,* the enactment of the classical ideal of integrating a working farm with a philosophical retreat. It represented the unity of beauty with profit—and use with pleasure—which were within the means of a person with modest income, writes Douglas Chambers in *The Planters of the English Landscape Garden* (1993).

Another design, one that Switzer published in *Ichnographia* (volume 3) as a depiction of his style, was a plan of a "rural and extensive garden." It shows a large estate divided into woodland and fields with some straight and some meandering roads. Some historians have suggested that it is remotely derived from Blenheim.

In 1727 Switzer moved to London and established a business as a seed merchant. Several years later he also had his own nursery at Millbank. He relied more and more on his abilities as an agricultural improver and continued to write.

Switzer helped John Boyle with improvements at his estate, Marston Bigot, in 1737. The design, which appears in the fourth volume of Colin Campbell's *Vitruvius Britannicus* (1739), shows fountains of the type with which Switzer was known to have been involved. Recently John Harris (1990) has suggested that Switzer designed the garden for Stamp Brooksbank's home (1728) in Clapton near London.

The advancement of silviculture during this time is documented by the great difference in diversity of species mentioned in Switzer's essays in *The Practical Husbandman* (1733) as opposed to those mentioned in the 1718 edition of *Ichnographia*. In the latter he mentions oak, ash, beech, chestnut, hornbeam, Scotch pine, silver spruce, elm, lime, and poplar, which is no more extensive than those described by John Evelyn a half-century earlier in *Sylva* (1706). By 1733 Switzer wrote, "Any one who would strive to bring the raising and planting of forest trees to their utmost Perfection . . . ought not to be content with treating barely on those Plants which grow at Home." By 1752 the techniques and principles described by Switzer had become convention.

Biography
Born in Hampshire, England, 1682. Writer, garden designer, nurseryman, best known for documentation of revolution in English garden design toward naturalistic style; trained according to school of George London and Henry Wise; served apprenticeship in the Brompton Park nursery with George London; worked with firm at Castle Howard and Blenheim; owned a nursery in Millbank and a seed shop in Westminster; owned small garden at Vauxhall; actively opposed to Scottish gardeners who came in increasing numbers to England. Died in 1745.

Selected Designs
1710	Grimsthorpe, countess of Lindsey, Lincolnshire, England
1718–40	Cirencester Park, Lord Alan Bathurst, Gloucestershire, England
1730s	Nostell Priory, West Yorkshire, England (unexecuted)

Selected Publications
Nobleman, Gentleman, and Gardener's Recreation, 1715; new edition, as *Ichnographia Rustica,* 1718
Practical Fruit Gardener, 1724
Practical Kitchen Gardener, 1727

Introduction to the General System of Hydrostaticks and Hydraulicks, 1729
editor, *Practical Husbandman and Planter,* 1733

Further Reading
Brogden, William A., "Stephen Switzer and the Garden Design in Britain in the Early 18th Century," Ph.D. diss., University of Edinburgh, 1973
Brogden, William A., "Stephen Switzer, 'La Grand Manier,'" in *Furor Hortensis: Essays on the History of the English Landscape Garden in Memory of H.F. Clark,* edited by Peter Willis, Edinburgh: Elysium Press, 1974
Brogden, William A., "The Ferme Ornée and Changing Attitudes to Agricultural Improvement," *Eighteenth-Century Life* 8 (1983)
Chambers, Douglas, *The Planters of the English Landscape Garden: Botany, Trees, and the Georgics,* New Haven, Connecticut: Yale University Press, 1993
Harris, John, "A Tour of London's Gardens with John Rocque," in *London's Pride: The Glorious History of the Capital's Gardens,* edited by Mireille Galinou, London: Anaya, 1990
Hunt, John Dixon, *Gardens and the Picturesque: Studies in the History of Landscape Architecture,* Cambridge, Massachusetts: MIT Press, 1992
Hunt, John Dixon, *Greater Perfections: The Practice of Garden Theory,* Philadelphia: University of Pennsylvania Press, and London: Thames and Hudson, 2000
Hussey, Christopher, *English Gardens and Landscapes: 1700–1750,* New York: Funk and Wagnalls, and London: Country Life, 1967
Jacques, David, *Georgian Gardens: The Reign of Nature,* London: Batsford, and Portland, Oregon: Timber Press, 1983
Turner, James, "Stephen Switzer and the Political Fallacy in Landscape Gardening History," *Eighteenth-Century Studies* 11 (1978)
Turner, Tom, *English Garden Design: History and Styles since 1650,* Woodbridge, Suffolk: Antique Collectors Club, 1986
Willis, Peter, *Charles Bridgeman and the English Landscape Garden,* London: Zwemmer, 1977

STEVIE O. DANIELS

Switzerland

Some kind of primitive gardening was probably being practiced in Switzerland during the late pre-Roman Age. During the Roman period, design ideas from the Mediterranean countries certainly influenced the layout of the gardens discovered in the 19th and 20th centuries in connection with archaeological excavations. Pollen, seeds, and other vegetable material found at the sites show that quite a number of garden plants were cultivated in Switzerland at that time. After the Roman occupation came to an end about A.D. 400, the cultivation of vegetables and medicinal herbs may have continued.

The Benedictine and Cistercian monks seem to have reintroduced the cultivation of fruit trees relatively early. For instance, peach trees are known to have been growing and fruiting in the Benedictine monastery of St. Gall as early as the 830s. A little later the famous plan of St. Gall was sent there, possibly from a nearby monastery on the island of Reichenau, in the Lake of Constanz. It is the only surviving document from the Middle Ages that records the layout of a monastery with the gardens and garden plants. The large parchment sheet shows a vegetable garden in front of the house where the gardener and his assistants lived and a smaller herb garden next to the infirmary. The cemetery was planted with fruit trees. The plan is on display in the monastery library. (The monastery of St. Gall was not built according to this plan, as has sometimes been maintained.)

In 1260 the Gardeners' Guild was founded in Basel, then the largest town in the country. Lindenhof in Zürich and Petersplatz in Basel date as public parks from the late Middle Ages and belong to the very earliest of their kind in Europe. The gardens of the burghers were small, often outside the town walls, and used mainly for the cultivation of vegetables and other useful plants. There is little information about the gardens of noble families from this era. However, some late medieval tapestries from the Basel area depict well-to-do people feasting, playing cards, and obviously enjoying themselves in gardens set up with turf seats, beautiful carved tables, and colorful tents for shelter.

The writings and plant drawings of Conrad Gessner, the 16th-century botanist and town physician of Zürich, show that he and his contemporaries delighted in growing ornamental plants and that they also took an interest in garden design. For example, Gessner had numerous oleanders, figs, laurels, and orange and lemon trees that had to be covered or brought indoors for the winter. His last garden was laid out in a Renaissance manner with a

CAMPVS DIVI PETRI, QVI EST BASILEÆ.   S. PETERS PLATZ IN BASEL.

An early public park, St. Peters Platz, Basel
Courtesy of Sammlung Alte Drucke und Graphische Sammlung, Zentralbibliothek, Zurich, Switzerland

round bed in the middle and other beds surrounding it in the form of a circle. Tree houses built in the boughs of linden and apple trees were popular and something of a Swiss specialty described enthusiastically by foreign visitors. The Reformation led to the dissolution of monasteries in many parts of the country, and their gardens were made over to apothecaries, hospitals, and other institutions. The garden of the Augustine monastery in Basel was given to the Faculty of Medicine of the university. It was reorganized as a proper botanic garden in 1776 by Professor Wilhelm von Lachenaal.

During the baroque era, many Swiss served in foreign armies, and after returning home they had their gardens fashioned in the French, Italian, or Dutch manner. Because of the mountainous topography of Switzerland these gardens were, however, usually smaller than the ones in the neighboring countries that had served as their models. They often consisted of one or more terraces with a formal box parterre in front of the garden facade of the castle or the manor house. The topiary trees were cut into bizarre forms, and the overall picture was enriched with pavilions, intricate wrought iron gates and railings, as well as ornamental pools with fountains and, occasionally, sculpture. Thanks to abundant water supply and natural pressure, even fairly modest Swiss gardens had small pools with jets of water.

The gardens of this era were most often designed by architects, but there were also some owner-designers who laid out or remodeled their gardens. *Le thresor des parterres de l'univers*, one of the first pattern books on the design of parterres in Europe, was written by Daniel Loris and published in Geneva in 1629; the text is in French, German, English, and Latin, reflecting the early international connections of garden art. Some monastery gardens were beautifully remodeled during the baroque era. The first Swiss books on flower gardening, published in German (instead of Latin) were written by a Capucine monk, Pater Timotheus von Roll, in the 1680s. Ostentation and public expenditure were frowned upon by the municipal authorities, but public promenades were planted in several towns. The Grabenpromenade in Bern was expressly laid out to benefit people living in the sunless back streets; it was made in 1740.

During the second half of the 18th century, people began to take a keen interest in importing and growing different kinds of foreign plants, initially out of consideration for their economic usefulness but later also for their aesthetic interest and ornamental qualities. The layouts of many baroque gardens were simplified at that time. New gardens were created in the geometric French manner, although less ornately than earlier. Three Swiss contributed greatly to the landscape garden movement on the European continent: Albrecht von Haller, the naturalist and physician; Salomon Gessner, the writer and artist; and Jean-Jacques Rousseau, the polemicist and philosopher. In their own country, although admired and appreciated, they do not seem to have had much influence on the development of landscape design. The natural views, with their waterfalls, forests, meadows, and mountains, were there for everybody to admire, and people did not find it necessary to emulate them in their gardens. Thus the first landscape gardens were designed in Switzerland only toward the end of the 18th century. The best known of them was the Eremitage in Arlesheim, near Basel, laid out by members of the owner family.

The Napoléonic Wars wreaked havoc on Switzerland, and they were followed by a new constitution with many political realignments in various cantons. Consequently gardening pursuits, always sensitive to social upheavals, came to a standstill for a while. Probably due to these events, designing in the landscape garden style began really to spread only in the 19th century. Several trends and influences seem to have contributed to the local developments of this style in Switzerland during the first half of the century, but they have not been studied in greater detail so far. Botanic gardens were established by the universities of Geneva in 1818, Zürich in 1834, and Bern in 1860.

During the second half of the 19th century, Switzerland became more prosperous, and large new suburbs began to cluster around old town centers. "Green belts" were planned for the areas vacated when the town walls began to be taken down from the 1830s onward, but due to financial pressures the plans were carried out only partially in most towns. The gardens of the new suburban villas built during this era were often landscaped like small parks. Foreign conifers became very popular, and they were planted in large numbers, especially in the gardens at the Swiss lakes, where the climate is relatively mild. Lakeside promenades with unusual conifers, other exotic trees, and colorful carpet beds were made in many towns. The best-known garden "artists" were Conrad Löwe, Theodor and Otto Froebel, and Evariste Mertens.

The beautification of churchyards became an issue; some impressive new cemeteries were designed, for example, Wolfgottesacker in Basel, and many older ones were enlarged and planted with trees. Horticultural journals and gardening books began to be published in much larger numbers than earlier, and they contributed to the more rapid spread of new design ideas than had earlier been the case. The numerous garden exhibitions from the 1840s onward had a similar influence. Rock gardens and alpine plants became fashionable toward the close of the century, although Gessner, for example, had collected them as early as in the 16th century, partly because of their medicinal properties and partly out of botanic interest. Henry Correvon (1854–1939), a genial nurseryman, became a sort of "father of the alpine garden," tirelessly promoting them as well as planting "flowery walls" in Switzerland and abroad. Part of his garden called Floraire survives in Chêne-Bourg, near Geneva.

The renewal of formal garden design in the spirit of the Arts and Crafts movement gathered pace toward the end of the 19th century. Rediscovery of the simple peasant gardens, with their small geometric beds for flowers, herbs, and vegetables edged neatly with box, came as a revelation to people who had gradually grown wary of the rarefied design concepts of the late landscape garden style. Straight lines, restraint in the use of exotic plants, and an overall simplicity of design became the tenets of the new "architects' gardens." Their spell was brief, and since the late 1920s the ideas of functionalism have been combined with reinterpreted landscape motives. Robert Froebel, Oskar and Walter Mertens, Paul Schädlich, Adolf Vivell, Ernst Klingelfuss, and Gustav Ammann were the best-known garden architects during the first half of the 20th century. The work of Johannes Schweizer, Ernst Baumann, and Edouard Neuenschwander was widely admired in the later decades of that century. Some foreigners—for example, Russell Page—have also designed noteworthy gardens in Switzerland.

Botanic gardens have been established in Brissago, Lausanne, Neuchâtel, and St. Gall in the 20th century; there are also several alpine gardens, the best known of which is the Schynige Platte, near Interlaken, at the height of about 2,000 meters (2,187 yd.) above sea level. The peasant gardens are still beloved by all and sundry, and they are quite a feature, especially in certain villages in the canton of Bern. Many other old gardens, especially in the towns, were irrevocably lost in the late 20th century. Some of them were built over, and some were made into public parks with consequent remodeling and simplified plantings.

Toward the close of the 20th century, the ecological movement contributed to new developments. For instance, the adherents of "wild" or "near to nature" gardening wished to use only native plants. Simultaneously, a growing interest in saving and restoring historical gardens as well as a trend toward a new kind of formalism in garden design were making themselves felt.

Further Reading

Ammann, Gustav, *Blühende Gärten; Landscape Gardens; Jardins en fleurs*, Erlenbach-Zurich: Verlag für Architektur, 1955

Baumann, Ernst, *Neue Gärten; New Gardens*, Zurich: Girsberger, and New York: Wittenborn, 1955

Beer, Roger, editor, *Les parcs de Genève: 125 ans d'histoire*, Geneva: Édition du Service, 1988

Bucher, Annemarie, editor, *Vom Landschaftsgarten zur Gartenlandschaft: Gartenkunst zwischen 1880 und 1980 im Archiv für Schweizer Gartenarchitektur und Landschaftsplanung*, Zurich: Hochschulverlag AG an der ETH, 1996

Correvon, Aymon, *Rocailles fleuries*, Geneva: L'imprimerie de "La Tribune de Genève," 1942; 4th edition, Paris: Delachaux et Nestlé, 1964

Correvon, Henry, *Les plantes alpines et de rocailles: Description, culture, acclimatation*, Paris, 1895; as *Rock Garden and Alpine Plants*, edited by Leonard Barron, New York: Macmillan, 1930

Fretz, Diethelm, *Konrad Gessner als Gärtner*, Zurich: Atlantis, 1948

Guillaume, Dr., "Notice historique sur les promenades publiques et les plantations d'arbres d'agrément dans le Canton de Neuchâtel," *Musée neuchatelois* 6, 8, and 9 (1869–72)

Hauser, Albert, *Bauerngärten der Schweiz: Ursprünge, Entwicklung und Bedeutung*, Zurich: Artemis, 1976

Heyer, Hans-Rudolf, *Historische Gärten der Schweiz: Die Entwicklung vom Mittelalter bis zur Gegenwart*, Bern: Benteli, 1980

Horn, Walter, and Ernest Born, *The Plan of St. Gall: A Study of the Architecture and Economy of and Life in a Paradigmatic Carolingian Monastery*, 3 vols., Berkeley: University of California Press, 1979

Keller, Heinz, editor, *Winterthur und seine Gärten*, Winterthur: Heimatschutzgesellschaft Winterthur, 1975

Meles-Zehmisch, Brigitte, and Anke Rogal, editors, *Gärten in Basel: Geschichte und Gegenwart*, Basel: Oeffentliche Basler Denkmalpflege, 1980

Ruoff, Eeva, editor, *Gärten in Riesbach: Beiträge zur Gartengeschichte Zürichs*, Zurich: Gesellschaft für Gartenkultur, 1984

Schwarz, Urs, *Der Naturgarten*, Frankfurt: Krüger, 1980

EEVA RUOFF

Sydney, Royal Botanic Gardens

Sydney, Australia

Location: Sydney harborside, south of the Sydney Opera House

The Royal Botanic Gardens, Sydney, are set on 35 hectares (86.5 acres) (including the Government House grounds) adjoining the Port Jackson Harbour of Sydney at Farm Cove. Within seven months of settlement at Sydney Cove in 1788 by the British, under Governor Arthur Phillip, convicts cleared some nine hectares (22 acres) to create a Government Farm at Farm Cove. These works instigated horticultural and botanical experiments and activities on the site. Although aesthetics and design considerations were minor factors at the time, the colonial government proceeded to develop an economic agricultural venue on a convenient location; the poor soils, salt-laden northeasterly winds, stony land with occasional tidal flooding, and reliable water still influence the setting of the Royal Botanic Gardens, Sydney, today.

Initially the gardens were poorly managed parcels sublet for various agricultural pursuits, and they only partially produced some of the vines, fruit trees, ornamental plants, and other useful exotics and economic botanical specimens for acclimatization and dissemination in the new colony. The gardens were also maintained—in contrast to other land subdivision and speculative activities by colonial governors Phillip (1788–95), John Hunter (1795–1800), Philip Gidley King (1800–1806), and William Bligh (1806–10)—until the arrival of Lieutenant-Colonel Lachlan Macquarie (1810–21) in 1810, as an expansive refuge from convict penal activities with the designation of "Government Domain," as it also hosted the Government House.

Macquarie changed the emphasis of the gardens and established its scientific and botanical foundations. He designated its role as a domain, revived its original purpose as intended by Phillip as a horticultural venue, and proclaimed laws to preserve its role as the "Governor's Demesne." He constructed Mrs. Macquarie's Drive and "Chair" lookout in 1816 in response to the ideas of his wife.

Succulent Garden at Sydney Royal Botanic Garden
Copyright Mel Watson/Garden Picture Library

The question of the foundation date of the gardens as being 1814 or 1816 is debatable given various ornamental tree donations to the Governor's Garden. A later director of the gardens, Joseph Henry Maiden (1896–1924), however, was adamant that 13 June 1816 is the "official birthday of the Botanic Gardens." This corresponds with the opening date of the Drive.

With Sir Joseph Bank's patronage in England British secretary of state Earl Bathurst appointed Allan Cunningham as the King's Botanist in the colony in December 1816. Cunningham was preceded by the arrival of Private Charles Fraser, who apparently had gardening experience with the Duke of Norfolk. Macquarie placed Fraser in charge of the Governor's Garden in early 1817 and later gave him the title of Colonial Botanist. Cunningham enthusiastically engaged in expeditions, collecting various specimens for return to England; Fraser also engaged in similar pursuits but had by 1820 established a rich plant collection in the gardens quite sepa-

rate from the Governor's kitchen garden. In 1821 Fraser was formally appointed Colonial Botanist and thereby Superintendent of the Garden; this title and the scientific charter of the gardens were encouraged by colonial governors Sir Thomas Brisbane (1821–25), Ralph Darling (1825–31), and Sir Richard Bourke (1831–38). Between 1825 and 1830 Fraser laid out the Lower Lawn based on Dr. Hooker's plan for the Glasgow Botanical Garden. Cunningham served as Colonial Botanist and Superintendent of the Botanic Gardens from 1837 to 1838.

With Fraser's death in December 1831, a series of temporary and ill-conceived appointments occurred before Charles Moore (1848–96) was appointed director of the botanic gardens in 1848. Under Moore a period of garden maturation, scientific management, and a long period of development was fostered by the patronage and support of various individuals and the gardens' Committee of Management. Moore commenced further botanical explorations in the colony, instigated plant and seed exchange correspondence with colleagues in European gardens, set about reclaiming land from the waters and silt of Farm Cove to extend the original gardens, established the genesis of a herbarium in 1854 and library in 1852, commenced trials of English fodder grasses, and proceeded to establish the landscape design foundations of the gardens. During the 1870s, as director he was sought after for several other public parks and government residence grounds, as well as with the Royal National Park and the University of Sydney campus, in their design, planting, and botanical management. His botanical expertise culminated in the significant *Handbook of the Flora of New South Wales* (1893), compiled with the assistance of Ernst Betche.

In 1878–79 Colonial Architect James Johnstone Barnett designed and erected the Garden Palace, consisting of 3.3 hectares (8 acres) of floor space, for the International Exhibition of Works of Industry and Art on land in the inner Domain. This structure was destroyed by fire on 22 September 1882, and an additional 7.68 hectares (19 acres) was annexed to the gardens. A sunken garden was erected on the palace site and opened by Governor Sir Roden Cutler in 1938.

In 1896 Joseph Henry Maiden (1859–1925) was appointed director of the gardens. Maiden's botanical reputation had been well established in New South Wales based on his research and his *Useful Native Plants of Australia* (1888), which foreshadowed a philosophical shift in the gardens' collections to give more weight to the study of Australian species. At the same time he reasserted a vision for the gardens, overhauled the medicinal plants garden, developed the systems garden, and commenced numerous planting and research programs, including the supervision of a new herbarium completed in 1899. The latter was incorporated within the Museum and National Herbarium opened in 1901 and enabled Betche to compile his *Census of Domain Plants* (1916).

Upon Maiden's retirement in 1924 Dr. George Percy Darnell-Smith (1868–1942) was appointed director. Much of Darnell-Smith's directorship was overshadowed by the depression. Upon his retirement in 1933 the gardens' functions were split between two curators—Edward Ward (1871–1915) in charge of the gardens and Edwin Cheel (1872–1951) in charge of the herbarium. George Hawkey succeeded Ward in 1934, and Cheel was succeeded by Robert Henry Anderson in 1936. Anderson had published *The Trees of New South Wales* (1932) and initiated the *Contributions from the NSW National Herbarium* in 1939. With the functions reunited in 1945, Anderson became director and restructured the gardens' operations. He steered the gardens into a phase of modernization, tempered by excisions due to the Cahill Expressway, and extensive systematic and taxonomic research. He hosted many dignitaries and royal guests and encouraged the surrender of land now comprising the Mount Tomah Garden to the gardens. The royal epithet was granted in 1959.

Becoming director in 1964, Herbert Knowles Charles Mair continued Anderson's programs and initiatives. Mair also renovated the grounds devastated by the Cahill Expressway and initiated the new pyramid glasshouse project. He was succeeded in 1970 by John Stanley Beard, previously foundation director of King's Park and Botanic Gardens in Perth, who became a strong advocate of a new *Flora of Australia* and witnessed the start of landscape works at Mount Tomah and the opening of the glasshouse. Beard was succeeded by his Deputy Chief Botanist, Dr. Lawrence A.S. Johnston in 1972, who continued the work to publish a *Flora of Australia* to succeed George Bentham's *Flora Australiensis* (1863–78). He, with his deputy Dr. Barbara Briggs, retitled the *Contributions from the NSW National Herbarium* as *Telopea* in 1973, started *Cunninghamia* in 1981, supported the publication of *Plants of New South Wales* (1981) by Dr. Surrey Jacobs and John Pickard—the first work of its kind since Maiden and Betche's *Census* of 1916—witnessed the opening of the new herbarium building in 1982, commenced fund-raising for the Sydney Tropical Centre, and orchestrated the selection of Mount Annan as a botanic garden and arboretum, before retiring in 1985. The unity and purpose of the gardens were redefined with the passage of the Royal Botanic Gardens and Domain Trust Act (1980).

The opening of extension botanic gardens at Mount Annan (1988) on 410 hectares (1,013 acres), Mount Tomah (1987) on 28 hectares (69 acres), and the Sydney Tropical Centre (1990) heightened the international standing and cultural significance of the gardens. Carrick Chambers succeeded Johnston in 1987 and brought a unique blend of skills in science and horticulture to the gardens. He designed the Rose Garden in 1988 and instigated the Sydney Garden Thematic Plan to strengthen the gardens' interpretive attributes. Chambers's deputy, Frank Howarth, succeeded him in 1997.

The Royal Botanic Gardens possess strong gardenesque design traditions with patches of the original Victorian structure, but they are skillfully sculptured around Farm Cove to enhance views out over Port Jackson. Mount Tomah features a wide range of cool-climate plants, especially rhododendrons. Mount Annan features Australian native plants.

Synopsis

1770	Joseph Banks collects plants on Botany Bay shore as part of *Endeavour* expedition
1788	Governor Arthur Phillip arrives at Botany Bay and establishes Sydney Town at Farm Cove on Port Jackson; first gardens at Farm Cove established
1792	Farm Cove gazetted a Crown reserve under Governor Phillip
1794	Superintendent of convicts, Nicholas Devine, leases Government Old Farm
1813	Landscape works commence in Government Gardens
1814	D'Arcy Wentworth donates an *Araucaria heterophylla* to Governor's Garden
1816	Mrs. Macquarie's Drive and Chair constructed and opened; Colonial Botanist Private Charles Fraser and King's Botanist Allan Cunningham arrive
1821	Botanic Garden well-established under Charles Fraser as superintendent
1825–30	Lower Lawn laid out
1848	Charles Moore arrives in Sydney and assumes management of gardens
1849	Moore presents first report and commences period of renovation and planting works and activities
1879	Garden Palace erected by Colonial Architect James Johnstone Barnet
1882	Garden Palace destroyed by fire
1889	Sandstone piers and gateway erected as memorial to Garden Palace
1899	New herbarium building completed
1901	Botanical Museum and National Herbarium opened
1933	Darnell-Smith retires and gardens' functions split; Edward Ward placed in charge of gardens and Edwin Cheel placed in charge of herbarium
1938	Sunken Garden established on site of Garden Palace for sesquicentennial of European settlement
1959	Royal epithet granted

1962	Garden Palace gates relocated due to siting of Cahill Expressway
1970–71	Pyramid Glasshouse erected
1971	Mount Tomah Garden started
1982	New herbarium constructed and opened
1984	Mount Annan selected as botanic garden and arboretum
1987	Mount Tomah Botanic Garden opened
1988	Mount Annan Botanic Garden opened; Sydney bicentennial celebrations
1990	Sydney Tropical Centre opened
1998	Rare and Threatened Display opened

Further Reading

Cambage, R.H., "Notes of the Late J.H. Maiden, History of the Sydney Botanic Gardens," *Journal of the Royal Australian Historical Society* 14, part 1 (1928)

Churches, David, *The Cultural Significance of the Royal Botanic Gardens, Sydney,* Sydney, 1990

Gilbert, Lionel, *The Royal Botanic Garden Sydney: A History, 1816–1985,* Melbourne and New York: Oxford University Press, 1986

Gilbert, Lionel, "Botanical Investigation of New South Wales, 1811–1880," Ph.D. diss., University of New England, 1971

Wilson, Edwin, *The Wishing Tree,* Kenthurst, New South Wales: Kangaroo Press, 1992

Wilson, Edwin, editor, *Royal Botanic Gardens Sydney,* Sydney: Royal Botanic Gardens, 1982

DAVID JONES

Symbolism in Eastern Gardens

While it can be said that all gardens are architectural, the Eastern, or Oriental, garden, unlike most modern Western garden styles, is purposefully crafted in the architectural context of Asian myth to serve as a spiritual center of humankind's existence. Although Eastern and Western garden styles both have their origins in the mystical *pairi-daeza,* or "paradises" of Persian Dar-al-Islam, the Eastern garden has retained its spiritual roots, crafting gardens that are in harmony with what Buddhists call *Gokurakujō*—obtaining paradise through human creation.

Most Westerners, when asked to name an Eastern garden style in terms of mythic context, would likely think of the Zen garden or perhaps in more general terms, the Japanese garden. The Zen garden is, however, but one style, or school, and the term *Japanese garden* is a generic designation of a variety of styles. Although the styles that are generically called "Japanese" or "Eastern" are divergent, certain elements derived from Asian myth are common to all. The Eastern garden, whatever the school, belongs equally and simultaneously to the realms of nature, architecture, and art.

Like gardens everywhere, the Eastern garden originated in the materialism and leisure of the affluent nobility. In these societies, whether Eastern or Western, nature came to be crafted to suit spiritual perspectives, becoming a symbiosis of the crafted and the natural and differing only in degree of artificiality. Human design found its expression in the right angle, while nature found its articulation in the unique and extraordinary. Yet it is not beyond the Eastern gardener to help nature along by enhancing the shape of a feature of nature to make it more unique, at least in the context of the garden. Simply put, nature was placed under the creative control of man, making the garden humankind's first effort to play God. In Buddhism *Gokurakujō,* or "attaining paradise," is not about entering heaven but becoming one with Creation and the Creator in a humanly crafted garden.

In the Eastern scheme of the universe, all extraordinary beauty—natural or man-made—is venerated. In the oldest of the indigenous Japanese religions, Shintoism, the uniqueness of nature is venerated as *go-shintai,* an abode of a deity. In most Shinto-inspired art the artist makes deliberate use of natural chance by crafting elaborate, "nature-inspired" flaws into the artwork. Such artistic license was not lost in the crafting of the garden or in building the classic Japanese teahouse or palace. Each was laid out according to fixed architectural rules to create what Japanese garden expert Günter Nitschke calls *unio mystica,* the perfect fusion of two opposites, opposites that Nitschke labels as "physical" and "intellectual."

In the blending of the physical and intellectual, the Eastern garden follows three basic architectural archetypes or paths: meditation, devotion, and magic. Although all three have similarities, each is derived from the "competing" cosmologies of *cakravala* Hinduism, Mahayana Buddhism, and Chinese Taoism.

When Buddhism arrived in the Far East, it brought with it the image of the cosmic mountain at the center of the universe, Mount Meru (*Shumi-sen* in Japanese).

Hindu cosmology, from which Buddhism derives, teaches that Mount Meru is a flat disk lying on golden earth, floating on water in the center of seven inner mountain ranges of gold and one outer range of iron, the *cakravala*. It is from this last range that *cakravala* Hinduism takes its name. Meru and each of the first seven of these ranges are separated by oceans containing a total of eight uninhabited islands. However, in the ocean between the seventh and the *cakravala* are four islands inhabited by humans.

The stupas (Buddhist shrines) and temples of central Asia follow the design of *cakravala* cosmology, the best example being Wat Phra Si Sanphet in Thailand. In the Far Eastern garden Meru is found not as a stupa but usually as a single towering rock at the center of the garden. Often, the *cakravala*-inspired garden depicts through symbolic design all nine ranges and eight oceans. An excellent example of *cakravala* influence is found in the garden fronting the Golden Pavilion in Kyoto, Japan. Here, the architect has re-created the mystical center of the universe, the place through meditation to achieve Nirvana.

The second path is rooted in popular Mahayana Buddhism. This sect, using the easier path of devotion—prayers, chants, and contemplations of images—rather than rigorous practices of *cakravala* meditation, originated in India between the second and fifth centuries A.D. Mahayana believes that space is divided into ten realms, each containing innumerable universes, most lying under the direction of a specific Buddha. The most significant of these universes for humans, *Sukhavati* (*Judo* in Japanese), the "Pure Land," is under the direction of Amida (Amitabha), the Buddha of light and eternal life, and lies at the "provisional limit of the worlds to the West." To be reborn in *Sukhavati* is a significant step toward becoming a Buddha. The "Pure Land" is a paradise where magnificent palaces are set amidst shady terraces and lotus ponds.

The fear of death runs deep in Mahayana Buddhism. With death nearby, one must therefore enjoy whatever pleasures the temporal has to offer, making Mahayana Nirvana worldly rather than heavenly both in practice and origin. Thus the gardens of Mahayana influence, best defined by the gardens of the Japanese Heian era (794–1185), closely resemble the pleasure gardens of the ancient Middle East. Perhaps this explains why the mythical land in Mahayana Buddhism lies to the west and the not the east.

Chinese Taoist myth, the third path, tells of five lofty peaked islands populated by humans who have obtained immortality and who reside in perfect harmony and fly about on the backs of cranes. The islands, borne on the backs of giant sea turtles, are located somewhere in the eastern ocean, far off the coast of China. Unfortunately, two of the islands were lost when

their turtles died doing battle with a sea monster. Several Chinese and Japanese emperors mounted massive expeditions hoping to find these islands and bring back the elixir of immortality. At the turn of the first century B.C., Emperor Wu, having failed in his expeditions, decided instead to lure the immortals to his own palace. To do so he built a garden resembling how he imagined these mythical isles by creating a lake containing four islands, each with a palace. To be able to communicate with the immortals whom Wu was sure would take up residence in the palaces, he built a platform approximately 61 meters (66.7 yd.) high.

In time the Japanese condensed the four islands of Taoism into one, the island of P'eng-lai, or Horai-zan, which was symbolized in the garden by a Horai mountain or crane or turtle island. Thus in time cranes and turtles became symbols of longevity not only in Japanese gardens but also in Japanese ritual.

Of particular significance to Japanese gardens is the triadic arrangement of rocks, a feature dating at least to the gardens of the Nara era (ca. 710–94). The oldest text on Japanese garden architecture, the *Sakutei-ki* (late 11th century; The Book of Garden Making) notes two different compositions: *hinbunseki-gumi*, the use of rocks to represent the shape of the Chinese character for "objects," with triadic composition developed along the horizontal plane, and *sanzonseki-gumi*, rock compositions that recall the Buddhist trinity. Here, like Buddhist stupas, the triads follow the vertical plane.

Triadic composition, as the name implies, uses three components, generally one large, one small, and one medium-sized, to create dynamic balance. Triadic composition is true not only of Japanese gardens but also of architecture, the *Noh* theater, and the *jkebana* school of flower arranging. The principles of *jkebana* carry over into garden design: *ten*, "the branch of truth" (the tallest), *chi*, "the accompanying branch" (slightly shorter), and *jin*, "the flowing one" (the shortest). Here is the archetypal Chinese tripartite structure of the universe, heaven, and earth and man, respectively. *Jkebana* has also been called a "trinity" of forces: horizontal, diagonal, and vertical.

Sakutei-ki also refers to the four heavenly animals, particularly the Blue Dragon and White Tiger, and their significance to the placement of the garden house. The waters of the Blue Dragon are to flow from the east to the southwest, under the house, which should be built upon the belly of the dragon (i.e., the water's bend), so as to wash away all of the evil spirits and carry them to the White Tiger).

In recent years *feng shui* has become popular in the West. *Feng shui*, literally "wind and water," is about connecting one's spirit with the harmony of a particular place. In gardening it is about the gardener and garden being in partnership not only with each other but also with the earth. *Feng shui* teaches that gardening is more about emotional and spiritual attitude than actual design.

Feng shui draws on four ancient Shinto archetypes, each of which enters equally into the design. The first of these archetypes is *shime,* the territorial archetype. *Shime* is about the garden plot itself. The word literally means "a bound artifact." In the *feng shui* or *horai* garden, "possession" is not about owning but about setting apart, literally "sanctifying," or making holy by becoming one with it—being "bound" to it. Such thinking gives rise to a whole "theology" of gardening, which must be considered in planning an Eastern garden. The second archetype is about binding. *Iwakora* (rock seat) and *iwaraka* (rock boundary) refer to mystically binding rock with *shime-nawa,* or "ropes of occupation." Such binding speaks to the significance of selection and placement of garden appointments. Appointments should not be selected and placed for eye appeal alone but primarily for their "heart appeal," their resonance within us. A significantly placed bench, a small pond of water with an island, or a large rock, as its *horai,* contributes to a sense of sanctity. The third archetype, *shinzen,* is about the "binding of agriculture," such as in the binding of sheaths of grain. The Japanese word for garden is *shima,* from which the word *shime* derives. The *shima* is "land that has been taken possession of."

In *feng shui*-inspired garden design it is important that the plants and the gardener each nurture the other. The particular choice of plants is relatively insignificant as long as the choices have spiritual value, in that they offer something to the heart. An unusual-shaped or exceedingly beautiful or fragrant tree or bush can become the garden's *go-shintai,* the symbol of both holiness and the One from which holiness flows. Thus, plot, appointment, and plants must all be in balanced relationship to each other and the gardener, which is the fourth archetype: the "one who binds."

Eastern gardens are endowed with what Zen Buddhism calls *yugen,* "a tranquillity of mysterious depth," a lingering resonance. A classic example of *yugen* is to be found in the *karesansui* garden of Saihō-ji. The term *karesansui* is formed from *kare* (dry), *san* (mountain), and *sui* (water), thus a "dry mountain water garden," that which we commonly call a "Zen garden." The *karenansui* at Saihō-ji, designed by the "father of Japanese contemplative garden design," Musō Kokushi (Muso Soseki), in the early 14th century is claimed to be

the first *karesansui* garden built and predates the rest of Saihō-ji by 400 years.

Cakravala Hinduism, Chinese Taoism, and Mahayana Buddhism all have one concern in common, that of outwitting nature, ironically, by the means of man-made nature. Shintoism, on the other hand, is about the veneration of nature and ancestral spirits, but even here, nature is manipulated to create harmony with the spirits of nature. It quickly becomes obvious to the student of Eastern garden expression that the various schools have in time intermingled, yet each school, in its own way, has given birth to its own unique Eastern garden style—styles that still dominate Eastern gardening.

Further Reading

Bennet, Steven J., "Patterns of the Sky and Earth—A Chinese Science of Applied Cosmology," *Chinese Science* 3, no. 1–26 (1978)

Hayakawa, Masao, *Niwa,* Tokyo: Heibonsha, 1967; 2nd edition, 1979; as *The Garden Art of Japan,* translated by Richard L. Gage, New York: Weatherhill, 1973

Inaji, Toshiro, and Pamela Virgilio, *The Garden As Architecture: Form and Spirit in the Gardens of Japan, China, and Korea,* New York and Tokyo: Kodansha, 1998

Kloetzli, Randy, *Buddhist Cosmology: From Single World System to Pure Land: Science and Theology in the Images of Motion and Light,* Delhi: Motilal Banarsidas, and Oxford: Motilal Books, 1983

Ledderose, Lothar, "The Earthly Paradise: Religious Elements in Chinese Landscape Art," in *Theories of the Arts in China,* by Susan Bush and Christian F. Murck, Princeton, New Jersey: Princeton University Press, 1983

Nitschke, Günter, *Gartenarchitektur in Japan: Rechter Winkel und natürliche Form,* Cologne, Germany: Taschen, 1991; as *Japanese Gardens: Right Angle and Natural Form,* translated by Karen Williams, Cologne, Germany: Taschen, 1993

Ross, Nancy Wilson, *Three Ways of Asian Wisdom: Hinduism, Buddhism, Zen, and Their Significance for the West,* New York: Simon and Schuster, 1966

Too, Lillian, *The Complete Illustrated Guide to Feng Shui for Gardens,* Boston and Shaftsburg, Dorset: Element, 1999

FRANK MILLS

Symbolism in Western Gardens

Symbolism in gardens is used to express an idea or evoke an emotional response. It naturally reflects the beliefs and philosophies of different periods and societies, whether in the form of adornments to the garden or in the concept of the design itself. For the most part, the symbolism deliberately suggests to the viewer the intended mood or association, but the symbolism of a garden design may only be perceived by later generations, as a reflection of the attitudes and beliefs of the earlier society.

Such symbolism is probably as old as our animist ancestors who, sensing a sacred quality to a woodland glade, dedicated it (in fear or veneration) to a local spirit and carved an effigy of that spirit at the glade's center. In the Judaeo-Christian tradition it is as old as the Garden of Eden where "in the middle of the garden [the Lord] set the tree of life and the tree of the knowledge of good and evil." Eden, meaning "the garden of delight," embodies the aspiration of later garden designers who sought to recreate what the Persians called a paradise garden (from the Persian *pairidaeza* for "enclosure") but which came to imply "heaven on earth." To the Persians, from whose work all Western (and Mogul) gardens descend, water was not only a welcome cooling element, it was also a channel for the spirits of the dead. Four canals divided the early Persian garden, symbolizing the four regions of the earth; under the influence of Islam, the number was increased to represent the eight divisions of the Koran. Cypresses often alternated with fruit trees to express mortality and rebirth, respectively.

To the Greeks, who were city dwellers for the most part, gardens were places for contemplation: Plato famously taught in a garden and Epicurus gathered his disciples as a "garden sect." Their formal colonnaded gardens, ornamented with statuary of gods and mythological heroes, set the mood for such activities, and it was here that water and shade became associated with poetry and the arts. The Romans inherited these concepts: Pliny the Younger described his own garden in Tuscany, where he aimed for harmony between the house and garden and which, too, was a place for contemplation and discussion. A number of "rooms," many with ornamental box topiary, set different moods. A miniature landscape garden was effected "in imitation of the negligent beauties of rural nature." In the small urban gardens of Pompeii, formality often included references to fertility (and by extension the garden) in the form of a statue of the god Priapus. Alternatively it might refer to revelry, symbolized by a statue of the god Bacchus. To extend the horizon, trompe l'oeil paintings on the walls often depicted wild, rocky, water-fed landscapes, perhaps reflecting the urban dweller's nostalgia for his rural past. A similar feeling for landscape, and a reverence for nature, can be seen in the only surviving sacred landscape garden at Tivoli and its Temple of Sibyl, which was the inspiration for many 18th-century gardens. These elements must have existed in parts of Hadrian's villa where a *nympheum,* grotto, and cascades of water defined the mood, and where a temple of Venus was set against the backdrop of the Vale of Tempe—a poetic reference to its Greek namesake.

The Dark Ages were a time of subsistence gardening, but monasteries kept alive the idea of colonnaded courtyard gardens. Both in the monastery and castle there was also often a *hortus conclusus,* a secret enclosed garden dedicated to, and symbolic of, the Virgin Mary. This concept was derived from Solomon's *Song of Songs:* "A garden enclosed is my sister, my spouse; a spring shut up, a fountain sealed." Such traditions, together with the Islamic garden influence brought back by the Crusaders, inspired the early Renaissance garden. At the end of the 14th century, the Medici court in Florence reintroduced the formal gardens of old, where fountains played and statuary, a *nympheum,* grottoes, avenues of cypress, and simple box parterres created a sense of calm orderliness, where discussions of poetry and philosophy could flourish, and where the concept of humanism developed. All was contained within a wall, but the garden, terraced and sited on a hill, commanded views over the open countryside (or, as with the Villa Medici at Fiesole, over the city of Florence). Such positions paralleled the all-embracing interests of the Renaissance.

The High Renaissance gardens of Rome were on a grander scale, reflecting the unbounded confidence of the "complete man" of the time. Following Renaissance ideals of symmetry and proportion, villa and garden design were coordinated; the garden radiated from a central axis and demonstrated Renaissance man's belief in his total mastery over nature. Nowhere is this displayed more theatrically than in the Villa d'Este's superb and exuberant terraced water gardens.

Toward the end of the 16th century, however, some of this confidence had seemingly eroded. In *The Quest for Paradise* Ronald King suggests that the Villa Lante, at Bagnaia, demonstrates this perception when the beautiful, delicate, terraced formal garden merges for the first time with woodland and wilderness. The Villa Lante was built for a cardinal but, as with all Renaissance gardens, contains predominantly pagan symbols. (Pagan references, however, were not universal: in the late 15th century in Portugal, for instance, water staircases, set within an avenue of trees, were bordered by the Stations of the Cross.) Of the same period as the Villa Lante is the Villa Orsini at Bomarzo, where fantastic monsters and giants are carved from irregular natural outcrops of rock. Whatever the intended contemporary symbolism (if any) of these strange carvings, they suggest a new sense of man's fragility in the natural world.

No such doubts assailed the French garden designers of the 17th century who began to dominate garden design at the end of the 16th century. The great designs of André Le Nôtre, above all those for Versailles, symbolized the power of Louis XIV: the great central axis led from the center of the palace (and the King's bedchamber) along a mile-long allée—apparently to infinity—as a visual confirmation of the king's power. Frequent references to Greek and Roman mythology inspired contemplation of the perceived Golden Age of the classical past and, by inference, to the glories of the contemporary age, just as statues of the Sun God invited comparison with the Sun King.

At the end of the 17th century, French planning came to England via the Netherlands, with the accession of William and Mary. The only known description of a symbolic garden of the period is that of William Lawrence. A Gloucestershire squire, he created a memorial garden at Shurdington dedicated to his beloved wife and son who, in 1692, had died within two months of each other. The garden was divided into compartments representing the Ages of Man, while the main plat had at its center a statue of Time, scythe in hand. A snake at his feet represented Aesculapius, the god of medicine, as a reference to the failure of the doctor to prevent the family deaths. The various gates, surmounted by pyramids and urns (Roman emblems of death), bore the initials of Roman inscriptions describing the attributes of the dead. A fishpond with heraldic devices on a central pavilion and a cupola on the house, surmounted by a globe of flint glass (seemingly burning incense to his son's memory), completed the design. The garden was to be an aid to contemplation, but proved to have therapeutic powers: in time, that which had been a "violent sorrow" turned into a "pleasing remembrance."

In 18th-century England, the dominance of formal gardens was weakened by the influence of Chinese gardens, spread by Jesuit missionaries, and by the influence of the landscape painters Claude Lorrain, Gaspard Poussin, and others. The designs of William Kent, from 1720, and the influence of the poet Alexander Pope, who satirized the symbolic topiary of the 17th century baroque garden, led to the early landscape gardens. Horace Walpole described Pope's own garden at Twickenham as leading, through a gloomy grotto to "opening day" and "dusky groves," to his mother's tomb and the "solemnity" of cypress. It was all managed, he said, with "exquisite judgement." (The *Cupressus sempervirens*, introduced by Inigo Jones early in the 17th-century, was still a symbol of death, as it had been for the Persians and the Romans.) During this period of garden mania, straight lines were replaced by Hogarth's serpentine "line of beauty." Kent perceived (according to Walpole)

that "all nature was a garden" and a "picturesque" setting for Arcadian or Elysian antiquity. The formal 17th century garden had been an enclosed world, relating to the house and turning in on itself. The sunken fence, known as a ha-ha, made an outward-looking attitude possible as walls and fences were swept away and the far prospect became part of the garden. Focal points were acquired, such as a Greek temple or Roman Pantheon; a winding path led to a statue or urn in a clearing, maintaining classical references. At Stowe, for instance, William Kent designed a Temple of British Worthies whose busts gazed reflectively over the river Styx (the local stream) to the Elysian Fields beyond. Later, hermitages, grottoes, or ruined Gothic-style buildings were incorporated to induce a gentle melancholy at the transience of man's efforts. Often the symbols had a didactic quality requiring a meditative response to a particular classical theme. In his garden at Leasowes, William Shenstone deliberately hinted to his spectators, by means of statues or poetic inscriptions, where their thoughts should turn or how they should react.

The serenity and naturalness of Lancelot (Capability) Brown's gardens reflected a reaction to the often over-contrived nature of such gardens and was something nearer to the thinking of the French philosopher Jean-Jacques Rousseau, whose ideal *Elysée* was a fertile, uninhabited island: in *La Nouvelle Héloïse (1761)* he suggested that efforts by man to "make nature more beautiful . . . disfigure her." At the latter end of the 18th century, the appropriate response turned from melancholy to awe, as the wild and "sublime" garden developed. Following Edmund Burke's definition that sublime (as opposed to beautiful) objects are vast, gloomy, violent, and inspire terror—rocks, waterfalls, and sheer precipices formed the new picturesque garden. Such gardens reflected 18th-century distancing from the Renaissance belief in man as the supreme master of the natural world and suggested his frailty when confronted by the forces of nature.

In colonial North America, Spanish settlers in the Gulf of Mexico introduced the Islamic-inspired gardens of Spain. In Virginia (for instance at Williamsburg or George Washington's house, Mount Vernon) and in the New England colonies, the settlers followed the formal style of 17th-century French and English gardens. As pioneers, these early Americans must have needed the psychological security of their fenced gardens and the reassurance of a familiar outlook. The landscape style of the 18th century, however, which had also spread to continental Europe, found its natural home in a new, expanding country where the horizons were seemingly limitless. Imaginatively, even in New York City, in the mid-19th century, Frederick Law Olmsted landscaped 800 acres of Central Park. Particularly after the American Revolution, the landscape style, with notable exceptions, had flourished. One exception was Washington, D.C., where the French formal style was echoed in straight lines, wide avenues, and regularly planted trees, perhaps symbolizing the disciplined guiding principles of the founding fathers.

Further Reading

Clark, H.F., *The English Landscape Garden,* London: Pleiades, 1948; 2nd edition, Gloucester, Gloucestershire: Sutton, 1980

King, Ronald, *The Quest for Paradise: A History of the World's Gardens,* New York: Mayflower Books, and Weybridge, Surrey: Whittet/Windward, 1979

Masson, Georgina, *Italian Gardens,* London: Thames and Hudson, and New York: Abrams, 1961; new edition, 1966

Moynihan, Elizabeth B., *Paradise As a Garden: In Persia and Mughal India,* New York: Braziller, 1979; London: Scolar Press, 1980

Sinclair, Iona, editor, *The Pyramid and the Urn: The Life in Letters of a Restoration Squire: William Lawrence of Shurdington, 1636–97,* Stroud, Gloucestershire, and Dover, New Hampshire: Sutton, 1994

Thacker, Christopher, *The History of Gardens,* London: Croom Helm, and Berkeley: University of California Press, 1979

Wilber, D.N., *Persian Gardens and Garden Pavilions,* Rutland, Vermont: C.E. Tuttle, 1962; 2nd edition, Washington D.C.: Dumbarton Oaks, 1979

IONA SINCLAIR

T

Taj Mahal

Agra, Uttar Pradesh, India

Location: on the south bank of the river Yamuna (Jamna), about 1 mile (1.6 km) from the Red Fort, and approximately 120 miles (193 km) south-southeast of Delhi

The Taj Mahal, the mausoleum that the Mogul emperor Shah Jahan (r. 1628–58) built for his favorite wife, Mumtaz Mahal, at Agra (1632–43 and later) expresses the characteristic Mogul concept of a tomb set in an architecturally planned garden in its most monumental and ideal form. The residential waterfront garden, a specific Mogul variant of the Persianate *chahar-bagh* (fourfold garden), was here introduced into a funerary context and brought to the grand scale of imperial mausoleums. Thus invested with an imperial connotation, the waterfront garden became the preferred form of Shah Jahan's palatial gardens and garden palaces (e.g., Red Fort, Delhi, 1648); it was not again used as a setting for tombs, however. As with most Mogul gardens, only the architectural elements of the Taj Mahal garden preserve the original design; less is known about its plants and trees.

The site of the Taj Mahal was originally occupied by a mansion (*haveli*) of Raja Man Singh of Amber (Jaipur), a high-ranking Rajput official in the Mogul administration who as a member of the indigenous Indian nobility had been allowed to own an inheritable property at Agra, a privilege then hardly ever granted to the ruling Muslim elite. After the death of Mumtaz Mahal in June 1631 at Burhanpur, the raja's grandson Jai Singh offered (or was induced to offer) Shah Jahan the site for the burial of the deceased queen and received in exchange four other properties at Agra. Work on the site of the Taj Mahal had started by January 1632, when the body of the dead queen arrived at Agra and was temporarily buried under a small dome in the area of the garden. The planting of the trees must have taken place at this time; this can be deducted from the reports of the foundation of other gardens of Shah Jahan, such as the Shalimar gardens of Lahore (1641–42). The historians of Shah Jahan mention the progress of the construction on the occasion of the celebrations of the death anniversaries of Mumtaz Mahal; they fail, however, to inform us about the development of the garden. The completion of the entire Taj Mahal complex is reported in 1643, but according to an inscription on the gateway of the garden, work went on at least until 1647.

The mausoleum is set at the northern end of the main axis of a vast oblong walled-in complex consisting of the tomb garden and to its south a forecourt and a bazaar and caravanserai unit, which survives only in fragments. The tomb garden consists of two main elements, a *chahar-bagh* (a cross-axially divided four-part garden) and, toward the river, a raised terrace on which was placed the mausoleum and its flanking buildings. With this configuration the garden follows the typical residential garden of Mogul Agra, the waterfront garden. It is a specific form of the *chahar-bagh*, developed by the Moguls in response to the geographical conditions of the Indo-Gangetic plain to take advantage of a large river as the main water supply of a garden. With the shift toward the river the main garden pavilions had the climatic advantages of running water and presented a carefully composed front to those who saw them from a boat or across the river. From the landward side the buildings offered an equally satisfying backdrop for the garden.

Mogul Agra consisted of two bands of such riverfront gardens lining the Yamuna, popularly called Jamna. The design of the Taj garden deviates from the classical *chahar-bagh* design with the mausoleum at its center; it follows the residential waterfront garden and expresses it in an ideal form, in perfect geometry and symmetry, enlarged to a scale beyond the reach of ordinary mortals, to create, as the sources tell us, here on earth an image of

Gate of the garden of the Taj Mahal seen from inside the garden
Copyright Mary Evans Picture Library

the house of Mumtaz Mahal in the garden of paradise, linked at the same time to the garden tradition of the city.

The waterfront garden scheme was also a key element in the planning of the entire Taj complex. To the south of the garden is an oblong complex that contains the forecourt, called Jilau Khana, framed by two smaller enclosures housing residential courtyards for the tomb attendants, *khawasspuras,* and two tomb gardens for lesser wives of Shah Jahan. These subsidiary tomb enclosures echo on a smaller scale the design of the main tomb garden.

South of the Jilau Khana was another complex whose arrangement reflected the scheme of the tomb garden. It was formed by open bazaar streets crossing each other, which corresponded to the walkways of the garden, and four-square caravanserai courtyards or inns, taking the place of the four garden quadrants. The *chahar-bagh* scheme was here transferred in a unique and creative way onto a complex of utilitarian civic architecture. The entire complex of the Taj Mahal consisted thus formally

of two components following the waterfront design, that of the tomb garden, a true waterfront garden, and that of the landlocked architectural variant of the two subsidiary complexes.

The components were also connected functionally. The subsidiary unit serviced the funerary unit of the tomb garden because by imperial command the upkeep of the tomb was financed by the income generated from its bazaars and caravanserais. The service unit was the counterpart of the tomb garden, linked to it by design and function. This scheme epitomizes in a unique way the connection to architecture that is generally characteristic of the Mogul garden. Architectural planning determines also the inner organization of the proper garden element of the complex, the *chahar-bagh* component of the tomb garden. The square of the garden measuring approximately 296 by 296 meters (326 by 326 yd.) is divided by two large walkways (*khiyaban*), approximately 31 meters (34 yd.) wide, into four quadrants. The *khiyabans* consist of several elements. In their center runs a shallow sunk

Mausoleum of the Taj Mahal seen from inside the garden
Copyright Mary Evans Picture Library

canal (*nahr*) containing a line of fountains (*farwara*). It is framed by narrow paved strips and by ornamental parterre borders formed of alternating square and oblong star patterns, a characteristic design of Mogul architectural decoration. These in turn are framed by wider strips paved with red sandstone slabs arranged in a geometrical design, used also for the flooring of Mogul buildings. At the crossing of the walkways in the center of the garden is a raised platform (*chabutra*) of white marble with an ornamental pool (*hauz*) containing five fountains.

The sources say very little about the plantation of the Taj garden. The main historians of Shah Jahan, Lahauri, and Salih Kanbo (translated by Begley and Desai), describe all the architectural features of the garden but mention only that it was planted with "various kinds of fruit bearing trees (*ashjar mewadar*) and rare aromatic herbs (*riyahin badi` a'in*)." European observers of the 17th century say little more about the plantation of the Taj garden. François Bernier, in *Voyages* (1670; translated in Begley and Desai), mentions merely "garden walks covered with trees and many parterres full of

flowers." An idea of what grew in 1632 in a typical residential Agra garden can be had from Peter Mundy's *Travels in Asia*. He notes that the walkways were lined on each side with cypress trees and the squares of the subdivisions were planted with

> litle groves of trees, as Apple trees (those scarse), Orenge Trees, Mulberrie trees, etts. Mango trees, Caco [cocoanut] trees, Figg trees, Plantan trees, theis latter in rancks, as are the Cipresse trees. In other squares are your [meaning English] flowers, herbes, etts., whereof Roses, Marigolds . . . to bee seene; French Mariegolds aboundance; Poppeas redd, carnation and white; and divers other sortes of faire flowers which wee knowe not in our parts, many groweinge on prettie trees, all watered by hand in tyme of drought, which is 9 monethes in the Yeare.

The naturalistically rendered flowers in *pietra dura* inlay work and marble, used to decorate the tomb stones

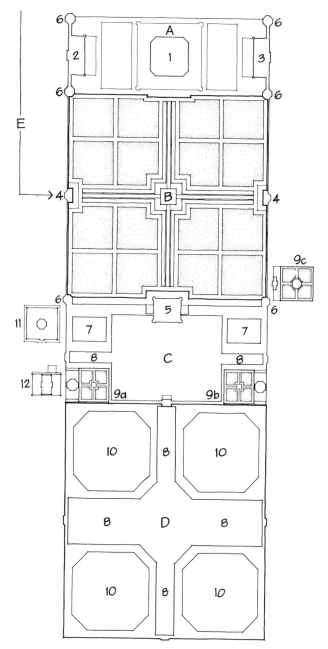

Site plan of the Taj Mahal: A—terrace; B—tomb garden (*chahar-bagh*); C—complex of forecourt (*jilau khana*); D—complex with cross axial bazaar and caravanserais; E—water works; 1—mausoleum; 2—mosque; 3—assembly hall (*mihman khana*); 4—garden pavilion; 5—gate; 6—tower pavilion; 7—quarters for tomb attendants (*khawasspura*); 8—bazaar street; 9—subsidiary tomb; 10—caravanserai; 11—tomb; 12—mosque
Copyright Ebba Koch

of Mumtaz Mahal and Shah Jahan and the dados of the mausoleum, show which plants the Moguls considered ideal in a funerary context. Poppies, crown imperial, martagon lilies, tulips, and irises feature here prominently.

Fruit trees in the Taj garden were observed by travelers in the late 18th and 19th centuries; this is confirmed

by an early 19th-century site plan in the Taj Museum. The subdivisions of the garden are inscribed as *takhta* (plots), in which were grown inter alia grapefruits or pomelos, lime, and guavas. That cypress trees lined the main walkways can be taken as an established fact; they were a characteristic lining of Mogul garden walkways and appear also on Mundy's 1632 drawing of Akbar's tomb (1613) at Sikandra in the outskirts of Agra.

The waterworks of the Taj garden are situated outside its western wall and still preserve the original design. They consist of an arched aqueduct running up to the middle of the garden, which brought the water from the Jamna to the height of the garden wall, from where it entered the garden through pipes with the necessary pressure to keep the fountains playing and the garden plots irrigated.

At the end of the 18th century, the Taj Mahal began to be visited by British travelers and artists in search of the picturesque; Thomas and William Daniell made the Taj Mahal and its garden, full of trees, known to a wider Western audience with the aquatint views in their *Oriental Scenery* (1801).

In 1803 Lord Lake conquered Agra for the directors of the East India Company, and the Taj Mahal became the focus of the selective preservation of monuments of the new British government. The Taj garden was used for picnics and as an encampment ground for British officials and travelers; the fruits grown there were sold for the benefit of the government. The earliest photographs of the Taj garden, taken in the 1850s, show the garden fully overgrown with trees.

Care of the Taj Mahal was put on a more systematic basis at the beginning of the 20th century when the Archaeological Survey of India, founded in 1860, also took on the agenda of conservation. The institution prevailed after India's independence in 1947; its Horticulture Branch is presently responsible for the plantation of the Taj garden, in which the cypress trees are kept small and trees are confined to certain areas so as not to obstruct the view to the mausoleum (see Plate 32).

Synopsis

1631	Death of Mumtaz Mahal, favorite wife of Mogul emperor Shah Jahan
1631	Raja Jai Singh of Amber offers site to Shah Jahan in exchange for four other properties at Agra, and development of garden begun at end of year or early 1632
1632	Body of Mumtaz Mahal arrives from Burhanpur and temporarily buried under small cupola on site of garden
1633	Celebration of second anniversary of death of Mumtaz Mahal on completed platform of mausoleum, her third and final burial place

1638–39	Completion of mausoleum building
1643	Completion of tomb garden and subsidiary complexes
1647	Completion of monumental gateway of garden
1666	Burial of Shah Jahan at side of his wife
1801	British artists Thomas and William Daniell publish two views of Taj Mahal and garden in *Oriental Scenery*
1803	Conquest of Agra by Lord Lake for East India Company
1808	Appointment of Taj Committee "for the care and preservation of the celebrated building nominated the Taj Mahal"
1815	Lord Hastings view of Taj Mahal obstructed by mango trees in garden
1828	Surveyor general of India, Colonel Hodgson, completes plan of complex
1835	Fanny Parks describes in her diary her impression of Taj garden and its use by British
1860	Foundation of Archaeological Survey of India
1873	Public Works Department of Government of India assigns to Local Governments duty to care for all buildings and monuments of historical or architectural interest
1873	Foundation of Agra Archaeological Society, which advises on repairs to Taj Mahal
1898–1905	Restoration of "water-channels and flower-beds of the garden more exactly to their original state" under Lord Curzon, governor general of India
1947	Archaeological Survey of India taken over by the new Indian government, its Horticulture Branch in charge of Taj garden

Further Reading

Begley, Wayne E., and Ziyaud-Din A. Desai, *Taj Mahal: The Illumined Tomb: An Anthology of Seventeenth-Century Mughal and European Documentary Sources*, Cambridge, Massachusetts: The Aga Khan Program for Islamic Architecture, 1989

Crowe, Sylvia, *The Gardens of Mughul India: A History and a Guide*, London: Thames and Hudson, 1972; Delhi: Vikas, 1973

Gurner, C.W., "Lord Hastings and the Monuments of Agra," *Bengal, Past and Present* 27, no. 1 (1924)

Koch, Ebba, *Mughal Architecture: An Outline of Its History and Development (1526–1858)*, New York and Munich: Prestel, 1991

Koch, Ebba, "The Mughal Waterfront Garden," in *Gardens in the Time of the Great Muslim Empires: Theory and Design*, edited by Attilio Petruccioli, Leiden, The Netherlands, and New York: Brill, 1997

Moynihan, Elizabeth, *Paradise As a Garden in Persia and Mughal India*, New York: Braziller, 1979; London: Scolar Press, 1980

Mundy, Peter, *The Travels of Peter Mundy in Europe and Asia, 1608–1667*, edited by Richard Carnac Temple, 5 volumes, London: Hakluyt Society, 1907–36; reprint, Nendeln, Liechtenstein: Kraus, 1967

Parks, Fanny, *Wanderings of a Pilgrim in Search of the Picturesque*, edited by Esther Chawner, 2 vols., London, 1850; reprint, Karachi, Pakistan, and London: Oxford University Press, 1975

Raleigh, Thomas, editor, *Lord Curzon in India: Being a Selection from His Speeches As Viceroy and Governor General of India, 1898–1905*, New York and London: Macmillan, 1906

Rawdon-Hastings, Francis, *The Private Journal of the Marquess of Hastings*, 2 vols., edited by Sophia Frederica Christina Chrichton-Stuart, London, 1858

Villiers-Stuart, Constance Mary, *Gardens of the Great Mughals*, London: Black, 1913; reprint, New Delhi: Cosmo, 1983

EBBA KOCH

Tao Qian 369?–427

Chinese Poet

Tao Qian was a great literary writer and poet of the Eastern Jin dynasty. He was also known as Tao Yuanming, his polite name of Yuanliang, and his posthumous title "Jingjie." Tao Qian was born in Cai-Shang, Xunyang County (today's southwest of Jiujiang City), Jiangxi Province. His great-grandfather Duke Tao Kan was a top official of the Eastern Jin dynasty, and his grandfather Tao Mao was a governor of Wuchang City.

His father, however, withdrew from society and lived in solitude. By the time Tao Qian was born, his family was already poor.

As a youth, Tao Qian was deeply influenced by the Confucian school of thought. He was also attracted by the philosophy of nature reflected in the social tendency of seclusion by the philosophical sect in the Wei and Jin dynasties. The general atmosphere of the times strongly affected the character and style of Tao Qian's poetry and literature.

In 396, when Tao Qian was 28 years old, he served as *Jijiu* of Jangzhou (honorary inspector-general of schools in Jangzhou) and Zhenjiang *Canjun* (honorary advisor to the military general stationed at Zhenjiang), among other positions. Distressed at the corruption of the government, he resigned several times. He held his final commission, as county magistrate of Peng-Ze in 405, for only about 80 days, when he finally retired from official life and secluded himself in the countryside. Tao Qian retired because he felt that his ideal of preventing society from becoming degraded was ruined and that his official career had been fraudulent. Against such hypocritical common customs, he hereafter lived an ordinary and hard life in the countryside. Occasionally involved in farm work, he mainly occupied himself with his writings, extolling the landscape, wine, and *Chrysanthemum*. In his remaining years he was quite poor and sometimes had to beg for food. Although in the 420s he was asked to return to work as an official, he refused. Nothing could shake his will in seclusion.

Part of Tao Qian's philosophical thought was that the universe is always in motion; it also included atheism and a natural outlook on life, which was reflected in his social ideals. This philosophy is reflected in his pastoral poetry and essays. Esteemed as a great pastoral poet by the people of his time, Tao Qian left more than 120 poems and about 20 essays. In his writings he depicts the beauty of the natural landscape with implied meanings. His writing style is elegant and reserved, and his plain and lucid language influenced the following generations of writers. His most influential writings include *Return Home*, *Peach-Blossom Source* (written in the author's later years), and *A Biography of the Gentleman of the Five Willows* (*Wu Liu Xian Sheng Zhuan*).

The poem *Return Home*, a representative work of Tao Qian, was finished after the author returned to his home. In this poem Tao Qian gives expression to his happy mood upon his resignation and homecoming. The work also exhibits the author's unsullied temperament after his career in government, his longing to live with nature, and his commendable sentiment of refusing to follow the times and his disdain of the corrupted government. A beautiful lyric poem, *Return Home* is a harmonious mingling of scenes and feeling.

Biography

Born in Caishang, Xunyang County (today Jiujiang County), Jiangxi Province, 369. Becomes an official, 396; designated magistrate of Pengzhe County, 405; after 80 days commission, retires and writes poem *Return Home*; writes *A Biography of the Gentleman of the Five Willows*, 420. Died 427.

Selected Publications

Return Home, 405
Biography of the Gentleman of the Five Willows, 420

Further Reading

Davis, A.R., *T'ao Yuan-ming, AD 365–427: His Works and Their Meaning*, Cambridge, and New York: Cambridge University Press, and Hong Kong: Hong Kong University Press, 1983

ZHENG SHILING

Tea Garden

The tea garden evolved with the Way of Tea—one of the ways within Zen Buddhism designed to facilitate spiritual growth. The tea garden, teahouse, and tea ceremony are a comprehensive system of ritual activity and symbolic environment that create the Way of Tea, *chado* in Japanese. The tea garden is designed to provide a transition from the day-to-day world to the spiritual world of the teahouse. The tea garden, *roji* in Japanese, is primarily a garden for ritual movement rather than an object of scenery.

Chado traces its beginnings to China, where during the T'ang dynasty (A.D. 618–907) tea was valued for its medicinal and metaphysical qualities; tea drinking had become part of temple ritual. The 12th-century Japanese monk Myoan Eisai is credited with founding Zen Buddhism in Japan after studying in China and being the first to grow tea for religious purposes (Tanaka). During the 14th century tea became associated with popular entertainments: contests where guests were invited to guess which particular type of tea was being served. Gardens were used in tea entertainments as the place of respite between the banquet and the tea, influencing the union of a garden with the Way of Tea.

Zen monks such as Murata Shuko in the 15th century became interested in returning tea to a more spiritual pastime. Shuko was instrumental in transforming tea, inventing the idea that the host himself should serve the tea, and the *soan* style of teahouse (or "grass-hut" style). This innovation took the tearoom out of the temple building or residence and gave it its own architecture and its own setting within a garden. This was an absolute revolution in design. Temple gardens at the time were visually compelling but physically inaccessible, viewed from a fixed vantage point along a wall. According to the architectural anthropologist Gunter Nitschke, the tea garden setting in Japan was the first Buddhist architecture independent of other influences (Nitschke).

Masters of Tea and Zen, Takeno Joo and Sen Rikyu in the 16th century were responsible for developing and perfecting the *wabi* style of tea: a teahouse, garden, and ritual exemplified by the aesthetics of simplicity and restraint and emphasizing the spiritual aspects of tea. Joo's tea garden was in two parts, the design motif that is still employed today. Gardens of his era typically contained no trees, but Joo's garden was said to have capitalized on the effect of trees adjacent to his garden.

As teahouses became walled on all four sides, the tea garden became more planted. (One was not distracted by views of the garden if the teahouse had no windows.) The two parts of the tea garden, the outer *roji* and the inner *roji,* are designed to look different. Typically, larger stepping stones are employed in the outer *roji,* and smaller stones in the inner *roji.* The outer *roji* contains trees and shrubs with a ground plane of sand or gravel and moss. The inner *roji* has more vegetation and moss. Brightly colored flowers, elaborate displays of rocks, and water features are considered to be too distracting in a tea garden.

While tea gardens are highly designed, restraint is key. The overall tone is that of a stylized wildness. Trees such as pines, cedars, and oaks were often selected to achieve this effect. Plants have symbolic meanings in Japan, and these meanings are employed in the tea garden: for example, pines symbolize longevity. A walk though a tea garden should remind one of a walk along a mountain path, with the teahouse reminiscent of a rustic hut. This sensibility resulted from city dwellers desiring a relationship with nature.

In order to understand the design and function of a tea garden, it is necessary to understand it as a part of the Way of Tea. After accepting the invitation to a tea ritual, guests arrive at the host's main gate at least 15 minutes before the invited time. The guests enter the host's open gate and proceed to the *yoritsuki*—an area where they leave coats and pocketbooks and don ritual attire. The guests then move to the *machai,* or waiting area, to drink a flavored seasonal beverage. After this refreshment the guests proceed to the garden waiting bench within the outer *roji.*

Hearing the host pouring water into the ritual basin is the guests' cue to prepare to arise from the waiting bench. When they see their host opening the middle gate, the guests stand and bow and walk through the outer *roji* to the middle gate. Tea gardens employ stepping stones as their walkways. The placement of the stones and their varying height above the ground necessitates that the guests pay attention to their step, noticing the rocks texture and position. This accomplishes two things: the walk through the outer *roji* will seem longer than by actual measurement, and the focus of the guest is directed, heightening one's attention on the moment and further removing one from the everyday world. The path through the *roji* is rarely straight, symbolizing that the path to enlightenment is a difficult one.

The middle gate's design is not prescribed, but it is typically a simple wooden structure, sometimes a freestanding wall. But none are gates in the usual sense; it is clear that one could simply walk around this gate. Middle gates are ritual objects, designed to mark the passage into the inner world of tea.

As the guests walk the path in the inner *roji,* they notice that the stones and moss have been sprinkled with water by their host. This evolved from Shinto rites in which water was equated with purity. The guests proceed to the low stone basin filled with water, and in another activity derived from Shinto they crouch one by one to rinse their mouths and hands. A nearby stone lantern is lit for evening ceremonies.

The guests may then proceed to the teahouse. It may be just a few steps away, but the path is not direct, and the teahouse is generally screened by vegetation. Often the guests' entrance to the teahouse is through a *nijiriguchi,* a feature invented by Rikyu. This entrance is an opening approximately 90 by 90 centimeters (35 by 35 in.) that must be crawled through. The *nijiriguchi,* like the ritual basin, promotes humbleness—one must bow to accomplish these acts—and focuses one's attention on the spiritual realm. As the guests enter the teahouse and close the door behind them, they have a sense of having left the world behind.

Further Reading

Bibb, Elizabeth, *In the Japanese Garden,* Washington, D.C.: Starwood, and London: Cassell, 1991

Houser, Preston L., and Mizuno Katsuhiko, *The Tea Garden: Kyoto's Culture Enclosed,* Kyoto, Japan: Mitsumura Suiko Shoin, 1992

Ito, Teiji, *Koto no dezain shakkei to tsuboniwa,* Tokyo: Tankosha, 1965; as *Space and Illusion in the Japanese Garden,* translated and adapted by Ralph Friedrich and Masajiro Shimamura, New York: Weatherhill, 1973; 2nd edition, 1980

Nitschke, Gunter, *From Shinto to Ando: Studies in Architectural Anthropology in Japan,* London: Academy Group, 1993

Okakura, Kakuzo, *The Book of Tea,* New York: Duffield, 1906; Rutland, Vermont, and Tokyo: C.E. Tuttle, 1956

Suzuki, Daisetz Teitaro, *Zen Buddhism and Its Influence on Japanese Culture,* Kyoto, Japan: The Eastern Buddhist Society, 1938; 2nd revised and enlarged edition, as *Zen and Japanese Culture,* Princeton, New Jersey: Princeton University Press, 1970

Tanaka, Sen'o, *The Tea Ceremony,* Tokyo and New York: Kodansha International, 1973; revised edition, 1998

Treib, Marc, and Ron Herman, *A Guide to the Gardens of Kyoto,* Tokyo: Shufunotomo, 1980

REBECCA KRINKE

Tenryū-ji

Kyoto, Japan

Location: approximately 6 miles (9.7 km) west-northwest of Kyoto Station

Tenryū-ji, a Zen Buddhist temple of the Rinzai sect, is at the heart of the Arashiyama district to the northwest of Kyoto proper. Although the present buildings date from the Meiji period (1868–1912), the quiet pond garden has changed little since its completion late in the first half of the 14th century. Then as now, the abbot's quarters afford the best vantage point of the garden, which is renowned for its rockwork, especially the dry waterfall, and the view across to Arashiyama, the mountain that gives the district its name.

The temple was born out of a tumultuous time in Japanese history, the Nanbokuchō period (1336–92), when two courts coexisted. In the preceding Kamakura period (1185–1336), power lay in the hands of the Kamakura-based shogunate. In 1333 a general from its ranks, Ashikaga Takauji, overthrew this regime and restored the imperial family's right to rule. Three years later, however, Takauji himself seized supreme authority, forcing Emperor Godaigo into exile in Yoshino, near Nara. Here the emperor established the southern Court around himself, holding firm to the imperial regalia. Takauji set up a rival northern Court in Kyoto, placing a puppet emperor on the throne and declaring himself the founder of the new Ashikaga shogunate.

Upon the death of Godaigo in 1339, the Zen priest Musō Soseki (1275–1351) petitioned Takauji to build a temple as an offering to ensure the repose of the emperor's spirit. Takauji concurred. By 1345 the temple Tenryū-ji and its garden were complete, with Soseki, often referred to by his posthumous title of Musō Kokushi, or national teacher, in place as the founding abbot.

The site chosen for the temple had long been associated with the imperial family. In the Heian period (785–1184), Prince Kaneakira (914–87) had a villa there, with the typical pond garden of that time. The low, rounded Kameyama, or Tortoise Mountain, was a significant feature of the garden, for the tortoise carries auspicious connotations of longevity. During the Kamakura period, Emperor Gosaga retired there in 1270, naming his newly built residence Kameyama Palace after this same mountain.

With the conversion of the site to a Zen temple, Kameyama came to play a more modest role. For now, the wider environs were embraced. Following the precedent set about a decade before by a Chinese priest appointed to Kennin-ji in eastern Kyoto, Soseki selected ten landmarks to be the *jikkyō* (literally ten stages or ten boundaries) for Tenryū-ji. Known as the Kameyama *jikkyō*, they included features within the temple grounds and beyond, such as the temple's main gate and the garden pond, the Oi River, and Arashiyama.

All ten were given new Chinese-style names derived from Buddhist lore, thereby imbuing them with fresh significance and creating for the temple an environment rich in allegorical references. Arashiyama, for instance, was renamed Nengerei, "peak of the picked flower" (Yamasaki). It is said that once when preaching Buddha plucked a single flower and held it out before those listening. This wordless gesture was sufficient for one of those present to grasp the Buddha's message. Those in the Tenryū-ji community would have readily recalled this story upon looking across to Arashiyama/Nengerei, now subtly incorporated into the garden.

Arashiyama is actually on the opposite side of the Oi River from Tenryū-ji and thus well outside the temple compound. Takau-ji had its slopes planted with cherry trees to recall the famous cherries of Yoshino, where Godaigo had spent his exile from Kyoto, and with maples from the Tatsuta River district. The virtual inclusion of Arashiyama into the garden is an early example of *shakkei*, the technique of "borrowing" or "capturing" a distant landform and seamlessly merging it into the garden space. Several centuries later, the magnificent stroll gardens of the Edo period (1603–1867), such as Shugaku-in and Ritsurin-kōen, would bring *shakkei* into its full expression.

Within the garden, another subtle spatial play was effected, drawing on the representation of mountainous landscape in scrolls of the Chinese Song dynasty (960–1279). Inspired by the successive layering of depth in these ink paintings, Tenryū-ji's rock placings lead the eye deep into the garden. The large, flat Reclining Moon Rock on the near shore functions as "a *repoussoir* or 'pushing off point'" (Slawson). In the middle distance, a peninsula to the right foils a clear view and serves to enhance the illusion of depth across to the garden's focal rock arrangement, the dry waterfall (*kare-taki*) at the base of Kameyama. A bridge that once allowed passage across the water just in front of the falls is now a national treasure and no longer walked upon. A cluster of tall rocks set in the pond just to the right is often said to represent Mount Horai, the Taoist Isles of the Blest.

The waterfall, an early Japanese example of a dragon's gate waterfall (*ryū-mon-baku*), is also of continental origin. An old Chinese legend tells of a three-tiered waterfall where any fish that achieved the extraordinary feat of swimming up the falls was transformed into a dragon. Accordingly, there is a tall, upright stone, the Carp Stone, halfway up the Tenryū-ji falls. In China the tale alluded to the difficulty of surmounting the rigorous examination system to advance in the civil service. When imported into the garden of a Zen temple such as Tenryū-ji, the falls became a metaphor for the difficult path to enlightenment.

Soseki is most commonly credited with the design of Tenryū-ji's garden; old texts speak of his profound love of gardens and his belief in their value along the path to enlightenment. However, some scholars (see especially Kuitert) argue that, given the early date of the garden, the strength and sophistication of the Chinese influence displayed in the rockwork, especially the dry waterfall, could not have been the work of a Japanese and that a Chinese designer is a more viable attribution. There is no decisive evidence with which to settle this question. Time has masked the facts just as surely as it has naturalized the rocks around the pond and the cherries on Arashiyama.

Synopsis

10th C.   Site of Prince Kaneakira's (914–87) villa with pond garden

Principal rock groupings, Tenryū-ji, Saga, Kyoto, Japan
Copyright Marc Treib

1270   Retired Emperor Gosaga moves into new Kameyama Palace
1339   Emperor Godaigo dies and, prompted by Musō Soseki, Ashikaga plans establishment of Zen temple to honor Godaigo's spirit
1341   Groundbreaking ceremony performed with Musō Soseki officiating
1345   Temple and garden complete
1347   Retired Emperor Kogon visits to view cherry blossoms on Arashiyama
1358   Main buildings destroyed by fire
1464   Ashikaga Yoshimasa visits to see maples on Arashiyama
1868–1912 Construction of present buildings (Meiji period)
1934   Severe storm brought down trees, restoring view of Arashiyama

Further Reading

Hayakawa, Masao, *Niwa*, Tokyo: Heibonsha, 1967; 2nd edition, 1979; as *The Garden Art of Japan*, translated by Richard L. Gage, New York: Weatherhill, 1973

Ito, Teiji, *Koto no dezain shakkei to tsuboniwa*, Tokyo: Tankosha, 1965; as *Space and Illusion in the Japanese Garden*, translated and adapted by Ralph Friedrich and Masajiro Shimamura, New York: Weatherhill, 1973; 2nd edition, 1980

Ito, Teiji, *The Gardens of Japan*, Tokyo and New York: Kodansha, 1984

Johnson, Norris Brock, "Geomancy, Sacred Geometry, and the Idea of a Garden: Tenryu-ji Temple, Kyoto, Japan," *Journal of Garden History* 9, no. 1 (1989)

Johnson, Norris Brock, "Japanese Temple Gardens and the Apprentice Training of Priests," in *Apprenticeship: From Theory to Method and Back*

Again, edited by Michael W. Coy, Albany: State
University of New York Press, 1989

Keane, Marc P., *Japanese Garden Design,* Rutland,
Vermont: C.E. Tuttle, 1996

Kuck, Lorraine E., *The World of the Japanese Garden:
From Chinese Origins to Modern Landscape Art,*
New York: Walker/Weatherhill, 1968

Kuitert, Wybe, *Themes, Scenes, and Taste in the History
of Japanese Garden Art,* Amsterdam: Gieben, 1988

Nitschke, Günter, *Gartenarchitektur in Japan: Rechter
Winkel und natürliche Form,* Cologne, Germany:
Taschen, 1991; as *Japanese Gardens: Right Angle and
Natural Form,* translated by Karen Williams,
Cologne, Germany: Taschen, 1993

Slawson, David A., *Secret Teachings in the Art of
Japanese Gardens: Design Principles, Aesthetic
Values,* Tokyo and New York: Kodansha, 1987

Yamasaki, Masafumi, editor, "Rakugai Landscape and
Zen Temples," in *Kyoto: Its Cityscape Traditions and
Heritage,* edited by Yamasaki, Tokyo: Process
Architecture, 1994

FRAN NOLAN

Terrace Garden

Throughout the history of gardening and garden design, the concept of terracing has gone through several evolutions. Traditionally the word *terrace* meant a raised, flat mound of earth with sloping sides, or any of a series of flat platforms of earth with sloping sides, rising one above the other, as in a hillside. This definition is most clearly seen in the ancient forms of terrace agriculture as practiced around 500 B.C. by Latin American cultures. Today the classification of terrace garden is often used to describe gardens found on the terrace of a home. The word *terrace* is now usually meant to describe either an unroofed, paved area immediately adjacent to a house or a small roofed balcony outside an apartment.

The use of terracing in agriculture is believed to have originated with the early Incas who, around 500 B.C., built hundreds, even thousands, of miles of terraces on the west faces of extremely high altitude mountains. These terraces were created to serve a vital purpose in addressing the shortage of space needed for food production in the small, fertile side valleys of the Andes foothills.

The first use of tiered terraces in garden design dates back to ancient Egypt. These terraces did not provide a utilitarian function but were created for an aesthetic purpose. Unlike ancient farming terraces, these terraces were created for the aristocracy, for kings and queens, and were a symbol of status, wealth, and power. Terraces continued to function as symbols of the holding classes until the late 18th century.

The first-known terrace garden is that surrounding a mortuary temple known as Deir El-Bahari, built for Queen Hatshepsut (1505–1483 B.C.). The Mortuary Temple of Hatshepsut is at the head of a valley beneath the Peak of Thebes. The temple was the work of the architect Senenmut, who was influenced by the architecture of the 12th dynasty, which built many monarchs' tombs in cliff-hanging terraces.

The temple is comprised of a series of three vast terraces continuing throughout the mountain, a tree-lined avenue of sphinxes leading up to the temple, and ramps leading from terrace to terrace. The terraces are reached via grand stairways or ramps of dressed stone with cloisters. They are laid out formally and incorporate flower beds, groups of trees, and ponds. The shrine is found on the uppermost terrace.

The only other documented use of terracing in ancient Egypt are the Hanging Gardens of Babylon, one of the seven wonders of the ancient world. These were terraced gardens built by King Nebuchadnezzar II around 600 B.C. for his wife, who missed the mountains of her homeland. The gardens were 400 square feet (37.2 sq. m), rising in a series of terraces from the river, and were laid out on a brick terrace nearly 75 feet (22.9 m) above the ground. An irrigation system was designed to lift water from the Euphrates River to the gardens.

There are no documented terraced gardens of this type in ancient Greece, but there were home gardens in the rear of a house that often had covered terraces on three sides of the house (with a formal garden), much like the patios or terraces of modern homes. The ground was banked up and lined with trees on the fourth side of the house.

The ancient Romans developed the terraced villa, which was greatly influenced by the great garden of Queen Hatshepsut. Here the house was built on a hillside, and the villa, a complex of gardens, buildings, and statuary, was below it in a series of terraces that finally led down to the academy at the bottom. The academy was a grove of trees, with statues, fountains, and seats or benches. A well-known example of the Roman villa can be seen in Hadrian's Villa (Tivoli, Italy) built from approximately A.D. 118 to 134. The terraces of Roman villas were also laid out with geometrical and formal patterns edged with clipped box and gardens of topiary animals.

A terrace garden at Foots Cray Place, designed by Thomas Mawson in 1902, from Mawson, *The Art and Craft of Garden Making,* 1900

Turning toward the east, the use of terracing began in China in the 12th century, particularly in Suzhou, which was known as the "city of gardens." Some of these gardens date back 1,500 years to the Eastern Jing dynasty. At one time Suzhou was home to over 200 gardens. The gardens were designed as a retreat from political life for those in power and to permit them to return to nature. Many of the Suzhou gardens incorporated hills and water, flowers, trees, pavilions, terraces, towers, and halls. These elements can be seen in gardens such as the Lion Grove Garden, a terraced temple garden designed in 1342.

The tradition of terrace gardening continued in the Middle Ages, particularly in castle gardens, with the construction of walks on the summits of castle walls. In addition terraces were used extensively by the Arabs in Spain, as illustrated by the 13th-century gardens of the Generalife in Granada. These gardens stretch along the hillsides along the Alhambra and consist of seven levels. The highest terrace is called the Court of the Canal and is enclosed on three sides by buildings and by an arcade on the fourth side. There is also a fountain, miniature mosque, and clipped box parterres.

In the 15th century the Villa Medici at Fiesole, overlooking Florence and the Arno Valley, became the first terraced garden of the Renaissance. Renaissance terraces continued to flourish well into the 17th century and also took advantage of the new plants that were discovered by world travelers, as well as from the introduction of botanical gardens. In 1550 perhaps the most famous terrace garden of all time was built: the Villa d'Este at Tivoli. This magnificent villa consists of a connected series of rising terraces, all surrounded by water, including fountains, fishponds, grottoes, and the "walk of a hundred fountains," a long promenade with hundreds of jets of water.

The Renaissance garden spread from Italy to Germany, Spain, Holland, and France. In France terrace gardens were first introduced in the early part of the 17th century; the garden that best illustrates the French Renaissance style is Dampierre, near Boissy-sur-Seine. This garden demonstrates all the elements of a classic French garden: a formal, geometrical parterre, a perfectly rectangular canal, rectangular rows of trees, a raised terrace, and a large, rectangular, formal lake. The later French gardens designed by the noted landscape architect André Le Nôtre were even grander than those seen in Italy. Unlike the terraces found in Italy, however, in France, the terraces lay along the land rather than being carved from it. This can be seen at such noted gardens as Versailles and at Saint-Germain, at which Le Nôtre created the "grand terrace."

The use of the terrace as a platform was not used extensively in England because of the strong influence of the celebrated architect Lancelot "Capability" Brown, who replaced the great formal gardens of England with more naturalistic gardens. In the latter part of the 18th century, terraces were reintroduced as part of the naturalistic English garden movement, which was practiced heavily by Humphry Repton. Repton, however, made terraces a part of the house, much like those in use today. It was during this period that terraces were no longer used strictly in garden designs only for the aristocracy but became part of public gardens and smaller, private homes as well.

During the Victorian era English architects embraced the Renaissance style of Italian gardens, and one of the most influential architects of the time was Sir Charles Barry. He created Italianate gardens with a series of balustrade terraces descending from the foot of a house to the lower level. One of his gardens, Shrubland Park, is particularly reminiscent of 16th-century Italian gardens with its architectural garden of terraces. These Italian-influenced terrace designs continued late into the 19th century and early into the 20th.

These English influences reached the United States and were adapted to meet the particular needs of Americans. The terrace was used in the same way as it was in England during the naturalistic period, as a part of the house. In this case a house terrace forms an architectural base for the house and has clearly defined boundaries. Today the typical terrace is a paved area against one wall of the house and provides a space for use as an outdoor living room.

Terraces also took on a uniquely American flavor during the 20th century when they began to be used in roof gardens. Roof gardens are an ancient art that was revived due to the architectural need to create setbacks in the upper stories of tall buildings to allow for sunlight on the lower floors of the building. To meet this need a series of flat terraces were created, with most of the plants being grown in pots or deep boxes of soil. These gardens are reminiscent of the techniques of the Babylonians when they made their hanging gardens.

Further Reading

Clifford, Derek Plint, *A History of Garden Design,* London: Faber, and New York: Praeger, 1962; 2nd edition, 1966

Douglas, William Lake, *Garden Design: History, Principles, Elements, Practice,* Scarborough, Ontario: Prentice Hall Canada, 1983; London: Macdonald, and New York: Simon and Schuster, 1984

Farrar, Linda, *Ancient Roman Gardens,* Stroud, Gloucestershire: Sutton, 1998; revised edition, 2000

Lloyd, Seton, Hans Wolfgang Müller, and Roland Martin, *Ancient Architecture: Mesopotamia, Egypt, Crete, Greece,* New York: Abrams, 1974

Loxton, Howard, editor, *The Garden,* London: Thames and Hudson, 1991

Morris, Edwin T., *The Gardens of China: History, Art, and Meanings,* New York: Scribner, 1983

Mosser, Monique, and Georges Teyssot, editors, *L'architettura dei giardini d'Occidente,* Milan: Electa, 1990; as *The Architecture of Western Gardens,* Cambridge, Massachusetts: MIT Press, 1991; as *The History of Garden Design,* London: Thames and Hudson, 1991

Plumptre, George, *The Garden Makers: The Great Tradition of Garden Design from 1600 to the Present Day,* London: Pavilion, and New York: Random House, 1993

Symes, Michael, *A Glossary of Garden History,* Princes Risborough, Buckinghamshire: Shire, 1993; 2nd edition, 2000

Taylor, Christopher, *The Archaeology of Gardens,* Aylesbury, Buckinghamshire: Shire, 1983

Thacker, Christopher, *The History of Gardens,* Berkeley: University of California Press, and London: Croom Helm, 1979

Wood, Arthur Denis Blachford, *Terrace and Courtyard Gardens for Modern Homes,* London: Collingridge, 1965; 2nd revised edition, as *Terrace and Courtyard Gardens,* Newton Abbot, Devon: David and Charles, 1970; as *English Terrace and Courtyard Gardens,* South Brunswick: Barnes, 1972

Wright, Richardson Little, *The Story of Gardening: From the Hanging Gardens of Babylon to the Hanging Gardens of New York,* London: Routledge, and New York: Dodd, 1934

JUDITH GERBER

Tessin Family

Swedish Architects

From the mid-17th to the mid-18th century, Swedish architecture was dominated by three members of the Tessin family: Nicodemus Tessin the Elder, his son Nicodemus Tessin the Younger, and his grandson Carl Gustaf Tessin. Their work represents the first important appearance of French baroque and classical Italian elements in the architectural and landscape designs of northern Europe.

During the reign of King Gustavus II Adolph (r. 1611–32), Sweden emerged as one of Europe's great powers and began to attract artists and tradesmen from across the continent. In 1636 Nicodemus Tessin the Elder, a military engineer by training who had entered the service of the Swedish chancellor Axel Oxenstierna, moved from his native Pomerania to Stockholm. There, he found the demand for military fortifications on the wane; however, with the power of the Swedish nobility and royal family on the rise, the need for impressive private residences and public buildings was growing. He found employment under Swedish royal architect Simon de la Vallee and completed, among other early works, Castle Tidö at Västerås for Oxenstierna in 1645.

The following year Tessin the Elder was appointed de la Vallee's successor. He designed a number of towns in the region of Norrland in the late 1640s but realized that in order to meet the increasing demands of his patrons he needed additional study. Supported by Queen Christina, he traveled to Italy, France, and Holland from 1651 to 1653, visiting important architectural sites, collecting numerous books, drawings, and prints, and meeting with some of the most prominent men in his field, including the French landscape architect André Le Nôtre.

Tessin the Elder returned to Stockholm confident that he could fulfill Sweden's ambitions for a grand architecture. In 1661 he was named city architect of Stockholm. His many designs for the capital included such major works as the Caroline Mausoleum in Riddarholm Church (1672) and the Bank of Sweden (1676). Among his other notable achievements was the huge cathedral at Kalmar (1660–70), which was inspired by Giacomo da Vignola's Il Gesù in Rome. Tessin the Elder's most significant work, however, was the magnificent Drottningholm Palace, a commission he received from the dowager queen Hedvig Eleonora.

Construction began on the palace in 1662. He designed the palace, located on an island in Lake Mälaren just outside central Stockholm, in a modified French baroque style. The central section has a square plan, with a monumental staircase in the main hall and richly decorated apartments on each of the three floors, including a dazzling green-and-gold state bedchamber whose floor is composed of six different types of wood and whose ceiling is supported by Corinthian pilasters. The palace is capped by a Nordic *sateri* roof, which features a raised center portion and round dormer windows. Tessin the Elder designed the formal gardens of the palace grounds in the style of Le Nôtre. Elegant parterres offer expansive vistas of the lake. Fountains, bronze statuary, and box hedges are among the gardens' prominent features.

Tessin the Elder died in 1681, five years before Drottningholm was completed by his son, Nicodemus Tessin the Younger. From an early age Tessin the Younger had been groomed to succeed his father. In addition to the education he received under his father's guidance, he studied for five years in Rome (1673–78) and for two years in Paris (1678–80). Upon his father's death Tessin the Younger was appointed Stockholm city architect. After completing Drottningholm he made a second visit to Rome and Paris in 1687–88. In Rome he was introduced by Christina (who had abdicated her throne in 1654) to sculptor and architect Giovanni Lorenzo Bernini and to Bernini's protégé, architect and engineer Carlo Fontana. The admiration that Bernini and Fontana had for ancient and baroque culture made a lasting impression on Tessin the Younger. His later works, including the palace that he built for himself in Stockholm in 1696–1700, were conspicuous for their Italian classical facades and French baroque interiors and gardens.

In 1697 the Royal Castle of Stockholm was destroyed by fire, and Tessin the Younger received the commission to design a new royal palace. His most impressive achievement, the Royal Palace of Stockholm is remarkable for its grace in proportion and sheer immensity in scale. With its 608 rooms the palace is one of the largest in Europe. Tessin the Younger gave each of the palace's four facades its own distinctive character. In contrast with the north facade, which is largely bare of ornament, the south and west facades are richly decorated. The south is adorned with a huge triumphal arch, while the central section of the west features Doric columns on the ground floor, caryatids with Ionic capitals on the first floor, and Corinthian pilasters on the second floor. Tessin the Younger patterned the east facade, with its nine-window-wide central section and colossal pilasters, after Bernini's Palazzo Odelscalchi in Rome. Also on the east Tessin the Younger placed the Logården Park, a miniature palace garden that, like the gardens at Drottningholm, is in the manner of Le Nôtre.

Because of a shortage of money and workmen during the reign of Karl XII, the construction of the Royal Palace of Stockholm was delayed for many years. Tessin the Younger turned his attention to other projects, including designing gardens for royal palaces at Ulriksdal and Karlberg. He also drew up plans for a remodeled Louvre in Paris and a Temple of Apollo in Versailles, but these proposals were rejected by Louis XIV. Not until the mid-1720s—just a few years before Tessin the Younger's death—did work resume on the Royal Palace of Stockholm. It was finally completed in 1754 under the supervision of his son, Carl Gustaf Tessin.

Carl Gustaf's main career was as a statesman and court official. A founder of the anti-Russian Hat Party, he became speaker of the Swedish parliament in 1738 after his party had won a parliamentary majority, and he later served as head of the Swedish state chancellery. Although his skill as an architect never approached the level of his father and grandfather, he made a number of significant contributions in the field. For many years he served as Stockholm's high commissioner of public buildings. Besides overseeing the enormous task of completing the Royal Palace of Stockholm, he designed with architect

Carl Hårleman an impressive country estate for himself at Åkerö. He also became a notable collector and expanded his family's vast collection of architectural prints, drawings, and books—an invaluable resource that is preserved today in the National Museum in Stockholm.

See also Drottningholm

Nicodemus Tessin the Elder 1615–1681

Biography
Born in Stralsund, Pomerania (now Stralsund, Germany), 7 December 1615. Trained as military engineer in Pomerania; emigrated to Stockholm, Sweden, 1636; employed under Swedish royal architect Simon de la Vallée, then succeeded Vallée as royal architect, 1646; sent by Queen Christina on tour of Italy, France, and Holland, 1651–53, after which his designs showed strong French and Italian influences; named city architect of Stockholm, 1661; most important work, Royal Palace of Drottningholm, Sweden, commissioned by dowager queen Hedvig Eleonora, 1662, and completed by son, Nicodemus Tessin the Younger, 1686. Died in Stockholm, Sweden, 24 May 1681.

Selected Designs
1645	Castle Tidö, Västerås, Sweden
1660–70	Cathedral of Kalmar, Sweden
1662–81	Gardens and palace (completed by Nicodemus Tessin the Younger), Royal Palace of Drottningholm, Lake Mälaren, Sweden
1672	Caroline Mausoleum, Riddarholm Church, Stockholm, Sweden
1676	Bank of Sweden, Stockholm, Sweden

Nicodemus Tessin the Younger 1654–1728

Biography
Born in Nykoping, Sweden, 23 May 1654. Father Nicodemus Tessin the Elder. Studied in Rome, 1673–78, and Paris, 1678–80; succeeded father as Stockholm city architect, 1682; completed Royal Palace of Drottningholm, Sweden, 1686; made second visit to Rome and Paris, 1687–88; in Rome, met Giovanni Bernini and Carlo Fontana, who had strong influence on him; excelled at garden design as well as architecture and became leader of group of artists-craftsmen; after Royal Castle of Stockholm destroyed by fire in 1697, designed new Royal Palace; construction of new palace completed by his son, Carl Gustaf Tessin, 1754. Died in Stockholm, Sweden, 10 April 1728.

Selected Designs
1694	Steninge Castle, Sweden
1696–1700	Gardens and palace, Tessin Palace, Stockholm, Sweden
1697–1728	Logärden Park and palace (completed by Carl Gustaf Tessin), Royal Palace of Stockholm, Sweden

Carl Gustaf Tessin 1695–1770

Biography
Born in Stockholm, Sweden, 5 September 1695. Father Nicodemus Tessin the Younger. Studied in France and Italy; entered Swedish diplomatic service, 1720s, and embarked on political career; completed Royal Palace, Stockholm, 1754; enlarged father and grandfather's collection of architectural prints, drawings, and books (now housed in National Museum, Stockholm). Died in Åkerö, Sweden, 7 January 1770.

Selected Designs
1740s	Country estate (with architect Carl Hårleman), Åkerö, Sweden

Further Reading
Josephson, Ragnar, *L'architecte de Charles XII, Nicodème Tessin à la cour de Louis XIV*, Paris and Brussels: Van Oest, 1930
Josephson, Ragnar, *Tessin: Nicodemus Tessin d. y.: Tiden, mannen, verket*, 2 vols., Stockholm: Norstedt, 1930–31

SHERMAN J. HOLLAR

Thailand

Thailand represents several different interconnected realities: a geographic place in Southeast Asia, the homeland of the Thai people, and a modern nation-state. Central to the development of the landscape and people of Thailand has been their setting, in particular the valley and lowlands of the Chao Phraya River. It is in this valley that the southward-moving sequence of Thai royal capitals, so central to the nation's history, was built. The Thai (or Tai, as the larger cultural group was called during this early period) arrived in the northern uplands of Southeast Asia, most likely from the Yunnan region of China, by the ninth century. From this mountainous homeland they gradually moved into lush riverine lowlands, reaching the Chao Phraya plains by the 13th century. Once there, a succession of royal capitals became the centers of Thai life: Sukhotai during the 13th and early 14th centuries, Ayudhya beginning in 1351, and finally the current capital, Bangkok, in 1782.

Due to their location the Thai received cultural influences from a variety of nearby groups. India and Ceylon provided the most conspicuous components of their material and metaphysical culture. These Indian impacts often arrived indirectly through neighboring kingdoms, the most important of which was the Angkor-centered Khmer kingdom (modern Cambodia). After the 14th century Europeans also affected the Thai. Despite all these foreign influences, the Thai people maintain traditional, animistic landscape beliefs and practices. These include geomancy practices akin to Chinese *feng shui* and the custom of appeasing spirits of place, through the construction of a small temple-like "spirit house," at any newly developed site.

Thai traditions of landscape design can be seen in three major areas. First is in the arrangement of cities, particularly the royal capitals. The second is in the grounds of Buddhist temples. The third is in the grounds of palaces and other upper-class homes. Although it may seem strange to discuss city plans in the context of gardens, the Thai conceived of plans for royal capitals as large gardens set against the verdant garden-like natural landscape. Particularly within the inner royal areas of cities, orchards and heavily forested blocks provided shady open spaces that were likely used as semipublic parks. The best example of a Thai royal garden-city can be found at Sukhotai. A stone inscription describes Sukhotai and its outskirts as having a "great lake" and groves of areca palm, betel nut, mango, tamarind, and coconut trees. Ponds provided places for growing aquatic vegetation, particularly the lotus and water lily, that so beautifully color the historic city today.

During the period up to the 19th century, there is little evidence to suggest that the Thai constructed gardens, in the Western sense of the word, at either temples or palaces. Temple paintings, the principal visual evidence for landscape design, show both temples and palaces as walled compounds, having many small buildings set around paved courtyards planted with a few clipped trees. Other ornamental features sometimes included ponds and sculpture-like rocks. An unusual mural from the Phra Singh Temple in the northern city of Changmai illustrates one of the few designed garden spaces shown in temple paintings but may only represent a mythical

Garden of Wat Bupharam, Thailand
Copyright Jochen Tack/Das Fotoarchiv

landscape. This small, irregularly shaped garden held a tall red-painted pavilion with a second-story viewing platform, a small circular pool, white-and-blue glazed planters, and a peripheral planting of heavily fruited and flowered small trees. Monks used temple gardens as a source of flowers and vegetation for offerings, as well as sites for symbolically important vegetation, such as the bohdi tree (*Ficus religiosa*), which was said to be the particular tree species under which the Buddha sat at the time he first received enlightenment. Palace gardens served as recreation spaces for the court but were still designed in the simple manner of the temple garden. Most garden courts had extensive paving, clipped trees, and both large shade and small flowering trees, such as frangipani *(Plumeria)*.

In the 19th century, as Thailand received greater influences from abroad, palace landscapes changed slightly with the introduction of miniaturized landscape scenes set either in containers or small beds. These miniature views were heavily planted with diverse species but also incorporated other features, such as sculpture, ornamental rocks, and water. Although the diminutive gardens have the appearance of Chinese tray gardens, they were widely used during a period of English influence and may have been inspired by the gardenesque style of design. One purely European introduction to Thailand was the use of lawn. Lawns were usually set out as rectangular stone-edged panels, such as those found at the Siwalai Garden of the Grand Palace in Bangkok.

In the 20th century Thailand continued to mix traditional design approaches with those borrowed from the West, particularly England. Victorian-style gardens with patterned planting beds and a great variety of trees and shrubs were common in royal gardens, temples, and the few early public parks of Bangkok. An example of this type of planting can be seen at Bangkok's Wat Benchamabophit. Since the 1950s Thai designers have increasingly been educated in the West, particularly the United States, leading to modern influences in design. At the same time these designers have a strong sense of their traditions and have attempted to reintroduce Thai concepts into professional landscape design. One landscape architect, Decha Boonkham (often called the father of landscape architecture in Thailand), was particularly important in this effort. His contributions have included the development plan for Sukhotai Historical Park and the establishment of the first degree program at a Thai university. More recently the team of landscape architects working for the Thai Fine Arts Department have continued this trend through their site plans and detailed designs for Phnom Rung and Si Satchanalai Historical Parks. Through the work of these designers and horticulturists, the contemporary Thai landscape remains as colorful a tapestry of old and new, natural and built, sacred and secular, as any vivid piece of Thai silk.

Further Reading

Gosling, Betty, "Reflections on a Golden Age," *Archaeology* 43, no. 5 (1990)

Matics, K.I., *Introduction to the Thai Mural*, Bangkok: White Lotus, 1992

Pendleton, Robert Larimore, *Thailand: Aspects of Landscape and Life*, New York: Duell Sloan and Pearce, 1962

Warren, William, *Thai Style*, New York: Rizzoli, 1989

Warren, William, *The Tropical Garden: Gardens in Thailand, Southeast Asia, and the Pacific*, Bangkok: Asia Books, and New York: Thames and Hudson, 1991; new edition, New York: Thames and Hudson, 1997

Wyatt, David K., *Thailand: A Short History*, New Haven, Connecticut: Yale University Press, 1984

NANCY J. VOLKMAN

Theater. *See* Amphitheater/Theater

Theophrastus ca. 371–ca. 287 B.C.

Greek Scholar of Botany

According to the biographer Diogenes Laertius (probably early third century A.D.) Theophrastus was born Tyrtamus to a fuller, Melantes, in Eresus and was renamed by Aristotle for his graceful literary style; but the new name may have been no more than hypocoristic teasing for Theophrastus's not altogether successful attempts to master the dialect of Athens, where uniquely the name was common. The tradition, also in Diogenes, that Theophrastus was, with Aristotle, a pupil of Plato in Athens is suspect. He probably first met Aristotle when the latter was at Assos after Plato's death in 347 B.C. and became his associate when Aristotle founded the Lyceum at Athens in 335 B.C. Theophrastus took over as head of the school from Aristotle (whose books he inherited) when the latter retired for political reasons to Chalcis in 323 B.C., and upon his own death was himself succeeded by Straton. Whereas Aristotle's Lyceum was largely a collection of people using rented property, Theophrastus, although also a metic (resident alien), was permitted through the influence of his pupil Demetrius of Phalerum (governor of Athens) to acquire property and thus established the school as a permanent material entity.

From a huge output (Diogenes lists 227 treatises, on a range of subjects almost as great as that of Aristotle) the most substantial surviving works of Theophrastus are his *Enquiry into Plants* (usually known by its Latin title, *Historia Plantarum*) and *Explanations of Plants* (*De Causis Plantarum*). The former consists now of nine books and the latter six. Diogenes states ten and eight, respectively, but the surviving *On Odors* is perhaps the eighth book of *Explanations,* the seventh possibly being the lost *On Wine and Oil,* which Diogenes mentions separately, as he does two further botanical works (*On Fruits* and *On Juices*), which were probably other versions or merely other names of parts of *Enquiry* and *Explanations*. These works are the author's lectures at the Lyceum, presumably augmented and revised through much of his lengthy career. Perhaps instigated by Aristotle, they are the botanical counterpart to the elder scholar's zoological researches. Their last firmly dated reference is to some time between 306 and 294 B.C.

Enquiry is largely an examination of the morphology, physiology, reproduction, and development of plants, based on minute observation and supported by description, with associated information on such topics as diseases and economic uses. Its resultant interest in classification laid the historical foundation for modern scientific plant taxonomy. Over 500 plants are mentioned, most native to Greece and many of which could be studied in the botanical garden attached to the Lyceum, but Theophrastus also adds examples from elsewhere in Europe, North Africa, and Asia. For knowledge of some Asiatic species, he was probably indebted to Alexander III of Macedon, who had sent specimens and information to Aristotle. In *Explanations* Theophrastus discusses common and peculiar characteristics, natural processes and human procedures, and flavors and odors. The surviving *Odors,* which deals with the animal in addition to the vegetal, is largely but not exclusively practical and includes the preparation of synthetic perfumes. While Theophrastus was familiar with the now largely lost philosophical and botanical work of predecessors and contemporaries (most notably Aristotle, whom he does not hesitate to correct, although never by name) and gained much information from woodcutters and *rhizotomoi* (root cutters; more generally gatherers of herbs), his treatises constitute the first comprehensive and rigorously scientific study of plants and range from detailed descriptions of species to highly theoretical arguments about causes.

The fundamental divisions of Theophrastus's classification, although he admits of overlapping, are trees, shrubs, undershrubs, and herbs, which were still being accepted by John Ray in the late 17th century. Theophrastus's observations, however, take him much further

through an interest in both the outward appearance and the anatomy of both permanent and transient parts and in their functions, thus enabling him to lay the basis of botanical morphology. For instance, he makes distinctions among flowering plants between not only the petaliferous and the apetalous (to use modern terms) but also between the hypogynous, epigynous, and perigynous and between the angiospermous and gymnospermous, the former further divided into monocotyledons and dicotyledons; he realizes that the laminal and filamentose materials about the fruit germ, although widely differing in appearance, are essentially the same thing and uses the term *fruit* for every form of encasement; in branch systems he notices the difference between monopodial and sympodial growth; and, again, in addition to differentiating between tap, adventitious, and lateral roots, he notes, contrary to the belief of his contemporaries, that roots on the one hand may be aerial and on the other do not necessarily comprise all the subterranean parts such as bulbs, corms, and other modifications of stems.

Theophrastus (or Aristotle) probably coined the term *pericarp* and one for internode (*mesogonation*), but he also employed the practice, still evident today, of naming botanical after zoological parts such as "rib," "flesh," "heart," and "nerve." His descriptions of root, stem, leaves, and fruit are frequently comparable with those of modern botanists, although the latter employ a technical Latinate vocabulary (which obscures the fact that such vocabulary is in origin frequently metaphorical) for characteristics and emphasize measurements, whereas the former in both regards are more dependent on comparisons with familiar botanical species and other phenomena (e.g., the sacred lotus has a "head" like a round wasp's nest and leaves the size of a Thessalian hat).

Theophrastus's descriptions often include ecological comments. Thus, while distinguishing between, for instance, xerophytes, hydrophytes, and halophytes, he is concerned also with the interaction of a plant's genotype and factors, both natural and anthropogenic, such as soil, moisture, temperature, elevation, and exposure to winds and sun, these both large-scale and in microhabitats. While necessarily ignorant of genetic mechanisms, he notes the mutation of plants (presumably annuals) in the third year after their introduction into a new environment. He shows awareness, too, of parasitism and symbiosis with both other plants and animals.

Less doctrinaire than Aristotle, Theophrastus openly evinces in his *Metaphysics* qualms over Aristotle's rigid and all-embracing hierarchical teleology, qualms that are perceptible also in his *Enquiry*. Again, he is more cautious than Aristotle in drawing functional and morphological analogies between the animal and vegetal kingdoms, between which he is consequently able to draw a far clearer distinction than does Aristotle. Furthermore, while not rejecting outright the commonly held belief in spontaneous reproduction, Theophrastus suggests that in some plants the development of seeds may have escaped observation and calls for more accurate investigation. Quotations in Galen's *On the Constitutions and Powers of Simple Drugs* (second century A.D.) supplement what is found in his surviving works on the relationship between flavors, which he classifies in *Explanations,* and odors. For Theophrastus flavors are a consequence of progressive concoction by both the plant's interior heat and external solar heat.

Explanations was translated into and commented upon in Arabic, and both of Theophrastus's main treatises were read in Byzantium (although the more practical Dioscorides was more popular there), but in the medieval west Theophrastus, while influential, was known only indirectly. In 1451 Theodore Gaza made Latin translations of Theophrastus's works, whose publication in 1483 was shortly followed by that of the Greek texts in 1497. Since, however, Theophrastus's example of inductive explanatory hypothesizing had stimulated emulation in neither antiquity nor the Middle Ages, no substantial advances upon his work in pure botany were made until the scientific awakening and the invention of a practical microscope two millennia after his time. Carl Linnaeus and more recent scholars have claimed Theophrastus as "the father of botany." His name has been given to the family Theophrastaceae, which comprises some 70 species of tropical and subtropical dicotyledonous trees and shrubs in the order *Primulales.*

Biography

Born at Eresus (modern Skala Eresou) on island of Lesbos, Greece, ca. 372–370 B.C. Associate of Aristotle and from 323 B.C. and his successor as head of Lyceum, a research institute he greatly expanded; wrote on many scientific and philosophical subjects, but surviving works are principally botanical; directly or indirectly most influential pure botanist in West until Renaissance. Died ca. 287 B.C., his will giving instructions for internment in his garden.

Selected Works

Enquiry into Plants, edited and translated by Arthur Hort, 2 vols., 1916
De Causis Plantarum, translated by Benedict Einarson and George K.K. Link, 3 vols., 1976–90

Further Reading

Arber, A., *The Natural Philosophy of Plant Form,* Cambridge and New York: Cambridge University Press, 1950
Diogenes Laertius, *Lives of Eminent Philosophers,* translated by R.D. Hicks, vol. 1, Cambridge, Massachusetts: Harvard University Press, and London: Heinemann 1925; reprint, 1991
Fortenbaugh, W.W., and R.W. Sharples, editors, *Theophrastean Studies on Natural Science, Physics and Metaphysics, Ethics, Religion, and Rhetoric,* Oxford and New Brunswick, New Jersey: Transaction Books, 1988
Fortenbaugh, W.W., P.M. Huby, and A.A. Long, editors, *Theophrastus of Eresus: On His Life and Work,* Oxford and New Brunswick, New Jersey: Transaction Books, 1985
Greene, E.L., *Landmarks of Botanical History,* 2 vols., edited by Frank N. Egerton, Stanford, California: Stanford University Press, 1983
Regenbogen, Otto, "Theophrastos von Eresos," in *Real-Encyclopädie der classischen Altertumswissenschaft,* Supplement 7, Stuttgart, Germany: Metzler, 1940
Strömberg, R., *Theophrastea: Studien zur botanischen Begriffsbildung,* Göteborg, Sweden: Wolflergren and Kerbers, 1937
Wörhle, G., *Theophrasts Methode in seinen botanischen Schriften,* Amsterdam: Grüner, 1985

A.R. LITTLEWOOD

Thijsse Park

Amstelveen, Amsterdam, Netherlands

Location: approximately 4 miles (6.4 km) southwest of Amsterdam

Dr. Jac. P. Thijsse Park, in Amstelveen, a suburb of Amsterdam, is the best-known example of the Dutch phenomenon of the *heem* park. These parks, and Thijsse

Park in particular, are now seen as inspirational examples of the creative approach to ecological landscape and garden design. The park itself is named after Jac. P. Thijsse, whose work in the 1920s provided inspiration for the *heem* park movement. Thijsse was an educationalist with a strong environmental consciousness.

Together with E. Heimans he wrote a number of books that resulted in much increased awareness among Dutch citizens of the need for nature conservation. He promoted the idea of the "instructive garden" in towns and cities, where native plants were displayed in attractive representations of natural plant communities for the educational benefit of the public.

These ideas were taken up and applied most famously in the 1940s by C.P. Broerse, the director of parks in Amstelveen. It was he who coined the term *heem park* (*heem* meaning "home" in the sense that the parks provided a refuge for species that were disappearing from the countryside). In addition to the educational and environmental principles set down by the likes of Thijsse, Broerse was equally concerned with aesthetics. The emphasis was still on the use of native species as the best choices for the wet peaty soils (although nonnatives were used in some cases where a more formal or ornamental effect was thought appropriate), but their use was not restricted to the imitation of natural plant communities. Rather, they were used to produce striking visual impressions with a highly naturalistic character.

Dr. Jac. P. Thijsse Park is one of a series of *heem* parks in Amstelveen that together form a green network of wildflower landscapes through the residential areas. Thijsse Park itself is linear in nature, twisting around a low-density housing development. The park is just over 12 acres (5 ha) and was laid out in three phases: 1940–41, 1943, and 1972 under the then director of parks, J. Landwehr, a former assistant of Broerse. Landwehr had a practical botanical background and was able to obtain and multiply much of the necessary plant material. Water is abundant, whether in small channels or large open expanses. The character of the park is predominantly woodland, within which sit large open glades, ponds, and lakes. A path system takes the visitor through the park, continuously crossing from deep shade to sunlit glade and across footbridges, through meadows, heathland, and woodland. A visit in spring is inspirational: spectacular sheets of woodland wildflowers such as primrose (*Primula vulgaris*), oxlip (*Primula elatoir*), bittercress (*Cardamine amara*), sweet bedstraw (*Galium odorata*), and wood anemone (*Anemone nemoralis*)stretch endlessly. In summer the park is heavier and more shaded in character, although the glades and waterside spaces are filled with meadow species, such as

tall growing bellflower (*Campanula rotundifolia*). There are some set-piece plantings of great character, such as the pioneer birch wood with its striking yellow ground layer of greater celandine (*Chelidonium majus*) and the big clumps of royal fern (*Osmunda regalis*)surrounded by bog asphodel (*Narthecium ossifragum*).

The current manager of the Amstelveen *heem* parks, Hein Koningen, continues the tradition of Broerse and Landwehr, taking an extremely sensitive approach to combining ecology and aesthetics. Along with the original *heem* park concept, it is this idea of creative ecological management that makes Thijsse Park, and the others nearby, so relevant to gardeners of today. *Heem* parks, and the vegetation they contain, are seen as dynamic sites rather than as static entities. Management is an extremely creative process, guiding natural processes of succession and colonization. Thijsse Park now attracts visitors from the world over to admire these beautiful examples of "creative conservation."

Synopsis

1925	Jac. P. Thijsse creates a scientific instructive garden (now called Thijsse's Hof) in Zuiderpark, The Hague
1939	C.P. Broerse lays out the first Amstelveen heem park (De Braak, immediately adjacent to Dr. Jac. P. Thijsse Park)
1940–41	The first phase of Thijsse Park completed, followed soon after by phase two
1972	Final part of the park added

Further Reading

Bos, H.J., "The Dutch Example: Native Planting in Holland," in *Nature in Cities*, edited by Ian Laurie, Chichester, West Sussex, and New York: Wiley, 1979

Hayter, S., "Painting the Town Green," *Horticulture Week* 6 January 1995

Koningen, H., "The Process of Managing Naturalistic Parks," in *Creative Ecology and Integral Landscape Design*, edited by R. Leopold, Amsterdam: Perennial Perspectives Foundation, 1996

Woudstra, J., "Jacobus P. Thijsse's Influence on Dutch Landscape Architecture," in *Nature and Ideology,* edited by Joachim Wolschke-Bulmahn, Washington D.C.: Dumbarton Oaks Research Library and Collection, 1997

NIGEL DUNNETT

Tiergarten Berlin. *See* Berlin, Tiergarten

Tivoli

Copenhagen, Denmark

Location: southwest of Copenhagen city center, adjacent to the central railway station

The Tivoli garden was inaugurated in 1843. Combining the traditional facilities of an amusement park with a romantic landscape layout and a rich floral display, Tivoli has for generations, to locals as well as to visitors, been synonymous with the Copenhagen summer season. The garden forms part of a semicircular row of public gardens laid out on Copenhagen's old city ramparts. Beyond Tivoli this green belt comprises the Ørsted Park (1876–79), the Botanical Garden (1871–74) and the Eastern Park (1873).

Although Tivoli underwent major alterations in the 1940s, the characteristics of the original plan still predominate. Starting at the entrance area, the main promenade occupies the easternmost part of the grounds. It closely follows the layout of the old escarpment. The zigzag flow of the walkway is bordered by double rows of trees and presents itself as a rather intimate space. En route the visitor discovers an unbroken succession of architectural and botanical scenes. Many of the buildings testify to the widespread exotic influences of the 19th century. The ground falls away to the west, and this area is dominated by a picturesque lake. Originally, the old city moat was here. The numerous attractions mingle with restaurants and outdoor as well as indoor facilities for the performing arts. The intermingling of a whole series of exotic styles calls to mind the Roman emperor Hadrian's villa at Tivoli outside Rome, a remote, yet important, paradigm.

Many of the garden's nearly 900 trees play a crucial role in the spatial organization and framing of the numerous separate gardens within the Tivoli ensemble. Lime, ash, chestnut, and flowering cherry occur in large quantities. A wealth of shrubs, flowers, pergolas, fountains, benches, sculptures, and rockeries border on the architectural elements. Supported by the many blooming shrubs (lilac and laburnum) the flower scenery changes several times during the season. It starts with tulips, hyacinths, narcissi, and other bulbs; then follow the roses, the perennials, and the annuals (400,000 are planted every year). Chrysanthemums and marigolds conclude the display. As a consequence of its picturesque and many-styled layout, the garden appears larger than it really is.

Thousands of incandescent lamps illuminate the grounds after dark. Over the years a variety of lamps have been designed especially for Tivoli, the oldest and most characteristic one being a cupola of red, white, green, blue, or yellow glass. Pathways, buildings, attractions, and fountains, as well as trees, are illuminated. The light orgy culminates at midnight with the fireworks. This tradition also goes back to the 1840s and includes parterre pyrotechnics (cascades, wheels, and whips) as well as Roman lights and rockets.

Tivoli's originator was Georg Carstensen, a widely traveled journalist and publisher who had earned himself a reputation as organizer of big public festivals. His idea was to create a Danish counterpart to the Parisian Tivoli-Vauxhall and the Kroll Garden within Berlin's Tiergarten. The project was furthered by the then-ruling absolute king, Frederik VIII, who declared Tivoli a useful tool for distracting the Danish citizenry from growing political activity. The garden was a great hit from its very early days, and in 1856 Carstensen began to create Europe's largest amusement park, the Alhambra at Frederiksberg, Denmark.

The young architect Harald Conrad Stilling was entrusted with the task of drawing up Tivoli's initial plan. The program evoked a fantasy world. Next to the larger buildings such as the bazaar (housing cafés, shops, and a restaurant), the concert hall, and the theater, a wealth of wooden pavilions, bowers, Chinese umbrellas, and tents were fitted in. A switchback, a merry-go-round, a swing, an icehouse, and a shooting gallery also formed part of the earliest attractions. In all respects, a cosmopolitan and elegant design was aimed at amid the lush plantation. Although none of the original structures has survived, much of the authentic atmosphere has been cherished in subsequent designs. Over the years some of the foremost representatives of Danish design have worked for Tivoli, and a blend of loyalty to the old traditions and innovation has been their common link, whether designing buildings, benches, railings, signboards, or posters. Some motifs appear again and again, for example, Moorish cupolas, Chinese pagodas, the Turkish crescent, the chestnut leaf, and the characters of the pantomime tradition. Pantomime was introduced at Tivoli in 1844, and the colorful Pantomime Theater (1874; by Wilhelm Dahlerup) is the oldest existing building in the garden. Dahlerup also designed the present main entrance area (1879–88).

Carstensen's involvement with large parts of the European entertainment business of the time soon determined Tivoli's reputation. From the early days music, dance, and acrobatics on a high international level formed part of Tivoli's performance program. In 1844 a boys' musical guard was founded. This institution is also still going strong.

Tivoli's plan was revised in the 1940s by a team including G.N. Brandt and the architects Poul Henningsen and Hans Hansen. The garden aspect was emphasized to the detriment of new architectural set pieces, and several new elements were incorporated with the existing scheme. The parterre garden (1943) on the edge of the Tivoli lake should be singled out, not so much for its rich floral display as for the geometric and spatial dynamics. A curved brick wall, lined with white benches, frames the rear part of the terrace and thus matches the irregular coastline. The flower beds are oblong, lined by flagged pathways and placed diagonally beneath a few deciduous trees. Tulips and other bulbs alternate with colorful perennials and roses. Thirty-two fountains in circular beechwood vessels, all placed irregularly, underline the oasislike atmosphere of this much-favored corner.

Erwin Langkilde and Simon Henningsen designed the illuminated hanging gardens (1955) as well as a playground (1958) with a series of sculptures. The latter was to set a fashion for many other public gardens. In 1961 Eigil Kjaer created the tall, transparent, cylindrical bubble fountains and the circular, partly gold-mounted pool, with the Nimb, Tivoli's largest Moorish-styled structure, as a suggestive backdrop. Another corner boasts several of Bjørn Wiinblad's Arab-inspired sculptures and fountains. One of the most recent garden designs (1985) is by Lin Utzon and Birgitte Fink and features 12 monumental blue-and-white porcelain cupolas and a lush planting of annuals.

The Tivoli season runs from May through September. Since 1994 part of the garden has been opened in December, and a Christmas fair takes place there.

Synopsis

1843   Construction of Tivoli garden, with bazaar, concert hall, theater, wooden pavilions, and Chinese umbrellas and tents, designed by Harald C. Stilling

1844   Pantomime created and musical guard of boys introduced, establishing garden as performance center

1874   Pantomime Theater, designed by W. Dahlerup

1940s   Remodeling of garden, including new designs by G.N. Brandt and P. Henningsen

1943   Parterre garden created

1955   Illuminated hanging gardens established, designed by Erwin Langkilde and Simon Henningsen

1958   Playground with sculptures built

1961   Fountain, pool, and Moorish-style Nimb created by Eigil Kjær

1985   Blue and white porcelain cupolas built, designed by Lin Utzon and Birgitte Fink

Further Reading

Haugsted, Ida, *Tryllehaven Tivoli: Arkitekten H.C. Stillings bygninger og den ældste have,* Copenhagen: Museum Tusculanums Forlag, 1993

Løppenthin, Ide, "Den københavnske forlystelseshave: Træk af dens oprindelse og udvikling," *Arkitekten 56* (1954)

Tivoli ved Kjøbenhavn—De Copenhague, établi en 1843 par une compagnie d'actionnaires sous la direction de George Carstensen (1845), Copenhagen: Antikvariat R. Levin, 1974

MARGRETHE FLORYAN

Tomb Garden

The English word *tomb* describes a wide range of burial structures, from caves and earthen mounds to architectural towers, often found within the same locale. Most types have had associated gardens attested from the most ancient historical periods. Idealized as places of eternal life, the home of the deity, or representations of the cycles of life and death, gardens offer a symbolically as well as vegetatively rich setting for the tomb. The tradition of the tomb garden is deeply rooted in the Near East but has had an enduring influence throughout Asia, Europe, North Africa, and the modern world. Other traditions have evolved independently in parts of Asia, Africa, and in the pre-Columbian Americas.

Tomb gardens throughout history respond to the faith that those who die find immortality and, frequently, that earthly possessions sustain the dead in the afterlife. This belief is famously true for ancient Egyptian tombs, as seen at the funerary complex of Queen Hatshepsut at Dier el Bahri, where archaeologists found the desiccated remains of *Ficus sycomorus* (Egyptian sycamore) planted outside the tomb and elaborate garden paintings adorning the interior, promising eternal luxury and commemoration of her great expedition to Punt to gather plants for the temple gardens of Amon.

An understanding of tomb gardens of the Near East begins with texts that describe gardens as the place of the deity. The essential elements of paradisaical places are abundant: life-giving waters, trees, and animal life. The god or gods hold council in the garden, begin pro-creation, and determine the course of human destiny. Yahweh himself inhabits the luxurious *gan-YHWH* (Genesis 13:10, Isaiah 5:13) or *gan-elohim* (Ezekiel 28:13, 31:8–9). Humans are simply invited to reside in the garden of Eden, entrusted to provide names for the plants and animals. Once expelled, an enclosing wall prevents their return to that eternal paradise. Other ancient Near Eastern texts similarly describe the gardens as the place of the deity, with springs and abundant life-giving water. In Mesopotamian texts the garden of Dilmun is described in the Sumerian story of Enki and Ninhursag. The pre-Islamic paradise garden (literally *pairidaeza*, enclosure) is also seminal, and David Stronach has recently shown at Pasargadae that by the end of the first millennium B.C. the Persians were using the geometric, quadripartite division of space as symbolic, reinforcing the contrast of irrigated, cultivated gardens and pavilions with the arid mountains. The tomb gardens engage these fundamental concepts of garden by re-creating that paradise, assembling collections of plants and animals, and providing water and abundant vegetation within a protective enclosure.

Specific examples of tomb gardens are found in the Bible. For example, II Kings 21:18 mentions the burial of the king Manasseh "in the garden tombs of his family, in the garden of Uzza," although this passage may indicate he was buried in the gardens of his house; how-ever, it may be the same burial place of Uzzia described by Josephus as being in a garden. The tomb of Jesus was a new one cut in the rock (John 19:41; Luke 23:53); many today regard the Garden Tomb on the north side of Jerusalem to be this site. Tombs are also located near sacred trees (Genesis 35:8).

The pre-Islamic Persian tomb garden set the ground for developments in Europe and in Asia. The tomb of the Persian king Cyrus the Great at Pasargadae (546 B.C.) was set into a garden grove with trees laid out in even rows and small buildings incorporated for the tomb's guardians. The most fabulous tomb in literary tradition was that of Mausoleus (353 B.C.), one of the seven won-ders of the classical world, whose name became a topos for all such monumental burial places. No garden has been identified as yet in the enclosing precinct, but this remarkable structure integrates Persian, Egyptian, and Greek traditions into a single monument, and some form of planting would have responded appropriately. In one of his characteristically inventive assemblages, Herod the Great set a fortified palace into a great tumulus and sur-rounded the artificial hill with unfortified gardens, pavil-ions, and pools to form the setting for his burial place.

The Persian *chahar-bagh*, or quadripartite garden, became a formal expression of an ordered world, with its geometric layout, formally arranged trees, and foun-tains. For the Arab conquerors of Persia, the garden was the Koranic Paradise expressed on earth. The form trav-eled east with the Moguls into India, integrating with Tartar traditions of garden tombs and the Indian tradi-tions of tomb and temples gardens to culminate in the monumental tomb gardens of the Mogul rulers. The first of the genre was the tomb garden of Babur (1508–30) at Baghi Babur, a simple walled garden laid on a single plane. As Elizabeth Moynihan has observed, the tomb and the garden are integrated into the geometry, the embodiment of the idealized paradise, with the tomb an idealized mountain. Humayun (1530–56) created a plea-sure ground near Delhi for use during his life, looked after by priests, with produce paying for maintenance. It is the oldest-surviving tomb garden. On his death the central pavilion became his mausoleum. The Taj Mahal (1632–54) culminates the sequence, an unforgettable testament to Shah Jahan's devotion to his wife. Elabo-rate and rich in its materials, the overall design is simple and graceful. An inscription on the main gate quotes the Koran, beckoning the visitor into paradise.

The tomb garden entered the European tradition through the Greek and Roman contacts with the cultures of Asia Minor, although a prehistoric tradition of tumuli is evident throughout Europe. Stonehenge, for example, is part of an integrated, designed landscape of burial mounds, trackways, and probably associated woods and fields. Relict tumuli were integrated into later landscape features. Marlborough School, an old manor house in Savernake Forest, Wiltshire, incorporated a prehistoric tumulus as a mount in the medieval period, the views across the downs being dramatic in both periods.

Literature made the classical monuments more influ-ential over time. The literary and artistic tradition of the Greek and Roman tomb gardens, however, provided a model for both public and private gardens in association with tombs and memorial shrines. The literature, art, and archaeological remains indicate that the tomb gar-den provided the place where remembrance of the dead was integrated with the daily life of the deceased's fam-ily. Roman tombs outside the gates of towns and cities possessed trees, gardens, and vineyards, as well as dining couches, ovens, and other provisions for family picnics at the tomb. As in earlier Etruscan tombs, the evocation of home inside as well as outside the tomb assumed that the deceased was present and involved in these events. For those of too modest means to afford a villa, the gar-den might provide the only escape from the density of the tenement districts of large cities, although over time the catacombs replicated that very density. Roman liter-ature celebrates tomb gardens from the splendors of Cyrus's tomb to the nouveau riche excesses of the freed-man Trimalchio's planned tomb gardens to the poet Martial's garden for a flea beloved by a shepherd.

Tomb of Humayun, Delhi, India
Copyright D. Fairchild Ruggles

The interaction between gardens and tombs has broadened in many cultures to provide for public interactions between the tombs of great public figures (politicians, military, athletes, etc.) within parklike settings, adding the dimensions of education and recreation to the cultural tradition of paying homage to the dead. The Roman emperor Augustus made his tomb in the Campus Martius into the centerpiece of a large public park for the Roman people. The earthen mound of the tumulus draws on the tradition of earthen tumuli in Etruria, still visible today at Cerveteri and Tarquinia, as well as that of Asia Minor. Augustus's tomb was planted with evergreen trees, usually thought to be cypresses, a symbol of memory. Pausanius's description of this park, along with other images from Greek and Roman culture, remained part of a classical education into the 20th century, influencing tomb and cemetery design throughout the Renaissance and modern periods.

These ancient traditions have been formative in conceptions of burial places in modern times. Pere La Chaise, outside Paris, is a landscape of monuments that provided not only a sanitary burial place for people of varied classes and religious denominations but also a public park and a venue that educated the visitors by commemorating the public figures buried there. This combination would form the early basis for public parks in the United States, notably Mount Auburn Cemetery in Cambridge, Massachusetts, created as an arboretum and park setting.

The pre-Columbian landscape offers its own examples of burial mounds in designed landscape settings. The Hopewell tradition along the Ohio River included the practices of various ethnic groups, but a shared trait was the creation of burial/ceremonial complexes with outdoor spaces that created the setting for the mounds.

The notion of a monument surrounded by gardens is complemented in many cultures by the idea of a burial within a forest clearing, often a less formal express of landscape design. Pre-Islamic India, northern Europe, Greece, and pre-Columbian North American and Asia offer examples of this tradition. Lawn cemeteries and forest cemeteries, generally regarded as a product of the 20th century, can be understood within this tradition.

Asplund's Forest Cemetery in Stockholm (1917–40) is perhaps the most famous example.

Symbols of power, places of pleasure and remembrance, markers of the movement of sun and stars, resources for the afterlife, botanical gardens, and places for education, tomb gardens include the dead in the lives of the living and offer the living an earthly evocation of a paradisaical afterlife.

Further Reading

Cleal, Rosamund, Karen E. Walker, and Rebecca Montague, *Stonehenge in Its Landscape: The Twentieth-Century Excavations,* London: English Heritage, 1995

Jashemski, Wilhelmina F., *The Gardens of Pompeii: Herculaneum and the Villas Destroyed by Vesuvius,* 2 vols., New Rochelle, New York: Caratzas, 1979–93

Kramer, Samuel N., editor and translator, *Enki and Ninhursag: A Sumerian "Paradise" Myth,* New Haven, Connecticut: American Schools of Oriental Research, 1945

Moynihan, Elizabeth B., *Paradise As a Garden: In Persia and Mughal India,* New York: Brazillier, 1979; London: Scolar Press, 1982

Pregill, Philip, and Nancy Volkman, *Landscapes in History: Design and Planning in the Western Tradition,* New York: Van Nostrand Reinhold, 1993

Stronach, David, "Parterres and Stone Watercourses at Pasargadae: Notes on the Achaemid Contribution to Garden Design," *Journal of Garden History* 14 (1994)

Wallace, Howard N., *The Eden Narrative,* Atlanta, Georgia: Scholars Press, 1985

Waywell, Geoffrey B., *The Free-Standing Sculptures of the Mausoleum at Halicarnassus in the British Museum,* London: British Museum, 1978

KATHRYN L. GLEASON

Tools, Garden

Throughout history, gardeners and farmers have desired more efficient tools to accomplish their gardening and agricultural tasks. In the last few centuries there has been little overall change in the appearance of most garden tools. The biggest modifications in tool design came with the development of new and stronger materials. But even as garden tools evolved and changed over time, gardening tasks have not. Gardeners still follow the annual routine of preparing the soil, sowing the seeds, cultivating, providing water and nutrients, pruning, and harvesting a bountiful crop of fruits, vegetables, or flowers.

Archaeologists discovered that early gardens were planted by humans with nimble hands, strong backs, and sturdy legs, along with very crude tools made of branches, bone, and horn. Digging sticks and crude mattocks, a tool that looks much like a pickax with a flat blade, are the first documented garden implements, dating back to 40,000 B.C. Variations of hoes were discovered in Egypt, Peru, and the area known as Mesopotamia, dating from 5000 B.C. to 4000 B.C. Predynastic Egyptians made hoes by tying a V-shaped branch to a thick piece of wood. A bronze hoe or mattock blade was found to be of Mycenean (southern Greece) origin and made about 1100 B.C. Today, there are two basic types of hoes, the draw hoe and push hoe. The draw hoe uses a chopping motion to dig into the soil and has its blade set at a 90-degree angle to the handle. Push hoes use a slicing effect with their blades pushing forward and pointing away from the user.

Romans designed the basic shapes of spades and shovels that gardeners are familiar with today. Medieval spades were rough heavy tools, often made of wood, with only the working edge in iron. Iron smelting became available with the invention of the blast furnace in the Middle Ages, allowing blades to be lighter and more precise.

A dibble is a planting tool dating back to Roman times. Dibbles are really nothing more than a digging stick with a pointed end. Their purpose is to poke a hole in the soil for placement of a seed, seedling, or bulb. Once in place, they are covered with a swipe of the hand. Earlier representations of the dibble, showing that they were made of mammoth's ribs, have been found in cave paintings in France dating to 40,000 B.C. Dibbles with stone heads dating back to 5000 B.C. were found in Mesopotamia. During the Renaissance dibbles were manufactured, leaving fewer styles to choose from. Iron was added to the tip to penetrate hard clay soils. By the 16th century dibbles had hammered tin or copper tips. By the 19th century they were made in a number of shapes.

During the Middle Ages writings about agriculture by the Roman poet Virgil were rediscovered, and European gardeners and farmers followed his recommendations for cultivating to bring nutrients to the plant. Later, during the Renaissance, scientists felt the reason for cultivating was to allow easier penetration of water into the soil and then to the roots of the plants. The 19th century brought about the humus versus chemical theories

The common or draw hoe, from Peter Henderson, *Gardening for Pleasure*, 1883

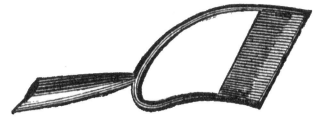

The Dutch or push hoe, from Peter Henderson, *Gardening for Pleasure*, 1883

of plant nutrition. There is still controversy today among professionals in horticulture and agriculture about the level of cultivation needed and the type of fertilizer necessary to apply for greater production.

The garden rake began as a tool for harvest. In Roman times a rake might have been made with an ash or willow handle, an oak head, and iron or wooden teeth screwed into the head. About the end of the 18th century, a rake was developed that could not only gather straw but also move soil and gravel. Rakes peaked in England just before the introduction of mechanized agriculture. Today, the rake's primary uses are to smooth the surface of soils (which requires a flathead rake with the head attached directly to the shaft) or to gather grass cuttings or leaves (which requires a bow-head rake with forged teeth in a metal bow and a handle with spring action).

Agricultural implements, the forerunners of garden tools, changed greatly with the introduction of metals. Metals were used mainly for weapons but also for farming and gardening tasks. By the end of the Middle Ages in Europe, the division between agricultural and garden tools became evident. Agriculture developed more elaborate hand tools for specific tasks, and the tools of the garden became more specialized and refined.

Moving water to the plant has also been an integral part of the gardening process. The annual flooding of the Nile basin in early Egypt was eagerly awaited because it brought needed water and nutrients to the crops. However, gardeners and farmers still needed to move the water from the source to the crops. For centuries water was lifted from rivers and streams by hand, using buckets or other contraptions that brought water to fields by channel, furrows, or pipes. Romans were most noted for the development of irrigation, using gravity to move water through lead or clay pipes, where it was then applied to the soil beside the plant. During the 18th century irrigation systems greatly improved, expanding the potential for supplying water to fields and gardens. Wheeled carts and buckets were another option for distributing water to smaller fields and gardens. But for the most part water was originally carried in animal-skin pouches, then vases, or vessels. During the 1880s cities developed their own water systems. This paralleled the development of the flexible garden hose and greatly aided the gardener in transporting water to the garden.

The watering can, which came about in the middle of the 17th century, has come in a great many shapes and sizes. Gardeners appreciate its ability to gently apply water to plants. The first watering cans were earthenware pots using a vacuum method to fill and pour water. The first spouted watering can with a rose (a round sprinkling nozzle with several holes allowing a gentle spray of water) and spout was also earthenware. Watering cans developed into their present shape in the late 17th century. In the 18th century most watering cans were made of copper. By the 19th century the cost of copper rose, and watering cans were made of zinc, iron, or galvanized tin. English watering cans of the 19th century were large, with two handles, one across the top and one at the back. Most French cans were oval in shape and had only one handle arched from the top front of the can to a point midway on the back of the can. In 1885 John Haws developed a watering can that combined design elements from both the French and English cans. Gardeners still use Haws watering cans today, along with watering cans resembling the English and French styles.

The Renaissance brought about new ideas about the art of living and garden tools. More sophisticated tools were developed to meet the needs of those new ideas. During the 15th and 16th centuries up to 70 different types of gardening tools were used by gardeners in England and France.

Before the industrial revolution, the majority of tools were custom-made by local blacksmiths; each tool was built to the strength and size of the gardener's hands. Oftentimes the blacksmith would decorate the tools with special designs, using religious symbols or botanicals as inspiration. Later, during the late 18th and 19th centuries, the industrial revolution brought high-temperature processes by which steel and other alloys could be made finer, lighter, and even more durable, making possible the development of even finer quality garden tools.

Tools designed for removing spent flowers, shaping shrubs, and maintaining trees benefited greatly from the development of the new techniques and materials. The first attempts at pruning were probably on grapevines in Armenia about 6000 B.C. This coincides with the spread of civilization through Babylonia, Egypt, Greece, and Rome. As the grapevine traveled through these areas, the pruning tools traveled as well, reaching Britain 100 years before the Christian era. Romans used the billhook as a pruning tool; it had a sharp curved blade with a handle and was in every gardener's pocket. Pruners as they are known today are a relatively recent invention developed in France in 1851. Hand pruners were a result of the new industrial era and an important entry in the 19th century. They rested in one hand and could cut stems more than one inch (2.5 cm) in diameter. However, it took some 50 years for the pruner to become an indispensable tool. By the end of the 19th century it was common.

The shaping of trees and shrubs became important as the Italians refined the art of topiary and the French in the 17th century gave Europe a taste for parterres and trimmed allées. The earliest garden shears were nothing more than oversized versions of sheep shears. It is unknown who invented the hedge shears, the first garden tool based on the scissor principle, but it was the forerunner for the modern shears, hand pruners, and loppers. Long-bladed hedge shears set a new standard for the garden.

The beginning of the 19th century also saw a response to the demands of the growing middle class, for whom gardening was a favorite leisure activity. During this time professional gardeners traveled from place to place and required two types of tools: smaller hand tools that they carried with them, such as pruners, trowels, dibbles, etc., and larger gardening tools that stayed in the garden, such as wheelbarrows, ladders, and water barrels, etc. By this time the wide range of tools and machines used for gardening provided easier working conditions and focused on specific gardening tasks.

Another major technological advance to have a significant impact on the availability of gardening tools was the development of improved printing. In the 1830s came the ability to reproduce entire pages of type through a molding process (stereotyping), which immediately increased the availability of garden books, periodicals, and catalogs. Later, the development of steam-powered printing presses once again increased the production capacity for producing printed garden materials.

European and U.S. mail-order catalogs for seeds, tools, and other gardening equipment proliferated from 1850 on. Often printed in color, catalogs were an efficient way for people living in isolated areas to obtain up-to-date tools and new varieties of seeds every year. Catalogs diminished in popularity only during World War II.

Some tools developed a regional style, as in England, where each county had a specific type and the tool could distinguish where the gardener lived. That did not happen in the United States. The only differences found among modern tools in the United States are practical ones, based on use. Today, gardeners value the development of stainless-steel tools, as well as tools made from

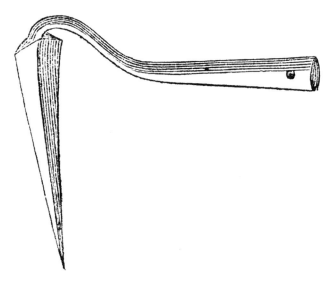

Common thrust hoe, from Peter Henderson, *Gardening for Pleasure,* 1883

recycled and other high-tech materials. Tools can be purchased at the local garden or hardware store, from catalogs, and over the internet. Gardeners across the globe today have access to more tools to accomplish any number of garden tasks than during any other time in history.

Further Reading

Biles, Roy E., *The Book of Garden Magic,* Cincinnati, Ohio: s.n., 1935; revised edition, as *The Complete Illustrated Book of Garden Magic,* edited by Marjorie J. Dietz, Chicago: Ferguson, 1970

Comte, Hubert, *Tools: Making Things around the World,* New York: Abrams, 1998

Crotz, D. Keith, "Science and Technology in American Gardens," in *Keeping Eden: A History of Gardening in America,* edited by Walter T. Punch, Boston: Little Brown, 1992

Huxley, Anthony Julian, *An Illustrated History of Gardening,* New York: Paddington Press, 1978; London: Macmillan, 1983

Logan, William Bryant, *Smith and Hawken, the Tool Book,* New York: Workman, 1997

Seymour, Edward Loomis Davenport, editor, *The Garden Encyclopedia: A Complete, Practical, and Convenient Guide to Every Detail of Gardening,* New York: Wise, 1936; as *The New Garden Encyclopedia: A Complete, Practical, and Convenient Guide to Every Detail of Gardening,* 1948

Slesin, Suzanne, et al., *Garden Tools,* New York: Abbeville Press, 1996

MARILYN MAGNUSON

Tourism and Gardens

Tourism's relationship with gardens has its origins in 15th-century Renaissance culture, which experienced a significant increase in spatial mobility. In 1495 the French king Charles VIII visited Naples as part of a military expedition but took the time to visit the city's gardens and to comment on their paradisiacal nature in correspondence home. When he returned to France he arrived not only with a keen admiration for Italian garden design but with the gardener Pasella da Mercigliano in tow, whose efforts were required for the design of the king's gardens at Ambroise.

Recreational gardening and the leisurely visiting of both public and private gardens became a more popular activity for the monarchy and aristocracy, a phenomenon linked to humanistic intellectual pursuits. In his *De Re Aedificatoria* (1452, fully published 1485; *On Architecture*) Leon Battista Alberti advises that city planners should cultivate urban spaces such as public squares and gardens for enjoyment. Humanist educators including the Dutch philosopher Justus Lipsius expounded the view that foreign-travel experiences served to broaden the minds of great men, and a generation of Netherlandish aristocrats, artists, and philosophers made the journey southward to the Italian peninsula. Knowledge pertaining to classical gardens and architecture was included in the gentleman's education, and illustrated books published in western Europe disseminated humanistic landscaping principles among the cultural elite, leading to the diffusion of classicizing estate gardens. One such publication, Jacques Androuet Du Cerceau's *Premier volume des plus excellentes bastiments de France* (1576; *First Volume of the Most Excellent Buildings in France*), included copper engravings illustrating the most beautiful gardens in 16th-century France. Appealing to its exclusive clientele, a second volume followed shortly thereafter in 1579.

The landed estate increasingly became a center of touristic and leisure activities, as royal or aristocratic spaces gradually became more accessible. London's Hyde Park opened to the public in 1635 and St. James's Park followed in the early 18th century. Elaborate pleasure gardens such as Vauxhall (1661) and Ranelagh (1742) limited public access with subscription fees but offered a range of amusements for visitors, including arbors for tea drinking, promenades, and evening musical entertainment. In France 17th-century visitors to Louis XIV's Versailles reveled in guidebooks and written descriptions intended to augment their experiences of the palace's magnificent gardens; copperplate engravings, poetic descriptions, and maps could be purchased and used on the site. André Félibien published the first official guidebook to the entire complex, *Description sommaire du chasteau de Versailles* (1674; *Summary Description of the Chateau of Versailles*); many others followed. In Germany Joseph Furttenbach's popular travelogue *Newes Itinerarium Italiae* (1627) introduced favored Italian estates and their landscaped green spaces to its readers and instilled in them an admiration for the Genoese gardens of the Prince Doria and the Roman gardens of the Villas Medici, Farnese, and Borghese. The Landgrave Karl traveled south in the late 17th century to visit Roman villas and their gardens; he, like Charles VIII before him, acquired a taste for Italianate gardens and ultimately returned to Kassel with the designer Giovanni Francesco Guerniero, from whom he commissioned plans to expand his family's landscape garden of Wilhelmshöhe.

During the 18th century the Grand Tour of Europe became a cultural phenomenon among the landed classes and significantly altered aesthetic sensibilities, along with those pertaining to gardening. At the same time a nostalgia derived from romantic novels and the *fêtes galantes* such as those by the French painter Antoine Watteau, effected in the aristocracy a desire to return to a pastoral existence and the "air of neglect" associated with picturesque gardens. Claude-Henri Watelet's garden Moulin-Joli combined the tendencies of the formal French Renaissance garden with a new taste for irregular planning and picturesque views of fields and water. Visitors during the garden's approximate 40-year history included Marie Antoinette, as well as the painters Hubert Robert and François Boucher, the latter credited with designing the Watelet house on the grounds. Interest in Chinese gardens, which stemmed from Jesuit missionary descriptions such as those of Jean-Denis Attiret, proliferated in both France and England and led to subsequent travelers' accounts of the pavilions, dragons, and serpentine paths associated with Eastern landscaping. At the same time French writers such as Denis Diderot and Jean-Jacques Rousseau (and subsequent French travelers) focused their attentions westward to England and to the "melancholic" gardens such as those of Richmond and Stowe.

The Enlightenment and Romanticism gradually resulted in new concepts regarding nature and travel. Thermalism experienced a revival, as "taking the waters" became a fashionable pursuit for the aristocracy. Gardens were closely associated with these medicinal spas, for walking was an important part of the cure; gardeners were employed to maintain the tree-lined promenades, formal hedges, and trellised flowers and vines. By the early 19th century the less affluent had begun to imitate the aristocracy, visiting suburban spas and pleasure gardens on Sundays.

The industrial revolution, the development of modern transportation systems, and the growing expansion of capitalism profoundly impacted 19th-century tourism, primarily by making leisure tourist pursuits easier. Municipal park spaces conceived by urbanists as public gardens became more numerous and accessible, with middle-class suburban gardens emerging outside London and other cities and large "central" parks realized in industrialized metropolises such as New York. England witnessed the largest increase in tourism at the same time the government adopted a more liberal attitude toward the estates of its monarchy. Hampton Court opened to public tourists, who were allowed to purview its gardens, walk its pathways, and admire its paintings and sculptures. Regional tourist societies that provided access to country estates and their gardens flourished, and descriptive travel literature such as William Howitt's *Visits to Remarkable Places* (1840) promoted the idea that the nation's formerly elitist spaces—including gardens—were public property. Such widespread accessibility prompted debates in *The Gentleman's Magazine* and *The Times* regarding the behavior of working-class tourists visiting such gardens. Criticisms notwithstanding, a new era of tourism had been inaugurated.

Further Reading

Berger, Robert W., *In the Garden of the Sun King: Studies on the Park of Versailles under Louis XIV,* Washington, D.C.: Dumbarton Oaks Research Library and Collection, 1985

Comito, Terry, *The Idea of the Garden in the Renaissance,* New Brunswick: Rutgers University Press, and Hassocks, West Sussex: Harvester Press, 1978

Curl, James Stevens, "Spas and Pleasure Gardens of London, from the Seventeenth to the Nineteenth Centuries," *Garden History* 7, no. 2 (Summer 1979)

Hall, Colin Michael, and Stephen John Page, *The Geography of Tourism and Recreation,* London and New York: Routledge, 1999

Mieczkowski, Zbigniew, *World Trends in Tourism and Recreation,* New York: Peter Lang, 1990

Mosser, Monique, and Georges Teyssot, editors, *L'architettura dei giardini d'Occidente,* Milan: Electa, 1990; as *The Architecture of Western Gardens,* Cambridge, Massachusetts: MIT Press, 1991; as *The History of Garden Design,* London: Thames and Hudson, 1991

Tinniswood, Adrian, *A History of Country House Visiting,* Oxford and Cambridge, Massachusetts: Blackwell, 1989

Towner, John, *An Historical Geography of Recreation and Tourism in the Western World, 1540–1940,* Chichester, West Sussex, and New York: Wiley, 1996

Towner, John, "Tourism History: Past, Present, and Future," in *Tourism: The State of the Art,* edited by A.V. Seaton, Chichester, West Sussex, and New York: Wiley, 1996

KELI E. RYLANCE

Town Garden. *See* Urban Garden/Town Garden

Tradescant Family

English Gardeners and Collectors

The Tradescants today are commemorated by the species *Tradescantia* because the blue Virginian variety of this plant, commonly known as Moses in the Bullrushes, was first recorded in England as growing in the South Lambeth garden of the elder Tradescant in 1629, having been brought from America by a friend. Tradescant subsequently also acquired the white- and pink-flowered forms. It was one of many plants received from overseas sources, some of them recorded by his friend and contemporary John Parkinson in his 1629 publication *Paradisi in sole Paradisus Terrestris* (Earthly Paradise of Park-in-Sun, a pun on his name). Tradescant subsequently listed in his own hand on a back page of his copy of Parkinson's book the names of the more than 200 plants he received between 1629 and 1633; among them were the first specimens of *Anthyllis barba-jovis,* the smoke tree (*Cotinus coggygria*), *Astragalus massiliensis,* the sad geranium (*Pelargonium triste*), the mastic tree (*Pistacia lentiscus*), the foam-flower (*Tiarella cordifolia*), *Achillea clavennae,* the giant reed (*Arundo donax*), shrubby orache (*Atriplex halimus*), *Aristolachia pistolachia,* the oleaster (*Eleagnus angustifolia*), the atamasco lily (*Zephranthes atamasco*), the Canadian goldenrod (*Solidago canadensis*), the coneflower (*Rudbeckia lacinata*), *Eupatorium ageratoides, Taxicodendrum radicans, Sedum cepaea, Erigeron annuus,* the tree germander (*Teucrum fruticans*), *Erythronium americanum,* the century plant (*Agave americana*), *Aeonium arboreum, Spiraea hypericifolia, Anagyris foetida,* and probably a number of other introductions. In the following year he printed his own plant list, *Plantarum in Horto Johannem Tradescanti nascentium Catalogus* (1634; Catalog of Plants Growing in the Garden of John Tradescant), which contains more than 750 plants, including more new varieties, as well as a large number of fruit trees. It was a remarkably comprehensive list for the time.

The elder Tradescant's first known employer was Robert Cecil, first earl of Salisbury, the greatest statesman of the day, who was rebuilding Hatfield House and laying out substantial gardens when Tradescant joined his workforce in 1610. Tradescant traveled to the Continent to buy plants for this garden on several occasions, as at that time it was only in the Low Countries and France that he could find the rare species that were wanted to fill the newly laid out beds. Among the plants recorded in his bills for overseas purchases were the first cherry laurel (*Prunus laurocerasus*) and double liverwort (*Hepatica nobilis* 'Flore Pleno') recorded in England. Tradescant also supervised the earl's gardens at Salisbury House in the Strand in London, where an extensive rose garden was laid out, and at Cranborne in Dorset, where he is known to have planted trees. In 1614, soon after the earl's death, Tradescant moved to St. Augustine's, Canterbury, to work for Edward, Lord Wotton in the old monastery garden. Here he became famous for growing melons.

Always an adventurous character, Tradescant took advantage of any opportunity to travel further afield. In 1618 he accompanied one of his employer's neighbors, Sir Dudley Digges, on a diplomatic mission to Archangel in Russia, leaving a detailed account of the long sea voyage and all that he encountered on arrival, and returning with various plants including the first *Rosa acicularis.* He also brought back souvenirs, one of which was a Russian *schety,* an abacus, now in the Ashmolean Museum, Oxford, and regarded as the oldest to survive.

Two years later Tradescant embarked on another adventure. This time he enrolled as a volunteer to quell the Barbary pirates who had been harassing British trading vessels in the Mediterranean as well as in the intervening seas. The expedition was a failure, but the various ports at which the ship called enabled him to go plant hunting, and he brought back the first recorded star clover (*Trifolium stellatum*) and probably the turpentine tree (*Pistacia terebinthus*), four varieties of rock rose (*Cistus*), and two of *Smilax* and *Ononis speciosa,* which are all native to the western Mediterranean area and are first recorded by Tradescant in his garden list of 1634. Another acquisition was the Algiers apricot, which was considered particularly sweet and delicate: "This with many other sorts John Tradescant brought with him returning from the Argier voyage, wither he went voluntary with the Fleete, that went against the Pyrates in the yeare 1620," his friend John Parkinson wrote in 1629.

Tradescant subsequently entered the service of the duke of Buckingham, supervising the gardens at New Hall in Essex, Burley-on-the-Hill, Rutland, and the duke's two London houses. Tradescant was entrusted as baggage master when, in 1625, the duke was dispatched to Paris with great ceremony to bring back Princess Henrietta Maria as the bride of Charles I; Tradescant took the opportunity to buy trees in Paris for the garden at New Hall. In the same year he became responsible for the duke's museum collection and wrote to the secretary to the navy asking for a comprehensive list of items to be collected and dispatched back by merchants and British residents abroad. No doubt Tradescant, as keeper of this collection, was in a position to take any duplicates for himself. In 1627 he enrolled as an engineer when the duke commanded an expedition to relieve the Huguenot stronghold of La Rochelle. The casualties were such that Tradescant was lucky to survive. The plants that he found there were similar to those growing at home, but stepping ashore at Plymouth he picked up the prickly strawberry (*Fragaria vesca*), which is a botanical freak, apparently acquiring it after a chance encounter with a woman who was throwing it out in disgust at finding she had grown an inedible variety. The failure of the expedition added to the duke's already fast declining popularity and subsequent assassination in the following year.

By 1629 Tradescant was in a position to establish his own botanic garden and museum at South Lambeth, the first in England to be open to the public. There was a charge of sixpence, and visitors came from far and wide to view the many rare and exotic plants that he grew, make purchases from his nursery garden, and admire the unusual items in the museum collection. In the following year he was appointed keeper of the gardens, vines, and silkworms at the royal palace of Oatlands, which had been granted to Queen Henrietta Maria on her marriage to King Charles I. The buildings covered 14 acres (5.6 ha) and overlooked the Thames between

Walton and Weybridge, Surrey, with extensive gardens, which included a 262-foot-long (80 m) orangery. In 1636 he also took on the supervision of the Oxford Physic Garden. Tradescant died in 1638 and is buried in the churchyard of St. Mary at Lambeth, now the Museum of Garden History.

The younger John Tradescant followed in his father's footsteps and is thought to have trained under him, leaving the King's School, Canterbury, where he would have received a classical education. He was made a freeman of the Worshipful Company of Gardeners in 1634 and was in Virginia on a plant-hunting expedition for Charles I when his father died. On his return the younger Tradescant took over the running of the garden and museum at South Lambeth as well as his father's appointment at Oatlands Palace, although it is not known how long he was able to continue in this; soon after 1650 the palace was dismantled and the materials from it were sold. With the start of the civil war and the subsequent interregnum, Tradescant had to adapt to different times; his garden now included many useful plants, such as vegetables and medicinal herbs, although he continued to cultivate the exotics alongside. He made two more voyages to Virginia, in 1642 and 1654, and his introductions included Virginian winter cherries (*Physalis pubescens*), American plane (*Platanus occidentalis*), swamp cyprus (*Taxodium distichum*), northern maidenhair fern (*Adiantum pedatum*), Virginian bladder nut (*Staphylea americanum*), pitcher plant (*Gelsemium sempervirens*), tulip tree (*Liriodendron tulipifera*), Virginian maple (*Acer rubrum*) and probably American liverwort (*Hepatica americana*), hackberry (*Celtis occidentalis*), red and yellow trumpet honeysuckle (*Lonicera sempervirens*), Virginian yucca (*Yucca filamentosa*), and *Glycyrrhiza lepidota*. The younger Tradescant died in 1662 and is buried in the same tomb as his father at Lambeth. His widow, née Hester Pooks, kept up the garden until her death in 1678, and the museum collection eventually went to found the Ashmolean Museum, Oxford.

The gardens in which the elder Tradescant worked have all been remodeled as later fashions dictated, with their small enclosed gardens of knots and parterres swept away to embrace the wider landscape. The east garden at Hatfield House likely bears the closest resemblance to its 17th-century counterpart, with its original terracing still in place. Only the mound at Burley-on-the-Hill still survives. Nothing remains of the garden at St Augustine's, Canterbury, where ruins now lie excavated and exposed, the earth in which Tradescant's plants once grew having been removed. All of them must have been among the finest gardens of their day.

Both father and son were essentially plantsmen interested in new and unusual varieties. Although few introductions can actually be said to have been collected with their own hands, possibly because not many records survive from the time, many more are recorded as first growing in England in their South Lambeth garden, having been received from friends and contacts overseas. The elder Tradescant exchanged plants with Jean Robin, gardener to successive French kings, and with the Paris nurserymen Rene and Pierre Morin. Tradescant also had contacts in Holland, Belgium, and as far afield as Constantinople. He may also have received some early American arrivals from his investment in the Virginia Company in 1627. His son probably maintained some of these contacts and no doubt established his own in Virginia. The Tradescants' main importance to gardening and horticulture lay in their skill at successfully nurturing newly arrived plants, distributing them to others, and displaying them to an interested public at a time when new and exciting species were still coming in from the Old World and starting to arrive from the New.

John Tradescant the Elder ca. 1570–1638

Biography
Born probably in Corton, Suffolk, ca. 1570. Worked and traveled to buy plants for eminent but unknown employer, before 1610; appointed gardener to Robert Cecil, first earl of Salisbury, 1610; in 1614, employed by Sir Edward Wotton at St. Augustine's Palace, Canterbury, Kent, and became famous for growing melons; subsequently entered service of duke of Buckingham; traveled to Archangel, Russia, collecting plants, 1618; joined expedition against pirates and traveled to Mediterranean, including Algiers, where he also collected plants, 1620; established botanic garden and museum at South Lambeth, London, ca. 1629, first in England open to public; appointed keeper of the gardens, vines, and silkworms at royal palace of Oatlands, Surrey, 1630. Died in South Lambeth, London, 1638.

Selected Publications
Plantarum in Horto Iohannem Tradescanti Nascentium Catalogus, 1634

John Tradescant the Younger 1608–62

Biography
Born in Meopham, Kent, England, 1608. Son of John Tradescant the Elder; educated at King's School, Canterbury, Kent, England, and subsequently believed to have trained under his father; sworn freeman of Worshipful Company of Gardeners, 1634; visited Virginia to collect plants for King Charles I, 1637, and for himself in 1642 and 1654, introducing many new plants; inherited family enterprise at South Lambeth,

London, and succeeded father's appointment at Oatlands Palace, Surrey, England, 1638. Died in South Lambeth, London, 1662.

Selected Publications
Musaeum Tradescantianum, 1656

Further Reading
Leith-Ross, Prudence, *The John Tradescants: Gardeners to the Rose and Lily Queen,* London: Owen, 1984

Leith-Ross, Prudence, and Henrietta McBurney, *The Florilegium of Alexander Marshal in the Collection of Her Majesty The Queen at Windsor Castle,* London: Royal Collection, 2000
MacGregor, Arthur, editor, *Tradescant's Rarities: Essays on the Foundation of the Ashmolean Museum, 1683, with a Catalogue of the Surviving Early Collections,* New York: Oxford University Press, and Oxford: Clarendon Press, 1983

PRUDENCE LEITH-ROSS

Training. *See* Plant Training

Trees

"It is the arrangement and management of trees and shrubs in that landscape gardening almost wholly consists," wrote John Claudius Loudon in 1804 (*Observations on the Formation and Management of Useful and Ornamental Plantations*).

In the Middle Ages woodland trees played no role in the garden. Only orchards (Latin, *viridaria*) contained a considerable variety of fruit trees. Trees without fruits were not interesting in the medieval garden, although they had great symbolic value.

In the early Islamic world date palms were greatly valued both for their fruit, an important source of food in an arid landscape, and as symbols of fertility. The exiled Syrian prince who became Abd Al-Rahman I (r. 756–88) of Spain, for example, composed a poem in which he identified one of the palms in his Rusafa palace with his homeland:

A palm tree stands in the middle of Rusafa, born in the West, far from the land of palms. I said to it, "How like me you are, far away and in exile, in long separations from family and friends."

Orange trees were popular in Islamic Spain from the 9th through the 15th centuries, grown in the courtyards of both gardens and mosques for their fragrance, beauty, and fruit. The mountainous and well-watered gardens of Kashmir in the Mogul period (1526–1858) were famed for their apple orchards, as well as for other fruit and nut trees. When Isfahan was made the capital of Iran under the Safavid dynasty in 1598, its transformation included a long gardened avenue called the *chaharbagh* that was lined with a double row of plane trees. The planting of these trees was personally directed by the shah, and their height and appearance were greatly admired by the English and French ambassadors and merchants who later saw them there.

Various peoples attributed mythological significance to trees in early European history. Holy trees were often trained, although not included in gardens. Clipped lime trees were recorded in Germany near churches or city halls since about the year 1200. They were trimmed into several levels and rooms. This was the only aspect honored by A.J. Dézallier d'Argenville in 1709 in his annotations on German gardening. Around 1238 Pietro de' Crescenzi recommended topiary-like trimmed trees forming whole houses. Yew, savin, juniper, elder, and hawthorn were associated with the dead and planted in cemeteries. Old yews are a significant feature in old Celtic cemeteries in Britain and Normandy. In the 17th century the symbolic value of trees was still very present in Germany, as theological writings such as Jan Meursius's *Arboretum sacrum* (1642; Holy Arboretum) and Johannes Ursinus's *Arboretum biblicum* (1663; Biblical Arboretum) demonstrate.

Trees and shrubs, mostly box and yew, trimmed into topiary according to antique models (*ars topiaria*) were placed in Renaissance gardens, especially in the central points of the square beds and hedges. This feature survived in the baroque garden and can still be found today as a folk art in some parts of Britain and northern Germany. The highest-valued trees of the Renaissance garden were Mediterranean species such as the orange and lemon tree, the cedar of Lebanon, laurel, pomegranate, or fig and Judas tree. These were mostly kept in tubs. Some newly introduced trees, such as the horse chestnut and Turkish hazel, remained rarities in the Renaissance garden.

Renaissance artists created the tree-lined avenue outside the garden. In the 17th century walkways edged with trees were introduced into gardens as well. The principal species were Dutch lime trees (*Tilia vulgaris*), elms, horse chestnuts, and hornbeams and in certain cases also firs, acacias, maples, sycamores, and others. They were pruned (French, *elagué*) if necessary to avoid clumping their crowns together. The height of the stem was generally high, often five to ten meters (5.5 to 11 yd.). The juvenile appearance of the tree with its greatest circumference in the lower third of the crown was aesthetically the ideal one. *Arbres en boule*, exactly round-shaped trees, provided special features near the parterres. Only in the outlying areas of a park were unclipped avenues to be found. Sometimes species alternated with each other, for example, firs with lime trees. Tree rows trimmed together as an elevated hedge were termed in French *en eventail*. They occurred bordering parterres or salons. Lime trees, elms, and hornbeams also served to build up architecture formed by trees, called *berceaux naturels, galeries, portiques de verdure,* and *cloîtres* (tunnels, galleries, porticoes, cloisters). Louis XIV's elm *berceau* in Marly was the most admired example of this kind. In the bosquets the trees could grow freely, but the rules of proportion required them to be cut down from time to time. Nevertheless, in the 18th century, particularly during the rococo period, the bosquet fillings often increased to a height greater than theoretically allowed.

As the first tree introduced from the New World, the arborvitae arrived in Europe around 1534, followed by the acacia before 1623 and the tulip tree in 1653. Most of the North American trees arriving into Europe were introduced in the 18th century, including the catalpa, red oak, box elder, silver maple, white pine, bald cypress, and hemlock spruce. Only a few species came from Asia, such as the Babylon willow, heaven's tree, and pagoda tree. The first varieties selected by gardeners in Europe were some variegated and double-flowered trees and shrubs such as variegated maples and double-flowered cherries, plums, and peaches.

One of the significant features of the rococo garden is the great assortment of trees and shrubs, whereby several species were arranged by height and regularly mixed into a grid. This arrangement was called a clump or shrubbery. Philip Miller described this feature in the article

"Wilderness" in his *Gardener's Dictionary* (1731). After the invention of the landscape garden, designers grouped trees according to picturesque principles. William Kent and Lancelot "Capability" Brown grouped trees by themselves in large, rounded clumps of one indigenous species. These large groups constituted the dark masses in the large-scale landscaped garden inspired by Italianate landscape paintings. Brown used few single trees, such as planes, chestnuts, scarlet oak, tulip tree, and cedar, in the park, but in smaller gardens his surviving plant lists contain a more ample assortment.

In the 18th-century sentimental garden, on the other hand, designers used trees to evoke emotions. As William Shenstone wrote in 1764 ("Unconnected Thoughts on Gardening"), "All trees have a character analogous to that of men." Oaks, for example, were understood as manly and as British (or in Germany, as German), and Lombardy poplars and Babylon willows were considered as harmful. William Chambers, the marquis de Girardin, and C.C.L. Hirschfeld excelled in coordinating trees, emblems, and emotions. The main sentimental categories were gay, melancholic, romantic, and sublime. The German authors Carl Gottlob Rössig, Christian Ludwig Stieglitz, and Christian Friedrich Ludwig compiled elaborate lists of suitable species for each emotion.

Thomas Whately, William Gilpin, Richard Payne Knight, and Sir Uvedale Price recommended more refined grouping. The distances had to alternate, and the species and heights were irregularly mixed according to the aim of variety. F.L. von Sckell in Germany and Jean-Marie Morel and Alexandre de Laborde in France, as well as others, followed these English models. Horace Walpole wrote in 1771 ("History of the Modern Taste in Gardening"):

The introduction of foreign trees and plants contributed essentially to the richness of colouring so peculiar to our modern landscape. The mixture of various greens, the contrast of forms between our forest-trees and the northern and West-Indian firs and pines, are improvements more recent than Kent, or little known to him. The weeping willow and every florid shrub, each tree of delicate or bold leaf, are new tints in the composition of our gardens.

For Whately and his contemporaries the connection between the trees was more important than the appearance of a single tree. The artful selection and combining of trees and other plants were regarded as constituting landscape gardening. The harmony of the whole was attained by combining similar leaves, tints, and habits. "No group," wrote Humphry Repton in 1803 (*Observations on the Theory and Practice of Landscape Gardening*), "will appear natural unless two or more trees are planted very near each other; whilst the perfection of a group consists in the combination of trees of different age, size and character." But variety, according to Repton, must not be overdone; one should avoid an "indiscriminate mixture of every kind of tree." Repton planted mostly a group of one prevailing kind of tree next to one of another kind.

The eclectic taste of the 19th century preferred single trees for beauty and strangeness. The tree was seen as an individual to be displayed. Trees were often planted by famous persons or at important occasions, and artists painted portraits of trees. The intended expression of the garden scene was no longer attained by combination but by individual species. Collecting became more fashionable than grouping and was attainable by any person, not just garden designers. In 1832 John Claudius Loudon termed this system the gardenesque style.

The assortment increased in the 19th century via many new introductions, mainly from the Pacific Coast of North America and from East Asia. From North America came many tall-growing conifers, such as the Douglas fir, the Wellingtonia, and the Lawson cypress. From China and Japan came the Paulownia, several magnolias, and the Japanese maples and cherries. Another vast assortment was generated by crossing plants. Typical sorts of the first half of the 19th century were *Robinia* 'Umbraculifera', *R.* 'Tortuosa', and the purple beech. In the second half of the century, the color-leaved varieties, such as the variegated box elder and the golden elm, came to a peak. In accordance with color theories by Issac Milner, Goethe, and Michel-Eugène Chevreul in the 19th century, contrasting colors are considered harmonious, for example, yellow and purple, green and red, and blue and orange, while neighboring colors, such as lime green and blue or green and yellow, are disharmonious. The tree combinations reflected these ideas of harmonious contrasts. Gardeners liked to combine white poplars with purple beeches and birches or catalpas with conifers, and so on.

A.J. Downing spread Loudon's ideas throughout the United States, slightly simplifying them. In *A Treatise on the Theory and Practice of Landscape Gardening, Adapted to North America* (1841), he established four categories of trees: round-headed (e.g., oak), oblong or pyramidal (Lombardy poplar), spiry topped (larch), and drooping (weeping willow). These types must not construct "indiscriminate mixture of forms." According to Downing there are two main principles of combination: "1. certain leading expression together with as great a variety as possible, 2. intermingling trees of opposite characters, discordance may be prevented and harmonious expression promoted, by interposing other trees of an intermediate character." More than a third of his book is devoted to trees growing in North America. He rejected the "dotting and scattering" found in Loudon's

Derby Arboretum, although in his own designs one can find many single trees on the lawn, "all striking in habit and foliage," as he explained.

British landscape gardeners in the middle of 19th century also took a position against the dotting of single trees (e.g., Charles Paxton, Edward Kemp, Joshua Major, and Charles H. Smith) and reconsidered the late 18th-century writings of Gilpin and Price on the Picturesque. Recently, Brent Elliot has named this phenomenon the "Pricean Revival." Gardeners remembered indigenous species, observing nature, and picturesque assembling. To use the vast assortment of indigenous species, however, new models were required. One possibility was plant geography, established by Alexander von Humboldt in 1805; another was the natural system of botany created by Bernard de Jussieu and Antoine-Laurent de Jussieu in the late 18th century. Each geographic region, according to Humboldt, has its own peculiar character, expressed in the physiognomy of the habit and leaves of the plants growing there. Several attempts to imitate natural plant societies according to the geographic regions of the world are recorded between 1850 and 1900. The garden section called "China" in James Bateman's estate, Biddulph Grange, was one famous example. Here, only Chinese plants and buildings were assembled. In Germany Gustav Meyer stated in 1859 (*Lehrbuch der schönen Gartenkünst* [Book of Advice for Garden Art]), "Only a planting according to nature-physiognomic manner can judiciously be called an imitation of nature and a perfect work of art." In 1879 the French landscape architect Edouard André also recommended planting according to the rules of nature, as researched by natural science. The grouping of trees in gardens therefore became almost a field of academic study.

Not all landscape designers were satisfied with such realistic planting. Out of this dissatisfaction arose the Impressionistic style in gardens. As in painting, one witnesses in planting a transition from realism to Impressionism around 1875. Some French Impressionists such as Pissarro, Caillebotte, and Monet did not restrict themselves to painting gardens but were themselves passionate gardeners. They chose trees and plants not geographically but according to the individual impressions they made. As a parallel phenomenon, the gardener William Robinson in England had recommended wild gardening since 1870, meaning Impressionistic planting beyond geographic restrictions. Woodland embellishment with rhododendrons and perennials became a popular topic. Among Robinson's numerous followers were Gertrude Jekyll, Willy Lange, Camillo Schneider, Alfred Rehder, Charles Sprague Sargent, Ernst Henry Wilson, Ernst Graf Silva Tarouca, Vita Sackville-West, Lanning Rooper, and Penelope Hobhouse.

The modernist reform movement aimed at reducing the vast assortment of trees and shrubs. While the British

Arts and Crafts architects Reginald Blomfield and John Sedding made use of old-fashioned and native flowers, the Silesian forest owner Heinrich von Salisch argued in his *Forstästhetik* (1885; Woodland Aesthetics) against the planting of any exotic tree in gardens, as well as in parks and avenues. In the *Gardener's Chronicle* for 1898 Alexander Dean declared a color-leaved garden to be a horror. Such varieties were now regarded as sick. Patriotic planting of simple, indigenous kinds was recommended. Several peoples claimed to have found their own national planting. In Germany Alfred Lichtwark propagated in 1909 the heath garden, after the model of the heathland near Luneburg. Especially under the National Socialist era (1933–45) some garden designers fought against nonindigenous trees and "unnatural" and "sick" varieties. In 1934 Alwin Seifert uttered with some irony, "We proclaim Picea pungens glauca as the public enemy number one" (*Süddeutsche Monatshefte*).

Most modernist garden architects generally preferred old-fashioned trees such as limes, horse chestnuts, and yews. Avenues, hedges, and topiary had an enormous renaissance. They served not only to copy traditional garden elements but also to form new, sometimes Expressionistic or Cubist forms. The German architect Hugo Koch emphasized in 1927 (*Der Garten* [The Garden]) that the tree functions through its cubic mass and that the garden designer has to use this mass for effect. The baroque garden was seen as a model for the use of trees to create rooms. Some trees with expressive forms were placed alone like sculptures. Grouping went out of fashion. In *Aristocrats of the Garden* (1928) E.H. Wilson prized individualistic trees and shrubs, particularly those from China, many of which he himself introduced. Popular singles included magnolias, ornamental apple and cherry trees, lilac varieties, and the striking laburnum.

Since 1910 the German garden architect Carl Heicke supported a reduction of the nursery assortment. This led to the so-called *Sichtung* (sighting for selection) of plants and to *Sichtungsgärten* (experimental gardens for sighting). The results are effective even today. Most nurseries restrict themselves to a narrow assortment in order to guarantee best sale. For example, one can find *Crataegus laevigata* 'Pauls Scarlet' easily, but where can one purchase the simple flowered scarlet hawthorn offered extensively in the 18th century?

Further Reading

Chambers, Douglas D., *The Planters of the English Landscape Garden: Botany, Trees, and the Georgics,* New Haven, Connecticut: Yale University Press, 1993

Downing, Andrew Jackson, *A Treatise on the Theory and Practice of Landscape Gardening, Adapted to North America,* New York and London, 1841; 4th edition, New York, 1850; reprint, Washington, D.C.: Dumbarton Oaks Research Library and Collection, 1991

Duhamel de Monceau, Henri Louis, *Traité des arbres et arbustes qui se cultivent en France en pleine terre,* 2 vols., Paris, 1755

Farrington, Edward I., *Ernest H. Wilson, Plant Hunter: With a List of His Most Important Introductions and Where to Get Them,* Boston: Stratford, 1931

Harvey, John Hooper, *The Availability of Hardy Plants of the Late Eighteenth Century,* Glastonbury, Somerset: Garden History Society, 1988

Jarvis, P.J., "The Introduced Trees and Shrubs Cultivated by the Tradescants at South Lambeth," *Journal of the Society for the Bibliography of Natural History* 9, no. 3 (1979)

Loudon, John C., *Observations on the Formation and Management of Useful and Ornamental Plantations,* Edinburgh, 1804; reprint, Edinburgh: Constable, 1904

Loudon, John C., editor, *The Landscape Gardening and Landscape Architecture of the Late Humphry Repton, Esq., Being His Entire Work on These Subjects,* London, 1825; 2nd edition, London, 1840 ; reprint, Farnborough, Hampshire: Gregg, 1969

Loudon, John C., *Arboretum et Fruticetum Britannicum,* 8 vols., London, 1838; 2nd edition, as *Arbotetum et Fruticetum Britannicum; or, The Trees and Shrubs of Britain,* 8 vols., London, 1844; abridged edition, as *An Encyclopaedia of Trees and Shrubs: Being the Arboretum et Fruticetum Britannicum Abridged,* New York, 1869

Michaux, Francois André, *Histoire des arbres forestiers de l'Amerique septentrionale,* 3 vols., Paris, 1810–13; as *The North American Sylva; or, A Description of the Forest Trees of the United States, Canada, and Nova Scotia,* translated by Augustus L. Hillhouse, 5 vols., Philadelphia, Pennsylvania: Rich and Hart, 1957

Rehder, Alfred, *Manual of Cultivated Trees and Shrubs Hardy in North America,* New York: MacMillan, 1927; 2nd edition, revised and enlarged, New York: MacMillan, 1940

Sargent, Charles Sprague, "The Artistic Aspect of Trees," *Garden and Forest* 1 (1888–89)

Silva Tarouca, Ernst Graf, and Camillo Schneider, editors, *Unsere Freiland-Laubgehölze,* Vienna: Tempsky, 1913; 3rd edition, Vienna: Hölder-Pichler-Tempsky, 1931

Silva Tarouca, Ernst Graf, and Camillo Schneider, editors, *Unsere Freiland-Nadelhölzer,* Vienna: Tempsky, 1913; 2nd edition, Vienna: Hölder-Pichler-Tempsky, 1922

Spongberg, Stephen A., *A Reunion of Trees: The Discovery of Exotic Plants and Their Introduction into North American and European Landscapes,* Cambridge, Massachusetts: Harvard University Press, 1990

Taylor, George, "The Contribution from America to British Gardens in the Early 19th Century," in *John Claudius Loudon and the Early Nineteenth Century in Great Britain*, edited by Elisabeth B. MacDougall, Washington D.C.: Dumbarton Oaks, 1980

Wein, Kurt, "Die erste Einführung nordamerikanischer Gehölze in Europa," *Mitteilungen der Deutschen Dendrologischen Gesellschaft* 42 (1930) and 43 (1931)

Wilson, Ernest H., *Aristocrats of the Garden*, Garden City, New York: Doubleday Page, 1917; London: Williams and Norgate, 1937

CLEMENS ALEXANDER WIMMER

Tresco Abbey Gardens

Tresco, Isles of Scilly, England

Location: 28 miles (45 km) west of Land's End, on island of Tresco

Tresco, one of the Isles of Scilly, benefits from warm sea currents, generating an equable climate averaging 350 days with air temperatures above the five degrees Celsius (41 degrees F) necessary for plant growth; humidity is high and frosts rare. Nevertheless, the granite islands, never exceeding 50 meters (55 yd.) altitude, are windswept, barren of trees, quick draining, and—except for Tresco—short of natural water. They form part of the Duchy of Cornwall and were leased in 1834 to Augustus Smith, a young philanthropist from Ashlyns near Berkhamsted in Hertfordshire, after the neglect by the former Lord Proprietors had caused a scandal. Already *Aeonium cuneatum* and *Echium* from the Canary Isles and mesembryanthemums had naturalized, and *Agave americana,* myrtles, fuchsias, and pelargoniums thrived in the open all year round.

By 1838 Smith had built at the top of a south-facing rocky slope, above the priory ruins, Tresco Abbey, a house to his own design, with a prospect across the inner lagoon to Saint Mary's, the main island. Few documents have survived, but the growth of the garden can be traced in his published correspondence with Lady Sophia Tower, a distant relative. He began by developing the area around the house, planting among the rocks new varieties of mesembryanthemums obtained from the Royal Botanic Gardens, Kew, enclosing the ruins, and creating a walled Pump Garden above the Hop Circle, where *Humulus lupulus* festooned ropes between wooden posts. The beds in the nearby Pebble Garden were shaped like the Union Jack. After his visit in 1857 Joseph Hooker wrote in the *Botanical Magazine* (1872) that he had been "astonished and delighted with the luxuriance and variety of the Cape and Australian vegetation . . . displayed." By that time the Long Walk had been constructed on the lower level, where Smith planted his rarer finds. He named one area here "Australia," which contained plants of the Aralia tribe, in particular acacias and cassias; another area he named "Mexico." His collection of agaves were the wonder of visitors; an illustration in the *Gardeners' Chronicle* of 1875 shows 13 flowering in one bed. The upper terrace, leading from the house, was next to be created, where the proteas have now become a feature. Midway, the lower walk and terraces above were connected by a path ending in steps leading up to *Neptune,* the figurehead of a ship, on the upper terrace. A fine collection of other figureheads was housed in a summerhouse, which became known as Valhalla. Among Smith's other eccentricities was the introduction of ostriches into the garden and a bizarre attempt to create a deer park on the treeless windswept island of Samson; in the end he had to rest content with black rabbits.

By the time of Smith's death in 1872, the basic layout and size of the garden (17 acres [7 ha]) was much as it remains today, planted in a way that Henry Alford, Dean of Canterbury, in 1868 felt gave "a curious foreign character to the place," recalling villas in Europe instead of England. Present knowledge of the planting during this period is much illuminated by 44 watercolors of sprays of flowers painted by Frances Le Marchant, Smith's sister and a talented artist.

Since he was not married, Augustus Smith left his estate to his nephew, Thomas Algernon Dorrien, who adopted the surname "Smith." Although inexperienced in horticulture, he used his organizing abilities to develop the Isles' trade in daffodils, for which as Proprietor he felt some responsibility. There were already several narcissi naturalized on the islands: *Narcissus tazetta,* perhaps dating from the monks at the priory, *N.* 'Soleil d'Or', *N.* 'Grand Monarque', and *N. biflorus* around the Garrison on St. Mary's, *N.* 'Scilly White' at

Newford, the previous Steward's residence, *N*. 'Telamonius Plenus', and *N*. × *odorus* (syn. *N*. *campernelli*) obtained from a French ship in 1820. Sales had already been successfully pioneered on the suggestion of Augustus Smith, but Dorrien Smith began methodical trials at Tresco of the commercial potential of nearly 350 varieties, of which around 150 he had newly imported from the Continent. As a result sales increased spectacularly, their progress closely followed in the major horticultural journals.

Since the hedges and shelterbelts were now established, Dorrien Smith could enlarge the collection of tender plants, many received from Kew, which attracted the attention of several writers in periodicals. The first semiofficial list of 827 plants did not appear until that of Teague in 1891; Dorrien Smith followed this with his own catalog of over 1,670 plants in 1906.

Major Arthur Dorrien Smith succeeded his father in 1918, but as a consequence of retrenchments after World War I, as well as his reluctance to increase his tenants' rents, he negotiated the return of the islands to the duchy, with the exception of Tresco, which is their status today. Unlike his father, Major Arthur had already by 1910 gained a reputation as a botanist from his collecting and travels in South Africa, Australia, New Zealand, and the Chatham Islands, from which the Abbey Gardens were to profit. He added a pergola and pond to the middle terrace, named the Grecian Rock Terrace, but perhaps his most lasting contribution was the inception of the card index, begun in 1935, which has been systematically updated and revised and is now computerized. A survey made in 1959, shortly after Major Arthur's death, lists 974 species of trees and shrubs, 503 succulents, bromeliads, etc., and 385 herbaceous and bulbous plants.

In 1987 and 1988 the garden suffered from icy gales that wreaked havoc on the shelterbelts and destroyed many tender plants. There had been several similar wrecks in the past, from which, as in this case, the garden soon recovered. Robert Dorrien Smith, the present owner, has added sculptures by David Wynne and has created a new Mediterranean Garden to the design of Carey Duncan-Haouach. Today, tourism has become the principal industry of the islands, but the essential character of the Abbey Gardens, which are unique in the British Isles, has remained intact.

Synopsis

1834	Augustus Smith (1804–72) granted first lease of Isles of Scilly by Duchy of Cornwall, for 39 years
1834–8	Augustus Smith resident at Heugh House on St Mary's
1838	Augustus Smith takes up residence at completed Tresco Abbey
1849	Received mesembryanthemums from Sir William Hooker, director of Royal Botanic Gardens, Kew
1850	First description of garden (North, 1850)
1851	Hop Circle enclosed within yew hedge
1852	Long Walk begun
1855	Rocky slope beneath the abbey at east end finished and greenhouses begun
1857	Garden visited by Joseph Hooker, assistant director of Kew
1858	Neptune Steps and Upper Terrace completed
1859	District named Australia created
1860	Abortive attempt to create a deer park on depopulated island of Samson
1863	First published list of plants on Scilly (Daubney, 1863)
1872	Thomas Algernon Dorrien (ca. 1845–1918), nephew of Augustus inherits the lease of the islands and adopts the surname Smith
1874	Obituary of Augustus Smith in *Pall Mall Gazette*
1875	*Gardeners' Chronicle* prints first illustrations and plant list published in any journal
1873–92	Frances Le Marchant, sister of Augustus, paints 44 sprays of flowers from garden
1881–7	Algernon Dorrien Smith conducted trials of around 350 narcissus varieties
1891	First semi-official list of plants (Teague 1891)
1906	Algernon Dorrien Smith privately prints first official list of plants
1907–9	Major Arthur Algernon Dorrien Smith plant collecting and botanizing in Antipodes
1918	Major A.A. Dorrien Smith (1876–1955) inherits lease of islands
1920–22	Negotiations with Duchy to relinquish lease on all inhabited islands except Tresco
1920s	Grecian rock terrace formed
1929	New lease of 99 years granted, for Tresco alone
1935	Plant card index begun, with dates of introduction from 1848, and sources
1955	Commander Thomas Mervyn Dorrien Smith (ca. 1913–73) inherits lease of Tresco
1959	Survey of plants, probably by Royal Botanic Gardens, Kew (copies available in their library and that of the Royal Horticultural Society, London)
1973	Robert Arthur Dorrien Smith inherits lease of Tresco

1982	"Catalogue of Plants" compiled by Peter Clough, head gardener, and K. Spencer
1993	Prize-winning design for Mediterranean Garden, by Carey Duncan-Haouach
2000	Mediterranean Garden completed

Further Reading

Bowley, R.L., *The Fortunate Islands: The Story of the Isles of Scilly*, St. Mary's, Isles of Scilly: Bowley, 1945; 8th edition, revised and enlarged, 1990

"The Crown of Scilly," *Pall Mall Gazette* (5 August 1872); reprint, in *Gardeners' Chronicle* 23 (17 August 1872), and in Tower (cited below)

Daubeny, Charles G.B., *Climate: An Inquiry into the Causes of Its Differences, and into the Influences on Vegetable Life*, Oxford and London, 1863; reprint of extract, "Tender Plant Growing at . . . Tresco, Scilly," *Journal, Royal Institution of Cornwall* 1, no. 1 (1864–65)

Hunkin, J.W., "Tresco under Three Reigns," *Journal of the Royal Horticultural Society* 72 (1947)

Inglis-Jones, Elisabeth, *Augustus Smith of Scilly*, London: Faber, 1969

King, Ronald, *Tresco: England's Island of Flowers*, London: Constable, and Salem, New Hampshire: Salem House, 1985

Nelhams, Mike, *Tresco Abbey Gardens*, Truro, Cornwall: Truran, 2000

North, Isaac William, *A Week in the Isles of Scilly*, Penzance, Cornwall: Rowe, and London: Longman, 1850

Pett, Douglas Ellory, *The Parks and Gardens of Cornwall*, Penzance, Cornwall: Hodge, 1998

Smith, T. Algernon Dorrien, *Tresco Abbey Gardens, Isles of Scilly*, S.l.: s.n., 1906

Teague, A. Henwood, "Plants Growing in Tresco Gardens," *Transactions of the Penzance Natural History . . . Society* 3 (1891)

Tower, Lady Sophia F., *Scilly and Its Emperor*, S.l.: s.n., 1873

DOUGLAS ELLORY PETT

Tsarskoye Selo

Pushkin, St. Petersburg Oblast, Russia

Location: approximately 15 miles (26 km) south of St. Petersburg

In the late 1710s, Peter the Great presented a small settlement called Sarskaya Myza to his future wife, Empress Catherine I. This land had previously been part of the ancient Russian town of Novgorod, and had, as a result of fighting between Novgorod and Sweden over the course of many years, become annexed by Sweden in the 17th century. When Peter returned this land to Russia after the Northern War, its name was changed to Tsarskoye Selo (the Czar's Village), and it belonged to Catherine until 1727. At the time of her reign, it was a modest feudal estate, much less lavishly decorated than other imperial residences near St. Petersburg.

In the early 18th century, the scant local population consisted primarily of hunters and fishermen. The climate and geography were unsuitable for farming: woods covered vast expanses of poor and marshy soil. Serfs moved by Peter from other parts of Russia worked to drain the marshes and build roads. New villages were built by the government for these people, and eventually agricultural lands and peasant settlements surrounded the imperial residence.

At first, there was just the modest palace for Catherine, designed by the architects J.F. Braunshtein and I. Ferster (1717–23). Its southern facade looks out on the old garden—a formal part of Catherine's (Yekaterininsky) Park. It was the first baroque garden in Russia; it was designed by the Dutch gardener Jan Roosen, and the project was supervised by Johann Focht. Initially the garden consisted of three parts: the upper garden, the lower garden, and the "wild growth." The upper garden, which was closest to the palace, was made of three wide terraces gradually sloping down to the south. The terraces were decorated with flower beds, bosquets, and *berceaus* (trellised arbors covered with climbing plants). On the lowest terrace there were rectangular ponds. The lower garden was designed as three radial allées cut through the original orchard. Further on there was a birch coppice, separated from the lower garden by the fish canal.

In the northern part of the estate, along the main axis of the palace and the old garden, there was the preserve—a large fenced part of the wood, rectangular with diagonal paths—which created a natural environment for the animals kept for the royal hunt. East of the palace and the garden, there was a small settlement for servants.

The second period of development of the park complex lasted from 1742 to 1761, after the estate passed to the Empress Elizabeth I. The palace was enlarged, rebuilt, and redecorated to become a masterpiece of Russian baroque architecture. The original design of the garden was kept but with more magnificence brought in. In the upper garden, parterres took the place of the flower beds, and an amphitheater supplemented the lower garden ensemble. Sculptures played an important role in adding to the splendor of the whole. The topiaries of the park made an excellent background for marble statues and busts. The beauty of the park was enhanced by new baroque park pavilions—the hermitage, *monbijou*, grotto, and tobogganing hill. In the 1750s a pond system, consisting of the big pond, five lower ponds, and connecting canals, completed the park ensemble.

While the old garden was being enlarged and redesigned, the new garden was laid out along the main axis of the palace, between the preserve and the parade court. Its square shape was emphasized by the Cross (Krestovy) canal. Inside, cross allées divided the garden into four parts, called the courtines, and the designers intended to have a shaped parterre with a pond at the spot where the allées crossed. The courtines vere decorated with all kinds of entertaining elements, typical for baroque gardens, including a maze, a mushroom-shaped summer house, a Parnassus hill, an open-air theater with turf benches, a *boulingrin* (sunken lawn bounded by sloping banks), and so on.

The ensemble of the garden street—the first street of the settlement that ran parallel to the eastern border of the garden—was mostly completed within the same period. It was comprised of private houses of the courtiers, stables and hothouses, and a church. In the palace hothouse, there were many rare and exotic plants from the Americas, India, Spain, and the Middle East. There were coffee trees, various cacti, orange trees, and a huge collection of pineapples (about 100 plants). In the summer, these potted plants were displayed in front of the palace and along the garden, parallel to the garden street. The Tsarskoye Selo was now a magnificent out-of-town residence for the court of Elizabeth I. The old garden ensemble represented a perfect setting for typical features of Russian baroque gardens in the 18th century: topiaries, water mirrors made by the ponds, park pavillions, and a hothouse with exotic plants.

Catherine II's reign brought the highest flourishing to the Tsarskoye Selo. The first English landscape garden in Russia (still very much in existence today) was laid out there during this period, and the Tsarskoye Selo became a setting for the empress's experiments, which were inspired by the ideas of the Age of Enlightenment.

The essence of ideas expressed in the Tsarskoye Park is reflected in a letter written by Catherine the Great to the great French philosopher Voltaire in 1772:

I am passionately in love with English gardens, their curves, slopes, lake-shaped ponds and on-land archipelagoes, and feel profound contempt for straight lines and bordered alleys. I detest fountains: they torture water, making it flow against its nature; all the statues are now in exile in galleries, entrance-halls, etc.; in a word, my plantomania is dominated by my Anglomania.

In 1770 the empress commissioned the project to the architect Vassily Neyolov and the gardener Trifon Ilyin. Later on they were joined by Johann Busch and his son Josef.

Busch came from England in 1771 by invitation of Catherine II and at first was demonstrating samples of English gardening in Pulkovo and other localities. He started working permanently in Tsarskoye Selo in 1775. Creating Catherine's Park took more than 20 years, continuing right until the death of Catherine II in 1796. More than 50 park pavilions, monuments, bridges, cascades, and piers were constructed within this period. Around these structures there were formed five landscape areas: the big pond area, the swan and upper ponds area, the rose field area, Kagulsky obelisk area, and the lower cascade ponds area. These areas were united into a single composition by picturesque landscape paths and allées and separated by thick courtines of trees and shrubs. The number of park structures does not seem excessive because they are dispersed over a sufficiently large area, the total of which is about 262 acres (106 ha), 40 (16 ha) of which are occupied by the big pond.

The landscape courtines, solitaires, and allée shrubbery mostly consist of broad-leaved trees: oaks (*Quercus robur*), lindens (*Tilia*), elms (*Ulmus*), ash trees (*Fraxinus*), and maples (*Acer platanoides*). Fewer, but most important decoratively, are larches (*Larix sibirica*), pines (*Pinus sibirica*), and spruce (*Picea abies*). Larch and fir seed for planting in the park, as well as seeds of tartar honeysuckle (*Lonicera*), wild almond (*Amygdalus communis*), Juniper (*Juniperus*), and heather (*Erica*), were sent from Siberia by the Imperial Academy of Sciences research party, headed by the well-known scientist P.S. Pallas. Silvery willows (*Salix alba*) were widely used for shore landscapes. Rose Field was composed of extensive meadows with courtines of roses and wild roses of various sorts. In 1789 Busch finished forming this area by planting a ken-cons oak wood. Busch ordered the oaks from England. Firs played a very important role in making the landscape near the ruined tower look romantic. A pine grove, quite rare for

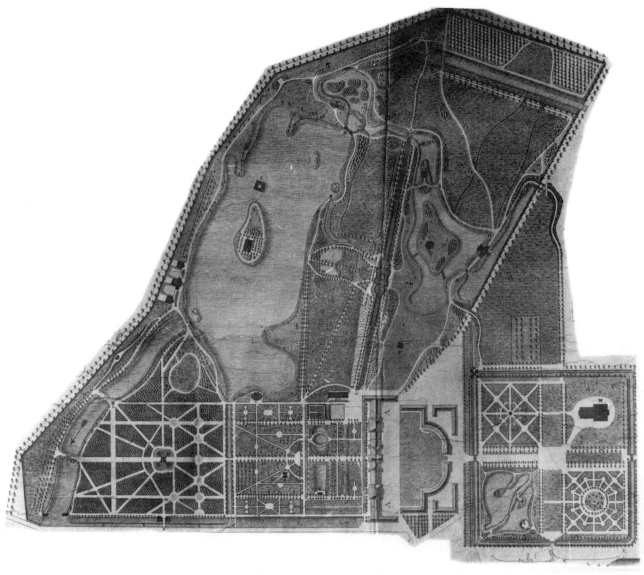

Part of John Busch's plan of Tsarskoye Selo
Courtesy of British Library

Tsarskoselsky parks, was planted around Trifon's hill (*Trifonova Gora*), erected by the lower ponds by Ilyin.

Water areas are a definitive detail in the park design. To create them, it was necessary to provide additional water supplies. This was accomplished with the help of the Taitsky free-flow water conduit, which delivered water from a place called Taytsy, 10 miles (16 km) from the parks. The construction of the Taitsky water conduit represented an oustanding engineering and technical achievement for 18th-century Russia. The construction of the first park buildings began in 1770, simultaneously with digging out the pond system designed by Neyolov. At the same time, the little folly was erected, the first stone arch with soil embankments connecting the park that was being designed to the new garden. The Yekaterinburgsky stone-cutting plant started making blocks of Siberian marble for the Palladian bridge over the canal connecting the big pond to the upper and swan ponds. The model for this was Wilton Park in England, well known at the time from pictures. Part of the English garden image is enhanced by the marble monuments of various colors, commemorating the victories of Russia in the Turkish war (for example, the Kagulsky Obelisk and the Chesmenskaya and Moreyskaya rostral columns).

Early classical style was used by Ilya Neyolov (son of Vassily Neyolov) in the design of two small pavilions for the regular old garden—upper and lower baths. For

Babolovsky Palace, erected between the Kuzminka river and the Taitsky water conduit, and considerably removed from the center of the Tsarskoye Selo, he chose the English version of the Gothic style. Together with the garden master Busch, he laid out around it a small English garden with the silver pond.

The last big construction event that occurred during the reign of Catherine II was the construction of the palace for her grandson Alexander, future Russian emperor, and the laying out of a landscape garden with ponds and cascades around it. The new, or Alexandrovsky, palace was situated outside the already existing palace-and-garden ensemble; it is well placed, being on the axis of the wide transverse alley of the new garden, which makes it a part of the existing composition. Alexander's Palace is one of the best country palaces in the St. Petersburg environs.

The last period in the history of Tsarskoye Selo's formation begins with considerable town planning transformations that were started during the reign of Alexander I and finished during the reign of Nicholas I in the middle of the 19th century.

The author of the new town plan was the architect V.I. Geste, a pupil and follower of Charles Cameron, and a well-known town planner. His project was the first and most striking example of exemplary settlements during Alexander's reign. Geste foresaw future extension of Tsarskoselsky parks and brought a measure of order into the chaotic structure of the old palace settlement by creating regular rectangular blocks of houses. On three sides the town is surrounded by imperial parks, and on the southeast side there is a boulevard connecting Catherine's and Alexander's parks.

Alexander's Park includes regular ensembles of the new garden with construction in the Chinese style, the Alexandrovsky palace with a landscape garden around it, the redesigned preserve, and new areas in the north and the northeast. Its total area is 625 acres (253 ha).

Work on extending the area of the imperial parks continued up to the middle of the 19th century. From 1820 to the 1860s Tsarskoselsky gardeners laid out Babolovsky landscape park, to the west of Alexander's and Catherine's parks. It was named after Gothic Babolovsky Palace and a little English garden, which were included in the expansion. This park was designed for riding. There were no garden pavilions planned for it. Its beauty was enhanced by the meandering Kuzminka stream and the open canal of the Taitsky water conduit. Babolov's, Alexander's, and Catherine's parks comprise a territorially whole palace-and-park ensemble, unified into a single compostion by a network of landscape park paths.

During the reign of Nicholas I, there appeared in Tsarskoye Selo the Separate Park, one of the last imperial parks built in the St. Petersburg environs. It was created around Colonists' Pond, an open canal, and the Pavlovsk waterworks by gardeners F. Lyamin and I. Piper. The design of the Separate Park combines the elements of a public park with the elements of an agro-park. The Separate Park is also of significance to the town plan as a link between the parks of Tsarskoye Selo and Pavlovsk. Its area is 375 acres (152 ha).

In the first half of the 19th century, there were some additions to Catherine's Park, completing the appearance of landscapes around the big pond. The granite terrace, intended for viewing the panorama of the big pond, was designed by Luiggi Rusk and built in 1809. Some years later under the terrace there was erected the famous fountain called "The Dairymaid," or "The Maid with a Jug," glorified many times by Russian poets. The last park pavilion—the Turkish Baths, designed to look like a miniature Turkish mosque—was built on the big pond in 1850–52. During the period 1855–65, the private garden with a fountain, a pergola, flower beds, and sculptures, designed by the architect F. Vidov, was created near the Zubovsky building of the palace for Alexander II.

In the 1900s Tsarskoselsky Alexandrovsky Palace became a permanent residence of the last Russian emperor, Nicholas II. There were no significant changes in the park's appearance, except putting an iron fence around the area surrounding the palace. Along the border of Alexander's Park there were built barracks for the private convoy and a complex of multipurpose buildings designed in traditions of ancient Russian architecture.

A synthesis of European styles and details peculiar to Russian culture and nature provided for creation of a unique palace-and-park ensemble and turned Tsarskoye Selo into an encyclopedia of park and garden art and architecture from the 18th century to the beginning of the 20th century.

During World War II the town was occupied by the German army. Catherine's Palace was destroyed by artillery bombardment and fires. Combat and tree cutting in the park reduced the number of trees and shrubs dramatically; about 60 to 70 percent of the ornamental coniferous trees were lost. In order to restore the losses, immediately after the war, trees were planted in both Catherine's and Alexander's parks without any system. Experimental restoration works and a working out of the general concept of restoration of the Tsarskoselsky parks were conducted by T.B. Dubyago. Restoration of the landscape part of Catherine's park began in 1979.

Synopsis

| late 1710s | Peter the Great presents estate to his wife, Catherine |
| 1717–23 | Construction of palace for Catherine I by architect J.F. Braunshtein; construction of formal part of Yekaterininsky Park (Catherine's Park) |

	and preserve, designed by gardener Jan Roosen
1727	Catherine I dies
1742–61	Creation of formal part of Alexandrovsky Park (Alexander's Park) for Empress Elizabeth I, designed by architect C.I. Tchevakinsky and gardener H. Girard
1762	Catherine II, "the Great," becomes empress
1770	Vassily I. Neyolov designs landscape part of Catherine's Park (English garden) and first constructions (pyramid, little folly, Palladian Siberian bridge); planning work, with participation of gardener Trifon Ilyin, begun
1770s	Creation of landscape pond system, construction of numerous bridges, dams, and cascades piers, designed by V.I. Neyolov and engineered by I.K. Gerard; design and construction of Chinese Village model by V.I. Neyolov and A. Rinaldi
1772	Construction started on admiralty and big folly, designed by V.I. Neyolov; Rinaldi designs Gatchina gates
1773	Construction of Taitsky water conduit
1774	Hermitage kitchen for old garden, designed by V.I. Neyolov, construction work begun
1780–87	Construction of C. Cameron's termae; planting of flowers by J. Busch
1783–85	I.V. Neyolov designs and builds Babolovsky Palace and English garden around palace, with help of gardener J. Busch
1785	Construction of upper hothouses
1789	Ken-cons oak wood laid out by J. Busch
1792–1811	Laying out of garden near Alexandrovsky Palace with ponds, dams, and cascades (designed by I.V. Neyolov, gardener Busch, and engineer P. von Tol)
1808	Extending of new garden and inclusion of preserve and garden star near Alexandrovsky palace; A.A. Menelas and J. Busch start work on redesigning preserve
1817–25	Creation of city boulevard by gardener F.F. Lyamin
1850–52	Construction of Turkish baths with pier on the pond, designed by I.A. Monigetti
1855–66	Laying out of Private Garden with fountain and pergola, designed by A.F. Vidor for Alexander II
1961–70	Restoration of Yekaterininsky Park, conceived by N.E. Tumanova and T.B. Dubyago
1979	N.E. Tumanova makes designs for restoration of landscape part of English garden in Yekaterininsky Park and work begins

Further Reading

Bardovskaia, L., "Anglyiskie gravyry i kollektsiy Ekaterininskogo dvortsa-museia i ikh vliyaniye na forminovaniye Ekaterininskogo parka v 70-e gody XVIII veka (English Engravings in the Collection of the Yekaterine Palace-Museum and Their Influence upon the Design of the Garden in the 1770s)," in *Russkaia khudozhestvennaia cultura XVIII veka i inostranniye mastera* (Russian Arts Culture of the 18th Century and Foreign Masters), Moscow: The Tretyakov Gallery, 1982

Dubiago, T.B., *Russkie reguliarnye sady i parki* (Russian Formal Gardens and Parks), Leningrad: Gos. Izd-vo Lit-ry po Stroitel'stvu, 1963

Ducamp, Emmanuel, editor, *Vues des palais impériaux des environs de Saint-Pétersbourg: Aquarelles, peintures et gravures du XVIIIᵉ et du XIXᵉ siècle*, 4 vols., Paris: Gourcuff, 1992; see especially vol. 3, *Tsarskoïe Selo*

Floryan, Margrethe, *Gardens of the Tsars: A Study of the Aesthetics, Semantics, and Uses of the Late 18th-Century Russian Gardens*, Aarhus, Denmark: Aarhus University Press, and Sagaponack, New York: Sagapress, 1996

Gross, A., "Russian Gardens, English Architect," *Journal of Garden History* 1 (1991)

Gross, A., "The History of the Ekaterininskii and Alexandrovskii Parks," in *A Sense of Place: Tsarskoe Selo and Its Poets*, edited by Lev Loseff and Barry P. Scherr, Columbus, Ohio: Slavica, 1993

Kennett, Audrey, *The Palaces of Leningrad*, London: Thames and Hudson, and New York: Putnam, 1973

Kosmian, G.K., editor, *Gorod Pushkin: Istoriko-krayevedcheskiy otcherk-putevoditel* (Town of Pushkin: A Historical Guidebook), St. Petersburg: Lenizdat, 1992

Lemus, Vera V., *Pushkin: Palaces and Parks,* translated by Boris Grudinsko, Leningrad: Aurora, 1984

Likhachev, Dmitrii Sergeevich, *Poeziia sadov: K semantike sadovo-parkovykh stilei* (A Poetry of Gardens: About the Semantic of Park and Garden Styles), St. Petersburg: Nauka, 1982; 3rd edition, Moscow: Soglasie, 1998

Liulina, Rimma Dmitrievna, Abram Grigor'evich Raskin, and Mikhail Pavlovich Tubli, *Dekorativnaia skul'ptura sadov i parkov Leningrada i prigorodov XVIII–XIX vekov; La sculpture décorative des jardins et des parcs de Léningrad et de ses environs XVIIIᵉ–XIXᵉ siècles; Decorative Sculpture in the Gardens and Parks of Leningrad and Its Environs, 18th and 19th Centuries,* Leningrad: Khudozhnik R.S.F.S.R., 1981 (with summaries in English, French, and German)

Petrov, Anatolii Nikolaevich, *Gorod Pushkin: Dvortsy i parki* (The Town of Pushkin: Palaces and Parks), Leningrad: Iskusstvo, 1964

Petrov, Anatolii Nikolaevich, and E.N. Petrova, "Gorod Pushkin (The Town of Pushkin)," in *Pamiatniki arkhitektury prigorodov Leningrada* (The Architectural Monuments of Suburbs of Leningrad), by Petrov et al., Leningrad: Stroiizdat, 1983

Semenova, G.V., "Otdelny park v Tsarskom Sele (The Separate Park in Tsarskoye Selo)," *Pamyatniki istoriy i kultury S. Peterburga* (Monuments and Memories of Culture, St. Petersburg) 4 (1998)

Shvidkovskii, Dmitrii Olegovich, *Gorod russkogo prosveshcheniya* (The Town of Russian Enlightenment), Moscow: Znanie, 1991

Shvidkovskii, Dmitrii Olegovich, "Prosveshcheniye i russky sad vtoroy poloviny XVIII veka (The Enlightenment and Russian Garden of the Second Part of the 18th Century)," *Istoriya sadov* (The History of Gardens) 1 (1994)

Stepanenko, E.G., "Palladianskiye motivi v arkhitecture Tsarskoselskikh Parkov (The Palladian Motives of Architecture of the Parks of Tsarkoye Selo)," in *Aleksandrovskii Dvorets: Briefs of the 4th Tsarskoselsky Scientific Conference,* St. Petersburg: The State Museum Tsarskoe Selo, 1998

Tumanova, Nataliia Evgenevna, *Ekaterininskii Park: Istoriia razvitiia i metodika vosstanovleniia* (Catherine's Park: The History of the Development and Methods of Reconstruction), St. Petersburg: Stroiizdat, 1997

Vilchkovskii, Sergei Nikolaevich, *Tsarskoe Selo,* St. Petersburg: Vil'borg, 1911; reprint, St. Petersburg: Titul, 1992

Voltaire, *Voltaire and Catherine the Great: Selected Correspondence,* edited and translated by Antony Lentin, Cambridge: Oriental Research Partners, 1974

GALINA V. SEMENOVA

Tuileries

Paris, France

Location: central Paris, on north bank of river Seine, between Place de la Concorde and Louvre Museum

The Tuileries is one of the most important and historic public parks in France. Like Versailles and Fontainebleau, it played a key role in French royal history. A popular large (25.5-hectare [63 acre]) open-air space at the very heart of Paris, often besieged by visitors, it has the distinction of being a major garden, of royal origins, that has been open to the public for almost four centuries. It also has the distinction of having been designed and maintained by the outstanding gardening dynasties of the late 16th and 17th centuries, particularly the Mollets and Le Nôtres. Until 1664 these families also had houses within the Tuileries, next to the river Seine. Although the garden had its origin in the 16th century and has had a complex history, its appearance today is largely the result of changes made in the mid-17th century by André Le Nôtre.

Like the Luxembourg Gardens, the Tuileries had its origin in a royal death, that of Henri II in 1559, and in a member of the Médicis family, Catherine, Henri's widow. After 1559 Catherine was free to indulge her extravagant tastes in building and garden making. Her main efforts were concentrated on Fontainebleau, near Paris, and on a new palace for herself, the Tuileries, west of the Louvre, on what was then the edge of Paris. The site of the latter was known as the "Sablonnière" and was occupied by tile kilns (*tuileries*). In 1564 Philibert de l'Orme began work on the palace, whose main block ran between the two present-day western pavilions of the Louvre. These were originally built in the late 16th century (Pavillon de Flore) and 1660–65 (Pavillon de Marsan) as part of the Tuileries palace.

At the same time a great formal garden, the Grand Jardin, was laid out on a rectangular area of farmland to the west of the palace, from which it was separated by a public road and the garden wall. Unusually, a woman was involved in the design process. This was Marie de Pierrevire, a favorite of Catherine's and married to a Florentine banker living at Saint-Cloud, near Paris. The design was a typical Renaissance one of rectilinear compartments divided by straight allées. The three main east-west allées were flanked by fir, elm, and sycamore. There was no clear hierarchy or unity of design. Each compartment was different, the more ornamental ones, laid out with geometric parterres, being at the palace end; further away were orchards, wooded areas, and a labyrinth. At the furthest end from the palace the garden was bounded by a wall with a central semicircular projection called the Echo. Bernardo Carnesecchi was in charge of the planting, and Pierre Le Nôtre, André's grandfather, was head gardener. The most important of the garden's architectural features, which included a theater, an aviary, and a menagerie, was a grotto, long since gone, built by Bernard Palissy in 1567. Palissy was an exceptionally skilled potter, and the interior walls of the grotto were covered with faience lizards, snakes, birds, and vegetation. Water fell into a pool, in which swam faience fish, from an artificial rock (*rocher*) covered with animals. Palissy also made the labyrinth out of bent and woven willows (*osiers ployés*).

The gardens were the venue for grand royal entertainments and diplomatic spectacles, of which Catherine de Médicis was very fond. In 1573, a year after she had abandoned the palace for superstitious reasons, the fete for the Polish ambassadors was held there. The entertainment included a procession of 16 nymphs, representing the provinces of France, who were carried in on a *rocher*, probably designed by Palissy. Although the gardens continued in use after 1572, they were neglected and damaged in the civil wars at the beginning of Henri IV's reign (1589–94).

After this hiatus, the gardens entered their second phase of development, during the reign of Henri IV. At this time Claude Mollet and Pierre Le Nôtre restored the gardens, while retaining the original layout. Le Nôtre laid out new parterres, and Mollet made a new private garden, the Petit Jardin, east of the palace in about 1600. In 1608 the parterres were remade again as *parterres de broderie*, with box and rue designs surrounded by *palissades* (green walls) of juniper. Further alterations were carried out by Pierre Le Nôtre's son Jean (André's father). The major lasting contribution of this phase was the making of the north terrace, now flanked by the Rue de Rivoli. It was planted with a double row of white mulberries (in all, 15–20,000 mulberries were planted in the gardens; Henri IV was keen to promote the silk industry). Against the wall was a *palissade* of Judas trees (*Cercis silaquastrum*), and parallel to it was a long woodwork tunnel arbor, or *berceau*, punctuated by eight pavilions on the cross axes. The intricacy and rich planting of the gardens—jasmine, quince, and pomegranate are mentioned—must have been a feast for the senses. However, despite the *parterres de broderie*, the gardens remained essentially 16th century in style and were not integrated with the palace. During this phase, in 1638,

the Petit Jardin was laid out with a huge *parterre de broderie* designed by Claude Mollet (the second; son of Pierre) for Mademoiselle de Montpensier, the daughter of Gaston d'Orléans, who lived in the palace until 1652. The Petit Jardin was removed in 1662.

It was André Le Nôtre, who had been working in the gardens since 1637, who transformed them for Louis XIV in 1665–72. While retaining the basic layout Le Nôtre gave the gardens the spacious, integrated, and hierarchical layout that largely survives today. He also integrated them with the palace by removing the public road and garden wall and replacing them with a terrace overlooking the gardens. Le Nôtre used sophisticated optics to achieve a sense of unity, harmony of scale, and balance. He made a strong central axis, on either side of which the layout was not symmetrical but balanced. Nearest the palace were two large flowing *parterres de broderie*, each with central round ponds and fountains, with cut-turf parterres beyond. There were only four statues in the gardens at this time. Next, the very wide central allée, flanked by chestnuts and planes, led past varied compartments and bosquets to a grand octagonal pool near the west end. At this end, where the garden boundary was extended to make it more symmetrical, curving ramps were made on either side of the central axis up to broad terraces. The north terrace, called the Terrasse des Feuillants from 1791, was balanced by one of the same height along the south side, the Terrasse du Bord-de-l'Eau. The main axis was continued beyond a grille on the garden boundary and a defensive ditch as the Avenue des Tuileries (later the Avenue des Champs-Elysées). This ran through open countryside right up to the heights of Chaillot (later the Place de l'Etoile), and Le Nôtre planned that it should extend all the way to Saint Germain-en-Laye. During the late 20th century it was extended to La Défense.

During the regency of Louis XV (1715–23), the young king lived at the Tuileries; aviaries and pavilions were made to amuse him, and in 1719 many statues by Guillaume and Nicholas Coustou, Antoine Coysevox, Pierre Le Pautre, Corneille Van Clève, and others were brought from the abandoned royal gardens of Marly, on the edge of Paris. These included the figures of the river gods Tiber and Nile, which were set up around the octagonal basin, and personifications of two groups of French rivers, the Seine and Marne, the Loire and Loiret. The equestrian statues of Fame and Mercury, by Antoine Coysevox, were placed at the west entrance. In 1757 the square subsequently called the Place de la Concorde, immediately west of the gardens, came into being as the site chosen for a statue of Louis XV. In 1794 the great equestrian statues, the *Chevaux de Marly* (now in the Louvre and replaced by replicas), made by Guillaume Coustou in 1745, were installed in the Place de la Concorde to frame the Avenue des Tuileries vista. Statues

View of the Tuileries Gardens, from an ink drawing by Israel Silvestre the Younger
Photo by J.G. Berizzi; copyright Réunion des Musées Nationaux/Art Resource, New York

from other royal gardens followed, and some remain in the gardens. More were added in the 19th century, including a collection by Aristide Maillol, now between the yew hedges in the neighboring garden of the Cour du Carrousel, which was designed by Jacques Wirtz and completed in 1996. The *parterres de broderie* were grassed over during the 18th century.

Although the main structure of the 17th-century gardens has survived, there have been some subsequent alterations. During the reign of Louis-Philippe, in the 1830s, the gardens were simplified, the ditch at the west end filled in, and a private, informal garden, the Jardin Réservé, was made at the east end, shut off from the public by railings. Paris grew rapidly around the Louvre and the Tuileries in the 19th century, and the development of the Avenue des Champs-Elysées axis, during the transformations of Georges-Eugène Haussmann in the 1850s and 1860s, was determined by Le Nôtre's main axis of the Tuileries gardens and Avenue des Tuileries. The Tuileries palace was demolished in 1884, after the Communards set fire to it in 1871. Its site was made into part of the informal garden in 1889. The two main buildings in the gardens, the Jeu de Paume, built as a tennis court but now used for temporary exhibitions, and the Orangerie, a greenhouse that now houses the famous "*Nymphéas*" (Water Lilies) by Claude Monet,

were added to the north and south terraces respectively in 1851 and 1853.

A monument to Charles Perrault, on the south terrace, is important in that it was he who persuaded Louis XIV's finance minister, Jean-Baptiste Colbert, that the gardens should remain open to the public. The gardens were a favorite promenade of the nobility until just before the Revolution and afterwards became the popular resort they remain today. Attempts were made to reserve them for the upper classes: in 1841 the *New Paris Guide* stated that "Persons in working habits or carrying any parcels, except books, are not allowed to enter."

An ambitious restoration program during the 1990s began to return the gardens to something of their 17th-century feel. The formality of the east end was restored, with a terrace overlooking the grass parterres; compartments were renewed, including one with a sunken canal, which may not have been an original feature. Bosquets of horse chestnuts were partly replanted with mixed species, including limes and Judas trees. The Tuileries is such an integral part of the history and fabric of central Paris that the city would be inconceivable without it.

Synopsis

1519   François I buys land that Tuileries are
                built on

1564	Catherine de Médicis begins Tuileries palace, with Philibert de l'Orme as architect
1564–72	Gardens made under supervision of Marie de Pierrevire and Bernardo Carnesecchi
1567	Bernard Palissy begins grotto
1572	Palace abandoned by Catherine de Médicis
1573	Fete for Polish ambassadors held in gardens
1594–1609	Claude Mollet and Pierre Le Nôtre renew parterres and add new features, including north terrace
ca. 1600	Petit Jardin made by Claude Mollet
1608	Parterres remade as *parterre de broderie*
1610–43	Some simplification of layout; by end of Louis XIII's reign (1643), Claude II Mollet and André Le Nôtre both working at Tuileries
1638	Huge *parterre de broderie* made in Petit Jardin, design by Claude Mollet
1662	Petit Jardin removed
1665–72	Gardens transformed by André Le Nôtre, Avenue des Tuileries planted to Chaillot
1719	Statues brought from Marly
1783	Gas-filled balloon ascent from gardens
1830s	Louis-Philippe alters west end of gardens by filling in ditch outside; garden simplified; informal private garden, Jardin Réservé, made at east end
1851	Jeu de Paume (real tennis court) built
1853	Orangery built
1871	Palace burned by Communards
1884	Palace demolished
1889	Palace site converted to garden
1990s	Restoration of gardens

Further Reading

Adams, William Howard, *The French Garden, 1500–1800*, London: Scolar Press, and New York: Braziller, 1979

Hazlehurst, F. Hamilton, *Gardens of Illusion: The Genius of André Le Nostre*, Nashville, Tennessee: Vanderbilt University Press, 1980

Woodbridge, Kenneth, *Princely Gardens: The Origins and Development of the French Formal Style*, London: Thames and Hudson, and New York: Rizzoli, 1986

Yates, Frances, *The Valois Tapestries*, London: Warburg Institute, University of London, 1959; 2nd edition, London: Routledge and Paul, 1975

ELISABETH WHITTLE

Tunnard, Christopher 1910–1979

Canadian Landscape Architect

Christopher Tunnard is best known to garden historians as Britain's enfant terrible of the late 1930s. He was born in Victoria, British Columbia, Canada. He received his advanced education at Victoria College, University of British Columbia, and later at the College of the Royal Horticultural Society at Wisley, England, and the Westminster Technical Institute, England, where he took building construction courses in 1932. From 1932 to 1935 he worked in the London office of Percy S. Cane, one of the preeminent garden designers in the tradition of the Arts and Crafts movement and author of *Modern Gardens* (1926–27). In 1936 Tunnard initiated his own practice of landscape architecture in London and on the former estate of Charles James Fox at St. Ann's Hill, Chertsey Surrey. His design work, which paralleled that of Oliver Hill, became somewhat better known when the next year he initiated a series of articles in *Architectural Review,* which he subsequently published as *Gardens in the Modern Landscape* (1938). He developed three approaches to what he saw as a new technique for 20th-century gardens that underpinned his theories: the functional, an overarching approach based on the concept that use determines form; the empathic, based on Japanese-inspired attitudes toward nature expressed symbolically as the use of materials in asymmetrical compositions; and the artistic, based on principles of modern art. His citation of architectural work by Peter Behrens, Le Corbusier, and Mies van der Rohe set his work apart, as did illustrations of several French gardens, including the garden at Hyeres by Gabriel Guevrekian and the work of Jean Canneel-Claes in Belgium. The Japanese work by Antonin Raymond and

Sutemi Horiguti illustrated contemporary expressions of the empathic. At this time Tunnard also formed relationships with key figures in art, including Paul Nash and Alexander Calder, whose work Tunnard illustrated in *Gardens in the Modern Landscape.*

Tunnard demonstrated his ideas of the "Garden into Landscape" in the building and planting of his home and studio, St. Ann's Hill (1936). His concept of "Garden into Landscape" foreshadowed his later interest in the wider planning of landscape. With his friend architect Raymond McGrath, Tunnard created an asymmetrical yet contextual design around the white concrete eroded cylindrical addition (1936) to the remains of the historic house. In this garden Tunnard wrapped a semicircular pool around an existing *Rhododendron ponticum,* punched through an existing curved brick wall to make an axis that drew the line of the garden through the center of the new house, and incorporated a now magnificent wisteria into the main facade of the house on the established 18th-century landscape garden designed by Charles Hamilton. Tunnard explained the evolution of his thinking in terms of a graphic history of the evolution of the site from the 17th century until the construction of the new building. These plan drawings were etched into the mirrored glass in the foyer of the house, where busts of Fox and Hamilton were also placed. This ensemble signified Tunnard's interest in the history of landscape design, the effects of which manifested themselves in the comparatively tentative experimental formal stance that Tunnard adopted during this period. Many of his design concepts could be considered contextual in their resonance with existing elements of the site.

Among other projects during this fertile period of domestic design, Galby (ca. 1937) for Sir Charles Keene, earl of Leicester, demonstrated another sort of historically informed design approach in the transformation of traditional Dutch parquet gardens to functional contemporary domestic design. The most photogenic of his consulting projects was Bentley Wood (1935), the site and garden at Halland, Sussex, with Serge Chermayeff, the house's owner and architect. The terrace of this house, largely created by Chermayeff, had a space frame terminus that framed a view of the Downs. Tunnard's design for the plantings around the house including a thinned birch wood planted with color fields of daffodils. Gordon Cullen, later the editor of the *Architectural Review* and author of *Townscape* (1961), made character sketches to illustrate these projects in Tunnard's book; H.F. Clark drew the plans.

Tunnard also espoused ideas of communal gardens and wider planning. He illustrated this larger urban-planning and design agenda with European projects such as Roemerstadt and Neubuehl; the Bos Park in Amsterdam; one of the Farm Security Administration Camps in

Texas designed by Garrett Eckbo (included in the second edition of *Gardens in the Modern Landscape*); and an unexecuted proposal of his own conception, a suggested redevelopment in a Corbusian approach to preserve the 18th-century landscape garden at Claremont, Surrey. Geoffrey Jellicoe reviewed *Gardens in the Modern Landscape* in *Architectural Review* (March 1939) and warned readers to prepare themselves for a "brave new world" of garden design. Just prior to World War II Tunnard undertook the site planning in London for Elizabeth Denby's "all-Europe house" for the Ideal Home Exhibition of 1939. This design was, in fact, a row structure with jagged setbacks of the type being designed by architect Sven Markelius. Tunnard also served as the garden architect for the Modern Architectural Research (MARS) group's utopian plan for the growth of London, the ideas of which were later published by architect Maxwell Fry in *Fine Building* (1944).

In the United States Tunnard's book also had a strong impact on three young American landscape architects: Dan Kiley, Garrett Eckbo, and James Rose. The three had persuaded Dean Joseph Hudnut to invite Tunnard to lecture at Harvard. When Tunnard arrived Walter Gropius led the architectural curriculum, which was strongly focused on the issues of urban planning and housing. Coming to Harvard's department of architecture directly from his MARS project with Fry, Gropius's former partner, Tunnard plunged straight into an architectural studio led by Gropius, with Hugh Stubbins, Martin Wagner, and himself as critics. He taught a course called "Site Planning," and among his students during his four years at Harvard were Lawrence Halprin, Edward Larrabee Barnes, and Philip Johnson. His modernist ideas, however, received little friendly reception among most landscape architects in the mainstream of practice in these years.

After serving in the Royal Canadian Air Force during World War II, Tunnard was a Wheelwright Fellow and briefly an editor of *Architectural Forum.* In 1945 he began teaching at Yale, where he had been attracted by the focus on what became his own developing interests in city planning and urban history, and specifically, the history of classicism in design. Tunnard's work in the 1950s, 1960s, and 1970s intensified this shift away from modernism. His books, including the *City of Man* (1953), *American Skyline* (with Henry Hope Reed, 1955), *Man-Made America: Chaos or Control* (1963) and *World with a View* (1978), and city-planning and preservation courses at Yale during this time signaled new dimensions in his thinking and work about landscape. He was one of the progenitors of the Venice Charter, the founding document of the International Committee on Monuments and Sites (ICOMOS), and a founder of the New Haven, Connecticut, Historic Preservation Commission. When he died in 1979, few

Americans knew about or understood his contributions to the rise of modernism in landscape architecture.

Biography
Born in Victoria, British Columbia, Canada, 1910. Educated at Victoria College, University of British Columbia, and College of Royal Horticultural Society, Wisley, England, until 1930; also trained at Westminster Technical Institute, England, 1932; employed in London office of garden designer Percy S. Cane, 1932–35; set up own London practice, 1936; lectured on site planning at Harvard University, Cambridge, Massachusetts, then taught at Yale University, New Haven, Connecticut, from 1945. Died in New Haven, Connecticut, 1979.

Selected Designs
1935   Bentley Wood (with architect Serge Charmayeff), Halland, East Sussex, England
1936   Christopher Tunnard's residence, St. Ann's Hill, Chertsey, Surrey, England

Selected Publications
Gardens in the Modern Landscape, 1938; 2nd edition, 1948
City of Man, 1953
American Skyline (with Henry Hope Reed), 1955
Man-Made America: Chaos or Control? (with Boris Pushkarev), 1963
World with a View, 1978

Further Reading
Brown, Jane, *The Modern Garden,* New York: Princeton Architectural Press, 2000
Cane, Percy Stephen, *Modern Gardens: British and Foreign,* London: The Studio, 1926
Chermayeff, Serge, *Design and the Public Good: Selected Writings, 1930–1980,* Cambridge, Massachusetts: MIT Press, 1982
Cullen, Gordon, *Townscape,* New York: Reinhold, and London: Architectural Press, 1961
Fry, Maxwell, *Fine Building,* London: Faber, 1944
Walker, Peter, and Melanie Simo, *Invisible Gardens: The Search for Modernism in the American Landscape,* Cambridge, Massachusetts: MIT Press, 1994

LANCE M. NECKAR

Turkey

Although the Turkish architectural tradition is one of the most original and powerful in the history of world architecture, it is not matched by an equally impressive landscape tradition. Indeed, evidence for an early Turkish landscape garden tradition is scant. The Turks settled in Anatolia in the seventh century A.D. The culture that they brought with them was that of a nomadic or seminomadic people, and they found few opportunities for settling gardens because of frequent wars and migrations. However, ample evidence indicates that these early Turks appreciated nature in its virgin state; their native plains, valleys, rivers, and mountains were enjoyed as if they were gardens. Although no designed gardens survive from this ancient time, Turkish art, in the form of tiles, miniatures, illustrations, and manuscripts, often uses the patterns of flowers, leaves, and trees, revealing the importance of nature and gardens in Turkish life. It was not until the Turks converted to Islam that they found the pale reflection of Muhammad's Garden of Paradise in their built gardens.

The oldest recorded examples of Turkish gardens, which were designed under the rule of the Anatolian Seljuk dynasty (1071–1243), were in the Kubadabad Palace near Beysehir and in the Keykubadiye Palace in Konya. Only the ruins of these palaces still survive. Garden designs were affected by Persian, Arabian, and Asian arts during this era. In the early Ottoman Empire period (1299–1453) gardens were usually functional and informal but strongly influenced by Seljuk and Byzantine arts. The gardens in Samarkand were the most wonderful examples of this time.

Turkish life in both the early and late Ottoman periods revolved around two types of open spaces: the naturalistic and the enclosed. The former were public open green spaces within dense urban areas where people would go to recreate and to picnic. Sometimes they were pasturelands, and they were often found beside a waterway. Unlike Chinese or English gardens, instead of imitating nature with manmade hills, valleys, and lakes, the Ottomans incorporated nature itself into their public open spaces. The enclosed gardens, on the other hand, were basically outdoor rooms, situated close to a house, with high walls or hedges ensuring privacy.

Early Ottoman gardens in Anatolia usually consisted of a backyard or courtyard within the house. The house was not always in the middle of the garden, and the garden was not always big. Although larger gardens might be divided into quarters, in the Persian manner, this was not usually the case for smaller gardens. Gardens often contained fruit trees, flower and vegetable beds, flowerpots, and sometimes a fountain or a pool surrounded by marble pavements, and such places were always considered as continuations of the house. In the garden, trees were used for their shade, water features for their cooling effect and their sound, and flowers for their fragrance and color. Residents of the house spent many hours in the garden during the long hot summer days. Gardens often featured large trees such as planes (*Platanus orientalis*), limes (*Tilia* spp.), horse chestnuts (*Aesculus hippocastanum*), and cypresses (*Cupressus sempervirens*).

Because the Turks cherished nature in itself, they always retained existing trees in their gardens. If there were no trees, they would often plant them in rows along both sides of a straight path. Climbing plants were trained up the trunks of trees or onto house walls. Trees were linked with each other by geometrical flowerbeds, each containing a single species. Because gardens became an important part of everyday life, and the time spent in gardens became correspondingly longer, kiosks for shade became an essential element in almost every garden, a tendency found in even the earliest Ottoman gardens.

Some impressive gardens still exist from the second era of the Ottoman Empire (1453–1703). The Topkapı Palace (Seraglio) and Üsküdar Palace gardens are the most important examples from this time, although they are simple and functional and Renaissance and baroque effects are hardly in evidence. After the conquest of Istanbul in 1453 by Mehmet II the Conqueror (r. 1451–81), the Ottoman capital moved from Edirne to Istanbul, where the magnificent Topkapı Palace was built, overlooking the Bosporus and the Golden Horn. The Topkapı Palace served the Ottoman sultans from the 15th century to the 19th century. With its several buildings and 12 different gardens, it became one of the main green spaces in Istanbul. To maintain the gardens, which contained recreational areas, orchards, and kitchen gardens, 920 gardeners were needed. From Bâb-ı Humayun, the main gateway to the palace, one enters the first courtyard, which once served as a field for riding horses. The second courtyard, Divan, where the palace proper began, is smaller than the first one and contains the palace kitchen and kitchen gardens to the east, shaded by cypress and plane trees. This courtyard also contains fountains, marbled pathways, and a large grassed area. Through Bâb-ı Saadat, the main gateway, one reaches another courtyard, which was more private for palace residents and contains the harem and harem's courtyard, and which may even be compared to the ordinary backyard of a house, with several pine trees, flowerbeds, and grassed areas. In addition to these three courtyards, the rest of the open area was regarded as the fourth courtyard, an extensive piece of land containing several kiosks, including the Baghdad kiosk. From the beginning of this era, the shores of the Bosporus became even more popular than it had been in Byzantine times. The first garden built on the Bosporus was called the Tokad Gardens and was created in 1458 at the wish of the Sultan Mehmet II. Istanbul's very first urban forests were created on the banks of the Golden Horn between 1450 and 1500.

The tulip, so often associated with Holland, has a longer association with Turkey. Originally cultivated by the Ottomans in the early 16th century, it spread from Turkey to Europe. However, the mania for tulips, which reached its peak period between 1634 and 1647 in Europe, especially in the Netherlands, did not start until the early 18th century in Turkey. The era between 1717 and 1730 is known as the "Tulip Age" here because of the penetrating influence of the tulip upon Turkish art and literature during this period. At this time the typical Turkish garden was still informal, often using a natural watercourse. Gardens remained places for outdoor entertainment. Tulips embellished gardens all over Istanbul and became a symbol of elegance and pleasure. During this period Sultan Ahmed III (r. 1703–30) began to imitate European court life and pleasures, holding seasonal garden parties and festivals in imitation of the pleasures of Versailles. Gardens of tulip beds were established, and a charming rococo pavilion called the Sofa Pavilion, or the Pavilion of Kara Mustafa Pasha, was built in the grounds of the Topkapı Palace to enable Ahmed III to obtain the most pleasure from his floral displays. At night tortoises with candles on their backs were set free among the palace tulip beds.

By the end of the 16th century, sultans, their close relatives, high officials, rich families, and distinguished foreign officers had begun to build summerhouses with large gardens beside the Bosporus. These often included formal terraces and parterres in the French manner. These *Yalı* (summerhouses) and *Kösk* (winter houses) usually had both an inner garden and an outer garden. The former can be described as an entrance garden, usually in the form of a quadrangle with fruit trees, chestnuts, hazelnut groves, and vegetable gardens. Near to the building more stylish plants would be used, such as pines, planes, and acacias. The outer garden was usually found behind the house where it could be reached from a connecting paved area. This area might be divided into separate areas for men and women, the harem garden for women and the *selamlık* garden for men. This was a more private garden, best described as a flower garden, replete with roses, jasmines, and honeysuckles, though it might also contain a small pool. The Sadabad Palace and Bebek Mansion were two of the most important examples of these outer gardens from this era. The

Sadabad Palace and its garden were strongly influenced by grand French gardens such as those at Versailles, Fontainebleau, and Marly. In this period, also known as the Golden Era of Horticulture, several groves were established in the valleys of the rivers Göksu and Kagıthane in Istanbul. Recreational areas were also created in natural forest areas on the outskirts of Istanbul, while throughout the city both natural and exotic species were planted for amenity. Similar works were carried out in Anatolian cities.

In the last Ottoman Era (1730–1923) formality and symmetry became important features of garden design. Examples of the most beautiful formal gardens, which were influenced by European gardens, include the Çıragan, Beylerbeyi, and Dolmabahçe Palaces. The landscape painter Antoine Ignace Melling designed the Halide Sultan Yalısı and Çıragan Palace gardens. The last palace to be built for a sultan in Istanbul was the Yıldız Palace, constructed in the 19th century with a garden designed by a Frenchman called Le Roi. Although created by a Frenchman, the design owes more to the principles of English park landscape gardening. It is the largest palace garden in Istanbul, covering 160 hectares (395 acres). Although the Ottoman Empire was in decline during this period and the sultan's family was burdened by debts, the Ottomans still built many other residences, the grounds of which were embellished with trees and shrubs brought from European nurseries. In order to satisfy the demand for plant material in the early 20th century, another Frenchman, Adolphe Deroin-Yenne, established a nursery in Ortaköy while a German, C.H. Koch, created another in Kadıköy.

The first European-style urban park in Istanbul was called Taksim Bahçesi (now Taksim Park) and was established in 1869. It was rectangular and designed in a symmetrical fashion. The center of the park was created according to Beaux-Arts principles, but the margins were done in a Picturesque style. One can still see the influence of this design in the existing park. During the same period another park, Tebebası Bahçesi, which no longer exists, was created entirely on Picturesque principles. Before World War I Cemil Pasha, the governor of Istanbul, opened the outer gardens of the Topkapı Palace to public access under the name of Gülhane Park, and he established the Sultanahmet, Fatih, and Dogancılar Parks.

When the Turkish Republic was established in 1923, under the leadership of Mustafa Kemal Ataturk, the country was reorganized in every respect. The young republic's most important aim was to accelerate the process of modernization that had begun in the late Ottoman period. Ataturk sent an officer, Sami Bey, to Europe to study gardening. Upon Sami Bey's return the Çankaya

Presidential Palace and Gardens were created in Ankara, the new capital of the Turkish Republic. A fine garden was also created for Ataturk at the Termal Hotel in Yalova. As a part of Ankara's first urban plan, prepared by Herman Jansen, a German town planner, in 1927, the first designed urban park in modern Turkey, Gençlik Park, was developed. A large forest farm, Ataturk Orman Çiftligi, was also created in Ankara in 1933. Also in the early 1930s an area was reclaimed from mosquito-infested derelict land to create the parkland setting for the Izmir International Fair.

Formal education in landscape architecture began in 1940, and several universities throughout Turkey now provide degree programs in landscape architecture. In the early years of the republic, slow economic development did not allow more urban parks to be created, and it was even a struggle to maintain the fine old ones, but after the 1950s the gardens of the palaces were restored, in particular Yıldız Park, Emirgan Park, and Çamlıca Park. The late 20th century saw a new phase for green space development and the establishment of a number of public parks, exhibition areas, holiday villages, hotels, as well as private gardens, in towns and cities. Maçka Demokrasi, Kuruçesme, and Ulus Parks in Istanbul, Kuglupark, Altınpark, and Botanik Bahçesi in Ankara, and Soganlı Botanik Bahçesi in Bursa are some of the new public parks opened to the public in the closing decades of the 20th century.

See also Islamic Gardens

Further Reading

Celik, Zeynep, *The Remaking of Istanbul: Portrait of an Ottoman City in the Nineteenth Century,* Berkeley: University of California Press, 1986

Cerasi, Maurice M., *La città del Levante: Civiltà urbana e architettura sotto gli Ottomani nei secoli XVIII–XIX,* Milan: Jaca, 1988

Eldem, Sedad H., *Türk Bahçeleri* (Turkish Gardens), Ankara: Kültür Bakanlığı, 1976

Evyapan, Gönül Aslanoğlu, "Anatolian Turkish Gardens," *Mimarlik Fakütesi dergisi* (Journal of the Faculty of Architecture) 1 (1975)

Titley, N.M., *Plants and Gardens in Persian, Mughal, and Turkish Art,* London: British Library, 1979

Yaltırık, Faik, Asuman Efe, and Adnan Uzun, *Tarih boyunca Istanbul'un park, bahçe ve koruları egzotik ağaç ve çalıları* (Inventory of Exotic Tree and Bush Species of Istanbul's Parks, Gardens, Groves), Istanbul: Isfalt, 1997 (with a summary in English)

MINE F. THOMPSON

Turner, Richard ca. 1798–1881

Irish Ironmaster

Richard Turner is remembered principally for his iron glasshouses, especially the magnificent "ornamental, light, useful and . . . everlasting" (Robinson, *Gardener's Chronicle,* 1864) Curvilinear Range in the National Botanic Gardens, Glasnevin (Dublin), and for the wings of the Palm House, designed by Charles Lanyon, in the Belfast Botanic Gardens. Turner also built the Great Palm House at the Royal Botanic Gardens, Kew, perhaps the most famous glasshouse in the world, a building that exemplifies the vigor and wealth of the Victorian era.

Nothing has yet been discovered about Turner's childhood or his training as a draftsman and engineer. He came from a family of ironmongers. Leixlip seems to have been his early home, and about 1816 he married a local girl, Jane Goodshaw. They had at least nine children, including William, who succeeded as head of the firm in 1863. Richard Turner took over the management of his family's ironmongery business, which from 1819 had been situated on St. Stephen's Green, Dublin, from his uncle, also named Richard. Turner engaged in building speculation in Dublin during the 1820s and 1830s and with the capital gained was able to acquire land at Ballsbridge, one of Dublin's southern suburbs, on which he established the Hammersmith Iron Works in 1834. There Turner forged his spectacular glasshouses and many other more mundane iron artifacts—heavy iron gates (e.g., at Donadea Castle, County Kildare, Ireland), railway station roofs (e.g., Broadstone Station, Dublin), and railings for Trinity College, Dublin.

Turner's earliest known commission (ca. 1833–34) for a glasshouse was at Colebrooke, County Fermanagh (now in Northern Ireland). The Curvilinear Range at the National Botanic Gardens, Glasnevin, was constructed in stages between 1843 and 1848 and then enlarged in 1868–69. The plans for the extension, dated January 1868, are in Turner's hand, although by this time his son William was in charge of the family iron foundry. The history of this glasshouse is complicated, but it is certain that Richard Turner influenced the design as well as the material used. He also forged and erected all of it apart from the earliest, south-facing half of the east wing.

The history of the Great Palm House at the Royal Botanic Gardens, Kew, is also complicated; again, Turner was directly involved in the design of it, collaborating with the architect Decimus Burton. Turner was entirely responsible for the construction of the building; all the ironwork was prefabricated at the Hammersmith Iron Works in Ireland. The Great Palm House in Kew is loftier and more extensive in plan than the Glasnevin range, yet the buildings are "sisters"—Turner worked on both during the late 1840s, while the famine was at its peak in Ireland.

What makes Richard Turner's glasshouses so remarkable? They are light, bright, and brilliantly constructed. The thin glazing bars and pierced pilasters let in as much light as possible. Although others, including John Claudius Loudon, had pioneered the use of iron glazing bars, Turner used iron in novel ways, creating freestanding, robust structures of hitherto unimaginable size. His innovations included a glazing bar of wrought iron, just one-and-a-half inches deep and a half-inch wide; more than that, he could curve these bars to create airy spaces.

Several of Turner's contemporaries have left pen portraits of him. John Charles Lyons, orchid grower and landowner of Ladiston, Mullingar, wrote in 1848 that Turner was "an ingenious, tasty, clever fellow, without a depth of science." In the late 1870s, by which time Richard Turner was advanced in age and retired, Thomas Drew remembered Turner as "ubiquitous, with a stock of daring and original projects always on hand . . . and his eloquent, plausible, and humourous advocacy of them." Turner's stock of "daring and original" schemes had included unsuccessful designs for "crystal palaces," including the Great Exhibition in London (1851) and the Dublin Exhibition (1853), as well as roofs for railway stations in England and Ireland.

As Drew also observed, Turner's innovative genius did not bring him much financial success, but he is distinguished as the builder—and should be fully credited as codesigner—of several of the world's finest buildings, including the sumptuous Curvilinear Range at Glasnevin.

Today, few of Richard Turner's buildings survive intact. The Glasnevin Curvilinear Range is an exception. It was faithfully restored to its original state for the bicentenary of the National Botanic Gardens in 1995 and is now the best and most complete example of Turner's work. The Great Palm House in the Royal Botanic Gardens, Kew, however, has been severely restored more than once and is virtually just a gross facsimile. Indeed, redundant ironwork from the Kew Palm House was used in the restoration program at Glasnevin.

See also Glasnevin, National Botanic Gardens; Kew, Royal Botanic Gardens

Biography
Born perhaps in Dublin, Ireland, ca. 1798. Married Jane Goodshaw, ca. 1816; speculated in buildings,

1820s and 30s, and accumulated capital to establish Hammersmith Iron Works, Ballsbridge, Dublin, Ireland, 1834; numerous commissions to build glasshouses; his son William Turner (1827–88) succeeded him as head of family business. Died in Dublin, 31 October 1881.

Selected Designs

1836	Peach House, Vice-Regal Lodge (now Aras an Uachtaráin), Phoenix Park, Dublin, Ireland
1839	Wings of Palm House, Belfast Botanic Gardens Park, Stranmillis, Belfast, Northern Ireland
1844–48	Great Palm House, Royal Botanic Gardens, Kew, Richmond, Surrey, England; Curvilinear Range, National Botanic Gardens, Glasnevin, Dublin, Ireland
1852	Victoria Regia House, Royal Botanic Gardens, Kew, Richmond, Surrey, England
1866	Longueville House, Mallow, Cork, Ireland
1868–69	Extension of Curvilinear Range, National Botanic Gardens, Glasnevin, Dublin, Ireland

Further Reading

Diestelkamp, E.J., "Richard Turner (c. 1798–1881) and His Glasshouses," *Glasra* 5 (1981)

Diestelkamp, E.J., "The Design and Building of the Palm House, Royal Botanic Gardens, Kew," *Journal of Garden History* 2 (1982)

Diestelkamp, E.J., "The Curvilinear Range at the National Botanic Gardens," *Moorea* 9 (1990)

Diestelkamp, E.J., "The Curvilinear Range National Botanic Gardens, Dublin," *Curtis's Botanical Magazine* 12 (1995)

Diestelkamp, E.J., and E.C. Nelson, "Richard Turner's Legacy—The Glasnevin Curvilinear Glasshouse," *Taisce Journal* 3, no. 1 (1979)

McCracken, Eileen M., *The Palm House and Botanic Garden, Belfast,* Belfast: Ulster Architectural Heritage Society, 1971

Nelson, E.C., "Richard Turner, an Introductory Portrait," *Moorea* 9 (1990)

Nelson E.C., and McCracken, Eileen M., *The Brightest Jewel: A History of the National Botanic Gardens, Glasnevin, Dublin,* Kilkenny, Ireland: Boethius, 1987

E. CHARLES NELSON

U

United States

The United States provided the setting for the evolution of landscape architecture (already well founded in garden design) as a land-planning profession. The relative youth of the country means that most of the development in garden design and landscape architecture has occurred within the past 300 years.

Pre-Columbian Era

The United States has diverse ecosystems and natural landforms. Examples include the Great Desert Basin, the Pacific and Atlantic coastlands, the Rocky Mountains, the Mississippi River lowlands, the Great Lakes, western canyon lands, and the Great Plains. Many pre-Columbian people traveled as hunters and gathers throughout these lands, although more settled agricultural communities such as Pueblo Bonito, Chaco Canyon, New Mexico also existed. Native American groups formed civilizations responsible for villages and elaborate settlements, as well as transportation routes that were often adapted by European settlers for their own use. For example, the Warrior's Path of the Cherokee and Shawnee became the settlers' Wilderness Road that crossed the Appalachians through the Cumberland Gap (Kostof).

Early Native American cultures had a close relationship with the land and great reverence for nature. Stunning built landscapes were created that have inspired contemporary artists and design professionals. Two examples include the Serpent Mound located in southern Ohio and the Anasazi cliff dwellings (A.D. 600–1300) at Mesa Verde National Park in Colorado. The Serpent Mound is one of the most noteworthy effigy mounds in North America. It is generally believed that the prehistoric Adena people (800 B.C.–A.D. 100) were the architects of this great work, since nearby burial formations have been attributed to the Adena. The Anasazi cliff dwellings illustrate the land-planning innovation of the prehistoric Anasazi, ancestral pueblo people with descendants who, according to the National Park Service, include 24 native American tribes still living in the South-

west. The Anasazi cliff dwellings were villages built along the Mesa and against the canyon walls. The site design exhibits advanced planning techniques, which use solar energy, wind protection, and spatial division according to specific applications. These prehistoric towns became the first cultural landscapes preserved by Congress through the establishment of the Mesa Verde National Park in 1906. (The National Park Service defines the cultural landscape as a "geographic area, including both cultural and natural resources and the wildlife or domestic animals therein, associated with a historic event, activity, or person or exhibiting other cultural or aesthetic values.")

Colonial America

Colonial settlement in the New World was characterized by expectations of personal freedom and the promise associated with great expanses of land. People from England, France, and Spain played a dominant role in the settlement and design of the built environment. As a new civilization evolved, these European cultures influenced land planning and garden design.

Early colonists cleared forested land for the preparation of agricultural crops; their initial concern was for survival. As habitation became stable in the late 17th century, design principles in site planning and garden design became a focused priority. European standards of classicism were the dominant stylistic approach emulated by the colonists. Edmund Bacon has suggested that the gridiron plan proposal for the ideal city published in Pietro di Giacomo Cataneo's *L'architettura* (1567; *Architecture*) may have provided the inspiration for Thomas Holme's 1683 design of Philadelphia for William Penn. This plan and other examples, including Williamsburg, Virginia (1699), designed by Francis Nicholson, and Savannah, Georgia (1733), by James Oglethorpe, epitomize the colonial American desire for geometric order and functional harmony.

As the new nation emerged use of the grid continued on a vast scale via President Jefferson's Land Ordinance

James Fanning, Museum of Modern Art Sculpture Garden (1955, 1964), New York, United States
Copyright Lauri Macmillan Johnson

of 1785 and the National Survey, which placed a grid upon great expanses of land within the United States. Unfortunately, this grid also imposed arbitrary conditions for development. Consequently, natural variations in topography, vegetation, and river configurations were often ignored. On a smaller scale residential lots and streets became standardized, and the centrally located village green, used for holding cattle, evolved to become the town square, or common, for public gatherings and events. Boston Common has become one of the most acclaimed of the colonial village squares. It was an early predecessor to the city park, which was introduced throughout the country as a result of social reform movements. Boston Common later became the starting point for the Olmsted-Eliot park system known as the Emerald Necklace (1894), which linked public gardens and parks (e.g., Arnold Arboretum and Franklin Park) along the Muddy River in a continuous series of open green spaces.

Colonial gardens were fashioned from the Renaissance prototypes, reflecting the cultural backgrounds of the settlers. Spanish-style gardens, created in residential courtyards within the interior of the home complex, often used the *chahar-bagh* pattern typical of Islamic gardens of Spain and the Middle East, in which pathways usually divided the enclosed patio into four quadrants, with a fountain placed in the center. The French and Dutch colonial gardens emphasized geometric order and topiary. They used, as did the English, ornamental parterres or knot gardens. English colonial gardens for modest residences were usually simple, functional plots that included herbs, medicinal plants, and flowers. These kitchen gardens were considered both functional and ornamental. The garden layout was usually symmetrical, with rectangular and occasionally circular forms; plantings were often asymmetrical. Located near the house, kitchen gardens were typically enclosed with wooden fences, stone walls, or low clipped hedges. In New England small "dooryard gardens" were developed adjacent to the front door of the house. These small fenced gardens held plant collections valued by the settlers. Colonists obtained specimens for their gardens through plant collecting, trade, and the importation of plants from Europe. According to Pregill and Volkman, dooryard gardens later evolved into cottage gardens, which became popular ornamental displays of irregular plantings of shrubs, annuals, and perennials.

In contrast, larger colonial residences with extensive agricultural lands, had elegant formal pleasure gardens. Southern gardens, associated with plantation estates, were magnificent displays of wealth and power. As self-sufficient farms, plantations relied on slave labor for the production of cash crops of tobacco, rice, and cotton. Houses were grand, and gardens were primarily symmetrical, using geometric patterns, long vistas, and a showy collection of indigenous and exotic trees and shrubs. This early American style is characterized in the homes of two U.S. presidents, George Washington (1732–99) and Thomas Jefferson (1743–1826).

Mount Vernon, the estate of Washington, the first president of the United States, sits on the Potomac River in Virginia and includes five farms with over 8,000 acres (3,237 ha) of grounds. The landscape of Washington's home, the Mansion House, is composed of woodlands, serpentine roads, a rolling meadow (bowling green), and two distinct gardens. The upper garden, a pleasure garden, features floral displays of rocket larkspur, foxglove, and sweet alyssum. Formal vistas are accentuated with fruit trees, boxwood topiary, and parterres. The lower garden, a kitchen garden, remains hidden behind plantings of weeping boxwood, buckeye, and Kentucky coffee trees. The overall landscape represents a transition in American garden design from formal to informal. The layout is symmetrical, but the walkways are curved, and the wide variety of plant species creates a natural and Romantic sense. From this early national period the "wilderness garden" arose, which may have originated in North America as an attempt to blend the classical with the natural. Wilderness gardens included formal terraces near the house and a wooded area of irregular plantings and meadows called the "wilderness," which became the terminus for the formal garden vista.

Thomas Jefferson was well recognized for the 1803 Louisiana Purchase, which doubled the size of the United States. He is also regarded as one of the country's first architects and garden designers. Through his scientific observations and travel to Europe, he became acquainted with the English "natural style" of garden design. Monticello, his Charlottesville, Virginia, estate reflects a sympathy toward the Romantic blended with French formality. Largely inspired by Renaissance aesthetics, the classical revival architecture of the home represents an American design standard that found maturity in the City Beautiful movement. Jefferson's plan for the University of Virginia in Charlottesville (1817–26) is another example of his diverse ability in architecture, planning, and landscape gardening.

Romantic Movement

In the early development of the country, the natural landscape and wilderness were feared places. Land was cleared for agricultural use and development. Town planning and garden design remained primarily formal during the 18th century; use of the grid offered a sense of control over nature. In the 19th century, as industrialization and transportation routes spread throughout North America, wilderness areas were settled, and the natural landscape eventually was viewed as a place of beauty. As an idealized image, the wilderness began to be associated with the American countryside; a tamed and romanticized view of nature emerged, and the American Romantic movement was launched.

The wilderness movement also helped in the creation of the National Park System. John Muir (1828–1914), the first president of the Sierra Club and a conservationist, helped to designate Yosemite as a national park in 1890. In addition, George Catlin, an artist who observed the wasteful slaughter of buffalo, urged the government in 1832 to preserve natural and cultural resources through the establishment of "wilderness parks." The U.S. National Park Service was established in 1916 to administer the country's national parks, which were created both for recreation and the preservation of scenic beauty. The U.S. Forest Service was established (in its present form in 1905) to administer national forests. Arthur Carhart, a landscape architect with the U.S. Forest Service, helped to create the Wilderness Act of 1964; millions of acres of land were set aside as "wild" land.

The American nurseryman André Parmentier (1780–1830) was one of the first, in the mid-1820s, to introduce the English Romantic garden style to the United States through his nursery operation in Brooklyn, New York. The importation of North American plants to Europe by horticulturists such as Englishman John Claudius Loudon, who wrote *An Encyclopedia of Gardening* (1822), made the American Garden (a collection of indigenous American plants) popular. American horticulturist Andrew Jackson Downing (1815–52) promoted the naturalistic landscape style for specific application in the United States. Author of several books, his *Treatise on the Theory and Practice of Landscape Gardening, Adapted to North America* (1841) gave Downing national acclaim. His theories, based on Humphry Repton's English garden style, emphasized asymmetrical plant arrangements with undulating paths and an exalted imitation of nature. As an architect, horticulturist, and nurseryman, Downing understood the need to integrate the cottage villa with the garden in artistic harmony. He promoted ideas for suburban living, which became one of the visionary premises for the "Country Place era" in the late 19th century.

Living along the Hudson River Valley, Downing, who was associated with the Hudson River school of intellectuals (including landscape painter Thomas Cole [1801–48] and writer Washington Irving [1783–1859]), promoted theories of Romantic beauty. He collaborated with William Cullen Bryant, poet and editor of the *New*

Daniel Urban Kiley and Eero Saarinen, Jefferson National Expansion Monument (designed 1948, with revisions through 1964; constructed 1971–81), St. Louis, Missouri, United States
Copyright Lauri Macmillan Johnson

York Evening Post, to campaign for a naturalistic park in New York City. They believed parks would improve humanity and alleviate the social problems caused by urban industrialization. This utopian idea, reflected in Romantic landscape paintings such as those by Thomas Doughty, Asher Durand, Frederic Edwin Church, George Inness, Thomas Moran, and Albert Bierstadt, as well as transcendentalist philosophy, became a strong foundation for the establishment of the profession of landscape architecture by Frederic Law Olmsted (1822–1903), who named the profession in 1863. Transcendentalists such as Ralph Waldo Emerson (1803–82) and Henry David Thoreau (1817–62) promoted values related to simple living and land stewardship and encouraged reform for greater egalitarianism.

Olmsted, superintendent of the proposed park, and English architect Calvert Vaux (1824–95), who came to the United States as Downing's partner, joined forces in a design competition for the park. Their design, "Greensward," was selected as the winning concept, and Central Park (1858–63, 1865–78), as it was officially named, became the first Romantic park in the United States. Olmsted and Vaux continued to work on other projects, including Prospect Park in Brooklyn, New York (1865–73), and the model suburb Riverside, Illinois (1868–70). The curving road patterns and large open green spaces of this suburb have been widely imitated throughout the United States. Other suburban villages designed by the Olmsted office include Roland Park in Baltimore, Maryland (1891), and Forest Hills Gardens (designed by Olmsted Brothers) in Long Island, New York (started in 1911).

Olmsted was a surveyor, nurseryman, journalist, book publisher, farmer, civil engineer, and international traveler. Like Downing and his contemporaries, Olmsted believed that natural landscape scenery had the power to cure the social evils of urban society. During the Civil War he participated in the organization of the U.S. Sanitary Commission, which eventually became the American Red Cross and U.S. Army Medical Corps. Under Lincoln's presidency, Olmsted helped to develop a proposal that ultimately led to the creation of the National Park System. Yellowstone, with boundaries largely in Wyoming but also Montana and Idaho, became the first national park in 1872.

Romantic American landscapes, often referred to as "Olmstedian landscapes," have their roots in the English natural style, with Victorian architectural influences that provide formal elements (e.g., buildings, bridges, steps) as works of art within the landscape setting. Curved land forms and water bodies with naturalistic plant compositions were used to create vistas and spatial sequences that provide beautiful scenery and recreational opportunities as a reprieve from city life. Previously, Romantic cemeteries filled the need for recreation as urban dwellers escaped to the tranquillity of the rural pastoral landscape. Usually located on the perimeter of the city, cemeteries such as Mount Auburn in Cambridge, Massachusetts (1835), Laurel Hill in Philadelphia (1836), Greenwood in Brooklyn, New York (1838), Arlington in Washington, D.C. (1864), Graceland in Chicago (1878), and Forest Lawn near Los Angeles (1906) were expansive pleasure grounds that have remained popular tourist attractions. Pioneers in the rural Romantic cemetery movement were H.W.S. Cleveland (1814–1900), author of *Landscape Architecture as Applied to the Wants of the West* (1873), and Jacob Weidenmann (1829–93), author of *Beautifying Country Homes: A Handbook of Landscape Gardening* (1870).

City Beautiful Movement

The World's Columbian Exposition (Chicago World's Fair) of 1893 was a commemoration of the 400th anniversary of Columbus's "discovery" of America. Also called the "Great White City," with its classical revival architecture and lavish gardens, the fair inspired national public interest in civic design. Under architect Daniel Burnham's leadership, and with the participation of many design professionals, the fair presented the "classical ideal" as prescribed by the École des Beaux-Arts. This resulted in the City Beautiful movement (1893–1940), which encouraged classical revival architecture and planning and led to the establishment of the American Academy in Rome (1894). Previously, American cities were unsanitary, coal-polluted places lacking public amenities or beauty. The McMillan Commission Plan (1901), which implemented Pierre L'Enfant's 1791 Versailles-inspired design for Washington, D.C., epitomizes the use of classical city planning, with axial and cross-axial geometries, magnificent vistas, parks, and promenades.

Olmsted, with partner Charles Eliot (1859–97), Warren H. Manning (1860–1938), and Olmsted's sons John C. Olmsted (1852–1920) and Frederick Law Olmsted Jr. (1870–1957)(who eventually established their own firm in 1898 called Olmsted Brothers), played a significant role in design and planning during this period of growth. Eliot created the Boston Metropolitan Park System with a methodology he developed using a scientific natural-systems approach. Manning developed a "National Plan for America," which directed planning toward environmental sensitivity. An expert plantsman, he prepared the planting plans for many of Olmsted's projects, including the World's Columbian Exposition and the Biltmore Estate in North Carolina. Other estate projects by the independent Manning office were for wealthy clients, including Rockefeller, McCormick, Peavy, and Seiberling. Manning's design for Frank A. Seiberling (Stan Hywet Hall, Akron, Ohio, started 1911) was a 70-acre (28.3-ha) site featuring a Tudor-style house and formal European garden. Separate garden rooms were created, such as the English garden, designed by Manning's collaborator, Ellen Biddle Shipman. Another garden room, the lagoon garden, located at an old quarry site, was designed to include native plantings of wildflowers and ornamental shrubs. The site features a 500-foot-long (152.4 m) white birch allée. A restoration plan of this historically significant Manning landscape was developed by Child Associates in 1984.

Other important designers who helped shape the development of landscape architecture and garden design in the United States during the first decades of 20th century include John Nolen (1869–1937), who promoted city and regional planning as a distinct profession; Frank Albert Waugh (1869–1943), who wrote *Landscape Gardening* (1899) and *Landscape Beautiful* (1910) and was professor of horticulture and landscape gardening at what is now the University of Massachusetts; Henry Vincent Hubbard (1875–1947), who in 1910 founded with Charles Downing Lay (1877–1956) and Robert Wheelwright (1884–1965) the journal of the American Society of Landscape Architects (*Landscape Architecture*) and coauthored with Theodora Kimball the important text *An Introduction to the Study of Landscape Design* (1917); Albert Davis Taylor (1883–1951), coauthor with Gordon D. Cooper, *The Complete Garden* (1921); Elbert Peets (1886–1968), who stressed classical planning and design and coauthored with Werner Hegemann (1881–1936) *Civic Art: The American Vitruvius* (1922); George Kessler (1862–1923), who created the widely celebrated master plan for Kansas City, Missouri, which incorporated parks, boulevards, and architecture with classically styled spatial geometries; and Arthur Shurcliff (1870–1957), who in the 1930s produced landscape reconstruction plans, including the Governor's Palace at Williamsburg, Virginia.

This period of social reform legislation described as the progressive movement (1900–1917) and, later, Franklin Delano Roosevelt's New Deal program of the 1930s initiated and strengthened comprehensive city planning. City master plans were created for Boston, Chicago, Denver, Portland, and San Francisco. In addition, the mass production of the automobile led to the popularization of recreational travel in the United States. Garden-style parkways such as the Bronx River Parkway (1923) and the Taconic State Parkway (1933), both in New York, the Blue Ridge Parkway in Virginia (1935), and the Garden State Parkway in New Jersey (1956) were developed as "pleasure roads" to incorporate scenic landscape beauty. These serpentine roadways were designed with wide medians, replete with picturesque plantings, to enhance driving pleasure as well as motorist safety. Parkway development became associated with the park movement, paralleling the widespread implementation of city, state, and national parks for scenic preservation and recreation. The period of growth after the Great Depression was aided by social-work programs created in 1933. These include the Civilian Conservation Corps, the Public Works Administration, the Works Administration Program, the Tennessee Valley Authority, and the Federal Housing Administration. Young people found jobs in the creation of public projects such as the new town Norris, Tennessee (1933–34), constructed to serve workers on the Norris Dam, the San Antonio, Texas, River Walk, Paseo del Rio (started 1937), the Blue Ridge Parkway in Virginia (1935), and many gardens, parks, zoos, and recreational facilities such as Lynd Saddle Trail in Itasca State Park, Minnesota, and Boerner Botanical Garden in Hales Corner, Wisconsin. Robert Moses (1888–1991), a New York City civic planner, directed the construction of numerous large-scale New York City and state public projects, including the Lincoln Center for the Performing Arts, Shea Stadium, and Jones Beach State Park, as well as 35 highways, 12 bridges, and numerous housing projects and playgrounds.

Advances in English town planning as presented by Ebenezer Howard's Garden City Diagram from *Tomorrow: A Peaceful Path to Real Reform* (1898) (retitled in the second edition *Garden Cities of Tomorrow* [1902]) influenced American town planning during the City Beautiful movement. A blending of city and country life, Howard's concept featured limited population growth and a "greenbelt" of open agricultural land surrounding the city. Separation of neighborhoods created identity and city parks were focal amenities. Examples of model garden cities include Letchworth and Welwyn in England and Radburn, New Jersey, in the United States. The plan for Radburn (1926), designed by Clarence Stein and Henry Wright, included garden courts, small parking areas, pedestrian open-space systems connecting shops, schools, and neighborhoods, or "superblocks," and a buffered industrial center. New towns, World War I factory towns, and garden cities based in part on Howard's model were created for self-sufficiency. The industrial town Chicopee, Georgia (1927), by Earle Draper (1893–1994), and garden cities Mariemont, Ohio (1925), by John Nolen, and Chatham Village (Pittsburgh), Pennsylvania (1932), by Ralph E. Griswold (1894–1981), are early examples. Later projects, sponsored by Roosevelt's New Deal administration, were Greenbelt, Maryland, by Hale J. Walker, Greenhills, Ohio, by Justin R. Hartzog and William A. Strong, and Greendale, Wisconsin, by Elbert Peets (1886–1968) and Jacob Crane. World War II subdivisions followed, and the Levittown communities located in New York (1947), Pennsylvania (1950), and New Jersey (1955) became American housing prototypes.

Country Place Era

The Country Place era originated with the work of Downing and the design of many estates along the

Lawrence Halprin, Franklin Delano Roosevelt Memorial (designed 1970s; constructed 1997)
Copyright Lauri Macmillan Johnson

Hudson River. It was in the later years of the 19th century, however, that interest in residential gardens became a focused movement. This was in part a result of the publication of the *Cyclopedia of American Horticulture* (four volumes; 1900–1902), by Liberty Hyde Bailey, Jr. (1858–1954), who promoted rural America and the idealized agrarian society. Industrialization also encouraged rural development for the managerial class, who could afford to buy suburban homes and commute to city work places.

The Victorian period was the transition between Romantic design and the classical Renaissance-inspired design of the early 20th century. Garden design in this period is often referred to as Victorian or Victorian Eclectic, since Victorian garden design was an eclectic medley of foreign styles. A "fear of voids" or "fear of unadorned space" (*horror vacui*) led to a desire to fill the garden open space with arbitrary placements of plants and ornamental objects. J.C. Loudon promoted this gardenesque style and emphasized horticultural variety and specimen plant displays, sometimes at the expense of spatial unity and simplicity in design. Exotic and unusual plants were favored, such as those with twisted or weeping forms or plants with double flowers, varie-

gated leaves, or exfoliating bark. Specialty gardens, such as tropical or alpine gardens and lily ponds, were fashionable, and rose hybridization became popular as well. Garden features, often isolated within the landscape, included stone lanterns, Japanese pagodas, and French Renaissance parterres. Mass-produced ornate garden objects—cast-iron corn stalk or grapevine fencing, decorative gnomes, and Italian classical figures—became commonly repeated motifs. Turf was used as a living carpet and background for these freestanding garden objects. Geometric beds in the shape of circles, diamonds, and stars were set as focal points within the lawn. This "bedding out" of herbaceous plants also took the form of "carpet bedding," which placed annuals and perennials in elaborate realistic layouts such as fleurs-de-lis, family crests, dogs, boats, and signs of the zodiac.

This was a period of enthusiasm in residential gardens for both modest suburban homes and the expensive country estates of high-society industrialists. Gardens were used for weddings, poetry reading, and recreational activities (e.g., croquet, tennis, softball, and badminton). Gardening during this period became a "home-based" hobby reflecting the new humanism characterized by social reform movements, including women's suffrage,

Steve Martino and Associates, Papago Park (1991), Phoenix, Arizona, United States
Copyright Lauri Macmillan Johnson

children's rights, and temperance movements cited as the beginning of the modern era.

The Hunt-Olmsted design of the Vanderbilt family's Biltmore Estate in Asheville, North Carolina (1893), is an example of an impressive upper-class residence. Inspired by French Renaissance aesthetics, the garden includes formal and informal features with perennial flower borders, rose gardens, intricate stonework, bowling green, conservatory, and stables. However, it was the natural areas that most interested Olmsted. Overworked farmland was eventually replaced with forested land through the management of Gifford Pinchot. As a result, the Biltmore site has been credited as the origin of the profession of forestry in North America.

Charles A. Platt (1861–1933), landscape painter and architect, wrote *Italian Gardens* (1894), the first book written in English on the subject of Italian Renaissance gardens. This publication, and the writings of contemporaries such as Edith Wharton, helped to trigger the revival of Italian gardens in the United States. Platt stressed the importance of integration between the house and garden through the use of axial geometry and the creation of garden rooms. His estate designs for Sprague, Rockefeller, McCormick, and Faulkner are examples of Italian classical revival gardens in the United States. This neoclassical approach eventually replaced Victorian design and set the stage for the transition to modern garden design.

Women landscape architects began to play an important role in the early decades of the 20th century. Gertrude Jekyll (1843–1932), English garden designer, made the herbaceous border popular in the United States. Ellen Biddle Shipman (1870–1950) and Beatrix Jones Farrand (1872–1959) were two prominent landscape architects whose garden designs have qualities of lasting importance. Shipman, who worked with Platt, had extensive knowledge of horticulture. She taught for many years at the Lowthorpe School of Landscape Architecture Gardening and Horticulture for Women (which later became affiliated with the Rhode Island School of Design) and the Cambridge School of Architecture and Landscape Architecture for Women. Farrand studied landscape horticulture under Charles Sargent, founder and director of Arnold Arboretum. Her designs include Dumbarton Oaks, Washington, D.C. (1921–47), the Abby Aldrich Rockefeller Garden, Seal Harbor, Maine (1926–50), the English Garden at Stan Hywet Hall, Akron, Ohio (1929), and a number of college campuses, including Princeton (1913–41) and Yale (1924–47). She was the only female founding member of the American Society of Landscape Architects, in 1899.

Modern Design

Artists at the turn of the 20th century introduced new modern styles of art characterized by an increase in freedom of expression within a wider range of subject matter and media. Advances in scientific knowledge and the shift from an agricultural society to the machine age, as well as political turmoil in Paris, the art center of the contemporary world, led to reactive art movements in the 20th century. Various forms of modern art, including Constructivism, Futurism, Cubism, Dadaism, Social Realism, Abstract Expressionism, Neoplasticism, and Surrealism, inspired a new aesthetic in the applied arts (industrial design, furniture design, architecture, landscape architecture, and garden design).

Cubism, developed by Pablo Picasso and Georges Braque, discarded representational conventions and eventually led to nonobjective expression. Modern technology produced new materials, methods of construction, and advances in structural engineering. Steel-frame construction made skyscrapers possible, and reinforced concrete gave rise to cantilevered buildings and suspension bridges. "Streamlined" forms with horizontal lines and teardrop shapes were used by industrial designers to create a new look characterized by machine forms and the feeling of motion. Airplanes, ships, and locomotives, as well as common household objects such as refrigerators and vacuum cleaners, were designed in accordance with this new aesthetic, which drew inspiration from the principles of aerodynamics.

Walter Gropius (1883–1969), German architect and educator, inspired by the De Stijl movement in Holland, founded the Bauhaus in 1926. His premise was to unite industrial design with architecture in the exploration of new materials, construction techniques, and built forms. The Bauhaus style, known also as the international style, was impersonal, geometric, and highly functional. In 1937 Gropius came to the United States as chair of architecture at the Graduate School of Design at Harvard.

The expression "form follows function," first used by the architect Louis Sullivan (1856–1924), became the slogan for modern architecture. Within the Chicago School (which included architects Daniel Burnham, William Le Baron, and John Root), Sullivan pioneered skyscraper design. His design extension of the Carson Pirie Scott and Company Department Store (1899–1904) is acclaimed as one of the first steel-frame structures that demonstrated the modern approach in architecture: only the window frames are decorated, and the underlying framework of steel girders determines the simple facade.

Frank Lloyd Wright (1867–1959), Sullivan's protégé, mastered the interplay between architecture and the natural landscape in what became known as organic architecture, as represented by Falling Water, in Bear Run, Pennsylvania (1935). Wright's architectural compositions were indicative of the Arts and Crafts movement (1870–1920), which stressed hand-crafted, one-of-a-kind pieces made from indigenous building materials. This reactive style was opposed to the impersonal mass production generated by the machine-age design of the Bauhaus. In keeping with the philosophies of the Arts and Crafts movement, Wright and landscape designer Jens Jensen (1860–1951) developed Prairie-style architecture and landscape architecture to reflect the natural qualities of the Midwestern landscape. Jensen stressed the use of native plants in his designs and became known for his use of stone council rings for gathering places. Examples include private estate gardens for Edward L. Ryerson in Lake Forest, Illinois (1912), and Henry Ford in Dearborn, Michigan. Jensen designed several parks in Chicago, as well as the Morton Arboretum, in Lisle, Illinois. Another Midwestern garden designer who promoted the use of native plants and nature as a source of inspiration for design was Ossian Cole Simonds (1857–1931). The use of native plants was advocated also by plant ecologist Edith A. Roberts and landscape architect Elsa Rehmann, coauthors of *American Plants for American Gardens* (1929). Wolfgang Oehme and James van Sweden are contemporary designers involved in native plant and natural habitat restorations. Their collaborative work can be seen in the New American Gardens at the U.S. National Arboretum.

In garden design it was perhaps the work and writing of Fletcher Steele (1885–1971) that first introduced the change from neoclassical expression and eclectic styles to modern. A critical analysis of the modern garden design experiments in Paris in the 1920s, Steele's landmark article "New Pioneering in Garden Design," published in 1930 in *Landscape Architecture,* marked the beginning of scholarly interest in modern gardens in the United States. Steele's engaging Blue Steps, in Naumkeag, Massachusetts (1926), and other estate gardens remained primarily classical, flavored with eclectic adornment and the decorative French Art Deco style. It was not until international-style architecture became popular at Harvard that American landscape architects began to reject classical plans and embrace new modern styles.

One of the first landscape architects to popularize the modern approach was Thomas Church (1902–78), who, living in the San Francisco Bay area, developed "California-style" landscape architecture. This organic style emphasized client needs, integration with existing site conditions, and the creation of garden rooms for outdoor living. In architecture the Japanese inspired bungalow designs and small gardens of Charles and Henry Green are examples of the California style blended with the Arts and Crafts style (e.g., the Blacker and Gamble [1908–9] houses in Pasadena, California). In garden design the formal Beaux-Arts layout was replaced with occult (asymmetrical) balance, which used modern art as a catalyst for innovation. Cubist theory may have influenced the design work of Church, resulting in gardens with multiple viewpoints. Modern gardens represent a departure from axial design, which emphasizes a single main sight line, characteristic of Beaux-Arts gardens. Modern garden plans resembled nonobjective or abstract art, such as paintings by Piet Mondrian, Joan Miró, Alexander Calder, and Picasso; these gardens are often referred to as abstract or Cubist gardens.

Church designed over 2,000 gardens for clients of various income levels. The Dewey Donnell garden, El Novillero (1947–48), exists as an American icon of modern landscape architecture. This private residence, located in Sonoma, California, features an organically shaped swimming pool with abstract sculpture by artist Adline Kent. Church's design integrates the geometries of the built environment with the dramatic views of San Pablo Bay and the adjacent live oak woodland plant community. In the beginning stages of his practice Church used a range of styles—often the French baroque, but also Romantic as well as modern. His modern garden layouts incorporate fluid curves and diagonal lines, which he used in small gardens to create the illusion of greater depth. Church paid particular attention to human scale and spatial sequence; his gardens are characterized by simplicity (in color, line, and form), ease of maintenance, appropriate plant selection, and innovative use of new materials. Several of his assistants, including Garrett Eckbo, Lawrence Halprin, Douglas Baylis, and Robert Royston, became well-known landscape architects following the modernist traditions.

As modern landscape architecture was advanced in the late 1930s by Harvard design students Garrett Eckbo, Daniel Urban Kiley, and James Rose, landscape design, including work by Church, became more asymmetrical, celebrating the departure from past eclectic styles that often disregarded natural site conditions. Abstract geometric patterns were used as symbolic representations of nature. Nature was no longer romanticized. The modern landscape forms, derived in part from modern art included obtuse triangular forms such as Halprin's Lovejoy Plaza, Portland Oregon (1961), occult rectangular ones such as Kiley's Oakland Museum, Oakland, California (1969), and amorphous fluid "plastic-like" curved forms such as Church's Dewey Donnell garden, El Novillero, Sonoma, California (1947–48).

The "Harvard Revolt" is the phrase often used to describe the experimentation by Eckbo, Kiley, and Rose during their landscape architectural studies at Harvard. Modern architecture in vogue, the three were inspired to exchange the traditional Beaux-Arts principles with modern design theories. Site-specific analysis encouraged ecological preservation, and a desire for function placed users' needs before arbitrary design configurations.

Garret Eckbo (1910–2000), author of *Landscape for Living* (1950) and *The Landscape We See* (1969), published student projects in *Pencil Points* magazine (now *Progressive Architecture*) in 1938. These were acknowledged as the first modern gardens published in the

United States. He became the founding partner (1964) of the landscape architectural firm Eckbo, Dean, Austin, and Williams (later known as EDAW). Continuing as a professor (eventually emeritus) at the University of California at Berkeley, his practice and numerous scholarly articles provided leadership for the profession for almost half a century.

Dan Kiley (b. 1912) used simple asymmetrical rectangular forms, but counter to modernist theories, he also drew inspiration from 17th-century French Renaissance garden geometry. The allée axis of the Miller Garden in Columbus, Indiana (1955), reflects this classical motif; as a result, this work is often cited as a source of inspiration for postmodern garden designers, who turned once again to classical references. The Jefferson National Expansion Monument, St. Louis, Missouri designed in the late 1940's (with Eero Saarinen), also reflects the simplicity and classical language of Kiley's modern style. (Construction drawings for the project were completed in 1948 with design revisions occurred through 1964 and construction phases occurring from 1971–81). Other significant Kiley projects include the United States Air Force Academy, Colorado Springs, Colorado (1968), the Chicago Art Institute South Garden, Chicago, Illinois (1962), the Oakland Museum, Oakland, California (1969), the National Gallery of Art, Washington, D.C. (1977, 1989), the Dallas Museum of Art, Dallas, Texas (1983), Fountain Place, Dallas, Texas (1985), the Henry Moore Sculture Garden, Nelson-Atkins Museum of Art Kansas City, Missouri (1988), and the Kimmel Residence, Salisbury, Connecticut (1996).

James Rose (1910–91) specialized in residential gardens primarily within the New Jersey/New York region. He was known to have been influenced by Zen Buddhism and Japanese garden design; his gardens exhibit a strong relationship with the interior spaces of the house. Significant articles were published in *Pencil Points* magazine (now *Progressive Architecture*)(1938–39).

Modern landscape architecture in the United States was impacted by Brazilian landscape architect Roberto Burle Marx (1909–94), and Mexican architect Luis Barragán (1902–88). Burle Marx approached garden design as a fine art and created landscape compositions that resembled three-dimensional paintings made with earth, water, sky, and plants. His garden layouts typically blended elaborate fluid curves with geometric angles. Horticulturist and plant collector, he promoted ecological biodiversity and rain-forest protection before the environmental trend became popular. Influenced by French international-style architect Le Corbusier (1887–1965) and the vernacular traditions of Mexico, Barragán designed a number of garden orchestrations with planes (walls, ground levels, and channels). Masterful and elegant use of color, texture, and light grace his landscape pieces. A well-known example from Mexico City is the Plaza del Bebedero de los Caballos, Las Arboledas (1958–62). Inspired in part by the work of Barragan is the contemporary landscape architect Mario Schjetnam, who's firm Grupo de Diseño Urbano designed the Museo de las Culturas del Norte, Paquimé, Casas Grandes, Chihuahua, and Parque Ecólogico Xochimilco, Xochimilco, Ciudad de Mexico.

After World War II and throughout the second half of the 20th century, the profession of landscape architecture developed rapidly throughout the United States. Diverse project types emerged, such as corporate projects, entertainment places, urban plazas and streetscapes, commercial waterfronts, beaches, stadiums, airports, landscape restorations, and places for ecotourism. Many recognized landscape architects made significant contributions to the evolution of the built environment of the United States.

Finding sources of inspiration in art and the natural beauty of the High Sierra Mountains, Lawrence Halprin (b. 1916) operated a California-based practice. His famous designs include Ghiradelli Square, San Francisco (1962), Ira's Fountain and Lovejoy Plaza in Portland, Oregon (1961), Sea Ranch, an ecologically planned community built in northern California (1965), Freeway Park, Seattle, Washington (1976), Levi Strauss Plaza, San Francisco (1982), and the more recent Roosevelt Memorial in Washington, D.C. (design work started in the 1970s with implementation in 1997). Features include four outdoor galleries: one for each of FDR's terms in office (spanning from 1933–45). Site symbolism and representational art works are used to tell the story of FDR's contributions through the Great Depression and World War II. Halprin's wife, Anna Halprin, a well-known dancer, worked with him to develop a system of recording human activities in urban settings. Based on dance notation, he called this methodology *motation*.

Hideo Sasaki (b. 1919–2000) approached landscape architecture as a collaborative venture among interdisciplinary planning and design professionals. The firm he founded in 1953, Hideo Sasaki and Associates in Watertown, Massachusetts, later became Sasaki, Dawson, DeMay Associates, now Sasaki Associates, participates in a wide variety of national and international projects. Samples include Stuart O. Dawson's design of the Deere and Company Administrative Center, Moline, Illinois (1961–64), the Frito-Lay Headquarters, Plano, Texas (1982), the Dallas Arts District (1984), Toledo Riverfront, Ohio (1984), and Euro Disneyland, Paris (1992).

Ecological design became the focus during the environmental movement of the late 1960s and 1970s, fueled by Aldo Leopold's *Sand County Almanac* (1949), Rachel Carson's *Silent Spring* (1962), and Rene Dubos's *So Human an Animal* (1968). Ian McHarg (1920–2001), who established the program of landscape architecture at the University of Pennsylvania, wrote the popular book *Design with Nature* (1967) which helped lead to the

1969 Environmental Protection Act. His innovative planning technique, similar to Charles Eliot's work in the 1890s, was eventually termed the *overlay system*. In this system recordings of site-specific data (soil, vegetation, slope, etc.) are mapped and overlaid with one another to ultimately create a composite image. Used to guide design decisions, McHarg's multidisciplinary approach toward regional planning created the foundation for sustainable development. His firm, Wallace, McHarg, Roberts, and Todd, created a number of ecologically based communities, including the housing project Woodlands, near Houston, Texas (1972), and Amelia Island Plantation, a resort in Florida (1973). The firm also prepared the master plan for Baltimore's Inner Harbor (1974). Other ecologically focused designers and scholars include Philip H. Lewis, Jr., John Lyle, Julius Fabos, Carl Steinitz, Frederick R. Steiner, Robert Thayer, and Andropogon Associates, who collaborated with Edward L. Blake, and Jones and Jennings as well as others to create the Crosby Arboretum in Picayune, Mississippi (1989).

Peter Walker, who coauthored with Melanie Simo *Invisible Gardens: The Search for Modernism in the American Landscape* (1994), designed the Foothill College campus in Los Altos, California (Sasaki Walker and Associates, 1961), which integrates buildings, pathways, and site topography with a modernist design approach. In the 1980s, as Walker began to explore classical forms and axial geometry blended with minimal art gestures, his experimental designs reflected the emerging postmodern approach. Examples include Tanner Fountain, Harvard University, Cambridge, Massachusetts (1983), Cambridge Center Roof Garden, Cambridge, Massachusetts (1984), Solana, Westlake, and Southlake, Texas (1984–89), and Herman Miller Company, Rockland, California (1987). Peter Walker has been associated with Sasaki, Walker Associates (1957), the SWA Group (1968), Peter Walker Martha Schwartz Landscape Architecture (1983), Peter Walker and Partners (1990), and Peter Walker William Johnson and Partners Landscape Architecture.

Gas Works Park in Seattle, Washington (1973), illustrates Richard Haag's (b. 1923) strong will and character as a designer. This industrial park was recycled into an urban art park. Historic reference to its past industrial use was preserved as the gas "towers" have become works of art in the landscape. Although public opposition was strong, other industrial artifacts were transformed into a playground maze of brightly painted machinery. Haag, known for his work in the Pacific Northwest, was involved in the historic preservation of Pike Place Market, Seattle, Washington, and the 140-acre (57 ha) nature preserve Bloedel Reservation, Bainbridge Island, Washington (1978–85). Another regionally focused landscape architect with projects in the Boston area is Carol R. Johnson (b. 1930). Her projects include Lechmere Canal Park

(1986), the revitalization of East Mystic River Reservation (1983), and John F. Kennedy Park (1984–89), located along the Charles River. Flowers in the park bloom at the end of May in remembrance of Kennedy's birthday, and fragments of his famous speeches are embossed in granite pillars that frame the park entrances.

Other significant projects from the modern era include James Fanning's Museum of Modern Art Sculpture Garden (1955, 1964), Zion and Breen's Paley Park (1965), and M. Paul Friedberg's Jacob Riis Plaza (1965) (all in New York City). Additional projects include Theodore Osmundson's design of the Kaiser Center Roof Garden, Oakland, California (1961), Sasaki, Dawson, DeMay Associates' Constitution Plaza, Hartford, Connecticut (1963), EDAW's design of the Tucson Community Center, Tucson, Arizona (1968), and Edward D. Stone, Jr., and Associates' design of PepsiCo World Headquarters, Purchase, New York (1972, 1981–85). Grant Jones's pioneering concepts for zoo habitats are seen in Woodland Park Zoo, Seattle, Washington (1976), and its recent additions, one example being the Elephant Forest Exhibit (1989).

Postmodern Design

Modernism created a new paradigm and made a fundamental break from eclectic and historic styles. In the 1960s and 1970s some examples of modern architecture and landscape architecture had lost their appeal as the forms were being recycled in uninteresting ways. Change seemed inevitable, and the sequence of experimentation initiated first in literature and art and followed by architecture and landscape architecture was repeated in the postmodern era. Pop art developed an eclectic perspective in the 1970s and was eventually replaced with photorealism. In general postmodern art was dominated by a realistic focus and pluralism of approach that led to specific trends. These include allegory, narrative, still-life and landscape, ornament, and pattern painting. In postmodern architecture, such as Charles Moore's Piazza d'Italia, New Orleans, Louisiana (1976–79), Michael Graves's Portland Public Services Building, Portland, Oregon (1980–82), and Robert Stern's Point West Place, Framington, Massachusetts (1983–84), there was a rebirth of classical style. A new design vocabulary arose, dominated by "freestyle" classicism, which used humor, artistic experimentation, and in some postmodern landscapes, occult modern geometries. Neoclassical planning returned, as exhibited in Andres Dùaney and Elizabeth Planter-Zyberk's design of the town of Seaside, Florida (1978).

Environmental artists and site artists created art within a landscape medium. Their innovative projects provided inspiration for landscape architecture. Some examples include Isamu Noguchi's *Sunken Garden for Chase Manhattan Bank Plaza*, New York, New York (1961–65), and *California Scenario*, Costa Mesa, California (1982);

Michael Heizer's *Double Negative*, Near Overton, Nevada (1969–71); Robert Smithson's *Spiral Jetty,* Great Salt lake, Utah (1970); Christo's (Christo Javachrff) *Running Fence*, American West Coast (1972–76), and *Surrounded Islands*, Biscayne Bay, Miami, Florida (1983); Nancy Holt's *Sun Tunnels*, Great Basin Desert, Utah (1973–76), and *Dark Star Park*, Arlington, Virginia (1984); Walter De Maria's *The Lighting Field*, New Mexico (1974–77); Carl Andre's *Stone Field Sculpture*, Hartford, Connecticut (1977); Herbert Bayer's *Mill Creek Canyon Earthworks*, Kent, Washington (1979–82); Richard Fleischner's *Wiesner Building Plaza*, Massachusetts Institute of Technology, Cambridge, Massachusetts (1979); Robert Irwin's *9 Spaces 9 Trees*, Seattle, Washington (1979); Doug Hollis's *A Sound Garden*, National Oceanic and Atmosphere Adminstration (N.O.A.A.), Seattle, Washington (1981); and Marry Miss's *Field Rotation,* Governors State University Park Forest South, Illinois (1981).

Early postmodern landscape architectural projects such as Martha Schwartz's Bagel Garden (a temporary parterre of lacquered pumpernickel bagels arranged on a bed of purple aquarium gravel), Cambridge, Massachusetts (1979), and George Hargreaves's Harlequin Plaza (a surrealistic courtyard with black and white, distorted, diamond-shaped paving and red and purple walls with diminishing heights, used to create false perspective and spatial illusion; the plaza was the showcase of several large harlequin statues), Greenwood Village, Colorado (1982), demonstrated that landscape architects could explore artistic and humorous directions. Personal expression within the designer's frame of reference became accepted practice. Michael R. Van Valkenburgh's exhibition and publication *Transforming the American Garden: Twelve New Landscape Designs* (1986) featured theoretical landscapes that reclaimed garden design as an art form. Landscape architects during the 1960s and 1970s were primary involved with large-scale public planning projects employing environmental and sociocultural scientific approaches; landscape architecture was not typically thought of as a form of art. *Progressive Architecture* created a special issue entitled the "New American Landscape" (1989), which highlighted postmodern landscape architecture. Garden design and related scholarly activity became avant-garde, and the term *green architecture* was used as a substitute name for gardens and the landscape (the term *green architecture* currently relates to environmentally sound architecture). Classical garden forms and historic reference became vogue.

During the 1980s and 1990s many types of projects with various stylistic approaches were created. A few celebrated built landscapes from these decades include the Maya Lin's Vietnam Veteran's Memorial, Washington, D.C. (1981); Cooper-Eckstut Association's (with many other landscape architects and artists) Battery Park City,

New York, New York (started 1982), including Child Associates' South Cove Park (1988) and Carr, Lynch, Hack and Sandell's Hudson River Park (1990); SWA Group's Refugio Valley Park, Hercules, California (1981), Williams Square, Las Colinas, Texas (1984), the gardens of the Arizona Center, Phoenix, Arizona (1990), and with the Office of Peter Walker and Martha Schwartz, Burnett Park, Fort Worth Texas (1983); Hargreaves Associates' Plaza Park, San Jose, California (1989); Michael R. Van Valkenburgh's Minneapolis Sculpture Garden Expansion, the Walker Art Center, Minneapolis, Minnesota (1988–92); Morgan Wheelock's Becton Dickinson and Company Headquarters, Franklin Lakes, New Jersey (1987); Hunter Reynolds Jewell's Crystal Park, Arlington, Virginia (1988); Jones and Jones's Newcastle Beach Park, Bellevue, Washington (1988); Danadjieva and Koenig Associates' Riverfront Promenade, Indianapolis, Indiana (1988); Murase Associates' Japanese American Historical Plaza, Portland Oregon (1990); Sasaki Associates Charleston Waterfront Park (1990); and Steve Martino and Associates' Papago Park, Phoenix, Arizona (1991).

Postmodern landscape architecture from the early 1980s sometimes ignored the principles that guided the environmental movement in order to explore the vision of landscape as art. This singular approach led to the development of landscape expressions that may have lacked practical qualities related to site conditions or community use. Such projects were often criticized for this neglect. The postmodern superficial application of past historic styles also caused concern. As postmodern landscape architecture matured landscape design became an integration of multiple principles including sustainable design, landscape as art, and regional history and culture. Examples include Hargreaves Associate's Byxbee Park, Palo Alto, California (1990), and the Louisville Waterfront Park, Louisville, Kentucky (started 1995); Hanna/Olin's Bryant Park Restoration, New York, New York (1991–94), and with Fong and Associates and Raymond Hansen Associates, the J. Paul Getty Center, Los Angeles, California (1997); Civitas' Commons Park, Denver, Colorado (2000); and Jones and Jones' Waterworks Garden, Renton, Washington (1996); as well as the master plan, coordinated under Hunter Interests, for the Río Nuevo Project in Tucson Arizona (started 2000). As this new paradigm continues to evolve, the term *new modern* is sometimes used to describe the design aesthetic that strives for deep understanding with respect to the complexities of site, region, and community. This term may be replaced with another more evocative label, but contemporary landscape architecture and garden design will continue to be shaped by numerous frameworks including art, ecology, regionalism, culture, history, past styles, lasting materials, and appropriate technology, all of which will become an interwoven fabric for creating enduring and meaningful landscapes.

See also Arnold Arboretum; Biltmore House; Brooklyn
Botanic Garden; Central Park; Dumbarton Oaks;
Huntington Library and Botanic Gardens; Missouri
Botanical Garden; Mount Auburn Cemetery; Mount
Vernon; Stanford University; Vizcaya Villa;
Williamsburg, Colonial

Further Reading
Bacon, Edmund N., *Design of Cities,* New York: Viking
Press, and London: Thames and Hudson, 1967;
revised edition, London: Thames and Hudson, 1982
Beardsley, John, *Earthworks and Beyond: Contempory
Art in the Landscape,* New York: Abbeville Press, 1984
Birnbaum, Charles A., and Christine Capella Peters,
*The Secretary of the Interior's Standards for the
Treatment of Historic Properties with Guidelines for
the Treatment of Cultural Landscapes,* Washington,
D.C.: U.S. Department of the Interior, National Park
Service, Cultural Resource Stewardship and
Partnerships, Heritage Preservation Services, Historic
Landscape Initiative, 1996
Birnbaum, Charles A., editor, *Preserving Modern
Landscape Architecture: Papers from the Wave Hill
National Park Service Conference,* Cambridge,
Massachusetts: Spacemaker Press, 1999
Birnbaum, Charles A., and Robin Karson, editors,
Pioneers of American Landscape Design, New York:
McGraw Hill, 2000
Carr, Ethan, *Wilderness by Design: Landscape
Architecture and the National Park Service,* Lincoln:
University of Nebraska Press, 1998
Crandell, Gina, and Heidi Landecker, editors, *Designed
Landscape Forum 1,* Washington, D.C.: Spacemaker
Press, 1998
Fletcher, Banister, *A History of Architecture on the
Comparative Method,* London, 1896; as *Sir Banister
Fletcher's A History of Architecture,* 19th edition,
edited by John Musgrove, London and Boston:
Butterworth Group, 1987
Francis, Mark, and Randolph Hester, *The Meaning of
Gardens: Idea, Place, and Action,* Cambridge,
Massachusetts: MIT Press, 1990
Frankel, Felice, and Jory Johnson, *Modern Landscape
Architecture: Redefining the Garden,* New York:
Abbeville Press, 1991
Haskell, Barbara, *The American Century: Art and
Culture, 1900–1950,* New York: Whitney Museum of
American Art, 1999
Hunt, John Dixon, and Peter Willis, editors, *The Genius
of the Place: The English Landscape Garden,
1620–1820,* New York: Harper and Row, and
London: Elek, 1975
Jellicoe, Geoffrey, and Susan Jellicoe, *The Landscape of
Man: Shaping the Environment from Prehistory to
the Present Day,* New York: Viking Press, and

London: Thames and Hudson, 1975; 3rd edition,
expanded and updated, New York: Thames and
Hudson, 1995
Jencks, Charles, *Post-Modernism: The New Classicism
in Art and Architecture,* New York: Rizzoli, and
London: Academy Editions, 1987
Jencks, Charles, *The New Moderns: From Late To Neo-
Modernism,* New York: Rizzoli, and London:
Academy, 1990
Karson, Robin, *Fletcher Steele, Landscape Architect:
An Account of a Gardenmaker's Life, 1885–1971,*
New York: Abrams/Sagapress, 1989
Kassler, Elizabeth B, *Modern Gardens and the
Landscape,* New York: Museum of Modern Art,
1964; revised edition, 1984
Kiley, Dan, and Jane Amidon, *Dan Kiley: The Complete
Works of America's Master Landscape Architect,*
Boston: Little Brown, 1999; as *Dan Kiley in His Own
Words: America's Master Landscape Architect,*
London: Thames and Hudson, 1999
Kostof, Spiro, *America by Design,* New York: Oxford
University Press, 1987
Landecker, Heidi, editor, *Martha Schwartz:
Transfiguration of the Commonplace,* Washington,
D.C.: Spacemaker Press, 1997
Laurie, Michael, *An Introduction to Landscape
Architecture,* New York: American Elsevier, and
London: Pitman, 1975; 2nd edition, New York:
Elsevier, 1986
Leszczynski, Nancy, *Planting the Landscape: A
Professional Approach to Garden Design,* New York:
Wiley, 1999
Lippard, Lucy R., *Overlay: Contemporary Art and the
Art of Prehistory,* New York: Pantheon, 1983
Lyall, Sutherland, *Designing the New Landscape,* New
York: Van Nostrand Reinhold, and London: Thames
and Hudson, 1991
Mann, William A., *Space and Time in Landscape
Architectural History,* Washington, D.C.: Landscape
Architecture Foundation, 1981
Moore, Charles Willard, William J. Mitchell, and
William Turnbull, Jr., *The Poetics of Gardens,*
Cambridge, Massachusetts: MIT Press, 1988
Mosser, Monique, and George Teyssot, *L'architettura
dei giardini d'Occidente,* Milan: Electa, 1990; as *The
History of Garden Design,* London: Thames and
Hudson, 1991; as *The Architecture of Western
Gardens,* Cambridge, Massachusetts: MIT Press,
1991
Newton, Norman T., *Design on the Land: The
Development of Landscape Architecture,*
Cambridge, Massachusetts: Harvard University
Press, 1971
Page, Robert R., Cathy Gilbert, and Susan Dolan, *A
Guide to Cultural Landscape Reports,* Washington

D.C.: U.S. Department of the Interior, National Park Service, Cultural Resource Stewardship and Partnerships, Park Historic Structures and Cultural Landscaps Program, 1998

Pregill, Philip, and Nancy Volkman, *Landscapes in History: Design and Planning in the Western Tradition,* New York: Van Nostrand Reinhold, 1993; as *Landscapes in History: Design and Planning in the Eastern and Western Traditions,* 2nd edition, New York: Wiley, 1999

Profiles in Landscape Architecture, Washington D.C.: American Society of Landscape Architects, 1992

Robins, Corinne, *The Pluralist Era: American Art, 1968–1981,* New York: Harper and Row, 1984

Simo, Melanie, *100 Years of Landscape Architecture: Some Patterns of a Century,* Washington, D.C.: American Society of Landscape Architects Press, 1999

Simo, Melanie, and David Dillon, *Sasaki Associates Integrated Environments,* Washington, D.C.: Spacemaker Press, 1997

Steele, Fletcher, "New Pioneering in Garden Design," *Landscape Architecture* 20, no. 3 (April 1930)

Thacker, Christopher, *The History of Gardens,* Berkeley: University of California Press, and London: Croom Helm, 1979

Tishler, William H., editor, *American Landscape Architecture: Designers and Places,* Washington, D.C.: Preservation Press, 1989

Tobey, George B., *A History of Landscape Architecture: The Relationship of People to Environment,* New York: American Elsevier, 1973

Treib, Marc, editor, *Modern Landscape Architecture: A Critical Review,* Cambridge, Massachusetts: MIT Press, 1993

Trieb, Marc, and Dorothée Imbert, *Garrett Eckbo,* Berkeley: University of California Press, 1997

Trulove, James G., editor, "Looking Back," *Landscape Architecture* 80, no. 10 (1990)

Van Valkenburgh, Michael R., curator, *Built Landscapes: Gardens in the Northeast,* Brattleboro, Vermont: Brattleboro Museum and Art Center, 1984

Van Valkenburgh, Michael R., Margaret B. Reeve, and Jory Johnson, *Transforming the American Garden: 12 New Landscape Designs,* Cambridge, Massachusetts: Harvard University Graduate School of Design, 1986

Walker, Peter, and Melanie Simo, *Invisible Gardens: The Search for Modernism in the American Landscape,* Cambridge, Massachusetts: MIT Press, 1994

Ward, Alan, *American Designed Landscapes: A Photographic Interpretation,* Washington, D.C.: Spacemaker Press, 1998

Wilkinson, Elizabeth, and Marjorie Henderson, *The House of Boughs: A Sourcebook of Garden Designs, Structures, and Suppliers,* New York: Viking Press, 1985

LAURI MACMILLAN JOHNSON

Uppsala Universitet Botaniska Trädgården

Sweden

Location: two gardens approximately 40 miles (64 km) northwest of Stockholm, in Uppsala, near royal castle; third garden at Hammarby, 9 miles (14.5 km) southeast of Uppsala

The University of Uppsala, founded in 1477, can claim to be the oldest in Scandinavia. Founded on the initiative of the archbishop primate of Uppsala, it foundered under political unrest after 30 years and was refounded as a specifically Protestant foundation with a new charter in 1595. Liberally endowed by the king, Gustavus II Adolph (r. 1611–32) and his chancellor Axel Oxenstierna, the institution flourished and under the powerful influence of its professor of medicine, the physician Olof Rudbeck, began to develop its preeminence in medical studies, which at this date still included botany.

A medical faculty had been established in 1620, and Rudbeck founded the botanical garden in 1653; a print of it appears in Rudbeck's *Atlantica* (1679). Then situated in the center of the town, the garden was near the river and was used for the teaching of botany and pharmacy, related disciplines, both then still under the umbrella of medicine. By the end of the century more than 1,800 species were being grown there, but the garden was destroyed by a great town fire in 1702, together with its 7,000 wood printing blocks to make hand-painted plates of specimens. The garden was left untended for 40 years until in 1741 Carl Linnaeus assumed charge of it as professor of medicine.

With Linnaeus to supervise the garden, Uppsala became the world center for the study of botany. He reorganized the garden to accord with his system of classification and lived with his small private zoo of animals in a corner of the garden. He sent students all over the world to examine the flora and himself led summer weekend "herbationes" with students to explore the flora of the Uppsala region.

The garden's location close to the river Fyrisån was unsuitable for gardening, as the grounds were swampy. In addition, through Linnaeus's contacts with fellow scientists around the world, the expanding plant collection needed more space. In 1787 Carl Peter Thunberg, Linnaeus's disciple and successor, persuaded King Gustav III to donate a part of his royal park to the university, which is the current site of the botanical garden. The royal park was designed in 1750 by the architect Carl Hårlemann. Gustav also donated a large sum of money, used to build the orangery building, Linneanum.

By 1807 all the plants and animals had been moved to the castle garden, and the new botanical garden was inaugurated on 21 May. The castle garden, or university botanical garden, now extends over 34 acres (14 ha), contains some 11,000 species and hybrids, and is heavily subdivided according to geographical provenance and affinity. A tropical greenhouse with approximately 4,000 species supplements the orangery. The baroque garden has itself been restored according to a plan from the 1750s. Four of Linnaeus's original laurel trees are still growing in the Linneanum.

The garden's herbaceous perennial and annual plant collections are some of the most extensive in the world. The vast collection of herbaceous perennial species were all raised from seed collected from wild plants all of known good provenance. The garden also includes a collection of garden herbaceous perennials, planted and grown as systematically as are the species. The annual plant collection includes almost 1,000 species.

The garden of which Linnaeus was himself prefect in the 18th century has been reconstructed from his original 1745 plan and is now called the Linnaeus Garden. It contains no plants not known to have been cultivated in Linnaeus's time. Oblong with a triangular extension at one end, it is split lengthwise and contains two large oblong beds lying side by side, one for annuals and biennials and the other for perennials, all arranged according to Linnaeus's sexual system. Two-thirds of the way up the garden toward the triangular extension are three ponds, two transverse oblongs containing the "river" pond and the "marsh" pond, with Linnaeus's own flower, *Linnaea borealis,* and a central star-shaped "lake" pond with white waterlilies and newts. Beyond

these are spring and autumn flower beds on either side of the semihardy plants from the orangery, which need winter shelter. Linnaeus's old home has been turned into a museum managed by the Linnaeus Society, which has handed the garden over to the university.

Together with the university botanical garden, which serves the strictly educational purposes of teaching and research, and the historically interesting reconstituted 18th-century garden of Linnaeus is a third related Uppsala University garden at Hammarby, approximately 9 miles (15 km) southeast of the town. Linnaeus bought a small estate here in 1758, and although the main building was pulled down and rebuilt in 1762, he had a small museum built to house his extensive natural history collections. His wife and two of their daughters continued living at Hammarby after his death, and in 1879 the Swedish state bought the estate from the Linnaeus family. The university now manages it as a partly open-air museum, its flower beds filled with species cultivated at Hammarby by Linnaeus. A Siberian plantation has been restored, and apple clones are cultivated for the Nordic gene bank. The Hammarby estate also contains a nature walk. The three gardens are known as the Botanska trädgården, Linnés Hammarby, and Linnéträdgården.

Synopsis

1477	University of Uppsala founded
1653	Botanical garden founded by physician Olof Rudbeck
1702	Destruction of garden, equipment, specimens, and records in town fire
1741	Carl Linnaeus appointed to University of Uppsala as professor of practical medicine and given charge of botanical garden
1758	Linnaeus acquires Hammarby estate outside Uppsala
1778	Death of Linnaeus
1787	Gift to university of castle garden site
1787–1807	Plants and animals moved from old site to new castle garden site
1807	Inauguration of new botanical garden
1879	Acquisition of Hammarby garden by Swedish state
1917	Reconstruction of Linnaeus's garden

Further Reading

Blunt, Wilfrid, *The Compleat Naturalist: A Life of Linnaeus,* London: Collins, and New York: Viking Press, 1971

Hunger, Friedrich Wilhelm Tobias, *Charles de l'Escluse (Carolus Clusius): Nederlandsch kruidkundige, 1526–1609*, Amsterdam: Nijhoff, 1927; reprint, 1943

Morren, Edouard, *Charles de l'Escluse: Sa vie et ses œuvres, 1526–1609*, Liège, Belgium: s.n., 1875

Roze, Ernest, *Charles de l'Escluse d'Arras*, Paris, 1899; reprint, S.l.: Landré et Meesters and Kew Books, 1976

ANTHONY H.T. LEVI

Urban Garden/Town Garden

The urban garden—or town garden as we know it today—has its roots in the Garden City movement of the early 20th century. Certainly in the United Kingdom the legacy of the industrial revolution of the late 18th and 19th centuries had been a dramatic increase in residential densities, urban squalor, and the elimination of garden spaces. The Garden City movement, initiated by Ebenezer Howard, championed the cause of lower-density housing, each house with its own generous garden plot, both at the front and back of the house. While the generous garden provision of early garden cities such as Letchworth and Hampstead in England is no longer widespread, the model has had profound influence on urban development internationally.

Surveys have shown that in the United Kingdom the majority of the population desire individual home ownership and tenure of a garden. In fact, studies of residents' satisfaction on urban housing estates show that this relates more to the external environment—the design, use, and maintenance of external spaces—than to the dwellings themselves.

The urban garden fulfills a wide range of roles, many of which are common to gardens in a general context but also assume special importance in towns and cities. Some of these functions are purely practical, such as provision of space for storage, clothes drying, car parking, and fruit and vegetable cultivation; however, many functions go far beyond the purely utilitarian.

Gardens in towns are associated with many potential social benefits. Private gardens are viewed as safe havens for children's play in contrast to the danger of the streets. Gardens can foster community feeling through encouraging acquaintances with neighbors, either as contact over the fence or through sharing of horticultural materials and knowledge. Gardens are now viewed as outdoor extensions of interior living space, and they have value for entertainment and outdoor leisure.

In recent times the value of urban gardens to feelings of personal well-being has been realized. Surveys have shown that the most favored attribute of the urban garden is its role in stress reduction, relaxation, and as an antidote to the pace of urban life and the harshness of the built environment. The therapeutic value of contact with nature and the act of cultivation assume special importance in cities. For many people gardens provide an outlet for creativity and personal expression.

Urban gardens, particularly the front garden, have a further use to the householder—they are a primary means for conveying a particular image to the rest of the world. As such they can enforce conformity (for example, in the United States local planning regulations can dictate the appearance and content of front gardens to maintain a particular neighborhood quality) or highlight individuality. They can be particularly important in conveying impressions of status and "territoriality."

When viewed in the context of other types of urban open space, gardens appear to be extremely important. As the smallest and most ubiquitous elements in the hierarchy of urban open spaces, private gardens offer residents a unique range of recreational opportunities: the space is accessible to all members of a household; it can be used spontaneously and without incurring travel costs; and it can be used without competition from other users (except other household members). Urban gardens also offer greater flexibility than other outdoor facilities and can be modified to meet the householder's requirements. The reduction or elimination of garden space in high-density developments can force householders to substitute some activities that cannot be carried out in public open spaces or to seek alternative locations for other activities (particularly recreational activities) and thus increase traffic burden and energy use.

While offering many benefits to the individual home owner, urban gardens have an important, wider role in enhancing environmental quality in cities. They are valuable in providing a "green" environment and have a crucial role in increasing wildlife and biodiversity. Urban gardens also offer opportunities for composting and recycling of organic waste, water retention and storage, and climate modification through greater tree cover.

Further Reading

Halkett, I.P.B., "The Recreational Use of Gardens," *Journal of Leisure Research* 10 (1978)

Kaplan, R., "Some Psychological Benefits of Gardening," *Environment and Behaviour* 5 (1973)

Kellet, J.E., "The Private Garden in England and Wales," *Landscape Planning* 9 (1982)

NIGEL DUNNETT

V

Vanbrugh, John 1664–1726

English Architect

John Vanbrugh was an architect active in England at the beginning of the 18th century and was most renowned for his two grandest buildings, Castle Howard and Blenheim Palace. He never lacked for work, yet his career was marked by many disputes, most famously that with Sarah, duchess of Marlborough. The style of his architecture was dramatic and new and seems to have been often difficult for many of his contemporaries to understand or admire. The forms he used were for the most part classical, but he also introduced into his designs elements that referred, sometimes very specifically, to traditions of Gothic and Elizabethan design and seemed to invite responses less of reasoning, as in the Renaissance theory of architecture, than of what in philosophy then was called fancy or association—as much of passion as truth, of history as of any ideal model of architecture.

Little is known of Vanbrugh's early life. In 1686 he received a military commission from the earl of Huntingdon, and in 1688 he was arrested in France for spying and subsequently imprisoned there for four years. It was then he began to write, and in 1696, four years after his release, his play *The Relapse; or, Virtue in Danger* was produced in London to great success, followed a year later by *The Provok'd Wife*. In 1704 he built a theater in the Haymarket, but by then his interests had turned to architecture.

How in 1700 he obtained the commission from the earl of Carlisle for the rebuilding of Castle Howard is not clear, but he knew the earl from their membership in the Kit-Kat Club, a group of Whigs. It was perhaps from this connection that in 1702 Vanbrugh was made comptroller of the Royal Works, becoming the colleague of Sir Christopher Wren at the Board of Works, a position he held until 1713 when he was dismissed by a new Tory government. Castle Howard was Vanbrugh's first important work, and here he was able to establish the rich, almost discordant architectural vocabulary he would use all his working life. In 1704 came the commission for Blenheim Palace, near Woodstock, the monument to the duke of Marlborough and the recent military victories over France. This was an extremely complex design, moving in its style from the grand, French manner of the north front to the plainer articulation of the parts of the garden front to the more idiosyncratic elements of the kitchen court, where emblem upon emblem of England was set around the gates and roofs. Vanbrugh also built or rebuilt a number of smaller aristocratic houses—Kings Weston, Kimbolton, Seaton Delaval, Eastbury, Grimsthorpe Castle, and Claremont—and these too were intended to speak of the history of England and, in the associative mode, to have what Vanbrugh called "the Castle air," or, as he also put it, "a Noble and Masculine shew." This was, of course, quite different from the imagery of the earlier classicizing work of Inigo Jones or of the immediately later designs of Lord Burlington and other neo-Palladian architects.

Vanbrugh's smaller designs were equally inventive, from the so-called Goose-Pie House on Whitehall to the buildings at Greenwich, including a deliberately asymmetrical house he designed for himself in the Gothic style. In the work he did after 1716 for the Board of Ordnance at various sites, including Greenwich, Chatham, Plymouth, and Upnor, he used another new style, plain and done in brick, anticipating what was to emerge in the later warehouse designs of architects such as Edward L'Anson and D.A. Alexander.

Vanbrugh himself was not a landscape gardener, and in some projects, such as Seaton Delaval and Kimbolton, he seems not to have concerned himself with anything of the surroundings. But on occasion he took great interest in the planning of the gardens of the houses he worked on, introducing something there of the asymmetry and allusion seen in his architecture. At Castle Howard he filled the grounds with pavilions and surrounded the garden with a thick, battlemented wall, marked with many Gothic details. It was at Blenheim that he first worked with Charles Bridgeman, the king's gardener, and he continued to work with Bridgeman at Eastbury, Claremont, and most notably, at Stowe. In its own way, Bridgeman's work was close to that of Vanbrugh, for he stood at the transition, in garden design, between the traditions of the French formal garden and that of the more natural garden, at a moment when there was great general interest in gardens in England and the growing idea that the house and garden be seen as artistically of a piece.

At Blenheim there was a vast park around the house and a river where Vanbrugh laid out a formal garden, a small lake with a bridge across it, and a long avenue of beeches, elements used to great effect by Lancelot "Capability" Brown when later in the century Brown laid out the magnificent natural garden to be seen there now. Similarly, at Stowe there were some formal parterres and symmetrical avenues, but within this Vanbrugh and Bridgeman introduced an asymmetry, partly derived from the shape of the estate. They also used, from France, the ha-ha, a concealed ditch that marked off the garden from the countryside without blocking the view. In arguing with the duchess of Marlborough about retaining the old, partly ruined manor of Woodstock, Vanbrugh referred to it as being something, if seen from the north front of Blenheim, that would be "One of the Most Agreable Objects that the best of Landskip Painters can invent." This sense of the picturesqueness of the garden and delight in ruins and their associations that Vanbrugh showed in this exchange was to be picked up, with similar effect, by many of the designers of the new gardens in England and throughout Europe in the later years of the 18th century.

See also Blenheim Palace; Castle Howard; Duncombe Park; Stowe

Biography

Born in London, 1664. Received military commission, 1686; arrested for spying in France and imprisoned, 1688–92; returned to England; obtained commission for the rebuilding of Castle Howard, North Yorkshire, England, 1700; comptroller of royal works, 1702–13; commissioned to design Blenheim Palace, Oxfordshire, England, 1705; worked with king's gardener, Charles Bridgeman, at Stowe, Buckinghamshire, England, and other sites. Died in London, 1726.

Selected Designs

1700–1728	Gardens and buildings, Castle Howard, North Yorkshire, England
1705–16	Gardens and buildings, Blenheim Palace, Oxfordshire, England
ca. 1719–24	Gardens (with Charles Bridgeman), Stowe, Buckinghamshire, England

Further Reading

Cast, D., "Seeing Vanbrugh and Hawksmoor," *Journal of the Society of Architectural Historians* 43 (1984)

Clarke, G.B., editor, *Descriptions of Lord Cobham's Gardens at Stowe, 1700–1750,* Aylesbury: Buckinghamshire Record Society, 1990

Dobrée, Bonamy, and Geoffrey Webb, editors, *The Complete Works of Sir John Vanbrugh,* 4 vols., London: Nonesuch Press, 1927; reprint, New York: AMS Press, 1967

Downes, Kerry, "The Kings Weston Book of Drawings," *Architectural History* 10 (1967)

Downes, Kerry, *Vanbrugh,* London: Zwemmer, 1977

Downes, Kerry, *Sir John Vanbrugh: A Biography,* London: Sidgwick and Jackson, and New York: St. Martin's Press, 1987

Green, David Bronte, *Blenheim Palace,* London: Country Life, 1951

Summerson, John, *Architecture in Britain, 1530 to 1830,* London and Baltimore, Maryland: Penguin, 1953; 9th edition, New Haven, Connecticut: Yale University Press, 1993

Vanbrugh, John, and Edward Lovett Pearce, *Architectural Drawings in the Library of Elton Hall,* edited by Howard M. Colvin and Maurice J. Craig, Oxford: Roxburghe Club, 1964

Whistler, Laurence, *Sir John Vanbrugh, Architect and Dramatist, 1664–1726,* London: Cobden-Sanderson, 1938; New York: Macmillan, 1939

Whistler, Laurence, *The Imagination of Vanbrugh and His Fellow Artists,* London: Arts and Technics, 1954

Willis, Peter, *Charles Bridgeman and the English Landscape Garden,* London: Zwemmer, 1977

DAVID CAST

Vaux, Calvert 1824–1895

English Architect and Landscape Architect

Architect and landscape designer Calvert Vaux is best known for his "pattern-book" domestic architecture, much of it built in the Hudson River Valley, and for pastoral parks ornamented with rustic gazebos, bridges, and pavilions. His partnership with Frederick Law Olmsted resulted in the creation of Central Park in New York City and Prospect Park in Brooklyn, New York, and laid the foundation for the American park movement. Vaux balanced "naked use" with beauty; his work combined landscape improvement and the spirit of republicanism with aesthetic concerns. Likened to a "poet and painter" he proposed a symbiotic handling of nature and architecture much like his colleague and arbiter of taste, Andrew Jackson Downing. In American landscape history Vaux links, both ideologically and by direct association, the work of Downing and Olmsted.

Vaux (rhymes with "fox") trained in England as an architect apprenticed to Lewis Nockalls Cottingham, who worked in the English Gothic Revival mode. Vaux's background in Gothic style and ornamentation, and an understanding of picturesque characteristics, influenced his domestic architecture. His 1857 publication *Villas and Cottages* contains variations of Gothic and Italianate designs, which employ irregularity of plan and outline, decorative verge boards, and brackets, turrets, verandas, and bay windows. Always sensitive to site and the manner in which buildings were adapted to their location, he believed that "nature should not be subservient to architectural composition." His buildings "fit" and respected the place. Vaux addressed the use of modern improvements, employing hot air furnaces, running water, and ventilators. His urban and institutional work was primarily high Victorian Gothic in flavor, evoking the polychrome stonework advocated by John Ruskin, including the Metropolitan Museum of Art, New York City (1874–80), and buildings for the Children's Aid Society (1879–92). Typical of the mid- to late 19th century, Vaux's work was a free interpretation of historical sources, adapted to site and use. An exercise in Islamic-Persian exoticism, his design for artist Frederic Church's house, Olana, overlooking the Hudson River, is an example of Vaux's ability to accommodate patron and place.

The ideological link between Downing and Vaux can be traced to English precedent. The picturesque aesthetic as defined by Sir Uvedale Price provided a reference for their ideas. Their interest in aesthetics and good taste reflects the recommendations of John Claudius Loudon, who shaped the field via his writings on suburban gardening, the laying out of public spaces, and in his architectural periodical. Loudon's seminal public parks, along with those of Joseph Paxton, provided models for Vaux to emulate. Vaux was particularly competent in the design and ornamentation of "tasty embellishments," garden architecture such as bridges, benches, and pavilions that provided artistic expression. Landscape projects included the grounds for Grace Church, New York City (1881), and for New York's Trinity Cemetery (ca. 1881). His understanding of larger design concerns is evident in the planned residential neighborhood of Riverside, Illinois (1868), outside Chicago.

The partnership of Vaux and Olmsted constitutes one of the more important associations of American landscape history. Of their joint projects, Central Park (1858–76) is their most famous. Vaux's proposal to Olmsted that they coauthor the "Greensward" plan for the park competition resulted in their winning entry, which was adopted in 1858. As partners in the general design, their contributions were "mutual, equal and indivisible," with Olmsted's work in an administrative capacity and Vaux overseeing artistic concerns. Conceived as an urban oasis and democratic space, the park was considered by *Harper's Monthly* (1862) to be the country's finest work of art, one that allowed visitors to "drive out of the city into the landscape." This successful handling of "Nature first and 2d and 3d—Architecture after a while" remains a masterful combination of vistas, lawns, and picturesque, rocky outcroppings intersected by vehicular and pedestrian circulation routes. Of all the architectural elements that decorate the park, the culminating achievement may be the classical terrace that terminates the promenade and serves as the park's formal centerpiece.

The 19th-century interest in urban parks prompted the popular success of Manhattan's Central Park and inspired similar undertakings, including one in nearby Brooklyn. Prospect Park (1866–73) is less well known but considered to be Vaux and Olmsted's finest artistic achievement. Spanning 526 acres (213 ha) (smaller than Central Park), its irregular shape dictated a particularly successful plan. (Unlike the long narrow rectangle of Central Park, Prospect Park's shape is reminiscent of Paxton's Birkenhead Park, England.) The Brooklyn park's three main components are the Long Meadow (a 90-acre [36-ha] manifestation of "the beautiful"), rugged, picturesque spots meant for "rambles," and a 60-acre (24-ha) spring-fed lake. The organization of plantings within the park heightens the physical and visual experience of the visitor: in the Long Meadow there is a rhythmic progression through space as the viewer is led into and through openings created by "gates" of trees. Knotty cedar arbors, sheltered seats of sassafras logs, and the cast-iron Concert Grove Pavilion of Hindu-Oriental flavor were ornamental additions. One of many tunnels and bridges, the Cleftridge Span was constructed of a new stonelike concrete, the interior richly patterned in polychrome block.

Assessing Vaux's contributions to the field is complicated by the fact that he worked with partners most of his professional life. Besides the business partnerships of Downing and Vaux, and Olmsted, Vaux, and Company, he worked with architects Frederick Clarke Withers and Jacob Wrey Mould, engineer George K. Radford, and landscape architect Samuel Parsons, Jr. Understandably, there is a question of precise authorship and creative accountability in the projects these partnerships produced. Recent scholarship has reassessed Vaux and his work, in particular, the long-held perception that he served as an assistant to Olmsted on the Central Park project. Olmsted's precise words prove the contrary. Although Vaux's early career has been studied, his later landscape and architectural work has yet to be assessed in depth. His solutions for urban apartment blocks (labeled by him "Parisian buildings") and tenement housing remain to be put into context. Vaux's training as an architect never eclipsed his vision as an artist who shaped the landscape. In this regard it is fitting he was the first professional to embrace and use the title of "landscape architect."

See also Central Park

Biography
Born in London, England, 20 December 1824. Attended Merchant Taylors' School, London; apprenticed to architect Lewis Nockalls Cottingham, 1839; hired as assistant by Andrew Jackson Downing, in London; departed for United States, 1850, and became Downing's partner; met Frederick Law Olmsted at Downing's home in Newburgh, New York, 1851; married Mary Swan McEntee, 1854 (four children); after Downing's death in 1852, continued to design rural residences at Newburgh office until move to New York City, 1856; published *Villas and Cottages,* 1857; worked as consulting architect and landscape architect adviser to board for Central Park, 1858–73; during 1860s and until 1872, in partnership with Frederick Law Olmsted, designing grounds and structures for major parks throughout United States, including Central Park and Prospect Park, New York, and park system for Buffalo, New York (1868–76), campus of University of California, Berkeley (1866), and South Park, Chicago (1871–73); served as landscape architect for city of New York, 1881–83 and 1888–95; later years were spent designing urban and institutional architecture (often with G.K. Radford) and designing landscapes in collaboration with Samuel Parsons, Jr. Died Brooklyn, New York, 19 November 1895.

Selected Designs

1850	Study for Springside, Matthew Vassar house (with A.J. Downing), Poughkeepsie, New York, United States (never executed)
1853	The Point, Lydig M. Hoyt house, Staatsburg, New York, United States
1858–76	Central Park (with F.L. Olmsted), New York City, New York, United States
1866–73	Prospect Park (with F.L. Olmsted), Brooklyn, New York, United States
1868	Town plan (with F.L. Olmsted), Riverside, Illinois, United States
1868–76	Park system (with F.L. Olmsted), Buffalo, New York, United States
1870	*Olana* (with F.C. Withers), Frederic E. Church house, Hudson, New York, United States
1872–78	American Museum of Natural History (with J.W. Mould), New York City, New York, United States
1873	Pavilion (with G.K. Radford), Centennial Exhibition, Philadelphia, Pennsylvania, United States
1873–79	Grounds, parliament buildings, Ottawa, Canada
1874–80	Metropolitan Museum of Art (with J.W. Mould), New York City, New York, United States
1876	Pavilions, Congress Park, Saratoga Springs, New York, United States
1881	Grounds, Grace Church, New York City, New York, United States
ca. 1881	Grounds, Trinity Cemetery, New York City, New York, United States
1882	Improved Dwelling Association Model Tenement (with G.K. Radford), New York City, New York, United States
1887	Downing Park (with F.L. Olmsted), Newburgh, New York, United States

Selected Publications
"Should a Republic Encourage the Arts?" *Horticulturalist* 7 (February 1852)

"American Architecture," *Horticulturalist* 8 (February 1853)

"Hints for Country House Builders," *Harper's New Monthly Magazine* 11 (November 1855)

"Parisian Buildings for City Residences," *Harper's Weekly* 1 (December 1857)

Villas and Cottages: A Series of Designs Prepared for Execution in the United States, 1857; 2nd edition, 1864

"A Plea for the Artistic Unity of Central Park," *New York Times* (27 August 1879)

"Landscape Gardening," in *Encyclopaedia Britannica: Supplement,* 1886

"Street Planning in Relation to Architectural Design," *Proceedings of the Architectural League of New York* (1889)

Further Reading

Alex, William, and George B. Tatum, *Calvert Vaux: Architect and Planner,* New York: Ink, 1994

"Calvert Vaux, Designer of Parks," *Park International* (September 1920)

Creese, Walter, "Calvert Vaux," in *American Landscape Architecture: Designers and Places,* edited by William H. Tishler, Washington, D.C.: Preservation Press, 1989

Francis, Dennis S., and Joy Kestenbaum, "Calvert Vaux," in *The MacMillan Encyclopedia of Architects,* edited by Adolf K. Placzek, vol. 4, New York: Free Press, and London: Collier MacMillan, 1982

Kowsky, Francis R., *Country, Park, and City: The Architecture and Life of Calvert Vaux, 1824–1895,* New York: Oxford University Press, 1997

"Return to Splendor: Oriental Pavilion, Prospect Park, Brooklyn, New York," *Architectural Record* 77, no. 8 (July 1989)

Rosenzweig, Roy, and Elizabeth Blackmar, *The Park and the People: A History of Central Park,* Ithaca, New York: Cornell University Press, 1992; London, 1998

Schuyler, David, and Jane Turner Censer, editors, *The Years of Olmsted, Vaux, and Company,* Baltimore, Maryland: Johns Hopkins University Press, 1992

Sigle, John D., "Calvert Vaux, an American Architect," master's thesis, University of Virginia, 1967

Stewart, John J., "Notes on Calvert Vaux's 1873 Design for the Public Grounds of the Parliament Buildings in Ottawa," *Bulletin of the Association for Preservation Technology* 8, no. 1 (1976)

Toole, Robert M., "Illustrated and Set to Music: The Picturesque Crescendo at Idlewild," *Journal of the New England Garden History Society* 4 (Spring 1996)

CAROL GROVE

Vaux-le-Vicomte

Seine-et-Marne, France

Location: a few miles east of Melun, southeast of Paris, on the D215 to Champeaux, Junction 15 on the A5 (E54) motorway

Vaux-le-Vicomte is the perfect example of the classical French garden of the 17th century and the first great one to be designed by André Le Nôtre. It demonstrates what could be achieved at the time by a team of highly skilled professional designers and artists, working in the classical tradition, when given a free hand and unlimited resources. Vaux-le-Vicomte is almost an abstract work of art, monumental in scale, where all the elements are integrated into the overall conception. Humans become insignificant here; it was built for the gods. And herein lay its initial downfall.

Vaux-le-Vicomte was created by Nicolas Fouquet, who inherited a small estate there from his father in 1640. Fouquet was a highly cultured "Renaissance man," a patron of the arts, and a favorite of Louis XIV's chief minister, Cardinal Mazarin, who made him joint superintendent of finance, along with Abel Servien, in 1653. Huge wealth and grandiose ideas followed: Ser-

vien built Meudon, Fouquet outdid him with Vaux-le-Vicomte. Fouquet already had a house, Saint-Mandé, near Vincennes, which had a 30-acre (12-ha) garden of standard Renaissance layout, filled with statues, fountains, rare plants, and 200 orange trees. Vaux-le-Vicomte, however, offered him the chance to do something on an altogether greater scale.

An artistic team of the highest quality was assembled to carry out the project of building a magnificent château, set in monumental grounds, which established a new and very high standard for such properties. The architect, Louis Le Vau, was the first to be hired; he was asked to draw up plans in 1655. Fouquet left the design to him but stipulated that the grounds were to be laid out by Le Nôtre, who was taken on in 1657. In 1658 the artist Charles Le Brun was contracted to carry out a sculpture program for the grounds. The genius of the scheme that these three men produced is in its integration; the château lies at the core of a hierarchy of scale, axes, and sight lines. Views and levels are carefully controlled to give an illusion of symmetry and enormous scale and to provide surprise. Water, which is a dominant element in

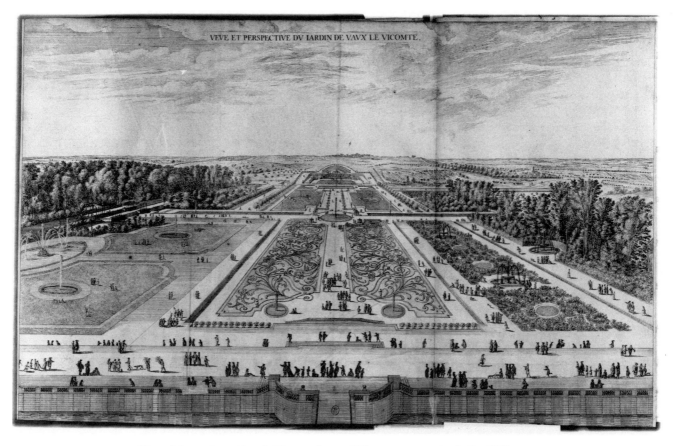

View of the garden at Vaux-le-Vicomte, from a 17th-century engraving by Israël Silvestre
Courtesy of Bibliothèque Nationale de France

the gardens, was also carefully integrated, the 1,200 fountains and complex waterworks being the work of Claude Robillard. Michel Anguier and Lespagnandel carved the sculptures, and the herm statues that originally decorated the parterres and other parts of the garden were designed by Nicolas Poussin. The role of plants, in particular trees, was mainly a structural one of controlling vistas and providing backdrops. However, there were areas of the gardens where flowers dominated, and the final key member of the creative team was Antoine Trumel, who had responsibility for the planting.

The gardens were laid out in an astonishingly short period, from 1657 to 1661. The cost was over 10 million francs, and the work force numbered as many as 18,000. The ground was uneven and gently sloping down to the small valley of the river Angueil, which ran east-west across the site. Much leveling took place, and three villages—Vaux-le-Vicomte itself, Jumeau, and Maison Rouge—were removed. Le Nôtre's design is dominated by a main axis, which runs north-south through the outer and inner forecourts, the center of the château, and the center of the gardens. The layout is not symmetrical but balanced about this axis. There are several transverse axes, which are of great importance to the scheme.

Although restored and in places simplified, Le Nôtre's gardens survive. The layout begins with a highly ornamented zone nearest the château, the central axis flanked by elaborate, mirror-image *parterres de broderie* in box on a background of crushed brick. To the right (west), looking from the château, is a formal flower garden backed by a bosquet; to the left, down a level, is a wider, simple parterre with an oval pool and gilt crown fountain—the Basin de la Couronne. Le Nôtre's subtle landscaping means that this area can be read as a unified whole either from the central axis or from left to right. The first transverse axis, at the end of this zone, has a round pool in the center, flanked by paths and canals. To the right the path leads to a gate into the kitchen garden (*potager*); to the left it terminates in the great broad steps of the Grille d'Eau. Originally these were flanked and crossed by rows of fountains, but the water has not been restored. The central walk continues, flanked by simple parterres and pools, outer paths and bosquets, and terminates at a large rectangular reflecting basin, the Arpent d'Eau, which covers about an acre (0.4 ha). The walk here was originally called the Allée d'Eau, as it was flanked by rows of fountains, now gone, which the novelist Mlle de Scudéry likened to a crystal balustrade. A transverse axis runs through the Arpent d'Eau and flanking pools to the "Confessional" to the right. This is a raised stone terrace, reached by flanking steps, with a three-arched cryptoporticus (partially concealed gallery) beneath it.

It is not until this part of the garden is reached that the masterstroke becomes apparent: hidden below is a vast, 900-meter-long (984-yd.) canal, the former river Angueil, forming one of the greatest transverse axes in the history of garden making. The coup de théâtre is heightened by the two great opposing water features on the main axis—on the near side, the Grandes Cascades, a recessed monumental wall of tiered cascades, and on the far side, the grotto. This is of a similar scale, with seven alcoves containing rockwork cascades, flanked by recesses containing representations of giant reclining river gods. Flanking steps lead to a terrace and pool above, with a central jet of water, La Gerbe, rising to over five meters (5.5 yds). The noise from all these fountains increases the sense of climax.

On the far side of the canal the central axis climbs the gentle slope above the grotto as a grass walk flanked by "wings" of woodland. At the top is the giant figure of the Farnese Hercules, leaning on his club. From the château and parterres the central axis appears to run continuously from the main walk up the slope to Hercules. Such was Le Nôtre's genius with optical illusion.

The date of 17 August 1661 was the famous and fateful day on which Fouquet entertained the king, Louis XIV, his mistress, and court at a fete at Vaux-le-Vicomte, the sumptuous extravagance of which excelled anything the king could contrive. In the gardens the king was offered ballets, Molière's play *Les Fâcheux* (with scenery by Le Brun), and spectacular fireworks and illuminations; an artificial whale appeared to rise from the canal. Molière was given only 15 days' notice and clearly wrote the play to be performed in the Vaux-le-Vicomte gardens; at one point in his prologue, stage directions indicate that dryads, fauns, and satyrs were to emerge from behind trees and the herm statues. Jean-Baptiste Colbert, ambitious assistant to Mazarin and jealous of Fouquet, had already sown the seeds of Fouquet's downfall, but this extreme demonstration of wealth and artistic patronage, far beyond any the king himself could command at that time, sealed his fate. Three weeks later Fouquet was arrested. He never saw Vaux-le-Vicomte again and spent the rest of his days languishing in the fortress of Pignerol.

Vaux-le-Vicomte then entered a period of plunder and neglect. Almost immediately the king began to purloin whatever he could remove: trees and shrubs from the nurseries, statuary, and most important, the creators themselves—Le Vau, Le Nôtre, and Le Brun—who were to be instrumental in the creation of Versailles, the royal riposte to Vaux-le-Vicomte. The king also plundered Fouquet's other garden, Saint-Mandé, removing its statuary and orange trees to Versailles. Poussin's herms went to Versailles in 1684, and the Hercules was removed by Colbert to his own château of Sceaux after 1670. In 1705 Vaux-le-Vicomte was sold to Marshal de Villars, whose son sold the lead of the waterworks. In 1764 the estate was bought by the Duc de Choiseul-Praslin, whose family continued there until the mid-19th century, when the last of the family committed suicide. A savior finally arrived in 1875 in the form of Alfred Sommier, a wealthy industrialist, who set about restoring the gardens with the help of the garden restorer Henri Duchêne. Much reconstruction work was necessary, but the bones of the garden remained. Some of the fountains were abandoned, but life was breathed back into the whole. A new Hercules was installed in place of the original. The work was continued by Duchêne's son Edmé, and in the late 20th century his great-grandson, Comte Patrice de Vogüé, kept up this noble family tradition.

The gardens of Vaux-le-Vicomte occupy a central position in the development of the grand, classical French garden. It was there that Le Nôtre developed his fully fledged, mature style, where the integration of architecture and garden reached its apotheosis and a team of professionals worked together to create a single work of art. Versailles stands firmly on the shoulders of Vaux-le-Vicomte.

Synopsis

1640	Nicolas Fouquet inherits Vaux-le-Vicomte
1655	Louis Le Vau asked by Fouquet to draw up plans
1657	André Le Nôtre hired to design gardens
1658	Charles Le Brun hired to design sculpture program
1661	Gardens finished on 17 August; Fouquet hosts sumptuous fete for Louis XIV in château and grounds; three weeks later Fouquet arrested by d'Artagnan, captain of the king's musketeers, and imprisoned for life
1665	Sale of contents begins
ca. 1670	Hercules statue moved by Colbert to Sceaux
1680	Fouquet dies in fortress of Pignerol
1684	Herm statues, designed by Poussin, moved from gardens to Versailles
1705	Vaux sold to Marshal de Villars
1764	Bought by Duc de Choiseul-Praslin
1875	Bought by Alfred Sommier, who restores gardens with help of Henri Duchêne;

Vaux-le-Vicomte remains in family's ownership

Further Reading
Adams, William Howard, *The French Garden, 1500–1800,* London: Scolar Press, and New York: Braziller, 1979
France, Anatole, and Jean Cordey, *Le chateau de Vaux-le-Vicomte,* Paris: Calmann-Lévy, 1933

Hazlehurst, F. Hamilton, *Gardens of Illusion: The Genius of André Le Nostre,* Nashville, Tennessee: Vanderbilt University Press, 1980
Woodbridge, Kenneth, *Princely Gardens: The Origins and Development of the French Formal Style,* London: Thames and Hudson, and New York: Rizzoli, 1986

ELISABETH WHITTLE

Vegetable Garden

In horticulture a vegetable is defined as an edible herbaceous plant commonly used for culinary purposes. Some vegetables can be eaten only after they are cooked, while others are eaten either cooked or raw. Therefore, anything that has to do with the growing of vegetables is popularly known as vegetable gardening. In general, vegetable gardening is usually considered a part of horticulture. However, certain vegetables, such as potatoes, that are grown in large areas alongside general farm crops are often included as a branch of agriculture rather than horticulture. Traditionally, vegetable gardens were viewed as being in one of two categories: commercial gardens or home or amateur gardens. Today, the term is most often associated with the home or amateur garden.

The earliest known cultivation of vegetables dates back to approximately 7000 B.C., with the peoples of Central America, who cultivated corn and other crops. Another early vegetable that was cultivated rather than simply growing wild was cabbage. These cabbages were cultivated by the pre-Celtic people of western Europe. Other early vegetable examples include the Greeks' growing of celery, which was mentioned in the *Odyssey,* and onions, which were grown in ancient Egyptian gardens.

Archaeological evidence dating to 4800 B.C. in Tehuacan, in south-central Mexico, shows that squash, maize, chili peppers, and avocados were cultivated. Archaeologists have also found evidence from the Ingus Valley region in Mesopotamia dating to 4000 B.C. that demonstrates extensive agricultural activity by the Sumerians, including crops such as peas, wheat, sesame seed, and barley. The Sumerians also developed scientific irrigation, which made such agriculture possible. In addition, evidence from 2000 B.C. shows that Native American civilizations of Mexico and the Andes grew many varieties of corn, beans, squash, and sunflowers and that they used many wild plants as foods as well. It is also believed that they created the tomato from wild species.

However, such early cultivation was very different from the vegetable gardens we think of today. Vegetable gardens as they are known today have their origins in ancient Egypt, whose vegetable gardens were part of a complete and elaborately planned garden. These early Egyptian gardens were planted in rectangles and lined with trees, grapevines, and vegetables.

During the Hellenistic period, the seventh century B.C., wealthy Greeks had extensive gardens, which included kitchen gardens in enclosed or walled courtyards and vegetable gardens that contained culinary and medicinal herbs. These vegetable and kitchen gardens continued well into the fifth century A.D.

From the second to the sixth century A.D., simple gardens resembling what were later called cottage gardens, and containing fruit trees, were also used extensively. These gardens contained vegetable and salad gardens, as well as some flowers. Descriptions of these gardens can be found in the romance novels of the time.

Early Roman gardens were predominantly fruit and vegetable gardens, called *hortus.* The typical *hortus* contained asparagus, beets, endive, leeks, and cabbage. The *hortus* was used not only to feed one's family but also as a market garden or kitchen garden to earn money. It was out of these kitchen gardens that the *villa rustica* of the wealthier Italian classes later developed. The *villa rustica* was a country house and garden that provided fruit, wine, and vegetables.

During the Middle Ages in Europe, monasteries became the centers of horticulture. As such, they were the first to include vegetable gardens, specifically kitchen gardens. They took over the tradition of the *villa rusticas* of early Rome and supported their communities with their fruits and vegetables. These gardens are exemplified by the Swiss monastery St. Gall, which includes a large vegetable garden consisting of 18 raised beds arranged in a square. Archaeologists have also found evidence in England of vegetables being grown in

An example of a vegetable garden, ca. 1754, from the *Encyclopédie* of Diderot and d'Alembert
Courtesy of Mary Evans Picture Library

the ninth and tenth centuries by the Vikings. Some of the Viking crops included carrots, parsnips, turnips, celery, spinach, brassicas, and cabbage.

Not until the 13th century did interest in vegetable gardening really begin to spread throughout Europe. This was due in part to the publication in 1260 of *De vegetabilibus* by Albert Magnus. The vegetable garden was also part of the gardens designed by noted Florentine architect Leon Battista Alberti, who wrote a textbook on gardening in the 1440s. Alberti's ideal garden design included a vegetable garden on the hillside beyond the straight, square flower and green garden.

World exploration also exerted a strong influence on the vegetable gardens of Europe. Columbus and the explorers who followed him were impressed with the abundance and uniqueness of the vegetables found in the New World. Some of the new vegetables and plants introduced to Europe from the Americas included tomatoes, beans, chili peppers, avocados, corn, pumpkins, squash, and sweet potatoes.

In the 14th century gardening began to spread from the noble classes to the lower classes. Just as in Italy, the French gardens of the day also included box-edged beds for vegetables. Gardening in England, including vegeta-

ble gardening, remained rather limited until the late 15th century.

During the Renaissance vegetable gardens in France were carefully planned as part of the entire garden. On one side of an alley of trees stood a square vegetable garden or kitchen garden with an entrance into the house and an entrance into the orchard beyond. The vegetables were grown in long beds with walks approximately 0.6-meters (0.66 yd.13) wide between them. Some of the beds contained table vegetables; others held pot herbs and physic herbs. The vegetables grown in this kitchen garden included leeks, garlic, turnips, and carrots. One of the grandest examples of French vegetable gardens can be found at Versailles. The enormous formal *potager* (fruit and vegetable garden) at Versailles was designed by Jean de La Quintinie, whose book on gardening was translated in 1693 by John Evelyn as *The Compleat Gardener. Potagers* spread from the French court to the French countryside, particularly to the gardens of the small country estate, in which the *potager's* beds were edged with flowers and included onions, turnips, radishes, beans, and asparagus. The style of the *potagers* also spread to other parts of Europe, including Italy and England.

The English gardens of the time featured very different vegetables than those found today, consisting mainly of pot herbs such as marjoram, sage, rosemary, and thyme. The herbs were grown in a private physic garden, on artificial hills to save space and to provide a variety of herbs. In 1629 John Parkinson published what is considered the first great English gardening book, *Paradisi in sole, Paradisus Terrestris*. In it he recommends that the English garden feature a kitchen or vegetable garden "furnished with herbs, roots and fruits for meat or sauce with us."

It was also during the 17th century that the first book devoted solely to vegetable gardening was published: Richard Gardiner's *Profitable Instructions for the Manuring, Sowing, and Planting of Kitchen Gardens* (1603). His ideal garden featured carrots, lettuce, beans, beets, turnips, peas, beets, cabbage, onions, parsnips, and gourds, as well as salad, stewing, and sauce herbs.

In the American colonies during the 17th century, agriculture dominated the use of the land, and early settlers focused on food crops, rather than planting pleasure gardens. Not surprisingly, their gardens resembled those from their homes in Europe, and during the early part of the century, herb, salads, and vegetable seeds were still being imported from Europe. They also planted wild forest and meadow plants. Early vegetable gardens typically contained pot herbs on one side of the path and vegetables such as turnips, parsnips, carrots, radishes, cucumbers, and onions on the other. By 1646 gardens and orchards were so commonplace that a law was passed punishing those who robbed them.

The use of imported seeds to North America from England, Holland, and France continued until the middle of the 18th century when in 1784 the first commercial seed-growing business was established in Philadelphia by David Landreth. He began to supply colonists with tomatoes, artichokes, cauliflower, eggplant, rhubarb, and sweet corn. Others followed suit, and soon seed companies sprang up in Philadelphia and New York.

It was in 18th-century England that the idea of vegetable gardening as we know it today was first initiated. Although the herb garden was still an important part of gardens, a square parcel containing medicinal plants and vegetables was now being featured. In the early part of the century, truck or market gardeners began growing many more kinds of vegetables and began to produce them out of season. It was also in England, on 1 January 1721, that a nurseryman presented George I with the first cucumber raised under glass.

In addition, new plants brought from explorers and plant traders were being used in gardens. The average garden contained beds of pot or kitchen herbs used for stewing and stuffing and in salads. English gardeners also began raising vegetables such as potatoes, artichokes, French beans, carrots, spinach, kidney beans, and sweet potatoes. Eventually, as the taste for vegetables increased, the kitchen garden grew and the herb garden diminished.

Both the English cottage gardens and the gardens of New England featured mixed flowers, vegetables, herbs, and salad, and were usually in front of the house, fenced or walled in. American kitchen gardens from 1600 to 1800 were planted based on astrology; they featured many herbs and included raised beds and fences to keep animals out.

In the United States vegetable gardens varied by region. In New England there were special beds for each vegetable or an association of vegetables. In the north rows were simply laid out straight across between side paths. In the south formal squares and borders were used extensively. However, the vegetables grown were similar in all of the regions. Regardless of the layout, the kitchen or vegetable garden was separate from the flower garden. Vegetables and herbs were usually planted in an area that was easily accessible to the house. There were no separate herb gardens; rather, culinary herbs were included with the vegetables. The most common vegetables found in early American gardens were artichokes, asparagus, beans, cabbage, carrots, celery, parsley, cucumber, broccoli, cauliflower, watercress, chamomile, endive, shallot, lavender, fennel, lettuce, horseradish, marjoram, onion, mint, parsnips, peas, spinach, sage, thyme, radishes, and turnip. The tomato was introduced later to American gardens because it was believed to be deadly. Not until 1820 was this myth proven untrue.

The first popular U.S. seed catalog was written by Bernard McMahon in 1804. He followed this with "The American Gardener's Calendar" in 1806, which listed 67 kitchen-garden vegetables. The popularity of American vegetable and kitchen gardens reached its peak in the mid-19th century. In 1867 Peter Henderson wrote *Gardening for Profit*, which focused on marketing and selling one's garden crops. Another popular book of the time was *The Southern Farmer and Market-Gardener* (1842) by Francis S. Holmes. In addition, the increasing demand for a steady supply of vegetables led to the use of greenhouses in both the colder seasons and in states with colder climates.

By the end of the 19th and beginning of the 20th centuries, the design of vegetable gardens, like all other types of gardens, was no longer inspired only by the designs of architects but by amateur botanists and gardeners themselves.

In the 1930s the herb garden began to reappear in the United States. Much of this appeal was attributed to an interest in herbs for cooking. In addition there was the increasing recognition that plants, particularly herbs, played a vital role in one's health. During the 1930s several books on herb growing and cooking were published.

In the United States vegetable gardening became extremely popular during the 1940s, due mostly to World War II. For example, in 1942, 40 percent of all vegetables were produced in so-called victory gardens. By the end of the 1940s and the war's end, gardening as a hobby took on an increased role. This trend continued as more and more people moved to the suburbs in the 1950s.

By the end of the 1960s the environmental movement had also led to an increased interest in gardening and organic produce. In addition the 1970s saw a resurgence in culinary herbs. By the mid-1970s gardening magazines, books, and television programs were widely available, which helped the amateur gardener grow better fruits and vegetables. Television shows such as the *Victory Garden*, which debuted in 1974, helped spur interest in vegetable gardening. In addition Bernard McMahon's 1857 *McMahon's American Gardener* was reprinted in 1976. In 1996 the *Kitchen Garden Magazine* debuted, focusing on growing and cooking with home-grown herbs and vegetables.

Further Reading

Arkin, Frieda, *The Essential Kitchen Gardener*, New York: Holt, 1990

Clarke, Ethne, *The Art of the Kitchen Garden*, New York: Knopf, 1987

Gorer, Richard, *The Growth of Gardens*, Boston: Faber, 1978

Leighton, Ann, *Early American Gardens: For Meate or Medicine*, Boston: Houghton Mifflin; as *Early English Gardens in New England: "For Meats or Medicine,"* London: Cassell, 1970

Leighton, Ann, *American Gardens in the Eighteenth Century: "For Use or for Delight,"* Boston: Houghton Mifflin, 1976

M'Mahon, Bernard, *The American Gardener's Calendar*, Philadelphia, Pennsylvania, 1857; reprint, as *McMahon's American Gardener*, New York: Funk and Wagnalls, 1976

Tucker, David M., *Kitchen Gardening in America: A History*, Ames: Iowa State University Press, 1993

Wright, Richardson Little, *The Story of Gardening: From the Hanging Gardens of Babylon to the Hanging Gardens of New York*, New York: Dodd Mead, and Garden City, and London: Routledge, 1934

JUDITH GERBER

Veitch Family

Scottish Family of Nurserymen

From the late 18th century to the middle of the 20th century, the Veitch nurserymen pushed back the frontiers of horticulture. They were active in the fields of plant hunting, publishing, exhibiting, and training, as well as developing a commercially successful empire and supporting the great horticultural institutions of the day. Of Norman descent, the family was living in Jedburgh, Scotland, at the time of the birth of John Veitch (1752–1839), the founder of the nursery firm. Following early horticultural experience at an Edinburgh nursery, John came south to London, working in a nursery garden until summoned to Killerton in Devon to lay out a park for Sir Thomas Dyke Acland. This early landscaping project was so successful that, during the latter part of the 18th century, John continued to take on commissions, including planting works at Luscombe Castle and Poltimore House, Devon, while working as land steward for the Acland Estates.

At the beginning of the 19th century, John Veitch established his own Killerton Nursery at Budlake, moving the business closer to Exeter, Mount Radford, in 1832. This move marked the beginning of the renowned Exeter Nursery. John's son, James Veitch (1792–1863), was by this time a partner in the firm, taking over in 1837, two years before his father died. In 1838 James Veitch, Jr. (1815–69), joined his father as a partner, and the firm was renamed James Veitch and Son. Their business acumen and horticultural skill quickly ensured them a reputation both at home and abroad. From early times James had realized the importance of searching for new and exotic plants and sent many plant hunters abroad. The Lobb brothers, Thomas and William, were two of the earliest and most successful travelers commissioned by him. In 1840 William set out for South America bringing back species such as *Berberis darwinii*, *Desfontainia spinosa*, *Embothrium coccineum*, *Escallonia macrantha*, and *Lapageria rosa*. He also collected seed from the monkey puzzle tree (*Aruacaria araucana*) and then, in California, from the *Sequoiadendron giganteum*, both of which were later established in Great Britain. His brother William was equally successful, traveling to Burma and the East Indies in 1843 and bringing back a wonderful range of orchids, hoyas, and rhododendrons.

On 16 April 1853 a London branch was added to the firm when James, Jr., acquired the already famous Royal Exotic Nursery of Knight and Perry at King's Road, Chelsea. The two nurseries were run together—James Veitch remaining in Exeter, and his son managing the London nursery until the elder Veitch died in 1863. James, Jr.'s, younger brother, Robert (1823–85), took over the Exeter firm, eventually moving to new premises and running it as a separate enterprise from 1864.

In Chelsea the Royal Exotic Nursery prospered, becoming the leading nursery in Great Britain. James Veitch, Jr. was not only a gifted nurseryman but was also dedicated to promoting the great horticultural organizations of the time. He was a trustee of the Gardeners' Royal Benevolent Institution and a member of the Council of the Royal Horticultural Society (RHS) from 1856 to 1864. Like the Exeter Nursery, the Chelsea Nursery became famous for new plant introductions, not only through plant hunting but by pioneering the hybridization of orchids, becoming one of the greatest orchid suppliers of the time. The first hybrid orchid, *Calanthe* × *dominii*, from *C. masuca* and *C. furcata*, was raised there in 1856 by one of its nurserymen, John Dominy. In later years his successor, John Seden, produced 490 hybrid plants including orchids, tuberous begonias, and roses.

Fame for the Chelsea Nursery was also garnered by James, Jr.'s, eldest son, John Gould Veitch (1839–70), who traveled through Japan, China, and the Philippines and later in Australia and the Pacific. Japan had only recently opened up to the West, and John Gould was one of the first Europeans to reach the summit of Mount Fujiyama. He brought back *Acer palmatum, Magnolia* × *soulangeana* 'Nigra', *Parthenocissus tricuspidata* 'Veitchii', the Japanese umbrella pine (*Sciadopitys verticillata*), and the spectacular golden ray lily of Japan (*Lilium auratum*).

In 1863 the nursery acquired land at Coombe Wood, Kingston Hill, Surrey, a site that was to specialize in hardy trees and shrubs, herbaceous perennials, and water plants. Further branches were added at Langley, near Slough and Feltham in Middlesex, to allow more experimental work, in particular with fruit trees and seeds. John Gould and his brother Harry James (1840–1924) became partners with their father in 1865, unfortunately for only a few years as John died at his home in Coombe Wood at the early age of 31, a year after his own father, leaving Harry to continue the nurseries with the help of his younger brother, Arthur (1844–80). On James Veitch, Jr.'s, death the RHS instituted the Veitch Memorial Medal, an annual award to be presented to a person who had made an outstanding contribution to horticulture in Great Britain.

Under the enthusiastic and inspiring leadership of Harry James, the Veitch empire prospered. During the period 1877–79 Charles Maries collected for the nursery from Japan and China, introducing species such as *Abies veitchii, Hamamelis mollis, Iris kaempferi,* and *Primula obconica.* The intrepid E.H. Wilson also worked for Veitch in China during the years 1899–1905 and introduced hundreds of seeds and plants to England, the most notable including *Davidia involucrata, Meconopsis integrifolia, Buddleia davidii* 'Veitchiana', and *Clematis montana* var. *rubens.*

The firm also ventured into publishing, producing a number of well-respected reference works, including *A Manual of the Coniferae* (1881) and *Manual of Orchidaceous Plants Cultivated under Glass in Great Britain,* first issued in nine parts between 1887 and 1894. John Gould's elder son, James Herbert Veitch (1868–1907), published *A Traveller's Notes* (1896) after plant hunting in Japan, Korea, China, India, and Australia. The most important work, *Hortus Veitchii* (1906), a history of the house of Veitch, was compiled by James Herbert's younger brother, John G. Veitch (1869–1914), and covers the development of the nurseries, the plant hunters, the hybridists, and the plants introduced.

Like his father, Harry was a council member of the RHS (1888–89, 1897–1919). He received the RHS Victoria Medal of Honor (VMH) for his services in 1906 and was knighted in 1912 for his role in the organization of the second Great International Horticultural Exhibition, the first Chelsea Flower Show. By 1914, however, Sir Harry was the sole survivor of the London branch of the Veitch family and decided to sell the nurseries. He died at Slough, Buckinghamshire, on 6 July 1924, at the age of 84. His obituary described him as "the most outstanding figure in contemporary horticulture" (*Gardener's Chronicle,* 12 July 1924).

The Exeter branch of the family continued as a Veitch enterprise until 1969. After the Exeter and Chelsea Nurseries separated in 1863, Robert ran the Exeter firm until joined by his son Peter (1850–1929) in 1880. Peter, who took over when his father died in 1885, was not only a well-traveled plant hunter and knowledgeable nurseryman, specializing in trees and shrubs, but was also very active in Exeter activities, serving on many local committees. He created a prosperous business and in 1917, like his cousin Harry, was awarded the VMH. Peter's daughter, Anna Mildred (1889–1969), assisted him in the business and ran the firm after his death in 1929. Illness forced her to sell the nurseries in 1969. Several hybrids have been named after Peter and Mildred, including *Magnolia* × *veitchii* 'Peter Veitch' and *Camellia* × *williamsii* 'Mildred Veitch'.

The Veitch family's invaluable contribution to horticulture is difficult to assess. As one author commented, "It may be said that whatever other nurserymen had done before them, the Veitch family did it more and better!" (Willson).

Veitch, John 1752–1839

Biography
Born in Jedburgh, Scotland, 1752. Worked at Edinburgh nursery before moving south to London; hired by Sir Thomas Dyke Acland to lay out park at Killerton, Devon; established Killerton Nursery, Budlake, Devon, 1808; moved nursery to Mount Radford, Exeter, Devon, 1832, and established renowned Exeter Nursery; succeeded by son, James Veitch (1792–1863), who had taken over nursery in 1837. Died in Mount Radford, Exeter, Devon, 1839.

Veitch, James 1792–1863

Biography
Born in Killerton, Devon, 1792. Father established nursery at Budlake, Devon, in 1808, where James became a partner; moved nursery closer to Exeter, Mount Radford, 1832, and renamed Exeter Nursery; James took over business in 1837, two years before father's death; with son, James Veitch, Jr., developed business, and in 1853 London branch added when James, Jr., acquired Royal Exotic Nursery of Knight and Perry, in Chelsea, London; James, Sr., remained in Exeter, while son managed London branch. Died in Exeter, Devon, 1863.

Selected Publications
A Manual of the Coniferae, 1881; 2nd edition, as *Veitch's Manual of the Coniferae*, edited by Adolphus H. Kent, 1900
A Manual of Orchidaceous Plants Cultivated under Glass in Great Britain, 2 vols., 1887–94
A Traveller's Notes, 1896
Hortus Veitchii: A History of the Rise and Progress of the Nurseries of Messrs. James Veitch and Sons, 1906

Further Reading
Heriz-Smith, Shirley, "The Veitch Nurseries of Killerton and Exeter c. 1780 to 1863, Part 1," *Garden History* 16, no. 1 (1988)
Heriz-Smith, Shirley, "James Veitch and Sons of Chelsea, 1853–1870," *Garden History* 17, no. 2 (1989)
Musgrave, Toby, Chris Gardner, and Will Musgrave, *The Plant Hunters: Two Hundred Years of Adventure and Discovery around the World*, London and New York: Ward Lock, 1998
Willson, Eleanor Joan, *West London Nursery Gardens: The Nursery Gardens of Chelsea, Fulham, Hammersmith, Kensington, and a Part of Westminster, Founded before 1900*, London: Fullham and Hammersmith Historical Society, 1982

BARBARA SIMMS

Veitshöchheim

Würzburg, Bavaria, Germany

Location: approximately 3 miles (4.8 km) northwest of Würzburg, approximately 60 miles (96.5 km) east-southeast of Frankfurt

The garden at Veitshöchheim was created in the third quarter of the 18th century as an elaborate allegorical journey through life from the cradle to the grave. It was laid out as a series of rococo garden enclosures populated by an exceptional collection of statues. Although heavily reconstructed, it presents almost intact a complex and inventive scheme without precedent (and virtually without offspring) in the history of garden design.

The prince bishops of Würzburg had maintained a rural retreat at Veitshöchheim, a village on the banks of the Main a few miles downstream from the city, since the 17th century. This house gradually acquired the comforts of refined rural living, and by the early 18th century it overlooked a small parterre, with a kitchen garden to one side and a large rectangular orchard projecting southward, which also served as cover for game birds. This layout, surrounded by a high wall, formed the framework within which the present layout was to be developed.

A curiously disjointed baroque garden was laid out on the site under Prince Bishop Johann Philipp von Greiffenclau in the early years of the 18th century, and the present layout of paths, hedges, balustrades, and lakes was established at this time. A plan of this *Boskettgarten* of 1721 shows the bones of the present layout in position: a large piece of water in the form of an elaborated

Rococo garden with Pegasus fountain, Veitshöchheim, Bavaria, Germany
Copyright John and Irene Palmer/Garden Matters

ellipse is the principal feature, linked to a grid of geometric enclosures by a network of paths.

During the 1750s a series of additions added richness and detail to the established layout. The magnificent residence was now essentially complete as the prince bishops' urban headquarters in Würzburg, and it was predictable that its architect, Balthasar Neumann, would be called in to make improvements to the house at Veitshöchheim. He duly added the two wings that give the house its present appearance: boldly swelling and baroque, but still with the essential character of a summer pavilion away from the business of state. At the same time the first cycle of 14 statues was added by Johann Wolfgang van der Auvera.

The unique character of the present garden was developed beginning in 1763 during the stewardship of Prince Bishop Adam Friedrich von Seinsheim. He conceived the idea of constructing an allegorical garden of astonishing complexity, symbolizing a complete journey through the trials and opportunities of life in a strict sequence and culminating in a choice between banishment to hell or a glorious ascent to paradise. In order to mark out the stations of the journey, Seinsheim commissioned the rococo sculptor Ferdinand Tietz to carve a sequence of several hundred life-size sandstone sculptures representing a tremendous range of characterizations. Tietz had just completed a comparable statue sequence at Seehof, the summer residence of the bishops of Bamberg, of which only a fraction now survive. At Veitshöchheim his figures draw on a wide range of sources, including classical mythology, scenes from everyday life, exotically oriental characters, and fables. The statues are carved in a quizzical and vigorous rococo style. Further statues were added after Tietz's departure by Peter Wagner, and the design was completed by 1773. Many of the present examples are copies of the originals.

A key feature of the garden, the cascade, which was destroyed in 1945, was flowing from the eastern side of the garden down the gentle axial slope toward the large lake. The cascade represented the wellspring of life, with the view to the statue group in the center of the lake being a glimpse of paradise, not to be attained until the experiences and trials of life, as represented by the incidents along the route through the garden, were completed. The visitor is then taken past a series of visual incidents symbolizing the choices to be made on the journey through life: some of these have Masonic as well as religious and mythical significance. The pavilion of light, for example, sits on top of a grotto of tufa, populated by dreadful beasts that represent darkness. Another sequence takes the visitor through childhood experiences (the fables) to the turf theater, representing university, with wings of hornbeam hedging. Walks through shady woodland groves, past Tietz's exotic "Chinese" pavilions, bring one to the Lindensaal, an outdoor room with a roof of lime foliage supported by the columns of the regularly spaced trunks. The whole space of the garden, which is by no means large, is visually divided and controlled by a network of hedges and trees, generating atmospheric effects and permitting specific views and delaying others until the optimum moment.

Another sequence is based on the idea of maturity and adult life: thus the statue groups refer to love, marriage, the "marketplace of life," and so forth. The layout is distinguished by a pair of open wooden pavilions, which permit views of one another and of other garden features by means of precisely clipped openings in the wall-like hedges. Thus each enfilade of such openings allows a view through several hedges at once to a terminating feature. There are periodic glimpses of paradise beyond, but the wise visitor is to approach it by following the full circuit and observing each "lesson" in turn.

The final choice occurs at the Sea of the Dead, a rectangular pond in the southwestern corner of the garden. The wise visitor proceeds from here to the large piece of water, now revealed as the Lake of Purification. In the center is a statue group representing Parnassus rising above the flood at the center of a new world order. The nine muses are gathered on the rock, and the winged Pegasus rears up at its peak, as if to transport a prince bishop to paradise. At intervals water jets shoot from the rock into the lake in elaborate patterns. In niches cut into the surrounding hedge are the assembled gods of Olympus.

This remarkable, emblematic rococo garden went into a decline soon after its completion but has survived changes of taste, political vicissitudes, and a general lack of appreciation of its special character to enjoy new favor as a perfect representative of a lost age of design and craftsmanship.

Synopsis

1682	First summer pavilion established
1686	Present boundaries established
1699–1719	Prince Bishop von Greiffenclau in office; rococo garden established with present layout of paths, hedges, and lakes
1721	Framework of present layout shown on plan (in Bavarian state archives)
1752	Johann Wolfgang van der Auvera's first series of statues
1755–79	Prince Bishop von Seinsheim in office
1763	Seinsheim oversees improvement plans
1765	Ferdinand Tietz's statue sequences begin to be installed
1773	Present layout completed
1776	Gardens opened to the public
1945	Cascade destroyed

Further Reading

Enge, Torsten Olaf, and Carl Friedrich Schröer, *Gartenkunst in Europa, 1450–1800*, Cologne, Germany: Taschen, 1990; as *Garden Architecture in Europe, 1450–1800*, translated by Aisa Mattaj, Cologne, Germany: Taschen, 1990

Reinhardt, Helmut, "The Garden of the Prince-Bishop at Veitshöchheim," in *The History of Garden Design: The Western Tradition from the Renaissance to the Present Day*, edited by Monique Mosser and Georges Teyssot, London: Thames and Hudson 1991

Tunk, Walter, editor, *Veitshöchheim: Schloss und Garten, amtlicher Führer*, Munich: Bayerische Verwaltung der Staatlichen Schlösser, Gärten und Seen, 1962; 4th edition, 1982

STEVEN DESMOND

Vernacular Garden

The definition of vernacular gardens—as with vernacular artifacts, architecture, settlements, and landscapes—is elusive. Vernacular has referred to the rural, the preindustrial, the local, the handmade, the unso-phisticated, the traditional, and the customary. It has referred to design and construction by common people and equated with folk and popular. The boundaries between the popular and commonplace and the elite and special are not sharp, however, and there is continuing debate over the meaning of all these terms, as well as with the relationship of the vernacular to mass culture.

The history of gardens before the modern era often does not make a rigid separation between the vernacular and so-called higher styles. Garden art, rooted in the pragmatics and techniques of agriculture and horticultural practice, naturally links the vernacular and the elite. It is essential to recall that before the industrial era most persons were farmers or familiar with agricultural practices. For example, the history of medieval or early American gardens demonstrates the connection well, where gardens were viewed as a continuum of expression and experience and not as a dichotomy between high and low.

Vernacular-garden research has followed a distinct course. Early studies recognized and described places and brought them within the purview of study, followed by documentation and then interpretation. Architectural historians often neglected anything beyond the building envelope, and garden historians neglected the commonplace garden. Recent studies intersect the work of landscape architects, geographers, historians, folklorists, and anthropologists. Interest in the vernacular represents a democratization of scholarship and a desire for a more comprehensive view of history and culture through a concern for ordinary everyday life.

What questions are asked of these places and their makers? How are they created, designed, and used? What do they mean? What attitudes, values, and perceptions do they communicate? Gardens most often sit between structures and the broader landscape, whether it be street, a rural setting, or wilderness, with their spatial position defining their function and meaning. Most research has focused on the gardens that are part of the pair of house and garden: house gardens, kitchen gardens, dooryard gardens, and yards. Geographers and anthropologists have focused their attention on the dooryard garden. Much of their investigation has been typological, describing, categorizing, and organizing places on the basis of an examination of morphology, spatial configuration, boundaries, territory, terminology, social class, location, function, plants, and other design elements. They have included the role of household activity, social life, the automobile, and symbolic artifacts. These typologies all show plants and space used for the production of food, fruit, and fiber, for medicinal purposes, building materials, ritual objects, and adornment, and as part of both a subsistence and developing market economies. The meaning to a person and a household spans diet to social space and ritual, personal expression, and artistry.

The anthropological perspective began with Bronislaw Malinowski's classic *Coral Gardens and Their Magic,* which considers the gardens of the Trobriand Islanders of the Pacific. Other ethnobotanical garden studies have researched the forest and desert gardens of peoples in the Amazon, Southeast Asia, and the American Southwest. Vernacular gardens have been shown to be powerful symbols of cultural identity and value transmission. Dooryard-gardens studies have looked at various ethnic, racial, and religious communities, including gardens in Puerto Rico, Martinique, and Peru, southern rural African-American gardens, and Amish gardens. Ethnicity and race have been a concern, but only selectively, with most groups and subcultures not addressed at all. In the United States the prototypical house and yard, including its lawn, are subject to much discussion and interpretation as a national landscape type with regional variations. There are also communal vernacular gardens including community gardens, allotment gardens, and victory gardens.

Taking the lead from the social sciences, explicit formal design analysis is rare in vernacular-garden study, with Albert Hauser's work on Swiss farm gardens a rare exception. Feminist scholarship has given its attention to landscape values and attitudes, but one must turn to the realm of literature and biography for garden insight such as Alice Walker's essay "In Search of Our Mother's Gardens" or the writings of Antiguan Jamaica Kincaid, which address questions of cross-cultural exchange and the conflicting meanings of gardens between the powerful and the powerless.

Definitions of the vernacular that privilege the native or indigenous are complicated by processes of migration and distribution, which transmit and disseminate design vocabulary, technique, ideology, or plants themselves. For example, much of North America is planted with migrants, both deliberate and opportunistic, from other continents, and oftentimes garden makers of all classes consciously introduce what is new or exotic. There are studies of migrant gardens in France, Italian folk-garden shrines, and Portuguese immigrant gardens in California. Questions of modes of dissemination, dispersion, and taste have been addressed, notably information gleaned from popular magazines.

A basic question in garden history is the relationship between the vernacular garden and design. A few regional and local studies have emphasized the relationship between high and elite garden art and the vernacular experience. For example, the vernacular Mediterranean and Middle Eastern design forms of *villa* (Italy and much of the Roman world), *quinta* (Portugal), *carmen* (Andalusia), and *bustan* (Middle East) are all garden types that cut across these boundaries. The connection is also obvious in examples such as the influence of the English cottage garden on the designs of William Robinson and Gertrude Jekyll or the evolution of the Palladian garden.

The paradox is that upon investigation the vernacular—the common and ordinary—often shows itself to be special. Vernacular gardeners are opportunistic, resourcefully taking advantage of found materials and recycling their form and meaning. At the extreme their designs are idiosyncratic displays of an extreme individualistic and expressionist spirit. Vernacular gardens remind one of the remarkable democracy and accessibility of garden art. A central theme in vernacular-garden studies is the recognition that garden is not only a noun, a place, but also a verb, an activity. Gardens are planned, constructed, and cared for, and the results are carefully monitored. Here lies the foundation of an aesthetic sensibility, an eye that registers subtleties and appreciates form, pattern, and a multiplicity of meanings. Highlighted in studies of gardens of the homeless or defiant gardens created in wartime and internment situations is the most profound reminder that the urge to transform one's surroundings for personal benefit is a basic human aspiration and a reminder that artistry is not confined to any one group or class.

Further Reading

Balmori, Diana, and Margaret Morton, *Transitory Gardens, Uprooted Lives,* New Haven, Connecticut: Yale University Press, 1993

Beardsley, John, *Gardens of Revelation: Environments by Visionary Artists,* New York: Abbeville Press, 1995

Butler, Francis, "Italian Folk Shrines: The Portuguese Immigrant Gardens in California," *Places* 4 (1987)

Gundaker, Grey, "Tradition and Innovation in African-American Yards," *African Arts* 26, no. 2 (1993)

Hauser, Albert, *Bauerngärten der Schweiz,* Zurich: Artemis, 1976

Helphand, Kenneth I., "Defiant Gardens," *The Journal of Garden History* 17, no. 2 (1997)

Hester, Randolph, and Mark Francis, editors, *The Meaning of Gardens,* Cambridge, Massachusetts: MIT Press, 1990

Hunt, John Dixon, and Joachim Wolschke-Bulmahn, editors, *The Vernacular Garden,* Washington, D.C.: Dumbarton Oaks Research Library and Collection, 1990

Hutchinson, Bernadette, "Amish Gardens: A Symbol of Identity," *Pennsylvania Folklife* 43, no. 3 (1994)

Jenkins, Virginia Scott, *The Lawn: A History of an American Obsession,* Washington, D.C.: Smithsonian Institution Press, 1994

Kimber, Clarissa, "Spatial Patterning in the Dooryard Gardens of Puerto Rico," *Geographical Review* 63 (1973)

Kincaid, Jamaica, "Flowers of Evil: In the Garden," *The New Yorker* 68, no. 33 (1992)

Lassus, Bernard, *Jardins imaginaires,* Paris: Presses de la Connaissance, 1977

Malinowski, Bronislaw, *Coral Gardens and Their Magic: A Study of the Methods of Tilling the Soil and of Agricultural Rites in the Trobriand Island,* London: Allen and Unwin, and New York: American Book, 1935; 2nd edition, London: Allen and Unwin, 1966

Prieto-Moreno, Francisco, *Los jardines de Granada,* Madrid: Ciqüeña, 1952

Schroeder, Fred, *Front Yard America: The Evolution and Meanings of Vernacular Domestic Landscape,* Bowling Green, Ohio: Bowling Green State University Popular Press, 1993

Walker, Alice, *In Search of Our Mothers' Gardens: Womanist Prose,* San Diego, California: Harcourt Brace Jovanovich, 1983; London: Women's Press, 1984

Warner, Samuel Bass, *To Dwell Is to Garden: A History of Boston's Community Gardens,* Boston: Northeastern University Press, 1987

Westmacott, Richard, *African-American Gardens and Yards in the Rural South,* Knoxville: University of Tennessee Press, 1992

Works, Martha Adrienne, "Dooryard Gardens in Moyobamba, Peru," *Focus* 40, no. 2 (1990)

KENNETH HELPHAND

Versailles

Versailles, Yvelines, France

Location: approximately 10 miles (16 km) southwest of Paris city center

What is particularly remarkable about the Château of Versailles, which was created in the 17th century, is that it was born out of such an unpromising environment. Early in the century, in 1624, Louis XIII decided to build a hunting lodge in an area of wild countryside to the west of the city of Paris, which he had visited previously in 1607. Traditionally the area is described at the time as being made up of dense forests and bogs, marshy ground, and dense tangles of fallen vegetation only inhabited by deer, wild boar, and other game. As an area for hunting, it was ideal. Some small hamlets existed in the area (Trianon, for example), but generally the land was unimproved agriculturally and was not thought to be a place of any charm. In 1631 the king decided to tear down the original lodge and had a small château built of brick and stone in the style of the period. (It should be noted that one of the niceties of the French is that a gentleman's residence is called a château to contrast with a château-fort or castle; the term *palais* is not used.) The new château was designed for Louis XIII by the architect Philibert Le Roi. Set within a moat, the house and outbuildings surrounded a courtyard but were not without formal gardens, laid out to the west. Later additional wings were continued eastward on either side of the approach. Louis XIII died in 1643, when his son was only five years old, and it was not for another 18 years that any major changes were to occur.

The reasons for Louis XIV's choice of Versailles as the site for his great château are not entirely clear. It has been suggested that it arose from fond memories of his father and the visits to the hunt in his extreme youth; others suggest that it was inspired by his amorous escapades here in his teens. Quite early in his reign the king decided that he would embark on a plan of refurbishing the various royal châteaux. Whatever the reason for concentrating so much on Versailles, the wish to build a modern structure was spurred in particular by the dissatisfaction with the royal château of Fontainebleau, which was seen as uncomfortable and inconvenient. The tale is told that it had been a matter of extreme displeasure for the young king to discover that at Vaux-le-Vicomte Fouquet, who was only a commoner, had created for himself a château that, although not particularly big, outshone in design and style all those of the nobility of France, even those of royalty. This was in 1661 at a great fete held on 17 August to which Louis XIV was invited. The king must have immediately decided that he would not be upstaged and put Fouquet's designers, the trio Louis Le Vau, Charles Le Brun, and André Le Nôtre, to work to create his own ideal royal château. Le Nôtre, after all, was already the holder of two royal appointments. This was the year in which Cardinal Mazarin, who had held sway during the king's regency, died, and Louis decided, at the age of 22, to take over the reigns of government personally. He had been married the previous year to his mistress Louise La Valliere.

One of the architectural constraints imposed by the king was the retention of the original château, which was not to be touched in the new development. The first phase of the development involved refurbishing the existing château and reconstructing the outbuildings to

provide additional accommodation. This was completed in 1662. Very soon there was need for still more room, and in 1668 a plan for enlarging the château was adopted. To achieve the king's requirement Le Vau built around the original château itself, although it is assumed that the other buildings were soon removed, with the exception of one of the later wings extending out and flanking the courtyard on the south side (the left as the château is approached). Le Vau's additions came to be known as "the envelope." This treatment ensured that the new and old buildings were interconnected; the original château remained intact, but a series of open air wells was created between the two.

The third principal phase of development of the château began in 1678 but was only completed in 1684. This was the new west facade commissioned from Jules Harduin Mansart, centered on the great Gallerie des Glaces. Both château and gardens were subject to change and development from 1662 until well into the 18th century.

Already by 1663 a new plan bearing Le Nôtre's signature for the layout of the Petit Parc had been prepared following the rebuilding by Le Vau. This incorporated the important central axis, although it was narrower where the Allée Royale is at present. Two parts of that plan appear to be the only elements of the design of that time that still exist; these are two rectangular bosquets crossed with allées on either side of the central axis, flanking the Allée Royale.

Versailles is a paramount example of axial design on both sides of the château. To the east the town is bisected by the Avenue de Paris, which it is said provided a view along this straight vista toward the city from the king's private chambers. Two other avenues create with it a *patte d'oie*, leading, the one southeast and the other northeast, from the great open space in front of the château. It is worth noting that, in order that the line of the design should be clear, these avenues were built up along parts of their length and set on shallow embankments above the buildings fronting them, where the natural ground drops away. Thus the layout of the town is all part of the greater design concept.

To the west the completed central axis extended well beyond the full length of the great central canal, some reports suggesting that it at one time exceeded 5 miles (approximately 8 km). The full extent of the park was developed over a period of over 60 years, and while the construction of the house began almost at once, it appears that for the first two years very little change took place in the park. In fact the royal designers were not only occupied with Versailles; the king had decided to improve all the royal châteaux, and so they were in fact working also on new plans for Fontainebleau as well as in the Tuileries and St. Germain-en-Laye. It must be remembered, too, that a parterre garden had already been laid out to the west of the old château of Louis XIII. Indeed, the present *parterre du nord*, although doubled in size from the original, retains the essential design outline attributed to Jacques Menours, the nephew of Jacques Boyceau de la Barauderie, from that period.

On the terrace immediately to the west of the château a *parterre d'eau* originally comprising a central circular pool was laid out. To this parterre four smaller interconnecting pools with cartouche outline were added in a design by Charles Le Brun completed in 1670. The *parterre d'eau* in its present form was laid out early in 1684 as shown in Perelle's illustration of 1685. This area for many years created problems for the designers attempting to reach a satisfactory solution. The new design followed the construction of the new west facade of the château designed by Jules Harduin Mansart between 1682 and 1683.

Farther west, before arriving at the Allée Royale, and on a lower level is the Latona fountain basin completed in 1666 and the parterre garden associated with it. The Allée Royale, with its central grass feature, the so-called *tapis vert*, was completed by widening the central axis in 1667 just after the completion of the Latona basin. The ground slopes down to the west through this whole area to the great basin in which is set a statue of Apollo driving his horse-drawn chariot of gold. This is a later piece of work dating from 1679, although the basin itself or something very like it was to be found as early as the 1663 Le Nôtre drawing.

To the south of the *parterre d'eau*, balancing the *parterre du nord*, was the *parterre du midi*, or *parterre des fleurs*, the only part of the garden devoted to displays of colorful flowers. Beyond this at a lower level was the orangery (see Plate 33). Both these features of the garden still exist in their original positions, although much increased in size and grandeur from their original designs. The *parterre du midi* also looks over the Swiss Lake, as it is called; this is farther south still and was excavated some time between 1678 and 1688. From early in the development of the park, there had been proposals for a water body in the same position; drawings exist showing a large hexagonal pool, but this had not been carried through. There was more than aesthetic reasoning behind this use of water features; the marshy conditions meant that it was necessary to create such water bodies to provide the means of drainage. Paradoxically Versailles suffered both from an excess of water and a deficiency—too much soil water but not enough to operate all the fountains in the Petit Parc. This has always been a problem. In Louis XIV's time it is said that armies of gardeners attended the king when he toured the garden to turn on the fountains where he was going and turn off those he had passed. Later an incredible exercise in engineering known as the Machine of Marly, incorporating 14 waterwheels, was created to

pump water into the reservoirs; although huge and complex it seems to never have worked satisfactorily.

The Petit Parc today extends over an area of 1,690 acres (684 ha); in earlier times it was nearly three times that area, encompassing 4,295 acres (1,738 ha). At its peak the Grand Parc extended over an incredible 16,343 acres (6,614 ha). Nearest to the château were the formal parterres beyond which on the south were the orangery and the Swiss Lake and on the north the Basin of Neptune. On either side of the central axis to the west were the bosquets dissected by walks lined with trelliswork and with a series of fountains at the intersections of these walks. Statues of Flora, Ceres, Bacchus, and Saturn were introduced among the changes that took place over the years. An early feature, which was later replaced was the Grotto of Thetis; the figures from it were subsequently placed in the later Bains d'Appollon. Other well-known features in this area are the Isle Royale, the Theatre d'Eau, L'Encelade, La Renomme, and the later Collonade designed by Mansart in 1685.

One of the largest features of the Petit Parc was the great canal, begun in 1668, which extended the central axis westward from the Basin d'Appollon. The main canal is 4,921 feet (1,500 m) in length and is intersected by a cross canal, with a southern branch 1,969 feet (600 m) long and a northern branch of 1,321 feet (400 km). At the southern end stood the menagerie created in 1663, which existed until it was sacked during the Revolution. At the northern end, at the same time as its excavation, work was beginning to pull down the manor house and the small village of Trianon to make room for a new private retreat for the king. This was the Trianon de Porcelaine, a small building clad in Normandy faience tiles, which predated the Grand Trianon that visitors now see in this position. The Trianon de Porcelaine was started in 1670 and remained in use for 17 years. In 1687 it was found to be inadequate for the royal purposes and was replaced by a new building designed by Mansart usually known as the Grand Trianon but alternatively called the Marble Trianon. This building has its own small garden, as did the Trianon de Porcelaine before it. The later garden featured one of Le Nôtre's most unusual and imaginative creations, the Garden of Sources, based on a network of streams over which it was possible to step from one grass island to another. Each of the islands was quite small but large enough to accommodate a gaming table and seats. This was a late work of Le Nôtre begun in 1687.

From quite early in its history under Louis XIV, Versailles, or its park, was destined to be the setting for spectacular events and entertainments. In May 1664 between the 7th and 13th of the month the "Pleasures of the Enchanted Isle" took place. This was a grand weeklong celebration with all sorts of entertainments, receptions, grand dinners, musical performances, firework displays, and the presentation of two plays by Molière: *The Princess of Elis* and *Tartuffe*. Four years later another great event was held, reputedly the most sumptuous of all. For this another play by Molière, *Georges Dandin,* was commissioned, as was a suite by the composer Jean-Baptiste Lully, *Les Fetes de l'Amour et de Bacchus*. In the previous year the digging of the great canal had begun. It is not clear whether the canal was filled with water by the time of this festival, but it is known that on other occasions the canal was used for the reenactment of sea battles for the amusement of the court. At this time the king was still living either at Fontainebleau or Paris, although as time went by his visits to Versailles became more frequent. The use of the grounds for great spectacles and entertainments of a less lavish kind on a regular basis throughout Louis XIV's reign illustrates the importance of the château and of the town of Versailles as the political center of France. The king was the absolute ruler of his country, and power was gathered round him; therefore, anyone who had any political, social, or other aspirations had to be in Versailles and accepted at court to achieve their ends. To be dismissed to the country, as happened to some of the nobility at various times, was quite literally to be cast into the wilderness. In 1682 Versailles was declared to be the official seat of government, regularizing a well-established state of affairs. As early as 1677 the king had revealed his intention that Versailles would become his residence.

Early in his life Louis XIV had expressed his intention to devote himself to the "pursuit of glory," and this he did in a way that had no precedent and no subsequent equal. Some of this is expressed in the park through the use of sculptures. Statuary was always a feature of this garden, as with other formal gardens of France and Italy. In this case the theme related to figures who could be compared to the king, whose sobriquet the "Sun King" was alluded to in the use of the statue of Apollo in the great central basin. Five years before this was completed, the project of the "great commission" was put into effect, whereby a large number of sculptures completed to initial designs by Le Brun (but executed by different artists) was begun. This developed the theme of power, associating the Sun King with the great supernatural figures of classical legends and mythical history. In the same year (1674) the last of the three great spectacular celebrations was held at the end of July and into August and enlivened by performances of new works by Molière, Lully, and Racine, among many other events.

One should not omit from any description of Versailles the small group of Picturesque late 18th-century buildings forming the "Hameau" associated with Marie Antoinette and dating from 1783. Earlier, in 1761, Louis XV had commissioned the architect Jacques-Ange Gabriel to build the Petit Trianon. Later Louis XVI presented the Petit Trianon to Marie Antoinette—who did not relish the public nature and formality of court life—as a private retreat. The building itself has a formal setting, but between it and the Hameau is an area that has something of the character of an English landscape park. Within the Hameau—which conforms to the ideas of the Picturesque as described by Sir Uvedale Price himself—are the Belvedere and the Temple of Love, both mid-18th-century buildings. On the other side between the Grand and Petit Trianons is the French Pavilion (1750), also by Gabriel.

Although the French Revolution resulted in the sacking of the château, with the removal of the furniture and great damage to the park, restoration began in the early years of the empire. As early as 1805 work began to refurbish and return the furniture to the château and to restore the park. In the latter case, however, many formal elements, including most of the extensive formal ornamental trelliswork that had lined the walks through the bosquets, were not replaced.

Synopsis

1607	Louis XIII first visits area on hunting expedition.
1624	Louis XIII builds small hunting lodge
1631	Original lodge torn down and replaced with small château of brick and stone, designed by Philibert Le Roi; parterre garden laid out to the west of the small château, designed by Jacques Menours
1661	Garden designer André Le Nôtre, painter and designer Charles Le Brun, and architect Louis Le Vau commissioned by Louis XIV to work at Versailles
1663	Menagerie created at southern end of cross canal
1664	Completion of the additional buildings at château for royal visits; labyrinth created, designed by Charles Perrault and Le Nôtre
1665	Le Nôtre's first plan for Petit Parc prepared
1666	Latona fountain basin and its parterre garden completed
1669	Excavation of grand canal begun, and enlargement of château to create "envelope" by La Vau; layout of Allée Royale
1670	Construction of Trianon de Porcelaine, displacing village of Trianon; transformation of Bassin des Cygnes into Bassin d'Apollon with sculptures by Jean-Baptiste Tuby
1677–83	New Potager du Roi built, designed by Jean-Baptiste de la Quintinie

1678	Excavation of the artificial lake Pièce d'Eau des Suisses begun
1678–85	Redevelopment of west front of château by Jules Harduin Mansart
1682	Development by Baron Arnold de Ville of "Machine de Marly" to supply water for fountains in park
1684	Parterre d'Eau laid out
1688	Replacement of Trianon de Porcelaine with Grand Trianon, designed by Mansart; Le Nôtre completes unique design for Jardin des Sources
1761	Petit Trianon constructed by architect Jacques-Ange Gabriel
1774	Labyrinth destroyed by Comte d'Angivilliers
1785	Creation of Marie Antoinette's Hameau by Mique
1789	Château sacked during Revolution, with great damage to park
1805	Restoration begun

Further Reading

Adams, William Howard, *The French Garden 1500–1800,* London: Scholar Press, and New York: Braziller, 1979

Friedman, Ann, "The Evolution of the Parterre d'eau," *Journal of Garden History* 8, no. 1 (1988)

Hazlehurst, F. Hamilton, *Gardens of Illusion: The Genius of André Le Nostre,* Nashville, Tennessee: Vanderbilt University Press, 1980

Lablaude, Pierre-André, *Les jardins de Versailles,* Paris: Scala, 1995; as *The Gardens of Versailles,* translated by Fiona Biddulph, London: Zwemmer, 1995

Marie, Alfred, *Naissance de Versailles,* 2 vols., Paris: Fréal, 1968

Marie, Alfred, and Jeanne Marie, *Mansart à Versailles,* 2 vols., Paris: Fréal, 1972

Marie, Alfred, and Jeanne Marie, *Versailles au temps de Louis XIV,* Paris: Impr. Nationale, 1976

Mitford, Nancy, *The Sun King, Louis XIV at Versailles,* London: Hamish Hamilton, and New York: Harper and Row, 1966; 2nd edition, London: Sphere Books, 1976

Pincas, Stéphane, *Versailles: Un jardin a la française,* Paris: Éditions de la Martinière, 1995; as *Versailles: The History of the Gardens and Their Sculpture,* translated by Fiona Cowell, New York: Thames and Hudson, 1996

Taylor-Leduc, Susan, "Louis XVI's Public Gardens: The Replating of Versailles in the Eighteenth Century," *Journal of Garden History* 14 (1994)

Van de Kemp, Gerard, *Versailles,* Versailles: Éditions d'Art Lys, 1977; as *Versailles,* New York: Vendome Press, and London: Sotheby Parke Bernet, 1978; 2nd edition, New York: Park Lane, 1981

Woodbridge, Kenneth, *Princely Gardens: The Origins and Development of the French Formal Style,* London: Thames and Hudson, and New York: Rizzoli, 1986

M.F. DOWNING

Vesuvian Gardens

Campania, Italy

Pompeii
Location: approximately 12 miles (19 km) southeast of Naples

Herculaneum
Location: approximately 5 miles (8 km) southeast of Naples

Torre Annunziata
Location: approximately 11 miles (18 km) southeast of Naples

Stabiae
Location: approximately 18 miles (29 km) southwest of Naples

Because of the way in which Pompeii and the surrounding Campanian sites were preserved by the sudden eruption of Vesuvius in A.D. 79, these sites are a unique and precious source of information about ancient gardens. Approximately 626 gardens have been found in Pompeii, Herculaneum, and the surrounding villas. The study of Italian gardens begins with these gardens.

The garden played an important role in the everyday life of the inhabitants of Pompeii and helped define many aspects of their culture, including art, architecture, horticulture, economics, and religion.

Gardens are found in many public buildings, but they were most important in homes, where they played a

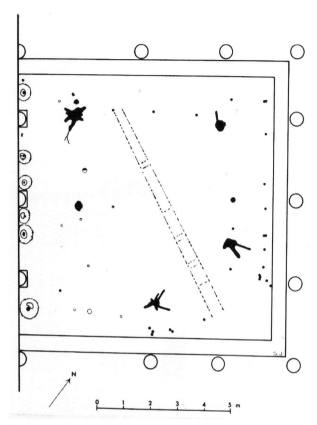

Plan of peristyle garden in House of Julius Polybius, Pompeii (roots
are indicated in solid black, stakes are indicated by circles)
Copyright Stanley A. Jashemski

central role. Located within the high walls broken only
occasionally by high, small windows, the garden was
the heart of the house, whether large or small, furnishing light, air, and ease of communication to rooms
opening on it. It served as an important room of the
house, a place to work and play, to cook and eat, and to
worship. These gardens differed greatly not only in size,
design, function, and plantings but also with respect to
the role of water, sculpture, and garden furniture.

At the time of the eruption of A.D. 79, Campania was
part of the Roman Empire. But the area had been previously successively settled by Oscans, Etruscans, and
Samnites. The homes of the earliest inhabitants are
largely unknown to us, for they lie below subsequent
construction and await subsoil excavation. The authorities are understandably reluctant to conduct extensive
excavations in the earlier levels, for that would mean
the destruction of the ruins preserved by the eruption,
which are still being studied by scholars and enjoyed by
millions of visitors every year.

Houses here were by no means as uniform as text-
books suggest. Only about 300 houses in the entire
Vesuvian area had a garden with a portico on one or

more sides. Approximately 38 interior courtyards had
no portico. Sometimes wide windows gave a view into
the gardens. Some of the larger, more luxurious houses
even had roof gardens. Pliny the Elder (A.D. 23–79) in
his *Natural History* tells of imported trees suitable for
such gardens. Seneca the Younger (died A.D. 65) in his
Epistles scathingly deplored such unnatural practices as
planting the tops of buildings with trees, with their
roots where the roofs should be.

Information about Vesuvian gardens, because of the
way in which they have been preserved, is rich and varied. Garden paintings are one important source of information (see Plate 34). A common technique was to
paint a picture of a garden on one or more of the garden
walls, thus increasing the apparent size of the garden.
Behind a painted fence, plants, trees, birds, statues,
pools (sometimes shown with fish), and fountains, often
too large for the actual garden, could be pictured. In a
few houses interior rooms were painted to appear as a
garden. These paintings furnish invaluable evidence
about the ancient flora and fauna, for the plants and
birds pictured are those that would have been found in
the ancient gardens.

The architectural context of a garden, its paintings,
and sculpture are important, but only careful excavation can tell how the garden actually looked in antiquity. In addition, soil contours, planting patterns,
fragments of carbonized roots, stems, seeds and fruits,
ancient pollen, bacteria, and even insects all contribute
to our knowledge of a site.

In 1973, the peristyle garden in the house of Julius
Polybius was uncovered and excavated using techniques
that had been newly developed at that time. It had a
portico on three sides. In such early houses rain water
collected in the *impluvium* (a shallow pool in the center
of the atrium) or in gutters around the garden was
stored in a cistern below and was the only source of
water for the family and garden. The small garden of
Polybius contained five large trees and many smaller
ones, including eight small trees espaliered against the
west wall. The tall trees were pruned high, for many
small plants grew at the edge of the garden. Stakes supported the branches of some trees heavy with fruit or
nuts. Fragments of terra-cotta pots with four holes
(three on the sides and one in the bottom), in which the
trees along the west wall had been started, suggest that
the trees might have been the exotic citron that Pliny
writes were transported "in pots with breathing holes
for the roots" (*Natural History*) or perhaps the lemon.
It is commonly stated that the Romans did not know
the lemon, but lemon trees are pictured in the garden
paintings in the House of the Fruit Orchard at Pompeii.
A mosaic (ca. A.D. 100) in the Terme Museum, Rome,
accurately portrays both a lemon and a citron, showing
their different characteristics and relative size.

View of garden and adjacent rooms in the House of the Bracelet, Pompeii
Drawing by Victoria I

Carbonized figs found around the tree root in the northwest corner of the garden of Polybius identify one of the trees. Marks left in the soil by an exceptionally long and narrow ladder, so shaped to fit into the dense branches, similar to the ones used in the area today to pick cherries and pears, suggest the garden had such fruit trees. Plentiful olive pollen indicates the presence of an olive tree. This informally planted garden was a great surprise to scholars; it was quite different from the replanted formal gardens in the excavations. Nonetheless, subsequent excavations showed that such informal gardens were common in the early houses. Trees in the Mediterranean area require little water once they are established.

When the aqueduct was introduced during the Augustan period (27 B.C.–A.D. 14), water became plentiful; pools and fountains became important parts of the garden, and low, formal plantings that required more water became possible. The small formal garden that stretched out at the rear of the lower level of the House of the Bracelet (or the House of the Wedding of Alexander) was such a garden. This beautiful three-story house was one of those built over the city walls after the walls were no longer needed for protection when Pompeii became a Roman city. This is the first formal garden in an elegant house to be scientifically excavated. A beautiful, high-vaulted garden room, its walls covered with exceptionally beautiful garden paintings, opened on the north end of the east side of the garden. Most of the adjacent exedra, with less well preserved garden paintings, was occupied by a marble water triclinium (three couches arranged in U shape, made comfortable with cushions, on which the family and their guests reclined to eat). Water from an apsed mosaic fountain fell down over water steps and rose in a jet in the middle of the couches. The water eventually emptied into a pool at the east end of the garden. Water rose in a jet from the low column in the middle of the pool and from the 28 jets around the rim of the pool. The shells and bones of fish, animals, and birds found along the north garden wall were probably debris left from meals eaten in the water triclinium. The garden was laid out with passageways on four sides, with a trapezoidal-shaped bed at each corner of the garden. The size and locations of the root cavities suggest a formal hedge, perhaps box.

With the exception of seasonal plants, such as oleander, rose, and violet, formal gardens contained mostly evergreens. The opium poppy was probably sometimes included, for it appears in the garden paintings, as do the large white morning glory and the corn marigold. Romans used flowers most often in garlands and crowns; most favored were the rose, Madonna lily, and violet. Many of the flowers used in garlands were wild flowers.

Small houses in Pompeii also included sizable cultivated areas. Among these is the large vineyard in the large city block across from the amphitheater. It was laid out as the Roman agrarian writers recommended, with arbored passageways, the vines and stakes precisely spaced. More informally planted vineyards, orchards, and a market-garden vineyard have also been excavated. The garden of Hercules was probably a commercial flower garden.

Gardens also were found in the luxurious villas at nearby Stabiae and in the villa of Poppaea, the wife of the Emperor Nero at Oplontis (modern Torre Annunziata). There are 13 remarkable gardens in the area available for excavation in the villa of Poppaea. The gardens inside the villa were much like those in city houses; some were informal, and most were formally planted. But the great exterior gardens, which took advantage of the magnificent view of the sea in front of the villa and the mountains in the rear, were unique.

The formal architectural layout of the large parklike garden at the rear of the villa of Poppaea reflected the plan of the villa itself. From its entrance the perspective through the atrium continued through the enclosed garden and the grand salon, with its monumental entrance at the rear of the villa, to a landscaped pathway on the central axis of the villa. Flanking the central passageway were four centaur fountains. Five marble shafts supporting white marble heads of Aphrodite, a woman of the Julian-Claudian period, a portrait of boy of the same period, the head of the child Dionysius, and a bearded Dionysius were set among flowering shrubs. At the east edge of the garden was a row of large trees, probably plane trees.

The east wing of the villa, which was built during the Roman Empire (A.D. 50–70) looked out on an Olympic-size swimming pool and a magnificent sculpture garden beyond. Along the east side of the swimming pool, a row of 13 statue bases has thus far been found. Behind each base was a tree. Oleanders grew in the beds behind these trees. The six marble statues thus far recovered, beginning from the south, were the head of Hercules, an ephebe (a Greek youth), and a Nike (Victory); balancing these on the north were another Nike (or Diana?) without a head, and a head of Hercules. At the south end of the swimming pool was a sculptured white marble group of a hermaphrodite and satyr; and further to the south was a small square pool in which stood a large white crater fountain. The limits of this magnificent garden, surely worthy of an empress, are not yet known.

Synopsis

2nd C. B.C.	Samnites begin building villas in Pompeii, with peristyle gardens
27 B.C.– A.D. 14	Aqueducts built to bring water to Pompeii, enabling use of pools and fountains in gardens, and making low, formal plantings possible
A.D. 79	Eruption of Mt. Vesuvius preserved gardens under lapilli and volcanic ash; at this time there were extensive gardens at Villa Poppaea at Oplontis (Torre Annunziata)
1973	Peristyle garden in Samnite house of Julius Polybius excavated using new archeological techniques to identify plants

Further Reading

Ciarallo, Annamaria, and M. Mariotti Lippi, "The Garden of Casa dei Casti Amanti," *Garden History* 21 (Summer, 1993)

De Caro, Stefano, "The Sculptures of the Villa of Poppaea at Oplontis," in *Ancient Roman Villa Gardens,* edited by Elisabeth B. MacDougall, Washington, D.C.: Dumbarton Oaks Research Library and Collection, 1987

Jashemski, Wilhelmina F., *The Gardens of Pompeii: Herculaneum and the Villas Destroyed by Vesuvius,* 2 vols., New Rochelle, New York: Caratzas, 1979–93

Jashemski, Wilhelmina F., and Frederick G. Meyer, editors, *The Natural History of Pompeii and the other Vesuvian Sites,* Cambridge and New York: Cambridge University Press, 2002

Mau, August, *Pompeji in Leben und Kunst,* Leipzig: Engelmann, 1900; 2nd revised edition, 1908; as *Pompeii, Its Life and Art,* translated by Francis W. Kelsey, New York and London: Macmillan, 1899; 2nd edition, 1902; reprinted, New Rochelle, New York: Caratzas, 1982

WILHELMINA F. JASHEMSKI

Victorian Period

Queen Victoria's long reign (1838–1901) defined an era dominated by the industrial revolution. An evolving social Darwinism condemned some to enslavement by science and technology, but the self-reliant and self-improving found a way up the economic ladder to swell the middle classes. Their newly rich values were manifest in the architecture of the new suburbs, where gardening, no longer an upper-class luxury, became a socially acceptable pursuit—especially for women.

Victorian engineering was highly innovative, but architecture reproduces historical styles in a relentless but largely unfulfilled search for aesthetic fulfillment in a material world. Gardens were equally eclectic, enriched by a preoccupation with exotic plants, whose novel forms, textures, and colors layered chaos upon aesthetic chaos, a situation that remained until the last quarter of the century. The Victorian era's greatest contributions to the landscape were, rather, social and scientific: the creation of public parks to ameliorate the stressful conditions in the industrial cities, and the introduction of new plants accompanied by new initiatives in horticultural science to make the new plants flourish in alien situations.

Suburban gardens blended the formal and informal. Principal rooms opened onto formal terraces often backed by conservatories containing tender exotics. Informal shrubberies lined curving carriage drives and blocked views of the suburban neighbors. Hedges, often elaborately topiaried, enclosed spaces that might feature a specimen tree or fountain. An abhorrence of plainness led lawns to be cut into scroll-shaped beds stuffed with brilliantly colored flowers. This practice, known as carpet bedding or bedding out, was costly because the tender plants had to be over wintered under glass. The mode survives in municipal gardens and wherever there are devotees of artificiality.

By the 1840s industrialized printing permitted the publication of modestly priced gardening books, journals, and alluringly colored nursery catalogs. They proclaimed the social acceptability of gardening and aimed to cultivate the showy varieties of plants arriving at the nurseries. Plant collecting, once an amateur activity, became a worldwide pursuit of professional plant collectors, sponsored by the horticultural societies or the larger commercial nurseries.

Of the professional gardeners, Humphry Repton (1752–1818) continued to work in the English landscape style but was the first to recognize the practical need for terraces and an aesthetic need for flowers. Ashridge (1813), the first of these gardens, had a formal terrace garden in the vicinity of an earlier mansion. Interest was provided by a "monks' garden," with a holy well feeding water to a *rosarium* with a fountain and a grotto. A visit by the German garden maker Prince Pückler in 1816 gathered inspiration for his garden at Muskau.

John Claudius Loudon (1807–43) and his wife, Jane Webb (1807–58), vigorously promoted the cause of gardening. Their spirited and pragmatic advocacy was found notably in the *Encyclopaedia of Gardening* (1822) and *The Gardener's Magazine* (from 1826). Gardens, they maintained, were works of art, not nature, and creating them was a highly edifying activity. There were, they advised, four styles to choose from: (1) the *geometric*, a popular style emulating Tudor, Jacobean, or Italian gardens; (2) the *picturesque*, inspired by mountainous scenery; (3) the *gardenesque*, popular with suburban gardeners because it enabled them to show off the

latest plants and parade their horticultural skills; and (4) the *rustic*, which imitated the simplicity of cottage gardens. This last found popularity late in the century with those weary of the elaboration of the other styles.

Public parks were arguably the most significant and certainly the longest enduring contribution to the designed landscape; their purpose was to ameliorate the disastrous environments created in the mushrooming industrial cities. Once again, the Loudons were spirited advocates. Their terrace garden at Gravesend (1835) was the first publicly owned space in England. Among the park makers were in England, Sir Joseph Paxton and his pupils; in North America, Andrew Jackson Downing, Frederick Law Olmsted, and Calvert Vaux; in Paris, Napoléon I and Napoléon III, with Baron Haussmann and Alphand; and in Germany, Peter Josef Lenné, and Prince Pückler-Muskau.

Sir Joseph Paxton (1803–65) was an outstanding park maker, gardener, writer, and publisher, whose boundless energy and versatility typified the Victorian ideal man. As head gardener at Chatsworth, Derbyshire, for the sixth duke of Devonshire, he created innovative glasshouses to shelter the duke's tender collections. These foreshadowed the huge glasshouse he conceived for the 1851 Great Exhibition in Hyde Park, which was later moved to the park he designed at Sydenham. Paxton's first park, Prince's Park, Liverpool (1842), was contained within a suburban residential development. He refined this concept at Birkenhead Park, Liverpool (1844), a planned residential suburb and his most influential park. Here he introduced lawns, lakes, garden structures, and shrubberies, integrating them with a system of paths and carriageways to create a recreational system with considerable visual diversity.

In the United States the Loudons' philosophy of "improvement and taste" found an equally energetic arbiter in Andrew Jackson Downing (1815–52). Virtually nothing remains of his executed projects along the Hudson River, but his books, including *A Treatise on the Theory and Practice of Landscape Gardening* (1841), were immensely influential. Traces of his style linger at Lyndhurst, Tarrytown, the Gothic Revival mansion designed by Alexander Jackson Davis (1803–1902), Downing's first architectural collaborator.

Downing met his new architectural partner, Calvert Vaux (1824–92), in England in 1850 and introduced him to his friend, the peripatetic journalist and social reformer, Frederick Law Olmsted (1822–1903). Upon Downing's premature death two years later, Vaux and Olmsted entered and won the design competition for Central Park in New York City (1857). Olmsted had visited Birkenhead Park, which he proclaimed a "people's park" because it was enjoyed by all classes, sexes, and age groups. Herein lay the inspiration for their winning entry, their first park and their most influential. It is a brilliant emulation of Repton's principles, mixing open and closed spaces varied by undulating topography and large expanses of water. Rich and varied plantings created "green lungs" to improve air quality, and the varied greens of plantings effectively countered Upper Manhattan's stark geometries.

A breath of refreshing simplicity came with the Arts and Crafts movement led by William Morris (1834–96). Tiring of high Victorian overelaboration, many reassessed the merits of the Loudons' fourth style, the rustic. Its principal polemicist was William Robinson (1838–1935), a gardener and voluminous writer. His *The English Flower Garden* (1883) and journal *The Garden* (1871) are still in print. He used simple but formal layouts of old-fashioned and hardy plants close to the walls of Gravetye Manor, his ancient home in Sussex. He then blended formality with naturalistic spaces farther away from the buildings enlivened with drifts of woodland species. Preferring natives or hardy plants with muted colors, he anticipated current approaches in ecological gardening.

For many, returning to the amiable but untutored lower-class informalities of the vernacular was unacceptable and led to an aesthetic storm in a teacup: the controversy of natural versus formal. E. Adveno Brooke's *The Gardens of England* (1857), for all its incredible eccentricities, demonstrates the popularity of the formal Italian Renaissance style. Paxton liked it, as did the landscape gardener Williams Andrew Nesfield (1793–1881) and his often-time architect collaborator, the great Sir Charles Barry (1856–1942). Robinson was joined by Henry Ernest Milner (1845–1906) and his *The Art and Practice of Landscape Gardening* (1890) to lead the naturalists. They argued that architects constricted nature, whereas the formalists, led by Sir Reginald Blomfield's *The Formal Garden in England* (1892), claimed that architecture should establish the form of the garden. Plants were to be only decorative adjuncts but with no brilliant hues, for they injured a building's integrity.

Both sides inclined toward simplicity with topiary in neutral forms to create architectural "rooms." There was no desire to replicate the spectacular sculptural topiary at Elvaston Castle created for the fourth earl of Harrington (from 1830) by William Barron, one of the foremost head gardeners. An American garden, directly inspired by Elvaston, can still be found at the Horatio Hollis Hunnewell estate, Wellesley, Massachusetts (1859).

Robinson's ideas reached a wider audience through his journal *The Garden,* which was subsequently taken over by his longtime contributor and champion of the English flower garden, Gertrude Jekyll (1843–1932). Her first book of many, *Wood and Garden* (1899), introduces her love of the natural and informal as seen in the English cottage gardens of southern England, a love she conveyed to the young architect Sir Edwin Lutyens (1869–1944), who designed her house, Munstead Wood (1893–97). This began a highly successful design collaboration: her naturalism with his easy formalism uniting the philosophical rift between the naturalists and the formalists. Goddards, Abinger, Surrey (1899), was a harbinger of a host of successful collaborations that would reach their creative peak in the first decade of the 20th century.

Further Reading

Alex, William, *Calvert Vaux, Architect and Planner,* New York: Ink, 1994

Beveridge, Charles E., and David Schuyler, editors, *Creating Central Park, 1857–1861,* Baltimore, Maryland: Johns Hopkins University Press, 1983

Briggs, Asa, editor, *The Nineteenth Century,* New York: McGraw-Hill, and London: Thames and Hudson, 1970

Chadwick, George F., *The Park and the Town: Public Landscape in the 19th and 20th Centuries,* New York: Praeger, 1966

Downing, Andrew Jackson, *A Treatise on the Theory and Practice of Landscape Gardening, Adapted to North America,* New York, London, and Boston, 1841; 4th edition, New York, 1850; reprint, Washington, D.C.: Dumbarton Oaks Research Library and Collection, 1991

Elliott, Brent, *Victorian Gardens,* Portland, Oregon: Timber Press, and London: Batsford, 1986

Lawrence, Elizabeth, *The Gardener's Essential Gertrude Jekyll,* Boston: Godine, 1986

Ledward, Daphne, *The Victorian Garden Catalog,* London: Studio, 1995

Leighton, Ann, *American Gardens of the Nineteenth Century,* Amherst: University of Massachusetts Press, 1987

Loudon, John C., *The Suburban Gardener, and Villa Companion,* London: Loudon, 1838; reprint, New York: Garland, 1982

Robinson, William, *The English Flower Garden,* London, 1883; 15th edition, London: Murray, 1933; reprint, Sagaponack, New York: Sagapress, 1995

Roper, Laura Wood, *FLO: A Biography of Frederick Law Olmsted,* Baltimore, Maryland: Johns Hopkins University Press, 1973

Scott-James, Anne, *The Cottage Garden,* London: Lane, 1981

Simo, Melanie Louise, *Loudon and the Landscape: From Country Seat to Metropolis, 1783–1843,* New Haven, Connecticut: Yale University Press, 1988

Stuart, David C., *The Garden Triumphant: A Victorian Legacy,* New York: Harper and Row, and London: Viking, 1988

Weidenmann, Jacob, *Beautifying Country Homes: A Hand Book of Landscape Gardening*, New York, 1870; reprint, as *Victorian Landscape Gardening*, Watkins Glen, New York: The American Life Foundation, 1978

Zaitzevsky, Cynthia, *Frederick Law Olmsted and the Boston Park System*, Cambridge, Massachusetts: Belknap Press, 1982

JOHN MARTIN

Victory Gardens: Russia

The origin of the appellation *victory garden* is found in the vocabulary developed by the Soviet Communist regime in the years following World War II. Guided by the ambition to create new public areas dedicated to the patriotism and heroism the Soviet army had demonstrated during the war, the term *park pobedij* (*pobeda* meaning "victory") was applied. From the late 1940s every Soviet town was furnished with monuments commemorating the heroes of what in the official Soviet terminology was called the Great Patriotic War, and victory gardens were laid out in most of the so-called Hero Cities. The Moscow Victory Garden in Leningrad (1945) counted among the very first. A number of cities throughout the former Eastern bloc were also supplied with gardens reflective of this ideology.

By their military meaning victory gardens are closely related to other garden genres that take the commemoration of war as their point of departure. Contrary to battle gardens and war-memorial gardens, which all aim at visualizing the sacrificial aspect of war, victory gardens have the unilateral celebration of the heroic as their semantic goal.

Most of the characteristics applying to monumental art and architecture are also valid to victory gardens, but the latter necessarily strike a propagandistic chord. Of basic importance are also the public aspect and the demonstrative staging of the emblems of power in an architecture based on well-known and highly connotative forms (triumphal arches, stelae, obelisks, mounds, sarcophaguses). Monumentality in size and clarity in plan are no less crucial for the heroic message to be communicated to the garden users, whether they be organized masses, small groups, or individuals. Ideological as well as aesthetic reasons account for the extensive use of elements from absolutist garden design and urban planning, trimmed with antique and neo-antique touches. Parts of the planting scheme often speak the same symbolic language as the architecture, and large-scale inscriptions are incorporated with the architectural or sculptural program. Individual and mass graves were integrated into some of the early designs, and some victory gardens have been placed where the victory was won, but this is rather unusual.

Although the ideology of the victory garden enjoyed the most favorable conditions of growth in the Soviet Union, different kinds of forerunners of such layouts can be determined. Pictorial testimonies linked to the death cult of the Egyptians, Sumerians, and Assyrians held a specific iconography of victory, and some aspects were later absorbed by European culture. A special cult of the fallen was established in Marathon, with the Great Mound commemorating the Greek soldiers who died in the battle against the Persians in 49 B.C. The Roman *via triumphalis* (triumphal procession) tradition exemplified the idolization of victory in a landscape setting including, for example, processions on Mons Latiaris in the Alban Hills. Moreover the Romans used the obelisk and the column as specific symbols of military victory, such as the trophy set up by Emperor Trajan in Adamklissi (A.D. 109) near the place where the Dacians were defeated.

Direct allusions to these ancient practices can be found in numerous gardens of postmedieval times in countries whose military records justified the festive staging of victory. One of the patrons excelling in this genre was the Russian empress Catherine the Great (1762–96), as shown in her garden at Tsarskoe Selo. The phenomenon literally boomed in the wake of the Napoleonic Wars and again after World War I. The erection of commemorative obelisks and stelae thus affected not only over Europe's public squares but also came to characterize whole areas of royal, noble, and public gardens, regardless of their dominant aesthetic and botanic patterns. The scale differed much from that applied in antiquity and later in the Soviet victory gardens. Yet in Berlin a hill was turned into a public garden in celebration of the efforts of Prussia against France in 1813 and 1815. Works began after a design by Karl Friedrich Schinkel on the Kreuzberg hill (1818), followed by a major remodeling directed by H. Mächtig (1879–80). Significantly enough, the garden was then renamed Victoria Garden.

Following World War II Soviet ideology was quickly and effectively transplanted to the Soviet sector of Berlin. A grandiose public space called the Soviet Memorial was created within the already existing Treptow Garden (inaugurated November 1945; designed by J.V. Vutchetitch).

According to the German and Russian inscriptions on the entrance, the garden is devoted to "the heroes who had fallen for the freedom and independence of the socialist motherland." The scene opens with two red granite blocks made to look like lowered Soviet flags. Within the strictly axial plan is a large parterre garden with raised grass-covered beds for mass soldier graves, terraces and slopes bordered by sarcophagi and decorated with reliefs, inscriptions and martial symbols, and finally a colossal mound that houses a mausoleum crowned by a gigantic soldier figure. A carefully thought-out planting scheme unites the heroic, the emotional, and the national, for example, with the use of poplars, willows, and birch trees.

Variations of this aesthetic and iconographic pattern characterize the Soviet victory gardens of the following decades. One of World War II's fiercest battles, Stalingrad (1942–43), formed the background for the layout of the staggering Mamaev Kurgan complex near the city, today Volgograd. Here the motif of the central mound (*kurgan*) again occurs, integrated with gigantic sculptural works devoted to heroic death, courage and heroism, and women and children (1963–67; design by E.V. Buchetich and Ya.B. Belopolsky).

Following years of planning and debate, the Victory Garden in Moscow was finally inaugurated on Victory Day, 9 May 1995—50 years after the end of World War II.

Designed by A.T. Polyanski, the garden was placed on the city outskirts and axially oriented toward the Triumphal Arch, which commemorates the Russians' successful effort against Napoléon (1813). The garden thus resumes several chapters of Russian and Soviet military history: it encompasses a domed church modeled in the old Russian tradition, a war museum, and an open-air exhibition of military vehicles and large-scale weapons. The extensive grounds are laid out in a strict geometric pattern, dominated by mastodon stone slopes and terraces and planted with alleys, flower beds, and bosquets of birch and fir. The overall language is much more temperate than in earlier victory gardens, the notion having obviously lost much of its ideological power with the collapse of the Soviet Union. Yet the very realization must be seen as an expression of the Russian will to perpetuate former military glory.

Further Reading

Borg, Alan, *War Memorials: From Antiquity to the Present*, London: Cooper, 1991

Floryan, Margrethe, *Gardens of the Tsars: An Analysis of the Aesthetics, Semantics, and Uses of the Late 18th-Century Russian Gardens*, Aarhus, Denmark: Aarhus University Press, and Sagaponack, New York: Sagapress, 1996

MARGRETHE FLORYAN

Victory Gardens: United States

"Food will win the war and write the peace. . . . We need more food than ever before in history. If a suitable space is not available at home, all who can do so are asked to obtain plots on community or allotment gardens that can be reached by bus or street car." These words by Agriculture Secretary Claude Wickard, in a press statement in 1943, illustrate the domestic effort of home and community gardens and their role in aiding in the war effort.

Food production was an important commodity during the era of World War II. Even before the United States entered the war in 1941, U.S. farmers were supplying food for the allies. After the bombing of Pearl Harbor, the strain of providing food and supplies to the troops became evident, as farm labor was in short supply because many workers left for military service. To that end, civilians were asked to aid in the war effort by farming small plots of land in their communities or at their homes to ease the demand for food.

According to the *Guide for Planning the Local Victory Garden Program*, the goals of the program were to

1. Increase the production and consumption of fresh vegetables and fruits by more and better home, school, and community gardens, to the end that we become a stronger and healthier nation.
2. Encourage the proper storage and preservation of the surplus from such gardens for distribution and use by families producing it, local school lunches, welfare agencies, and for local emergency food needs.
3. Enable families and institutions to save on the cost of vegetables and apply this saving to other necessary foods which must be purchased.
4. Provide through the medium of community gardens, an opportunity for gardening by urban dwellers and others who lack suitable home garden facilities.
5. Maintain and improve the morale and spiritual well-being of the individual, family, and Nation.

Rationing had proven ineffective during World War I. After the beginning of the U.S. involvement in World War II, homemakers rushed the grocery store shelves for sugar. This led to the rationing of several key food items, the first being sugar (5 May 1942), the second coffee (29 November 1942), and butter and other fats, canned and frozen goods, and red meat to follow. Milk was never rationed, although canned milk was (because of the metal in the can).

In an address to the nation, President Roosevelt stated that "Every single man, woman and child" was to become "a partner in the most tremendous undertaking of our American History . . . [The] front is right here at home, in our daily tasks." This call to action manifested itself in stamp and bond drives, scrap and salvage collection, and the creation of victory gardens.

The Department of Civil Defense headed up a campaign to convince non-farming families to produce and preserve some of their own food at home. Along with the Office of War Information and private partnership, the Department of Civil Defense mounted a publicity campaign to promote victory gardens. Articles and advertisements ran in popular magazines such as *Good Housekeeping* and *House and Garden*.

Victory gardens were encouraged in four main locations: farms, town and suburban areas, allotment gardens, and school lunch gardens. Gardens sprang up in backyards, vacant lots, and community spaces. Local governments reduced water rates, changed zoning laws to allow chickens and rabbits to be kept in towns, and passed stronger laws to punish theft and vandalism. The summer of 1943 saw the peak of victory garden activity with 20 million victory gardens in America producing one third of all vegetables used, an average of over 13 pounds per week per garden. This became increasingly important as one fourth of the total food production was needed for the armed forces and the allies.

The program assisted the layman in three main areas. First the timing of the campaign planning, how to cultivate and prepare the soil, how to plant a garden, and what to plant. Second, the preserving, canning, drying, freezing and storing of the goods. Third, the protection of resources such as garden tools, fertilizers, insecticides, and other supplies.

Fruit and vegetable production varied by region of the country and urban/rural situation. The recommended list included leafy vegetables (lettuce, cabbage, kale, turnip greens, chard, collards, and spinach), root vegetables (potatoes, sweet potatoes, turnips, parsnips, beets, carrots, and rutabaga), and miscellaneous items such as tomatoes, bush and pole beans, lima beans, peas, onions, radishes, cucumbers, squash, rhubarb, and sweet corn. Over one third of the fruits and vegetables produced were tomatoes. This was due to the small amount of space required to grow tomatoes as well as to shortages.

The Victory Garden movement had an impact on women and children. Women were encouraged to enter the workforce, volunteered for the Red Cross, Civil Defense and War Bond drives, and responded to the wartime programs of rationing and Victory Gardens. Children cultivated gardens at school and home. "Victory Squadrons" were groups of students released from school for portions of days to assist in other community agricultural efforts. School victory gardens directly attributed at least 168,000 acres (67,990 ha) of gardens during the first year of war.

A similar program was conducted during World War I in England. The Woman's Land Army (1918–20) enlisted women in the war effort and allowed them to fight at home by producing food needed at the front. In 1917, 42,000 women enrolled and 8,000 were accepted. This was part of an agricultural effort that led to a total of 300,000 agricultural workers enlisted in the English army.

The Victory Garden program was officially dropped in 1946 because of the perceived lack of threat. This action led to food shortages because the agriculture industry had not yet come back into full production.

Further Reading

Baars, Patricia, Wynell Burroughs, and Jean Mueller, editors, "Victory Gardens in World War II," *Social Education* 50, no. 4 (April/May 1986)

Field, Sherry L., "Roosevelt's World War II Army of Community Service Workers," *Social Education* 60, no. 5 (September 1996)

Hayes, Joanne Lamb, *Grandma's Wartime Kitchen: World War II and the Way We Cooked*, New York: St. Martin's Press, 2000

Laughlin, Margaret, "The Woman's Land Army, 1918–1920," *Social Education* 58, no. 2 (February 1994)

McIntosh, Minnie B., and Frances C. Fox, "City Gardens in Wartime," *Monthly Labor Review* 61 (October 1945)

United States Department of Agriculture, Commission on Victory Gardens, *The 1943 Victory Garden Program*, Washington, D.C.: United States Office of Civilian Defense, 1943

United States Office of Civil Defense, *Guide for Planning the Local Victory Garden Program*, Washington, D.C.: United States Office of Civilian Defense, 1942

United States Office of War Information, Bureau of Campaigns, *The U.S. Campaign to Promote the Production, Sharing, and Proper Use of Food*, Washington, D.C.: Bureau of Campaigns, 1943

JOSEPH C. BLALOCK, JR.

Vienna Stadtpark. *See* Stadtpark

Vignola, Giacomo Barozzi da 1507–1573

Italian Architect

Giacomo Barozzi da Vignola was a painter, architect, and theorist, the most important architect after Michelangelo in Rome in the 1550s and 1560s. On his death Vignola was buried with great honor in the Pantheon, and his two books, the *Regola delli cinque ordini d'architettura* (1562; The Rule of the Five Orders of Architecture) and the posthumously published *Le due regole della prospettiva pratica* (1583; The Two Rules of Practical Perspective), preserved his fame for generations afterward. Yet he did not find it easy working with other architects and artists. Nor was he helped by a decline in patronage in the mid-16th century or by often contentious behavior to his patrons and colleagues. But his achievements were obvious. He established a type of the new church for the Counter-Reformation, and in his secular commissions he produced buildings of a design that were at once original and yet grounded firmly in the principles of antique art and the models of his immediate architectural predecessors. If Leon Battista Alberti had concerned himself only with theory, all Vignola wrote came from the direct study of ancient monuments. With their detailed engravings, Vignola's writings were clearly directed to working architects and to the standardization of the processes of design, now that architecture itself was becoming a recognized practice.

Barozzi was born the son of architects in Vignola, near Bologna, and it was in Bologna that he was first trained as a painter. It was while there working for Baldessare Peruzzi that he probably first showed an interest in architecture. In the late 1530s he moved to Rome, and by 1538 he was at the Vatican. In 1541 he collaborated with Perino del Vaga on sets for a performance of Niccolò Machiavelli's play *Clizia* at the Palazzo Farnese, and in the same year he traveled to France to work with Francesco Primaticcio on casting copies of antique statues to decorate the fountains and gardens of Fontainebleau. On his return Vignola went to Bologna to work on the uncompleted facade of San Petronio. After many disputes, however, especially with the other architect of the project, all his designs were left unexecuted. But while there, he worked on the Palazzo Bocchi (1545–55), a complex, emblematic design, done for the humanist Achille Bocchi, and a

striking columnar portal in the Palazzo Comunale (1547).

By late 1549 Vignola was back in Rome. In 1555 he received a commission from Pope Julius III to design a casino, or small house, on land on the outskirts of the city at the Porta del Populo. Other architects and artists were involved at the Villa Giulia, notably Giorgio Vasari and Bartolommeo Ammannati, but the design for the facade, for which Vignola alone was responsible, became the most important model for the *villa suburbana* in the 16th century, with its tripartite vertical division and arched entrance portico with a balcony above, framed by columns and pilasters. Behind the entrance was a so-called Corinthian room, which led to a semicircular arcade running around the whole garden court. Within this at the lower level was a *nymphaeum*, fed by the recently restored Aqua Vergine; beyond this, on axis, was a view to the garden, seemingly set at the height of the third terrace of the villa, filled with statues that suggested from the courtyard a distinct, distant vanishing point.

Vignola also worked on ecclesiastical projects, the small church of Santa Anna dei Palafrenieri (1565–76) at the Vatican, and the church of Il Gesu (1568–75), a commission from Cardinal Alessandro Farnese. The design here was for a Latin-cross plan with no aisles, allowing larger side chapels and a broader nave to make the cupola at the crossing the dominant visual element. In the end the designs for the facade were not grand enough for Cardinal Farnese, who passed the commission on to Giacomo della Porta. Despite this setback Vignola continued to be busy; he is recorded at the Villa Gambara (Lante), Bagnaia (1568), at the Villa Tuscolana, Frascati (1569), and at Castel Gandolfo (1570). The plan also at the Villa Lante seems to embody his ideals, with its organized design and the classicizing pavilions and parterres at the far end of the garden.

It was again Cardinal Farnese who gave Vignola his greatest commission, the design for a villa at Caprarola (1555–79), a small town northwest of Rome, part of the Farnese fiefdom. There was already on the site a large pentagonal fortress with full bastions, designed by Antonio da Sangallo and Peruzzi. It was on this that Vignola set his design for the palace. A straight street on axis to the main entrance of the palace was cut through the town of Caprarola, and the approach continued beyond balanced semicircular ramps that led to a trapezoidal piazza and flights of stairs to the main portal. Access to the house was also possible from a tunnel cut at the lower level through the exterior bastions. Inside, the upper floor was reached by a long spiral staircase, based on the ramp staircase by Bramante at the Belvedere at the Vatican. Beyond the facade Vignola laid out a sequence of staterooms and a circular chapel and further, a remarkable courtyard, completely round and decorated with 10 bays of superimposed arches, rusticated piers below, and above on the *piano nobile* (main floor) paired Ionic half-columns, a strict circular plan in contrast to the ever-shifting geometry of the pentagonal sides.

Beyond this was the garden, separated from the palace by a deep defensive ditch, divided into two square plans, with plantations of trees between them, encircled by a wall such that they seemed part of the forested hillsides beyond. The gardens were formal, with fountains and parterres, carefully designed to be seen from the palace itself. The whole design, symbolically and scenographically, was an extraordinary achievement. Cardinal Farnese was reproved by Paul III for using his money this way rather than for charity; but even as critical a traveler as Montaigne could say that he had seen "none in Italy that may be compared to it."

See also Giulia, Villa

Biography

Born in Vignola, Emilia-Romagna, Italy, 1507. Trained as painter, Bologna, Italy; moved to Rome, 1530s; traveled to France and worked with Francesco Primaticcio copying antique statues for fountains and gardens of Fontainebleau, Seine-et-Marne, France, 1541; returned to Bologna, then Rome, 1549; employed by Pope Julius III to work on Villa Giulia, Rome, 1555; employed on many other ecclesiastical and private projects; created gardens and villa at Caprarola, Viterbo, Italy, for Cardinal Farnese, 1555–73. Died in Rome, 1573.

Selected Designs

1545–1550   Palazzo Bocchi, Bologna, Emilia-Romagna, Italy

1551–1555   Gardens and casino, Villa Giulia, Rome, Italy
1559–73   Gardens and villa, Palazzo Farnese, Caprarola, Viterbo, Italy
1561   Orto Farnesiani, Rome, Italy
1568   Pavilions and parterres, Villa Gambara (Lante)(now the Villa Lante), Bagnaia, Viterbo, Italy
1569   Villa Tuscolana (now Villa Vecchia), Frascati, Roma, Italy

Selected Publications

Regola delli cinque ordini d'architettura, 1562; as *Vignola: or, The Compleat Architect, Shewing in a Plain and Easie Way the Rules of the Five Orders in Architecture,* 1655; as *Canon of the Five Orders of Architecture,* 1999
Le due regole della prospettiva practica, 1583

Further Reading

Bassi, Elena, editor, *Trattati: Con l'aggiunta degli scritti di architettura,* Milan: Polifilo, 1985
Casotti, Maria Walcher, *Il Vignola,* 2 vols., Trieste: s.n., 1960
Labrot, Gérard, *Le palais Farnese de Caprarola: Essai de lecture,* Paris: Klincksieck, 1970
Lotz, Wolfgang, *Vignola-Studien,* Würzburg, Germany: Triltsch, 1938
Lotz, Wolfgang, *Studies in Italian Renaissance Architecture,* Cambridge, Massachusetts: MIT Press, 1977
Masson, Georgina, *Italian Gardens,* New York: Abrams, and London: Thames and Hudson, 1961; 2nd edition, 1966
Tuttle, R.J., "Vignola," in *The Dictionary of Art,* edited by Jane Turner, vol. 32, New York: Grove, and London: Macmillan, 1996
Vighi, Roberto, *Il nuovo Museo nazionale di Villa Giulia,* Rome: Tipografia Artistica, 1955

DAVID CAST

Villa Aldobrandini. *See* Aldobrandini, Villa

Villa d'Este. *See* Este, Villa d'

Villa Garzoni. *See* Garzoni, Villa

Villa Lante. *See* Lante, Villa

Villa Madama. *See* Madama, Villa

Villa Orsini. *See* Orsini, Villa

Vine

The earliest vine, and still one of the most popular today, is the grapevine. Grapes have been a staple in Western gardens since the earliest gardeners started to grow plants. The common grape (*Vitis vinifera*) is native to southeastern and south-central Europe. The oldest written description of a garden was from the reign of Snefru in Egypt (2600 B.C.) and describes a 2.5-acre (1-ha) core garden belonging to the governor of the northern delta district as having a very large lake and fine trees. An additional thousand acres (404 ha) of vineyards were nearby. Grapevines provided fruit for liquid refreshment, edible leaves, and, in the core garden, much-needed shade to protect the garden visitors. Plants cultivated in gardens during this time were grown for many purposes. They were used for food, cosmetics, herbal properties to cure ailments, and as cut flowers to appease the gods; some were even grown just for decorative purposes.

Grapes continued to be popular in ancient Egypt during the reign of King Tutankhamen (r. 1361–1352 B.C.) and were held in high favor, so much so that they were portrayed on the casket of the king when he died. The Egyptians loved flowers and often grew vines on trellises where shade would also add to the enjoyment of the garden. Another Egyptian king was also fond of vines: Ramses III (r. 1198–1166 B.C.) was known for sending gifts to the people of Heliopolis (now Baalbek, the ancient ruined city north of Cairo). Among these gifts were great gardens planted with trees and vines. In total Ramses donated 514 gardens or their sites to various temples.

The first written record of a Greek garden is found in Homer's *Odyssey* (ninth–eighth century B.C.) and also included a fertile vineyard. One of the most sumptuous gardens, created about 250 B.C., was that of the powerful Greek Hiero II in the Sicilian port city of Syracuse. It was laid out on his boat. In it were shade arbors of white ivy and grapevine planted in casks that were filled with earth. This innovative garden was watered by lead pipes that were hidden from view.

During the same century the Greek naturalist Theophrastus was teaching students about the medicinal uses of plants. He is also the first person in Western literature to document this information. Plants from Egypt particularly interested Theophrastus, but he also identified ivy as a desirable plant in the garden. Expeditions such as those by Alexander the Great to Asia Minor probably brought back jasmine, which was used with ivy and honeysuckle to enclose the walls around many garden perimeters. Trellises were also used to grow these plants.

Roman cloister gardens with a covered passage around a courtyard often had ivy growing up the colonnade or interior wall. These courtyard gardens were an extension of the house. Roman gardeners of the first century A.D. were very fond of plants (including vines) and had them in the house, in the courtyard, and on apartment balconies and roofs, as is done today.

Wisteria played an important part in Renaissance garden designs. Many terraces included wisteria extending up support walls. Wisteria was used as a prominent accent plant at the Villa Gamberaia, a Renaissance Tuscan garden overlooking the Arno valley of Italy. The garden has trompe l'oeil windows painted on the side of the villa wall. The wisteria adds an element of realism to the effect.

Many other Italian Renaissance gardens contained porticoes, which were colonnades or covered main entrances. These were ideal architectural features for growing vines. These twining, informal plants also were used to cover arbors. Architectural wooden pergolas clothed in living green can be found in the Medici villas located around Florence.

French Renaissance gardens also used vine-covered arbors. The restored garden of the 16th-century Château de Villandry in Indre-et-Loire (Tours) contains rose-covered arbors that are strategically situated in the Jardin Potager. The four corners of the center areas of the nine quadrants are the locations for these arbors. Grapes adorn square arbors that line the terrace walks.

A Portuguese garden called Quinta Dos Azulejos built two hundred years later, in the mid-18th century, contains wisteria growing on an arbor structure that resembles a tunnel. This garden has a Mediterranean-style traditional Islamic garden featuring a totally enclosed interior. The purpose of this style of garden is to provide a location for an *ambulatio* (a leisurely walk). Part of this journey takes place under the very shady, tunnel-like, wisteria arbor.

Victorian-era gardening involved much eclecticism, with gardeners tending to use plants in exuberance. Garden beds contained as many plants as possible and were designed for impact. The more bizarre the better. Although vines were not in the forefront of this era that saw the bedding plant achieve prominence, ivy and honeysuckle were important for climbing the walls of homes and were used to add all-important character to the picture. Vines were used to give an image of shadowy foliage demurely hiding the architecture of a house. They were prized more than paint or gilding as an adornment for houses. People hid unsightly fences with delicate foliage and brilliant flowers of climbing vines. Scarlet runner beans (*Phaseolus coccineus*) were used over pantry windows, hop (*Humulus lupulus*) and grapevines over a kitchen garden wall, and morning glory (*Ipomoea purpurea*) for dining-room windows.

These new arrivals to the Victorian garden were also used on trellises. Virginia creeper (*Parthenocissus quinquefolia*) from eastern North America was a fast-growing hardy vine that was ideal for covering the outer walls of homes or as a ground cover. Fragrant tropical jasmine vines could be used for the same purposes in the southern parts of England. English ivy (*Hedera helix*), ideal for bordering flower beds, was the most-admired evergreen vine at this time. It would easily cling to walls and buildings and gave a structure a look of elegance, dignity, and charm. It also was used to cover rustic buildings (cottages) in an informal style. Additionally, English ivy was popular in floral arrangements for its attractive, glossy, dark-green foliage and dark-blue fruit. A new plant to the Victorian garden was the Japanese honeysuckle (*Lonicera japonica*), which was brought to England and then to the United States in the 1870s. The fragrance of this vine made it an instant success. Unfortunately, it is now naturalized in many parts of the United States and is considered a noxious weed.

At the turn of the 20th century, new vines were still being introduced from exotic locations into English gardens. The eminent English garden designer and author Gertrude Jekyll recommended using Dutchman's pipe (*Aristolochia*) and Virginia creeper from the United States, Boston ivy (*Parthenocissus tricuspidata*) from China and Japan, porcelain vine (*Ampelopsis*) from Asia, and Chinese gooseberry (*Actinidia chinensis*) from China in the garden. Wisteria from China or Japan had arrived in the United States and England many years before, in 1816, and was already a staple of the garden. Large-leaved grape and other grapevines, roses, and clematis were also suggested as coverings for pergolas. These provided shady rest sites for garden visitors.

Victorian gardeners enjoyed a huge influx of plants from the many plant hunters traveling the world in search of new and exotic specimens to bring back to English nurseries and botanical gardens. Robert Fortune, a Scottish plant collector who collected in China (for the Royal Horticultural Society) and Japan, is credited with bringing back and introducing 120 prominent species of plants. One of these plants was a clematis with white star-shaped flowers that he brought back in the 1870s. It was said that nothing was prettier on a Victorian porch or veranda.

Powis Castle in Wales is an early English interpretation of an Italian Renaissance garden built in the late 17th century. One of the terrace gardens contains a semicircular vine arbor in the center of the turf lawn. This feature was probably taken from the terraces of the 16th-century Château de Villandry.

Garden designs in England changed dramatically after 1861 when an Irish gardener named William Robinson joined the staff of the Royal Botanic Garden in London. Robinson's preferences had an immense influence on gardens of the time, and reflections of his style can still be seen in most modern gardens today. His gardens exhibited a more informal, naturalistic style than the previously designed Victorian gardens. Vines were a natural way to achieve this style. Robinson used honeysuckle and ivy in many of his gardens designed in the late 19th and early 20th centuries. A prolific author, he wrote a book on clematis entitled *The Virgin's Bower* (1912).

The interest in vines at this time was so strong, due in part to the writings of Robinson and Jekyll, that special structures were being built in gardens to house this group of plants. A vinery is a brick and stone garden house in which vines are cultivated. One of the most attractive is in the garden at Holkham Hall in Norfolk, England. This estate is considered one of the greatest in the country. William Kent, who started as an interior designer and architect and later ventured into garden design, is credited with freeing the garden from formality. By using woodland and lawn, water and shade, he created picturesque scenes in the landscape. Lancelot "Capability" Brown would later continue the work of Kent to create a park-like garden at this site. The gardens of Holkham Hall were constructed over 120 years during the height of the exuberant Victorian gardening era. The vinery, designed by the architect Samuel Wyatt, was completed in 1870. It has a central entrance flanked by two columns and a wrought iron fan overhead. The large building was used for evening parties in the summer and contained fruit trees with the vines.

Vines continue to gain popularity as gardeners enter the 21st century. They are especially useful in small city and suburban gardens. Growing plants vertically to maximize the usefulness of these spaces has led to a continued interest in these plants.

Further Reading

Elliott, Brent, *Victorian Gardens*, Portland, Oregon: Timber Press, and London: Batsford, 1986

Hobhouse, Penelope, *Plants in Garden History*, London: Pavilion Books, 1992; as *Penelope Hobhouse's Gardening through the Ages*, New York: Simon and Schuster, 1992

Huxley, Anthony Julian, *An Illustrated History of Gardening*, New York: Paddington Press, 1978

Jellicoe, Geoffrey, and Susan Jellicoe, *The Landscape of Man: Shaping the Environment from Prehistory to the Present Day*, London: Thames and Hudson, and New York: Viking Press, 1975; 3rd edition, expanded and updated, New York: Thames and Hudson, 1995

Leopold, Allison Kyle, *The Victorian Garden*, New York: Clarkson Potter, 1995

Masson, Georgina, *Italian Gardens*, New York: Abrams, and London: Thames and Hudson, 1961

Phillips, Roger, and Nicky Foy, *A Photographic Garden History*, London: Macmillan, 1995

Plumptre, George, *The Garden Makers: The Great Tradition of Garden Design from 1600 to the Present Day*, London: Pavilion Books, and New York: Random House, 1993

Plumptre, George, *Great Gardens, Great Designers*, London: Ward Lock, 1994

Smit, Daan, and Nicky den Hartogh, *Barokke siertuinen*, The Hague: Atrium, 1995; as *Baroque Gardens*, New York: Smithmark, 1996

Stroud, Dorothy, *Capability Brown*, London: Country Life, 1950

Symes, Michael, *A Glossary of Garden History*, Princes Risborough, Buckinghamshire: Shire, 1993; 2nd edition, 2000

Thacker, Christopher, *The History of Gardens*, Berkeley: University of California Press, and London: Croom Helm, 1979

Wilkinson Barash, Cathy, *Vines and Climbers*, Avenel, New Jersey: Crescent Books, 1997

ANNE MARIE VAN NEST

Vista Garden

Historians generally assign the inception of the vista garden to the 17th century, when classical tastes in villa design demanded long axial avenues that gave a strict order to the garden and directed vision through the immediate garden toward distant landscape elements. However, the vista garden was by no means the invention of European classicism; its roots begin at least as early as ancient Rome, and the vista was a fundamental design determinant in the gardens of Islam and the Far East.

In urban dwellings Roman architects created subtle views that passed from an atrium through a *tablinum* (a central room attached to the atrium's far end) into a peristyle garden; in smaller houses wall paintings gave the illusion of such vistas. The scale was more imposing at the Porticus of Pompey (Rome, 55 B.C.), a vast public court in which the long axial view from the Senate House to the theater was framed by colonnades and rows of shade-giving plane trees. Although Roman patrons sought escape from the city in country villas, they brought the principles of axial organization and climactic vistas with them. For example, at Horace's Sabine Villa (Licenza, Italy, first century B.C.), a viewer standing on the steps of the manor house could gaze down the length of an enormous garden toward a high mountain that, although beyond the perimeter of the property, was the vista's intended finale.

Although Chinese garden designers also liked to contrast the carefully contrived beauty of the garden with the sublime majesty of a distant mountain or valley, unlike the Romans they avoided axiality. The combination of intimate garden with the natural world invited discovery by the viewer, and indeed the only point of juncture between the two was the human eye. For example, Gen Yue (Henan Province, China, 1117–23) was a huge park with a pavilion on a rocky peak from which the emperor could survey the entire manmade and natural landscape below. In a different manner gardens such as Zhuo Zheng (Suzhou, Jiangsu Province, China, 1506–21) united disparate landscape elements—pagodas, trellises, bridges, ponds, and trees—in a balanced arrangement in which the viewer moved sequentially from one scene to another. Paths and landscape elements were manipulated to invite close-range and distant—or "borrowed"—perspectives (respectively called *diu jing* and *jie jing*). From China this interest in the creation of an irregular landscape viewed within garden walls as well as above and beyond them was exported to Japan.

Clearly, a vista can take many forms. While in Asian gardens the view usually avoids the rigid symmetry of the axis, in French classical gardens such as Vaux-le-Vicomte (Seine-et-Marne, France, 1656–61), the view followed a long penetrating axis that united the close at hand with the far away so that the eye integrated the whole in one grand act of looking. The château of the patron Nicolas Fouquet (minister of finance to Louis XIV) at Vaux occupied a central and elevated position, and the view extended from it, descending through the gardens until it reached an enormous statue of Hercules.

But the dominance of the totalizing vista can also be nonaxial, taking the form of a wide panorama that the viewer enjoys as a contrast to the narrow, occluded space preceding it. This is the case in the Alhambra Palace (Granada, Spain, 13th–14th centuries), where vision was contained within the high walls of courtyards, such as the Court of the Myrtles and the Partal (formerly an enclosed space), and then released via a window offering a dramatic view of the surrounding landscape. Poised on the perimeter walls of the Alhambra and the summer estate next door, the Generalife, are more than a dozen such belvederes (the Spanish equivalent is *mirador*, literally, a place for viewing) and towers that offer extensive, all-encompassing views from the hilltop palace to the city and countryside at its feet.

Such vistas had symbolic meaning that were written about and acted on by contemporary patrons and viewers. Chinese gardens represented the natural world in microcosm as well as a symbolic retreat from it, variously reflecting Confucian and Daoist philosophy. At Vaux-le-Vicomte the inflexible axis that stretched from one end of the property to the other gave the illusion of infinite domain, an attribute of supreme power that more properly belonged to Louis XIV himself. Indeed, Fouquet was imprisoned soon after the estate's completion, and members of his design team, most notably André Le Nôtre, were then commissioned to redesign the gardens of Versailles on an even more grandiose scale. To realize the new concept at Versailles, a vast and costly hydraulic infrastructure of waterwheels, canals, reservoirs, and an aqueduct was built, the land was reterraced, and the central axis was directed toward the setting sun, all at an enormous expense of money and human life. The axial avenue that led from the king's apartment in the center of the palace through the garden of parterres and fountains toward the western horizon was a powerful metaphor for absolute rule.

In the Islamic gardens of the Alhambra, the formidable towers and elevated miradors positioned the eye to see a view of the inhabited landscape that was a metaphor for sovereignty. The intended eye was that of the patron, the ruler; and the mirador represented him even in his absence. As at Versailles, although a person other than the ruler might site himself temporarily to experience the full effect of the view (which could not be seen in its entirety except from the designated central position), the adoption of that central viewing place was a temporary transgression that merely emphasized the sovereign's legitimate and permanent possession of it.

Further Reading

Adams, William Howard, *The French Garden, 1500–1800,* New York: Braziller, and London: Scolar Press, 1979

Gleason, Kathryn, "Porticus Pompeiana: A New Perspective on the First Public Park of Ancient Rome," *Journal of Garden History* 14, no. 1 (1994)

Hayakawa, Masao, *Niwa,* Tokyo: Heibonsha, 1967; 2nd edition, 1979; as *The Garden Art of Japan,* translated by Richard Gage, New York: Weatherhill, 1973

Jashemski, Wilhemina F., *The Gardens of Pompeii: Herculaneum and the Villas Destroyed by Vesuvius,* 2 vols., New Rochelle, New York: Caratzas, 1979–93

Keswick, Maggie, *The Chinese Garden: History, Art, and Architecture,* London: Academy Editions, and New York: Rizzoli, 1978; 2nd revised edition, London: Academy Editions, and New York: St. Martin Press, 1986

Ruggles, D. Fairchild, *Gardens, Landscape, and Vision in the Palaces of Islamic Spain,* University Park: Pennsylvania State University Press, 2000

Walton, Guy, *Louis XIV's Versailles,* Chicago: University of Chicago Press, and London: Viking, 1986

D. Fairchild Ruggles

Visual Arts, Garden in

Gardens are found as subject matter in the visual arts for many purposes. While sculpture has long had a significant place in gardens, two-dimensional art forms such as painting, drawing, printmaking, and photography are the media more commonly concerned with garden subjects. All of these arts have re-created ideal or imaginary gardens, have been the inspiration for garden designs, or have recorded a particular aspect of a garden. Most have also been used to present a proposed garden design to a patron or to reproduce on the walls of a room the experience of being in a garden.

In many cultures garden imagery is associated with paradise or heaven, and gardens are sometimes symbolic of more specific meanings, such as the *hortus conclusus* in its association with the Virgin Mary. Gardens have also been the stimulus for other arts—Claude Monet's great series of paintings of his own garden at Giverny records the garden he created as ideal subject matter for his own impressionist art. These many aspects of gardens in the visual arts can be loosely grouped into two categories, representing either imaginary or actual gardens.

Imaginary gardens, whether representations of paradise or simply generalized and idealized garden images, usually communicate aesthetic principles associated with the design of gardens in a particular time and place. From the Western Paradise of the Amida Buddha in Japanese art to the paradise gardens of Persian miniatures, such images present what was most admired in garden art. Similarly, European baroque images of Eden show it as large, geometric, and axial—just as it might have been if designed by André Le Nôtre.

Gardens can be found in the visual arts at least since early in the second millenium B.C. The Egyptians, representing the goods and benefits of earthly life for use in the afterlife, included gardens in tomb paintings and other funerary art, for example, the model of a house and garden from Thebes (11th Dynasty, ca. 2009–1997 B.C.), now in the Metropolitan Museum of Art. Relief sculp-

ture decorating the palaces of Assurbanipal at Ninevah and Darius and Xerxes at Persepolis show aspects of ancient Near Eastern gardens. Gardens play a major role in the illusionistic wall painting of Rome, which often reproduced garden scenes inside houses, sometimes seeming to "paint away" the wall and leaving the viewer in a painted garden. Perhaps the most famous example is the garden scene in the Villa of Livia at Primaporta (late first century B.C.). Illusionistic paintings or mosaics were also included in Roman gardens to extend their views or include imaginary garden features, as for example in the House of Venus at Pompeii (before A.D. 79).

The arts of the medieval world frequently include garden imagery, usually in symbolic or imaginary settings. Garden imagery could represent the Virgin Mary, heaven, Eden, or the sinful world of luxury and materialism. There is rarely any sense that an actual garden is represented; rather, the artist is depicting an idealized garden of the general type known in medieval Europe, usually relatively small in scale, geometric in layout, and enclosed by walls or cloisters.

As mentioned above, gardens are part of the legend and history of the ancient Near East, and they also have a strong place in the arts of the Islamic world. From the 14th century onward, there are few manuscripts of Persian legend or poetry that do not represent a garden someplace, usually as a site of human activity. The format of the gardens is consistent with the layout of actual gardens—walled gardens with two intersecting canals dividing them into four parts—but they too are types rather than images of actual gardens, and like most images mentioned so far, contain mostly fantastic plants and trees, with only a few recognizable species.

Since the Renaissance in Europe, Western art has included topographical views of actual gardens as well as ideal gardens of many different sorts. Many of these were estate views, depicting a great house in its surroundings. Estate views, such as a well-know series of 14 paintings of the villas of the Medici family by Giusto

The Orange Tree Garden at Chiswick, by Pieter Andreas Rysbrack, ca. 1728
Courtesy of Devonshire Collection, Chatsworth, by permission of the Duke of Devonshire and the Chatsworth Settlement Trustees. Photograph courtesy of Photographic Survey, Courtauld Institute of Art

Utens (ca. 1599–1602), often occupied decorative locations inside Italian villas. Mostly these images were taken from a very high viewpoint, emphasizing the scale, geometry, and boundaries of the gardens. Prints, too, recorded great Italian gardens, such as those included in the late-17th-century *Li Giardini di Roma* of Giovanni Battista Falda. The inclusion of gardens as subject matter in the visual arts was closely related to a contemporary understanding that garden design itself was pictorial, with relations to both painting and the creation of theatrical stage sets.

Estate views continue to the present day and are one of the major categories of garden depictions. From the great European estates of the 17th century to English and American country houses in the 18th and 19th centuries, gardens were regularly depicted as elements of great estates. An American example is Benjamin Henry Latrobe's painted watercolor views of George Washington's estate at Mount Vernon (1796).

Baroque gardens in France, those of André Le Nôtre and his contemporaries, were often illustrated in bird's-eye views, the elevated viewpoints helping to emphasize the grand scale, geometric design, and major axes of the gardens. Individual sections of the garden at Versailles were frequently depicted in paintings and prints, and the many prints, for example those of Adam Perelle and Pierre Le Pautre, were often aimed as much at viewers who might never visit the garden as those who knew it well. Dutch gardens of the same period share the geometric focus of French gardens and were also sometimes represented in bird's-eye views.

As European garden design moved from more geometric to more irregular styles, emphasizing variety and surprise, the point of view of painting and prints was generally lowered. Elevated viewpoints lend themselves to the emphasis of geometry and boundaries, while lower viewpoints are better suited to a more pictorial approach to both painting and garden design.

Eighteenth-century England was known for developing the landscape garden, and scholars have long discussed the pictorial aspects of these gardens. Perhaps because of the frequent contemporary associations between painting and gardening, English gardens are some of the most commonly depicted. A number of gardens were painted in multiple views, whose different foci emphasize the variety found in the garden and whose compositional conventions, borrowed from Italianate landscape painting, accentuate the pictorial nature of the garden. In 18th-century England, the relationship between gardening and painting was such a commonplace that even ordinary visitors wrote of the views in gardens in the language of painting.

Despite major differences in Eastern and Western understanding of the purpose and meaning of gardens, the perceived relationship between garden design and other visual arts crosses temporal and cultural boundaries. The great Chinese garden designer Ji Cheng in his garden manual *Yuan ye*, published in 1634, describes the similarity of aesthetics of gardens and paintings. In Chinese painting, as in European and American painting, both ideal and actual gardens are frequent subjects. These paintings generally respect the boundaries that maintain the identity of a garden as a world apart and are attentive to structures and overall design rather than to detail and plant materials. The work of the painter Yüan Chiang (active ca. 1690–1746) includes imaginary representations of famous destroyed palaces and their gardens as well as portraits of existing gardens.

Given the frequency with which pictorial representations of actual gardens are used as historical documentation of garden features or as illustrations in discussions of gardens, it is important to note their limitations as historical evidence. Most views of gardens serve a purpose determined by the audience or patron for the views. In many cases, they flatter, reconstruct, and conform to contemporary pictorial conventions. Even views of particular gardens seldom reproduce what a viewer in a specific location would have seen. Rather, they present characteristic views concentrating on what would have been considered the garden's most important features. Most often, these are the buildings, bodies of water, and other structural elements, not the plants. Details are often ignored or added in the studio rather than on the spot and may therefore be less than faithful to the original. Plant materials are often indistinguishable in species.

Photography would seem to provide more true-to-life representations of gardens, but the relationship between the crafted photographic image and the garden that is its subject is, in reality, very similar to that in other visual arts. A photographer is as careful in selecting viewpoint and presents as personal an interpretation of any garden as a painter or printmaker. Some of the most powerful photographs of gardens are Eugène Atget's evocative images of Versailles and other French gardens—yet these have as little in common with other viewers' experiences of these same gardens as most paintings would. By focusing on a single urn or statue and avoiding the large vistas and grand axes of the gardens, Atget is often able to create a far more intimate and personal experience than many viewers achieve on site.

Not surprisingly, as the hierarchies of subject matter in Western art relaxed in the 19th and 20th centuries, gardens became more likely to be featured in the works of major artists. Monet is the most famous Impressionist painter to paint gardens, but Edouard Manet, Pierre-Auguste Renoir, Mary Cassatt, Gustave Caillebotte, and others also painted garden subjects. At the same time, these artists were less likely than their predecessors to paint or draw or photograph a garden primarily to communicate some aspect of its design than to employ garden imagery as a focus for personal artistic statements. In the 20th century, gardens occasionally appeared in the work of artists as diverse as Howard Hodgkin and Jennifer Bartlett, but their works seldom communicated about gardens themselves at the same level as in previous centuries.

Further Reading

Adams, William Howard, *Atget's Gardens: A Selection of Eugène Atget's Garden Photographs,* London: Fraser, and Garden City, New York: Doubleday, 1979

Arbitman, Kahren, *Gardens of Earthly Delight: Sixteenth- and Seventeenth-Century Netherlandish Gardens,* Pittsburgh, Pennsylvania: Frick Art Museum, 1986

Babelon, Jean Pierre, and Simone Hoog, editors, *Les jardins de Versailles et de Trianon d'André Le Nôtre à Richard Mique,* Paris: Réunion des Musées Nationaux, 1992

Barnhart, Richard M., *Peach Blossom Spring: Gardens and Flowers in Chinese Paintings,* New York: Metropolitan Museum of Art, 1983

Brown, Jane, *The Art and Architecture of English Gardens: Designs for the Garden from the Collection of the Royal Institute of British Architects, 1609 to the Present Day,* New York: Rizzoli, and London: Weidenfeld and Nicolson, 1989

Cayeux, Jean de, *Hubert Robert et les Jardins,* Paris: Herscher, 1987

Clayton, Virginia Tuttle, *Gardens on Paper: Prints and Drawings, 1200–1900,* Philadelphia: University of Pennsylvania Press, and Washington, D.C.: National Gallery of Art, 1990

Fagiolo, Marcello, *Lo specchio del Paradiso: L'immagine del giardino dall'antico al Novecento,* Milan: Silvana, 1996

Griswold, Mac, *Pleasures of the Garden: Images from the Metropolitan Museum of Art,* New York: Metropolitan Museum of Art, 1987

Halpern, Linda Cabe, "The Uses of Paintings in Garden History," in *Garden History: Issues, Approaches, Methods,* edited by John Dixon Hunt, Washington, D.C.: Dumbarton Oaks Research Library and Collection, 1992

Harris, John, *The Artist and the Country House: A History of Country House and Garden View Painting in Britain, 1540–1870,* London: Sotheby Parke Bernet, 1979; revised edition, London: Sotheby, and New York: Harper and Row, 1985

Hobhouse, Penelope, *Painted Gardens: English Watercolours, 1850–1914,* New York: Atheneum, 1988; London: Pavilon, 1991

Holme, Bryan, *The Enchanted Garden: Images of Delight,* New York: Oxford University Press, and London: Thames and Hudson, 1982

Jackson-Stops, Gervase, *An English Arcadia, 1600–1990: Designs for Gardens and Garden Buildings in the Care of the National Trust,* Washington, D.C.: American Institute of Architects Press, 1991; London: National Trust, 1992

Laing, Ellen Johnston, "Quin Ying's Depiction of Sima Guang's Duluo Yuan and the View from the Chinese Garden," *Oriental Art* 33, no. 4 (1987–88)

Titley, Norah M., *Plants and Gardens in Persian, Mughal, and Turkish Art,* London: British Library, 1979

Treib, Marc, "Frame, Moment, and Sequence: The Photographic Book and the Designed Landscape," *Journal of Garden History* 15, no. 2 (1995)

LINDA CABE HALPERN

Vizcaya Villa

Miami, Florida, United States

Location: approximately 2 miles (3.2 km) southwest of central Miami

The gardens of Villa Vizcaya are perhaps the finest expression of 16th-century Italianate garden design in America. The villa, which once encompassed 180 acres (73 ha) and created a veritable media frenzy when it was completed in 1916, was built by James Deering, a wealthy industrialist and heir to the International Harvester fortune. Deering, a quiet and intensely private bachelor, sought a tropical retreat from the icy winters of his Michigan home. After seeking recommendations from his wealthy friends, Deering hired Paul Chalfin to oversee building a suitable estate on the shores of Biscayne Bay. Chalfin, a painter who had trained in Europe and served as the protégé of famed interior designer Elsie de Wolfe, formed the idea of re-creating a 16th-century Italian villa.

During the period between 1910 and 1915, Deering and Chalfin traveled through Europe to study architectural design and to collect, on a massive scale, antiquities and statuary for Deering's residence. At the same time, work was proceeding on the house, and in December 1916, Deering moved into his Italianate palazzo. The house, which held one of the most extensive collections of 15th- through 19th-century decorative arts in America, was complete in every detail, but outside its doors the grounds and gardens-to-be lay in shambles.

In 1914 Chalfin had hired Diego Suarez to design the Vizcaya gardens. Suarez, a native of Columbia, studied architecture in Italy and had absorbed the intricacies of garden design from his friend Arthur Acton, who owned Villa la Pietra outside of Florence.

Suarez initially designed the Vizcaya gardens to resemble a typical Italian hillside with descending levels dropping to a lake or other body of water. However, when Suarez traveled to Miami, he was immediately dismayed. The harsh Florida sun was totally unlike the soft ambient light of the Italian countryside; indeed, the glare off the lagoon at the southern edge of the Vizcaya property was blinding. Standing on the construction site, Suarez drastically changed his plans. Instead of having the gardens descend to the lagoon, there would be a sculpted landscape with an artificial hillock at the water's edge, leading the viewer's eye up rather than down. In addition, to visually open up the garden, two long axial paths would fan out at angles to the left and right—an idea Suarez borrowed from Villa Gamberaia at Settignano.

Suarez's plans were complete by 1917, when Chalfin was ready to begin construction of the formal gardens, but by then World War I was absorbing all available manpower. Chafin dismissed Suarez from Deering's employment, and when the gardens were completed in 1921, Chalfin claimed credit for their design. Indeed, for the next 45 years, Suarez's name was not associated with Vizcaya. Only in the mid-1950s was the record set straight, and Suarez received the recognition he deserved.

The southern gardens, covering ten acres (4 ha), remain today essentially as they were in 1921. Formal and baroque in design, they are crafted around controlled views, precise geometric configurations, evergreen shrubbery, stonework (as evidenced in statuary and other architectural aspects), and water features. The plant material is adapted to the realities of Vizcaya's subtropical climate, with live oak (*Quercus virginiana*),

Jasminum simplicifolium at Vizcaya Villa, Miami, Florida
Copyright Garden Matters

evergreen jasmine (*Jasminum simplicifolium*), and palms playing prominent roles.

The main axis of the south garden is aligned with the main axis of the house. It runs across an elevated reflecting pool that is flanked by an allée of clipped live oaks and up a water staircase to the casino on the mount. The staircase, composed of two flights of stairs between which there is a channel of splashing water, is flanked by shell-lined grottoes and is reminiscent of the water staircase at Villa Lante. The casino, or house in miniature, not only forms the major focal point of the garden but also is a characteristic Renaissance conceit. From it, garden visitors could look over the quiet blue waters of the lagoon or back toward the impressive palazzo, adding yet another dazzling contrast within the garden.

On both sides of the main axis, the garden is carpeted with intricate parterres, frankly imitative of the French-style *broderie* patterns at La Reggie outside of Naples. The two axial walkways that fan out from the terrace are lined with antique statuary depicting mythological gods and goddesses. Nestled beyond the walkways are several smaller, more intimate gardens: a walled secret garden (*giardino segretto*), a theater garden with seats of grass, a maze garden, and the fountain garden. The latter garden features a 17th-century travertine fountain that once served as the village fountain for Bassano di Sutri outside of Rome. Deering had acquired the fountain on one of his trips to Italy by agreeing to build a modern water supply system in exchange for the sculpture.

The eastern terrace of the villa overlooks Biscayne Bay. Although there was no room for Suarez to design a garden per se, one of Suarez's most celebrated landscape elements lies in the water on the eastern side of the house. A rubble pile had arisen in the bay during the

Reflected plinth at Vizcaya Villa, Miami, Florida
Copyright Garden Matters

course of the construction of the house, and Deering and Chalfin had determined that it should be turned into a breakwater in the shape of a boat. Inspired by Isola Bella in northern Italy, where the entire gardens are built in the shape of a barge, Suarez's splendid breakwater is about 53 meters (57 yd.) long and 11 meters (12 yd.) wide and is graced by massive sculptures created by the noted artist Alexander Calder.

Deering was to enjoy the gardens for only four years, from 1921 until his death in 1925. At that time, the entire 180-acre (73-ha) estate—complete with island gardens extending beyond the formal gardens, a private yacht basin, gondola canals, a small farm, a dairy, and a tropical forest—were to remain virtually neglected for nearly 30 years. Beginning in the mid-1940s, Deering's heirs sold all but the core 28 acres of the estate, which were acquired by Dade County. In 1952, Villa Vizcaya

was opened to the public, and the grounds remain an authentic example of Renaissance garden design.

Synopsis

1910	James Deering and Paul Chalfin begin to travel through Europe purchasing antiquities and statuary for estate
1911	Deering hires Chalfin as artistic director for Florida building project
1912	Deering purchases initial acreage along Biscayne Bay
1914	Diego Suarez hired as landscape architect to design gardens for Vizcaya; construction of house begun
1916	Construction of house completed and Deering moves in on Christmas Day

1916–19	Chalfin dismisses Suarez; garden construction interrupted by World War I
1919	Work on garden recommenced
1921	Gardens completed
1925	Deering dies and nieces and nephews inherit Vizcaya
1925–34	Vizcaya largely neglected
1926	Hurricane causes substantial damage
1934–35	Vizcaya opened to public during two winter seasons
1945	Catholic Church purchases 130 acres (53 ha) of Vizcaya estate as hospital site
1952	Dade County, Florida, acquires Vizcaya's remaining acreage; Vizcaya opened to public as museum
1994	Vizcaya designated National Historic Landmark

Further Reading

Harwood, Kathryn Chapman, *The Lives of Vizcaya: Annals of a Great House*, Miami, Florida: Banyan Books, 1985

Maher, James T., *The Twilight of Splendor: Chronicles of the Age of American Palaces*, Boston: Little Brown, 1975

SUSAN GARRETT MASON

von Anhalt-Dessau, Franz. *See* Anhalt-Dessau, Franz von

von Sckell, Friedrich Ludwig. *See* Sckell, Friedrich Ludwig von

Vrtba Garden

Prague, Malá Strana, Czech Republic

Location: Karmelitská Street 25, Malá Strana, 0.25 mile (0.4 km) south of Prague Castle

The Petřín Mountain, with its many gardens, plays an important role in the picture of the Czech Republic's capital, showing a captivating configuration of houses, palaces, and churches and enhanced by a dominating feature, its many towers. In the place where the eastern slopes of the hill turn to the north, the Vrtba Garden, one of the best creations of Central European landscaping and Prague baroque style, is set into the slope. This garden is part of the Vrtba Palace, in Malá Strana. Visitors and admirers come into the garden through a carriageway and the two courtyards of the house behind which it is hidden.

Two Renaissance houses and a vineyard of the lords of Lustenek are the basis of a palace complex whose building development has been complicated. These properties were bought between 1627 and 1631 and the houses reconstructed by a member of an ancient Czech aristocratic family, Count Sezima of Vrtba.

Laying out the Vrtba garden (0.31 hectares [0.76 acres]) between 1715 and 1720 was part of the second important construction period of the palace after 1709. Connected with the development of a magnificent baroque garden, the reconstruction of the palace was decided on by their owner at that time, Count Jan Josef of Vrtba, the supreme burgrave of the Prague Castle and a bearer of the Order of the Golden Fleece. Jan Josef, Sezima's grandson, entrusted the Czech architect and builder František Maxmilián Kaňka (1674–1766) with carrying out this work. Kaňka had Italian training and at first collaborated with artists of Italian origin, such as Santini-Aichl or Alliprandi. Besides Italian training,

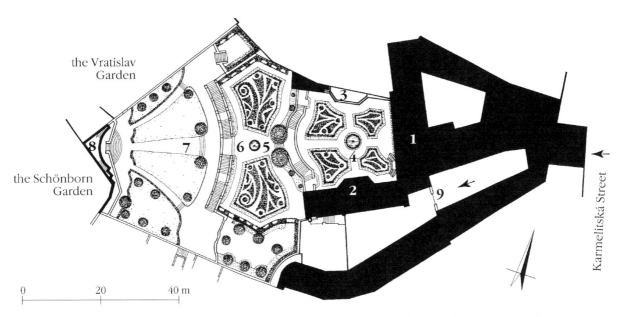

Plan of Vrtba Garden: 1—Vrtba Palace; 2—*sala terrena;* 3—*voliére* for birds; 4—parterre in front of *sala terrena;* 5—middle terrace;
6—supporting wall with double-armed staircase, gallery of sculptural vases and figures representing classical gods; 7—upper terrace; 8—*theatron;*
9—entrance gate
Copyright Karin Dienstbierová

Kaňka, a native of Prague, also had an unusual sense of the Bohemian environment and Prague that showed in his work. In the case of the Vrtba Garden it manifested itself through immense inventiveness in space arrangement and certainty in shaping the garden as a space and a layout. On an irregularly shaped building plot ascending a steep slope, he attained a surprising effect in composition, especially due to the gradation of the mass of three levels of the garden, which were held by convexly or concavely shaped retaining walls and culminating in a *theatron* shaped like an arc. It is also interesting to see the way in which the baroque style made the most of axes, using the short one between the *sala terrena* and the aviary in the low part of the garden as a basis for tangentially meeting the axis that is the backbone of the garden's composition. He closed the axis at the highest level of the garden by the *theatron,* linked with the other elements by two ramp roads. Thus, he cleverly called to memory the modified link of stairs or ramps with palaces, casinos, or *gloriettas* (a pavilion away from the house) on the highest terraces of Italian gardens and, more important, preserved the ancient domestic tradition of a towerlike lookout grape press; this tradition dates back to some time during the 16th century.

Sculptural decoration by Matyáš Bernard Braun (1684–1738) and frescoes by Václav Vařvinec Reiner (1689–1743) certainly contributed to Kaňka's convincing interpretation of the garden's style. A sculptor and wood carver, Braun was a native of Oetz near Innsbruck in the Tyrol and probably was trained in Salzburg by B. Mandl,

a native of Prague. Braun subsequently sojourned in Italy, where he came to know especially Bernini's dynamic works and drew lessons from them. He settled in Prague in 1710 and introduced himself by means of his now famous St. Luitgarde's sculptural group on Charles's Bridge. Thereafter, he was not short of orders and was able to establish his workshop. He created a set of statues and sculptural vases for the Vrtba Garden. The landing and the massive retaining hall with double-flight stairs between the second- and the third-highest levels of the garden came to be decorated with vases with plentiful reliefs and statues of ancient gods: Apollo with a bow, Mercury, Diana with a dog, Juno with a peacock, Minerva with a shield, Jupiter with an eagle, and Vulcan with a hammer. The originals, made from 1720 to 1735, are now kept in a collection of sculptures elsewhere, with copies in their stead on the bridge. As to the other originals, two statues have been left in the *sala terrena,* namely those of Bacchus and Ceres. Two other originals, those of Flora and of an unidentified goddess, are located laterally on the gate between the first and the second courtyards. Atlas, erected on the gable molding of the gate, is a copy.

The way in which the problem of colors in the architecture of the garden has been solved is another proof of the inventiveness of, and mutual collaboration between, the members of the creative team. The painted windows of the aviary and the color treatment of the retaining wall between the medium and the highest levels of the garden have been reconstructed according to the results of research, except for the paintings on the free fields of this wall, which have disappeared. Rainer's 1720 fresco on the face wall of the final *theatron* at the highest level of the garden has disappeared as well, while it has been possible to reconstruct the plastic decoration of the *theatron* with reliefs showing sea gods and virgins. The plastic and painted decoration of the *sala terrena* and the little *salon* adjacent to it in the west have been preserved, too. The plastic and painted decoration of the central area of the *sala terrena* produces the impression of romantic architectural works with mythological scenes and vistas of landscape. Showing a scene with Venus and Adonis, the fresco on the vault of the *sala terrena* is authentic evidence of the collaboration of Reiner, one of the most important painters of the high baroque style in Bohemia, who was trained by Michael Václav Halbax and Petr Brandl and who has become especially famous as a fresco painter.

Unlike the preserved structures of the garden—that is, those from the baroque or later additions, especially in the form of two small pavilions built after 1839 in the central part and plastic decoration and sculptural and to some extent even painted decoration—the original approach to vegetation and its original structure as to the individual species are known only from indefinite descriptions and later iconography. Therefore, when preparing the rehabilitation of the garden, which was carried out between 1990 and 1998, it was necessary to come to terms with this reality. To approach the assumed original state, substitutions having a reminiscent character have been chosen. Clipped low borders consisting of common box (*Buxus sempervirens*) were used to frame the vegetation fields. Box also forms the basis of the clematis *broderie* of the parterre in front of the *sala terrena*, mentioned as a flat *giardinetto*. Box and common yew and Japanese yew (*Taxus baccata* and *Taxus cuspidata*) have also been used to emphasize the shaped accents in the forms of balls and cones. Cube forms, including one with cut-out arcs, have been made of clipped hornbeam (*Carpinus betulus*). At the leveling stairs leading to the central part of the garden, two preserved Oriental arborvitae (*Thuja orientalis*) continue to show off. Flowers, both estival plants and biannuals, are used to emphasize plant decoration and enrich it. Roses and perennials have a durable effect as to colors.

An ascent to the highest parts of the garden gradually unveils unique vistas of the city, many churches, neighboring gardens, and the picturesque configuration of the Malá Strana and Hradčany roofs. From the *theatron*, especially from the observation point set up on its roof during the modifications carried out between 1826 and 1835, a large segment of the panorama of the city may be seen, with the dominant features formed by Hradčany, the dome of St. Nicholas's Church on the Malá Strana Square, and the towers of the Church of Our Lady Victorious in Karmelitská Street. Consequently, the Vrtba Garden can be said to be an extraor-dinary garden work and an open-air gallery of statues, as well as an observation point showing a city that cannot be forgotten.

Synopsis

1588	Area of future palace complex comes under Malá Strana jurisdiction
1591	Imperial architect Oldřich Avostalis de Sala builds house next to that of famous Bohemian Lord Kryštof Harant of Polžice and Bezdružice
1598	Avostalis dies, house bought by E. Schmidgrabner of Lustenek
1621	Houses of Lord Harant and Schmidgrabner confiscated
1627–31	Houses and vineyard bought by Count Sezima of Vrtba, who joins them and creates Vrtba palace complex
1650	Vineyard destroyed by phylloxera
1687	Count Jan Josef of Vrtba inherits houses and land of former vineyard, preserves late-Renaissance facade and begins to cultivate land
1709	Second great building period of palace complex begun
1715–20	Vrtba Garden laid out, designed by Frantisek Maxmilián Kaňka, for Count Jan Josef and wife, M.J. of Heisenstein
1720–35	Matyáš Bernard Braun creates set of statues and vases for garden, Václav Vavřinec Reiner works on painted decoration
1723	Jan Josef welcomes Emperor Charles VI on visit to garden
1799	Palace complex bought by university professor J. Mayer
1800	Palace reconstructed to design by Josef Klement Zobel
1825–40	*Theatron* repaired and observation point constructed on roof; garden redesigned in English landscape style; two small Empire pavilions built in central part of garden (eastern one rented by painter Mikuláš Aleš)
1911	House and garden bought by wholesale merchant Felix Lüftner from Judge Vokaun, who had let garden go to waste at turn of the century
1945	Palace complex becomes property of Czechoslovak state
1952–90	Garden administered by enterprise Gardening Centers of City of Prague, and subsequently by Parks, Woods, and Gardening Centers of City of

Prague, while house administered by District Enterprise for Management of Houses; parterre between *sala terrena* and aviary used as playground by a nursery school, remaining part of garden opened to public

1990–98   Renovation of garden

Further Reading

Bašeová, Olga, *Pražské zahrady* (Prague Gardens), Prague: Panorama, 1991

Birnbaumová, Alžběta, and Miroslav Volek, "Dvě nejkrásnájší zahrady severního svahu Petřína (The Two Most Beautiful Gardens on the Northern Slope of Petřín)," in *Staletá Praha* (Prague Hundreds of Years Old), vol. 4, Prague: Orbis, 1969

Dokoupil, Zdenek, et al., *Historické zahrady v Čechách a na Moravě* (Historic Gardens in Bohemia and Moravia), Prague: Nakl. Československých Výtvarných Umělcu, 1957

Lejsková-Matyášová, Milada, "Altány, gloriety, saly terreny prazských zahrad (Bowers, Gloriettas, and Salas Terrenas in Prague Gardens)," in *Staletá Praha* (Prague Hundreds of Years Old), vol. 4, Prague: Orbis, 1969

Pacáková-Hoštálková, Božena, et al., *Zahrady a parky v Čechách, na Moravě a ve Slezsku* (Gardens and Parks in Bohemia, Moravia, and Silesia), Prague: Libri, 1999

Petrů, Jaroslav, and Antonín Marián Svoboda, "Pražské zahrady (Prague Gardens)," in *Zahradnický slovník naučný* (Gardening Encyclopedia), vol. 4, Prague: ÚZPI, 1999

Poche, Emanuel, "Zahrada domu Vrtbovského v Praze III (The Garden of the Vrtba House in Prague III)," *Umění* 10 (1927)

Wirth, Zdeněk, *Pražské zahrady* (Prague Gardens), Prague: Poláček, 1943

BOŽENA PACÁKOVÁ-HOŠŤÁLKOVÁ

W

Wales

United Kingdom

Wales is a small, largely upland country, with a population that has always been concentrated in its more fertile lowland fringes. It had been thought that Wales had very few historic parks and gardens or that most of those created had long since disappeared. Recent research has shown that this is far from the case; Wales is now known to have a wealth of parks and gardens of all periods, from the medieval to the 20th century. Some, such as Powis Castle and Bodnant, are of international importance and well known, but many more have survived in relative obscurity.

In a general way the development and style of Welsh parks and gardens follow those of England. What sets the Welsh gardens apart is the landscapes in which many of them are set—the spectacular mountains of Snowdonia and northwest Wales, the dramatic Wye valley, the steep and picturesque Ystwyth valley, the Menai Strait, the gentler Conwy valley, and Vale of Clwyd, the intricate estuaries of Pembrokeshire. The utilization and borrowing of this scenery is what gives these historic parks and gardens their special Welsh character. Makers of notable gardens tended to come from the higher social strata, to be wealthy, or both. In early periods this meant noblemen and church leaders; later, particularly in the 18th century onward, many gentry landowners ventured into landscaping. Mineral wealth, including lead, copper, iron ore, and coal, played a part in creating sufficient wealth to build and landscape on a grand scale. In the 19th century industrialists, many of them incomers to Wales, played an important part.

The earliest parks and gardens to survive in Wales date to the medieval period. During this time the wealthy created many deer parks, a few of which remain. Those at St. Donat's Castle and Ewenny Priory (Glamorgan) are walled, while that of Abergavenny Priory (Monmouthshire) is surrounded by a bank and ditch. A survival of great rarity is the layout of beds and paths of a monastic garden of the 15th century at Haverforwest Priory (Pembrokeshire). Other gardens of the period are known only from records, for example the gardens made for Queen Eleanor of Castile while on campaign with Edward I, in the north Wales castles of Conwy, Caernarfon, and Rhuddlan.

Wales has some important formal gardens from the Tudor and Stuart periods. During this time some of the noblemen of Wales occupied prominent positions at court. They were well versed in the latest fashions and created grand and notable gardens, some of which survive. The most outstanding are the large-scale terraced gardens at Raglan Castle (Monmouthshire) and St. Donat's Castle, the formal gardens and bowling green of Gwydir Castle (Conwy), and the small but well-preserved gardens at Vaynol (Gwynedd) and Garthgynan (Denbighshire). The walled garden of Chirk Castle (Whitehurst Gardens, Denbighshire) was built in the 1650s.

In the late 17th century a more expansive, but still formal, style developed. Great axial arrangements of avenues, rides, and canals were laid out, often to be removed by the next, more informal phase of landscaping. Some of the greatest historic parks and gardens of Wales are of this era and style. The most famous is Powis Castle (Powys), whose baroque terraces, probably of the 1690s, cascade down the steep slope below the castle. Erddig (Wrexham) includes a grand canal; Llangedwyn Hall (Powys) has terraces contemporary with those of Powis Castle. Tredegar House (Newport) retains its walled gardens and one great avenue; Llanfihangel Court (Monmouthshire) has beautiful terraces and an original sweet chestnut avenue. Magnificent lime avenues survive at Mostyn Hall (Flintshire) and Soughton Hall (Flintshire). An elaborate Italianate garden,

Powis Castle, Wales
Copyright Kevin Richardson/Garden Picture Library

complete with water tricks, was made at Llannerch (Denbighshire), but it has long since gone.

Formal landscaping survived for slightly longer in Wales than in England; the "natural" landscape park did not generally take root until the late 18th century, and most examples are from the early 19th century. There are a few ornamental landscapes of transitional type from the mid-18th century, which are of great significance. The most important are Leeswood (Flintshire), laid out by Stephen Switzer in 1728–32, and The

Gnoll (Glamorgan), in which a formal cascade was made in the 1720s and an informal one in the 1740s. Many parks were designed in a low-key manner by their owners or agents, but some employed fashionable designers of the day. Chief among these was William Emes, who worked on the parks of Chirk Castle, Erddig, Powis Castle, Penrice Castle (Swansea), and others between 1760 and 1790. Lancelot "Capability" Brown did a little work in Wales. His major commission here was at Wynnstay (Wrexham), where in 1777–83 he laid out a park and pleasure ground, which survive, and made a great lake and cascade, without water since the dam burst in the 19th century. Humphry Repton had only three definite Welsh commissions, at Plas Newydd (Anglesey), Rug (Denbighshire), and Stanage Park (Powys). All are exceptionally fine landscape parks in beautiful and varied landscape settings. Repton admitted that "appropriation of landscape" was the key to his landscaping at Rug, and the same could be said for both Plas Newydd, which has magnificent views across the Menai Strait to Snowdonia, and Stanage. Of the numerous other landscape parks, special mention should be made of Clytha Park (Monmouthshire), which contains a famous folly, Clytha Castle, and Dynevor Park (Carmarthenshire), on the edge of the beautiful Tywi valley.

The discovery of the picturesque and romantic qualities of the Welsh landscape during the second half of the 18th century led to the creation of the most famous picturesque landscapes in Wales. The first was Piercefield (Monmouthshire), where a spectacular walk was made by Valentine Morris along the lip of the Wye valley in the 1750s. In the 1780s and 1790s Thomas Johnes created the picturesque domain of Hafod in the Ystwyth valley. Very soon both were famous destinations of travelers in search of the picturesque, Piercefield being incorporated into what became known as the Wye Tour—a boat trip down the river Wye from Ross-on-Wye to Chepstow. Perhaps the most eccentric use of the Welsh landscape in this way was at Plas Newydd, Llangollen, where Eleanor Butler and Sarah Ponsonby, the "Ladies of Llangollen," led a life of "sweet retirement" in their rural cottage and romantic garden.

The Victorian era of the 19th century produced great parks and gardens of a rather different kind. Formality returned around the house, and new plant introductions, such as American conifers (wellingtonia [*Sequoiadendron giganteum*], monkey puzzle [*Araucaria araucana*], Douglas fir [*Pseudotsuga douglasii*]) and rhododendrons, changed the face of pleasure grounds. The wealthy built grandiose mock castles, such as Penrhyn Castle (Gwynedd), Margam Castle (Glamorgan), Bodelwyddan Castle (Denbighshire), and Gwyrch Castle (Conwy), the last perhaps the ultimate romantic Gothic extravaganza, complete with matching park and garden walls, lodges, and farm buildings. Many others followed suit on a smaller scale. Some of the great Victorian designers worked in Wales: W.E. and W.A. Nesfield worked on Kinmel Hall (Denbighshire) and Bodelwyddan (Denbighshire), both of which have outstanding formal gardens. Edward Milner designed the gardens of Dingestow Court (Monmouthshire) and Bryn-y-neuadd (Conwy), where an impressive mid-19th-century French fountain survives. Wales has the dubious distinction of being the birthplace of the Leyland cypress (x *Cupressocyparis leylandii*), which arose as a natural cross at Leighton Hall (Powys), where the grand Victorian gardens were designed by Edward Kemp, a pupil of Sir Joseph Paxton.

The Edwardian period was an eclectic one, with examples in Wales of many different styles, including Japanese. The outstanding site of the period is Bodnant (Conwy), a garden of enormous horticultural interest, created by several generations of the Aberconway family. Designers such as T.H. Mawson, H. Avray Tipping, C.E. Mallows, Percy Cane, and Clough Williams-Ellis have left a valuable legacy of imaginative formal gardens, often in spectacular situations. Mawson's Dyffryn (Glamorgan) is the most important formal Edwardian garden in Wales. Williams-Ellis's own garden of Plas Brondanw draws in the mountain peaks around it through the clever channeling of views.

Public parks from the Victorian and Edwardian eras are an integral part of the legacy of historic parks and gardens in Wales. They are mainly concentrated in the urban, industrial cities of Cardiff and Swansea, with most of the remainder in seaside resorts. Cardiff has two great public parks—Bute Park, which was formerly the private park of the marquesses of Bute, and Roath Park, the first municipal park in the city. In Swansea the principal public parks of Singleton and Clyne, which contain planting of exceptional botanical interest, were formerly the private grounds of houses of the Vivian family.

While this brief review only skims the surface of the wealth and diversity of historic parks and gardens in Wales, it demonstrates that the historic parks and gardens of Wales can stand in comparison to those in the rest of Britain.

Further Reading

Briggs, C.S., "The Fabric of Parklands and Gardens in the Tywi Valley and Beyond," *Carmarthenshire Antiquary* 33 (1997)

Lloyd, Thomas, *The Lost Houses of Wales: A Survey of Country Houses in Wales Demolished since c. 1900*, London: Save Britain's Heritage, 1986; 2nd edition, 1989

Whittle, Elisabeth, "The Renaissance Gardens of Raglan Castle," *Garden History* 17, no. 1 (1989)

Whittle, Elisabeth, *The Historic Gardens of Wales,* London: H.M.S.O., and Cardiff, Wales: Cadw, Welsh Historic Monuments, 1992

Whittle, Elisabeth, "The Historic Parks and Gardens of Gwent, 1: Medieval to *c.* 1720," *Monmouthshire Antiquary* 10 (1994)

Whittle, Elisabeth, "The Tudor Gardens of St. Donat's Castle, Glamorgan, South Wales," *Garden History* 27, no. 1 (1999)

ELISABETH WHITTLE

Walled Garden

The walled garden is perhaps the archetype of the garden: an enclosed space definitively set apart from the surrounding land. Walled gardens are found in many parts of the world and in many different cultural traditions. Certainly for those that inherited something of the early Persian traditions, the Garden of Eden or paradise (*pairidaeza* in ancient Persian) is known to have been defined by its enclosure. The reasons for enclosure are complex and have no doubt included psychological and symbolic factors, as well as the practical, from earliest times. A key virtue of the surrounding barrier is that it keeps things out—unwanted animals, people, and, perhaps most important of all, wind. The walls modify the microclimate and, in particular, can ameliorate the effects of potentially damaging and drying winds, so that conditions are created conducive to plant growth and human comfort.

The walled garden's pedigree goes back as far as the record of human settlement, and there is archaeological evidence of walled gardens (some very small) in the Neolithic settlements of the Near East and in Bronze Age settlements from Mesopotamia to northern Europe. The shape of early gardens derived from the structure of dwellings and the spaces between and around them (often rectilinear) or from the traditions of animal herding and ease of construction (mostly circular). A beautiful early example of an extensive walled garden is shown in a tomb painting at Thebes, dating from Egypt's New Kingdom (1567–1085 B.C.), which shows a tile-capped wall around a rectangular space, lined internally with date palms, pomegranates, and other trees and containing four lotus-filled duck ponds and a central vine-covered arbor or trellis.

The courtyard garden, where the house creates the enclosure, is a special type of walled garden that particularly favors the integration of indoor and open-air living and the exclusion of the outside world. It is therefore well suited to warm climates and to societies that place emphasis on privacy or segregation—for example, of women from men or for those in religious orders. The courtyard garden has found many expressions throughout history and across cultures: Chinese urban development was organized around courtyards and larger walled enclosures for millennia, and the traditional urban form of the Near and Middle East was evidently an Islamic refinement of much earlier courtyard house traditions in the region. The ancient Roman peristyle court was an elegant expression of the type, as seen in the remains of the House of the Vettii at Pompeii, and remained part of the vocabulary of the Roman monastic tradition (perhaps also benefiting from experience of the Moorish courtyards of Spain)—the cloister—for centuries thereafter.

Medieval gardens in Europe were almost exclusively walled, whether or not they contained further internal subdivisions such as the *hortus conclusus.* Manuscript illustrations of secular landscapes show walled pleasure gardens or *herbers* containing flowery meads (meadows) and fruit trees, plant trellises and arbors. More utilitarian kitchen and physic gardens contained regular, rectangular plant beds for vegetables and herbs, together with fruit and nut trees that were sometimes trained against the walls. The monastic tradition included the walled orchard, often combined with a cemetery as shown in a ninth century illustration of Saint Gall, Switzerland, which parallels and contrasts with the Moorish tradition evident in the early-12th-century Patio de Los Naranjos (Court of Orange Trees), Córdoba, a mosque courtyard of orange trees with an elegant irrigation system of water channels set into the paving.

The most sophisticated use of walled gardens, in horticultural terms, was probably developed between the 17th and 19th century in northern Europe, and in Scotland in particular. It drew upon the medieval walled garden tradition, enhanced by Renaissance sophistication of layout and, eventually, 19th century engineering and technological ingenuity. Walled gardens in all climates can give protection from wind damage, whether the hot, drying winds of the Mediterranean or the cold and salt-laden ones of the North Sea. The added benefit in northern latitudes is the storage and reradiation of

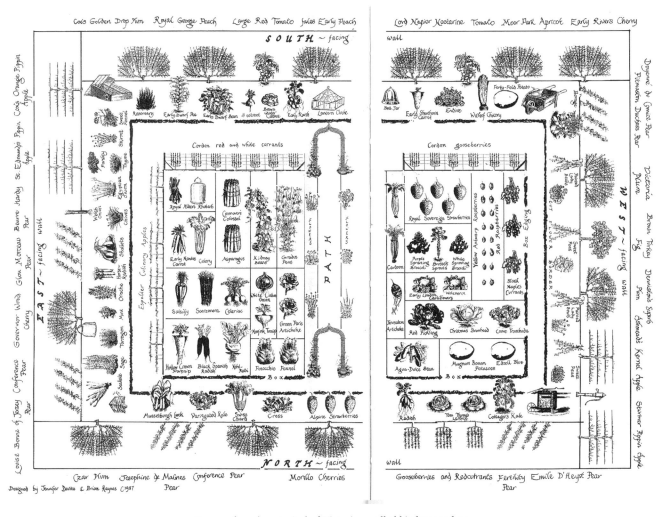

Range of produce typical of Victorian walled kitchen gardens
Courtesy of Jennifer Davies

heat where vertical walls receive greater insolation than horizontal ground for over half the year. During and after the Renaissance, the elaborate terraced gardens of Italy and the extensive parterres of French gardens were matched in Britain by walled pleasure gardens that survived much later than their southern counterparts, well into the 18th century, partly because of the benign microclimate they bestowed. Such gardens often made use of *claires-voies*, fenced gaps or windows in the walling, to offer extensive vistas between compartments or to the surrounding countryside without sacrificing the benefits of enclosure. Although the 18th century English landscape style swept the walled garden away from the house, banishing it out of sight as a utilitarian kitchen garden, the skilled horticultural use of walled gardens was maintained, largely through the tradition of Scottish-trained gardeners.

In many kitchen gardens where stone was the primary building material, some of the walls were lined with brick in order to conduct more heat, especially important for the ripening of fruit such as grapes, peaches, nectarines, and apricots. Writing in 1822 the great Scottish horticulturist and writer John Claudius Loudon recommended the use of brick and, failing that, whinstone (a blackish basalt that absorbs heat better than a lighter-colored stone), and an aspect up to 20 degrees east of south as the best for fruit-growing. The ideal garden, Loudon said (quoting Walter Nicol's 1818 *Gardener's Kalendar*), has north walls 14 to 18 feet (4.3 to 5.5 m) high, south walls of 10 to 12 feet (3 to 3.7 m), and east and west walls at intermediate height. Shelter tree planting around the garden helped reduce wind turbulence, and by the mid-18th century, elaborate glasshouses and heating systems along the north wall gave exotic growing conditions. Even without these technological advances, the creation of a walled garden on a south-facing slope could create growing conditions in Great Britain the equivalent of those hundreds of miles south.

Espaliered fruit trees and walled garden at Pitmedden, Scotland
Photo by Brinsely Burbridge, courtesy of Royal Botanic Garden, Edinburgh

Loudon claimed the effect of a south-facing wall alone to be worth seven degrees of latitude (just under 500 miles [80 km]). The recommended slope was a fall of 1-in-25 or -30, and the siting of a metalwork gate at the lowest point was advised to allow the cold air to drain out at night.

The productivity of walled gardens served to supply the large households that even modest country estates of the 18th or 19th century entailed and provided a great variety of fresh fruit and vegetables in even the most unpromising of latitudes. The kitchen garden was often sited next to the stables, for easy manuring, and the soil was further enriched by the products of hunting and game shooting: blood, bone, and feather. Skill was involved in choosing a range of cultivars that greatly extended the productive seasons for fruit and in creating the pattern of espaliers to maximize coverage of each wall and optimize the aspect appropriate for each kind of fruit. The head gardener would conventionally be housed in a bothy, or hut, on the north side of the walled garden, allowing him ready access to the fires

and flue controls of the heating system within the walls, used for frost protection and ripening of fruit.

Such kitchen gardens drew in part on agricultural expertise and traditions that stretched back many centuries in different parts of Europe, from the vineyard terraces of the Mediterranean and the kailyards (cabbage patches) of northern Scotland to the extraordinary peach walls of Montreuil, near Paris, where 18th-century writers commented on the finely tuned use of minute variations in wall aspect to ensure that the espaliered peach fruits ripened at different times. Since World War I, however, the labor and cost involved in constructing, maintaining, and cultivating elaborate, productive walled gardens has become prohibitive for most landowners, and many of the skills have also been lost. Walled gardens survived better into the late 20th century as a source of aesthetic pleasure, with the walls themselves often a prime focus. Different construction materials, renderings, coursing patterns, copings, and decorative or sculptural inserts have all left their mark as evidence of the local geology, culture, craftsmanship, and education of the owners and workmen who built them. The meditative Zen Buddhist space of the 500-year-old dry landscape at Ryoan-ji, in Kyoto, Japan, has enclosing clay walls, designated a national treasure in their own right, which have been echoed in the late-20th-century use of rammed earth walls for private gardens by Swiss landscape architect Dieter Kienast. At the start of the 20th century, English and Continental traditions of stone, tile, and brick construction were drawn on in creative new ways by architect Edwin Lutyens, in collaboration with Gertrude Jekyll, to build walled garden spaces that have been mirrored on a diminutive scale in countless suburban English gardens over the subsequent decades.

Further Reading

Campbell, Susan, *Walled Kitchen Gardens,* Princes Risborough, Buckinghamshire: Shire, 1998

Davies, Jennifer, *The Victorian Kitchen Garden,* London: BBC Books, 1987; New York: Norton, 1988

Jellicoe, Geoffrey, and Susan Jellicoe, *The Landscape of Man: Shaping the Environment from Prehistory to the Present Day,* London: Thames and Hudson, and New York: Viking Press, 1975; 3rd edition, expanded and updated, New York: Thames and Hudson, 1995

Little, G. Allen, editor, *Scotland's Gardens,* Edinburgh: Spurbooks, 1981

Loudon, John Claudius, *An Encyclopaedia of Gardening,* 2 vols., London, 1822; new edition, 1835; reprint, New York: Garland, 1982

Manley, G., "Climate and Landscape Architecture," *Journal of Institute of Landscape Architects* 14, no. 2 (1966)

Saville, Diana, *Walled Gardens: Their Planting and Design,* London: Batsford, 1982

Ward Thompson, Catharine, "International Prototypes and Local Identity: The Walled Garden of Scotland As Heritage Landscape," *International Journal of Heritage Studies* 4, no. 2 (1998)

CATHARINE WARD THOMPSON

Walling, Edna 1895–1973

Australian Garden Designer

The influence of the English garden designer Gertrude Jekyll was quite strong on Edna Walling, for she eventually abandoned the perfect lawn, difficult to maintain in Australia's hot dry climate, and abandoned also the formal garden bed filled with colorful annuals, proposing a more natural and romantic type of garden. Walling was an excellent painter in watercolors and produced beautifully crafted plans for her gardens that showed the owners how the garden would be in its mature state. Much more than working drawings, they were in effect beautiful works of art and had considerable influence on the garden owners, who often framed the designs and hung them on their walls. Walling's early gardens displayed her talent for semiformal gardens, with dry stone walls, stone steps, and pergolas softened by natural plantings. There is a feeling of repose and space in even her smallest gardens.

Walling's influence was extended by the publication of four books beginning in the 1940s. These were *Gardens in Australia: Their Design and Care* (1943), *Cottage and Garden in Australia* (1947), *A Gardener's Log* (1948), and *The Australian Roadside* (1952). The first two books used her own photographs of the village she developed at Blicking Vale (Mooroolbark), an outer suburb of Melbourne, where she not only designed the garden settings but also designed and built the charming small cottages. It was here that she began to develop her interest in using Australian native plants in a natural setting.

Walling began to design larger country gardens in rural Victoria and New South Wales. These still retained her signature design concepts of dry stone walls, circular steps, and pergolas but included a greater use of water and pools as well as shrub groupings and trees while still retaining open grass spaces. Even small buildings such as pavilions were included. They all managed to give the impression of space. An outstanding early garden (1931) in Victoria was Cruden Farm for Dame Elizabeth Murdoch, which has a wonderful curved entrance drive lined with the white trunks of lemon-scented gum trees (*Eucalyptus citriodora*). It is the successful use of curved groups of shrubs and trees that gives Walling's gardens a sense of space while still retaining a feeling of intimacy.

Later Walling began to use more Australian native plants and maintained an abiding interest in Australian flowers and trees. Her book *The Australian Roadside,* in which she argued to retain the natural bushland, had an enormous influence on the Australian countryside. The grouping of eucalyptus along country roads owes much to her writing on the subject. Even the softening and beautifying of those engineering feats, the super-highways, through the extensive planting of Australian native plants owe most of their effect to her pleas for the planting of native plants. Walling's last book, *On the Trail of Australian Wildflowers,* was not published until 1984; the manuscript, together with her photographs, was uncovered by her friend Jean Galbraith after Walling died. These books opened many Australian eyes to the beauty of Australian native plants. Thus, her contribution and influence were felt not only in the design of Australian gardens of lasting beauty but on the wider landscape of Australia's countryside.

Biography

Born in Yorkshire, England, 4 December 1895. At age of 16, emigrated with family to New Zealand, then Australia; studied at Burnley Horticultural College, Melbourne, Australia, from 1916; started working in suburban gardens, and began in 1920s to design and write about garden design in Australian magazines, particularly in *Australian Home Beautiful,* writing a regular column from 1937 to 1950; her articles were often illustrated with her sketches and photographs; designed over 200 gardens in peak period of career, mostly in Melbourne; fame spread when she built cottage for herself and organized village of similar simple, charming cottages in landscape setting at Mooroolbark, near Melbourne; which became inspiration for *Gardens in Australia,* 1943; designed larger country gardens in both Victoria and New South Wales; became enthusiastic environmentalist and strongly advocated preservation of Australian landscape; gave up Melbourne headquarters and practice and, in 1967, moved north to Buderim in southern Queensland, Australia; planned new career using plants of tropical landscape, and planned new village of terraces and courtyards quite different from earlier one near Melbourne; plans came to nothing due to deteriorating health. Died in Queensland, Australia, 8 August 1973.

Selected Designs

1931	Cruden Farm, Victoria, Australia
before 1946	Blicking Vale village, Mooroolbark, New South Wales, Australia

Selected Publications

Gardens in Australia: Their Design and Care, 1943
Cottage and Garden in Australia, 1947
A Gardener's Log, 1948
The Australian Roadside, 1952
On the Trail of Australian Wildflowers, 1984

Further Reading

Dixon, Trisha, *The Vision of Edna Walling: Garden Plans, 1920–1951,* Hawthorn, Victoria: Bloomings Books, 1998
Guest, Sarah, *Private Gardens of Australia,* New York: Harmony Books, and London: Weidenfeld and Nicolson, 1990
Watts, Peter, *The Gardens of Edna Walling,* Melbourne: National Trust of Australia (Victoria), Women's Committee, 1981; 2nd edition, as *Edna Walling and Her Gardens,* Rozell, New South Wales: Florilegium, 1991

VICTOR CRITTENDEN

Walpole, Horace 1717–1797

English Writer and Landscape Designer

Son of Sir Robert Walpole, who virtually created the position of Britain's prime minister, Horace Walpole in his many writings made pithy observations on landscape history and discussed scores of English layouts. He also dramatized the effects of architecture and atmosphere in his pioneering Gothic novel *The Castle of Otranto* (1764). Walpole approached landscaping with an eye trained by close inspection of Italian paintings, effecting what he liked on his own Thameside property.

In his chatty historical survey "On Modern Gardening" (1770), which covers time from Eden to Lancelot "Capability" Brown, Walpole argues that landscape design merits establishment among the other respected arts of painting, sculpture, and literature that share a symbiotic relationship with it. He felt that this art form, originating from such humble concerns as vernacular herb gardens, had by his time matured enough to allow such functions to be unthreatening, even enhancing, to

Engraving of Strawberry Hill by Joseph Farington, ca. 1793
Courtesy of the Print Collection, Lewis Walpole Library, Yale University

its aesthetic agendas—as Charles Bridgeman demonstrated in admitting farmed fields into Queen Caroline's vistas within Richmond Park. On the other hand, Walpole contended, conspicuous nonorganic embellishment ruptures a garden's link with nature: "pride and desire of privacy" had imperceptibly sophisticated "the idea of a kitchen-garden" into an artful enclosure "dignified by walls," ornamented "by costly marbles," even "opposing nature" with fountains wasting the water plants needed, in order to parade the owner's power.

Although 17th-century England had featured landscaped deer parks remote from homes—"contracted forests, and extended gardens"—Walpole states in "On Modern Gardening" that it was John Milton's "prophetic eye of taste," in his description of Eden in *Paradise Lost,* that foresaw how spontaneous natural beauty could surpass "trim gardens"—a vision anticipating by half a century the work of Bridgeman and William Kent. Walpole includes in this essay a warning against the overreaction of contemporary English fads; the whimsical irregularities of so-called Chinese gardens—

their fussily sited pierced stones and their serpentizing bridges—seemed to him as unnatural as the formality of Versailles or Hampton Court. For Walpole, Kent played the Messiah to Milton's John the Baptist: adoption of the ha-ha by Bridgeman and others marked the paradigm shift "when nature was taken into the plan," and Kent "leaped the fence, and saw that all nature was a garden." Walpole's discussion of Kent, comprising about an eighth of the essay, stresses how Kent's prior work as painter and set designer shaped his landscapes' originality.

Turning to horticulture, Walpole finds that "improvements more recent than Kent, or but little known to him" address the commingling of the forms and colors of trees, and lists several happy combinations. He welcomes the ways Thomas Whateley's *Observations on Modern Gardening* (1770), by positing the genres and instrumentalities of landscape design, established the craft of modern gardening. Walpole's essay builds toward a millenarian optimism: "We have discovered the point of perfection. We have given the true model of gardening to the world," and only a weakness for novelty, privacy, or formality would thwart the spread of landscapes to "every quarter of our island." Walpole was confident that England's aristocracy was the healthiest taste setter: when owners exert year-round experience of their property while improving it, such changes both respect the genius of the place and dramatize the genius of a nation.

For the last 50 years of his life, Walpole saw to it that the actual layout of his Strawberry Hill home was at least as well known as his oft-published opinions. He contrived that his growing Gothic castle of a house and all his grounds would remain visible from the two major highways circling them and, in turn, that from his windows or well-sited benches the passing traffic of river barges, animals, carts, and pedestrians were always in view. Across the Thames he could discern Richmond Hill and upstream and down the villages of Kingston and Twickenham. From the natural terrace of his slight hilltop, he overlooked pastures animated by his own cattle in meadows sequestered by ha-has. Perhaps a Whiggish pride in English productivity seconded his connoisseurship in landscape painting, satisfying him with outward signs of successful husbandry on this *ferme ornée* (ornamental farm).

The only statues erected at Strawberry Hill, a bronze replica of Bernini's *Apollo and Daphne,* represent a sublimation of human beauty in arboreal nature; perfumed acacias, syringas, almond, lilacs, Virginia cedars, cypress, Weymouth and Norfolk pines, and Scotch firs were Walpole's favored trees, with tulips, nectarine, honeysuckle, and jonquils adding the cheerful note he sought. From his nursery he often shared specimens with friends.

Along adjoining borders of Walpole's property, to the west and south, rose the plantings for his Serpentine Walk, its trees thick toward the outside but otherwise thinly enough planted to allow strollers to catch inward views back toward his house. This green palisade at his property's verge could in turn be viewed from the house, loosely screened by other trees that, "while they called in the distant view between their graceful stems, removed and extended the perspective by delusive comparison" (his praise of Kent, "On Modern Gardening"). Across one of the bordering highways, a round goldfish pond, Po-Yang, formed the focus for a walled flower garden beside his nursery. Strawberry Hill received some 60 visitors (anyone who applied) each of the five summer months it was open each year.

Other audiences reached by Walpole's enthusiasm for the new English styles were those receiving his thousands of letters or members of his wide social acquaintance. Wilmarth Lewis's edition of *The Correspondence* uses five volumes merely to index those letters, citing each opinion or landscape visited. Walpole's thorough engagement when observing the unfolding English garden may be gauged from private notes after a 1760 visit to Rousham: "The best thing I have seen of Kent. Gothic buildings, Arcade from ancient baths, temples, old bridge, palladian [bridge], river, slender stream winding in a stone channel thro grass walks in wood, cascades overgrown with Ivy; grove of Venus of Medici. The whole, sweet." Later on the same tour, regarding another residence, Blenheim, four years before Capability Brown began his work there, Walpole wrote: "Blenheim. Execrable within, without, & almost all round" ("Journals of Visits to Country Seats").

Biography

Born in London, 1717. Youngest son of Sir Robert Walpole, England's Prime Minister (1721–42); with Cambridge classmate and poet Thomas Gray, visited France and Italy, 1739–41; private and published notes on father's and other great art collections mark the connoisseurship of painted landscapes that helped shape "Strawberry"; purchased leasehold on property near London, 1747, which he named Strawberry Hill and began to landscape its eventual 46 acres (18.6 ha) beside the Thames; member of Parliament, 1742–68; purchased the freehold for Strawberry, 1749; recorded visits to some 45 English country houses, 1751–84; became fourth Earl of Orford, 1791. Died in London, 1797.

Selected Designs

1747–97   Walpole's Strawberry Hill, Twickenham, Middlesex, England

Selected Publications

Aedes Walpolianae; or, A Description of the Collection of Pictures at Houghton-Hall in Norfolk, 1747
Essays on the work of William Kent, in *The World* (1756)
The Castle of Otranto, 1764
A Description of the Villa of Horace Walpole at Strawberry Hill, 1774
"On Modern Gardening," in *Anecdotes of Painting in England,* vol. 4, edited by George Vertue, 1780
Satirical Poems by William Mason with Notes by Horace Walpole, edited by Paget Toynbee, 1926
"Journals of Visits to Country Seats," edited by Paget Toynbee, 1927–28
The Yale Edition of Horace Walpole's Correspondence, edited by Wilmarth S. Lewis, et al., 48 vols., 1937–83

Further Reading

Chase, Isabel W.U., editor, *Horace Walpole, Gardenist: An Edition of Walpole's The History of the Modern Taste in Gardening, with an Estimate of Walpole's*

Contribution to Landscape Architecture, Princeton, New Jersey: Princeton University Press, 1943

Hunt, John Dixon, "Writing the English Garden: Horace Walpole and the Historiography of Landscape Architecture," *Interfaces: Image texte langage* 4 (1993)

Kallich, Martin, *Horace Walpole*, New York: Twayne, 1971

Lewis, Wilmarth S., *Horace Walpole*, New York: Pantheon Books, 1960; London: Hart-Davis, 1961

Mowl, Timothy, *Horace Walpole: The Great Outsider*, London: Murray, 1996

Quaintance, Richard E., "Walpole's Whig Interpretation of Landscaping History," *Studies in Eighteenth-Century Culture* 9 (1979)

Snodin, Michael, "Strawberry Hill, Part Two: The Site," *Architectural History* 38 (1995)

Walpole, Horace, *Essay on Modern Gardening*, Strawberry-Hill, Middlesex, 1785; reprint, as *On Modern Gardening: An Essay by Horace Walpole*, edited by Wilmarth S. Lewis, New York: Young Books, 1931

RICHARD QUAINTANCE

Wang Chuan Bie Ye

Shaanxi Province, China

Location: original location (the garden no longer exists) in Lantian, Shaanxi Province, about 31 miles (50 km) southwest of Changan, now Xian, capital of the Tang dynasty, China

Wang Chuan Bie Ye (Refuge by the River Wang) was a country retreat of Wang Wei (706–61), a famous Tang poet and painter in his private life and an imperial official in his professional life who solved the contradiction between his Confucian duty to serve the emperor and his Chan Buddhist desire to live in seclusion close to nature by building himself a retreat far away from the capital. It was located on the site of the former estate of the early Tang poet Song Zhiwen (650?–713?). By the time Wang settled there, the garden had been long deserted and devastated. Wang had it restored according to his taste and in harmony with the surrounding landscape of mountains, valleys, springs, brooks, and rich fauna and flora. His concept of a garden and the emotional attitude of man toward it was a crucial influence on the Chinese art of gardening.

Wang Chuan Bie Ye comprised 20 *jing* (scenic units) with rustic huts and pavilions, each distinguished by a special natural feature, such as a hill, a stream, a bamboo grove, etc. The division of the garden into *jings* started a new tradition in Chinese gardening. Their composition had much in common with horizontal scroll painting in which the landscape was also divided into *jings*. Although it has not existed for many centuries, Wang left the testimony of the garden to future generations through his poetry and painting. The scenic

units of the retreat are the main theme of his *Wang Chuan Ji* (Wang Chuan Collection). It has a preface and 20 *jue ju* (quatrains), each devoted to one *jing* of the garden. Another 20 poems were written by his friend Pei Di (b. 716), a minor Tang poet. The pleasures of life in seclusion are also described in Wang's famous "Letter from the Mountains to Candidate Pei." Wang painted a horizontal scroll of the garden simulating a stroll through its nooks and views. The original of this work is not extant, and it exists only in later copies. Both Wang's poetry and painting give an intimate record of the garden interwoven with the poet's moods, feelings, and philosophy.

The retreat (Wang moved there ca. 746) was located deep in the mountains on the banks of the winding river Wang. The main entrance was at the moat by the *Meng dong yung* (Meng walls), *jing* 1. It had an air of antiquity and was renowned for its old pine trees and willows with soft branches. Behind it rose the *Hua ze gana* (Flower Hill), *jing* 2, from which there was a view of the surrounding countryside, which was especially lovely when "autumn dressed the mountains into colors" or when the moonlight "was tossed up and thrown down by the waves of the Wang river." After crossing the mountains, the narrow path brought the traveler to the *Wen zing guan* (Hut Built from the Wood of the Apricot Wen), *jing* 3, the most important building in the garden. Its roof was made of fragrant grasses, and in the valley it was protected by the mountains from the north. Toward the south it had a view of Yi Lake.

Up in the hills there was the *Jin zhu ling* (Slope Covered with Bamboo Jin), *jing* 4. The reflection of the stems in the mountain stream followed by a narrow path gave the water a sapphire tint. The *Lu zhai* (Dear Enclosure), *jing* 5, deep in the mountains, evoked the feeling of man's unity with nature. The *Mu lan zhai* (Magnolia Enclosure), *jing* 6, with magnolias as the main feature and a stream, was endowed with the spirit of the unknown and mysterious. The *Shu wu pian* (Dogwood Waterside), *jing* 7, was an ideal place to offer a drink to anyone willing to share it with the host. The *Guan huai mo* (Path among Locusts), *jing* 8, had a special charm in the autumn when it was covered with fallen multicolored leaves. It brought the traveler to the *Lin hu ting* (Pavilion on the Shore of the Lake), *jing* 9, where he could rest and wait for a long expected guest approaching from afar in a small boat.

The *Nan ni* (Southern Moat), *jing* 10, on the southern shore of the lake, served as an anchorage for boats. *Yi hu* (Lake Yi), *jing* 11, with its changing surface, was a source of poetical inspiration all year round. *Yang Lan* (Waves under the Willows), *jing* 12, imparted the atmosphere of parting with friends. The scenery of the *Luan Jia* (Hut among the Trees), *jing* 13, changed dramatically after the autumn rains when the brook became more like a roaring river. The *Jin xie yuan* (Spring with Golden Sand), *jing* 14, lured one to drink a gulp of its water in the hopes of becoming immortal. The *Bai shi tan* (Shallow Rapids among the White Stones), *jing* 15, was a place to enjoy the cold breeze coming from the water on hot summer days. The *Bei ni* (Northern Hill), *jing* 16, served as a wharf for boats. The *Zhu li guan* (Hut in the Bamboo Grove), *jing* 17, was the poet's favorite retreat to play his lute under the moonlit sky. The *Qi Yuan* (Lacquer Tree Garden), *jing* 19, was a reminder of the philosopher Zhuang Zi, who once performed the humble function of overseer of the lacquer tree orchard. The *Shu Yuan* (Pepper Tree Garden), *jing* 20, according to Wang's quatrain based on Qu Yuan's (340?–278 B.C.) poetry, suggests that the garden was a paradise on earth.

The garden offered many pleasures to the poet and his friends whom he took boating on the lake, composing poetry, observing the changing views, and drinking wine. For the future generations, it became an ideal of life in retirement in harmony with nature.

Synopsis

680?–713?	Poet Song Zhiwen owns estate with garden on land
713?–744?	After Song's death, estate deserted and devastated
746?	After acquiring land, Wang Wei moves into newly rebuilt garden; in winter of same year, writes prose piece, "A Letter from the Mountains to Candidate Pei," espousing joy in leisurely life
after 746	Wang Wei and Pei Di write 40 quatrains on the 20 *jings* of the garden; later Wang converts part of estate into monastery

Further Reading

Hrdlicka, Zdenek, and Venceslava Hrdličková, *Chinoisische Gartenkunst*, Prague: Aventinum, and Hanau, Germany: Dausien, 1998

Hu, Dongchu, *The Way of the Virtuous: The Influence of Art and Philosophy on Chinese Garden Design*, Beijing: New World Press, 1998

Keswick, Maggie, and Charles Jencks, *The Chinese Garden: History, Art, and Architecture*, London: Academy Editions, and New York: Rizzoli, 1978

Weng, Wei, and Pauline Yu, *The Poetry of Wang Wei: New Translations and Commentary*, Bloomington: Indiana University Press, 1980

VĚNA HRDLIČKOVÁ

Wangshi Yuan

Suzhou, Jiangsu Province, China

Location: approximately 50 miles (80 km) west of Shanghai, in Southern District of Suzhou

A typical residential garden of the classical Chinese tradition, Wangshi Yuan (The Retired Fisherman's Garden) measures 5,400 square meters (1.3 acres) in total area, one-third of which is occupied by architectural elements. The primary section of the house-garden complex was organized along an axis starting with a formal entrance leading to the sedan chair hall, lounge, and the main hall. Xiexiu Lou (Picking-Elegant-View Two-Storied Building) serves as a point of departure

Dianchunyi (Late Spring Chamber) at Wangshi Yuan (Retired Fisherman's Garden)
Copyright Joseph C. Wang

where one could enter the garden in the north and the west.

There are numerous buildings in the garden that, when grouped together, may be viewed as two large sets of courtyards. On the south, Xiaoshanconggui Xuan (Little-Hillock-and-Laurel-Grove Hall) plus the area of Daohuo Guan (Pursuance-of-Harmony House) and Qin Shi (Music Room) constitute a small courtyard to serve as living quarters and places for banqueting and assemblage. On the north, Wufeng Shuwu (Five-Peak Study), Jixuzhai (Gathering-the-Void Study), Kansongduhua Xuan (Looking-at-the-Pine-and-Painting Hall), and Dianchuanyi (Late-Spring Chamber) form another set of larger courtyards with the study as a major attraction. At the central part of the garden, trees and flowers, hills and rocks, and buildings of all types make up the major scenic area with the pool at its center.

Xiaoshanconggui Xuan is the principal building in the garden, but it is relatively small compared to the flower halls of other private gardens in Suzhou. In front

of the hall and at its back are piled stones. On the south, laurel trees are planted in a low, dwarfish parterre made of lake stones. However, on the north, the yellow stone rockery called "Yungang" (Cloudy Heights) is rather lofty and steep. On top of the rockery are several maples, laurels, and magnolias, producing a variety of colors. From the hall, where hilly rocks are scattered about in apparent disorder, one passes through a stretch of narrow, dim, and winding corridors to reach the central area of the garden. There, the garden pool drifts about and, working with its tortuous surroundings, suddenly appears bright and spacious. This illustrates the device of using dimness in contrast with brightness, and a hillock and rocks in opposition to the water in the pool.

The pool, measured at about 330 square meters (395 sq. yd.), occupies the geometric center of the garden. The shape of the surface is somewhat square and is seen as one continuous whole instead of being divided up, such as those found in other Chinese gardens. From the square shape, there are only two branches extending out into bays at the southeastern and northwestern corners. The pavilions and covered corridors, the two-story waterside pavilion, and the stone bridges built on the shores of the pool are all low lying and seem to bend down over the surface of the water. The expanse of the pool is bright and spacious, and its shores are low. On its yellow stone embankments, stones are piled to form the shape of caves, so the surface of the pool seems to consist of broad and extensive waves coming from a remote, indiscernible source. No water lilies are planted in the pool, so the light from the sky, colors of the hills, corridors and halls, and shadows of trees may all be reflected in the water to make the whole scene rich and full of variety.

To the south of the pool there is the light and delicate Zhuoying Shuige (Washing-Tassel Waterside Pavilion). The simple and vigorous rock precipice Yungang stands in strong contrast to the pavilion. To the east of the pool and immediately next to the residence there stands a stretch of high walls. There, open pavilion, open corridors, horizontal architrave, and fake tracery windows are used. Also, a rockery is piled there, and creeperlike wisteria and climbing figs are planted to avert the feeling of stiffness and relieve the monotony of the wall surfaces.

In the northern part of the garden, two-story halls for reading and chambers for painting, such as Kansongduhua Xuan, Jixuzhai, and Dianchunyi (Late Spring Chamber), form courtyards by themselves. In the courtyards are parterres with piled stones, groves of bamboo, flowers and trees, and stone peaks for scenery. The studies and courtyards are in the northwestern corner of the garden, known for the many Chinese herbaceous peonies planted there. Peaked rocks stand in prominence in these courts, trees appear sparse and bright, and everything is arranged simply and elegantly. With the addition of the newly constructed Lengquan Ting (Cold-Springs Pavilion) and Hanbi Quan (Enclosing-Emerald Springs) in the courtyard of Dianchunyi, the scene has become more enriched. The Astor Court in the Metropolitan Museum of Art in New York City is a faithful copy of Dianchunyi and its courtyard.

Their attractive and charming structures and their delicate and exquisite details in construction distinguish the buildings in Wangshi Yuan. The pavilions and two-story pavilions around the pool especially are known for their characteristics of petite scale, low height, and transparency. The furniture and interior decoration are also tastefully exquisite. The stones in the garden are used in different surroundings according to their qualities. For instance, yellow stones are used for rockeries, the parterre around the pool, and the embankment of the pool. Lake stones are employed in the courtyards. The two kinds are rarely mixed in use. As for flowers and trees, only a few kinds are planted. The total number of trees in the garden is relatively small and includes sweet gum, maple, laurel, lacebark pine, pine, Chinese wisteria, and magnolia.

Synopsis

1174–89	Government official Shi Zheng-zhi builds house-garden complex and names it Wan Juan-Tang; garden sold to Mr. Ting upon Shi's death and left deserted when Ting dies
1765–70	Song Zong Yuan buys property, rebuilds it, and renames it Wangshi Yuan; again deteriorates into ruins after Song's death
1796	Acquired by millionaire merchant Qu Yuan-cun who renovates and expands garden with new buildings and scenes
1862–74	Li Hong Yi claims ownership
1911	Rapid transfer of ownership from Da Xin-shan to Zhang Shi-luan
1932	Artists Zhang Shan-zi, Zhang Da-qian, and Kun Zhong take residence and keep tiger cub in garden as life subject for painting
1940	He Ya-nong purchases garden and donates it to state ten years later
1958	Opened to public following extensive repairs and renovation
1963	Listed in Jiangsu province Cultural Relics Register
1982	Listed in People's Republic of China National Cultural Relics Register
1997	Listed in World Cultural Heritage Register

Further Reading

Fang, Pei-he, "Jiangnan Yuanlin De Dianfan" (A Model of Garden Design in the South of Yangzi River) *Suzhou Yuanlin* (Gardens of Suzhou) 2 (1995)

Liu, Tun-chen, *Su-chou ku tien yüan lin,* Beijing: Chung-kuo chien chu kung yeh ch'u pan she, 1979; as *Chinese Classical Gardens of Suzhou,* translated by Chen Lixian, edited by Joseph C. Wang, New York: McGraw-Hill, 1993

Zhou, Wei-quan, *Zhongguo Gudian Yuanlin Shi* (History of Chinese Classical Gardens), Beijing: Qinghua Daxue Chubanshe, 1990

XU DEJIA AND JOSEPH C. WANG

Wardian Case

The Wardian (or Ward's) case consists of a sealed but not airtight glass cover over a container of well-drained soil that provides a closed environment for growing plants. An accidental discovery in 1829 led to its invention by the London physician and amateur naturalist Nathaniel Bagshaw Ward. In *The History of Gardens* (1979), Christopher Thacker names the Wardian case as one of the greatest inventions in garden history. It is the precursor of what became known in the United States as a terrarium.

Ward describes the circumstances of the discovery and his subsequent experiments in an 1834 *Gardeners' Magazine* article entitled "On growing Ferns and other plants in glass cases, in the midst of the smoke of London." Interested in observing the metamorphosis of a hawk moth, he buried the chrysalis in moist soil inside a large bottle and covered it with a lid. A month passed before the insect was fully formed, and during that time minute specks of vegetation became visible on the surface of the soil. Ward was curious to investigate the development of the plants in such a closed situation in which light, heat, moisture, and moderate air circulation kept the interior at a constant humidity, and he placed the bottle outside a north-facing window and left it unattended. The fern and grass grew well for more than three years, until the lid rusted and the plants died after being exposed to rainwater and the sooty, smoky London air. Ward continued to experiment successfully with many species of ferns and other plants, which he placed in variously sized and shaped boxes with glazed sides and lids. The bottom of each box was filled with a mixture of bog-moss, vegetable mold, and sand; the ferns and other specimens were planted and thoroughly watered, the excess being drained through a plug-hole; the plug was replaced, the lid put on, and no further care was given. After eight years Ward and Joseph Paxton (who had just completed the Great Conservatory at Chatsworth) inspected the collection and found the plants healthy. Ward also filled two cases with plants and shipped them to Sydney, Australia, in the summer of 1833, and the plants were flourishing when they arrived after five months at sea. Previous efforts to transport live specimens to and from distant parts of the world had encountered immense difficulties; only a small percentage survived the extremes of temperature and humidity, lack of care, and shortage of fresh water during the long voyages. Ward published the results of his investigations in *On the Growth of Plants in Closely Glazed Cases* (1842).

Wardian cases were immediately put to practical use by the Horticultural Society of London (later the Royal Horticultural Society) when Robert Fortune was sent to China in 1843 as the society's plant collector, with

Example of a Wardian case, from Henry T. Williams, editor, *Window Gardening*, 14th ed., 1878

instructions to observe the effects of the voyage on plants contained in three cases and, on arrival, to offer the contents as propitiatory gifts. Three years later he set sail for London with the cases refilled with Chinese exotics. Fortune is considered the pioneer of the tea industry in India, for he returned to China and conveyed 20,000 tea plants in Wardian cases from Shanghai to the Himalayas. Ward's invention allowed many other plant migrations, including the quinine-producing cinchona from Brazil to India and bananas from China to Samoa and Fiji.

Nurserymen and horticulturists in all parts of the world took advantage of the Wardian case to ease the importation of young trees, shrubs, and plants from distant countries. In 1848 the U.S. physician William W. Valk described its practical uses to readers of *The Horticulturist* and also recommended Wardian cases for the cultivation of plants in parlors and drawing rooms. Valk's prediction that these tasteful containers would soon become fashionable was borne out in the following decades. In Great Britain the newly affluent middle class, living in houses polluted by gaslights and coal fires, was seized by "fernmania," and Ward's invention allowed delicate ferns and other rare exotics to flourish indoors. Shirley Hibberd's *Rustic Adornments for Homes of Taste* (1856) presents the cases in various guises, both heated and unheated. These "fern-cases" ranged from a flowerpot containing a lone fern covered with a bell jar to an extravagant miniature greenhouse containing a rockery and more than 20 different ferns. In *The American Woman's Home* (1869), the Beecher sisters praise the Wardian case as the best and cheapest of home decorations. Although ornate ones with plate glass were expensive, they advised that a small-scale Wardian case could be had by simply turning a tumbler over a plant, and they gave instructions for a homemade version fabricated from common window glass mounted on a frame with a zinc-lined bottom.

Richardson Wright identifies the terrarium—made possible by Ward's discovery—as the most recent American garden enthusiasm in his 1934 *The Story of Gardening*. According to the *Oxford English Dictionary*, terrarium was first used in 1890 in reference to a glass case in which small land animals were kept for scientific observation; in the 1930s the term was adopted in the United States to mean a sealed transparent container in which plants are grown. Dubbed "terrariamania," the renewed popular interest in the 1970s spawned numerous books that presented the "balanced ecosystem" of the terrarium as an educational tool for understanding the Earth's environment and as a means of therapeutic gardening and creative expression. The natural processes duplicated within the container—the water cycle, the nitrogen and carbon cycles, and photosynthesis—were explained in detail, and the advantages of glass versus plastic containers were discussed. The numerous edifying experiments that could be conducted with terrariums included observing the effect of a daily five-minute talk to the plants. The lesson: plants grow faster as a result of the increased carbon dioxide (CO_2) forced into the container by breathing—not from the greater attention paid to them. As the 20th century ended, a Victorian-style Wardian case of glass and metal with a grow light fixed within an ogee-arched roof could be found in garden supply catalogs under the name of "tabletop conservatory."

Further Reading

Beecher, Catharine E., and Harriet Beecher Stowe, *The American Woman's Home; or, Principles of Domestic Science,* New York and Boston, 1869; 2nd edition, as *The New Housekeeper's Manual,* New York, 1873; reprint, Hartford, Connecticut: Stowe-Day Foundation, 1996

Hadfield, Miles, *Pioneers in Gardening,* London: Routledge and Paul, 1955; New York: MacMillan, 1956

Hibberd, Shirley, *Rustic Adornments for Homes of Taste,* London, 1856; new edition, revised by Thomas William Sanders, London, 1895; reprint, London: Century, 1987

Kayatta, Ken, and Steven Schmidt, *Successful Terrariums,* Boston: Houghton Mifflin, 1975

Morgan, Joan, and Alison Richards, *A Paradise out of a Common Field: The Pleasures and Plenty of the Victorian Garden,* New York: Harper and Row, and London: Century, 1990

Scourse, Nicolette, *The Victorians and Their Flowers,* London: Croom Helm, and Portland, Oregon: Timber Press, 1983

Thacker, Christopher, *The History of Gardens,* London: Croom Helm, and Berkeley: University of California Press, 1979

Valk, William W., "Remarks on Gardening as a Science.—No. 7," *Horticulturist* 2 (January 1848)

Ward, Nathaniel Bagshaw, *On the Growth of Plants in Closely Glazed Cases,* London, 1842; 2nd edition, 1852; reprint, 1985

Wilson, Charles L., *The World of Terrariums,* Middle Village, New York: Jonathan David, 1975

JUDITH K. MAJOR

Water Garden

Water gardens are known to have existed since Egyptian times, when the precious substance not only served the practical purpose of irrigating the oases but was also intended to evoke the aura of a sheltered paradise. As the first archaeological excavations that began in 1910 of gardens close to Pompeii have shown, Roman terrace gardens were intersected with a technically highly sophisticated system of canals, which ran lengthwise. The heyday of ornamental water gardens or water parterres paralleled the rise of the Ottoman Empire during late antiquity, culminating in the Arabic pool gardens in the Alhambra and the palaces of the Moors around Palermo. Spreading from there, the island and pool gardens in Italy continued to develop throughout the late 15th century and the whole of the 16th century, a trend that was no doubt influenced to a large degree by Francesco Colonna's famous book *Hypnerotomachia Polyphili* (Venice, 1499).

One of the best surviving examples is the water garden of the Villa Bagnaia (1566–ca. 1600) in Tuscany. Its islandlike fountain, which is isolated by water segments, is reminiscent of the Villa Marittima (built ca. 100 B.C.)

in Tivoli, which had been rediscovered only a few generations earlier. Bagnaia served as a model for a number of draft plans that included ornamental pools, such as du Cerceau's sketches for "Les plus excellents bastiments de France." The spatial solutions used in France were usually directly imported from Italy, as was the case in the summer residence of Henry IV in Saint-Germain-en-Laye (ca. 1600) with its water garden on the lower terrace that—as a direct influence of Bagnaia—encompasses a round island with a fountain.

Pool courtyards, with enclosing side wings, evoke the atmosphere of a *vita contemplativa* while reflections from the water are designed to convey spaciousness and transcendence. The Turkish-Asmanli gardens and those influenced by the Moors and the *reyes de taifas* deserve particular mention: the Palace of the Caliph (9th–11th centuries; later the Palace of the Normans) in Palermo was once ornamented by canals, basins, and pools; Favara (Sicily) even had a pavilion in the midst of a pond, which was fed by various artificial cascades—an efficient way of producing cool air. Toledo (Spain) is supposed to have had a similar garden. Still open to the public is the famous myrtle garden in the Alhambra in Granada, which consists of a rectangular pool surrounded by aromatic myrtle (13th–14th centuries). The pool courtyard was particularly typical of Islamic residences.

Far and near eastern elements are often found in the bizarre and fantastic etchings after the designs of Hans Vredeman de Vries (1526–1606), which depict dozens of water courts, among them the famous *grottoe-cortile* of the Villa Giulia (Rome). These were not built north of the alps because such arrangements were too costly. Already in the 1640s this type of classical atrium, trimmed mostly with tub flowers, became old-fashioned, although it reached new heights within neo-Renaissance and classic modernist movements. The Bungalow Garden of today with its oblong swimming pool is the descendent of the water court.

The canal garden made a convincing room experience without any embellishments of tubs or even flanking allées. During Renaissance times it mostly appeared in a corner of the bosquet (e.g., the Eremitage de Gaillon); later, however, it became the main attraction in the middle axis of the great baroque gardens (e.g., Versailles, Nymphenburg, and Westbury Court Garden), connecting the realm of art with that of untouched nature. The layout of the basins in the canal garden was very often in the form of a cross (e.g., Versailles) and was large enough to give room for boating (even small sailboats).

The special ornamental ponds that stood in high esteem during mannerist England were shaped in strict geometrical patterns, as demonstrated in the important remains at Tackley (Oxfordshire), Old Modelay Manor, Gorhambury (Hertfordshire), and Chatsworth (Yorkshire). An artificial mound was sometimes built in the

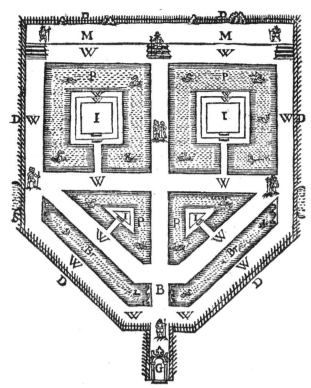

FIG. 28.—From Markham's *Cheape and Good Husbandrie.*

G. The Gate.	P. The Ponds.
D. The Ditch and quickset hedge.	I. The Peniles.
W. The Walkes.	M. The Mount.
B. The Bridge.	Br. The Brooke.	S. The Springhead.

The walkes about the pond may be planted with fruit-trees or willows.

Site design for a water garden, taken from Gervase Markham's *Cheape and Good Husbandrie,* 1638

center of the main pond (e.g., Chatsworth). William Lawson contributed some interesting designs to this late Elizabethan and Jacobean fashion with his housefather book *Cheape and Good Husbandry,* in which the practical was convincingly fused with the aesthetic. In Tackley, whose owner was a friend of Lawson, there still exist surprisingly large remains of a design for an ornamental fish pond shown in Lawson's book.

The zenith of water gardens came in the early 17th century, when one saw the segments of the *parterre à pièces coupés* filled with water instead of earth or lawn. Sometimes these "moving mirrors" were interconnected, so that fish could enjoy a labyrinthian life inside them. The best-known water parterre may have been that of the sunken Hortus Palatinus at Heidelberg Castle. The Palatine elector allowed in print both a perspective and a ground plan of the garden in 1620. With few alterations only it was re-created at Schlackenwert Garden (Bohemia), a Saxonian possession in the early 17th century. Isaac de Caus, the younger brother of Salomon de Caus, designed a water garden for Wilton House (Wiltshire), which was clearly influenced by Heidelberg.

Some especially small-sectioned water parterres were created at Raglan Castle (Wales) and at Saint-Germain-en-Laye (both ca. 1600) when, after the death of Henry IV, some minor alterations were effectuated in keeping with the new protobaroque style. At the Villa Suburbana Hellbrunn near Salzburg, the idea of the island garden was combined with the modern water parterre. It was from experiences such as these that the classical French water parterre was developed during the reign of Louis XIV.

The development of the French water parterre was already apparent in the 1640s, in some of Joseph Furttenbach's engravings of his "Architectura." In most cases the water arrangements of Furttenbach are island gardens with fountains or rocks in the center.

During the baroque era French ideas prevailed in the architectonic styles within Europe. The original water parterre of the mannerist period, which existed only of water and small narrow paths, began to disappear. In its place lavishly bordered water spaces served as virtual mirrors within the floral *parterre de broderie* of the *compartiment* garden in front of the castle. Perhaps the most magnificent of these baroque water parterres was designed by André Le Nôtre for Chateau Chantilly in 1666: the *compartiment* here consists of two parterre pieces, each with five fountains that are bound together by *tapis verts* (segments of lawn). Starting at the "Great Channell," a broad cross channel pushes between this arrangement.

A late imitator of this style is the luxurious water garden at Blenheim Palace (Oxfordshire), which was laid out from 1926 to 1928 after a design by Achille Duchêne. The water garden of Stanway, Gloucestershire, has been re-created in an authentic baroque style.

The water parterre went out of fashion beginning about 1700; neither d'Aviler, Florinus (Count von Sulzbach), nor Dezaillier d'Argenville noticed it in their influential treatises.

Further Reading

Androuet du Cerceau, Jacques, *Les plus excellents bastiments de France*, 2 vols., Paris, 1576–79; reprint, Paris: Sand and Conti, 1988

Currie, C.K., "Fishponds As Garden Features, c. 1550–1750," *Garden History* 18, no. 1 (1990)

Dennys, John, *The Secrets of Angling*, London, 1620; reprint, New York: Freshet Press, 1970

Estienne, Charles, *Praedium rusticum*, Paris, 1554; as *Maison Rustique; or, The Countery Farme*, London, 1616

Everson, P., "The Gardens of Campden House, Chipping Campden, Gloucestershire," *Garden History* 17, no. 2 (1989)

Hazlehurst, F. Hamilton, *Gardens of Illusion: The Genius of André Le Nostre*, Nashville, Tennessee: Vanderbilt University Press, 1980

Mansfield, Kenneth, *The Fisherman's Companion*, London: Eyre and Spottiswoode, 1968

Skilliter, S.A., compiler, *William Harborne and the Trade with Turkey, 1578–1582: A Documentary Study of the First Anglo-Ottoman Relations*, Oxford and New York: Oxford University Press, 1977

Walton, Izaak, *The Compleat Angler; or, The Contemplative Man's Recreation*, London, 1653; 5th edition, London, 1676; reprint, Leicester, Leicestershire: Charnwood, 1988; New York: Modern Library, 1996

Weber, Gerhard, *Brunnen und Wasserkünste in Frankreich im Zeitalter von Louis XIV*, Worms, Germany: Werner'sche Verlagsgesellschaft, 1985

Wells-Cole, Anthony, *Art and Decoration in Elizabethan and Jacobean England: The Influence of Continental Prints, 1558–1625*, New Haven, Connecticut: Yale University Press, 1997

Whittle, Elizabeth H., "The Renaissance Gardens of Raglan Castle," *Garden History* 17, no. 1 (1989)

Whittle, Elizabeth H., "The Early Seventeenth-Century Gardens of Tackley, Oxfordshire," *Garden History* 22, no. 1 (Summer 1994)

Woodbridge, Kenneth, *Princely Gardens: The Origins and Developments of the French Formal Style*, London: Thames and Hudson, and New York: Rizzoli, 1986

THOMAS SCHELIGA

Water in the Landscape

Water is ubiquitous; it supports life and shapes continents. Not surprisingly, in all societies water carries with it not just practical significance but also profound cultural meaning.

In the murals of ancient Egypt, from about 3000 B.C., can be found the oldest known pictures of gardens, in which water played a central role. The climate of Egypt is exceedingly dry, and harnessing the annual inundation from the Nile was critical to the success of food production. Scarce water was carefully husbanded. Thus, canals bringing water from the river and rectangular storage pools were features of any settlement and became valued elements of individual gardens.

In the Persian empire, established in the sixth century B.C. by Cyrus the Great, water was similarly scarce. Gently sloping underground channels, or *qanats,* were built to carry water long distances from the water table to the surface canals that distributed the precious fluid to cultivated ground. The symbol of the pool of life feeding the four channels that quartered the world became a potent artistic image in Persian gardens—the paradise gardens, or *paradeisoi,* that were to become so widely influential.

From such early control of water supply there developed the hydraulic systems that raised water to support the terraced gardens of Mesopotamia, most famously the Hanging Gardens of Babylon, one of the seven wonders of the ancient world. Although the actual form and date of these gardens remain in debate, sources are agreed that the gardens were constructed on stone vaults and watered from the Euphrates.

While water bodies such as these were a response to the natural paucity of water, it was plenty that inspired in China one of the oldest continuous traditions of garden design in the world. Taoist philosophy was formative, and it often found its most powerful expression in a love of natural scenery. Gardens reflected such imagery, with rocks representing the elemental masculine principle, or *yin,* and water the feminine, or *yang.* From the fifth century A.D., Buddhism, gradually spreading into China from the west, also reiterated this association of landscape imagery with the essence of life.

In the Western world there is scattered information about the shape of gardens in ancient Greece. Culinary and medicinal demands were the imperative in private gardens. It was in the public domain that the notion of a garden for spiritual sustenance and pleasure held sway. In the eighth century B.C. Homer's responses to the beauties of nature seem to reflect such attitudes. In particular, gushing springs of water were the focus of delight and dedication, associated with the gods.

In the fourth century B.C., when Alexander the Great returned from his victories in Persia, the Greeks began to copy those great royal hunting grounds, the paradise gardens. Inspired by this model, from the Hellenistic period and throughout the classical world, more elaborate gardens were created, with pools, fountains, and ornamentation signifying both worldly status and spiritual sustenance. Gardening became a fashionable pursuit among the Romans, reflected in treatises, notably Pliny the Elder's *Naturalis historia* (Natural History) in the first century A.D.

Pliny the Younger cast more light on the elaboration of garden forms when, at the end of the first century A.D., he published his literary letters, including descriptions of his Tuscan villa, to the north of Rome. Water was central to its layout and character, from the tiny courtyard with a fountain and plane trees to the swimming baths and features that were fed from a spring on high ground. Similarly, Emperor Hadrian's Villa, built between A.D. 118 and 138 at the foot of the Tivoli hills, proclaims its status by an extravagant use of water in baths, pools, fountains, and most magnificently, the Canopus Canal, a sacred enclosure dedicated to the god Serapis.

By this date it is clear that gardens, often with water features, had become an integral part of Roman lifestyle. As demonstrated by the archaeological investigations of Pompeii, the town that was buried in A.D. 79 following Vesuvius's catastrophic eruption—and in which Pliny the Elder lost his life—elaborate water gardens were found in association with even relatively small villas.

It was increasingly important to be able to employ water that was not immediately dependent on a natural source. To this end, the Romans invented the aqueduct to bring water into the cities, the Aqua Appia being the first to bring water into Rome, in 312 B.C.

This facility proved to be of enormous significance in the development of some of the major gardens of the Italian Renaissance. The Villa d'Este, built in Tivoli in the mid-16th century for Cardinal Ippolito II d'Este, is perhaps the most astonishing of these. Its gardens were created with the advice of Pirro Ligorio, a scholar of ancient Rome. They featured spectacular water displays, made possible by an aqueduct tunneled through the hill, from the distant Monte Sant'Angelo, and a conduit, almost a mile (1.6 km) long, diverting water from the river Aniene. Over 300 gallons of water a second were thus made available to power displays that included the famous Fountain of the Organ, the Fountain of the Owl, the Pathway of One Hundred Fountains, the *giochi d'acqua* (water games) and all the other effects that so impressed visitors.

Throughout the centuries the influence of the paradise garden had also continued to evolve. From the seventh century they were adapted to Islam, with the geometric convention of water channels issuing from a central pool and dividing gardens into quadrants (*chaharbagh*), the perpetual movement of water transforming the temporal and spiritual desert.

In the mid-13th century the Alhambra was built outside Granada, Spain, as a residence for the Moorish king, Mohammed ben Al-Ahmar. Many changes were effected over the following centuries, but the gardens remain essentially Islamic, the enclosed courts featuring canals, basins, fountains, and jets. Like the contemporary gardens of the nearby summer palace, the Generalife, the numerous water features and lush vegetation are supported by the water from the distant Sierra Nevada, conserved in large cisterns and reservoirs, distributed by a system of channels and fountains.

Gardens with similar motifs could be found throughout the Islamic world. For example, in the 16th century Babur, the first important Mogul emperor of northern India, was renowned as a great warrior. He was also a patron of the arts; in his capital at Agra he established a center of culture. Contemporary miniature paintings, as well as his chronicle of his life, reveal that gardens were his passion. His favorite garden, the Bagh-i-Wafa, featured reservoirs, fountains, and channels, which in turn supported flowers, birds, and the ceaseless murmuring of running and splashing water.

The precise whereabouts of Babur's gardens remain unclear, but his successors carried on the tradition. In particular, commemorative tomb gardens became increasingly magnificent. The supreme example of this is the Taj Mahal, completed in 1654 by Shah Jahan, in memory of his favorite wife. The Taj itself lies not at the heart of the *chahar-bagh,* as was the tradition, but at one end of the garden, on a platform overlooking the river Jumna, invoked as a representation of perpetual life. The facade of the tomb appears at the heart of the geometric garden, where it is mirrored in the square, marble pool and thus tied into an elusive world of perfect order.

The poetic possibilities of reflecting pools were also an inspiration for the great gardens of 17th- and 18th-century France, then becoming the most powerful country in Europe. The topography around Paris lent itself to the creation of vast, flat expanses of formal water, stretching as far as the eye could see—nature subjugated by an absolute power. One of the finest of such gardens is Vaux-le-Vicomte, laid out in the 1650s and 1660s for Louis XIV's finance minister, Nicholas Fouquet. This was the first great garden by André Le Nôtre. The influence of the philosopher René Descartes, who speculated about the nature of consciousness and perception, is evident at Vaux-le-Vicomte, where readings of its "reality" are so various. As one moves through the garden, the evidence of the eye is constantly revised: elliptical basins of water become circles, circles become ovals, reflections carry the château far into the garden and bring the sky down to earth. In 1661 Fouquet held a banquet for Louis XIV. It was the magnificence of Vaux-le-Vicomte that caused the minister's downfall. The king ordered Fouquet's arrest and confiscated the property. Appropriating many of the artifacts of the garden, as well as its designer, Le Nôtre, Louis XIV began to devote himself to creating something even bigger and better at Versailles.

The landscape of Versailles is structured around the great cruciform canal. Contemporary illustrations reveal that many richly ornamented miniature craft, from pleasure boats to warships, carried members of the court on trips along the canal. One of the boats was reserved for the composer Jean-Baptiste Lully's orchestra. In addition to this great expanse of water, there were also well over a thousand fountains, some with great basins and programs of sculpture, some much smaller, encountered throughout the bosquets. The difficulty was to find an adequate supply of water.

In this context the French court benefited from skills developed in Italy. Thomas Francini, a remarkable hydraulic engineer who had worked in the mannerist gardens at Pratolino, had arrived in France in the 1590s to superintend the fountains, grottoes, and automata for the royal garden at Saint-Germain-en-Laye. In 1623 Francini became superintendent of the waters and fountains of France. He and his descendants remained in charge of all the major royal waterworks until the 18th century; their expertise facilitated the creation of the array of fountains at Versailles. The water supply was first provided by a network of reservoirs. In 1680 this was supplemented by an enormous hydraulic pressure pump, the "Machine de Marly," constructed at Bougival to bring water from the Seine up approximately 530 feet (162 meters) of hillside to an aqueduct and from there to Versailles. Even this was insufficient, however, and in the 1680s there was a scheme, never completed, to carry water from the river Eure along an aqueduct for over 62 miles (100 km) to the royal court.

The water effects characteristic of Italy and France clearly influenced the landscapes of Britain in the late 17th and early 18th centuries. In addition, the more reserved formality of the canals and water features of the Netherlands, manifest in the famous gardens laid out at the end of the 17th century at Het Loo by Prince William of Orange, were enormously important. Water bodies had been included in English gardens since the Roman period. Sometimes these were defensive moats. More often they were fishponds, including the large *vivarium,* or breeding pond, and the small *servatorium,* or holding pond. The freshwater fish thus available were a status symbol, associated with both secular and religious institutions throughout the medieval period. Gradually, the keeping of fish became a secondary attraction, and the ornamental possibilities of water became more significant. By the 17th century the static, utilitarian pond was often replaced with features that revealed the impact of Renaissance Europe, including fountains, canals, cascades, and baths. Royal gardens, in particular, revealed this change. They became impressive statements of authority—essential in such politically uncertain times. The gardens at Hampton Court were redeveloped, first by Charles II, who had been exiled in France, and then by William of Orange, who had become William III of England in 1688. He commissioned Christopher Wren to transform the palace and added a grand *parterre de broderie,* enlivened by 13 fountains, linked with Charles II's great canal stretching through the park.

The model of such splendor inspired great aristocratic families. The first duke of Devonshire created extensive formal gardens at Chatsworth, in Derbyshire. There, in 1694, M. Grillet, a pupil of Le Nôtre, created fountains and an exquisitely designed cascade. The sound of the falling water was musically orchestrated by subtle differences in the stone profile of each step. At the top of the cascade is the cascade house, by Thomas Archer. The composition remains one of the most splendid baroque effects in Britain.

By the 18th century the baroque style was no longer fashionable. At Chatsworth most of the baroque gardens were replaced with a magnificent example of the English landscape school, a vision of perfected nature that was cast over so many parks and gardens in England at this time. Chatsworth's transformation was effected by the most famous exponent of the style, Lancelot "Capability" Brown. Water was of supreme importance in such landscapes. At Blenheim Palace, in 1764, Brown dammed the small river Glynde to form a great, sinuous lake, the scale of which effectively provides a balance to the massive architectural pile of the palace itself. Lakes such as this are poetic images of perfect peace and were certainly influenced by the paintings of Nicolas Poussin and Claude Lorraine, which were collected by aristocrats as they made their Grand Tours of the classical world. Other cultural and political themes were also encoded in these gardens, which were read as an expression of tranquil social and political order, as opposed to the extravagant display or totalitarian authority of other countries, notably the ancien régime in Catholic France.

The influence of the English landscape school was widespread, portraying Enlightenment ideals, especially in central Europe. Examples can be found in the garden of Arkadia, near Lowicz, in Poland, created for Princess Helena Radziwill beginning in 1775, and the gardens at Tsarskoye Selo, outside St. Petersburg, remade for the anglophile Catherine the Great of Russia. Princess Helena wrote her own guide to Arkadia; it reveals the classical-Romantic themes embedded in the layout, with evocations of order and perfection together with love, beauty, happiness, memory, and death. Central to the experience was the lake, fed by the waters of the river Lupi, reflecting several of the main eye-catching structures and representing the principle of natural continuity.

By the end of the 18th century in England, water was once again manipulated in a variety of ways to signify a changing climate of political opinion and personal taste. In 1794, with his poem *The Landscape,* Richard Payne Knight launched his crusade for the picturesque ideal. Inspired by the Romantic movement and by the excitement of revolution in France, Knight despised the grandiose scale of water bodies associated with Brown and his followers. For him, natural, rushing streams presaged a challenge to the old order and invoked instead a sense of freedom and individuality. Hence, there was an increasing fashion for traveling in the wilds of the English Lake District, Scotland, or the Swiss Alps, where narrow streams, dramatic gorges, and natural waterfalls could excite with an awesome suggestion of primitive power.

Scenes such as this even made their way into public landscapes that were created in the 19th century for the newly urbanized communities of the burgeoning towns and cities of the West. In England one of the most important public parks was laid out in Birkenhead, on the banks of the river Mersey, ambitiously planned as the first city of a new age. Here, Joseph Paxton—also head gardener at Chatsworth—laid out a magnificent park, opened in 1847. The two lakes that lie at the heart of the park are roughly irregular in outline, their long, narrow arms snaking around high banks overhung with vegetation. The composition dramatically suggests the infinite continuity and irrepressible energy of nature.

The influence of Birkenhead Park is discernible in Central Park, New York, designed by Calvert Vaux and Frederick Law Olmsted in 1857. Here, the stretch of the lake next to the formal terrace—described by Vaux as the park's "drawing room"—is smooth and polite. Farther afield, it extends long, irregular arms toward the rough naturalism of the ramble. In the north of the park the Harlem Meer and the rugged ravine and waterfall evoke a much wilder environment, appropriate to the pioneering spirit of the nation. The lake also served a practical purpose: boating became popular, and in winter ice skating attracted immense crowds in the 1860s. It was an opportunity afforded to all members of society, and contemporary newspapers celebrated this evidence of American democracy.

Lakes such as these were carefully constructed. Where possible, a river or spring was harnessed to good effect. Perhaps more often, public park lakes were created on boggy ground that was unfit for building development. This is true of both Birkenhead Park and Central Park where, in the late 1850s, the young engineer George Waring worked with a work gang, laying miles of drain tiles in trenches three to four feet deep. These directed the surface water downward to collecting drains and from there to brick channels, which fed the lakes.

The bed of a lake usually required excavation. It had to be puddled to make it watertight, unless the subsoil was heavy clay. This involved working a mixture of wet clay so that it became malleable and impervious and could be used to line the base and sides of a lake. Laid in a layer at least one foot thick and rammed to a homogeneous finish, this type of lining will usually only crack if it dries out or is eroded.

The 19th and 20th centuries saw experimentation with materials for lining pools and lakes. Various concrete mixes, often reinforced with metal, became less popular than linings of rubberized or plasticized material. Such techniques allow the creation of informal water bodies of all kinds. Molded concrete, to form the bed of lakes and streams, was employed in the 20th century by one of the leading modernists, Roberto Burle Marx. His early career as a painter influenced his landscape designs, dominated by flowing, abstract compositions of water and the lush plants of his native Brazil. In the 1960s the combination of modernist architecture and Burle Marx's landscape and water settings was the dramatic expression of the thrusting new capital, Brasilia.

Water intended to enrich and civilize urban settings has been a recurrent theme. The late 20th-century taste for informal pools and naturalistic streams must also be seen as a reflection of the "green" debate that so passionately informed political discourse at this time. "Natural" ponds, with indigenous flora and fauna, were seen as the ideal—perhaps an inevitable reaction in a society that grows increasingly urban. Associated with this is the examination of the cleansing properties of water. Since the mid-1980s there has been a gathering interest in the use of constructed wetlands for the treatment of pollution. The early experiments were conducted in Germany, where there was extensive research into the methods by which organic wastes, nutrients, and a variety of chemical compounds can be broken down and stabilized. Carefully managed, such a system can be highly effective.

Water has been a literally vital element of designed landscapes through time and across the world. Formal or informal, large or small, it appears in numerous guises, including canals, pools, lakes, streams, waterfalls, and fountains. It continues to serve a multiplicity of functions, reverberating with practical, personal, political, spiritual, and aesthetic meanings.

Further Reading

Plumptre, George, *The Water Garden*, New York: Thames and Hudson, 1993
Rosenzweig, Roy, and Elizabeth Blackmar, *The Park and the People: A History of Central Park*, Ithaca, New York: Cornell University Press, 1992

HILARY A. TAYLOR

Webb, Jane. *See* Loudon, John Claudius and Jane Webb Loudon

Weed

From the 18th to the 20th century, gardeners have agreed that plants growing where they are not wanted are weeds. *Merriam-Webster's Collegiate Dictionary* (10th ed., 1993) defines a weed as "a plant that is not valued where it is growing." In 1740, however, the English horticulturist Philip Miller wrote of some plants esteemed "bad Weeds" that their virtues "are not at present known." According to Miller "all plants noxious in gardening and agriculture are weeds," but many useful plants are also weeds "because they are out of their proper place, or occupy the room of still better things." Early in the 20th century the American horticulturist Liberty Hyde Bailey echoed a similar sentiment: "A weed is a plant that is not wanted. There are, therefore, no species of weeds, for a plant that is a weed in one place may not be in another." The United States Department of Agriculture considers plant species weeds when they interfere with human activities or welfare: "Such plants grow where they are not wanted."

Weeds are not wanted primarily because of their objectionable habits. They survive adverse environmental conditions and often produce rank and unattractive growth. Many spread invasively throughout the garden, field, or landscape by vegetative plant parts such as rhizomes. Others produce enormous quantities of seed each year, which commonly remain viable for 10, 20, or even 40 years. Special seed structures, like the hairy appendages of a dandelion, enable their dispersal over great distances.

Miller recognized that the reproductive cycles of weeds affect their tenacity and control:

It appears that the annual weeds infest arable lands and that the perennials chiefly flourish in grass. The reason is obvious: in the former the roots of perennials are continuously disturbed and cut up by ploughing and other operations of agriculture; and the seeds of annuals find a ready entrance into land where the parts are constantly undergoing a separation. In the latter, the perennials are often made to spread by cutting or eating down the stems; and the seeds of annuals are not easily received into the closely compacted turf.

To eradicate weeds it is necessary to know their life cycle in order to know when they reproduce by seed or spread by other propagules. Based on their reproductive cycle, weeds are classified into four groups: annuals, winter annuals, biennials, and perennials. Annuals germinate in spring or summer, flower, seed, and then die in the same season. Winter annuals germinate in autumn, form a foliar rosette before winter, then flower, seed, and die the next spring or summer. Biennials differ from winter annuals in that they germinate in spring or summer. Perennials germinate at any time, may flower and seed in their first year, but usually wait until their second year, overwinter, then flower and seed in subsequent years.

Weeding, as defined by the early 19th century English horticulturist John Claudius Loudon, "is the operation of drawing, or digging out such plants from any given bed as are foreign to those cultivated there." They "are drawn out of the ground by the hand or by pincers, or they are dug or forked out by weeding tools." Loudon recognized that the best time to weed was after it rained, and he identified the tools to use to eliminate weeds.

The draw hoe consisted of a six- or seven-inch-long by two- or three-inch-wide plate of iron, attached to a four-foot-long handle, at an angle less than a right angle. It was used to cut down weeds by drawing earth towards the gardener. The thrust hoe, sometimes called a Dutch hoe, was different; it consisted of a thin plate of iron attached to the end of a handle by a bow. According to Loudon, heavier work was more easily accomplished by a draw hoe than a thrust hoe, since a man could draw more than he could thrust or push. It required more skill to kill weeds with a thrust hoe than with a draw hoe. An English gardener by the name of Barnes, who lived at Bicton near Exeter, invented the Bicton crane-necked hoe to stir the soil surface near growing crops and to destroy weeds.

Other weeding implements Loudon mentions include the dock weeder, the thistle extirpator, the French weed extirpator, and the Guernsey weeding-prong, all tools with a similar forked or clawed end by means of which weeds are grubbed up. The dock weeder was used to dig pasture weeds with long conical roots, such as dock. When the Guernsey weeding-prong was used, the hands

of women and children, who provided a great part of the weeding labor, were kept clean.

Usually a weed is not native to the area where it grows. At some point in its history it was introduced to that locale, established itself, and became an "exotic" plant. Weeds can be relocated by being carried on the fur of animals or through their droppings after the animal or bird has grazed on the plant. Most likely, it was transported by humans, either intentionally or accidentally. Once in its new home, it began to change the fabric of the landscape through its reproductive vigor.

The pungent common mugwort or chrysanthemum weed, *Artemisia vulgaris,* is an example. This perennial plant is frequently seen along roadsides and in waste places where its vigorous, rhizomatous rootstock spreads and strongly takes hold. Its persistent rhizomes make mugwort difficult to eradicate. It adapts to mowing and cultivation and is relatively tolerant of most herbicides. As a plant of some medicinal value, however, it has historically had a kinder reception.

Because *Artemisia vulgaris* is used chiefly in the treatment of women's diseases, Pliny the Elder recorded that it took its name from Artemis, who is the Roman goddess Diana. It was called *vulgaris* because it is common in all countries. The English herbalist Nicholas Culpeper observed in 1788, "Providence has placed it everywhere about our doors." John Parkinson's (1640) prescribed herbal remedy was to boil a hot decoction "for women to sit over to draw down their courses, to help the delivery of the birth, to expel the afterbirth, as also for the obstructions and inflammations of the mother."

According to Pliny, travelers who bound the herb to themselves would not be weary on their journey, nor would evil medicines or beasts hurt them. It was fitting, therefore, that 17th-century settlers in the New World would bring mugwort with them to grow in their gardens as medicine. From their gardens it escaped and began to naturalize throughout the countryside, only to become a persistent weed. Many other plants common in the 20th-century American landscape, such as dandelion, mulberry, tree-of-heaven, Norway maple, bittersweet, porcelain berry, kudzu, Japanese knotweed, and purple loosestrife, have traveled to North America similarly, and each has a fascinating tale to tell. However, by their tenacious reproductive vigor these plants have made a nuisance of themselves, frequently choke out existing vegetation, and therefore have become weeds.

Further Reading

Allan, Mea, *Weeds: The Unbidden Guests in Our Gardens,* New York: Viking Press, 1978

Bailey, Liberty H., editor, *Cyclopedia of American Horticulture,* 4 vols., Toronto, Ontario: Virtue, and New York: Macmillan, 1900–1902; revised edition, as *The Standard Cyclopedia of Horticulture,* 6 vols., New York: Macmillan, 1914–17

Culpeper, Nicholas, *The English Physician; or, An Astrologo-Physical Discourse of the Vulgar Herbs of This Nation,* London, 1652; new edition, as *The English Physician Enlarged,* London, 1826; reprint, as *Culpeper's Complete Herbal and English Physician,* London: Parkgate, 1997

Fogg, John M., *Weeds of Lawn and Garden: A Handbook for Eastern Temperate North America,* Philadelphia: University of Pennsylvania Press, 1945

Georgia, Ada, *A Manual of Weeds: With Descriptions of All the Most Pernicious and Troublesome Plants in the United States and Canada, Their Habits of Growth and Distribution, with Methods of Control,* New York: Macmillan, 1914; reprint, 1938

Loudon, John Claudius, *An Encyclopaedia of Gardening,* 2 vols., London, 1822; new edition, 1835; reprint, New York: Garland, 1982

Miller, Philip, *The Gardener's Dictionary, Containing Methods of Cultivating and Improving the Kitchen, Fruit, and Flower-Garden,* London, 1731; 8th edition, as *The Gardener's Dictionary, Containing the Best and Newest Methods of Cultivation and Improving the Kitchen, Fruit, Flower Garden, and Nursery,* 2 vols., London, 1768; reprint, London: Miller, 1992

Muenscher, Walter C., *Weeds,* New York: Macmillan, 1935; second edition, New York: Macmillan, 1955

Parkinson, John, *Theatrum Botanicum: The Theatre of Plants; or, An Herball of a Large Extent,* London, 1640

Reed, Clyde Franklin, *Selected Weeds of the United States,* Washington, D.C.: Agricultural Research Service, 1970; as *Common Weeds of the United States,* New York: Dover, 1971

Uva, Richard H., Joseph C. Neal, and Joseph H. Di Tomaso, *Weeds of the Northeast,* Ithaca, New York: Cornell University Press, 1997

RICHARD R. IVERSEN

Wellington Botanic Garden

Wellington, New Zealand

Location: Kelburn; accessible by cable car from Wellington city center

When the New Zealand Company planned a town belt for Wellington in 1840, 12 acres (4.9 ha) of land were put aside for a botanic garden. By the time the Colonial Botanic Gardens, as they were then called, were developed in 1868 by the New Zealand Institute, the area had become "the camping ground of all the goats and cows, . . . and the native forest was being cut down for firewood and several squatters . . . had cottages on it" (Tritenbach).

The new gardens were managed by leading scientist James Hector. He was director of the Geological Survey Department and the Colonial Museum and manager of the New Zealand Institute (later to be called the Royal Society of New Zealand). Hector was to influence scientific thinking in New Zealand for the next 30 years. No doubt he heeded the advice of Sir Joseph Dalton Hooker, director of Kew Gardens, who wrote, "I am heartily glad you have started the Museum at Wellington; there is nothing like a Museum and Gardens to screw money out of the public for science" (Shepherd and Cook).

Hector set up the gardens as a trial ground for exotic timbers and potential commercial crops such as flax, hops, olives, and sugarcane. Some of the conifers planted over the following 20 years are still standing, although many were felled when the emphasis changed to recreation in the early 1900s and flower beds became a priority.

The gardens were vested in the city council in 1891. By then the Wellington Botanic Garden contained a pinetum, 15 acres (6 ha) of natural bush, an area devoted to botany, and collections of camellias, rhododendrons, magnolias, ferns, and exotic trees. Change of management saw a shift from scientific interest to interest in a pleasure garden, and the hilly terrain, with its contrasts of shelter and exposure, created opportunity for diverse plantings. Seasonal massed bedding displays of single species and elaborately designed formal bedding were major features of the main gardens from 1904 through the late 1960s. Support from the Norwood family saw the development of the Lady Norwood Rose Garden in 1953 and the Begonia House in 1960. The Wellington Herb Society helped develop a fine herb garden, which includes a bed of native species used for medicinal purposes. Another recent development is the sculpture walk, featuring spectacular large-scale works by New Zealand sculptors, as well as a piece by Henry Moore, *Bronze Form*.

In the 1980s it was decided to develop the garden as an educational facility. The area of native forest took on new significance, and plantings of New Zealand's endangered species around the new Education and Environment Center (now known as The Treehouse) proved hugely successful.

Wellington Botanic Garden lies alongside the historic non-Catholic cemetery for colonial Wellington. During the 1970s an urban motorway was pushed through the cemetery, causing the reinterment of 3,700 bodies in a mass burial. One positive outcome was that the cemetery was turned into Bolton Street Memorial Park, administered by the Wellington Botanic Garden. The grounds are now home to a significant heritage rose collection, creating a nostalgic setting for the old headstones and a delightful oasis of tranquility within the city environment.

Synopsis

1840	New Zealand Company sets aside land in Wellington town belt for botanic garden
1867	Change in law allowed land dedicated for Botanic Reserve to become Crown Domain under Public Domains Act, and James Hector given authority to manage it
1868	New Zealand Institute develops Colonial Botanic Gardens
1869	The garden's board, with financial support from Wellington Philosophical Society, establishes collection of native plants from New Zealand and its offshore islands
1874	Main path is formed, with two bridges crossing Pipitea Stream, and natural pond developed into swan pond at junction of Pipitea and Pukatea Streams
1875	Garden's pinetum contains 127 species
1882–83	Large collections of native seeds and plants sent to botanic gardens at Kew, Jamaica, Hobart, Washington, and Melbourne
1886	Teaching garden established as botanical garden (primarily for native species)
1891	Botanic Garden passed from government to City Council ownership, and land appropriated for observatory and cable car to city, leaving garden with 63 acres (25.5 ha)
1905	Children's playground completed
1907	Band rotunda constructed near duck pond
1910	Park recreation ground completed a northern end of Botanic Garden by extensive cutting and filling
1911	Fernery constructed, surviving until late 1950s
1930	Cutting and filling a ridge at the southern end of the Botanic Garden created Magpie Lawn
1953	Lady Norwood Rose Garden created on infill from Anderson Park development
1960	Begonia House completed, sponsored by Sir Charles Norwood
1968	Wahine Storm caused considerable damage and loss of number of tall trees
1972	Dwarf conifer collection begun near main entrance
1991	Treehouse (education and administration center) built overlooking duckpond
1995	Cable Car Lookout over Wellington redeveloped and grass collection established
1997	Wellington Botanic Garden Advisory Board established

Further Reading

Alington, Margaret, *Unquiet Earth: A History of the Bolton Street Cemetery*, Wellington, New Zealand: Wellington City Council, 1978

Gabites, Isobel, *Wellington's Living Cloak: A Guide to the Natural Plant Communities*, Wellington, New Zealand: Victoria University Press and Wellington Botanical Society, 1993

Shepherd, Winsome, and Walter Cook, *The Botanic Garden, Wellington: A New Zealand History, 1840–1987*, Wellington, New Zealand: Millwood Press, 1988

Tritenbach, P., *Botanic Gardens and Parks in New Zealand*, Auckland: Excellence Press, 1987

ISOBEL GABITES

Whately, Thomas d. 1772

English Author and Politician

Thomas Whately's contribution to the history of gardening consists of his book *Observations on Modern Gardening,* first published in 1770. The treatise may have circulated in manuscript form among garden enthusiasts since 1765. It was a well-received and influential work in England, as well as in France and Germany. The third edition appeared already in 1771, and that same year it was also published in French and German editions. It became a standard reference work, giving a systematic and complete treatment of the English style in gardening that had been wanting for many years. The treatise greatly influenced subsequent gardening treatises in France and Germany by Watelet, Morel, Girardin, and Hirchfeldt. It was also criticized, however, for being too metaphysical and obscure and for not illustrating its concepts with pictures and drawings. Other important English works in gardening theory written about the same time include George Mason's *An Essay on Design in Gardening* (1768), Horace Walpole's *The History of the Modern Taste in Gardening* (1771), William Mason's *The English Garden* (1772–81), and William Chambers's *A Dissertation on Oriental Gardening* (1772). Of these only Chambers's dissertation became as much debated and translated as Whately's treatise.

With his treatise Whately aimed to provide the art of ("modern") gardening with a position among the liberal arts. The first sentence of the work reads: "Gardening, in the perfection to which it has been lately brought in England, is entitled to a place of considerable rank among the liberal arts." In order to be counted as a liberal or fine art, as opposed to a mechanical art, gardening had to acquire an independent body of theory that proved gardening to be an art form that involves the mind and the imagination. In his introduction Whately states that the pleasure gardening gives is not primarily related to utility but to "an exertion of fancy [and] a subject for taste." In 1762 Lord Kames (Henry Home) had included gardening among the art forms in his *Elements of Criticism,* stating that the advantage of gardening over almost any other art form was its capacity for stirring the imagination through a great variety of means. As is Lord Kames's general art theory, Whately's theory of gardening appears to have been largely inspired by Lockean philosophy as it had been developed into an associationist aesthetic by Edmund Burke. It was crucial that the designer manage to create scenes with strong character in order to make a real impression on the visitor's mind.

Garden historical references to *Observations on Modern Gardening* often mention Whately's use of the concept of character. He uses this concept in various ways, on the one hand to indicate a specific quality of a scene and on the other to categorize different methods of representing in the garden. In this latter use he distinguishes between *emblematic, imitative,* and *original* characters. The emblematic is the lowest form: "They make no immediate impression; for they must be examined, compared, perhaps explained, before the whole design of them is well understood." The imitative character arises "when a scene, or an object, which has been celebrated in description, or is familiar in idea, is represented in a garden. . . . They are all representations; but the materials, the dimensions, and other circumstances, being the same in the copy and the original, their effects are similar in both." Whately values original characters the most: "But the art of gardening aspires to more than imitation: it can create original characters, and give expressions superior to any they can receive from allusions." Original character is directed toward immediate recognition: "They require no discernment, examination, or discussion, but are obvious at a glance, and instantaneously distinguished by our feelings."

The work is structured as a classical treatise with 14 chapters in a systematic order. In the introduction Whately provides a key to understanding the structure of the treatise. He writes that the gardener should know how to select and discover the advantages of a place, how "to supply its defects, to correct its faults, and to improve its beauties." The only materials the gardener may use for these operations are "the objects of nature," which the gardener must study. The treatise begins with four chapters on the principles of the materials that nature employs "in the composition of her scenes, ground, wood, water and rocks," and a fifth chapter on the material of buildings. These materials are treated from a strictly aesthetic viewpoint. For example, Whately considers the different shades of green and shapes of trees, but never which kind of soil the different kinds may require. Throughout the book the emphasis is entirely on the experience of the garden, that is, the impression the qualified designer should be able to "calculate." Whately discusses the notions of art, picturesque beauty, and character in the following three chapters and then continues in five chapters with what he calls the "general subjects," which are garden, park, *ferme ornée,* and riding. The last chapter deals with the effects of time and seasons on the expression of the garden.

Observations on Modern Gardening was originally only illustrated with verbal descriptions. In 1798

Horace Walpole published an annotated edition illustrated with engravings. The initial lack of illustrations seems to have been a conscious attempt at capturing the poetic experience of the garden, to represent temporal and imaginary aspects that an ordinary engraving would not be capable of. Rather than providing the reader with a quick glance of one view (as an engraving would do), the descriptions assisted the reader in providing an imaginary experience of particular scenes. The gardens and scenes described by Whately include Caversham, Claremont, Dovedale, Enfield Chace, Esher Place, Hagley, Ilam, The Leasowes, Matlock Bath, Middleton Dale, Moor-Park, New Weir on the Wye, Painshill, Persfield, Stowe, Tintern Abbey, Woburn, and Wotton. Travel guides for tours around England also quoted his description, such as, *The Ambulator or the Stranger's Companion in a Tour Round London* (1774).

Biography

Place and date of birth unknown. Early training unknown; credited with assisting in the modernization of his brother's garden at Nonesuch Park, Epsom, Surrey, England; author of *Observations on Modern Gardening,* 1770. Died 26 May 1772.

Selected Publications

Observations on Modern Gardening, 1770

Further Reading

Chase, Isabel Wakelin Urban, *Horace Walpole: Gardenist,* Princeton, New Jersey: Princeton University Press, 1943

Dent, John, *The Quest for Nonsuch,* London: Hutchinson, 1970

Grillner, Katja, "Ramble, Linger, and Gaze: Dialogues from the Landscape Garden," Ph.D. diss., Royal Institute of Technology, Stockholm, 2000

Johnson, George William, *A History of English Gardening,* London: Baldwin and Cradock, 1829

Wiebenson, Dora, *The Picturesque Garden in France,* Princeton, New Jersey: Princeton University Press, 1978

KATJA GRILLNER

Wiepking-Jürgensmann, Heinrich Friedrich 1891–1973

German Landscape Architect

Heinrich Friedrich Wiepking-Jürgensmann was one of the outstanding landscape architects in Germany in the first half of the 20th century. (Wiepking-Jürgensmann used this hyphenated name until the end of National Socialism in 1945. After that he used the name Wiepking only.) His only formal training in landscape architecture was his apprenticeship in the parks department of the city of Hannover, Lower Saxony, from 1907 to 1909. He then served in the military and traveled to England and France. In 1912 he was given a position in Hamburg in the well-known business of Jacob Ochs, who not only designed gardens, parks, cemeteries, and other open spaces in Germany and Austria but also worked as a landscape contractor executing his own designs and operating his own tree nurseries.

By 1914 Wiepking had become a director in Ochs's firm and remained so until 1922. In this position he designed gardens in various countries in Europe, such as Russia, Bohemia, and Italy. His career was interrupted by his military service in World War I from 1914 to 1918. From 1920 to 1922 Wiepking headed the Berlin branch of Ochs's business. In 1922 he formed a team with the architect Theodor Merrill and worked as a freelance landscape architect in Berlin and Cologne. The private garden he designed in 1929 for Erich Mendelsohn in Berlin-Pichelsberg falls into this period. In 1934 Wiepking succeeded Erwin Barth, in the chair in garden design at the Agricultural University Berlin.

Early on, Wiepking had shown his National Socialist orientation and thus proved to be the right person to fill the chair according to the National Socialist law for the reconstruction of German civil service of 7 April 1934, which allowed only "Aryans" and those who clearly were in favor of National Socialism to be civil servants. In 1936 Wiepking designed the open spaces around the Olympic village and around the *Reichs* track and field stadium in Berlin. Whereas Wiepking's predecessor Barth had focused on design and planning issues in an urban environment in his university courses, Wiepking directed the interest of his students to the landscape. This is reflected in the name change—to institute for landscape and garden design—which Wiepking effected in 1939.

Following National Socialist expansion politics, especially in Poland and the Soviet Union, Wiepking envisioned a "spring of life for the German landscape and garden designer which exceeds all which even the hottest hearts amongst us have ever dreamed of." Alwin Seifert, a landscape architect and architect who was made *Reichslandschaftsanwalt* (Reichs-landscape attorney) in 1940 and who tried to outdo Wiepking in National Socialist landscape architecture, held a similar view. The National Socialist Reichs-leader SS (Schutz-Staffel) Heinrich Himmler, who also was Reichs-commissioner for the "Strengthening of Germanness" in the so-called incorporated eastern areas (i.e., the land taken from Poland after September 1939), appointed Wiepking *Sonderbeauftragter* (special mandatory) for landscape design issues within his planning authority.

In this position Wiepking actively promoted anti-Semitic, racist, and National Socialist thinking in landscape architecture. He actively cooperated with Professor Konrad Meyer, an outspoken National Socialist and director of the Institut für Agrarpolitik und Agrarwesen (Institute for Agrarian Policy and Agrarian Issues). Meyer, who was a high ranking SS leader, conceived the Generalplan Ost (General Plan East), which provided for the expulsion of millions of people from Poland and Russia in order to "re-Germanize" their land so that Germans would settle there and defend it as their "homeland." Wiepking's book *Die Landschaftsfibel* (Landscape Primer), which appeared in 1942, and his contributions to journals such as *Neues Bauerntum* (New Farming) and the SS weekly *Das Schwarze Korps* (The Black Corps), which propagated anti-Semitism and racism, reflect these ideas. They culminated in the concept of a military landscape (*Wehrlandschaft*) structured by hedges of shrubs and hardwood trees as well as by deep ditches running from north to south, which would inhibit surprise attacks by tanks from the East. How closely Wiepking was connected to the sites of the Holocaust is demonstrated by a diploma thesis on the greening of Auschwitz, a rural site in Poland where one of the largest National Socialist concentration camps was established, which he issued to one of his students in 1943. As a member of the Gesellschaft Reichsarboretum (*Reichs*-arboretum Association) since 1938, Wiepking planned the spatial arrangement of this area in Frankfurt on Main in 1940.

Wiepking was a member of the highest National Socialist nature protection authority from 1942 to 1945 and led the group for landscape maintenance in the so-called incorporated eastern areas in the newly established department of nature protection and land maintenance in the *Reichs*-forestry authority in 1942. He served as a deputy for the position of nature protection and land maintenance in the Warthegau in 1943. However, Wiepking's great aspirations for landscape design and landscape planning eroded due to the events of World War II.

Although Wiepking talked about research as a prerequisite for landscape planning and landscape design, his activities in this respect were negligible. He introduced into landscape architecture thinking that was hostile toward science and that spoiled the discipline for a long period even after the end of World War II. When the Russians came to Berlin and thus ended World War II, Wiepking left his position and went west.

In spite of his clear National Socialist orientation he managed to establish, together with others, the Higher School for Horticulture in Osnabrück, Germany, and the College for Horticulture and Land Culture in Hannover, Germany, in 1946. In the latter he was given a position as acting chair for land maintenance, landscape, and garden design from 1948 to 1949 and as chair from 1949 to 1959. He also served as acting director of this college from 1950 to 1952, when it became incorporated into the Technical University of Hannover, Germany. In 1949 he designed the private Deilmann garden in Bentheim, Germany, and in 1963 the Frommeyer garden in Bad Iburg. In 1966 he received an honorary Ph.D. from the University of Lisbon, Portugal, where one of his students from the Nazi period had a teaching position. Wiepking died in 1973. From 1970 to 1995 the Deutsche Gartenbau Gesellschaft (German horticulture association) awarded a prize that Wiepking had established for students of landscape architecture who promised to continue to work in the field as he had understood it.

See also Barth, Erwin

Biography
Born in Hanover, Lower Saxony, Germany, 1891. After apprenticeship in municipal parks department of city of Hanover, Germany, 1907–9, traveled to London and Oxford, England, and Paris, France, 1910–12; with horticultural enterprise of Jacob Ochs in Hamburg and Berlin, Germany, 1912–13, and was director, 1914; in Hamburg, 1918–20; in Berlin, 1920–22; worked as free-lance landscape architect in Berlin and Cologne, Germany, where he formed team with architect Theodor Merrill, 1922–34; professor and director of institute for garden design at Agricultural University Berlin, 1934–45; charged especially with landscape design issues by National Socialist Reichs-leader SS Heinrich Himmler, who also was Reichs-commissioner for the Strenghtening of Germanness in so-called incorporated eastern areas (land taken from Poland after September 1939); took over deputy position for nature protection and land maintenance in Warthegau, 1943; founded together with others Higher School for Horticulture, Osnabrück, Germany, and College for Horticulture and Land Culture, Hanover, Germany, 1946; acting chair for land maintenance, landscape, and

garden design at newly established College for Horticulture and Land Maintenance, Hanover, Germany, 1948; chair and director of institute for land maintenance, landscape, and garden design at same institution, 1949–59; acting director of College for Horticulture and Land Maintenance, Hanover, 1950–52, when it became incorporated into Technical University of Hanover, Germany; received honorary Ph.D. from University of Lisbon, Portugal, in 1966. Died in Osnabrück, Germany, 1973.

Selected Designs

1929	Private garden Erich Mendelsohn in Berlin-Pichelsberg, Germany; Wieseck park in Gießen, Germany
1935	Open space, airport Berlin-Tempelhof, Germany
1936	Olympic village and open spaces around the Reichs-track and field stadium in Berlin, Germany; open space around the Reichs-memorial Tannenberg, Germany
1939–45	Land development plans for reconstruction work after World War II in the so-called incorporated eastern areas
1949	Private garden for Deilmann, Bentheim, Germany
1951	Opening show, first federal garden exhibition in Hanover, Germany
1963	Private garden for Frommeyer, Bad Iburg, Germany
1966	Private garden for Vornbäumen, Bad Iburg, Germany
1972	Private garden for Deilmann, Montagnola, Italy

Selected Publications

Die Landschaftsfibel, 1942
Umgang mit Bäumen, 1963

Further Reading

Andreae, J., "Gärten Wiepkings im Kölner Stadtteil Marienburg," Diplomarbeit, Gesamthochschule Essen, 1991

Buchwald, Konrad, et al., editors, *Festschrift für Heinrich Friedrich Wiepking,* Stuttgart: Eugen Ulmer, 1963

Gröning, Gert, and Joachim Wolschke-Bulmahn, *Die Liebe zur Landschaft,* vol. 3, *Der Drang nach Osten: Zur Entwicklung der Landespflege in den "eingegliederten Ostgebieten,"* Munich: Minerva, 1987

Gröning, Gert, and Joachim Wolschke-Bulmahn, *Grüne Biographien: biographisches Handbuch zur Landschaftsarchitektur des 20. Jahrhunderts in Deutschland,* Berlin: Patzer, 1997

Kellner, Ursula, "Heinrich Friedrich Wiepking (1891–1973): Leben, Lehre und Werk," doctoral dissertation, University of Hannover, 1997

Poblotzki, Ursula, *Menschenbilder in der Landespflege, 1945–1970,* Arbeiten zur sozialwissenschaftlich orientierten Freiraumplanung, Munich: Minerva, 1992

GERT GRÖNING

Wilanów

Wilanów, Warsaw, Poland

Location: approximately 6 miles (9.7 km) southeast of Warsaw city center

Wilanów is a palace-garden ensemble in the 13th-century village called Milanów. It is situated in the postglacial valley of the Vistula River on a terrace characterized by a flat grassland plain, streams, and the remains of an old river bed, which forms small lakes. One of these lakes has been incorporated into the garden composition.

The park represents two design styles. The older part, formal and well preserved, surrounds the baroque palace built during the reign of King Jan III Sobieski (1629–96) and developed in the 18th century. Wilanów, 11 kilometers (6.8 mi.) from the king's palace in Warsaw, was a summer residence with the character of a Roman *villa suburbana.* The newer part, located on the periphery of the old, is informal and was established at the beginning of 19th century when Wilanów belonged to the Potockis.

In the uniaxial baroque *entre cour et jardin* conception, the *avantcour* and the *cour d'honeur,* garden salon, bosquets, and the willow alley leading into the valley landscape are situated on the main axis, intentionally running across the postglacial valley from the slope through the floodland terraces reaching the river. The access alley falls into a triple goose foot. The *avant-cour* and the *cour d'honeur* were joined in 1801 to romanticize the composition, and the result was a large garden interior between the extended wings of the palace. This area was decorated with an oval lawn and a fountain in the middle. The two-story baroque palace was designed by A. Locci and K. Bay (1690–1745) and decorated by A. Schlüter, C. Callot, J.E. Szymonowicz-Siemiginowski, and M.A. Palloni. It was later extended with two more wings in the first half of 17th and in the 19th centuries (by Ch.P. Aigner and F.M. Lanci). The palace came about as result of extending the 16th-century walled manor house belonging then to the Milanowskis. It was later bought by King Jan III Sobieski in 1677 and extended by a summer residence and garden and a manor house, and it was named *Villa Nova*.

In 1720 Wilanów was ruled by Princess E. Sieniawski and became a residence of barons; it was at this time that the late baroque wing was built, rendering the palace into a rectangular horseshoe-shaped structure. In 1730 the palace and the garden were leased for life to King Augustus II (1670–1733). Later it was passed on to the Czartoryskis (1729–99). From 1785 to 1799 it belonged to the Lubomirskis, from 1799 to 1892 to the Potockis, and finally to the Branickis. S.K. Potocki opened a gallery in the richly decorated interior of the palace, and it became the first public museum in Poland (1805). The late baroque and rococo look of the palace is attributed to the Princess Lubomirski. The rich sculptural arrangement (gilded lead) was replaced by stone sculptures of mythological figures.

The garden salon is situated to the east of the palace on two terraces. The upper terrace lies directly by the palace and is attached to a supporting wall with a stone balustrade, springs, vases, and sculptures. The *parterre de broderie* is located here with single, formed trees, sculptures of ancient gods, and fountains. The upper terrace is connected to the lower terrace by two symmetrical flights of stairs. There is a grotto underneath the stair platform. The lower terrace is similarly decorated. It is delimited with tall hedges of covered bosquets built with trimmed hornbeams, limes, and elms. The embroidery parterre, arbor with creepers, formed lime hedges, flower bowling green, and orangery are on the northern side of the palace. The decorative work around the palace was done by talented artists, architects, and gardeners (J. Ziedler, J. Fontana, and probably Tylman from Gameren).

The landscape park was developed in phases. An informal part in Romantic style was built between 1784 and 1791 by transforming Sobieski's farm according to Sz. B. Zug's plan. The garden work was done by two

brothers, G. and K. Symon, and J.K. Schuch and K. Bartel. In 1815–21 S.K. Potocki enlarged the park surrounding the palace by partly transforming it into a landscape style garden. The central residence of Wilanów is a perfect ornamental farm with a Dutch hamlet, brewery (1770–90), St. Ann's church, and a blacksmith's shop (1780), school (1807), and cemetery (1815). Orchards, protective green belts, and avenues were set in the open landscape.

On the south side of the palace, built in 1856, lies the neo-Renaissance Italian garden consisting of a rosarium and a flower garden joined together in an eclectic manner by a low box hedge border and a fountain. The entrance to the Italian garden led through a trelliswork covered with knotweed (*Fallopia baldschuanica*). In place of the kitchen garden, a Bacchus Hill was raised and covered with grape vines and statuary.

The landscape park surrounding the baroque palace-garden ensemble benefits from two water sources, the Wilanów stream and the Służew brook with a cascade. Among the garden structures, the Roman bridge, a patriotic monument of the battle of Raszyn, a Chinese arbor, and a mausoleum remain to the present day; a sarcophagus and an obelisk were added later.

In the 18th and 19th centuries, the residence and village developed rapidly and became well known for its splendid composition of a park landscape. Summer residences of the rich, built at different times and in various styles but possessing a common origin, fitted nicely into the landscape. The borders of the Potocki dominion was marked by boundary posts in the form of obelisks with the family coat of arms and Polish eagle on top. Residences of other family members were established nearby, including Natolin, Ursynów, Królikarnia, and Morysin.

During World War II the Germans looted the artwork and destroyed the historical garden at Wilanów. After the war the palace and garden came under the ownership of the National Museum and were opened to the public. Most of the artwork and historical memorabilia were returned. The palace was restored in 1955–65 and turned into a museum housing Polish portraiture from the 16th to the 19th centuries. A unique poster museum was organized in the riding school, and a permanent exhibition of arts and crafts in the orangery. The garden has been reconstructed according to the plans of G. Ciołek. From 1964 to 1981 the palace served as a residence for distinguished guests of the Polish government. Wilanów has endured and has become an object of national pride.

By the 1970s and 1980s the arborvitaes on the parterre had become too big and were out of proportion to the surrounding area. Although conservation work around the garden and palace intensified, the state of the whole ensemble left much to be desired. The garden was slowly being swallowed by the expanding city; the views of the other family residences were becoming obscured. Light and sound performances were organized in the 1970s and 1980s.

Among crucial threats to the palace and its garden at the turn of the century were air pollution and intensive vehicle traffic, contaminated water in the Służew brook, the unsightly chimneys of a nearby power station, and plans to construct a new highway near the park. The palace and garden of Wilanów and its residences are included under the monument protection act. The open areas around the park are part of the local and European ecological system (Econet), and steps are being taken to protect this horticultural and cultural treasure.

Synopsis

1667	Jan III Sobieski, King of Poland, buys estate
1681	Deer park, Pheasantry, later called Natolin
1696	Baroque *villa suburbana* of the *entre-cour-et-jardin* type (terrace garden, *cour d'honeur*)
1720	Wilanów bought by Princess Elżbieta Sieniawski
1729–33	Lifelong tenure by King Augustus II of Poland
1733	Intensive development of residence and garden by the Czartoryskis, including the *patte d'oie* and the canal along the western part of the main axis
1772	August Czartoryski founds a new church in Wilanów
1775	Duchess Izabela Czartoryski-Lubomirski creates the Roskosz palace-garden complex
1780	Development of the deer park, called Pheasantry (later Natolin), into Roskosz palace-garden ensemble
1784	S.K. Potocki buys Roskosz (today called Ursynów), develops and transforms the garden, designed by Szymon Bogumil Zug
1799	Dam, artificial island, and Roman Bridge built
1805	Development of residence, extension of garden, and creation of gallery
1812	Morysin garden complex created
1815–21	S.K. Potocki enlarges the park, partly in landscape style
1816	Cemetery and Potocki's Mausoleum built
1817	Gucin-Gaj residence, new farm and farm villages of Wilanów, Wolica, Kabaty created
1845	Reconstruction of the St. Catherine's Church
1846	Yellow Tavern, peacock house in the village Potok
1857	Reconstruction of St. Ann's Church in Wilanów
1892	Wilanów bought by Branickis
1939	Devastation during World War II
1945	Garden taken over by National Museum
1947–64	General conservation and restoration of garden and park, by Gerard Ciołek
1955–65	General conservation of the palace

Further Reading

Cydzik, Jacek, and Wojciech Fijałkowski, *Wilanów,* Warsaw: Arkady, 1975; 2nd edition 1989

Fijałkowski, Wojciech, *Wilanów: Palac i ogród,* Warsaw: Sztuka, 1954; as *Wilanów: The Palace and Garden,* Warsaw: Krajowa Agencja Wydawnicza, 1954

Fijałkowski, Wojciech, *Wilanów, Past and Present,* Warsaw: Interpress, 1985

Fijałkowski, Wojciech, *Królewski Wilanów,* Warsaw: Tow. Opieki nad Zabytkami, 1998

Fijałkowski Wojciech, and Krzysztof Jablonski., *Wilanów,* Warsaw: Arkady, 1967 (with English summary)

MAREK SIEWNIAK

Wildflower

Wildflower is a term that continues to defy definition. Once considered to be the flower of a plant that was not in cultivation, this designation fails when one includes plants such as coneflowers, poppies, lupines, columbines, trillium, and even orchids that are often grouped as wildflowers yet are widely cultivated. A more accurate definition might be a plant that has not been changed, hybridized, or improved by humans and usually is still found growing natively somewhere in the region where it is being cultivated. But not all so-called wildflowers are necessarily natives. Purple loosestrife (*Lythrum salicaria*) now grows naturally in the northeastern United States, but it was imported from overseas. All nonhybridized or cloned plant varieties were at one time wildflowers. Although the typical modern garden flower tends to be a hybrid bred for display purposes, the ephemeral, delicate qualities associated with wildflowers have kept them in some favor in the gardening world.

The idea of gardening with wildflowers or of allowing a portion of property to naturalize or go native is hardly a new concept. In 1625 Francis Bacon devoted six acres (2.4 ha) of his 30-acre (12-ha) garden to heath or wild meadow. In his essay *Of Gardens* he describes his heath as containing thyme, violets, and primroses. His garden may have been a precursor of present-day wild gardens, although the term *wild garden* is a bit of an oxymoron since by definition a garden is cultivated. Bacon defined the garden as an escape from nature. Now that nature is scarce, gardens serve as a substitute.

Two centuries later Scottish garden designer and historian John Claudius Loudon suggested that the lawn at Scone Palace should be left unmown to allow the clover, thyme, daisies, and saxifrage to take over. This type of wildflower gardening made use of native plants. Plants are considered native if they were growing naturally in the area before human intervention. Native plants usually grow in groupings or communities with other species adapted to similar soil and climate conditions. They have evolved and adapted to their local conditions over thousands of years, making them able to withstand cold, heat, and drought and making them resistant to pests and diseases common to that area. Among these groupings or communities are forests, prairies, bogs, flood plains, savannas, alpine areas, and freshwater marshes. Such communities act as ecosystems, and native species kept in their native habitat will remain in balance and noninvasive.

Such balance, unfortunately, has not always been the case with wildflower gardens. It is a common misconception that wildflowers are considered hardy and maintenance free wherever they are grown. Wildflowers taken out of their native environment often will not thrive without attention. In recent years many people have tried to establish maintenance-free wildflower lawns and gardens by simply scattering a canister of seeds, only to be disappointed by the unsightly mishmash that resulted. A wild garden represents a specific plant community and is most successful when the site is appropriate and unifying. Woodlands lend themselves to the creation of wildflower gardens, as do heathlands and streamsides.

By the late 19th century William Robinson and Gertrude Jekyll were advocating a naturalized landscaping that blended with the surrounding woodlands. Robinson rallied against artificial garden styles and promoted the use of hardy plants. Foreign plants were acceptable if they behaved like natives and did not require special attention. In this he was really advocating ecological gardening. He wanted the gardener to understand a plant's needs and growing tendencies and to plant accordingly. Both Robinson and Jekyll felt that, once established, the plant material should be allowed to naturalize into drifts. While often referred to as wild gardens, such landscapes still involved a great deal of design and maintenance.

The Netherlands and West Germany pioneered the creation of wildflower parks. Jaques P. Thijsse felt parks failed to give visitors a sense of nature. In 1925 he opened Bloemendaal near Haarlem, a natural garden based on the design of landscape architect Leonard Springer. It contains a small woodland, pond, marsh, heathland, dune landscape, and even a cereal field and is still used as a demonstration tool by teachers. In 1940 designers Christiaan Broerse and later Koos Landwehr developed the Jaques P. Thijsse Park in Amstelveen as a series of woodland glades. By developing the public park, Landwehr hoped to expose as many people as possible to wild flora, thereby making them aware that nature is something that cannot be done without or replaced. However, these gardens are still fighting nature by creating a garden that would not otherwise be there.

Madestein in The Hague opened in 1982. To create this natural or wildflower garden the top soil layer down to sand and dunes was removed. The topography has been a bit exaggerated, and drainage ditches and dikes have been constructed to create a naturalized dune landscape that will require only annual mowing of the grasses and perhaps some thinning of trees.

The natural approach has moved a little slower in Great Britain. The William Curtis Ecological Park on a former lorry park near London's Tower Bridge was conceived as a spontaneous development of vegetation. Over 200 species have since established there. While the area is educational, the question remains whether a spontaneously developed planting can still be considered a garden.

In the United States landscape designer Jens Jensen, a Danish immigrant, worked with Frank Lloyd Wright to help create the Prairie style using indigenous plant material. Reestablishing native prairies has remained at the forefront of wildflower gardening in the United States. But with the advent of bedding plants, wildflowers began to be taken for granted, often looked upon as weeds to be eradicated. In 1982 Lady Bird Johnson donated land and money toward the creation of a National Wildflower Research Center to study wildflowers with the same degree of inspection given to cultivated plants.

The current interest in ecology, xeriscaping, and regional identity has renewed interest in wildflowers and natural gardening. Many wildflowers, such as lady's slipper (*Cypripedium calceolus*), are now greatly prized by plant collectors. But having been out of favor for so long, many of these same plants are now on threatened or endangered lists and cannot be dug and removed from the wild unless the native location is being destroyed for some reason. This situation has made the plants and true wildflower gardens all that much more rare.

Further Reading

Art, Henry Warren, *A Garden of Wildflowers: 101 Native Species and How to Grow Them,* Pownal, Vermont: Storey Communications, 1986

Bruce, Hal, *How to Grow Wildflowers and Wild Shrubs and Trees in Your Own Garden,* New York: Knopf, 1976; reprint, New York: Lyons Press, 1998

Burrell, C. Colston, *A Gardener's Encyclopedia of Wildflowers: An Organic Guide to Choosing and Growing over 150 Beautiful Wildflowers,* Emmaus, Pennsylvania: Rodale Press, 1997

Druse, Kenneth, and Margaret Roach, *The Natural Habitat Garden,* New York: Potter, 1994

Jones, Samuel B., Jr., and Leonard E. Foote, *Gardening with Native Wild Flowers,* Portland, Oregon: Timber Press, 1997

Johnson, Lady Bird, and Carlton B. Lees, *Wildflowers across America,* New York: Abbeville Press, and Austin, Texas: National Wildflower Research Center, 1988

Wilson, James Wesley, *Landscaping with Wildflowers: An Environmental Approach to Gardening,* Boston: Houghton Mifflin, 1992

MARIE IANNOTTI

Wild Garden. *See* Natural Garden (Wild Garden)

Wilhelmshöhe

Kassel, Hesse, Germany

Location: a mountain park in the nature reserve of Habichtswald, approximately 6 miles (9.6 km) west of Kassel and 75 miles (120 km) south-southwest of Hanover

Wilhelmshöhe (formerly known as Weissenstein, Winterkasten, and Karlsberg), Europe's largest hillside park, rises above the city of Kassel. A dramatic site, it boasts a colossal monument of Hercules at its summit, a neoclassical palace below, a large Gothic Revival castle at its perimeter, an abundance of cascades, fountains, and jets of water, and exotic plant species.

Originally an Augustinian convent called Weissenstein (named for the white quartz rock from which it was built), it reverted to the ruling Hesse-Kassel family following the Reformation. Its site, halfway up the mountain, established the location of future residences.

In 1606 Landgrave Moritz supplanted the convent with a Renaissance residence and gardens, which included parterres, geometric flower beds, and kitchen gardens at the perimeter. Above and to the west of the house, about one-third of the way to the summit, Moritz built a grotto and cascade.

Moritz's successor, Landgrave Karl, was greatly influenced by the Villa Aldobrandini at Frascati and had his architect, Guerniero, transform Weissenstein into a grand baroque garden. An extension of the palace, the main axis now began at the very top of the mountain, with a 233-foot (71 m) monument whose rustic base, octagon, and pyramid culminated in a copper sculpture of a Farnese-type Hercules. In front of the monument's base, a pool fed a stone cascade that surged down to a grotto and pool known as Neptune's Basin. From here, Guerniero had planned a second cascade, flowing to the Moritz grotto beneath, but this waterfall was never built. Instead, additions were made around the grotto: a parterre with fountains, a wide road running at right angles to the mountain, and six subsidiary paths radiating out

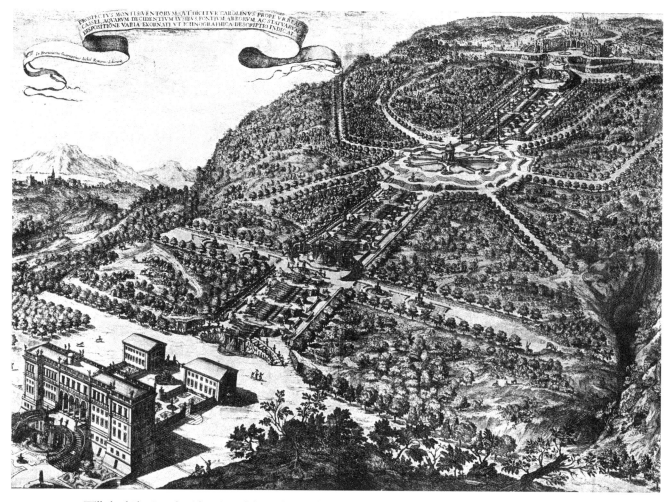

Wilhelmshöhe Cassel, with a view of the Karlsburg, from Giovanni Francesco Guernieri, *Delineato Montis*, 1706

to the wooded gardens. (Guerniero had also determined that the Moritz grotto was to be changed to a mannerist *teatro d'acqua* similar to that at the Villa Aldobrandini, but this work was only undertaken in the 1770s when it was rebuilt as a Pluto grotto.) Below this, closer to the palace, a circular fountain basin was constructed. As at Frascati, antique elements were incorporated into the landscape: colonnades, statuary, grottoes, and pools. In recognition of this massive transformation, Weissenstein was renamed Karlsberg.

Karl's other famous creations were the orangery (1703) and the gardens of Karlsaue at Kassel. The prohibitive costs of these projects, the loss of interest by his children, and the Seven Years' War precluded implementation of additional changes at Karlsberg.

A second era of improvements was undertaken in the second half of the 18th century by Landgrave Friedrich II. Strongly influenced by English gardens (particularly William Chambers's ideas of separate picturesque views and his exotic buildings for the Royal Botanic Gardens,

Kew), Friedrich softened the baroque axis, making the side areas more informal, breaking them up into numerous small scenes, and ornamenting them with vases, statues, hedges, trellises, fences, and gates. He built a Turkish mosque, Chinese village, an Egyptian pyramid, temples of Mercury and Apollo, tombs of Homer and Virgil, hermitages, a valley of philosophers, an Elysian field, and a Pluto grotto. Most renowned was the circular fountain basin that produced a jet rising over 170 feet. Rustic seats were picturesquely arranged throughout the park, offering resting points and places to enjoy the beauty. Finally, extending the dominant axis of the cascades, he linked the palace to the town of Kassel by an ash- and linden-lined avenue. And in Kassel itself he built the Bellevue palace, notable for the earliest *anglo-chinois* garden in Europe.

Karlsberg was covered with decomposed volcanic soil; its fertility and the high humidity of the area made the growth of exotic plants possible. Friedrich imported numerous species of trees from North America: groves of pines and larch, wild chestnut, and all species of rose trees were planted to the left of the palace front. Unfortunately, in order to effect many of these changes and to provide suitable space for viewing the buildings, large tracts of indigenous forest were cut down.

Wilhelm IX was critical of his father's eclectic tastes and particularly bitter about the destruction of native oaks and beeches, symbols of earlier centuries. Christian Cay Lorenz Hirschfeld, the garden theorist, had already commented on Wilhelmshöhe's lack of historical associations. Wilhelm's legacy would not be the small inconsequential structures of his father but rather, more exalted structures. First came the magnificent neoclassical palace (1786–92), which survives today, followed by an enormous ruined Roman aqueduct with formidable waterfalls, situated halfway between the palace and the Pluto grotto. Near the latter another torrent of water was created, spanned by a Devil's Bridge. Such sublime and romantic ideas culminated in the construction of Löwenburg, the colossal Gothic Revival castle, symbol of Wilhelm's absolute authority. Henceforth, Karlsberg would be known as Wilhelmshöhe (Wilhelm's Heights).

During Napoleonic times Kassel was ruled by Jerome Bonaparte, who made the palace his headquarters. During the early 19th century trees from the rich forests of the North Pacific coast of North America were introduced, followed by Asian plants from the Himalayas to the Far East. A ballroom, guardhouse, and botanical greenhouse were constructed.

Bombing attacks in World War II destroyed much of the gardens and the palace. Restoration was completed by 1974.

Synopsis

1143	Augustine convent of Weissenstein built where current palace stands
1277	Kassel became seat of House of Hesse-Kassel
1527	Reformation resulted in dissolution of the convent
1596–1627	Reign of Landgrave Moritz
1606	Weissenstein palace (then called Mauritiolum Leucopetraeum) built for Moritz in Renaissance style (as *corps de logis* flanked by two wings)
1615–17	Cascade and Moritz grotto built marking first east-west axis
1670–1730	Reign of Landgrave Karl who renames estate Karlsberg
1701–18	Hercules monument and cascade built on Karlsberg, designed by Roman architect Giovanni Francesco Guerniero
1703	Orangery building in Aue at Kassel begun
1740	Future landgrave Friedrich II marries Mary, George II's daughter
1751–60	Reign of Landgrave Wilhelm VIII
1760–85	Reign of Landgrave Friedrich II who made extensive changes influenced by English gardens
1767	Simon du Ry appointed Kassel's court architect; allée linking town to palace created
1770s	Pluto Grotto built (replacing Moritz Grotto)
1775	Tombs of Virgil, Cestius, Homer, and Ovid built
1778–92	Roman Aqueduct built
1779	Elysium created
1780	Socrates Hermitage built
1782–83	Mercury temple built
1782–85	Chinese Village constructed
1785–1821	Reign of Landgrave Wilhelm IX (Elector Wilhelm I of Hesse-Kassel from 1803)
1785–91	Lake constructed
1786–90	Southern wing of palace built
1786–92	Weissenstein Palace built (De Wailly's ideas embodied in final version), designed by Simon du Ry and Heinrich Christoph Jussow (*corps de logis* with separate wings set at 45-degree angle to main body)
1787–89	Fountain basin enlarged
1787–92	Northern (church) wing of palace built
1788–92	Aqueduct built
1790–92	Jussow cascade built
1791	Marstall built
1793	Jussow's Devils' Bridge and Carl Steinhöer's waterfall created
1793–1801	Löwenburg built
1794	Bowling Green and Felseneck (Gothic tower) begun
1798	Weissenstein renamed Wilhelmshöhe
1799	Jussow succeeds Simon Louis du Ry as court architect
1806–13	During French occupation, Kassel became capital of Jerome Bonaparte's Kingdom of Westphalia
1808–9	Dancing hall built
1813–18	House of Socrates built
1817	Jussow's Temple of Apollo by fountain basin rebuilt
1821–31	Reign of Landgrave Wilhelm II
1824–26	J.C. Bromeis's Watch House built
1826–28	Steinhöfer's new waterfall built
1829	Connecting building between main palace and side wings built

1943–45   Bomb attacks destroyed middle section
           of building and much of gardens
1974   Restoration of palace and gardens
           completed

Further Reading

Badenoch, Teresa S., "Wilhelmshöhe: A Unique Record
    of a Changing Landscape," *Journal of Garden
    History* (Spring 1986)
Bromeis, Johann Conrad, *Johann Conrad Bromeis,
    1788–1855: Ein Kurhessischer Architekt* (exhib. cat.),
    Kassel: Kunstsammlungen, 1988
Dittscheid, Hans-Christoph, *Kassel-Wilhelmshöhe und
    die Krise des Schlossbaues am Ende des Ancien
    Régime: Charles de Wailly, Simon Louis Du Ry und
    Heinrich Christoph Jussow also Architekten von
    Schloss und Löwenburg in Wilhelmshöhe*
(1785–1800), Worms, Germany: Werner
    Verlagsgesellschaft, 1987
Hirschfeld, Christian Cajus Lorenz, *Theorie der
    Gartenkunst,* 5 vols., Leipzig, 1779–85; 2nd edition,
    Hildesheim, Germany, and New York: Olms, 1985;
    see especially vols. 4 and 5
Holtmeyer, A., *Kreis Cassel-Land,* Marburg, Germany:
    Elwertsche, 1910
Lukatis, Christian, and Hans Ottomeyer, editors,
    *Herkules: Tugendheld und Herrscherideal: Das
    Herkules-Monument in Kassel-Wilhelmshöhe,*
    Eurasburg, Germany: Edition Minerva, 1997
Paetow, Karl, "Klassizismus und Romantik auf
    Wilhelmshöhe," Ph.D. diss., University of Leipzig,
    1929

TERESA S. WATTS

Williamsburg, Colonial

Williamsburg, Virginia, United States

Location: at the center of Williamsburg, Virginia

Colonial Williamsburg is a 20th-century living museum restoration of the architecture and gardening of 18th-century colonial Virginia's capital. The 1699 town plan and subsequent 18th-century development reflect ideals of urban planning and the role of public and private gardens in defining the character of a town. The colonial area restoration of Williamsburg, begun in 1927, marked the beginning of the Colonial Revival Movement in the United States. John D. Rockefeller, Jr.'s, agreement to underwrite the restoration project spurred national development in several areas: historic preservation, city planning, commercial rehabilitation, architectural training and research, historic archeology, and colonial landscape design. It was the first major instance of archeological methods being used to direct garden restoration plans by locating and identifying garden elements, including plant species.

Royal Governor Francis Nicholson's 1699 plan for the new capital at Middle Plantation incorporated aspects of urban planning reaching from Christopher Wren and Indigo Jones to Renaissance England and Europe. Duke of Gloucester Street, the town's main axis, runs along a ridge between the York and James Rivers, important colonial trade routes. The College of William and Mary (established in 1695) terminates the western end, and the Capitol Building marks its eastern terminus. The axial plan encouraged symmetry, balance, and harmony in subsequent townscape developments. An approximately 76-meter (83 yd.) modulus determined the blocks, ratios of vista lengths, and size of the palace green and courthouse green. Nicholson, and later Lieutenant Governor Alexander Spotswood, incorporated the human dimension when arranging public and private buildings in relationship to streets, neighborhoods, vistas, public green spaces, and individual gardens. Market Square, near the center of the axis, functions as a roundpoint in a landscape garden with radiating streets creating vistas into the landscape and defining distinct residential areas. The town plan evokes a sense of visual unity and creates interplay of pictorial vistas through deliberate placement of buildings, open spaces, and trees. Vistas were important considerations early on, compelling decisions to relocate buildings and remove trees to create or enhance pictorial vistas through town and into the surrounding landscape. Market Square and the octagonal Magazine function as a landscape park and focal point into which several buildings face or view. A secondary axis crossing Duke of Gloucester Street at the Bruton Parish Church established the location of the Palace Green with the Governor's Palace at its terminus. Buildings were placed to visually terminate other traverse streets as well.

A formal garden at the Governor's Palace, Williamsburg, Virginia
Copyright Archive Photos

Williamsburg remained a vital political center until the capital was moved in 1780. It was a quiet college and market town until the 1920s. At the instigation of the Reverend W.A.R. Goodwin, rector of Bruton Parish Church, John D. Rockefeller, Jr., sponsored the restoration of Colonial Williamsburg. Viewed primarily as an architectural restoration, the project interpreted colonial town life for visitors. The Boston firm of Perry, Shaw, and Hepburn, Architects, served as project architects during the initial restoration (1927–37). Boston landscape architect Arthur A. Shurcliff directed landscape and garden restorations throughout the colonial area.

Researchers investigated the layout and design of specific gardens and buildings using the best methods available in the early 1930s. These archeological methods proved accurate for locating the major structural form of the 18th-century town and its major buildings, as well as garden walks, piers, and wall foundations. Researchers gathered information from a 1782 survey known as the *Frenchman's Map;* site surveys of boundary lines, and building, walkway, and fence locations; detailed inventory of existing plant species and locations; historical documents and other texts; former

owners' accounts; and insurance maps. Shurcliff also visited numerous representative old southern sites such as the University of Virginia, and the plantations of Claremont, upper Brandon, Shirley, and Westover. When the town restoration was completed in 1935, 442 postcolonial buildings were demolished, 8 moved out of the restoration area, 66 colonial buildings repaired or restored, and 84 reproduced on colonial foundations.

Lacking specific information on plants and planting layouts, Shurcliff created gardens as regional and period interpretations rather than horticulturally correct restorations. Coupled with a desire to create pleasurable places for visitors, the restoration garden plans are more ornate than the original gardens are believed to have been. Shurcliff also included period elements known not to have been in Williamsburg. He successfully argued for their inclusion because of visual interest, ease of planting and maintenance, and anticipated visitor pleasure.

The College of William and Mary formal garden follows a European approach to framing important buildings. Simple, regular lines and symmetric, geometric patterns organize the garden court between three college buildings. Shurcliff's boxwood, holly, and seasonal flower plantings were reminiscent of 18th-century European garden forms, pleasant to view and easy to maintain.

Researchers based the restoration of the Governor's Palace and the Palace Green on a copperplate engraving, the *Bodleian Plate* (ca. 1740), discovered at Oxford University in 1929. As English public-building gardens signified their importance, the Governor's Palace reflects the political and social roles of a propertied country squire. The restoration depicts the palace gardens and the aristocracy alongside the utilitarian landscapes of kitchen gardens, pastures, and streetscapes. The reconstructed garden includes a bowling green, a labyrinth planted in holly, and a mount for viewing the gardens and adjacent landscape park, which extends into the surrounding countryside. The ravine west of the palace includes a canal, its slope faced with terraced kitchen gardens. Many of these garden elements are discussed in Sir Francis Bacon's 1625 garden treatise *On Gardens*. French garden elements present in the reconstruction also reflect John Evelyn's 1693 *The Complete Gardener*.

The developers of Colonial Williamsburg valued historical accuracy in architectural restoration and reconstructions. Desires to revive the past as a picture of beauty within a romantic setting influenced landscape and garden restoration decisions. Although more advanced archeological research revealed the inaccuracies of Shurcliff's work, they are historically important examples of classic 20th-century Colonial Revival gardens. In response to more contemporary concerns of landscape authenticity, the Colonial Williamsburg Foundation has rebuilt a few of the individual residential gardens in keeping with historical accuracy. In recognition of visitor expectations, other areas are referred to as Shurcliff's Colonial Revival gardens and interpreted as early 20th-century landscapes.

As a testing ground for historic landscape and garden restorations, many of the representation decisions at Colonial Williamsburg have influenced public and private restorations across the United States since the 1930s.

Synopsis

1633	Williamsburg settled as Middle Plantation
1674	Bruton Parish established
1693	College of William and Mary established
1699	Act of Assembly created capital at Williamsburg
1705–18	Governor's Palace built under direction of Governor Alexander Spotswood; gardens (1712–20) exploited "borrowed scenery" from palace to meadows and canal
1722	Williamsburg incorporated as city, including restrictions on buildings to be located on half-acre lots and providing greens and squares to emphasize public buildings
1780	State capital moves to Richmond
1926	John D. Rockefeller, Jr., underwrites restoration of Williamsburg to 18th C. colonial appearance
1928	Rockefeller commissions Reverend William A.R. Goodwin to begin purchasing properties within colonial city area
1928–37	Restoration effort begins, continues after World War II; funding provided by Rockefeller Foundation

Further Reading

Bazin, Germain, *Paradeisos, ou, L'art du jardin*, Paris: Chêne, 1988; as *Paradeisos: The Art of the Garden*, London: Cassell, and Boston: Little Brown, 1990

Brinkley, M. Kent, and Gordon W. Chappell, *The Gardens of Colonial Williamsburg*, Williamsburg, Virginia: Colonial Williamsburg Foundation, 1996

Colonial Williamsburg Official Guidebook and Map, Williamsburg, Virginia: Colonial Williamsburg Foundation, 1979

Griswold, Mac, Eleanor Weller, and H.E. Rollins, *The Golden Age of the American Gardens: Proud Owners, Private Estates, 1890–1940*, New York: Abrams, 1991

Hosmer, Charles B., Jr., "The Colonial Revival in the Public Eye: Williamsburg and Early Garden Restoration," in *Colonial Revival in America*, edited by Alan Alexrod, New York: Norton, 1985

Martin, Peter, *The Pleasure Gardens of Virginia: From Jamestown to Jefferson*, Princeton, New Jersey: Princeton University Press, 1991

Olmert, Michael, *Official Guide to Colonial Williamsburg*, Williamsburg, Virginia: Colonial Williamsburg Foundation, 1998

Shurcliff, Arthur A., "The Gardens of the Governor's Palace, Williamsburg, Virginia," *Landscape Architecture* 27 (January 1937)

Shurcliff, Arthur A., "The Ancient Plan of Williamsburg," *Landscape Architecture* 28 (January 1938)

Weishan, Michael, *The New Traditional Garden: A Practical Guide to Creating and Restoring Authentic American Gardens for Homes of All Ages*, New York: Ballantine, 1999

TERRY L. CLEMENTS

Wilson, Ernest Henry 1876–1930

English Plant Collector

Ernest Henry Wilson was born in Gloucestershire, England. After leaving school with little direction, he took a job with the Hewitt Nurseries at Solihull, Warwickshire. Although new to horticulture, he showed an affinity for the work and was singled out to work at the Birmingham Botanical Gardens. While there he also enrolled in botany studies at the Birmingham Technical School, where his achievements earned him the Queen's Prize and the attention of the Royal Botanic Gardens, Kew. In 1897, at 21 years of age, Kew offered him a position, and shortly thereafter he became a teacher of botany in the Royal College of Science at South Kensington, which is now a part of the University of London.

About this time British plant exploration had reached its peak. The firm of James Veitch and Sons was looking for someone to explore inland China in search of a source for the dove tree (*Davidia involucrata*), which had been reported on by Augustine Henry, an earlier explorer to China. They asked at Kew for a recommendation, and Wilson was offered and accepted the assignment. He stayed in China for three years, returning with approximately 400 plants new to British botanists. Wilson had found his niche and would spend the remainder of his career exploring and collecting new plant species.

Veitch sponsored a second trip to China. Wilson's assignment this time was to locate the yellow poppy *Meconopsis integrifolia*. He found the poppy and a good deal more. Many of the seeds collected during his explorations were sent back to the Veitch nursery, including *Meconopsis integrifolia*, *Astilbe davidii*, *Pheum alexandrae*, *Senecio clivorum*, *Paeonia veitchii*, and *Clematis Montam rubens*.

A trip to America allowed him to spend a great deal of time exploring the Arnold Arboretum in Massachusetts and the gardens of its first director, Charles Sprague Sargent, a man known for sending his staff to the far corners of the world in search of new and exotic plant material. Sargent himself had been on several expeditions, and the two men became lifelong friends and colleagues.

On his return to England, Wilson accepted a position as a botanical assistant at the Imperial Institute in London. However, his new friend Sargent asked him to make yet another trip to China on behalf of the Arnold Arboretum. He started for China with instructions to locate trees and shrubs of value to American gardens. This was the beginning of his employment by the Arnold Arboretum. Among his introductions were the paperbark maple (*Acer griseum*), the hardy silk tree (*Albizia julibrissin*), the beauty bush (*Kolkwitzia amabilis*), the dove tree (*Davidia involucrata*), *Magnolia wilsonii*, the giant dogwood, and the Korean Stewartia. His discoveries were particularly embraced by the American South because it shared a similar climate with parts of China, allowing these varieties to adapt and thrive. There is now an Ernest Henry "Chinese" Wilson Collection within the International Garden at the State Botanical Garden of Georgia.

Although Wilson remained based in the United States, Great Britain was still able to benefit from his discoveries. Plant material considered too tender for Boston's harsh climate was sent to the Dawyck Arboretum near Peebles in the Scottish Borders. Many species can still be seen there.

Wilson also introduced the West to the kiwifruit, or Chinese gooseberry (*Actinidia chinensis*). New Zealand's kiwifruit industry can be traced back to Wilson's plant material. His introduction of the Korean forsythia (*Forsythia ovata*), arguably the hardiest species of forsythia at the time, has been used in hybridization to develop even hardier cultivars capable of spring flowering in colder northern climates.

On his fourth exploration of China, again initiated by the Arnold Arboretum, Wilson returned with a vast assortment of seeds and bulbs. There were reportedly thousands of lily bulbs among his introductions, including the royal lily, Sergeant's lily, Henry's lily, and the Wilmott lily. Wilson also rediscovered and reintroduced *Lilium davidii*. His success exploring China garnered him the nickname "Chinese" Wilson, a name with which he was never comfortable. His usual good luck was interrupted on this fourth trip, when he was caught in a landslide in the Min River valley and broke his leg in two places, forcing him to return home briefly to heal.

Once recovered, Wilson set his sights on Japan with the intention of collecting Japanese cherries. He returned with 63 named forms of Japanese cherries, then, being restless, took off again to further his explorations of Asia, expanding into Korea and Formosa.

Returning to the Arnold Arboretum in 1919, Wilson was appointed its associate director but continued traveling and collecting. Three years later, he was off yet again, spending the next two years scouting plants around the world in Australia, New Zealand, India, Central and South America, and East Africa.

Eventually Wilson was made director of the Arnold Arboretum. Among the many prestigious awards bestowed on him were the Victoria Medal of Honor of the Royal Horticultural Society of London in 1912, the Veitch Memorial Medal, and the George Robert White Memorial Medal of the Massachusetts Horticultural

Society. He was made a fellow of the American Academy of Arts and Sciences and received an honorary M.A. degree from Harvard University and a Doctor of Science degree from Trinity College in Connecticut.

All totaled, Wilson discovered an impressive 3,356 species and varieties. Over 100 plants introduced by Wilson received the First-Class Certificate or Awards of Merit of the Royal Horticultural Society of London. He lent his name to 60 species and varieties of Chinese plants.

Both Wilson and his wife died in an automobile accident in Worcester, Massachusetts in 1930. His birthplace, Chipping Camden, Gloucestershire, is now home to the Wilson Memorial Garden. The garden's plantings are exclusively Wilson introductions and include the paperbark maple, *Acer griseum,* and the plant for which he reportedly wished to be remembered, the *Lilium regale.*

See also Arnold Arboretum

Biography

Born in Gloucestershire, England, 1876. Began horticultural career at Hewitt Nurseries in Solihull, Warwickshire; offered job at Birmingham Botanical Gardens and began botany studies at Birmingham Technical School, 1892; offered employment at Royal Botanic Gardens, Kew, 1897; undertook first of his explorations of China in search of dove tree, 1899; returned to China to search for *Meconopsis integrifolia,* 1903; visited Arnold Arboretum in Boston, Massachusetts, and made acquaintance of Charles Sprague Sargeant, 1904; set off for China again and became botanical assistant at Imperial Institute in London on his return, 1905; another trip to China on behalf of Arnold Arboretum to look for shrubs and trees suitable for American gardens, 1907; returned to China for Arboretum, bringing back seeds, tubers, and thousands of lily bulbs, 1910; explored Japan for Japanese cherries, 1911; scouted Korea and Formosa, 1917; appointed associate director of Arnold Arboretum, 1919; set off for Australia, New Zealand, India, Central and South America, and East Africa, 1922; made director of Arnold Arboretum, 1927. Died 1930.

Selected Publications

Naturalist in Western China, 1913
Plantae Wilsonianae, 1913–17
Cherries of Japan, 1916
Conifers and Taxads of Japan, 1916
Aristocrats of the Garden, 1917
Monograph of Azaleas (with Alfred Rehder), 1921
America's Greatest Garden: The Arnold Arboretum, 1925
Lilies of Eastern Asia, 1925
Plant Hunting, 1927
More Aristocrats of the Garden, 1928
China, Mother of Gardens, 1929
Aristocrats of the Trees, 1930

Further Reading

Briggs, Roy W., *"Chinese" Wilson: A Life of Ernest H. Wilson, 1876–1930,* London: HMSO, 1993

Cox, Euan Hillhouse Methven, *Plant-Hunting in China: A History of Botanical Exploration in China and the Tibetan Marches,* London: Collins, 1945

Farrington, Edward I., *Ernest H. Wilson, Plant Hunter: With a List of His Most Important Introductions and Where to Get Them,* edited by Alfred Rehder, Boston: Stratford, 1931

Turrill, William Bertram, editor, *Recent Researches in Plant Taxonomy,* New York: Pergamon Press, 1964

MARIE IANNOTTI

Winter Garden

The term *winter garden* has several meanings. Originally it referred to a garden for winter display, especially using attractive conifers. Later it meant a domestic hothouse or forcing house. The most important use of the term, however, was to describe a garden in a greenhouse meant for leisure, recreation, and entertainment amid yearly or evergreen scenery. It was called an exotic garden and related to the Renaissance conception of an ever-green and ever-alive garden. It was a symbol of durability and nonvariability of nature's cycles: *Ver perpetuum,* that is, uninterrupted spring. These domestic conservatories allowed for the collection, cultivation, and display of exotic plants obtained through travel, discovery, and war. The obtaining of exotic fruits was treated almost like black magic. Fruits that appeared from this contest with nature, independent of the seasons, increased the splendor of residences. Orangeries, first seen in the 17th century, were the precursor to the conservatories and winter gardens of Victorian times.

The areas in front of and around the orangeries became a continuation of the exotic garden connected by a view from the interior. They were set up as parterres on which potted orange trees were exposed with sculptures on large *gazon*. The lack of flowers in these areas was meant to eliminate unwanted competition for the splendid exotic plants. In special compositions the atmosphere of an antique world was re-created together with the islands of happiness, *insulae beatae*. The antique atmosphere was created with the help of Mediterranean plants. The basic plant materials used were orange trees, laurel, boxwood, and roses. Neither geographical nor plant systematic criteria were employed, and variety was entirely allowed. The use of Chinese vases or faience vases from Delf with a touch of the Far East stressed the exotic climate of the composition. Chinese details were introduced and used in the decoration of garden furniture and fences. Exotic garden scenes became very popular in the 19th century, symbolizing fantastic land or paradise, and were associated with the popularization of various wintergreen exotic plants. The Frenchman Edouard André in the second half of the 19th century was the great perpetuator of the exotic garden scene. Additional impetus came from the technical possibilities (e.g., fabricated metal constructions and large glass sheets) in constructing and heating even larger greenhouses called glass palaces, for example, the Crystal Palace built in 1851 in Hyde Park in London for large exhibitions. Specialist hothouses also appeared, such as palm houses, camellia houses (Pilnitz, Germany), orchid houses (Vienna, Austria; Łańcut, Poland), and cactus houses.

The introduction and development of garden exhibitions in conservatories accelerated the development of winter gardens. Winter gardens could demonstrate scientific and technical achievements. Plants were usually grown in picturesque groups, basically in the ground, and supplemented with other potted plants (such as orchids and ferns) placed on the ground or hung on tree trunks. Attractive exotic trees such as palms, fig, coffee, cacao, ficus, and euphorbia were planted. Winding paths were irregular and usually covered with sand or strengthened with stone or ceramic slabs. An exotic atmosphere prevailed, which was stressed by the use of succulents (e.g., *Hoya, Euphorbia, Passiflora, Opuntia,* and many others), accompanied by exotic birds in cages. Due to the wide variety of plant material used, climate zones were separated into tropic, subtropic, and desert.

Classical winter gardens appeared in the program of large palace-garden ensembles (e.g., Łazienki and Łańcut, both in Poland) and were at that time separate impressive compositions with ponds, pavilions, canals, and bridges, such as at King Ludwig II's winter garden in Munich. Winter garden greenhouses could be connected to the palace by a passage (e.g., Łańcut). In the 19th century, in the outer part of the exotic garden, exotic coniferous plants were introduced such as *Picea, Pinus, Abies, Torreya, Cryptomeria, Sciadopitys,* and

especially *Thuja occidentalis,* which was to replace the delicate *Cupressus sempervirens,* a symbol of Italy. Other plants included *Ilex, Mahonia, Jasminum,* myrtle, and rosemary. As in the 18th century, the passage between the external and interior parts had to be carefully arranged; the view from the greenhouse was made to end in the shadows of exotic trees and shrubs exposed on homogeneous lawns.

These ideas also appeared at small country residences and were arranged as part of the residential building. Similarly, winter gardens became part of town palaces and even residences. They were then reduced to "green rooms," verandas, flower windows, window greenhouses, or Wardian cases. Aquariums and terrariums followed later in homes. For the middle class winter gardens were a symbol of the elite.

Because of their popularity, winter gardens began appearing in public places. The winter garden at Crystal Palace was an unparalleled example. Besides their scientific and educational roles, winter gardens in botanical gardens were a place for social events, as in the palm houses of town parks (e.g., Poznań, Poland). Winter gardens also were created at health resorts, acting as part of the therapeutic programs even during bad weather. They were made more attractive by adding restaurants, confectioneries, and band shells. Winter gardens were also found in greenhouses built in towns (e.g., Champ Elysees, Paris, 1846). The winter garden program, besides providing tropical promenades, also offered cafes, elegant restaurants, volières, art galleries, ballrooms and billiard rooms. Productive town greenhouses are still at times made available to the public as winter gardens.

Also during the 19th century some styleless exotic gardens reflected a crisis in garden forms in their tendencies to create unbridled nature and in an increasing interest in plants and their properties. Such gardens became a gathering of rare and exotic plants, planted with no clear thought of composition, in a spontaneous manner. Lack of consideration of the habitat and biological properties of plants led to overpopulation, deformation of habit, and consequentially loss of the exotic character of the plant. In the 20th century the admiration of winter gardens gradually faded and with it the innovativeness and originality of its forms and impressions.

Greenhouses are very labile elements of gardens and are usually expensive to run. Remnants of the greenhouse winter garden are the popular cultivation of rare exotic plants in homes and offices. Reminiscents are found also in exotic interior decorations in restaurants, cafes, and shopping centers, and in bank vestibules and waiting rooms at railway stations or airports. Winter gardens today can be found in residences and villas of various scales, from small *cache pots, jardinieres,* or indoor gardens to flower windows to perfect green rooms. They are set up in stainless, transparent, and resistant constructions that have good isolation parameters and are usually made from artificial material. They are equipped with modern heating and thermoregulation systems. The current eco-house concept tries to integrate its functions completely into the natural cycles of matter and energy.

Further Reading

Dubbini, R., "Glasshouses and Winter Gardens," in *The Architecture of Western Gardens: A Design History from the Renaissance to the Present Day,* edited by Monique Mosser and Georges Teyssot, Cambridge, Massachusetts: MIT Press, and London: Thames and Hudson, 1991

Hix, John, *The Glass House,* Cambridge, Massachusetts: MIT Press, and London: Phaidon, 1974

Saudan-Skira, Sylvia, and Michel Saudan, *Orangeries: Palaces of Glass—Their History and Treatment,* translated by Alayne Pullen, Cologne, Germany: Taschen, 1998

MAREK SIEWNIAK

Wise, Henry 1653–1738

English Gardener

Henry Wise joined George London as the junior partner at the Brompton Park Nursery in Kensington in 1687 after the death and retirement of the three other senior partners. Although it is difficult to assess their precise roles, Wise seems to have quickly assumed a managerial position, while London toured the country advising clients. After the accession of William of Orange to the English throne, and for nearly 30 years, the partnership played a significant part in the development of the formal garden in England.

A portrait of Henry Wise by Kneller suggests a kindly, authoritative man, described by the diarist John Evelyn, a patron of Brompton Park Nursery, as both "industrious" and "knowing." Wise seems to have had a particular expertise with trees, his work frequently involving the maintenance and replacement of mature trees. He was responsible for providing the horse chestnuts backed by four rows of limes for the avenue in Bushey Park, designed by Christopher Wren as the state approach to Hampton Court. As ranger of St. James's Park, Wise replaced some 350 mature limes.

After Queen Mary's death in 1694, Wise increasingly took over from George London the role of royal gardener, and in 1702 Queen Anne appointed him superintendent of the Royal Parks and Gardens, a post that commanded a high salary and a lodge in Windsor Park. Some of the work involved modifying earlier schemes carried out by London for William and Mary, removing all box from the parterres, replacing it with gravel and cut turf. Wise also undertook the extension of the gardens to the north of Kensington Palace. The Sunk Garden, with its formal terraces, cabinets, and niches, reminiscent of garden features at Versailles and Marly, has been attributed to his assistant, Stephen Switzer.

In general, it seems that Wise's job in the royal gardens was chiefly to plant and maintain. At Blenheim, however, he undertook his most ambitious scheme, the work being completed over a period of four years from 1705 to 1709. The site of Woodstock Park in Oxfordshire was granted to the duke of Marlborough by Queen Anne in 1705 as a reward for his defeat of the French army at Blindheim, and the building of a new palace and gardens was initially to be financed by the government. The architect chosen was Sir John Vanbrugh, and the team included his assistant, Nicholas Hawksmoor, and Queen Anne's gardener, Henry Wise. The military nature of the plan drawn by Wise, with the trees of the Grand Avenue facing each other in battle formation, together with the form of the Bastion Garden to the south of the house suggest that Vanbrugh himself was involved in the design. There is no evidence that Wise was paid for designs or drafts. In the account books for the project (preserved in the British Museum manuscript collection), Wise is described as a master gardener, responsible for its making, planting, and maintenance. It was he who employed day laborers, carters, and weeders, paying them out of his own fee.

The account books provide unique evidence concerning the construction and planting of a formal garden of this scale. Work began with the digging out of bad earth and the laying of drains. Discarded earth was used to build up the terraces, which were laid with a coat of flat stones ready to receive the gravel. Bushes and trees that blocked vistas had to be grubbed out, and borders and quarters had to be dug, leveled, and raked, ready for planting.

Huge consignments of trees, plants, and flower roots were sent by carrier from Brompton Park Nursery. These included hedge yews of various heights, pyramid yews, and hollies for the Bastion Garden; fruit trees, vines, and figs for the kitchen garden; flowering shrubs for the wilderness; and roots of lemon and striped thyme for edging, together with bulbs of every variety, especially tulips—an indication of the range of stock available at Brompton Park Nursery at the time. The kitchen garden alone grew 28 different kinds of peaches and nectarines, as well as 72 kinds of figs, mulberries, apples, quinces, and cherries. Many exotics were introduced by plant collectors and botanical gardens from countries such as North America and even the Cape. As the hard-working nurseryman-contractor, Wise clearly promoted the type of garden that would bring business to the nursery, at the same time keenly aware of the prevailing fashion of his day. Whether the style originated from France or Holland was not his concern, and together with his partner, he seems to have been content to use the pattern books of his day, eventually drawing on his experience to build up a pattern book of his own.

A garden on the scale of Blenheim required enormous maintenance. It lasted only 50 years before Lancelot "Capability" Brown was brought in to replace the formal garden with a more economical landscape garden.

Nonetheless, the evident success of Blenheim brought the partnership of Wise and London a commission to design a new garden for the Marlboroughs's town house in London, which was completed in 1711, as well as a small garden for Marshal Tallard, a defeated French general who had been exiled to Nottingham. Here they worked on a very small scale, introducing all the elements of a London and Wise garden, with two tiny parterres laid out with colored sands in the emblem of the French king. After London's death in 1714, it appears that Wise did not take on any major commissions himself. He sublet Brompton Park Nursery to two of his gardeners, keeping Brompton Park House for himself, together with certain pieces of land that held his most valued plants. By 1724, less than 20 years after the Blenheim project, when the nursery was reputed to stock 10 million plants, it no longer figured as a leading nursery. By the time Wise retired to Warwickshire in 1727, the formal style of gardening that the partnership had done so much to promote was already being replaced by the more economical and finally more "English" landscape design promoted by writers such as Joseph Addison and Horace Walpole.

The only remaining evidence of the partnership of London and Wise are the canals in the school grounds of Stonyhurst, the neglected but recognizable avenue and Octagon Canal in Wanstead Park, and the over-grown topiary and weed-covered ponds of the surviving garden at Melbourne Hall in Derbyshire. The contemporary engravings of Knyff and Kip are some indication of what has been lost.

See also Blenheim Palace; Chatsworth Gardens; Hampton Court Palace and Bushy Park; Kensington Gardens

Biography

Born 1653. Claimed to be descended from well-established family in Warwickshire, England; joined Brompton Park Nursery, Kensington, London, as junior partner to George London, 1687; worked at Hampton Court, from 1699; appointed superintendent of Royal Parks and Gardens by Queen Anne, 1702; extended and renovated gardens at Kensington Palace, London; undertook most important project at Blenheim, Oxfordshire, England, 1705–9; purchased Warwick Priory, Warwick, Warwickshire, England, 1709; collaborated with George London on many gardens, including Marshal Tallard's garden, Nottingham, Nottinghamshire, England; after death of London in 1714, sublet Brompton Park to two of his gardeners, retaining house for himself; retired to Warwick Priory, 1727. Died at Warkwick Priory, Warwick, Warwickshire, England, 1738.

Selected Designs

1695–1700	Stonyhurst, Lancashire, England (of which canals survive)
1699–1707	Renovation and maintenance, Hampton Court, Middlesex, England
1702–4	Maintenance and renovation at Kensington Palace, London, England
1704	Melbourne Hall (with George London), Derby, Derbyshire, England
1705	Marshal Tallard's garden, Nottingham, Nottinghamshire, England
1705–9	Blenheim Palace, Oxfordshire, England, for Duke and Duchess of Marlborough
1707	Design for Lower Wilderness, Hampton Court, Middlesex, England
1710–11	Gardens, Marlborough House, London, England

Selected Publications

Compleat Gard'ner, translated (with George London), from the French by Jean de la Quintinie, 1699
The Retir'd Gard'ner, translated (with George London), from the French by François Gentil, 2 vols., 1706

Further Reading

Blomfield, Reginald, *The Formal Garden in England*, London, 1892; 3rd edition, London and New York:

Macmillan, 1901; reprint, New York: AMS Press, 1972

Campbell, Colen, *Vitruvius Britannicus*, 3 vols., London, 1715–25; reprint, 1 vol., New York: Blom, 1967

Chittenden, Frederick James, "Henry Wise and the Royal Gardens in Queen Anne's Time," *Journal of the Royal Horticultural Society* (1939)

Green, David Brontë, *Gardener to Queen Anne: Henry Wise (1653–1738) and the Formal Garden*, London and New York: Oxford University Press, 1956

Jacques, David, and Arend Jan Van der Horst, *The Gardens of William and Mary*, London: Croom Helm, 1988

Mollet, André, *Le jardin de plaisir*, Stockholm, 1651; reprint, Paris: Éditions du Moniteur, 1982

Switzer, Stephen, *The Nobleman, Gentleman, and Gardener's Recreation*, London, 1715; new edition, as *Ichnographia Rustica: The Nobleman, Gentleman, and Gardener's Recreation*, 3 vols., London, 1718; reprint, New York: Garland, 1982

SANDRA MORRIS

Wisley

Surrey, England

Location: approximately 25 miles (40 km) southwest of central London, near Woking

Wisley (see Plate 35) is the garden of the English Royal Horticultural Society, which is orientated toward practical horticulture and one of whose main aims is to train the gardeners of the future. The Wisley Garden therefore serves a different purpose to that of the Royal Botanical Society at Kew. The society itself was incorporated by royal charter in 1804, and its purpose was specified "to promote horticulture in Britain and around the world." It runs the celebrated annual Chelsea Flower Show.

The Wisley estate was given to the Royal Horticultural Society in 1903. At that time only a small part of the 24 hectares (59 acres) was actually cultivated as a garden, with the rest devoted to wooded farmland. The first garden had been the creation of George Ferguson Wilson, a keen horticulturist, who had purchased the site in 1878 and established the Oakwood experimental garden there, attempting to make "difficult plants grow successfully." He specialized in lilies, gentians, Japanese irises, primulas, and water plants, and Oakwood is the direct antecedent of the present Wild Garden.

When Wilson died in 1902 Sir Thomas Hanbury bought Oakwood and the adjoining Glebe Farm. He was a wealthy Quaker who, with his botanist brother Daniel, had already in 1867 established a famous hillside garden at La Mortola on the Italian Riviera, and it was he who in 1903 presented the Wisley estate to the Royal Horticultural Society. For at least 30 years the society had been looking for a garden away from London's smoke ring to replace the Chiswick garden it had leased since 1822. The Wisley benefaction also came appropriately to celebrate the 100th anniversary of the society's foundation in 1804, for which it was building its new London office headquarters.

The move of the garden from Chiswick was completed by May 1904, and the garden was formally opened by Edward VII that year. Although it was still primarily an ornamental garden, the society did not forget its scientific and educational aspirations, and it opened a small laboratory, as well as a horticultural school for the formation of future gardeners. The society's trials of flowers, vegetables, and fruit resumed and expanded, epitomizing, it claimed, "the Society's endeavour to show to the public the best kinds of plants to grow."

The gardens are now largely devoted to horticultural experiment. They attract visitors for the borders, rose gardens, and glasshouses but are chiefly devoted to testing new varieties of flowers and vegetables, as well as new methods of cultivation. Of particular interest at present is a half-acre (0.2 ha) country garden by the English garden designer Penelope Hobhouse, with a formal rectilinear path layout, terracing natural contours. Color-themed beds surround a central pond.

The Temperate Glasshouse has been remodeled and divided into three sections, one for plants thriving on dry, bright conditions, one for temporary plant displays, and another for a new waterfall and pools for plants requiring warm, damp conditions. A large new benefaction has recently made possible the creation at Wisley of a bonsai collection, with the bonsai displayed Japanese-fashion on pedestals in a gravel garden with lanterns, rocks, water basin, and bamboo fences.

The half-timbered, mock-Tudor laboratory building, where pests, diseases, and other garden problems are investigated, looks older than it is, but its style suits much else in the garden. The soil is acid sand, which drains fast but is poor in nutrients. Wisley includes a canal, rock garden, formal garden, and a walled garden together with rose gardens, richly packed herbaceous borders, summer, winter, and woodland gardens, an orchard, and an arboretum. In addition are also an alpine garden, model vegetable gardens, and an area in which different styles of model gardens can be compared. Comparisons are a feature of Wisley, with trial areas of collections of cultivars displayed together for assessment.

Wisley holds national collections of *Crocus, Colchicum, Daboecia, Epimedium, Erica, Daphne, Galanthus, Hosta,* and *Pulmonaria.* Its stated purpose is to "use and occupy the estate for the purpose of an experimental garden and the encouragement and improvement of scientific and practical horticulture in all its branches." It fulfills this purpose largely by its field trials but also partly by its commercial operations. It has commenced internet marketing, and its shop contains the largest collection of new gardening books in Britain. It has since 1907 been running horticultural courses for future gardeners, providing nationally recognized professional qualifications. It is establishing itself as the preeminent professional body and is expanding its examining. The education department runs a full program of lectures, demonstrations, workshops, and guided walks throughout the year.

Among the many roles filled by Wisley in the gardening world, its educational activities may merit greatest acclaim. The field trials, model gardens, available comparisons, and research into pest control are all ultimately determined by the resolve to remain practical and horticultural rather than abstractly scientific and botanical. It has at present an annual income of over £25 million and keeps its administrative costs down to almost 3 percent of income, employing over 40 full-time staff.

Synopsis

1804	Foundation of Royal Horticultural Society
1878	George Ferguson Wilson purchases Wisley estate and establishes experimental garden
1902–3	Thomas Hanbury buys estate and donates it to Royal Horticultural Society
1904	Opening of Wisley after transfer of Royal Horticultural Society garden from Chiswick in London
1907	Royal Horticultural Society begins horticultural training at Wisley
1911	Rock garden built, designed by Edward White

Further Reading

Dickson, A., et al., *Four Essays Written by Students at Wisley, 1913,* London: Spottiswoode, 1913

Gould, N.K., *Guide to Wisley Gardens,* Rochester, Kent: Stanhope Press and Royal Horticultural Society, 1947; 7th edition, London: Royal Horticultural Society, 1954

Rix, Martyn, and Alison Rix, *Wisley: The Royal Horticultural Society's Garden,* Baltonsborough, Somerset: Holland, 1989

Sharman, Fay, *Wisley Garden,* London: Royal Horticultural Society, 1989

ANTHONY H.T. LEVI

Women as Gardeners

The history of the garden is inextricably tied to the history of women's work. The figuration of nature-as-female and the garden as a feminine domain dates from the beginning of historical record. The findings of archaeologists and anthropologists conclusively assert the key role played by women in the cultivation of domestic gardens in most parts of the world from the earliest periods of Neolithic society. Throughout time women of all classes gardened to produce food for the family table and herbs for medicinal and cosmetic purposes, and engaged in floriculture as a genteel art form. Although women were largely restricted from gardening professionally until the late 19th and early 20th centuries, the poorest women weeded European castle gardens for very modest remuneration from medieval times, extracting nettles and other unwanted plants. The Medici queens have long been credited with bringing Italian garden traditions to France during the 16th century, their interest in gardening proving a decisive factor in the development of that country's garden arts.

Although women would not find a place in the landscape professions for another 300 years, William Lawson's *The Country Housewife's Garden* of 1617 became one of the first publications to recommend gardening as

Frontispiece of Frances Wolseley, *Gardening for Women,* 1908
Courtesy of Dumbarton Oaks, Trustees for Harvard University

an activity especially suited to women. A hundred years later, Charles Evelyn wrote *The Lady's Recreation* (1717), a publication that coincided with a period in which women of economic and social prominence began to think of gardening as an aristocratic and highly skilled accomplishment. At the same time many women of lesser means were tending parsonage gardens, much in the manner of Jane Austen. Although gardening books written by and for women appeared infrequently in the 18th century, unpublished manuscripts such as Sylvia Streatfield's *Sylvia's Flower Garden* (1735) demonstrate the depth of horticultural knowledge some women possessed. Her "little treatise," as she called it, contains detailed instructions about soils, root treatments, planting schedules, and general horticultural knowledge for the propagation of flowers and shrubs, and it is part of a literary genre that has continued uninterrupted to the present with the ever-popular writings of Vita Sackville-West, Rosemary Verey, and Penelope Hobhouse.

By the end of the 18th century, women's magazines featured gardening articles, but women could also seek gardening advice in their own libraries by turning to books such as Elizabeth Blackwell's *A Curious Herbal* (1737–39), Margaret Meen's *Exotic Plants from the Royal Garden at Kew* (1790), and Mary Lawrance's *A Collection of Roses* (1799). They could also instruct themselves and their children in botanical science with the aid of books such as Maria Elizabeth Jackson's *Botanical Dialogues* (1797), a text later endorsed by Erasmus Darwin. As a discipline for study, botany became popular among English women who believed it instructed the young in the wonders of nature and allowed health benefits since it entailed work out of doors in the fresh air and at least a degree of exercise. Botanical publications by and for women began to slowly alter the standards of education for women by interjecting science into the accepted curriculum of the period. An indication of the dispersion of botanical and horticultural knowledge among 18th-century women appears in their contributions to agronomy. As Alice Morse Earle indicated in her 1901 *Old Time Gardens,* Eliza Lucas Pinckney of Charleston, South Carolina, contributed to the introduction of indigo propagation in her state.

Numerous 19th-century publications advocated gardening as an acceptable activity for women on the grounds that it improved health and helped women avoid the numerous nervous disorders associated with the upper classes. Aside from the produce it could contribute to the home, gardening also kept women safely occupied and away from the perceived dangers and vices of urban life and political agitation. Among the most renowned female authors of the period, Jane Loudon produced books that instructed her readers on appropriate attire and comportment as well as horticultural information. The wife of the well-known landscape gardener John Claudius Loudon, she enjoyed a degree of name recognition associated with the field that most female authors of the time must have envied, and her books sold quite briskly, reaching a large audience.

During this period, when gardening literature for women reached its pinnacle, such books served a variety of functions, most of which contributed to the formation of a network of women's specialized knowledge and support. The literature provided an important outlet for women to assert their opinions and identity at a time when few others existed. After 1870 the books contain increasing numbers of pleas and carefully phrased arguments for female access to the gardening or landscape profession. Career choices were severely restricted for 19th-century women, particularly for those of the middle class. As in earlier times, earning a living was a difficult task, one that was not socially sanctioned and that was to be avoided through marriage if at all possible.

But gardening became a vocation that allowed women to earn a modest income through the sale of surplus produce and seeds. In 1872 Anna Warner published her didactic novel *Miss Tiller's Vegetable Garden and the Money She Made by It,* which contained lessons in business, accounting, and customer relations. In the United States after 1870, statutes modeled after the 1848 Married Women's Property Act proliferated, making it increasingly possible for married women to own their own property and gardens. But even when actual proprietary rights could not be claimed, the women's gardening literature encouraged women to take control of a piece of land in their yards, appropriating the terrain through gardening endeavors.

As a literary corpus these books comprised an important educational resource for two of the best-known female designers of the late 19th and early 20th centuries: Gertrude Jekyll and Beatrix Jones Farrand, who became a founding member of the American Society of Landscape Architects (ASLA). Neither woman had the opportunity for formal education in botany, horticulture, or landscape architecture since such formal training for women did not commence until the turn of the century. Among the first schools of landscape architecture open to women were England's Swanley College, which admitted women to study horticulture in 1900, the Lowthorpe School of Landscape Gardening for Women, which opened in 1901, and the Cambridge School of Architecture and Landscape Architecture, which began enrolling women in 1915. Since their practices commenced in the closing decades of the 19th century, Jekyll and Farrand had to turn to alternate educational sources. In addition to their clear talents, intelligence, and ability to self-educate, their professional success was predicated on their placement within the upper classes of British and American society, which gave them access to wealthy and influential clients. Moreover, each had access to important mentors or colleagues. Jekyll benefited from her close relationships with William Robinson and Sir Edwin Lutyens; Farrand made connections through her well-known aunt, the novelist Edith Wharton. Despite their fame and the large number of important gardens each created, Jekyll and Farrand are somewhat anomalous for their times, the exception rather than the rule; most of their contemporaries—Ellen Wilmott, Ellen Biddle Shipman, Marjorie Sewell Cautley, and Marian Coffin aside—struggled to attain any degree of professional recognition or success. Additionally, female clients often played an important role in decisions related to garden layout and plant selection, so that the number of women involved in garden design extends well beyond the names of the few well-known practitioners to include office staff, hobbyists, part-time practitioners, and countless others.

Equally important at the end of the 19th century was the founding of the Garden Clubs of America, an outgrowth of the General Federation of Women's Clubs, founded in 1889. Women first organized local chapters of garden clubs, which initially dealt exclusively with domestic gardening issues. The local chapters later coalesced to form a national organization that continues to thrive today and which has long served the needs of women who used club memberships as a means of expressing personal identity and attaining community involvement.

The years before World War II witnessed the emergence in England of at least three additional female landscape architects who attained a significant degree of prominence as the century progressed. Both Brenda Colvin and Sylvia Crowe graduated from Swanley College and became important members of the professional societies and educational institutions of their countries, and they established practices that extended beyond residential design to include design of parks, new towns, regional plans, and reclamation projects. They also served as founding members of the International Federation of Landscape Architects and as presidents of the Landscape Institute. Both women published important books: Colvin's *Land and Landscape* (1947) and Crowe's *Garden Design* (1958), *Landscapes of Power* (1958), and *Forestry in the Landscape* (1966). Susan Jellicoe, wife and partner of Sir Geoffrey Jellicoe, forged a reputation as a planting designer in her husband's firm and as coauthor of their still-popular survey of landscape history, *The Landscape of Man* (1975).

In the United States the West Coast provided fertile ground for the flourishing of women-owned landscape architectural firms. Among the first firms owned and operated by female landscape architects on the West Coast was the partnership of Edith Schryver and Elizabeth Lord, whose practice commenced in 1929 in Salem, Oregon. But the combination of concentrated wealth, liberal attitudes, and booming growth made southern California the ideal environment for women to succeed in practice. In the first half of the 20th century, Lutah Maria Riggs and Florence Yoch built reputations for the design of estate gardens for wealthy clients in the areas in and around Los Angeles; they both specialized in the regional adaptation of forms through the use of native plant species and Mediterranean embellishments. In San Diego, California, Kate Sessions developed an extensive nursery of plants especially suited to that region's climate and worked closely with architects such as Irving Gill to create gardens that were integrated with their architectural framework. In the postwar period northern California took the lead with the emergence of Mai Arbegast and Geraldine Knight Scott, who both specialized in planting design. Among her many important projects, Arbegast consulted in the mid-1960s on the planting for Seattle's Freeway Park, designed by another woman—Angela Danadjieva—

working in the firm of Lawrence Halprin and Associates. Scott served as the local planting consultant to Dan Kiley on his design for the Oakland Museum gardens. She built a significant practice based in the design of suburban residential gardens.

These women are a very few among the thousands who practice as professional landscape architects today. A 1999 report on women in the ASLA records steady growth in female membership, although women have seldom attained the status of Fellow and only entered the governing structure of the society in the 1970s. The study indicates that 2,000 women were ASLA members in 1988, although this number does not account for the many women in practice who are not members, those involved in the design/build professions, or those who continue to garden as amateurs and hobbyists today.

Further Reading

Barber, Elizabeth Wayland, *Women's Work: The First 20,000 Years: Women, Cloth, and Society in Early Times,* New York: Norton, 1994

Bell, Susan Groag, "Women Create Space in Male Landscapes: A Revisionist Approach to Eighteenth-Century Garden History," *Feminist Studies* 16 (1990)

Beneš, Mirka, and Dianne Harris, editors, *Villas and Gardens in Early Modern Italy and France,* Cambridge and New York: Cambridge University Press, 2001

Bennett, Jennifer, *Lilies of the Hearth: The Historical Relationship between Women and Plants,* Camden East, Ontario: Camden House, 1991

Birnbaum, Charles, and Lisa E. Crowder, editors, *Pioneers of American Landscape Design: An Annotated Bibliography,* Washington, D.C.: U.S. Department of the Interior, National Park Service, 1993

Close, Leslie Rose, "A History of Women in Landscape Architecture," in *The Gardens of Ellen Biddle Shipman,* edited by Judith B. Tankard, Sagaponack, New York: Sagapress, 1996

Doumato, Lamia, *Women and Landscape Architecture: A Bibliography,* Monticello, Illinois: Vance Bibliographies, 1986

Doumato, Lamia, *Architecture and Women: A Bibliography Documenting Women Architects, Landscape Architects, Designers, Agricultural Critics and Writers, and Women in Related Fields Working in the United States,* New York: Garland, 1988

Fabricant, Carol, "Binding and Dressing Nature's Loose Tresses: The Ideology of Augustan Landscape Design," in *Studies in Eighteenth-Century Culture,* vol. 8, edited by Roseann Runte, Madison: University of Wisconsin Press, 1979

Haraway, Donna Jeanne, "Situated Knowledges: The Science Question in Feminism and the Privilege of Partial Perspective," in *Simians, Cyborgs, and Women: The Reinvention of Nature,* by Haraway, London: Free Association Books, and New York: Routledge, 1991

Harris, Dianne, "Cultivating Power: The Language of Feminism in Women's Garden Literature, 1870–1920," *Landscape Journal* 13, no. 2 (1994)

Hennigan, Valeri, and Jot Carpenter, "Women in ASLA: A Descriptive Analysis," *Landscape Journal* 17, no. 1 (1998)

Kellaway, Deborah, editor, *The Illustrated Book of Women Gardeners,* Boston: Little Brown, and London: Virago, 1997

Krall, Dan, "Early Women Designers and Their Work in Public Places (Ellen Shipman, Beatrix Farrand, Marjorie Cautley, and Helen Bullard)," in *Landscapes and Gardens: Women Who Made a Difference,* compiled by Miriam Easton Rutz, East Lansing: Michigan State University, 1987

Macleod, Dawn, *Down-to-Earth Women: Those Who Care for the Soil,* Edinburgh: Blackwood, 1982

Merchant, Carolyn, *The Death of Nature: Women, Ecology, and the Scientific Revolution,* San Francisco: Harper and Row, 1980

Morris, Mandy, "'Tha' It Be Like a Blush Rose': English Cultural and Gendered Identity in the Secret Garden," *Environment and Planning D: Society and Space* 14 (1996)

Rose, Gillian, "Geography As a Science of Observation: The Landscape, the Gaze, and Masculinity," in *Human Geography: An Essential Anthology,* edited by John Agnew, David N. Livingstone, and Alisdair Rogers, Cambridge, Massachusetts, and Oxford: Blackwell, 1996

Schenker, Heath, "Feminist Interventions in the Histories of Landscape Architecture," *Landscape Journal* 13, no. 2 (1994)

Shteir, Ann B., *Cultivating Women, Cultivating Science: Flora's Daughters and Botany in England, 1760–1860,* Baltimore, Maryland: Johns Hopkins University Press, 1996

Taboroff, June, "Wife Unto Thy Garden: The First Gardening Books for Women," *Garden History* 11, no. 1 (1983)

DIANNE HARRIS

Woodland Cemetery

Stockholm, Sweden

Location: Enskede, 2 miles (3.2 km) miles south of Stockholm city center

In their collaborative design for the Woodland Cemetery in Stockholm's southern outskirts of Enskede, architects Erik Gunnar Asplund and Sigurd Lewerentz rejected traditional European prototypes for the cemetery—the city of the dead or paradise garden—as well as 19th-century secularized forms based on the English landscape garden. Their starting point was the site itself, a wooded tract within agricultural environs that was punctuated by a granite ridge and scarred by quarrying operations. By enhancing attributes of the site—ridge and valley, earth and sky, forest and clearing, meadow and marsh—they transcended the limitations of conventional Christian iconography to evoke associations of death and rebirth in a landscape of spiritual dimension.

Woodland Cemetery was the first of a series of cemeteries developed in Sweden during the first half of the 20th century to engage issues of burial reform. After Gustav III prohibited the sale of burial sites within urban churchyards for hygienic reasons in 1783 (anticipating a similar Napoleonic decree of 1804), responsibility for burial reverted to the state. The large municipal cemeteries that resulted from this legislation were situated outside the cities and laid out as parks to reflect their hygienic intent. Asplund and Lewerentz countered this tendency toward secularization in municipal cemeteries with an affirmation of the sacred value of the site. In a conscious effort to counteract the modern eschewal of death, they amplified the cemetery's symbolic resonance through a direct appeal to essential experiences.

Formal allées of pollarded lime trees line a broad suburban avenue, screening high stone walls that obscure any inward view. To the south a grassy forecourt, semicircular in form and bounded by retaining walls of dressed stone, interrupts the sequence, providing access to the cemetery within. Swedish whitebeams atop the walls are profiled against a backdrop of pine trees, reinforcing the transition from built to natural. The forecourt's bold semicircular form leads to an entry route that is channeled between retaining walls of ashlar masonry. A fountain to one side—a fieldstone wall bathed in a steady trickle of water and screened by a Doric colonnade—suggests eternity as well as tears of mourning. This wall of tears marks the gateway to the sacred enclosure, while the gradual ascent of the entry drive reinforces a sense of departure from the realm of the living. A clearing framed by the break of the entry drive is punctuated by a granite cross, which is the only object to interrupt the horizon—the boundary between earth and sky, visible and invisible.

Within the cemetery the architects transmuted this celebration of boundary to the relationship of earth to sky. The open lawn viewed upon entry is free of burial markers, imparting serenity to the setting. This uninterrupted expanse provides a view of the cemetery's broader organization and choice of route. To the east a broad walk of rough paving stones—the Way of the Cross—leads through the carpet of grass; in a gradual ascent this walkway passes a columbarium and a series of small funerary chapels that culminate in the monumental porch of Asplund's Chapel of the Holy Cross (1940) as it extends to the horizon. Near the main chapel a sweep of paving stones set in the open lawn culminates in a low mound surmounted by a catafalque, marking an outdoor setting for funeral rites. A lily pond at the crest of the hill is deliberately isolated from any natural source of water; singled out to reinforce its symbolic reference to the eternal cycles of life and death, the pool serves as a backdrop to the outdoor ceremonial plaza.

To the west a long segmented flight of stairs ascends a steep earthen mound to a low-walled precinct, where a grove of weeping elms is dramatically profiled against the sky. This grass-covered knoll topped by a Meditation Grove draws on a variety of sources, ranging from ancient Swedish burial mounds, such as those of the Swedish kings at Old Uppsala (fifth–seventh centuries), to the garden mounts depicted in Eric Dahlberg's *Svecia Antiqua e Hodierna* (late 17th century; Ancient and Contemporary Sweden). While the hill's massive form suggests the difficulties of the mourner's task, the ascent comprises successive flights of steps, decreasing in height to ease the approach to the summit.

To the south a birch grove marks the forest edge, providing a colonnade to the burial grounds that lie within the fir forest beyond. The architects had the forest thinned to create a visual continuum, eliminating deciduous trees to enhance the impression of uniformity. Toward this end they had the undergrowth cleared and the ground planted with grass, modifications that distinguish this wooded landscape as a human construct and thus a symbolic act. A unified aesthetic also characterizes the treatment of the grave markers; their subordination to the effect of the whole is ensured by dimensional restrictions as well as a mandatory design-review process. The primary impression of the forest's expanse is reinforced by its uniform carpet of grass dotted with simple grave markers, unlike the characteristic demarcation of family burial plots with curbs and fences in traditional Swedish cemeteries. At Enskede the ground plane is public, its continuity broken only by modest memorials of stone, iron, and wood, oriented with the chapels toward the setting sun.

The forest is pierced by a long straight path, the Way of the Seven Wells, that extends from the Meditation Grove to the airy columnar forehall of a small solitary chapel. Lined with spruces and pressed into the forest floor, this footpath suggestively simulates descent into the earth and gradual reemergence on approaching Lewerentz's Resurrection Chapel (1925). A crosswalk leads through the pine trees to a second individual chapel within a low-walled precinct. This is Asplund's Woodland Chapel (1921), the cemetery's first structure to be completed. Its primitive overhanging roof shelters an open porch, in contrast to the freestanding forehalls of the chapels encountered earlier, while its surrounding burial quadrant is a microcosm of the cemetery landscape. A rectangular area sunken into the earth is dotted with small memorials dedicated to children, beyond which a low circular mound lined with miniature willows provides a welcome respite from the burial grounds.

This ritualized landscape communicates with little recourse to representation. The cemetery's meaning does not rely on the intermediary authority of the church; instead it builds on the common, private experience of mourning to convey a sense of oneness with nature and with humankind.

Synopsis

1909	Stockholm City Council sets aside 50 hectares (123 acres) for an extension to Sandsborg Cemetery (established 1895), south of Stockholm
1914	Stockholm Cemetery Authority announces International Design Competition for new South Cemetery
1915	Competition won by Swedish architects Erik Gunnar Asplund and Sigurd Lewerentz
1918–21	Woodland Chapel built, designed by Asplund
1921–25	Resurrection Chapel built, terminating the Way of the Seven Wells, designed by Lewerentz
1922–24	Workers' Building completed, designed by Asplund
1924	Service road cut through gravel ridge west of cemetery entrance created mound later developed as Meditation Grove
1923–32	Cemetery walls erected by public relief workers
1935	Collaboration between Asplund and Lewerentz ends, and Asplund is engaged to design crematorium complex
1935–1940	Crematorium complex completed, including Chapels of Hope, Faith, and Holy Cross, the Way of the Cross, and outdoor ceremonial plaza, designed by Asplund; development of Way of the Seven Wells and Meditation Grove, designed by Lewerentz
1940	Stone cross added beside the Way of the Cross, opening of crematorium complex celebrated 14 June; Asplund dies 20 October and is buried in columbarium near Chapel of the Holy Cross
1951–56	Pedestrian entry gate built, designed by Lewerentz
1952–61	Service buildings for the Resurrection Chapel built to design by Lewerentz
1958–61	Memorial Ground for cremated remains established, designed by Lewerentz

Further Reading

Constant, Caroline, *The Woodland Cemetery: Toward a Spiritual Landscape: Erik Gunnar Asplund and Sigurd Lewerentz, 1915–61*, Stockholm: Byggförlaget, 1994

Gunnar Asplund, 1885–1940: The Dilemma of Classicism (exhib. cat.), London: Architectural Association, 1988

Johansson, Bengt O.H., *Tallum: Gunnar Asplund's and Sigurd Lewerentz's Woodland Cemetery in Stockholm*, Stockholm: Byggförlaget, 1996

Lerup, Lars, "Asplund's Stockholm Crematorium," *Lotus International* 38, no. 2 (1983)

Porphrios, Demetri, "Classical, Christian, Socialdemocrat: Asplund and Lewerentz's Funerary Architecture," *Lotus International* 38, no. 2, (1983)

Sigurd Lewerentz, 1885–1975: The Dilemma of Classicism (exhib. cat.), London: Architectural Association, 1989

Treib, Marc, "Woodland Cemetery—A Dialogue of Design and Meaning," *Landscape Architecture* 76, no. 2 (March/April 1986)

CAROLINE CONSTANT

Wörlitz Park

Dessau, Saxony-Anhalt, Germany

Location: approximately 10 miles (16 km) east of Dessau

The park at Wörlitz is at the heart of the former model principality of Anhalt-Dessau, transformed during the second half of the 18th century by Prince Leopold Friedrich Franz in an unprecedented and sustained effort to establish a new social and artistic order in his small state, based on the principles of the Enlightenment.

Prince Franz was a determined and thoroughgoing anglophile, and through a series of tours of Britain, the first in 1764, he developed a philosophy of landscape design that drew on English models involving the ideas of Lancelot "Capability" Brown and Andrea Palladio and the image of a gentleman's estate that combined use and beauty and where progressive agricultural practices would take place in ornamental surroundings: in short, a *ferme ornée*.

Franz showed his commitment to the realization of his ideals by establishing a model state in Anhalt-Dessau, a "Garden Kingdom" where the practical results of his reforms could be experienced. Several estates were remodeled or newly established in this process, including those at the Luisium, the Georgium, and Oranienbaum, all grouped in the countryside east of the court city of Dessau; but the centerpiece was to be the rural estate at Wörlitz in the floodplain south of the Elbe.

The earliest developments at Wörlitz took place around the house, itself a former hunting lodge. The first known garden feature was the English Seat of 1765, a Palladian structure copying Henry Flitcroft's Venetian Seat of 1744 at Stourhead (the latter no longer extant). Work on improvements clearly must have started immediately after the English tour of the previous year. The construction of the English Seat was supervised by Franz's friend, companion, and court architect Friedrich Ludwig von Erdmannsdorff, who was to be responsible for most of the buildings on the Anhalt-Dessau estates.

Erdmannsdorff was responsible for the new *Landhaus* (country house, as opposed to castle or palace) at Wörlitz in 1769, its Palladian facade based on Brown's design at Broadlands, Hampshire. Franz and Erdmannsdorff were no mere copyists, however: the roof of the house carries a belvedere, serving both as a viewing platform for the park and as part of the district's flood-warning defenses. Thus, at the house, as everywhere else in the Garden Kingdom, use and beauty were bound together.

The house looks north across a large lake formed by an isolated meander of the Elbe, and Franz was quick to

exploit the pictorial potential of this feature, siting Erdmannsdorff's Nymphaeum on the opposite shore as early as 1768. The great flood of 1770–71, however, inundated much of the early garden layout and necessitated the raising of the dike wall to prevent future disasters. Undaunted, Franz used the opportunity to implement revised designs.

Schoch's garden, named after the court gardener Johann Leopold Ludwig Schoch, occupies a large island on the northern side of the main lake and comprises an informal layout focused on the Gothic House. This, the first Gothic-revival building in Germany, was Franz's favored retreat on the grounds and features two contrasting facades. Facing into the garden is the brick "English" facade, drawing its inspiration from Horace Walpole's Strawberry Hill. The opposite facade, looking toward the kitchen garden, represents an Italian chapel, delicately painted in yellow and white.

Walking toward the Temple of Flora, derived from Flitcroft's structure of the same name at Stourhead, the visitor is led between the kitchen garden on the one side and an arable field on the other. An awareness gradually builds that the journey is not merely ornamental but educational. Each sequence introduces scenes of production as well as art, and each feature is viewed from several others, thus building expectation in advance and encouraging the visitor to see the park as an integrated whole, rather than a series of separate incidents. Crossing the numerous canals, the visitor is led across bridges, each of a different design and inviting framed views along the watercourses to pleasures yet to come.

The flood dike forms the northern boundary of the pleasure ground and was brought into use as a raised promenade walk. Looking into the park reveals a network of vistas. At one point a series of sight lines lead from the Golden Urn, commemorating Franz's stillborn first child, to a range of design features including the apparently adjacent village church and synagogue, from which the viewer is to draw the moral of religious tolerance. In the opposite direction the view takes in a huge expanse of flood meadow bounded by oak forest, the habitat of storks and beavers.

The northeastern parts of the park are more sparingly populated by design features, reflecting the development of Franz's taste over time. The Pantheon stands in isolation, its pediment illustrating Minerva, goddess of wisdom, while statues of Apollo and the nine muses line the walls within. The Iron Bridge is a miniature replica of the English original and stands alongside a ford, allowing the visitor to contrast the most primitive form of river crossing with the most advanced.

The island called the Stein (rock) allowed Franz to combine an homage to Pompeii with Masonic devices, in this instance a progression through temples of darkness and light. A copy of Sir William Hamilton's villa housed Franz's collections of Roman artifacts, and a "ruined" amphitheater is built into the island. The rock is capped by a volcano, which in Franz's day was made to belch fire and smoke and even to spew "lava" for the benefit of guests viewing the spectacle at night in gondolas in a part of the lake modeled on the Bay of Naples.

An island of poplars commemorates Franz's admiration for Rousseau; South Sea pavilions recall the travels of Georg Forster and Captain Cook; and a wayside altar reminds the visitor to respect nature and care for her works. The many messages of Wörlitz combine to form an emblematic and didactic garden crowded with features, where the visitor is constantly called on to pause, compare, reflect, and consider. Even the road from Dessau is lined with avenues of fruit trees, at once beautiful and useful, and free for all to help themselves.

The Wörlitz Park, as its creator intended, introduced a whole series of new ideas into landscape design in Germany and further afield in Europe. It was the first large-scale landscape garden in Germany; the house was the first neoclassical building in Germany; the Gothic House established a similar precedent for the use of a revived national style. The journey to Wörlitz became a prerequisite for privileged landowners across central Europe. Its admirers included Johann Wolfgang von Goethe, who recorded his view on one visit at dusk that "the park is now infinitely beautiful. . . . It is as if one were being told a fairytale. . . .The whole place has the character of the Elysian Fields."

Synopsis

1740	Prince Franz of Anhalt-Dessau born
1764	First tour of England
1765	English Seat
1765–67	Neumark's Garden
1767–68	Nymphaeum
1769	Golden Urn
1769–73	Schloss Wörlitz
1770–71	Great flood
1771–90	Schoch's Garden
1773–1813	Gothic House
1781–88	Romantic Area
1782	Rousseau's Island
1783	Labyrinth
1788–92	Stein with Villa Hamilton and Volcano
1790	Synagogue
1791	Iron Bridge
1795–97	Pantheon
1797–98	Temple of Flora
1800	Death of Erdmannsdorff
1817	Death of Prince Franz

Further Reading

Bode, Ursula, Michael Stürmer, and Thomas Weiss, *For the Friends of Nature and Art: The Garden Kingdom of Prince Franz von Anhalt-Dessau in the Age of Enlightenment*, Ostfildern-Ruit, Germany: Hatje, 1997

Bowe, Patrick, *Gardens in Central Europe*, Woodbridge, Suffolk: Antique Collectors' Club, and New York: Train/Scala, 1991

Hirsch, Erhard, et al., *Das Gartenreich Dessau-Wörlitz*, Hamburg, Germany: L und H Verlag, 1996

Rode, August, *Beschreibung des Fürstlichen Anhalt-Dessauischen Landhauses und englischen Gartens zu Wörlitz*, Dessau, Germany, 1788; new edition, Dessau, Germany: Dünnhaupt, 1928

Trauzettel, Ludwig, *Wörlitz: Führer durch die englischen Anlagen*, Berlin: RV Verlag, 1991

Trauzettel, Ludwig, "Wörlitz: England in Germany," *Garden History* 24, no. 2 (1996)

STEVEN DESMOND

X

Xeriscape

The term *xeriscape* originates from the combination of the Greek word *xeros*, meaning dry, with the suffix *scape*. This term emerged following an extensive drought throughout the southwestern United States in 1977; the devastating effects of this event forced widespread reassessment of water use in landscapes. In particular landscape professionals realized that it was erroneous to assume an endless supply of water for existing and future landscapes. Although the practice of xeriscape is a recent effort in the United States, it was realized long ago in the Mediterranean countries that even in a hot, dry climate, gardens could offer shade and refreshment yet use a minimum amount of water. The Moorish influence on garden design with an emphasis on minimal planting (usually in conjunction with a water feature such as a fountain or canal) in small walled gardens and courtyards could certainly be considered an early form of xeriscaping.

Xeriscape was created by the Denver Water Department in 1981 as an educational concept to convey effective water conservation in combination with creative landscape designs. Since then, the term has become the common identity for landscape water conservation programs in many parts of the United States. By 1984 the concept had spread to other cities with water shortages, particularly in California, Texas, Arizona, and Nevada. Many local governments and water authorities adapted the program to address local agendas, and commercial landscapers began using the term "xeriscape" in marketing and even incorporating it into their business name. Concern over maintaining the integrity of the original xeriscape program resulted in the name and process being registered as a trademark in 1986 and given to the National Xeriscape Council, a nonprofit organization that distributes information about xeriscaping. In early 1990 there were active xeriscape education programs in more than 60 cities in 42 states and three foreign countries.

Colorado Springs and Denver in Colorado have developed prototypical water-conserving landscapes. The Denver Water Department organized, planned, designed, and constructed a xeriscape demonstration garden outside the department offices in Denver that has received wide recognition and a number of awards and citations. Other examples of water conservation gardens can be found in Sacramento, California, developed by the Department of Water Resources of the State of California, and at the Marin County Civic Center in Corte Madera, California.

Xeriscape incorporates seven principles presented in clear, concise language to encourage their use in designs in regions where water conservation is important. The first principle of xeriscape pertains to planning landscapes for water conservation. It provides a foundation from which the other six principles are applied and focuses users on organizing a site in a water-efficient manner. Importance is placed on starting the planning process with a site analysis that involves shade and sun patterns, topography, soil patterns, and wind flow. This is followed by an organization of the site in terms of zones of water use. For example, intended high-water-use areas, often referred to as "mini-oases," are typically recommended for and placed in zone 1. These zones are near buildings (commercial or residence) and in areas such as small entries, courtyards, or backyard patios and are considered the areas of highest outdoor use. The principle stresses the importance of grouping relatively high-water-use plants in these zones compared to other areas in the landscape. This capitalizes on the significant cooling effect for users created from the relatively high evapotranspiration of the lush plants in zone 1. The second zone, often referred to as a "transition area," is developed beyond mini-oasis areas. Plants in this zone use less water than those found in zone 1 but require more irrigation than plants used outside this area in zone 3. The second zone typically includes plant groupings in backyards or areas along entry walkways. Plants in zone 2 may consist of medium-textured, gray-green foliaged species, thereby providing a transition between predominantly coarse-textured, lush plants from zone 1 to drought-adapted species in zone 3 that tend to have sparser and more fine-textured foliage. Zone 3 involves plants that are the lowest water users in the landscape and may require no supplemental water after establishment.

The second principle relates to the specific water use of the plants used in xeriscapes. It emphasizes the importance of selecting appropriate species for the site, including regional species. The principle also stresses the significance of creating energy-saving microclimates within the landscape through careful placement of tree species that shade structure walls and windows, thereby potentially reducing the use of water and that of electricity for cooling a building. It also focuses on creating shaded microclimates for understory species and, hence, reducing their evapotranspiration and water use.

Limiting turf-covered areas is the emphasis of the third principle. Historically, turfgrasses have dominated landscapes in urban areas; however, this typically involves high water use. Reiterating ideas presented in the first principle, this principle recommends placement of turfgrasses near areas of high use, thereby optimizing benefits to users because of the cooling effect from high evapotranspiration and the lush appearance of turf.

The fourth principle relates to harvesting runoff water for plant use within and around landscapes whenever possible. Water catchment techniques are suggested for a variety of sites, including use of swales for directing runoff, channeling of water from sloped areas using topography, and shallow contouring for retention. This principle also emphasizes use of runoff from downspouts and walkways, roadway runoff, and collection of water using storage containers such as cisterns.

Efficient irrigation design and operation are the emphases of the fifth principle. Examples of appropriate irrigation systems include drip emitter irrigation for small to medium shrubs, spray (sprinkler) irrigation for turfgrasses, and bubbler or drip emitter irrigation for trees. The use of an appropriate watering schedule (frequency and duration) for each season is also stressed in this principle. Watering during cooler times of the day, such as early morning, also reduces loss of water to evapotranspiration.

The sixth principle relates to the use of mulches to reduce soil erosion and moisture loss and weed germination and establishment. Typical mulches associated with xeriscape designs include inert materials, such as decomposed granite or streambed rock, in the most arid regions and compost and bark chips in more mesic climates.

The last principle relates to the use of proper maintenance practices. This concept is considered just as important as the other more design-oriented principles of xeriscape. Regular maintenance of the irrigation system and plants is reinforced. For example, the use of slow-release fertilizer or no fertilization is stressed in these arid regions since most appropriate plants are adapted to low-fertility soils. The key to this principle is effective maintenance, which leads to fewer disease and long-term maintenance problems as the landscape matures.

Landscape architects and designers, contractors, and educators use xeriscape principles to inform the public about water conservation in combination with attractive landscapes. Xeriscape has been an effective educational tool largely because of the simplicity of the concept and its component principles. Since its creation in 1981, this concept has been embraced by landscape users and creators of Southwest designs and other water-scarce environments in the United States and continues to serve as a critical guide for design development of future landscapes in these areas today.

Further Reading

Duffield, Mary Rose, and Warren D. Jones, *Plants for Dry Climates: How to Select, Grow, and Enjoy,* Tucson, Arizona: HP Books, 1981

Ellefson, Connie Lockhart, Thomas L. Stephens, and Douglas Welsh, *Xeriscape Gardening: Water Conservation for the American Landscape,* New York: Macmillan, and Toronto, Ontario: Macmillan Canada, 1992

Johnson, Eric A., and Scott Millard, *The Low-Water Flower Gardener,* Tucson, Arizona: Ironwood Press, 1993

Knopf, Jim, *The Xeriscape Flower Gardener: A Waterwise Guide for the Rocky Mountain Region,* Boulder, Colorado: Johnson Books, 1991

McClure, Susan, *Water,* New York: Workman, 2000

Millard, Scott, *Gardening in Dry Climates,* edited by Cedric Crocker, San Ramon, California: Chevron Chemical, 1989

O'Keefe, John M., *Water-Conserving Gardens and Landscapes: Water-Saving Ideas, Plant Selection List, Home Drip Irrigation Guide, Easy-Care Landscapes, All-Region Zone Maps,* Pownal, Vermont: Storey Communications, 1992

Peace, Tom, *Sunbelt Gardening: Success in Hot-Weather Climates,* Golden, Colorado: Fulcrum, 2000

Perry, Bob, *Trees and Shrubs for Dry California Landscapes: Plants for Water Conservation,* San Dimas, California: Land Design, 1981

Robinette, Gary O., *Water Conservation in Landscape Design and Management,* New York: Van Nostrand Reinhold, 1984

Robinson, Peter, *Water-Wise Gardening,* New York: DK, 1999

Shuler, Carol, *Low-Water-Use Plants: For California and the Southwest,* Tucson, Arizona: Fisher Books, 1993

Wasowski, Sally, and Andy Wasowski, *Native Gardens for Dry Climates*, New York: Potter, 1995

Weinstein, Gayle, *Xeriscape Handbook: A How-to Guide to Natural, Resource-Wise Gardening*, Golden, Colorado: Fulcrum, 1999

Winger, David, editor, *Xeriscape Color Guide: 100 Water-Wise Plants for Gardens and Landscapes*, Denver, Colorado: Denver Water, and Golden, Colorado: Fulcrum, 1998

MARGARET LIVINGSTON

Xiequ Yuan

Beijing, China

Location: East of Wanshou Hill in Yiheyuan Garden

Xiequ Yuan, an enclosed garden in Yiheyuan, is a garden near the east end of Wanshou Hill, covering more than one hectare (2.5 acres). Emperor Qianlong built Qingyiyuan (later renamed Yiheyuan); Xiequ Yuan was one of the important gardens in this garden.

Xiequ Yuan was first built during the reign of Emperor Qianlong, who copied the idea from the famous Jichangyuan in Wuxi, Jiangsu province, inspired by a visit to Jichangyuan during his first southern tour in 1751. The emperor ordered the painters, who accompanied him, to make sketches of Jichangyuan for reference in order to build imperial gardens in Beijing. Xiequ Yuan, whose original name was Huishanyuan, was completed in 1754. Emperor Jiaqing changed the name after he rebuilt Huishanyuan. During the invasion of the Anglo-French forces in 1860, Qingyiyuan, including Xiequ Yuan, was destroyed. Emperor Guangxu rebuilt the entire garden in 1891.

Emperor Qianlong had chosen the east side of Wanshou Hill to build the garden in order to capture the spirit of Jichangyuan. The shoreline of Xiequ Yuan is low, and the view, as well as water, can be borrowed from Wanshou Hill. The lake water spreads out south below Wanshou Hill just like Jinhui Lake and Hui Hill in Jichangyuan. The steep shoreline of the back lakes, which is two meters (2.2 yd.) above ground level, shaping the long gorge, is similar to Bayinjien in Jichangyuan. The water zigzagging through bridges is another imitation of Qixinqiao Bridge in Jichangyuan.

Emperor Qianlong first built Huishanyuan with fewer pavilions and corridors surrounding the lake. In particular Momiaoxuan Hall, located on the north side of the lake, was smaller than the present-day Hanyuantang Hall. With the open view another pavilion, Qiqingxuan Hall, located at the top of rockeries at the north side, could be seen clearly. The balanced mountain and water view presented a harmonious whole. However, Hanyuantang Hall, bigger in size, now blocks most of the view after the rebuilding of Xiequ Yuan.

Located on the north side of the lake, overlooking the entire garden, Hanyuantang Hall is the main pavilion in Xiequ Yuan. The main entrance is at the corner of the southeast garden. Other pavilions linked by open galleries surround the lake. At the east end of the lake is Zhizhuntang Hall, and at the west end is Chengshuangjai Hall, as well as Zhuxinlou Tower. The south side includes three pavilions, Yinjing, Xiqiu, and Yinlu. Another canal, 20 meters (22 yd.) long, Yuqinxia, located on the west side of Hanyuantang Hall, with planted bamboo along it, was in imitation of gardens south of the Yangzi River.

Synopsis

1751	Following visit to famous Jichangyuan, Wuxi, Jiangsu Province, Emperor Qianlong orders design and construction of new garden at eastern front of Wanshou Shan in Qingyiyuan; new royal gardens patterned after Jichangyuan
1754	Construction completed and garden named Huishanyuan
1811	Emperor Jiaqing expands garden and changes name to Xiequ Yuan
1860	Anglo-French allied forces burn down and destroy Xiequ Yuan and Qingyiyuan
1888	Qingyiyuan rebuilt and renamed Yihe Yuan
1891	Xiequ Yuan reconstructed

Further Reading

Chi, Ch'eng, *The Craft of Gardens* (1634), translated by Alison Hardie, New Haven, Connecticut: Yale University Press, 1988

Johnston, R. Stewart, *Scholar Gardens of China: A Study and Analysis of the Spatial Design of the*

Chinese Private Garden, Cambridge and New York: Cambridge University Press, 1991

Keswick, Maggie, and Charles Jencks, *The Chinese Garden: History, Art and Architecture,* New York: Rizzoli, and London: Academy Editions, 1978

Liu, Tun-chen, *Su-chou ku tien yüan lin,* Beijing: Chung-kuo chien chu kung yeh ch'u pan she, 1979; as *Chinese Classical Gardens of Suzhou,* translated by

Chen Lixian, edited by Joseph C. Wang, New York: McGraw Hill, 1993

Tsu, Frances Ya-Sing, *Landscape Design in Chinese Gardens,* New York: McGraw Hill, 1988

Wang, Joseph Cho, *The Chinese Garden,* Oxford and New York: Oxford University Press, 1998

CHENG LIYAO AND JOSEPH C. WANG
TRANSLATED BY SYLVIA CHOI

Xi Yuan

Suzhou, Jiangsu Province, China

Location: outside Suzhou's Changman Gate, opposite the Liu Yuan

Xi Yuan, or West Garden, is generally the designation for both a Buddhist (Jiedonglu) monastery and the Xi Hua Yuan, a smaller flower garden to its west. By western standards of dating, the Xi Yuan is a complex of 19th-century buildings and sculptures from the late Qing dynasty and originating from 1869–1903. It is, however, both a monastery and a traditional Chinese garden with a history reaching back to the 14th century. Constructed during the Yüan dynasty, approximately 1327, it was originally called Guiyuan Monastery. Two hundred years later, in the Ming dynasty and during the reign of Emperor Jia Jing (1522–66), a court minister named Xu Shitai, superintendent imperial groom, acquired the monastery, converted it to his private residence, and named it Xi Yuan. Liu Yuan, or the Lingering Garden, considered one of the four great gardens of China and located across the road from Xi Yuan, was then part of Xu Shitai's estate and was known as East Garden. Xu Rong, Xu Shitai's son, returned the residence and small garden to Buddhist monks for their monastery and reclaimed the original name, Guiyuan. Additional buildings were added in 1635 during the reign of Emperor Chong Zhen when the monastery was renamed Jeidonglu Monastery. In 1860, however, the monastery was a casualty of war and burned down. The actual building fabric and sculptures of Xi Yuan, therefore, are about 130 years old. The complex is highly significant as the largest collection of religious architecture and art in Suzhou.

Xi Yuan presents eastern and western sections of distinctive character. In the eastern half monastery buildings are arranged axially, from the main gate to the Scripture Repository, in a layout recalling imperial complexes organized as a sequence of axial courtyards and aligned halls. Immediately inside the main gate is the Tian Wang Dian (Hall of Heaven Kings), sometimes known as the Jin Gang Dian, or Celestial Warriors Hall. Here, the four guardians of a Buddhist monastery are represented as painted clay sculptures. Considered Buddha's warrior attendants, these guardians rule the east, west, north, and south and protect the monastery from danger from the four directions of heaven. A smiling pot-bellied Monk Maitreya sits bare-chested in the middle of the hall. Behind him is General Wei Tuo, protector of Buddhism; indeed, outside, two iron armored generals of fierce mien also guard the exterior.

Passing beyond the Hall of Heaven Kings, one crosses a court and the Xiang Hua Qiao (Fragrant Flowers Bridge) to the terrace and the central hall of the monastery, the Da Xiong Bao Dian, or Prayer Hall. Three large wooden Buddhas sit inside protected by 20 guardian angels. The Sakyamuni, or Patriarch, Buddha is flanked by the Eternal Buddha Amitabha and Vaidurya Buddha, reliever of stress and curer of disease. Two disciples of Sakyamuni, the founder of Buddhism, attend: the elder Kasyapa Buddha and the Most Learned Ananda Buddha, the latter said to have authored the Buddhist Sutras, having memorized the Sakyamuni Buddha's teachings after the master ascended to heaven.

While the main axis of the monastery continues northward across another courtyard to the Scripture Repository, one of the most noteworthy features of the monastery is sited off to the left, or west, of the Xiang Hua Qiao and central Da Xiong Bao Dian. This is the Hall of Arhats containing gilt statues of 500 Buddhist monks who have attained Nirvana, a number mentioned in Chinese Buddhist canon as a sign that Buddhism was flourishing. These arhats fill 48 galleries and display remarkable individuality of expression and artistic creativity. Unlike Buddhas, which are portrayed in conventional ways in China, the 500 arhats are human and display wide artistic freedom of execution. Some are scholarly and contemplative, others aged and decrepit, still others muscular and aggressive, and the Monk Ji Gong (said to have ridiculed high officials) appears from one profile with a grin on his face, and from the opposite side he appears sad. His popularity made Monk Ji Gong a frequent subject in Chinese novels. A Thousand-Armed Guan Yin standing on a lotus blossom is a remarkable statue carved in camphor wood and gilt. In the center of the Arhat Hall, a miniature clay mountain with seated Buddhas represents the four sacred mountains of China: Wutai in Shanxi, Emei in Sichuan, Jiuhua in Anhui, and Putuo in Zhejiang. A monk who bowed before the four sides of this clay mountain is said to have fulfilled his vow to visit the four sacred mountains, without having to take the difficult pilgrimage to the real mountain sites.

Equally famous in Xi Yuan as the Monk Ji Gong is the so-called Mad Monk; both were associated with the famed Lingyan Monastery in nearby Hangzhou. Ji Gong was a high-ranking monk there during the southern Song dynasty (1127–79), while the Mad Monk is a fictitious character linked to the story of Qin Hui, a traitor and disloyal official of the late southern Song dynasty. Qin Hui is said to have made a pilgrimage to Hangzhou beyond the West Lake and over the hill to the Lingyan Monastery, where monks greeted him at the gate. The Mad Monk stood there with a broom and a blowpipe, and when Qin Hui asked the purpose of these, the Mad Monk answered, "In addition to sweeping away dust, the broom can also drive disloyal officials out of the court. The pipe, open at both ends, is like a traitorous official who communicates with the enemy; when the pipe blows, smoke rises to warn the people of foreign invaders." Fearing this response might provoke trouble, the head of the monastery quickly told Qin Hui the monk was mad.

The large amount of Xi Yuan given over to Buddhist monks and monastic use points to the reverence Buddhism had for nature, seeking some of the most beautiful natural sites for the erection of their monasteries. The Lingyan Monastery above West Lake in Hangzhou is among China's most famous and is considered one of the nation's most historic sites. In addition, artificially created gardens brought nature to man. The classic Chinese garden was filled with miniature mountains, Taihu rocks, rockeries, and hills, all symbolic of sacred mountains, and was accented with islands in ponds representing the sacred isles of the Eastern Sea. Here, the distillers of the *elixir vitae* dwell, the gods whose breath force, or *Qi*, was the essential element of all things and the very vitality of China. Thus, the western section of Xi Yuan contains a small fish pond with a lake-centered double-eaved pavilion (Hu Xin Ting), an island in the sea joined to land by zigzag bridges, so shaped in broken lines in order to protect from evil spirits who travel in straight lines. In the Xi Hua Yuan the monks might release fish "to save them from the cooking pot" or merely retire in order to contemplate eternal truths, meditate, or enjoy poetic musings in a paradisiacal oasis at the edge of the now bustling city of Suzhou.

Synopsis

1327	Guiyuan Monastery constructed on site of Xi Yuan or West Garden
ca. 1522–66	Xu Shitai, Ming dynasty official in charge of emperor's horses and vehicles, buys Guiyuan Monastery and builds, east of it, Liu Yuan, known as East Garden; Xu Shitai's son, Xu Rong, gives West Garden (Xi Yuan) estate back to Buddhist monks for monastery
1635	Guiyuan Monastery renamed Jeidonglu Monastery, and additional buildings erected
1796–1819	During reign of Emperor Jia Qing of Qing dynasty, Liu Rongfeng, an official in charge of province's finances and taxes, takes control of East Garden; rebuilt, East Garden renamed Hanbi Shanzhuang but also known as Liu's Garden of Liu Yuan
1860	Jeidonglu Monastery burns down
1869–1903	Jeidonglu Monastery rebuilt; Xi Yuan includes Xi Hua Yuan, small garden west of monastery
1875	Sheng Xuren, during reign of Emperor Guang Xu of Qing dynasty, acquires Liu's Garden, renovates it, and renames it Liu (meaning "linger[ing]") Yuan
1894–95	Liu Yuan reduced to ruins
1949	People's Revolution
1953	People's Republic of China rebuilds Liu Yuan

Further Reading

Suzhou: A Garden City, Beijing: Foreign Language Press, 1984

Zhong, Junhua, *Sights and Scenes of Suzhou,* Beijing: Zhaohua, 1983

ROBERT M. CRAIG

Y

Yi Yuan

Suzhou, Jiangsu Province, China

Location: in city of Suzhou near intersection of
Ganjiang and Renmin roads

Tradition and continuity are the central themes of Chinese garden art, and to note that Yi Yuan (Garden of
Ease), built in 1875, is little different in its major features
from other Suzhou gardens of a much earlier date merely
gives evidence of this persistence of character. Garden
design is also the most ephemeral of art forms, and it
should likewise be noted that the actual fabric of gardens
experienced today represents historic elements more frequently reconstructed than preserved. Significant and
defining features of ancient gardens such as Suzhou's
Canglang Ting Yuan (Garden of the Surging Wave Pavilion), whose history reaches back to the 10th or 11th century, were destroyed and rebuilt, often several times, and
as recently as the Qing dynasty (1644–1911).

Yi Yuan, one of Suzhou's most recent gardens, pays
homage to such predecessors. In particular, Canglang
Ting Yuan, one of the city's oldest gardens, is referenced
by the siting and naming of Yi Yuan's Xiaocanglang Ting
(Little Surging Wave Pavilion) amid the main Yi rockery,
where it is prominently visible from the central pool.
Flowers and trees, artificial rocks, pavilions with poetic
names, and continual references to nature characterize
this "Garden of Ease," "Garden of Joy," or "Happy Garden," as Yi Yuan has been variously translated.

Beyond historic architecture and land forms, the idea
and content embodied in the traditional Chinese garden
(whether from antiquity or modernity) constitute the significant meaning of the Chinese garden. In this sense Yi
Yuan, one of Suzhou's newest gardens, is also one of its
oldest in spirit. Like all classic Chinese gardens, Yi Yuan is
essentially a "hill-and-water garden". Indeed, the Chinese
word for landscape, *shan shui,* means mountains and
water. The earth, excavated for a pond, is piled up to form
an adjacent hill, and so it is that, in the western portion of

the Yi Yuan, a natural hill-and-water garden is formed of
pools, rockeries, and small pavilions, while the more
architectonic character of the eastern section is defined by
galleries, courtyards, larger pavilions, and halls.

This eastern part was originally the site of a Ming
dynasty (1368–1644) official's residence, Wu Kuande,
who served under Emperor Hong Zhi (r. 1488–1505).
(Other sources indicate that ancestral halls were west of
the garden and that the "owner's residence" was located
across an alley to the south of Yi Yuan.) Wu Kuande
may well have been a mere "humble administrator"; the
nearby Zhuo Zheng Yuan (Humble Administrator's
Garden) was typically associated with these scholar gardens. However, it was centuries later that the western
garden was developed by Gu Wenbin, an official in the
Ch'ing dynasty who spent some seven years and
200,000 taels of silver to build Yi Yuan. Thus emerged a
private pleasure garden, in the tradition of the historic
gardens of the Suzhou literati, where Gu Wenbin
brought together the best and most characteristic elements of Chinese garden art.

A double corridor (wall with covered walkways on
either side) at Yi Yuan is modeled on the partitioned
gallery at the water's edge of Canglang Ting Yuan; here,
it divides the two sections of the Yi garden without dis-
connecting them. Much as the canal outside Canglang
Ting Yuan is brought into view through ornamental
windows accenting the boundary wall, so the *lou
chuang,* or leaking windows, open the Yi Yuan wall
with grilled windows of various patterns to provide
visual glimpses from one space into another. Thus, the
Yi Yuan galleried wall separating the east and west gardens both divides and connects. As its solid form is
pierced by dematerializing filtered light, one is reminded
of the yin and yang of ever-becoming opposites (soft
and hard, light and shadow, man-made and natural)
that find complementary embodiment in garden art.

Little Surging Wave Pavilion and zig zag bridge at Yi Yuan garden
Copyright Robert M. Craig

Whether outside the garden walls or visible from one interior space "leaking" into another, Chinese decorative doors, windows, moon gates, and lattice-framed openings punctuate the garden and offer framed impressions that a garden designer has orchestrated to benefit the observer. Windows of varied profile shape and in-fill pattern serve to compose selected scenes throughout the Chinese garden and effectively paint artistic views in stop-action much as might a painter or photographer.

The concept of borrowing a view, in which a scene from beyond the wall is brought into the experience of an observer, is characteristic of the subtlety of design and choreography of visual experience that informs Chinese gardens. The garden maker directs both man and nature. It has been noted that openings along garden walls mark the pace of perambulations as space, light, color, and textural contrasts leak through ornamental windows and permit a filtering of natural elements from one part of the garden into another. In a similar way a "water gate" forms a natural rock bridge under which flows water connecting the main eastern pond of Yi Yuan to the rambling and more tightly girdled rivulets beyond.

Other borrowed elements at Yi Yuan include a land boat (the Han Chuan, or Painting Landboat Study) modeled on that at the Zhuo Zheng Yuan, a lotus pond of a character and scale reminiscent of that at Wang Shi Yuan (Garden of the Retired Fisherman), and rockeries laid out in emulation of the best of lake-stone rockeries in Suzhou, those at Huan Xiu Shan Zhuang (Mountain Villa of Encircled Elegance), the masterpiece of the famous rockery artist Ge Yuliang. Also noteworthy at Yi Yuan is a lake-stone parterre located behind the main hall, a mandarin duck- or twin-hall-patterned building whose southern half is called Chuyue Xuan (Hoeing-on-the-Moon Hall) and which overlooks the stone parterre. Unlike French or Italian geometric floral parterres, the stone parterre at Yi Yuan is irregular, with fieldstone paving laid within boundary rocks and recalling lotus-surfaced water flowing irregularly among edging rockeries. The whole is planted with peonies, Chinese herbaceous peonies, Chinese firs, laurels, and lace-bark pines.

The north half of this same main twin-hall is the Oux-iang Xie, or Lotus-Root-Fragrance Waterside Pavilion, a building joined to the pond by a waterside terrace and reminiscent of the Distant Fragrance Hall at Zhuo Zheng Yuan.

In a total area of less than one-half hectare (1.2 acres), Yi Yuan provides a "melody of green ravines" and the "shade of ancient pines," as the eight characters written by Yu Yue (1821–1907), a scholar of the Qing dynasty, give evidence on a wooden tablet over the door of the Han Chuan (Land Boat). The garden designers of classic Chinese gardens intended to provide aesthetic experiences, moments of poetic contemplation, diversions from everyday cares, and places of natural beauty in which the art of life and the contented life of art might be enjoyed. Hence, Yi Yuan is a "Happy Garden," a "Garden of Ease," embodying the quintessential elements of traditional Chinese garden art.

Synopsis

ca. 1500	Eastern section of Yi Yuan residence of Wu Kuan, Ming dynasty minister under Emperor Hong Zhi
1700–1800	Wood carvings with inscriptions in calligraphy (now displayed in a pavilion of paintings) executed by Qing dynasty painter Zheng Banqiao (1693–1756)
ca. 1875	Yi Yuan developed as private garden by Gu Wen Bin under Emperors Tong Zhi and Guang Xu of late Qing dynasty
late 19th c.	Yu Yue, Qing dynasty scholar, poet, novelist, dramatist, and author of some 250 volumes, including *Records of Yi Yuan,* writes eight calligraphic characters on wooden tablets over the door of Han Chuan
World War II	Interior of Ouxiang Xie destroyed
1949	During People's Revolution, private gardens, including Yi Yuan, opened to public

Further Reading

Chi, Ch'eng, *The Craft of Gardens* (1634), translated by Alison Hardie, New Haven, Connecticut: Yale University Press, 1988

Craig, Robert M., "The Garden of Ease (Yi Yuan), Suzhou: Designed Diversions, Picture Views, and Objects of Contemplation in a 19th Century Chinese Garden," *Nineteenth Century Studies* 1 (1987)

Craig, Robert M., "Passages to a Different Universe: The Three Gardens of Zhuo Zheng Yuan, Suzhou," *SECAC Review* 11, no. 3 (1988)

Johnston, R. Stewart, *Scholar Gardens of China: A Study and Analysis of the Spatial Design of the Chinese Private Garden,* Cambridge and New York: Cambridge University Press, 1991

Keswick, Maggie, and Charles Jencks, *The Chinese Garden: History, Art, and Architecture,* London: Academy, and New York: Rizzoli, 1978

Liu, Tun-chen, *Su-chou ku tien yüan lin,* Beijing: Chung-kuo chien chu kung yeh ch'u pan she, 1979; as *Chinese Classical Gardens of Suzhou,* translated by Chen Lixian, edited by Joseph C. Wang, New York: McGraw Hill, 1993

Qian, Yun, editor, *Classical Chinese Gardens,* Hong Kong: Joint, 1982

Suzhou: A Garden City, Beijing: Foreign Language Press, 1984

Tsu, Frances Ya-Sing, *Landscape Design in Chinese Gardens,* New York: McGraw Hill, 1988

Zhong, Junhua, *Sights and Scenes of Suzhou,* Beijing: Zhaohua, 1983

ROBERT M. CRAIG

Yoch, Florence 1890–1972

United States Landscape Architect

Florence Yoch's early landscape architectural practice, to which she brought the sophistication of a formal professional education and European travel, centered in Pasadena, California, beginning in 1921. She was joined in 1926 by her lifelong partner, Lucile Council, in a personal and professional relationship that would last until Council's death in 1964. Yoch was the principal garden designer, while Council suggested plant materials and handled office-related matters. Both supervised installations with exacting standards and attention to detail, frequently working out significant parts of the plans on location. Yoch often spent several days walking a site to familiarize herself with its character and was highly intuitive in developing the concepts that emerged out of her natural sensitivity.

Yoch and Council's firm developed a reputation for highly original adaptations of the vocabulary of the Mediterranean Basin—especially Italy and Spain—to California's terrain and growing conditions, frequently on sites that were difficult or confined. It also tended to favor informality within a strong ordering geometry in its designs-reminiscent, perhaps, of Lawrence Johnson's earlier work in the English Cotswalds. Yoch was also noted for transplanting full-grown trees using large trucks and cranes. In 1927 she specified that 40 oak trees and 87 Italian cypresses be moved for Il Vescovo, the extensive Los Angeles garden of Mr. and Mrs. W.T. Bishop, on which she collaborated with architect Gordon Kaufmann. She also installed extensive lawn areas.

Yoch believed foreign travel to be a necessary adjunct of her profession and frequently went to Europe with Council in search of inspiration, attributing the originality of her work to this influence. The combination of intellectual and experiential knowledge enabled her to achieve a strong environmental accord between her clients' cultural preferences and the physical context of southern California. She used European source material extensively, including even the ceramic pots she and Council habitually collected during their travels, which lent even her most up-to-date gardens a sense of credibility and permanence. Freely adapting the eclecticism that had dominated landscape design for decades, their firm created innovative and surprising variations on historical themes.

Il Brolino, which she designed for lumber heiress Mary Stewart in Montecito in 1922, allowed Yoch to work on a large scale for the first time. The mountainous setting contrasted sharply with George Washington Smith's severely plain Italianate design for the house. Yoch mediated between the dramatic landscape and simple domestic architecture by designing a series of outdoor Italianate garden rooms to create spatial structure, order, and a sense of human scale. She also made use of fanciful topiary to provide focus and a note of whimsy, not attempting to compete with the rugged landscape, views of which were enframed by the monumental "Water Gate," groupings of oak and eucalyptus, and clipped pittosporum hedges.

Yoch was equally comfortable working on a more modest scale. Intimate spaces often loomed large, even in her most elaborate compositions, and she was able to accommodate complex design programs in small areas. In 1925 she collaborated with architect Roland E. Coate on a house and garden occupying a flat site of less than an acre for the A. Parley Johnsons. Yoch designed a series of floral parterres arranged around a central lawn panel providing a sense of openness vertically anchored by Italian cypresses, stone pines, and two fountains. Small gardens of differing size, level, and character provided variety and included a shady raised terrace, secret garden, kitchen garden, orchard, and an arbor covered with jasmine, roses, and clematis. The design clearly reveals Yoch's often-expressed admiration for the medieval garden as an appropriate model for the lifestyle and climate of southern California.

Yoch and Coate were again at work in 1927 on an Andulusian-style townhouse and garden for Mrs. Richard B. Fudger. Located on a hilly irregular lot in the Los Angeles enclave of Hancock Park, the Moorish-inspired garden, now considerably altered, was sheltered from the street by a double row of olives. A walled motor court accommodated the newly important automobile and did double duty as a patio. Stairs led to an upper level and loggia on which the front door and a pergola leading to a rose garden opened. The main rooms of the house wrapped around a formal garden of boxwood hedges and two olive trees to the south; a semicircular terrace overlooked an existing olive orchard to the west that Yoch retained. Olives also reinforced the site's visual boundaries and created a sheltered, introverted quality for the rambling, multilevel complex. The design received an American Institute of Architects award in 1930 for "skill and interest of design in a peculiarly shaped lot." Yoch herself used it to illustrate her talk "Fitting the Land for Human Use, an Art That Is Closely Allied to Architecture," which was published in *California Arts and Architecture* in July of the same year.

Yoch and Council did not confine their work to the private sphere. From the earliest days they produced park designs for locations as diverse as Shoshone Falls, Idaho, Orange County in California, and Los Mochis on the west coast of Mexico. The latter was a design for a botanical garden created in 1929–30 on 19 acres (7.7 ha) owned by B.F. Johnston, president and founder of United Sugar. Mr. and Mrs. Johnston wished to create a garden exhibiting plants from places hospitable to sugar cane, including Spain, Cuba, California, the Hawaiian Islands, the Philippines, Java, and Sumatra. The bilaterally symmetrical plan was organized around a major axis and minor cross axes, with canals and allées reminiscent of Versailles. Moving outward from the house, informality ruled within the quadrants defined by the main and cross axes; rows of Indian laurel trees intersected at a circular basin. The symmetrical plan included an asymmetric array: a meadow, citrus garden, water labyrinth, and tropical grove. Yoch also reinterpreted the traditional European plant vocabulary, using tropical species from around the world. The garden's scale and vigor, combined with its experimental quality, make it stand out from the firm's other work. It now exists as a public park, with over 75 species of palms still extant.

In her many smaller public projects featuring atria, courtyards, and patios, Yoch was an acknowledged expert. Her design for the Los Angeles Women's Athletic Club (1925) re-created the look of pastoral Italy and required the hoisting of five Italian cypresses weighing several tons apiece to a roof location 40 feet (12.2 m) above the ground. In Pasadena she met equal success with the Vroman Bookstore (1921), Serendipity Antique Shop (1927–28), and the Athenaeum at the California Institute of Technology (1930–31), again working with Gordon Kaufmann.

Yoch's ability to create a sense of age and permanence was especially useful in the designs she made for the Hollywood motion-picture community during the 1930s. A romantic hilltop garden overlooking Los Angeles for the innovative director Dorothy Arzner led to major commissions from David O. Selznick, Jack Warner, and George Cukor, for whom she designed splendid estates in West Los Angeles. Through the enormous popularity of the medium during the years of the Great Depression, motion-picture makers had amassed huge personal fortunes. True to the spirit of the film industry, they sought landscape designs with immediate visual impact and a sense of "authenticity," reflecting both their personal and professional goals. These landscapes also had to accommodate the inevitable flow of Hollywood visitors, serving as screens on which wealth and professional status could be projected. Yoch proved herself able to meet the unique needs of this group, and her design philosophy by necessity expanded to include immediate as well as long-term goals.

Yoch's knowledge of history and historical design precedents had served her well, but her designs for the film community now incorporated new and specific client requirements. A more pronounced functionalism infused her design philosophy (always responsive to utilitarian needs), reflecting the new aesthetic of modernism. Her Hollywood landscapes were lavish and forward looking and employed immediately dramatic effects. The Selznicks's grounds included expansive lawns and motor courts to serve as stages for family life and entertaining. Irene Selznick commented that the patience that Yoch counseled was difficult to practice in an "overnight town." The Warners's grounds were larger and more elaborate, focusing on public display and the accommodation of large crowds. The Cukor garden was less grand but more distinctive, extending along a hillside, its form dictated by the steep slope and a long, narrow house. It had an intimate, organic feeling and was less formalistic and historically derivative.

The film industry would provide another outlet for Yoch's expanding vision; her most unusual work proved to be as a film set designer for five highly prestigious Hollywood productions. In 1935 research for the early Technicolor film The Garden of Allah (1936) took Yoch to Europe and North Africa, where she found many sights worthy of recording both with a camera and in her sketchbooks. She also made detailed observations of native plants, many of which she was able to find in southern California. In this instance the Villa Landon in Algiers provided botanical inspiration in the varied forms of date palm, olive, ficus, pepper tree, carob, oleander, pomegranate, cistus, Spanish broom, lantana, philodendron, amaryllis, cassia, helianthus, scarlet poppy, thyme, pink convolvulus, and white tree mallow.

Over the next five years Yoch was extremely active in film set design. The first sound version of Romeo and Juliet (1936) featured the Capulet courtyard, site of the famous balcony scene, in which Yoch evoked the Italian Renaissance but used asymmetrically placed details typical of California gardens-an instance, perhaps, of art imitating life. She also designed a courtyard garden for The Good Earth (1937) and transformed a large part of the Metro Goldwyn Mayer Ranch in the San Fernando Valley into a Chinese agricultural landscape. Her most famous creation, however, was the landscape of "Tara," the antebellum plantation in Gone with the Wind (1939). Her last set design, for How Green Was My Valley (1941), featured a meadow in which over ten thousand daffodils bloomed simultaneously. She created these scenic illusions at full scale on sound stages, studio back lots, or in rural locations.

Film required Yoch to be not only creative and contextual but ephemeral as well, her natural thrift and materials of her craft notwithstanding. Her ability to produce immediate, strong dramatic effects infused with a sense of permanence exemplified her innovativeness and adaptability, the results of an open mind combined with comprehensive knowledge of historical precedents. Her ideas and work were widely disseminated through the then dominant medium of film and subtly influenced the aesthetic ideas of an entire generation.

Yoch continued to blend old and new even as she moved toward modernism. By the 1940s she was experimenting with simplified angular layouts in which space and circulation no longer existed in easily recognizable curved or rectilinear patterns. To accompany a modern ranch house owned by R.B. Honeyman in San Juan Capistrano, Yoch and Council created yet another contemporary variation on Moorish geometry (1946–47). In a courtyard a rill and font set off four angled, asymmetric floral parterres in which gardenias, cycads, Australian tree fern, hibiscus, begonias, agapanthus, and camellias peacefully coexisted; unity was provided by repetition. Four different trees (southern magnolia, Arnold crabapple, coral, white oleander) distinguished the individual beds. Unusual choices such as banana and bird of paradise were featured, but old favorites such as sweet olives and Italian cypresses also made their appearance.

Yoch and Council also began to make more use of native trees and shrubs, adapting ideas gleaned from sources as diverse as California meadows and Australian plant habitats. Later planting plans were simpler and less lavishly developed, especially in the northern California gardens. While its adoption of modernism was wholehearted, their firm continued to incorporate historical references in its designs. As late as 1969 Yoch was again working in Pasadena on a fourth garden for the C.E. Davises. Contemporary and starkly abstract in its use of form, color, and materials, the design also incorporated a Spanish fountain and highly ornamental pool for swimming. In contrast, the garden also featured a magnolia walk leading to a curved flight of cantilevered steps that descended to an oval terrace. Yoch achieved unity through the use of white-flowering plants throughout, including wisteria, crape myrtle, and several species of magnolia.

In 1958 Yoch began collating notes for a projected book encompassing her design philosophy, but she only completed a draft of the first chapter. Yoch was known for the flexibility and innovativeness of her ideas; the insights and support of Council and the sensitive, well-traveled clientele with whom they worked, rather than worked for, contributed to her success. A new eclecticism that blended changing lifestyles, old and new forms, and native and imported plant materials marked her later designs. The homes and gardens that Yoch and Council built for themselves, variously located in south Pasadena (a garden designed in the early 1920 for Council's parents, whose garage served as their office until 1934), San Marino, north Pasadena, and Carmel, also functioned as proving grounds for their ideas. Throughout the firm's history Yoch and Council's work emphasized comfort, intimacy, accessibility, attention to detail, and personal supervision. Yoch's creative energy and involvement with clients continued unabated even after Council's death. In a letter dated 14 June 1971, the year before she died, Yoch wrote to a longtime friend, Thomas C. Moore, "I am having fun this year doing the garden for the oldest wooden house in Monterey," an appropriate closing comment, perhaps, on a unique career that produced over 250 highly individualized designs.

Biography

Born in Laguna Beach, California, 1890. Attended University of California, Berkeley, and Cornell University, Ithaca, New York; graduated from University of Illinois, Urbana-Champaign, 1915; established landscape architecture practice centered in Pasadena and Orange County, beginning 1921; later extended practice north to Santa Barbara and Monterey areas, and south to Mexico; joined by Lucile Council as apprentice in 1921; formed lifelong personal and professional partnership with Lucile Council; work profoundly influenced by extensive travel and study abroad; active in Hollywood film community as landscape architect and film set designer in 1930s and early 1940s; explored and adopted modernism in 1940s, but continued to use historical details freely; during her career produced over 250 garden designs; relocated to Carmel, California, 1960; continued in active practice after Council's death in 1964. Died 1972.

Selected Designs

1921	Vroman Bookstore courtyard, Pasadena, California, United States
1922–23	Il Brolino garden, Mrs. Mary Stewart residence, Montecito, California, United States
1925	Women's Athletic Club roof garden, Los Angeles, California, United States
1925–27	Mr. and Mrs. A. Parley Johnson residence, Downey, California, United States
1927	Il Vescovo garden, Mr. and Mrs. W.T. Bishop residence (with architect Gordon Kaufmann), Bel Air, California, United States
1927–28	Mrs. Richard B. Fudger residence, Los Angeles, California, United States; Serendipity Antique Shop courtyard, Pasadena, California, United States
1929–30	Jardin Botanico Las Palmas, Mr. and Mrs. B.F. Johnston residence, Los Mochis, Sinaloa, Mexico
1930–31	Athenaeum (faculty club) garden, California Institute of Technology, Pasadena, California, United States
1932–33	Dorothy Arzner residence, Los Angeles, California, United States
1934–39	Mr. and Mrs. David O. Selznick residence, Beverly Hills, California, United States
1935–37	Mr. and Mrs. Jack Warner residence, Beverly Hills, California, United States
1936	Mr. George Cukor residence, Beverly Hills, California, United States; set design for *The Garden of Allah* (film), Selznick International Pictures; Capulet courtyard for film *Romeo and Juliet*, Metro-Goldwyn-Mayer
1937	Courtyard garden for film *The Good Earth*, Metro-Goldwyn-Mayer
1939	Landscape of the plantation Tara for film *Gone with the Wind*, Selznick International Pictures
1941	Meadow for film *How Green Was My Valley*, Twentieth Century-Fox Film Corporation

1946–47   Mr. and Mrs. R.B. Honeyman, Jr., residence, Rancho Los Cerritos, San Juan Capistrano, California, United States

1969   Mr. and Mrs. C.E. Davis residence, Pasadena, California, United States

Selected Publications

"Fitting the Land for Human Use: An Art That Is Closely Allied to Architecture," *California Arts and Architecture* (July 1930)

Further Reading

"Architectural Digest Visits George Cukor," *Architectural Digest* 35 (January–February 1978)

Church, Thomas D., *Gardens Are for People: How to Plan for Outdoor Living*, New York: Reinhold, and London: Chapman and Hall, 1955; 3rd edition, by Church, Grace Hall, and Michael Laurie, Berkeley: University of California Press, 1955

Goldsmith, Margaret Olthof, *Designs for Outdoor Living*, New York: Stewart, 1941

Griswold, Mac K., and Eleanor Welles, *The Golden Age of American Gardens: Proud Owners, Private Estates, 1890–1940*, New York: Abrams, 1991

Myrick, Susan, *White Columns in Hollywood: Reports from the GWTW Sets*, edited by Richard Harwell, Macon, Georgia: Mercer University Press, 1982

Power, Nancy Goslee, and Susan Heigee, *The Gardens of California: Four Centuries of Design from Mission to Modern*, New York: Potter, 1995

Selznick, Irene Mayer, *A Private View*, New York: Knopf, and London: Weidenfeld and Nicolson, 1983

Streatfield, David C., *California Gardens: Creating a New Eden*, New York and London: Abbeville Press, 1994

Wharton, Edith, *Italian Villas and Their Gardens*, New York: Century, and London: Lane, 1904; reprint, New York: Da Capo Press, 1976

Yoch, James J., *Landscaping the American Dream: The Gardens and Film Sets of Florence Yoch, 1890–1972*, New York: Abrams/Sagapress, 1989

ROBERT A. BENSON

Yuan Ming Yuan

Beijing, Hobei Province, China

Location: northwest suburbs of Beijing

Yuan Ming Yuan, now for the most part in ruins, was the largest and most luxurious of the imperial gardens built during the Qing dynasty (1644–1911). It was the culmination of almost 2,000 years of Chinese gardening as an art and enjoyed worldwide fame for its grandeur and beauty. Tragically, it was to be looted and burned down by foreign armies in 1860 and again in 1900.

The water garden of 350 hectares (865 acres) surrounded by a wall was considered by the Chinese the "garden of gardens" (*wan yuan zhi yuan*). It took more than 130 years to establish during the reign of five emperors, who spent most of their time in the garden and executed their official duties there, returning to the capital only in winter and on special occasions. The garden thus became an extension of the imperial palace in Beijing.

The complex known as Yuan Ming Yuan encompassed three gardens: Yuan Ming Yuan (The Garden of Perfect Brightness), Chang Chun Yuan (the Garden of Long Spring), and Wan Chun Yuan (the Garden of Eternal Spring, originally called Yi Chun Yuan, the Garden of Lovely Spring). The whole was later known as Yuan Ming Yuan or Yuan Ming San Yuan (the Three Gardens of Yuan Ming). The beginnings of the first garden, Yuan Ming Yuan, fall into the reign of Emperor Kang Xi (1662–1722). This second ruler of the Manchu dynasty, who was captivated by Chinese culture, was impressed during his travels to southern China by the gardens of Suzhou, Hangzhou, and other cities in that region. Returning to Beijing he decided to lay out similar gardens, "like paintings," in his capital to give him pleasure in the hot summers and to remind him of the southern landscape. For this purpose he chose the locality known as "Three gardens and five mountains" (San yuan wu shan) west of Beijing at the foot of the Xi Shan (Western Mountains). In 1690 he began to lay out a typical southern garden on a former Ming garden site and in 1701 gave it to his son, the future emperor Yong Zheng (1723–35) as a gift of great spiritual value. Kang Xi bestowed on it the name Yuan Ming Yuan, signifying moral integrity, the greatest merit of a ruler. Yong Zheng continued with enthusiasm the layout of the garden, even though he had to work with considerable economy "not to burden his people with unnecessary expenses." His successor, Emperor Qian Long (1736–95), an able statesman who visited the southern regions several times, continued in his predecessor's work. He did so on a grand scale, for during his reign the country achieved great economic prosperity. He soon gained the reputation of a connoisseur of gardens and their design. To reach the desired effect he was willing to "move the sky and turn the earth" (*yi tian shu di*), as a contemporary poet commented. It is well known that whenever anything caught the emperor's fancy during his southern journeys he ordered his painters to draw a detailed picture of it for the landscape gardeners.

Qian Long added 12 more views to his father's 28 in Yuan Ming Yuan and thus finished the task, which brought him much joy and satisfaction. In 1744 he commissioned the artists Tang Dai and Shen Yuan to draw all the 40 views of this splendid garden. (The pictures are now in the Bibliothéque Nationale in Paris.)

In 1745 Qian Long started to landscape the Garden of Long Spring, which bordered on Yuan Ming Yuan to the east. He decided to lay out a European section along the northeastern boundary, covering four hectares (10 acres) and commonly called Xi Yang Lou. It was the first project of this kind in China and therefore marks a special chapter in the history of Sino-European contacts. The emperor's interest in Western gardens and waterworks was probably aroused by chance by a European engraving showing a fountain. He then commissioned the Italian Jesuit missionary Castiglione to design the foreign buildings and French fellow Jesuit Michel Benoist to construct garden fountains in the European style. The project took a long time to complete, from 1745 until 1759. The palaces erected there, including the Palace of the Calm Sea (Hai Yan Tang), the Palace of Harmony and Delights (Xie Qi Qu), the Big Fountains (Da Shui), the Aviary (Yang Qiao Long), and others were built in a mixture of Italian baroque and Chinese style. The fountains were arranged with considerable skill, and according to the Jesuit missionaries the large ones could compare with those in Versailles and St. Cloud. This western section was depicted in a series of 20 copper-plate engravings made in China in 1783. (Now in the Bibliothéque Nationale, Paris).

The construction of the third garden of the complex, Wan Chun Yuan, started in 1769 and continued under Qian Long's successor, Jia Qing (1796–1820).

Teams of competent garden architects and artisans created a garden complex unique in the world. It not only continued the traditions of northern gardens but also embodied the style of residential gardens of the south. The most important element in the composition of these three gardens was the *jing* (view, vista), each comprised by smaller units, *jing chu*. This was called "creating a garden in a garden" (*yuan zhong you yuan*) and was typical for Chinese garden style. The vistas were inspired by Chinese mythology, literature, and southern gardens. Each vista enshrined the idea of the next and thus linked together so that they unrolled before one's eyes like a horizontal scroll painting. The lakes and streams were connected by paths winding through picturesque valleys, and everything seemed to be the work of nature. There were no straight lines, the hills were covered with trees and shrubs, and on the banks of the streams and lakes there were flowers growing out of the rocks and changing with the seasons. Something was always hidden from the view, and something revealed. The main feature of the garden was the square shaped Fu Hai (Sea of Fortune), covering 28 hectares (70 acres), with Peng Lai Islands of the Immortals, an essential motif in Chinese imperial gardens since ancient times. On the Fu Hai there was a variety of dragon boats and arks with poetic names. The buildings covered 160,000 square meters (191,400 sq. yd.) and varied in size and shape, thus adding to the diversity of the garden. Each detail of the buildings suggested their functions, such as the Hut of Repose (An Wen Chuan), the Place Where to Wait for the Fish (Guan Yu Yue), the Study Where the Willows Bow Down (Shen Liu Du Shu Dan Gu), and many others. Other names were inspired by flowers and trees planted nearby.

There was a great library as well, housing all 79,333 volumes of the monumental collection of Chinese works known as the Complete Library of Four Branches (Ssu ku chuan shu). Rare antiques and works of art from imperial collections were displayed in the pavilions.

The garden was the scene of many ceremonial occasions. According to an eye-witness account, the favorite pastime of the emperor Kang Xi was to gaze at the reflection of the full moon in the lake. On these evenings lanterns were lit on the islands and lights twinkled on the slopes of the hills. It was an unforgettable experience. The garden was a miniature embodiment of the empire, and as the ruler strolled there his mind attained harmony with the "music of the universe" and his creative ability was restored.

The garden was described by the Jesuits Benoist and Attiret. In a letter dated 1 September 1743, Attiret praised the natural impression the garden made, contrasting it with geometric stiffness of the formal French parks. The Chinese model appealed to Europeans especially in the "beauty of irregularity" and was most congenial to the English with their liking for natural gardens.

The grandiose project of the Chinese emperors, including the "European episode," became a tragic ruin in the autumn of 1860 when the British and French armies overran China, defeated in the Opium Wars. The garden was looted and burned in a fire that lasted three

Engraving of the European Garden at Yuan Ming Yuan

days and nights. Approximately 80 percent of the buildings were destroyed, and priceless objects were carried away. Thirteen years later the emperor Tong Zhi initiated a reconstruction of the garden to celebrate his mother's 40th birthday, but because of lack of funds he was forced to stop. In 1900 the destruction was completed when the armies of eight Western powers again passed through, pillaging after the defeat of the Boxer Rebellion.

After that there followed a period of desolation. The ruins of marble columns and buildings in the western part were all that remained of the former glory. Nevertheless, the whole layout of the original garden with the foundations of the buildings remained. After the establishment of the People's Republic of China, Premier Zhou Enlai issued a degree that the whole area of the original garden should be preserved with a view to eventual restoration. In 1980 a Petition of Protection, Recovery, and Utilization of the Ruined Site of the Yuan Ming Yuan sponsored by Madame Song Qingling was signed by 1,583 important Chinese personalities, and the Society of Yuan Ming Yuan was established. In 1988 Wang Jing Zhi and Zhang De Xiang, after more than seven years of work, finished the Pictorial of All Views of Yuan Ming Yuan (Yuan Ming Yuan Quan Jing Tu) consisting of eight large pictures of rectangular-shaped silk sheets. It is based on serious research of all accessible materials. Since then a wall along the eastern part of the garden has been built, the Sea of Fortune excavated with the main island and the Jade Terrace (Yao Tai) renovated, as well as the Imperial Gate to the Wan Chun Yuan, the Green Watching Pavilion (Jian Bi Ting), and the western section of the Wanhua Maze. Thus a considerable part of the garden has been restored to life and has become a favorite place of entertainment and leisure for the people of Beijing.

Synopsis

1690	Kang Xi, second emperor of Qing dynasty, begins landscaping imperial garden northwest of Beijing
1701	Kang Xi gives garden to his son, future emperor Yong Zheng, and names it Yuan Ming Yuan
1723–1735	Yong Zheng continues father's activities and finishes landscaping of Yuan Ming Yuan
1743	Jesuit priest U.D. Attiret describes the garden in a letter, thus introducing it to Europe
1744	Forty views of Yuan Ming Yuan painted by Tang Dai and Shen Yuan

	(now in Bibliothéque Nationale, Paris)
1745	Emperor Qian Long begins landscaping Chang Chun Yuan (Garden of Long Spring), including Xi Yang Lou, the European section
1759	Xi Yang Lou is finished
1783	Qian Long begins landscaping the third garden of the complex, Wan Chun Yuan (Garden of Eternal Spring); all three gardens later become known as Yuan Ming Yuan
1784	20 copperplate engravings of the European section are produced
1860	Yuan Ming Yuan razed and burned by British and French armies
1900	Remnants of Yuan Ming Yuan are plundered by united armed forces of eight foreign nations
1980	Petition of Protection, Recovery and Utilization of ruined site of Yuan Ming Yuan issued
1980s–1990s	Yuan Ming Yuan partially reconstructed and made accessible to the public

Further Reading

Budde, Hendrik, Christoph Müller-Hofstede, and Gereon Sievernich, *Europa und die Kaiser von China* (exhib. cat.), Frankfurt: Insel, 1985

Chan, Charis, *Imperial China*, London: Viking, and San Francisco: Chronicle Books, 1991

Hrdlička, Zdenek, and Věnceslava Hrdličková, *Chinesische Gartenkunst*, Prague: Aventinum, and Hanau, Germany: Dausien, 1998

Hu, Dongchu, *The Way of the Virtuous: The Influence of Art and Philosophy on Chinese Garden Design*, Beijing: New World Press, 1998

Keswick, Maggie, and Charles Jencks, *The Chinese Garden: History, Art, and Architecture*, London: Academy Editions, and New York: Rizzoli, 1978

Titley, Norah, and Frances Wood, *Oriental Gardens*, London: British Library, 1991; San Francisco: Chronicle Books, 1992

Wang, Jing Zhi, and De Xiang Zhang, *Yuan Ming Yuan: The Pictorial*, Xinjiang: People's Publishers, 1990

Wang, Wei, *Yüan Ming Yüan*, Beijing: Pei-ching ch'u pan she, 1957

VĚNA HRDLIČKOVÁ

Z

Zeist

Utrecht, Netherlands

Location: approximately 5 miles (8 km) east of Utrecht

The castle gardens of Zeist, known chiefly from 18th-century prints, not only are themselves remarkable works of garden layout but also reflect the influence of French garden design, and particularly of the designs of J. Boyceau de la Baraudière for the Luxembourg gardens in Paris, in such a way as to make it possible to date the design to within a year or two from its appearance alone. For example, modifications were clearly made to the garden's architecture between its original creation by the architect and garden designer Jacob Roman in 1677, when the castle was built, and the prints of D. Stoopendaal (in or soon after 1700) and prints of a later date by Johannes de Bosch. The garden's style and its architectural modifications also reflect the dramatic political changes that South Holland and neighboring Utrecht were undergoing.

In 1677 Willem Adriaan I, lord of Odijk, Kortgene, Zeist, and Dreibergen and in 1679 to become count of Nassau, commissioned the architect Jacques Roman to build in the "high domain of Zeist and Dreibergen," Zeist Castle, intended to be a miniature replica of Versailles and its gardens. The famous garden underwent augmentation but no substantial change until in 1745 the castle was sold to Cornelis Schellinger, who opened it to the Moravian brethren, to whom Schellinger gave the gardens. They added the two square gardens in front of the castle, considerably derogating from the magnificence of the original baroque concept.

The Stoopendaal print of the classical French-style garden at Zeist in the university library at Wageningen shows the two large square gardens in front of the house, one on each side of the central axis. One has a sunken elliptically shaped interior walk; the other includes straight walks radiating from the center of the square to the middle of each side. The two wings of the house extend forward to form a courtyard with the facade; two oblong gardens extending backward, one divided into two squares and the other with another elliptical walk, flank the house.

Behind the house itself extending to each side slightly beyond the wings are two symmetrically arranged square gardens on each side of the axis, bordered by trees and ending in a semicircular garden enclosure. Beyond the enclosure lies the moat, which here breaks from its rectilinear lines into a semicircle, protected by a rear wall. The two external canals with their rows of trees, presumably not only decorative but also functionally strengthening the sides of the canals, extend forward to enclose not only the house and its flanking oblong gardens but also the moat and the large square gardens in front of the house. Behind the garden's closing hemisphere to the rear of the house are double rows of a half-dozen square gardens on each side of the axis. The final 16 squares, two rows of four side by side on each side of the axis, are joined together by radiating paths to each corner and to the middle of each side of each group of eight. Outside the perimeter are outhouses and a kitchen garden. The whole impressive ensemble contains as much formal decoration as can reasonably be fitted into its classically formal elongated structure.

Synopsis

1677	Willem Adriaan I commissions architect and garden designer Jacob Roman to build Zeist castle and gardens as replicas of Versailles
1745	Castle and gardens sold to Cornelis Schellinger, and damage to gardens follows
1924	Castle acquired by municipality of Zeist

Further Reading

Groen, Jan van der, *Den nederlandtsen hovenier,* Amsterdam, 1668

Jacques, David, and Arend Jan van der Horst, *The Gardens of William and Mary,* London: Helm, 1988

Kuyper, W., *Dutch Classicist Architecture: A Survey of Dutch Architecture, Gardens, and Anglo-Dutch Architectural Relations from 1625 to 1700,* Delft, The Netherlands: Delft University Press, 1980

Oldenburger-Ebbers, Carla S., "The Anglo-Dutch Garden in the Age of William and Mary," *Journal of Garden History* 8, nos. 2–3 (1988)

Oldenburger-Ebbers, Carla S., "Garden Design in the Netherlands in the Seventeenth Century," in *The History of Garden Design,* edited by Monique Mosser and Georges Teyssot, London: Thames and Hudson, 1991

ANTHONY H.T. LEVI

Zen Garden

The expression *Zen garden* is a catchall term used to refer to any of number of garden styles, the design of which may have been influenced by Zen Buddhism. *Zen garden* is a common expression in the West but is rarely used in Japan, where more accurate terms exist. The gardens most often associated with this expression are tea gardens (*cha-niwa* or *roji*) and the sand and stone gardens (see Plate 36) found in Zen Buddhist temples and some residences. The latter, which are more properly called *karesansui,* which literally means "dry mountain water," are the focus of this essay. While the development of *karesansui* was related to Zen Buddhism as a religion and as a social force, they also derived from other social and artistic influences.

Buddhism is a religion based on the teachings of an Indian sage, Śākyamuni (Japanese, Shakamuni), who preached in northern India in the sixth or fifth century B.C. His teachings of paths to enlightenment were written down as sutras in later years by his disciples and spread throughout Asia, where they inspired the development of various sects. In the sixth century A.D., the priest Bodhidharma (Japanese, Daruma) took his own vision of Buddhist thought from India to China. Rather than focusing on the written doctrine of the Buddha, Bodhidharma concentrated on meditation as a means to enlightenment, even as Śākyamuni had himself done.

In China Bodhidharma's teaching developed into a sect called Chan, which is the Chinese pronunciation of *dhyāna,* the Sanskrit word meaning meditation. The introduction of this teaching from Japan is attributed primarily to two Japanese priests, Eisai and Dōgen, who made pilgrimages to China and returned with teachings in 1168 and 1223, respectively. The Japanese pronunciation of Chan is *Zen;* thus Zen Buddhism literally means "meditation Buddhism." The development of *karesansui,* however, was not coincident with the introduction of Zen Buddhism to Japan; the gardens do not appear until the end of the Muromachi period (1333–1568).

Although Chan priests were involved in arts such as ink painting, they did not build gardens such as those found now in Japanese Zen temples, and Kamakura-period Japan (1185–1333) was not fertile ground for such development. It should be noted that the term *karesansui* was used in Japan long before the introduction of the Zen Buddhist religion (initially pronounced *karasenzui*) and was even mentioned in the *Sakuteiki,* a gardening treatise written in the mid-11th century, as a gardening style in which neither ponds nor streams were employed. The *karasenzui* of that earlier era, however, were quite different from the enclosed courtyard gardens (*karesansui*) that developed during Japan's medieval period.

During the Kamakura period most large-scale temple and residential gardens were stylistic outgrowths of the gardens of Heian-period (794–1185) aristocratic residences. One new development during the Kamakura period, however, was the inclusion of new types of Buddhist allegory in some temple gardens. Although not strictly limited to Zen Buddhist thought, these allegorical images were imported from China and used in garden design by Zen Buddhist priests. One example is the rock arrangement in the upper garden of Saihō-ji (Moss Temple) in front of a meditation hall called Shitōan. The name given to the hill area, the name of the meditation hall, and the rock arrangement itself are all drawn from a particular Chinese parable that describes the meeting of two high priests, Yū Shūsai (Chinese, Xiong Xiucai) and Ryō Zasu (Chinese, Liang Zuozhu). Another Chinese metaphor often used in Zen temple gardens at that time was the dry waterfall arrangement called *ryūmon baku* (dragon's-gate waterfall), such as the one found at Tenryūji temple. This image stems from a Chinese tale of a carp that persists in swimming up nine great waterfalls and thus becomes a dragon. In China this alluded to the rewards of persisting at the stringent exams for government positions, and in Japan the allegory was applied by Zen priests to symbolize the benefits of perseverance at meditation as the route to enlightenment.

The development of courtyard *karesansui* gardens as we know them today derives not only from Zen Buddhism but also from the fact that in the Muromachi period the seat of government, and thus the focus of society, shifted back to Kyoto from Kamakura. In Kyoto the combined influence of long-established aristocratic culture, the wealth of newly ascendant merchants, and the austerity of the military class, as well as the influx of Chinese thought from Zen priests, gave rise to a society that had a strong interest in arts, especially those that expressed the aesthetics of reserve and paucity. All of these social groups supported the arts, and some of Japan's best-known cultural attributes developed during this period, for instance theater (*noh*), flower arranging (*ikebana*), and tea ceremony (*sadō*). As a result, *karesansui* gardens developed primarily at temples of the Rinzai sect, which had its power base in Kyoto, but not in temples of the Sōtō sect, which tended to be situated in provincial mountain areas.

Two classic examples of *karesansui* are the gardens at the temples Daisenin and Ryōanji. To understand these gardens, it is necessary to realize that earlier temples (and aristocratic residences) had central main halls that were entered by crossing an open sand-covered courtyard to the south of the hall. The hall itself had a central room, the focus of which was southward, toward the exterior court where various events took place. Through the Kamakura and Muromachi periods, the main hall began to be divided into a "public" southern half and a private northern half. These public and private aspects are referred to as *hare* and *ke*, respectively. The first *karesansui* were developed in conjunction with the private area; the northeastern garden at Daisenin is a good example of this. There we find an arrangement of plants, rocks, and sand created so as to depict an image of wild mountains exactly as found in the ink landscape paintings that were popular at the time.

Through the medieval period, as public functions gradually began to be performed inside the southern half of the main hall rather than outside in the southern court, and with the development of a new architectural entryway that allowed for formal access to the main hall from the side, the use of the southern court gradually shifted from entry court to viewing garden, of which the famous stone garden at Ryōanji is such an example. This garden contains only stones set in sand, with no plants other than some moss that has grown about the base of some stones. The design of the gardens, like that of the ink landscape paintings of the time, gives as much preference to space (*ma*) as to objects, is based on triangular relationships between the objects, and employs a paucity of palette that is in keeping with the aesthetics of the time as well as the tenets of Zen Buddhism, which shuns outward ornamentation in favor of inward spirit.

Further Reading

Keane, Marc Peter, *Japanese Garden Design*, Rutland, Vermont: C.E. Tuttle, 1996

Kuck, Loraine E., *The World of the Japanese Garden: From Chinese Origins to Modern Landscape Art*, New York: Walker/Weatherhill, 1968

Kuitert, Wybe, *Themes, Scenes, and Taste in the History of Japanese Garden Art*, Amsterdam: Gieben, 1988

Nitschke, Günter, *Gartenarchitektur in Japan: Rechter Winkel und natürliche Form*, Cologne, Germany: Taschen, 1991; as *Japanese Gardens: Right Angle and Natural Form*, translated by Karen Williams, Cologne, Germany: Taschen, 1993

MARC PETER KEANE

Zhan Yuan

Nanjing, Jiangsu Province, China

Location: southeastern part of city center, on east side of Zhonghua Road, and approximately 170 miles (274 km) west-northwest of Shanghai

Originally the site of Zhan Yuan was the West Garden of the residence of Xu Da, Zhongshan duke and a general of the Ming dynasty, located at Dagong Fang (a lane of Nanjing city). Xu Pengju, a seventh-generation relative of Xu Da, built it as a garden in the late 15th century. When Emperor Qianlong visited Nanjing, he lived in this garden and named it Zhan Yuan (Viewing Garden), from a poem of Su Shi, a famous poet of the Song dynasty: "viewing the hall, as in the heaven." Emperor Qianlong ordered a copy of the garden to be made in Changchun Yuan of Beijing and named it Ru Yuan.

During the Qing dynasty Zhan Yuan was occupied by the office of the military department and then became the office of the civil administration department. It was recorded in a landscape painting of Yuan Jiang in the early 18th century. During the Taiping Heavenly Kingdom it was the residence of the East King Yang Xiuqing. After Yang's death it became the residence of a vice prime minister, Summer Official Lai Hanying. After the kingdom was suppressed in 1864, the garden was also destroyed and the stonework was scattered in other gardens. The garden was rebuilt in the 1870s and 1890s. The east part of the garden became the residence of a government official, and the west part remained unoccupied and became almost wild. In 1960 it was rebuilt under the supervision of architectural historian Liu Dun-zhen.

The garden covers an area of 5,280 square meters (6,315 sq. yd.) and has a simple rectangular layout. The main entrance is located at the eastern side of the garden and faces the main hall with a unexpectedly open effect. The main hall, Jingmiao Hall (Silence and Excellence Hall) is located at the south end of the garden, which is also the site of the main part of the garden.

The southern part of the garden is mainly stonework; it is said the stonework remains from the Song dynasty. The northeast part of the stonework presents an artistic conception of a cliff. The stone is combined with a pond, which flows into the main hall and becomes a stream and then again a pond. The main hall is nearly surrounded by the water, which approaches the meadow in front of the hall with waves lapping against the bank, creating a unique effect of an open country in a classical Chinese garden.

Synopsis

1370s	Site is West Garden of Xu Da, Zhongshan duke and general of Ming Dynasty
1470s	Garden built by 7th generation grandson of Xu Da, Xu Pengju
late 18th C.	Emperor Qianlong visits and renames garden Zhan Yan (Viewing Garden)
1850–64	Residence of East King Yang Xiuqing and then Vice Prime Minister Lai Hanying
1864	Garden destroyed by military campaign
1870s	Garden rebuilt
1890s	Garden rebuilt
1960	Garden renovated under supervision of Professor Liu Dun-zhen

Further Reading

Chi, Ch'eng, *The Craft of Gardens* (1634), translated by Alison Hardie, New Haven, Connecticut: Yale University Press, 1988

Johnston, R. Stewart, *Scholar Gardens of China: A Study and Analysis of the Spatial Design of the Chinese Private Garden*, Cambridge and New York: Cambridge University Press, 1991

Keswick, Maggie, and Charles Jencks, *The Chinese Garden: History, Art and Architecture*, New York: Rizzoli, and London: Academy Editions, 1978

Liu, Tun-chen, *Su-chou ku tien yüan lin*, Beijing: Chung-kuo chien chu kung yeh ch'u pan she, 1979; as *Chinese Classical Gardens of Suzhou*, translated by Chen Lixian, edited by Joseph C. Wang, New York: McGraw Hill, 1993

Tsu, Frances Ya-Sing, *Landscape Design in Chinese Gardens*, New York: McGraw Hill, 1988

Wang, Joseph Cho, *The Chinese Garden*, Oxford and New York: Oxford University Press, 1998

ZHENG SHILING

Zocher, Jan David 1790/91–1870

Netherlands Architect

Jan David Zocher and his father of the same name were both architects. Both designed buildings, but the son is better known for his landscape designs and paintings. The son of Jan David Zocher, Jr., Louis, also worked as a landscape architect in the family firm. Louis also worked on projects with his father, with the result that much confusion has arisen, particular through the mistaken attribution to Jan David, Jr., of the work of his father. Furthermore, while it seems certain that Jan David, Sr., was born in 1763 and died in 1817, and that Jan David, Jr., died in 1870, it is not clear whether Jan David, Jr., was born in 1790, as all major reference works and the Nederlands Architectuurinstitut state, or in 1791, which is the date most recently preferred, with no reason given, in publications of the Amsterdam Rijksmuseum, normally authoritative in such matters.

The architect of interest in the present context is Jan David, Jr., principally because of his responsibility for the design of the Vondelpark in Amsterdam, as well as for the Soestbergen Cemetery in Utrecht and the 1836 Amsterdam stock exchange in the shape of a Greek temple, found unsuitable in 1848 and since destroyed and replaced by the 1903 building by H.P. Berlage. Zocher also created parks at Haarlem—the original Agnetapark in Delft where that created by his son now stands—and painted watercolor designs for small residential gardens. The paintings effectively highlight a multitude of focal points and intimate private spaces by combining a bird's-eye with a frontal view. An example is exhibited at the Cooper-Hewitt National Design Museum in New York. The chief characteristic of Zocher's designs for larger landscape spaces is their break with formal French classicism and their adaptations of English landscape style, making plentiful use of meandering streams and serpentine lakes with an almost exaggerated number of irregularities in the shapes of their sinuous edges. Zocher shows a fondness for the untamed forms of nature and for assemblages of winding paths between bushes and randomly placed clusters of trees to form intimate private enclaves.

The Soestbergen Cemetery in Utrecht opened in 1830 as a result of Napoléon's decree that for reasons of hygiene burials should no longer take place in the churches or elsewhere in the center of Utrecht. Zocher was invited to devise the cemetery layout and used the English landscape style on which his father had already begun to draw, and which by the end of the 18th century had established itself as the dominant English style. Zocher, however, blended with this English inspiration the empathy with nature explored by Jean-Jacques Rousseau and others of his generation. Zocher employed at Soestbergen the winding paths and random tree clumps later to become a characteristic of his park designs. At its center the cemetery has an unusual mound, intended no doubt to elevate the imaginations of mourners to the ascent of the soul on death.

Zocher's fame rests on the Vondelpark in Amsterdam. He studied in Paris before succeeding his father as landscape architect to Willem I. There followed the numerous contracts for town parks of which the principal, most celebrated, and most successfully executed was the Vondelpark, undertaken with the help of his son. In the mid-19th century the town was bursting beyond the boundary imposed by its largest canal, the Singelgracht, and in 1864 a group of 24 patrician citizens led by Christiaan Pieter van Eeghen initiated a move to build beyond it to the west a park of drives and walks in what was to become the center of an upscale residential area.

The Zochers moved away from the formality of earlier symmetrical Dutch gardens, creating an English-style park with lengthy winding paths, open lawns, ponds and ornamental lakes, meadows, and woodland. The park includes enclosures for animals to graze. Exotic birds were imported, its parakeets became famous, and it is claimed that, in addition to 100 plant species, approximately 120 types of tree were introduced. When the park opened on 15 June 1865, it was not quite eight hectares (20 acres), 1,500 meters long by about 300 meters wide (1,640 yd. by 328 yd.). Known as the Nieuwe Park until 1868, by 1877 it had grown to 45 hectares (111 acres), having been renamed Vondelpark in 1868 after the city's best-known playwright, Joost van den Vondel, who had died in 1679 in poverty and disgrace after the production of his controversial play *Lucifer*. Containing a pavilion and inspired by the green area in the middle of the town known as the Plantage, where the botanical garden, founded in 1632, has been situated since 1682, the Vondelpark has become the city's favorite outside recreation area.

Biography

Born ca. 1790. Son of architect Jan David Zocher, Sr. Studied in Paris before succeeding father as landscape architect to Willem I; known mostly for city parks, especially Amsterdam's Vondelpark; his son Louis Zocher worked with him and continued family landscape architecture firm after his death. Died 1870.

Selected Designs

1830	Soestbergen cemetery, Utrecht, Netherlands
1864–65	Vondelpark, Amsterdam, Netherlands

Further Reading

Helmink-Habes, Hanneke, "Zakelijk Talent: De firma Zocher en de ontwikkeling en financiering van het stedelijk groen," *Nederlands jaarboek voor de geschiedenis van tuin- en landschapsarchituur* 3 (1997)

Immerseel, Ronald H.M. van, and Peter F.M. van Oosterhout, "Dordwijks aanleg in landschapsstijl: J.D. Zocher jr en Chr. Eggink," *Nederlands jaarboek voor de geschiedenis van tuin- en landschapsarchituur* 3 (1997)

ANTHONY H.T. LEVI

Zoological Garden

Animals have been an integral part of gardens and parks since ancient times. Mesopotamian, Egyptian, and Chinese garden parks contained native and exotic animals as early as ca. 3000–2000 B.C. These collections served several purposes: food for the table, game for the hunt, symbols of power and prestige for impressing guests, and luxuries for the pleasure of their collectors.

These collections were followed by similar ones in Greco-Roman societies, Persian and Arabic societies, Aztec and Inca societies, and as part of medieval monarchies, monasteries, and municipalities. These ancient and medieval collections were often kept in large natural areas; however, individual animals, such as lions, were kept in cages, and other smaller mammals and birds were kept as pets. These collections were the privilege of royalty and wealthy individuals.

As Europe entered its Renaissance during the 16th century, in tandem with the age of exploration, the discovery of many new species coincided with the proliferation of private menageries. Menageries remained the privilege of royalty and the wealthy class, but the number of wealthy individuals was increasing, as were the number of collections. Menageries were arranged taxonomically and characterized by rows of cages containing related species. The emphasis was on having as many species as possible, so the space was devoted to the animals and their cages, not to the animal's environment. However, a menagerie's setting was often among an estate's gardens.

Toward the end of the 18th century, large royal menageries opened to the public, although little else about them changed. The most important of these were the Tiergarten Schönnbrunn in Vienna (established in 1752 but continuing the royal collection established in 1569), the Menagerie du Jardin des Plantes, Muséum National d'Histoire Naturelle in Paris (established in 1793 but continuing the Menagerie Royale de Versailles established in 1665), and the Tower of London Menagerie (established in 1235 but continuing the royal collection established about 1100).

It was during the early 19th century that the menagerie evolved into the zoological garden (or zoological park). At that time knowledge about animals and their habitats was increasing, transportation was improving, the public was becoming better educated, and improved husbandry was possible. All of this and more affected the menagerie as it began its transition into a public cultural institution. Although the larger established European menageries were changing, it was a newly established collection in London that arguably was the first zoological garden.

In 1828 the Zoological Society of London established its zoological garden in Regent's Park. Although the animals remained in taxonomically arranged cages, the grounds were landscaped, education of the visitors was improved, and science was an important part of the staff's work. Many other zoological gardens soon appeared throughout Europe. While many of these were transformed European menageries that were part of royal estates, the London Zoo was built in one of London's new public parks.

In the United States most zoological gardens have been located in urban parks. The first known urban menagerie was established informally at Central Park in the early 1860s (it did not become a responsibility of New York City until the early 1870s), followed by a menagerie at Lincoln Park in Chicago in 1868. The Philadelphia Zoological Garden, located in Fairmount Park, began its existence as a zoological garden in 1874, although it was chartered in 1859, the Civil War and other difficulties delaying its opening. American zoos and aquariums followed suit in the 19th and 20th centuries, becoming ubiquitous features of municipal urban parks.

Colonial zoos of the 19th century often began at botanical collecting stations or in botanical gardens. Several were part of agricultural acclimatization programs, since the husbandry of exotic species for agricultural purposes was important to the economy of the colonies. Many of these colonial zoos were well landscaped, and the animal exhibits were usually open, natural areas since climate was not a concern. Often the landscaping had the appearance of a botanical garden, or the native vegetation was simply allowed to grow.

It was not until the latter part of the 20th century that animal exhibits became landscaped natural habitats. With improved husbandry, better knowledge about the animals' biological and social needs, an increased emphasis on conservation and propagation, and an increased sensibility toward animal welfare, it was finally possible to exhibit animals in social groups within natural settings. This type of exhibit evolved into the immersion exhibit, whereby the exhibit and its surroundings appear to be a continuous landscaping. In larger zoological gardens the plant collection can be almost as valuable as the animal collection.

In 1952 the Arizona-Sonora Desert Museum in Tucson opened as a living museum. It exhibited animals native to this desert region in open exhibits landscaped with native desert plants. The few buildings that were needed were built into the landscape in order to be barely noticeable. As much attention has been paid to educating the public about the plants and desert environment as about the animals. It has been an environmental center and a was precursor to the zoo biopark (or conservation park) concept of the 1990s.

As the natural environments of zoological gardens have become more extensive and valuable, both on the zoo grounds and in the animal exhibits, the care of these areas has become increasingly important. In response to the need for a more professional care of the zoo landscape, the Association of Zoological Horticulture was formed in 1980. Its purposes are to promote horticulture as an integral part of zoo design, to promote the conservation of endangered species, to share ideas and information about plants and their role in zoos, and to promote zoo horticulture as a profession.

Zoological gardens have become re-creations of the natural world. Exhibits use both exotic and native plant species to simulate natural habitats for the animals, while the public areas of the zoos are landscaped. The natural effect often extends beyond the zoos since they are often set within parks. While the emphasis is on the animals, they are but one component of the natural world, and the modern zoological garden exemplifies this integration of animals, plants, and other natural elements.

Further Reading

Bridges, William, *Gathering of Animals: An Unconventional History of the New York Zoological Society,* New York: Harper and Row, 1974

Fisher, James, *Zoos of the World: The Story of Animals in Captivity,* Garden City, New York: Natural History Press, 1967

Hanson, Elizabeth Anne, "Nature Civilized: A Cultural History of American Zoos, 1870–1940," Ph.D. diss., University of Pennsylvania, 1996

Hoage, R.J., and William A. Deiss, editors, *New Worlds, New Animals: From Menagerie to Zoological Park in the Nineteenth Century,* Baltimore, Maryland: Johns Hopkins University Press, 1996

Hyson, Jeffrey Nugent, "Urban Jungles: Zoos and American Society," Ph.D. diss., Cornell University, 1999

Kisling, Vernon N., "Colonial Menageries and the Exchange of Exotic Faunas," *Archives of Natural History* 25, no. 3 (1998)

Kisling, Vernon N., editor, *Zoo and Aquarium History: Ancient Animal Collections to Zoological Gardens,* Boca Raton, Florida: CRC Press, 2001

Loisel, Gustave, *Histoire des ménageries de l'antiquité à nos jours,* Paris: Doin, 1912

Ponsonby, Doris Almon, *It Began Before Noah,* London: Joseph, 1972

Rogers, Chuck, "A History of the Association of Zoological Horticulture," *International Zoo Yearbook* 29 (1990)

Stott, R. Jeffrey, "The American Idea of a Zoological Park: An Intellectual History," Ph.D. diss., University of California—Santa Barbara, 1981

Wemmer, Christen M., editor, *The Ark Evolving: Zoos and Aquariums in Transition,* Front Royal, Virginia: Smithsonian Institution Conservation and Research Center, 1995

Wirtz, Patrick, "Zoo City: Bourgeois Values and Scientific Culture in the Industrial Landscape," *Journal of Urban Design* 2, no. 1 (1997)

Zuckerman, Solly, editor, *The Zoological Society of London, 1826–1976, and Beyond,* London: Academic Press, 1976

VERNON N. KISLING, JR.

Zwinger

Dresden, Saxony, Germany

Location: in the center of Dresden, next to the Opera House and Palace, near the river Elbe

When a fire destroyed large parts of the palace in Dresden in 1702, plans for a completely new building were made. Friedrich August I, duke of Saxony, elector of the Holy Roman Emperor from 1694, and since 1697 August II, king of Poland, decided to create an extension to the palace. The term used to describe the area between two ramparts, *Zwinger,* was to be its name. During his travels in the France of Louis XIV,

August II had been impressed by the gardens of Versailles. In 1709 he ordered Matthäus Daniel Pöppelmann, appointed state architect in 1705, to create a building that was to house the ruler's collection of exotic plants, his extensive—and valuable—stock of orange and laurel trees in particular.

Pöppelmann thus started out to design an orangery but soon had to transform the ensemble of pavilions and galleries planned and erected between 1709 and 1732 to fulfill another important function: the square around which the buildings were grouped was to serve as an arena for courtly festivities, a demonstration of wealth and power in the style of absolutist monarchs. At first, construction was hurried in order to have an appropriate stage ready for the sumptuous festivities accompanying the marriage of August II's son to the emperor's daughter Maria Josepha in 1719. The costly celebrations reduced the king's funds considerably so that in the following years construction proceeded more slowly. Some of the original magnificent designs had to be abandoned or put into effect on a smaller scale. The architect's initial concept of a rectangle of buildings could not be realized in his lifetime.

When initiating the project August II had sketched out his idea of an orangery and garden he wanted to call the Garden of the Hesperides; he sent Pöppelmann to study the palaces and gardens in other European countries, including those in Prague, Vienna, Salzburg, Rome, and Versailles. Balthasar Permoser, a master sculptor from Bavaria, was to work on the decoration of the buildings and grounds. He and his colleagues added an army of figures, about 130 in all until 1726, as well as all the sandstone ornaments that enhanced the distinctly baroque style of Zwinger. An ideal partner to Pöppelmann, Permoser helped him create Zwinger's Nymph's Bath, a room separated from the courtyard, in accordance with the architect's design, inspired by his visits to Italian gardens, especially those of the villas in Frascati. Its fountains drew heavily on those in Rome.

In 1713 and 1714 respectively, the first buildings to be structurally completed were the Mathematical-Physical Salon and the French Pavilion. The Bowed Galleries with another pavilion in the middle—the Wall Pavilion (completed 1719)—connected them to form one end of the rectangle. The Long Gallery with the glistening Crown Gate was erected between 1714 and 1718. The year 1718 also saw the scaling down of the idea to create Zwinger as a huge garden building annexed to a new palace. As the plans for a new palace were given up, the ensemble had to become something on its own. In 1728 the function as an arena for festivities changed when the galleries became a place for the library and collections of the dynasty, a museum, and the Palais Royal des Sciences.

While some of the buildings put up temporarily as wooden constructions to be ready for the celebrations in 1719 were built from sandstone until 1732, the edifice to mirror the Long Gallery and close the rectangle remained only an idea up until the middle of the following century. In 1847 construction work began on the gallery designed by Gottfried Semper, architect of the Dresden Opera House. Although he wanted the new gallery to fit into the overall design, he modeled his building according to Italian Renaissance, not baroque, styles. Although he was criticized for this only a few decades later, today the Semper Gallery is praised as a

successful completion of the ensemble. Construction work did not end here, however; even after five phases of restoration work on Zwinger between 1783 and 1963, the work continues. In 1990 the reconstruction of the Crown Gate was completed, with a restoration of the cupola decorations that had been gone for a hundred years.

From the beginning Pöppelmann had in mind for Zwinger a lavish garden scheme in the style of French gardens. It was to be an essential part of the palace area, consisting of the new palace building, the gardens and the orangery. His consecutive designs until the publication of his ideas in 1729 all follow the same structural concept. The square in the middle of the area between the two ends of the 107-meter-wide (117 yd.) rectangle, with Wall Pavilion on one side and Town Pavilion on the other, was to consist of four water basins with a colorful *parterre de broderie* behind each of them. Parterres with lawn and box trees parallel to the Long Gallery and between the Bowed Galleries next to the Wall Pavilion were to attract the view to the fountains in the middle of the yard. The choice and arrangement of plants and the symmetrical layout would invest the ensemble with an air of festivity while at the same time enhancing the impression of an architecturally orientated design, that of a highly ordered area. The scenery was to be completed by an allée of lime trees placed behind the Wall Pavilion.

The plans were not put into practice before 1719 because the area was needed for the wedding festivities of August II's son. In the following years funds were reduced drastically, and interest in taking the ambitious plans to completion dwindled. It would be another 100 years before Zwinger's courtyard acquired a more elaborate layout. From 1819 onward small round ponds with fountains were created, lined by orange trees in tubs that were placed along the paths. The garden was newly laid out in 1876 when C.F. Krause, as garden director, had roses and clematis planted to line the lawn parterres. The original baroque garden designs of Pöppelmann were far from being put into effect. Not even Hubert Ermisch, who supervised the fourth and first true phase of restoration work on Zwinger in the 1920s and 1930s, carried out the initial plans. Today, visitors find a symmetrically ordered courtyard with the four ponds and their fountains and parterres dominated by lawn.

Synopsis

1702	Fire destroys large parts of palace
1709	Elector of Saxony, Friedrich August I, orders Matthäus Daniel Pöppelmann to build orangery within castle walls (in so-called Zwinger), as part of rebuilding after fire

1709–32	Pavilions and galleries completed by Pöppelmann and Balthasar Permoser
1711–16	Nymph's Bath
1712–13	Mathematical-Physical Salon
1713–14	French Pavilion built
1714–18	Crown Gate and Long Gallery
1716–19	Wall Pavilion
1718–19	Pavilion on southern end and German Pavilion
1718–28	Town Pavilion and Bowed Galleries
1728	Concept of Zwinger as orangery given up, and Zwinger used to house library and various scientific and art collections
1759–60	Zwinger damaged during the Seven Years' War, and courtyard turned into timber depot
1783–95	In first phase of "restoration," some elaborate ornaments, stone vases on the balustrades, cherubs, and other figures taken away
1806–13	Zwinger damaged during Napoleonic Wars
1819–30	Gardens in Zwinger courtyard laid out for first time
1847–55	Rectangle closed with erection of gallery designed and partially built by Gottfried Semper
1849	Some pavilions and bowed galleries destroyed by fire
1852–57	Reconstruction of destroyed buildings
1857–63	In second phase of "restoration," buildings painted with varnish
1876	Courtyard adorned with roses and clematis, by C.F. Krause
1880–98	In third phase of "restoration," Portland cement instead of sandstone used to repair buildings and figures
1924–36	Fourth phase of "restoration," first true restoration based on scientific and architectural principles according to original designs
1945	All Zwinger pavilions destroyed during bombing of Dresden
1945–63	Fifth phase of restoration
1990	Restoration of Crown Gate completed

Further Reading

Hempel, Eberhard, *Der Zwinger zu Dresden: Grundzuge und Schicksal seiner künstlerischen Gestaltung*, Berlin: Deutscher Verein für Kunstwissenschaft, 1961

Kirsten, Michael, *Dresden, der Zwinger*, Leipzig: Seemann, 1991

Löffler, Fritz, *Der Zwinger in Dresden*, Leipzig: Seemann, 1976; 4th edition, 1992

Man, John, *Zwinger Palace, Dresden*, London: Tauris Parke Books, 1990

Pöppelmann, Matthäus Daniel, *Vorstellung und Beschreibung des Zwingersgarten zu Dresden*, Dresden, 1729; reprint, Dortmund: Harenberg Kommunikation, 1980

ANGELA SCHWARZ

INDEX

INDEX

Page numbers in **boldface** indicate article titles; page numbers in *italics* indicate illustrations.

NOTES ON ADVISERS
AND CONTRIBUTORS

Abbs, Barbara. Freelance garden writer. Author of *Gardens of the Netherlands and Belgium*, 1999, *The Conservatory Month by Month*, 1997, and *French Gardens: A Guide*, 1994. Contributor to many publications, including *Garden History*, 1993, *New Plantsman*, 1994, 1996, and *Sussex Archaeological Society Collections*, 1994. **Essay:** Beloeil.

Alanen, Arnold R. Professor, Department of Landscape Architecture, University of Wisconsin, Madison. **Essays:** Bullard, Helen Elise (with Lynn Bjorkman); Manning, Warren H. (with Lynn Bjorkman); Peets, Elbert.

Armstrong, Paul. Associate Professor, School of Architecture, University of Illinois, Urbana-Champaign. Editor of *Space, Light, and Movement: the Architecture of Jack Sherman Baker*, 1997, *Architecture of Tall Buildings*, 1995, *CBTUH Review*, 1998–present, *Reflections*, 1989–95, and *Urbanism*, 1990, 1992. Contributor to numerous books and journals. **Essay:** Paradise Garden.

Baskervyle-Glegg, Diana. Garden designer, freelance garden writer. Contributor to *Country Life, The Field, The Garden, English Garden, Country Homes,* and *New Dictionary of National Biography.* **Essays:** Douglas, David; Herbs: Culinary (with Judith Gerber); Levens Hall; Edwardian Period.

Benson, Robert A. Professor, Department of Landscape Architecture, Ball State University. **Essays:** Film, Garden in (with David Doz); Literature, Garden in; Yoch, Florence.

Bevington, Michael J. Archivist, Stowe School, Buckingham. Author of several books, including *Stowe Church: A Guide,* 1995, *Stowe: The Garden and the Park,* 1994, and *Stowe: A Guide to the House,* 1990. Contributor to many publications, including *New Arcadian Journal,* 1997 and *Buckinghamshire Landscapes, 1444 to 1997,* edited by Sir Timothy Raison, 1997. **Essay:** Stowe.

Bjorkman, Lynn. Architectural Historian, Keweenaw National Historical Park, Calumet, Michigan. **Essays:** Bullard, Helen Elise (with Arnold R. Alanen); Manning, Warren H. (with Arnold R. Alanen).

Black, Brian. Assistant Professor, Department of History, Altoona College, Pennsylvania State University. **Essays:** Amusement Park; Lawn; Prairie Style.

Blalock, Joseph C., Jr. Assistant Professor, Department of Landscape Architecture, Ball State University. **Essays:** Paxton, Joseph; Victory Gardens: United States.

Boewe, Charles. Freelance writer and editor. Author of *Fitzpatrick's Rafinesque,* 1982, and *Prairie Albion,* 1962. Editor of *Précis ou Abrégé des Voyages, Travaux, et Recherches de C.S. Rafinesque,* 1987, and Rafinesque's *The World,* 1956. Contributor to numerous books and journals, including *American National Biography,* edited by John A. Garraty, 1999, and *Biographical Dictionary of American and Canadian Naturalists and Environmentalists,* 1997. **Essay:** Bartram Family; Lahore, Shalamar Bagh.

Bowe, Patrick. Freelance writer. Author of *Houses and Gardens of Portugal,* (co-author), 1998, *Gardens of the Caribbean,* (co-author), 1998, *The Complete Kitchen Garden,* 1996, and other books. Contributor to many collections and journals, including *Country Life Gardens,* edited by T. Robertson, 1998, *House and Garden,* and *Garden History.* **Essays:** Calcutta Botanic Garden; India; Sutherland, John.

Bramlage, Georgene A. Owner, Cave Hill Garden Design, freelance writer, photographer, and lecturer. **Essay:** Sargent, Charles Sprague.

Briggs, C. Stephen. Freelance Writer. **Essays:** Aranjuez; Archaeology.

Brighton, John Trevor. Department of Continuing Education, Sheffield University. Author of numerous books, including *Recollections of Bakewell,* 1994, *A Portrait of Bishop Otter College, Chichester,* 1992, and *Henry Gyles, Virtuoso and Glasspainter of York,* 1984. Editor of several books and journals including *150 Years: The Church Colleges in Higher Education,* 1983, and *Bakewell Historical Society Journal,* 1972–present. Contributor to many journals, including *Journal of Garden History,* 1994, and *Journal of the Walpole Society,* 1998. **Essay:** Chatsworth Gardens.

Bueno, Juan Antonio. Director and Associate Professor, Graduate Program in Landscape Architecture, Florida International University. Contributor to numerous books and journals, including *Greenways: The Beginning of an International Movement,* edited by J.G. Fabos and J. Ahern, 1995, *Landscape and Urban Planning,* 1995, *Places in Time: Historic Architecture and Landscapes of Miami,* edited by L. Alvarez and J.D. Fora, 1994, and *Landscape Journal,* 1993. **Essays:** Chinampas; El Escorial; Seville, Real Alcázar.

Burley, Jon Bryan. Assistant Professor, Landscape Architecture Program, Michigan State University, East Lansing. Editor of *DesignNet,* 1995–99. Contributor to *Landscape Research,*1996, *Journal of Natural Resource Life Science Education,* 1996, *Journal of Environmental*

Planning and Management, 1995, *Landscape and Urban Planning,* and *Greenways: The Beginning of an International Movement,* edited by J.G. Fabos and J. Ahern, 1995. **Essays:** Ecology; Pre-Columbian Gardens.

Butler, Peter. Graduate student, Department of Landscape Architecture, Iowa State University. **Essay:** Ruins.

Campbell, Susan. Freelance garden writer. Author of *Walled Kitchen Gardens,* 1998, *Charleston Kedding: A History of Kitchen Gardening,* 1996, *Cottesbrooke, an English Kitchen Garden,* 1987, and *A Calendar of Gardeners' Lore,* 1983. Contributor to several books and journals, including *The Country House Kitchen Garden 1600–1950,* edited by C. Anne Wilson, 1998, and *Garden History,* 1984, 1985. **Essays:** Frames and Pits; Pests and Diseases, Combating of; Potager (Kitchen Garden).

Cast, David. Professor, Department of History of Art, Bryn Mawr College. Author of *The Calumny of Apelles,* 1981. Editor of *Word and Image,* 1997–2000. Contributor to numerous book collections and journals, including *Journal of Society of Architectural Historians,* 1993, 1998, *Encyclopedia of Interior Design,* 1997, and *The Dictionary of Art,* 1996. **Essays:** Boboli Gardens; Bridgeman, Charles; Chelsea Physic Garden; Curtis, William; Garzoni, Villa; Knight, Richard Payne; Ligorio, Pirro; Marot, Daniel; Medici Family (with Charlotte Johnson); Prior Park; Studley Royal and Fountains Abbey; Vanbrugh, John; Vignola, Giacomo Barozzi da.

Cheng Liyao. Senior Editor, China Architecture and Building Press. Author of *Chinese Classical Gardens,* 1999, *Scholar's Garden,* 1992, *Imperial Garden Architecture,* 1992, and *Classical Chinese Gardens,* 1982. Editor of *Journal of Environmental Art,* 1991, *Eight Essays on Gardens,* 1990, *Commercial Environment,* 1988, and *An Analysis of Traditional Chinese Gardens,* 1986. Contributor to numerous anthologies and journals. **Essays:** Ban Mu Yuan (with Joseph C. Wang); Bei Hai Park (with Joseph C. Wang); Xiequ Yuan (with Joseph C. Wang).

Clark, Elizabeth Cernota. Graduate student, Mayborn Graduate Institute of Journalism, University of North Texas. Editor of *Gardens* 1994–2000, and many other publications. Contributor to many books, magazines and newspapers, including *Growing Fruits and Vegetables Organically,* 1994, *Texas Gardener,* 1982–88, *Horticulture,* 1987, and *Dallas Times-Herald,* 1983–89. **Essay:** Milotice.

Clayden, Andrew. Department of Landscape, University of Sheffield. **Essay:** Cemetery (with Jan Woudstra).

Clements, Terry L. Associate Professor, Department of Landscape Architecture, Virginia Polytechnic Institute and State University. **Essays:** Cautley, Marjorie Sewell; Steele, Fletcher; Williamsburg, Colonial.

Coffin, David. Howard Crosby Butler Memorial Professor of the History of Architecture, Emeritus, Department of Art and Archaeology, Princeton University. Author of *The English Garden: Meditation and Memorial,* 1994, *Gardens and Gardening in Papal Rome,* 1994, *The Villa in the Life of Renaissance Rome,* 1979, and *The Villa d'Este at Tivoli,* 1960. Editor of many collections and journals, including *Journal of Garden History,* 1981–91 and *The Italian Garden,* 1972. Contributor to numerous publications. **Essays:** Alberti, Leon Battista; Orsini, Villa.

Collett, Jill. Freelance garden historian and photographer. Author of *Bermuda: Her Plants and Gardens, 1609–1850,* 1987, and *Gardens of the Caribbean,* 1998. Contributor to *Cayman Airways Magazine,* 1989, *Bermudian,* 1987, and *Bermuda: A Living Museum of Roses,* edited by Elizabeth Carswell, 1984. **Essays:** Andromeda Gardens; Bermuda; Caribbean Islands and West Indies; Fortune, Robert; Michaux Family; Miller, Philip.

Constant, Caroline. Professor, Department of Architecture, University of Florida. Author of *A Non-Heroic Modernism: The Architecture of Eileen Gray,* 2000. Co-editor of *Eileen Gray: an Architecture for all Senses,* with Wilfried Wang, 1996. Contributor to many books and journals, including *Relating Architecture to Landscape,* edited by Jan Birksted, 1999, *Scandinavia: Luoghi, figure, gesti di una civiltà del paesaggio,* edited by Domenico Luciani and Luigi Latini, 1998, and *Casabella,* 1998. **Essay:** Woodland Cemetery.

Correy, Allan. Retired landscape architect and retired senior lecturer in landscape architecture, University of Sydney. Contributor to *Landscape Australia,* 1998, *Historic Environment,* 1996, *Planner,* 1987, *Planning Outlook,* 1977, and *Architecture in Australia,* 1972. **Essays:** Brown, Jocelyn; Sorensen, Paul.

Couch, Sarah. Freelance garden writer. Contributor to *Arboricultural Journal,* 1994, *Garden History,* 1992, and *Landscape Design,* 1992. **Essay:** Avenue and Allée.

Cowell, Fiona. Freelance writer. Author of *Arkadia: The Illusion and the Reality,* 1995. Contributor to *Garden History,* 1986, 1987, 1998. **Essay:** Arkadia.

Craig, Robert M. Professor, College of Architecture, Georgia Institute of Technology. Author of *John Portman:*

An Island on an Island, 1997, *Atlanta Architecture: Art Deco to Modern Classic, 1929–1959,* 1995, *From Plantation to Peachtree Street: A Century and a Half of Classic Atlanta Homes,* 1987. Editorial Board Member of *Nineteenth Century Studies,* 1987–present. Editor of *SECAC Review,* 1983–87. Contributor to numerous collections and journals. **Essays:** Xi Yuan; Yi Yuan.

Crane, Howard. Professor, Department of History of Art, Ohio State University. Author of *The Garden of Mosques: Hafiz Hüseyin Ayvansarayi's Account of the Muslim Religious Monuments of Ottoman Istanbul,* 1999. Board Member of *Muqarnas,* 1997–present. Contributor to *Journal of the Economic and Social History of the Orient,* 1993, *Bulletin of the Asia Institute,* 1987, and *Muqarnas,* 1983. **Essay:** Babur.

Crittenden, Victor. Director, Mulini Press. **Essays:** Australia; Shepherd, Thomas; Walling, Edna.

Cull, Gillian. Chinese Language Department, Beijing Normal University. **Essay:** China.

Daniels, Stephen. Professor of Cultural Geography, University of Nottingham. Author of *Joseph Wright,* 1999, *Humphry Repton: Landscape Gardening and the Geography of Georgian England,* 1999, and *Fields of Vision: Landscape Imagery and National Identity in England and the United States,* 1993. Editor of many books and journals, including *The Picturesque Landscape,* 1994. Contributor to several anthologies and periodicals. **Essays:** Picturesque; Repton, Humphry.

Daniels, Stevie O. Director of Publications, Lafayette College and freelance horticultural writer. Author of *The Wild Lawn Handbook: Alternatives to the Traditional Front Lawn,* 1995. Editor of several books and journals, including *Easy Lawns: Low Maintenance Native Grasses for Gardeners Everywhere,* 1999, and *Journal of Interdisciplinary History,* managing editor, 1991–94. Contributor to *Natural Home,* 2000, *Pennsylvania Magazine,* 1993–present. **Essays:** Africa; Fruit; Switzer, Stephen.

Das, Jana. Faculty member India Studio 2000, Department of Built Environment, University of New South Wales. Contributor to *Ivory,* 1998, *Indian Architect and Builder,* 1998, and *Pioneer,* 1997. **Essays:** Enclosure; Mogul Gardens.

Dass, Nirmal. Freelance writer. Author of *The Songs of the Saints from the Adi Granth,* 1999, *Rebuilding Babel: The Translations of W.H. Auden,* 1993, *Songs of Kabir from the Adi Granth,* 1991, and *The Avowing of King Arthur: A Modern Verse Translation,* 1987. Con-

tributor to *Studies in Medievalism,* 1998. **Essays:** Alexandria, Gardens of Ancient; Baba Wali, Garden of; Chashma Shahi; Iran; Mesopotamia, Ancient.

de Courtois, Stéphanie. Associate Professor, École Nationale Supérieure du Paysage, Versailles. Author of *Le potager du roi,* 1998. **Essay:** André, Edouard François.

de Jong, Erik A. (adviser). Professor, Faculty of Letters, Vrije Universiteit, Amsterdam.

de las Rivas Sanz, Juan Luis. Professor Titular, Instituto de Urbanisnica, Universidad de Valladolid. Author of *Planeamiento Urbano en la Europa Comunitaria,* 1994, *El Espagio Como Lugar. Sobre la Naturaleza de la Forma Urbana,* 1992, and *Arquitectura Urbana. Elementos de Teoria y Diseño,* 1990. Editor of several publications including *Territorio,* 1999 and *Avance de Directrices de Ordenacion Territorial de Valladolid y Entorno,* 1998. Contributor to many books and journals. **Essays:** La Granja; Spain.

Del Tredici, Peter. Director of Living Collections, Arnold Arboretum, Harvard University. Author of *Early American Bonsai,* 1989, *St. George and the Pygmies,* 1984, and *A Giant among the Dwarfs,* 1983. Contributor to many publications, including *Gingko biloba,* edited by T. Van Beek, 2000, *Science,* and *American Journal of Botany.* **Essay:** Arnold Arboretum (with Stephen A. Spongberg).

Dernie, David. Lecturer, Department of Architecture, University of Cambridge. Author of *Villa d'Este at Tivoli,* 1996, and *Victor Horta,* 1995. Contributor to *Architectural Review Quarterly,* 1997, *SCROOPE,* 1993–94, *Timeless Architecture,* edited by D. Cruickshank, 1985, and *Architects' Journal,* 1985. **Essay:** Este, Villa d'.

Desmond, Steven. Landscape consultant. Contributor to *The Garden,* 1995, and *Historic Garden,* 1994. **Essays:** Eremitage; Rievaulx Terrace; Schinkel, Karl Friedrich; Schwetzingen; Veitshöchheim; Wörlitz Park.

Downing, M.F. Reader in Landscape Design, University of Newcastle Upon Tyne. Author of several books including *Teaching Landscape Architecture in Europe,* 1992, and *Landscape Construction,* 1977. Editor of *Journal of Environmental Planning and Management,* 1991–92, and *Planning Outlook,* 1972–91. Contributor to many journals including *Ekistics,* 1996. **Essays:** Adam, William; Amsterdamse Bos; Bois de Boulogne; Chantilly; Chenonceaux; Crowe, Sylvia, Dame; Du Cerceau, Androuet; Evelyn, John; Gilpin, William Sawrey;

Het Loo Palace; Le Nôtre, André; Little Sparta; Mount; National Trust Gardens; Sissinghurst Castle Garden; Versailles.

Doz, David. Essay: Professor of Architecture, Head, Division of Architecture and Art, Norwich University. **Essay:** Film, Garden in (with Robert A. Benson).

Dunnett, Nigel. Lecturer, Department of Landscape, University of Sheffield. Contributor to *Landscape and Sustainability,* 1999, *Readers Guide to the Social Sciences,* 1999, *The Garden,* 1996–99, and *Landscape Design,* 1997–98. **Essays:** Natural Garden (Wild Garden); Thijsse Park; Urban Garden/Town Garden.

Edmondson, John. Head of Botany, National Museum and Galleries on Merseyside, Liverpool. Author of *James Bolton of Halifax,* 1995. Editor of *Index Nessensis,* 1998, *European Garden Flora,* 1997, *Flora Europaea,* 1993, and *Watsonia,* 1987–98. Contributor to numerous journals and anthologies. **Essays:** Bradley, Richard; Collinson, Peter.

Ehrlich, Marek. Department of Historic Gardens, Institute of Historic Monument Care, České Budějovice, Czech Republic. **Essays:** Červený Dvůr (with Marie Pavlátová); Hluboká (with Marie Pavlátová).

Evans, Susan Toby. Adjunct Professor, Department of Anthropology, Pennsylvania State University. Author of *Out of the Past,* 1992. Editor of *Ancient Mexico and Central America: An Encyclopedia,* 2000, *The Tectihuacan Valley Project Final Report,* 2000, and *Excavations at Cihuatecpan,* 1984. Contributor to many books and journals, including *The Seventy Wonders of the Ancient World,* edited by Chris Scarre, 1999. **Essays:** Chapultepec Park; Huaxtepec Park.

Ezhov, Valery. Director, Doctor of Technical Sciences, Nikita Botanical Gardens, National Scientific Center. **Essay:** Nikitsky Botanical Garden.

Farrar, Linda. Freelance garden writer. Author of *Ancient Roman Gardens,* 1998, and *The Gardens of Italy and the Western Provinces of the Roman Empire from 400 BC to 400 AD,* 1996. **Essays:** Pliny Family; Roman Gardens.

Fatsar, Kristóf. Assistant Professor, Department of Garden Arts, Szent Istvan University. **Essays:** Hungary; Petri, Bernhard.

Firsov, Gennady A. Botanic Garden, Komarov Botanical Institute. **Essay:** Komarov Botanical Institute Botanic Garden.

Floryan, Margrethe. Curator, Thorvaldsen Museum. Author of *Gardens of the Tsars: A Study of the Aesthetics, Semantics, and Uses of Late 18th Century Russian Gardens,* 1996. Contributor to *Dutch Yearbook for Garden and Landscape Architecture,* 1999, and *Landskab,* 1991, 1994. **Essays:** Bolotov, Andrei Timofeevich; Branitz; Denmark; Frederiksberg; Hirschfeld; Christian Cay Lorenz; København Botanisk Have; Krieger, Johan Cornelius; Liselund; Pavlovsk; Tivoli; Victory Gardens: Russia.

Fujii, Eijiro. Faculty of Horticulture, Chiba University. Author of several books including *Gardens as a Life-Style,* 2000, and *New Waves of Landscape,* 1999. Editor of *Journal of the Academic Society of Japanese Gardens,* 1997–2000, *Landscape Ecology,* 1999, and other publications. Contributor to numerous publications, including *Journal of the Japanese Institute for Landscape Architecture,* 1978–2000. **Essay:** Kokushi (Muso Soseki).

Gabites, Isobel. Freelance garden writer. Author of *The Native Garden: Design Themes from Wild New Zealand,* 1998, *Wellington's Living Cloak: A Guide to the Natural Plant Communities,* 1993, and *Roots of Fire: A Guide to the Plant Ecology of Tongariro National Park,* 1987. **Essays:** Otari-Wilton's Bush Native Botanic Garden and Forest Reserve; Wellington Botanic Garden.

Galbraith, David Allan. Manager of Biodiversity Projects, Royal Botanical Gardens. Editor of *Partnerships for Plants: Conservation, Biodiversity, and Botanical Gardens in Canada,* 1997. Contributor to many books and journals, including *Encyclopedia of the World's Zoos,* 2001, *The Public Garden,* 1998, and *Encyclopedia of Molecular Biology,* 1994. **Essay:** Ontario, Royal Botanical Gardens.

Ganapathy, Kartik Ram. Lecturer, Department of Architecture, Vastukala Academy, Indraprastha University; visiting faculty, India Studio 2000, Faculty Built Environment, University of New South Wales. Editor of *The Taj Mahal of Agra "Heaven on Earth,"* 1999. Contributor to *Ivory,* 1998. **Essays:** Agra Fort; Red Fort.

Gaponenko, Nikolay B. Scientific Secretary, M.M. Grishko National Botanic Garden, National Academy of Sciences of Ukraine. **Essay:** Grishko National Botanic Gardens.

Garland, Anne. Freelance writer. Author of *The Way We Grow,* 1993, *Safe Food,* 1993, and *Women Activists,* 1988. Editor of *Brooklyn Botanic Garden Twenty-First Century Garden Guides,* 1996. Contributor to

Brooklyn Botanic Garden's Gardener's Desk Reference, 1998. **Essay:** Brooklyn Botanic Garden.

Gerber, Judith. Freelance writer. Contributor to *American National Biography,* 1997, 1999, *A-Z Encyclopedia of 20th Century Music,* 1997, *International Dictionary of University Histories,* 1996, *Encyclopedia of Fictional People,* edited by Seth Godin, 1996, and *Encyclopedia of Global Industries,* 1995. **Essays:** Burbank, Luther; Herbs: Culinary (with Diana Baskervyle-Glegg); Journalism; Magazine; Market Garden; Terrace Garden; Vegetable Garden.

Gladigau, Ute-Harriet. Ph.D. candidate, Institute of Art History, Ludwig-Maximilians-University. Contributor to *Es muss nicht immer Rembrandt sein,* exhib. cat., edited by Robert Stalla, 1999. **Essay:** Girard, Dominique.

Gleason, Kathryn L. Associate Professor, Department of Landscape Architecture, Cornell University. Editor of *Archaeology of Garden and Field,* with Naomi F. Miller, 1994, and *Journal of the Conservation and Management of Archaeological Sites,* 1993. Contributor to *Journal of Roman Archaeology,* 1998, *Caesarea Maritima: A Retrospective after Two Millennia,* edited by Avner Raban and Kenneth Holum, 1996, and *Journal of Garden History,* 1994, and other publications. **Essay:** Tomb Garden.

Glenn, John. Department of Archaeology, University of York. **Essay:** Derby Arboretum.

Goodman, Emily N. Freelance writer and gardener. Editor of and contributor to *Wandering South,* forthcoming. **Essays:** Animals in Gardens; Fruit Garden.

Gottesleben, Tilman. Institute of Greenplanning and Garden Architecture, University of Hannover. **Essay:** Sanspareil.

Grillner, Katja. Researcher, Department of Architecture, Royal Institute of Technology, Stockholm. Author of *Ramble, Linger, and Gaze: Dialogues from the Landscape Garden,* 2000, *Four Essays Framed: Questions of Imagination, Interpretation and Representation in Architecture,* 1997, and *Automata, Perspectives and Music: Poetic Instruments in the Written Garden of Salomon de Caus,* 1995. Editorial board member of *Nordic Journal of Architectural Research* and guest editor of *Nordic Journal of Architectural Research,* 1998. Contributor to numerous books and journals. **Essay:** Whately, Thomas.

Gröning, Gert. Professor, Institute for History and Theory of Design, University of Arts, Berlin. Co-author of several books including *Grüne Biographien,* with

Joachim Wolkschke-Bulmahn, 1997, *Die Liebe zur Landschaft,* with Joachim Wolkschke-Bulmahn, 1986, 1995, and *Von der Stadtgärtnerei zum Grünflächenamt,* with Joachim Wolkschke-Blumahn, 1990. Editor of various book collections and journals including *Arbeiten zur sozialwissenschaftlich orientierten Freiraumplanung,* with Ulfert Herlyn, 1980–present, *Landscape Research,* 1995–present, and *Journal of Garden History,* 1996. Contributor to many publications. **Essays:** Barth, Erwin; Germany (with Joachim Wolschke-Bulmahn); Lange, Willy (with Joachim Wolschke-Bulmahn); Lesser, Ludwig; Pniower, Georg Béla; Wiepking-Jürgensmann, Heinrich Friedrich.

Grove, Carol. Landscape historian. Contributor to *Albion,* 1999, and *Journal of the New England Garden History Society,* 1998. **Essays:** Missouri Botanical Garden; Vaux, Calvert.

Hahn, Hazel. Lecturer, Department of History, University of California, Berkeley. Contributor to *Encyclopedia of Historians and Historical Writing,* 1999, and *Makers of Western Culture, 1800–1914,* edited by John Powell, 1999. **Essays:** Jardin Anglais; Jardin des Plantes; Le Blond, Alexandre-Jean-Baptiste; Philosopher's Garden.

Hajós, Beatrix. Art historian. Author of *Die Schönbrunner Schlossgärten,* 1995. Contributor to *Dehio-Handbuch der Kunstdenkmäler Österreichs,* 1996, and *Historische Gärten in Österreich,* 1993. **Essays:** Austria (with Géza Hajós); Hellbrunn; Laxenburg; Schönbrunn.

Hajós, Géza (adviser). Associate Professor, Department of Historic Gardens, Bundesdenkmalamt, Vienna. Author of several books including *Park Laxenburg,* 1998, and *Romantische Gärten der Aufklärung,* 1989. Editor of *Die Gartenkunst,* 1989–2001, *Journal of Garden History,* 1988–93, and *Historische Gärten in Österreich,* 1993. Contributor to numerous journals and anthologies. **Essay:** Austria (with Beatrix Hajós).

Halpern, Linda Cabe (adviser). Associate Professor of Art History, Dean of General Education, James Madison University. Contributor to *Journal of Garden History,* 1995, *Garden History: Issues, Approaches, Methods,* 1992, and *Classic Ground: British Artists and the Landscape of Italy, 1740–1830,* edited by Duncan Bull, 1981. **Essays:** Pope, Alexander; Visual Arts, Garden in.

Harris, Dianne. Assistant Professor, Department of Landscape Architecture, University of Illinois, Urbana-Champaign. Editor of *Situating Villas and Gardens in Early Modern Italy and France,* with Mirka Benes, forthcoming. Contributor to *Landscape Journal,* 1994,

1998, *Regional Garden Design in the United States,* 1995, and *Journal of Garden History,* 1990. **Essays:** Women as Gardeners.

Heinrich, Vroni. Institut für Landschaftsarchitektur, Technische Universität Berlin. Editor of *Stadtgrün,* with Goerd Peschken, 1985, *Hermann Mattern. Gärten, Gartenlandschaften, Häuser,* 1982, and *Gustav Meyer zum 100. Todestag,* with Goerd Peschken. 1978. Contributor to numerous books and journals, including *Gartenpraxis,* 1996, and *History of Garden Design,* edited by Monique Mosser and Georges Teyssot, 1991. **Essay:** Mattern, Hermann.

Helphand, Kenneth. Professor of Landscape Architecture, University of Oregon. Co-author of *Yard Street Park: The Design of Suburban Open Space,* 1994, and author of *Colorado: Visions of an American Landscape,* 1991. Editor of *Landscape Journal,* 1995–present. Contributor to *Journal of Garden History, Landscape,* and other journals. **Essays:** Israel; Vernacular Garden.

Henderson, Paula. Freelance writer. Contributor to *Garden History,* 1992, 1999, *Patronage, Culture, and Power: The Early Cecils, 1558–1612,* 1999, *Apollo,* 1997, and *Albion's Classicism,* edited by Lucy Gent, 1995. **Essays:** Arbor; Bacon, Francis; Buildings, Garden; Formal Garden Style; Furniture, Garden; Pleasance.

Herrington, Susan. Assistant Professor, Department of Landscape Architecture, University of British Columbia. Contributor to *Built Environment,* 1999, *Landscape and Urban Planning,* 1998, *Studies in the History of Gardens and Designed Landscapes International Quarterly,* 1998, and *Landscape Journal,* 1997. **Essays:** Children and Gardening; Furttenbach, Joseph; Meyer, Gustav; Sckell, Friedrich Ludwig von.

Hollar, Sherman J. Assistant Editor, Encyclopedia Britannica. Editor of *Britannica Book of the Year,* 1995–2001, and *Yearbook of Science and the Future,* 1999–2000. **Essays:** Lutyens, Edwin; Tessin Family.

Hoyles, Martin. Senior Lecturer, Department of Cultural Studies, University of East London. Author of several books, including *Remember Me: Achievements of Mixed-Race People—Past and Present,* with Asher Hoyles, 1999, *The Gardener's Perpetual Almanack,* 1997, and *The Story of Gardening,* 1991. Editor of many anthologies and journals, including *The Politics of Childhood,* 1989 and *More Valuable than Gold,* 1985. **Essays:** Cobbett, William; Gardener in Society; Kensal Green Cemetery; Poetry, Garden in; Politics of Gardening.

Hrdličková, Věna. Professor Emeritus, Far Eastern Department, Charles University, Prague. Author of many volumes with Zdeněk Hrdlička, including *Chinesische Garten Kunst,* 1998, *Umění Čínských Zahrad,* 1997, and *The Art of Japanese Gardening.* Editor of several books and journals, including *O Kultuře Čaje V Číně,* 1998, and *Bonsai Zpravodaj,* 1992–94. Contributor to numerous anthologies and periodicals. **Essays:** Shi Zi Lin; Wang Chuan Bie Ye; Yuan Ming Yuan.

Hunt, Martha A. Assistant Professor, Department of Landscape Architecture, Ball State University. Contributor to *Pioneers of American Landscape Design: An Annotated Bibliography,* edited by Margherita Tarr, 1995. **Essay:** Grass.

Hutcheon, Jane. Librarian, Royal Botanic Garden, Edinburgh. **Essays:** Addison, Joseph; Aiton, William; Pisa, Orto Botanico dell'Università di.

Iannotti, Marie. Freelance garden writer. Editor of *The Gardener's Guide to Ulster and Dutchess Counties,* 1997–99. Contributor to *Ulster Home Gardener,* 2000, *Dig,* 1996–97, and *Dutchess Land and Living,* 1996. **Essays:** Cottage Garden; Garden Club; Garden Show and Flower Show; Hooker, William Jackson and Joseph Dalton Hooker; Wildflower; Wilson, Ernest Henry.

Iversen, Richard R. Associate Professor, Department of Ornamental Horticulture, State University of New York, Farmingdale. Author of *The Exotic Garden: Designing with Tropical Plants in Almost Any Climate,* 1999. Contributor to *American Gardener,* 1996, *Fine Gardener,* 1996, *American Horticulturist,* 1994, *Public Garden,* 1994, and *Hortechnology,* 1994. **Essays:** Indoor Garden; Hothouse Plant; Rose Garden; Weed.

Jashemski, Wilhelmina F. (adviser). Professor, Department of History, University of Maryland. **Essay:** Vesuvian Gardens.

Johnson, Charlotte. Freelance garden writer. Contributor to *New Dictionary of National Biography,* 2001, *Surrey Gardens Trust Newsletter,* 1999, and *Essex Gardens Trust Journal,* 1999. **Essays:** Cane, Percy S.; Lante, Villa; Medici Family (with David Cast).

Johnson, Lauri MacMillan. Associate Professor, School of Landscape Architecture, College of Architecture, Planning, and Landscape Architecture, University of Arizona.

Essays: Burle Marx, Roberto; Design Fundamentals; Rose, James; United States.

Jones, David. Senior Lecturer, Landscape Architecture, School of Architecture, Landscape Architecture, and Urban Design, University of Adelaide. Author of *Gardens in South Australia 1840–1940*, 1998, and *Designed Landscapes of South Australia*, 1997. Editor of *Landmark*, 1990–present, and *Landscape and Urban Planning*, 1993–present. Contributor to many publications, including *Urban Design Studies*, 1998. **Essays:** Forest Lodge; Indonesia; Kebun Raya Botanic Garden; Malaysia; Singapore Botanic Gardens; Sydney, Royal Botanic Gardens.

Jones, Tresa. Freelance garden writer. **Essay:** Ornamental Plant.

Jørgensen, Karsten. Professor, Department of Landscape Planning, Agricultural University of Norway. Author of *Formspråk: Landskapsarkitekturen*, 1989. Contributor to many journals, including *Landscape Review*, 1998, and *Garden History*, 1997. **Essays:** Andersson, Sven-Ingvar; Moen, Olav Leif; Norway; Reistad, Karen; Sørensen, Carl Theodor.

Joselow, Evie T. Adjunct Professor, New York University. **Essay:** Garden City.

Katen, Brian. Assistant Professor, Landscape Architecture, Virginia Polytechnic Institute. Contributor to *Landscape Journal*, 1999. **Essay:** Guévrékian, Gabriel.

Keane, Marc Peter. Guest Lecturer, Department of Landscape Architecture, Kyoto University of Art and Design. Author of *Sakuteiki: Translation and Annotation*, with Jiro Takei, 2001, and *Japanese Garden Design*, 1996. **Essays:** Japan; Joruri-ji; Sakuteiki; Zen Garden.

Kenworthy, Richard. Associate Professor, Landscape Architecture, College of Architecture, Design, and Construction, Auburn University. Author of *Writings on the Gardens of Italy, 1800–1939*, 1990, and *Italian Gardens Transplanted: Renaissance Revival Landscape Design in America, 1850–1939*, 1988. Contributor to *Journal of Garden History*, 1990, 1991. **Essays:** Eliot, Charles William; Platt, Charles A.

King, Julia. Freelance garden writer. **Essays:** Biltmore House; Giulia, Villa; Madama, Villa.

Kiriushina, Ludmila. State Museum Estate Archangelskoye. Contributor to *Istoria Sadova*, edited by D. Shvidkovsky, 1994, and numerous other publications. **Essay:** Archangelskoye.

Kisling, Vernon N., Jr. Collection Management Coordinator, Marston Science Library, University of Florida. **Essays:** Park; Zoological Garden.

Koch, Ebba. Adjunct Professor, Institute of Art History, University of Vienna. Author of *Mughal Art and Imperial Ideology*, 2000, and *Mughal Architecture*, 1991. Contributor to many books and journals, including *Gardens in the Time of the Great Muslim Empires: Theory and Design*, edited by Attilio Petruccioli, 1997, *Muqarnas*, 1997, 1994, and *Environmental Design*, 1986, 1991. **Essay:** Taj Mahal.

Köhler, Marcus. Professor, Fachhochschule Neubrandenburg. Co-author of *Gartenkunst in Braunschweig. Von fürstlichen Gärten des Barock zum Bürgerpark der Gründerzeit*, with Hans-Joachim Tute, 1989. Contributor to multiple books and journals including *Encyclopedia of Interior Design*, 1996, *Garden History*, 1997, *Gartenkunst*, 1995, and *Museums Journal*, 1996. **Essays:** Busch Family; Caserta, La Reggia di.

Kolšek, Alenka. Conservationist advisor, Institute for the Conservation of Cultural Heritage, Celje, Slovenia. Contributor to numerous publications, including *Piranesi*, 1999, *Vestnik*, 1998, and *Historical Parks and Gardens in Slovenia*, 1995. **Essay:** Dornava.

Komara, Ann E. Assistant Professor, Landscape Architecture, University of Colorado, Denver. Contributor to *Landscape Journal*, 1998–99, *Landscape Architecture*, 1991, and *Abstracting the Landscape: The Artistry of Landscape Architect A.E. Bye*, edited by Eliza Pennypacker, 1991. **Essays:** Alphand, Jean-Charles Adolphe; Buttes Chaumont.

Krinke, Rebecca. Assistant Professor, Department of Landscape Architecture, University of Minnesota. Contributor to *Manufactured Sites: Rethinking the Post-Industrial Landscape*, edited by Niall Kirkwood, 2001, and *Land Forum*, 2000. **Essays:** Noguchi, Isamu; Tea Garden.

Kvashny, Alon. Professor and Chair, Landscape Architecture Program, Division of Resource Management, West Virginia University. Contributor to several publications, including *Journal of Landscape and Urban Planning*, and *Landscape Journal*. **Essays:** Education: Garden Design; Landscape Architecture; Lighting.

Lack, H. Walter. Professor, Director, Botanic Garden and Botanical Museum Berlin-Dahlem, Freie Universität, Berlin. Author of numerous books, including *The Flora Graeca Story*, 1999, and *A Garden for Eternity: The Codex Liechtenstein*, 2000. Contributor to numerous collections and journals. **Essays:** Belvedere Palaces; Berlin-Dahlem, Botanischer Garten; Botanical Illustration; Collecting, Plant; Padova, Orto Botanico dell'Università di; Palermo, Orto Botanico dell'Università di.

Laird, Mark (adviser). Adjunct Professor, Faculty of Architecture, Landscape, and Design, University of Toronto. Author of *The Flowering of the Landscape Garden: English Pleasure Grounds, 1720–1800*, 1999, and *The Formal Garden: Traditions of Art and Nature*, 1992. Contributor to numerous anthologies and journals, including *John Evelen's "Elysium Britannicum" and European Gardening*, 1998, and *Mark Catesby and the Natural History of Carolina, Florida, and the Bahama Islands*, 1998. **Essays:** American Garden; Nuneham Courtenay; Parterre and Plate-Bande; Shrubbery.

Laurie, Michael. Professor Emeritus, Department of Landscape Architecture, University of California, Berkeley. Author of *75 Years of Landscape Architecture at Berkeley*, 1988–92, *An Introduction to Landscape Architecture*, 1975, 1986. Contributor to numerous books and journals, including *Landscape*, 1993, and *Ecological Design and Planning*, edited by G. Thompson and F. Steiner, 1997. **Essays:** Eckbo, Garrett; Farrand, Beatrix Jones.

Lauterbach, Iris. Research Department, Zentralinstitut für Kunstgeschichte, Munich. Author of *Der französische Garten am Ende des Ancien Regime*, 1987. Editor of several collections, including *Die Landshuter Stadtresidensz*, 1998, *Jacques Boycean, Traité du Jardinage*, 1997, and *Le Fontane di Roma*, 1996. Contributor to many books and journals, including *Interieurs der Goethezeit*, edited by Christoph Hölz, 1999. **Essays:** Aldobrandini, Villa; Blondel, Jacques-François; Boyceau, Jacques de la Barauderie; Hortus Palatinus; Mollet Family; Neugebäude; Parc Monceau.

Lawalree, André. Chef de département honoraire, Jardin botanique national de Belgique, Meise. Author of *Plantes sauvages protégées en Belgique*, 1981, *Introduction à la flore de la Belgique*, 1978, *Flore générale de Belgique, Spermatophytes*, 1952, and *Flore générale de Belgique, Ptéridophytes*, 1950. Editor of *Bulletin de la Société royal de Botanique de Belgique*, 1950–65. Contributor to several anthologies and journals. **Essays:** Belgique, Jardin Botanique National de.

Leach, Helen. Associate Professor, Department of Anthropology, University of Otago, Dunedin. Author of *1,000 Years of Gardening in New Zealand*, 1984. Contributor to *Antiquity*, 1997, *Journal of the Royal New Zealand Institute of Horticulture*, 1991, 1994, 1996, *Garden History*, 1982, 1995, and *Oxford Companion to Gardens*, edited by A. Jellicoe et al., 1986. **Essay:** New Zealand.

Leith-Ross, Prudence. Author of *The Florilegium of Alexander Marshal in the Collection of Her Majesty the Queen*, 1999, and *The John Tradescants: Gardeners to the Rose and Lily Queen*, 1984. Contributor to *Garden History*, 1993, 1997, *British Heritage*, 1985, and *Apollo*, 1984. **Essay:** Tradescant Family.

Levi, Anthony H.T. Freelance writer. Author and editor of numerous books and contributor to many scholarly journals. **Essays:** Alhambra; Enghien; Herbal; Italy (with Candice A. Shoemaker); Kleve; Landscape Garden Style; Leiden, Universiteit Hortus Botanicus; Oraienbaum (Lomonosov); Oxford Botanic Garden; Polonnaruwa Gardens; Restoration, Landscape; Stadtpark; Uppsala Universitet Botaniska Trädgården; Wisley; Zeist; Zocher, Jan David.

Libby, Valencia. Associate Professor, Department of Landscape Architecture and Horticulture, Temple University. Contributor to *Pioneers of American Landscape Design*, edited by C. Birnbaum, 2000, *Breaking Ground: Examining the Vision and Practice of Historic Landscape Restoration*, 1999, and *The Influence of Women on the Southern Landscape*, 1997. **Essay:** Coffin, Marian.

Littlewood, A.R. Professor, Department of Classical Studies, University of Western Ontario. Author of *The Progymnasmata of Ioannes Geometres*, 1972. Guest Editor of *Journal of Garden History*, 1992. Contributor to many books and journals, including *Byzantine Court Culture from 829 to 1204*, edited by H. Maguire, 1997, *Journal of Garden History*, 1992, and *Der Garten von der Antike bis zum Mittelalter*, edited by M. Carroll-Spilleche, 1992. **Essays:** Byzantium; Dioscorides, Pedanius; Greece; Linnaeus, Carl; Theophrastus.

Liu Dun-zhen. Essays: Canglang Ting (with Joseph C. Wang and Xu Dejia); Wangshi Yuan (with Joseph C. Wang and Xu Dejia).

Livingston, Margaret. Assistant Professor, School of Landscape Architecture, University of Arizona. Editor of *Journal of Arid Environments*, 2001, and *Plants for Dry Climates*, 2000. Contributor to several publications, including *Aridus*, 2000, *Urban Ecosystems*, 1998, and *Journal of Arid Environments*, 1997. **Essay:** Xeriscape.

Luferov, Alexander N. Docent, Department of Botany, Sechenov Moscow Medical Academy. Author of *Botanical Nomenclature*, 1995. Contributor to many journals, including *Botanical Journal*, 1999, 2000, and *Komarovia*, 1999. **Essay:** Kolomenskoye Palace and

Gardens (with Loubov I. Lyashenko and Arkadiy Vergunov).

Lundquist, Kjell. Lecturer, Department of Landscape Planning, Swedish University of Agricultural Sciences, Alnarp. Author and editor of many publications. Contributor to numerous books and journals, including *Parks and Gardens in Sweden,* 1997, and *Museologia Scientifica,* 1998. Essays: Abelin, Carl Rudolf Zacharias; Box; Hårleman, Johan; Sweden.

Lyashenko, Loubov I. Museum-reserve Kolomenskoye. Author of *Application of Piretroids and Dimilin in Forestry in USSR and Abroad,* 1986, and *Application of Chemical Means of Combating Needle and Leaf-Gnawing Pests,* 1984. Editor of *Science and Advanced Experience Achievements in Wood Protection from Pests,* 1987. Contributor to multiple publications, including *World Home,* 1996. Essays: Kolomenskoye Palace and Gardens (with Alexander N. Luferov and Arkadiy Vergunov).

Magallanes, Fernando. Associate Professor, Department of Landscape Architecture, North Carolina State University. Essays: Barragán, Luis; Parque Güell.

Magnuson, Marilyn. Temporary Instructor, Department of Horticulture, Iowa State University. Essays: Ornament, Garden; Tools, Garden.

Major, Judith K. Professor, School of Architecture and Urban Design, University of Kansas. Author of *To Live in the New World: A.J. Downing and American Landscape Gardening,* 1997. Contributor to many books and journals, including *Journal of Garden History,* 1990, 1991, 1995, and *The Architecture of Western Gardens,* edited by Monique Mosser and Georges Teyssot, 1991. Essays: Downing, Andrew Jackson; Wardian Case.

Mann, William A. Professor, School of Environmental Design, University of Georgia, Athens. Editor of *Landscape Architecture: An Illustrated History in Timelines, Site Plans, and Biography,* 1993, and *Space and Time in Landscape Architectural History,* 1982. Contributor to *Landscape and Urban Planning,* 1998, and *Landscape,* 1986. Essay: Cameron, Charles.

Manning, Martin J. Librarian, United States Department of State. Contributor to numerous publications, including *Encyclopedia of New England Culture,* 2000, *American National Biography,* edited by John A. Garraty, 2000, and *Encyclopedia of Europe since 1945,* 2000. Essays: Drottningholm; History; Mount Vernon; Pleasure Garden; Regency Gardening.

Martin, John. Professor, Department of Landscape Architecture and Regional Planning, University of Massachusetts, Amherst. Contributor to numerous books and journals, including *Portugese Studies Review,* 1994, *Grolier Academic Encyclopedia,* 1992, and *Historical Atlas of Massachusetts,* 1991. Essays: Atget, Eugène; Bridge; Generalife; Howard, Ebenezer; Portugal; Victorian Period.

Mason, Susan Garrett. Freelance writer. Author of *Southwinds Gourmet,* 1998, and *Costal Erosion and Archeological Resources on National Wildlife Refuges in the Southeast,* 1983. Editor of *Southeastern Flower Show Guide,* 1997, and *Peachtree Papers,* 1992. Contributor to *Icons of Garden Design,* 2001, and other publications. Essay: Vizcaya Villa.

Mawson, David. Retired conservation architect. Contributor to *Royal Society of the Arts Journal,* 1984, and *Landscape Design,* 1979. Essay: Mawson, Thomas Hayton.

McBurney, Henrietta. Deputy Curator, Print Room, Royal Library, Windsor Castle. Essay: Catesby, Mark.

McCracken, Donal P. Professor, Department of History, University of Durban, Westville. Author of several books including *Gardens of Empire,* 1997, *A New History of Durban Botanic Gardens,* 1996, and *Natal the Garden Colony,* with P.A. McCracken, 1990. Contributor to numerous journals. Essays: Botanic Station; Labels, Plant; South Africa.

McNeur, Lorna Anne. Lecturer, Department of Architecture, University of Cambridge. Contributor to numerous books and journals, including *Architects' Journal,* 1991, 1995, SCROOP, 1990, 1994, 1999, and *The International Dictionary of Architecture,* 1993. Essays: Central Park; Renaissance Garden Style.

McPeck, Eleanor M. Radcliffe Institute for Adanced Studies, Harvard University. Co-author of *Beatrix Farrand's American Landscapes,* with Diana Balmori and Diane McGuire, 1985. Contributor to numerous journals and exhibition catalogs. Essay: Dumbarton Oaks.

Mejía, Cecilia (adviser). Independent consultant, Bogotá, Colombia. Author of *Gardens of Colombia,* 1996.

Messer Diehl, Elizabeth R. Assistant Professor, Landscape Architecture Program, West Virginia University. Editor of *Journal of Therapeutic Horticulture,* 1999, 2000. Contributor to *Regional Planning Journal,* 2000, and *Journal of Therapeutic Horticulture,* 1996, 1998. **Essays:** Hospital Garden; Saiho-ji; Sculpture Garden.

Meyers, Karen. Assistant Professor, Department of English, Heidelberg College. **Essays:** Belgium; Kingdon-Ward, Francis.

Miles, Paul. Freelance garden writer. Author of *The Mitchell Beazley Pocket Guide to Garden Plants,* with Hugh Johnson, 1981, and *Garden Britain,* 1980. Contributor to numerous books and journals. **Essays:** Alpine Garden (with Candice Shoemaker).

Miller, William C. Professor and Dean, Graduate School of Architecture, University of Utah. Author of *Alvar Aalto: An Annotated Bibliography,* 1984. Editor of *The Architecture of the In-Between,* 1990, *Journal of Architectural Education,* 1984–87, guest editor 1980, and *Reflections,* 1984–87. Contributor to numerous collections. **Essay:** Aalto, Alvar.

Mills, Frank. Faculty, Celtic Studies Program, Marylhurst University. Author of *Oran Mór: Celtic Wisdom for a New Millennium,* 1999. Editor and publisher of *Bright's Feast: The Journal of Celtic Thought.* Contributor to *Bright's Feast,* 1996–99, and *Encyclopedia of Monasticism,* 1999. **Essays:** Egypt: Medieval; Medieval Garden Style; Monastic Garden; Sanctuary Garden; Symbolism in Eastern Gardens.

Morris, Sandra. Landscape historian and Lecturer, AA School of Architecture, London. Contributor to *Between Architecture and Landscape,* edited by Jan Birkstead, 1999 and *Garden History,* 1991, 1993. **Essays:** Annevoie, Jardins d'; London, George; Wise, Henry.

Müller, Ulrich. Professor, Friedrich Schiller Universität, Jena, Germany. **Essays:** Kent, William; Rousham House.

Murta, Kenneth Hall. Professor Emeritus, School of Architecture, University of Sheffield. **Essay:** Jones, Inigo.

Myers, Mary E. Assistant Professor, Department of Landscape Architecture, College of Design, North Carolina State University, Raleigh. Contributor to *Design News,* 1999, and *Great American Learning Vacations,* 1994. **Essays:** Parkway; Shugaku-in.

Nadenicek, Daniel Joseph. Associate Professor of Landscape Architecture, Pennsylvania State University. Editor of *What Do We Expect to Learn from Our History,* 1996. Contributor to *Landscape and Urban Planning,*

1997, *Nature and Ideology: Natural Garden Design in the Twentieth Century,* edited by Joachim Woschke-Bulmahn, 1997, and *Pioneers of American Landscape Design II,* edited by Charles Birnbaum and Julie Fix, 1995. **Essays:** Cleveland, Horace William Shaler (with William H. Tishler); Copeland, Robert Morris (with William H. Tishler); Greenough, Horatio.

Neckar, Lance M. Professor, Department of Landscape Architecture, University of Minnesota. Author of *Built in Milwaukee,* 1981. Editor of *Landscape Journal,* special edition, 1988. Contributor to many books and journals, including *Midwestern Landscape Architecture,* 2000, *The Regional Garden in the United States,* 1995, and *Garden History,* 1991. **Essay:** Tunnard, Christopher.

Nelson, E. Charles (adviser). Independent scholar and freelance writer. Author of numerous books and articles. **Essays:** Bog Garden; Darwin, Charles, and Down House; Glasnevin, National Botanic Gardens; Herbarium; Ireland; Mount Stewart; Niven, James; Turner, Richard.

Nicholson, Sandra. Senior Lecturer, Faculty of Horticulture, Writtle College. **Essays:** Allotment; Plants in Garden Design and Gardens.

Nolan, Fran. Ph.D. candidate, Department of Art History, University of Queensland. Author of *"Fuzei": A Breeze of Feeling,* 1995. Contributor to *Landscape Australia,* 1997. **Essays:** Katsura Imperial Villa; Ryōan-ji; Shisen-dō; Tenryū-ji.

Novák, Zdeněk. Freelance writer. **Essay:** Lednice-Valtice Cultural Landscape.

Orgler, Lisa Nunamaker. Landscape Architect, Facilities Planning and Management, Iowa State University. **Essay:** Nymphenburg, Palace of.

Pacáková-Hošt'álková, Božena. Specialist for historic gardens and landscape, State Institute for the Preservation of Historic Monuments, Prague, Czech Republic. Author of *Zahrady a parky v Čechách, na Moravě a ve Slezsku,* with Jaroslav Petrů, Dušan Riedl, and Antonín M. Svoboda, 1999, and *Bratislavské parky,* 1973. Editor of *Portál,* 1987, 1988, and *Pražské zahrady a parky,* 2000. Contributor to many books and journals, including *Zahradnický slovník naučný,* edited by František Mareček, 1996–2000. **Essays:** Ledebour Garden; Vrtba Garden.

Palazzo, Danilo. Researcher, Dipartimento di Architettura e Pianificazione, Politecnico di Milano. Author of

Sulle spalle di giganti. Le matrici della pianificazione ambientale negli Stati Uniti, 1997. Contributor to numerous anthologies and journals, including *Landscape and Urban Planning,* 2000, and *Il senso del paesaggio,* edited by Paolo Castelnovi, 2000. **Essay:** Rastrelli, Bartolomeo Francesco.

Parshin, Artyom. Deputy Director, Aptekarsky Ogorod, Moscow University Botanic Garden. **Essays:** Moscow University Botanic Garden; Russian Academy of Sciences, Main Botanic Garden.

Paterson, Allen. Independent scholar and freelance writer. Author of *Designing a Garden,* 1992, *Herbs in the Garden,* 1985, *A History of the Rose,* 1983, *Plants for Shade,* 1980, and *Gardens of Southern England,* 1978. Consulting editor of *Guide to Creative Gardening,* 1984. Contributor to several book collections and journals. **Essays:** Bulb; Canada; Climber; Herb Garden.

Pavlátová, Marie. Department of Historic Gardens, Institute of Historic Monument Care, České Budějovice, Czech Republic. Author of *Hluboká nad Vltavou,* with I. Popelová, 1994. Co-contributor to *Garden - Park - Landscape, the Journal of the Landscape and Garden Society of Czech Republic,* with I. Popelová, 1991. **Essays:** Červený Dvůr (with Marek Ehrlich); Hluboká (with Marek Ehrlich).

Perrotta, Marc. Freelance writer. Contributor to forthcoming *Encyclopedia of Twentieth Century Architecture.* **Essay:** Amphitheater/Theater.

Pett, Douglas Ellory. Freelance writer. Author of *Parks and Gardens of Cornwall,* 1998, and *Historic Gardens of Cornwall,* with D. Hunt, 1991. Contributor to *Cornish Garden,* 1992–99. **Essay:** Tresco Abbey Gardens.

Philippon, Daniel J. Assistant Professor, Department of Rhetoric, University of Minnesota. Editor of *The Friendship of Nature: A New England Chronicle of Birds and Flowers,* by Mabel Osgood Wright, 1999, and *The Height of Our Mountains: Nature Writing from Virginia's Blue Ridge Mountains and Shenandoah Valley,* with Michael P. Branch, 1998. Contributor to numerous books and journals, including *Southern Literary Journal,* 1998, *Appalachian Heritage,* 1998, and *The Literature of Nature: An International Sourcebook,* edited by Patrick Murphy, 1998. **Essay:** Bailey, Liberty Hyde.

Pullan, Wendy. Lecturer, Department of Architecture, University of Cambridge, and Fellow, Clare College, Cambridge. Author of *Urban Order Transformed,* forthcoming. Editor of *Making Architecture,* forthcom-

ing, and *Structure in Science and Art,* 2000. Contributor to many book collections, including *Text and Artifact in the Religions of Mediterranean Antiquity,* edited by S. G. Wilson and M. Desjardins, 2000, and *Memory and Oblivion,* edited by W. Reinink and J. Stumpel, 1999. **Essays:** Hortus Conclusus; Islamic Gardens; Religion, Garden in.

Purchas, Anne. Freelance writer. Contributor to *Georgian Group Journal,* 1994, 1995, and *Architectural History,* 1994. **Essays:** Chambers, William; Gatchina.

Quaintance, Richard. Professor Emeritus, Department of English, Rutgers University, New Brunswick, New Jersey. Editor of *An Explanatory Discourse by Tan Chet-qua (1773),* by Sir William Chambers, 1978. Contributor to *Country and the City Revisited: England and the Politics of Culture, 1550–1850,* edited by Gerald MacLean et al., 1999, *Studies in Eighteenth-Century Culture,* 1998, *Persuasions,* 1997, and numerous other books and journals. **Essays:** Kew, Royal Botanic Gardens; Walpole, Horace.

Räckers, Beate. Freelance writer. Author of *Stadtfriedhof Seelhorst,* 2000. **Essay:** Duchêne Family.

Rich, Paul. Professor of International Relations and History, University of the Americas, Puebla, Mexico. Author of *Stanford Patriarchs,* 1993, *Invasions of the Gulf,* 1992, *Chains of Empire,* 1992, and *Elixir of Empire,* 1991. Editor of several publications, including *Annals of the American Academy of Political and Social Science,* 1997, 1999, and *Policy Studies Review,* 1998. Contributor to many books and journals. **Essays:** Mexico; Roof Garden; Sculpture in the Garden.

Ridgway, Christopher. Curator, Castle Howard. Editor of *William Andrews Nesfield, Victorian Landscape Architect,* 1994. Contributor to *Country Life Art and Antiques,* special issue, 1999, *European Gardens,* 1996, *Garden History,* 1993, and *Country Life,* 1989. **Essays:** Castle Howard; Nesfield, William Andrews.

Riedinger, Edward A. Professor and Head, Latin American Library Collection, Ohio State University. Author of *Turned-on Advising,* 1995, *Where in the World to Learn,* 1995, *Como se faz um presidente,* 1988, and other books. Editor of *História ciências, saúde—Manguinhos,* 1995–present, and other publications. Contributor to numerous books and journals. **Essays:** College Campus; Fronteira, Palace of; Les Cèdres; Père Lachaise Garden Cemetary.

Riedl, Dušan. Architect and emeritus research worker, Research Institute for Building and Architecture, Brno,

Czech Republic. Author of many books, including *The Villa of the Tugendhats, Created by Ludwig Mies van der Rohe in Brno*, 1997, *Brněská architektura 20. Století*, 1992, and *Rekonstrukee historických jader měst*, 1987. Editor of *Zahrady a parky v Čechách, na Moravě a ve Slezsku*, 1999, and other books. Editorial Board Member of *Projekt*, 1965–68, 1992–2001 and *Ceskoslovenský architekt*, 1983–87. Contributor to multiple journals and book collections. **Essay:** Czech Republic; Kroměříž.

Rohde, Michael. Landscape architect and Associate Professor, Institut für Grünplanung und Gartenarchitektur, Universität Hannover. Author of *Von Muskau bis Konstantinopel*, 1998, *Eduard Petzold*, 1998, *Parkpflegewerk Hinüberscher Garten in Hannover-Marienwerder*, 1997, and *Mariannenpark Leipzig-Parkpflegewerk*, 1993. Editor of *Stadt und Grün*, with H.-J. Liesecke, 1996–98. Contributor to numerous anthologies and journals. **Essays:** Jäger, Hermann; Petzold, Eduard.

Ruggles, D. Fairchild (adviser). Visiting Assistant Professor, South Asia Program and Department of Architecture, Cornell University. Author of *Gardens, Landscape, and Vision in the Palaces of Islamic Spain*, 2000. Editor of *Women, Patronage, and Self-Representation in Islamic Societies*, 2000, and *Journal of Garden History*, guest co-editor 1994. Contributor to *The Cambridge History of Arabic Literature: The History of Al-Andalus*, edited by Maria Menocal, Michael Sells, and Raymond Scheindlin, 2000, *Gesta*, 1997, and many other books and journals. **Essays:** Córdoba, Great Mosque of; Madinat al-Zahra'; Nishat Bagh; Srinagar, Shalamar Bagh; Vista Garden.

Ruoff, Eeva. Professor, Department of Architecture, Helsinki University of Technology. Author of several books including *Kularanta - Gullranda - A Summer Home in Finland*, 1996, and *Monrepos - muistojen puutarha*, 1993. Editor of *Mitteilungen der Schweizerischen Gesellschaft für Gartenkultur*, 1989–present, *Rooman maisema: Forumit, puistot, piazzat*, 1995, and other journals and book collections. Contributor to numerous journals and anthologies. **Essays:** Finland; Froebel Family; Switzerland.

Rusnak, Cecilia. Assistant Professor, Department of Landscape Architecture, Pennsylvania State University. Editor of *Perspectives in Landscape History*, 2000. Contributor to *New England Journal of Garden History*, 1999, *Journal of Preservation Technology*, 1999, and *Archbridges: History, Analysis, Assessment*, edited by Anna Sinepoli, 1998. **Essay:** Jefferson, Thomas.

Rylance, Keli E. Assistant Professor, Department of Art and Design, University of Wisconsin, Stout. Contributor to *Memory and Oblivion: 29th International Congress of Art*, edited by Wessel Reinink and Jeroen Stumpel, 1999. **Essay:** Tourism and Gardens.

Sales, John. Gardens consultant, formerly Head of Gardens, The National Trust. **Essays:** Biddulph Grange; Stourhead.

Salmen, Walter. Professor Emeritus, Department of Musicology, University of Freiburg. Author of many books including *Der Weimarer Musenhof*, 1998, *Der Tanzmeister*, 1997, and *Beruf: Musiker*, 1997. Editor of *Terpsichore: Tanzhistorische Studien*, 1997–present, *Mozart in der Tanzkultur seiner Zeit*, 1990, and other books and journals. Contributor to several anthologies and journals. **Essay:** Music in the Garden.

Salza Prina Ricotti, Eugenia. Architect, Archaeologist, corresponding member, Pontificia Accademia Romana di Archeologia. Author of *Villa Adriana: Il sogno di un imperatore*, 2001. Contributor to numerous journals and anthologies. **Essay:** Adriana, Villa.

Scheliga, Thomas. Herzog August Bibliothek Wolfenbüttel. Author of *Schloesser und Schlossgärten in Deutschland*, 1995. Editor of *Salzthalischer Mayen-Schluss*, 1994. Editorial board member of *UniArt*, 1992. Contributor to numerous books and journals including *Johann Royer (1574–1655) und die Flora des Nordharzes*, 1998. **Essays:** De Caus Family; de Vries, Hans Vredeman; Water Garden.

Schwarz, Angela. Assistant Professor, Department of History, Gerhard Mercator University, Duisburg. Author of *Der Schlüssel zur modernen Welt*, 1999, and *Die Reise ins Dritte Reich*, 1993. Editor of *Vom Industriebetrieb zum Landschaftspark*, 2001, *Kein Boden für Sozialdemokraten am Niederrhein*, 1999, and *Politische Sozialisation und Geschichte*, 1993. Contributor to many books and journals. **Essays:** Hampton Court Palace and Bushy Park; Olmsted Family; Painshill; Zwinger.

Šćitaroci, Bojana Bojanić Obad. Scientific Researcher. Co-author of *Manors and Gardens in Northern Croatia*, with Mladen Obad Šćitaroci, 1998, and author of *Traditional Architecture of Island Hvar*, 1997. Contributor to numerous collections and journals. **Essays:** Croatia (with Mladen Obad Šćitaroci); Dubrovnik Renaissance Gardens (with Mladen Obad Šćitaroci); Maksimir (with Mladen Obad Šćitaroci).

Šćitaroci, Mladen Obad. Professor, Department of Town Planning, Faculty of Architecture, University of Zagreb.

Co-author of *Manors and Gardens in Northern Croatia, Slavonia*, with Bojana Bojanić Šćitaroci, 1998, *Croatian Garden Architecture Heritage: Protection and Renovation*, 1992, and *Castles, Manors, and Gardens of Croatian Zagorje*, 1991. Editor of *Traditional Architecture of Island Hvar*, 1997, *Croatian Lexicon*, 1993–94, and *Croatian Encyclopedia*, 1993–94. Contributor to several anthologies and journals. **Essays:** Croatia (with Bojana Bojanić Obad Šćitaroci); Dubrovnik Renaissance Gardens (with Bojana Bojanić Obad Šćitaroci); Maksimir (with Bojana Bojanić Obad Šćitaroci).

Semenova, Galina V. Art critic and chief specialist, Department of History, Architecture Information, and Scientific Examination, Committee of State Inspection on Using and Protection of Monuments of History and Culture, St. Petersburg. Contributor to *The Monuments of History and Culture of St. Petersburg*, 1998, *St. Petersburg's Readings*, 1997, *Russian Country Estate*, 1995, *Gardens of St. Petersburg*, 1994, and *Planning of Cultural Landscapes*, 1993. **Essay:** Tsarskoye Selo.

Shiling, Zheng. Professor, Department of Architecture, Tongji University. Author of several books, including *The Evolution of Shanghai Architecture in Modern Times*, 1999, *Kisho Kurokawa*, 1997, and *On Rationality of Architecture, the Value System and Symbolism*, 1996. Editor of *Chinese Architecture of the Twentieth Century*, 1999, *Encyclopedia of Contemporary Art*, 1997 and other book collections. Contributor to numerous books and journals. **Essays:** Gen Yue; Ge Yuan; Ji Chang Yuan; Liu Yuan; Shi Tao; Tao Qian; Zhan Yuan.

Shoemaker, Candice A. (editor). Formerly Director, School of the Chicago Botanic Garden. Currently Associate Professor, Department of Horticulture, Forestry, Recreation Resources, Kansas State University. **Essays:** Alpine Garden (with Paul Miles); England; Italy (with Anthony H.T. Levi); Maze; Netherlands; Plant Training.

Shorban, Ekaterina. Senior Research Fellow and Curator, General Inventory of Historical Monuments of Russia, State Institute of Art History. Author of *Moscow Mansions*, 1996. Editor of *Archive of Architectural Russia*, 1990–present. Contributor to numerous collections. **Essays:** Semenov, Vladimir Nikilayevitch.

Shvidkovsky, Dmitry (adviser). Professor and Chairman, Department of Architectural History, Moscow Institute of Architecture. Author of several books including *The Empress and the Architect: British Architecture and Gardens at the Court of Catherine the Great*, 1996, *St. Petersbourgh: The Architecture of the Tsars*, 1997. Editor of many journals including *Archive of Architecture, Russia*, 1990–present, *Russian History*, 1989–present,

and *Journal of Garden History*, 1993–96. Contributor to numerous books and journals. **Essays:** Kuskovo; Lvov, Nikolai Alexandrovitch; Russia; Summer Garden.

Siciliano, Paul C., Jr. Assistant Professor, Department of Horticulture and Landscape Architecture, Purdue University. Contributor to *Indiana Nursery and Landscape Association Journal* and *American Nurseryman*. **Essays:** Informal Garden; Kiley, Daniel Urban.

Siewniak, Marek. Professor, Department of Landscape Architecture, Technical University, Cracow. Author of several books, including *Tezaurus sztuki ogrodowej*, 1998, *Baumpflege heute*, 1984, 1987, 1988, 1994, and *Öregfāk diszfāk Apolāsa*, 1979. Editor and contributor to various books and journals. **Essays:** Aviary; Łazienki Park; Poland; Wilanów; Winter Garden.

Sim, Jeannie. Lecturer in Landscape Architecture, Queensland University of Technology. Author of *Inventory of Historical Cultural Landscapes in Queensland*, 1997. Contributor to *Theoretical Framework for Designed Landscapes in Australia*, edited by Richard Aitken et al., 1998. **Essays:** Botanic Garden; Fernery.

Simms, Barbara. Garden designer and historian, Garden Tales, Kingston, Surrey. Author of *Intimacy and Splendour: Six Gardens through Time*, 1999, and *The Role of Gardens in Suburban Development, 1800–1914*, 1999. **Essays:** Arts and Crafts Gardening; Beaton, Donald; Brown, Lancelot; Hill, Thomas; Jellicoe, Geoffrey Alan; Loudon, John Claudius and Jane Webb Loudon; Sackville-West, Victoria (Vita) Mary; Veitch Family.

Sinclair, Iona. Editor of *The Pyramid and the Urn, the Life in Letters of a Restoration Squire: William Lawrence of Shurdington, 1636–1697*, 1994. Contributor to *Garden History*, 1996, and *The Gloucestershire Gardens and Landscape Trust Newsletter*, 1995. **Essay:** Symbolism in Western Gardens.

Sobti, Manu P. Doctoral Candidate, Ph.D. program, College of Architecture, Georgia Institute of Technology. Contributor to several books and journals, including *Proceedings of the 6th International Seminar on Urban Form at Florence*, 1999, *Fluid Migrations: The Immigration of Peoples and Cultures*, edited by Nezar Alsayyad, 1996, and *Paris-Architektur und Utopie*, edited by Kristin Fiereiss, 1989. **Essays:** Automata; Hydraulics.

Solman, David. Freelance writer. Author of *Loddiges of Hackney: The Largest Hot-House in the World*, 1997, and *Clissold Park*, 1992. Contributor to *The Hackney Terrier*, 1991, 1992, and *Junior Education Magazine*,

1989. **Essays:** Fairchild, Thomas; Lawson, Thomas; Lawson, William; Loddiges Family; London Parks; Mount Auburn Cemetery.

Spongberg, Stephen A. Director, Polly Hill Arboretum. **Essay:** Arnold Arboretum (with Peter Del Tredici).

Spreiregen, Paul D. (adviser). Architect, planner, and author. Author of several books including *Pre-Design*, 2 vols., 1985, 1990, *Design Competitions*, 1979, and *Building a New Town: The Storm of Finland's New Garden City, Tapiola*, 1971. Editor of *Metropolis and Beyond: Selected Essays of Hans Blumenfeld*, 1979, and *Competitions*. Contributor to many book collections and journals.

Steiner, Frederick. Professor, School of Planning and Landscape Architecture, Arizona State University. Author of several books including *The Living Landscape*, 1991, and *Soil Conservation in the United States: Policy and Planning*, 1990. Editor of many books and journals including *Environmental Management*, 1999–present, *Journal of the American Planning Association*, 1998–present, and *To Heal the Earth*, 1998. Contributor to numerous journals and anthologies. **Essay:** Education: Landscape Architecture.

Streatfield, David C. Professor, Department of Landscape Architecture, University of Washington. Author of *California Gardens: Creating a New Eden*, 1994, *Seventy-five Years of Landscape Architecture at Berkeley: An Informal History*, 1993, *Landscape and the Gardens and Literature of Eighteenth Century England*, 1981, and *Early Warning System: The Santa Cruz Mountains Regional Pilot Study*, 1970. Contributor to several book collections. **Essays:** Brandt, Gudmund Nyeland; Church, Thomas Dolliver; Huntington Library and Botanic Gardens; Stanford University.

Sullivan, Jack. Assistant Professor, Department of Natural Resource Sciences and Landscape Architecture, University of Maryland. **Essay:** Duncombe Park.

Svoboda, Antonín Marián. Researcher-dendrologist, Arboretum Průhonicianum, Prague, Czech Republic. Author of numerous studies, including *The Ornamental Cultivars of the Common Beech—Fagus silvatica L.—in the Czech Republic*, 1988. Editor of *Gardens in South Bohemia—European Landscape Parks—Červený Dvůr*, with L. Helebrant, 1991, and other books. Contributor to various journals. **Essay:** Průhonický Park.

Swaffield, Simon. Professor of Landscape Architecture, Lincoln University, New Zealand. Editor of *Landscape Review*, 1995–99, and *Garden Design: A New Zealand Guide*, 1993. Contributor to *Journal of Environmental Planning and Management*, 1998, *Environmental Politics*, 1997, and *Harvard Design Journal*, 1997. **Essay:** Christchurch.

Szafrańska, Malgorzata. Royal Castle of Warsaw. Author of *Ogród polski w XIX wieku. Antologia tekstów*, 1998, *Ogród renesansowy. Antologia tekstów*, 1998, and *Ogród Zamku Królewskiego w Warszawie*, 1994. Editor of *Ogród. Forma-Symbol-Marzenie*, 1998. Contributor to *Arte-Documento*, 1996, and other journals. **Essays:** Nieborów; Puławy.

Tankard, Judith B. Instructor, Graduate Program in Landscape Design History, Radcliffe Seminars. Author of *A Place of Beauty: Artists and Gardens of the Cornish Colony*, 2000, *Gertrude Jekyll at Munstead Wood*, 1996, *The Gardens of Ellen Biddle Shipman*, 1996, and *Gertrude Jekyll: A Vision of Garden and Wood*, 1989. Editor of *Journal of the New England Garden History Society*, 1990–93, 1997, 1999. Contributor to numerous books and journals. **Essays:** Jekyll, Gertrude; Munstead Wood; Robinson, William; Shipman, Ellen Biddle.

Taylor, Hilary A. Director, HTLA Ltd., historic landscape consultants. Author of *British Impressionism: Landscape, Images and Attitudes*, exhibition catalog, 1989. Contributor to *Regeneration of Public Parks*, edited by Jan Woudstra and Ken Fieldhouse, 1999, *Garden History*, 1995, *Historic Garden*, 1992, and *Country Life*, 1991. **Essays:** Birkenhead Park; Water in the Landscape.

Thompson, Catharine Ward. Head, School of Landscape Architecture, Edinburgh College of Art, Heriot-Watt University. Editor of *A Woody Plant Selection Guide*, by D. Skinner, 3rd ed., 1994. Editorial advisory board member of *Landscape Research*, 1996–present. Contributor to numerous journals, including *Landscape Review*, 1998, *International Journal of Heritage Studies*, 1998, and *Arboricultural Journal*, 1997. **Essays:** Edinburgh, Royal Botanic Garden; Scotland; Walled Garden.

Thompson, Mine F. Former Research Assistant, Department of Landscape Architecture, University of Istanbul. Editor of *Journal of Landscape Architecture*, 1997–99. Contributor to *Conservation of Istanbul's Monumental Trees*, with A. Uzun, edited by Ellas Conference Comity, 2000, *The Development of Waterfront Parks on Reclaimed Land*, 1997, and *Usage of Plant Material on Pedestrian Zones*, edited by MSU Urban Design Group, 1996. **Essay:** Turkey.

Tishler, William H. Professor, Department of Landscape Architecture, University of Wisconsin, Madison. Editor of *Shaping Heartland Landscapes*, 1999, *American Landscape Architecture: Designers and Places*, 1989, and *Index to Graduate Work in the Field of Landscape Architecture*, 1974. Contributor to numerous books and journals, including *Landscape Journal*, 1999, and *Swiss Vernacular Landscape*, 1998. **Essays:** Cleveland, Horace William Shaler (with Daniel Joseph Nadenicek); Copeland, Robert Morris (with Daniel Joseph Nadenicek); Jensen, Jens; Simonds, Ossian Cole.

Trauzettel, Ludwig. Head gardener, Kulturstiftung, Dessau-Wörlitz, Germany. Author of *Wörlitz, Führer durch die Englishen Anlagen*, 1991. Co-Author of *Der Englische Garten zu Wörlitz*, with A. Rode and H. Ross, 1987, and other books. Contributor to numerous journals, including *Das Gartenreich Dessau-Wörlitz. Ein Reiseführer*, 1996, *Stadt und Grün*, 1998, and *Garten Der Goethezeit*, 1993. **Essay:** Anhalt-Dessau, Franz von.

Treib, E. Marc (adviser). Professor of Architecture, College of Environmental Design, University of California, Berkeley. Co-author of *Garrett Eckbo: Modern Landscapes for Living*, with Dorthée Imbert, and author of numerous books and articles.

Troeva, Vesselina. Associate Professor, Head, Department of Urban Planning, University of Architecture, Civil Engineering and Geodesy, Sofia. Author of *Landscape Planning*, 1997. Editorial Board Member of numerous journals, including *Architecture*, 1990–present. Contributor to many books and journals, including *Our Home*, 1995 and *The Urban Experience: A People Environment Perspective*, edited by S.Y. Neary, M.S. Symes, and F.E. Brown, 1994. **Essays:** Boris Gardens; Bulgaria.

van Groeningen, Isabelle. Landscape design consultant. Contributor to *The Essential Gardenbook*, 1998, *Gartenpraxis*, 1998, *The Garden*, 1995, 1998, *Gardens Illustrated*, 1997, and *The Hardy Plant*, 1995. **Essays:** Color; Hidcote Manor Garden; Perennials.

Van Nest, Anne Marie. Instructor, Niagara Parks Botanical Gardens. **Essays:** Clusius, Carolus; Container Gardening; Ground Cover; Keukenhof; Vine.

van Zuylen, Gabrielle (adviser). Independent scholar and freelance writer. Author of *The Alhambra*, 1999, *Tous les jardins du monde*, 1994, *The Gardens of Russell Page*, 1991, and *Gardens of France*, 1983. Editor of *Small Books of Great Gardens*, 1999. Contributor to numerous books and journals. **Essay:** Page, Russell.

Vávrová, Věra. Archivist, Archives of Prague Castle. Contributor to many books and journals including *Josef Navrátil (1798–1865). Katalog výstavy Správy Pražského hradu a Národní galerie*, 1998, *Pražský hrad*, 1998, *Víno*, 1997, *Klenot města*, 1997, and *Umění a řemesla*, 1997. **Essay:** Prague Castle Gardens.

Vergunov, Arkadiy. Professor of Architecture, Moscow Architecture Institute. **Essay:** Kolomenskoye Palace and Gardens (with Alexander N. Luferov and Loubov I. Lyashenko).

Volkman, Nancy J. Associate Professor, Department of Landscape Architecture and Urban Planning, Texas A and M University. Author of *Landscapes in History: Eastern and Western Traditions in Design and Planning*, 1998. Contributor to *Palms and Pomegranates: Heirloom Plants of the Southeast*, 1995, *International Dictionary of Architects and Architecture*, 1993, *Kansas History*, 1987, and *Land Use Policy*, 1987. **Essays:** Daisen-in; Parmentier, André Joseph Ghislain; Thailand.

von Rath, Ulrich. Medical doctor. Gemeinschaftskrankenhaus Herdecke, Germany. Author of *Botanik und Pharmakologie in der Renaissance*, 1998. Contributor to *Polish Botanical Studies. Studies in Renaissance Botany*, 1998, *Zandera*, 1998, *Museologia scientifica*, 1998, *Lustgården*, 1995, and *Bulletin historique de la ville de Montpellier*, 1994. **Essay:** Montpellier Botanic Garden.

Wang, Joseph C. (adviser). Professor, Department of Architecture, Virginia Polytechnic Institute. Author of *Chinese Classical Gardens of Suzhou*, 1993, and *The Chinese Garden*, 1998. Contributor to *Places*, 1992, *MIMAR*, 1992, *Design Book Review*, 1994, and *Jianzhushi*, 1995, as well as to *Chinese Landscapes: The Village as Place*, edited by Ronald Knapp, 1992. **Essays:** Ban Mu Yuan (with Cheng Liyao); Bei Hai Park (with Cheng Liyao); Canglang Ting (with Liu Dun-zhen and Xu Dejia); Gu Yi Yuan (with Xu Dejia); Hu Qiu (with Xu Dejia); Wangshi Yuan (with Liu Dun-zhen and Xu Dejia); Xiequ Yuan (with Cheng Liyao).

Warner, Pamela J. Doctoral candidate, Department of Art History, University of Delaware. Co-author of *The Romance of Transportation: Vehicle and Voyage in North American Art*, with Ellen A. Plummer, 1993. Contributor to *Laszlo Moholy-Nagy: From Budapest to Berlin, 1914–1923*, edited by Belena Chapp, 1995. **Essay:** Chinoiserie.

Watts, Teresa S. Professor, Art History, Art Department, Potsdam College, State University of New York. Contributor to numerous collections and journals, including *The Dictionary of Art*, 1996, *Dictionary of National Biography*, 2000, and *The Journal of Garden History*, 1986. **Essay:** Wilhelmshöhe.

Weaver, Karol K. Instructor, Bloomsburg University of Pennsylvania. **Essays:** Colonialism and Gardening; Herbs: Medicinal.

Webster, Constance A. Associate Professor of Landscape, Rutgers University. Contributor to *Journal of the New England Garden History Society*, 1996, *33rd IFLA World Congress Proceedings*, 1996, *Revue d'Architecture de Paysage*, 1987, *Landscape Journal*, 1986, and *Journal of Garden History*, 1986. **Essays:** Anet; Ermenonville; France; Rambouillet.

Weilacher, Udo. Landscape Architect, Federal Institute of Technology, Zurich, Switzerland. Author of *Between Landscape Architecture and Land Art*, 1996. Contributor to *Aussenräume*, edited by Dieter Kienast, 2000, *Topos*, 2000, *Garten und Landschaft*, 2000, *Archithese*, 1999, and other books and journals. **Essays:** Ammann, Gustav; Cramer, Ernst; Kienast, Dieter.

Weimarck, Gunnar. Professor, Göteborg Botanic Garden, Region of Västra Götaland, Sweden. Author of *Att hålla ordning på arter och släkten, en familjeangelägenhet*, 1997 and *Atlas över Skånes flora*, with H. Weimarck, 1985. Editor of several books and journals including *Nordiskt ljus och italiensk hetta*, 1996, *Det blommar i Botaniska*, 1992, and *Nordic Journal of Botany*, 1981–84. Contributor to many journals and anthologies. **Essay:** Göteborgs, Botaniska Trädgård.

Westmacott, Richard. Professor, School of Environmental Design, University of Georgia, Athens. Author of *African American Gardens and Yards in the Rural South*, 1992, *Water Resources Protection Technology*, 1981, and *New Agricultural Landscapes*, 1974. Editor of *Stormwater Management Alternatives*, 1980, and *The Nature of Landscape Design*, 1974. Contributor to several journals. **Essays:** African-American Gardening; Kensington Gardens.

Whalley, Robin. Freelance writer. Author of *Knot Gardens and Parterres*, 1998. Editor of *The Boke of Iford*, 1993. Contributor to *Gardens Illustrated*, 1998, *Hortus*, 1995, 1996, and *Bath History*, 1994. **Essays:** Knot Garden; Peto, Harold Ainsworth.

Whelan, Agnieszka. Independent scholar and freelance writer. Contributor to numerous books and journals, including *Art and Politics*, 1998, and *Biuletyn Historii Sztuki*, 1996. **Essays:** Konchi-in; Kyoto Botanic Garden; Shoden-ji.

Whitehead, David. Freelance writer. Author of *James Wathen's Herefordshire, 1777–1820*, 1994. Editor of *Journal of Picturesque Society*, 1997, and *Medieval Art and Architecture of Hereford*, 1995. Contributor to *The Picturesque Landscape*, edited by Charles Watkins and Stephen Daniels, 1994, and other books and jounals. **Essays:** Ferme Ornée; Gardenesque Style; Georgian Period; Hestercombe; Kemp, Edward; Langley, Batty; Leasowes; Mason, William Hayton.

Whittle, Elisabeth. Inspector of Historic Parks and Gardens, Cadw, Cardiff. Author of *Guide to the Antiquities of Gwent and Glariorgan*, 1992, and *The Historic Gardens of Wales*, 1992. Joint editor of *Garden History*, 1989–97. Contributor to *Garden History*, 1999, 1994, 1996, 1999 and *Monmouthshire Antiquary*, 1994. **Essays:** Blenheim Palace; Fontainebleau; Giverny; Luxembourg Gardens; Marly; Sceaux; Tuileries; Vaux-le-Vicomte; Wales.

Wilkinson, Alix. Independent scholar, freelance writer. Author of *Ancient Egyptian Jewellery*, 1972. Contributor to *Encyclopedia Britannica*. **Essay:** Egypt: Ancient.

Wimmer, Clemens Alexander. Garden historian, Potsdam. Author of *Geschichte der Gartentheorie*, 1989, and *Die Gärten des Charlottenburger Schlosses*, 1985. Editor of *Zandera: Mitteilungen aus der Bücherei des Deutschen Gartenbaues*, 1990–present. Contributor to many books and journals, including *Garden History*, 1998, and *Mid den Bäumen sterben die Menschen*, edited by Jost Hermand, 1993. **Essays:** Arboretum; Baroque Style; Bed and Bedding System; Berlin, Tiergarten; Books, Gardening; Charlottenburg; Cultivar; Großsedlitz; Klein-Glienicke; Lenné, Peter Joseph; Neoclassicism; Nurserymen; Rococo Style; Sanssouci; Trees.

Winter, John. Deputy Director, Horticulteral Services, National Botanical Institute, Kirstenbosch, Cape Town. **Essay:** Kirstenbosch National Botanical Garden.

Wolschke-Bulmahn, Joachim (adviser). Professor, Department of Landscape Architecture, University of Hannover. Author of several books, including *American Garden Literature in the Dumbarton Oaks Collection (1785–1900)*, with Jack Becker, 1999, and *Grünen Biographien: Biographisches Handbuch zur Landschaftsarchitektur des 20. Jahrhunderts in Deutschland*, with Gert Gröning, 1997. Editor of numerous books and journals, including *Places of Commemoration: Search for Identity and Landscape Design*, 1999, and *Journal of Garden History*, 1992–94, 1997–present. Contributor to many journals and anthologies. **Essays:** Allinger, Gustav; Germany (with Gert Gröning); Hammerbacher, Herta; Lange, Willy (with Gert Gröning); Migge, Leberecht; Seifert, Alwin.

Woods, May. Garden historian. Author of *Visions of Arcadia*, 1996, and *Glass Houses*, 1988. Contributor to

Historic Gardens Review, 2000, and *Follies,* 1999. **Essay:** Greenhouse.

Woudstra, Jan. Lecturer, Department of Landscape, University of Sheffield. Editor of *Garden History,* 1998–present. Contributor to *Nature and Ideology,* edited by J. Wolschke-Bulmahn, 1997, *Tuinkunst: Dutch Yearbook of the History of Garden and Landscape Architecture,* 1996, *Groen,* 1996, *Architects' Journal,* 1996, and numerous other books and journals. **Essays:** Bijhouwer, Jan Thijs Pieter; Boer, Willem Christiaan Johannes; Cemetery (with Andrew Clayden); Container; Grove; Modernism; Pathways and Paving; Ruys, Mein.

Wye-Rodney, Kristin. Editor of *Dangerous Crossings: The First Modern Polar Expedition, 1925,* 2000, *Cold War at Sea,* 2000, *Most Secret and Confidential,* 2000, *Jane's Sentinel: Central America and the Caribbean,* 1999, and *Jane's Chemical and Biological Defense Guidebook,* 1999. **Essays:** Anuradhapura Gardens; Egypt: Modern; Grosser Garten; Petrodvorets; Rio de Janeiro, Jardim Botânico do; Romania; Schleissheim; South America.

Xu Dejia. Department of Architecture, Suzhou Institute of Urban Construction and ENV. Protection, China. Author of *Planting Arrangement in the Classical Gardens of China,* 1997, and *Technique of Landscape Nursery,* 1985. Contributor to *Journal of Suzhou Institute of Urban Construction and ENV. Protection,* 1995–97, and *International Symposium on Horticulture Germplasm, Cultivated and Wild,* 1988. **Essays:** Canglang Ting (with Liu Dun-zhen and Joseph C. Wang); Gu Yi Yuan (with Joseph C. Wang); Hu Qiu (with Joseph C. Wang); Wangshi Yuan (with Liu Dun-zhen and Joseph C. Wang).